CCIE

Cisco Certified Internetwork Expert

Study Guide

Second Edition

CCIE™:
Cisco® Certified Internetwork Expert
Study Guide
Second Edition

Rob Payne, CCIE #8325
Kevin Manweiler, CCIE #5269

San Francisco • London

SYBEX

Associate Publisher: Neil Edde
Acquisitions and Developmental Editor: Maureen Adams
Production Editor: Kelly Winquist
Technical Editors: Justin Menga, Pavan Reddy
Copyeditor: Judy Flynn
Compositor: Scott Benoit, Judy Fung
Graphic Illustrator: Jeff Wilson, Happenstance Type-O-Rama
CD Coordinator: Dan Mummert
CD Technician: Kevin Ly
Proofreaders: Emily Hsuan, Nancy Riddiough, Eric Lach, Laurie O'Connell, Monique Vandenberg, Yariv Rabinovitch, Sarah Tannehill
Indexer: Lynnzee Elze
Book Designer: Bill Gibson, Judy Fung
Cover Designer: Archer Design
Cover Photographer: Andrew Ward, Life File, PhotoDisc

Library of Congress Card Number: 2002116883

ISBN: 0-7821-4207-9

SYBEX®

To Our Valued Readers:

Thank you for looking to Sybex for your CCIE exam prep needs. CertCities.com recently ranked the CCIE as the #1 certification in its list of the "10 Hottest Certifications for 2003," and it's no wonder. Developed by Cisco to validate expertise with Cisco's internetworking technology, the CCIE certification well deserves its reputation as one of the toughest certification exams in the world of IT.

We at Sybex are proud of the reputation we've established for providing certification candidates with the practical knowledge and skills needed to succeed in the highly competitive IT marketplace. It has always been Sybex's mission to teach individuals how to utilize technologies in the real world, not to simply feed them answers to test questions. Just as Cisco is committed to establishing measurable standards for certifying those professionals who work in the cutting-edge field of internetworking, Sybex is committed to providing those professionals with the means of acquiring the skills and knowledge they need to meet those standards.

The Sybex team of authors, editors, and technical reviewers have worked hard to ensure that this Study Guide is comprehensive, in-depth, and pedagogically sound. We're confident that this book, along with the collection of cutting-edge software study tools included on the CD, will meet and exceed the demanding standards of the certification marketplace and help you, the CCIE certification exam candidate, succeed in your endeavors.

Good luck in pursuit of your CCIE certification!

Neil Edde
Associate Publisher—Certification
Sybex, Inc.

This book is dedicated to my loving wife, Kelly, who is not just my wife, but also my best friend, as well as my two sons, Christopher and Joshua, for the endless understanding and support throughout the development of this book. Also, for teaching me good values and the importance of continuous learning throughout my lifetime, thanks to my parents, Randall and Beverly; my brother, Larry; and my sisters, Juanita, Cheryl, and Lorretta. Thank you Kevin, for working on this project with me. And finally, thanks to all my family and friends—as the true value of a person can be measured by the friendships they keep, and I feel blessed and rich to have so many wonderful friends whom I have laughed and cried with over the years.
—Rob Payne

This book is dedicated to helping network engineers work 9 to 5 instead of 5 to 9 and to my wonderful and supportive family, Lynne, Kyle, and Katherine—you are truly the greatest! Thanks also to my parents, Nancy and Allan, who stressed the importance of education, and to my twin brother, Kurt, who often showed up at work for me when I was busy writing. Rob, thank you for the opportunity to work with you on this. And to the reader, may God be with you as you study, pass the exams, and continue in your networking experiences.
—Kevin Manweiler

Acknowledgments

We would especially like to thank Francis Ferguson, Ken Sexton, and Simon Tipper for their significant contribution in the development of material throughout this book. We could not have completed this book without your contributions. Thanks to John Bess, Francisco Vigil, Dave Bilberry, Paul Vieira, Dean Olson, and Mark Breedlove (CCIE #8657) for their review of the material and various subject matter input. Likewise, thanks to John Cavanaugh, CCIE #1066; Darell Godeaux, CCIE #1830; Reed Streifthau, CCIE #3115; Luis Salcido, CCIE #1440; Nimish Desai; Junnie Sadler, CCIE #7028; Dave Knuth, CCIE #7961; Cesar Obediente, CCIE #5620; Troy Hall, CCIE #7412; Mike O'Shea, CCIE #5308; Scott Frisby, CCIE #5059; Thomas Easow, and the rest of the Raleigh (RTP), N.C., Cisco Advanced Services (NSA) Engineering Group—your combined experience and knowledge dramatically improved the quality of this book.

Thanks to our bosses—Bob Hartinger, Dave Knuth, and Rick Crawford—for all the support during this project.

Thanks to Justin Menga, CCIE #6640, and Pavan Reddy, CCIE #4575, for their thorough and comprehensive technical editing. Working with both of you raised the level of technical accuracy as well as increased the breadth of topics within this book.

And a special thanks to Neil Edde, Maureen Adams, Kelly Winquist, Scott Benoit, and Judy Flynn at Sybex for their outstanding support and guidance throughout the writing of this book. *Thanks* for believing in and supporting this project.

About the Authors

Rob Payne

Rob Payne, CCIE #8325, has been working, lecturing, and teaching within the networking industry for over 20 years. He has degrees in computer science, computer information systems, and business administration, and he holds 13 major industry certifications. Currently, Rob is a network consulting engineer for Cisco Systems, where he provides network consulting services to the world's largest Fortune 1 company. Formerly, Rob worked at Galileo International, where he assisted in designing a global ATM/MPLS network, and at MCI/Worldcom as a network engineer in the Advanced Network Engineering Group, as well as Raytheon Systems Corporation. In addition, Rob has worked as a member of the U.S. Presidential White House Staff, where he dealt with networks for the CIA, FBI, NSA, FEMA, and the White House, in support of the president of the U.S. as well as the vice president, first lady, Secret Service, and White House senior staff.

Kevin Manweiler

Kevin Manweiler, CCIE #5269, started life as a software developer working on secure phone systems for the Air Force and White House after graduating from Rice University with a BS in electrical engineering. While working as a test engineer at Matrix Corporation, Kevin stumbled into networking by building a home-grown router out of spare VME-bus boards and learning IP subnetting from a few cryptic pages in a Sun workstation manual. The router segmented the flat, accident-prone network in place at the time. Kevin then worked as a contractor at IBM, providing support and education for their router products. In this capacity, he taught over 2,000 customers, developers, and field support personnel as an instructor in a two-week networking boot camp and was deployed as an onsite troubleshooter to customer sites around the world. For the past four years, Kevin has worked as a network consulting engineer in Cisco's Advanced Services (NSA) group supporting a number of Cisco's largest enterprise customers.

Contents at a Glance

Contents

Introduction

So, you are ready to achieve the CCIE certification. Well, there is definitely good reason to do so, since the CCIE certification is regarded as the most difficult and rewarding within the internetworking industry. The Cisco Certified Internetworking Expert (CCIE) is the premiere, or Expert Level, of Cisco certification.

If you find the CCIE examination topics too overwhelming, then perhaps you may want to use a stepping stone approach by progressing through the pyramid of Cisco certifications. The pyramid starts with the beginning, or Associate Level, courses:

- Cisco Certified Network Associate (CCNA)
- Cisco Certified Design Associate (CCDA)

    Then it progresses to the Professional Level courses:

- Cisco Certified Network Professional (CCNP)
- Cisco Certified Design Professional (CCDP)
- Cisco Certified Internetwork Professional (CCIP)
- Cisco Certified Security Professional (CCSP)

    Then finishes with the Expert Level:

- Cisco Certified Internetworking Expert (CCIE)

All of the Associate and Professional Level certifications can be achieved by only passing written exams. The Associate to Professional certification process is hierarchical; all the exams build upon each other. For example, the CCDP can only be obtained after first achieving CCNA and CCDA certification.

Cisco Systems also offers many specialist certifications within various networking topics, such as Content Networking, Wireless, IP Telephony, Optical, and Security. More information about the Associate, and Professional Level of Cisco certifications, as well as the Specialist certifications, can be found at the Cisco website, known as Cisco Connection Online (CCO):

www.cisco.com/en/US/learning/le3/learning_career_certifications_and_learning_
paths_home.html

The CCIE examination program currently comprises four separate CCIE certifications: Routing and Switching, Communications and Services, Security, and Voice. Each of these CCIE certifications must be independently obtained.

CCIE Certifications

As we just mentioned, there are currently four CCIE certifications, which are as follows:

- CCIE Routing and Switching (CCIE R&S)
- CCIE Communications and Services (CCIE C&S)
- CCIE Security
- CCIE Voice

This book is intended to prepare you for the CCIE R&S written (qualification) examination as well as the CCIE R&S lab examination.

CCIE R&S—Taking the Exams

The CCIE R&S certification is the traditional, de facto, and best known CCIE certification, which is based on routing and LAN/WAN switching. As Cisco Systems has approximately 80% of the router and switch market worldwide, the Routing & Switching CCIE certification is the most sought after.

The CCIE certification comprises a two-part examination process, the first part is a two-hour written examination (also known as the qualification exam) that includes all topics covered in the CCNA, CCDA, CCNP, and CCDP along with additional internetworking technologies. The second part of the examination is a one-day, hands-on, practical lab examination, which covers every aspect of configuring internetworking in a Cisco Systems equipment environment.

R&S Written Examination

The CCIE R&S written examination (Exam #350-001), which is also known as the qualification examination, is made up of a 100-question, closed-book examination and costs $300 US. You are given two hours to complete the examination, which can be scheduled and taken at Prometric (`www.2test.com`) or VUE (`www.vue.com/cisco`) testing centers.

The passing score for the written examination is set using statistical analysis, which usually varies between 50 and 75 percent. The more people that pass the examination, the higher the passing score; if the number of people passing the examination decreases, the passing score will decrease accordingly.

In preparing for the CCIE written exam, we recommend that along with studying the material provided to you in this book, you review other documentation (books, white papers, etc.), RFCs, and the Cisco Connection Online (CCO) website for additional information. Likewise, be sure to complete the chapter review questions and the CD-ROM questions in this book.

R&S Lab Examination

The Routing and Switching lab exam is a full, one-day practical exam and costs $1250 US. The CCIE candidate will be presented with a complex design to implement from the physical layer up. Candidates are not required to configure any end-user systems but are responsible for any device residing in the internetwork, routers, switches, hubs, etc. Network specifics, point values, and testing criteria used to assess correctness of the individual configurations are provided. Each configuration scenario and problem has preassigned point values. The candidate must obtain a minimum mark of 80% to pass.

Currently, the Routing and Switching lab exam tests any feature up to and including IOS version 12.1 that can be configured on the 2600 series routers, 3600 series routers, and Catalyst 3550 series switches. The following topics have been removed from the lab exam content:

LAT	Banyan VINES
DECnet	Token Ring
AppleTalk	Token Ring Switching
ISO CLNS	IPX
XNS	IGRP
X.25	ATM LANE

These changes only affect the Routing and Switching lab exam. Some of the test topics may continue to appear on the Routing and Switching written exam. Readers are advised to consult the Qualification Blueprint for the Routing and Switching written exam for a detailed list of topics tested on the written exam.

The lab examination is 100% based on the Cisco networking philosophies and the implementation of internetworking technologies as it pertains to Cisco network implementations. The lab examination requires that a CCIE candidate spend several hundred hours researching and studying technologies and solutions as they pertain to Cisco equipment. Because the CCIE lab is 100% hands-on, it is extremely unlikely that a candidate can pass the examination without having access to a Cisco lab environment.

In preparing for the CCIE lab exam, we recommend that along with studying the material provided to you in this book, you review other documentation (books, white papers, etc.), RFCs, and the Cisco Connection Online (CCO) website for additional information. Likewise, be sure to review the hands-on lab scenarios provided in this book in Chapters 7, 11, and 12, as well as the seven chapter supplements on the CD-ROM (Chapters 7, 12, 14, 15, 19, 20, and 21 supplements).

If you are preparing for the CCIE lab examination, it is crucial that you get as much time/experience on actual routers/switches as possible. If you are not able to physically get access to routers and switches, then it is a good idea to gain access to an equipment rack via Internet access. There are many websites that offer Web and/or Telnet access to routers and switches, usually on a pay-per-hour basis.

Lab Equipment List

Table I.1 lists the equipment we used in our test rack to develop and verify the hands-on lab scenarios in this book.

TABLE I.1 Test Rack Lab Equipment

Router	Model and interface type	Memory and interface name
R1	Cisco 2610 Router	48MB DRAM/16MB FLASH
	12.1.5 Enterprise Plus IPSEC 56	
	1 Ethernet	E0/0
	1 Serial WIC	S0/0
	1 ISDN BRI WIC	BRI0/0
R2	Cisco 3640 Router	64MB DRAM/32MB FLASH
	12.1.7 Enterprise Plus	
	1 FastEthernet	Fa0/0
	1 Serial WIC	S0/0
	1 ISDN BRI WIC	BRI0/0
	2 FXS VWIC	Voice-port1/0, Voice-port1/1
	1 ATM OC-3	ATM3/0
R3	Cisco 2501 Router	16MB DRAM/16MB FLASH
	12.1.5 Enterprise Plus IPSEC 56	
	1 Ethernet	E0
	2 Serial	S0, S1
R4	Cisco 2501 Router	16MB DRAM/16MB FLASH
	12.1.5 Enterprise Plus	
	1 Ethernet	E0

TABLE I.1   Test Rack Lab Equipment *(continued)*

Router	Model and interface type	Memory and interface name
	2 Serial	S0, S1
R5	Cisco 2620 Router	64MB DRAM/32MB FLASH
	12.1.5 Enterprise Plus	
	1 FastEthernet	Fa0/0
	1 Serial WIC	S0/0
	1 NM-2V, 2 FXS VWIC, 1 FXO VWIC	Voice-port1/0, Voice-port1/1, Voice-port1/2
R6	Cisco 2610 Router	48MB DRAM/16MB FLASH
	12.1.5 Enterprise Plus	
	1 Ethernet	E0/0
	1 Serial WIC	S0/0
S1	Cisco Catalyst 3550-24 Switch	64MB DRAM/16MB FLASH
	12.1.11.EA1 (EMI version)	
	2-port Gigabit Ethernet based on Gigabit Interface Converter (GBIC)	
	24-port 10/100Base-TX Ethernet	

We also used an additional separate router as our Frame Relay switch (FS). The equipment is listed in Table I.2.

TABLE I.2   Frame Relay Switch

Router	Model and interface type	Memory and interface name
FS	Cisco 2522 Router	16MB DRAM/16MB FLASH
	12.1.5 Enterprise Plus	

TABLE I.2 Frame Relay Switch *(continued)*

Router	Model and interface type	Memory and interface name
	1 Ethernet	E0
	10 Serial	S0, S1, S2, S3, S4, S5, S6, S7, S8, S9

Table I.3 lists additional equipment that we used to fully develop the scenarios. However, you do not actually need it to complete the scenarios.

TABLE I.3 Additional Test Rack Lab Equipment

Equipment type	Description
Terminal Access Server (TAS)	Cisco 2511 Router with 16 asynchronous ports
ATM Switch	Cisco LightStream 1010 with ATM OC-3 interfaces
ISDN Simulator Switch	Adtran Atlas 550 with 4-port BRI-U

The Origin of This Book

In studying for the lab examination, we researched through over 30 Cisco-specific publications relating to the CCIE certification program/technologies. We also researched through the entire Cisco website known as Cisco Connection Online (CCO), as well as white papers and RFCs, for information and solutions that pertain to the technologies presented in the CCIE lab examination. In doing this research and practicing for the lab examination, we realized that it is virtually impossible to quickly access the necessary information to perform the router and switch configurations required.

 In conducting research for this book, we utilized the Cisco Connection Online (CCO) website as a reference resource, and just as we found it as an invaluable resource, we are sure you will also find it a great asset to assist you in studying as well as performing your day-to-day work-related duties.

To pass the CCIE lab examination, a candidate must not only be extremely knowledgeable in all networking technologies, they must also be extremely proficient in implementing these technologies in a Cisco environment.

The command structure for configuring Cisco devices is often cryptic and not always intuitive. Large portions of research and study time are often spent just researching the command syntax. On several occasions, we had to re-research the exact syntax for configuring the Cisco equipment, even though we already understood the technology. It was at this point that we realized that we needed to document, for our own benefit, these commands in an abbreviated format that we could quickly reference when practicing for the lab examination.

The documentation would show the syntax of each command and its function as it pertains to the configuration of a Cisco router or switch. It also identifies nuances and intricacies within the technologies that may not necessarily be outwardly apparent to the candidate.

We then were presented with the concept of creating a single book that is targeted at preparation for both the CCIE R&S written examination and the CCIE R&S lab examination. The result is this book, which we feel will provide a good solid foundation of the required material for both of these exams.

We feel that two different groups of network engineers would benefit from this book's contents. The first group is the CCIE R&S candidates, who are inundated with the need for detailed technology and configuration information in preparation for the CCIE R&S written and lab examinations. The second category includes any network engineer who requires a quick reference and/or practical configuration examples of Cisco internetworking technologies while on the job.

How to Use This Book

Within each chapter of this book, you are provided partial router configurations. They are not meant to be actual real-world router configurations; they are only intended to show the possible commands that can be implemented and to provide a short description of the purpose of each command. Notice that when the command syntax is displayed, the commands will be displayed on the left side of the page, and opposite the command (on the right side of the page) will be a brief description of the command itself.

Here is an example of how the command syntax is displayed:

```
interface Serial0/0
```

encapsulation ppp	This configures ppp encapsulation on a serial interface
ppp authentication chap	Configures PPP authentication of the serial connection, requires a username/password defined for the remote router
bandwidth 56	Defined in Kbps. 56 Kbps = 56000 bps
clockrate 56000	Defined in bits per second 56,000bps=56Kbps. The clock rate command must be used on the physical DCE interface to generate a clock

Some of the various commands that you will see within a configuration would never be implemented at the same time on a single router or even a single interface. However, within this book they may be displayed together only as a means of showing the various commands within the fewest numbers of pages possible. Exceptions to this are in Chapters 7, 11, and 12, which contain hands-on lab scenarios, as well as the seven chapter supplements on the CD-ROM (Chapters 7, 12, 14, 15, 19, 20, and 21 supplements), which all contain hands-on lab scenarios.

What This Book Covers

This book contains detailed internetworking technology information, router and switch configuration information, and some hands-on lab scenarios designed to prepare you for the CCIE R&S written and lab examinations.

The CCIE R&S blueprint, as posted on the Cisco website known as Cisco Connection Online (CCO), is a guideline of the examination objectives on which the questions on the written examination might be based. The exam objectives include Cisco device operation, general networking theory, bridging and LAN switching, IP, IP routing, desktop protocols, QoS, WAN and LAN media, security, multiservice, and IP multicast.

This book covers all of the exam objectives for the CCIE Routing and Switching (R&S) written (qualification) examination. We have developed examination objectives based on the CCIE R&S blueprint posted on the website, CCO. These examination objectives are listed at the beginning of each chapter. You can find out more information, and view the Qualification Blueprint for the CCIE R&S at the following website (select CCIE from the pull-down menu):

www.cisco.com/warp/public/10/wwtraining/

As you read through this book, you will probably notice that we have tried to place the core topic material emphasized for the written and lab examinations (WAN/IP routing and Ethernet switching) at the beginning of the book and the secondary material (bridging, IPX, ISDN, multicast, HSRP, NTP, etc.) toward the end of the book.

What's on the CD

We worked hard to provide some great tools to help you with your CCIE certification process. All of the following tools should be loaded on your workstation when studying for the test.

The All-New Sybex Test Preparation Software

The test preparation software, made by experts at Sybex, prepares you to pass the CCIE R&S exam. In this test engine you will find all the review and assessment questions from the book, plus two additional bonus exams that appear exclusively on the CD. You can take the assessment exam, test yourself by chapter or topic, take the practice exams, or take a randomly generated exam comprising all the questions.

Electronic Flashcards for PC and Palm Devices

So to prepare for the exam, you do...what? Okay, let's summarize. Well first, you read this book. Then you proceed to study the review questions at the end of each chapter and work through the practice exams included in the book and on the CD. And afterward you test yourself with the flashcards included on the CD. Having done these things, you're now unshakably confident because you know that if you can get through these difficult questions and understand the answers, you're truly a formidable force. You can take the worst the CCIE R&S exam can do to you.

That's because the flashcards include 150 questions designed to hit you harder than Jet Li and make sure you're the Terminator of test takers—meaning you *are* ready for the exam. Between the review questions, practice exams, and flashcards, you'll be ready to rock with everything you need and more to pass!

Chapter Supplements

The seven chapter supplements on the CD-ROM (Chapters 7, 12, 14, 15, 19, 20, and 21 supplements) are designed to provide hands-on lab scenarios for you to build and practice your configuration skills on.

The hands-on lab scenarios that we have developed for this book are by no means presented as real-world best practices. These scenarios have been designed to challenge you in as many aspects of the specified technologies as possible. They are intended to test your comprehension of the material and to aid you in your own self-assessment as you progress through this book. Hopefully, the scenarios are helpful in your preparation for the CCIE lab examination and within your day-to-day real-world job. Please remember that we do not recommend configuring your live network as we have done in the scenarios. Once again, these scenarios have been developed for this book to allow us to present as many complex routing and switching technology issues as possible.

Try to build the scenarios in this book before reading the solutions. These hands-on lab scenarios are intended to test your knowledge of routing and switching. CCIE candidates must remember that in the CCIE lab examination, 99-percent right is 100-percent wrong; there is no partial credit. If either the tasks themselves or the solutions presented does not make sense, stop, investigate the problem, and do not move on until you have a firm understanding of the problem and the solution.

CCIE Glossary

We've compiled a Glossary of terms used throughout the book to help strengthen your foundation of Cisco and networking terminology. The Glossary is in PDF format. Acrobat Reader 5 is also included on the CD.

CCIE Study Guide, 2nd Edition in PDF

Sybex offers the *CCIE Study Guide, 2nd Edition* in PDF format on the CD so you can read the book on your PC or laptop if you travel and don't want to carry a book or if you just like to read from the screen computer.

To you, the reader, we wish that God may be with you in all your endeavors!

"Success is a journey... not a Destination...." by Anonymous

Assessment Test

1. Which of the protocols listed below is used for signaling on ISDN?
   A. LAPB
   B. LAPD
   C. LAXD
   D. ITU I.430

2. Which of the following are not token ring functions? (Choose all that apply.)
   A. Ring Parameter Server (RPS)
   B. Ring Purge Detector (RPD)
   C. Active monitor (AM)
   D. Ring Error Monitor (REM)
   E. Token generator (TG)

3. Which types of queuing can be configured using Modular QoS CLI (MQC)? (Choose all that apply.)
   A. Priority queuing (PQ)
   B. Custom queuing (CQ)
   C. Class-based weighted fair queuing (CBWFQ)
   D. Low latency queuing (LLQ)
   E. All of the above

4. Which of the following are valid Data Link Connection Identifiers (DLCIs)?
   A. 0
   B. 1
   C. 1022
   D. 1023
   E. None of the above

5. Which of the following routing protocols use multicast addresses to advertise updates? (Choose all that apply.)
   A. RIP version 1
   B. RIP version 2
   C. IGRP
   D. EIGRP
   E. OSPF

6. If you have a network with 2 LANs with 50 hosts and 2 point-to-point WANs, which mask should you use on the LANs and which mask should you use on the WANs? Your network address is 192.168.10.0.

   A. LANs /26, WANs /30

   B. LANs /27, WANs /30

   C. LANs /26, WANs /29

   D. LANs /30, WANs /26

7. Host 1 communicates to Host 2 by first crossing Data Link Switching (DLSw) router 1 and then crossing DLSw router 2. Host 1 sends out an LLC2 frame. Which device is responsible for acknowledging the LLC2 frame?

   A. Host 1

   B. Host 2

   C. Router 1

   D. Router 2

   E. LLC2 is unacknowledged.

8. Under which of the following situations is BGP commonly used? (Choose all that apply.)

   A. When multi-homing

   B. When connecting multiple ISPs

   C. When connecting routers within the same autonomous system

   D. When configuring backup links

9. A Frame Relay switch is getting congested. What type of message would it transmit to the sender of the frame?

   A. BECN

   B. FECN

   C. DE

   D. CIR

   E. CR

10. Router A learns about the 172.16.0.0 network via ISIS, IGRP, and OSPF. Which routing protocol would the router choose for the network?

   A. RIP

   B. OSPF

   C. IGRP

   D. None of the above

11. An SNA station wants to locate network resources. The SNA station transmits an explorer frame that is received by the Data Link Switching (DLSw) router. The DLSw router sends a query to the remote DLSw router. Assuming the remote DLSw router can reach the resource, what type of reply would the remote DLSw router send?

    A. All-routes explorer

    B. Single-route explorer

    C. RARP

    D. ARP

    E. ICANReach

12. Router A and Router B are on the same Ethernet segment and configured for HSRP, and no virtual MAC address has been configured. The standby IP address is 200.1.1.1. Router A initially becomes the active router. If router A should fail, what will Router B do?

    A. Assume the IP address of Router A

    B. Assume the IP address 200.1.1.1

    C. Assume the MAC and IP address of Router A

    D. Assume the MAC address of Router A and IP address 200.1.1.1

    E. Nothing

13. How could you prevent an OSPF router from learning about network 192.168.1.0 via OSPF while preserving other OSPF routes? (Choose all that apply.)

    A. Access group on the interface

    B. Route filter

    C. Modify administrative distance for OSPF to 255 for that network

    D. Disable OSPF

    E. Cannot be done

14. The command `ip nat inside static 10.1.3.2 200.4.2.5` is an example of which type of NAT translation?

    A. Static NAT

    B. Dynamic NAT

    C. Overlapping NAT

    D. Port mapping

15. The command `Debug ISDN Q.931` provides information about which of the following?

    A. TEI negotiation

    B. Bearer capability

    C. B channel ID

    D. B and C

16. Which of the following commands can be used to verify the NAT configuration? (Choose the two best answers.)

    A. `show ip nat statistics`

    B. `show ip nat configuration`

    C. `show ip nat all`

    D. `show ip nat translation`

17. Which of the following cannot be used by IGRP for calculating the metric?

    A. Bandwidth

    B. Delay

    C. Reliability

    D. Loading

    E. MTU

18. If you wanted to convert the IP address 224.215.145.230 to a multicast address, which of the following would it be?

    A. 01-00-5E-57-91-E6

    B. 01-00-5E-D7-91-E6

    C. 01-00-5E-5B-91-E6

    D. 01-00-5E-55-91-E6

19. You wish to run a routing protocol over a dial-up link but do not want the link to stay up all the time. What would be the best solution?

    A. Floating route

    B. Proxy ARP

    C. Backup interface

    D. HSRP

    E. OSPF demand circuit

20. You have two routers that will be participating in a single HSRP group on a common subnet. How many IP and MAC addresses will the workstations use for their default router?

    A. None; they communicate with the phantom router.

    B. One.

    C. Two.

    D. Three.

21. What command allows a round-robin load balance using IPX?

   A. `Standby`

   B. `maximum-hops`

   C. `hsrp`

   D. `maximum-paths`

22. Which type of interface allows you to have multiple virtual circuits on a single serial interface and yet treat each as a separate interface?

   A. LANE

   B. Ethernet

   C. Secondary

   D. Subinterfaces

23. What is the reverse Telnet port range on a 2509 router (which has eight native async interfaces)?

   A. 1800–1899

   B. 1990–1999

   C. 2001–2008

   D. 2010–2020

24. Which command will allow a router to act as a TFTP server for a local flash image?

   A. `tftp-server flash:c2500-js-1_120-8.bin`

   B. `copy tftp flash`

   C. `copy flash tftp`

   D. `server-tftp flash:c2500-js-1_120-8.bin`

25. If a host wants to subscribe to a multicast group, which of the following protocols can be used? (Choose all that apply.)

   A. IBMP

   B. IGMPv1

   C. IGMPv2

   D. CGMP

   E. DVMRP

   F. MOSPF

   G. PIM (DM/SM)

   H. CBT

26. Which type of voice interface acts like a central office (CO) by providing dial tone to a POTS device?

    A. Foreign Exchange Office (FXS)

    B. Foreign Exchange Station (FXO)

    C. Ear & Mouth Type 1 (E&M Type 1)

    D. An Analog Subscriber Loop (ASL)

27. How are ATM LANE transmissions to unknown stations performed?

    A. LECS

    B. LES

    C. BUS

    D. LEC

28. An H.323 gatekeeper performs which function?

    A. Terminates H.323 sessions

    B. Translates between H.323 terminals and conference bridges

    C. Initiates real-time transport protocol sessions between H.323 devices

    D. Call admission control

29. In the RIF field C410 0047 00A0, in which direction should the route descriptor be read?

    A. Left to right

    B. Right to left

    C. Top to bottom

    D. Bottom to top

    E. None of the above

30. You observe the source MAC address of several frames on your network using a protocol analyzer. Which of the following source MAC addresses indicate that RIF information is contained in it?

    A. A000.0C11.2222

    B. 1111.1111.1111

    C. 1000.1212.FFFF

    D. 2222.2222.2222

    E. 0000.0000.000F

31. What performs MAC-to-ATM address resolution?

   A. LECS

   B. LES

   C. BUS

   D. LEC

32. Network Address Translation (NAT) will provide what level of security against IP spoofing attacks?

   A. Complete

   B. None

   C. Some protection, but not complete

33. Which encryption algorithm provides the strongest security?

   A. DES

   B. DSS

   C. Kerberos

   D. 3DES

   E. RADIUS

34. If you have a network with 4 LANs with 10 hosts and 6 point-to-point WANs, which VLSM should you use on the LANs and which mask should you use on the WANs? Your network address is 192.168.10.0.

   A. LANs /26, WANs /30

   B. LANs /27, WANs /30

   C. LANs /28, WANs /30

   D. LANs /29, WANs /30

35. What type of VLAN membership assigns VLANs to a port when a host is attached to a switch?

   A. Cut-through

   B. Static

   C. Dynamic

   D. Administer assigned

36. What is an autonomous system between two other autonomous systems called?

   A. Transfer AS

   B. Forwarding AS

   C. Transit AS

   D. Transmitting AS

37. Which of the following can provide an encrypted Telnet session?

    A. RADIUS

    B. Kerberos

    C. TACACS+

    D. Local

38. Which of the following access lists dynamically create a reciprocal inbound access list based on outbound traffic?

    A. Standard access lists

    B. Extended access lists

    C. Dynamic access lists

    D. Reflexive access lists

    E. Enhanced access lists

39. In EIGRP, what is the next hop router on the path to a given destination prefix known as?

    A. Designated router (DR)

    B. Backup designated router (BDR)

    C. Successor

    D. Feasible successor

40. In BGP, what rule states that a router will not install a route into the BGP route table learned from an iBGP neighbor unless that route is local (a connected network) or unless that route is also learned by the router from an IGP?

    A. Next hop reachability

    B. Synchronization

    C. Next-hop-self

    D. Atomic aggregate

Answers to Assessment Test

1. B.   Link Access Procedure on the D Channel (LAPD) is used to carry ISDN signaling information over the D channel. For more information about LAPD, see Chapter 15.

2. B, E.   The Ring Parameter Server (RPS), active monitor (AM), and Ring Error Monitor (REM) functions are all valid. The Ring Purge Detector (RPD) and token generator (TG) functions are not. For more information, see Chapter 5.

3. C, D.   Class-based weighted fair queuing (CBWFQ) and low latency queuing (LLQ) are configured using MQC. Priority queuing (PQ) and custom queuing (CQ) are legacy queuing methods. For more information, see Chapter 18.

4. E.   Valid DLCIs are 16–1007. For more information, see Chapter 3.

5. B, D, E.   RIP version 2 uses 224.0.0.9, EIGRP uses 224.0.0.10, and OSPF uses both 224.0.0.5 and 224.0.0.6. For more information, see Chapter 9.

6. A.   You need two block sizes of 64 and two block sizes of 4. For the LANs, you would need /26 and the WANs are /30. See Chapter 8 for more information.

7. C.   Data Link Switching (DLSw) locally terminates the connection, preventing time-outs across the WAN. For more information, see Chapter 14.

8. A, B.   Border Gateway Protocol (BGP) should be used when connecting multiple ISPs to an autonomous system or when multihoming ISPs. See Chapter 12 for more information.

9. A.   Backward Explicit Congestion Notification (BECN) is sent against the flow of traffic. For a comparison of different WAN technologies, see Chapter 3.

10. C.   The router will choose the protocol with the lowest administrative distance. Interior Gateway Routing Protocol (IGRP) has the lowest administrative distance of 100. For more information, see Chapter 9.

11. E.   The Data Link Switching (DLSw) requesting router would send a CANUReach. The remote DLSw router would use explorer frames on the local segment to determine whether the resource is available. If it is available, the switch replies with an ICANReach message. For more information, see Chapter 14.

12. B.   The virtual MAC address will be 0000.0c07.ac01 since one isn't manually configured. The standby router will assume the virtual IP address of 200.1.1.1. Please see Chapter 22 for more information.

13. B, C.   A route filter is the most common method. However, setting the administrative distance to 255 would cause the route to be ignored. Setting the administrative distance to 0 is rarely done. For more information, see Chapter 17.

14. A.   The `ip nat inside static 10.1.3.2 200.4.2.5` command is an example of a manually configured static NAT table entry. For more information, see Chapter 10.

15. D. The command Debug ISDN Q.931 provides information about the ISDN layer 3, including information about bearer capability and channel ID. For more information about Q.931, see Chapter 15.

16. A, D. The two best commands that can be used to verify the NAT configuration are show ip nat statistics and show ip nat translation. You can also use the keyword verbose with show ip nat translation. For more information, see Chapter 10.

17. E. By default, Interior Gateway Routing Protocol (IGRP) uses only bandwidth and delay, but you can configure IGRP to use reliability and loading too. For more information, see Chapter 9.

18. A. The MAC prefix is 01-00-5E. Because the second octet is greater than 127, it is possible that the value in the high-order bit will be discarded, which leaves a binary value of 1010111 that needs to be converted to hex. In turn, that leaves 57 as the value for the fourth octet of the MAC address. For more information, see Chapter 21.

19. E. Open Shortest Path First (OSPF) demand circuits bring up the link initially, trade information, and then tear the link back down. The link will come up only when needed. Please see Chapter 15 for more information.

20. B. Hot Standby Router Protocol (HSRP) routers provide redundant default gateways to clients. For more information on workstation IP and MAC addresses used with default routers in HSRP, see Chapter 22.

21. D. The maximum-paths command is used to provide load balancing with IPX and AppleTalk network. See Chapter 13 for more information on load balancing with IPX.

22. D. Subinterfaces allow you to create multiple VCs yet configure them on one interface. See Chapter 3 for more information on VCs used with Frame Relay.

23. C. Simply add 2000 to the line numbers for async, which are 1–8 on a Cisco 2509 router. For more information, see Chapter 2.

24. A. The tftp-server command allows the routers to listen to UDP port 69 and serve the specified image to any other device, which creates a tftp session with this router. For more information on flash updates from a router, see Chapter 2.

25. B, C. Cisco Group Management Protocol (CGMP) is Cisco's proprietary version of Internet Group Management Protocol (IGMP). IBMP is not a valid protocol. The other protocols are for routing purposes and group management within a network. For more information, see Chapter 21.

26. A. An FXS port on a Cisco router provides dial tone to an analog device. For more information about interface types, see Chapter 20.

27. C. When interfacing to the emulated LAN (ELAN), the broadcast and unknown server (BUS) establishes a bidirectional connection, allowing forwarding of multicast and unknown-destination unicast frames. For more information, see Chapter 4.

28. D. An H.323 gatekeeper controls access to the network using Registration, Admission, and Status (RAS). For more information about H.323, see Chapter 20.

29. A. The direction bit in the Routing Control portion of the Routing Information Field (RIF) is set to 0, so the RIF is read left to right. In this case C410 converts to binary 1100 0100 <u>0</u>001 0000 where the bolded and underlined bit is the direction bit. For more information, see Chapter 14.

30. A. The first bit of the source MAC address will be set to 1 for a frame containing a Routing Information Field (RIF). Thus, the value of the first character will always be greater than 0x8. For more information, see Chapter 14.

31. B. The LAN Emulation Server (LES) acts as traffic control for all LAN Emulation Clients (LECs) connecting to the emulated LAN, providing the address resolution, registration, and broadcast and unknown server information that guide communication among LECs. For more information, see Chapter 4.

32. B. Even though the clients use private address space, packets with a spoofed private address will still be propagated. See Chapter 10 for more information.

33. D. Triple DES (3DES) provides 168-bit encryption. See Chapter 19 for more information.

34. C. You need four block sizes of 16 and six block sizes of 4. The LANs use /28 and the WANs /30. See Chapter 8 for more information.

35. C. Dynamic VLANs are created by an administrator on a VMPS server and then assigned dynamically to ports on a switch when a host is attached. Please see Chapter 6 for more information.

36. C. An autonomous system between two other autonomous systems is referred to as a transit AS. Traffic from one autonomous system must traverse through a transit AS to get to another autonomous system. See Chapter 12 for more information.

37. B. Kerberos can provide for encrypted logins and encrypted services such as Telnet and rsh. See Chapter 19 for more information.

38. D. Reflexive access lists monitor outbound traffic and create a corresponding inbound access list. See Chapter 16 for more information.

39. C. A successor is the next hop router on the path to a given destination prefix. Based on the feasible distance (FD), it is the forwarding path to which packets are sent for a given destination network prefix. See Chapter 9 for more information.

40. B. When synchronization is turned on, a router will not install a route learned from an internal Border Gateway Protocol (iBGP) neighbor unless that route is local (a connected network) or unless that route is also learned by the router from an IGP. See Chapter 12 for more information.

Chapter

1

Network Design and Concepts

THE CCIE QUALIFICATION EXAM TOPICS COVERED IN THIS CHAPTER INCLUDE THE FOLLOWING:

- ✓ General routing protocol concepts
- ✓ Know the OSI reference model
- ✓ Understanding hierarchical topologies
- ✓ Designing scalable networks
- ✓ Increasing fault tolerance
- ✓ Understand binary, decimal, and hexadecimal conversion

When designing networks, it is extremely important to start with a good, solid network topology. The thought you put into this initial step will determine how well your network design will perform in the future.

In this chapter, we'll discuss network topology designs that help you optimize network features. We'll teach you how to design a hierarchical topology using the Cisco three-layer model and show you how to build an internetwork that is scalable, manageable, and cost effective with improved performance. This chapter will also teach you how to build fault-tolerant internetworks and how to perform load balancing for both LANs and WANs. We will also review some of the fundamentals of networking.

Although some of the topics in this chapter may seem to be extremely basic to most readers, they are topics that will be covered in the CCIE qualification examination. Likewise, it is extremely important to have a solid foundation of the networking environment prior to discussing the higher-level technologies. For this reason, we most certainly must discuss these topics.

General Routing Concepts

First we'll discuss routing within the network environment. Keep in mind the difference between switching and routing. Switching occurs at the OSI Data-Link layer (layer 2), and routing occurs at the OSI Network layer (layer 3). Switches forward *frames* based on MAC addresses, and routers forward *packets* based on a logical layer 3 address, such as an IP address. With that said, we should note that the single topic of routing in itself is multifaceted. We'll discuss aspects such as static versus dynamic routing and briefly cover interior and exterior routing protocols. Finally, we will discuss distance vector versus link-state routing protocols.

Static vs. Dynamic Routing

Routing protocols are dynamic, meaning that they can make forwarding decisions based on changes to network topology, whereas static routes are manually configured on the routers and can only make a static forwarding decision. However, if a static route's next-hop goes down (drops out of the routing table), that static route will be removed from the routing table.

Static routing is efficient in a hub-and-spoke network, which has no redundant paths forming any type of a mesh or partial mesh topology. Dynamic routing protocols can determine the best routes to a destination network automatically. Dynamic routing protocols use metrics to make their routing decisions. Also, because dynamic routing automatically adds and deletes routes as the network topology changes, the network administration is greatly simplified.

Interior vs. Exterior Routing Protocols

Routing protocols can be divided into two separate categories: interior gateway protocols (IGPs) and exterior gateway protocols (EGPs). IGPs are used to perform routing within a single autonomous system (AS) or a single administrative network domain. EGPs are used to communicate, or route traffic, between separate autonomous systems (separate administrative network domains). Border Gateway Protocol (BGP) is the main EGP in use today, and most other routing protocols are IGPs (RTMP, RIP, IGRP, EIGRP, OSPF, IS-IS, NLSP).

Distance Vector vs. Link-State Routing Protocols

The early routing protocols were all distance vector, based on the Bellman-Ford routing algorithm. They advertise routes to destination networks based on the distance and direction required to reach the destination network. The most popular vector or metric is hop count. All routers that are configured with hopcount-based distance vector routing protocol must advertise their full routing tables to each of their neighbor routers at specified intervals (for example, every 30 seconds, 60 seconds, 90 seconds, etc.). This advertisement of the full routing table is accomplished by broadcasting the packets out every interface in the router, which results in a lot of broadcast in the network using up valuable wide area network (WAN) bandwidth.

The following are some examples of distance vector routing protocols:

- Routing Table Maintenance Protocol (RTMP)—AppleTalk
- Routing Information Protocol (RIPv1 and RIPv2)
- Interior Gateway Routing Protocol (IGRP)
- DEC DNA Phase IV

To correct some of the inefficiencies of the distance vector routing protocols, link-state routing protocols were developed. Link-state routing protocols are based on the shortest path first (SPF also known as Djikstra) algorithm. Routers running a link-state routing protocol compile information about themselves (their IP addresses, directly connected links, and the up or down status of those links). This compiled information is sent to every other router in the network, and then each router independently calculates the best path to each destination network and maintains a map or topology of the entire network. Routers will transmit a partial or incremental routing update only when and if a directly connected link to a router changes its up or down status, thus the issue with all the broadcast traffic in the network is avoided.

The following are some examples of link-state routing protocols:

- Open Shortest Path First (OSPF)
- Intermediate System-to-Intermediate System (IS-IS)
- NetWare Link Services Protocol (NLSP)
- DECnet Phase V

Now that you understand general routing protocol concepts, it is imperative that you understand the networking environment. The most important aspect of the networking environment is the OSI model, because it provides a reference by which all networking functions can be understood.

OSI Reference Model

The topic of the Open System Interconnection (OSI) model is covered in just about every networking course and book, so we will provide a quick review of the seven-layered model. The OSI model was developed by the International Organization for Standardization (ISO) in 1984 to describe the flow of data on a network. The seven layers (from bottom to top) are as follows: Physical, Data-Link, Network, Transport, Session, Presentation, and Application. You can remember the layers with the statement "Please Do Not Throw Sausage Pizza Away."

Each layer is self-contained, meaning that each layer can be implemented independently. If you run IP (layer 3), it can ride on top of various layer 2 protocols, such as Ethernet, Frame Relay, High-Level Data Link Control (HDLC), Point-to-Point Protocol (PPP), and so on. In the following sections, we'll review each layer.

Physical Layer (OSI Layer 1)

The Physical layer describes the transportation of the bits over the physical media (metallic cable, fiber, air waves). Keep in mind that the bits (1s and 0s) can be represented by either digital or analog signals. It also defines the signaling specifications, cable types, and interfaces as well as voltage levels, data rates, and maximum transmission distances. Repeaters and hubs operate in the Physical layer because they do not delineate broadcast or collision domains.

The following are some examples of the Physical layer standards:

- RJ-45
- EIA/TIA-232
- V.35

Data-Link Layer (OSI Layer 2)

The Data-Link layer provides reliable transport of the bits across the Physical layer. It formats the bits into frames for transmission. The Data-Link layer provides sequencing of frames, flow control, synchronization, and physical addressing. Bridges and layer 2 switches operate in the

Data-Link layer and make forwarding decisions based on a MAC address. The following are some examples of the Data-Link layer standards:

- Frame Relay
- Asynchronous transfer mode (ATM)
- High-level Data Link Control (HDLC)
- Ethernet
- Integrated Services Digital Network (ISDN)
- Point-to-Point Protocol (PPP)

And remember that, especially when discussing Ethernet, the Data-Link layer is divided into two sublayers for a local area network (LAN). The upper sublayer is the Logical Link Control (LLC) sublayer, which manages communications between devices. The lower sublayer is the Media Access Control (MAC) sublayer, which manages the protocol access to the physical media. Devices that operate in this layer can utilize a unique physical MAC address.

Network Layer (OSI Layer 3)

The Network layer is responsible for data forwarding and methods to determine the best forwarding path to a destination. At this layer, data is forwarded in units called packets. This layer specifies routing protocols, logical network addressing, and packet fragmentation. Routers and layer 3 switches operate at this layer and make forwarding decision based on a layer 3 address, such as an IP address. Routers and layer 3 switches both define collision and broadcast domains. As a CCIE, this is where you will really prove your worth!

The following are some examples of the Network layer standards:

- Internet Protocol (IP)
- Routing Information Protocol (RIP)
- Open Shortest Path First (OSPF)
- Internetwork Packet Exchange (IPX)

Transport Layer (OSI Layer 4)

The Transport layer provides transport of the data from the upper layers. It can provide end-to-end error checking and recovery, multiplexing, virtual circuit management, and flow control. Messages are assigned a sequence number at the transmission end. At the receiving end the packets, or segments, which are also called Transport layer protocol data units (PDUs), are reassembled and checked for errors. And when TCP is used on the Transport layer, additional functionality such as flow control is included. Flow control, which is also known as windowing, manages the data flow to ensure that the transmitting device does not send more data than the receiving device can handle. The following are some examples of the Transport layer standards:

- Transmission Control Protocol (TCP)
- User Datagram Protocol (UDP)

- Sequenced Packet Exchange (SPX)
- Real-Time Transport Protocol (RTP)

 NOTE   Real-Time Transport Protocol (RTP) is actually a special Transport layer protocol that rides on top of UDP, but it is considered a Transport layer protocol.

Session Layer (OSI Layer 5)

The Session layer provides a control structure for communication between various applications. It establishes, manages, and terminates communication connections called *sessions*. The management of these sessions involves the synchronization of dialog control by using checkpoints in the data stream.

The following are some examples of the Session layer standards:

- NetBIOS
- Session Control Protocol (SCP)
- Real-Time Control Protocol (RTCP)

Presentation Layer (OSI Layer 6)

The Presentation layer is responsible for code conversion functions. These functions ensure that data sent from one application on one device is readable by an application on another device. This is accomplished through converting the character representation formats, *data compression,* and encryption. Voice encoding schemes are also specified at this layer.

The following are some examples of the Presentation layer standards:

- ASCII
- Moving Picture Experts Group (MPEG)
- Graphics Interchange Format (GIF)
- Voice CODECs (e.g., G.711, G.729a, G.726, G.728)

Application Layer (OSI Layer 7)

The Application layer provides the user and operating system with access to the network services. This layer interacts with the software applications by identifying communication resources, determining network availability, and distributing information services. It also provides synchronization between the peer applications that reside on separate systems.

The following are some examples of the Application layer standards:

- Telnet
- File Transfer Protocol (FTP)

- Simple Mail Transfer Protocol (SMTP)
- Simple Network Management Protocol (SNMP)

Now that you understand the seven layers of the OSI model, you can conceptually rationalize the flow of data across a network environment. Next, we'll turn our attention to the many aspects of a good, reliable network design. An architect must design a solid foundation on which to build a skyscraper. A network must also be designed with a good solid foundation; if not, it will surely crumble in a matter of time.

Hierarchical Topologies

Hierarchy helps us to understand where things belong, how things fit together, and what functions go where. It brings order and understanding to otherwise complex models. If you want a pay raise, hierarchy dictates that you ask your boss, not your subordinate. The boss is the person whose role it is to grant (or deny) your request.

Hierarchy has many of the same benefits in network design that it does in other areas. When a hierarchical model is used to design a network, the network is more predictable. Using a hierarchical model, you can define the levels at which certain functions should be performed. For example, you would ask your boss, not your subordinate, for a raise because of their relative positions in the business hierarchy. Likewise, you can use tools such as access lists at certain levels in hierarchical networks and avoid them at others.

Let's face it: large networks can be extremely complicated, with multiple protocols, detailed configurations, and diverse technologies. Hierarchy helps you to summarize a complex collection of details into an understandable model. Then, as specific configurations are needed, the model dictates the appropriate manner in which to apply them.

Benefits of Hierarchical Topologies

Hierarchy can be applied to network topology in many ways, and Cisco has long encouraged using the hierarchical approach when designing the network topology. The benefits of hierarchy to network topology include improvements in the following areas:

- Scalability
- Manageability
- Performance
- Cost

We'll look at each of these in a bit more depth.

Scalability

Hierarchical networks, which are easier to scale than other models (such as a flat network model), are actually composed of many individual modules, each with a specific position within the hierarchy. Because their design is modular, expansion can often be as simple as adding new modules into the overall internetwork. A flat network model does not lend itself to future physical growth or additional segmentation of business functionality.

Manageability

Hierarchical networks are easier to manage than other types of networks because they are easier to troubleshoot. For example, anyone familiar with Ethernet will know what great fun it is to troubleshoot 10Base2 (a coaxial network infamous for poor troubleshooting avenues). If the network is down, where do you begin (assuming you lack sophisticated diagnostic tools)? You'll need more cable when installing 10BaseT, but the cost is almost always justified because troubleshooting a star network is so much easier than troubleshooting a bus network. Hierarchical networks offer similar advantages in troubleshooting. It is much simpler to isolate problems within a hierarchy than in other models, such as meshed networks. In a flat network, you have to search for issues within a single, large network, and in a hierarchical network, the large network is segmented into separate partitions, making it easier to isolate the issue.

Performance

Improvements to network performance may well justify hierarchical network design. Networks that use hierarchical design can take advantage of advanced routing features such as *route summarization,* which results in smaller routing tables and faster convergence in large networks. Fully meshed networks require larger routing tables and converge slower because of the greater number of possible paths.

Cost

In the end, overall cost is often the driving force when building networks. Due to the properties we just discussed, hierarchical networks generally require fewer administrator hours to maintain and can make more efficient use of hardware and other resources. You can anticipate hardware needs more readily than in nonhierarchical networks, which will be explained more in the next section. In addition, you can more accurately purchase and share WAN bandwidth between layers of hierarchy.

As you can see, there are many benefits of a hierarchical approach to network design as it pertains to scalability, manageability, performance, and cost. Now we'll mix things up a little bit by discussing the Cisco three-layer hierarchical model.

The Three-Layer Hierarchical Model

Just when you finally memorized all the aspects of the OSI reference model, Cisco created its own hierarchical model that you now need to learn. This model is used to help you design a scalable, reliable, cost-effective hierarchical internetwork. Cisco defines three layers of hierarchy. The Cisco three-layer hierarchical model refers to a conceptual guideline to follow in your network design; it does not refer to the network data flow, as the OSI model does. The three layers are as follows:

- Core
- Distribution
- Access

Each layer has specific responsibilities. Remember, however, that the three layers are logical and not necessarily physical. Three layers do not necessarily mean three separate devices. In the OSI model, another logical hierarchy, the seven layers describe functions but not necessarily protocols, right? Sometimes a protocol maps to more than one layer of the OSI model, and sometimes multiple protocols communicate within a single layer. In the same way, when you build physical implementations of hierarchical networks, you may have many devices in a single layer or you might have a single device performing functions at two layers. The definition of the layers is logical, not physical.

The *core layer* provides high-speed transport between locations. It provides low latency, high availability, and redundancy. No compression, access lists, or encryption should be performed at this layer because they will introduce latency.

The *distribution layer* provides route policies/filtering. It typically provides access lists, distribution lists, route summarization, security policies, compression, and encryption. Layer 3 switches can be implemented in this layer.

The *access layer* provides local and remote access to the network. This layer provides shared and switched layer 2 bandwidth, MAC filtering, and virtual local area network (VLAN) segmentation. Typically, remote access servers and virtual private network (VPN) concentrators are also implemented at this layer.

Figure 1.1 depicts a network in which the three-layer hierarchy model has been implemented.

FIGURE 1.1   A three-layered hierarchical network

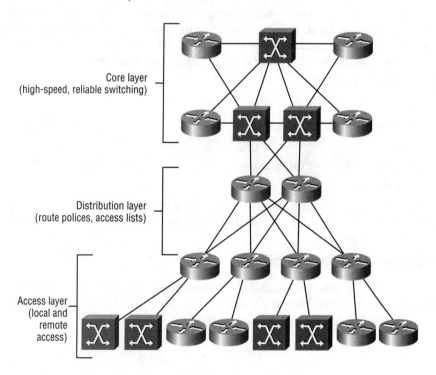

Core layer
(high-speed, reliable switching)

Distribution layer
(route polices, access lists)

Access layer
(local and
remote
access)

You should not add new routers below the access layer. To do so would expand the diameter of the network, which breaks the predictability of the topology. If you need to add new routers to support additional workgroups, they should communicate through the distribution layer and thus be peers (instead of subordinates) to the other access layer routers.

As already noted, having three separate levels does not have to imply the use of three separate routers. It could be fewer, or it could be more. Remember, this is a logical approach, and in some networks, two layers may be combined. Therefore, as in smaller networks, the core and distribution layers will probably be combined.

At this point, we have covered hierarchical topologies as they pertain to network design as well as good design characteristics to implement into your network design. But when you design a network, you also have a responsibility to take into account factors such as reliability and availability, efficiency, adaptability, and security. These are all criteria that will add value to your network design and ensure the longevity of the network.

Scalable Internetworks

Increasing demands for connectivity both in businesses and at home has led to extraordinary growth of today's internetworks, and because of this growth, it's important for internetworks to be scalable.

A scalable internetwork is continually growing, so it has to be flexible and it has to be easy to add components to it. An ideal design is based on the hierarchical model to simplify its management and to permit well-planned growth that honors the network's requirements.

Following are mandatory characteristics of a scalable internetwork:

- It's reliable and available.
- It's responsive.
- It's efficient.
- It's adaptable.
- It's easily accessible while being secure.
- It's cost effective.

But that's enough of an introduction! In the following sections, we'll discuss these topics and help you understand the role each of these functions plays in the overall network design.

Reliability and Availability

When it comes to reliability, the internetwork's core layer is the most critical. The Cisco definition of *reliable* is "an internetwork that can respond quickly to changes in the network topology and accommodate failures by rerouting traffic."

The following list includes some Cisco internetwork operating system (IOS) features that serve to provide reliability and availability:

Reachability   Open Shortest Path First (OSPF), Enhanced Interior Gateway Routing Protocol (EIGRP), and NetWare Link Services Protocol (NLSP) use expanded metrics that can go beyond the hop count limitations of distance vector routing algorithms. These routing protocols (OSPF, EIGRP, and NLSP) analyze a combination of factors to establish the real cost of a path to a network, making Cisco routers capable of supporting very large internetworks.

Convergence   Scalable routing protocols can converge quickly because of each router's complete understanding of the internetwork and ability to quickly detect problems.

Alternate paths routing   Because OSPF and EIGRP build a complete map of the internetwork, a router can dynamically reroute traffic to an alternate path if a problem occurs.

Load balancing   Through static routes and dynamic routing protocols (such as EIGRP, OSPF, RIP, etc.), the Cisco IOS is able to perform *load balancing*. This allows for redundant links and for more bandwidth to be available to locations needing more than just one link. For example, if two T1 WAN links were installed between buildings, the actual bandwidth between them would reach approximately 3 megabits per second (Mbps). In addition, this helps convergence time.

Tunneling   Running a *tunneling protocol* affords the ability to communicate across WAN links previously unreachable. For example, if you have a WAN link that supports only TCP/IP and you want to manage a Novell NetWare server that supports only IPX across it, you could tunnel IPX packets inside IP packets and achieve your goal. However, remember that this causes overhead on the router.

Dial backup   You can configure dial backup links for redundancy on your WAN links. This can also be configured as bandwidth on demand, providing extra bandwidth whenever a link becomes saturated, enhancing the link's reliability and availability as well as its performance.

Responsiveness

Because the network administrator is responsible for ensuring that users don't experience delays in responsiveness as the internetwork grows, they must be keenly aware of the latency factor that each piece of equipment (routers, switches, and bridges) contributes to the internetwork.

The Cisco IOS provides mitigation for the latency needs of each protocol running on your internetwork with various queuing techniques. We will discuss the various queuing and quality of service (QoS) techniques in Chapter 18.

Efficiency

The task of creating smoothly running, efficient LANs and internetworks is obviously important, but optimizing the bandwidth on a WAN can be difficult. The best way to reduce the bandwidth usage is to reduce the amount of update traffic on the LAN that will be sent over your WAN.

The following Cisco IOS features are available to help reduce bandwidth usage:

Access control lists (ACLs)   These are used to permit or deny certain types of traffic from entering or exiting a specific router interface. ACLs can stop basic traffic, broadcasts, and protocol updates from saturating a particular link. TCP/IP, IPX, and AppleTalk can all be filtered extensively. ACLs can also be implemented to control access to devices in the network.

Snapshot routing   Commonly used for ISDN connections when running distance vector protocols, *snapshot routing* allows routers to exchange full distance vector routing information at an interval defined by the administrator.

Compression over WANs   The Cisco IOS supports TCP/IP header and data compression to reduce the amount of traffic crossing a WAN link. You can configure link compression so that header and data information are compressed into packets. This is accomplished by the Cisco IOS prior to sending the frame across the WAN. Cisco IOS also provides PPP compression and header compression for the RTP protocol.

Dial-on-demand routing (DDR)   This allows wide area links to be used selectively. With it, the administrator can define "interesting" traffic on the router and initiate point-to-point WAN links based on that traffic. Interesting traffic is defined by access lists, so there's a great deal of flexibility afforded the administrator. For instance, an expensive ISDN connection to the Internet could be initiated to retrieve e-mail but not retrieve a web resource. DDR is an effective tool if WAN access is charged according to a quantified time interval, and it's best to use it in situations in which WAN access is infrequent.

Reduction in routing tables entries   By using route summarization and incremental updates, you can reduce the number of router processing cycles by reducing the entries in a routing table. Route summarization, which summarize all the routes advertised into one entry, occurs at major network boundaries. Incremental updates save bandwidth by sending only topology changes instead of the entire routing table when transmitting updates.

Adaptability

Another important goal for an administrator is to design an internetwork that responds well to change. To achieve this, internetworks need to be able to do the following:

- Pass both routable and nonroutable network protocols. For example, TCP/IP is routable, and Microsoft's NetBIOS Enhanced User Interface (NetBEUI) is not routable, only bridgeable.

- Create islands of networks using different protocols. This allows you to add protocols used by the network islands to core layer routers or to use tunneling in the backbone to connect the islands, thus eliminating the necessity of adding unwanted protocols to the core backbone.

- Balance multiple protocols in a network. Each protocol has different requirements, and the internetwork must be able to accommodate the specific issues of each.

The Cisco IOS also has many features that contribute to network adaptability:

EIGRP   Cisco's proprietary EIGRP allows you to use multiple protocols within one routing algorithm. EIGRP supports IP, IPX, and AppleTalk. It also allows unequal cost load balancing, which we will discuss in Chapter 9, "IP Interior Gateway Protocols."

Redistribution   This allows you to exchange routing information between networks that use different routing protocols. For example, you can update a routing table from a network running IGRP on a router participating in a RIP network.

Bridging   By using source-route bridging and integrated routing and bridging, you can integrate your older networks and protocols that do not support routing into the new internetwork.

Accessible but Secure

Access layer routers must be both accessed and used to connect to a variety of WAN services while maintaining security to keep hackers out.

The following Cisco IOS features support these requirements:

Dedicated and switched WAN support   You can create a direct connection with Cisco routers using basic or digital services (a T1, for example). Cisco routers also support many different switched services such as Frame Relay, Switched Multimegabit Data Services (SMDS), X.25, and ATM to give you options to meet cost, location, and traffic requirements.

Exterior Gateway Protocol support   Both exterior gateway protocol (EGP) and Border Gateway Protocol (BGP) are supported by the Cisco IOS. BGP, discussed in detail later in this book, is used mostly by Internet Service Providers (ISPs) and has mostly replaced EGP.

Access control lists   These are used to prevent specific kinds of traffic from either entering or leaving a Cisco router.

Authentication protocols   Cisco supports both Password Authentication Protocol (PAP) and Challenge Handshake Authentication Protocol (CHAP) for providing authentication on WAN connections using Point-to-Point Protocol (PPP).

Hopefully, you now have a better understanding of what is required for a good solid foundation in your network design, as well as some of the additional factors—such as reliability and availability, efficiency, adaptability, and security—that must also be taken into account in a good network design. Next we'll discuss fault tolerance, or assuring that a host is able to find a path to the internetwork.

Fault-Tolerant Topologies

Some networks are more important than others. Of course, *all* networks are important, right? In some situations, however, network availability (or the lack thereof) can be much more costly.

When you're designing networks, the use of many features can significantly increase fault tolerance and decrease the possibility of network outages. Perhaps you have worked with servers that included disk mirroring or Redundant Array of Inexpensive Disks (RAID) or even redundant servers. These all use one form of protection. In this section, we will discuss techniques that ensure that, first, hosts can find a path to the internetwork, and second, once they find a path, the path actually works! Remember to always keep the three-layer hierarchical model in mind and that to properly implement fault tolerance, you must consider fault tolerance at each layer of the network.

Redundant LAN Configurations

It does little good to install routers at the access level if the workstations cannot find and use them. This leads us to the issue of investigating how different workstations find routers that lead to the internetwork and how you can help those workstations find redundant paths out of the LAN. We'll consider this problem for the following protocols:

- Transmission Control Protocol/Internet Protocol (TCP/IP)

- Internetwork Packet Exchange (IPX)

- AppleTalk

Transmission Control Protocol/Internet Protocol (TCP/IP)

Most network administrators have configured a default router (or default gateway) on a host when setting up TCP/IP. This, along with configuring the IP address, the subnet mask, and perhaps the DNS server, is standard when setting up any TCP/IP device.

In Figure 1.2, Workstation A and Workstation B are assigned the default gateway of 172.16.10.1. Server A, which has two NICs, also gets a default gateway of 172.16.10.1. Workstation C, however, must be assigned a default gateway of 172.16.20.1, which is the first (and only, in this diagram) router that it sees. It cannot contact the router at 172.16.10.1 directly because they are on separate data-link networks! Once the administrator has this all mapped out, they can configure all the devices with TCP/IP information.

Some implementations of TCP/IP will allow for multiple default gateways; others provide for the workstation to listen to routing updates to learn of routers. Either method will provide the client with redundant paths out if the primary router should fail and should be considered when available. Unfortunately, the most common method of default router configuration is to statically assign the default router at the client. This means that should the router fail, there are two options: either fix the router or reconfigure the workstation. Hardly fault tolerant! We will look at two Cisco solutions to this problem: Hot Standby Router Protocol (HSRP) and proxy Address Resolution Protocol (ARP) support.

FIGURE 1.2   A sample internetwork

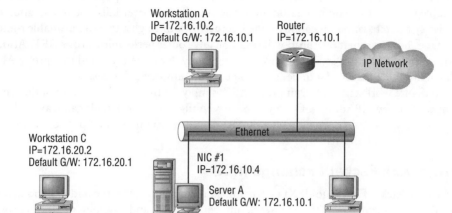

Default Gateway and HSRP

Hot Standby Router Protocol (HSRP) can allow IP devices to keep working through their default router even when that router fails. It does this by creating what Cisco calls a virtual router, or *phantom router,* on the network. This phantom router does not exist physically, but it does have a Media Access Control (MAC) address and an IP address. Workstations are configured to use the phantom router's IP address as a default gateway. The phantom addresses are actually passed among the physical routers participating in HSRP. If the physical router hosting the phantom router's MAC and IP addresses fails, another physical router automatically answers to the phantom's MAC and IP addresses and accepts the traffic. The workstations need never be aware that the hardware they are talking to has changed, and the MAC and IP addresses they have been using continue to function as if nothing had ever happened.

We will discuss HSRP and the various ways of configuring this functionality in Chapter 22, "IP Services."

Default Gateway and Proxy ARP

You can configure some IP stacks to take advantage of proxy ARP. Under normal circumstances, workstations will use the Address Resolution Protocol (ARP) to find the hardware addresses that are on their local network. When using proxy ARP, however, these workstations will send out ARP requests for *every* IP device that they want to communicate with, regardless of whether or not it is on their local network. Any router that is hearing this request and that is able to reach the desired IP address can respond to the ARP with its own MAC address. From the workstation's view, it looks like the whole world is one big LAN. The routers take care of the details of reaching remote segments. Proxy ARP is now enabled by default in all Cisco routers.

The end result is that workstations can dynamically locate redundant paths out of the LAN. When the proxy ARP request (which is a broadcast) is sent out, a response can come from any router able to reach the required destination, and thus if one router fails, the workstation can immediately begin to communicate with the internetwork through any other available routers. Understand, however, that overhead will result on any router performing proxy ARP. Also, be aware that proxy ARP is a security concern because any device can respond to a proxy ARP, which could enable that traffic to be intercepted by unauthorized devices.

To configure workstations to run proxy ARP, simply set the default gateway of the workstations to their own IP address. Once you have reconfigured your default gateway to the IP address of the workstation, try pinging a remote device. Turn on `debug ip packet` on the router and see what happens.

Internetwork Packet Exchange (IPX)

Internetwork Packet Exchange (IPX) is dynamic in the assignment of the address and default router. IPX clients can issue a "find network number" request, and any router that can provide access to the requested network answers it. If that particular router goes away, the client will automatically reissue the request. If there is a different path out, the new router will answer the client request and the client can then take advantage of the new path. Once again, it's completely dynamic.

What this means is that at the access layer, anytime you provide two paths out, AppleTalk and IPX clients will automatically find them and use them, and that increases the fault tolerance of your network. As we mentioned, if the clients cannot find paths out, the internetwork is not much use to them. IP clients are typically more challenging because they generally are not as dynamic at finding paths out as IPX or AppleTalk clients.

AppleTalk

Have you ever wondered why you don't have to play these little gateway games with Apple-Talk? The reason is that both addressing and default router configuration are dynamic with this protocol. With AppleTalk, the workstations actually listen to the Routing Table Maintenance Protocol (RTMP) routing updates. They don't build routing tables as routers do, but they do pay attention to the source AppleTalk address of the update. They then use that address as their default gateway. RTMP updates are broadcast every 10 seconds, which means that if you lose your default router on a network, workstations will take a maximum of 10 seconds to learn any redundant router address.

Redundant WAN Connections

As you have just seen, you can provide redundancy in the links between clients and servers on the LAN using several techniques. Now we will look at ways to provide redundancy inside the WAN.

Consider the network illustrated in Figure 1.3. This is a full mesh network, in which every node has a direct link to every other node. For fault tolerance, this is great, but it is far from efficient and does not scale well. Also, it has departed from the hierarchical topology we looked at earlier. There is a solution, however, that will preserve hierarchy while providing redundancy in the WAN. A full mesh is commonly used within a layer (especially the core layer); do not implement a full mesh between layers.

FIGURE 1.3   A full mesh network

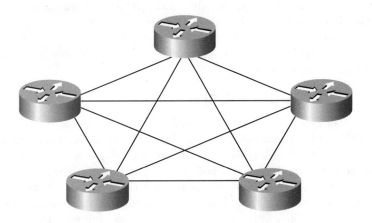

Partial Mesh Topology

We have implemented a partial mesh in the network shown in Figure 1.4. Notice that we have preserved our hierarchy, yet each node has a redundant link to the layer above it. This design provides all the advantages of hierarchical design, is scalable, and can take advantage of load balancing.

FIGURE 1.4   Redundant hierarchical network

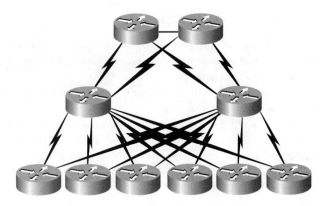

You can add the additional WAN connections in several ways. You could add them in identical pairs—that is, you could install two T1 lines rather than one. This provides the ultimate in redundancy. If one T1 fails, another is waiting to go. From a cost perspective, however, this can be similar to buying two new cars just in case one gets a flat tire. True, you will probably never have to walk to work, but that security will certainly cost you.

An alternative to identical connections to the next layer is using links that are not the same, that is, perhaps a T1 and a 56Kbps backup line. Should the primary line fail, internetwork connectivity can be preserved, although generally at a reduced level. Once again, cost will most likely determine the capacity of the backup line.

Cisco has a solution that is similar to this second example, in which the two connections are not the same. In this case, the second, or backup, line is not even running until the primary line fails! We will look at this solution next.

Dial-on-Demand Routing (DDR) Backup

Not all redundant links have to be dedicated lines. In many cases, an ISDN Basic Rate Interface (BRI) is used to back up a dedicated leased line. This can be a great advantage because you will probably not want to bring the ISDN up unless the primary line fails (or becomes overloaded). Cisco's DDR allows this configuration. The ISDN line can be configured to become active only when the primary line either fails or is under heavy load. Of course, should the primary line fail and you have to depend on your backup, you will likely not have your normal bandwidth available. You will, however, likely be paying significantly less than you would to have a pair of dedicated lines.

We will discuss the various configurations and functionality of DDR in Chapter 15, "Integrated Services Digital Network (ISDN) and Dial Backup."

As you just saw, you can provide redundancy inside the WAN environment by using both redundant links or circuits and DDR. Both of these functions come with a financial cost to you, so you will most likely want to assure the best possible return on investment (ROI). To do so, you will want to use all the bandwidth that you are paying for, which brings us to the topic of load balancing.

Performance: Load Balancing

Redundant links are not cheap to operate, but they are called for in some situations. If you are going to pay for redundant links, you would likely want to use both lines when they are both available, and that involves load balancing.

A good design rule is to keep bandwidth consistent within a layer of hierarchy whenever possible and to use technologies such as DDR when it's not possible to purchase equal links.

In the following sections, we'll discuss various methods of utilizing load balancing in the WAN environment with three different protocols: Internet Protocol (IP), Internetwork Packet Exchange (IPX), and AppleTalk.

Load Balancing with Internet Protocol (IP)

With most IP routing protocols, load balancing is automatic. Dynamic routing protocols are supposed to find the redundant paths, and dynamic IP routing protocols will use both available paths. This is not, however, always be a good thing.

Some routing protocols (for example, those that use hop count) could see these two paths and load-balance across them just fine until the 56Kbps line is full. At that point, the traffic is equally balanced. These protocols, however, are not smart enough to realize that more than 90 percent of the total bandwidth is going unused on the T1! Once any link is operating at capacity, these routing protocols are not capable of sending additional traffic across links still not at capacity because they do not understand capacity as a metric. This problem is called pinhole congestion, and you can avoid it by using advanced routing protocols such as EIGRP.

Load Balancing with Internetwork Packet Exchange (IPX)

By default, IPX will not load-balance across multiple links; however, Cisco provides a way to enable IPX load balancing. You can use the `ipx maximum-paths` command, which specifies a number of links to load-balance across. We will discuss this command when we cover the IPX protocol later on in this book.

Load Balancing with AppleTalk

AppleTalk, like IPX, considers only one path to a remote network. You can set the number of parallel routing paths that can be used by AppleTalk by using the `appletalk maximum-paths` command. Remember to set this on all your routers, not just one router.

We've been discussing various methods of utilizing load balancing in the WAN environment. Fault tolerance is also needed in the multiaccess or LAN environment.

Fault Tolerance on Multiaccess Segments

LAN segments are very reliable when compared with their wide area counterparts. However, failure occurs on LANs as well, making fault tolerance an important issue. The most well-known fault tolerance mechanisms on a LAN are the dual rings encountered in Fiber Distributed Data Interface (FDDI) networks, where upon primary ring failure, a secondary backup fiber link will automatically take over, and the Spanning-Tree Protocol (STP) encountered in Ethernet networks, where upon a path failure, a redundant path can automatically take over.

In this section, you will also learn about fault tolerance methods that occur at the Data-Link and Network layers of the OSI reference model. We'll look at the following two types of fault tolerance:

- Internet Control Message Protocol (ICMP) redirects
- Proxy Address Resolution Protocol (proxy ARP)

Internet Control Message Protocol (ICMP) Redirects

The Internet Control Message Protocol (ICMP) is used primarily for error handling and testing; however, one of the processes it uses can provide fault tolerance. Here's how this type of fault tolerance works: When a packet is received by a router on a particular interface and the destination for the packet is outside that interface, an ICMP redirect tells the sender of that packet to send the packet to a different router. The sender should then update its local routing table so that further packets are sent directly to the correct address.

Proxy ARP

Proxy Address Resolution Protocol (proxy ARP) is a variation on the ARP protocol in which an intermediate device, such as a router, sends an ARP response on behalf of an end node to the requesting host. Proxy ARP has been defined and referenced in many Requests for Comments (RFCs). This technology once had a strong following, and one of the benefits is that it can reduce bandwidth usage on slow-speed WAN links. As networks grew, however, proxy ARP did not scale with them.

Enabling Proxy ARP on Cisco Routers

By default, proxy ARP is enabled on Cisco routers, as displayed in the results of the following show ip interface command:

```
RouterA#show ip interface ethernet 0
Ethernet0 is up, line protocol is up
  Internet address is 10.1.0.1/16
  Broadcast address is 255.255.255.255
  Address determined by setup command
  MTU is 1500 bytes
  Helper address is not set
  Directed broadcast forwarding is disabled
  Multicast reserved groups joined: 224.0.0.9
  Outgoing access list is not set
  Inbound  access list is not set
  Proxy ARP is enabled
  Security level is default
  Split horizon is enabled
  ICMP redirects are always sent
  ICMP unreachables are always sent
  ICMP mask replies are never sent
  IP fast switching is enabled
  IP fast switching on the same interface is disabled
  IP Null turbo vector
  IP multicast fast switching is disabled
  IP multicast distributed fast switching is disabled
  Router Discovery is disabled
  IP output packet accounting is disabled
```

```
    IP access violation accounting is disabled
    TCP/IP header compression is disabled
    Probe proxy name replies are disabled
    Policy routing is disabled
    Network address translation is disabled
    Web Cache Redirect is disabled
    BGP Policy Mapping is disabled
RouterA#
```

Disabling Proxy ARP on Cisco Routers

To disable Proxy ARP on a Cisco router, use the no ip proxy-arp command, as follows:

```
RouterA(config)#interface ethernet 0
RouterA(config-if)#no ip proxy-arp
RouterA(config-if)#^Z
RouterA#
```

Most Cisco routers default to a four-hour ARP time-out.

The Advantages and Disadvantages of Proxy ARP

Proxy ARP has the following advantages:

- Simple configuration, no need to configure clients with gateway
- Load balancing, although it's somewhat random
- Immediate fault tolerance, if addresses have not been recently contacted

    Using proxy ARP involves the following disadvantages:

- Creation of a lot of broadcast traffic
- Waiting for ARP cache on the workstation to time out in event of failure
- Lack of control over which router is primary and which is secondary

    Proxy ARP does provide some fault tolerance on a multiaccess segment, but it does not give the level of control that most administrators want. A more robust and flexible method is needed. In response to this need, Cisco developed the Hot Standby Router Protocol (HSRP). We will discuss HSRP in Chapter 22.

    Now let's shift gears and discuss the basic aspect of networking, We're of course referring to the 1s and 0s and how they represent data information.

Binary, Decimal, Hexadecimal Conversion

As a CCIE candidate, you must know how to perform conversions between decimal, binary, and hexadecimal numbers. This is the aspect of networking that is most important for you to thoroughly understand. The digital world comprises bits of information represented by a series of 1s and 0s, and if you are going to exist in this digital world, you must understand how the 1s and 0s are able to represent bits of information. A numbering system that uses 1s and 0s is known as a binary system, meaning that two states exist: a 1 or a 0. Now to make it easier to understand 1s and 0s, we represent them as either decimal or hexadecimal values. Because of this, it is imperative that you know how to convert binary to decimal and then to hexadecimal.

The decimal numeric system is based on 10 digits, 0 through 9. After 9, you use 2 digits starting at 10 and then cycle the rightmost digit from 0 to 9 again. At this point, the left digit is incremented to the next higher value; thus, after 19 comes 20.

The binary number system uses two digits, a 0 and a 1. Binary numbers are the language of computer systems. IP addresses and MAC addresses are represented by binary numbers. Each digit (0 or 1) is a *bit,* thus the binary number 10110110 is a binary number with 8 bits. An IP (version 4) address comprises 32 bits, and a MAC address comprises 48 bits. IP addresses are usually displayed in a dotted decimal format, meaning that each 8-bit number is represented as a decimal number. Likewise, a MAC address is displayed in hexadecimal format, meaning that it takes two hexadecimal characters to represent the original 8-bit number.

Binary to Decimal Conversion

To convert a binary number to decimal, multiply each digit by a power of 2. Each digit, or bit, has a decimal equivalent of from 1 to 128 (reading right to left), which is based on the location of the bit in the binary number. This is similar to converting decimal numbers based on 1s, 10s, 100s, and so on. In decimal format, the number 111 is 100+10+1. In binary format, the number 11111111 is the sum of 128+64+32+16+8+4+2+1, or 255. For the binary 8 bits 10110110, the result of the conversion is 128+0+32+16+0+4+2+0=182.

Figure 1.5 an X is used to represent the 8 bits within the binary word. Notice that, starting from the right to left, each digit is multiplied by 2 (1, 2, 4, 8, 16, 32, 64, and 128). The number is the value that the digit position holds. A 1 means that you use that digit position value, and a 0 means that you do not use that digit position value. So, if you add up the digit values with a 1, you will get 128+32+16+4+2=182.

FIGURE 1.5   Binary to decimal conversion

```
Digit position value ───────▶    128  64  32  16   8   4   2   1

                                  X   X   X   X   X   X   X   X

Binary value for the ───────▶      1   0   1   1   0   1   1   0
decimal number 182

                                 128 + 32 + 16 + 4 + 2 = 182
```

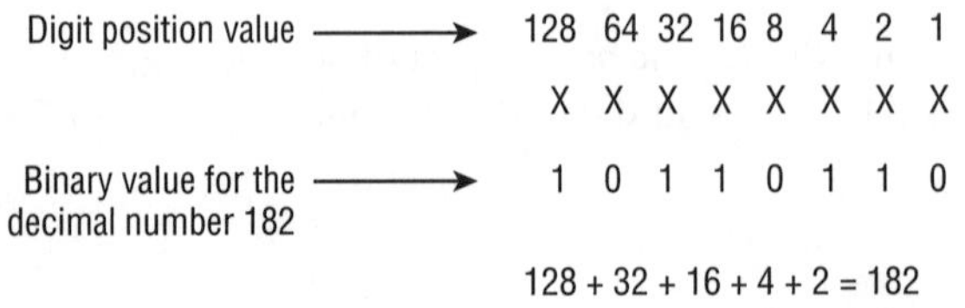

To convert decimal to binary, you simply need to figure out which digit position values are needed, so that when the values are added up, they equal the required decimal number.

Memorize 1, 2, 4, 8, 16, 32, 64, and 128. Use this as you read a binary number from right to left. It should be helpful in converting faster.

Binary to Hexadecimal Conversion

To convert a binary number to its hexadecimal equivalent, you must first divide the 8 bits of the binary word into two *nibbles* of 4 bits each. This is because with hexadecimal representation, there is only 16 possible values for the 4 bits to represent (0 through 15), thus each of the four digit positions represents a value the same as it does in the binary world. In hexadecimal format, the number 1111 is the sum of 8+4+2+1, or 15. For the binary 4 bits 0110, the result of the conversion is 0+4+2+0=6. So, the binary 8 bits of 01100111 become two nibbles of 0110 and 0111. The first nibble, 0110, is equal to 6, and the second nibble, 0111, is equal to 7 (0+4+2+1=7), thus the hexadecimal equivalent of the 8 binary bits is 67.

This all works well until the total value reaches from 10 through 15 because you only have one digit to represent the nibble (4-bit value). When this happens, you can perform the conversion by switching to letters after the number 9, thus the number 10 equals *A*, and the number 11 equals *B*, and so on until the highest possible number, 15, which equals *F*.

In Figure 1.6, we show the decimal numbers 0 through 15 with their binary and hexadecimal equivalents.

FIGURE 1.6   Decimal to binary to hexadecimal conversion

Decimal	Binary	Hex
0	0000	0
1	0001	1
2	0010	2
3	0011	3
4	0100	4
5	0101	5
6	0110	6
7	0111	7
8	1000	8
9	1001	9
10	1010	A
11	1011	B
12	1100	C
13	1101	D
14	1110	E
15	1111	F

A decimal number of **182** equals a binary number of **10110110**. This binary number can be broken into two nibbles: 1011 and 0110.

Here's how to convert the binary into hexadecimal:
1011=11=**B**
0110=6=**6**

Therefore, the decimal number 182 equals the hexadecimal value **B6**.

The hexadecimal format is used with MAC addressing, IPX addressing, and token ring addressing. It is common to represent a hexadecimal number with 0x before the number so that it is not confused with a decimal number. The hexadecimal number 16 is written as 0x10, not 10. It is also common to use the term *hex* when referring to hexadecimal.

We will discuss how to convert binary to decimal and to hexadecimal further in Chapter 8, "IP Addressing, and Subnetting," when we actually discuss the IP version 4 (IPv4) as well as the new IP version 6 (IPv6) standard.

Summary

A good network topology design makes it much easier to design and deploy network applications that run over the top of the network. Cisco recommends using a hierarchical design, which offers many benefits, including predictability, scalability, efficiency, cost control, and security.

Further, Cisco recommends that medium to large businesses use a three-layered hierarchical model consisting of core, distribution, and access layers. Each layer has clearly defined functions, and once the network is established, it can scale significantly before it needs to be reengineered.

Topologies that enhance network fault tolerance are often required. IPX and AppleTalk dynamically find their gateways to the internetwork, but IP features such as HSRP and proxy ARP can improve fault tolerance in workstation-to-router communication. Redundant WAN links can provide additional fault tolerance and can be used inside hierarchical designs. Technologies such as DDR provide for backup links. When redundant links are used, design consideration should be given to load balancing. You should also identify and avoid issues such as pinhole congestion.

In this chapter, we discussed decimal to binary to hexadecimal conversion. We also reviewed the basic features of the Cisco internetwork operating system (IOS). It is important that you have a firm understanding of the basics offered in this chapter before you move on to the other chapters in this book.

Exam Essentials

Understand the difference between static routing and dynamic routing.   Static routing is efficient in a hub-and-spoke network that has no redundant paths forming any type of a mesh or partial mesh topology. However, static routes must be manually configured. Dynamic routing protocols can determine the best routes to a destination network automatically. Dynamic routing protocols use metrics to make their routing decisions.

Know the seven layers of the OSI model.   The seven layers (from bottom to top) are as follows: Physical, Data-Link, Network, Transport, Session, Presentation, and Application. You can remember the layers with the statement "Please Do Not Throw Sausage Pizza Away."

Know the benefits of the hierarchical network model.   The benefits of hierarchy to network topology include improvements to scalability, manageability, performance and cost.

Know the three layers of the Cisco three-layer hierarchical model   Cisco defines three layers of hierarchy: core, distribution, and access.

Understand binary to decimal conversion.   To convert a binary number to decimal, multiply each digit by a power of 2. Each digit, or bit, has a decimal equivalent of from 1 to 128 (reading right to left), which is based on the location of the bit of the binary number. This is similar to decimal numbers based on 1s, 10s, 100s, and so on. In decimal format, the number 111 is 100+10+1. In binary format, the number 11111111 is the sum of 128+64+32+16+8+4+2+1, or 255.

Key Terms

Before you take the exam, be certain you are familiar with the following terms:

access layer	nibbles
bit	packets
core layer	phantom router
data compression	route summarization
distribution layer	sessions
frames	snapshot routing
hierarchy	tunneling protocol
load balancing	

Review Questions

1. Which of the following are advantages of hierarchical design?
    A. Fault tolerance
    B. Scalability
    C. Ease of management
    D. Predictability
    E. All the above

2. Which of the following are layers in Cisco's three-layer hierarchical design? (Choose all that apply.)
    A. Backbone
    B. Core
    C. End node
    D. Access
    E. Distribution

3. Which of the following should be included at the core layer? (Choose all that apply.)
    A. Packet filtering
    B. Firewalling
    C. Fast throughput
    D. Fault tolerance
    E. Additional devices

4. How many layers of hierarchy should you add below the access layer?
    A. None
    B. One
    C. Two
    D. Three
    E. Four

5. Which of the following are recommended at the distribution layer? (Choose all that apply.)
    A. Packet filtering
    B. Access lists
    C. Queuing
    D. Redundant WAN connections
    E. Firewalls

6. Which of the following protocols allow for dynamic location of default routers? (Choose all that apply.)

    A. IP

    B. IPX

    C. AppleTalk

    D. NetBEUI

7. Which of the following methods will allow IP workstations to locate routers dynamically? (Choose all that apply.)

    A. HSRP

    B. Workstation listening to routing protocols

    C. Proxy ARP

    D. RTMP

8. You need to add a new site to your hierarchical network. Which of the following are possible places to connect the new site into your existing network? (Choose all that apply.)

    A. Access layer

    B. Distribution layer

    C. Core layer

    D. Backbone

9. What is the hexadecimal equivalent of decimal 182?

    A. 67

    B. 92

    C. B6

    D. 1A

10. You have a T1 link from an access layer router to a distribution layer router, and you have a BRI DDR connection to another distribution layer router. The DDR is configured to run in case of failure. Which of the following do you have?

    A. Proxy ARP

    B. Fault tolerance

    C. Load balancing

    D. HSRP

    E. None of the above

Answers to Review Questions

1. E.   Hierarchical design provides fault tolerance, scalability, manageability, and predictability.

2. B, D, E. The three layers of the Cisco hierarchical model are core, distribution, and access.

3. C, D. The core layer should not do anything to hinder packet flow through the network. It should provide fast throughput and fault tolerance.

4. A. No network should be installed below the access layer.

5. A, B, C, D, E. Access lists, queuing, redundancy, and firewalls should be used in the distribution layer.

6. A, B, C. IP, IPX and Appletalk protocols all allow clients to locate gateways dynamically. NetBEUI is not a routable protocol.

7. A, B, C. HSRP, dynamic routing protocols, and proxy ARP can be used to allow IP hosts to find and use alternate default gateways.

8. B, C. If the new site might be a future hub, it can be connected directly to the core. It should never be connected through the access layer.

9. C. Decimal 182 equals the binary equivalent of 10110110, which becomes the two nibbles 1011 and 0110. So, 1011=B, and 0110=6.

10. B. ISDN BRI can provide backup in case of failure.

Chapter 2

Configuration and IOS Commands

THE CCIE QUALIFICATION EXAM TOPICS COVERED IN THIS CHAPTER INCLUDE THE FOLLOWING:

- ✓ Understand how the CLI is used to configure Cisco routers
- ✓ Create and verify passwords using the Cisco CLI
- ✓ Configure the router interfaces using the Cisco CLI
- ✓ Create and verify banners using the Cisco CLI
- ✓ Understand the configuration register settings
- ✓ Perform password recovery techniques
- ✓ Accessing the device with reverse Telnet

In this chapter, we will discuss various IOS commands and their functionality. The material presented in this chapter is extremely relevant to the CCIE qualification exam; however, you must know how to use and apply this information thoroughly for the CCIE lab exam as well. It's essential that you know how to use the CLI to perform certain tasks, and we'll cover them thoroughly in this chapter.

Cisco Router User Interface

The Cisco Internetwork Operating System (IOS) is the heart and soul of Cisco routers and most Cisco switches. In the following sections, we'll take a look at some different routers and how they are configured using the command-line interface (CLI).

Cisco Router IOS

When you first bring up a Cisco router, it will look for and load the first Cisco IOS in flash memory if a file is present. The IOS will load and then look for a valid configuration called startup-config that is stored by default in *nonvolatile RAM (NVRAM)*. The type of Central Processing Unit (CPU), the amount of random access memory (RAM) and flash memory and NVRAM, the router operational uptime, installed interfaces, the current running IOS image, and so on can all be verified with the show version or show hardware command:

```
Router#show version
Cisco Internetwork Operating System Software
IOS (tm) 2500 Software (C2500-JS-L), Version 12.0(8), RELEASE SOFTWARE (fc1)
Copyright (c) 1986-1999 by cisco Systems, Inc.
Compiled Mon 29-Nov-99 14:52 by kpma
Image text-base: 0x03051C3C, data-base: 0x00001000

ROM: System Bootstrap, Version 11.0(10c), SOFTWARE
BOOTFLASH: 3000 Bootstrap Software (IGS-BOOT-R), Version 11.0(10c), RELEASE
```

```
SOFTWARE (fc1)

RouterA uptime is 5 minutes
System restarted by power-on
System image file is "flash:c2500-js-l_120-8.bin"

cisco 2522 (68030) processor (revision N) with 14336K/2048K bytes of memory.
Processor board ID 15662842, with hardware revision 00000003
Bridging software.
X.25 software, Version 3.0.0.
SuperLAT software (copyright 1990 by Meridian Technology Corp).
TN3270 Emulation software.
Basic Rate ISDN software, Version 1.1.
1 Ethernet/IEEE 802.3 interface(s)
2 Serial network interface(s)
8 Low-speed serial(sync/async) network interface(s)
1 ISDN Basic Rate interface(s)
32K bytes of non-volatile configuration memory.
16384K bytes of processor board System flash (Read ONLY)
Configuration register is 0x2102
```

Notice that this router has 14336K/2048K bytes of memory installed (14336K is processor memory and 2048K is I/O memory) and that the total system memory is the sum of these two (16384K). Some configurations require adjustment of the processor and I/O memory ratios depending on the number and type of interfaces installed (more I/O memory required) or if you have large images installed (more processor memory required); the adjustments are made using the memory-size iomem command. Also, this router has 16384K of flash memory and 32K of NVRAM.

If there is no configuration in NVRAM, then the router will first attempt AutoInstall, and if not configured on the back end, it will eventually fault and then bring up what is called setup mode. This is a step-by-step process to help you configure a router for the first time if you are just getting started with Cisco routers. You can also enter setup mode by typing the command setup from global configuration mode. Setup only covers some very global commands, but it will help you if you don't know how to configure certain protocols like bridging or DECnet, for example. Next we'll take a look at the most powerful way to configure Cisco routers, and that is with the CLI.

Command Line Interface (CLI)

The command-line interface (CLI) is really the best way to configure a router because it gives you the most flexibility.

To use the CLI, just answer no when asked if you want to enter the initial configuration dialog. The router will come back with messages that display the status of all the router interfaces:

```
Would you like to enter the initial configuration dialog? [yes]: no
Would you like to terminate autoinstall? [yes]:<press Enter key>


Press RETURN to get started!


00:00:42: %LINK-3-UPDOWN: Interface Ethernet0, changed state to up
00:00:42: %LINK-3-UPDOWN: Interface Serial0, changed state to down
00:00:42: %LINK-3-UPDOWN: Interface Serial1, changed state to down
00:00:42: %LINEPROTO-5-UPDOWN: Line protocol on Interface
Ethernet0, changed state to up
00:00:42: %LINEPROTO-5-UPDOWN: Line protocol on Interface
Serial0, changed state to down
00:00:42: %LINEPROTO-5-UPDOWN: Line protocol on Interface
Serial1, changed state to down
00:01:30: %LINEPROTO-5-UPDOWN: Line protocol on Interface
Ethernet0, changed state to down
00:01:31: %LINK-5-CHANGED: Interface Serial0, changed state
to administrativelydown
00:01:31: %LINK-5-CHANGED: Interface Ethernet0, changed state
to administratively down
00:01:31: %LINK-5-CHANGED: Interface Serial1, changed state
to administratively down
00:01:32: %IP-5-WEBINST_KILL: Terminating DNS process
00:01:38: %SYS-5-RESTART: System restarted --
Cisco Internetwork Operating System Software
IOS (tm) 2500 Software (C2500-DS-L), Version 11.3(9), RELEASE SOFTWARE (fc1)
Copyright (c) 1986-1999 by cisco Systems, Inc.
Compiled Tue 06-Apr-99 19:23 by dschwart
```

Logging into the Router

Press <Enter> after the messages and the Router> prompt will appear. You are now in exec mode, which is mostly used to view statistics. Exec mode is a basic, restricted mode that is a stepping stone to logging into enable mode, which provides access to all commands in Cisco IOS and allows you to perform all operations possible (enable mode is the Cisco equivalent to the root or administrator). You can only view and change the configuration of a Cisco router in enable mode, which you enter with the command `enable`:

```
Router>
Router>enable
Router#
```

You end up with a `Router#` prompt, which indicates that you are in enable mode. You can now both view and change the configuration. You can go back to exec mode from enable mode by using the `disable` command:

```
Router#disable
Router>
```

At this point, you can type `logout` to exit the console, or you could just type `logout`, `exit`, or ^Z (Ctrl+Z) from the enable mode prompt in order to log out:

```
Router>logout

Router con0 is now available
Press RETURN to get started.

Router>enable
Router#logout

Router con0 is now available
Press RETURN to get started.
```

Overview of Router Modes

You can make global changes to the router from a CLI by typing `configure terminal` (`config t` for short), which puts you in global configuration mode and changes what is known as the running-config. You can type `config` from the enable mode prompt and then press <Enter> to take the default of terminal, as follows:

```
Router#config
Configuring from terminal, memory, or network [terminal]?<Return>
Enter configuration commands, one per line.  End with CNTL/Z.
Router(config)#
```

At this point you can make changes that affect the router. This is known as the global configuration mode, which is used to configure features that apply globally to the router as a whole.

To make changes to an interface, you use the `interface` command from global configuration mode, as in the following:

```
Router(config)#interface ?
  Async            Async interface
  Dialer           Dialer interface
  FastEthernet     FastEthernet IEEE 802.3
  Group-Async      Async Group interface
  Lex              Lex interface
  Loopback         Loopback interface
  Null             Null interface
Router(config)#interface fastEthernet 0/0
Router(config-if)#
```

Notice the prompt changed to `Router(config-if)#` to tell you that you are in interface configuration mode.

There are also subinterfaces, which allow you to create virtual interfaces within the router. In subinterface configuration mode, the prompt changes to `Router(config-subif)#`:

```
Router(config)#interface fastethernet0/0.?
  <0-4294967295>  FastEthernet interface number
Router(config)#interface fastethernet0/0.1
Router(config-subif)#
```

To configure user access to a device (like setting exec mode passwords), you use the `line` command to enter `line` configuration mode. The prompt then becomes `Router (config-line)#`. Lines are used to provide connectivity to a device, such as Telnet (vty), asynchronous (TTY), console port (CON), and auxiliary port (AUX):

```
Router#config t
Enter configuration commands, one per line.  End with CNTL/Z.
Router(config)#line ?
  <0-70>   First Line number
  aux      Auxiliary line
  console  Primary terminal line
  tty      Terminal controller
  vty      Virtual terminal

Router(config)#line console 0
Router(config-line)#
```

The `line console 0` command is known as a major or global command, and any command typed from the `(config-line)` prompt is known as a subcommand.

It is not important that you understand what each of these commands do at this time. These will all be explained later in great detail. What is important here is that you are familiar with the prompts that are available.

Editing and Help Features

You can use the Cisco advanced editing features to help you configure your router. By typing a question mark (?) at any prompt, you can see the list of commands that are available from that prompt:

```
Router#?
Exec commands:
  access-enable    Create a temporary Access-List entry
  access-profile   Apply user-profile to interface
  access-template  Create a temporary Access-List entry
  bfe              For manual emergency modes setting
  clear            Reset functions
  clock            Manage the system clock
  configure        Enter configuration mode
  connect          Open a terminal connection
  copy             Copy configuration or image data
  debug            Debugging functions (see also 'undebug')
  disable          Turn off privileged commands
 --More-
```

At this point, you can press the spacebar to get another page of information or press <Enter> to display one command at a time. You can also press any other key to quit and return to the prompt.

To find commands that start with a certain letter, use the letter and the question mark (?) with no space between them, like this:

```
Router#c?
clear  clock  configure  connect  copy
```

In this example, typing c? displays all the commands that start with *c*. Also notice that the Router# prompt appeared with the command still present. This is helpful when you have long commands and need the next possible one—as opposed to retyping the entire list every time you use a question mark!

To find the next command in a string, type the first command and then a question mark:

```
Router#clock ?
  set  Set the time and date

Router#clock set ?
  hh:mm:ss  Current Time

Router#clock set 10:30:10 ?
  <1-31>  Day of the month
  MONTH    Month of the year
Router#clock set 10:30:10 28 ?
  MONTH  Month of the year
Router#clock set 10:30:10 28 jan ?
  <1993-2035>  Year
Router#clock set 10:30:10 28 jan 2000 ?
  <cr>
Router#
```

By typing the command clock followed by a space and then a question mark, you will get a list of the next possible commands and what they do. Notice that you just continue to type a command, a space, and then a question mark until <cr> (carriage return) is your only option. If you are typing commands and receive this message, then you know that the command is not complete:

```
Router#clock set 10:30:10
% Incomplete command.
```

Just press the Up arrow key to receive the last command entered and continue by using the question mark.

Also, you may receive an error message like the following:

```
Router(config)#access-list 110 permit host 1.1.1.1
                                           ^
% Invalid input detected at '^' marker.
```

Notice that the caret symbol (^) marks the point where you have entered the command incorrectly. This can be very helpful. Press the up arrow key and use a question mark at the ^ to get your options.

If you receive the following error message, it means you did not enter all of the keywords or values required by this command:

```
Router#show te
% Ambiguous command:  "sh te"
```

Use the question mark to find the command you need:

```
Router#show te?
WORD  tech-support  terminal
```

An editing feature we need to mention is the automatic wrapping of long lines. In the following example, the command as typed had reached the right margin and automatically moved 10 spaces to the left. The dollar ($) sign indicates that the line has wrapped to the left:

```
Router#config t
Enter configuration commands, one per line.  End with CNTL/Z.
Router(config)#$ 110 permit host 171.10.10.10 0.0.0.0 host
```

Setting the Passwords

There are two types of passwords used to secure your Cisco router: enable passwords and line passwords. Enable passwords are used to control access to enable mode. Line passwords are used to control access to exec mode. An enable password can be configured with either the enable password or enable secret command. Either of these will prompt a user for a password when the command enable is used.

You set the enable passwords from global configuration mode:

```
Router(config)#enable ?
  password      Assign the privileged level password
  secret        Assign the privileged level secret
```

password   This command is used to set the enable password in plain text (required on older, pre-10.3 systems). This password will be ignored if an enable secret is set.

secret   This command will store a hash of the enable password. It overrides the enable password if set.

If you try to use the same password for enable secret and enable password, you'll get a nice, polite warning that this would be a security risk, but the password will be accepted anyway

```
Router(config)#enable secret kelly
Router(config)#enable password kelly
The enable password you have chosen is the same as your enable secret.
```

```
This is not recommended.  Re-enter the enable password.
```

Even though the enable secret password will override the enable password, it won't provide any protection if a wannabe hacker can guess the enable secret from the plaintext enable password. It is recommended that you use different enable and enable secret passwords, or you use only an enable secret password (if IOS permits).

 You can protect your enable password and other line passwords by using the `service-password encryption` command; however even in the encrypted format, these passwords are easily cracked using tools freely available on the Internet. The enable secret command password uses a secure hashing algorithm called Message Digest 5 (MD5), which is much much harder to break, but it's still vulnerable to dictionary attacks (in which an attacker tries common dictionary words in an attempt to guess the enable secret). When using enable secret, make sure you use strong passwords that are not vulnerable to dictionary attacks (for example, use a combination of letters, numbers, and symbols that are long and difficult to guess).

Exec mode passwords can be assigned after entering `line` configuration mode:

```
Router(config)#line ?
  <0-4>    First Line number
  aux      Auxiliary line
  console  Primary terminal line
  vty      Virtual terminal
```

There are three types of ports one can configure:

Aux   This is used to enter config-line mode for the auxiliary port. This is typically used for configuring a modem on the router, but it can be used as a console as well.

Console   This is used to enter config-line mode for the console port.

Vty   This is used to enter config-line mode for the vty ports. Vty ports are virtual ports that can terminate telnet and other connectivity. With default configuration, telnet (and other vty connectivity) if the password is not set.

 An enable password must also be set if you wish to gain enable mode access from a Telnet session.

To configure the exec mode passwords, you configure the line you want and use either the `login` or `no login` command to tell the router to prompt for authentication.

> **Timesaving Tip**
>
> You can use the no `login` and `privilege level 15` commands to allow you to telnet to a router and immediately gain enable mode access:
>
> ```
> line vty 0 4
> no login
> privilege level 15
> exec-timeout 0 0
> ```
>
> The `exec-timeout 0 0` command means the Telnet session will never time out. Never use this technique in the real world, only in the lab examination.

Auxiliary Password

The auxiliary port (line) can be used for alternate user access to a device, such as connecting an external analog dial-up modem for out-of-band management/recovery capabilities. To configure the auxiliary password, go to global configuration mode and type the `line aux ?` command. Notice that you only get a choice of 0-0 because there is only one port:

```
Router#config t
Enter configuration commands, one per line.  End with CNTL/Z.
Router(config)#line aux ?
  <0-0>  First Line number
Router(config)#line aux 0
Router(config-line)#login
Router(config-line)#password josh
```

It is important to remember the `login` command or the auxiliary port won't prompt for authentication. Also, if you use the `login` command and do not issue a password, then the aux port will disallow any sessions. If you try to log on as a user with no password set, the router will respond with `Password required, but none set.` and terminate the session.

Console Password

To set the console password, use the command `line console 0`. However, notice that when we tried to type `line console 0` from the AUX line configuration, we got an error. You can still type `line console 0` and the router will accept it; however, the help screens do not work from that prompt. Type `exit` to get back one level, as follows:

```
Router(config-line)#line console ?
% Unrecognized command
```

```
Router(config-line)#exit
Router(config)#line console ?
  <0-0>  First Line number
Router(config)#line console 0
Router(config-line)#login
Router(config-line)#password chris
```

Because there is only one console port, we can only choose line console 0.

There are a few other important commands to know with regard to the console port:

```
Router(config)#line con 0
Router(config-line)#exec-timeout 0 0
Router(config-line)#logging synchronous
```

The exec-timeout 0 0 command sets the time-out for the console EXEC session to 0 (zero). To have fun with your friends at work, set it to 0 1, which makes the console time out in one second! The way to fix that is to continually press the Down arrow key while changing the time-out time.

The logging synchronous is a nice command, and although we think it should be a default command, it's not. It stops console messages from popping up and disrupting the input that you are trying to type. This makes reading your input messages much easier.

VTY Password

To set the exec mode password for Telnet access into the router, use the line vty command. Because most routers default to only five lines, the vty lines are 0 4, as shown:

```
Router(config-line)#line vty 0 4
Router(config-line)#login
Router(config-line)#password kelly
```

If you try to telnet into a router that does not have a vty password set, you will receive an error stating that the connection is refused because the password is not set. You can tell the router to allow Telnet connections without a password by using the no login command:

```
Router(config-line)#line vty 0 4
Router(config-line)#no login
```

After your routers are configured with an IP address, you can use the Telnet program to configure and check your routers instead of having to use a console cable. You can use the Telnet program by typing telnet from any command prompt (DOS or Cisco). Remember that the vty passwords must be set on the routers for this to work. If not, you must use the no login command.

Once you telnet into any router, you can return to your router by using the Ctrl+Shift+6, then X keystroke sequence. Once you are back at your original router prompt, you can type show sessions to display the sessions. Press the number next to the session on the far left of the screen. This process will be discussed further in the "Using a Reverse Telnet Session" section.

By using the show user command, you can see the connections made to your router. You can use the clear line command to disconnect the Telnet session.

Banners

Banners allow you to display information. You can set a banner on a Cisco router so that when either a user logs into the router or an administrator telnets into the router, a banner will give them information you want them to have. Another reason for having a banner is to add a legal notice to users dialing into your internetwork. There are four different banners available:

```
Router(config)#banner ?
  LINE      c banner-text c, where 'c' is a delimiting character
  exec      Set EXEC process creation banner
  incoming  Set incoming terminal line banner
  login     Set login banner
  motd      Set Message of the Day banner
```

The Message of the Day (MOTD) is the most commonly used banner. It gives a message to every person dialing into or connecting to the router, whether they access via vty, auxiliary port, or console port:

```
Router(config)#banner motd ?
  LINE  c banner-text c, where 'c' is a delimiting character
Router(config)#banner motd ~
Enter TEXT message.  End with the character '~'.
$ized to be in Acme.com network, then you must disconnect immediately.
~
Router(config)#^Z
Router#
00:25:12: %SYS-5-CONFIG_I: Configured from console by console
Router#exit

Router con0 is now available

Press RETURN to get started.

If you are not authorized to be in Acme.com network, then you must
  disconnect immediately.
Router>
```

This MOTD banner tells anyone connecting to the router that they must be authorized or they must disconnect. The key part to understand is the delimiting character, which is ~ in the preceding example. You can use any character you want, and it is used to tell the router when the message is done. Therefore, you can't use the delimiting character in the message itself. Once the message is complete, press <Enter>, then the delimiting character, then <Enter> again. If you don't do that, the message will still work, but if you have more than one statement, they will be combined as one message and put on one line. The other banners are as follows:

Exec banner You can configure a line-activation (exec) banner to be displayed when an EXEC process (such as a line activation or incoming connection to a vty line) is created.

Incoming banner You can configure a banner to be displayed on terminals connected to reverse Telnet lines. This banner is useful for providing instructions to users who use reverse Telnet. (For more on reverse Telnet, see "Using a Reverse Telnet Session" later in this chapter.)

Login banner You can configure a login banner to be displayed on all connected terminals. This banner is displayed after the MOTD banner but before the login prompts. The login banner cannot be disabled on a per-line basis. To globally disable the login banner, you must delete it with the `no banner login` command.

Router Interfaces

As stated earlier, lines are used to provide various methods of user access to a device, such as Telnet (vty), asynchronous (TTY), console port (CON), and auxiliary port (AUX). Interfaces are used to provide LAN or WAN access.

Interface configuration is one of the most important configurations of the router. Without interfaces, the router is useless. Interface configurations must be exact to allow the router to communicate with other devices. Some of the tools available for configuring an interface are Network layer addresses, media-type, bandwidth, and other administrator commands.

Different routers use different methods to select interfaces on a router. For example, the following command shows a 2522 router with 10 serial interfaces:

```
Router(config)#interface serial ?
  <0-9>  Serial interface number
```

At this point, you must choose the interface you want to configure. Once you do that, you need to be in interface configuration mode for that interface. The command to choose serial port 5, for example, would be as follows:

```
Router(config)#interface serial 5
Router(config-if)#
```

The 2522 router has one Ethernet 10BaseT port. Typing the `interface ethernet 0` command configures the interface:

```
Router(config)#interface ethernet ?
  <0-0>  Ethernet interface number
```

```
Router(config)#interface ethernet 0
Router(config-if)#
```

The 2500 router, as demonstrated earlier, is a *fixed configuration router,* which means that you buy a certain model router and you are stuck with that physical configuration. To configure an interface on a fixed configuration router, you always use the command `interface type number`. However, on a 2600, 3600, 4000, or 7000 series router, there is a physical slot in the router and a port number on the module plugged into that slot. For example, on a 2600 router, the configuration would be `interface type slot/port`, as follows:

```
Router(config)#interface fastethernet ?
  <0-1>  FastEthernet interface number
Router(config)#interface fastethernet 0
% Incomplete command.
Router(config)#interface fastethernet 0?
/
Router(config)#interface fastethernet 0/?
  <0-1>  FastEthernet interface number
```

Notice that you cannot just type `int fastethernet 0`. You must type the full command, which is `type slot/port`, or `int fastethernet 0/0`.

To set the type of connector, use the command `media-type`, which is typically auto-detected:

```
Router(config)#interface fastethernet0/0
Router(config-if)#media-type ?
  100BaseX  Use RJ45 for -TX; SC FO for -FX
  MII       Use MII connector
```

NOTE   The `media-type` command is required only on routers that provide multiple physical media connectors for an interface (e.g., Cisco 4000).

You can turn an interface off with the interface command `shutdown` or turn it on with the `no shutdown` command. If an interface is shut down, it will appear administratively down when using the `show interface` command, and the `show running-config` command will indicate that the interface is shut down. All interfaces are shut down by default:

```
Router(config-if)#no shutdown
Router(config-if)#
00:57:08: %LINK-3-UPDOWN: Interface FastEthernet0/0, changed state to up
00:57:09: %LINEPROTO-5-UPDOWN: Line protocol on Interface
    FastEthernet0/0, changed state to up
```

VIP Cards

If you have a 7000 or 7500 series router with Versatile Interface Processor (VIP) cards, you define an interface by using the `interface type slot/port adapter/port number` command as follows, for example:

```
7000(config)#interface ethernet 2/0/0
```

Serial Interface Commands

To configure a serial interface, there are a couple of specifics that need to be addressed. Typically, the interface will be attached to a *channel service unit/data service unit (CSU/DSU)* type of device that provides clocking for the line. However, if you have a back-to-back configuration in a lab environment, for example, one end must provide clocking. This is the *data communication equipment (DCE)* end of the cable. Cisco routers by default are all *data terminal equipment (DTE)* devices, and you must tell an interface to provide clocking if it is to act as a DCE device.

 You can use the `show controllers` command to determine the cable type (DCE or DTE) attached to a serial interface.

You configure a DCE serial interface with the `clock rate` command:

```
Router#config t
Enter configuration commands, one per line.  End with CNTL/Z.
Router(config)#interface serial0
Router(config-if)#clock rate ?
       Speed (bits per second)
  1200
  2400
  4800
  9600
  19200
  38400
  56000
  64000
  72000
  125000
  148000
  250000
  500000
  800000
  1000000
  1300000
```

```
       2000000
       4000000

       <300-4000000>    Choose clockrate from list above
Router(config-if)#clock rate 64000
%Error: This command applies only to DCE interfaces
Router(config-if)#interface serial1
Router(config-if)#clock rate 64000
```

It does not hurt anything to try to put a clock rate on an interface. Notice that the clock rate command is in bits per second.

> Be careful when configuring clock rate to ensure that the interface and/or cable for *both* ends of the connection can support the configured rate. For example, the Cisco 2522 router includes 10 serial interfaces, but only two of these (serial0 and serial1) are high speed (operate at up to 2Mbps) and the remaining are low speed (operate at up to 115Kbps). If you set the speed too high for the low-speed serial interfaces, the interface will not come up properly. Similarly, if you use RS-232 back-to-back serial cables, you can configure a maximum clock rate of only 250000bps.

The next command you need to understand is the bandwidth command. Every Cisco router ships with a default serial link bandwidth of a T1, or 1.544Mbps. However, you must understand that this has nothing to do with how data is transferred over a link. The bandwidth command does not restrict the amount of bandwidth available to an interface. The bandwidth of a serial link is used by routing protocols such as IGRP, EIGRP, and OSPF to calculate the best cost to a remote network. If you are using RIP routing, then the bandwidth setting of a serial link is irrelevant. Here is an example of using the bandwidth command:

```
Router(config-if)#bandwidth ?
  <1-10000000>  Bandwidth in kilobits

Router(config-if)#bandwidth 64
```

Notice that unlike the clock rate command, the bandwidth command is configured in kilobits.

Hostnames

You can set the hostname of the router with the hostname command:

```
Router#config t
Enter configuration commands, one per line.  End with CNTL/Z.
Router(config)#hostname Arkansas
Arkansas(config)#
```

The hostname command is only locally significant, which means it has no bearing on how the router performs name lookups on the internetwork. Even though it is tempting to configure the hostname after your own name, you are better served by naming the router something significant to the location.

Descriptions

Setting descriptions on an interface is helpful to the administrator, and like the hostname, it is only locally significant. This is a helpful command because it can be used to keep track of circuit numbers, for example:

```
Arkansas(config)#interface ethernet0
Arkansas(config-if)#description Sales Lan
Arkansas(config-if)#interface serial0
Arkansas(config-if)#description Wan to Bentonville circuit:6fdda4321
```

You can view the description of an interface either with the show running-config command or the show interface command:

```
Arkansas#show running-config
[cut]
interface Ethernet0
 description Sales Lan
 ip address 172.16.10.30 255.255.255.0
 no ip directed-broadcast
!
interface Serial0
 description Wan to Bentonville circuit:6fdda4321
 no ip address
 no ip directed-broadcast
 no ip mroute-cache

Arkansas#show interface ethernet0
Ethernet0 is up, line protocol is up
  Hardware is Lance, address is 0010.7be8.25db (bia 0010.7be8.25db)
  Description: Sales Lan
  [cut]
Arkansas#show interface serial0
Serial0 is up, line protocol is up
  Hardware is HD64570
  Description: Wan to Bentonville circuit:6fdda4321
[cut]
Arkansas#
```

Viewing and Saving Configurations

If you run through setup mode, it will ask you if you want to use the configuration you created. If you answer yes, then it will copy the configuration running in DRAM, known as running-config, to NVRAM and name the file startup-config.

You can manually save the file from DRAM to NVRAM by using the `copy running-config startup-config`. You can use the shortcut `copy run start` also:

```
Router#copy running-config startup-config
Destination filename [startup-config]? <cr>
Warning: Attempting to overwrite an NVRAM configuration previously
  written by a different version of the system image.
Overwrite the previous NVRAM configuration?[confirm]<cr>
Building configuration...
```

Notice that the message warned that we were trying to write over the older startup-config. We have just upgraded the IOS to version 12.0.8, and the last time we saved the file, we were running 11.3.*x*.

You can use the command `write memory` or just `wr` to save your running configuration to startup configuration. This command is a legacy command but is still supported and will save time in the CCIE lab exam

You can view the files by typing the command `show running-config` or `show startup-config` from enable mode. The `sh run` command, which is the shortcut for `show running-config`, tells us that we are viewing the current configuration:

```
Router#show running-config
Building configuration...

Current configuration:
!
version 12.0
service timestamps debug uptime
service timestamps log uptime
no service password-encryption
!
hostname Router
ip subnet-zero
frame-relay switching
!
[cut]
```

The sh start command, which is the shortcut for the show startup-config command, shows us the configuration that will be used the next time the router is reloaded. It also shows us how the amount of NVRAM used to store the startup-config file:

```
Router#show startup-config
Using 4850 out of 32762 bytes
!
version 12.0
service timestamps debug uptime
service timestamps log uptime
no service password-encryption
!
hostname Router
!
!
ip subnet-zero
frame-relay switching
!
[cut]
```

You can delete the startup-config file by using the command erase startup-config. Once you perform this command, you will receive an error message if you try to view the startup-config file:

```
Router#erase startup-config
Erasing the nvram filesystem will remove all files! Continue? [confirm]
[OK]
Erase of nvram: complete
Router#show startup-config
%% Non-volatile configuration memory is not present
Router#
```

Verifying Your Configuration

Obviously, the show running-config would be the best way to verify your current configuration. The show startup-config would be the best way to verify the backup configuration used the next time the router is reloaded.

However, once you take a look at the running-config, and it appears that everything is in order, you can verify your configuration with utilities like ping and Telnet.

You can ping with different protocols, and you can see a list of these by typing ping ? at the router exec mode or enable mode prompt:

```
Router#ping ?
  WORD      Ping destination address or hostname
  appletalk  Appletalk echo
```

```
decnet     DECnet echo
ip         IP echo
ipx        Novell/IPX echo
srb        srb echo
<cr>
```

You can also perform an extended ping, which allows increased functionality, such as setting the repeat count (number of pings), varying the datagram size, specifying a source IP address (a ping will automatically have the source IP address of the outgoing interface it flows through), and setting many other optional features:

```
Router#ping
Protocol [ip]:
Target IP address: 147.19.1.1
Repeat count [5]: 15
Datagram size [100]:
Timeout in seconds [2]:
Extended commands [n]: y
Source address or interface: 10.1.1.1
Type of service [0]:
Set DF bit in IP header? [no]:
Validate reply data? [no]:
Data pattern [0xABCD]:
Loose, Strict, Record, Timestamp, Verbose[none]:
Sweep range of sizes [n]:
Type escape sequence to abort.
Sending 15, 100-byte ICMP Echoes to 10.1.1.1, timeout is 2 seconds:
!!!!!!!!!!!!!!!!
Success rate is 100 percent (15/15), round-trip min/avg/max = 1/3/1 ms
```

To find a neighbor's Network layer address to use for the ping command, you need to either go to the router or switch or type show cdp neighbor detail (this will be discussed later).

You can also use the Trace program to find the path that a packet takes as it traverses an internetwork. Trace can also be used with multiple protocols:

```
Router#trace ?
  WORD       Trace route to destination address or hostname
  appletalk  AppleTalk Trace
  clns       ISO CLNS Trace
  ip         IP Trace
  oldvines   Vines Trace (Cisco)
  vines      Vines Trace (Banyan)
  <cr>
```

Telnet is a good tool to use when creating sessions with a remote host because it uses IP at the Network layer and TCP at the Transport layer:

```
Router#telnet ?
  WORD  IP address or hostname of a remote system
  <cr>
```

From the router prompt, you do not need to type the command `telnet`. If you just type a hostname or IP address, the router will assume you want to telnet.

There are several options that can be used in conjunction with the `telnet` command. Just as with the `ping` command, the Telnet session you initiate will automatically have the source IP address of the interface that the session flows out of. It is possible to use the `/source-interface` option with the `telnet` command to change the source IP address. Likewise, if you just type a hostname or IP address, the router will assume you want to telnet (TCP port 23); you can specify a specific port number after the `telnet` command to use a different port number:

```
Router#telnet 147.19.30.1 ?
  /debug            Enable telnet debugging mode
  /line             Enable telnet line mode
  /noecho           Disable local echo
  /quiet            Suppress login/logout messages
  /route:           Enable telnet source route mode
  /source-interface Specify source interface
  /stream           Enable stream processing
  <0-65535>         Port number
  bgp               Border Gateway Protocol (179)
  chargen           Character generator (19)
  cmd               Remote commands (rcmd, 514)
  daytime           Daytime (13)
  discard           Discard (9)
  domain            Domain Name Service (53)
  echo              Echo (7)
  exec              Exec (rsh, 512)
  finger            Finger (79)
  ftp               File Transfer Protocol (21)
  ftp-data          FTP data connections (used infrequently, 20)
  gopher            Gopher (70)
  hostname          NIC hostname server (101)
  ident             Ident Protocol (113)
  irc               Internet Relay Chat (194)
  klogin            Kerberos login (543)
```

```
kshell            Kerberos shell (544)
login             Login (rlogin, 513)
lpd               Printer service (515)
nntp              Network News Transport Protocol (119)
pim-auto-rp       PIM Auto-RP (496)
pop2              Post Office Protocol v2 (109)
pop3              Post Office Protocol v3 (110)
smtp              Simple Mail Transport Protocol (25)
sunrpc            Sun Remote Procedure Call (111)
syslog            Syslog (514)
tacacs            TAC Access Control System (49)
talk              Talk (517)
telnet            Telnet (23)
time              Time (37)
uucp              Unix-to-Unix Copy Program (540)
whois             Nicname (43)
www               World Wide Web (HTTP, 80)
<cr>
```

Verifying with Show Commands

Another way to verify your configuration is by typing show interface commands. The first
command is show interface ?, which lists all the available interfaces to configure. Here is an
example of show interface ?:

```
Router#show interface ?
  Ethernet    IEEE 802.3
  Null        Null interface
  Serial      Serial
  accounting  Show interface accounting
  crb         Show interface routing/bridging info
  irb         Show interface routing/bridging info
  <cr>
```

The next command is show interface ethernet 0. It shows the hardware address, logical
address, and encapsulation method, as well as statistics on collisions:

```
Router#show interface ethernet0
Ethernet0 is up, line protocol is up
  Hardware is Lance, address is 0010.7b7f.c26c (bia 0010.7b7f.c26c)
Internet address is 172.16.10.1/24
  MTU 1500 bytes, BW 10000 Kbit, DLY 1000 usec,
    reliability 255/255, txload 1/255, rxload 1/255
```

```
Encapsulation ARPA, loopback not set, keepalive set (10 sec)
ARP type: ARPA, ARP Timeout 04:00:00
Last input 00:08:23, output 00:08:20, output hang never
Last clearing of "show interface" counters never
Queueing strategy: fifo
Output queue 0/40, 0 drops; input queue 0/75, 0 drops
5 minute input rate 0 bits/sec, 0 packets/sec
5 minute output rate 0 bits/sec, 0 packets/sec
   25 packets input, 2459 bytes, 0 no buffer
   Received 25 broadcasts, 0 runts, 0 giants, 0 throttles
   0 input errors, 0 CRC, 0 frame, 0 overrun, 0 ignored, 0 abort
   0 input packets with dribble condition detected
   33 packets output, 7056 bytes, 0 underruns
   0 output errors, 0 collisions, 1 interface resets
   0 babbles, 0 late collision, 0 deferred
   0 lost carrier, 0 no carrier
   0 output buffer failures, 0 output buffers swapped out
```

The most important status of the `show interface` command is the output of the line and Data-Link protocol status. If the states change to `Ethernet 0 up`, `line protocol up`, then the line is up and running:

```
RouterA#show interface ethernet0
Ethernet0 is up, line protocol is up
```

The first parameter refers to the Physical layer, which is up when it receives carrier detect. The second parameter refers to the Data Link layer and looks for keepalives from the connecting end.

If you see that the line is up but the protocol is down, you are having a keepalive or framing issue:

```
RouterA#show interface serial0
Serial0 is up, line protocol is down
```

Check the keepalives on both ends to make sure they match, that the clock rate is set (if needed), and that the encapsulation type is the same on both ends.

If you see that the line interface and protocol are both down, it is a cable or interface problem:

```
RouterA#show interface serial0
Serial0 is down, line protocol is down
```

Also, if one end were administratively shut down, then the remote end would show line down and protocol down:

```
RouterB#show interface serial0
Serial0 is administratively down, line protocol is down
```

To turn on the interface, type the command no shutdown in interface configuration.

The show interface serial0 command shows us the serial line and the *maximum transmission unit (MTU)*, which is 1500 bytes by default. It also displays the default bandwidth (BW) on all Cisco serial links: 1544Kbit. This information is used to determine the bandwidth of the line by routing protocols such as IGRP, EIGRP, and OSPF. Another important configuration to notice is the keepalive, which is 10 seconds by default. Each router sends a keepalive message to its neighbor every 10 seconds. If both routers are not configured for the same keepalive time, then the command will not work.

You can clear the counters on the interface by typing the clear counters command. Here is the output of the show interface serial0 and clear counters commands:

```
Router#show interface serial0
Serial0 is up, line protocol is up
  Hardware is HD64570
  MTU 1500 bytes, BW 1544 Kbit, DLY 20000 usec,
     reliability 255/255, txload 1/255, rxload 1/255
  Encapsulation HDLC, loopback not set, keepalive set (10 sec)
  Last input never, output never, output hang never
  Last clearing of "show interface" counters never
  Queueing strategy: fifo
  Output queue 0/40, 0 drops; input queue 0/75, 0 drops
  5 minute input rate 0 bits/sec, 0 packets/sec
  5 minute output rate 0 bits/sec, 0 packets/sec
     0 packets input, 0 bytes, 0 no buffer
     Received 0 broadcasts, 0 runts, 0 giants, 0 throttles
     0 input errors, 0 CRC, 0 frame, 0 overrun, 0 ignored, 0 abort
     0 packets output, 0 bytes, 0 underruns
     0 output errors, 0 collisions, 16 interface resets
     0 output buffer failures, 0 output buffers swapped out
     0 carrier transitions
     DCD=down  DSR=down  DTR=down  RTS=down  CTS=down
Router#clear counters ?
  Ethernet  IEEE 802.3
  Null      Null interface
  Serial    Serial
  <cr>
Router#clear counters serial0
Clear "show interface" counters on this interface [confirm]return
Router#
00:17:35: %CLEAR-5-COUNTERS: Clear counter on interface Serial0 by console
Router#
```

The `show controllers` command displays information about the physical interface itself. It will also give you the type of serial cable plugged into a serial port. Typically this will only be a DTE cable, which then plugs into a type of data service unit (DSU):

```
Router#show controllers serial 0
HD unit 0, idb = 0x1229E4, driver structure at 0x127E70
buffer size 1524  HD unit 0, V.35 DTE cable
cpb = 0xE2, eda = 0x4140, cda = 0x4000


Router#show controllers serial 1
HD unit 1, idb = 0x12C174, driver structure at 0x131600
buffer size 1524  HD unit 1, V.35 DCE cable
cpb = 0xE3, eda = 0x2940, cda = 0x2800
```

Notice that serial 0 has a DTE cable, whereas the serial 1 connection is a DCE cable. Serial 1 would have to provide clocking with the `clock rate` command. Serial 0 would get its clocking from the DSU. Also, keep in mind that with some IOS versions, `show controllers` is the only command that needs to have a space after the command word serial:

```
Router#show controllers serial 1
```

The Configuration Register

In addition to understanding the major aspects of the CLI, you need to understand how to control the router's bootup process. This can be accomplished by changing the configuration register. All Cisco routers have a 16-bit software register, which is written into the nonvolatile memory. The configuration register is set by default to load the Cisco IOS from flash memory and to look for and load the `startup-config` file from NVRAM.

You can change the configuration register to do the following:

- Force the system into the bootstrap monitor.
- Select a boot source and default boot filename.
- Enable or disable the Break function.
- Control broadcast addresses.
- Set the console terminal baud rate.
- Load operating software from ROM.
- Enable booting from TFTP server.

The default configuration setting on Cisco routers is 0x2102. This means that bits 13, 8, and 1 are on, as shown in Table 2.1. Table 2.2 lists the software configuration bit meanings.

TABLE 2.1 Configuration Register Bit Numbers

Configuration register	2			1			0			2			
Bit number	15	14	13	12	11	10	9	8	7	6	5	4	3	2	1	0
Binary	0	0	1	0	0	0	0	1	0	0	0	0	0	0	1	0

 Add the prefix *0x* to the configuration register address (0x2102) to indicate hexadecimal numbering or unpredictable results will occur!

TABLE 2.2 Software Configuration Meanings

Bit No.	Hex	Description
0–3	0x0000–0x000F	Set boot field (see Table 2.3).
6	0x0040	Ignore NVRAM contents.
7	0x0080	Enable OEM.
8	0x0100	Disable Break.
10	0x0400	Use all zeros for IP broadcast.
11–12	0x0800–0x1000	Set console line speed.
13	0x2000	Boot default ROM software if network boot fails.
14	0x4000	Do not use net numbers with IP broadcasts.
15	0x8000	Enable diagnostic messages and ignore NVM contents.

Notice that bit 6 can be used to ignore the NVRAM contents. We'll come back to that in the password recovery section. Let's take a look at the boot field, which is made up of bits 0–3 in the configuration register. In Table 2.3, we show the boot field bits and what each value means. There are three main values to use, 00, 01, or 02–0F:

- To boot to ROM monitor mode, set the configuration register to 0x2100. You must manually reboot the router with the i command. The router will show the rommon> prompt. On newer routers, you must use the reset command.

- To boot a mini-IOS image stored on the ROM (referred to as RXBOOT), set the configuration register to 0x2101. The router will show the router(boot)> prompt if it is an older router, or it will show the rommon 1 > prompt if it is a newer RISC-based router with a "smart ROM" instead of a mini-IOS.

- Any value from 0x2102 through 0x210F tells the router to use the boot commands specified in NVRAM. Remember that in hex, the scheme is 0–9 and A–F. (A=10, B=11, C=12, D=13, E=14, and F=15). So you really are setting the configuration register to 210(15), or 1111 in binary.

TABLE 2.3   Boot Field (Configuration Register Bits 00-03)

Boot Field	Meaning
00	Sets the router to ROM monitor mode
01	Boot image from ROM
02-0F	Specifies a default netboot filename

Changing the Configuration Register

In the preceding section, we discussed what type of changes you can make to the configuration register, but how do you know what its current value is? Make sure you know before you make any changes. You can find out with the show version command as shown:

```
Router#show version
Cisco Internetwork Operating System Software
IOS (tm) C2600 Software (C2600-I-M), Version 12.0(3)T3,  RELEASE SOFTWARE (fc1)
Copyright (c) 1986-1999 by cisco Systems, Inc.
Compiled Thu 15-Apr-99 15:41 by kpma
Image text-base: 0x80008088, data-base: 0x80693A88
ROM: System Bootstrap, Version 11.3(2)XA4, RELEASE SOFTWARE (fc1)
Router uptime is 1 minute
System restarted by power-on
System image file is "flash:c2600-i-mz.120-3.T3"
cisco 2621 (MPC860) processor (revision 0x102) with 24576K/8192K bytes of memory
```

```
Processor board ID JAB034800PC (2306277002)
M860 processor: part number 0, mask 49
Bridging software.
X.25 software, Version 3.0.0.
2 FastEthernet/IEEE 802.3 interface(s)
32K bytes of non-volatile configuration memory.
8192K bytes of processor board System flash (Read/Write)

Configuration register is 0x2102
```

Notice that the last information given from this command is the value of the configuration register.
    You can change the value of the configuration register with the config-register command:

```
Router(config)#config-register 0x2101
Router(config)#^Z
Router#show version
[cut]
Configuration register is 0x2102 (will be 0x2101 at next reload)
```

Notice that when we changed the configuration register to boot from ROM, the show version command shows us what the current running configuration register is as well as what it will be when we reboot the router. Any change to the configuration register will not take effect until the router is reloaded.

Password Recovery

Using the configuration register, you are able to change the mode into which the router will boot up. The configuration register is also used to assist in the password recovery process.
    Remember the bit 6 in the configuration register we mentioned earlier? That bit is used to tell the router to either use or ignore the contents of NVRAM to load a router configuration.
    The default configuration register is 0x2102, which means that bit 6 is off (see Table 2.1). The router will look for and load a configuration stored in the NVRAM (startup-config). To perform a password recovery, you need to turn on bit 6, which will tell the router to ignore the NVRAM contents.
    If you are locked out of a router because you forgot the password, you can change the configuration register to help you recover the password. Here are the steps for password recovery:

1.   Boot the router and perform a break using the Ctrl+Break sequence. Note that the Windows NT default HyperTerminal program must be upgraded to version 3.0 or higher or Ctrl+Break will not perform the voltage change properly.

```
System Bootstrap, Version 11.3(2)XA4, RELEASE SOFTWARE (fc1)
Copyright (c) 1999 by cisco Systems, Inc.
TAC:Home:SW:IOS:Specials for info
PC = 0xfff0a530, Vector = 0x500, SP = 0x680127b0
```

```
C2600 platform with 32768 Kbytes of main memory

PC = 0xfff0a530, Vector = 0x500, SP = 0x80004374

monitor: command "boot" aborted due to user interrupt
rommon 1 >
```

2.   Notice the boot aborted due to user interrupt. At this point you will be at the rommon 1> prompt on some routers. You can change the configuration register with the confreg command. If you turn on bit 6, the configuration register will be 0x2142.

```
rommon 1 > confreg 0x2142
You must reset or power cycle for new config to take effect
```

The commands in this step and step 1 were issued on a Cisco 2600 series router. To change the configuration register on an older platform (such as the 7000, 7500, 3000, or 2500 series routers), type o after creating a break sequence on the router. This will give you the menu for changing the configuration register. To change the configuration register from this point, use the command o/r and then enter the register setting you want.

```
System Bootstrap, Version 11.0(10c), SOFTWARE
Copyright (c) 1986-1996 by cisco Systems
2500 processor with 14336 Kbytes of main memory
Abort at 0x1098FEC (PC)
>o
Configuration register = 0x2102 at last boot
Bit#    Configuration register option settings:
15      Diagnostic mode disabled
14      IP broadcasts do not have network numbers
13      Boot default ROM software if network boot fails
12-11   Console speed is 9600 baud
10      IP broadcasts with ones
08      Break disabled
07      OEM disabled
06      Ignore configuration disabled
03-00   Boot file is cisco2-2500 (or 'boot system' command)
>o/r 0x2142
```

3.   At this point, you need to reset the router. From the 2600 series router, type reset. From the 2500 series, type I for *initialize*. The router will reload, but it will not load a configuration or come up into setup mode because no startup-config is used. Answer **no** to entering setup mode, press **<Enter>** to go into exec mode, and then type enable to go into enable mode.

4. You are now past the point of the exec mode and enable mode passwords in a router, and you can copy the `startup-config` file to `running-config` (`copy run start`). The configuration is now running in DRAM and you are in enable mode, which means you can view and change the configuration.

5. You cannot view the enable secret password, but you can change it. Be careful not to log out or you'll have to start over.

```
Router#Config t
Router(config)#Enable secret kelly
```

6. After you change all the passwords you want to change, set the configuration register back to the default with the `config-register` command.

```
Router#Config t
Router(config)#Config-register 0x2102
```

7. Be sure to save your configuration by running the command `copy run start` to save your new password!

8. Reload the router.

9. Reenable all interfaces with the `no shutdown` command because every interface will be back in the default shutdown state.

10. Save your config one last time with the `copy run start` command to save the interfaces in the enabled state.

We've discussed the CLI and the configuration register and looked at how to use the configuration register to control which mode the router will boot up into as well as how to perform a password recovery. Now we'll shift gears a little and discuss flash memory and how the router utilizes it.

Managing Flash Files

Flash is an electronically erasable programmable read-only memory (EEPROM). It is the default location for the IOS on all Cisco routers.

You can type the `show flash` command to see the contents of flash. Here is an example on a 2600 router:

```
Router#show flash

System flash directory:
File  Length   Name/status
  1   3612344  c2600-i-mz.120-3.T3
```

```
[3612408 bytes used, 4776200 available, 8388608 total]
8192K bytes of processor board System flash (Read/Write)
```

Here is an example of flash on an 800 series router.

```
800Router#show flash
Directory of flash:/

0  ----        49096   Nov 03 1998 01:14:21  TinyROM-1.0(2)
1  -r-x      2314996   Dec 30 1998 21:37:19  c800-g3-mw.120-1.XB1
3  -r-x      2931536   Dec 30 1998 20:55:54  c800-g3n-mw.120-1.XB1

8388608 bytes total (3014656 bytes free)
800Router#
```

Notice that both routers have only 8MB of flash, but that the 800 router has three images stored in flash. We use different images for different protocol support with the 800 series router and store backups of smaller code that support fewer features. You can store multiple images in flash only if you have the room in flash memory. This is typically done in case a new version of IOS creates more problems than it solves when it's loaded into flash. If this happens, you can just boot from the original IOS image quickly.

If you issue the show flash command, you will notice that the 2600 router will boot the only image available. However, which one does the 800 series router boot? We'll take a look at that in the following sections. But first we'll briefly discuss the dir, delete, undelete, and squeeze commands.

You can also display a list of files on a file system using the dir (directory) command. This will list deleted files, undeleted files, and files with errors. Here is the output of a dir command on a 7200 series router:

```
7206Router#dir
Directory of slot0:/

1  -rw-     3689020   Aug 15 2000 13:30:19  c7200-dr-mz_111-30_CA.bin
2  -rw-    11506908   Sep 18 2002 16:06:12  c7200-a3js-mz.121-13.bin

16384000 bytes total (1187816 bytes free)
```

After you display the files you have in the router's file system, what if you want to delete a file? To delete a file, you would use the delete command:

```
7206Router#delete slot0:c7200-dr-mz_111-30_CA.bin
Delete filename [c7200-dr-mz_111-30_CA.bin]?
Delete slot0:c7200-dr-mz_111-30_CA.bin? [confirm]
```

When you use the dir command again and look at the output, you'll notice that the file you just deleted does not appear in the file system directory anymore:

```
7206Router#dir
Directory of slot0:/

    2  -rw-   11506908    Sep 18 2002 16:06:12  c7200-a3js-mz.121-13.bin

16384000 bytes total (1187816 bytes free)
```

Although, if you issue a show flash command, you'll notice that the deleted file is still listed but is marked with a *D* (under the ED column); this means the file is marked for deletion:

```
7206Router#show flash
-#- ED --type-- --crc--- -seek-- nlen -length- -----date/time------ name
1   .D unknown 0A9886EC 3A4ABC   25  3689020 Aug 15 2000 13:30:19
    c7200-dr-mz_111-30_CA.bin
2   .. unknown F15B658C E9E018   24 11506908 Sep 18 2002 16:06:12
    c7200-a3js-mz.121-13.bin

1187816 bytes available (15196184 bytes used)
```

Now, if you decide you did not want to delete that file, you can reverse what you just did by using the undelete command. Notice that we designate to undelete file 1 in slot0:, and in the output above, file 1 is the deleted file (under the # column):

```
7206Router#undelete 1 slot0:
```

If you issue the show flash command again, you'll see that the file is no longer marked for deletion:

```
7206Router#show flash
-#- ED --type-- --crc--- -seek-- nlen -length- -----date/time------ name
1   .. unknown 0A9886EC 3A4ABC   25  3689020 Aug 15 2000 13:30:19
    c7200-dr-mz_111-30_CA.bin
2   .. unknown F15B658C E9E018   24 11506908 Sep 18 2002 16:06:12
    c7200-a3js-mz.121-13.bin

1187816 bytes available (15196184 bytes used)
```

And if we issue a dir command, the file now shows up in the file system:

```
7206Router3#dir
Directory of slot0:/
```

```
    1  -rw-     3689020    Aug 15 2000 13:30:19  c7200-dr-mz_111-30_CA.bin
    2  -rw-    11506908    Sep 18 2002 16:06:12  c7200-a3js-mz.121-13.bin
```

```
16384000 bytes total (1187816 bytes free)
```

By the way, when you have files marked for deletion, they are still in flash memory and taking up space. The file system must be squeezed in order to finally remove the files marked for deletion from memory. This is accomplished with the **squeeze** command:

```
7206Router#squeeze slot0:
```

The file deletion and squeeze process is kind of like the process for deleting files in the Macintosh and Windows operating systems. You can delete files, but the files are not really gone until you empty the Trash can or Recycle Bin.

Flash Partitions

The flash memory can be partitioned with the **partition** command. If you insert new flash into a router, it may already be partitioned, as the **show flash** command demonstrates here:

```
Router#show flash

System flash directory, partition 1:
File  Length   Name/status
  1   8121000  c2500-js-1.112-18
[8121064 bytes used, 267544 available, 8388608 total]
8192K bytes of processor board System flash (Read ONLY)


System flash directory, partition 2:
File  Length   Name/status
  1   5248188  c2500-i-1.113-7.t.bin
[5248252 bytes used, 3140356 available, 8388608 total]
8192K bytes of processor board System flash (Read/Write)
```

The flash had been used in other routers so it had already been configured. Notice in the output that the router has two partitions, each holding a different IOS version. We need to erase one of those partitions and then combine the partitions into one so we have more room in flash to load a larger version. To do that, we must first delete the files with the `erase flash` command:

```
Router#erase flash
Partition   Size    Used    Free    Bank-Size   State       Copy Mode
   1        8192K   7930K    261K    8192K       Read ONLY   RXBOOT-FLH
   2        8192K   5125K   3066K    8192K       Read/Write  Direct

System flash directory, partition 2:
File  Length    Name/status
  1   5248188   c2500-i-1.113-7.t.bin
[5248252 bytes used, 3140356 available, 8388608 total]

Erase flash device, partition 2? [confirm]
Are you sure? [yes/no]: y
Erasing device... eeeeeeeeeeeeeeeeeeeeeeeeeeeeeeeeee ...erased
```

We typed the `erase flash` command and, by default, were asked if we want to delete partition 2. We confirmed that and the file was erased. The IOS in partition 1 was in use, so the only file we could delete was the IOS in partition 2.

Once the file in the second partition is deleted, we can add the second partition to the first partition to give us one large partition. Use the `partition flash` command to change the partitions:

```
Router#config t
Enter configuration commands, one per line.  End with CNTL/Z.
Router(config)#partition flash ?
  <1-8>  Number of partitions in device
Router(config)#partition flash 1 16
Router(config)#
```

The command is a little convoluted, but basically it asks, how many partitions do you want to make and how large do you them to be? In this example, we chose to use partition 1 at 16MB in size. By using the `show flash` command, you can see that the flash partition is now one large flash partition of 16MB.

```
Router#show flash
%SYS-5-CONFIG_I: Configured from console by console
System flash directory:
File  Length    Name/status
  1   8121000   /c2500-js-1.112-18
```

```
[8121064 bytes used, 8656152 available, 16777216 total]
16384K bytes of processor board System flash (Read ONLY)
Router#
```

Configuring Boot Files

If you have only one file in flash memory, that file will boot by default. If you have more than one image in flash, you need to tell the router which file to boot. First, you can find out which file is booted by using the show version command:

```
800Router(config)#show version
[cut]
System image file is "flash:c800-g3n-mw.120-1.XB1"
[cut]
```

This tells you that the router booted an IOS from flash and gives the filename. You can change the file used to boot by using the boot system command:

```
800Router(config)#boot system ?
  WORD   TFTP filename or URL
  flash  Boot from flash memory
  mop    Boot from a Decnet MOP server
  rcp    Boot from a server via rcp
  rom    Boot from rom
  tftp   Boot from a tftp server
```

A boot system configuration command used by the router configuration in NVRAM will override the default netboot filename.

At this point, we can type boot system flash ios-name and then reboot the router. If you use the boot system flash IOS_file_name command and it still boots the old file, you'll have to change the filename in the configuration register also:

```
boot#set ?
set baud           ={1200|2400|4800|9600|19200|38400|57600|115200}
set data-bits      ={7|8}
set parity         ={none|even|odd}
set stop-bits      ={1|2}
set console-flags  ={cts|dsr}
set mac-address    =X.X.X
set unit-ip        =N.N.N.N
set serv-ip        =N.N.N.N
```

```
set netmask         =N.N.N.N
set gate-ip         =N.N.N.N
set pkt-timeout     =N (seconds)
set tftp-timeout    =N (seconds)
set boot-action     ={flash|tftp|none}
set file-name       ="file-name"
set watchdog        ={off|on}
set prompt          ="prompt-string"
set ios-conf        =N
boot#set file-name = ios-name
```

Setting a Fallback Routine

You can set up a fallback routine to get the router up in the event your flash memory becomes corrupted and won't load. If flash fails, you can tell the router to load an IOS file from a Trivial File Transfer Protocol (TFTP) host. Use the **boot system** command:

```
Router#config t
Enter configuration commands, one per line.  End with CNTL/Z.
Router(config)#boot ?
  bootstrap   Bootstrap image file
  buffersize  Specify the buffer size for netbooting a config file
  host        Router-specific config file
  network     Network-wide config file
  system      System image file

Router(config)#boot system ?
  WORD   TFTP filename or URL
  flash  Boot from flash memory
  mop    Boot from a Decnet MOP server
  rcp    Boot from a server via rcp
  tftp   Boot from a tftp server
```

The commands will work in the order in which you type them. Add the default **boot system flash** command and then add the **boot system tftp** command. If you do it in the reverse order, the router will always try to load an IOS image from a TFTP host first:

```
Router(config)#boot system flash ?
  WORD  Configuration filename
  <cr>
Router(config)#boot system flash c2500-js-l_120-8.bin
Router(config)#boot system ?
  WORD   TFTP filename or URL
```

```
    flash  Boot from flash memory
    mop    Boot from a Decnet MOP server
    rcp    Boot from a server via rcp
    tftp   Boot from a tftp server
Router(config)#boot system tftp ?
  WORD  Configuration filename
Router(config)#boot system tftp c2500-js-l_120-8.bin ?
  Hostname or A.B.C.D  Address from which to download the boot config file
  <cr>
Router(config)#boot system tftp c2500-js-l_120-8.bin 172.16.30.2
```

Using a Cisco Router as a TFTP Host

If you don't have a PC or Unix host nearby to upload an IOS version to a router, you can copy an IOS version directly from a Cisco router using the Trivial File Transfer Protocol (TFTP) by making a router into a TFTP server.

The command to copy from/to a TFTP server changed a little in 12.*x*, but it still has 100-percent compatibility with IOS 11.*x* commands. The command **tftp-server flash** now allows you to add an access list to control access. However, you can just remove the command from the router's configuration instead of using an access list. In the following listing, we show a router being set up to accept TFTP requests for flash download (thus, the router will act as a TFTP server):

```
Router(config)#tftp-server flash:?
flash:c2500-js-l_120-8.bin
Router(config)#tftp-server flash: (press the tab key, and the file available in
  flash shows up)
Router(config)#tftp-server flash:c2500-js-l_120-8.bin ?
  <1-99>      IP access list of requesting hosts
  <1300-1999> IP expanded access list of requesting hosts
  alias       file alias
  <cr>
```

At this point you can press <Enter> to allow any TFTP requests or add an access list to limit requests:

```
Router(config)#tftp-server flash:c2500-js-l_120-8.bin 10
Router(config)#access-list 10 permit 172.16.30.5 ?
  A.B.C.D  Wildcard bits
  log      Log matches against this entry
  <cr>

Router(config)#access-list 10 permit 172.16.30.5 log
```

> You can use the `log` command to find out when the access-list is being hit. However, we don't recommend doing so during production because the log keyword causes extra CPU processing for each matching packet. Likewise, you can use the `show access-list` command; the number of matches to the access list for each entry will be indicated regardless of whether `log` is configured or not.

Cisco Discovery Protocol (CDP)

Cisco Discovery Protocol (CDP) is a Cisco-proprietary protocol that uses a Sub-Network Access Protocol (SNAP) frame at the Data-Link layer to gather information about neighboring Cisco devices like routers and switches. CDP allows Cisco devices to communicate information to each other; for example, Cisco IP phones and Cisco switches can communicate information such as voice VLAN ID and inline power requirements.

CDP starts by default on any router version 10.3 or later and discovers which neighboring Cisco routers are running CDP by doing a Data-Link multicast. It doesn't matter which protocol is running at the Network layer because CDP does not use Network layer information.

Once CDP has discovered a router, it can display information about the upper-layer protocols, such as IP and IPX. A router caches the information it receives from its CDP neighbors. Anytime a router receives updated information that a CDP neighbor has changed, it discards the old information in favor of the new broadcast.

Let's take a look at a network trace and examine a CDP frame:

```
Flags:          0x80  802.3
  Status:       0x00
  Packet Length:305
  Timestamp:    12:09:42.623000 06/09/1998
802.3 Header
  Destination:  01:00:0c:cc:cc:cc
  Source:       00:00:0c:8d:5c:9d
  LLC Length:   287
802.2 Logical Link Control (LLC) Header
  Dest. SAP:    0xaa  SNAP
  Source SAP:   0xaa  SNAP
  Command:      0x03  Unnumbered Information
  Protocol:     00-00-0c-20-00  Cisco DP
  Packet Data:
  . .}....RouterA.01 b4 9f 7d 00 01 00 0b 52 6f 75 74 65 72 41 00
  ............ ...02 00 11 00 00 00 01 01 01 cc 00 04 ac 10 0a 01
```

```
....Ethernet0...00 03 00 0d 45 74 68 65 72 6e 65 74 30 00 04 00
........ Cisco I08 00 00 00 01 00 05 00 d4 43 69 73 63 6f 20 49
nternetwork Oper6e 74 65 72 6e 65 74 77 6f 72 6b 20 4f 70 65 72
ating System Sof61 74 69 6e 67 20 53 79 73 74 65 6d 20 53 6f 66
tware .IOS (tm) 74 77 61 72 65 20 0a 49 4f 53 20 28 74 6d 29 20
3000 Software (I 33 30 30 30 20 53 6f 66 74 77 61 72 65 20 28 49    GS-I-L),
   Version    47 53 2d 49 2d 4c 29 2c 20 56 65 72 73 69 6f 6e    11.0(18), RELEA
   20 31 31 2e 30 28 31 38 29 2c 20 52 45 4c 45 41    SE SOFTWARE (fc153 45 20
   53 4f 46 54 57 41 52 45 20 28
```

Notice in the EtherPeek trace that the frame is a SNAP frame and the protocol is a Cisco DP. Also notice that Network layer information isn't present in the frame. Make special note that the destination MAC address starts with 01, indicating a multicast, and also notice the all-*c* hardware address, indicating CDP.

Changing the CDP Timers

You can execute the commands that display the results of the CDP broadcast on a router that's configured to run CDP on its interfaces—but you can see only the directly physically connected routers and switches because no routing information is contained in the CDP packet. On Cisco devices, CDP packets are not routed or switched to any other interfaces.

From a router prompt, type sh cdp to see a list the CDP timers:

```
Router>show cdp
Global CDP information:
        Sending CDP packets every 60 seconds
        Sending a holdtime value of 180 seconds
```

Notice that CDP packets are being sent out to all active interfaces every 60 seconds by default and any CDP packets received from neighboring Cisco devices will be held for a maximum of 180 seconds. If no packets are received from a neighbor device within 180 seconds, that neighbor information will be discarded.

You can change the packet update frequency as well as the holdtime with the global configuration command cdp timer and cdp holdtime:

```
Router#config t
Enter configuration commands, one per line.  End with CNTL/Z.
Router(config)#cdp ?
 holdtime  Specify the holdtime (in sec) to be sent in packets
 timer     Specify the rate at which CDP packets are sent(in sec)
 run

Router(config)#cdp timer 90
Router(config)#cdp holdtime 240
```

```
Router(config)#^Z
Router#
00:47:54: %SYS-5-CONFIG_I: Configured from console by console
Router#show cdp
Global CDP information:
        Sending CDP packets every 90 seconds
        Sending a holdtime value of 240 seconds
```

Turning Off/On CDP

You can turn the CDP protocol off completely on a Cisco device or you can just turn it off on a certain interface or selection of interfaces.

To turn it off completely, use the **no cdp run** global configuration command, as in the following example:

```
Router#config t
Enter configuration commands, one per line.  End with CNTL/Z.
Router(config)#no cdp ?
 holdtime  Specify the holdtime (in sec) to be sent in packets
 timer     Specify the rate at which CDP packets are sent(in sec)
 run

Router(config)#no cdp run
Router(config)#^Z
Router#
00:57:05: %SYS-5-CONFIG_I: Configured from console by console
Router#show cdp
% CDP is not enabled
```

To turn CDP off on only one interface, use the **no cdp enable** command from interface configuration mode:

```
Router#config t
Enter configuration commands, one per line.  End with CNTL/Z.
Router(config)#cdp run
Router(config)#^ZRouter#show cdp
Global CDP information:
        Sending CDP packets every 90 seconds
        Sending a holdtime value of 240 seconds
Router#config t
Enter configuration commands, one per line.  End with CNTL/Z.
Router(config)#interface ethernet0
```

```
Router(config-if)#no cdp ?
  enable  Enable CDP on interface
Router(config-if)#no cdp enable
Router(config-if)#^Z
```

We'll show you how to look at CDP per interface in the next section.

CDP Commands

To display a list of commands available on a router or switch, use the sh cdp ? command:

```
RouterB#show cdp ?
  entry      Information for specific neighbor entry
  interface  CDP interface status and configuration
  neighbors  CDP neighbor entries
  traffic    CDP statistics
  <cr>
```

show cdp interface

By typing sh cdp interface, you can view the interface information. Notice our timers are set to 90 and 240 instead of the default of 60 and 180. Also missing is the Ethernet 0 interface:

```
Router#show cdp interface
Serial0 is up, line protocol is up
  Encapsulation HDLC
  Sending CDP packets every 90 seconds
  Holdtime is 240 seconds
Serial1 is up, line protocol is up
  Encapsulation HDLC
  Sending CDP packets every 90 seconds
  Holdtime is 240 seconds
```

Let's turn Ethernet 0 back on:

```
Router#config t
Enter configuration commands, one per line.  End with CNTL/Z.
Router(config)#interface ethernet0
Router(config-if)#cdp enable
Router(config-if)#^Z
Router#
01:04:47: %SYS-5-CONFIG_I: Configured from console by console
Router#show cdp interface
Ethernet0 is administratively down, line protocol is down
```

```
  Encapsulation ARPA
  Sending CDP packets every 90 seconds
  Holdtime is 240 seconds
Serial0 is down, line protocol is down
  Encapsulation HDLC
  Sending CDP packets every 90 seconds
  Holdtime is 240 seconds
Serial1 is down, line protocol is down
  Encapsulation HDLC
  Sending CDP packets every 90 seconds
  Holdtime is 240 seconds
Router#
```

show cdp entry

The sh cdp entry command can give you the CDP information received from all routers if you type an asterisk (*) after the command or for a specific router if you type the router name after the command (note that the command is case sensitive):

```
Copyright (c) 1986-1999 by Cisco Systems, Inc.
Compiled Tue 02-Feb-99 05:04 by dschwart


-------------------------
Device ID: 2621
Entry address(es):
  IP address: 172.16.10.5
Platform: cisco 2621,  Capabilities: Router
Interface: Ethernet0,  Port ID (outgoing port): FastEthernet0/0
Holdtime : 151 sec

Version :
Cisco Internetwork Operating System Software
IOS (tm) C2600 Software (C2600-DOS-M), Version 12.0(4)T,  RELEASE SOFTWARE (fc1)
Copyright (c) 1986-1999 by cisco Systems, Inc.
Compiled Wed 28-Apr-99 17:29 by kpma


-------------------------
Device ID: 003080C7CD40
Entry address(es):
  IP address: 172.16.10.200
Platform: cisco 1900,  Capabilities: Trans-Bridge Switch
Interface: Ethernet0,  Port ID (outgoing port): 12
```

```
Holdtime : 129 sec

Version :
V8.01
```

Notice that you receive the IP address of the interface from which you receive the information. This can help you create a network diagram, because you can now telnet into the router if you know the passwords. By typing show cdp entry *, we were able to find all our directly connected neighbors. We found one 2501 router, a 2621 router and a 1900 switch.

You can type show cdp entry *hostname* to gather the information about only one neighboring device:

```
router#show cdp entry 2621
-------------------------
Device ID: 2621
Entry address(es):
  IP address: 172.16.10.5
Platform: cisco 2621,  Capabilities: Router
Interface: Ethernet0,  Port ID (outgoing port): FastEthernet0/0
Holdtime : 166 sec

Version :
Cisco Internetwork Operating System Software
IOS (tm) C2600 Software (C2600-DOS-M), Version 12.0(4)T,  RELEASE SOFTWARE (fc1)
Copyright (c) 1986-1999 by cisco Systems, Inc.
Compiled Wed 28-Apr-99 17:29 by kpma
```

show cdp neighbors

The show cdp neighbors command gives you information about directly attached Cisco devices:

```
router#show cdp neighbors
Capability Codes: R - Router, T - Trans Bridge, B - Source Route Bridge S -
    Switch, H - Host, I - IGMP, r - Repeater
```

Device ID	Local Intrfce	Holdtme	Capability	Platform	Port ID
2621	Eth 0	161	R	2621	Fas 0/0
Router	Eth 0	139	R	2500	Eth 0
003080C7CD40	Eth 0	140	T S	1900	12

```
router#
```

For each neighbor, `show cdp neighbors` displays the following:

Neighbor device ID   The hostname of the neighbor router that this router exchanges CDP information with.

Local interface   The local interface on the local router that the device is attached to. Notice that everything is being heard from Ethernet 0.

Holdtime   How much longer the device will hold the neighbor information before discarding.

Capability   The router's capability code—*R* for router, *S* for switch, and so on.

Platform   Which type of Cisco device the neighbor is.

Port ID   The neighboring interface from which the CDP information is broadcasted.

The `sh cdp neighbor detail` command will give you the same information as the `sh cdp entry *` command:

```
router#show cdp neighbor detail
-------------------------
Device ID: 2621
Entry address(es):
  IP address: 172.16.10.5
Platform: cisco 2621,  Capabilities: Router
Interface: Ethernet0,  Port ID (outgoing port): FastEthernet0/0
Holdtime : 151 sec

Version :
Cisco Internetwork Operating System Software
IOS (tm) C2600 Software (C2600-DOS-M), Version 12.0(4)T,  RELEASE SOFTWARE (fc1)
Copyright (c) 1986-1999 by cisco Systems, Inc.
Compiled Wed 28-Apr-99 17:29 by kpma

-------------------------
Device ID: Router
Entry address(es):
  IP address: 172.16.10.51
Platform: cisco 2500,  Capabilities: Router
Interface: Ethernet0,  Port ID (outgoing port): Ethernet0
Holdtime : 129 sec

Version :
Cisco Internetwork Operating System Software
```

```
IOS (tm) 2500 Software (C2500-D-L), Version 11.3(8), RELEASE SOFTWARE (fc1)
Copyright (c) 1986-1999 by cisco Systems, Inc.
Compiled Tue 02-Feb-99 05:04 by dschwart


-------------------------
Device ID: 003080C7CD40
Entry address(es):
  IP address: 172.16.10.200
Platform: cisco 1900,  Capabilities: Trans-Bridge Switch
Interface: Ethernet0,  Port ID (outgoing port): 12
Holdtime : 130 sec


Version :
V8.01
```

 Real World Scenario

CDP Neighbors

The use of CDP can actually be a great troubleshooting tool to use day to day. If you are responsible for a large network environment, and if you are like most of us in that good documentation of the network infrastructure is an almost unreachable dream, then we're sure you can probably relate to this issue. We are of course referring to getting the dreaded call that there is a problem in the network, and it always seems that the 3:00 AM calls are always dealing with an obscure remote site for which nobody has any documentation or even any idea of what equipment is installed.

That is when our good old friend CDP comes to the rescue. You can work your way, one device at a time, through the network by discovering via CDP all the devices that connect to or are neighbors with the device you are telnetted into. You can telnet to the neighbor device, discover its neighbors via CDP, then telnet to the next neighbor, and so on until you are able to create a network diagram for that remote site.

Once you have the site diagram, troubleshooting the actual issue becomes greatly simplified. After all, a picture is worth a thousand words.

 A CCIE lab tip for you is use CDP to determine the IP or IPX addresses of devices that are attached to a device.

Hopefully you are feeling comfortable with CDP now, because it can be a great troubleshooting tool to allow you to verify equipment connectivity. Next we will discuss how to control who is allowed to telnet into the router. This can be a good first-line security mechanism. An ACL can also be a great tool. You can use them to control who is allowed to telnet into the router. This can be a good first-line security mechanism and is the topic we'll discuss next.

WARNING Where routers are attached to public networks, CDP is considered a security risk and should be disabled.

Using an ACL to Control Vty Access

If you can avoid configuring access control lists (ACLs) on your router, so much the better because access lists can waste precious CPU cycles. However, if you need to control access to telnet to your router and you don't trust passwords alone to manage your security, you can set up an access list to give you that extra security.

But if you were to add a standard or extended IP access list to your router to control port 23 access (Telnet), to which interface would you add the access list? All of them? You would have to because Telnet can be used on any active interface.

Cisco has created a way to control vty (Telnet) access on your router without wasting precious CPU cycles and without having to put an access list on every interface; you create an IP standard or extended access list, but you don't apply it to the interfaces, you apply it to the vty lines:

```
Router#config t
Enter configuration commands, one per line.  End with CNTL/Z.
Router(config)#access-list 10 permit 172.16.30.0 0.0.0.255
Router(config)#line vty 0 4
Router(config-line)#access-?
access-class

Router(config-line)#access-class ?
  <1-199>  IP access list
  <1300-2699>  IP expanded access list
Router(config-line)#access-class 10 in
```

NOTE Newer releases of Cisco IOS and particular Cisco IOS–based switches can have 16 vty lines configured (as opposed to 5), so you may need to use the `line vty 0 15` command to apply the access class to all lines.

Notice that the command to add the access list to the vty lines is `access-class`. We created a standard access list, but as the help screen shows, you can use either a standard or an extended access list. In the previous example, we limited the Telnet access to only hosts from network 172.16.30.0. Because we don't have a second line, the default is `deny any`.

You don't have to add the `access-class` command to all lines, but it is recommended because you can't control what line you enter the router on. Also, be sure you don't lock yourself out. For better security, it would be better to add just the hosts that need to access the routers. However, always put a second host in the access list in case the first one goes down. Of course, you could simply change the IP address on a different host, but just adding the hosts might be easier:

```
Router(config)#access-list 10 permit 172.16.30.4 0.0.0.0
Router(config)#access-list 10 permit 172.16.30.5 0.0.0.0
```

Notice that we only permitted two hosts, instead of a whole network.

As was stated earlier, using the `access-class` command can be a good first-line security mechanism. Now we'll talk about what a terminal access server (TAS) is and how it can be a welcome addition to a network infrastructure, not to mention that you must be knowledgeable on the use of a TAS to prepare for the CCIE lab examination.

Terminal Access Server

This section focuses on the correct configuration to provide terminal access server functionality within a router. A *terminal access server* is also referred to as a TAS. You must know the proper configuration and procedure for performing a reverse Telnet for the CCIE qualification exam, but you also must know how to use the reverse Telnet capability for the CCIE lab exam. In the actual lab examination, the terminal access server may already be configured for you, but we wanted to include this information so that you are familiar with the configuration and functionality for everyday use. Also, you should configure a terminal access server in your own lab environment so that you are comfortable with its use and maneuvering around the various routers and switches.

Speed is very important in the CCIE lab exam. You are expected to perform a large amount of complex configurations within an extremely limited amount of time. By feeling comfortable with this test environment, you will be able to quickly perform the simpler tasks and allow more time for the complex tasks that may take longer to configure and verify.

Cisco provides four 2500 series routers that can be configured to provide the access server functionality. These are the 2509, 2510, 2511, and 2512 routers. It is also possible to use a 2600 or 3600 series routers with a 16- or 32-port asynchronous network module installed. We are going to specifically address the terminal access sever functionality. The terminal access server is used to provide reverse Telnet capability to all of your equipment console ports. A *reverse Telnet* is a Telnet session that is initiated out of an asynchronous port on the terminal access server to a console port on the destination device console port. The destination console port is connected directly to one of the terminal access server's asynchronous ports with a standard Cisco rolled cable.

Terminal Access Server Functionality

To perform a reverse telnet, there must be an active IP address on the terminal access server. Then, you perform a Telnet to the active IP address followed by a 20*XX* (where *XX* is the number of the asynchronous port, or line, that the console cable is connected to). In Figure 2.1, the terminal access server has been configured with an active interface loopback0 and IP address of 147.19.24.1. So, we are able to perform a reverse telnet to router R1 by issuing the command `telnet 147.19.24.1 2001`:

FIGURE 2.1   Terminal access server

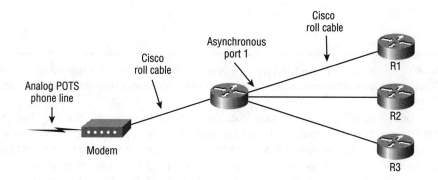

Notice that we used the command `telnet 147.19.24.1 2001`; we did so because R1 is connected to the asynchronous port (line) #1 on the terminal access server. If R2 had been our destination, we would have used the command `telnet 147.19.24.1 2002` because R2 is connected to the asynchronous port (line) #2 on the terminal access server. Using the same basic concept, you can also set up local host addresses for each connected device and then you will be able to reverse-telnet by the device name.

Using a Reverse Telnet Session

After you have created a reverse Telnet session to a destination router, you can return to the terminal access server prompt and keep the session to the destination router active. This can be done by using the escape sequence followed by the letter *x*, the keystroke is Ctrl+Shift+6, then X.

You can use the `escape-character` command on the line used for reverse Telnet to modify the escape sequence.

At this point, you are at the terminal access server prompt but the session to R1 is still active. You can perform a reverse telnet to R2 as previously explained. Now you are at the R2 prompt, but the terminal access server has active sessions open to both R1 and R2.

If you back out of your session from R2 with the key sequence Ctrl+Shift+6, then X, you will be back at the terminal access server prompt. If you issue the command show sessions, you will notice that the session to R1 is now connection (Conn) #1 and the session to R2 is now connection (Conn) #2. The asterisk denotes the current active session, and pressing <Enter> takes you right back to the R2 router prompt. If you want to return to R1 using the active session, simply type the number 1 and you will be back at the R1 prompt. Shown here is the output of a show sessions command:

```
TAS#show sessions
Conn Host            Address          Byte  Idle Conn Name
   1 R1              1.1.1.1             0     0 R1
*  2 R2              1.1.1.1             0     0 R2
```

 If you are at the TAS prompt and you press <Enter> without specifying a command, you will be connected to the most recent active connection from which you escaped.

To disconnect or kill an active session from the terminal access server, use the disconnect connection number command. So, to kill the active session to R1, from the terminal access server prompt, issue the command disconnect 1. Remember, when you use the exit command, it will kill all active sessions as well as take you out of the terminal access server.

When you're using a terminal access server and reverse Telnet sessions to practice for the CCIE lab examination, we recommend that you connect (initiate the reverse Telnet sessions) in sequential order. By this we mean that router R1 is the first connected session (session 1), router R2 is the second connected session (session 2), and so on.

Out-of-Band Management

Terminal access servers are typically utilized to provide an *out-of-band management* function. In case you lose network connectivity to a remote site, you can use an analog *plain old telephone service (POTS)* or *public switched telephone network (PSTN)* phone line to dial into the terminal access server and then reverse-telnet into the desired destination device. The following is a basic configuration to support an external modem connected off of the Auxiliary port of the terminal access server:

```
line aux 0
    password cisco            Password to use in conjunction with the
                              Login command
    autoselect ppp            Enable dial in users to bypass the EXEC
                              facility, and automatically start PPP
    login                     All connections must be logged in
                              (authenticated) with the password
```

```
modem InOut                    Drop connection on loss of DCD, allows
                               outbound connections to the modem
transport input all            Allow outbound connections to this line
stopbits 1                     Improve throughput by reducing async
                               framing overhead  (Default stopbits = 2)
speed 38400                    Set to the highest speed in common
                               between the modem and the port
flowcontrol hardware           RTS/CTS flow control
```

Likewise, you can configure a LAN connection (Ethernet or token ring) to the terminal access server, which will provide you the capability to telnet to the terminal access server. Then you can perform your reverse telnets from the terminal access server to all the devices at that remote site while maintaining only one Telnet session from your workstation.

Terminal Access Server Configuration

To properly configure the terminal access server, you must configure the asynchronous lines to accept network protocols; this is accomplished with the `transport input all` command. Also, you must ensure that the terminal access server does *not* allow any incoming traffic to spawn a virtual EXEC session from the destination device; this is accomplished with the `no exec` command.

Although we used the interface Loopback0 as our active IP address in the example in the section "Terminal Access Server Functionality" earlier in this chapter, any active IP address can be used for the reverse Telnet function (e.g., IP address on the interface Ethernet0, interface Tokenring0, and so on). It is preferred to use a loopback interface for the reverse Telnet function because it is a stable interface that will never go to an unreachable DOWN state.

When configuring the terminal access server, you can use an `ip host` command to statically map a destination device to an asynchronous port. This allows you to perform a reverse telnet session from the terminal access server to the destination device by simply typing the destination device's name. Notice in the sample configuration commands from a Cisco 2511 router that follows that the `ip host` command is in the form of the destination device's name (R2), the asynchronous port it is connected to (2002), and then the active IP address of the terminal access server (147.19.24.1):

```
interface Loopback0            Create an interface loopback0
  ip address 147.19.24.1 255.255.255.255   Assign the interface IP
                               address 147.19.24.1

ip host R2 2002 147.19.24.1    Router R2 is connected off of port
                               2 using Loopback 0, IP address
                               147.19.24.1. This sets up a local
                               host name for router R2
```

```
line 1 16
    transport input all          Allows the asynchronous ports to
                                 accept all network protocols
    no exec                      This will NOT allow any inbound
                                 EXEC sessions on the lines
```

 The no exec command is very important because it prevents the TAS from interpreting data sent from the lines and spawning an EXEC session. If you don't use this command, very strange things can happen with your TAS sessions.

Terminal Access Server Troubleshooting

Sometimes an asynchronous port (line) may get hung up and require you to return it to an idle state. This can be accomplished by using the clear line *asynchronous port number* command. So, to return asynchronous port #1 to an idle state, issue the command clear line 1 (you *must* be in privileged "enable" mode). You are able to view the status of all the asynchronous lines by performing a show line command, as shown in the following output (* indicates which lines are supporting active connections):

```
TAS#show line
```

	Tty	Typ	Tx/Rx	A	Modem	Roty	AccO	AccI	Uses	Noise	Overruns	Int
*	0	CTY		-	-	-	-	-	0	0	0/0	
	1	TTY	9600/9600	-	-	-	-	-	0	0	0/0	
*	2	TTY	9600/9600	-	-	-	-	-	3	0	0/0	
*	3	TTY	9600/9600	-	-	-	-	-	1	0	0/0	
	4	TTY	9600/9600	-	-	-	-	-	0	0	0/0	
	5	TTY	9600/9600	-	-	-	-	-	0	0	0/0	
	6	TTY	9600/9600	-	-	-	-	-	0	0	0/0	
	7	TTY	9600/9600	-	-	-	-	-	0	0	0/0	
	8	TTY	9600/9600	-	-	-	-	-	0	0	0/0	
	9	TTY	9600/9600	-	-	-	-	-	0	0	0/0	
	10	TTY	9600/9600	-	-	-	-	-	0	0	0/0	
	11	TTY	9600/9600	-	-	-	-	-	0	0	0/0	
	12	TTY	9600/9600	-	-	-	-	-	0	0	0/0	
	13	TTY	9600/9600	-	-	-	-	-	0	0	0/0	
	14	TTY	9600/9600	-	-	-	-	-	0	0	0/0	
	15	TTY	9600/9600	-	-	-	-	-	0	0	0/0	
	16	TTY	9600/9600	-	-	-	-	-	0	0	0/0	

At times, you may receive a reply message such as `Connection refused by remote host`. It may be necessary to use the `disconnect` and `clear line` commands in conjunction to completely return the asynchronous port to an idle state. Also, make sure the `no exec` command is applied to the asynchronous lines on the terminal access server. Without this command, the destination devices can initiate EXEC sessions from themselves to the terminal access server, which locks up the line and prevents you from performing a reverse telnet to the destination device.

Summary

In this chapter, we showed you how to set your passwords and how to manipulate the configuration register settings, as well as how to copy a Cisco IOS to an IOS server as a backup and how to restore or upgrade a Cisco IOS from a TFTP server.

This chapter also gave you a good review of how Cisco Discovery Protocol (CDP) functions and how to use it to gain information about other Cisco devices throughout your internetwork.

The terminal access server is an important piece in the total network architecture. Through the use of a POTS (PSTN) dial-in connection, it allows for out-of-band management in case of a network outage and loss of connectivity. It also provides a central point to launch reverse Telnet sessions at each remote site. This functionality can be useful even when there is no network outage or loss of connectivity.

As stated earlier, the terminal access server may already be configured for you in the actual CCIE lab examination. However, this is an important concept to understand and use in an everyday on-the-job application.

Exam Essentials

Understand the three types of memory in a Cisco router.   Flash memory is used to hold the full IOS image, NVRAM is used to store the startup configuration file, and DRAM is used as the working memory that holds the running-config, routing tables, ARP tables, and so on.

Be able to explain how the configuration register works.   All Cisco routers have a 16-bit software register, which is written into the nonvolatile memory. The configuration register is set by default to load the Cisco IOS from flash memory and to look for and load the startup-config file from NVRAM.

Know what Cisco Discovery Protocol (CDP) is.   Cisco Discovery Protocol (CDP) is a Cisco-proprietary protocol that uses a SNAP frame at the Data-Link layer to gather information about neighboring Cisco devices like routers and switches.

Know how to enable and disable CDP.   You can turn the CDP protocol off completely on a Cisco device or you can just turn it off on a certain interface or selection of interfaces. To turn it off completely, use the `no cdp run` global configuration command. To turn CDP off on only one interface, use the `no cdp enable` command from interface configuration mode.

Know how to perform a reverse Telnet session.   To perform a reverse telnet, there must be an active IP address on the terminal access server. Then, you perform a telnet to the active IP address followed by a 200*X* (where *X* is the number of the asynchronous port, or line, that the console cable is connected to).

Key Terms

Before you take the exam, be certain you are familiar with the following terms:

channel service unit/data service unit (CSU/DSU)	out-of-band management
Cisco Discovery Protocol (CDP)	plain old telephone service (POTS)
data communication equipment (DCE)	public switched telephone network (PSTN)
data terminal equipment (DTE)	reverse Telnet
maximum transmission unit (MTU)	terminal access server
nonvolatile RAM (NVRAM)	

Review Questions

1. When a router is first booted, where is the IOS loaded from by default?

   A. Boot ROM

   B. NVRAM

   C. Flash

   D. ROM

2. Which command will give you the same information as the `sh cdp entry *` command?

   A. `sh cdp neighbor detail`

   B. `sh cdp entry all`

   C. `sh cdp neighbor`

   D. `show cdp traffic`

3. Which configuration register setting will boot the router to ROM monitor mode?

   A. 0x2100

   B. 0x2101

   C. 0x2102

   D. 0x210F

4. Which configuration register setting will tell the router to use the boot command specified in NVRAM? (Choose all that apply.)

   A. 0x2100

   B. 0x2101

   C. 0x2102

   D. 0x210F

5. If you are in enable mode and want to return to exec mode, which command do you use?

   A. `exit`

   B. `quit`

   C. `disable`

   D. Ctrl+Z

6. Which command will show you the contents of the EEPROM in your router?

   A. `show flash`

   B. `show flash file`

   C. `show ip flash`

   D. `sh ver`

7. Which of the following commands will load an IOS image from a TFTP host?

    A. `load flash tftp 172.16.30.2 IOS_Name`

    B. `copy tftp flash IOS_Name 172.16.10.2`

    C. `boot system flash 172.16.30.2 IOS_Name`

    D. `boot system tftp IOS_Name 172.16.10.2`

8. Which command will allow users to telnet into a router and not be prompted to enter an exec mode password?

    A. `login`

    B. `no login`

    C. `You can be default, no command needed`

    D. `no password`

9. What is the proper command to perform a reverse telnet out of async port (line) number 2?

    A. `telnet 147.19.24.1 2001`

    B. `telnet 147.19.24.1 2002`

    C. `telnet 147.19.24.2`

    D. `147.19.24.2`

10. What is the proper command to view the status of all the asynchronous lines within the TAS?

    A. `show sessions`

    B. `show async sessions`

    C. `show hosts`

    D. `show async line`

    E. `show line`

Answers to Review Questions

1. C. Flash memory is used by default on all Cisco routers to hold the IOS.

2. A. The `show cdp neighbor detail` and `show cdp entry` * are equivalent commands.

3. A. The configuration register setting of 0x2100 will tell the router to boot from ROM.

4. C, D. The configuration register setting of 0x2102-F tells the router to boot the IOS from flash and load the configuration from NVRAM.

5. C. The command `disable` will take you from enable mode to exec mode.

6. A. The flash memory is an EEPROM. The command `show flash` will show you all the files in flash memory.

7. D. The question asks which command will load an image, not copy one. `Boot system flash ios-name ip-address` is the command used to load an IOS from a TFTP host.

8. B. The command `no login` allows users to telnet into a router without an exec mode password.

9. B. You perform a telnet to the active IP address followed by a 200*X* (where *X* is the number of the asynchronous port that the console cable is connected to).

10. E. You are able to view the status of all the asynchronous lines by performing a `show line` command.

Chapter 3

WAN Technologies and Configuration

THE CCIE QUALIFICATION EXAM TOPICS COVERED IN THIS CHAPTER INCLUDE THE FOLLOWING:

- ✓ How packet switching compares with other technologies
- ✓ T1/E1 encoding
- ✓ SONET and POS
- ✓ Leased line protocols
- ✓ X.25 theory
- ✓ Frame Relay theory and terminology
- ✓ Types of compression
- ✓ Frame Relay enhancements
- ✓ Frame Relay switching
- ✓ Frame Relay with point-to-point and multipoint circuits

This chapter focuses on building wide area networks (WANs) and providing IP connectivity using synchronous serial interfaces. We will discuss Physical layer technologies, such as T1/E1 encoding and framing, Synchronous Optical Network (SONET), and Packets over SONET (POS). We will briefly discuss packet switching and the X.25 protocol suite as an introduction to Frame Relay. However, we will mainly focus on the following layer 2 encapsulation protocols:

- High-Level Data Link Control (HDLC), which is Cisco proprietary

- Point-to-Point Protocol (PPP)

- Frame Relay

WAN technologies is a core topic for CCIE, in the qualification exam and especially in the lab exam. The CCIE candidate must not be weak in this area. Although this would appear to be a relatively easy topic, if you don't have a strong foundation in layer 2 technologies and their operation, their interdependencies with layer 3 technologies will introduce hidden complexities in the lab examination. And of course, you must understand the Physical layer (layer 1) technologies.

It is pretty much a certainty that WAN technologies will be part of the CCIE qualification and lab exams, so getting a layer 2 network built and configured correctly is essential in the lab examination. All other upper-layer technologies require that layer 2 is configured properly. If layer 2 is not configured properly, unexpected symptoms will appear in your network.

Again, because it is a CCIE core technology, any weakness in this area will severely hinder a candidate's chances of passing the CCIE lab exam.

Physical Layer Technologies

The Physical layer is responsible for transporting the bits across the physical media, such as metallic cable, fiber, air waves, and so on. It is important that you understand the basic characteristics of synchronization and T1/E1 encoding/framing/line speeds. In the following sections, we'll take a look at each of these technologies.

Synchronous Lines (T1/E1)

Most networks are made up of leased lines and use time-division multiplexing (TDM), so they are synchronous in nature. *Synchronous* means that the transmitting and receiving ends of the circuit are both utilizing the same clock source.

The building block of synchronous circuits is the digital signal level 0 (DS0), which is 64Kbps. In North America and Japan, the most common carrier is the T1. It is has an aggregate speed of 1.544Mbps: there are 24 channels and each channel is a DS0, or 64Kbps, so 24×65Kbps = 1.536 Mbps; add 8Kbps of framing, so 1.536Mbps + 8Kbps = 1.544Mbps.

In Europe and other countries, the E1 carrier is the most common. The E1 has an aggregate speed of 2.048Mbps. The DS0 is still 64Kbps. The E1 is actually 32 channels (32×64Kbps = 2.048Mbps). One 64Kbps DS0 channel is used for framing and another is normally used for out-of-band signaling (leaving 30 channels, or 1920Kbps of data bandwidth), but the signaling channel can also be used as a data channel (leaving 31 channels, or 1984Kbps of data bandwidth).

In order to provide increased bandwidth, 28 T1s can be multiplexed into a DS3, which is 44.736Mbps. So, the DS3 is actually made up of 672 separate DS0s. Sometimes the DS3 signal is also referred to as a T3 (just as T1 and DS1 are used interchangeably). Actually, the T-carrier is the carrier signal the digital signal (DS) is transported on top of.

Encoding and Framing

A T1 can use either *alternate mark inversion (AMI)* or *bipolar 8-zero substitution (B8ZS)* encoding. With AMI encoding, 1s are represented by positive or negative voltage, alternating back and forth or flip-flopping. A 0 is represented as 0 voltage. The problem with AMI is that voltage levels are needed to maintain timing across a circuit. If you have too many 0s (no voltage) in a row, the circuit could loose timing and no longer be in sync. The solution to this problem is B8ZS.

The B8ZS encoding scheme deliberately inserts bipolar violations (two consecutive 1s at the same polarity) into the data stream to replace a series of eight consecutive 0s. At the receiving end of the circuit, the deliberate bipolar violation is removed and the eight consecutive 0s are reinserted, thus the proper data has been transmitted successfully.

A T1 circuit can implement Super Frame (SF, also known as D4 framing) or Extended Superframe Format (ESF). In SF, a series of 12 D4 frames are packaged as a super frame, and in ESF, a series of 24 D4 frames are packaged as an Extended super frame. You typically find an AMI circuit using SF (or D4) framing and a B8ZS circuit using ESF.

Timing

In order for devices at both ends of a circuit to remain synchronized, they must have a common clocking source. Usually when configuring devices for serial communication, you will source your clock (timing) from the line (the telco circuit) and the DTE interface device will loop back the transmit clock.

However, it is possible that the serial cable length is too far (causing delay), which will cause the data received at the far end to be phase-shifted. By default, the clock phase is not inverted, so it may be necessary to use the `invert txclock` command to correct for the phase-shifting. You may also have the DTE interface end of the circuit loop back the transmit clock. In that case, use the `dce-terminal-timing` command on the far-end DCE device to synchronize the received data at the DCE interface with the looped-back clock and do not use the `invert txclock` command.

SONET and SDH

Synchronous Optical Network (SONET) is of course a synchronous carrier, which can be multiplexed to several different aggregate speeds. SONET uses the Synchronous Transport Signal (STS) as its framing format. SONET is a Physical layer protocol for optical media, as opposed to T1/T3, which is a Physical layer protocol for copper media. Each SONET frame comprises 9 rows by 90 columns of octets for a total of 810 octets ($9 \times 90 = 810$). These 810 octets are transmitted in 125 microseconds, or 8000 frames per second (8000 x 125 microseconds = 1 second). So the basic aggregate rate of a STS-1 is 51.84Mbps (810 bytes per frame × 8 bits per byte × 8000 frames per second = 51.84Mbps).

The following are the SONET aggregate speeds:

- OC-1 = 51.84Mbps
- OC-3 = 155.52Mbps
- OC-12 = 622.08Mbps
- OC-24 = 1.244Gbps
- OC-48 = 2.488Gbps
- OC-192 = 9.952Gbps

Synchronous Digital Hierarchy (SDH) is the international equivalent of SONET. SDH is the international standard as defined by the International Telecommunications Union (ITU). SDH does not have the equivalent of the SONET OC-1 because SDH starts with an aggregate speed of 155.52Mbps.

The following are the SDH aggregate speeds:

- STM-1 = 155.52Mbps
- STM-2 = 622.08Mbps
- STM-3 = 2.488Gbps

Packet over SONET (PoS)

One method of transmitting data on top of SONET is asynchronous transfer mode (ATM). Another method is to use Packet over SONET (PoS). PoS maps IP directly into the SONET/SDH frames and is made up of three parts:

- Link-layer protocol
- Octet framing to map onto the SONET payload
- Data scrambling for security and reliability

PoS specifies STS-3c/STM-1 (155Mbps) as the standard aggregate speed, with a usable bandwidth of 149.760Mbps.

PoS also provides for the automatic protection switching (APS) feature, which is supported on Cisco 7500 series routers and Cisco 12000 series routers. This feature allows switchover of

POS circuits in the event of circuit failure and is often required when connecting SONET equipment to telco equipment. APS refers to the mechanism of using an `aps protect` POS interface in the SONET network as the backup for the `aps working` POS interface. When the working interface fails, the `aps protect` interface quickly assumes its traffic load. The following is an example of how to configure the POS1/1 interface to protect the POS1/0 interface:

```
interface POS1/0
 ip address 10.1.1.1 255.255.255.0
 crc 16
 aps group 10
 aps working 1

interface POS1/1
 ip address 10.1.1.3 255.255.255.0
 no keepalive
 crc 16
 aps group 10
 aps revert 1
 aps protect 1 100.1.1.1
```

Dynamic Packet Transport (DPT)/Spatial Reuse Protocol (SRP)

Dynamic Packet Transport (DPT) is a Cisco-developed resilient optical packet ring technology that is optimized for packet transmission. DPT uses dual, counter-rotating rings that are referred to as inner and outer and can be used for data and control packets concurrently. DPT operates by transmitting the data packets across one ring in one direction and the control packets across the other ring in the other direction. DPT is now referred to as resilient packet ring (RPR).

DPT uses Spatial Reuse Protocol (SRP), a MAC layer protocol. According to Cisco, SRP was designed to be scalable and provide optimized IP packet aggregation/transport in LANs, MANs, and WANs. It can support 128 nodes running at high speeds (OC-48c/STM-16c and OC-192c/STM64c).

SRP is more efficient than older technologies such as token ring and FDDI, which use source stripping, meaning that packets transverse the entire ring before being stripped by the source. SRP uses destination stripping, meaning that the packets travel across the ring from source to destination and are striped at the destination. This frees up bandwidth on other segments of the ring and it can be used by other stations.

Now that we have discussed the predominate Physical layer technologies, we'll work our way up the OSI model to the Data-Link layer technologies, such as HDLC, PPP, and Frame Relay.

Data-Link Technologies

The Data-Link layer provides reliable transport of the bits (which are represented as electrical, optical, or frequency signals) across the Physical layer. This layer formats the bits into frames for transmission. It is important that you understand the layer 2 technologies most commonly used in the WAN environment:

- High-Level Data Link Control (HDLC)
- Point-to-Point Protocol (PPP)
- Frame Relay

In the following sections, we'll take a look at each of these technologies, but first we'll discuss the X.25 protocol suite, which was the first major deployed packet-switched technology. You can actually think of X.25 as the father of Frame Relay.

Packet Switching and X.25

The development of WAN technology has followed a path of consistently providing more bandwidth, flexibility, and reliability. The need for WAN data circuits was apparent even during the development of the first commercial computers in the 1960s. The real question was how to make the best use of the very limited bandwidth available and how to ensure reliability.

Before we get into a discussion of the X.25 protocol suite, let's take a look at packet switching.

Packet Switching

Packet switching makes maximum use of available bandwidth and can handle bursty traffic (prone to periods of high activity followed by periods of inactivity). Packet switching relies heavily on buffering. In a dedicated line or time-division multiplexing, available bandwidth is strictly allocated among different conversations, and the bandwidth utilized by conversation cannot exceed its allocated bandwidth. POTS telephony is an example of this. This brings us to this packet switching rule: the sum of the input lines' bandwidth can, and often does, exceed the bandwidth of the output line.

 An important concept in packet switching is that the aggregate bandwidth required for all conversations can be greater than the actual bandwidth of the line.

At first glance, this rule sounds impossible, but consider the nature of data traffic. Data traffic, unlike voice traffic, is bursty. Instead of traveling in a steady stream, data travels in relatively unpredictable large chunks. This factor makes packet switching possible.

Frame Relay and X.25 are the two most popular implementations of packet-switching networks. Although they use the same fundamental technology, they vary greatly in theory and in function.

Now we'll discuss the X.25 protocol suite.

X.25 Protocol Suite

In 1976, the CCITT (currently named the ITU) released the X.25 specification, which addressed the need for standardization of WAN connection. *X.25* is similar to Frame Relay in several ways, but the most striking difference is that X.25 is defined in three layers of the OSI reference model whereas Frame Relay is defined only at layer 2.

The X.25 protocol suite specification has three layers. The packet layer of X.25 stacks up to the Network layer of the OSI model, the link layer to the Data-Link layer, and the physical layer to the Physical layer.

X.25 is widely implemented not only because it was the first standardized WAN packet-switching protocol, but because it is an extraordinarily reliable and surprisingly robust protocol. In this section, we will examine each of the X.25 layers, from the bottom up. X.25 uses both permanent virtual circuits (PVCs) and switched virtual circuits (SVCs).

The Physical Level Layer

The physical layer is concerned with the electrical and procedural interface between a DTE device and a DCE device. The ITU's three recommendations for the X.25 physical layer are as follows:

X.21   The recommended standard for digital circuit operation

X.21-bis   The recommended standard that defines the analog interface to allow access to the digital switched network

V.24   The standard that provides procedures that enable the DTE to operate over leased analog circuits

We will discuss X.21 because it is by far the most popular implementation. The other two standards are rarely used with X.25.

X.21 STANDARD

X.21 handles the activation and deactivation of the physical layer between the DCE and DTE devices. Table 3.1 shows the eight channels defined by X.21. X.21 supports point-to-point connections at various speeds.

TABLE 3.1   The X.21 Interchange Circuit

Line	Name	From DTE	From DCE
G	Signal ground		
Ga	DTE return	X	
T	Transmit	X	
R	Receive		X

TABLE 3.1   The X.21 Interchange Circuit *(continued)*

Line	Name	From DTE	From DCE
C	Control	X	
I	Indication		X
S	Signal timing		X
B	Byte timing		X

The Link Layer

The link layer establishes next-hop connectivity. The X.25 standard allows several protocols at layer 2. *Link Access Procedure Balanced (LAPB)* is derived from HDLC and is the most commonly used. In addition to all the features of HDLC, it also allows for the establishment of a logical connection. *Link Access Procedure* is an earlier version of LAPB and is rarely used. *Link Access Procedure D Channel (LAPD)* is used with ISDN. *Logical Link Control (LLC)* allows for the transmission of X.25 across LANs. The link layer for X.25 is usually implemented as LAPB. LAPB guarantees the delivery of data between the DTE and the DCE.

The LAPB protocol is responsible for the following:

- Delivering the data efficiently
- Synchronizing the link
- Detecting and recovering transmission errors
- Identifying and reporting procedural errors to higher layers

The LAPB frame begins and ends with the same flag sequence (01111110) as Frame Relay. The Address field indicates whether the frame contains a command or a response. The Control field contains sequence numbers, commands, and responses for controlling the data flow.

There are three types of LAPB frames:

Information   Carries the actual data across the network. Also uses sequence numbers to maintain flow control and ordered delivery. Information frames send and receive sequence numbers.

Supervisory   Carries control information (flow control), includes RECEIVE READY (RR), REJECT (REJ), and RECEIVE NOT READY (RNR) signals. Supervisory frames only receive sequence numbers; they do not transmit sequence numbers. The Control field inside the LAPB frame includes the sequence number that refers to the point of the communications session that the Supervisory frame relates to.

Unnumbered   Used for control purposes only, such as link setup or disconnection and error reporting. The Control field does not carry sequence numbers (hence the term *unnumbered*). Instead, it carries commands that indicate the control event represented by the unnumbered frame.

The implication of using LAPB at the link layer is that the circuit should be much more reliable because LAPB provides guaranteed delivery, out-of-order frame delivery, data integrity, and flow control services.

The Packet Layer

Packet level protocol (PLP) is the X.25 packet level protocol. PLP manages the transmission of data through the virtual circuits. It is also responsible for the error detection and recovery process at the network layer. PLP has five modes of operation (one more than Frame Relay) to initialize the virtual circuit:

Call Setup   Initiates and establishes the call.

Data Transfer   Transmits data traffic across traffic.

Idle   Indicates that the virtual circuit is active but data is not transmitted.

Call Clearing   Terminates the call.

Restarting   Resets the call to resynchronize communication.

Network Address at the Packet Layer

One of the most important features of the packet layer is the network address. X.25 uses the *X.121 address specification* to identify network entities. The X.121 address specification provides a globally unique addressing scheme. In some ways, X.121 addresses are similar to phone numbers and are used in establishing connections.

The X.121 address contains a maximum of 14 digits and is called the *International Data Number (IDN)*. The first four digits constitute the *Data Network Identification Code (DNIC)*. The DNIC is composed of a three-digit country code and a one-digit public switched network identifier. The remaining digits (as many as 10 of them) make up the *National Terminal Number (NTN)*, indicating the particular device on the public switched network.

X.25 allows for extraordinary reliability across the network. Error checking and correction occurs at both layer 2 and layer 3. X.25 will continue to be popular wherever a reliable protocol is needed.

Now that we've given you a brief run-through packet switching and the X.25 protocol suite, we'll discuss the layer 2 encapsulation protocols that we mentioned at the beginning of this chapter.

Protocol Translation

Cisco routers can also be configured as protocol translators, which enable communication between X.25 and IP devices. However, the only supported IP-based application is Telnet. An IP host can telnet to a specific IP address, which will get translated by the router (acting as a protocol translator) to an X.121 address and forwarded to the X.25 end station.

The protocol translation function can be configured with the `translate tcp` *ip-address* `x25` *x.121-address* global command. To translate X.25 to IP (Telnet), the command is reversed: `translate x25` *x.121-address* `tcp` *ip-address*.

High-Level Data Link Control (HDLC) Protocol

The *High-Level Data Link Control (HDLC) protocol* is a popular ISO-standard, bit-oriented, Data-Link layer protocol that specifies an encapsulation method for data on synchronous serial data links using frame characters and checksums.

In byte-oriented protocols, control information is encoded using entire bytes. Bit-oriented protocols, on the other hand, may use single bits to represent control information. Other byte-oriented protocols include SDLC, LLC, Transmission Control Protocol (TCP), and Internet Protocol (IP).

HDLC has three operating (transfer) modes:

Normal Response Mode (NRM)   Used in unbalanced configurations. In this mode, slave stations (or secondary stations) can transmit only when specially instructed by the master (primary station). The link may be point-to-point or multipoint. In the latter case, only one primary station is allowed.

Asynchronous Response Mode (ARM)   This mode is used in unbalanced configurations. It allows a secondary station to initiate a transmission without receiving permission from the primary station. This mode is normally used with point-to-point configurations and full duplex links and allows the secondary station to send frames asynchronously with respect to the primary station.

Asynchronous Balanced Mode (ABM)   Used mainly on full duplex point-to-point links for computer-to-computer communications and for connections between a computer and a packet switched data network. In this case, each station has an equal status and performs the both primary and secondary functions. This mode is used in the protocol set known as X.25.

HDLC is the default encapsulation used by Cisco routers over synchronous serial links. Cisco's HDLC is proprietary—it won't communicate with any other vendor's HDLC implementation—but don't give Cisco grief for it; everyone's HDLC implementation is proprietary.

HDLC is used in the PPP stack, which is discussed in the next section. However, this is the ISO version of HDLC, and it has a nonproprietary method of identifying the Network layer protocol through Link Control Protocol (LCP). If LCP is not used and only HDLC is used at the MAC sublayer of the Data-Link layer, however, there must be a way to identify the Network layer protocol being transmitted. This is why HDLC is proprietary per vendor. Each vendor has created its own way of encapsulating the Network layer packets into the HDLC format for transmission on point-to-point links. If you need to communicate between the serial interfaces of various vendors, you must use the ISO standard HDLC, which is utilized in Point-to-Point Protocol (PPP).

Point-to-Point Protocol (PPP)

Point-to-Point Protocol (PPP) is a Data-Link protocol that can be used over either asynchronous serial (dial-up) or synchronous serial (ISDN or leased line) media and that uses LCP to build and maintain data-link connections.

The basic purpose of PPP is to transport layer 3 packets across a Data-Link layer point-to-point link. Figure 3.1 shows the protocol stack compared with the OSI Reference model.

FIGURE 3.1   The Point-to-Point Protocol (PPP) stack

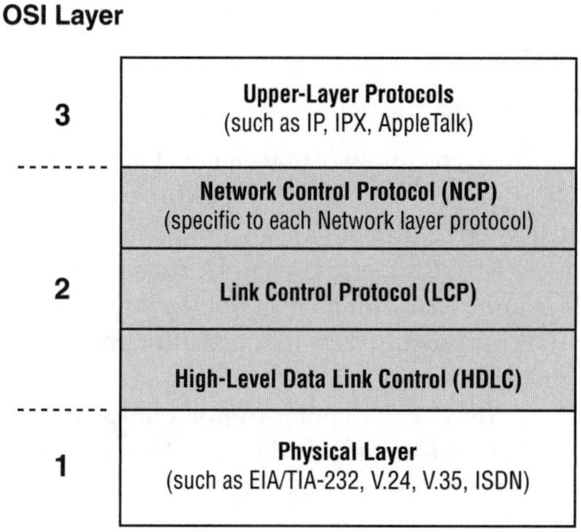

OSI Layer

3	**Upper-Layer Protocols** (such as IP, IPX, AppleTalk)
	Network Control Protocol (NCP) (specific to each Network layer protocol)
2	**Link Control Protocol (LCP)**
	High-Level Data Link Control (HDLC)
1	**Physical Layer** (such as EIA/TIA-232, V.24, V.35, ISDN)

PPP contains four main components:

EIA/TIA-232-C   Physical layer international standard for serial communication. Other possible Physical layer standards are EIA-449, EIA-530, and V.35.

HDLC   A method for encapsulating datagrams over serial links.

LCP   A method of establishing, configuring, maintaining, and terminating the point-to-point connection.

Network Control Protocol (NCP)   A method for establishing and configuring different Network layer protocols. PPP is designed to allow the simultaneous use of multiple Network layer protocols. Some examples of protocols here are Internet Protocol Control Program (IPCP) and Internetwork Packet eXchange Control Program (IPXCP).

It is important to understand that the PPP stack is specified at the Physical and Data-Link layers only. NCP is used to allow multiple Network layer protocols to be encapsulated across a PPP link.

Multilink PPP

By using ISDN with PPP encapsulation, Cisco routers can support multiple connections over the same physical interface. Thus, Cisco routers can use dial-up connections to establish more than one connection at a time to an access server. Why would you want a router to be able to do that? You would because, if it can, you're granted twice the bandwidth of a single dial-up line. The capacity to increase bandwidth between point-to-point dial-up connections by grouping interfaces and then splitting and recalculating packets to run over that group of interfaces is called *multilink*.

Before you can run multilink, you must define the interesting packets using the `dialer-list` global command. This command directs the router to search for specific network protocols for making and keeping a link active. You can apply a dialer list to an interface using the subcommand `dialer-group`. We will discuss this more in depth when we talk about dial connections in Chapter 15, "Integrated Services Digital Network (ISDN) and Dial Backup."

Frame Relay

Frame Relay is a packet-switched technology that emerged in the early 1990s. It is a Data-Link and Physical layer specification that provides high performance, operates on the assumption that the facilities used are less error prone than when X.25 was used, and transmits data with less overhead. Because modern transmission circuits are considered much more reliable than circuits in the days of X.25, Frame Relay omits many of the reliability features of X.25, leaving these functions to upper-layer protocols. This means that Frame Relay transmits data with less overhead than its X.25 predecessor.

Frame Relay is more cost effective than point-to-point links and can typically run at speeds from 64KB to 1.544Mbps (1.984Mbps outside the U.S.). However, Frame Relay can operate at as high a speed as a DS3. Frame Relay networks provide features for dynamic bandwidth allocation and congestion control.

Frame Relay is used with a variety of network protocols. Cisco Frame Relay supports the following protocols:

- IP
- DECnet
- AppleTalk
- Xerox Network Service (XNS)
- Novell IPX
- Connectionless Network Service (CLNS)
- International Organization for Standardization (ISO)
- Banyan VINES
- Transparent bridging

Frame Relay provides a communications interface between data terminal equipment (DTE) and data circuit-terminating equipment (DCE) devices. DTE devices include terminals, PCs, routers, and bridges (customer-owned end node and internetworking devices), and DTE devices are devices such as packet switches.

Popular opinion maintains that Frame Relay is more efficient and faster than X.25 because it assumes error checking will be done through higher-layer protocols and application services.

Frame Relay provides connection-oriented, Data-Link layer communication via virtual circuits. These virtual circuits are logical connections created between two DTEs across a packet-switched network, which is identified by a Data Link Connection Identifier, or DLCI (we'll get to DLCIs in a bit). Also, like X.25, Frame Relay uses both PVCs and SVCs, although most Frame Relay networks use only PVCs.

Frame Relay Terminology

To understand the terminology used in Frame Relay networks, first you need to know how the technology works. Figure 3.2 is labeled with the various terms used to describe the parts of a Frame Relay network.

FIGURE 3.2   Frame Relay technology and terms

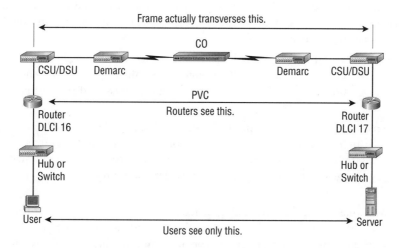

The basic idea behind Frame Relay is to allow users to communicate between two DTE devices through DCE. Users should not see the difference between connecting to and gathering resources from a local server and a server at a remote site connected with Frame Relay. Because the maximum speed is a DS3 (45Mbps), the connection will be slower than a 100Mbps Ethernet LAN, but the difference in the connection should be invisible to the user.

Figure 3.2 illustrates everything that must happen in order for two DTE devices to communicate. Here is how the process works:

1. The user's network device sends a frame out on the local network. The hardware address of the router (default gateway) will be in the header of the frame.

2. The router picks up the frame and extracts the packet. It then looks at the destination IP address within the packet and checks to see if it knows how to get to the destination network by looking in the routing table.

3. After looking up the destination network, the router needs to determine the dlci/pvc corresponding to the next-hop in the routed path. It typically can find the DLCI number of the next-hop router by looking up an IP-to-DLCI mapping. Frame Relay mappings are often created statically, but can also be created dynamically using the Inverse Address Resolution Protocol (IARP, or Inverse ARP) by the router. It then forwards the data out the interface corresponding to the dlci/pvc it has already determined. Because this will be a serial interface encapsulated with Frame Relay, the router puts the packet onto the Frame Relay network encapsulated within a Frame Relay frame. It will add the DLCI number associated with the virtual circuit to the destination. The DLCI identifies the virtual circuit (PVC or SVC) to the routers and switches participating in the Frame Relay network.

4. The channel service unit/data service unit (CSU/DSU) receives the digital signal and encodes it into the type of digital signaling that the switch at the packet switching exchange (PSE) can understand. The PSE receives the digital signal and extracts the 1s and 0s from the line.

   The CSU/DSU is connected to a demarcation (demarc) installed by the service provider, and its location is the service provider's first point of responsibility (the last point on the receiving end). The demarc is typically just an RJ-48S jack installed close to the router and the CSU/DSU in the U.S. Internationally, the point of demarcation varies because some service providers include the CSU/DSU with the circuit at the time of installation, which would make the CSU/DSU the point of demarcation.

5. The demarc is typically a twisted-pair cable that connects to the local loop. The local loop connects to the closest central office (CO), sometimes called a point of presence (POP). The local loop can connect using various physical mediums, but twisted-pair or fiber-optic cable is common.

6. The CO receives the frame and sends it through the Frame Relay "cloud" to its destination. This cloud can be dozens of switching offices—or more! Frame Relay switches in the cloud forward the frame based on its DLCI. As the frame traverses Frame Relay switches, its DLCI may change but it will still follow the provider-configured path (PVC) until it reaches the destination router.

7. Once the frame reaches the switching office closest to the destination office, it is sent through the local loop. The frame gets to the demarc and then to the CSU/DSU. Finally, the router extracts the packet, or datagram, from the frame and puts it in a new LAN frame to be delivered to the destination host. The frame on the LAN will have the final destination hardware address in the header. This address was found in the router's ARP cache or by performing an Address Resolution Protocol (ARP) broadcast. Whew!

The user and the server do not need to know, nor should they know, everything that happens as the frame makes its way across the Frame Relay network. The remote server should be as easy to use as a locally connected resource

Frame Relay with Cisco Routers

When configuring Frame Relay on Cisco routers, you need to specify it as an encapsulation on serial interfaces. The two encapsulation types are Cisco and Internet Engineering Task Force (IETF).

The default encapsulation is Cisco (indicating the original Frame Relay encapsulation created by Cisco Systems, StrataCom, Northern Telecom, and Digital Equipment Corporation, which became known as the Gang of Four) unless you manually type in IETF, and Cisco is the type used when connecting two Cisco devices. You'd opt for the IETF-type encapsulation if you needed to connect a Cisco device to a non-Cisco device with Frame Relay. If the provider is translating from Frame Relay to ATM, they might specify the type of encapsulation to use.

Data Link Connection Identifier (DLCI)

A Frame Relay virtual circuit (PVC) is identified by a DLCI (a 10-bit PVC identifier). A Frame Relay service provider, such as the telephone company, typically assigns DLCI values, which are used by Frame Relay to distinguish between different virtual circuits on the network. Because many virtual circuits can be terminated on one multipoint or one subinterface point-to-point Frame Relay interface, many DLCIs are often affiliated with it.

For the IP devices at each end of a virtual circuit to communicate, their IP addresses need to be mapped to DLCIs. This mapping can function as a multipoint device—one that can identify to the Frame Relay network the appropriate destination virtual circuit for each packet that is sent over the single physical interface. The mappings can be done dynamically by the router through Inverse ARP or manually through the `frame-relay map` command.

Every DLCI number is generally locally significant. What does this mean? It means that DLCI numbers do not necessarily need to be unique across the entire internetwork. Two DLCI numbers can be the same on different sides of a link because Frame Relay maps a local DLCI number to a virtual circuit on each interface of the telco's switch. The DLCI is defined by 10 noncontiguous bits in the header and can be a value of 16–1007.

Local Management Interface (LMI)

The Local Management Interface (LMI) was developed in 1990 by Cisco Systems, StrataCom, Northern Telecom, and Digital Equipment Corporation and became known as the Gang-of-Four LMI or Cisco LMI. This gang took the basic Frame Relay protocol from the Consultative Committee for International Telephony and Telegraphy (CCITT)—now known as the International Telecommunication Union (ITU)—and added extensions onto the protocol features that allow internetworking devices to communicate easily with a Frame Relay network.

The LMI is a signaling standard between a customer-premises equipment (CPE) device and a frame switch and is responsible for managing and maintaining status between these devices. LMI messages provide information about the following:

Keepalives   Verifies data connectivity to the telco (Frame Relay service provider)

Multicasting   Provides a local DLCI PVC

The status of virtual circuits   Provides DLCI status

There are three possible LMI types: Cisco, ansi, and q933a. Beginning with IOS version 11.2, the LMI type is determined automatically with the autosense feature. This enables the interface to determine the LMI type supported by the switch. If you're not going to use the autosense feature, you'll need to check with your Frame Relay provider to find out which type to use instead.

The default type is Cisco (Gang-of-Four), but you may need to change to ANSI or Q.933A. The three LMI types are depicted in the following router output:

```
RouterA(config-if)#frame-relay lmi-type ?
  cisco
  ansi
  q933a
```

As seen in the output, all three standard LMI signaling formats are supported:

- Cisco: LMI defined by the Gang of Four (default), uses DLCI 1023
- ANSI: Annex D defined by ANSI standard T1.617, uses DLCI 0
- ITU-T (q933a): Annex A defined by Q.933, uses DLCI 0

Committed Information Rate (CIR) and Discard Eligible (DE)

Usually when you lease Frame Relay services from a service provider, you receive a guaranteed amount of bandwidth up to a predefined maximum limit. Although the *committed information rate (CIR)* guarantees the rate, the user traffic can burst to higher rates if the service provider's Frame Relay network is underutilized. The CIR is defined in two ways, and its use depends on the Frame Relay provider's implementation. The CIR is either the maximum speed that the Frame Relay provider transfers information for each PVC, or it is the average rate (in bps) at which the network guarantees to transfer data over a specified time period.

Any packets which exceed the CIR are marked as *discard eligible (DE)*, which means that they can be thrown away if the service provider's Frame Relay cloud is congested.

Committed Burst, Excess Burst, and Committed Rate Measurement Interval

In order to understand Frame Relay, you must understand these three mechanisms:

Committed burst size (Bc)   The maximum amount of data (in bits) that the network agrees to transfer, under normal conditions, during a time interval (Tc).

Excess burst size (Be)   The maximum amount of uncommitted data (in bits) in excess of Bc that a Frame Relay network can attempt to deliver during a time interval Tc. This data (Be) generally is delivered with a lower probability than Bc. The network treats Be data as discard eligible.

Committed rate measurement interval (Tc)   The time interval during which the user can send only Bc committed amount of data and Be excess amount of data. In general, the duration of Tc is proportional to the "burstiness" of the traffic. Tc is computed (from the subscription parameters of CIR and Bc) as Tc = Bc/CIR. Tc is not a periodic time interval. Instead, it is used only to measure incoming data, and as the data is coming in, it acts like a sliding window. Incoming data triggers the Tc interval, which continues until it completes its commuted duration.

We will discuss these in further detail in Chapter 18, "Quality of Service (QoS)," when we discuss Frame Relay traffic shaping (FRTS).

FECN and BECN

Frame Relay provides a mechanism for alerting that there is congestion within the Frame Relay network and that the nodes need to start throwing away packets marked DE. This mechanism is the use of congestion notifications, such as Forward-Explicit Congestion Notification (FECN) and Backward-Explicit Congestion Notification (BECN).

A FECN notifies the receiving DTE that the frame experienced congestion within the service provider's Frame Relay network, whereas a BECN notifies the sending DTE that frames heading toward the destination are experiencing congestion within the network.

Compression

With Cisco routers, you can configure payload compression on point-to-point or multipoint interfaces. Either the Stacker method or FRF.9 using the Stacker method can be configured. The Stacker method uses an encoded dictionary to replace a stream of characters with codes.

The following is an example of a point-to-point Stacker configuration:

```
frame-relay payload-compress packet-by-packet
```

The following is an example of a multipoint subinterface Stacker configuration:

```
frame-relay map protocol protocol-address dlci payload-compress packet-by-packet
```

Frame Relay Forum 9 (FRF.9) uses higher compression ratios, which allows more data to be compressed for faster transmission. FRF.9 is recognized by the Frame Relay Forum as the standards-based compression.

The following is an example of a point-to-point FRF.9 configuration:

```
frame-relay payload-compress frf9 stac
```

The following is an example of a multipoint subinterface FRF.9 configuration:

```
frame-relay map protocol protocol-address dlci payload-compress frf9 stac
```

Subinterfaces

You can have multiple virtual circuits on a single serial interface and yet treat each as a separate point-to-point or multipoint interface. These are known as *subinterfaces*. Think of a subinterface as a virtual hardware interface defined by the IOS software.

An advantage gained through using subinterfaces is the ability to assign different Network layer characteristics to each subinterface and virtual circuit, such as IP routing on one virtual circuit and IPX on another or even different IP subnets per subinterface.

Now that you have a good understanding of HDLC and Frame Relay encapsulation, let's take a look at how to configure them on a router.

Configuring HDLC on a Cisco Router

Synchronous serial interfaces are supported on various serial network interface cards on Cisco router systems. Proprietary Cisco interfaces support full-duplex operation at T1 (1.544Mbps) and E1 (2.048Mbps) speeds. By default, synchronous serial lines use the High-Level Data Link Control (HDLC) encapsulation. This implementation of HDLC is Cisco proprietary and will not interoperate with non-Cisco devices.

As in any synchronous serial connection, a DTE must communicate with a DCE. In a real-world telecommunication environment, the telco equipment performs the function of the DCE; these functions include providing signaling as well as providing a clock source.

First, we will discuss how to view the controllers in the router to determine what type of cable is connected to the interface; then we will discuss the required commands to actually configure the HDLC encapsulation on an interface.

Physical Connectivity

In a lab environment where routers are connected back-to-back, a DTE-to-DCE cable must be used to connect two routers. To verify which side of a connection is the DCE side, use the show controller command. The following is the output from a show controller command:

```
show controller serial0/0
CD2430 Slot 0, Port 0, Controller 0, Channel 0, Revision 15
Channel mode is synchronous serial
idb 0x6101DF5C, buffer size 1524, V.35 DCE cable, clockrate 56000
```

As can be seen from this output, the serial0/0 interface has a V.35 DCE cable connected and the interface has a clock rate of 56000bps. This must be configured using the clock rate 56000 command on the specified serial interface.

```
show controller serial0/0
CD2430 Slot 0, Port 0, Controller 0, Channel 3, Revision 15
Channel mode is synchronous serial
idb 0x61031D20, buffer size 1524, V.35 DTE cable
```

As you can see, the serial0/0 interface has a V.35 DTE cable connected. The interface has no clock rate listed because the clock rate is being provided by the DCE side.

HDLC Configuration Commands

The following lines of code are the required commands to configure HDLC encapsulation on a router interface. Notice that we show the `encapsulation hdlc` command, but you don't need to type this command in the router because it is the default setting within Cisco IOS:

```
interface serial0/0
```

`encapsulation hdlc`	This is the default synchronous serial encapsulation type, and does not display when showing a router configuration.
`bandwidth 56`	Defined in Kbps. 56 Kbps = 56000 bps. Used by routing protocols for metric Calculation
`clockrate 56000`	Defined in bits per second 56,000 bps=56Kbps. The clock rate command must be used on the physical DCE interface to generate a clock

NOTE   Don't forget that all physical interfaces on the Cisco IOS are shut down by default, so you must use the no shutdown command to explicitly enable them.

That was a quick explanation of HDLC encapsulation and how to configure it on a router. Next we'll discuss PPP encapsulation and how to configure it.

Configuring PPP on a Cisco Router

Point-to-Point Protocol (PPP), described in RFC 1661, is a point-to-point encapsulation layer 2 protocol used to carry Network layer protocol information over point-to-point links. This is an open standard protocol and can be used to provide interoperability between different vendor equipment. PPP has Link Control Protocol (LCP), which provides a method of establishing, configuring, maintaining, and terminating the point-to-point connection. LCP enables connections to negotiate additional services, such as authentication, multilink PPP, and PPP callback.

PPP authentication can also be implemented on any PPP-encapsulated connection. This allows two routers to authenticate a serial connection. The available authentication methods are Challenge Handshake Authentication Protocol (CHAP) and Password Authentication Protocol (PAP). With PAP, the remote router attempting to connect to the local router is required to send an authentication request. PAP passes the password and the hostname or username in clear text (unencrypted). CHAP, on the other hand, sends a 64-bit hashed signature instead of the clear text password. So, CHAP is far more secure than PAP. However, PPP authentication is primarily used in PPP dial-up environments, not in point-to-point dedicated circuits.

PPP has a feature called Multilink PPP. This feature allows a router to logically bundle two or more physical interfaces into one logical interface connection. The reason for doing this is to provide a higher aggregate bandwidth connection, which can then be used as an alternative to router protocol load-sharing mechanisms. Multilink PPP can also be used with ISDN to bundle B channels together (this will be covered later on in Chapter 15).

PPP Configuration Commands

Unlike HDLC encapsulation, PPP is not the default encapsulation setting, so the `encapsulation ppp` command must be configured on the router interface. Also, the following example shows the optional functionality of configuring CHAP authentication and configuring the interface to be a member of a PPP multilink bundle:

```
interface Serial0/0
```

encapsulation ppp	This configures ppp encapsulation on a serial interface
ppp authentication chap	Configures PPP authentication of the serial connection, requires a username/password defined for the remote router
bandwidth 56	Defined in Kbps. 56 Kbps = 56000 bps
clockrate 56000	Defined in bits per second 56,000bps=56Kbps. The clock rate command must be used on the physical DCE interface to generate a clock
ppp multilink	Enable ppp multilink on physical interface
username R2 password cisco	This is the username and password used to authenticate a connection to router R2, R2 will need a reciprocal username/password configured to authenticate R1

Remember that if you use PPP CHAP authentication, you must configure a username/password command for each remote end device that will be authenticating with this interface. Likewise, the remote devices must also have a username/password configured for this router. Now we'll discuss Frame Relay encapsulation and how to configure it.

Configuring Frame Relay on a Cisco Router

Frame Relay is an example of a packet-switched technology. Devices attached to a Frame Relay WAN fall into two general categories: DTE and DCE. The connection between a DTE device and a DCE device consists of both a Physical layer component and a Data-Link layer component. The physical component defines the mechanical, electrical specifications for the connection between the devices. The link layer component defines the protocol that establishes the connection between the DTE device, such as a router, and the DCE device (the Frame Relay switch).

Frame Relay uses a virtual circuit (VC) to connect a DTE (router) to another DTE (router). Frame Relay virtual circuits fall into two categories: *switched virtual circuits (SVCs)* and *permanent virtual circuits (PVCs)*. Frame Relay VCs are uniquely identified to the DTE (router) using a *Data-Link Connection Identifier (DLCI)*.

Local Management Interface (LMI) is a set of enhancements to the basic Frame Relay specification LMI status messages provide communication and synchronization between Frame Relay DTE and DCE devices. LMI includes support for a keepalive mechanism, which verifies connectivity to the frame relay switch. This keepalive also allows synchronization between the DTE and DCE devices, which provide a periodic status report on the DLCIs known to the Frame Relay switch. DTE sends out a status inquiry, and the DCE responds with a status response. Keepalives are sent every 10 seconds, and a full status message is generated every 60 seconds by the Frame Relay switch, which indicates all the DLCIs (PVCs) available for the interface. This is how routers can learn DLCI information without being configured. Cisco routers support three different LMI types:

Cisco LMI   This is the default LMI on a Cisco router. This is also propriety to Cisco devices.

ANSI T1.617 LMI   Referred to as Annex D. Defined by American National Standards Institute (ANSI).

ITU-T Q.933 LMI   Referred to as Annex A.

A Cisco router will automatically sense the LMI type configured on the Frame Relay switch. LMI autosensing is accomplished by the router sending LMI messages of each type, which solicits a response that will include the correct LMI type. This capability was introduced in IOS 11.2. The LMI type does not have to be configured on a Cisco router that is acting as a Frame Relay DTE.

Because Frame Relay is an extremely popular technology as well as a core topic for both the CCIE qualification and lab examinations, we will devote the remainder of this chapter to discussing how to properly configure Frame Relay.

First, we will discuss how to configure a router to act as a Frame Relay switch. Then we will discuss how to properly configure router interfaces to operate as Frame Relay. Keep in mind that in the Frame Relay environment, you must be knowledgeable on how to configure point-to-point and point-to-multipoint circuits on both physical interfaces and subinterfaces.

Frame Relay Switch Configuration Command

A multiple serial interface router can be used to simulate a Frame Relay switch. The Frame Relay switch function performs a logical switching of DLCI. The incoming dlci is mapped to an outgoing interface and dlci combination. On the Frame Relay switch (FS), dlci 102 on serial port S0 is mapped to dlci 201 on serial port S1.

The following sections cover the configuration commands on the Frame Relay switch to provide the Frame Relay DLCI connectivity that is shown in Figure 3.3.

FIGURE 3.3   Frame Relay DLCI mapping

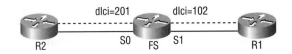

Global Commands

The `frame-relay switching` global command is required to enable the router to function as a Frame Relay switch:

frame-relay switching	Allows a router to perform Frame relay switching functions

Interface Commands

The following interface commands are required to configure Frame Relay encapsulation on the interfaces as well as to statically map the dlcis internally within the router to the proper interfaces:

```
interface Serial0
```

Encapsulation frame-relay	Default to Cisco encapsulation, available options are Cisco and IETF. Must be configured to IETF to connect to a non-Cisco Frame relay Switch
frame-relay lmi-type ansi	Default to Cisco LMI, the available options are cisco, ansi and q933a
frame-relay intf-type dce	Default to DTE, must be set to DCE to provide Frame relay Switching functions
bandwidth 2000	Defined in Kbps. 2,000 Kbps = 2 megabits
clockrate 2000000	Defined in bits per second 2,000,000 bps=2 meg. The clock rate command must be used on the physical DCE interface to generate a clock

```
frame-relay route 201 interface Serial1 102
```

	Used to create Frame PVC mapping. This command switches traffic that enters the local interface serial 0 on DLCI 201 to outbound interface Serial1 which uses DLCI 102

```
interface Serial1
    Encapsulation frame-relay          Default to Cisco encapsulation,
                                       available options are Cisco and IETF.
                                       Must be configured to IETF to connect
                                       to a non-Cisco Frame relay Switch

    frame-relay lmi-type ansi          Default to Cisco LMI, the available
                                       options are cisco, ansi and q933a

    frame-relay intf-type dce          Default to DTE, must be set to DCE to
                                       provide Frame relay Switching functions

    bandwidth 2000                     Defined in Kbps. 2,000 Kbps = 2 megabits

    clockrate 2000000                  Defined in bits per second 2,000,000
                                       bps=2 meg. The clock rate command must
                                       be used on the physical DCE interface
                                       to generate a clock

    frame-relay route 102 interface Serial0 201

                                       Used to create Frame PVC mapping.  This
                                       command switches traffic that enters
                                       the local interface serial 1 on DLCI
                                       102 to outbound interface Serial0 which
                                       uses DLCI 201
```

When troubleshooting problems with a Frame Relay switch, a useful command to troubleshoot the Frame Relay switch configuration is show frame-relay route. This command is used on a Frame Relay switch only to examine the static PVC mappings within the switch:

```
Router#show frame-relay route
```

Input Intf	Input Dlci	Output Intf	Output Dlci	Status
Serial0	102	Serial1	201	*active*
Serial0	103	Serial2	301	*inactive*
Serial0	104	Serial3	401	*active*
Serial1	201	Serial0	102	*active*
Serial1	203	Serial2	302	*inactive*
Serial1	204	Serial3	402	*active*
Serial2	301	Serial0	103	*active*
Serial2	302	Serial1	203	*active*
Serial2	304	Serial3	403	*active*
Serial3	401	Serial0	104	*active*
Serial3	402	Serial1	204	*active*
Serial3	403	Serial2	304	*inactive*

With the preceding command, the status that we are looking for is as follows:

- Inactive. If the Frame Relay switch is configured correctly, then all DLCIs defined on an interface should show `inactive` if the line protocol or port is down. If only one dlci shows `inactive` and the port is up, then there is most likely a configuration issue. Check to see that the interface is in an UP/UP state

- Active. Everything is good; move on.

Frame Relay Router Configuration Commands

The following is a concise list of configuration commands that are used to configure a router as a Frame Relay DTE. The commands listed are the commands required to build a Frame Relay network with an IP infrastructure. These commands *do not* customize Frame Relay for other technologies such as voice, bridging, routing, and so on. The specific commands to configure individual technologies are covered later on in this book, within their appropriate chapters. Here are the configuration commands:

`encapsulation frame-relay`	Default to Cisco encapsulation, the available options are Cisco, IETF. The encapsulation must be set to IETF if the Frame relay Switch is non-Cisco
`frame-relay lmi-type ansi`	Default to Cisco LMI type, but will auto detect the LMI type of the Frame Relay switch the available LMI types are Cisco, ansi and q933a
`bandwidth 2000`	Defined in Kbps. 2,000 Kbps = 2 meg, the bandwidth statement is used by routing protocols to calculate the Metric for the interface
`clockrate 2000000`	Defined in bits per second 2,000,000 bps=2 meg. The clock rate command must be used on the physical DCE interface to generate a clock
`no frame-relay inverse-arp`	Disables Inverse ARP on the applied interface
`ip address 172.16.4.1 255.255.255.0`	Maps a local IP address to an Interface

```
frame-relay map ip 172.16.4.2 102 broadcast
```
                                         Maps a remote IP address to a local
                                         DLCI of 102

```
frame-relay interface-dlci 102
```
                                         Maps a Frame relay DLCI to a
                                         interface, This command is used
                                         in a point-to-point environment.
                                         It cannot be used in conjunction
                                         with a frame-relay map command

Configuring Frame Relay for Specific Interface Types

This section of the chapter outlines the minimum commands required to configure specific Frame Relay implementations. This section identifies possible configuration options for Frame Relay and identifies for each option the required commands. It also documents for each configuration option issues with Inverse ARP and split-horizon.

Physical Interface: Point-to-Point Configuration

Figure 3.4 depicts a point-to-point Frame Relay network. Router R1 will send data out local dlci 102 and the data will arrive at router R2 on its local dlci of 201. The Frame Relay Switch was configured with these dlci mappings in Figure 3.3.

FIGURE 3.4   Frame Relay point-to-point

The following are the minimum configuration commands needed to configure point-to-point on a physical serial interface of both routers R1 and R2:

```
interface Serial0/0
  ip address 172.16.4.1 255.255.255.0
  encapsulation frame-relay

  frame-relay lmi-type ansi
```
                                         OPTIONAL, if specified it must
                                         match the Frame Relay Switch

INVERSE ARP ON A PHYSICAL FRAME RELAY INTERFACE

On a physical Frame Relay interface, Inverse ARP will automatically figure out the IP address of the remote router on the other end of the Frame Relay link.

SPLIT-HORIZON ON A PHYSICAL FRAME RELAY INTERFACE

For distance vector protocols, IP split-horizon is disabled; RIP/IGRP will send back all routes learned with a hop count of x+1.

> We will discuss split-horizon in detail in Chapter 9, "IP Interior Gateway Protocols."

Physical Interface Point-to-Multipoint Configuration at the Hub

Figure 3.5 depicts a point-to-multipoint network (also known as a hub-and-spoke network) with router R1 configured as the hub.

FIGURE 3.5   Frame Relay point-to-multipoint

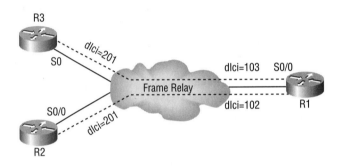

The following are the minimum configuration commands needed to configure point-to-multipoint on a physical serial interface:

```
interface Serial0/0
  ip address 172.16.4.1 255.255.255.0
  encapsulation frame-relay

  frame-relay lmi-type ansi        OPTIONAL, if specified it must
                                   match the Frame Relay Switch
```

INVERSE ARP ON A PHYSICAL FRAME RELAY INTERFACE

On a physical Frame Relay interface, Inverse ARP will automatically figure out the IP address of the remote router on the other end of the Frame Relay link.

Keep in mind that both PVCs are assigned to the same interface and that Inverse ARP is used on both to determine remote device layer 3 addressing. This is referred to as a nonbroadcast multiaccess (NBMA) network, so all routers must be on the same IP subnet (which causes issues for routing protocols that use broadcasts/multicasts). We will discuss this is further detail in Chapter 9 of this book.

SPLIT-HORIZON ON A PHYSICAL FRAME RELAY INTERFACE

For distance vector protocols, IP split-horizon is disabled; RIP/IGRP/EIGRP send back all routes learned with a hop count of x+1.

Subinterface Point-to-Multipoint Configuration at a Hub

The following are the minimum configuration commands needed to configure point-to-multipoint on a subinterface:

```
interface Serial0/0
```

```
  encapsulation frame-relay
```

```
  frame-relay lmi-type ansi
```
OPTIONAL, but if it is specified it must match the Frame relay Switch

```
interface Serial0/0.1 multipoint
```
Create a sub-interface as a point-to-multipoint type

```
  ip address 172.16.4.1 255.255.255.0
```
Assign IP address to the sub-interface

```
  frame-relay map ip 172.16.4.2 102 broadcast
```

Where 102 is the local DLCI of the router and 172.16.4.2 is the serial interface IP of the other spoke router R2

```
  frame-relay map ip 172.16.4.3 103 broadcast
```

Where 103 is the local DLCI of the router and 172.16.4.3 is the serial interface IP of the other spoke router R3

INVERSE ARP ON A POINT-TO-MULTIPOINT SUBINTERFACE

Inverse ARP is enabled on a multipoint subinterface. Therefore, to limit the dlcis that are automatically learned, configure the `no frame-relay inverse-arp` command and apply a unique Frame Relay MAP statement for each spoke.

SPLIT-HORIZON ON A POINT-TO-MULTIPOINT SUBINTERFACE

For distance vector protocols, IP split-horizon is enabled, RIP/IGRP/EIGRP will not send out any routes learned on this interface.

Configuring a Spoke Router with a Physical Interface

The following are the minimum configuration commands needed to configure the spoke router R2 that is shown in Figure 3.5 with a physical serial interface (when the hub router R1 is configured with a physical interface or multipoint subinterface dlcis):

```
interface Serial0/0
```

`ip address 172.16.4.2 255.255.255.0`	Assign an IP address to the interface
`encapsulation frame-relay`	
`frame-relay lmi-type ansi`	OPTIONAL, if specified it must match the Frame relay Switch
`frame-relay map ip 172.16.4.3 201 broadcast`	Where 201 is the local DLCI of the router and 172.16.4.3 is the serial interface IP of the other spoke router (R3)
`frame-relay map ip 172.16.4.1 201 broadcast`	Where 201 is the local DLCI of the router and 172.16.4.1 is the serial interface IP of the Hub (R1)

PROVIDING SPOKE-TO-SPOKE CONNECTIVITY

In this case, a `frame-relay map` command is needed to get access to any other spoke connected off the hub (R1) because Inverse ARP only provides address resolution of directly connected neighbors.

INVERSE ARP ON A PHYSICAL FRAME RELAY INTERFACE

On a physical Frame Relay interface, Inverse ARP will automatically figure out the IP address of the remote router on the other end of the Frame Relay link. If a `frame-relay map` command is used, then this will disable Inverse ARP for the dlci and protocol specified in the `frame-relay map` command.

If you specify the `frame-relay map` command, the current Inverse ARP mappings will remain in place, which can give you a false indication that the appropriate layer 3 to Frame Relay address resolution is occurring. These mappings will be removed after the router is rebooted or if the mappings were cleared manually via the `clear frame-relay in arp` command, at which point connectivity will fail if you have not implemented the appropriate static mappings.

SPLIT-HORIZON ON A PHYSICAL FRAME RELAY INTERFACE

For distance vector protocols, IP split-horizon is disabled; RIP/IGRP/EIGRP will send back all routes learned with a hop count of x+1.

Configuring a Spoke Router with a Point-to-Point Subinterface

The following are the minimum configuration commands needed to configure the spoke router R2 depicted in Figure 3.5 with a subinterface (when the hub router R1 is configured with point-to-point subinterfaces). When configuring frame relay point-to-point subinterfaces, subnetting occurs on a per subinterface basis, as opposed to having all frame relay routers interfaces on the same subnet:

```
interface Serial0/0

  encapsulation frame-relay

  frame-relay lmi-type ansi
```
OPTIONAL, if specified it must match the Frame relay Switch

```
interface Serial0/0.1 point-to-point

  ip address 172.16.4.2 255.255.255.0

  frame-relay interface-dlci 201
```
Use the interface DLCI command to associate a DLCI with a sub-interface, there can be only one interface DLCI assignment per point-to-point sub-interface. In this case, DLCI 201 is network 172.16.4.x/24. All traffic destined to this network will be sent down DLCI 201

INVERSE ARP ON A POINT-TO-POINT SUBINTERFACE

Inverse ARP is *not* utilized on a point-to-point subinterface.

SPLIT-HORIZON ON A POINT-TO-POINT SUBINTERFACE

For distance vector protocols, IP split-horizon is enabled, RIP/IGRP/EIGRP will not send out any routes learned on this interface.

Configuring a Spoke Router with a Point-to-Multipoint Subinterface

The following are the minimum configuration commands needed to configure the spoke router R2 depicted in Figure 3.5 with a point-to-multipoint sub-interface (when the hub router R1 is configured with physical interface or multipoint subinterface dlcis):

```
interface Serial0/0

  encapsulation frame-relay
```

`frame-relay lmi-type ansi`	OPTIONAL, if specified it must match the Frame relay Switch
`interface Serial0/0.1 multipoint`	Create a sub-interface as a point-to-multipoint type
`ip address 172.16.4.2 255.255.255.0`	
`frame-relay map ip 172.16.4.3 201 broadcast`	Where 201 is the local DLCI of the router and 172.16.4.3 is the serial interface IP of the other spoke router (R3)
`frame-relay map ip 172.16.4.1 201 broadcast`	Where 201 is the local DLCI of the router and 172.16.4.1 is the serial interface IP of the Hub (R1)

This option we just configured uses the `frame-relay map` command. This requires one Map statement for each router, including the head-end router that the spoke needs a connection to.

PROVIDING SPOKE-TO-SPOKE CONNECTIVITY

In this case, a `frame-relay map` command is needed to get access to any other spoke connected off the hub. Actually, by default Inverse ARP is enabled, and the IP address of R1 would be resolved this way. However, as soon as we applied a map statement, Inverse ARP was disabled for the DLCI and protocol, meaning R1 won't be learned via Inverse ARP anymore, so to enable connectivity to R3, a map statement is required for R3 as well as R1.

INVERSE ARP ON A POINT-TO-MULTIPOINT SUBINTERFACE

Inverse ARP is enabled on a point-to-multipoint subinterface. Therefore, use a `frame-relay interface-dlci` command to dynamically map the protocol to the dlci or to limit the dlcis that are automatically learned, configure the `no frame-relay inverse-arp` command, and apply a unique `frame-relay map` command for each spoke. See the section "Frame Relay Configuration Gotcha" for more details.

SPLIT-HORIZON ON A POINT-TO-MULTIPOINT SUBINTERFACE

For distance vector protocols, IP split-horizon is enabled; RIP/IGRP/EIGRP will not send out any routes learned on this interface

Frame Relay Configuration Gotcha

In the following sections, we'll discuss some of the subtle mechanics of Frame Relay that can cause a lot of misunderstanding and lost time in troubleshooting.

Inverse ARP and Frame Relay Map Statements

When a `frame-relay map` command is configured on an interface, Inverse ARP is then disabled. Because the router dynamically learned the hub router IP address using Inverse ARP (we didn't configure a `frame-relay map` command for the hub site), it will continue to work until the router is rebooted. After the router is rebooted, Inverse ARP is disabled and the router will not be able to ping the hub. The solution is to statically map both the hub and spoke routers.

> **NOTE**   Many people make the mistake of configuring a `frame-relay map` command for only another spoke router and forget about the hub router because they can still ping it until the next reboot.

If multiple DLCIs exist on the interface, then Inverse ARP is disabled only for the specific DLCI and layer 3 protocol that the Map statement is applied against (Inverse ARP would still be enabled for another layer 3 protocol on the same DLCI). To stop the router from dynamically learning any IP address via Inverse ARP, Inverse ARP must be disabled on the physical interface using the `no frame-relay inverse-arp` command.

Subinterface to a Physical Interface and Split-Horizon

When you're connecting two routers, one with a Frame Relay point-to-point subinterface and the other with a Frame Relay physical interface, the physical interface needs to have split-horizon enabled. Otherwise, the routes will be continuously learned and flushed on the router with the physical interface.

Troubleshooting Frame Relay

You must take a systematic approach to troubleshooting any network problem. The "cause and effect" approach is one of the most effective.

When you make a configuration change on a router, you should have an expectation of what the results of the change will be. If the results are not what you expect, then you should not move forward until you understand why you got the results you did. You'll have to deal with the problem sooner or later, and problems are easier to identify and solve when the network is in its simplest form. It will only get more complex and harder to identify the root cause of the problem when routing protocols and other technologies are added.

A layered approached is the best approach. First, verify physical connectivity, then layer 2 connectivity, and then layer 3 connectivity. Using this approach will enable you to quickly isolate the location of the problem.

Using Ping on Frame Relay

Ping is an extremely useful tool to help identity network problems, but in a Frame Relay environment, there are a few nuances when trying to ping local interfaces:

- On a physical interface configured for point-to-point and on a subinterface configured for point-to-point, you should be able to ping both local and remote IP addresses.

- On a physical interface (which is configured for multipoint by default) and on a subinterface configured for point-to-multipoint, you should be able to ping remote IP address.

 A ping request to the local interface will fail. For this ping to be successful, a `frame-relay map` command must exist for the locally configured IP and it must be mapped to a local active DLCI.

Troubleshooting Commands

The following commands are extremely useful when troubleshooting Frame Relay problems:

```
show ip interface brief
```

```
show frame-relay route
```

```
show frame-relay lmi
```

```
show frame-relay pvc
```

```
show frame-relay map
```

```
clear frame-relay inarp          clears the contents of the frame-relay
                                 inverse-arp cache
```

```
show controller
```

```
debug frame-relay lmi
```

```
debug frame-relay packet
```

show ip interface brief

The first command to identify the cause of a problem is the command `show ip interface brief`. This command shows the status of the physical and subinterfaces as well as status of the line protocol:

```
Interface       IP-Address      OK?   Method  Status    Protocol

Ethernet0       unassigned      YES   NVRAM   down      down

Serial0         172.16.32.1     YES   NVRAM   up        down

Loopback0       1.1.1.1         YES   NVRAM   up        up
```

Table 3.2 provides a description of the possible line and protocol states.

TABLE 3.2   Line and Protocol states

Interface	Protocol	Troubleshooting...
Down	Down	This is a physical problem.
		Is the port cabled correctly?
		Is the local Frame Relay switch port active?
Up	Down	This is not a physical connectivity problem, but there is a protocol problem.
		Is the encapsulation set correctly on both ends?
		Is the LMI-type set on the router to match the Frame Relay switch?
		Has the DCE end of the connection been configured with a `clock rate` command?
Up	Up	Everything is good. Move on.

show frame-relay lmi

The command `show frame-relay lmi` shows the status of Local Management Interface (LMI). This command is issued on a router (DTE). The command shows the operational state of LMI. Status inquiries are sent from the Frame Relay DTE to the Frame Relay switch; LMI `Status msgs Rcvd` are sent from the Frame Relay Switch to the Frame Relay DTE (router).

The following is the output of a show frame-relay lmi command from a router with Frame Relay fully operational. Please note that the Status enquiry messages sent and receive should increment equally when this is operating correctly.

A show frame-relay lmi command will have a protocol status of UP with the following router output:

```
LMI Statistics for interface Serial 0
(Frame-Relay DTE) LMI TYPE = ANSI

  Invalid Unnumbered info 0           Invalid Prot Disc 0

  Invalid dummy Call Ref 0            Invalid Msg Type 0

  Invalid Status Message 0            Invalid Lock Shift 0

  Invalid Information ID 0            Invalid Report IE Len 0

  Invalid Report Request 0            Invalid Keep IE Len 0

  Num Status Enq. Sent 8             Num Status msgs Rcvd 8

  Num Update Status Rcvd 0           Num Status Timeouts 0
```

A show frame-relay lmi command will have a protocol status of DOWN with the following router output:

```
LMI Statistics for interface Serial 0
(Frame-Relay DTE) LMI TYPE = ANSI

  Invalid Unnumbered info 0           Invalid Prot Disc 0

  Invalid dummy Call Ref              Invalid Msg Type 0

  Invalid Status Message 0            Invalid Lock Shift 0

  Invalid Information ID 0            Invalid Report IE Len 0

  Invalid Report Request 0            Invalid Keep IE Len 0

  Num Status Enq. Sent 7             Num Status msgs Rcvd 0

  Num Update Status Rcvd 0           Num Status Timeouts 7
```

show frame-relay pvc

The show frame-relay pvc command shows the DLCIs that were learned via LMI from the Frame Relay switch. It will also show the locally configured PVCs if they are different from the learned PVC via LMI. The following is the output of the show frame-relay pvc command:

```
PVC Statistics for interface Serial0/0 (Frame-Relay DTE)
```

	Active	Inactive	Deleted	Static
Local	0	0	1	0
Switched	0	0	0	0
Unused	2	1	0	0

```
DLCI = 201, DLCI USAGE=UNUSED, PVC STATUS=INACTIVE, INTERFACE=Serial0
   input pkts 0          output pkts 0          in bytes 0
   out bytes 0           dropped pkts 0         in FECN pkts 0
   in BECN pkts 0        out FECN pkts 0        out BECN pkts 0
   in DE pkts 0          out DE pkts 0
   out bcast pkts 0      out bcast bytes 0      Num Pkts Switched 0

DLCI = 203, DLCI USAGE=UNUSED, PVC STATUS=ACTIVE, INTERFACE=Serial0
   input pkts 0          output pkts 0          in bytes 0
   out bytes 0           dropped pkts 0         in FECN pkts 0
   in BECN pkts 0        out FECN pkts 0        out BECN pkts 0
   in DE pkts 0          out DE pkts 0
   out bcast pkts 0      out bcast bytes 0      Num Pkts Switched 0

DLCI = 204, DLCI USAGE=UNUSED, PVC STATUS=DELETED, INTERFACE=Serial0
   input pkts 0          output pkts 0          in bytes 0
   out bytes 0           dropped pkts 0         in FECN pkts 0
   in BECN pkts 0        out FECN pkts 0        out BECN pkts 0
   in DE pkts 0          out DE pkts 0
   out bcast pkts 0      out bcast bytes 0      Num Pkts Switched 0
```

A properly configured and operational PVC should have a DLCI usage of LOCAL and PVC status of ACTIVE. Also. on a Frame Relay switch, the DLCI usage will be SWITCHED.

Notice that the three PVCs each show a different PVC status. The following are descriptions for the three possible states of the dlcis:

Active   Both the local and remote ports are in a UP/UP state and the PVC is defined in the Frame Relay switch.

Inactive   The local port is in an UP/UP state, but there is something wrong with the remote end or the configuration of the Frame Relay switch. The Frame Relay switch port is down or the remote router's port is down.

Deleted   The PVC is defined in the local router but is not configured in the Frame Relay switch.

🌐 Real World Scenario

Understand DLCIs and LMI States

Author Rob Payne shares a short story about an experience he had many years ago:

"I was attempting to configure Frame Relay on a Cisco router, and I was using map commands to statically map the remote IP address to the dlci. Now, I was dealing with a major telco service provider as the Frame Relay provider, and the telco technicians would always refer to the local dlci for my local circuit at the home office as the remote dlci when in reality the remote dlci was serving my remote site. Thus, I was configuring my map commands to use the remote IP address of the circuit along with what I thought was the local dlci but was in fact the remote dlci. So, my PVCs were never becoming active, and I troubleshot this issue with the telco technicians for two days.

"Then, thanks to a good friend, and excellent engineer, Francis Ferguson, I was shown the light and the mystic cloud was raised from the issue of Frame Relay dlcis. Francis taught me how to read the LMI messages that I was receiving from the Frame switch and what each of the three PVC states meant. I was then able to ascertain that the telco technicians were referring to the dlcis incorrectly, and I was able to configure my Frame Relay map commands to point to the remote IP address and the local dlci. And as if by total magic, all the PVCs came up in an active state.

"I guess the moral to the story would be to never rely on someone else to tell you what your problem is, especially someone who is trying to point the finger back in your direction. Know the technology that you are implementing because it will surely save countless hours of unnecessary troubleshooting. *Thanks Francis."*

---

show frame-relay map

The command `show frame-relay map` shows the output of the command entered on the spoke router with one static mapping and one dynamic mapping:

```
Serial0 (up): ip 172.16.32.1 dlci 201(0x12C,0x48C0), static,
            broadcast, CISCO, status defined, active
```

Notice the output shows `static` because this is the result of having a manual `frame-relay map ip` command configured. Notice the following output shows `dynamic` because this is the result of Inverse ARP resolving the dlci to a layer 3 address automatically, without a `frame-relay map ip` command configured:

```
Serial0 (up): ip 172.16.32.2 dlci 301(0x12C,0x48C0), dynamic,
            broadcast, CISCO, status defined, active
```

show controller

To verify which side of a connection is the DCE side, use the show controller command. The following is the output from a show controller command:

```
show controller serial1/0
CD2430 Slot 1, Port 0, Controller 0, Channel 0, Revision 15
Channel mode is synchronous serial
idb 0x6101DF5C, buffer size 1524, V.35 DCE cable, clockrate 56000
```

As can be seen, the serial1/0 interface has a V.35 DCE cable connected, and the interface has a clock rate of 56000bps. This must be configured using the clock rate 56000 command on the specified serial interface:

```
show controller serial1/3
CD2430 Slot 1, Port 3, Controller 0, Channel 3, Revision 15
Channel mode is synchronous serial
idb 0x61031D20, buffer size 1524, V.35 DTE cable
```

As you can see, the serial1/3 interface has a V.35 DTE cable connected. The interface has no clock rate because the clock rate is provided by the DCE side.

debug frame-relay lmi

The command debug frame-relay lmi shows the incremental updates received from the DCE (Frame Relay switch):

```
02:28:02: Serial0/0(out): StEnq, myseq 97, yourseen 96, DTE up
02:28:02: datagramstart = 0x2C4C254, datagramsize = 14
02:28:02: FR encap = 0x00010308
02:28:02: 00 75 95 01 01 00 03 02 61 60
02:28:02: Serial0/0(in): Status, myseq 97
02:28:02: RT IE 1, length 1, type 0
02:28:02: KA IE 3, length 2, yourseq 97, myseq 97
02:28:02: PVC IE 0x7 , length 0x3 , dlci 102, status 0x2
02:28:02: PVC IE 0x7 , length 0x3 , dlci 103, status 0x2
02:28:02: PVC IE 0x7 , length 0x3 , dlci 104, status 0x2
02:28:02: Serial0/0(out): StEnq, myseq 98, yourseen 97, DTE up
02:28:02: datagramstart = 0x2C4BFD4, datagramsize = 14
02:28:02: FR encap = 0x00010308
02:28:02: 00 75 95 01 01 01 03 02 62 61
02:28:18: Serial0/0(out): StEnq, myseq 98, yourseen 97, DTE up
02:28:18: datagramstart = 0x2C4BFD4, datagramsize = 14
02:28:18: FR encap = 0x00010308
```

```
02:28:18: 00 75 95 01 01 01 03 02 62 61
02:28:18: Serial0/0(in): Status, myseq 98
02:28:18: RT IE 1, length 1, type 1
02:28:18: KA IE 3, length 2, yourseq 98, myseq 98
02:28:18: Serial0/0(out): StEnq, myseq 99, yourseen 98, DTE up
02:28:18: datagramstart = 0x2C4C254, datagramsize = 14
02:28:18: FR encap = 0x00010308
02:28:18: 00 75 95 01 01 01 03 02 63 62
```

Both sequence numbers increment in the preceding commands. Note that the DTE is in an UP status, and that the router received FULL status information about dlci 102, 103, and 104.

A status of 0x2 means the DLCI is ACTIVE (as per a show frame-relay pvc command), 0x0 means DLCI is programmed on the switch but is not usable for some reason (i.e., DLCI is INACTIVE as per a show frame-relay pvc command), and 0x4 means the DLCI is not programmed on the switch (i.e., DLCI is DELETED as per a show frame-relay pvc command).

debug frame-relay packet

The command debug frame-relay packet is used to determine if the Frame Relay mappings correctly exist. For instance, in the following example, a spoke router tried to ping another spoke router, but a local frame-relay map command did *not* exist:

```
02:25:13: Serial0:Encaps failed--no map entry link 7(IP).
02:25:15: Serial0:Encaps failed--no map entry link 7(IP).
```

In the following output, the frame-relay map command existed in both spoke routers, and thus the ping was successful. As with all traffic passing through a network, the packet is sent in a simplex fashion, meaning that the router looks for a local mapping and if it exists will send the packet accordingly. The remote router *must* go through the exact same lookup and mapping process to return the response:

```
02:25:05: Serial0(o): dlci 103(0x48C1), pkt type 0x800(IP), datagramsize 104
02:25:05: Serial0(i): dlci 103(0x48C1), pkt type 0x800, datagramsize 104
02:25:05: Serial0(o): dlci 103(0x48C1), pkt type 0x800(IP), datagramsize 104
02:25:05: Serial0(i): dlci 103(0x48C1), pkt type 0x800, datagramsize 104
```

An (o) means an outgoing frame and (i) means an incoming frame. Also, Cisco Frame Relay encapsulation uses Ethernet-style protocol codes for layer 3 protocols (e.g., 0x800 for IP), and IETF encapsulation uses NLPID (e.g., 0xCC for IP).

Summary

To achieve any degree of success in the CCIE qualification and lab examinations, it's essential that you know the information in this chapter. Layer 1 and layer 2 technologies are a core topic that you must know inside and out.

We discussed physical layer technologies, such as T1/E1 encoding and framing, Synchronous Optical Network (SONET), and Packets over SONET (POS). We then discussed packet switching and the X.25 protocol suite. We finished up the chapter by discussing layer 2 encapsulation protocols such as High-Level Data Link Control (HDLC), Point-to-Point Protocol (PPP), and Frame Relay.

You should be comfortable with all the variations of the technology and be able to implement any combination, with any restrictions and at any time. A good rule of thumb to use as a gauge is that you should be able to completely configure six blank routers to any given Frame Relay scenario within 15 minutes.

And now with a good solid understanding of Frame Relay, it is time to move on to the next chapter and discuss asynchronous transfer mode (ATM). You will see that by knowing Frame Relay, ATM is rather easy to understand (at least from the PVC perspective).

Exam Essentials

Understand the encoding and framing standards for a T1.   A T1 can use either alternate mark inversion (AMI) or bipolar 8-zero substitution (B8ZS) encoding. Likewise, a circuit can implement Super Frame (SF), also known as D4 framing, or Extended Superframe (ESF) Format.

Understand the Point-to-Point Protocol (PPP).   Point-to-Point Protocol (PPP) is a Data-Link protocol that can be used over either asynchronous serial (dial-up) or synchronous serial (ISDN or leased line) media and that uses LCP (Link Control Protocol) to build and maintain data-link connections.

Know what Frame Relay LMI is.   Local Management Interface (LMI) is a set of enhancements to the basic Frame Relay specification. LMI status messages provide communication and synchronization between Frame Relay DTE and DCE devices. LMI includes support for a keepalive mechanism, which verifies that data is flowing.

Know what the Data Link Connection Identifier (DLCI) is.   A Frame Relay virtual circuit (PVC) is identified by a DLCI (a 10-bit PVC identifier). A Frame Relay service provider, such as the telephone company, typically assigns DLCI values, which are used by Frame Relay to distinguish between different virtual circuits on the network.

Know what the committed information rate (CIR) is.   Usually when you lease Frame Relay services from a service provider, you receive a guaranteed amount of bandwidth up to a predefined maximum limit. Although the committed information rate (CIR) guarantees the rate, the user traffic can burst to higher rates if the service provider's Frame Relay network is underutilized.

Key Terms

Before you take the exam, be certain you are familiar with the following terms:

alternate mark inversion (AMI)

bipolar 8-zero suppression (B8ZS)

committed information rate (CIR)

Data Network Identification Code (DNIC)

Data-Link Connection Identifier (DLCI)

discard eligible (DE)

Dynamic Packet Transport (DPT)

Frame Relay

High-Level Data Link Control (HDLC) protocol

International Data Number (IDN)

Link Access Procedure

Link Access Procedure Balanced (LAPB)

Link Access Procedure D Channel (LAPD)

Local Management Interface (LMI)

Logical Link Control (LLC)

multilink

National Terminal Number (NTN)

packet switching

packet-lever protocol (PLP)

Permanent virtual circuits (PVCs)

Point-to-Point Protocol (PPP)

subinterfaces

switched virtual circuits (SVCs)

synchronous

Synchronous Optical Network (SONET)

X.121 address specification

X.25

Review Questions

1. What SONET aggregate carrier speed equals 622.08Mbps?

   A. OC-3

   B. OC-6

   C. OC-12

   D. OC-24

   E. OC-48

2. What are the two most common encoding/framing schemes for a T1?

   A. B8ZS/ESF

   B. B8ZS/D4

   C. AMI/ESF

   D. AMI/D4

3. Which two Frame Relay encapsulation types are supported on Cisco routers?

   A. ANSI

   B. q933a

   C. Cisco

   D. IETF

   E. shiva

4. Which three Frame Relay LMI types are supported on Cisco routers?

   A. ANSI

   B. q933a

   C. Cisco

   D. IETF

   E. shiva

5. A provider can sell more bandwidth than the actual Frame Relay network can supply. What is this called?

   A. Illegal

   B. Zero-sum multiplexing

   C. Frame stealing

   D. Over subscription

   E. XOT

6. The DLCI is located in the Frame Relay header. How many bits are in the DLCI?

    A. 8

    B. 16

    C. 32

    D. 4

    E. 10

7. Which of the following is a feature of LMI?

    A. Status inquiry

    B. BECN

    C. FECN

    D. CIR

    E. DE

8. Your central site has a single serial connection to the Frame Relay cloud. You have five virtual circuits from your central site to the remote site. Your remote sites are not receiving routing updates. You suspect a problem with split-horizon. What would be a typical solution? (Choose all that apply.)

    A. Static routes

    B. Subinterfaces

    C. Disable split-horizon

    D. Route filtering

    E. Modify administrative distance

9. You want to configure your router so that it forwards frames based on their DLCI. What is this process known as?

    A. IP routing

    B. Frame routing

    C. Impossible

    D. Frame switching

    E. Frame tagging

10. What is the proper command to implement the Stacker compression on a point-to-point Frame Relay interface?

    A. `frame-relay compress packet-by-packet`

    B. `frame-relay payload-compress packet-by-packet`

    C. `frame-relay payload-compress`

    D. `frame-relay payload-compress stac`

Answers to Review Questions

1. C. OC-12 = 622.08Mbps

2. A, D. You typically find an AMI circuit using SF or D4 framing and a B8ZS circuit using ESF.

3. C, D. The two types that are available are Cisco and IETF. Cisco is the default Frame Relay encapsulation type.

4. A, B, C. The three LMI types supported are ANSI, q933a, and Cisco. Cisco is the default LMI type.

5. D. Over subscription occurs when the combined committed information rate exceeds the back-bone capabilities.

6. E. The DLCI is defined by 10 noncontiguous bits in the header.

7. A. Local Management Interface provides for status inquiry. Inverse ARP provides a mechanism to map DLCIs to IP addresses.

8. A, B, C. Most IP routing protocols support disabling split-horizon; however, IPX RIP, and Apple RTMP do not. Static routes are a popular but inflexible solution. Subinterfaces are the most popular and the best solution.

9. D. Cisco routers can be configured as Frame Relay switches.

10. B. The following is an example of a point-to-point Stacker configuration: `frame-relay payload-compress packet-by-packet`

Chapter 4

Asynchronous Transfer Mode (ATM)

THE CCIE QUALIFICATION EXAM TOPICS COVERED IN THIS CHAPTER INCLUDE THE FOLLOWING:

- ✓ The ATM Protocol Model
- ✓ The physical layer, ATM layer, and ATM adaptation layer (AAL)
- ✓ LAN emulation
- ✓ The LAN emulation components
- ✓ The startup procedure of a LAN Emulation Client (LEC)

Asynchronous Transfer Mode (ATM) is used only as a backbone protocol, so you don't need to worry about your packet-based, broadcast LANs trying to communicate with the cell-based ATM networks, right? Unfortunately, nothing could be further from the truth. What you need is a way to resolve the difference between ATM's connection-oriented, point-to-point protocol and the connectionless, broadcast domains of a LAN medium.

Cisco, a founding and leading member of the ATM Forum LAN Emulation Sub-Working Group, has implemented LAN emulation (LANE) in its core products. Cisco designed LANE to hide ATM and look like 802.3 Ethernet and 802.5 Token Ring networks to end stations on a broadcast-oriented LAN. LANE works by making the ATM network emulate a broadcast-oriented multiaccess environment, all the way down to the Media Access Control (MAC) broadcast level. Before LANE, a proprietary conversion device was needed to convert from LAN to ATM.

Because it is possible that upper-layer protocols expect the lower layer to use a connectionless service, LANE is used to allow an upper-layer protocol to make connections to lower-layer ATM connection-oriented services. What this means is that LANE provides a switching service that is transparent to the 802.*x* networks.

In this chapter, you will learn about the ATM protocol suite and also ATM LANE, the components that make up LAN emulation, and how LANE emulates a broadcast medium (such as Ethernet).

The ATM Protocol Model

The ATM protocol dictates how two end devices communicate with each other across an ATM network through switches. The ATM protocol model contains three functional layers:

ATM physical Layer   Bit timing and the physical medium

ATM layer   Generic flow control, generation of cell header, multiplexing and demultiplexing

ATM adaptation layer (AAL)   Support for higher-layer services such as signaling, circuit emulation, voice, data, and video

These layers are very similar to layer 1 and layer 2 of the OSI reference model, as you can see in Figure 4.1.

FIGURE 4.1 The ATM model compared to the OSI reference model

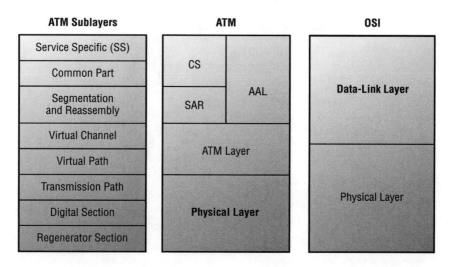

Although ATM is cell based, it is extremely closely related to the frame-based world of Frame Relay. Both are based on the use of nonbroadcast multiple access (NBMA) topologies utilizing virtual circuits to implement congestion avoidance mechanics, burst rates, and traffic management functionality.

ATM has two types of interfaces, the User-Network Interface (UNI) and the Network-to-Network Interface (NNI). The headers for these two comprise the following fields:

Generic flow control (GFC) 4-bits. Specific to UNI. Not currently used and is always set to the value 0000

Virtual path identifier (VPI) 8-bits = UNI and 12-bits = NNI. Identifies the virtual path connection

Virtual circuit identifier (VCI) 16-bits. Along with the VPI, uniquely identifies a cell as belonging to a specific virtual connection

Payload type indicator (PTI) 3-bits. Identifies the cell as user data or a management cell; contains the EFCI bit and the end-of-frame bit

Cell loss priority (CLP) 1-bit. Identifies the cell as being high or low priority

Header error control (HEC) 8-bits. Performs error checking in the cell header only, not in the payload

Figure 4.2 shows the 5-byte header for a UNI, and Figure 4.3 shows the 5-byte header for a NNI. The difference between the two is how they use the 5-byte cell header. If you only look at the first 12 bits of the header, an NNI will use all the bits for the VPI value, whereas the UNI will use the first 4 bits for the Generic Flow Control (GFC), then the next 8 bits for the VPI value. The remainder of the header is identical; it includes 16 bits for the VCI, providing 65,536 possible virtual circuits (VCs).

FIGURE 4.2   The UNI 5-byte header

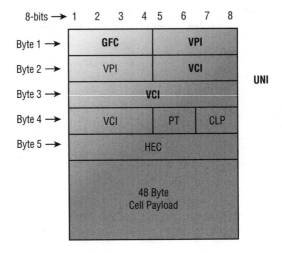

FIGURE 4.3   The NNI 5-byte header

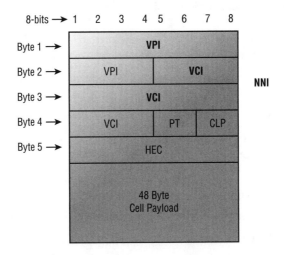

UNI is an interface that is being used between an ATM edge device and an ATM switch. Routers and workstations fall into this type of interface. Because the UNI includes the first 4 bits for GFC, there are only 8 bits for VPI values, thus a UNI can provide up to 256 virtual paths.

NNI is an interface that resides between two ATM switches and between ATM networks. Because the NNI does not use the GFC, it can provide all 12 bits for VPIs, or 4096 virtual paths.

Of course, both the UNI and NNI header format include 12 bits for the VCI values, so they both provide up to 4096 virtual circuits. NNI is suitable for service providers because it provides many more virtual circuits, which is important in a service provider environment for scalability purposes.

ATM is predictable and can be tightly controlled because of its use of 53-byte cells. ATM takes the frames of data from the upper layers of the OSI model and segments them into smaller sections in order to build them into cells with a fixed length of 53 bytes (5-byte header with 48-byte payload. This allows ATM to carry real-time, sensitive traffic like voice and video at much higher quality than a frame-based protocol would, which in turn allows ATM to provide fixed delay (i.e., little or no jitter) and it does not suffer from serialization delays caused by placing big frames on the network.

In the Frame Relay technology, a Data Link Connection Identifier (DLCI) is used as a locally significant virtual circuit (VC) identifier. The use of a DLCI allows multiple VCs to travel inside a single physical circuit. ATM utilizes a locally significant VC identifier just as Frame Relay does, although ATM refers to these VC identifiers as virtual path identifier/virtual circuit identifier (VPI/VCI) pairs. As Figure 4.4 depicts, ATM is a multiplexing technology, meaning that several virtual circuits can travel inside a single path. The VPI indicates the path or large pipe, and the VCIs indicate the VCs inside the path.

FIGURE 4.4   ATM VPI/VCI multiplexing

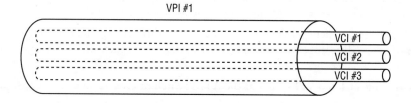

The ATM Physical Layer

The *ATM physical layer* is in charge of sending and receiving bits on the physical level. This layer also manages ATM cell boundaries and controls the cell packaging in the correct frame type for the ATM media you use. The ATM physical layer consists of two sublayers:

- The *physical medium dependent (PMD)* sublayer
- The transmission convergence (TC) sublayer

The PMD sublayer sends and receives a constant flow of bits that contain associated timing information to synchronize transmission and reception. The PMD sublayer relies on the media used for transport, and thus, ATM works only on ATM-specific media. Standards include DS-3/E3, 155Mbps local fiber, and SONET (Synchronous Optical Network)/Synchronous Digital Hierarchy (SDH). The ATM Forum also released 25Mbps ATM over twisted pair (although it's very unpopular).

The TC sublayer maintains several functions. It mainly extracts and inserts ATM cells within either a plesiochronous or synchronous time-division multiplexed frame and passes them to and from the ATM layer. The other functions of the TC sublayer are listed here:

Cell delineation   The TC sublayer maintains ATM cell boundaries.

Header error control sequence generation and verification   It creates and checks header error control to ensure valid data.

Cell rate decoupling   It inserts or suppresses unassigned ATM cells to adapt the rate of valid ATM cells to the payload capacity of the transmission system.

Transmission frame adaptation   It packages ATM cells in appropriate frames for physical layer implementation.

Transmission frame generation and recovery   It generates and maintains the given physical layer frame structure.

The ATM Layer

Through the use of virtual connections, the *ATM layer* connects and carries ATM cells through the network. It accomplishes this by using information contained within the header of each ATM cell. The ATM layer is responsible for the following:

- Multiplexing and demultiplexing ATM cells from different virtual connections. You can identify these different connections by their virtual circuit identifier (VCI) and virtual path identifier (VPI) values.

- Translating VCI and VPI values at the ATM switch or cross-connect.

- Extracting and inserting the header before or after the cell is delivered from or to the ATM adaptation layer.

- Governing the implementation of a flow-control mechanism at the UNI, which is basically two ports connected by a pair of wires, typically fiber.

- Passing and accepting cells from the AAL.

 A VCI (virtual channel identifier) can also be called a virtual circuit. This is simply the identifier for the logical connection between the two ends of a connection. A VPI (virtual path identifier) is the identifier for a group of VCIs that allows an ATM switch to perform operations on a group of VCs.

The ATM Adaptation Layer

The *ATM adaptation layer (AAL)* translates between the ATM cells and the larger service data units of the upper layers of the OSI reference model. This function works by receiving packets from the upper-level protocols and breaking them into 48-byte segments to be dumped into the payload of an ATM cell. As shown in Figure 4.1, the AAL has two sublayers: segmentation and reassembly (SAR) and the convergence sublayer (CS). The CS has further sublayers: the common part (CP) and the service specific (SS). Like protocols specified in the OSI reference model, protocol data units are used to pass information between these layers.

Specifications exist for a few different ATM adaptation layers:

AAL1 (Class A)   Used for transporting traffic that is continuously sent at regular intervals, such as voice traffic and uncompressed video traffic. Known as constant bit rate (CBR) service. Uses end-to-end timing and is connection oriented. Examples are DS1, E1, and Nx64Kbps emulation. AAL1 will provide a 47-byte payload in each cell; it steals 1 byte at the beginning of the payload (4 bits = sequence number and 4 bits = sequence number protection).

AAL2 (Class B)   Does not use the CS and SAR sublayers. Multiplexes short packets from multiple sources into a single cell. Uses a variable bit rate (VBR) and end-to-end timing and is connection oriented. Examples are packet, video, and audio.

AAL3/4 (Class C and Class D)   Designed for network service providers; uses VBR with no timing required but is still connection oriented. Examples are Frame Relay and X.25. AAL3/4 will provide a 44-byte payload in each cell; it steals 4 bytes from the payload (2 bytes = sequence number/MUX ID and 2 bytes = CRC at the end of the payload).

AAL5 (Class C and Class D)   Used to transfer most non-SMDS data and LAN emulation. Also uses VBR with no timing required. Serves connectionless protocols. Examples are IP and SMDS. AAL5 will provide the entire 48 bytes of payload in each cell.

ATM networks can provide the transport for several different, independent *emulated LANs (ELANs)*. When a device is attached to an ELAN, its physical location no longer matters to the administrator or implementation. This process allows you to connect several LANs in different locations, with switches, to create one large emulated network. This can make a big difference because attached devices can now be moved easily between ELANs. Thus, an engineering group can belong to one ELAN and a design group to another ELAN, even if the members of both groups are scattered across multiple locations.

LANE also provides translation between multiple media environments, allowing data sharing. Token Ring or FDDI networks can share data with Ethernet networks as if they were part of the same network.

Signaling ATM Adaptation Layer (SAAL)

The SAAL is made up of two parts: the Service Specific Connection Oriented Protocol (SSCOP), and the Service Specific Coordination Function (SSCF).

SSCOP provides the reliable transport of signaling messages between peer entities. Signaling requests are encapsulated in SSCOP frames and are carried across the ATM network in AAL5 packets using a well-known PVC. The ATM Forum PVC for UNI signaling uses the VCI of 5 (QSAAL). SSCF provides the interface between the Q.2931 protocol and the SSCOP.

Now that we have discussed the ATM protocol, we'll move on to talk about LAN emulation (LANE). LANE is not included in the CCIE lab examination (it used to be, but it has been removed as an objective), but it is listed in the blueprint for the CCIE qualification examination, so it's good foundational material for you to know.

Introduction to LAN Emulation

LAN Emulation (LANE) is an ATM service defined by the *ATM Forum* specification *LAN Emulation over ATM, ATM Forum 94-0035*. Members of the ATM Forum sat down together and devised a specification for LANE services across ATM to include three important characteristics:

- Connectionless service between LANs
- Ability to emulate broadcast services
- Media Access Control (MAC) address support

LANE services must provide connectivity between all ATM devices and all LAN devices. This connectivity extends to devices that are attached ATM stations as well as attached LAN devices that are crossing the ATM network. Connectivity between ATM devices and all other LAN devices is done through emulated LANs (ELANs).

ELANs are also used to create independent broadcast domains that are similar in concept to Ethernet segments or token rings. ELANs also allow ATM to work with existing older equipment.

ELANs have some similarities to VLANs because ELANs map to VLANs. ELAN workstations are independent of physical location, and ELANs must be connected to a bridge or router in order to communicate with each other.

Connectivity begins at the MAC sublayer of the Data-Link layer, allowing Windows upper-level network driver interface specification (NDIS) and open Data-Link interface (ODI) driver interfaces to transmit layer 3 protocols like TCP/IP, IPX, AppleTalk, and APPN, as well as allowing existing applications to continue operating without disturbance.

LANE provides a conversion process that allows you to emulate the connectionless environment of a LAN into the connection-oriented world of ATM. The LAN frames are encapsulated in RFC2684 (LLC/SNAP) encapsulation. The LANE converter receives LAN packets, places a 5-byte ATM specific identification header on the front of the cell, and removes the checksum (frame check sequence) from the packet. It then fragments the packets into a 48-byte payload with a 5-byte header, creating a 53-byte cell. After the packet has traveled the ATM network, the ATM information is removed and the packet is reassembled and returned to the LAN environment.

The LANE 1.0 specification is basically a software interface for the layer 3 protocols that is identical to existing LANs; this specification encapsulates user data in either Ethernet or Token Ring frames. It doesn't actually become the media access method of Ethernet or Token Ring, but it uses three servers that clients access over ATM connections.

Fiber Distributed Data Interface (FDDI) can be used with LANE 1.0 but is not really as well defined as Ethernet and Token Ring. ATM devices map FDDI packets into either Ethernet or Token Ring using existing translational bridging techniques. LANE 1.0 defines operation over ATM with best-effort delivery. LANE 2.0 has added quality of service (QoS) guarantees and support for multiple LECS, LES, and BUS services for redundancy. These are features that give ATM with LANE a benefit over existing LANs.

LANE Components

LANE consists of several components that interact and relate in different ways to provide network connectivity based upon the client/server model. The interaction of these components allows broadcast searching, address registration, and address caching. The LANE model is made up of the following components:

LAN Emulation Client (LEC or LANE Client)   A LANE Client emulates a LAN interface to higher-layer protocols and applications. It proxies for users attached into ATM via a non-ATM path.

LAN Emulation Server (LES or LANE Server)   This element provides address resolution and registration services to the LANE Clients in its ELAN. Each LES keeps a database of all LESs on other ELANs; it also manages the stations that make up its own ELAN.

LAN Emulation Configuration Server (LECS)   Using a database, the LECS keeps track of which LES serves an ELAN (each configuration server can have a different named database). The main function of a LECS is to inform a LEC about the ATM address of the LES.

Broadcast and unknown server (BUS)   This component is used for broadcasting, sequencing, and distributing multicast and broadcast packets. The BUS also handles unicast flooding. The main function of a BUS is to broadcast data from a LEC until the destination ATM address has been learned (and added to the LES). Actually, there is also the Selective Multicast Server (SMS), which provides multicast services only. If an SMS is not available on an ELAN, the BUS performs the SMS tasks.

WARNING   Make careful notice that LEC and LECS are completely different terms and components!

Figure 4.5 illustrates the components of LANE and their relationships, which we will discuss in the following sections. First we'll define all the components before talking about how they work together within LANE.

FIGURE 4.5 LANE components

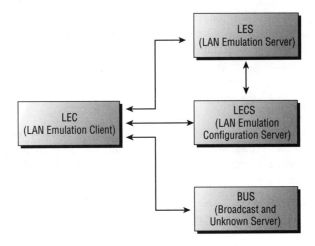

Simple Server Redundancy Protocol (SSRP) is a Cisco-proprietary protocol that provides redundancy for the LECS or the LES/BUS services. If the active LES or BUS fails in your ATM LANE network, another device will assume the role of the active LES or BUS. Also, if the LECS fails, another device assumes the role of the LECS.

The LAN Emulation Client

The *LAN Emulation Client (LEC)* provides the emulation of the Data-Link Layer interface that allows all higher-level protocols and applications to operate and communicate. The LEC runs in all ATM devices, which include hosts, servers, bridges, and routers, It is responsible for providing the following:

- Address resolution
- Data transfer
- Address caching
- An interface to the ELAN
- Driver support for higher-level services

The LEC enables both ATM-attached devices and ATM-capable systems (non-LANE systems such as Token Ring and Ethernet systems, legacy LAN hosts, and so on) to coexist within an ATM emulated LAN environment.

The address resolution function provides address registration and resolution services. This function is used for address and route descriptor types based on the LANE specification. The architecture can support resolution for other services. LANE specifications include support for MAC address registration (for non-Token Ring LANs) and for MAC address and route descriptor registration (for Token Rings).

Each LEC can be a member of only one emulated LAN. You can assign routers to exist within different ELANs by using multiple clients for each ELAN the router belongs to. The Cisco IOS provides the functionality to route information between multiple ELANs.

The data transfer function is aptly named. It allows the transport of frames between other LECs and the BUS. If a LEC does not have a corresponding LEC address to send unicast frames to, the frames are forwarded to the BUS for distribution between the remaining LECs.

Address caching gives each LEC a "directory" of LAN (MAC) addresses and their respective ATM addresses. The information is contained within a database, with tags pointing to other existing stations using different LECs.

Another function, interfacing to the ELAN, requires each LEC to establish connectivity to the LECS and receive the initial configuration services. These services can include receiving the LES ATM address based upon the LANE identifier. Usually the connection to the LECS is broken for continued operation after initial configuration has been received; after receiving the LES address, the LEC communicates directly with the LES. The initial conversation with the LES allows the LEC to join its ELAN and to register and resolve MAC addresses. The LEC also establishes communications with the BUS for all broadcast and unicast data.

Finally, the LEC provides driver interface support. This support allows existing higher-level applications and protocols to continue operation on the ELAN without change.

The LANE Server

The *LANE Server (LES)* is the central LANE component that provides the initial configuration data for each connecting LEC. The LES typically is located on either an ATM-integrated router or a switch. Responsibilities of the LES are as follows:

- Configuration and support for the LEC

- Address registration for the LEC

- Database storage and response concerning Mac-to-ATM address mappings

- An interface to the ELAN

The LES acts as traffic control for all LECs connecting to the emulated LAN, providing the address resolution, registration, and broadcast and unknown server information that guide communication among LECs. Figure 4.6 shows an example of a typical LANE design.

FIGURE 4.6   The role of the LES

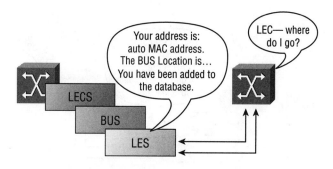

The LEC registers its addressing—network service access point (NSAP) and media access control/end system identifier (MAC/ESI)—with the LES. This information contains the ATM address the LEC will use, a LAN identifier, and if configured, an optional MAC address. Verification of each LEC also occurs in the initial connection, with the server checking and ensuring that each LEC has permission to join the requested ELAN.

The LES also handles address registration. The LES maintains a database of addresses needed for resolution. Registration occurs after the LEC joins the ELAN. Each LEC is allowed to have one registered address, so it can use the join request and no separate registrations are necessary.

The LES contains the ATM address database that responds for address resolution queries attempting to locate partner LECs. The LES responds in kind with the ATM addresses for the targeted ELANs. If no address can be found, the request is forwarded to all registered LECs on the *same* ELAN via the control distribute VCC.

Ultimately, the LES arranges control connections with the LEC. These connections are commonly known as either the *control direct ATM VCCs* (virtual channel connections) or the *control distribute ATM VCCs*. They handle address resolution and registration responses. The LES also establishes communication with the LECS, providing verification for LECs that are joining. The only item with which the LES does not maintain a constant connection is the BUS; instead, it provides each LEC with the ATM address of the BUS for forwarding.

The LAN Emulation Configuration Server

The *LAN Emulation Configuration Server (LECS)* is an important part of ELAN services, providing the configuration data that is furnished upon request from the LES. These services include address registration for *Interim Local Management Interface (ILMI)* support and configuration support for the LES addresses and their corresponding ELAN identifiers and for their NSAP addresses.

The LECS supplies the following:

- The LES ATM (NSAP address)

- Configuration support for the LES

- An interface to the ELAN

The registration of a LECS ATM address uses ILMI functions connecting to the ATM network, usually based on a switch. After registration, the network can supply the LEC with the address using ILMI on the return trip. Figure 4.7 shows the relationship of the LECS to the overall design.

FIGURE 4.7   The role of the LECS

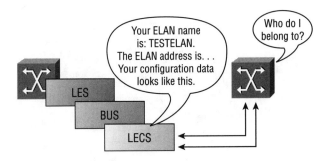

Support for configurations from the LECS ensures that the correct LES address is supplied to the LEC. Configurations can be as simple as providing a single LES address, or they can be more complicated, providing attributes for correlation. These entries can include the following:

- The ELAN name and the corresponding ATM address of a LANE Server
- The LANE Client MAC address and the corresponding ELAN name
- The LANE Client ATM template and the corresponding ELAN name
- The default ELAN name
- The LEC address and the LES
- The ELAN name and the LES
- The ATM address prefix and the LES
- The ELAN type and the LES

The LECS supplies configuration data directly to the LECs. A LEC queries for configuration data and then receives the LES address. The LECS, based upon the attributes received, assigns the correct LES address for each LEC. The LES can also establish a connection with the LECS, verifying each LEC's request to join the LES.

The Broadcast and Unknown Server

The *broadcast and unknown server (BUS)* provides broadcast management support necessary for LANs. The BUS must supply the following services:

- Distribution of broadcast multicast data to all LECs on an ELAN
- Distribution of unicast data
- An interface to the ELAN

The BUS must sequence and distribute multicast and broadcast data to all LECs. Broadcasting such data to all LECs can impact the overall performance of the system and network. Figure 4.8 shows the BUS and the communication sequence by which it exists in LANE.

FIGURE 4.8   The role of the BUS

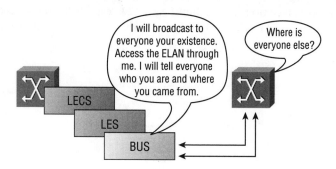

Distribution of unicast data includes the support and transmission of data to the LEC. A LEC will be able to establish a direct connection to another LEC only after the LEC has learned the correct NSAP-address-to-MAC-address mapping from the LES.

Until this occurs, the LEC forwards unicast data to the BUS. The BUS receives the data and must, in turn, broadcast the data to each LEC on the ELAN. (Again, you should configure this option carefully so that the expense of network travel is not increased by broadcasts to each LEC.)

When interfacing to the ELAN, the BUS establishes two connections. Each LEC has a multicast send point-to-point VC established to the BUS. This allows individual LECs to send to the BUS. The BUS also maintains a point-to-multipoint multicast forward VC, which includes all LECs. This allows the BUS to forward data sent from a LEC over a multicast send VC on to the multicast forward VC for delivery to all destinations.

LEC Communication

We have just reviewed the individual pieces that make up the LANE model; now let's examine the communication process. LANE components communicate by *switched virtual circuits (SVCs)*. LANE configurations use virtual channel connections (VCCs), which can also be called virtual circuit connections. SVCs and VCCs can be bidirectional or unidirectional, point-to-point or point-to-multipoint.

When a client first joints an ELAN, it must build an ATM-address-to-Ethernet-MAC-address table. These are the steps that occur to build that table:

1. The LEC sends an LE_ARP_REQUEST to the LES (a point-to-point VCC).

2. The LES forwards the LE_ARP to all clients on the ELAN (a point-to-multipoint control distribute VCC) unless the LES knows the MAC address of the LEC.

3. Any client that recognizes the MAC address responds with an LE_ARP_REPLY to the LES.

4. The LES forwards the response (a point-to-multipoint control distribute VCC) to the LEC.

Once the address-translation table is built, each LEC establishes a connection with the emulated LAN and another LEC; Figure 4.9 shows the path taken to do this.

FIGURE 4.9   Complete LEC–LEC communication

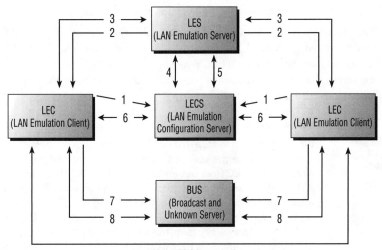

LEC-to-LEC Communication

In the next couple of pages, we'll examine each step in this LEC–LEC communication, after which we'll go into more detail about the internetworking and the mechanics behind what's happening. Figure 4.9 summarizes the following process, showing how each connection is accomplished and where it is going.

The LEC will attempt to determine the LECS using these steps:

A.   Look for a locally configured LECS ATM address.

B.   Use ILMI to query the local ATM switch for the NSAP of the LECS.

C.   Use a fixed address defined by the ATM Forum.

D.   Access PVC 0/17, a well-known VPI/VCI pair.

1.   Using ILMI, a query is made to the ATM switch containing the LECS. The query requests the ATM address of the LES for its emulated LAN. The switch contains a management information base (MIB) variable containing the requested ATM address. This connection is a bidirectional point-to-point *configure direct* VCC.

2.   The LECS responds across the established connection, providing the ATM address and name of the LES for the LEC's ELAN.

3. The LEC then establishes a connection with the LES based upon the configuration data received in the previous connection. The connection is a bidirectional point-to-point control direct VCC, one that remains up for the duration of the process.

4. While the connection is established with the LEC requesting entry (a configure direct VCC) to the emulated LAN, the LES makes a bidirectional connection to the LECS asking for verification so that the requesting LEC may enter the ELAN. The server configuration that was received in the first connection is now verified against the LECS database, determining authenticity and allowing membership.

What's going on in step 4? The LEC creates another packet now with the correct ATM address for the LES, again causing the control direct VCC to establish a connection. The LEC fires out an LE_JOIN_REQUEST to the LES containing the LEC ATM address and the MAC address to register with the emulated LAN. The LES makes a quick check with the LECS verifying the LEC. The LES receives the data, creates a new branch for the LEC, and issues an LE_JOIN_RESPONSE back to the LEC. This response contains the LANE Client identifier (LECID), a unique identifier for each client. This ID is used to filter return broadcasts from the BUS.

5. The LES replies to the LEC's request (through the existing configure direct VCC) by either allowing or denying membership in the ELAN.

6. If the LES allows the connection, the LEC is added to the point-to-multipoint control distribute VCC. Then the LEC is granted a connection using the point-to-point data direct VCC to the corresponding LEC or service it was searching for originally, and the higher-level protocols take over. If the LES rejects the LEC's request, the session is terminated.

7. After being given permission by the LES, the LEC must now find the ATM address for the BUS and become a member of the broadcast group.

What is going on in step 7? The LEC must locate the BUS, so an LE_ARP_REQUEST packet containing the MAC address 0xFFFFFFFF is sent. This packet is sent down the control direct VCC to the LES, which understands the request for the BUS. The LES then responds with the ATM address for the BUS.

8. Eventually the BUS is located and the LEC becomes a member of the emulated LAN.

   What will you get by going through this whole process? LANE provides an ATM forwarding path for unicast traffic between LECs. This forwarding path enables you to move data across the ATM network to unknown destinations.

Accomplishing this means the LEC issues an LE_ARP_REQUEST to the LES using the control direct VCC. If the LES does not know the address mapping requested in the LE_ARP_REQUEST, it forwards the request out the control distribute VCC to all the LECs listening. At the same moment, the unicast packets are forwarded to the BUS, where they are forwarded out to all endpoints. Remember, this sudden influx of unicast traffic isn't great for the network and will continue passing through until the LE_ARP_REQUEST is answered.

As the ARP request is translated and forwarded out the control distribute point-to-multipoint VC to each LEC, hopefully another LEC down the line resolves everything by replying with an LE_ARP_RESPONSE. The response is forwarded back to the LES and the address is added to the database, relating a new MAC address to an ATM address. Because of the two separate initial data forwarding mechanisms, *two* data direct VCs are established. The VC established by the LEC with the *lowest* NSAP address is maintained, and the other VC is torn down.

Once it receives the LE_ARP_RESPONSE, the LEC immediately does two things. First, it requests a data direct VCC that will carry the unicast traffic between the LECs. As soon as the data direct VCC becomes available, the LEC performs its second duty: sending the flush over the multicast send, allowing the BUS to forward the packet on the multicast forward VC. After passing through the network, the flush packet will return to the sending LEC, signaling that the LEC can begin communication with the located LEC.

We have now covered both the ATM protocol and ATM LANE. Let's now discuss how to configure the different kinds of ATM functionality on Cisco routers. Remember, because ATM LANE is not a topic for the CCIE lab examination, we will not be covering the configuration of ATM LANE.

Configuring ATM

This section of the chapter focuses on the correct configuration to provide asynchronous transport mode (ATM) connectivity with a Cisco router. It is a safe bet that in the CCIE lab examination you will have to configure ATM support. You will not have to configure the LS1010 ATM switch because the lab proctor will already have it configured for you. But you must be able to configure the router ATM interfaces properly. The problem is that there are several methods of configuring ATM, so you must be prepared to configure ATM in any of the possible methods the examination directs you to use. Configuring the router ATM interfaces properly is important whether you are practicing this configuration for the CCIE lab examination or for use in the real world of everyday networking.

Cisco has many products that support ATM, including the LightStream 1010, BPX, IGX, MGX, and ATM interfaces of routers. We are primarily looking at the router ATM interfaces in this chapter. In the CCIE lab examination, the proctor will probably use a LightStream 1010 to simulate the ATM cloud. The ATM switch will probably already be configured for you by the lab proctor, just as the Frame Relay switch will probably already be configured for you. ATM LAN emulation (LANE) is not included as part of the CCIE lab examination, so we will not be covering the ATM LANE technique in this hands-on scenario section of this chapter.

Figure 4.10 shows a typical lab environment configuration for ATM VCs. Notice that R1 has a single physical ATM interface that is supporting two VCs. VC #1 is connecting R1 to R2, VC #2 is connecting R1 to R3, and VC #3 is connecting R2 to R3. We will use this diagram as a reference as we discuss the various ATM PVC and SVC configuration methods.

FIGURE 4.10 Typical ATM lab environment

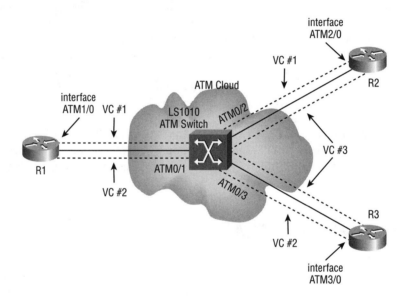

The following is a portion of the LightStream 1010 configuration, which is supporting the example in Figure 4.10. This configuration is supporting a full mesh topology (versus a hub-and-spoke topology):

```
hostname ls1010
!
atm address 47.0091.8100.0000.0061.7171.7171.9999.0000.0000.00
!
interface ATM0/1
 no ip address
 no atm ilmi-keepalive
```

```
atm pvc 1 100   interface  ATM0/2 2 100
atm pvc 1 200   interface  ATM0/3 3 200
!
interface ATM0/2
 no ip address
 no atm ilmi-keepalive
 atm pvc 2 100   interface  ATM0/1 1 100
 atm pvc 4 100   interface  ATM0/3 4 100
!
interface ATM0/3
 no ip address
 no atm ilmi-keepalive
 atm pvc 3 200   interface  ATM0/1 1 200
 atm pvc 4 100   interface  ATM0/2 4 100
```

Now that we have covered how to set up the ATM environment, we can move on to actually configuring the routers to support both PVCs and SVCs.

Configuring ATM Permanent Virtual Circuits (PVCs)

As you remember from Chapter 3 on Frame Relay, in certain circumstances all that is required to make a Frame Relay interface active is the command `encapsulation frame-relay` because LMI will take care of the rest of the configuration for you dynamically. In configuring ATM PVCs, it is not that easy. You must manually configure the VPI/VCI pair on your router interface, then Inverse ARP can dynamically map your local VPI/VCI pair to a remote network layer address. This is usually used in a full mesh environment.

 Inverse ARP is supported only for IP and IPX.

What if you do not want to rely on Inverse ARP to perform the local VPI/VCI pair to remote network layer address dynamically? Well then, you have two options.

Option 1 is to create an ATM map list, which is basically the same as the Frame Relay map statements that you used in the preceding chapter. ATM utilizes a virtual circuit designator (VCD), which is the VPI/VCI pair to distinguish individual VCs. Figure 4.11 shows an example of an ATM PVC configuration utilizing an ATM map list to statically perform the VPI/VCI pair mapping to remote network layer addresses. The following three listings all based on Figure 4.11.

FIGURE 4.11   Configuring an ATM map list

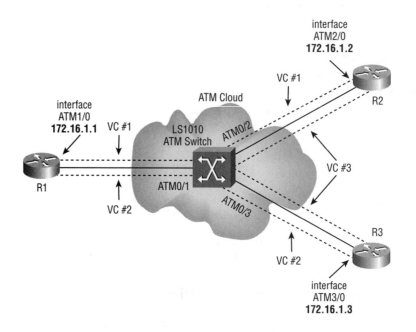

Router R1, ATM PVC with Physical Interface and Map List

```
interface ATM1/0
```

`ip address 172.16.1.1 255.255.255.0`	The local network layer address
`atm pvc 1 1 100 aal5snap`	Defines VPI= 1, VCI= 100 values for the PVC #1
`atm pvc 2 1 200 aal5snap`	Defines VPI= 1, VCI= 200 values for the PVC #2
`map-group kelly`	Applies ATM map-list kelly to the interface
`map-list kelly`	Map-list is the same as frame-relay map command
`ip 172.16.1.2 atm-vc 1 broadcast`	Static mapping of PVC #1 to the R2 IP Address of 172.16.1.2
`ip 172.16.1.3 atm-vc 2 broadcast`	Static mapping of PVC #2 to the R3 IP Address of 172.16.1.3

Broadcast = allows broadcast/multicast packets for routing protocols

Router R2, ATM PVC with Physical Interface and Map List

interface ATM2/0

ip address 172.16.1.2 255.255.255.0	The local network layer address
atm pvc 1 2 100 aal5snap	Defines VPI= 2, VCI= 100 values for the PVC #1
atm pvc 3 4 100 aal5snap	Defines VPI= 4, VCI= 100 values for the PVC #3
map-group chris	Applies ATM map-list chris to the interface

map-list chris — Map-list is the same as frame-relay map command

ip 172.16.1.1 atm-vc 1 broadcast	Static mapping of PVC #1 to the R1 IP Address of 172.16.1.1
ip 172.16.1.3 atm-vc 3 broadcast	Static mapping of PVC #3 to the R3 IP Address of 172.16.1.3

Broadcast = allows broadcast/multicast packets for routing protocols

Router R3, ATM PVC with Physical Interface and Map List

interface ATM3/0

ip address 172.16.1.3 255.255.255.0	The local network layer address
atm pvc 2 3 200 aal5snap	Defines VPI= 3, VCI= 200 values for the PVC #2
atm pvc 3 4 100 aal5snap	Defines VPI= 4, VCI= 100 values for the PVC #3
map-group josh	Applies ATM map-list josh to the interface

map-list josh — Map-list is the same as frame-relay map command

ip 172.16.1.1 atm-vc 2 broadcast	Static mapping of PVC #2 to the R1 IP Address of 172.16.1.1
ip 172.16.1.2 atm-vc 3 broadcast	Static mapping of PVC #3 to the R2 IP Address of 172.16.1.2

Broadcast = allows broadcast/multicast packets for routing protocols

Option 2 is to use the "New Way" of defining ATM PVCs on an interface (use the newer pvc command as opposed to the atm pvc command). This way utilizes the PVC vpi/vci command to create a separate subconfiguration for each PVC. In the following example, we are configuring separate point-to-point PVCs for each remote destination. This is the most efficient configuration because it resolves any routing (split-horizon) issues that you may encounter later on when configuring your IGP protocols. The configurations shown in the following three listings are based on Figure 4.12.

FIGURE 4.12   Defining individual ATM PVCs

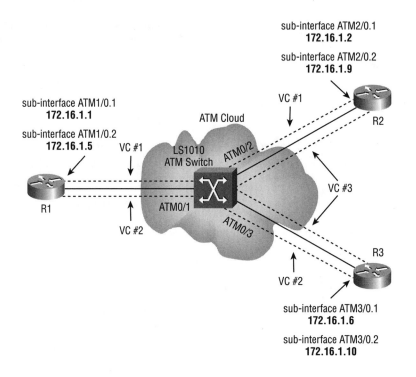

Router R1, ATM PVC with a Subinterface for Each PVC

interface ATM1/0	Physical ATM interface with no IP address applied
no ip address	
interface ATM1/0.1 point-to-point	Create a point-to-point sub-interface for PVC #1
ip address 172.16.1.1 255.255.255.252	The local network layer address

pvc 1/100   Defines VPI= 1, VCI= 100 values for the PVC#1

  protocol ip 172.16.1.2 broadcast   Static mapping of PVC #1 to the R2 IP Address of 172.16.1.2

                  Broadcast = allows broadcast/multicast packets for routing protocols

interface ATM1/0.2 point-to-point   Create a point-to-point sub-interface for PVC #2

  ip address 172.16.1.5 255.255.255.252   The local network layer address

  pvc 1 /200   Defines VPI= 1, VCI= 200 values for the PVC#2

    protocol ip 172.16.1.6 broadcast   Static mapping of PVC #2 to the R3 IP Address of 172.16.1.6

Router R2, ATM PVC with a Subinterface for Each PVC

interface ATM2/0   Physical ATM interface with no IP address applied

 no ip address

interface ATM2/0.1 point-to-point   Create a point-to-point sub-interface for PVC #1

  ip address 172.16.1.2 255.255.255.252   The local network layer address

  pvc 2/100   Defines VPI= 2, VCI= 100 values for the PVC#1

   protocol ip 172.16.1.1 broadcas   Static mapping of PVC #1 to the R1 IP Address of 172.16.1.1

interface ATM2/0.2 point-to-point   Create a point-to-point sub-interface for PVC #3

  ip address 172.16.1.9 255.255.255.252   The local network layer address

  pvc 4/100   Defines VPI= 4, VCI= 100 values for the PVC#3

   protocol ip 172.16.1.10 broadcast   Static mapping of PVC #3 to the R3 IP Address of 172.16.1.10

Router R3, ATM PVC with a Subinterface for Each PVC

`interface ATM3/0`	Physical ATM interface with no IP address applied no ip address
`interface ATM3/0.1 point-to-point`	Create a point-to-point sub-interface for PVC #2
`ip address 172.16.1.6 255.255.255.252`	The local network layer address
`pvc 3/200`	Defines VPI= 3, VCI= 200 values for the PVC#2
`protocol ip 172.16.1.5 broadcast`	Static mapping of PVC #2 to the R1 IP Address of 172.16.1.5
`interface ATM3/0.2 point-to-point`	Create a point-to-point sub-interface for PVC #3
`ip address 172.16.1.10 255.255.255.252`	The local network layer address
`pvc 4/100`	Defines VPI= 4, VCI= 100 values for the PVC#3
`protocol ip 172.16.1.9 broadcast`	Static mapping of PVC #3 to the R2 IP Address of 172.16.1.9

Configuring PVC Auto Discovery

If you do not know what the proper VPI/VCI pair is for your PVC, then you must discover the VPI/VCI pair dynamically. This can be accomplished with the `atm ilmi-pvc-discovery` command in conjunction with the `atm pvc 1 0 16 ilmi` command on the physical ATM interface.

Interim Local Management Interface (ILMI) is a standards-based protocol for setting and learning Physical layer and ATM layer parameters on ATM interfaces. By using ILMI, a router can interrogate an ATM switch and dynamically learn the configured ATM PVCs from it. This mechanism is referred to as ILMI auto discovery.

With ILMI auto discovery, the router and ATM switch exchange ILMI packets (SNMP messages) across the physical ATM connection. The ATM interfaces encapsulate these messages in ATM adaptation layer 5 (AAL5) cells. By default, ILMI messages are exchanged using a well-known PVC that uses VPI=0 and VCI=16.

Once these two commands (`atm ilmi-pvc-discovery` and `atm pvc 1 0 16 ilmi`) are placed on the physical ATM interface, you can use the `show atm vc` command to determine your PVC's VPI/VCI pair. Once you learn the proper VPI/VCI pair, reconfigure your ATM interface to support the required PVC. Use either option 1 or option 2 in the preceding section for this configuration. The configuration shown in the following listing is based on the example in Figure 4.11.

Router R3, ATM PVC Auto Discovery
```
interface ATM3/0
 ip address 172.16.1.3 255.255.25.0        The local network layer
                                           address
 atm pvc 1 0 16 ilmi                       SVC-NSAP address
                                           registration, must be applied
 atm ilmi-pvc-discovery                    Used when the PVC is not
                                           known
```

The following is the output of the show atm vc command:

Interface	VCD	VPI	VCI	Type	AAL/ Encapsulation	Peak Kbps	Avg. Kbps	Burst Cells	Status
ATM3/0	1	3	2	PVC	AAL5-SNAP	155000	155000	94	Active
ATM3/0	2	4	1	PVC	AAL5-SNAP	155000	155000	94	Active

From the output of the show atm vc command, we now know that there are two PVCs that have the VPI/VCI pairs of 3/2 and 4/1.

 Real World Scenario

OSPF over ATM

Remember that ATM was developed from Frame Relay, and thus, ATM has many of the same characteristics that Frame Relay has. Both of these technologies are based on the use of virtual circuits (VCs). So, certain layer 3 routing protocols that have specific requirements when implemented on top of Frame Relay will have the same requirements when implemented on top of ATM.

Consider the Open Shortest Path First (OSPF) routing protocol. When implementing OSPF on top of Frame Relay, it is imperative that you make sure that the OSPF network type configured on the interfaces at each end of the VCs match each other because, if the OSPF network types do not match, the interfaces will never form an OSPF neighbor adjacency.

ATM has the same issues with OSPF routing. So be sure to verify that the OSPF interface network types match up on both ends of the ATM VC or OSPF will not be able to form neighbor adjacencies.

Configuring ATM Switched Virtual Circuits (SVCs)

An ATM switched virtual circuit (SVC) is established only when needed. Just as with any SVC, the virtual circuit must be set up, then the data is transferred, then the virtual circuit is torn down. The process requires coordination or signaling from end to end. And in order to accomplish the signaling, each end device must be distinguished with a unique address. This is accomplished with the 20-byte NSAP address. An NSAP address is a layer 2 ATM address that can be thought of as kind of like a layer 2 Media Access Control (MAC) address.

Keep in mind that PVCs are locally significant, meaning you can reuse the same PVC numbers throughout the network as long as they are unique on a specific interface. NSAPs, in contrast, are globally unique within the context of the ATM network, providing a mechanism similar to telephone numbering, with the ability to locate any ATM device anywhere in the network.

The NSAP address is 160 bits (20 bytes) long and comprises the following:

- The initial domain part (IDP)
- The authority and format identifier (AFI)
  - 39 = DCC ATM format
  - 47 = ICD ATM format
  - 45 = E.164 format
- The initial domain identifier (IDI). The IDI is coded as follows:
  - A data country code (DCC) in conformance to ISO 3166
  - An International Code Designator (ICD)
  - An E.164 address
- Domain Specific part (DSP)
  - High-Order Domain Specific Part (HO-DSP)—10 bytes from the ATM switch
  - End System Identifier (ESI) —6 bytes from the end switch/router
  - Selector byte—1 byte. Usually the 13 byte combination of AFI, IDI, and HO-DSP is called the prefix (network portion of the address), while the ESI and Selector byte comprise the host portion of the address.

Cisco Systems uses the ICD format of NSAP address. In fact, Cisco ATM switches always have a prefix of 47.0091.8100.0000.<switch-mac-address> (e.g., 47.0091.8100.0000.1111.2222.3333). Figure 4.13 is an example of a full ICD NSAP address.

FIGURE 4.13 NSAP address format

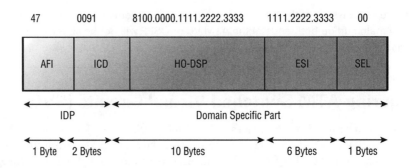

ATM SVC Signaling

There are two PVCs required to allow SVC connections to be established using Q2931 signaling:

- QSAAL, which uses the VPI/VCI pair of 0 5
- ILMI, which uses the VPI/VCI pair of 0 16

ILMI was explained in the previous section, so we'll talk about QSAAL. ATM end systems and network switches use signaling protocols to establish switched virtual circuits (SVCs) between two end routers. The ATM signaling components used for this are Q.2931 and the signaling ATM adaptation layer (SAAL).

A fundamental concept is that a SVC is actually a dynamic PVC after Q.2931 signaling is complete. In other words, the Q.2931 signaling dynamically builds a PVC between calling party and called party.

QSAAL is the signaling mechanism used by an ATM end system (router) to communicate to the local ATM switch. The router will use QSAAL to request an ATM SVC to another ATM end system. The ATM end systems can be connected anywhere on the ATM network and each ATM end system is uniquely identified on the ATM network by its NSAP address.

Signaling is required for dynamically built SVCs, and to provide the required ILMI and QSAAL signaling, the following two PVC commands must be applied to an ATM interface:

```
Interface ATM3/0
 atm pvc 1 0 5 qsaal
 atm pvc 2 0 16 ilmi
```

QSAAL takes care of SVC call setup requests but does not define how ATM end devices actually determine the appropriate NSAP of destination systems. It's kind of like the POTS—QSAAL is the PSTN, but you need to know the number of the person you are calling by some other mechanism (for example, the telephone directory).

ESI Addressing

One method of configuring ATM SVC connections is with the use of the ESI address and a map list. Refer back to the listings in the section "Configuring ATM Permanent Virtual Circuits (PVCs)" to see how to implement the map list. In this type of configuration, you statically place your local ESI address on your interface along with the two required signaling PVCs and then point the interface to a map list using the map-group command.

The map list will then statically map to the remote end NSAP address and Network layer address. Refer to Figure 4.14 for the listing that follows, which is an example of an ATM SVC configuration utilizing an ATM map list to statically perform the NSAP address mapping to a remote Network layer address.

FIGURE 4.14   ATM SVC with NSAP map list

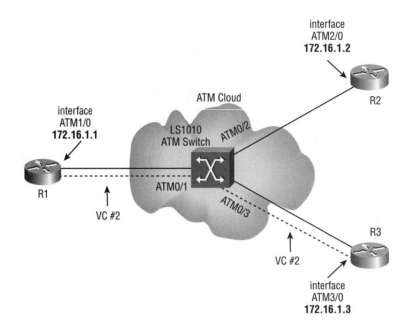

Remember that following the ESI section of the NSAP address is the selector byte, which is used to differentiate between multiple subinterfaces on the same physical interface.

Router R3, ATM SVC Utilizing Only the ESI Address and Map List

```
interface ATM3/0
```

```
  ip address 172.16.1.3 255.255.255.0
```
The local network layer address

```
  atm pvc 1 0 5 qsaal
```
Mandatory SVC for Q.2931 signalling

```
  atm pvc 2 0 16 ilmi
```
SVC-NSAP address registration

```
  atm esi-address 333300000000.00
```
Configure on originating multipoint interface

```
  map-group kelly
```
Applies ATM map-list kelly to the interface

```
map-list kelly
```

```
  ip 172.16.1.1 atm-nsap 47.009181000000006171717171.111100000000.00 broadcast
```

The preceding map list is used to statically map the R1 IP address of 172.16.1.1 to its layer 2 NSAP address of 47.00918100000006171717171.111100000000.00.

The ATM signaling (ILMI and QSAAL) allows router R3 to learn the location of the destination layer 2 NSAP address (47.00918100000006171717171.111100000000.00).

Then, through the use of the static map list, layer 3 protocols (IP in this example) are able to be routed without the requirement of an ARP function.

Classical IP (CLIP)

Another method of ATM SVC connections is the use of Classical IP, more commonly referred to as CLIP. This provides a mechanism to dynamically map the Network layer address with the NSAP address without having to use the static map list.

Classical IP can only be used to map the IP address to a NSAP address. It cannot operate with other Network layer protocols, such as IPX. To configure Classical IP, all you need to do is create an ATM ARP server. All other clients will then be configured as ATM ARP clients.

Figure 4.15 is an example of the Classical IP (CLIP) configuration between routers R1, R2, and R3, which are shown in the following three commands.

FIGURE 4.15   Classical IP

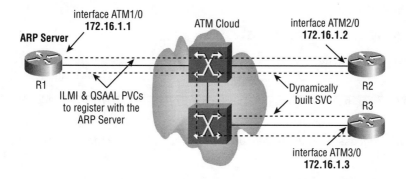

Router R1, ARP Server Side of the SVC Connection

```
interface ATM1/0

 ip address 172.16.1.1 255.255.255.0

 atm pvc 1 0 5 qsaal

 atm pvc 2 0 16 ilmi

 atm esi-address 111100000000.00

 no atm ilmi-keepalive

 atm arp-server self
```

The command atm arp-server self must be on the server

Router R2, ARP Client Side of the SVC Connection

```
interface ATM2/0
  ip address 172.16.1.2 255.255.255.0
  atm pvc 1 0 5 qsaal                          Mandatory SVC for Q.2931
                                               signaling

  atm pvc 2 0 16 ilmi                          SVC-NSAP address
                                               registration

  atm esi-address 222200000000.00             Place on originating
                                               multipoint interface

  no atm ilmi-keepalive
  atm arp-server nsap 47.009181000000006171717171.111100000000.00
```

Router R3, ARP Client Side of the SVC Connection

```
interface ATM3/0
  ip address 172.16.1.3 255.255.255.0
  atm pvc 1 0 5 qsaal                          Mandatory SVC for Q.2931
                                               signaling

  atm pvc 2 0 16 ilmi                          SVC-NSAP address
                                               registration

  atm esi-address 333300000000.00             Place on originating
                                               multipoint interface

  no atm ilmi-keepalive
  atm arp-server nsap 47.009181000000006171717171.111100000000.00
```

When configuring any of the routers for CLIP, you will have to configure the two mandatory signaling PVCs on the physical interface and your local ESI address on the physical interface. Then on the ARP client router, issue the show atm ilmi-status command to find the ARP server's NSAP address (prefix). Once you learn the ARP server's NSAP address, you can enter the atm arp-server nsap command, which points the client to the server. You can use the show atm arp command to verify that the SVC is operational.

WARNING   The preceding commands would only work if the ATM ARP server is connected to the same ATM switch as the client. The NSAP prefix changes between ATM switches and is impossible to determine via ILMI.

In the previous ESI addressing configuration, the ARP function was not required because we utilized the map list to statically map the layer 2 NSAP address to the layer 3 IP address. Classical IP uses an ARP function to dynamically map the layer 2 NSAP address to the layer 3 IP address. This provides a dynamic any-to-any topology—any device that is registered with the ARP server is able to dynamically build a SVC with any other device that is also registered with the ARP server.

The Classical IP process flow to allow R3 to dynamically build a SVC to R2 is as follows:

- Classical IP client R3 registers with the ARP server R1 (builds a SVC to the ARP server based on the NSAP address of the ARP server).
- Classical IP client R2, registers with the ARP server R1 (builds a SVC to the ARP server based on the NSAP address of the ARP server).
- Classical IP client R3 sends an ATM-ARP request for R2 to the ARP server R1.
- ATM ARP server R1 responds to the ATM-ARP request from R3 with the NSAP address of R2.
- Classical IP client R3 directly connects to Classical IP client R2 with a dynamic SVC.

Now that you know how to configure routers for the various functions of the ATM protocol, we'll briefly discuss good troubleshooting techniques and useful debug commands.

Troubleshooting ATM

When troubleshooting ATM, you can use the same techniques that you would use with Frame Relay or ISDN. As mentioned in the discussion at the beginning of this chapter, ATM evolved from Frame Relay and narrowband ISDN.

Just as you would do in troubleshooting Frame Relay or ISDN, assure that the packets are being transmitted out the proper interface using the `debug ip packet` command and the `debug atm packet` command.

If you have a good understanding of Frame Relay, ATM should be a natural progression and an easy concept to grasp.

Summary

In this chapter, you learned about the ATM protocols suite and how ATM LANE, the components that make up LAN emulation, emulates a broadcast medium (such as Ethernet).

We closely examined ATM LANE implementation and poked around inside the ATM network to try to figure out exactly what is going on and when. This has given you a fundamental understanding of how ATM works.

We indicated that as specified by the ATM Forum, three services must be emulated: connectionless services, multicast services, and LAN Media Access Control driver services. We also looked at the separate components that make up an emulated LAN, including the LEC, the LES, the LECS, and the BUS.

Finally, you learned how to configure ATM on a Cisco router. The design of ATM was discussed during the configuration examples, including how to design your network with ATM LANE.

ATM is a protocol that naturally progressed from Frame Relay and narrowband ISDN. It can be used to support virtually all types of end user services to include data, voice video, and so on. And with the QoS capabilities of ATM, it is easy to build in service level agreements (SLAs) for your customers.

Exam Essentials

Know the three layers of the ATM protocol.   The ATM protocol dictates how two end devices communicate with each other across an ATM network through switches. The ATM protocol model contains three functional layers: ATM physical layer, ATM layer, and ATM adaptation layer (AAL).

Understand the purpose of the VPI and VCI.   ATM utilizes a locally significant VC identifier just like the Frame Relay DLCI, although ATM refers to these VC identifiers as virtual path identifier/virtual circuit identifier (VPI/VCI) pairs. The virtual path identifier (VPI) identifies the virtual path connection, and the virtual circuit identifier (VCI), along with the VPI, uniquely identifies a cell as belonging to a specific virtual connection.

Know the size of an ATM cell.   ATM is efficient because of its use of 53-byte cells. ATM takes the frames of data from the upper layers of the OSI model and segments them into smaller sections in order to build them into cells with a fixed length of 53-bytes (5-byte header with 48-byte payload, based on AAL5). This allows ATM to carry real-time, sensitive traffic like voice and video at much higher quality than a frame-based protocol can.

Know the four components that are utilized in ATM LANE.   LANE consists of several components that interact and relate in different ways to provide network connectivity based upon the client/server model. The interaction of these components allows broadcast searching, address registration, and address caching. The LANE model is made up of the following components: LAN Emulation Client (LEC or LANE Client), LAN Emulation Server (LES or LANE Server), LAN Emulation Configuration Server (LECS), and broadcast and unknown server (BUS).

Know what the signaling ATM adaptation layer (SAAL) is made up of.   The SAAL comprises two parts: the Service Specific Connection Oriented Protocol (SSCOP) and the Service Specific Coordination Function (SSCF). SSCOP provides the reliable transport of signaling messages between peer entities. Signaling requests are encapsulated in SSCOP frames and are carried across the ATM network in AAL5 packets using a well-known PVC. The ATM Forum PVC for UNI signaling uses the VCI of 5. SSCF provides the interface between the Q.2931 protocol and the SSCOP.

Key Terms

Before you take the exam, be certain you are familiar with the following terms:

Asynchronous Transfer Mode (ATM)

ATM adaptation layer (AAL)

ATM Forum

ATM layer

ATM physical layer

broadcast and unknown server (BUS)

control direct ATM VCCs

control distribute ATM VCCs

emulated LANs (ELANs)

Interim Local Management Interface (ILMI)

LAN Emulation (LANE)

LAN Emulation Client (LEC)

LAN Emulation Configuration Server (LECS)

LAN Emulation over ATM, ATM Forum 94-0035

LANE Server (LES)

physical medium dependent (PMD)

switched virtual circuits (SVCs)

Review Questions

1. What is the primary function of the LAN Emulation Server (LES)?
   A. To provide the IP address for the ELAN the LEC is attempting to connect to
   B. To provide the initial configuration data for each connecting LEC
   C. To function as the director of all LEC functionality
   D. To configure all the emulated LANs on the network

2. What is the primary function of the BUS?
   A. To distribute multicast data to all LECs
   B. To distribute unicast data
   C. To interface to the emulated LAN
   D. All of the above
   E. None of the above

3. What is the primary function of the LAN Emulation Configuration Server (LECS)?
   A. To support configuration for the BUS addresses and their corresponding LANE identifiers
   B. To inform a LEC about the ATM address of the LES
   C. To configure all the emulated LANs on the network
   D. To support the driver interface for high-level applications

4. What is the well-known PVC used by LECs to contact the LECS?
   A. PVC 0/18
   B. PVC 0/71
   C. PVC 0/16
   D. PVC 0/17

5. How many bytes long is an ATM cell?
   A. 45
   B. 48
   C. 52
   D. 53
   E. 64

6. What is a VCI?

    A. Virtual circuit identifier

    B. Virtual channel identifier

    C. Virtual connection integration

    D. Both A and B

    E. Both A and C

7. How many ELANs can a single LEC belong to?

    A. Any amount configured

    B. 5

    C. 1

    D. None

    E. 10

8. What does the address 0xFFFFFFFF do?

    A. It is a request for the location of the BUS from the LEC.

    B. It is the broadcast address.

    C. Both A and B.

    D. None of the above.

9. How many VPI values can an NNI represent?

    A. 256

    B. 1024

    C. 4096

    D. None of the above

10. What field in the cell header identifies the cell as user data or a management cell and contains the EFCI bit and the end of frame bit?

    A. GFC

    B. VPI

    C. VCI

    D. PTI

    E. CLP

    F. HEC

Answers to Review Questions

1. C. The LES acts as traffic control for all LECs connecting to the emulated LAN, providing the address resolution, registration, and broadcast and unknown server information that guides communication among LECs.

2. D. One of the main functions of a BUS is to broadcast data from a LEC until the destination ATM address has been learned and added to the LES.

3. B. One of the main functions of the LECS is to inform a LEC about the ATM address of the LES.

4. D. LECs use PVC 0/17 for connections.

5. D. An ATM cell is 53 bytes long.

6. D. An ATM VCI is identified as both a virtual circuit identifier and a virtual channel identifier.

7. C. A single LEC can only belong to one LANE at a time; however, a single Cisco device can support multiple LECs.

8. C. 0x says the next characters are in hex. All F characters in hex is a broadcast.

9. C. Because the NNI does not use the GFC, it can provide all 12 bits for VPIs, or 4096 virtual paths.

10. D. Payload type indicator (PTI) identifies the cell as user data or a management cell and contains the EFCI bit and the end of frame bit.

Chapter 5

Token Ring

THE CCIE QUALIFICATION EXAM TOPICS COVERED IN THIS CHAPTER INCLUDE THE FOLLOWING:

- ✓ Token Ring topology
- ✓ Token Ring frame format
- ✓ Token Ring specialized functions
- ✓ Token Ring insertion process
- ✓ Hard and soft errors

Token Ring was developed by the IBM Corporation in the early 1980s as an outgrowth of ring topologies in multi-drop Synchronous Data Link Control (SDLC) and an answer to Ethernet as a high-speed LAN. It was then standardized as IEEE 802.5 in 1985.

Because the manufacture of Token Ring chipsets has been discontinued, one might puzzle over the need to study token ring at all. If even IBM is converting to Ethernet, what is the importance of learning Token Ring? The answer lies in the data center where mainframes reside. A larger number of mainframes still communicate with devices in the network with Systems Network Architecture (SNA) via token ring–attached front-end processors. Despite the fact that pundits have been predicting the demise of SNA and mainframes, both are still viable, and you are liable to encounter them at some point in your networking career.

In this chapter, we explore the fundamentals of Token Ring operation including token passing, the IEEE 802.5 frame format (which is key to understanding all the functions of Token Ring), the Token Ring insertion process into the ring, and the configuration and troubleshooting of Token Ring interfaces. We also look at the additional roles some Token Ring stations undertake in order to ensure orderly Token Ring operation.

Chapter 14 focuses on bridging and further investigates Token Ring networking by covering source-route bridging (SRB), wherein lies the true strength of Token Ring technology.

Token Ring Operation

The basic concept behind Token Ring (and FDDI, for that matter) is that a station must possess the token in order to transmit a frame. Because only one station at a time can transmit a frame, there is no chance for collisions and back-offs. Therefore, a Token Ring is said to be deterministic. This determinism is also enhanced by priority bits in the token frame, which allow certain devices such as bridges the ability to transmit frames before other devices on the ring do. When a station has control over the token, it will start transmitting its frame on the ring, changing the Token bit in the token ring frame header to indicate that the frame is a data frame. The frame will proceed to every station on the ring until it comes back to the originating station, which will remove the frame from the ring and transmit a new token. A feature called *Early Token Release* enables the originating station to circulate a new token before it has received back its frame. This allows for greater ring utilization, especially on larger rings, but is supported only on 16Mbps rings.

Token Ring LANs run at data rates of either 4Mbps or 16Mbps. The physical signal used by token ring is *differential Manchester encoding,* which is self-clocking and runs at twice the frequency of the data; therefore, a 16Mbs token ring LAN is actually clocked at 32Mbps. Differential Manchester encoding represents a logical zero as two signal transitions during a bit period and represents a logical one as a single-bit transition. Unlike Manchester encoding, which represents zero as a mid-bit transition from a low signal level to a high and a one as a mid-bit transition from a high signal level to a low, differential Manchester encoding does not suffer from signal polarity inversions.

A token ring frame is sent as a logical byte stream with the bits of each byte sent from the most significant bit (bit 0 or the leftmost bit) to the least significant bit (bit 7 or the rightmost). This is somewhat different from Ethernet, which also transmits its frames in a byte-wise fashion but with the least significant bit (rightmost) being transmitted on the wire first. The reason to note this difference comes into play when performing source-route transparent (SRT) bridging or source-route translational bridging (SR/TLB) and will be discussed further in Chapter 14.

Token Ring Frame Format

All of the elements of token ring operation are contained in the token ring frame. When compared with the Ethernet frame format discussed in Chapter 6, "Ethernet LAN Technologies," you'll see that the token ring frame has many more fields. The additional fields provide greater functionality for end stations to verify frame receipt, detect errors, and ensure orderly ring operation. Some of the fields are used solely by the special ring function devices discussed in the next section. A good knowledge of the frame format will enable you to understand the special functions of token ring and know how everything fits together.

There are two basic types of frames found on a token ring in addition to circulating tokens: *Media Access Control (MAC) frames* and Logical Link Control (LLC) frames. MAC frames are used for ring maintenance and reporting errors, and LLC frames are used for data communications. By looking at each of the fields in the token ring frame and what their values are used for, you'll get a better idea of how the token ring works. Figure 5.1 shows the token ring frame. A token frame is composed of the Starting Delimiter (SD), Access Control (AC), and Ending Delimiter (ED) fields only, as shown in Figure 5.2.

FIGURE 5.1   Token Ring frame

Token Ring Frame Format

Starting delimeter 1 byte	Access control 1 byte	Frame control 1 byte	Destination MAC address 6 bytes	Source MAC address 6 bytes

Routing Information Field (RIF) 0-18 bytes	Information field 3 - MTU	Frame check sequence 4 bytes	Ending delimeter 1 byte	Frame status 1 byte

FIGURE 5.2   Token frame

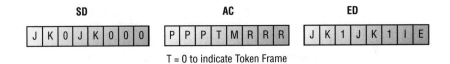

SD   AC   ED

| J | K | 0 | J | K | 0 | 0 | 0 | | P | P | P | T | M | R | R | R | | J | K | 1 | J | K | 1 | I | E |

T = 0 to indicate Token Frame

The following describe each of the fields in a token ring frame.

Starting Delimiter (SD)   The SD is a 1-byte set pattern of J, K, 0, J, K, 0, 0, 0, where *J* and *K* are code violations in differential Manchester encoding, which marks the beginning of a token ring frame.

Access Control (AC)   AC is a 1-byte field that contains the Priority and Reservation bits, the Token bit, and the Monitor bit.

The Priority bits indicate the priority of the current frame. If a station's priority is greater than or equal to the token's value, it may use the token. Table 5.1 lists the values of the priority bits and their meanings.

The Token bit is set to 0 to indicate a token and 1 to indicate a MAC/LLC frame.

The Monitor bit is set to 0 when a frame is originated by a station. As the frame passes the active monitor, the Monitor bit is set to 1. If the active monitor sees a frame with the Monitor bit set, it assumes that there is a problem with the originating station and strips the frame off the ring to prevent it from circulating endlessly around the ring.

The Reservation bits are set by a station to reserve the token for future use. A bridge with priority of 100 may want to use the token and ensure that a station with lower priority does not transmit before it does. The logic in the token ring chipset will remember lower-priority reservation settings and eventually reverts to the lowest setting to allow all stations to transmit.

TABLE 5.1   Token Priorities

Priority Value	Priority/Use
000	Normal user priority
	Tokenless MAC frames
	Response MAC frames
001	Normal user priority

TABLE 5.1   Token Priorities *(continued)*

Priority Value	Priority/Use
010	Normal user priority
011	Normal user priority
	MAC frames requiring tokens
100	Bridge
101	Reserved for future use
110	Reserved for future use
111	Station management

Frame Control (FC)   This 1-byte field contains the Frame Type and Control bits as well as two reserved bits.

The two Frame Type bits indicate whether the frame is a MAC frame (00) or an LLC frame (01).

The four Control bits indicate how the frame is to be buffered if it is a MAC frame. If the frame is an LLC frame, these bits are set to 0.

Destination MAC (DMAC) address   The Destination MAC address is a 6-byte field and is the target address of the frame. It can house either a single station MAC address, an all-stations broadcast address, a *functional address*, or a group address.

The most significant bit (bit 0) of the most significant byte of the Destination MAC address is the Individual/Group address indicator.

The next most significant bit (bit 1) is the U/L that indicates whether the address is universally administered or locally administered. When set to a 1, the address is locally administered; 0 indicates that the address is provided by the adapter vendor and should be unique.

The Functional Address Indicator bit resides in the most significant bit (bit 0) of the second most significant byte. If set to a 0, it signifies that a locally administered group address is a functional address; if set to a 1, the address is a group address.

Table 5.2 shows the Token Ring functional addresses.

TABLE 5.2 Token Ring Functional Addresses (Noncanonical Representation)

Function Name	Functional Address
Active monitor	C000.0000.0001
Ring Parameter Server	C000.0000.0002
Ring Error Monitor	C000.0000.0008
Configuration Report Server	C000.0000.0010
NetBIOS	C000.0000.0080
Bridge	C000.0000.0100
LAN Manager	C000.0000.2000
IP multicast	C000.0004.0000
User defined	C000.0008.0000–C000.4000.0000

Source MAC (SMAC) address The source MAC address is a 6-byte field that contains the MAC address of the station originating the frame. The source MAC address cannot be a broadcast or functional address; it is always a single-station address.

The most significant bit of the most significant byte of the source MAC address is the Routing Information Identifier (RII). If it is set to a 1, it means that there is a Routing Information Field (RIF) following the SMAC. If the RII is 0, there is no RIF and the Information Field directly follows the source MAC address.

Routing Information Field (RIF) This field has a variable length from 0 to 18 bytes (in the IEEE 802.5 specification this is 0 to 30 bytes) and is depicted in Figure 5.3.

If the RII bit is not set in the source MAC address (SMAC), the RIF will be 0 bytes and the Information field will follow the source MAC address.

The first 2 bytes/16 bits of the RIF are for the Routing Control (RC) field composed of the 3 Broadcast bits, 5 Length bits, a single Direction bit, 3 maximum transmission unit (MTU) bits, and 4 Reserved bits. The remaining bytes of the RIF are composed of 12-bit segments that list Ring Number/Bridge Number pairs. Table 5.3 lists the fields of the RIF.

FIGURE 5.3   Token Ring RIF

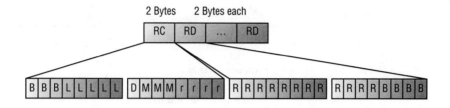

Routing Control (RC)

B - Broadcast bits
  000 - Specifically routed (non-broadcast)
  100 - All routes explorer
  110 - Spanning tree explorer
L - Length bits
  Length of RIF (including the RC itself)
D - Direction bit
  0 - Read RIF left to right
  1 - Read RIF right to left
M - MTU bits (Maximum Transmission Unit)
  000-516 bytes
  001-1500 bytes
  010-2052 bytes
  011-4472 bytes
  100-8144 bytes
  101-11407 bytes
  110-17800 bytes
  111-unknown
r - reserved (should be set to 0)

Route Descriptor (RD)

R - Ring bits (12 bits)
  Rings 1-4095 (decimal)
  0x001-0xFFF (hex)
B - Bridge bits (4 bits)
  Bridges 0-15 (decimal)
  0x0-0xF (hex)

TABLE 5.3   Routing Information Field (RIF) Routing Control (RC) Field

Field	Length	Meaning
BBB	3 bits	Broadcast bits
		000 = nonbroadcast
		100 = all-routes explorer
		110 = spanning tree explorer

TABLE 5.3 Routing Information Field (RIF) Routing Control (RC) Field *(continued)*

Field	Length	Meaning
LLLLL	5 bits	RIF length (in bytes)
D	1 bit	Direction bits
		0 = read RIF left to right
		1 = read RIF right to left
MMM	3 bits	Maximum transmission unit (MTU) bits
		000 = 516 bytes
		001 = 1500 bytes
		010 = 2052 bytes
		011 = 4472 bytes
		100 = 8144 bytes
		101 = 11,407 bytes
		110 = 17,800 bytes
		111 = unknown
rrrr	4 bits	Reserved

The IEEE 802.5 specification uses 6 bits for MTU size definition: the 3 regular MTU bits plus 3 of the reserved bits. This gives 64 MTU values and allows greater granularity of MTU sizes.

The RIF is like a trail of bread crumbs showing the path a frame takes from one end of the bridged network to its destination. A source-route bridge makes a forwarding decision based only on the RIF, not on IP addresses or MAC addresses. It finds its place in the RIF, looks for the next ring number, and forwards the frame out that interface. Nothing mysterious. We'll go over this in Chapter 14, so it'll seem like déjà vu.

Information (INFO) field   The Information field is of variable length and contains the data to be transmitted by the LLC frame.

At the start of the Information field is the IEEE 802.2 header. This can be either 3 or 8 bytes, depending on the upper-layer protocol that is using the frame. If the service access point (SAP) values are not 0xAA, the 802.2 header consists of the destination SAP (DSAP), the source SAP (SSAP), and control field that is set to 0x03. If the SSAP and DSAP values are 0xAA, then the first 5 bytes of the Information Field are allocated for the SNAP (Subnetwork Access Protocol) header, which includes the OUI and Ethertype. Figure 5.4 shows the IEEE 802.2 header.

FIGURE 5.4   IEEE 802.2 header

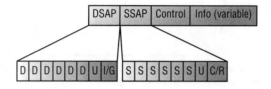

DSAP - Destination Service Access Point

D - Destination address bits
U - User/Standards assigned
   0 - User defined
   1 - Assigned by standards organization

I/G - Individual/Group address
   0 - Individual address
   1 - Group address

SSAP - Source Service Access Point

S - Source address bits
U - User/Standards bits
   0 - User defined
   1 - Assigned by standards organization

C/R - Command/Response
   0- Command
   1- Response

Frame Check Sequence (FCS)   This field contains a 4-byte cyclic redundancy check (CRC) calculated on the Frame Control (FC) field, Destination MAC (DMAC) address field, Source MAC (SMAC) address field, Routing Information Field (RIF), Information (INFO) field, and the Frame Check Sequence (FCS) field.

The FCS does not cover the starting and ending delimiters, nor does it cover the Access Control (AC) and Frame Status (FS) fields because of their variability.

Ending Delimiter (ED)   The ED is a 1-byte field consisting of a 6-bit set pattern J, K, 1, J, K, 1 and two 1-bit fields, I and E.

The E field (Error Detected bit) is set to 0 when the frame is transmitted. It is set to 1 if an error has been detected in the frame, such as a CRC error, a code violation in the middle of frame, or a nonintegral number of bytes in the frame.

The I field (Intermediate Frame bit) indicates whether this frame is a single-frame transmission or the first of multiple frames. When set to 0, it indicates a single-frame transmission or end of a multiple-frame transmission. When set to 1, the I field indicates that this is the first frame of a multiple-frame transmission.

Frame Status (FS)   This 1-byte field contains the *Address Recognized (A) bits* and *Frame Copied (C) bits* as well as four reserved bits that are set to 0.

A station sets the A bit as a 1 if the DMAC is either a single address or a group address destined for it or, in the case of a bridge, if the RIF indicates that the bridge should forward the frame.

A station sets the C bit to a 1 if it recognizes the frame and has copied it to an internal buffer.

Because the Frame Status (FS) field is not included in the FCS, the A and C bits are repeated twice. If sets of values do not match, the frame is considered invalid.

Table 5.4 shows the four combinations of the Address Recognized and Frame Copied bits.

TABLE 5.4   Address Recognized and Frame Copied Bit Combinations

AC	Interpretation
00	No station recognized the DMAC address and hence the frame was not copied. No bridge forwarded the frame to another segment.
01	Invalid combination.
10	The address was recognized but the target station or bridge was unable to copy the frame.
11	The target station received the frame successfully, or in the case of bridging, the bridge forwarded the frame to another segment.

Now that we've looked at the different fields in the token ring frame, we can look at some of the specialized token ring functions that use a number of these fields.

Token Ring Specialized Components

Unlike Ethernet, which is fairly democratic with all devices pitching in equally to maintain networking law and order, token ring calls upon some stations to assume special roles:

- Active monitor
- Standby monitor(s)
- Ring Parameter Server (RPS)
- Ring Error Monitor (REM)
- Configuration Report Server (CRS)

Although they enhance token ring manageability, the RPS, REM, and CRS are not essential to token ring operation. In the following sections, we'll take a closer look at each of these functions.

Active Monitor

The active monitor roles are as follows:

- Maintain the master clock

- Maintain ring delay

- Maintain regular neighbor notification actions

- Detect lost tokens and frames

- Strip frames if originator fails to do so

The *active monitor* is responsible for maintaining the ring and ensuring that everything runs in a smooth fashion. It is generally the ring station with the highest MAC address present when the ring initializes. The active monitor provides the master clock for the ring as well as inserts a 24-bit (one token frame's length) delay to frame passing. This prevents the originating station from seeing the token arrive before it is completely sent out.

The active monitor looks for the absence of tokens and frames by setting a timer when a starting delimiter is noticed. If another frame or token does not appear before the timer pops, the active monitor will purge the ring and regenerate another token.

When a station sends a frame, it sets the Monitor bit in the Access Control field to 0. As the frame gets repeated by the active monitor, the Monitor bit gets set to a 1. If the originating station fails to strip the frame off the ring and send out a token, the frame will reach the active monitor which sees the Monitor bit set and strips the frame off the ring, preventing it from circling endlessly.

The active monitor is also responsible for starting and maintaining the neighbor notification process. The active monitor will periodically send Active Monitor Present MAC frames as an all-stations broadcast. The first station to receive this broadcast will note that the A and C bits are still 0 and thus will assume that the active monitor is its *nearest active upstream neighbor (NAUN)*. It will set the A and C bits to 1 so that no other stations assume that the active monitor is their neighbor and then sets a timer to transmit a Standby Monitor Present MAC frame a short time later. When this first station transmits a Standby Monitor Present MAC frame, the next station on the ring notes that the A and C bits are not set and thus assumes that the first station is its neighbor (NAUN) and sets the A and C bits to 1. This sequence will continue until it reaches the active monitor again and all stations are aware of their neighbors.

If the current active monitor fails, the new active monitor is elected in a process called token claiming. This process is also applicable if the current active monitor or a standby monitor detects a loss of signal or if a station attaches to the ring and does not see an active monitor. A token ring station initiating token claiming inserts its clock as the master ring clock and broadcasts Claim Token MAC frames at regular intervals to all devices on the ring.

The other devices on the ring will inspect the Claim Token MAC frames. If a station's MAC address is lower than that of the current source of the Claim Token frames, it will pass along the MAC frame unchanged. However, if the receiving station's MAC address is higher than that of the source, it will insert its master clock and transmit Claim Token MAC frames. When the originating station receives back its own Claim Token MAC frame, it will then transmit three more Claim Token MAC frames. If these three frames are returned intact, the source station becomes the new active monitor, purges the ring, starts a new token, and sends a Report New Active Monitor MAC frame to the Configuration Report Server (CRS).

Standby Monitor(s)

Like a vice president, the standby monitor is there to take over in case "the Big Guy" takes a bullet. In this case, standby monitors check for the timely arrival of Active Monitor Present MAC frames. If the active monitor is not seen, a standby monitor will initiate the token claiming process to elect a new active monitor.

Ring Parameter Server

The Ring Parameter Server (RPS) serves to make newly inserted ring stations aware of the ring's operational parameters such as source-route bridge number and soft error report timer. The RPS also reports new station insertions to LAN network managers.

Ring Error Monitor

The Ring Error Monitor (REM) is responsible for collecting and analyzing hard and soft error information on the ring. Periodically, each station on the ring will send its soft error counts to the REM functional address (C000.0000.0008) via Report Soft Error MAC frames. Hard error events, when they occur, are sent to the all-stations MAC address (C000.FFFF.FFFF) as *beacon* MAC frames and are inspected by the REM.

See more on hard and soft errors later in this chapter.

Configuration Report Server

The Configuration Report Server (CRS) is largely a tool of the LAN Network Manager (LNM) and is used to gather station information and allow the LNM to set station parameters or have stations removed from the ring.

   The additional responsibilities undertaken by some of the stations on the ring not only help to manage the ring and keep statistics; in the case of the active monitor, they are essential to ring operations. For instance, in the next section you'll see the role the active monitor and Ring Parameter Server play when a station inserts itself on the ring.

LNM was developed by IBM as a way to monitor and manage token ring networks. Although this feature can be useful for troubleshooting in some cases, it is probably a good idea to turn it on only when necessary. On by default, it can be turned off via the `lnm disabled` global command.

Station Insertion

You can think of a device inserting into a token ring LAN much in the same way a person would join a fraternity—there are certain rites of initiation that must be observed. However, in the case of token ring activation, there are fewer robes and candles involved. Here is the five-step process to joining the Fellowship of the Ring:

Phase 0: Lobe Test   With the media attachment unit (MAU) relay closed, the transmit and receive wires of the cable are connected and the port is effectively wrapped. The adapter transmits 2047 Lobe Check MAC frames that must be received.

Phase 1: Monitor Check   At this stage, the station checks for the presence of an active monitor by looking for Active Monitor Present, Standby Monitor Present, or Ring Purge MAC frames. If any of these frames are detected, the station proceeds to Phase 2. If it does not detect these frames, it assumes it is the first station on the ring, there is no active monitor, or there is a problem with the ring and initiate the claim token process.

Phase 2: Duplicate Address Test (DAT)   The inserting station sends out a Duplicate Address Test MAC frame and checks the A and C bits in the Frame Status field when it takes the frame off the ring. If the address has been recognized and copied, there is another device using the same MAC address—in which case the inserting station removes itself from the ring. (Wouldn't it be cool if the two stations battled it out to see who gets to keep the MAC address? Something like in Highlander: "There can be only ONE!")

Phase 3: Neighbor Notification/Ring Poll   The station then looks for the periodic Active Monitor Present and Standby Monitor Present MAC frames, which constitute the neighbor notification process. Once the station has learned its nearest active upstream neighbor (NAUN) and identified itself to its downstream neighbor, it proceeds to Phase 4.

Phase 4: Request Initialization   Here the station registers its token ring microcode level and NAUN with the Ring Parameter Server (RPS) to pass on to LAN Network Managers. It also requests ring operating parameters from the RPS to ensure that it is in sync with other stations on the ring.

Now that the station is in the ring, life is good, right? In most cases, the answer is yes. However, sometimes faulty equipment or overloaded bridges/switches/routers can cause problems on the ring. In these cases, token ring has robust error reporting and fault detection, as you'll see in the next section.

Hard and Soft Errors

One of the strengths of token ring is its error detection and reporting capabilities. Built into the token ring chipset are all of the functions necessary to sense and respond to various types of error conditions. Errors are classified as either hard or soft errors depending on their severity. A *hard error* is usually something very disruptive to ring operation, like a break in topology, a station transmitting at the wrong rate (4Mbps versus 16Mbps), or a station with a faulty transmitter streaming frames or bits. A station detecting the presence of a hard error will broadcast Beacon MAC frames to alert other stations to the error. This process is called *beaconing*. *Soft errors* are more transient in nature than hard errors and generally only disrupt normal ring operations temporarily. Soft errors are usually dealt with through normal ring recovery procedures.

Token Ring Configuration

The basic configuration of a token ring interface is pretty straightforward. The major parameter to configure is the ring speed. This must match what the other devices on the ring are set to, otherwise a beaconing condition will ensue. Source-route bridging parameters, IP address, early token release, and MTU are all optional. The following lines show a token ring interface configured to route IP and bridge other traffic via source-route bridging.

`interface TokenRing1/0`	Chooses token ring interface
`ring-speed 16`	Sets the operating speed of this interface [16 Mbps or 4 Mbps] Must match other devices on the ring.
`ip address 172.16.1.1 255.255.255.0`	Assigns IP address.
`multiring all`	Enables a routable protocol to interoperate in a source-route bridged environment. [optional]
`mtu 4472`	Sets the maximum transmission unit on the interface. [optional]

early-token-release	On a 16Mbps ring, allows the router to give up the token before its transmitted frame returns to it. [optional]
source-bridge 100 1 2000	Defines a source-route bridging ring number. [optional]
no shut	Ensures the interface is not in an Administratively Down state

 If a router is configured for source-route bridging and the ring number is not consistent with what is already configured on the ring, the interface will not come up.

 The ring number configured on a Cisco router is in decimal, not hexadecimal.

Token Ring Troubleshooting

The following commands are useful when troubleshooting problems with token ring interfaces:

show interface TokenRing x/y	Displays interface.
show controller tokenring x/y	Not only shows internal status of the token ring interface, also displays useful information about the ring's health.
show source	Displays source-route bridging information. Displays known Routing Information Fields – useful for multi-ring and RSRB troubleshooting.
show lnm station	Displays error counts and information about the devices on the ring.
debug token event	Allows you to see token ring controller events and good for troubleshooting ring insertion problems.
debug token ring	Allows you to see LLC frames arriving on the ring.

Real World Scenario

Ring Insertion Problem

A recent problem we encountered with a customer's token ring interface serves as a good example of some of the issues you might run into. The router code at a remote location was upgraded to implement a new feature. In the process, one of its token ring interfaces failed to come up. Checking the syslog showed the following message:

```
%TR-3-OPENFAIL: Unit 1, open failed: Init Request, request params not answered
```

This made it appear that the RPS didn't respond. This particular interface was plugged into an active hub that had only one other station (a satellite back-up device) inserted. The sh int and sh controller commands didn't reveal anything, nor did debugs:

```
TokenRing1/0 open failed, ret_code 0007, error_code 0059, version 000001.CT17C4
```

Changing the ring speed as well as doing shut and no shut commands on the interface didn't fix the problem. Replacing the cable and moving it to a spare router also didn't help, nor did changing ports on the hub.

Finally, we unplugged the satellite device from the hub and inserted just the router's interface. Boom! Up it came. When we plugged the satellite back-up unit back in, it wouldn't come up. Hmmmm...head scratching time. After a few attempts, we were able to get both the router interface and the satellite device inserted. However, we noticed burst, lost frame, and token errors on the interface when we did a show controller.

At this point, the customer stopped pushing for the router cards to be replaced and shifted attention to the hub. Several days later, after a change window was negotiated, the hub was replaced. Both the router and the satellite device inserted without problems, and there were no new input errors logged by the router.

The point here is that people are generally not putting in new token ring equipment and that existing installations are getting old and may experience failures or partial failures. Also, sometimes router show and debug commands may not be overly helpful, and you have to try shaking things up a bit to get to the root cause of a problem.

Summary

In this chapter, we covered the essentials of token ring operation including token ring frame format, specialized ring functions, and station insertion.

Token Ring was developed by IBM and standardized as IEEE 802.5. Although minor differences such as Routing Information Field size and maximum transmission unit size definitions exist between the IBM and 802.5 specifications, the two are virtually indistinguishable.

Source-route bridging will be covered in depth in a later chapter. The important thing about SRB from a token ring frame perspective is the Routing Information Field containing the Routing Control field and segments composed of ring numbers and bridge numbers.

Specialized device functions on the token ring include an active monitor, standby monitors, a Ring Error Monitor, a Ring Parameter Server, and a Configuration Report Server. Of these functions, the most important is the active monitor, which provides the master clock to all devices on the ring, generates lost tokens, handles ring disruptions, and ensures that frames are taken off the ring so they do not circle endlessly.

Token ring station insertion must follow a five-step process:

- Lobe test
- Active monitor search
- Duplicate address test
- Neighbor notification
- Request initialization

Exam Essentials

Know the basic operation of Token Ring and how it differs from Ethernet. On a token ring network, a station must have control of the token to transmit on the shared media. Because no two devices can transmit at the same time, there are no collisions and token ring is said to be deterministic. Token ring networks run at 4Mbps and 16Mbps. A transmitted frame travels from station to station around the logical ring until it returns to the sender, who is supposed to remove it from the ring and transmit a new token.

Know the purpose of the A and C bits. The Address Recognized (A) and Frame Copied (C) bits allow a transmitting station to know whether its frame reached its destination and whether the target station was able to copy the frame into a buffer.

Know that Token Ring has specialized functions assumed by some stations. The active monitor on the ring is responsible for providing the master clock, ensuring that frames don't circle endlessly on the ring and that tokens are regenerated if they are lost, initiating ring recovery procedures, and maintaining the neighbor notification process.

Know the insertion process for a device to come active on a Token Ring. The five phases of the insertion process are the lobe test, search for an active monitor, duplicate address check, neighbor notification, and request for initialization from the RPS.

Key Terms

Before you take the exam, be certain you are familiar with the following terms:

active monitor	Frame Copied (C) bit
Address Recognized (A) bit	functional address
beacon	hard error
beaconing	Media Access Control (MAC) frames
differential Manchester encoding	nearest active upstream neighbor (NAUN)
Early Token Release	soft errors

Review Questions

1. At what speed(s) does token ring operate?

    A. 4Mbps

    B. 16Mbps

    C. 100Mbps

    D. A and B

    E. B and C

2. IBM's implementation of token ring diverges from IEEE 802.5 in which ways? (Choose all that apply.)

    A. The speeds that the ring can be clocked

    B. The number of stations allowed on the ring

    C. The size of the RIF field in the frame

    D. The maximum transmission unit (MTU) sizes for source-route bridging

3. In Phase 2 of token ring insertion, how does a station know if another station on the ring is using its same MAC address?

    A. The Ring Parameter Server alerts it.

    B. The active monitor requests that it remove itself from the ring.

    C. The A and C bits in the Frame Status (FS) field are set on the returned frame.

    D. The M bit in the Access Control (AC) field is set on the returned frame.

4. What is the largest frame that can be transmitted on a 16Mbps token ring LAN?

    A. 576-byte frame

    B. 1500-byte frame

    C. 1518-byte frame

    D. 4472-byte frame

    E. 17,800-byte frame

5. Which of the following is not a function of MAC frames?

    A. Report hard errors

    B. Report soft errors

    C. Allow Apple Macintoshes to communicate

    D. Perform lobe media tests

6. Which of the following are considered locally administered MAC addresses? (Choose all that apply.)

    A. 4000.1234.0001

    B. C000.1234.0001

    C. C000.FFFF.FFFF

    D. 6000.1234.0001

    E. None of the above

7. Which of the following token ring station MAC addresses is most likely to become the active monitor on the ring?

    A. 4000.1234.0001

    B. 0000.FFFF.0001

    C. 6000.1234.0001

    D. 8000.1234.0001

    E. C000.FFFF.FFFF

8. How can MAC frames be distinguished from LLC frames?

    A. MAC frames use the Type field, whereas LLC frames set the same field to Length.

    B. MAC frames are always sent to the all-stations MAC address of C000.FFFF.FFFF.

    C. MAC frames are always sent to the broadcast MAC address of FFFF.FFFF.FFFF.

    D. MAC frames set the Frame Type bits in the Frame Control (FC) field to 00.

    E. MAC frames set the Frame Type bits in the Frame Control (FC) field to 01 and are sent to the all-stations MAC address of C000.FFFF.FFFF.

9. When a station receives a frame destined for its MAC address, it will set which of the following bits under normal circumstances? (Choose all that apply.)

    A. Address Recognized

    B. Monitor

    C. Frame Copied

    D. Token

10. What is the Frame Check Sequence (FCS) on a token?

    A. 0000 0000 0000 0000

    B. FFFF FFFF FFFF FFFF

    C. Random, and depends on the source MAC address of the originating station

    D. None

Answers to Review Questions

1. D. Token ring runs at data rates of 4Mbps and 16Mbps.

2. C, D. The main differences with the IBM and IEEE 802.5 implementation of Token Ring lie in the area of source-route bridging.

3. C. The Address Recognized (A) and Frame Copied (C) bits are set in the FS field of the returned test frame that has the station's MAC address as both the source and destination.

4. E. 17,800 bytes is the largest token ring data MTU size.

5. C. AppleTalk data packets would use LLC token ring frames instead of MAC frames. The lobe media test and reporting of hard and soft errors is accomplished using MAC frames.

6. A, D. Bit 1 in the most significant byte of the MAC address indicates whether the address is locally administered (set to 1) or not.

7. C. 6000.1234.0001 is the largest single-station address listed and would win the token-claiming process to become the active monitor.

8. D. A setting of 00 in the two Frame Type bits in the FC field indicates a MAC frame. LLC frames have a setting of 01.

9. A, C. When a station receives a frame sent to its MAC address, it sets the Address Recognized and Frame Copied bits in the Frame Status field. Only the Active Monitor sets the monitor bit. The token bit will not be set in an LLC frame.

10. D. A token is composed of just a Starting Delimiter (SD), Access Control (AC) field, and Ending Delimiter (ED); there is no FCS.

Chapter

6

Ethernet LAN Technologies

THE CCIE QUALIFICATION EXAM TOPICS COVERED IN THIS CHAPTER INCLUDE THE FOLLOWING:

- ✓ Ethernet technologies
- ✓ CSMA/CD
- ✓ MAC address format
- ✓ Fast Ethernet technologies
- ✓ Gigabit Ethernet technologies
- ✓ VLAN, VTP, and trunking
- ✓ Spanning-Tree Protocol (STP)
- ✓ EtherChannel
- ✓ 802.11b Wireless LAN (WLAN)

Ethernet is undeniably the single most important medium in today's networks. As such, it is important to have a clear understanding of how Ethernet operates, its frame format, and its addressing scheme. Ethernet has evolved from the original 10Mbps standard to 100Mbps, 1Gbps, and finally 10Gbps and has made the jump to wireless with IEEE 802.11b.

Ethernet devices are predominantly interconnected using switches rather than shared media. Switches group Ethernet devices together in Virtual LANs (VLANs) and limit the collision domain to each device and its associated switch port. Switches can be connected to one another to provide redundancy and extend the reach of VLANs. A trunk connection between switches can carry encapsulated frames from multiple VLANs, and multiple physical switch-to-switch connections can be joined logically into an EtherChannel.

The Spanning Tree Protocol (STP) is essential to redundant layer 2 switching designs to prevent loops and subsequent meltdowns. Switches implementing STP communicate using Bridged Protocol Data Units (BPDUs) to establish and maintain the spanning tree to ensure that there is only one active path between any two segments in a VLAN. Cisco has increased the functionality of STP with features such as PortFast, Uplink Fast, and Backbone Fast.

Because this chapter covers the "S" in the R&S CCIE written and lab exams, the CCIE candidate is advised to study the material carefully and practice the Catalyst 5000 and 3550 configurations until they become second nature.

Ethernet

Ethernet was created in the early 1970s at Xerox PARC as a way to connect computers together using shared media running at 10Mbps. It has evolved over the last 30 years to become the most ubiquitous networking media, reaching speeds of 1000 times greater than before. The advent of switches in the 1990s, along with Fast Ethernet and full-duplex capability, removed/mitigated the collision weakness of Ethernet and helped accelerate its growth and spread.

It is essential that the CCIE candidate be thoroughly familiar with Ethernet and switching. The basic operation of Ethernet, its physical media, and frame formats will be examined in the following sections. Switching functions and features will be discussed later in the chapter.

Carrier Sense Multiple Access with Collision Detect (CSMA/CD)

Ethernet is based on *Carrier Sense Multiple Access with Collision Detection (CSMA/CD)*. This sounds like a mouthful, but it's not that complicated if we break it down into its component pieces:

Carrier Sense   Ethernet transceivers have the capability to detect if anything is being transmitted on the media. If nothing is being transmitted, they just pick up the carrier signal.

Multiple Access   This simply means that all devices share the same physical media. In the earlier days of Ethernet, devices were connected with thicknet or thinnet cabling and did share the same media. With switches, this is no longer technically true, but we'll overlook that for now...

Collision Detection   As a transceiver sends a frame, it also monitors its receive data pair to make sure that what was sent out is what everyone else is receiving. If the receive and transmit signals don't match, someone else must be transmitting as well and a collision occurs.

Now let's put this all together. When an Ethernet host wants to transmit, it first listens to the wire. If there is only the carrier signal, the host starts transmitting the frame. The beginning of the frame is the preamble, which is an alternating pattern of binary 1s and 0s that is 62 bits long. The preamble is a 5MHz square wave pattern in Manchester encoding that serves to synchronize the transmit and receive data clocks of the transceivers. Because of the time it takes for the clocks to enter the correct phase, the preamble is followed by 2 bits of 1s, which signal the start of the frame delimiter. This lets the transceivers know that the preamble is over and it's time to start MAC-level processing of the bits into bytes.

During transmissions on the shared media, two hosts may start transmitting simultaneously. If this happens, a collision is said to take place and special processing must be done. The first step is to alert all other stations to the collision. A jam signal consisting of 32 bits is sent by both hosts to ensure that the CRC of the received frame will be incorrect and hence discarded. The next step is that both hosts will set timers to wait before trying to retransmit their respective frames. These "back-off" timers are set to random values from 1 to 1024 times the minimum frame time slot period of 51.2 microseconds and are used to help prevent further collisions if the two hosts tried to retransmit at the same time. A host will attempt to retransmit a frame 15 times before giving up and discarding the frame and logging an error. This process is called the truncated *binary exponential backoff algorithm*. The amount of collisions varies with the traffic rate and the number of devices sharing the media. In practice, a shared media Ethernet environment achieves a top utilization of 70 percent before collisions become excessive.

10Mbps Ethernet has been implemented in a number of different physical formats. Table 6.1 lists some of the transmission media and their ranges and specifications.

TABLE 6.1 10Mbps Ethernet

Designation	Distance	Further Specifications
10Base5 (thicknet)	500 meters	Baseband Ethernet specification using standard (thick) 50-ohm base-band coaxial cable. Maximum 100 nodes per segment.
10Base2 (thinnet)	185 meters	10Mbps baseband Ethernet specification using 50-ohm thin coaxial cable. Maximum 30 nodes per segment.
10Base-T	100 meters	Point-to point specification for 10Mbps Ethernet over two pairs of Category 3, 4, or 5 UTP wire (one pair for transmitting data and the other for receiving data).
10Base-F	2000 meters	10Mbps Ethernet over multimode fiber.

Now that you've seen how Ethernet works, we'll look into Ethernet addressing and framing.

Ethernet Addressing

Ethernet stations are addressed by a 48-bit identifier known as a MAC address. Independent of any upper-layer protocol identifiers such as an IP or AppleTalk address, this 6-byte MAC address is used for one Ethernet station to send frames to another and is generally a unique value. When a network interface card (NIC) or Ethernet adapter is manufactured, its address is burned into a prom or similar component. For this reason, the MAC address is also referred to as the burned-in or hardware address.

Figure 6.1 shows the MAC address and how the 48 bits are divided. To make it easier to deal with, MAC addresses are generally written in hexadecimal format.

FIGURE 6.1   Ethernet addressing using MAC addresses

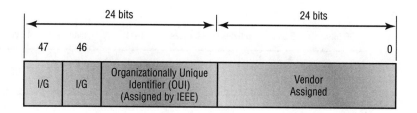

Ethernet transceivers transmit data 1 byte at a time and transmit it from the least significant bit to the most significant bit. This method is called canonical addressing (as opposed to the noncanonical addressing—used by Token Ring—in which bytes are transmitted from most significant bit to least significant bit). The only real time that this becomes important is when there is translational bridging between devices on Ethernet and Token Ring LANs, which we'll cover in Chapter 14, "Bridging and Data Link Switching."

If bit 46 is 0 (zero), the upper 24 bits of the MAC address are what's known as the *Organizationally Unique Identifier (OUI)*. The OUI is assigned by the Institute of Electrical and Electronics Engineers (IEEE) to an organization or company. The organization or company then pairs up the OUI with a unique bottom half of the MAC address when they manufacture a NIC/adapter. Because the MAC address allocated to an adapter by the manufacturer was historically burned into a PROM on the adapter, this address is also referred to as the burned-in address, or BIA. If bit 46 of the address is set to 1, this means the address is locally administered and overrides the BIA.

You can change the MAC address used by an Ethernet port on a router by using the mac-address command. Although locally administrating addresses on Ethernet ports is not widely done, it can make reading traces easier and make things more orderly if a port has to be replaced.

Ethernet Frames

Frames are used at the Data-Link layer to encapsulate packets handed down from the Network layer for transmission on a type of media access. The function of Ethernet stations is to pass data frames between each other by using a group of bits known as a MAC frame format. The 802.3 frame and the Ethernet frame are shown in Figure 6.2.

FIGURE 6.2   802.3 and Ethernet frame formats

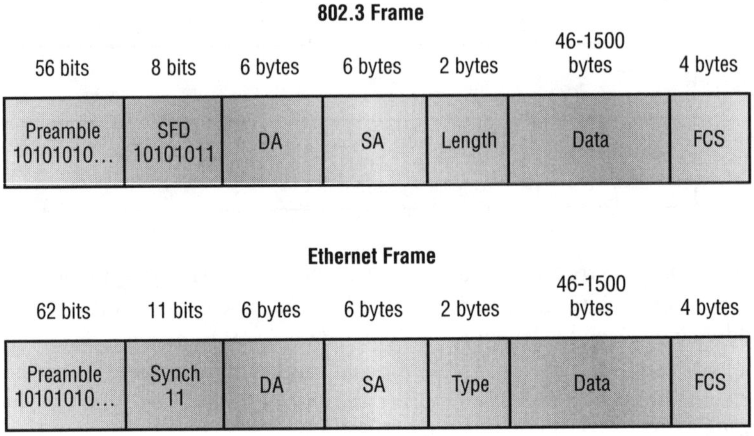

802.3 Frame

56 bits	8 bits	6 bytes	6 bytes	2 bytes	46–1500 bytes	4 bytes
Preamble 10101010...	SFD 10101011	DA	SA	Length	Data	FCS

Ethernet Frame

62 bits	11 bits	6 bytes	6 bytes	2 bytes	46–1500 bytes	4 bytes
Preamble 10101010...	Synch 11	DA	SA	Type	Data	FCS

Here is a description of the fields in the 802.3 and Ethernet frame types:

Preamble (Ethernet II)   An alternating 1,0 pattern provides a 5MHz clock at the start of each packet, which allows the receiving devices to lock the incoming bit stream. Uses either a 2-bit SFD (start frame delimiter) or a Synch field of binary 1s to indicate to the receiving station that the data portion of the message will follow.

Preamble/SFD (802.3)   The preamble is 7 octets of 10101010 followed by the SFD, which is 10101011. The combination of preamble and SFD in an 802.3 frame is identical to the preamble in an Ethernet II frame.

Destination address (DA)   The destination address transmits a 48-bit value using the least significant bit (LSB) first. Used by receiving stations to determine if an incoming packet is addressed to this particular node. The destination address can be an individual address, a broadcast address, or a multicast MAC address. Remember that a broadcast is all 1s, or Fs in hex, and is sent to all devices, whereas a multicast is sent to only a similar subset of nodes on a network.

Source address (SA)   The source address is a 48-bit MAC address supplied by the transmitting device. It uses the least significant bit (LSB) first. Broadcast and multicast address formats are illegal within the SA field.

Length or type   This 2-byte field is used in 802.3 frames to indicate the length of the frame and is used in Ethernet II frames to indicate the protocol type.

802.3 frames use a Length field (to indicate the length of the entire data field that is to follow) at the same location, whereas Ethernet II frames use a Type field to identify the Network layer protocol. 802.3 frames, however, can use a portion of the LLC header to identify the upper-layer protocol, borrowing bytes farther into the Data field.

Data   The data portion is the packet sent down to the Data-Link layer from the network layer, which can be anywhere from 46 to 1500 bytes. Note that the data portion of an IEEE 802.3 frame is in the 802.2 header and follows the SAP and SNAP fields discussed in the next section.

Frame check sequence (FCS)   The FCS is the field used to hold the CRC. After the frame is computed using a CRC, the answer is put into the FCS field.

IEEE 802.2 Service Access Point (SAP) and Sub-Network Access Protocol (SNAP)

Ethernet II frames use the 2-byte Type field to specify what upper-layer protocol the frame contains. IEEE 802.3 frames use the 1-byte service access point (SAP) value to identify the upper-layer protocol. Figure 6.3 shows the format of the source and destination SAP values. The most significant 6 bits of both the source and destination SAP values are used to identify the protocol address, and the penultimate least significant bit of the value denotes whether the SAP is defined by a standards body (set to 1) or whether it's user defined (set to 0).

FIGURE 6.3   IEEE 802.2 SAP and SNAP

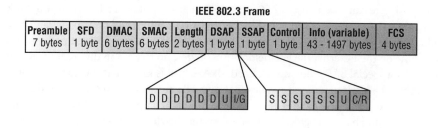

The IEEE adopted the IBM Systems Network Architecture (SNA) concept of service access point, which functioned similarly to a TCP or UDP port number to route frames to the correct application once the target host had been reached. Because of this, the values 0x04–0xEC are reserved for IBM SNA. Also, because these are user-defined SAP values, they are in increments of 4: 0x04, 0x08, 0x0C, and so on to 0xEC. In contrast, the Spanning-Tree Protocol (STP) SAP value is 0x42, which labels it as assigned by a standards organization. Some other protocol SAP values include 0xE0 for Novell IPX, 0xF0 for NetBIOS, 0xBC for Banyan VINES, and 0x80 for Xerox XNS. The least significant bit of the destination SAP is the individual/group bit. When set to a 0, it denotes an individual; when set to a 1, it's a group SAP. The least significant bit on the source SAP is the command/response bit (this is logical link control, after all). If set to a 1, it is a response; when set to 0, it is a command.

 Although SNA SAP values range from 0x04 through 0xEC, the majority of SNA traffic uses SAP 0x04 and to a lesser extent 0x08 and 0x0C. SNA source and destination SAP values do not have to match. SNA and NetBIOS utilize the logical link control (LLC) facilities of the 802.2 header. For this reason, you'll see the Command/Response bit set in the source SAP for these protocols.

Although 1 byte can specify up to 256 individual protocols, it isn't a lot when you think about how many protocols were being spawned in the 80s by companies and universities and how many SAP values are taken up by SNA. Therefore, the IEEE borrowed once more upon a proven concept, this time on the Ethernet II Type field. With 2 bytes, up to 65,536 different protocols could be labeled. So a special SAP value was defined, 0xAA, and is known as the Sub-Network Access Protocol (SNAP) SAP. If the source and destination SAP values in a frame are set to 0xAA and the control field is 0x03, the first 5 bytes of the Info field are taken up by the SNAP header. The SNAP header is 5 bytes and has two fields. The first field is the 3-byte OUI that labels who developed the protocol. The second field is 2 bytes and is the Type field. The values in the Type field are equal to the values that would be in an Ethernet II frame for the same protocol. Figure 6.3 also shows the format of the SNAP header.

SAP and SNAP values are revisited in Chapter 16 when we look at access lists and ways to control traffic.

Novell IPX Packets

Novell Internetwork Packet Exchange (IPX) packets can have one of four formats on Ethernet:

802.3   SAP 0xE0.

802.2   SAP 0xAA, Type 0x8137.

Ethernet II   Type 0x8137.

Novell Raw   A proprietary frame format similar to 802.3 with a length field. The first two bytes of the data field are 0xFFFF.

IBM SNA Services on Ethernet: Ethertype 80D5

Like the concept of SNAP in IEEE 802.3 frames, there is a special ethertype in Ethernet II frames used to indicate that further packet identification information is contained at the start of the data section. If the ethertype is 80D5, the first 3 bytes of the data field will contain the LLC header for SNA or NetBIOS traffic including the SSAP, DSAP, and control field. Although it is not widely used, you may come across it with some older IBM devices or emulators.

Broadcasts

A *broadcast* is a frame sent to all network stations at the same time. Remember that broadcasts are built into *all* protocols. Following is the dissected frame of an EtherPeek trace so that you can see the destination hardware address, the IP address, and more. Notice the Type field under the Ethernet header. The following is an Ethernet II frame:

```
Ethernet Header
   Destination:  ff:ff:ff:ff:ff:ff Ethernet Broadcast
   Source:        02:07:01:22:de:a4
   Protocol Type:08-00  IP
IP Header - Internet Protocol Datagram
   Version:              4
   Header Length:        5
   Precedence:           0
   Type of Service:      %000
   Unused:               %00
   Total Length:         93
   Identifier:           62500
   Fragmentation Flags:  %000
   Fragment Offset:      0
   Time To Live:         30
   IP Type:              0x11   UDP
   Header Checksum:      0x9156
   Source IP Address:    10.7.1.9
   Dest. IP Address:     10.7.1.255
   No Internet Datagram Options
```

As you can see, the source hardware and the IP address are from the sending station that knows its own information. Its hardware address is 02:07:01:22:de:a4, and its source IP address is 10.7.1.9. The destination hardware address is FFFFFFFFFFFF, a MAC layer broadcast that is monitored by all stations on the network. The destination network address is 10.7.1.255—an IP-directed broadcast for network 10.7.1.0—meaning all devices on network 10.7.1.0. We'll look at IP addressing in detail in Chapter 8.

A frame addressed in this manner tells all the hosts on network 10.7.1.0 to receive it and process its data. This can be both a good thing and a bad thing. When servers or other hosts need to send data to all the other hosts on the network segment, network broadcasts are useful indeed. But, if a lot of broadcasts are occurring on a network segment, network performance can be seriously impaired. This is one big reason that it is so important to segment your network properly with routers.

Full-Duplex Ethernet

Full-duplex Ethernet can both transmit and receive simultaneously and uses point-to-point connections. It is typically referred to as collision-free because it doesn't share bandwidth with any other devices. Frames sent by two nodes cannot collide because there are physically separate transmit and receive circuits between the nodes.

If you have a full-duplex 10Mbps Ethernet operating bidirectionally on the same switch port, you can theoretically have 20Mbps aggregate throughput. Full duplex can be used in 10Base-T, 100Base-T, and 100Base-FL media, but all devices (NIC cards, for example) must be able to support full-duplex transmission. Gigabit and 10 Gigabit Ethernet do not support half-duplex mode and run full duplex.

Figure 6.4 shows how full-duplex circuitry works. Full-duplex Ethernet switch (FDES) technology provides a point-to-point connection between the transmitter of the transmitting station and the receiver of the receiving station. Half-duplex, standard Ethernet can usually provide 40 to 50 percent of the bandwidth available. In contrast, full-duplex Ethernet can provide upwards of 80 to 90 percent (there is still overhead) because it can transmit and receive simultaneously and because collisions don't occur.

FIGURE 6.4   Full-duplex circuitry

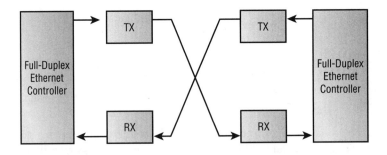

Figure 6.5 shows the circuitry involved in *half-duplex Ethernet*. When a station is sending to another station, the transmitting circuitry is active at the transmitting station and the receive

circuitry is active at the receiving station. This configuration uses a single cable similar to a narrow one-way bridge.

FIGURE 6.5   Half-duplex circuitry

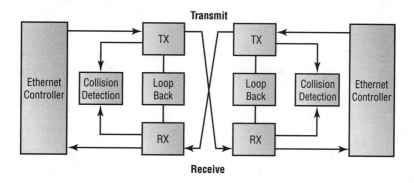

  Ethernet interfaces on Cisco routers default to half duplex. Starting with 12.0(4)T, 10Mbps Ethernet interfaces have the capability to be full duplex if the `full-duplex` command is used and the hardware supports it.

 Real World Scenario

Duplex Mismatch

A certain international WAN connection in our network had been having issues and causing EIGRP neighbor drop problems. Because of this, the router endpoints were being monitored closely. A few days into the monitoring, the U.S. router showed it had dropped EIGRP neighbors that morning, but with two local routers—not its international peer.

The syslog showed that the reason for the EIGRP neighbor drops was an SIA event (stuck-in-active event, covered in Chapter 9). SIA events are often caused by slow or problematic links that are usually serial connections. The two local routers had downstream serial neighbors that hadn't dropped due to SIA events. This meant that the problem existed between the U.S. router and its two neighbors.

A quick check of the interfaces on the routers and their common switch showed a number of input/output errors. Looking at the interface definitions in detail, it was noticed that the switch ports were set to full duplex while the router interfaces were set to half. Once the duplex mismatch was cleared up, the EIGRP neighbor drops stopped.

Fast Ethernet

Fast Ethernet supports a data rate of 100Mbps. The IEEE approved the 802.3u standard in 1995. Table 6.2 shows a listing of Fast Ethernet physical implementations.

TABLE 6.2   Fast Ethernet

Designation	Distance	Further Specifications
100Base-TX	100 meters	4B/5B block encoding, Cat5 UTP.
100Base-T4	200 meters	Uses four pairs of wire. Can use Cat 3 and Cat 4 cabling in addition to Cat 5 and Cat 1 STP. Does not support full duplex.
100Base-FX	2000-meter MMF, 10,000-meter SMF	4B/5B block encoding over fiber.
100VG (AnyLan)	100-meter Cat 3/4 200-meter Cat 5, 500-meter fiber	Based on IEEE 802.12 and supports Ethernet and token ring formats.

Now that we've looked at Fast Ethernet, we'll look at the advantages of going an order of magnitude faster with Gigabit Ethernet.

Gigabit Ethernet

Gigabit Ethernet retains the same basic frame format as 10Mbps and 100Mbps Ethernet but just changes the Physical layer to update the speed to 1000Mbps. Gigabit Ethernet is detailed in the IEEE 802.3z and 802.3ab specifications. IEEE 802.3ab details Gigabit Ethernet on Cat 5 UTP copper cabling, and IEEE 802.3z covers Gigabit Ethernet over fiber and coaxial cable. Because the Physical layer for 802.3z borrowed heavily from ANSI X3T11 Fibre Channel, it uses an 8B/10B signaling scheme where 8-bit bytes are coded as 10-bit symbols on the media. The encoding helps spread out the transmission of 1s that can cause laser overheating and helps prevent a DC component bias. Table 6.3 shows the different physical implementations of Gigabit Ethernet.

TABLE 6.3   Gigabit Ethernet

Designation	Distance	Further Specifications
1000Base-T	100 meters	IEEE 802.3ab Gigabit Ethernet over copper Cat 5 UTP.
1000Base-CX	25 meters	IEEE 802.3z Gigabit Ethernet over 150-ohm balanced shielded copper cable.
1000Base-SX (850 nm)	Up to 550 meters	IEEE 802.3z Gigabit Ethernet over multimode fiber.
1000Base-LX (1300 nm)	Up to 5 kilometers	IEEE 802.3z Gigabit Ethernet over single mode fiber.

10 Gigabit Ethernet (802.3ae)

The IEEE 802.3ae specification was ratified on June 12, 2002, which clears the way for high-speed backbones in the LAN and MAN. 10 Gigabit Ethernet is specified to run on fiber and only in full-duplex mode. Although it is not a CCIE lab or written topic, it is still good to be aware of this new performance enhancement. Table 6.4 lists some of the 10 Gigabit physical specifications.

TABLE 6.4   10 Gigabit Ethernet

Designation	Distance	Further Specifications
10Gbase-SR, 850 nm	2-300 meters (MMF)	Short wavelength. Designed for use over dark fiber.
10Gbase-SW, 850 nm	2-300 meters (MMF)	Short wavelength. Used to connect to SONET using WIS (WAN Interface Sublayer).
10Gbase-LR, 1310 nm	2-10 kilometers (SMF)	Long wavelength. Used over dark fiber.
10Gbase-LW, 1310 nm	2-10 kilometers (SMF)	Long wavelength. Used to connect to SONET using WIS (WAN Interface Sublayer).

TABLE 6.4   10 Gigabit Ethernet *(continued)*

Designation	Distance	Further Specifications
10GBase-ER 1550 nm	2-40 km (SMF)	Extra-long wavelength. Designed for use over dark fiber.
10Gbase-EW, 1550 nm	2-40 km (SMF)	Extra-long wavelength. Used to connect to SONET using WIS (WAN Interface Sublayer).
10Gbase-LX4, 1310 nm	2-300 m (MMF), 2-10 km (SMF)	Utilizes four wavelengths of light via wave division multiplexing.

Wireless Ethernet IEEE 802.11b

Ethernet has been freed from STP, UDP, and fiber and is now wireless. With the 802.11 standard ratified in 1997, the IEEE has adopted a frame format compatible with Ethernet. As you can see in Figure 6.6, the 802.11 frame format looks very similar to Ethernet with a few additions. Although there are a number of standards for *Wireless LANs (WLANs)*, because of the Wireless Ethernet Compatibility Alliance (WECA) Wireless-Fidelity (Wi-Fi) certification given to products that adhere to the 802.11b standard, 802.11b is the most prevalent standard for WLANs today.

FIGURE 6.6   802.11b data frame

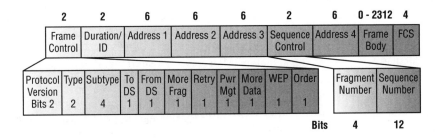

802.11b PHY

Like wired Ethernet, the 802.11b MAC layer stays constant despite the underlying physical transport. The 802.11 specification calls for 3 PHY (physical) transport methods: Direct Sequence Spread Spectrum (DSSS), Frequency Hopping Spread Spectrum (FHSS), and Infrared. The supported data rates are

1 and 2Mbps using Differential Binary Phase Shift Keying (DBPSK) and Differential Quadrature Phase Shift Keying (DQPSK). The two radio frequency (RF) PHY methods operate in the 2.4–2.4835 GHz range. 802.11b supplements the original 802.11 standard with higher data rates for the DSSS PHY specification. In particular, it uses an 8-chip complementary code keying (CCK) to achieve 5.5 and 11Mbps data rates.

Unlike Ethernet, which uses CSMA/CD, 802.11 uses Carrier Sense Multiple Access with Collision Avoidance (CSMA/CA). The primary reason for this is that the cost of an RF device that can listen and monitor its own transmissions is much more expensive than one that merely transmits. Therefore, the 802.11 standard uses an RTS/CTS scheme in which stations must request the right to transmit and then are granted use of the media.

WLAN Groupings

The grouping of 802.11 wireless devices is defined by the Basic Service Set (BSS). The simplest BSS is the Independent BSS (IBSS), which consists of two devices communicating directly with one another in what is known as ad hoc mode. Figure 6.7 shows two laptops with wireless adapters communicating in ad hoc mode. For two wireless devices to be in the same BSS, they must share the same configured Service Set Identifier (SSID). The SSID can range from 0 to 32 bytes in length.

FIGURE 6.7   802.11b ad hoc mode

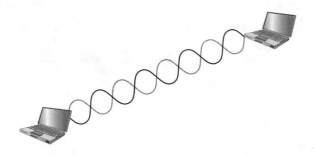

Figure 6.8 shows another type of BSS; the wireless devices are operating in infrastructure mode. Here, the wireless stations may be too far apart to associate with one another or need to access devices on the wired network. In this case, there is a special wireless device called an access point (AP) that not only participates in the BSS but also has a connection to the distribution system (DS). The DS is not defined by the 802.11 specification but is typically the switch and router networks we're accustomed to. A further extension of the infrastructure mode BSS is the Extended Service Set (ESS). The ESS is a grouping of interconnected BSSs via the DS that appear to the LLC layer of the wireless devices as a single BSS. This allows wireless devices to "roam" between access points and still be in the same logical network.

FIGURE 6.8 802.11b infrastructure mode

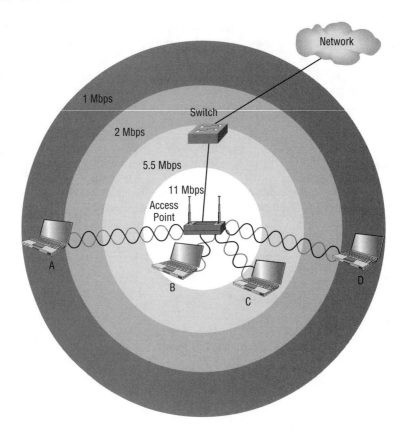

802.11b Security

Security is a major issue with WLANs because data transmission is not confined to wires or fibers. The 802.11b standard uses Wired Equivalent Privacy (WEP) to protect transmissions from casual eavesdropping and provide the same subjective level of confidentiality as a wired LAN. WEP uses the RC4 encryption algorithm with static 40-bit keys. A newer, although nonstandard, WEP2 uses 104-bit static keys.

Cisco offers the use of the Lightweight Extensible Authentication Protocol (LEAP) combined with 802.1x and Remote Access Dial-In User Service (RADIUS) to increase security. Central authentication and per-user WEP session keys are used to provide better security as well.

WLAN Standards

The Wireless LAN environment is a growing area, and new standards are emerging to extend wireless capability and deal with some issues. Table 6.5 shows a range of wireless standards that have already been developed or are evolving.

TABLE 6.5   IEEE Wireless Standards

Standard	Definition
IEEE 802.11	Base Wireless Specification in the 2.4 GHz band. Specifies data rates up to 2Mbps.
IEEE 802.11a	OFDM in the 5GHz Band. Support for higher-speed data transfer up to 54Mbps.
IEEE 802.11b	High Rate DSSS in the 2.4 GHz Band. Extends the original 802.11 specification to 11Mbps.
IEEE 802.11c	Bridge Operations Procedures. Ensures proper Access Point bridge operations and interoperability.
IEEE 802.11d	Global Harmonization.
IEEE 802.11e	MAC Enhancements for QoS. Extends the MAC layer to permit prioritization for voice and video traffic. Will remain backward compatible with existing MAC layer.
IEEE 802.11f	Inter Access Point Protocol. Sets a standard protocol for roaming between multiple vendors' access points.
IEEE 802.11g	Higher Rate Extensions in the 2.4 GHz Band. Will extend 802.11b to 54Mbps max data rate and support backward compatibility.
IEEE 802.11h	Spectrum Managed 802.11a. Provides Dynamic Channel Selection (DCS) and Transmit Power Control (TPC) to the 5GHz band so it won't interfere with satellite transmissions.
IEEE 802.11i	MAC Enhancements for Enhanced Security. Incorporating 802.1x and stronger encryption standards like AES to overcome the shortcomings of WEP.
IEEE 802.15	Wireless Personal Area Networks (WPANs) for devices such as PDAs, cell phones, pagers, and personal electronics.
IEEE 802.16	Working group for Broadband Wireless Access Standards including 802.16d Mobile Wireless MANs.

Now that we've covered some of the different forms Ethernet can assume, we'll look at how Ethernet devices are connected together with Cisco Catalyst switches, specifically the Catalyst 5000 and 3550 as seen in the CCIE lab.

Configuring the Catalyst 5000 and 3550 Switches

This section focuses on configuring local area networks on Cisco Catalyst 5000 and Catalyst 3550 switches. The Catalyst product family supports two version of operating code:

IOS   IOS code uses the standard IOS commands associated with configuring Cisco routers.

Catalyst OS   CAT OS code uses set and clear commands to configure the Catalyst switch.

Although Cisco is moving toward all Catalyst switches using an IOS-based command structure, the Catalyst 5000, 4000, and 6000 switches still use the CAT OS commands. The following sections focus on configuring the Catalyst 5000 switch using CAT OS commands. And because the CCIE lab exam now utilizes Catalyst 3550 switches, we will also discuss how to use the IOS commands for the same functionality.

The Catalyst switches can be used to create and support a virtual LAN (VLAN) architecture. The VLAN architecture segments layer 2 broadcast domains to the assigned Catalyst port in a given VLAN. The Catalyst switches can support up to 1000 VLANs per switch or per switch domain.

A Route Switch Module (RSM) can be installed in the Catalyst 5000 to provide multilayer services. The RSM is a router on a blade that gives the Catalyst 5000 routing functionality. It also allows the Catalyst to perform layer 3 switching functions at wire speed if there is a Net-Flow feature card II (NFFC II) on the Supervisor3 module.

The switches in the Cisco Catalyst 3550 Series Intelligent Ethernet Switch line are stackable, multilayer switches that give you high availability, quality of service (QoS), and security for better network operations. With a range of Fast Ethernet and Gigabit Ethernet configurations, the Catalyst 3550 Series can serve as both a powerful access layer switch for medium enterprise wiring closets and a backbone switch for mid-sized networks.

Because Catalyst switches are a CCIE core technology, any weakness in configuring them will severely hinder a candidate's chances of passing the CCIE lab exam.

Catalyst Configuration Commands

The configuration of the Catalyst switch for layer 2 services is a relatively simple task and can be broken down into five different topics:

- Port configuration
- VTP configuration
- VLAN configuration
- Spanning tree configuration
- Switch administration

We'll take a detailed look at each in the following sections.

Port Configuration

The following examples show the basic commands used to configure switch ports for operation as access ports for end users on the Catalyst 5000 and 3550.

Configuration Commands for the Cat OS-Based Switches: Catalyst 5000

`set port speed 2/10 100`	This command sets the port speed to 100 Mbps [100|10|auto], default setting is auto-negotiate
`set port duplex 2/10 full`	This command sets port 2/10 to full duplex [full|half], default setting is to auto negotiate
`set port name 2/10 server1`	Set the name of the port 2/10 to "server1"
`set port broadcast  2/10 1500`	Limit the broadcast traffic bandwidth to no more than 6 MB on port 2/10 of the Catalyst Switch. Assumes the average packet size is 500 Bytes
	Packet rate * average packet size in bits/sec. (1500 *(500*8))
`set port security 2/5 enable 00-0c-22-22-33-33`	Set security on port 2/5 to only allow MAC address 00-0c-22-22-33-33 to attach to the network on this port
`set port security 2/5 shutdown 100`	Sets security on port 2/5 to disable the port for 100 minutes in the event of a violation. By default, the shutdown time is indefinite
`set port qos 2/5 cos 3`	Colors all traffic that comes from port 2/5 with a cos of 3

The following is the output from `show port 2/2`:

Port	Name	Status	Vlan	Level	Duplex	Speed	Type
2/2	server1	connect	2	normal	half	100	

Port 2/2 has its name modified and has its speed and duplex and speed set.

Configuration Commands for the IOS-Based Switches: Catalyst 3550

```
interface fastethernet 0/12
```

`description server1`	Set the name of the port to "server1"
`speed 10`	Set interface to 10 Mbps
`duplex half`	Set interface to half-duplex mode
`switchport mode access`	Set port to access mode
`switchport port-security`	Enable port security on this port
`switchport port-security mac-address 000c.2222.3333`	
	Set a secure MAC address for this port

The following is the output from the **show interface** command:

```
FastEthernet0/12 is up, line protocol is up
  Hardware is Fast Ethernet, address is 0009.432c.908c (bia 0009.432c.908c)
  Description: server1
  MTU 1500 bytes, BW 10000 Kbit, DLY 1000 usec,
      reliability 255/255, txload 1/255, rxload 1/255
  Encapsulation ARPA, loopback not set
  Keepalive set (10 sec)
  Half-duplex, 10Mb/s
  input flow-control is off, output flow-control is off
  ARP type: ARPA, ARP Timeout 04:00:00
  Last input never, output never, output hang never
  Last clearing of "show interface" counters never
  Input queue: 0/75/0/0 (size/max/drops/flushes); Total output drops: 0
  Queueing strategy: fifo
  Output queue :0/40 (size/max)
  5 minute input rate 0 bits/sec, 0 packets/sec
  5 minute output rate 0 bits/sec, 0 packets/sec
    0 packets input, 0 bytes, 0 no buffer
    Received 0 broadcasts, 0 runts, 0 giants, 0 throttles
```

```
0 input errors, 0 CRC, 0 frame, 0 overrun, 0 ignored
0 watchdog, 0 multicast, 0 pause input
0 input packets with dribble condition detected
0 packets output, 0 bytes, 0 underruns
0 output errors, 0 collisions, 1 interface resets
0 babbles, 0 late collision, 0 deferred
0 lost carrier, 0 no carrier, 0 PAUSE output
```

VTP Configuration

The Cisco-proprietary VLAN Trunking Protocol (VTP) is a layer 2 protocol used to communicate which set of VLANs are in use across a group of switches by centralizing the database of VLAN values on one switch and pushing them out to the rest of the group. VTP eases administration and helps to ensure VLAN coherency across a group of switches. Typically, one switch will be configured as a VTP server, store the VLANs in its NVRAM, and be responsible for the VLAN database. Other switches are configured as VTP clients and learn which VLANs to trunk from configuration updates sent by the server. Every time the database is updated, the database revision is incremented.

For two Catalyst switches to share VLAN information, they must be configured with the same VTP domain name and must be connected to each other by active trunk ports. VTP information is sent out all trunk ports of a Catalyst switch using VLAN 1 and the destination MAC address of 01-00-0C-CC-CC-CC with an ethertype of 0x2003. An adjacent Catalyst switch only processes VTP information if the VTP message is from a switch in the same VTP domain.

VTP has a number of operating modes, and the switch can be configured to operate in any one of these VTP modes:

Server   In VTP server mode, the server switch is allowed to create, modify, and delete VLANs as well as other configuration parameters.

Client   A client cannot add or change the VLAN configuration information on the switch. The client switch within the same VTP domain receives VTP advertisements from a VTP server and modifies its configuration accordingly. VLAN information is not stored in NVRAM. If a client reboots, it will have to learn the VLANs from the server again.

WARNING   Care should be taken when you add a new switch to an existing network. If the configuration revision is higher on the new switch and it does not have the correct VLANs configured on it, the existing VLAN database can get wiped out. Always check to make sure that a new switch's configuration revision is less than the target network's.

Transparent   When you configure the switch as VTP transparent, the switch does not participate in VTP. However, a VTP transparent switch running VTP version 2 will forward received

VTP advertisements out all of its trunk ports. A switch in transparent mode running VTP version 1 will also forward advertisements, but only if they have the same VTP domain configured on the switch.

In Figure 6.9, if VLAN 222 is configured on SW1, this VLAN will automatically appear in both SW2 and SW3. VLANs can be added or deleted from SW1 or SW2 as they are configured as a VTP server. SW3 will only see all added VLANs, but it will not be able to add or delete any.

FIGURE 6.9 VTP example 1

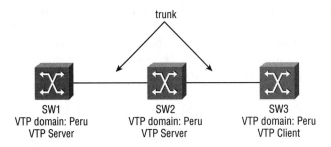

In Figure 6.10, if VLAN 222 is configured on SW1, this VLAN automatically appears in SW2. SW3 does not see the VLAN because it is configured with a different VTP domain name.

FIGURE 6.10 VTP example 2

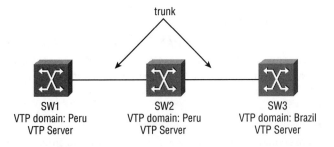

In Figure 6.11, if VLAN 222 is configured on SW1, this VLAN will not appear in SW2 because SW2 is configured in VTP transparent mode. The VLAN will appear in SW3 because SW2, which is configured as transparent mode, will flood all VTP messages out all operational trunk ports.

FIGURE 6.11   VTP example 3

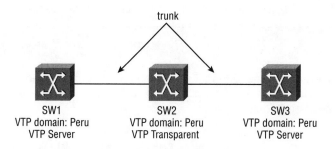

trunk

SW1	SW2	SW3
VTP domain: Peru	VTP domain: Peru	VTP domain: Peru
VTP Server	VTP Transparent	VTP Server

VTP Pruning

In a multiswitch VTP domain, VTP pruning would prune (eliminate) unnecessary traffic, such as broadcast, multicast, and flooded unicast packets from being sent to a switch that has no port configured in that specific VLAN.

The following listings show how to configure VTP on the Catalyst 5000 and Catalyst 3550 switches. Note that you must be in vlan database configuration mode to configure VTP on the 3550.

Configuration Commands for the Cat OS-Based Switches: Catalyst 5000

set vtp domain Lab	Set the domain name for this switch to Lab. All switches within this domain will exchange VTP information
set vtp mode transparent	Set the VTP mode of this specific switch to transparent [server|client|transparent]
set vtp passwd kyle	Set a VTP password of kyle All switches in this VTP domain will now authenticate VTP information
set vtp pruning enable	Enable VLAN pruning on this switch
clear vtp pruneeligible 200-300	Stop VTP pruning on vlans 200-300
set vtp pruneeligible 400-500	By default vlans 2-1005 are pruning eligible, this allows pruning on only VLANs 400-500

The following is the output from a **show vtp domain** command:

```
Domain Name        Domain Index  VTP Version  Local Mode  Password
--------------------------  ------------ -----------  -----
Lab              1         2          server    configured


Vlan-count Max-vlan-storage Config Revision Notifications
---------- ---------------- --------------- -------------
8          1023              0               disabled


Last Updater   V2 Mode    Pruning    PruneEligible on Vlans
---------------  --------  --------  ------------------------
0.0.0.0         disabled   disabled    2-1000
```

Configuration Commands for the IOS-Based Switches: Catalyst 3550

(vlan)# vtp domain Lab	Set the domain name for this switch to Lab. All switches within this domain exchange VTP information
(vlan)# vtp mode transparent	Set the VTP mode of this specific switch to transparent [server|client|transparent]
(vlan)# vtp password kyle	Set a VTP password of kyle, all switches in this VTP domain now authenticate VTP information
(vlan)# vtp pruning	Enable VLAN pruning on this switch, must be VTP Server to modify pruning
(config)# interface fastethernet 0/1	
(config-if)#switchport trunk encapsulation isl	
	Specify the encapsulation for the trunk as isl
(config-if)#switchport mode trunk	Set the port to trunk uncondit-ionally. Instead of trunk, you can use the dot1q-tunnel option to set the port as a 802.1q tunnel port

```
(config-if)#switchport trunk pruning vlan remove 200-300
                                        Stop VTP pruning on vlans 200-
                                        300
(config-if)#switchport trunk pruning vlan add 400-500
                                        By default vlans 2-1005
                                        are pruning eligible, this
                                        allows pruning on only VLANs
                                        400-500
```

The following is the output from a show vtp status command:

```
VTP Version                  : 2
Configuration Revision       : 0
Maximum VLANs supported locally : 1005
Number of existing VLANs     : 6
VTP Operating Mode           : Transparent
VTP Domain Name              : Lab
VTP Pruning Mode             : Enabled
VTP V2 Mode                  : Disabled
VTP Traps Generation         : Disabled
MD5 digest                   : 0xF2 0xD1 0xFB 0x83 0x42 0x56 0x95
Configuration last modified by 172.16.1.10 at 3-14-03 00:06:5
```

Trunk Configuration

Trunks on a Catalyst switch carry the traffic of multiple VLANs and can extend VLANs across an entire Catalyst network (VTP domain). Trunks can be configured to use either Inter-Switch Link (ISL) or 802.1q as the trunking protocol. Because ISL is a Cisco-proprietary protocol, it is generally recommended to use the standards-based 802.1q as the trunking protocol for Catalyst networks.

ISL tags each frame to identify the VLAN it belongs to. As shown in Figure 6.12, ISL encapsulates the trunked frame with a 26-byte header and a 4-byte FCS. The header includes a 15-bit VLAN ID that identifies each VLAN. Although ISL primarily encapsulates and transports Ethernet frames, it can also carry FDDI, Token Ring, and ATM in its payload.

FIGURE 6.12 ISL frame format

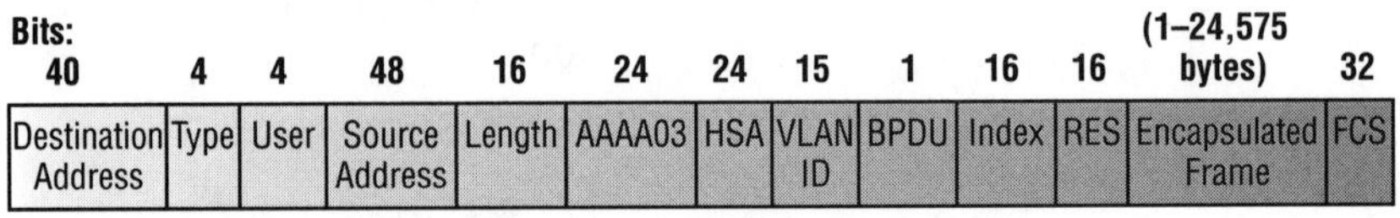

Bits:

40	4	4	48	16	24	24	15	1	16	16	(1–24,575 bytes)	32
Destination Address	Type	User	Source Address	Length	AAAA03	HSA	VLAN ID	BPDU	Index	RES	Encapsulated Frame	FCS

Destination Address

5 byte multicast address set to
  10-00-0C-00-00 or
  03-00-0C-00-00
to indicate this is an ISL frame

Type

Indicates type of frame encapsulated
  0000 - Ethernet
  0001 - Token Ring
  0010 - FDDI
  0011 - ATM

User

Extends Type field.
For Ethernet frames the User field
specifies priority of packets
  xx00 - Normal Priority
  xx01 - Priority 1
  xx10 - Priority 2
  xx11 - Highest Priority

Source Address

Set to the MAC address of the switch
port sending the encapsulated frame

Length

Length of the encapsulated packet minus
18 bytes since the DMAC, SMAC, length,
and FCS fields are not included.

AAAA03 (SNAP & LLC)

Constant value set to 0xAAAA03

HSA - High Bits of Source Address

Equal to the manufacturer's id in the
Source Address and set to 00-00-0C

VLAN

15-bit VLAN ID

BPDU/CDP Indicator

0 = encapsulated frame is not an STP
    BPDU or a CDP packet
1 = encapsulated frame is either an
    STP BPDU or a CDP packet

Index

Port index of sending switch's port ignored
by receiving switch; used for troubleshooting.

RES - Reserved

Used to hold additional information for
Token Ring and FDDI encapsulated frames.
For Ethernet frames it is set to 0.

Encapsulated Frame

The entire encapsulated frame including
original FCS.

FCS - Frame Check Sequence

32-bit CRC on entire ISL packet. FCS in the
encapsulated packet does not change.

The IEEE 802.1q implementation on Cisco switches uses one instance of STP for each VLAN allowed in the trunk. This practice is referred to as Per VLAN Spanning Tree (PVST). Similar to ISL, 802.1q uses a tag on each frame with a VLAN identifier, as shown in Figure 6.13. Unlike ISL, 802.1q uses an internal tag within the Ethernet frame by inserting a 4-byte field after the ethertype (0x8100 for 802.1q). IEEE 802.1q also provides support for the IEEE 802.1p priority standard. A priority field is included in the 802.1q frame.

FIGURE 6.13   802.1q frame format

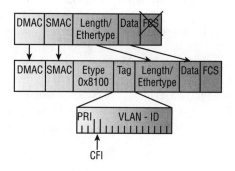

PRI - Priority
3 bits to denote 802.1p priority
CFI - Canonical Format Identifier
0 = MAC address is in Canonical format
1 = MAC address is in Non-Canonical
     (Token Ring) format
VLAN - ID
Identifies VLAN the frame has been assigned to.
0 indicates the Native VLAN is assumed.

If only a layer 2 switch is used, trunk ports are also used when connecting to routers that are configured to support "one arm routing" and "routing on a stick." By default, all switch ports are configured as trunk ports, which will try to form trunks with the remote device connected to the port using the Dynamic Trunking Protocol (DTP) discussed in the next section.

The ISL tag has provisions to hold the token ring source-route bridging Routing Information Field (RIF), which is used for the tr-isl feature in Catalyst 5000 switches. Because of this, the ISL tag is much larger than the 802.1q tag. Most of the time this is not an issue, but if you are performing wire-speed testing over trunked ports with a 64-byte packet stream, remember that the packets are now 94 bytes and you'll only get about 70 percent of the throughput you might have expected.

Dynamic Trunking Protocol (DTP)

The Dynamic Trunking Protocol (DTP) is an outgrowth of the original Dynamic ISL (DISL) protocol and is used by switches to ensure that different parameters used in the sending of 802.1q or

ISL tagged frames are consistent on both sides of the trunk. These parameters include the VLAN encapsulation type, hardware capability, native VLAN, and VTP domain. DTP uses the Cisco Discovery Protocol (CDP) multicast MAC address of 01-00-0C-CC-CC-CC and an ethertype of 0x2004 in its frames. As with CDP, information is transferred in packets using Type Length Value (TLV) objects.

When a port is configured as a trunk port, the encapsulation type can be specified as 802.1q, ISL, or negotiate. If it's set to negotiate, DTP tries to match up the encapsulation type on both sides. If both sides are set to negotiate, DTP favors ISL encapsulation. The DTP mode can be set to one of the values listed in Table 6.6. The trunk encapsulation type and whether the port and its remote counterpart form a trunk depends on the DTP settings on both sides.

TABLE 6.6 DTP Modes

Mode	Definition
Auto (default mode for most Catalyst switches)	Enables the port to convert the link to a trunk link. The port becomes a trunk port if the neighboring port is set to on or desirable mode.
On	Puts port into permanent trunking mode and negotiates to convert the link into a trunk. The port becomes a trunk port even if the neighbor does not agree to the change.
Nonegotiate	Port is in a permanent trunking mode but prevented from generating DTP frames. The neighboring port must be configured manually as a trunk port to establish a trunk link.
Desirable (default for IOS-based switches/routers)	This port actively attempts to convert the link to a trunk link. The port becomes a trunk port if the neighboring port is set to on, desirable, or auto.
Off	Puts this port into permanent nontrunking mode and negotiates to convert the link into a nontrunk link. The port becomes a nontrunk port even if the neighboring port does not agree to the change.

The following configuration examples show how to set up a trunk connection on Catalyst 5000 and 3550s.

Configuration Commands for the Cat OS-Based Switches: Catalyst 5000

set trunk 2/1 on dot1q

Configures port 2/1 as a trunk using 802.1q [isl|dot1q|negotiate] as the trunk encapsulation protocol. This command also sets the trunk mode to "on"[on|off|desirable|auto| negotiate].

clear trunk 2/1 2-1001

This command limits the number of VLANs on a trunk by removing VLANs from the allowed list. VTP information and data packets for VLANs 2-1000 will not be sent across this trunk (VLAN 1 cannot be cleared from an 802.1q trunk) and set trunk commands to specify the allowed VLANs

set trunk 2/1 100-200

The previous command clear trunk 2/1 1-1001 was use to clear every VLAN from the allowed list. This command will add VLANs 100-200 back into the allowed VLANs list for this trunk

clear trunk 2/1 2-99,201-1001

Optionally, this command performs the same task as the two previous commands. The end result is that only VLANs 100-200 are in the allowed list

By default, all VLANs are added to the allowed VLANs list for a trunk. To modify the allowed VLANs list, use a combination of the clear trunk and set trunk commands.

> The VTP domain name is sent in DTP messages when a trunk port is configured as desirable or auto. A trunk will not form if VTP domains do not match. If a trunk port is configured in on, off, or nonegotiate mode, no VTP domain information is sent.

The following is the output from the show trunk 2/1 command:

```
Port      Mode           Encapsulation  Status        Native vlan
--------  -------------  -------------  ------------  -----------
 2/1      on             dot1q trunking 500
```

```
Port      Vlans allowed on trunk
--------  -----------------------------------------------------------
 2/1      100-200
```

```
Port      Vlans allowed and active in management domain
--------  -----------------------------------------------------------
 2/1      100
```

```
Port      Vlans in spanning tree forwarding state and not pruned
--------  -----------------------------------------------------------
 2/1      100
```

The only active VLAN on port 2/1 between 100 and 200 is VLAN 100, therefore it is the only one displayed in the allowed, active, and spanning tree output.

Configuration Commands for the IOS-Based Switches: Catalyst 3550

```
interface fastethernet 0/1

switchport access vlan 2                 specify the default vlan, which is
                                         used if the interface stops
                                         trunking

switchport trunk encapsulation dot1q

                                         Specify the encapsulation for the
                                         is as 802.1q
```

switchport mode trunk on   Set the port to trunk
                                            unconditionally.

switchport trunk allowed vlan remove 2-1001

                                            This command limits the number of
                                            VLANs on a trunk by removing VLANs
                                            from the allowed list. VTP
                                            information and data packets for
                                            VLANs 2-1001 will not be sent
                                            across this trunk (VLAN 1 cannot be
                                            cleared from a trunk as it is used
                                            for VTP) and set trunk commands to
                                            specify the allowed VLANs

switchport trunk allowed vlan add 10-200

                                            The previous command switchport
                                            trunk allowed vlan remove 2-1001
                                            was use to clear every VLAN from
                                            the allowed list. This command
                                            adds VLANs 100-200 back into the
                                            allowed VLANs list for this trunk

The following is the output from the show interfaces fastethernet0/1 trunk
command:

Port   Mode   Encapsulation Status   Native vlan
Fa0/1   on   802.1q   trunking   1

Port   Vlans allowed on trunk
Fa0/1   1,10-200

Port   Vlans allowed and active in management domain
Fa0/1   1,10-200

Port   Vlans in spanning tree forwarding state and not pruned
Fa0/1   1,10-200

When a port is configured as an 802.1q tunnel port, spanning tree bridge protocol data unit (BPDU) filtering is automatically enabled, and Cisco Discovery Protocol (CDP) is automatically disabled.

Configuration Commands for a Cisco Router

A router can be configured to support layer 2 trunking. This is also referred to as "one arm routing" or "router on a stick." This functionality is accomplished through creating subinterfaces under the physical LAN interface and assigning the individual subinterfaces to the respective VLAN:

```
Interface FastEthernet0/0

 no ip address
```

`interface FastEthernet0/0.2`	creates sub-interface 0/0.2
`  encapsulation dot1q 2`	Assigns 802.1q trunking for VLAN 2
`ip address 172.16.1.1 255.255.255.0`	
	Assigns IP address
`interface FastEthernet0/0.100`	creates sub-interface 0/0.100
`  encapsulation dot1q 100`	Assigns 802.1q trunking for VLAN 100
`ip address 172.16.2.1 255.255.255.0`	
	Assigns IP address

EtherChannel

EtherChannel is a method of collecting individual ethernet ports between switches or routers into a logical group to achieve greater bandwidth and redundancy. EtherChannel is configured on switches using either the Cisco-proprietary Port Aggregation Protocol (PAgP) or the IEEE standard 802.3ad Link Aggregation Protocol (LACP). Up to eight ports can be joined logically as an EtherChannel.

The algorithm for packet distribution across the links in a channel group differs between switches and ranges from a simple XOR in the Catalyst 5000 on the least two significant bits in the source MAC and destination MAC addresses to a 17th order polynomial in the Catalyst 6000 using MAC addresses and layer 3 and 4 information. However, in all cases, traffic for the same "stream" is carried across the same physical link to ensure orderly packet delivery.

PAgP makes use of the CDP multicast destination MAC address 01-00-0C-CC-CC-CC and uses ethertype 0x0104. Table 6.7 calls out the different PAgP configuration modes a port can be placed in and Table 6.8 shows the different combinations of PAgP modes between two switch ports and their results.

TABLE 6.7   PAgP Configuration Options

Mode	Action
Off	The port will not channel regardless of how the peer's port is configured.
On	The port is set to channel regardless of what peer it is configured for. PAgP is not running. If peer port is set to On, a channel will form.
Auto	PAgP is in a passive state. If PAgP packets are received from the peer, PAgP will start negotiating EtherChannel formation.
Desirable	PAgP is in an active state. PAgP will initiate EtherChannel formation with the far side.
Silent	The silent keyword is used when the port is set to Auto or Desirable mode and the attached device is expected to transmit less often than PAgP's 30-second time-out period. This option is frequently set when performing EtherChannel to a server.

TABLE 6.8   PAgP Mode Combinations

Near Side Mode	Far Side Mode	Result
Off	Off	No channel
Off	On	No channel; port placed in errdisable state
Off	Auto	No channel
Off	Desirable	No channel
On	Off	No channel; port placed in errdisable state
On	On	Channel established
On	Auto	No channel; port placed in errdisable state
On	Desirable	No channel; port placed in errdisable state

TABLE 6.8 PAgP Mode Combinations *(continued)*

Near Side Mode	Far Side Mode	Result
Auto	Off	No channel
Auto	On	No channel; port placed in errdisable state
Auto	Auto	No channel
Auto	Desirable	Channel established
Desirable	Off	No channel
Desirable	On	No channel; port placed in errdisable state
Desirable	Auto	Channel established
Desirable	Desirable	Channel established

There are a number of restrictions on the configuration of ports in a channel group. All ports in the EtherChannel must belong to the same VLAN or must all be configured as trunk ports that are trunking the same VLANS. Ports are not allowed to be configured with dynamic VLANs. All ports must also have the same speed and duplex settings as well as spanning tree parameters. Once a channel is formed, if any settings are changed on one port, they are propagated to all ports in the channel.

The following short examples show how to configure EtherChannel on the Catalyst 5000 and Catalyst 3550 as well as a Cisco router.

Configuration Commands for the Cat OS–Based Switches: Catalyst 5000

```
set port channel 1/1-2 desirable        Assigns ports 1/1 and 1/2 as members
                                         of the channel
```

Configuration Commands for the IOS-Based Switches: Catalyst 3550

```
interface f0/6
  switchport trunk encapsulation isl       set trunk encapsulation type to ISL
  switchport mode trunk                     Assign all interfaces as static-
                                            access ports in the same VLAN, or
                                            configure them as trunks
```

`switchport access vlan 2`	If you configure the interface as a static-access port, assign it to only one VLAN. The range is 1 to 4094
`channel-group 1 mode desirable`	Assigns interface vlan 3 as a member of channel-group 1 and sets the DTP mode to desirable. [on|auto| desirable]

On a router, FEC is configured by assigning interfaces to a port channel with the `channel-group number mode on` command. The virtual interface is created with the `interface port-channel number` command:

`interface port-channel 14`

`interface fastethernet 4/0`

`channel-group 14`	Assigns interface f4/0 as a member of channel-group 14

`interface fastethernet 4/1`

`channel-group 14`	Assigns interface f4/1 as a member of channel-group 14

`ip address 172.16.10.15 255.255.255.0`

VLAN Configuration

The following sections detail the basic configuration of VLANs on the Catalyst 5000 and 3550 and, where appropriate, on an IOS-based router.

Standard VLANs

On a Catalyst switch, a VLAN allows you to group ports on the same or different switches, thereby confining unicast, multicast, and broadcast traffic to only the ports in that VLAN. Broadcast/multicast traffic originating from a particular VLAN is only flooded out other switch ports belonging to that VLAN. Table 6.9 shows the preconfigured and user-definable VLANs in Cisco switches.

TABLE 6.9 VLAN IDs

VLAN Number	Use
VLAN 1	Default VLAN, used by VTP
VLAN 2–1001	Open
VLAN 1002	FDDI
VLAN 1003	TrCrf
VLAN 1004	FDNET
VLAN 1005	TrBrf

The following are the commands needed to configure a VLAN on a Catalyst switch, and assign a port to the VLAN.

Configuration Commands for the Cat OS-Based Switches: Catalyst 5000

```
set vlan 100                    Create VLAN 100
set vlan 100 segment1           Set the name on VLAN 100 to "segment1"
set vlan 100 2/3-5              Assign ports 2/3, 2/4 and 2/5 to
                                VLAN 100
```

The following is the output from show vlan:

```
VLAN Name                         Status     IfIndex Mod/Ports,Vlans
---- -------------------------- --------- ------- ---------------
1    default                    active     5        1/2
                                                    2/6-12
2    green                      active     10       2/2
3    VLAN0003                   active     11       2/1
100  segment1                   active     12       2/3-5
1002 fddi-default               active     6
1003 token-ring-default         active     9
1004 fddinet-default            active     7
1005 trnet-default              active     8
```

As can be seen from the output, VLANs 2 and 100 have both had their default VLAN name changed; the default VLAN name is assigned to VLAN 3.

Configuration Commands for the IOS-Based Switches: Catalyst 3550

(vlan)#vlan 100 name segment-1 mtu 1600   Create VLAN 100

Set the name on VLAN 100 to segment-1

[optional] changes the mtu size to 1600 byte, from the defualt of 1500

interface fastethernet 0/2

 switchport mode access

 switchport access vlan 100   Assigns interface fastethernet 0/2 to VLAN 100

The following is the output from show vlan:

VLAN	Name	Status	Ports
1	default	active	Fa0/3, Fa0/4, Fa0/5, Fa0/6
			Fa0/7, Fa0/8, Fa0/9, Fa0/10
			Fa0/11, Fa0/12, Fa0/13, Fa0/14
			Fa0/15, Fa0/16, Fa0/17, Fa0/18
			Fa0/19, Fa0/20, Fa0/21, Fa0/22
			Fa0/23, Fa0/24, Gi0/1, Gi0/2
2	VLAN0002	active	Fa0/1
100	segment-1	active	Fa0/2
1002	fddi-default	active	
1003	token-ring-default	active	
1004	fddinet-default	active	
1005	trnet-default	active	

VLAN	Type	SAID	MTU	Parent	RingNo	BridgeNo	Stp	BrdgMode	Trans1	Trans2
1	enet	100001	1500	-	-	-	-	-	0	0
2	enet	100002	1500	-	-	-	-	-	0	0
100	enet	100100	1600	-	-	-	-	-	0	0
1002	fddi	101002	1500	-	-	-	-	-	0	0
1003	tr	101003	1500	-	-	-	-	-	0	0

VLAN	Type	SAID	MTU	Parent	RingNo	BridgeNo	Stp	BrdgMode	Trans1	Trans2
1004	fdnet	101004	1500	-	-	-	ieee	-	0	0
1005	trnet	101005	1500	-	-	-	ibm	-	0	0

As can be seen from the output, VLAN 100 has had its default VLAN name changed to segment-1 and VLAN 100 has an MTU size of 1600.

EXTENDED RANGE VLAN IDS

You can create an extended range of VLANs in the Catalyst 3550. These extended VLANs can range from 1006 to 4094. Extended-range VLANs are not saved in the VLAN database because they are saved in the switch running-config file. To configure extended range VLANs, you must be in VTP transparent mode.

```
vtp mode transparent
vlan 2048                                    Create extended range VLAN 2048
```

Dynamic Port VLAN Membership

Dynamic port VLAN membership uses a VLAN Management Policy Server (VMPS) to assign nontrunking ports dynamically to a specific VLAN. Each port is dynamically assigned to a VLAN based on the MAC address of the device that is connected to that port. When a Catalyst port becomes active, the MAC address is checked against a VMPS database (which contains a mapping from a MAC address to a VLAN name) and assigns the port to the appropriate VLAN.

Dynamic VLAN membership requires the use of a VMPS database server and also requires that the interface SC0 of a VMPS server switch is able to access to this server. Therefore, the Catalyst switch needs the database server to be attached to the same VLAN as the interface SC0 is assigned to, or it needs to be able to have access to the server via its default gateway. This switch will be assigned as the VMPS server switch, and any additional switches in the VTP domain are set up to point to the VMPS server Catalyst switch as opposed to the database server itself.

In Figure 6.14, the interface SC0 of the VMPS server switch is configured with IP address 172.16.1.10. The VMPS server's IP address is 172.16.1.2 and is connected to the same VLAN as the SC0. SW2 is configured as a secondary VMPS switch and points to the SC0 address of SW1 using the set vmps server command. Both SC0 interfaces of the Catalyst switches must be able to communicate to share VMPS information; therefore, they must share the same VLAN or IP routing connectivity has to exist between the Catalyst SC0 interfaces.

FIGURE 6.14   VMPS diagram

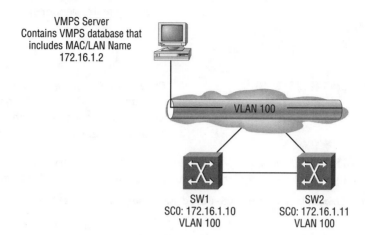

The following are the commands needed to configure dynamic VLAN membership.

Configuration Commands for the Cat OS-Based Switches: Catalyst 5000

SW1:

```
set vmps downloadserver 172.16.1.2 mac-addr.txt
```

Define the IP address of the VMPS database servers, and the VMPS configuration file (mac-addr.txt) that contains the MAC address to VLAN mapping. The switch will try and connected to the VMPS download server, and if it cannot find it VMPS operation will go inactive

```
set vmps state enable
```

Enable VMPS policy server on the switch

```
set vmps downloadmethod tftp
```

Set the VMPS download method from the server to TFTP [rcp|tftp]

```
set port membership 2/8 dynamic          Assign port 2/8 as a port that can
                                          have dynamic membership


SW2:

set vmps server 172.16.1.10              On a secondary switch, define the
                                          IP address of the VMPS enabled
                                          switch as opposed to the VMPS
                                          database server
```

The Catalyst 3550 cannot act as a VMPS server; it can only use the services of a VPMS server. However, a Catalyst 5000 series or Catalyst 6500 series can act as a VMPS server.

Configuration Commands for the IOS-Based Switches: Catalyst 3550

```
SW2:

vmps server 172.16.1.2 primary           Enter the IP address of the
                                          primary vmps server

vmps server 172.16.1.5                    Enter the IP address of the
                                          secondary vmps server


interface fastethernet 0/10

 switchport mode access                   Set port to access mode

 switchport access vlan dynamic           Configure port as eligible for
                                          dynamic VLAN membership
```

The following is the output from show vmps:

```
VQP Client Status:
--------------------
VMPS VQP Version:   1
Reconfirm Interval: 60 min
Server Retry Count: 3
VMPS domain server: 172.16.1.5
                    172.16.1.2 (primary, current)
```

Spanning-Tree Protocol (STP)

The purpose of the spanning-tree algorithm is to take a meshed, redundant topology and turn it into a spanning tree having only one active path between any two given segments. This prevents loops that can cause broadcast storms leading to network meltdowns and prevents multiple packets from arriving at a destination. Certain bridge ports are selected to go into a blocking state in which they do not forward traffic, although they are still connected to the network and active in case a forwarding port fails.

The STP chooses which ports are blocking in a two-step process:

1. Elect one bridge to be the root bridge.

2. Select only one bridge port per segment to forward frames back to the root bridge. This port is known as the designated port.

The bridges on each segment calculate their cost back to the root bridge. The port on each bridge that has the best cost back to the root bridge is selected as the bridge's root port and is always in a forwarding state. The root path cost for a bridge is the learned path cost plus the path cost set on the root port. The bridge with the lowest root path cost forwards frames for that segment; all other bridges' ports go into a blocking state unless the port is the bridge's root port. If two bridges advertise the same root path cost, the bridge with the higher-priority bridge identifier (lower numeric value) forwards. When two ports on a segment have the same root path cost and bridge ID, they must be on the same bridge. The tiebreaker then is the port ID. The lower port ID wins and forwards packets for the segment. The following list summarizes how a designated port is chosen on a segment:

1. Select the lowest root path cost.

2. Select the lowest bridge ID.

3. Select the lowest port ID.

Now that we've seen what the spanning-tree algorithm does, let's see how the spanning tree protocol implements it.

Spanning-Tree Protocol Details

Bridges communicate spanning tree information through the use of bridge protocol data units (BPDUs). As defined by the IEEE 802.1d standard, BPDUs use a multicast address of 0180.C200.0000 and SSAP/DSAPs of 0x42. Figure 6.15 shows the format of a Configuration BPDU. The Configuration BPDU contains information about the sender of the BPDU as well as the spanning tree parameters set by the root bridge.

FIGURE 6.15   Spanning tree Configuration BPDU

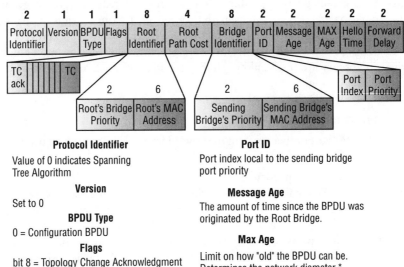

Protocol Identifier

Value of 0 indicates Spanning
Tree Algorithm

Version

Set to 0

BPDU Type

0 = Configuration BPDU

Flags

bit 8 = Topology Change Acknowledgment
bit 1 - Topology Change Flag

Root Identifier

Bridge Priority and MAC address of the
Root Bridge

Root Path Cost

Cost of the path to the Root Bridge.
Set to 0 if the sender is Root.

Bridge Identifier

Bridge Priority and MAC address of the
bridge sending the BPDU.

Port ID

Port index local to the sending bridge
port priority

Message Age

The amount of time since the BPDU was
originated by the Root Bridge.

Max Age

Limit on how "old" the BPDU can be.
Determines the network diameter.*

Hello Time

Time (in seconds) between Configuration
BPDU transmissions.*

Forward Delay

Time a port waits between the learning
and forward states. Also used to set the
filtering database time during Topology
Change Notifications.*

*Set by the Root Bridge

The root bridge is selected by the Bridge Electoral College... er, scratch that. The root bridge is the bridge that advertises the numerically lowest bridge identifier. The bridge identifier is the combination of a 2-byte bridge priority and the bridge's identifying MAC address. When a bridge powers up, it sends out BPDUs at regular intervals advertising itself as the root bridge. It will keep advertising these Configuration BPDUs until it receives a BPDU whose root identifier shows a bridge with a higher priority (lower numeric value) than it has. If two bridges share the same bridge priority, whichever bridge has the lower MAC address becomes the root bridge. Once a bridge hears a BPDU with a higher-priority root bridge identifier, it will stop sending out BPDUs with its values and send out copies with the root bridge's values, such as Max Age, Hello Time, and Forward Delay, which we'll cover shortly.

The root bridge sends out BPDUs periodically according to the Hello Time, which is 2 seconds by default. This lets the other bridges in the network know that the root bridge is still up and functioning and lets any freshly powered-up bridges know quickly who the root bridge is.

All bridges on segments connected to the root bridge forward copies of the received BPDUs out any nonblocking ports, inserting their own IDs in the Bridge Identifier field. Bridges connected to these segments then forward out copies of the BPDUs in turn on their nonblocking ports with their IDs inserted. When a bridge receives a BPDU, it checks the value in the Message Age field against the Max Age field. If they are equal, the BPDU is discarded; otherwise, the bridge adds 1 to the value of the Message Age field. The STP diameter is the number of bridges between any two segments in the network. The IEEE generally recommends having a network diameter of 7 or less.

Another field that is modified as the BPDU is passed through a bridge is the Root Path Cost field, initially set to 0 (zero) by the root bridge. When a BPDU is received, the path cost of the receiving port is added to the root path cost when transmitted downstream.

Here are some further points about the Spanning-Tree Protocol. All ports on the root bridge are in the forwarding state by definition (except if there are two ports configured for the same segment). The STP was designed to scale well and require few resources on bridges and switches. Unlike routing protocols such as OSPF and EIGRP that hold link-state and route information, the Spanning-Tree Protocol does not require switches to learn about other switches and hold topology information. As the network diameter grows, there is no further memory required on switches for STP; however, the Forwarding Delay and Max Age parameters should be adjusted accordingly.

Five different port states exist in STP and are shown in Table 6.10. Each port on a bridge or switch operates in its own STP state.

TABLE 6.10   Spanning Tree Port States

State	Meaning
Disabled	The port does not participate in STP. BPDUs received on this port are not processed, nor are received frames' source addresses added to the filtering database.
Blocking	Frames are not forwarded out a blocking port, nor is location information added to the filtering database. Received BPDUs are processed, but the port does not send BPDUs.
Listening	This transitory state is entered from the blocking state after STP determines this port needs to forward. It provides the opportunity for superior BPDUs to be received in case of network congestion or reconvergence.
Learning	Entered from the listening state. The port does not forward traffic but does add location information to the filtering database. Waits the Forwarding Delay time before entering the forwarding state.
Forwarding	In this state, the port forwards received frames and processes received BPDUs. Station location information is added to the filtering database. BPDUs are transmitted in this state.

When a bridge or a switch starts up, it transitions through these states. This process can take up to 50 seconds (blocking = 20 seconds, listening to learning = 15 seconds, learning to forwarding = 15 seconds, total = 50 seconds), assuming default parameters for a network diameter of 7.

In Figure 6.16 (before), SW1 is configured with the `set spantree root` command, making this the root switch. SW2 and SW3 have dual paths back to SW1, so either SW2 or SW3 has to place one of its ports in a blocking state to prevent a loop. SW4 has two paths to the root switch via SW2 and SW3. Therefore, spanning tree l puts one of these ports into a blocking state. After spanning tree has run and converged, each switch will have only one path back to the root switch; all other paths will be in a blocking state. Figure 6.16 (after) shows the effective forwarding topology after spanning tree has run and converged.

FIGURE 6.16 Spanning tree (before and after)

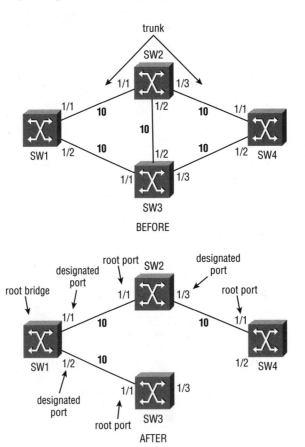

Topology Change Notifications

To shorten the time for possible misrouting of packets after a spanning tree topology change, the 802.1d specification calls for bridges to shorten their filtering database timers to the Forwarding Delay time set by the root bridge. The method for signaling the bridges in the network when to adjust their timers is handled with bits in the Flag portion of the Configuration BPDU and an additional BPDU called a Topology Change Notification (TCN) BPDU, shown in Figure 6.17. The TCN BPDU is much smaller than the Configuration BPDU and does not include as much information.

FIGURE 6.17   Spanning tree TCN BPDU

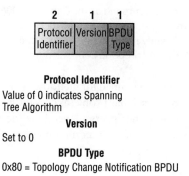

Protocol Identifier
Value of 0 indicates Spanning
Tree Algorithm
Version
Set to 0
BPDU Type
0x80 = Topology Change Notification BPDU

A bridge initially detecting a topology change sends TCN BPDUs out its root port toward the root bridge until it receives a Configuration BPDU with the Acknowledgment bit set from the designated bridge on the segment. The designated bridge follows the same procedure and sends TCN BPDUs until it receives a Configuration BPDU with the TCN Ack bit set. The TCN BPDUs are sent based on the locally configured Hello Timer on the bridge. When the root bridge receives a TCN BPDU, it sets the Topology Change flag and TCN ACK flag in the Config BPDUs it transmits. This forces the bridges to change their filtering database aging timers to the Forwarding Delay value, causing entries to age out faster. After a period of time (Forward Delay + Max Age), the root bridge resets the TCN flag, causing the bridges in the network to revert to using their configured filtering database aging timers.

The TCN process itself does not cause a "recalculation" of the spanning tree but is in turn a product of a change in the spanning tree topology and, as its name implies, signals that there may be instabilities in the network. In some instances, it may be undesirable to have filtering database entries aged prematurely. Therefore, the TCN process should only be used when an actual topology change between bridges is involved. By default, all ports on a bridge generate TCNs when they go up or down.

PortFast and BPDU Guard

PortFast is a proprietary Cisco feature that keeps ports from generating TCNs when they go down or come up. It also causes a port to skip the listening and learning port states when it comes up. PortFast should only be used on ports that are not connecting to other bridges. Although a port configured with PortFast still listens to BPDUs and participates in the spanning tree, because it goes into a forwarding state almost immediately, it may cause a spanning tree loop and overrun the switch's CPU before there is a chance to put the port in a blocking state. Because of this, there is an additional Cisco feature called BPDU Guard that causes a port configured with PortFast to go into an errdisabled state if it receives a BPDU.

The set port host command on the Catalyst 4000/5000/6000s enables PortFast, sets the channel mode to off, sets the trunk mode to off, and disables dot1q tunneling on a port. It significantly reduces the amount of time it takes a port to come up, but it should be used only on ports connected to a single host.

The Spanning-Tree Protocol is often blamed for meltdowns in redundant layer 2 environments. However, it is rare that the protocol itself has problems or is the cause of the problem. More often, bad hardware, cabling, or configuration triggers a layer 2 meltdown, which is termed a spanning tree meltdown. Nevertheless, it is strongly recommended to avoid layer 2 redundancy and design networks with layer 3 redundancy.

Uplink Fast

Uplink Fast is a Cisco-proprietary feature used to reduce the spanning tree convergence time after a direct link failure. It is intended for use by access switches that have no downstream bridge connections and operates by placing an alternate link directly into the forwarding state after the root port has failed, bypassing the listening and learning states. When the root port comes back up, the alternate port does not abdicate its role immediately because the original root port link could fail again or flap. Instead, it waits 2*Forwarding Delay + 5 seconds (35 seconds by default) for the original port to stabilize before switching over. Additionally, Uplink Fast sets the STP bridge priority value to 49152 (0xC000) to help ensure that the switch does not become the root bridge and increases the path cost values on the ports by 3000.

To further enhance network convergence, Uplink Fast sends a packet for each local entry in its CAM table up toward the distribution layer with the source MAC address set to the CAM entry value. This allows the upstream switches to quickly learn the new location of the access switch's devices. These packets use a multicast MAC destination address of 01-00-0C-CD-CD-CD with a type value of 0x200A.

Backbone Fast

Like Uplink Fast, Backbone Fast is a Cisco-proprietary feature used to reduce the spanning tree convergence time after an outage. However, Backbone Fast is designed to deal with indirect failures rather than the direct link failure Uplink Fast handles and, as its name implies, is more suited for switches in the backbone than at the access layer. The theory is to bypass the Max Age timer when the symptoms of a link outage are detected and actively query if the root bridge is still reachable. In the case of Figure 6.16, SW4's designated port is its link to SW2. If SW2's link to the root bridge (SW1) fails, the resultant spanning-tree topology would have SW4 going across its link to SW3 to reach the root bridge. Backbone Fast facilitates the switch to this alternate link by inspecting incoming STP BPDUs.

By the 802.1d standard, if a port receives a BPDU that's inferior to what it currently has stored, the port should discard it if it has heard a Configuration BPDU within Max Age seconds. Backbone Fast allows the switch to compare the root identifier on the received inferior BPDU to what is cached. If they are the same, the switch prepares to choose a new designated port and not wait the Max Age time to discard the current root bridge BPDU.

Before cutting over, the switch sends out special Root Link Query (RLQ) requests. These requests are in the form of Configuration BPDUs except with a different type. If a switch can reach the root bridge, it replies with an RLQ response indicating this. If it cannot, it replies with a negative RLQ response.

Because Backbone Fast uses special PDU packets (RLQ request and replies) to determine root bridge reachability over a path, all switches in the backbone must run Backbone Fast.

 On Cisco switches, there are other factors that add additional port startup delays, including auto-negotiations, PAgP, and DTP. All of these factors combined can cause approx. 27–30 seconds delay, before the port even comes up at a layer 2 level and is seen by STP. When configuring PortFast, configure a DTP mode of nonegotiate and a PAgP mode of off or use the set port host macro. You normally should leave auto-negotiation on for workstation ports.

Spanning Tree Port Priority and Port Cost

It is possible to force a certain switch to perform the role of the root switch for a specific VLAN. This forced election can be accomplished through the use of the set spantree commands. Using the set spantree root command sets the STP priority of the entire switch to 8192; therefore, each unique VLAN SPT will have a priority of 8192. If no VLAN number is specified, then VLAN 1 is the configured VLAN.

Because the Spanning-Tree Protocol uses different costs (port cost, path cost, port priority, etc.) in determining the best path to the root switch, the Catalyst software allows you to manually configure and decide which ports should be in forwarding mode as well as which ports should be in blocking mode. Both port cost and port priority can be changed on a per-port basis or on a per-VLAN basis. Selection of the root switch and the paths to the root switch should be taken into careful consideration before making any changes from the default parameters.

Configuration Commands for the Cat OS–Based Switches: Catalyst 5000

set spantree root 100	Set the switch to the root for VLAN 100
set spantree root 100-200	Set the switch to the root switch for VLANs 100 to 200. This command sets the STP bridge priority to 8192. [default is 32768]

set spantree root secondary 100-200	Set the switch as the backup root bridge switch for VLANs 100-200, in the event that the root fails
set spantree priority 12000 100	Set the spanning tree priority to 12000 for VLAN 100
set spantree portpriority 2/7 31	Set the spanning tree port priority to 31 for port 2/7, the default is 32
set spantree portvlanpriority 2/7 100 31	Set the spanning tree vlan priority for VLAN 100 on port 2/7 to 31, the default is 32. This command applies to trunk ports only
set spantree hello 4 100	Set the BPDU hello timer, the default is 2 [1|10] seconds. This should be consistent across the entire SPF domain
set spantree fwddelay 20 100	Sets the spantree Forward Delay time on VLAN 100 to 20 [4|30. This is the time the switch waits to transition from one STP state (listening) to the STP state (forwarding).]. Default is 15 seconds.
set spantree portfast 2/7-9 enable	Enable PortFast on ports 2/7, 2/8 and 2/9
set spantree portcost 2/7 20	Changes the global port cost of switch port 2/7 to a cost of 20. Ports with lower port costs are more likely to be chosen to forward frames. The default port cost for a port is 19 for FastEthernet

set spantree portvlancost 2/7 22 100-150	This command sets the STP cost of specific VLANs 100-150 on port 2/7 to a cost of 22. You should assign lower numbers to ports attached to faster media. This command applies to trunk ports only
set spantree maxage 10 100	Sets the Maximum age timer to 10 seconds for VLAN 100. This is the time spanning tree will wait to clear its cache and initiate a spanning tree recalculation in the event of a network failure. This command must be constant across the entire SPT domain. The default is 20 seconds. This should be consistent across the entire SPT domain

The following is the output from the **show spantree 100** command:

```
VLAN 100
Spanning tree enabled
Spanning tree type          ieee

Designated Root             00-e0-fe-65-fc-63
Designated Root Priority    8192
Designated Root Cost        0
Designated Root Port        1/0
Root Max Age    20 sec    Hello Time 2  sec   Forward Delay 15 sec

Bridge ID MAC ADDR          00-e0-fe-65-fc-63
Bridge ID Priority          8192
Bridge Max Age 20 sec    Hello Time 2  sec   Forward Delay 15 sec

Port     Vlan Port-State     Cost   Priority Fast-Start Group-Method
-------- ---- ------------- ----- -------- ---------- -----------
 1/1     100  forwarding      19       32   disabled
```

In the preceding output, the SPT VLAN can be seen to be VLAN 100 . It can also be seen that the designated root and the bridge id MAC ADDR are the same, which implies that this bridge is the root bridge. The bridge priority is set to 8192, and the SPT timers are shown. The only port on the Catalyst switch that STP 100 is running is on port 1/1.

The following is the output from the show spantree 1/1 command:

Port	Vlan	Port-State	Cost	Priority	Fast-Start	Group-Method
1/1	1	forwarding	19	32	disabled	
1/1	2	forwarding	19	32	disabled	
1/1	3	forwarding	19	32	disabled	
1/1	100	forwarding	19	32	disabled	
1/1	1003	not-connected	19	32	disabled	
1/1	1005	not-connected	19	4	disabled	

Port 1/1 is a trunk port and STP is being forwarded for VLANs 1–3 and VLAN 100. The port cost for these STP instances is 19, and the port priority is 32.

Configuration Commands for the IOS-Based Switches: Catalyst 3550

spanning-tree vlan 100 root primary	Set the switch to the root for VLAN 100
spanning-tree vlan 100 root secondary	Set the switch as the backup root bridge switch for VLAN 100, in the event that the root fails
spanning-tree vlan 100 hello-time 4	Set the BPDU hello timer, the default is 2 [1|10] seconds. This should be consistent across the entire SPF domain
spanning-tree vlan 100 forward-time 20	Sets the spantree Forward Delay time on VLAN 100 to 20 [4|30. This is the time the switch waits to transition from one STP state (listening) to the STP state (forwarding).]. Default is 15 seconds

`spanning-tree vlan 100 max-age 10`	Sets the Maximum age timer to 10 seconds for VLAN 100. This is the time spanning tree will wait to clear its cache and initiate a spanning tree recalculation in the event of a network failure. This command must be constant across the entire SPF domain. The default is 20 seconds. This should be consistent across the entire SPF domain

`Interface fastethernet 0/14`

`spanning-tree portfast`	Enable PortFast on port 0/14
`spanning-tree cost 20`	Changes the global port cost of switch port 0/14 to a cost of 20. Ports with lower port costs are more likely to be chosen to forward frames. The default port cost for a port is 19 for FastEthernet
`spanning-tree vlan 100 cost 22`	This command sets the STP cost of VLAN 100-150 on port 0/14 to a cost of 22. You should assign lower numbers to ports attached to faster media. This command applies to trunk ports only
`spanning-tree port-priority 31`	Set the spanning tree port priority to 31 for port 0/14. Valid range is 0 to 255. The default is 128
`spanning-tree vlan 100 port-priority 33`	Set the spanning tree vlan priority for VLAN 100 on port 0/14 to 33, the default is 128. This command applies to trunk ports only

Managing the Catalyst Switch

The examples in this section deal with configuring the Catalyst switch to allow both management and configuration access to the switch. Access to the Catalyst switch is provided via two mechanisms: interface SC0 and the Console port. The Catalyst 4000 also has an ME0 Ethernet interface that can be used for out-of-band management. The interface SC0 is an internal management interface that is used to allow IP access to the Catalyst. This interface is assigned an IP address and is assigned to a VLAN within the Catalyst. Once the SC0 is configured, an individual can have Telnet access directly to the Catalyst for management purposes.

The examples in this section deal with both the system and enable passwords as well as the control of access to the Catalyst from an administrative perspective.

Configuration Commands for the Cat OS-Based Switches: Catalyst 5000

`set prompt SW1`	Sets the system prompt to SW1
`set system name SW1`	Sets the system name to SW1; this is the system name that will be retrieved by SNMP
`set system location RTP`	Sets the system location to RTP
`set system contact 24 Hour Operation x5000`	Sets the contact information to 24 HourOperation x5000
`set interface sc0 100 172.16.1.10 255.255.255.0`	Assigns the SC0 interface to VLAN 100 with an IP address of 172.16.1.10 and with a 24 bit network mask
`set ip route 0.0.0.0 172.16.1.100`	Sets the default route (0.0.0.0) for the SC0 to a IP address
`172.16.1.100`	
`set password`	Sets the VTY password to Kyle, the password is case sensitive.

```
        Enter old password:

        Enter new password: Kyle

        retype new password: Kyle
```

set enablepass   Sets the Enable or configuration
                                        password to Katherine, the
                                        password is case sensitive.

    Enter old password:

    Enter new password: Katherine

    retype new password: Katherine

set ip permit enable   Enables restriction of telnet
                                        access to the Catalyst

set ip permit 172.16.1.0 255.255.255.0

                                        Restricts telnet access to the
                                        Catalyst from only hosts on
                                        the 172.16.1.0 "class C"
                                        Subnet.

set ip permit 10.2.25.1 255.255.255.255

                                        Allows a single host, 10.2.25.1
                                        telnet access to the Catalyst.

The following is the output from the show interface command:

```
sl0: flags=51<UP,POINTOPOINT,RUNNING>
        slip 0.0.0.0 dest 0.0.0.0
sc0: flags=63<UP,BROADCAST,RUNNING>
        vlan 100 inet 172.16.1.10 netmask 255.255.255.0 broadcast 172.16.1.255
```

The following is the output from the show system command:

PS-Status	Fan-Status	Temp-Alarm	Sys-Status	Uptime d,h:m:s	Logout
ok	ok	off	ok	0,00:03:22	20 min

Modem	Baud	Traffic	Peak	Peak-Time
disable	9600	0%	0%	Mon Nov 24 2002, 17:04:23

System Name	System Location	System Contact
SW1	RTP	24hr operation x5000

Because the Catalyst is a layer 2 forwarding switch, it is important to be able to look at the MAC forwarding tables. The CAM table is the MAC forwarding table for the Catalyst switch. The CAM table is VLAN specific, and a unique CAM table exists for each VLAN. It is possible to change the amount of time that the CAM entries will remain active in the table. By default, unused CAM entries remain in the CAM table for up to 300 seconds (5 minutes).

Content Addressable Memory (CAM) Tables

set cam agingtime 100 600	Changes the CAM age time from VLAN 100 only from the default 300 seconds, to 600 seconds
show cam dynamic 100	Displays the dynamically learned MAC for VLAN 100

The following is the output from show cam dynamic command:

```
VLAN   Dest MAC/Route Des   Destination Ports or VCs / [Protocol Type]
----   ------------------   ------------------------------------------
100    00-01-46-66-57-d0    1/1                        [ALL]
100    00-01-96-85-d7-20    2/1                        [ALL]
100    00-00-0c-91-9a-e8    2/5                        [ALL]
Total Matching CAM Entries Displayed = 2
```

The output shows a list of all the MAC addresses and the associated catalyst ports to which they are connected. For example, frames received with a MAC address of 00-00-0c-91-9a-e8 will be forwarded out port 2/5 according to the CAM table.

Configuration Commands for the IOS-Based Switches: Catalyst 3550

hostname SW1	Sets the system hostname to "SW1"
snmp-server contact 24 Hour Operation x5000	Sets the contact information to 24 Hour Operation x5000
snmp-server location Colorado	Sets system location to Colorado
enable password Kyle	Sets the VTY password to Kyle password is case sensitive
enable secret Katherine	Sets the Enable or configuration password to Katherine, password is case sensitive
ip default-gateway 172.16.1.100	Sets the default route (0.0.0.0)to IP address 172.16.1.100

```
interface vlan 100

ip address 172.16.1.10 255.255.255.0
```

> Assigns the interface to VLAN 100
> with an IP address of 172.16.1.10
> and a /24 bit mask

 To control Telnet vty access to the switch, you must invoke an access list with the `access-class` command just as is required on a router.

Logging Commands

The Catalyst switch is set up by default to log normal system messages to its internal buffer as well as to the console port. The default level of logging to the console port can be changed, and the level of logging can be configured to send log messages to a System Logging (Syslog) server, buffer, or console. When configuring the logging function, you can configure the facility and the severity of the message processed by the switch. The facility is the switch components such as VTP, CDP, STP, and so on. The severity is the level of message for each of these facilities that will be processed by the switch and sent as a log message. Syslog messages will be covered in Chapter 22, "IP Services".

Configuration Commands for the Cat OS-Based Switches: Catalyst 5000

`set logging server enable`	Enable the logging of console and system message to a log server.
`set logging server 172.16.2.25`	Define the IP address of the logging server.
`set logging level all 4`	Sets the logging for all facilities to level to 4 (warnings) for log messages sent to the logging server. All syslog messages from level 0 through 4 (warnings) will now be sent to the syslog server. The default logging level will vary depending on the facility. The available logging levels options are:

```
Level 0    =    Emergency

Level 1    =    Alert

Level 2    =    Critical
```

Level 3	=	Error
Level 4	=	Warning
Level 5	=	Notification
Level 6	=	Informational
Level 7	=	Debugging

Configuration Commands for the IOS-Based Switches: Catalyst 3550

logging 172.16.2.25	Define the IP address of the logging server
logging console warnings	Sets the logging for all facilities to level to 4 (warnings) for log messages sent to the logging server. All syslog messages from level 0 through 4 (warnings) are now sent to the syslog server. The default logging level varies depending on the facility. The available logging levels options are the same as on the example for the Catalyst 5000 above.

Simple Network Management Protocol (SNMP)

The configuration of SNMP allows for the standard SNMP information to be configured, such as a trap destination(s), SNMP community strings, and contact and location information. The following commands are only a subset of the SNMP set commands but are the most widely used configuration commands.

Configuration Commands for the Cat OS-Based Switches: Catalyst 5000

set snmp community read-only public	Sets the read community string to public
set snmp community read-write private	Sets the read-write community string to private
set snmp community read-write-all private	Sets the read write all community string to private
set snmp trap enable module	Configures the Catalyst to send traps to the SNMP server for all events and traps associated with the modules.

`set snmp trap enable  chassis`	Configures the Catalyst to send traps to the SNMP server for all traps associated with this event (chassis), and trap for the chassis.
`set snmp trap enable  syslog`	Sends all Syslog events to the SNMP trap server
`set snmp trap 172.16.8.15 public`	Sends all traps to a server with IP address of 172.16.8.15 , and sets the community string to "public" in the traps that are sent.

Configuration Commands for the IOS-Based Switches: Catalyst 3550

`snmp-server community public ro`	Sets the read community string name to public
`snmp-server community private rw`	Sets the read-write community string name to private
`snmp-server enable traps`	Sends all Syslog events to the SNMP trap server
`snmp-server host 172.16.8.15 traps public`	Sends all traps to a server with IP address of 172.16.8.15, and sets the community string to public in the traps that are sent.

SPAN and RSPAN

SPAN and RSPAN are features used to direct traffic from a single port, series of ports, or an entire VLAN to a single port for monitoring and/or troubleshooting purposes. SPAN is used on a single switch and copies traffic from the source port(s)/VLAN to a destination port. The traffic monitored can be ingress traffic (packets coming into the source ports/VLAN), egress traffic (packets being sent out the source ports/VLAN), or both.

SPAN and RSPAN do not interfere with normal switch operation but do have a few limitations. BPDUs are not copied, the destination port cannot be part of an EtherChannel and does not participate in the spanning tree, and the output traffic of an entire VLAN cannot be monitored. Also note that if a SPAN or RSPAN destination port is configured as a trunk port, the configured encapsulation method (ISL or 802.1q) will be used regardless of what the SPAN'ed port's encapsulation is. A Catalyst 5000 supports five SPAN sessions and does not support RSPAN, while the 3550 supports SPAN and RSPAN but only two sessions.

The next two examples illustrate configuring SPAN and RSPAN on the Catalyst 5000 and Catalyst 3550.

SPAN Configuration Commands for the Cat OS-Based Switches: Catalyst 5000

```
set span enable                  Enables SPAN on the Catalyst Switch

set span 2/8 2/5 both            Configures SPAN so that all traffic (rx and
                                 tx) to/from port 2/8 is copied to and sent
                                 out monitor port 2/5
```

The following is the output of a show span:

```
sw1 (enable) sh span
Status          : enabled
Admin Source    : 2/8
Oper Source     : Port 2/8
Destination     : Port 2/5
Direction       : transmit/receive
Incoming Packets: disabled
```

The output shows that the probe is connected to 2/5 and that port 2/8 is configured as a source and is also operational. The output also shows that incoming packets are disabled on the destination port. The inpkts enable optional parameter on the set span command enables the switch to process incoming packets from the destination port; however, this is rarely needed and cautioned against.

Configuration Commands for the IOS-Based Switches: Catalyst 3550

```
monitor session 1 source interface
fastethernet 0/19

                                 Configures SPAN such that all traffic
                                 from port 0/19 is SPAN'd to the
                                 destination interface

monitor session 1 destination
interface fastethernet 0/23

                                 Configures SPAN such that all
                                 captured traffic is spanned to the
                                 destination interface 0/23
```

The following is the output of a show monitor command:

```
Session 1
---------
 Type          : Local Session
```

```
Source Ports:
    RX Only:          None
    TX Only:          None
    Both:             Fa0/19
Source VLANs:
    RX Only:          None
    TX Only:          None
    Both:             None
Source RSPAN VLAN: None
Destination Ports: Fa0/23
    Encapsulation: Native
Reflector Port:    None
Filter VLANs:      None
Dest RSPAN VLAN:   None
```

Additional Functionality of the Catalyst 3550 Switch

The following sections detail some additional layer 2 and layer 3 features on the 3550 switch you should be aware of, including controlling the boot process, UDLD, and BPDU Root Guard.

Layer 2 Functionality

First, we'll briefly discuss the how to control the boot process for the Catalyst 3550. If you have multiple IOS versions loaded on the Catalyst 3550 switch, then you must specify which IOS version the switch should boot up with. If you are used to dealing with routers, you are probably used to using the boot system flash: command. Then you are able to view the command in the running configuration file.

Well, on the Catalyst 3550 the process is a little different. You must enter the boot system flash: command just as you did in the router, but you will not see the command in the configuration file. Instead, you must use the show boot command to view which IOS image the switch will boot up on.

The following is the output of a boot system flash:c3550-i5q3l2-mz.121-11.EA1.bin command:

```
Switch#show boot
BOOT path-list:        flash:c3550-i5q3l2-mz.121-11.EA1.bin
Config file:           flash:config.text
Private Config file:   flash:private-config.text
Enable Break:          no
Manual Boot:           no
HELPER path-list:
NVRAM/Config file
    buffer size:       393216
```

UniDirectional Link Detection (UDLD) is a layer 2 protocol that enables devices connected through fiber-optic or twisted-pair Ethernet cables to monitor the physical configuration of the cables and detect when a unidirectional link exists. When UDLD detects a unidirectional link, it administratively shuts down the affected port and notifies you. The following are the commands to implement UDLD:

```
udld enable                     Enable UDLD on all fiber-optic interfaces, it
                                is disabled by default


interface vlan 100
  udld enable                   Enable UDLD on this specific interface
```

Bridge Protocol Data Unit (BPDU) Guard can be implemented globally or on a per-interface basis.

At the global level, you can implement BPDU Guard on PortFast-enabled ports by using the `spanning-tree portfast bpduguard default` global command. PortFast-enabled ports should not receive BPDUs. Receiving a BPDU on a PortFast-enabled port signals an invalid configuration, such as the connection of an unauthorized device, and the BPDU Guard feature will put the port into the error-disabled state.

At the interface level, you can implement BPDU Guard on any port using the `spanning-tree bpduguard enable` command without also enabling the PortFast feature.

Layer 3 Functionality

Since the Catalyst 3550 is a multilayer switch, it provides not only the traditional layer 2 functions of a Catalyst switch but also many of the same features a Cisco router provides:

- IP routing using Routing Information Protocol (RIP), Interior Gateway Routing Protocol (IGRP), Enhanced Interior Gateway Routing Protocol (EIGRP), Open Shortest Path First (OSPF), and Border Gateway Protocol (BGP)
- Hot Standby Router Protocol (HSRP)
- ICMP Router Discovery protocol (IRDP)
- IP multicasting
- Quality of service (QoS)

IP ROUTING

Layer 3 IP routing can be implemented on a physical port (configured as a layer 3 port with the `no switchport` command) or a Switched Virtual Interface (SVI), which is a VLAN interface created with the `interface vlan vlan-id` command. Then the global `ip routing` command must be configured.

All the layer 3 IP routing functionality is implemented in the Catalyst 3550 using the same CLI commands that are used to configure a Cisco router. Refer to the appropriate chapter of this book to reference the correct commands required to configure the desired layer 3 functionality.

QUALITY OF SERVICE (QOS)

Packet classification and marking can be done at layer 2 on the 3550. The following is a quick example of how to set the 802.1p CoS value on incoming packets on an interface:

```
interface fastethernet 0/6
```

switchport priority extend cos	set the 802.1p CoS value to 4 on incoming packets overriding what is currently on the packets.

Just as with routers, you can configure queuing methods on the Catalyst 3550 utilizing policy maps containing multiple class maps to classify traffic. In conjunction with the class maps, you can also use route maps to identify and change the IP Precedence and DSCP values. Queuing techniques and classification will be discussed in Chapter 18.

Troubleshooting the Catalyst Switch

The following commands are useful when troubleshooting problems with the Catalyst switch.

Configuration Commands for the Cat OS-Based Switches: Catalyst 5000

show vtp domain	Display VTP configuration information
show vlan	Displays VLAN information
show port	There are multiple options that can be added to this command to get more specific information
show cam dynamic 222	Displays the MAC address table for VLAN 222
show logging buffers	Displays the logging level set on the switch
show spantree	Displays spanning tree information, optional extensions allow you to view specific information about VLANs and ports.

Configuration Commands for the IOS-Based Switches: Catalyst 3550

`show controllers cpu-interface`	Show the state of the CPU, and send/receive packets reaching the cpu
`show controllers ethernet-controller`	Display trasmit/receive statistics per interface
`show vtp`	Shows information about VTP – management domain, status, and counters
`show vlan`	Displays all configured VLANs
`show interface`	Shows Administrative and operational status of all interfaces
`show mac-address-table`	Shows the MAC address table, both static and dynamic entries
`show spanning-tree`	Displays spanning-tree information

Summary

In this chapter, we provided you with an introduction to the many different Ethernet technologies used today in an internetwork, including 10, 100, and 1000Mbps Ethernet. We discussed the origins of Ethernet and its progress through Gigabit Ethernet. Wireless 802.11b was also introduced in this chapter.

The Catalyst switch is a core component in any campus environment, and a strong understanding of its operations is needed. Spanning tree is one area that you should thoroughly understand. It is a key component in a layer 2 switching environment, and although spanning tree appears to be a relatively simple protocol, it is often overlooked and misunderstood. We will see spanning tree again when it raises its ugly head again in Chapter 14, "Bridging and Data Link Switching," so it is best to get a firm understanding of its operation.

In addition to knowing how to properly configure the Ethernet switches for multiple VLANs, you must be comfortable in configuring VTP and trunking. Hopefully, you now have a better understanding of those topics.

The final part of this chapter was dedicated to explaining both the Catalyst OS (as implemented in a Catalyst 5000) and the IOS (as implemented in a Catalyst 3550) and how to set up the lab switches for basic operation.

Exam Essentials

Know that Ethernet uses Carrier Sense Multiple Access with Collision Detection (CSMA/CD) and how it works.   The CSMA/CD protocol works like this: When a host wants to transmit over the network, it first checks for the presence of a digital signal on the wire. If all is clear (if no other host is transmitting), the host will then proceed with its transmission. And it doesn't stop there. The transmitting host constantly monitors the wire to make sure that no other hosts begin transmitting. If the host detects a special voltage change on the wire, indicating that a collision has occurred, it sends out an extended jam signal that causes all nodes on the segment to stop sending data. The nodes respond to that jam signal by waiting a random amount of time before attempting to transmit again. If after 15 tries collisions continue to occur, the nodes attempting to transmit will time out.

Know what an Ethernet address or MAC address is.   Ethernet addressing uses the MAC address burned into each and every Ethernet network interface card (NIC). The MAC address, sometimes referred to as a hardware address, is a 48-bit (displayed in hexadecimal) address written in a canonical format to ensure that addresses are at least written in the same format, even if different LAN technologies are used.

Understand VTP.   In a LAN switch trunking environment, the Virtual Trunking Protocol (VTP) enables central control of which VLANs are allowed to be trunked. Switches can be configured in either VTP server, client, or transparent mode. In server mode, the switch is responsible for maintaining the list of trunked VLANs and propagating this information to the other switches in the domain. A switch in VTP client mode requests VLAN trunk information from the server upon boot-up. A switch in VTP transparent mode learns trunked VLANs from its own configuration but will pass along VTP messages between servers and clients. VTP pruning is a feature that allows switches that have no ports in a particular VLAN and no connections to downstream switches with ports in that VLAN to remove the VLAN from its trunk ports.

Know what a Wireless LAN is.   Wireless LANs (WLANs) provide the capability to access internetworking resources without having to be wired to the network. Some of the functionality that WLANs provide are inside-building access, LAN extension, and outside building-to-building communications.

Understand the difference between ISL and 802.1q trunking.   ISL tags each frame to identify the VLAN it belongs to. The tag is a 30-byte header and CRC that is added around the FE frame. The IEEE 802.1q standard trunks VLANs over FE and GE interfaces and can be used in a multivendor environment. Cisco's implementation of 802.1q uses one instance of STP for each VLAN allowed in the trunk. Similar to ISL, 802.1q uses a tag on each frame with a VLAN identifier. Unlike ISL, 802.1q uses a 4-byte internal tag, which is inserted after the source MAC address.

Know what the Spanning-Tree Protocol (STP) is.   Spanning-Tree Protocol (STP) is a layer 2 protocol that runs on bridges and switches to provide a loop-free network when there are redundant layer 2 paths in the network.

Key Terms

Before you take the exam, be certain you are familiar with the following terms:

binary exponential backoff algorithm	full-duplex Ethernet
broadcast	half-duplex Ethernet
Carrier Sense Multiple Access with Collision Detection (CSMA/CD)	Organizationally Unique Identifier (OUI)
frames	Wireless LANs (WLANs)

Review Questions

1. What type of Ethernet frame uses a Type field?

    A. 802.2

    B. SNAP

    C. Ethernet II

    D. 802.3

2. Which technology allows Ethernet segments up to 185 meters using 50 ohms? (Choose all that apply.)

    A. 10Base2

    B. Thicknet

    C. 10Base5

    D. Thinnet

3. How many bits make up a MAC address?

    A. 24

    B. 48

    C. 94

    D. 96

4. What was created to overcome the problem of collisions that occur when packets are transmitted simultaneously from different nodes? (Choose all that apply.)

    A. Collision detection and jamming patterns

    B. CSMA/CD

    C. TCP/IP

    D. Ethernet

5. In a MAC address, how many bits does the IEEE assign?

    A. 24

    B. 48

    C. 94

    D. 96

6. Which of the following is true regarding half-duplex Ethernet?

   A. Uses a point-to-point connection between the transmitter of the transmitting station and the receiver of the receiving station

   B. Uses a single cable similar to a narrow one-way-bridge road

   C. Is not compatible with 100Base-T

   D. Works only with Cisco switches

7. Gigabit Ethernet 802.3z utilizes which type of coding?

   A. 4B/5B

   B. 8B/6T

   C. 8B/10B

   D. 10B/6T

8. The IEEE 802.11b standard provides speeds of 11, 5.5, 2, and 1Mbps and uses what type of frequency management?

   A. DSSS

   B. BSSS

   C. FHSS

   D. FDSS

9. Which trunking protocol efficiently inserts a 4-byte tag after the Source Address field (before the Type/Length field) of Ethernet frames.

   A. 802.1q

   B. 802.1d

   C. ISL

   D. VTP

10. What mechanism does Spanning-Tree Protocol (STP) use to detect and prevent possible loops in the network. This mechanism contains parameters that the switches use in the selection process for electing the root bridge/switch?

   A. Hello

   B. CDP

   C. HSRP

   D. BPDU

Answers to Review Questions

1. C. The Ethernet II standard uses a Type field to identify the Network layer protocol.

2. A, D. 10Base2 and Thinnet are the same thing. 10Base means 10Mbps of baseband technology.

3. B. A MAC address is 6 bytes, or 48 bits, long.

4. A, B. Collision detection and jamming patterns are used within the CSMA/CD protocol to control collisions in a network segment.

5. A. A MAC address is 6 bytes (48 bits) long. The IEEE assigns the first 3 bytes to the manufacturer.

6. B. Half-duplex is one twisted-pair wire in which the signal travels in both directions down the wire, but just one direction at a time.

7. C. Gigabit Ethernet 802.3z utilizes 8B/10B coding with simple NRZ, which encodes each 8-bit word (byte) as a 10-bit symbol.

8. A. IEEE 802.11b uses DSSS and is backward compatible with 802.11 systems that use DSSS.

9. A. ISL tags each frame to identify the VLAN it belongs to. The tag is a 30-byte header and CRC that is added around the FE frame. This includes a 26-byte header and 4-byte CRC. The IEEE 802.1q standard inserts a 4-byte tag after the Source Address field (before the Type/Length field) of Ethernet frames.

10. D. Spanning-Tree Protocol (STP) uses bridge protocol data units (BPDUs) to detect and prevent possible loops in the network. BPDUs contain parameters that the switches use in the selection process for electing the root bridge/switch.

Chapter 7

Building the Layer 2 Network

This chapter is a little different than the previous chapters because is not really aimed at preparation for the qualification exam. It is instead meant to be preparation for the lab examination and a day-to-day layer 2 environment reference.

Because this chapter does not directly focus on qualification exam preparation, we will not be specifying specific chapter objectives as they relate to the qualification exam; likewise, the end of the chapter will not include the regular exam essentials or questions.

For those of you who want to tackle both the written exam and the lab exam, this chapter takes what you've learned thus far and applies it in practice in a way that's consistent with how you'll be tested during the lab examination. For those of you focusing solely on the written exam (and isn't that a big enough hurdle?!), this chapter will serve as an exercise, building on what you've learned thus far. It will help you solidify the concepts and you'll see examples of how these protocols work in the real world.

In this chapter, you will use the layer 2 technologies discussed in the previous chapters to build configuration examples. The wording in the configuration examples may appear to be somewhat abstract, but this is intentional. The wording of the questions in a CCIE lab examination are also not straightforward. The wording will require you to analyze and derive a specific solution based on what is and is not stated because this will test your understanding of the technologies.

Getting the layer 2 infrastructure working correctly is an absolute must, and it must be 100-percent correct because all other technologies (routing, bridging, ISDN) will run on top of it. This point can never be stressed enough.

Knowing that layer 2 is working as it should be is important; therefore, you need to have a strategy for testing it and verifying that everything is working. If it is not working as expected, there is most likely a reason, and you must not move on until you resolve the problem or understand why it is happening. Leaving the problem unresolved will only cloud the issue when routing protocols are configured on top of the network.

To make troubleshooting easier, wherever possible router R1 will have all of its interfaces configured with dot 1 (.1) IP addresses, router R2 will have all of its interfaces configured with .2 IP addresses, and so on. This numbering scheme will be continued to all routers in the scenario to help standardize the configurations.

If you are preparing for the CCIE lab examination, it is crucial that you get as much time/experience on actual routers/switches as possible. If you are not able to physically get access to routers and switches, then it is a good idea to gain access to an equipment rack via Internet access. There are many websites that offer web and/or telnet access to routers and switches, usually on a pay-per-hour basis.

Now we'll take a look at the list of equipment that we used to develop these hands-on lab scenarios.

Lab Equipment List

Table 7.1 lists the equipment we used in our test rack to develop and verify the hands-on lab scenarios in this book:

TABLE 7.1   Test Rack Lab Equipment

Router	Model and interface type	Memory and interface name
R1	Cisco 2610 Router	48MB DRAM/16MB FLASH
	12.1.5 Enterprise Plus IPSEC 56	
	1 Ethernet	E0/0
	1 Serial WIC	S0/0
	1 ISDN BRI WIC	BRI0/0
R2	Cisco 3640 Router	64MB DRAM/32MB FLASH
	12.1.7 Enterprise Plus	
	1 FastEthernet	Fa0/0
	1 Serial WIC	S0/0
	1 ISDN BRI WIC	BRI0/0
	2 FXS VWIC	Voice-port1/0, Voice-port1/1
	1 ATM OC-3	ATM3/0
R3	Cisco 2501 Router	16MB DRAM/16MB FLASH
	12.1.5 Enterprise Plus IPSEC 56	
	1 Ethernet	E0
	2 Serial	S0, S1
R4	Cisco 2501 Router	16MB DRAM/16MB FLASH
	12.1.5 Enterprise Plus	

T A B L E   7 . 1   Test Rack Lab Equipment *(continued)*

Router	Model and interface type	Memory and interface name
	1 Ethernet	E0
	2 Serial	S0, S1
R5	Cisco 2620 Router	64MB DRAM/32MB FLASH
	12.1.5 Enterprise Plus	
	1 FastEthernet	Fa0/0
	1 Serial WIC	S0/0
	1 NM-2V, 2 FXS VWIC, 1 FXO VWIC	Voice-port1/0, Voice-port1/1, Voice-port1/2
R6	Cisco 2610 Router	48MB DRAM/16MB FLASH
	12.1.5 Enterprise Plus	
	1 Ethernet	E0/0
	1 Serial WIC	S0/0
S1	Cisco Catalyst 3550-24 Switch	64MB DRAM/16MB FLASH
	12.1.11.EA1 (EMI version)	
	2-port Gigabit Ethernet based on Gigabit Interface Converter (GBIC)	
	24-port 10/100Base-TX Ethernet	

We also used an additional separate router as our Frame-Relay switch (FS). The equipment used for it is listed in Table 7.2.

T A B L E   7 . 2   Frame Relay Switch

Router	Model and interface type	Memory and interface name
FS	Cisco 2522 Router	16MB DRAM/16MB FLASH
	12.1.5 Enterprise Plus	

TABLE 7.2   Frame Relay Switch *(continued)*

Router	Model and interface type	Memory and interface name
	1 Ethernet	E0
	10 Serial	S0, S1, S2, S3, S4, S5, S6, S7, S8, S9

Table 7.3 lists additional equipment that we used to fully develop the scenarios; however, you do not actually need them to complete the scenarios.

TABLE 7.3   Additional Test Rack Lab Equipment

Equipment type	Description
Terminal Access Server (TAS)	Cisco 2511 Router with 16 asynchronous ports
ATM Switch	Cisco LightStream 1010 with ATM OC-3 interfaces
ISDN Simulator Switch	Adtran Atlas 550 with 4-port BRI-U

As we stated in the beginning of this book, please keep in mind that within each chapter you are provided with partial router configurations, but they are not meant to be actual real-world router configurations; they are only intended to show the possible commands that can be implemented and to provide a short description of the purpose of each command. Some of the various commands that you will see within a configuration would never be implemented at the same time on a single router or even a single interface. However, within this book, they may be displayed together only as a means of showing the various commands within the fewest numbers of pages possible.

Likewise, the scenarios that we have developed for this book are by no means presented as real-world best practices. These scenarios have been designed to challenge you in as many aspects of the specified technologies as possible; they are intended to test your comprehension of the material and to aid you in your own self-assessment as you progress through this book. Hopefully, the scenarios are helpful in your preparation for the CCIE lab examination and within the day-to-day duties of your real-world job. So, please remember that we do not recommend configuring your live network as we have done in the scenarios. Once again, these scenarios have been developed for this book to allow us to present as many complex routing and switching technology issues as possible.

Try to build these scenarios before reading the solutions. This chapter is intended to test your knowledge of layer 2 protocols. CCIE candidates must remember that 99-percent right is 100-percent wrong; there is no partial credit. If either the tasks themselves or the solution presented does not make sense, stop, investigate the problem, and do not move on until you have a firm understanding of the problem and the solution.

Layer 2 Configuration Task 2.1

The first scenario that we will attempt is based on all the layer 2 technologies that have been presented to you in the previous chapters of this book. Figure 7.1 shows the layer 2 layout that must be built.

FIGURE 7.1 Network diagram for Task 2.1

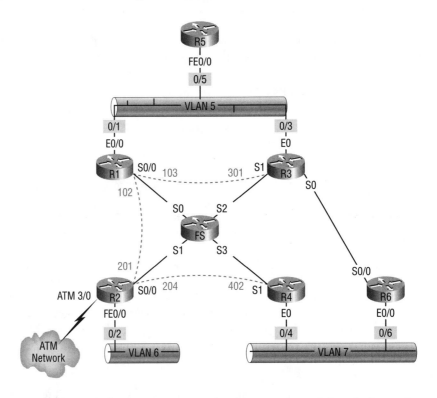

The following list includes the requirements for this scenario, and the solution to the scenario is presented in the next section. As stated earlier, try to complete the scenario without looking at the solution and then review the solution to gauge your comprehension of the material presented thus far in the book. Here are the requirements:

- Configure the Frame Relay switch (FS) with PVC mapping between routers R1, R2, R3, and R4, as shown in Figure 7.1. The FS will be the DCE for all Frame Relay connections.

- Configure R1, R2, and R4 in a hub-and-spoke configuration, using network 10.1.1.0/24 and configuring R2 as the hub router. Provide spoke-to-spoke connectivity. R2 must not be configured with a subinterface.

- Configure R1 and R3 as a Frame Relay point-to-point connection using network 10.1.2.0/24.

- Configure the link between R3 and R6 as a point-to-point using HDLC. Use network 10.1.20.0/24. R3 is the DCE end.

- Configure R2 to connect to a remote router using a PVC connection over the ATM interface (you cannot use Inverse ARP for layer 3 address resolution). Use network 10.1.21.0/24. R2 will connect to the remote router using VPI 10 and VCI 55; the IP address of the remote router is 10.1.21.9.

- Configure VLAN 5 on the Catalyst S1; connect R1, R3, and R5 to VLAN 5. Configure R5 to use ISL trunking to connect to VLAN 5. Use network 10.1.3.0/24.

- Configure VLAN 6 on the Catalyst S1; connect R2 to this VLAN. Use network 10.1.16.0/25.

- Configure VLAN 7 on the Catalyst S1; connect R4 and R6 to VLAN 7. Use network 10.1.17.0/25.

- Ensure that all Catalyst switch ports have fixed port speeds and duplex settings. Configure the Catalyst S1 interface VLAN 6 to use IP address 10.1.16.100.

Solution 2.1: Frame Relay Switch (FS) Configuration

The Frame Relay switch (FS) configuration requires the following configuration commands. Remember, when configuring a Frame Relay PVC, both ends of the PVC must be mapped and all PVCs are locally significant.

Configuration for Router FS

The FS configuration is listed here. Remember to perform a no shutdown command on all interfaces:

`frame-relay switching`	Enables the router to perform frame relay switching
`interface Serial0`	Connected to R1
`encapsulation frame-relay`	Set the Encapsulation as frame relay, The default encapsulation is Cisco, the other frame relay encapsulation option is IETF.
`frame-relay intf-type dce`	Required on the DCE Serial interface
`clockrate 128000`	Required on the DCE Serial interface. When configuring a router clock rate 128000 (two separate words) command is used to configure the router, but when the show run command is used to display the router configuration, the command will appear as clockrate 128000 (all one word).

```
frame-relay route 102 interface Serial 1 201    Map local DLCI 102 to Serial
                                                 port S1 DLCI 201

frame-relay route 103 interface Serial 2 301    Map local DLCI 103 to Serial
                                                 port S2 DLCI 301


interface Serial1                               Connected to R2

  encapsulation frame-relay

  frame-relay intf-type dce

  clockrate 128000

  frame-relay route 201 interface Serial 0 102  Map local DLCI 201 to Serial
                                                 port S0 DLCI 102

  frame-relay route 204 interface Serial 3 402  Map local DLCI 204 to Serial
                                                 port S3 DLCI 402


interface Serial2                               Connected to R3

  encapsulation frame-relay

  frame-relay intf-type dce

  clockrate 128000

  frame-relay route 301 interface Serial 0 103  Map local DLCI 301 to Serial
                                                 port S0 DLCI 103


interface Serial3                               Connected to R4

  encapsulation frame-relay

  frame-relay intf-type dce

  clockrate 128000

  frame-relay route 402 interface Serial 1 204  Map local DLCI 402 to Serial
                                                 port S1 DLCI 204
```

The following is the output from a show frame-relay route command:

Input Intf	Input Dlci	Output Intf	Output Dlci	Status
Serial1	201	Serial0	102	inactive
Serial1	204	Serial3	402	inactive

Serial0	102	Serial1	201	inactive
Serial0	103	Serial2	301	inactive
Serial3	402	Serial1	204	inactive
Serial2	301	Serial0	103	inactive

Solution 2.1: Router Configurations

In this section, we'll discuss the required router configurations for each of the routers to fulfill the requirements for Task 2.1. Remember to perform a no shutdown command on all interfaces.

Router R1 Configuration

Router R1 must be configured with two subinterfaces, one subinterface for the hub and spoke, the other for the point-to-point connection to R3. R1 will be configured as a spoke router on the Frame Relay hub-and-spoke scenario. Inverse ARP is enabled on a multipoint subinterface by default, but to provide spoke-to-spoke connectivity, it will need frame-relay map commands to both the R4 and R2.

The second subinterface on R1 is configured as a point-to-point network and needs a frame-relay interface-dlci command to map to R3. Router R1 also needs interface Ethernet E0 configured for network 10.1.3.0/24:

interface Serial0/0	Connected to FS Serial 0
Encapsulation frame-relay	Set the encapsulation as frame relay. No frame relay LMI statements need to be configured, as the router will auto sense the LMI type from the frame relay switch
interface Serial0/0.1 multipoint	Add sub-interface Serial 0/0.1 as a multipoint
ip address 10.1.1.1 255.255.255.0	
bandwidth 128	Inverse-arp is enabled on a multipoint sub-interface. But to provide spoke-to- spoke connectivity frame-relay map commands must be used
frame-relay map ip 10.1.1.2 102 broadcast	Map IP address to Hub R2 to local DLCI 102
frame-relay map ip 10.1.1.4 102 broadcast	Map IP address to Spoke R4 to local DLCI 102

```
                               Broadcast, is needed to
                               specify that broadcast
                               traffic will be sent
                               over this PVC, this is a
                               must when using routing
                               protocols such as RIP,
                               IGRP, EIGRP or OSPF.

interface Serial0/0.2 point-to-point      Add Sub-Interface Serial 0/0.2
                                           point-to-point

 ip address 10.1.2.1 255.255.255.0

 frame-relay interface-dlci 103            Assign Local DLCI 103 to this
                                           interface, for connection to
                                           router R3

 bandwidth 128

interface Ethernet0/0                      Ethernet interface is connected
                                           to Catalyst S1 port 0/1

 ip address 10.1.3.1 255.255.255.0
```

Here is the output of a show frame-relay map command:

```
Serial0/0.1 (down): ip 10.1.1.2 dlci 102(0x66,0x1860), static,
    broadcast, CISCO, status defined, inactive
Serial0/0.1 (down): ip 10.1.1.4 dlci 102(0x66,0x1860), static,
    broadcast, CISCO, status defined, inactive
Serial0/0.2 (down): point-to-point dlci, dlci 103(0x67,0x1870),
    broadcast, status defined, inactive
```

This output shows the static mapping under subinterface 0/0.2 and shows the point-to-point connection assigned to DLCI 103. The reason that the PVC also shows (down) is because the other end of the connections on R2, R3, and R4 are not yet configured.

Router R2 Configuration

Router R2 is the configured as the hub router in the hub-and-spoke network. R2 must be configured to use the physical interfaces. Because R2 is configured as the hub, it will dynamically learn the IP addresses of both R1 and R4. No frame-relay map commands are needed. R2 needs to have its ATM interface configured to connect to network 10.1.21.0/24. Remember that you cannot use Inverse ARP for layer 3 address resolution for the ATM PVC, so for this task to be completed, an ATM PVC needs to be configured and a map-group needs to be applied to the ATM interface. The map-list is used to map the remote router to the configured ATM PVC. R2 also needs to have interface FastEthernet0 configured to connect to network 10.1.16.0/25.

```
interface Serial0/0                    Connected to FS Serial 1

  encapsulation frame-relay            On a physical interface, inverse
                                       -arp is automatically enabled,
                                       the router will dynamically learn
                                       the addresses of the spokes using
                                       inverse arp, no frame-relay map
                                       commands are needed on R2

  ip address 10.1.1.2 255.255.255.0

  bandwidth 128

interface FastEthernet0/0              Interface FastEthernet is
                                       connected to port 0/2 on VLAN 6
                                       of the Catalyst S1

  ip address 10.1.16.2 255.255.255.128

interface ATM3/0                       Connected to Remote ATM switch

  ip address 10.1.21.2 255.255.255.0

  atm pvc 1 10 55 aal5snap             Define ATM PVC#1 with a VPI 10
                                       and VCI 55, uses aal5snap as the
                                       encapsulation mechanism

  map-group kelly                      Assigns a map group of kelly to
                                       this ATM interface

map-list kelly                         Creates a ATM map list called kelly

  ip 10.1.21.9 atm-vc 1 broadcast      Configures a ATM mapping for IP
                                       address 10.1.21.9 to ATM PVC#1
```

The following command is the output of a show frame-relay map command:

```
Serial0/0 (up): ip 10.1.1.1 dlci 201(0xC9,0x3090), dynamic,
            broadcast,, status defined, Active
Serial0/0 (up): ip 10.1.1.4 dlci 204(0xCC,0x30C0), dynamic,
            broadcast,, status defined, Active
```

This shows that the hub router R2 has dynamically learned the IP address of the both spokes routers R1 and R4. The following is the output of the show atm vc command:

Interface	VCD	VPI	VCI	Type	AAL/Encapsulation	Peak Kbps	Avg. Kbps	Burst Cells	Status
ATM3/0	1	10	55	PVC	AAL5-SNAP	155000	155000	94	Active

Router R3 Configuration

Router R3 is connected to R1 with via the Frame Relay network. R3 will dynamically learn the IP address of R1. No `frame-relay map` commands are needed.

Router R3 is also connected to R6 via an HDLC point-to-point. R3 is the DCE and therefore must provide clocking. R3's Ethernet interface is also configured to connect to network 10.1.3.0/24:

`interface Serial0`	Connected to Router R6
`ip address 10.1.20.3 255.255.255.0`	
	No encapsulation protocol needs to be specified as the default for a Serial Interface is HDLC. The DCE end of the cable must be connected to interface Serial 0
`clockrate 128000`	Clock rate must be specified on the DCE
`bandwidth 128`	
`interface Serial1`	Connected to FS Serial 2
`ip address 10.1.2.3 255.255.255.0`	
`encapsulation frame-relay`	Set encapsulation to frame relay
`bandwidth 128`	
`interface Ethernet0`	Interface Ethernet0 is connected to port 0/3 on VLAN 5 of the Catalyst S1
`ip address 10.1.3.3 255.255.255.0`	

Router R4 Configuration

Router R4 is the second spoke router in the hub-and-spoke network. For the network to provide spoke-to-spoke connectivity, R4 will need `frame-relay map` commands to connect to both R1 and R2. R4's Ethernet interface also needs to be configured to connect to network 10.1.17.0/25:

`interface Serial1`	Connected to FS Serial 3
`encapsulation frame-relay`	
`ip address 10.1.1.4 255.255.255.0`	
`frame-relay map ip 10.1.1.1 402 broadcast`	Map to the IP address of Spoke R1
`frame-relay map ip 10.1.1.2 402 broadcast`	Map to the IP address of Hub R2
`bandwidth 128`	

```
interface Ethernet0                    Interface Ethernet0 is
                                       connected to port 0/4 on
                                       VLAN 7 of the Catalyst S1

 ip address 10.1.17.4 255.255.255.128
```

Router R5 Configuration

Router R5 is connected to network 10.1.3.0/24, but it must be configured as an ISL trunk port. To configure the router to support ISL trunking, no IP address is configured under the physical interface but a Fast Ethernet subinterface must be configured. Under the subinterface, the encapsulation (ISL) must be specified, and the VLAN number that the subinterface is assigned to must also be specified.

The IP address associated with the VLAN is then configured under the subinterface. To support the ISL router connection, the Catalyst S1 port that this router is connected to must also be configured as an ISL trunk port:

```
interface FastEthernet0/0     Interface Fast Ethernet is connected to port
                              0/5 on the Catalyst S1. Note, no IP Address
                              is configured on the physical interface

interface FastEthernet0/0.5   A sub-interface is defined, it is not required
                              to have the sub-interface and the VLAN number
                              the same.

 encapsulation isl 5          ISL encapsulation is specified, and the assoc-
                              iated VLAN with this sub-interface is VLAN 5

 ip address 10.1.3.5 255.255.255.0
```

Router R6 Configuration

Router R6's serial interface is configured for HDLC and is connected to R3 using network 10.1.20.0/24. R6's Ethernet is connected to network 10.1.17.0/25:

```
interface Serial0             Connected to Router R3

                              No encapsulation protocol needs to be spec-
                              ified as the default for a Serial Interface
                              is HDLC. This the the DTE end of the cable

 ip address 10.1.20.6 255.255.255.0

 bandwidth 128

interface Ethernet0           Interface Ethernet is connected to port
                              0/6 on VLAN 7 of the Catalyst S1

 ip address 10.1.17.6 255.255.255.128
```

Solution 2.1: Catalyst Switch Configuration

In this section, we will discuss the required switch configuration for each of the routers to fulfill the requirements for Task 2.1.

Switch S1 Configuration

The Catalyst switch (S1) must be configured to support VLANs 5, 6, and 7. For the VTP/VLAN configuration, you need to be in vlan database mode, not in config mode. Port 0/5, which is connected to router R5, must be configured with ISL trunking. Once port 0/5 is configured as a trunk port, this port cannot be added to a specific VLAN 5. Ports 0/1 and 0/3 need to be added to VLAN 5. Port 0/2 needs to be added to VLAN 6. Ports 0/4 and 0/6 need to be added to VLAN 7. All switch ports need to be configured for port speed and duplex:

`vtp mode transparent`	Set the VTP mode of this specific switch to transparent [server|client|transparent]
`vlan 5`	Create VLAN 5
`  name VLAN5`	Set the name to VLAN5
`vlan 6`	Create VLAN 6
`  name VLAN6`	Set the name to VLAN6
`vlan 7`	Create VLAN 7
`  name VLAN7`	Set the name to VLAN7
`interface FastEthernet0/1`	
`  switchport access vlan 5`	Assign FastEthernet0/1 to VLAN 5
`  duplex full`	Set the port to full duplex
`  speed 100`	Set the port to 100 Mbps
`interface FastEthernet0/2`	
`  switchport access vlan 6`	Assign FastEthernet0/2 to VLAN 6
`  duplex full`	Set the port to full duplex

speed 100	Set the port to 100 Mbps
interface FastEthernet0/3	
switchport access vlan 5	Assign FastEthernet0/3 to VLAN 5
duplex half	Set the port to half duplex
speed 10	Set the port to 10 Mbps
interface FastEthernet0/4	
switchport access vlan 7	Assign FastEthernet0/4 to VLAN 7
duplex half	Set the port to half duplex
speed 10	Set the port to 10 Mbps
interface FastEthernet0/5	
switchport trunk encapsulation isl	Configures port 0/5 as a
switchport mode trunk	trunk port, and sets the encapsulation to ISL
interface FastEthernet0/6	
switchport access vlan 7	Assign FastEthernet0/6 to VLAN 7
duplex full	Set the port to full duplex
speed 100	Set the port to 100 Mbps
interface Vlan6	
ip address 10.1.16.100 255.255.255.128	Assigns the 10.1.16.100 address to VLAN 6
ip default-gateway 10.1.16.2	Sets the default route to use router R2 as its default gateway

Before creating VLANs, you must either configure a VTP domain name or configure VTP mode transparent.

The following shows the output of the show vlan command:

```
VLAN Name                       Status    Ports
---- -------------------------- --------- ------------------------------
1    default                    active    Fa0/7, Fa0/8, Fa0/9, Fa0/10
                                          Fa0/11, Fa0/12, Fa0/13, Fa0/14
                                          Fa0/15, Fa0/16, Fa0/17, Fa0/18
                                          Fa0/19, Fa0/20, Fa0/21, Fa0/22
                                          Fa0/23, Fa0/24
5    VLAN5                      active    Fa0/1, Fa0/3
6    VLAN6                      active    Fa0/2
7    VLAN7                      active    Fa0/4, Fa0/6
1002 fddi-default               active
1003 trcrf-default              active
1004 fddinet-default            active
1005 trbrf-default              active
```

VLAN	Type	SAID	MTU	Parent	RingNo	BridgeNo	Stp	BrdgMode	Trans1	Trans2
1	enet	100001	1500	-	-	-	-	-	1002	1003
5	enet	100005	1500	-	-	-	-	-	0	0
6	enet	100006	1500	-	-	-	-	-	0	0
7	enet	100007	1500	-	-	-	-	-	0	0
1002	fddi	101002	1500	-	-	-	-	-	1	1003
1003	trcrf	101003	4472	1005	3276	-	-	srb	1	1002
1004	fdnet	101004	1500	-	-	1	ibm	-	0	0
1005	trbrf	101005	4472	-	-	15	ibm	-	0	0

The output shows that VLANs 5, 6, and 7 have been created and that the appropriate ports have been added.

Port 0/5 will not show up in the output of the show vlan command because it was defined as a trunk.

Solution 2.1: Testing the Configuration

Once all of the configuration examples are complete, it is extremely important to test that all connectivity is working correctly. Again, because no routing protocol is configured, routers will be able to ping only directly adjacent router(s). You should be able to perform the following ping test:

- R1 should be able to ping R2's (10.1.1.2) and R4's (10.1.1.4) Frame Relay IP addresses and the IP address of R3's (10.1.2.3) Frame Relay link. R1 should also be able to ping the Ethernet IP address of R3 (10.1.3.3) and R5 (10.1.3.5).

- R2 should be able to ping R1's (10.1.1.1) and R4's (10.1.1.4) Frame Relay IP addresses, as well as the IP address of the VLAN 6 (10.1.16.100) interface of S1. ATM remote router 10.1.21.9 should also be pingable.

- R3 should be able to ping R1's (10.1.2.1) Frame Relay IP address and the serial IP address of R6 (10.1.20.6) on the HDLC link. R3 should also be able to ping the Ethernet IP addresses of R1 (10.1.3.1) and R5 (10.1.3.5).

- R4 should be able to ping R1's (10.1.1.1) and R2's (10.1.1.2) Frame Relay IP addresses and the Ethernet IP address of R6 (10.1.17.6).

- R5 should be able to ping the Ethernet IP addresses of R1 (10.1.1.1) and R3 (10.1.1.3).

- R6 should be able to ping the IP address of the HDLC interface of R3 (10.1.20.3) and should also be able to ping the Ethernet IP address of R4 (10.1.17.4).

Troubleshooting

The following commands can be used to troubleshoot this scenario:

```
show ip interface brief
show frame-relay pvc
show frame-relay map
show frame-relay lmi
clear frame-relay-inarp
show ports
show vlan
```

Layer 2 Configuration Task 2.2

The second scenario that we will attempt is based on all the layer 2 technologies that have been presented to you in the previous chapters of this book. Figure 7.2 shows the Layer 2 layout that must be built.

FIGURE 7.2   Network diagram for Task 2.2

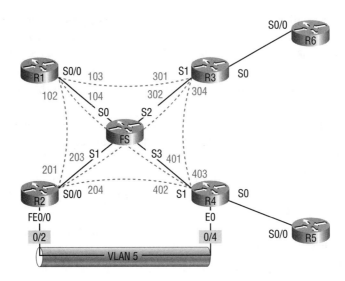

The following list includes the requirements for this scenario. The solution to the scenario follows in the next section. As stated earlier, try to complete the scenario without looking at the provided solution. Then review the provided solution to gauge your comprehension of the material presented thus far in the book. Here are the requirements:

- Configure the Frame Relay switch (FS) with a full PVC mesh between routers R1, R2, R3, and R4, as shown in Figure 7.2. The FS will be the DCE for all Frame Relay connections.

- Routers R1, R2, R3, and R4 should use ANSI as the LMI type.

- Configure R1, R2, and R4 in a hub-and-spoke configuration. Use network 172.16.32.0/24. Configure R4 as the hub and provide spoke-to-spoke connectivity (R1 must be able to ping R2).

- Configure R4 and R3 as a Frame Relay point-to-point connection. Use network 172.16.33.0/24.

- Routers R1, R2, and R3 must not be configured with subinterfaces.

- Ensure that all routers connected to the Frame Relay network use only the required DLCIs.

- Connect R4 and R5 using PPP. Configure R4 as the DCE. Use network 172.16.34.0/24.

- Connect R3 and R6 using PPP. Configure R3 as the DCE. Use network 172.16.35.0/24.

- Connect R2 and R4 using VLAN 5 on the Catalyst switch (S1). Use network 172.16.40.0/24.

Solution 2.2: Frame Relay Switch (FS) Configuration

The configuration for the Frame Relay switch (FS) is shown in the following section. Remember, when configuring a Frame Relay PVC, both ends of the PVC must be mapped and all PVCs are locally significant. On port S0 of the FS, which connects to router R1, three Frame Relay PVCs are defined: the first PVC 102 will be used to connect to R2, the second PVC 103 will be used to connect to R3, and the third PVC 104 will used to connect to R4. The rest of the configured PVCs follow along the same lines and should be self-explanatory.

Configuration for Router FS

Here is the configuration for Router FS:

`frame-relay switching`	Enables the router to perform frame relay switching
`interface Serial0`	Connected to R1
`  encapsulation frame-relay`	Set the Encapsulation as frame relay. The default encapsulation is Cisco; the other frame relay encapsulation option is IETF
`  frame-relay lmi-type ansi`	Set the LMI-type on the port to ANSI
`  frame-relay intf-type dce`	Set the interface as frame relay DCE
`  clockrate 128000`	Required on the DCE Serial interface
`  frame-relay route 102 interface Serial 1 201`	Map local DLCI 102 to Serial port S1 DLCI 201
`  frame-relay route 103 interface Serial 2 301`	Map local DLCI 103 to Serial port S2 DLCI 301
`  frame-relay route 104 interface Serial 3 401`	Map local DLCI 104 to Serial port S3 DLCI 401
`interface Serial1`	Connected to R2
`  encapsulation frame-relay`	
`  frame-relay lmi-type ansi`	
`  frame-relay intf-type dce`	
`  clockrate 128000`	
`  frame-relay route 201 interface Serial 0 102`	Map local DLCI 201 to Serial port S0 DLCI 102
`  frame-relay route 203 interface Serial 2 302`	Map local DLCI 203 to Serial port S2 DLCI 302

`frame-relay route 204 interface Serial 3 402`	Map local DLCI 204 to Serial port S3 DLCI 402
`interface Serial2`	Connected to R3
`  encapsulation frame-relay`	
`  frame-relay lmi-type ansi`	
`  frame-relay intf-type dce`	
`  clockrate 128000`	
`  frame-relay route 301 interface Serial 0 103`	Map local DLCI 301 to Serial port S0 DLCI 103
`  frame-relay route 302 interface Serial 1 203`	Map local DLCI 301 to Serial port S1 DLCI 203
`  frame-relay route 304 interface Serial 3 403`	Map local DLCI 304 to Serial port S3 DLCI 403
`interface Serial3`	Connected to R4
`  encapsulation frame-relay`	
`  frame-relay lmi-type ansi`	
`  frame-relay intf-type dce`	
`  clockrate 128000`	
`  frame-relay route 401 interface Serial 0 104`	Map local DLCI 401 to Serial port S0 DLCI 104
`  frame-relay route 402 interface Serial 1 204`	Map local DLCI 402 to Serial port S1 DLCI 204
`  frame-relay route 403 interface Serial 2 304`	Map local DLCI 403 to Serial port S2 DLCI 304

Following are some useful commands to troubleshoot the Frame Relay switch configuration:

```
show frame-relay pvc
show frame-relay route
```

Solution 2.2: Router Configurations

Figure 7.3 shows a more logical network diagram of the networks that will need to be configured on the routers. Even though the Frame Relay switch is configured in a full mesh, the router must be configured to allow only the connectivity that is shown in Figure 7.3. Therefore, R1,

R2, and R3 will need to be configured such that these routers do not dynamically learn about each other through the full mesh.

FIGURE 7.3   Logical network diagram for Task 2.2

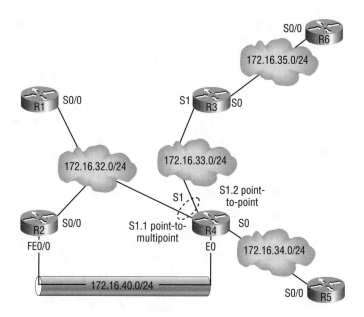

Router R1 Configuration

This section includes the interface configuration of router R1. R1 will be configured as a spoke router in the Frame Relay hub-and-spoke environment. R1 will automatically learn both R4's and R2's IP addresses because a full Frame Relay mesh network exists. But R1 and R2 must be configured in hub-and-spoke configuration. Therefore, R1 must be configured such that to communicate with R2, it must send all traffic to the hub router R4. To do this, R1 must have Frame Relay Inverse ARP disabled. This will ensure that R1 does not learn about R2 over the directly connected Frame Relay PVC 102 as well as R3 over PVC 103. Therefore, to provide connectivity to both R2 and R4, frame-relay map commands are required on R1's serial interface:

`interface Serial0/0`	Connected to FS Serial 0
`encapsulation frame-relay`	Set the Encapsulation as frame relay
`ip address 172.16.32.1 255.255.255.0`	Configured IP address on the interface
`bandwidth 128`	Specify the interface speed in Kbps, this can be used by routing protocols for metric calculation

```
frame-relay lmi-type ansi
```
This specifies the LMI type to ANSI, the command is optional, but if it is specified it must match the Frame Relay switch

```
no frame-relay inverse-arp
```
Disables the interface from dynamically learning remote router IP addresses using inverse arp. In this scenario, R1 only needs to know about connectivity to the Hub router R4 and to spoke R2. R1 should have no mapping for R3. Because inverse arp is disabled, frame-relay map commands must be used to map to the Hub router R4 and the Spoke R2

```
frame-relay map ip 172.16.32.4 104 broadcast
```
Map to Hub R4

Broadcast is needed to specify that broadcast traffic will be sent over this PVC, this is a must when using routing protocols such as RIP, IGRP, EIGRP or OSPF.

```
frame-relay map ip 172.16.32.2 104 broadcast
```
Map to Spoke R2 via the Hub router R4

Router R2 Configuration

Router R2 must also be configured as a spoke router and therefore must also have Inverse ARP disabled on the serial interface. Again, R2 needs a `frame-relay map` command for both routers R1 and R4. Router R2 also has FastEthernet0 configured to connect to network 172.16.40.0/24 on the Catalyst switch (S1):

```
interface Serial0/0
```
Connected to FS Serial 1

```
encapsulation frame-relay
```
Specify the encapsulation as frame relay

```
ip address 172.16.32.2 255.255.255.0
```

```
bandwidth 128
```

```
frame-relay lmi-type ansi
```
This specifies the LMI type to ANSI, the command is optional, but if it is specified it must match the Frame Relay switch

`no frame-relay inverse-arp`	Disables the interface from dynamically learning remote router IP addresses using inverse arp. Because inverse arp is disabled, frame-relay map commands must be used to map to the Hub router R4 and the Spoke R1
`frame-relay map ip 172.16.32.4 204 broadcast`	Map to Hub R4
`frame-relay map ip 172.16.32.1 204 broadcast`	Map to Spoke R1 via the Hub router R4
`interface FastEthernet0/0`	Interface FastEthernet0/0 connects to Port 0/2 of the Catalyst switch S1

`ip address 172.16.40.2 255.255.255.0`

Here is the output of the `show frame-relay map`:

```
Serial0 (up): ip 172.16.32.1 dlci 204(0xCC,0x30C0), static,
          broadcast,
          CISCO, status defined, active
Serial0 (up): ip 172.16.32.4 dlci 204(0xCC,0x30C0), static,
          broadcast,
          CISCO, status defined, active
```

The output shows static mapping to both R1 and R4. Both routers are mapped to DLCI 204. This is the DLCI that connects directly to R4. Note that the output will be true only after router R4 has been configured. It was used here as an example to clarify the static mappings.

Here is the output of a `debug frame-relay map` when a ping was sent from R2 to R1:

```
Ping 172.16.32.1
Type escape sequence to abort.
Sending 5, 100-byte ICMP Echos to 172.16.32.1, timeout is 2 seconds:
!!!!!
Success rate is 100 percent (5/5), round-trip min/avg/max = 64/67/68 ms
R2#
01:59:40: Serial0/0 (o): dlci 204(0x30C1), pkt type 0x800(IP), datagramsize 104
01:59:40: Serial0/0 (i): dlci 204(0x30C1), pkt type 0x800, datagramsize 104
01:59:40: Serial0/0 (o): dlci 204(0x30C1), pkt type 0x800(IP), datagramsize 104
```

As can be seen, the traffic from R2 to R1 is sent via R4, which is the hub router in this hub-and-spoke configuration. Note that the output will be true only after router R4 has been configured. It was used here as an example to clarify spoke-to-spoke reachability via DLCI 204.

Router R3 Configuration

Router R3 is connected with a Frame Relay point-to-point connection to router R4. Inverse ARP is disabled to stop R3 from learning about R1 and R2. Because Inverse ARP is disabled, a `frame-relay map` command is needed for Router R4.

R3 is also connected via a PPP connection to router R6. R3 has the DCE cable plugged into its serial interface, therefore R3 needs to be configured with a `clock rate` command to provide the clock:

`interface Serial0`	Connected to Serial 0/0 of router R6
`  encapsulation ppp`	Specify the encapsulation as PPP
`  ip address 172.16.35.3 255.255.255.0`	
`  clockrate 128000`	Clock rate must be specified on the DCE interface
`  bandwidth 128`	
`interface Serial1`	Connected to FS Serial 2
`  encapsulation frame-relay`	Encapsulation specified as frame relay
`  ip address 172.16.33.3 255.255.255.0`	
`  bandwidth 128`	
`  frame-relay lmi-type ansi`	Specific the LMI type to ANSI
`  no frame-relay inverse-arp`	Stops the router from learning IP address of remote routers dynamically
`  frame-relay map ip 172.16.33.4 304 broadcast`	Map to router R4

The following is the output of a debug frame-relay map when a ping was sent from R3 to R4. This ping was executed when the frame-relay map ip 172.16.33.4 304 broadcast was *not* configured on the interface but no frame-relay inverse-arp was configured on R3 interface:

```
01:21:28: Serial1:Encaps failed--no map entry link 7(IP).
01:21:30: Serial1:Encaps failed--no map entry link 7(IP).
```

R3 must have a frame-relay map to be able to connect to R4.

Router R4 Configuration

Router R4 is configured as the hub router in the hub-and-spoke environment. R4 also has a point-to-point Frame Relay connection to R3. R4 needs to be configured with two sub-interfaces, one as point-to-multipoint and the other as a point-to-point. R4 will learn the IP addresses of the spoke routers using Frame Relay Inverse ARP, but spoke connectivity can also be statically configured using frame-relay map statements.

R4 has a PPP connection to R5, and R4 has the DCE cable plugged into its serial interface, therefore R4 needs to be configured with a clock rate command to provide the clock. R4 also has its Ethernet interface configured to connect to the Catalyst switch (S1):

interface Serial0	Connected to Serial 0/0 or router R5
encapsulation ppp	Specify the encapsulation as PPP
ip address 172.16.34.4 255.255.255.0	
clockrate 128000	Clock rate must be specified on the DCE interface
bandwidth 128	
interface Serial1	Connected to FS Serial 3
encapsulation frame-relay	Frame relay encapsulation must be set on the physical interface
frame-relay lmi-type ansi	
interface Serial1.1 multipoint	Add sub-interface Serial 1.1 as a multipoint

```
ip address 172.16.32.4 255.255.255.0
```

Frame-relay map statements are used to connect to the spoke routers

```
frame-relay map ip 172.16.32.1 401 broadcast     Map to Spoke R1
frame-relay map ip 172.16.32.2 402 broadcast     Map to Spoke R2
```

```
interface Serial1.2 point-to-point
```

Add sub-interface Serial 1.2 as a point-to-point

```
ip address 172.16.33.4 255.255.255.0
frame-relay interface-dlci 403
```

On a Point-to-Point the Interface DLCI command is used to assigns DLCI 403 to this sub-interface, only one Interface DLCI can be assigned per sub-interface

```
interface Ethernet0
```

Interface Ethernet0 connects to the Catalyst switch S1 on port 0/4

```
ip address 172.16.40.4 255.255.255.0
```

The following is the output from show frame-relay map:

```
Serial1.1 (up): ip 172.16.32.1 dlci 401(0x191,0x6410), static,
           broadcast, CISCO, status defined, active
Serial1.1 (up): ip 172.16.32.2 dlci 402(0x192,0x6420), static,
           broadcast, CISCO, status defined, active
Serial1.2 (up): point-to-point dlci, dlci 403(0x193,0x6430),
           broadcast, status defined, active
```

This shows static maps to both the spoke routers R1 and R2 and the point-to-point connection to R3.

Router R5 Configuration

Router R5 is a very simple configuration; all that is needed is a PPP connection to R4:

```
interface Serial0                    Connected to Serial 0 to
                                     router R4

 encapsulation ppp                   Specify the encapsulation
                                     as PPP

 ip address 172.16.34.5 255.255.255.0

 bandwidth 128
```

Router R6 Configuration

Router R6 is also a very simple configuration; all that is needed is a PPP connection to R3:

```
interface Serial0/0                  Connected to Serial 0/0 to
                                     router R3

 encapsulation ppp                   Specify the encapsulation
                                     as PPP

 ip address 172.16.35.6 255.255.255.0

 bandwidth 128
```

Solution 2.2: Catalyst Switch Configuration

On the Catalyst switch S1, VLAN 5 must be configured. R2 is connected to port 0/2 and R4 is connected to port 0/4.

Switch S1 Configuration

The Catalyst switch (S1) must be configured to support VLAN 5. For the VTP/VLAN configuration, you need to be in vlan database mode, not in config mode. Ports 0/2 and 0/4 need to be added to VLAN 5. All switch ports need to be configured for port speed and duplex:

```
vtp mode transparent         Set the VTP mode of this specific switch to
                             transparent [server|client|transparent]


vlan 5                       Create VLAN 5
 name VLAN5                  Set the name to VLAN5
interface FastEthernet0/2
```

```
    switchport access vlan 5        Assign FastEthernet0/2 to VLAN 5


interface FastEthernet0/4
    switchport access vlan 5        Assign FastEthernet0/4 to VLAN 5
```

 Before creating VLANs, you must either configure a VTP domain name or configure VTP mode transparent.

The Issue of Frame Relay and Inverse ARP

If a router uses Frame Relay Inverse ARP, the router will automatically learn all the IP addresses of any router that has a direct Frame Relay PVC. Here is the output from a show frame-relay map on router R2 when Inverse ARP is enabled:

```
Serial0/0 (up): ip 172.16.32.1 dlci 201(0xC9,0x3090), dynamic,
            broadcast,, status defined, active
Serial0/0 (up): ip 172.16.32.4 dlci 204(0xCC,0x30C0), dynamic,
            broadcast,, status defined, active
Serial0/0 (up): ip 172.16.33.3 dlci 203(0xCB,0x30B0), dynamic,
            broadcast,, status defined, active
```

This output was taken when the Frame Relay network was built *without* disabling Inverse ARP on any router. From the output, it can be seen that R2 has learned via Inverse ARP the IP addresses of R1, R3, and R4.

R2 must be configured as a spoke router. This implies that when R2 pings R1, and vice versa, the traffic will go through the hub R4 to reach R1.

Here is the output of a debug frame-relay packet when a ping was sent from R2 to R1 when Inverse ARP was enabled:

```
ping 172.16.32.1
Type escape sequence to abort.
Sending 5, 100-byte ICMP Echos to 172.16.32.1, timeout is 2 seconds:
!!!!!
Success rate is 100 percent (5/5), round-trip min/avg/max = 36/37/40 ms
R2#
01:54:58: Serial0(o): dlci 201(0x3091), pkt type 0x800(IP), datagramsize 104
01:54:58: Serial0(i): dlci 201(0x3091), pkt type 0x800, datagramsize 104
01:54:58: Serial0(o): dlci 201(0x3091), pkt type 0x800(IP), datagramsize 104
01:54:58: Serial0(i): dlci 201(0x3091), pkt type 0x800, datagramsize 104
```

As can be seen, the packets are sent out DLCI 201, which is the direct frame PVC to R1; this is incorrect because the traffic should go through R4.

Solution 2.2: Testing the Configuration

Once all configuration examples are complete, it is extremely important to test that all connectivity is working correctly. Again, because no routing protocol is configured, routers will be able to ping only directly adjacent router(s). The following ping test should be able to be performed:

- R1 should be able to ping R2's (172.16.32.2) and R4's (172.16.32.4) Frame Relay IP addresses.

- R2 should be able to ping R1's (172.16.32.1) and R4's (172.16.32.4) Frame Relay IP addresses and the Ethernet IP address of R4 (172.16.40.4).

- R3 should be able to ping R4's (172.16.33.4) Frame Relay IP address and the IP address of the PPP interface of R6 (172.16.35.6).

- R4 should be able to ping R1's (172.16.32.1), R2's (172.16.32.2), and R3's (172.16.33.3) Frame Relay IP addresses. R4 should also be able to ping the Ethernet IP address of R2 (172.16.40.2) and the IP address of the PPP interface of R5 (172.16.34.5).

- R5 should be able to ping the IP address of the PPP interface of R4 (172.16.34.4).

- R6 should be able to ping the IP address of the PPP interface of R3 (172.16.35.3).

 R1, R2, and R4 *will not* be able to ping their own IP address assigned to their local interface in the hub-and-spoke network. This is because there is no `frame-relay map` statement for the local IP address. If you wish the ping to work to the local address, map the local address to any of the defined local DLCIs on each router.

It is important that layer 2 is working correctly. When troubleshooting any network-related problem, and before you enter a troubleshoot command, you should formulate a mental note of what the expected results of the command should be. If the results are different than expected, do not move on until you have analyzed this and can explain the anomaly. A good habit to get into for preparing for the CCIE lab is to save the configurations and reboot all the routers. Once the routers have rebooted, test the network connectivity once again.

Summary

It is truly important to have a strong understanding of how to implement layer 2 technologies. This is the network foundation on which all other technologies will reside. The most important thing to understand about building these scenarios is not the implementation itself, but when, where, and why certain commands must be used to achieve a certain objective. If something does not make sense, then research it, and do not move on until you understand it. Without a solid foundation in layer 2, it is very difficult to move forward and build a complex layer 3 network because things just get more difficult from here on.

Also, if you would like to try to implement a third layer 2 scenario, refer to Chapter 7 Supplement on the CD-ROM that accompanies this book.

Chapter

8

IP Addressing and Subnetting

THE CCIE QUALIFICATION EXAM TOPICS COVERED IN THIS CHAPTER INCLUDE THE FOLLOWING:

- ✓ The IP stack and the protocols within it
- ✓ The TCP and UDP protocols
- ✓ Windowing, handshaking, and fragmentation
- ✓ IP addressing
- ✓ Configuring complex subnet masks
- ✓ Address summarization
- ✓ Classless Inter-Domain Routing (CIDR)
- ✓ Using Variable Length Subnet Masking (VLSMs)
- ✓ IP version 6 (IPv6)

In this chapter, we are going to dig into the details of Transmission Control Protocol/Internet Protocol (TCP/IP). The U.S. Department of Defense (DoD) began to fund research for TCP/IP in 1969 and established it as a standard in 1976. Luckily, the DoD did not privately finance the research but used public tax money instead. Thus, the American people owned the project, and the rest is history.

We are going to start this chapter by explaining the IP version 4 (IPv4) protocol stack and how host data is encapsulated. Then we will discuss ARP, TCP windowing, handshaking, and fragmentation. We will discuss the programs and protocols used in the upper layers of the DoD stack such as Telnet, FTP, TFTP, SNMP, and so on.

Once we have finished our discussion of how the protocols work in the *DoD protocol stack* to reliably build data streams from host to host, we'll move to a discussion of IP addressing and subnetting. After subnetting is conquered, we will discuss how to create a supernet with a group of networks, which can help create efficient routing tables. Both Classless Inter-Domain Routing (CIDR) and Variable Length Subnet Mask (VLSM) will be discussed. We will finish off this chapter with a brief discussion of IP version 6 (IPv6).

If you are already familiar with IP addressing and subnetting techniques, you can skip ahead to the more advanced supernetting, VLSM, and IPv6 sections in this chapter. However, it is always nice to read another chapter on IP, just as a refresher.

IPv4 is described in RFC 791; IPv6 is described in RFC 2460.

TCP/IP and the DoD Model

The DoD model is a condensed version of the OSI model. It is made up of four, instead of seven, layers:

- The Process/Application layer
- The Host-to-Host layer
- The Internet layer
- The Network Access layer

Figure 8.1 shows a comparison of the four-layer DoD model and the seven-layer OSI reference model. As you can see, the two are similar in concept, but each has a different number of layers with different names.

FIGURE 8.1   The DoD model and the OSI model

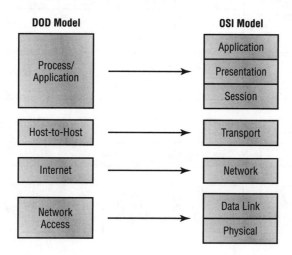

A vast array of protocols combine at the DoD model's *Process/Application layer* to integrate the various activities and duties of the OSI's corresponding top three (Session, Presentation, and Application) layers. (We'll be looking closely at those protocols in the next part of this chapter.) The Process/Application layer defines protocols for node-to-node application communication and also controls user interface specifications.

The *Host-to-Host layer* parallels the functions of OSI's Transport layer, defining protocols for setting up the level of transmission service for applications. It tackles issues such as creating reliable end-to-end communication and ensuring the error-free delivery of data. It handles packet sequencing and maintains data integrity.

The *Internet layer* corresponds to the OSI's Network layer, designating the protocols relating to the logical transmission of packets over the entire network. It takes care of the addressing of hosts by giving them an Internet Protocol (IP) address and handles the routing of packets among multiple networks.

At the bottom of the model, the *Network Access layer* monitors the data exchange between the host and the network. The equivalent of the Data-Link and Physical layers of the OSI model, the Network Access layer oversees hardware addressing and defines protocols for the physical transmission of data.

Although the DoD and OSI models are alike in design and concept and have similar functions in similar places, *how* those functions occur is different. Figure 8.2 shows the TCP/IP protocol suite and how its protocols relate to the DoD model layers.

FIGURE 8.2   The TCP/IP protocol suite

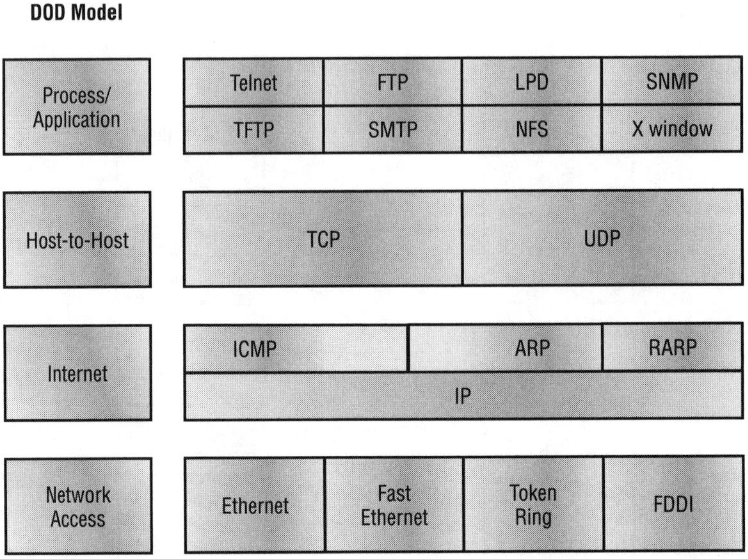

DOD Model

Process/Application	Telnet	FTP	LPD	SNMP
	TFTP	SMTP	NFS	X window

| Host-to-Host | TCP | | UDP | |

| Internet | ICMP | | ARP | RARP |
| | IP | | | |

| Network Access | Ethernet | Fast Ethernet | Token Ring | FDDI |

We are not going to discuss the Network Access layer in this chapter, so we'll jump to the Internet layer.

The Internet Layer Protocols

There are three main reasons for the Internet layer's existence: routing, providing a single network interface to the upper layers, and providing a globally unique identity, which allows global reachability.

None of the upper-layer protocols, and none of the ones on the lower layer, have any functions relating to routing. The complex and important task of routing is the job of the Internet layer. The second reason for the Internet layer is to provide a single network interface to the upper-layer protocols. Without this layer, application programmers would need to write "hooks" into every one of their applications for each different Network Access protocol. This would not only be a pain in the neck, but it would lead to different versions of each application—one for Ethernet, another one for Token Ring, and so on. To prevent this, IP provides one single network interface for the upper-layer protocols. Once that's accomplished, it's then the job of the IP and the various Network Access protocols to get along and work together.

All network roads don't lead to Rome—they lead to the IP. And all the other protocols at this layer, as well as all those at the upper layers, use it. Never forget that. All paths through the model go through the IP. The following sections describe the protocols at the Internet layer.

The protocols that work at the Internet layer are as follows:

- Internet Protocol (IP)
- Internet Control Message Protocol (ICMP)
- Address Resolution Protocol (ARP)
- Reverse Address Resolution Protocol (RARP)

The Internet Protocol (IP)

The *Internet Protocol (IP)* essentially *is* the Internet layer. The other protocols found here merely exist to support it. The IP contains the Big Picture, and it could be said to "see all" in that it is aware of all the interconnected networks. It can do this because all the machines on the network have a software—or logical—address called an IP address, which we'll cover more thoroughly later in this chapter.

The router looks at each packet's IP destination address. Then, using a routing table, it decides where a packet is to be sent next, choosing the best path. This process is performed on a hop-by-hop basis; that is, this routing process is performed independently on each router (or hop) between a source and destination. The Network Access–layer protocols at the bottom of the model don't possess IP's enlightened scope of the entire network; they deal only with physical links (local networks).

Remember that switching/bridging occurs at layer 2 of the OSI model, because switching defines collision domains and identifies individual devices with MAC addresses. Routing occurs at layer 3 of the OSI model and defines broadcast domains. Routing is accomplished through the implementation of logical addressing (a network and host portion of an address). The network portion of an address is used to route a datagram across the WAN environment, and once the datagram is delivered to the proper destination network, then the host portion of the address is used to deliver the datagram to the destination device.

The IP receives segments from the Host-to-Host layer and fragments them into datagrams (packets). The IP then reassembles datagrams back into segments on the receiving side and hands the segments up to the Host-to-Host layer. Each datagram is assigned the IP address of the sender and the IP address of the recipient. Each router (layer 3 device) that receives a datagram makes routing decisions based upon the packet's destination IP address.

Figure 8.3 shows an IP header. This will give you an idea of what the IP protocol has to go through every time user data is sent from the upper layers and wants to be sent to a remote network.

FIGURE 8.3 IP header

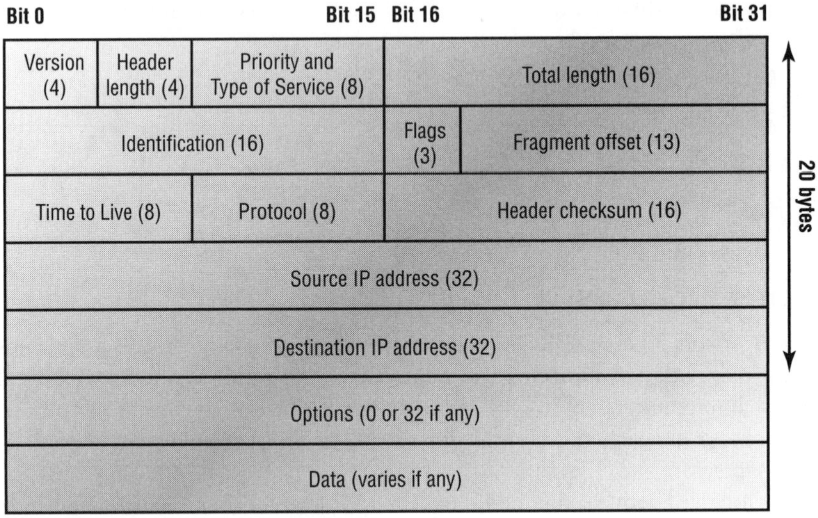

The following fields make up the IP header:

Version   IP version number. 4 bits long. For IPv4, the value is 0100.

HLEN   Header length in 32-bit words. 4 bits long. The minimum value for a correct IP header (five 32-bit words) is 5 (0101).

Priority or ToS   Type of Service. 8 bits long. Tells how the datagram should be handled. The first three bits are the precedence bits.

Total length   The length of the packet including header and data. 16 bits long for a maximum length of an IP packet = 65,535 bytes.

Identification   Unique IP packet value. 16 bits long. Identifies fragments for reassembly.

Flags   Specifies whether fragmentation should occur and shows more or last fragments. 3 bits long. Bit 0 is reserved and set to 0. Bit 1 indicates May Fragment (0) or Do Not Fragment (1). Bit 2 indicates Last Fragment (0) or More Fragments (1) to follow.

Frag offset   These provide fragmentation and reassembly if the packet is too large to put in a frame. Allows different maximum transmission unit (MTU) sizes on the Internet.

TTL   Time to live is 8 bits long. TTL is set into a packet when it is originally generated and gives the packet a time to live. If the packet doesn't get to where it wants to go before the TTL expires, boom, it's gone. This stops IP packets from continuously circling the network looking for a home.

Protocol   Port of upper-layer protocol (TCP is port 6, or UDP is port 17 [hex]). 8 bits long.

Header checksum   Cyclic redundancy check on header only. 16 bits long, and it is recomputed and verified at each point that the IP header is processed.

Source IP address   32-bit IP address of the sending station.

Destination IP address   32-bit IP address of the station this packet is destined for.

IP options   Used for network testing, debugging, security, and more. Variable in length.

Data   Upper-layer data.

Table 8.1 is a list of some popular protocols that can be specified in the protocol field.

TABLE 8.1   Possible Protocols Found in the Protocol Field of an IP Header

Protocol	Protocol number
Internet Control Message Protocol (ICMP)	1
Transmission Control Protocol (TCP)	6
Interior Gateway Routing Protocol (IGRP)	9
User Datagram Protocol (UDP)	17
IP version 6 (IPv6)	41
Generic Routing Encapsulation (GRE)	47
Enhanced Interior Gateway Routing Protocol (EIGRP)	88
Open Shortest Path First (OSPF)	89
Protocol-Independent Multicast (PIM)	103
Internetwork Packet Exchange in Internet Protocol (IPX in IP)	111
Layer 2 Tunneling Protocol (L2TP)	115

IP Fragmentation

It is important to understand IP packet fragmentation and reassembly. Although the maximum length of an IP packet can be over 65,535 bytes, many lower-level protocols do not support such large packets because they have a maximum size packet that they can transmit. This limitation is known as the maximum transmission unit (MTU). For example, the payload MTU for Ethernet is 1500 bytes. When the IP layer receives a packet to send, it first queries the outgoing interface to get the MTU. If the size of the packet is greater than the MTU of the outgoing interface, the packet is fragmented.

When a packet is fragmented, it is not reassembled until it reaches the destination IP layer. The destination IP layer performs the reassembly. Any router within the path can fragment a packet, and any router in the path can fragment a fragmented packet again. Each fragmented packet receives its own IP header and is routed independently from all other packets. If one or more fragments are lost, the entire packet must be retransmitted. Retransmission is the responsibility of the higher-layer protocols, such as TCP. Also, the flags field in the IP header might be set to not fragment the packet. If so, the packet is discarded if the outgoing MTU is smaller than the received packet.

The Internet Control Message Protocol (ICMP)

The *Internet Control Message Protocol (ICMP)*, described in RFC 792, works at the Network layer and is used by IP for many different services. ICMP is a management protocol and messaging service provider for IP. Its messages are carried as IP datagrams. RFC 1256, ICMP Router Discovery Protocol (IRDP), is an annex to ICMP that affords hosts extended capability in discovering routes to gateways.

Periodically, router advertisements are announced over the network, reporting IP addresses for the router's network interfaces. Hosts listen for these network infomercials to acquire route information. A *router solicitation* is a request for immediate advertisements and may be sent by a host when it starts up. We will discuss IRDP further in Chapter 22, "IP Services."

The following are some common events and messages that are related to ICMP:

Destination unreachable   If a router can't send an IP datagram any further, it uses ICMP to send a message back to the sender advising it of the situation. For example, if a router receives a packet destined for a network that the router doesn't know about, it will send an `ICMP destination unreachable` message back to the sending station.

Buffer full   If a router's memory buffer for receiving incoming datagrams is full, it will use ICMP Source Quench to send out this message.

Hop Count   Each IP datagram is allotted a certain number of routers that it may go through, and each time it goes through a router, it's called a *hop*. If it reaches its limit of hops before arriving at its destination, the last router to receive the datagram deletes it. The executioner router then uses ICMP TTL Expired to send an obituary message, informing the sending machine of the demise of its datagram.

Ping   Packet Internet groper (Ping) uses ICMP echo/reply messages to check the physical connectivity of machines on an internetwork.

The Address Resolution Protocol (ARP)

The *Address Resolution Protocol (ARP)*, described in RFC 826, is used to find the hardware (MAC) address of a host from a known IP address. Here's how it works: When IP has a datagram to send, it has already been informed by upper-layer protocols of the destination's IP address. However, IP must also inform a Network Access protocol, such as Ethernet or Token Ring, of the destination's hardware address on the local network. If IP doesn't find the destination host's hardware address in the ARP cache, it uses ARP to find this information.

As IP's detective, ARP interrogates the local network by sending out a broadcast asking the machine with the specified IP address to reply with its hardware address. In other words, ARP translates the software (IP) address into a hardware address—for example, the destination machine's Ethernet board address—and from the hardware address, deduces the machine's whereabouts. This hardware address is technically referred to as the *Media Access Control (MAC) address,* or the physical address. Figure 8.4 shows how an ARP might look to a local network.

FIGURE 8.4   Local ARP broadcast

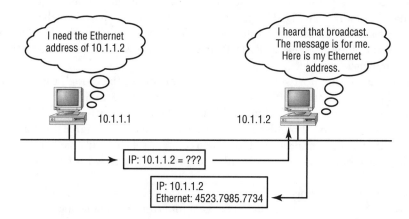

The Reverse Address Resolution Protocol (RARP)

When an IP machine happens to be a diskless machine, it has no way of initially knowing its IP address, but it does know its MAC address. The *Reverse Address Resolution Protocol (RARP),* described in RFC 903, discovers the identity of a diskless machine by sending out a packet that includes its MAC address and a request to be informed of what IP address is assigned to that MAC address. A designated machine, called a RARP server, responds with the answer and the identity crisis is over. RARP uses the information it does know about the machine's MAC address to learn its IP address.

Now we'll move up to the Host-to-Host layer as we continue our discussion of the protocol stack.

The Host-to-Host Layer Protocols

The Host-to-Host layer's main purpose is to shield the upper-layer applications from the complexities of the network. This layer says to the upper layer, "Just give me your data stream, with any instructions, and I'll begin the process of getting your information ready for sending."

The following sections describe the two protocols at this layer:

- The Transmission Control Protocol (TCP)
- The User Datagram Protocol (UDP)

The Transmission Control Protocol (TCP)

The *Transmission Control Protocol (TCP)* takes large blocks of information from an application and breaks them into segments. TCP is described in RFC 793. It numbers and sequences each segment so that the destination's TCP protocol can put the segments back into the order that the application intended. After these segments are sent, TCP (on the transmitting host) waits for an acknowledgment of the receiving end's TCP virtual circuit session; it then retransmits the segments that aren't acknowledged.

Before a transmitting host starts to send segments down the model, the sender's TCP protocol contacts the destination's TCP protocol in order to establish a connection. What is created is known as a *virtual circuit*. This type of communication is called *connection oriented*. During this initial handshake, the two TCP layers also agree on the amount of information that's going to be sent before the recipient's TCP sends back an acknowledgment. With everything agreed upon in advance, the path is paved for reliable communication to take place.

TCP is a full-duplex, connection-oriented, reliable, accurate protocol, and establishing all these terms and conditions in addition to checking for errors and managing flow control is no small task. TCP is a very complex protocol.

TCP Segment Format

The upper layers just send a data stream to the protocols in the Transport layers, so we'll demonstrate how TCP segments a data stream and prepares it for the Network layer. The Network layer then routes the segments as packets through an internetwork. The packets are handed to the Transport layer protocols on the receiving host, and the Transport layer protocols rebuild the data stream to hand to the upper-layer applications or protocols.

Figure 8.5 shows the TCP segment format. The figure shows the different fields within the TCP header.

FIGURE 8.5   TCP segment format

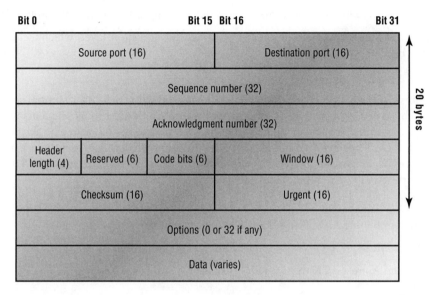

The TCP header is 20 bytes long. You need to understand what each field in the TCP segment is. The TCP segment contains the following fields:

Source port   Port number of the host sending the data. Port numbers will be explained a little later in this section. 16 bits long.

Destination port   Port number of the application requested on the destination host. 16 bits long.

Sequence number   Used to put the data back in the correct order or to retransmit missing or damaged data, which is called sequencing. 32 bits long.

Acknowledgment number   Defines which TCP octet is expected next. 32 bits long.

HLEN   Header length defines the number of 32-bit words in the header. 4 bits long.

Reserved   Always set to zero. 6 bits long.

Code bits (flags)   Control functions used to set up and terminate a session. 6 bits long.

Window   The window size that the sender is willing to accept, in octets. 16 bits long.

Checksum   TCP doesn't trust the lower layers and checks everything. The checksum protects the header and data fields. 16 bits long.

Urgent pointer Indicates the end of urgent data. 16 bits long.

Option Sets the maximum TCP segment size to either 0 or 32 bits, if any. Variable in length.

Data The data handed down to the TCP protocol at the Transport layer, which includes the upper-layer headers.

TCP Three-Way Handshake

Two systems establish TCP connections by synchronizing with each other's initial sequence numbers. This is accomplished by an exchange of connection-establishing segments with the SYN bit set and initial sequence numbers. The TCP connection is full duplex; each side has its own initial sequence number and must receive an acknowledgment from the other side.

This process is known as the three-way handshake, because the ACK (in step 2) and the SYN (in step 3) are actually sent in the same segment:

Step 1 System A sends a SYN with sequence number X to System B.

Step 2 System B must ACK that System A's sequence number is X.

Step 3 System B sends a SYN with sequence number Y to System A.

Step 4 System A must ACK that System B's sequence number is Y.

Windowing

TCP uses a window of sequence numbers to implement flow control. The receiver indicates the amount of data to be sent. The receiver sends with every ACK a window size that indicates a range of acceptable sequence numbers beyond the last received segment. The window allows the receiver to tell the sender how many bytes to transmit, and the window defines the amount of data that can be sent before an acknowledgment is required.

Sliding Window

After a connection is established, the sending TCP sends segments no larger than the received window size. The sender waits for the acknowledgment of sent segments before sending additional data. Each acknowledgment also has the window size, which indicates the amount of data that the receiver is willing to accept. The window can change in size, therefore the name *sliding window*.

The User Datagram Protocol (UDP)

Application developers can use the *User Datagram Protocol (UDP)* in place of TCP. UDP is the scaled-down economy model and is considered a *thin protocol*. Like a thin person on a park bench, a thin protocol doesn't take up a lot of room—or in this case, much bandwidth on a network. The UDP header is 8 bytes in length.

UDP also doesn't offer all the bells and whistles of TCP, but it does do a fabulous job of transporting information that doesn't require reliable delivery—and it does so using far less overhead. (Please note that UDP is covered thoroughly in RFC 768.)

There are some situations in which it would definitely be wise for application developers to opt for UDP rather than TCP. Remember the watchdog SNMP up there at the Process/Application layer? SNMP monitors the network, sending intermittent messages and a fairly steady flow of status updates and alerts, especially when it's running on a large network. The cost in overhead necessary to establish, maintain, and close a TCP connection for each one of those little messages would reduce what would be an otherwise healthy, efficient network.

Another circumstance calling for using UDP instead of TCP is when the matter of reliability is already accomplished at the Process/Application layer. For example, *Network File System (NFS)* handles its own reliability issues.

UDP receives upper-layer blocks of information, instead of streams of data as TCP does, and breaks them into segments. Unlike TCP, UDP does *not* sequence the segments and does not care in which order the segments arrive at the destination. UDP sends the segments off and forgets about them. It doesn't follow through, check up on them, or even allow for an acknowledgment of safe arrival—complete abandonment. Because of this, it's referred to as an *unreliable* protocol. This does not mean that UDP is ineffective, only that it doesn't handle issues of reliability.

Further, UDP doesn't create a virtual circuit, nor does it contact the destination before delivering information to it. It is, therefore, also considered a *connectionless* protocol. Because UDP assumes that the application will use its own reliability method, it doesn't use any. This gives an application developer a choice when running the Internet Protocol stack: TCP for greater reliability or UDP for less overhead.

UDP Segment Format

The very low overhead of UDP, because UDP does not use windowing or acknowledgments, is shown in Figure 8.6.

FIGURE 8.6   UDP segment

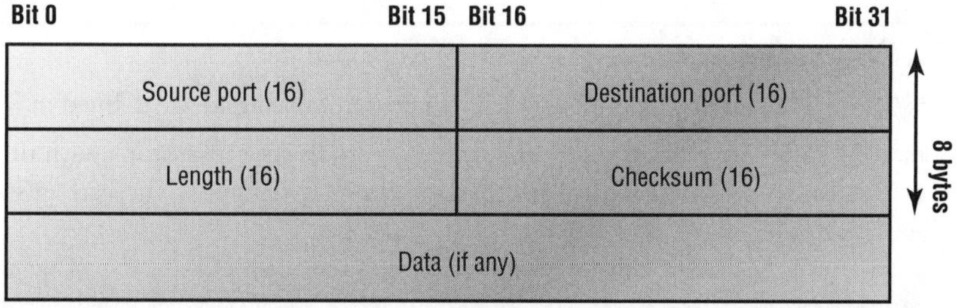

You need to understand what each field in the UDP segment is. The UDP segment contains the following fields:

Source port   Port number of the host sending the data. 16 bits long.

Destination port   Port number of the application requested on the destination host. 16 bits long.

Length of the segment   Length of UDP header and UDP data. 16 bits long.

Checksum   Protects both the UDP header and UDP data fields. 16 bits long.

Data   Upper-layer data.

UDP, like TCP, doesn't trust the lower layers and runs its own checksum. Remember that UDP has low overhead because it does not utilize a sequence number, an ACK number, and window size.

Port Numbers

TCP and UDP must use *port numbers* to communicate with the upper layers. Port numbers are used to keep track of different conversations crossing the network simultaneously. Originating source port numbers, 1024 and above, are dynamically assigned by the source host; 1023 and below are defined in RFC 1700, which discusses what are called well-known port numbers.

Virtual circuits that do not use an application with a well-known port number are assigned port numbers randomly chosen from within a specific range instead. These port numbers are used to identify the source and destination host in the TCP segment.

Figure 8.7 illustrates how both TCP and UDP use port numbers.

FIGURE 8.7   Port numbers for TCP and UDP

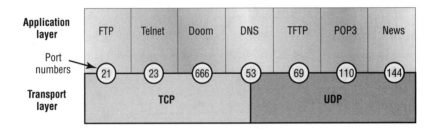

The different port numbers that can be used are explained here:

- Numbers below 1024 are considered well-known port numbers and are defined in RFC 1700.

- Numbers 1024 and above are used by the upper layers to set up sessions with other hosts and by TCP as source and destination addresses in the TCP segment. These are also referred to as client port numbers.

   Some vendors do use numbers above 1023 for their application in order to make them unique.

When a TCP or UDP session is initiated, the application will be issued a client port number (above 1023) by the IP protocol stack. The combination of the host IP address and the port number makes each session unique. The combination of the IP address and port number is known as a socket. The server will always listen for inbound packets for the specific well-known port number (1 through 1023), which is assigned for the application it is providing (for example, port 80 for HTTP, port 23 for Telnet, etc.).

The existence of sockets is what allows a single device to have multiple IP-based applications running concurrently. Sockets also allow multiple web browser windows (sessions) to open concurrently because each browser window is actually a different port number, thus a different socket number. This is accomplished because HTTP 1.1 pipelining allows multiple windows (sessions) from a single browser window. So even though all the IP packets are being received by the same NIC (in other words, the same IP address), each web browser window (each instance of an IP-based application) is unique.

With the discussion of the Host-to-Host layer completed, we will now move up the protocol stack and discuss the Process/Application layer.

The Process/Application Layer Protocols

In this section, we will talk about and describe the different applications and services typically used in IP networks. We'll cover the following protocols and applications:

- Telnet
- FTP
- TFTP
- SMTP
- SNMP
- DNS
- BootP
- DHCP

Telnet

Telnet, described in RFC 854, is the chameleon of protocols. It utilizes TCP port 23. Telnet's specialty is terminal emulation. It allows a user on a remote client machine, called the Telnet client, to access the resources of another machine, the Telnet server. Telnet achieves this by pulling a fast one on the Telnet server and making the client machine appear as though it were a terminal directly attached to the local server. This projection is actually a software image, a virtual terminal that can interact with the chosen remote host.

The emulated terminals are of the text-mode type and can execute refined procedures such as displaying menus that give users the opportunity to choose options and access the applications on the duped server. Users begin a Telnet session by running the Telnet client software and then logging on to the Telnet server.

The name Telnet comes from *telephone network,* which is how most Telnet sessions used to occur.

File Transfer Protocol (FTP)

The *File Transfer Protocol (FTP)*, described in RFC 959, uses TCP port 20 for data connection and 21 as the server port. It is the protocol that actually lets us transfer files; it can facilitate file transfers between any two machines that are using it. But FTP isn't just a protocol; it's also a program. Operating as a protocol, FTP is used by applications. As a program, it's employed by users to perform file tasks by hand. However, in both capacities, an FTP client is accessing an FTP server according to the rules of FTP.

Accessing a host through FTP is only the first step. Users must then be subjected to an authentication login that's probably secured with passwords and usernames placed there by system administrators to restrict access. You can get around this somewhat by adopting the username *anonymous*—only you'll be limited in what you can access once you are in there. For security reasons, not all FTP servers allow the anonymous username.

Trivial File Transfer Protocol (TFTP)

The *Trivial File Transfer Protocol (TFTP)*, described in RFC 1350, is the stripped-down, stock version of FTP, though it's the protocol of choice if you know exactly what you want and where it's to be found. It doesn't give you the abundance of functions that FTP does, though. TFTP, which uses UDP port 69, has no directory browsing capabilities; it can do nothing but send and receive files. This compact little protocol also skimps in the data department, sending much smaller blocks of data than FTP. Also, there's no authentication as there is with FTP, so it's insecure.

TFTP is used extensively by Cisco devices, because it simplifies the code required to support image and other file transfers.

Simple Mail Transfer Protocol (SMTP)

Simple Mail Transfer Protocol (SMTP), which is defined in RFC 821, answers our ubiquitous call to e-mail and uses a spooled, or queued, store-and-forward method of mail delivery, utilizing TCP port 25. Once a message has been sent to a destination, the message is spooled to a device—usually a disk. The server software at the destination posts a vigil, regularly checking this queue for messages. When it detects them, it proceeds to deliver them to their destination. Typically, SMTP is used to send mail and Post Office Protocol, version 3 (POP3) is used to receive mail. However, some SMTP servers allow the Internet Messaging Application Protocol (IMAP) for receiving mail.

Simple Network Management Protocol (SNMP)

Simple Network Management Protocol (SNMP), which is defined in RFC 1157, is the protocol that provides for the collection and manipulation of valuable network information. It gathers data by polling the devices on the network from a management station at fixed or random intervals, requiring them to disclose certain information. SNMP uses UDP ports 161 and 162. When all is well, SNMP reveals the network *baseline*—the operational traits of a healthy network. This protocol can also stand as a watchman over the network, quickly notifying managers of any sudden turn of events. These network watchmen are called *agents*, and when aberrations occur, agents send an alert called a *trap* to the management station.

Domain Name Service (DNS)

Domain name service (DNS) is used to resolve hostnames and was specifically used to resolve Internet names, such as www.cisco.com. You don't have to use DNS; you can just type in the IP address of any device you want to communicate with. An IP address is used to identify hosts on a network and on the Internet as well. DNS is implemented using both TCP and UDP port 53 because workstations use UDP port 53 and DNS servers use TCP port 53 for DNS zone transfers.

However, DNS was designed to make our lives easier. Also, what would happen if you want to move your web page to a different service provider? The IP address will change and no one will know what it is. DNS allows you to use any IP address to specify a domain name. You can change it as often as you want and no one should know the difference.

DNS is used to resolve *fully qualified domain names (FQDNs)*, for example, www.cisco.com. An FQDN is a hierarchy that can logically locate a system based on its domain identifier.

Bootstrap Protocol (BootP)

BootP stands for *Bootstrap Protocol*, described in RFCs 951, 1395, 1497, 1532, and 1542. When a diskless workstation is powered on, it broadcasts a BootP request on the network. A BootP server hears the request (UDP port 67) and looks up the client's MAC address in its BootP file. If it finds an appropriate entry, it responds by telling the machine its IP address (UDP port 68) and the name of the file—usually via the TFTP protocol—that it should boot from.

BootP is used by a diskless machine to learn its own IP address, the IP address and hostname of a server machine, and the filename of a file that is to be loaded into memory and executed at bootup.

If the BootP server is located one or more router hops from the local subnet, the local default gateway router must be configured to forward the BootP request. The interface command `ip helper-address x.x.x.x` is configured on interfaces with devices connected that acquire their IP address information via BootP. The `ip helper-address x.x.x.x` command allows the router to proxy the BootP/DHCP request and forwards the request to the BootP/DHCP server as a directed unicast packet. Fields in the request are also used to indicate the correct scope that the IP address should be assigned from to ensure that hosts get the correct subnet addressing. When an IP helper address is configured, UDP forwarding is enabled on all the default UDP ports, which are as follows:

- TFTP (UDP 69)
- DNS (UDP 53)
- Time service (UDP 37)
- NetBIOS name server (UDP 137)
- NetBIOS datagram server (UDP 138)
- BootP server and client (UDP 67 and 68)
- TACACS service (UDP 49)
- IEN-116 name service (UDP 42)

To prevent and control the forwarding of other protocols, you use the `no ip forward-protocol udp [port number]` global command.

You might believe that BootP is an old program and not used anymore, right? Wrong. BootP is still around, but now we just call it the Dynamic Host Configuration Protocol, which you will learn about in the next section.

Dynamic Host Configuration Protocol (DHCP)

The *Dynamic Host Configuration Protocol (DHCP)*, described in RFC 1531, is used to give IP addresses to hosts. It allows easier administration and works well in small to even very large network environments. Many types of hardware can be used to be a DHCP server, including a Cisco router.

DHCP differs from BootP in that BootP is used to give an IP address to a host but the host's hardware address must be put in by hand in a BootP table.

You can think of DHCP as a dynamic BootP. However, remember that BootP is also used to send an operating system that a host can boot from. DHCP cannot perform this function. DHCP uses the same UDP ports 67 and 68 that BootP uses.

There is a lot of information a DHCP server can provide to a host when the host is registering for an IP address with the DHCP server. Notice all the information that can be provided by the DHCP server:

- IP address
- Subnet mask
- Domain name
- Default gateway (routers)
- DNS
- WINS information

A DHCP server can provide even more information, but the items in this list are the most common.

This ends our discussion of the different applications and services that typically are used in IP networks. In the next section, we'll discuss IP addressing, an extremely important topic to thoroughly understand.

IP Addressing

One of the most important topics in any discussion of TCP/IP is IP addressing. An *IP address* is a numeric identifier assigned to each machine on an IP network. It designates the location of a device on the network. An IP address is a software address, not a hardware address—the latter is hard-coded on a network interface card (NIC) and used for finding hosts on a local network.

IP addressing was designed to allow a host on one network to communicate with a host on a different network regardless of the type of layer 2 network the hosts are participating in.

Before we get into the more complicated aspects of IP addressing, you need to understand some of the basics. In this section, you will learn about some of the fundamentals of IP addressing and about its terminology. Later, you will learn about the hierarchical IP addressing scheme and subnetting.

 To understand IP addressing and subnetting, it's very important that you have already mastered binary-to-decimal conversion and the powers of 2. If you need to review these topics, refer back to Chapter 1, "Network Design and Concepts."

IP Terminology

Throughout this chapter, you will learn several terms that are critical to understanding the Internet Protocol. To start, here are a few of the most important:

Bit   One digit, either a 1 or a 0.

Byte   7 or 8 bits, depending on whether parity is used. For the rest of this chapter, always assume a byte is 8 bits.

Octet   Always 8 bits.

Network address   The designation used in routing to send packets to a remote network, for example, 172.16.0.0 and 10.0.0.0.

Broadcast address   Used by applications and hosts to send information to all nodes on a network. Examples include 255.255.255.255, which is all nodes on the local network and 192.168.223.255, which is all subnets and hosts on network 192.168.223.0.

The Hierarchical IP Addressing Scheme

An IP address is made up of 32 bits of information. These bits are divided into four sections, referred to as *octets*, each containing 1 byte (8 bits). You can depict an IP address using one of three methods:

- Dotted-decimal, as in 172.16.30.56
- Binary, as in 10101100.00010000.00011110.00111000
- Hexadecimal, as in AC 10 1E 38

All of these examples represent the same IP address. Although hexadecimal is not used as often as dotted-decimal or binary when IP addressing is discussed, you still might find an IP address stored in hexadecimal in some programs. For example, the Windows Registry stores a machine's IP address in hex.

The 32-bit IP address is a structured, or hierarchical, address, as opposed to a flat, or nonhierarchical, address. Although either type of addressing scheme could have been used, the hierarchical variety was chosen for a good reason.

The advantage of this flat-addressing scheme is that it can handle a large number of addresses, namely 4.2 billion (a 32-bit address space with two possible values for each position—either 0 or 1—gives you 2^{32}, or approximately 4.2 billion). The disadvantage of this scheme, and the reason it's not used for IP addressing, involves routing. If every address were unique, all routers on the Internet would need to store the address of each and every machine on the Internet. This would make efficient routing impossible, even if only a fraction of the possible addresses were used.

The solution to this dilemma is to use a two- or three-level hierarchical addressing scheme that is structured by network and host or by network, subnet, and host.

This two- or three-level scheme is comparable to a telephone number. The first section, the area code, designates a very large area. The second section, the prefix, narrows the scope to a local calling area. The final segment, the customer number, zooms in on the specific connection. IP addresses use the same type of layered structure. Rather than all 32 bits being treated as a unique identifier, as in flat addressing, a part of the address is designated as the network address and the other part is designated as either the subnet and host or just the node address.

Network Addressing

The *network address* uniquely identifies each network. Every machine on the same network shares that network address as part of its IP address. In the IP address 172.16.30.56, for example, 172.16 may be configured as the network address.

The *node address* is assigned to, and uniquely identifies, each machine on a network. This part of the address must be unique because it identifies a particular machine (an individual) as opposed to a network (which is a group). This number can also be referred to as a *host address*. In the sample IP address 172.16.30.56, the node address is 30.56.

The designers of the Internet originally decided to create classes of networks based on network size. For the small number of networks possessing a very large number of nodes, they created the rank *Class A network*. At the other extreme is the *Class C network*, which is reserved for the numerous networks with a small number of nodes. The class distinction for networks between very large and very small is predictably called the *Class B network*.

How an IP address is subdivided into a network and node address is determined by the class designation of one's network. Figure 8.8 provides you with a summary of the three classes of networks plus the D and E class addresses not used for assigning hosts in production networks. Although Class D addresses are not assigned as the primary IP number of a node, they are used for multicast applications (for instance, some routing protocols). Class A, B, and C will be described in much more detail throughout this chapter.

FIGURE 8.8   Summary of the five classes of networks

	8 bits	8 bits	8 bits	8 bits
Class A:	Network	Host	Host	Host
Class B:	Network	Network	Host	Host
Class C:	Network	Network	Network	Host
Class D:	Multicast			
Class E:	Research			

(To ensure efficient routing, Internet designers defined a mandate for the leading bits section of the address for each different network class. For example, because a router knows that a Class A network address always starts with a 0, the router might be able to speed a packet on its way after reading only the first bit of its address.) This is where the address schemes define the difference between a Class A, a Class B, and a Class C address.

Network Address Range: Class A

The designers of the IP address scheme said that the first bit of the first byte in a Class A network address must always be off. This means a Class A address must be between 0 and 127.

Here is how those numbers are defined:

0xxxxxxx

If you turn the other 7 bits all off and then turn them all on, you will find your Class A range of network addresses:

00000000=0
01111111=127

So, a Class A network is defined in the first octet between 0 and 127. It can't be less or more. (Don't worry; we'll talk about illegal addresses in a minute.)

If you are having any difficulty with the binary-to-decimal conversions, please refer to Chapter 1.

Network Address Range: Class B

The RFCs state that in a Class B network, the first bit of the first byte must always be turned on but the second bit must always be turned off. In other words, the first 2 bits are always 10. If you turn the other 6 bits all off and then all on, you will find the range for a Class B network:

<u>10</u>000000=128
<u>10</u>111111=191

As you can see, this means that a Class B network can be defined when the first byte is configured from 128 to 191.

Network Address Range: Class C

For Class C networks, the RFCs define the first 2 bits of the first octet as always turned on but the third bit can never be on. In other words, the first 2 bits are always 110. Following the same process as the previous classes, convert from binary to decimal to find the range. Here is the range for a Class C network:

<u>110</u>00000=192
<u>110</u>11111=223

So, if you see an IP address that starts at 192 and goes to 223, you'll know it is a Class C IP address.

Network Address Ranges: Classes D and E

The addresses between 224 and 255 are reserved for Class D and E networks. Class D is used for multicast addresses and Class E for scientific purposes. Multicast addressing and configuration are covered in Chapter 21, "IP Multicast."

Network Addresses: Special Purpose

Some IP addresses are reserved for special purposes, and network administrators shouldn't assign these addresses to nodes. Table 8.2 lists the members of this exclusive little club and why they're included in it.

TABLE 8.2   Reserved IP Addresses

Address	Function
Network address of all 0s	Interpreted to mean "this network or segment."
Network address of all 1s	Interpreted to mean "all networks," or reserved per RFC 790.
Network 127.0.0.1	Reserved for loopback tests. Designates the local node and allows that node to send a test packet to itself without generating network traffic.

TABLE 8.2   Reserved IP Addresses *(continued)*

Address	Function
Node address of all 0s	Interpreted to mean "this network or possible broadcast."
Node address of all 1s	Interpreted to mean "all nodes" on the specified network, for example, 128.2.255.255 means "all nodes" on network 128.2 (Class B address).
Entire IP address set to all 1s (same as 255.255.255.255)	Broadcasted to all nodes on the current network; sometimes called an "all 1s broadcast."

You can use a subnet of all 0s with the `ip subnet-zero` global command on a Cisco router.

Class A Addresses

In a Class A network address, the first byte is assigned to the network address and the 3 remaining bytes are used for the node addresses. The Class A format is as follows:

`Network.Node.Node.Node`

For example, in the IP address 49.22.102.70, 49 is the network address and 22.102.70 is the node address. Every machine on this particular network would have the distinctive network address of 49.

Class A network addresses are 1 byte long, with the first bit of that byte reserved and the 7 remaining bits available for manipulation. As a result, the maximum number of Class A networks that can be created is 128. Why? Because each of the seven bit positions can be either a 0 or a 1, thus 2^7, or 128.

To complicate matters further, the network address of all 0s (0000 0000) is also reserved to designate the default route. Additionally, the address 127, which is reserved for diagnostics, can't be used either, which means that you can use only the numbers 1 to 126 to designate Class A network addresses. This means the actual number of usable Class A network addresses is 128 minus 2, or 126. Got it?

Each Class A address has 3 bytes (24-bit positions) for the node address of a machine. Thus, there are 2^{24}—or 16,777,216—unique combinations and, therefore, precisely that many possible unique node addresses for each Class A network. Because addresses with the two patterns of all 0s and all 1s are reserved, the actual maximum usable number of nodes for a Class A network is 2^{24} minus 2, which equals 16,777,214.

Class A Valid Host IDs

Here is an example of how to figure out the valid host IDs in a Class A network address:

- In the address 10.25.0.0, all host bits off are the network address (remember, the second byte, 25, is a host byte) because the actual network address is 10.0.0.0.

- In the address 10.255.255.255, all host bits on are the broadcast address.

But how did we know that the last 3 bytes were the host portion of the address? Well, we knew this because the first bit of the first byte is a 0. However, discovering the host address is actually accomplished through a binary-ANDing process, which is also known as the logical or Boolean AND operation, in which a 0 and a 1 equals a 0, a 1 and a 1 equals a 1, and a 0 and a 0 equals a 0. Let's look at it:

```
00001010.00011001.00000000.00000000    10.25.0.0 in binary
11111111.00000000.00000000.00000000    MASK is 255.0.0.0
00001010.00000000.00000000.00000000    End result is 10.0.0.0
```

Notice that the second byte, 00011001, did not fall through the mask; either a 0 or a 1 plus a 0 equals a 0. The end result is the network portion of the address because the host portion of the address, or host bits, are all set to 0. So, as you can see, the network mask is simply used to distinguish the network portion of the address from the host portion of the address.

The valid hosts are the numbers between the network address and the broadcast address: 10.0.0.1 through 10.255.255.254. Notice that 0s and 255s are valid host IDs. All you need to remember when trying to find valid host addresses is that the host bits cannot all be turned off (0s) or on (1s) at the same time because they are reserved (as shown earlier in Table 8.2).

Class B Addresses

In a Class B network address, the first 2 bytes are assigned to the network address and the remaining 2 bytes are used for node addresses. The format is as follows:

`Network.Network.Node.Node`

For example, in the IP address 172.16.30.56, the network address is 172.16 and the node address is 30.56.

With a network address being 2 bytes of 8 bits each, there would be 2^{16} unique combinations. But the Internet designers decided that all Class B network addresses should start with the binary digit 1 followed by 0. This will leave 14 bit positions to manipulate, therefore 16,384 (2^{14}) unique Class B network addresses.

A Class B address use 2 bytes for node addresses. This is 2^{16} minus the two reserved patterns (all 0s and all 1s), for a total of 65,534 possible node addresses for each Class B network.

Class B Valid Host IDs

Here is an example of how to find the valid hosts in a Class B network:

- In the address 172.16.5.0, all host bits turned off are the network address (remember, the third byte, 5, is a host byte); the actual network address is 172.16.0.0.

- In the address 172.16.255.255, all host bits turned on are the broadcast address.

Once again, how did we know that the last 2 bytes were the host portion of the address? Well, we knew because the first 2 bits of the first byte is a 10. However, we can verify this through a binary ANDing process, in which a 0 and a 1 equals a 0, a 1 and a 1 equals a 1, and a 0 and a 0 equals a 0. Let's look at it:

```
10101100.00001000.00000101.00000000    172.16.5.0 in binary
11111111.11111111.00000000.00000000    MASK is 255.255.0.0
10101100.00001000.00000000.00000000    End result is 172.16.0.0
```

Notice that the third byte, 00000101, did not fall through the mask because either a 0 or a 1 plus a 0 equals a 0. The end result is the network portion of the address because the host portion of the address, or host bits, are all set to 0. As you can see, then, the network mask is simply used to distinguish the network portion of the address from the host portion of the address.

The valid hosts would be the numbers between the network address and the broadcast address: 172.16.0.1 through 172.16.255.254.

Class C Addresses

The first 3 bytes of a Class C network address are dedicated to the network portion of the address, with only 1 measly byte remaining for the node address. Here is the format:

```
Network.Network.Network.Node
```

Using the example IP address 192.168.100.102, the network address is 192.168.100 and the node address is 102.

In a Class C network address, the first 3 bit positions are always the binary 110. The calculation is as follows: 3 bytes, or 24 bits, minus 3 reserved positions leaves 21 positions. There are therefore 2^{21} (or 2,097,152) possible Class C networks.

Each unique Class C network has 1 byte to use for node addresses. This leads to 2^8 (or 256) minus the two reserved patterns of all 0s and all 1s, for a total of 254 node addresses for each Class C network.

Class C Valid Host IDs

Here is an example of how to find a valid host ID in a Class C network:

- In the address 192.168.100.0, all host bits turned off are the network ID (remember, the default Class C mask is 255.255.255.0, so the first, second and third bytes are make up the network portion of the address, leaving only the fourth byte as the host portion of the address).

- 192.168.100.1 is the first host.

- 192.168.100.254 is the last host.

- In the address 192.168.100.255, all host bits turned on are the broadcast address.

The valid hosts would be the numbers between the network address and the broadcast address: 192.168.100.1 through 192.168.100.254.

There are certain ranges of Class A, Class B, and Class C address space that have been reserved for private addressing space. In the following section, we'll discuss what the purpose of this private address space could be.

Private IP Addresses

Another aspect of TCP/IP routing has to do with private networks. You can use private IP addresses within a network if the network doesn't need to be reached by outside machines. Internet Assigned Numbers Authority (IANA) allocated three blocks of IP addresses for private network use, as described in RFC 1918 and shown next in Table 8.3.

TABLE 8.3   IANA Assigned Private Networks

Network	Mask	Block
10.0.0.0	255.0.0.0	1 Class A network
172.16.0.0	255.240.0.0	16 Class B networks
198.168.0.0	255.255.0.0	256 Class C networks

Corporate networks that don't connect to the global Internet can use these addresses. However, if you use these addresses within a network that also contains a globally unique IP address, you must filter the addresses with access lists to avoid advertising them to the Internet. Many companies use private IP address space, and it's imperative that these routes not be announced to the Internet. Although ISPs will not allow private networks to be advertised by their routers, it is a good practice to make sure that your enterprise or campus routers do not advertise private networks to the ISP.

So if a host machine is assigned a private IP address, it won't be able to communicate via TCP/IP to the outside world because private network advertisements aren't included in Internet routing tables—unless you provide the privately addressed host with a proxy server that has a globally unique address or use a Network Address Translation (NAT) service. (NAT is discussed in Chapter 10, "Protocol Redistribution and NAT.") All the clients' requests for information will then have the source IP address of the proxy machine and will be able to communicate through it.

You should implement private addressing schemes using the same plan you used with global IP addressing schemes—assign contiguous addresses to defined regions so that you can apply summarization. Use Variable Length Subnet Masking (VLSM) for subnetting to more efficiently utilize allocated networks (we will discuss subnetting and VLSM in the remainder of this chapter). Finally, don't forget to run routing protocols that support classless routing.

Always consider the future of the network when you implement private addresses—someday, some of those machines on what is currently a private network will likely need access to the Internet. Once a network moves from not needing global connectivity to needing globally unique IP addresses, you'll have to readdress.

Using private addresses really helps to conserve your allotment of valid, registered IP addresses. Because every computer on the network probably doesn't need to access the outside world directly, it's wise to make good use of those private addresses and save the unique ones for machines that require global connectivity.

Now that you understand IP addressing and the fact that an IP address is a numeric identifier assigned to each machine on an IP network, it's a good time to move on to the topic of subnetting.

Subnetting

In the previous section, you learned how distinguish the network and host portions of an address with the applied mask and the binary ANDing process. You also learned how to distinguish a Class A, Class B, and Class C address by looking at the first few bits of the first byte of the address. We also discussed how to define and find the valid host ranges used in a Class A, a Class B, and a Class C network address by turning the host bits all off (0s) and then all on (1s). However, in that section we were defining one network. What happens if you wanted to take one network address and create six networks from it? You would have to perform what is called *subnetting*, which allows you to take one larger network and break it up into many smaller networks.

There are many reasons to perform subnetting. The following list includes some of the benefits of subnetting:

Efficient use of IP address allocation   From the layer 3 routing perspective, a single IP address network can reside in only one single location in the network or off of one interface of a router. Therefore, having a Class A network (16,777,216 host addresses) configured on a WAN serial interface, which requires only two IP host addresses (one at each end of the link), is not efficient. So we divide the large Class A network into multiple, smaller subnetworks.

Reduced network traffic   We all appreciate less traffic of any kind. Networks are no different. Without trusty routers, packet traffic could grind the entire network down to a near standstill. With routers, most traffic will stay on the local network; only packets destined for other networks will pass through the router. Routers terminate broadcast domains. The smaller the broadcast domains you create, the less network traffic on that network segment.

Optimized network performance   This is a result of reduced network traffic.

Simplified management   It's easier to identify and isolate network problems in a group of smaller connected networks than it is to identify them within one gigantic network.

Efficient spanning of large geographical distances   Because WAN links are considerably slower and more expensive than LAN links, a single large network that spans long distances can create problems in every area mentioned in this list. Connecting multiple smaller networks makes the system more efficient.

To create subnetworks, you take bits from the host portion of the IP address and reserve them to define the subnet address. This means fewer bits for hosts, so the more subnets, the fewer bits available for defining hosts.

In this section, you will learn how to create subnets, starting with Class C addresses. However, before you implement subnetting, you need to determine your current requirements and plan for future conditions. To do so, follow these steps.

1. Determine the number of required network IDs.
   A. One for each subnet
   B. One for each wide area network connection
2. Determine the number of required host IDs per subnet.
   A. One for each TCP/IP host
   B. One for each router interface
3. Based on the preceding requirements, create the following:
   A. One subnet mask for your entire network
   B. A unique subnet ID for each physical segment
   C. A range of host IDs for each subnet

Subnet Masks

For the subnet address scheme to work, every machine on the network must know which part of the host address will be used as the subnet address. This is accomplished by assigning a *subnet mask* to each machine. This is a 32-bit value that allows the recipient of IP packets to distinguish the network ID portion of the IP address from the host ID portion.

The network administrator creates a 32-bit subnet mask composed of 1s and 0s. The 1s in the subnet mask represent the positions that refer to the network or subnet addresses.

Not all networks need subnets, meaning they use the default subnet mask. This is basically the same as saying that a network doesn't have a subnet address. Table 8.4 shows the default subnet masks for Classes A, B, and C. These cannot change. In other words, you cannot make a Class B subnet mask read 255.0.0.0. The host will read such an address as invalid and typically won't even let you type it in. For a Class A network, you cannot change the first byte in a subnet mask; it must read 255.0.0.0 at a minimum. Similarly, you cannot assign 255.255.255.255 because it is all 1s and is a host address mask. A Class B address must start with 255.255.0.0, and a Class C must start with 255.255.255.0.

TABLE 8.4 Default Subnet Mask

Class	Format	Default subnet mask
A	Net.Node.Node.Node	255.0.0.0
B	Net.Net.Node.Node	255.255.0.0
C	Net.Net.Net.Node	255.255.255.0

Subnetting Class C Addresses

There are many different ways to subnet a network. The right way is the way that works for you. First you will learn to use the binary method, and then we'll look at an easier way to do the same thing.

In a Class C address, only 8 bits are available for defining the hosts. Remember that subnet bits start at the left and go to the right, without skipping bits. This means that subnet masks can be as follows:

11111111.11111111.11111111.00000000	255.255.255.0
11111111.11111111.11111111.10000000	255.255.255.128
11111111.11111111.11111111.11000000	255.255.255.192
11111111.11111111.11111111.11100000	255.255.255.224
11111111.11111111.11111111.11110000	255.255.255.240
11111111.11111111.11111111.11111000	255.255.255.248
11111111.11111111.11111111.11111100	255.255.255.252
11111111.11111111.11111111.11111110	255.255.255.254

(Now, the RFCs state that you cannot have only 1 bit for subnetting because that would mean that the bit would always be either off or on, which would be illegal. So the first subnet mask that you can legally use is 192, and the last one is 252 because you need at least 2 bits for defining hosts.) This requirement is very much historical and is totally ignored today. In fact, you are likely to be asked to configure something like a 255.255.255.128 mask in the CCIE lab.

> The RFCs state that you cannot have only 1 bit for subnetting, but the exception to this rule is through the use of the `ip subnet-zero` command, which allows the use of the 0s subnet. Likewise, starting with IOS version 12.0S and 12.2T, a Cisco router with a point-to-point link can be configured with a 31 bit mask (255.255.255.254).

The Binary Method: Subnetting a Class C Address

In this section, you will learn how to subnet a Class C address using the binary method. We will take the first subnet mask available with a Class C address, which borrows two bits from subnetting.

For this example, we are using 255.255.255.192. We know that 192 = 11000000: 2 bits for subnetting and 6 bits for defining the hosts in each subnet. What are the subnets? Because the subnet bits can't be both off or on at the same time, there are only two valid subnets. In the first subnet, all host bits are off:

<u>01</u>000000 = 64

All host bits are also off in the second subnet:

<u>10</u>000000 = 128

The valid hosts would be defined as the numbers between the subnets, minus the all host bits off and all host bits on.

To find the hosts, first find your subnet by turning all the host bits off. Then turn all the host bits on to find your broadcast address for the subnet. The valid hosts must be between those two numbers. Table 8.5 shows the 64 subnet, valid host range, and broadcast addresses.

TABLE 8.5 Subnet 64

Subnet	Host	Meaning
01	000000=64	The network (do this first)
01	000001=65	The first valid host
01	111110=126	The last valid host
01	111111=127	The broadcast address (do this second)

Table 8.6 shows the 128 subnet, valid host range, and broadcast addresses.

TABLE 8.6 Subnet 128

Subnet	Host	Meaning
10	000000=128	The subnet address
10	000001=129	The first valid host
10	111110=190	The last valid host
10	111111=191	The broadcast address

As you can see, that wasn't really all that hard. However, the example we showed you used only 2 subnet bits. What if you had to subnet using 9, 10, or even 20 subnet bits? In the next section, we'll show you an alternate method of subnetting that makes it easier to subnet larger numbers.

Subnetting Class B Addresses

We have discussed Class C subnets, so we'll take a look at subnetting a Class B network. First, we'll look at all the possible Class B subnet masks. Notice that we have a lot more possible subnets than we did with a Class C network address:

```
11111111.11111111.10000000.00000000     255.255.128.0
11111111.11111111.11000000.00000000     255.255.192.0
11111111.11111111.11100000.00000000     255.255.224.0
11111111.11111111.11110000.00000000     255.255.240.0
11111111.11111111.11111000.00000000     255.255.248.0
11111111.11111111.11111100.00000000     255.255.252.0
11111111.11111111.11111110.00000000     255.255.254.0
```

```
11111111.11111111.11111111.00000000        255.255.255.0
11111111.11111111.11111111.10000000        255.255.255.128
11111111.11111111.11111111.11000000        255.255.255.192
11111111.11111111.11111111.11100000        255.255.255.224
11111111.11111111.11111111.11110000        255.255.255.240
11111111.11111111.11111111.11111000        255.255.255.248
11111111.11111111.11111111.11111100        255.255.255.252
11111111.11111111.11111111.11111110        255.255.255.254
```

The Class B network address has 16 bits available for host addressing. This means you can use up to 12 bits for subnetting because you must leave at least 2 bits for host addressing.

> (You must leave at least 2 bits for host addressing in a Class B network.) The exception to this rule is through the use of the `ip subnet-zero` command, which allows the use of the 0s subnet. Additionally, starting with IOS version 12.0S and 12.2T, a Cisco router with a point-to-point link can be configured with a 31 bit mask (255.255.255.254).

Do you notice a pattern in the subnet values? This is why we showed you the binary-to-decimal numbers in Chapter 1. Subnet mask bits start on the left and move to the right and cannot skip bits, so the numbers are always the same. Memorize this pattern.

> Actually, you can skip bits in subnet masks, but it is not a common practice. We will cover this in Chapter 16, when we discuss access control lists (ACLs).

The process of subnetting a Class B network is the same as the process for subnetting a Class C except you just have more host bits. Use the same subnet numbers you used with Class C but add a 0 to the network portion and a 255 to the broadcast section in the fourth octet. For example, here is a host range of two subnets used in a Class B subnet:

16.0	32.0
16.255	32.255

Just add the valid hosts between the numbers and you're set.

Let's look at an example. We will take the second subnet mask available with a Class B address, which borrows three bits from subnetting.

For this example, we are using 255.255.224.0. We know that 224.0 = 11100000.00000000: 3 bits for subnetting and 13 bits for defining the hosts in each subnet. What are the subnets? Because the subnet bits can't be all off (0s) or on (1s) at the same time, there are only six valid subnets, 001 through 110.

This is all 0s and *not a valid* subnet:

<u>000</u>00000=0

In the six valid subnets, all host bits off:

<u>001</u>00000=32
<u>010</u>00000=64
<u>011</u>00000=96
<u>100</u>00000=128
<u>101</u>00000=160
<u>110</u>00000=192

This is a broadcast and *not a valid* subnet:

<u>111</u>00000=224

The valid hosts would be defined as the numbers between the subnets, minus the all host bits off and all host bits on.

To find the hosts, first find your subnet by turning all the host bits off. Then turn all the host bits on to find your broadcast address for the subnet. The valid hosts must be between those two numbers (the subnet and the broadcast address). Table 8.7 shows the 32 subnet, valid host ranges, and broadcast addresses.

TABLE 8.7   Subnet 32

Subnet	Host	Meaning
001	00000=32	The network (do this first)
001	00001=33	The first valid host
001	11110=62	The last valid host
001	11111=63	The broadcast address (do this second)

Table 8.8 shows the 64 subnet, valid host ranges, and broadcast addresses.

TABLE 8.8   Subnet 64

Subnet	Host	Meaning
010	00000=64	The subnet address
010	00001=65	The first valid host

TABLE 8.8   Subnet 64 *(continued)*

Subnet	Host	Meaning
010	11110=94	The last valid host
010	11111=95	The broadcast address

Table 8.9 shows the 96 subnet, valid host ranges, and broadcast addresses.

TABLE 8.9   Subnet 96

Subnet	Host	Meaning
011	00000=96	The subnet address
011	00001=97	The first valid host
011	11110=126	The last valid host
011	11111=127	The broadcast address

Table 8.10 shows the 128 subnet, valid host ranges, and broadcast addresses.

TABLE 8.10   Subnet 128

Subnet	Host	Meaning
100	00000=128	The subnet address
100	00001=129	The first valid host
100	11110=158	The last valid host
100	11111=159	The broadcast address

Table 8.11 shows the 160 subnet, valid host ranges, and broadcast addresses.

TABLE 8.11   Subnet 160

Subnet	Host	Meaning
101	00000=160	The subnet address
101	00001=161	The first valid host
101	11110=190	The last valid host
101	11111=191	The broadcast address

Table 8.12 shows the 192 subnet, valid host ranges, and broadcast addresses.

TABLE 8.12   Subnet 192

Subnet	Host	Meaning
110	00000=192	The subnet address
110	00001=193	The first valid host
110	11110=222	The last valid host
110	11111=223	The broadcast address

The example we showed you used only 3 subnet bits. What if you had to subnet using 9, 10, or even 20 subnet bits? It is actually the exact same process, so don't let the number of bits intimidate you.

Subnetting Class A Addresses

Class A subnetting is not performed any differently from Class B and Class C subnetting. The primary difference is that there are 24 bits to play with instead of the 16 that are in a Class B address and the 8 in a Class C address.

Let's look at all the Class A subnets:

```
11111111.10000000.00000000.00000000    255.128.0.0
11111111.11000000.00000000.00000000    255.192.0.0
11111111.11100000.00000000.00000000    255.224.0.0
11111111.11110000.00000000.00000000    255.240.0.0
11111111.11111000.00000000.00000000    255.248.0.0
11111111.11111100.00000000.00000000    255.252.0.0
```

```
11111111.11111110.00000000.00000000      255.254.0.0
11111111.11111111.00000000.00000000      255.255.0.0
11111111.11111111.10000000.00000000      255.255.128.0
11111111.11111111.11000000.00000000      255.255.192.0
11111111.11111111.11100000.00000000      255.255.224.0
11111111.11111111.11110000.00000000      255.255.240.0
11111111.11111111.11111000.00000000      255.255.248.0
11111111.11111111.11111100.00000000      255.255.252.0
11111111.11111111.11111110.00000000      255.255.254.0
11111111.11111111.11111111.00000000      255.255.255.0
11111111.11111111.11111111.10000000      255.255.255.128
11111111.11111111.11111111.11000000      255.255.255.192
11111111.11111111.11111111.11100000      255.255.255.224
11111111.11111111.11111111.11110000      255.255.255.240
11111111.11111111.11111111.11111000      255.255.255.248
11111111.11111111.11111111.11111100      255.255.255.252
11111111.11111111.11111111.11111110      255.255.255.254
```

That's it. You must leave at least 2 bits for defining hosts. You can probably see the pattern by now. Remember, we're going to do this the same way as a Class B or C subnet, but we have more host bits, that's all.

> You must leave at least 2 bits for defining hosts. Starting with IOS version 12.0S and 12.2T, a Cisco router with a point-to-point link can be configured with a 31 bit mask (255.255.255.254).

Hopefully, you now have a good understanding of subnetting. Just as you can take address space and subnet, or divide it, you can also take multiple small address networks and combine them. This process is known as supernetting, or summarization.

Supernetting

Supernetting, which is also called *summarization*, is the process of combining networks to save routing table entries. For example, it is typically more efficient to advertise 172.16.0.0 instead of 254 subnets, starting with 172.16.1.0 going to 172.16.254.0. Supernetting can save a lot of room in a routing table!

You can use supernetting in a variety of networks (typically those that are large) using all types of routers and routing protocols. In this section, we will show you how to create a supernet and then how to apply it to Cisco routers running both EIGRP and OSPF, the routing protocols usually used in larger networks.

Creating a Supernet

To create a summarized entry, you gather the networks you want to combine and then write them out in binary. We'll combine in an effort to save routing table entries:

10.1.0.0 through 10.7.0.0

172.16.16.0 through 172.16.31.0

192.168.32.0 through 172.16.63.0

First, notice that the networks can easily be summarized because they are contiguous. An example of a group of networks that would be a poor choice for summarization is 172.16.10.0, 172.16.14.0, and 172.16.44.0. Noncontiguous networks make for an inefficient summarization entry.

Supernetting 10.1.0.0 through 10.7.0.0

First, put everything into binary, and then follow the bits, starting on the left and stopping when the bits do not line up. Notice where we stopped underlining the following:

```
10.1.0.0     00001010.00000001.00000000.00000000
10.2.0.0     00001010.00000010.00000000.00000000
10.3.0.0     00001010.00000011.00000000.00000000
10.4.0.0     00001010.00000100.00000000.00000000
10.5.0.0     00001010.00000101.00000000.00000000
10.6.0.0     00001010.00000110.00000000.00000000
10.7.0.0     00001010.00000111.00000000.00000000
```

Now, create a network number using only the underlined bits. Do not count the bits that are not underlined. The second octet has no bits on (1s in the underlined section), so we get this:

10.0.0.0

To come up with the mask, now count all the underlined bits as 1s. Because 8 bits in the first octet and 5 bits in the second are underlined, we'll get this:

255.248.0.0

Supernetting 172.16.16.0 through 172.16.31.0

Let's put the network addresses into binary and underline the bits starting on the left and moving to the right until they stop lining up:

```
172.16.16.0   10101100.0001000.00010000.00000000
172.16.17.0   10101100.0001000.00010001.00000000
172.16.18.0   10101100.0001000.00010010.00000000
172.16.19.0   10101100.0001000.00010011.00000000
172.16.20.0   10101100.0001000.00010100.00000000
172.16.21.0   10101100.0001000.00010101.00000000
```

```
172.16.22.0 10101100.0001000.00010110.00000000
172.16.23.0 10101100.0001000.00010111.00000000
172.16.24.0 10101100.0001000.00011000.00000000
172.16.25.0 10101100.0001000.00011001.00000000
172.16.26.0 10101100.0001000.00011010.00000000
172.16.27.0 10101100.0001000.00011011.00000000
172.16.28.0 10101100.0001000.00011100.00000000
172.16.29.0 10101100.0001000.00011101.00000000
172.16.30.0 10101100.0001000.00011110.00000000
172.16.31.0 10101100.0001000.00011111.00000000
```

Count only the underlined bits and only the bits that are on (1s) to get the network address:

```
172.16.16.0
```

Now, create the mask by counting all the bits that are underlined up to the point where they stop lining up. We have 8 bits in the first octet, 8 bits in the second octet, and 4 bits in the third octet. That is a /20, or this network address:

```
255.255.240.0
```

Boy, that sure seems like a pain in the pencil, huh? Try this shortcut. Take the first number and the very last number and put them into binary:

```
172.16.16.0 10101100.0001000.00010000.00000000
172.16.31.0 10101100.0001000.00011111.00000000
```

Can you see that we actually came up with the same numbers? Using the shortcut is a lot easier than writing out possibly dozens of addresses. We'll do another example, but we'll use our shortcut.

Supernetting 192.168.32.0 through 192.168.63.0

By using only the first network number and the last, we'll save a lot of time and come up with the same network address and subnet mask as if we wrote out all the numbers.

Here is the first number:

```
192.168.32.0 = 11000000.10101000.00100000.00000000
```

Here is the last number:

```
192.168.63.0 = 11000000.10101000.00111111.00000000
```

Here is the network address:

```
192.168.32.0
```

And here is the subnet mask:

```
255.255.224.0
```

Now that you understand the concept of summarization, we'll look at some of the possible ways of implementing summarization on Cisco routers.

Applying Supernets to Cisco Routers

You can use either Enhanced Interior Gateway Routing Protocol (EIGRP) or Open Shortest Path First (OSPF), among others, to advertise a supernet, but EIGRP and OSPF are the most popular. IGRP and Routing Information Protocol (RIP), along with EIGRP, will automatically summarize on classful boundaries. If you have noncontiguous networks—a classful network separated by another classful network—you'll need to turn off auto-summarization. Here is how to do that:

```
Router(config)#router eigrp 1
Router(config-router)#no auto-summary
```

Not really difficult, but if you don't type that in, your EIGRP routing process will not work. If you have a contiguous network and it is not separated by a discontiguous design, then EIGRP will auto-summarize and you're done. This command can also be used with RIP version 2.

However, if you want to manually configure a summary router using EIGRP, you use an interface command:

```
Router(config)#int ethernet0
Router(config-int)#ip summary-address eigrp 1 192.168.32.0 255.255.224.0
```

The EIGRP routing process will now advertise networks 192.168.32.0 through 192.168.63.0 as available through interface Ethernet0. This command can also be used with RIP version 2, using the `ip summary-address rip` command.

To configure a summary route advertised by OSPF, you use a routing process command:

```
Router(config)#router ospf 1
Router(config-router)#area 1 range 172.16.0.0 255.255.240.0
```

The OSPF routing process will find the interfaces assigned to this address range and advertise the summary route out those interfaces for area 1.

Configuring summarization within interior gateway protocols (IGPs) will be discussed in Chapter 9. Next, we'll discuss Classless Inter-Domain Routing (CIDR) and how it is implemented in the Cisco network environment.

Classless Inter-Domain Routing (CIDR)

Classless Inter-Domain Routing (CIDR) is primarily designed to address the issue of exhausting IPv4 address space. It also removes all of the restrictions associated with classful addressing and classful routing, and it is an industry standard for displaying the number of subnet bits used with the IP address of a host or a network. If, for example, you have a 172.16.10.1 address with a 255.255.255.0 mask, instead of writing the IP address and subnet mask separately, you can combine them. For example, 172.16.10.1/24 means that the subnet mask has 24 out of 32 bits on.

The following list shows all the possible CIDR addresses:

```
255.0.0.0=/8
255.128.0.0=/9
255.192.0.0=/10
255.224.0.0=/11
255.240.0.0=/12
255.248.0.0=/13
255.252.0.0=/14
255.254.0.0=/15
255.255.0.0=/16
255.255.128.0=/17
255.255.192.0=/18
255.255.224.0=/19
255.255.240.0=/20
255.255.248.0=/21
255.255.252.0=/22
255.255.254.0=/23
255.255.255.0=/24
255.255.255.128=/25
255.255.255.192=/26
255.255.255.244=/27
255.255.255.240=/28
255.255.255.248=/29
255.255.255.252=/30
255.255.255.254=/31
```

Cisco and CIDR

Cisco has not always followed the CIDR standard. Take a look at the way a Cisco 2500 series router asks you to put the subnet mask in the configuration when using the setup mode:

```
Configuring interface Ethernet0:
  Is this interface in use? [yes]:return
  Configure IP on this interface? [yes]:return
    IP address for this interface: 1.1.1.1
    Number of bits in subnet field [0]: 8
    Class A network is 1.0.0.0, 8 subnet bits; mask is /16
```

Notice that the router asks for the number of bits used only for subnetting, which does not include the default mask. This is nothing short of idiotic.

The newer Cisco routers, however, run a setup script that no longer asks you to enter the number of bits used only for subnetting. Here is an example of a 1700 series router in setup mode:

```
Configure IP on this interface? [no]: y
    IP address for this interface:1.1.1.1
    Subnet mask for this interface [255.0.0.0]:255.255.0.0
    Class A network is 1.0.0.0, 16 subnet bits; mask is /16
```

Notice that the setup mode asks you to enter the subnet mask address. It then displays the mask in CIDR format. Much better.

Configuring Subnet Mask Display Formats

When configuring IP addresses in a Cisco router, you cannot enter the number of bits used in a subnet mask in a router—for example, 172.16.10.1/24. It would be nice to be able to do that, but you must type out the mask: 172.16.10.1 255.255.255.0.

By default, the router displays a CIDR output for the number of bits used in the mask. If you want the router to display the full mask, use the ip netmask-format command as follows:

```
Router#sh int fastethernet0
FastEthernet0 is up, line protocol is up
  Hardware is PQUICC_FEC, address is 0050.547d.1787 (bia 0050.547d.1787)
  Internet address is 172.16.10.20/24
Router#ip netmask-format ?
  bit-count    Display netmask as number of significant bits
  decimal      Display netmask in dotted decimal
  hexadecimal  Display netmask in hexadecimal
Router#ip netmask-format decimal
Router#show interface fastethernet0
FastEthernet0 is up, line protocol is up
  Hardware is PQUICC_FEC, address is 0050.547d.1787 (bia 0050.547d.1787)
  Internet address is 172.16.10.20 255.255.255.0
```

If you want to have fun with your friends at work, you can always change the format to hexadecimal, like this:

```
Router#ip netmask-format hex
Router#show interface fastethernet0
FastEthernet0 is up, line protocol is up
  Hardware is PQUICC_FEC, address is 0050.547d.1787 (bia 0050.547d.1787)
  Internet address is 172.16.10.20 0xFFFFFF00
```

Boy, would that make for an interesting day!

We have discussed a lot of material so far in this chapter. And hopefully, you are feeling confident about your understanding of the TCP/IP protocol and subnetting. Now we'll discuss VLSM and how it is beneficial in the network environment.

Variable Length Subnet Masking (VLSM)

We could easily devote an entire chapter to Variable Length Subnet Masking (VLSM), but instead we're going to show you a simple way to take one network and create many networks using subnet masks of different lengths on different network designs.

The purpose of VLSM is to conserve IP addresses because, when you subnet, IP addresses are lost in the math. For example, if you have a Class C network address and need 14 subnets, 12 of them WAN links that use only 2 IP addresses, you'll waste a lot of address space if all interfaces on your router use the same mask. Take a look at Figure 8.9, which shows two routers with seven interfaces each, all using the same subnet mask.

FIGURE 8.9   Fourteen subnets with no VLSM applied

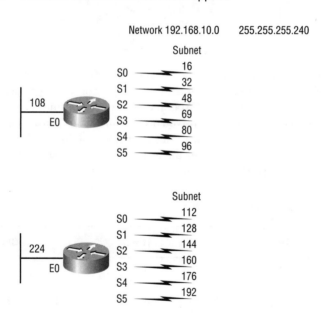

Notice that we have 14 subnets, each with 14 hosts on each interface. Our only option is to use the 255.255.255.240 mask because this will give us 14 subnets, but we get only 14 hosts on each LAN or WAN because of the bits reserved for subnetting. However, the WAN links are point-to-point and use only two IP addresses. Each WAN link is assigned 14 host IDs, which can be inefficient. Now take a look at Figure 8.10.

FIGURE 8.10 Fourteen subnets with VLSM applied

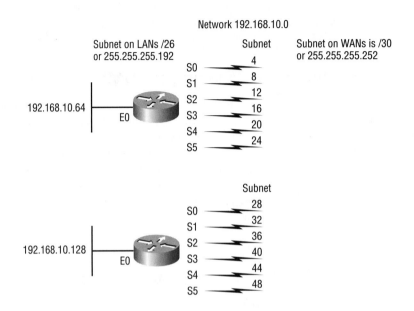

Because we can use different size masks on each interface, we now get 2 hosts per WAN interface and 64 hosts per LAN interface! What a difference. Not only can you get more hosts on a LAN, you still have room to add more WANs and LANs on the same network. Very efficient.

To create VLSMs quickly and efficiently, you need to understand how block sizes and charts work together to create the VLSM masks. Table 8.13 shows you the block sizes used when creating VLSMs with Class C networks. For example, if you need 25 hosts, you'll need a block size of 32. If you need 11 hosts, you'll use a block size of 16. Memorize the block sizes in this table.

TABLE 8.13 Block Sizes

Prefix	Mask	Hosts	Block Size
/26	192	62	64
/27	224	30	32
/28	240	14	16
/29	248	6	8
/30	252	2	4

The next thing to do is to create a VLSM table. Figure 8.11 shows you the three steps used in creating a VLSM table.

FIGURE 8.11   The three steps in creating a VLSM table

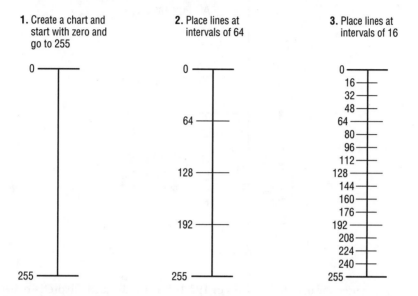

You can be thorough and create a fourth and fifth step; doing so will build the table in groups of 8 and 4, which is necessary for your WAN links.

Let's take our block size and VLSM table and create a VLSM using a Class C network address for the network in Figure 8.12. Now, fill out the VLSM table, as shown in Figure 8.13.

FIGURE 8.12   A VLSM network example

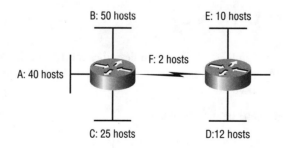

FIGURE 8.13   A VLSM table example

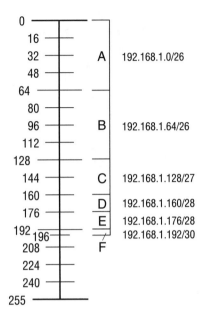

Notice that we used the network address of 192.168.1.0 and added the prefix of each block size used. Now, take those addresses and masks and apply them to the router interfaces. We still have plenty of room for growth. We never could accomplish this with one subnet mask.

Make sure you have a good understanding of IP addressing and subnetting because they are core topics for both the qualification exam and the lab exam. In the next section, we'll briefly discuss the IPv6 format because it is a topic for the qualification examination.

IP Version 6 (IPv6)

IPv6 addressing is covered in RFC 2373, which describes the 128-bit-long addressing format. The IPv6 addresses are displayed in hexadecimal format, divided into eight 16-bit segments. Here is an example of an IPv6 address:

FE11:3CB8:000E:0000:0000:3B00:0230:00A9

As you can see, it's a long address format, but any groups of 0s (four 0s) can be shortened to a single 0, or multiple groups of 16-bit 0s (four 0s) can be represented with a ::, which can appear only once in the address. Also, any leading 0s in a 16-bit segment do not need to be shown. So the preceding example of an IPv6 address can also be displayed as shown in the following two examples:

```
FE11:3CB8:E:0:0:3B00:230:A9
FE11:3CB8:E::3B00:230:A9
```

If you have both IPv4 and IPv6 addressing within the same network environment, the IPv4 address can be represented by six hexadecimal 16-bit segments that are combined with the dotted-decimal format, as the following two examples show:

```
0000:0000:0000:0000:0000:0000:147.19.1.1
::147.19.1.1
```

Using the CIDR format, IPv6 network addresses are represented the same as IPv4, which means they are represented in the address/prefix format. The following is an example of an IPv6 network with a 40-bit prefix (mask):

```
FE11:3CB8:E:0:0:3B00:230:A9/40
FE11:3CB8:E::3B00:230:A9/40
```

IPv6 Address Allocation

Just as the leading bits of an IPv4 address define the class of the address, the leading bits of the IPv6 address define the address type. These leading bits are of variable length and are called the format prefix (FP). Table 8.14 shows some of the IPv6 prefix allocations.

TABLE 8.14   IPv6 Prefix Allocation

Binary format prefix	Hexadecimal	Allocation
0000 0000	00	Unspecified, loopback, IPv4 compatible
001	2 or 3	Summarizable global unicast addresses
1111 1110 10	FE8	Link-local unicast addresses
1111 1110 11	FEC	Site-local unicast addresses
1111 1111	FF	Multicast addresses

And with our discussion of IPv6 completed, we conclude this chapter. If you are not feeling comfortable with the material presented in this chapter, please take the time to review it. It is important to thoroughly understand IP addressing and subnetting before you move on to the next chapter, where we will discuss all the major interior gateway protocols (IGPs) that are used to route the IP packets in a network.

Summary

This was a long but informative chapter. We started by discussing the various protocols and programs that can be used in the upper layers of the Internet Protocol stack.

We then covered the Internet Protocol suite of protocols and how to address hosts in an internetwork. We also showed you how to subnet, and hopefully, you can now do it in your head. It's OK if you can't, but you need to be able to subnet on paper at least.

We also showed you how to create a supernet by combining multiple contiguous networks and configuring them on a Cisco router running both EIGRP and OSPF. CIDR and VLSM were discussed, as well as the new IPv6 address format.

Exam Essentials

Know the four layers of the DoD model. The DoD model is a condensed version of the OSI model. It is made up of four, instead of seven, layers: the Process/Application layer, the Host-to-Host layer, the Internet layer, and the Network Access layer.

Know what IP is. The Internet Protocol (IP), which is connectionless, looks at each packet's IP address. Then, using a routing table, it decides where a packet is to be sent next, choosing the best path. The Network Access layer protocols at the bottom of the model don't possess IP's enlightened scope of the entire network; they deal only with physical links (local networks).

Know what TCP is. The Transmission Control Protocol (TCP), which is connection oriented, takes large blocks of information from an application and breaks them into segments. It numbers and sequences each segment so that the destination's TCP protocol can put the segments back into the order that the application intended. After these segments are sent, TCP (on the transmitting host) waits for an acknowledgment of the receiving end's TCP virtual circuit session and then retransmits those that aren't acknowledged.

Know what UDP is. UDP, which is connectionless, receives upper-layer blocks of information, instead of streams of data as TCP does, and breaks them into segments. Unlike TCP, UDP does *not* sequence the segments and does not care in which order the segments arrive at the destination. UDP sends the segments off and forgets about them. It doesn't follow through, check up on them, or even allow for an acknowledgment of safe arrival—complete abandonment. Because of this, it's referred to as an *unreliable* protocol. This does not mean that UDP is ineffective, only that it doesn't handle issues of reliability.

Understand what an IP address is.   An IP address is a numeric identifier assigned to each machine on an IP network. It designates the location of a device on the network. An IP address is a software address, not a hardware address—the latter is hard-coded on a network interface card (NIC) and used for finding hosts on a local network. IP addressing was designed to allow a host on one network to communicate with a host on a different network regardless of the type of LANs the hosts are participating in.

Understand supernetting.   Also called summarization, supernetting is the process of combining networks to save routing table entries.

Know what CIDR is.   Classless Inter-Domain Routing (CIDR) allows address allocation of the limited IPv4 address space to be managed in a much more tightly controlled and efficient way. It's also is an industry standard for displaying the number of subnet bits used with the IP address of a host or a network.

Understand the purpose of VLSM.   The purpose of Variable Length Subnet Masking (VLSM) is to conserve IP addresses because, when you subnet, IP addresses are lost in the math. For example, if you have a Class C network address and need 14 subnets, 10 of them WAN links that use only 2 IP addresses, you'll waste a lot of address space if all interfaces on your router use the same mask. VLSM also allows you to create subnets for larger networks, choosing a subnet mask that meets the size requirements of the network and reducing address wastage.

Key Terms

Before you take the exam, be certain you are familiar with the following terms:

Address Resolution Protocol (ARP)

Bootstrap Protocol (BootP)

Class A network

Class B network

Class C network

DoD protocol stack

domain name service (DNS)

Dynamic Host Configuration Protocol (DHCP)

File Transfer Protocol (FTP)

fully qualified domain names (FQDNs)

host address

Host-to-Host layer

Internet Control Message Protocol (ICMP)

Internet layer

Internet Protocol (IP)

IP address

Network Access layer

network address

Network File System (NFS)

node address

octets

port numbers

Process/Application layer

Reverse Address Resolution Protocol (RARP)

router solicitation

Simple Mail Transfer Protocol (SMTP)

Simple Network Management Protocol (SNMP)

subnet mask

subnetting

summarization

supernetting

Telnet

thin protocol

Transmission Control Protocol (TCP)

trap

Trivial File Transfer Protocol (TFTP)

User Datagram Protocol (UDP)

Review Questions

1. You have a network ID of 192.168.55.0 and you need to divide it into multiple subnets. You need 25 host IDs for each subnet and the largest number of subnets available. Which subnet mask should you assign?

    A. 255.255.255.192

    B. 255.255.255.224

    C. 255.255.255.240

    D. 255.255.255.248

2. If you have a subnet mask of 255.255.255.252, what is the equivalent /nn notation?

    A. /16

    B. /24

    C. /30

    D. /32

3. Which command will change the way the subnet mask is displayed on your Cisco router?

    A. Router(config)#`term ip netmask-format`

    B. Router#`ip netmask-format`

    C. Router(config-if)#`terminal ip netmask-format`

    D. Router#`terminal ip netmask-format hex`

4. What is domain name service (DNS) used for?

    A. To resolve XNS names

    B. To resolve DEC names

    C. To resolve fully qualified domain names (FQDNs)

    D. To build a hosts table

5. If you have an IP address of 172.16.10.5/25, what is the broadcast address that the host will use?

    A. 255.255.255.255

    B. 172.16.10.127

    C. 172.16.10.255

    D. 172.16.10.128

6. If you have an IP address of 172.16.10.5 with an 8-bit subnet mask, what is the valid host range this host is a member of?

    A. 10.1 through 10.126

    B. 10.5 through 255.255

    C. 10.1 through 10.255

    D. 10.1 through 10.254

7. How many usable hosts will the mask 255.255.255.252 provide?

    A. 16,384

    B. 2

    C. 4094

    D. 6

8. What is the valid host range of 172.16.10.5/27?

    A. 172.16.10.1 through 172.16.10.30

    B. 172.16.10.1 through 172.16.10.31

    C. 172.16.10.1 through 172.16.10.62

    D. 172.16.10.1 through 172.16.10.63

9. What is the valid host range of 172.16.10.5/26?

    A. 172.16.10.1 through 172.16.10.30

    B. 172.16.10.1 through 172.16.10.31

    C. 172.16.10.1 through 172.16.10.62

    D. 172.16.10.1 through 172.16.10.63

10. Which layer of the DoD model corresponds to the OSI's Network layer?

    A. The Network Access layer

    B. The Host-to-Host layer

    C. The Internet layer

    D. The Process/Application layer

Answers to Review Questions

1. B. The only answer that will give you 25 or more hosts is B, with 6 subnets and 30 hosts. A gives you 62 hosts, but only 2 subnets. C gives you 14 subnets with 14 hosts, and D gives you 30 subnets with 6 hosts.

2. C. Count the amount of bits on in each octet. The first octet use 8 bit, as do the second and third octets. The fourth octet uses 6 bits, which makes the total 30 bits.

3. B. The command `ip netmask-format` is the command used to change the way the subnet mask information is displayed.

4. C. DNS resolves hostnames to IP addresses.

5. B. First, figure out the mask, which is 255.255.255.128. The fourth octet has a value of 5, which means the subnet bit in the fourth octet must be off. The subnet is 0; the next subnet is 128. The broadcast address for the 0 subnet is 127.

6. D. First figure out the mask: 255.255.255.0. The question is really just asking you to add 8 bits to the default mask. The third octet is all subnet bits, and the fourth octet is all host bits.

7. B. Regardless of whether a Class A, B, or C address is associated with this mask, you'll get only two hosts.

8. A. First, figure out the mask: 255.255.255.224 is 27 bits. So, the subnet block size is 1–32. However, because subnet bits are in the third and fourth octet, the subnet bit in the fourth octet can be off, or 0. We have block sizes of 32, so the subnet is 0 and the broadcast address must be 31.

9. C. The mask is 255.255.255.192. So the subnet range is 1–62, with a 63 broadcast address.

10. C. The Internet layer corresponds to the OSI's Network layer, designating the protocols relating to the logical transmission of packets over the entire network.

Chapter 9

IP Interior Gateway Protocols

THE CCIE QUALIFICATION EXAM TOPICS COVERED IN THIS CHAPTER INCLUDE THE FOLLOWING:

- ✓ Static routes
- ✓ Understanding and modifying Administrative Distance
- ✓ The metrics, mechanics, and design of the Routing Information Protocol (RIP) and RIP v2
- ✓ Interior Gateway Routing Protocol (IGRP)
- ✓ Enhanced Interior Gateway Routing Protocol (EIGRP)
- ✓ Intermediate System-to-Intermediate System (IS-IS) protocol
- ✓ Open Shortest Path First (OSPF) protocol design

The two primary categories of routing protocols are interior gateway protocols and exterior gateway protocols. Typically, interior gateway protocols (IGPs) are used within an organization or a single autonomous system (AS) and exterior gateway protocols (EGPs) are used between multiple autonomous systems (ASs). IGPs for Transmission Control Protocol/Internet Protocol (TCP/IP) include the Routing Information Protocol (RIP), the Interior Gateway Routing Protocol (IGRP), the Enhanced Interior Gateway Routing Protocol (EIGRP), the Intermediate System-to-Intermediate System (IS-IS) routing protocol, and the Open Shortest Path First (OSPF) routing protocol.

Interior routing protocols are the mainstay for many CCIEs in the field. It is imperative that a CCIE candidate understand the theory behind these protocols and know how to configure each of them.

Back in Chapter 1, we briefly discussed static versus dynamic routing, interior versus exterior routing protocols, and distance vector versus link-state routing protocols. In this chapter, we are going to discuss these topics in much further detail. We'll start out by discussing static routing and how to configure static routes.

Static Routing

Static routes are manually configured on each router, and they are required at each hop along a path so that each routing device knows where to forward to the next hop. Routers route packets based upon the next hop to the destination IP address. Every time a change in the network topology is made, a network administrator must manually change the static routes throughout the entire network as required to correspond with the changes to the network topology. You can use static routes in hub-and-spoke networks with low-bandwidth links so that the bandwidth is not used by dynamic routing protocols. You can also use static routes in network firewall architectures and at connections with external partners.

Static Route Configuration

Static routes are configured with the `ip route` global configuration command. The command syntax is as follows:

```
ip route destination-network mask destination-ip
ip route destination-network mask outbound-interface
```

For example, if you want all traffic that is destined to the 147.19.24.0/24 network to be sent to the next hop IP address of 10.1.1.1, you would use the following command:

```
ip route 147.19.24.0 255.255.255.0 10.1.1.1
```

And if you want to route all traffic destined to the 147.19.24.0/24 network out of the local serial0/0 interface, then the following command would be used:

```
ip route 147.19.24.0 255.255.255.0 serial 0/0
```

Always keep in mind that you can create a catchall default route by using the network 0.0.0.0. So, if you wanted all traffic for which you do not have a more specific route in the routing table to be sent to the next hop IP address of 10.1.1.1, you would use the following command:

```
ip route 0.0.0.0 0.0.0.0 10.1.1.1
```

Because static routes have an administrative distance (AD) or believability of 1, if they reference the IP address of the next hop and of 0 if they reference the outbound local interface, they are always preferred over routes learned through a dynamic routing protocol.

We will discuss the AD in the next section, but for now keep in mind that a static route has an AD of 1. If you would like the static route to be used only if the dynamic routing protocol does not have a specific route, you can attach the new administrative distance to the end of the static route. This is also known as a floating static route. The following example is changing the administrative distance from 1 to 210 so that it floats above the dynamic routing protocols:

```
ip route 147.19.24.0 255.255.255.0 10.1.1.1 210
```

 Real World Scenario

Recursive Static Routes

Many Network Engineers have implemented recursive static routes within network designs in order to provide a stable network. Let's discuss what a recursive static routes is, because they are very useful in overcoming unique routing requirements within the network. A recursive static route actually points to a next hop that is either learned through a dynamic routing protocol (most useful) or defined in another static route statement. This next hop is most often more than one hop away from the router on which this route is being configured. In a dynamic routing environment, recursive static routes can be a very effective alternative to route maps or other possibly risky solutions. For example, look at these static routing statements:

```
ip route 192.168.1.1 255.255.255.255 192.168.2.1
ip route 10.0.0.0 255.0.0.0 192.168.1.1
```

> The actual next hop from the router is 192.168.2.1. The second statement uses the first statement in order to find the next hop. This "dual lookup" is what makes the route recursive.
>
> Here is the issue: A standard static route that points to a next hop will not be aware of any circuit failures. Therefore, the solution is to implement recursive static routes, because even though static routes are being used, all failures are still detected and traffic is rerouted. This is because the router will lose its route to the remote WAN interface whenever the circuit or intermediate LANs go down, and it will easily reroute through any other redundant path.

Keep in mind that a static route, although manually configured within a router, will not be placed into the routing table if the next hop associated with the route is not reachable. You should have a good understanding of static routing at this point and be ready to move on to dynamic routing protocols. But first, we'll show you what the administrative distance (AD) is and how you can use it in your network environment.

Administrative Distance for All Routing Protocols

For routers running multiple IP routing protocols, two or more of the routing protocols might have a route to the same destination. Which routing protocol should the router use to send the traffic to the destination? Cisco routers assign each routing protocol an *administrative distance (AD)*. In the event that two or more routing protocols have routes to the same destination network, the router must decide which one to place into the routing table. The Cisco IOS will select the route from the routing protocol with the lowest AD.

Table 9.1 shows all the administrative distance values for all routing protocols that Cisco supports. Refer back to this list when reading about all the other routing protocols.

TABLE 9.1   Administrative Distance

Route Source	Default Distance Values
Connected interface	0
Static route	1
Enhanced Interior Gateway Routing Protocol (EIGRP) summary route	5
External Border Gateway Protocol (BGP)	20

TABLE 9.1   Administrative Distance *(continued)*

Route Source	Default Distance Values
Internal EIGRP	90
Interior Gateway Routing Protocol (IGRP)	100
Open Shortest Path First (OSPF)	110
Intermediate System-to-Intermediate System (IS-IS)	115
Routing Information Protocol (RIP)	120
Exterior gateway protocol (EGP)	140
On Demand Routing (ODR)	160
External EIGRP	170
Internal BGP	200
Unknown	255

When using route redistribution, occasionally there may be a need to modify the administrative distance of a protocol. To change the administrative distance for routing protocols, use the `distance number` routing process command. The `number` value ranges from 0 to 255.

Now that you understand the administrative distance, let's discuss the difference between classful and classless.

Classful vs. Classless

The story about classless and classful is a long one. Basically, *classful* is the old way of doing routing. You had Class A, B, and C networks. The restriction was that you could use only one subnet. For example, for your Class B network 147.19.0.0, you use mask 255.255.0.0. This means that the mask 255.255.0.0 must be used for 147.19.0.0 everywhere. Classful routing protocols do not transmit subnet mask information in the routing updates; instead, they rely on classful address boundaries to determine this information. The router assumes the subnet mask is the same as the outbound interface, so all interfaces within the autonomous system (AS) must utilize subnet masks of the same length. However, with *classless* routing, you can use several masks for the same Class A, B, or C network because they transmit subnet mask information in their routing updates. This we call Variable Length Subnet Masking (VLSM). Another plus with classless routing is the use of supernetting, which is creating networks that have a shorter mask than the natural one. Supernetting allows you to group subnets together to form a larger address range for a network.

For example, natural masks for Class A network 255.0.0.0 would be networks 1.0.0.0–127.255.255.255; for Class B network 255.255.0.0, they would be networks 128.0.0.0–191.255.255.255; and for Class C network 255.255.255.0, they would be networks 192.0.0.0–223.255.255.255. Some examples of supernets are 146.128.0.0 255.128.0.0 and 194.94.0.0 255.255.0.0. You will see that the number of bits in the mask is less than the number of bits in the natural mask for Class A, B, or C networks.

On older versions of Cisco IOS (11.3 and prior), classless routing is not enabled by default and must be enabled explicitly using the `ip classless` global configuration command. If this command is not configured, any packets received for classful routes that are in the routing table will be matched against only the classful network and will be dropped (not subjected to the default route) if no match is found.

Now we'll move on to discuss operation of distance vector routing protocols.

Distance Vector Operation

RIP and IGRP are *distance vector* routing protocols. The distance vector algorithm (often called the Bellman-Ford algorithm) is designed for simplicity. Routers periodically announce all known routes to directly connected neighbors, including the distance associated with each route. The receiving router analyzes the information received, determines the best (lowest cost) path to each destination network, and places that entry in the routing table.

In this section, we'll look at the following five features of distance vector routing protocols:

- Defining a maximum
- The split horizon algorithm and route poisoning
- Holddown timers
- Triggered updates

Defining a Maximum

Defining a maximum was designed to prevent the count to infinity problem. In the count to infinity situation, the advertised distance of a particular network increases because incorrect routing information is being propagated. By defining a maximum, you allow for a route to increase to a certain value; once that value is reached, the route is no longer considered viable. RIP uses a maximum hop count of 16, and IGRP/EIGRP has a maximum hop count of 255.

In Figure 9.1, if network A fails, router R2 will eventually remove its entry from the routing table. R1 still has the cached route from R2 with a hop count of 1. R1 will advertise this route back to R2, which will treat this route as new and place an entry in the routing table with a hop count of 2. R2 will advertise this route to R1 with a hop count of 2. R1 considers this an update and corrects the routing table so that it contains a hop count of 3. This process continues forever if you don't define a maximum.

FIGURE 9.1   The count to infinity problem

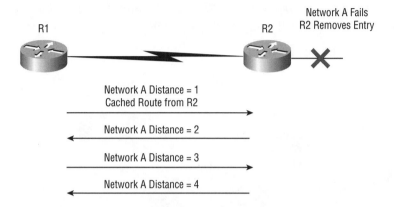

There are other methods to deal with this issue, such as split-horizon and holddown timers. Defining a maximum hop count provides additional protection.

Rule of Split-Horizon and Route Poisoning

The primary purpose of the *split-horizon* algorithm is to prevent routing loops between adjacent routers. The basic premise is that "it's never useful to send information out the interface from which it was learned," or in other words, "don't tell me, what I told you."

The rule of split-horizon always applies in a single, multipoint interface environment. All nodes attached to a multipoint interface belong to the same network number, thus for one spoke router to communicate with another spoke router, the packets must flow into the hub router and back out of the hub router through the same multipoint interface. Remember that the rule of split-horizon states that any routed packet that is received in through an interface *cannot* be transmitted out the same interface, or simply stated, never advertise a route out of the interface through which you learned it. The default setting of split-horizon is different for the different types of interfaces:

- On a physical interface with no Frame Relay encapsulation, split-horizon is enabled.

- On a physical interface with Frame Relay encapsulation, split-horizon is disabled.

- On multipoint and point-to-point subinterfaces with Frame Relay encapsulation, split-horizon is enabled.

For hub-and-spoke topology, disable split-horizon at the hub, although keep in mind that you *cannot* disable split-horizon for IPX RIP.

In Figure 9.2, router R3 will propagate a route for the 147.19.3.0 network, but because the path to router R1 is through the single, multipoint subinterface of router R2, router R1 will never receive the route advertisement for 147.19.3.0. This because the route will need to be advertised out of the same interfaces it was learned on.

FIGURE 9.2   The split-horizon issue

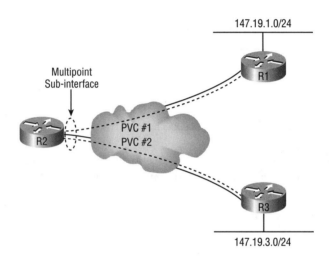

Route poisoning, also known as poison reverse updater, is another way of avoiding routing loops. Its rule states that once you learn of a route through an interface, advertise it as unreachable back through that same interface. Route poisoning decreases convergence time when a route fails. Normally, when a route fails, the router removes the route from the routing table. Other routers, after a period of time, also remove this route from their routing tables. A route can take a long time to age out of a large network. Route poisoning sets the distance of the failed route to infinity on the next routing update, and all the router's neighbors will know that the route has become inaccessible immediately.

Holddown Timers

Holddown times prevent a flapping route from generating huge amounts of traffic on the network and can prevent large routing loops. When a change occurs in the routing table, that entry is temporarily "frozen." Any new information about this route is ignored until the holddown timer expires. However, the "frozen" information is still used to forward packets. Keep in mind that although holddown timers are extremely effective in preventing routing loops, the use of them will greatly increase the network's convergence time. Holddown timers act as a dampening mechanism to improve network stability—setting timers aggressively (including holddown) can improve convergence time, but at risk of network instability.

Triggered Updates

Triggered updates can be used to decrease the convergence time. Distance vector routing protocols exchange information at periodic intervals. Triggered updates allow information to be exchanged anytime a change occurs instead of at periodic intervals.

Distance vector routing protocols are simple and somewhat efficient. Now let's discuss RIP.

Routing Information Protocol (RIP)

The *Routing Information Protocol (RIP)* was originally designed for the Xerox Network Systems (XNS) protocol suite. Developed at the Xerox Palo Alto Research Center (PARC), RIP was initially named the Gateway Information Protocol (GWINFO). In 1982, RIP was introduced to the TCP/IP suite of protocols in the Berkeley Software Distribution (BSD) of Unix. Despite its age, RIP remains an amazingly popular protocol.

RIP is supported by almost every major manufacturer of network equipment as well as by popular network operating systems such as Windows NT. RFC 1058, which describes Routing Information Protocol (RIP), was published in 1988.

How does RIP know which routes to keep in the routing table? Well, RIP uses timers to keep track of the usable routes.

RIP Timers

The following are descriptions of the timers that are utilized by RIP:

30 update timer   Every 30 seconds, the router sends a response message (update) out every RIP-enabled interface. To prevent synchronization issues (routers send updates at exactly the same time), a random variable (RIP_JITTER) will send an update between 25.5 and 30 seconds. RIP updates broadcasts use 255.255.255.255.

180 (Cisco) invalid timer   The invalid timer sets the amount of time a route can stay in a routing table without being updated. When the Invalid timer expires, the route update is not heard within 180 seconds, the route(s) is marked "possibly down," and a RIP update is sent out *all* RIP-enabled interfaces, with each route having a metric of 16. The RIP update will be sent out *all* interfaces every 30 seconds until the route(s) is flushed. Each neighbor receiving this update will immediately send out its RIP-enabled interfaces (including back to the original sender) the same routes marked as "inaccessible." The original route(s) is still used until the route is flushed.

180 Holddown timer   An update with a hop count higher than the metric recorded in the routing table will cause the route to go into holddown for 180 seconds.

240 (Cisco) flush timer   A route will be advertised with a metric of 16 until the flush timer expires. At this time, the route is removed. The RFC states that the Flush timer = 120 seconds in addition to the holddown timer, for Cisco, the Flush timer = 60 seconds + the invalid timer = 240 seconds. Use the `timers basic` command to change the update, invalid, holddown, and flush timer settings. All routers within the RIP domain must be configured with this command and have the identical timer values.

Triggered update timer   A triggered update occurs whenever the metric for a route is changed. It may include only those routes affected and does not cause the receiving router to reset its update timer. To avoid a "storm" of triggered updates after a topology change, subsequent triggered updates cannot be sent until the update timer expires (between 1 to 5 seconds).

Now we are ready to start discussing the specific types of RIP. RIP is available in two flavors, the original RIP version 1 and the newer RIP version 2. When people refer to RIP, they often mean RIP version 1. In the next section, we'll discuss the features and shortcomings of the first version, and then we'll discuss version 2 in the section that follows.

RIP Version 1 (RIPv1)

RIP uses the User Datagram Protocol (UDP) on port 520 to send and receive routing updates. RIP advertises the entire routing table to the local broadcast address (255.255.255.255) every 30 seconds.

> Instead of waiting for the route to disappear, you can issue the `clear ip route *` command.

RIP uses the hop count metric. Metrics are used to determine the best path to a particular destination. A hop count of 5 indicates that a packet must traverse five routers to get to the destinations. Only routers count toward hop count; Ethernet switches, hubs, and Frame Relay switches are transparent and are not included in the hop count. A hop count of 0 (zero) indicates that the network is directly connected to the router's physical interface; a hop count of 16 indicates that the network is unreachable.

A *default route* is the path on which the router sends traffic if it cannot locate any other matching route in the routing table. In RIP, the route is represented by 0.0.0.0.

RIP version 1 is the simplest IP routing protocol we will discuss. RIP version 1 works great on small networks for which security, Variable Length Subnet Masks (VLSMs), and broadcast traffic are not issues. Table 9.2 lists the features of RIP version 1 and their values.

TABLE 9.2   The Features of RIP Version 1

Feature	Value
Category	Distance vector
Class type	Classful
Advertising address	Broadcast; 255.255.255.255

TABLE 9.2 The Features of RIP Version 1 *(continued)*

Feature	Value
Metric	Hop count
Max hop count	15
Periodic interval	30 seconds

RIP Version 1: Classful (FLSM) Example

The rules of Fixed Length Subnet Mask (FLSM) are as follows:

- Routes that are members of a directly connected major network are only advertised out interfaces of the same major network if the subnet masks of the route and interface match.

- Routes with major networks that match the major network of the interface they were received will be given the same subnet mask as the interface.

- Routes are summarized to their class A, B, C major network when advertised over an interface addressed with a different major network.

- Routes received over interfaces of a different major network should be summarized classfully.

- If a route of a certain major network is received over an interface with a different major network and it is not summarized classfully, it will enter the routing table as a host route.

- It is advisable to use the same subnet mask consistently through a major network and to keep the entire major network contiguous.

Let's look at the output of show ip route commands on routers R1 and R2.

```
R1#show ip route

Gateway of last resort is not set

     147.19.0.0/16 is variably subnetted, 5 subnets, 3 masks
C       147.19.32.0/24 is directly connected, Serial0/0
C       147.19.33.0/24 is directly connected, Loopback0
C       147.19.34.0/23 is directly connected, Loopback1
C       147.19.32.2/32 is directly connected, Serial0/0
R       147.19.36.0/24 [120/1] via 147.19.32.2, 00:00:02, Serial0/0

R2#show ip route

Gateway of last resort is not set

     147.19.0.0/16 is variably subnetted, 5 subnets, 3 masks
```

```
C      147.19.32.0/24 is directly connected, Serial0
R      147.19.33.0/24 [120/1] via 147.19.32.1, 00:00:14, Serial0
C      147.19.32.1/32 is directly connected, Serial0
C      147.19.36.0/24 is directly connected, Loopback1
C      147.19.37.0/25 is directly connected, Loopback0
```

Notice in the preceding output that router R1 and router R2 are running RIP version 1, which is a classful routing protocol. Because RIP version 1 is classful, each of the routers will advertise routes without subnet mask information. Notice that the 147.19.37.0/25 network on router R2 does *not* show up in the routing table for router R1. This is because the subnet mask of 147.19.37.0/25 does not match the subnet mask of interface Serial0 (even though they belong to the same major network), thus router R2 will not advertise. However, the 147.19.36.0 network on router R2 will show up in the routing table of router R1 because its major network and mask of 255.255.255.0 matching that of interface Serial0, thus router R2 will advertise the route to router R1.

FIGURE 9.3   Classful (FLSM) example

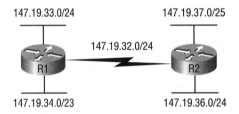

Likewise, the 147.19.34.0 network with a 255.255.254.0 mask on router R1 does *not* show up in the routing table for router R2. Once again, this is because router R1 does *not* recognize the 255.255.254.0 mask because it is *not* classful, so router R1 will *not* advertise the route to router R2. However, the 147.19.33.0 network on router R1 will show up in the routing table of router R2 because it has a classful mask of 255.255.255.0, thus router R1 will advertise the route to router R2.

Manipulating Routes with RIP

As with any routing protocol, there must be mechanisms to allow the router to prefer one route over another route. With RIP, the `offset-list` command can be utilized for this purpose. An offset list is a method of increasing the inbound or outbound hop count metric of routes learned by the router through RIP. You can specify only certain routes to apply the offset amount to by using an access list to specify the actual routes (networks) that the offset will be applied to. The command specifies an offset to add to the metric of a route entry and references an access list to determine entries to modify. If no ACL is called (by using a 0 as the access list number), all updates incoming or outgoing will be modified. If no interface is stated, the list will modify all incoming and outgoing updates specified by the ACL on any interface. The command is applied within the routing process on the router.

Here is an example of the `offset-list` command configuration:

```
router rip

network 147.19.0.0

offset-list 1 out 5 serial0/0
```
Add metric 5 [hop-count of 5] to all routes that match ACL 1 on interface serial0/0

```
access-list 1 permit 147.19.2.0 0.0.0.255
```

Configuring RIP Version 1

RIPv1 is classful, meaning that it will not advertise the subnet mask with the network address in the routing update messages that it periodically broadcasts to each of its adjacent neighbor routers. RIP is also a distance vector routing protocol, meaning that it uses the hop count (number of routers from source to destination) as the criteria to make its routing decisions. It is limited to 15 hops.

RIPv1 Process Commands

Let's take a look at some of the possible commands, which can be configured within the RIP routing process.

`network 147.19.0.0`
Specify interfaces that will advertise and listen for RIP updates. Major network on which RIP will run, only major class A, B or C

`passive-interface e0/0`
Specify which interface will not send RIP broadcasts, but will listen for RIP broadcasts; interface becomes a silent-host. Use routing filter if no inbound routes are desired

`neighbor 172.31.6.30`
Send a unicast advertisement/update to specified neighbor. Example: set passive-interface on e0/0, no RIP broadcasts are sent; if a neighbor on that same segment still needs to see routing updates, then enter neighbor command. Another use for the neighbor command is to enable unicast updates on non-broadcast media such as Frame-Relay

output-delay 30	Useful when a high speed router is sending multiple RIP messages to a low-speed router. Low speed router may not be able to process updates as fast as they are received, and routing info may be lost. output delay may be used to set an interpacket gap of between 8 - 50 milliseconds. Default - 0 milliseconds
input-queue 100	If a high-end router is sending at high speed to a low-speed router that might not be able to receive at the high speed. Configuring this command will help prevent the routing table from losing information. Use in conjunction with the output-delay command 100 = depth of the RIP input queue. Values = 0 – 1024, Default is 50
maximum-paths [1-6]	Allows equal-cost, load-balancing by forwarding packets over 1 to 6 multiple paths. The default = 4

RIP Troubleshooting Commands

Here are a few of the possible commands, which can be used to troubleshoot RIP.

```
debug ip rip
debug ip rip events
debug ip rip trigger
debug ip rip database
show ip rip database
show ip protocols
```

Now we'll move on to discuss RIPv2.

RIP Version 2 (RIPv2)

RIP version 2 was designed to address the shortcomings of version 1. RIP version 2 supports plain text and Message Digest 5 (MD5) authentication, route summarization, and Variable Length Subnet Masks (VLSMs).

On large networks, the broadcast used by RIP version 1 may be unacceptable. Version 2 uses multicast addresses for communication between routers and also supports the ability to use unicast updates between routers.

RIP version 2 uses the multicast 224.0.0.9.

RIP version 1 believes all routing updates that are received (RIP discards updates from a source not on the same subnet, unless no validate-update-source is used). An incorrectly configured device running RIP version 1 can cause severe network problems. RIP version 2 supports authentication using clear text or MD5 encryption.

Perhaps the biggest difference between the two versions of RIP is that version 1 is *classful* and version 2 is *classless* by virtue of including subnet mask information in routing updates. (Refer back to the section "Classful vs. Classless" earlier in this chapter to review the difference between the two.)

RIP provides a functional open standards solution for many environments. RIP is, nevertheless, still limited because of the nature of the hop count metric (which also does not take into account different speed links) and because the entire routing table is advertised every 30 seconds. Table 9.3 lists the features of RIP version 2 and their values.

TABLE 9.3   The Features of RIP Version 2

Feature	Value
Category	Distance vector
Class type	Classless
Advertising address	Multicast; 224.0.0.9
Metric	Hop count
Max hop count	15
Periodic interval	30 seconds

RIP Default Route Propagation

The following applies to both RIPv1 & RIPv2, ignore the "version 2" command for RIPv1 implementations.

Here is an example of the `ip route` command:

```
router rip
 version 2
 redistribute static
 network 10.0.0.0
ip route 0.0.0.0 0.0.0.0 Null0          Sets the Gateway of last resort on
                                        this router to Null 0
```

Here is an example of the `ip default-network` command:

```
router rip
 version 2
```

`ip default-network` `147.19.0.0`	Specify network address to be used as a default network. The classful network may be directly connected, specified by a static route, or discovered by a dynamic protocol. No network command is needed for 147.19.0.0

Here is an example of the `default-information originate` command:

```
router rip
 version 2
 default-information originate    Generate a default route into this RIP process
```

The following example originates a default route (0.0.0.0/0) over a certain interface when 147.19.0.0/16 is present. This is called conditional default origination:

```
interface Serial 1/0
  ip address 147.19.16.4 255.255.255.0


router rip
  version 2
  network 147.19.0.0
  default-information originate route-map kelly


route-map kelly permit 10
  match ip address 10
  set interface serial 1/0 serial 1/1    Used to specify which interface(s)
                                         the 0.0.0.0 default is to be sent on
access-list 10 permit 147.19.16.0 0.0.0.255
```

Configuring Authentication

Cisco's implementation of RIPv2 message authentication includes the choice of simple passwords or MD5 authentication and the option of defining multiple keys, or passwords, on a key chain. The router may then be configured to use different keys at different times.

The steps for setting up RIPv2 authentication are as follows:

- Define a key chain with a name.
- Define the key or keys on the chain.
- Enable authentication on an interface and specify the key chain to be used.
- Specify whether the interface will use clear text or MD5 authentication.

To configure RIP authentication, use the following interface and global commands:

```
interface serial0/0
```

`ip rip authentication key-chain chris`	Enable RIPv2 authentication on interface and specify which key-chain chris to use
`ip rip authentication mode {text | md5}`	Configure the interface to use MD5 digest authentication, or let it default to plain text authentication
`key chain chris`	Define key chain chris. Local Significance only. Name may be different on other routers
`key 1`	
`key-string josh`	Specify password josh - MUST be the same on both interfaces at each end of the link

Address Summarization with RIPv2

The `ip summary-address rip` command (available starting with IOS 12.1) causes the router to summarize a given set of routes learned via RIPv2 or redistributed into RIPv2. Host routes are especially applicable for summarization. To configure IP summary addressing, use the following command on the outbound interface:

```
int serial 0/0
```

`ip summary-address rip 147.19.4.0 255.255.252.0`	Specifies the IP address and network mask that identify the routes to be summarized.

This example will summarize the following four networks:

- 147.19.4.0
- 147.19.5.0
- 147.19.6.0
- 147.19.7.0

Now only one route is advertised for all four of these networks.

Configuring RIP Version 2

Routing Information Protocol version 2 (RIPv2), described in RFC 1723, is a classless routing protocol, meaning that the subnet mask is carried with each destination route entry. Because RIPv2 is classless, it supports Variable Length Subnet Masking (VLSM), which means that RIP version 2 does *not* have the same classful (FLSM) issue that RIP version 1 has. Also, RIPv2 supports authentication of its routing updates.

By default, the router IOS receives RIP version 1 and version 2 packets but sends only version 1 packets. You can configure the router IOS to receive and send only version 1 packets. Also, you can configure the router IOS to receive and send only version 2 packets. This can be accomplished with the following commands on the outbound/inbound interface:

ip rip send version 1	RIPv1 Only - Specify on interface which version to send
ip rip receive version 1	RIPv1 Only - Specify on interface which version to receive
ip rip send version 1 2	BOTH - Send both v1 (broadcast) and v2 (multicast) updates

RIPv2 Global Commands

Let's take a look at some of the possible commands, which can be implemented with RIPv2.

ip classless	Default is FLSM, router doesn't pay attention to the Class of the destination address, instead it performs bit-by-bit best match between the destination address and its known routes. Newer versions of IOS have this command enabled by default
ip subnet-zero	By default, Cisco IOS rejects an attempt to configure an all-zeros subnet as an invalid address/mask combo even if a classless routing protocol is running. To override this default use this command. Newer versions of IOS have this command enabled by default

RIPv2 Process Commands

Let's take a look at some of the possible commands, which can be implemented under the RIPv2 routing process.

```
router rip
 passive-interface Serial0/0
 network 147.19.0.0
```

`version 2`	Specify RIPv2 RIP process. Default =RIPv1 (change back = no version 2)
`distance 125`	Distance command changes administrative distance on all routes that are received (not transmitted)
`no auto-summary`	By default Cisco IOS will summarize at network boundaries the same as RIPv1. Turn off summarization by this Command

 See RIPv1 documentation for additional commands.

RIPv2 Troubleshooting Commands

Here are a few of the possible commands, which can be used to troubleshoot RIP.

```
debug ip rip
debug ip rip events
show ip protocols
```

In the next section, we'll look at another distance vector routing protocol—IGRP.

Interior Gateway Routing Protocol (IGRP)

This chapter focuses on one of the many network layer routing protocols, specifically the *Interior Gateway Routing Protocol (IGRP)*. IGRP was developed in the mid-1980s by Cisco Systems, Inc. with the primary purpose of providing a stable routing protocol that could be implemented within an autonomous system (AS). Prior to the development of IGRP, RIP was the most popular implemented IGP routing protocol. Although RIP is a reliable routing protocol, it has certain limitations, such as 16 hop count limitation that soon began to impede network growth. IGRP is a classful distance vector routing protocol. The most important aspect of IGRP to always remember is that it is classful and thus utilizes Fixed Length Subnet Masks (FLSMs). You can refer back to the beginning of this chapter for an explanation of classful versus classless.

IGRP uses the five path vector metrics of bandwidth, delay, reliability, load, and maximum transmission unit (MTU) to form a composite metric, which is the criteria used by routers to make their routing decisions. By default, only the bandwidth and delay metrics are utilized in the routing decision process. The composite metric will be calculated using the smallest bandwidth of all the outbound interfaces along the path to a destination network and the sum of the delay of all the outbound interfaces within a path to a destination network. Therefore, IGRP has a major benefit over other distance vector protocols such as RIP. RIP is limited to a router hop count of 16 (IGRP has a maximum hop count of 255), thus the network size is limited. Also, RIP makes its preferred routing decision based solely on the hop count, which means that a router running RIP will choose a one-hop path to a destination network over a two-hop-count path even though the two-hop path may have more bandwidth and better performance. When IGRP is utilizing its composite metric, a router will use the two-hop-count path to the destination network because the additional bandwidth, along with less delay, will cause the two-hop-count path to out-perform the one-hop-count path.

In Figure 9.4, if the routers were running RIP, the preferred path for R1 to R3 would be Link #1 because it is only one hop. However, it is not the best path for traffic to flow across because it is only a 56Kbps link. If the routers were running IGRP, the preferred path from R1 to R3 would be via R2 because even though this is a two-hop path, it is a T1 (1.544Mbps) link and can therefore handle the traffic more efficiently.

FIGURE 9.4 IGRP metrics versus RIP metrics

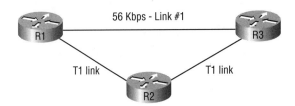

Next we'll discuss the metrics used by IGRP.

The Five Path Vector Metrics for IGRP

When IGRP sends out its periodic route updates (every 90 seconds), there are five path vector metrics that are sent to describe each destination prefix (network). IGRP uses a composite metric that can be based on bandwidth, delay, reliability, and loading. If the default metric weights are left at their default values, the bandwidth and delay metrics will be used only to calculate the composite metric. The calculation for the IGRP initially looks complex:

```
Metric = [K1 * Bandwidth + (K2 * Bandwidth)/(256-load) + K3*Delay ]*[K5/(reliability
+ K4)].
```

In this formidable equation, by default, K2, K4, and K5 are valued at 0 and K1 and K3 are valued at 1. This greatly simplifies the equation:

```
K2 = K4 = K5 = 0   and K1 = K3 = 1
```

Therefore, the following is true:

```
Metric = Bw + Delay
```

The bandwidth (Bw) and delay factors are calculated as follows:

```
Bw = 10,000,000/(bandwidth in Kbps)
Delay = delay in microseconds/10
```

The following is the final metric used in production:

```
Metric =[10,000,000/(minimum path bandwidth in Kbps)] + [(cumulative delay in
us)/10]
```

Bandwidth

The bandwidth metric has two constituents:

Bandwidth   Outgoing interface bandwidth, referenced in kilobits and based on media type. To change media type defaults, you must use the interface `bandwidth` command; otherwise, the metric will be calculated based on the default bandwidth of the interface.

$BW_{IGRP\,(MIN)}$ The formula for $BW_{IGRP\,(MIN)}$ is 10^7 / smallest *bandwidth* statement of any *outgoing* interface along the path to the destination prefix. Measured in Kbps for IGRP/EIGRP. This value is sent with each route prefix in the periodic route update and used to determine the composite metric for each destination prefix. Here is an example: A serial interface has a default of 1544 kilobits and a default bandwidth metric of 6476. To change the bandwidth to 512K, use interface command `bandwidth 512`. Bandwidth metric will now equal 10,000,000 / 512 = 19531.

Delay

The delay metric has three constituent parts:

Delay (DLY)   Outgoing interface delay metric, referenced in microseconds and based on media type. This value is displayed when using the `show interface` command. (i.e., DLY 5000 usec).

$Delay_{(IGRP)}$ Outgoing interface delay divided by 10. (Expressed in 10-microsecond units, or usec). This value is sent with each route prefix in the periodic route update. Default can be changed using the `delay` command on the interface. Here is an example: delay 5 (($Delay_{IGRP}$) 5×10 (usec) = 50 usec (DLY). Values for the `delay` command are 1 to 16777215 (maximum of 167 seconds).

$Delay_{IGRP\,(SUM)}$ End-to-end travel time. Total sum to any destination prefix using the $Delay_{IGRP}$ metric for each outgoing interface along the path toward the destination prefix. Used to determine the composite metric for each destination prefix. Maximum end-to-end delay is 167 seconds.

Total sum of any route can be displayed using the `show ip route A.B.C.D.` (i.e., `show ip route 172.16.0.0`). If the maximum hop count is exceeded (default of 100 hops), the route will be marked unreachable by setting the delay to 16777215 (0xFFFFFF).

OSPF also uses the bandwidth statement on the interface. Use the delay command if you want to influence IGRP routing when OSPF is also used on the same router.

Each enabled IGRP interface will have the bandwidth and delay parameters associated with the type of interface. Table 9.4 shows a listing of common media types and their associated metric values.

TABLE 9.4   IGRP Metric Examples

interface Media	Bw command	Bw IGRP	Delay command	DLY IGRP
FastEthernet (100M)	100000	100	100	10
FDDI (100M)	100000	100	100	10
16M Token-Ring	16000	625	630	63
10M Ethernet	10000	1000	1000	100
T1 (1.544M)	1544	6476	20000	2000
512K	512	19531	20000	2000
DS0 (64K)	64	156250	20000	2000
56K	56	178571	20000	2000
Loopback	8000000	8000	5000	500

Reliability

The reliability metric reflects the total outgoing error rates on the interfaces along the route, calculated on a 5-minute weighted average. Values are 1–255 (255 is 100-percent reliable, 128 is 50-percent reliable). The lowest value along the path is used for this metric. This metric is not used in the composite metric calculation unless the metric weights command is used.

To display route reliability use show ip route A.B.C.D. To show interface reliability, use show interface command.

Load

The load metric reflects the total load of outgoing interfaces along the route, calculated on a 5-minute weighted average.

Values are 1–255 (1 is minimally loaded and 255 is a 100-percent loaded link). The highest load along the path is used for this metric. This metric is not used in the composite metric calculation unless the `metric weights` command is used. To display route load, use `show ip route A.B.C.D`. To show interface load, use the `show interface` command.

Maximum Transmission Unit (MTU)

IGRP tracks the minimum MTU along the entire path to the destination network. This metric is not used in the composite metric calculation. To display minimum MTU for a route, use `show ip route A.B.C.D`.

Hop Count

Although not used as part of the five path vector metrics but included in each prefix update, the hop count is simply the number of gateways that a packet will have to go through to get to the destination. A router will advertise a directly connected interface with a hop count of 0 (zero). The default maximum hop count, or network diameter, is 100.

The hop count can be changed using the `metric maximum-hops` command. Values are 1–255. To display hop count for a destination prefix, use the command `show ip route A.B.C.D`.

IGRP Timers

The following are descriptions of the timers that are utilized by IGRP:

Update timer   Every 90 seconds, the router sends a response message (update) out every IGRP-enabled interface. To prevent synchronization issues (routers sending updates at exactly the same time), a random variable (20 percent subtracted from each update time) is used, which causes the updates to be sent between 72 and 90 seconds.

(Cisco) invalid timer   The invalid timer defines the amount of time a route can stay in a routing table without being updated. If a route is not heard within 270 seconds, the route is marked as unreachable until the flush timer expires, at which time the route will be deleted from the table. See the explanation for the holddown timer to see what happens in the route is marked unreachable.

Holddown timer   The holddown timer is used if a route is marked unreachable or if an update with a hop count higher than the metric recorded in the routing table will cause the route to go into holddown for 280 seconds The 280 seconds is 3× update (270) + 10 seconds. No new entry will be accepted during this period. You may disable holddown by using the `no metric holddown` command.

(Cisco) flush timer   A route will be advertised as unreachable until the flush timer expires. At this time, the route is removed. The flush timer equals 7× update timer which = 630 seconds.

Any of the default timers in the preceding list can be changed using the `timers basic` command. All routers within the same IGRP AS must have the identical settings for the timer values. Table 9.5 lists the features of IGRP and their values.

TABLE 9.5 The Features of IGRP

Feature	Value
Category	Distance vector
Class type	Classful
Advertising address	Broadcast; 255.255.255.255
Metric	Composite (bandwidth, delay, reliability, loading)
Max hop count	100 is default (maximum is 255)
Periodic interval	90 seconds

IGRP: Classful (FLSM) Example

The rules of Fixed Length Subnet Mask (FLSM) are as follows:

- If the destination address is a member of a directly connected major network, the subnet mask configured on the interface attached to that network will be used to determine the subnet of the destination address. Therefore, the same subnet mask must be used consistently throughout the major network.

- If the destination address is not a member of a directly connected major network, the router will try to match only the major Class A, B, or C portion of the destination address.

Let's look at the output of show ip route commands on routers R1 and R2.

```
R1#show ip route

Gateway of last resort is not set

     172.13.0.0/24 is subnetted, 1 subnets
C       172.13.32.0 is directly connected, Loopback1
     147.19.0.0/24 is subnetted, 3 subnets
C       147.19.32.0 is directly connected, Serial0/0
I       147.19.33.0 [100/8976] via 147.19.32.2, 00:00:03, Serial0/0
C       147.19.34.0 is directly connected, Loopback0
I    10.0.0.0/8 [100/8976] via 147.19.32.2, 00:00:03, Serial0/0
```

```
I    192.168.100.0/24 [100/8976] via 147.19.32.2, 00:00:03, Serial0/0

R2#show ip route

Gateway of last resort is not set

I    172.13.0.0/16 [100/8976] via 147.19.32.1, 00:00:00, Serial1
     147.19.0.0/24 is subnetted, 3 subnets
C       147.19.32.0 is directly connected, Serial1
C       147.19.33.0 is directly connected, Loopback1
I       147.19.34.0 [100/8976] via 147.19.32.1, 00:00:00, Serial1
     10.0.0.0/24 is subnetted, 1 subnets
C       10.1.1.0 is directly connected, Loopback2
C    192.168.100.0/24 is directly connected, Loopback3
```

In Figure 9.5, both router R1 and router R2 are running IGRP, which is a classful routing protocol. Because IGRP is classful, the subnet mask is not sent in the routing updates between routers. Therefore, the receiving router will assign the proper classful mask to each route that matches what class of address the route (network) is (Class A, Class B, or Class C). The only exception to this rule is if the network matches the major network of the receiving router's interface, it will place the route into the routing table with the mask of the receiving interface.

FIGURE 9.5   Classful (FLSM) example

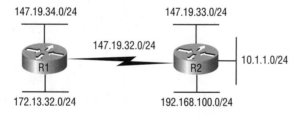

Router R2 has the 10.1.1.0 255.255.255.0 network configured, but router R1 receives the route and places it into its routing table as 10.0.0.0 255.0.0.0. The route is changed from a 24-bit mask to an 8-bit mask because router R2 summerizes to a classful boundary when sending the route and router R1 assigns a Class A mask to the Class A network. Likewise, the 192.168.100.0 network looks good on router R1 because the 24-bit mask is the natural mask for a Class C network. The 147.19.33.0 network is added to the routing table of router R1 because it is part of the same natural Class B network (147.19.0.0) as the interface (147.19.32.0 network) over which it was received.

Manipulating Routes with IGRP

As with any routing protocol, there must be mechanisms to allow the router to prefer one route over another route. With IGRP, the `offset-list` command can be utilized for this purpose. An `offset-list` command is a method of increasing the inbound or outbound composite metric of routes learned by the router through IGRP. You can specify only certain routes to apply the offset amount to by using an access list to specify the actual routes (networks) that the offset will be applied to. The command is applied within the routing process on the router. As mentioned earlier, the composite metric value is never sent with the prefix updates. The offset values actually increase the delay metric, whereby an offset of 1 will add an additional 10 microsecond units.

Let's take a look at some of the possible commands, which can be configured within the IGRP routing process.

```
router igrp 100

  network 147.19.0.0

  offset-list 1 out 37972 Serial0
```

Route metrics can be manipulated using the offset command. This command will add an additional 379720 microseconds to the delay metric to affect the overall composite metric for the route entry matched in Access List 1. If no ACL is called, by using a zero as the access list number. all updates incoming or outgoing will be modified, offset-list 0 selects all networks

Out – Perform offset on outgoing updates.

In – Perform offset on incoming updates.

Offset – Values for offset are 0-2147483647.

Manipulate the delay metric.

If no interface is stated, the list will modify all incoming or outgoing updates specified by the ACL on any interface.

```
access-list 1 permit 147.19.2.0 0.0.0.255
```

Rule of Split-Horizon for IGRP

Because IGRP is a distance vector routing protocol, it must follow the rule of split-horizon, which basically states that any routed packets that enter a router through an interface cannot be routed back out of the same interface. This is an important concept to keep in mind with everyday networking and in the CCIE lab examination. Refer back to the beginning of this chapter for an explanation of split-horizon.

Unequal-Cost Load-Balancing Traffic

IGRP is one of a few routing protocols that allow for equal and unequal load cost balancing. IGRP can load-balance traffic across multiple paths (up to six) to a destination, which will allow for greater throughput and reliability to a destination network. One method of allowing paths with different composite metrics to load-balance traffic across each other is the use of the `variance` command. The variance is a multiplier that is used to calculate the maximum acceptable metric of another unequal cost route to the same prefix. If the prefix composite metric of the second destination path is within the variance (multiple) of the metric of the lowest-cost path, then the router can use the second path along with the first path and load-balance traffic across both paths to the destination network. The router will load-balance the traffic proportionately to the metric of each route. To figure out the variance threshold, divide the highest received metric with the metric of the route currently installed in the routing table (i.e., lowest received metric + metric associated with the interface on which the route was received). By default, the variance is equal to 1, which means that only equal-cost load-balancing can occur. The `variance` command is applied within the routing process on the router.

Let's take a look at some of the possible commands, which can be used to configure load balancing across multiple paths.

```
router igrp 100
 network 147.19.0.0
```

`variance 3`	Any path composite metric equal to or less than three times the routers composite metric is considered a valid path
`maximum-paths 2`	Limit the number of possible valid, equal or unequal cost paths to two. The router can handle a value of 1 to 6 multiple paths

Configuring IGRP on a Router

The first step to implementing IGRP within your network is of course to configure the routing process on the routers. This is accomplished with the `router igrp 100` command (in this example, the autonomous system is 100). It is not necessary to have a registered autonomous system number to use IGRP. If you do not have a registered number, you are free to create your own within the range of 1–65,535. We recommend that if you do have a registered number, you use it to identify the IGRP process. Either way, all routers within your network that are expected to share routing information must belong to the same AS. There are exceptions when performing route redistribution, but that is a topic for further discussion in Chapter 10 of this book.

IGRP will broadcast routing updates out the interfaces that are within the specified networks. If any of the router interface IP addresses do not belong to the networks that are specified in the IGRP routing process, they will not be advertised in any IGRP routing update. Use the `passive-interface` command to limit IGRP broadcast traffic out the interface. Updates will still be received on a passive interface.

Let's take a look at some of the commands required to configure the IGRP routing process.

`router igrp 100`	Enable the IGRP routing process and assign an AS number, AS = 100 in this example
`network 147.19.0.0`	Associate networks with an IGRP routing process. The networks should follow the natural class boundary

Default Network

The IGRP routing protocol does not understand address 0.0.0.0 (quad 0). So, to perform the function of a default route, the router will advertise an actual address, which already exists in the routing table, as an exterior route. Destination networks that are advertised as exterior routes in IGRP are understood to be default routes. The network may be specified by a static route or discovered by a dynamic routing protocol.

In Figure 9.6, we want router R1 to have a default network of 192.167.1.0. Router R3 is propagating dynamically through its RIP routing protocol the 192.167.1.0 network, and router R2 will recognize this network as a "classful" network and assign the correct "classful" mask of 255.255.255.0. As shown in the output of the show ip route command on router R2, you can see that the 192.167.1.0 network is in the routing table.

FIGURE 9.6   Default network diagram

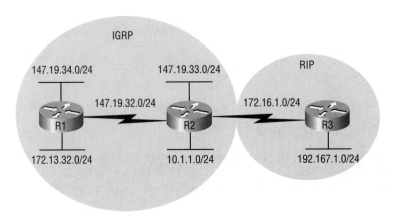

We'll configure the `ip default-network 192.167.1.0` command on router R2. Once again, as shown in the output of the **show ip route** command on router R2, you can see that the 192.167.1.0 network has been placed into the routing table as the gateway of last resort:

```
R2#show ip route
Gateway of last resort is 172.16.1.1 to network 192.167.1.0

I     172.13.0.0/16 [100/8976] via 147.19.32.1, 00:00:03, Serial1
      172.16.0.0/24 is subnetted, 1 subnets
C        172.16.1.0 is directly connected, Serial0
      147.19.0.0/24 is subnetted, 3 subnets
C        147.19.32.0 is directly connected, Serial1
C        147.19.33.0 is directly connected, Loopback1
I        147.19.34.0 [100/8976] via 147.19.32.1, 00:00:03, Serial1
      10.0.0.0/24 is subnetted, 1 subnets
C        10.1.1.0 is directly connected, Loopback2
R*    192.167.1.0/24 [120/1] via 172.16.1.1, 00:00:02, Serial0
```

However, if you view the output of a **show ip route** command on router R1, you'll notice that there is no gateway of last resort set and that the 192.167.1.0 network is not in the routing table:

```
R1#show ip route
Gateway of last resort is not set

      172.13.0.0/24 is subnetted, 1 subnets
C        172.13.32.0 is directly connected, Loopback1
      147.19.0.0/24 is subnetted, 3 subnets
C        147.19.32.0 is directly connected, Serial0/0
I        147.19.33.0 [100/8976] via 147.19.32.2, 00:00:03, Serial0/0
C        147.19.34.0 is directly connected, Loopback0
I     10.0.0.0/8 [100/8976] via 147.19.32.2, 00:00:03, Serial0/0
```

Likewise, the output of a **debug ip igrp events** on router R1 shows that it is not receiving the default network from router R2. Remember that the default network will be sent as an exterior route, and router R1 is not receiving any exterior routes from router R2:

```
R1#debug ip igrp events
R1#00:39:22: IGRP: Update contains 0 interior, 3 system, and 0 exterior routes.
  00:39:22: IGRP: Total routes in update: 300:39:22: IGRP: Update
  contains 0 interior, 3 system, and 0 exterior routes.
00:39:22: IGRP: Total routes in update: 3
```

In order for router R1 to have the default network, it must have the classful route that is being used as the default network in its routing table. For this to happen, we must perform route redistribution on router R2 so that the 192.167.1.0 network will be propagated from router R2 to router R1. Once the route redistribution has been configured, the output of a debug ip igrp events on router R1 shows that it is now receiving the default network from router R2:

```
R1#debug ip igrp events
00:41:18: IGRP: Update contains 0 interior, 2 system, and 1 exterior routes.
00:41:18: IGRP: Total routes in update: 3
```

Now that router R1 is receiving the 192.167.1.0 network, it will place the network into its routing table. Remember that router R2 has the ip default-network 192.167.1.0 command configured and is still sending the route to router R1 as an exterior route. Therefore, router R1 will use the 192.167.1.0 network as its default network.

As shown in the output of the show ip route command on router R1, you can see that the 192.167.1.0 network is in the routing table and it is set as the gateway of last resort. Notice that in the routing tables for router R2 and router R3, the 192.167.1.0 network will be flagged with *, indicating that it is a default route candidate to be used:

```
R1#show ip route
Gateway of last resort is 147.19.32.2 to network 192.167.1.0

      172.13.0.0/24 is subnetted, 1 subnets
C        172.13.32.0 is directly connected, Loopback1
I     172.16.0.0/16 [100/10476] via 147.19.32.2, 00:00:03, Serial0/0
      147.19.0.0/24 is subnetted, 3 subnets
C        147.19.32.0 is directly connected, Serial0/0
I        147.19.33.0 [100/8976] via 147.19.32.2, 00:00:03, Serial0/0
C        147.19.34.0 is directly connected, Loopback0
I     10.0.0.0/8 [100/8976] via 147.19.32.2, 00:00:03, Serial0/0
I*    192.167.1.0/24 [100/180671] via 147.19.32.2, 00:00:05, Serial0/0
```

IGRP Troubleshooting

When troubleshooting IGRP routing issues, you should verify that the routers are broadcasting their routing updates to each other and that the metrics are configured correctly. If you perform a show ip route command and do not see the required destination network route in the table, then routing cannot occur. The following are some of the recommended commands to assist in the troubleshooting of IGRP routing issues:

debug ip igrp events	Verify the source/destination of each update, and the number of routes in each update
debug ip igrp transactions	Monitor and verify IGRP routing update transaction information between routers
show ip protocols	Display IGRP process parameters

show interface	This will allow the verification of the metric values
show ip route	Shows the contents of the entire routing table
show ip route 147.19.25.3	Shows IGRP metrics for a specific route, 147.19.25.3 in this example

If you have a good understanding of the operation of IGRP within the routing environment and how IGRP derives its routing decision, then resolving any routing issues should be a quick process.

IGRP, a natural evolution of the distance vector protocol concept, is waning in popularity because Cisco developed an even better protocol called Enhanced IGRP.

Enhanced Interior Gateway Routing Protocol (EIGRP)

Enhanced Interior Gateway Routing Protocol (EIGRP) was developed by Cisco Systems from its IGRP routing protocol. Because EIGRP never developed into an open standards routing protocol, it is still considered a Cisco proprietary protocol that is understood only among other Cisco devices. EIGRP has been classified as a hybrid distance routing protocol. It incorporates features that are exhibited in a distance vector routing protocol, but it is more advanced because it associates characteristics of a link-state routing protocol without the additional overhead. The reason for its development was to overcome some of the limitations of traditional distance vectors routing protocols while still providing and maintaining a loop-free environment. It is not our intent in this chapter to describe in depth the full functionality of EIGRP, but it is important to describe some of the major characteristic and differences as compared to IGRP.

 In older literature, you will see EIGRP called a hybrid protocol. In more recent documents, EIGRP is referred to as an advanced distance vector routing protocol.

There are only a few similarities between EIGRP with IGRP and many major differences. First we'll look at some of the similarities:

- As stated earlier, EIGRP, like IGRP, is a Cisco Systems proprietary routing protocol.

- EIGRP uses the same five path vector metrics as IGRP to make the best routing decision to each given destination. Metrics such as bandwidth, delay, reliability, load, and maximum transmission unit (MTU) can be used to calculate a composite metric for each given destination prefix. However, by default, Cisco routers only utilize the bandwidth and delay metrics, which, unlike IGRP, are multiplied by 256 when the composite metric is computed.

As you can see, there aren't very many similarities between the two protocols. Therefore, by describing some of the differences, we'll also define the major characteristics of EIGRP.

Differences between EIGRP and IGRP

EIGRP is considered a classless, advanced distance vector routing protocol that uses the Diffusing Update Algorithm (DUAL) for routing calculations. The term *classless* is used because EIGRP supports Variable Length Subnet-Masking (VLSM) as well as discontiguous networks. IGRP is a *classful* routing protocol that does not allow for network subnet masks in the update. EIGRP has the following four components:

- Protocol Data Modules
- Reliable Transport Protocol (RTP)
- Neighbor Discovery/Recovery
- Diffusing Update Algorithm (DUAL)

Let's take a look at each.

Protocol Data Modules

EIGRP supports multiple protocols such as IP, IPX, and AppleTalk using Protocol Data Modules that are responsible for the protocol-specific routing tasks.

Reliable Transport Protocol (RTP)

RTP manages reliable and ordered delivery of EIGRP packets (which guarantees that each packet is delivered in the order sent) as well as the reception of EIGRP packets. As reliable packets are exchanged between neighbors, each packet sent includes a sequence number. If packets are not seen or are delivered out of order, packet retransmissions may be necessary. EIGRP packets are classified as either multicast or unicast and reliable or unreliable. RTP ensures that every single packet that is classified as reliable is acknowledged before the next packet in the sequence can be sent.

Neighbor Discovery/Recovery

Using hello packets, EIGRP dynamically discovers and maintains directly connected neighbors. Because there are no periodic updates to maintain the adjacent neighbor relationships, EIGRP establishes neighbor adjacencies by sending multicast (address 224.0.0.10) hello packets. Once neighbor adjacencies are formed, periodic hello packets are sent to each discovered neighbor to maintain that relationship. The frequency of the hello packet is dependent upon the bandwidth of the outbound interface the hello is being sent from. Hellos are sent every 5 seconds for the following:

- Broadcast media, such as Ethernet, token ring, and FDDI
- Point-to-point serial links, such as PPP or HDLC circuits, Frame Relay point-to-point subinterfaces, and ATM point-to-point subinterfaces
- High bandwidth (greater than T1) multipoint circuits, such as ISDN PRI and Frame Relay

Hellos sent every 60 seconds for multipoint circuits with a T1's bandwidth or lower, such as Frame Relay multipoint interfaces, ATM multipoint interfaces, ATM switched virtual circuits, and ISDN BRIs.

In order to determine if a neighbor adjacency is no longer valid, hello packets or other EIGRP packets must be seen within the times stated previously. In order to declare the neighbor down, a holddown timer of three times the hello interval is used.

The hello interval can be changed using the `ip hello-interval eigrp x` and `ip hold-time eigrp x` commands, where *x* is the EIGRP autonomous system processes number. These commands are placed on the outbound interface:

```
ip hello-interval eigrp 10 30        EIGRP AS 10 will use a hello interval
                                     of 30 seconds on the applied interface

ip hold-time eigrp 10 120            EIGRP AS 10 will use a hold time of 120
                                     seconds on the applied interface
```

Diffusing Update Algorithm (DUAL)

Diffusing Update Algorithm (DUAL) allows the router to receive routes advertised by all neighbors and make route computations based on the received metrics to decide the best route to any given destination prefix while still maintaining a loop-free environment. All best-known paths are stored in the routing table. If there is a topology change or current known metrics have changed, DUAL looks for a feasible successor (alternate path). Whenever a router chooses a new successor (or next hop for the IP prefix) due to an update that is equal to or better than the current metric, the router will select the new route and inform all of its other neighbors about the new reported distance.

An EIGRP router faced with an increased metric from its successor can find a better route immediately if the new best route goes through a feasible successor. The switchover is immediate and local to the router. The route stays "passive" (no diffusing computation for the route) and no other routers are involved, with the exception of the local router updating its neighbors. If there is no feasible successor, then the router sends a query to all adjacent neighbors for an alternate route. Any query request sent must be acknowledged. Once a new successor has been chosen, the new route is installed in the routing table.

- EIGRP uses 32 bits to describe destination address prefixes; IGRP uses 24 bits.

- EIGRP supports only internal and external routes; IGRP supports interior, system, and exterior routes. Routes that are considered internal are routes within the same EIGRP autonomous system. Routes that are considered external are routes that have been redistributed from another EIGRP AS or another routing protocol.

- Compared to IGRP, whose administrative distance is 100 for all routes, EIGRP's administrative distances are as follows:

  - 90 for routes that are internal, same EIGRP AS

- 170 for routes that are external, from another EIGRP AS or redistributed from another routing protocol

- 5 for routes that have been summarized, also known as an EIGRP summary route

- EIGRP route updates are sent to all EIGRP neighbors using the multicast address 224.0.0.10 for IP only. Updates in an AppleTalk environment use cable range broadcasts and IPX broadcasts on IPX-related networks (network ffff.ffff.ffff).

- EIGRP routing updates are characterized by the following three characteristics:

  - Nonperiodic updates are sent only when a path metric or topology change occurs. IGRP updates are classified as periodic and sent using a broadcast address (255.255.255.255).

  - Partial updates include only routes that have changed and not the entire routing table.

  - Bounded updates are sent only to specified routers based on a query request.

- EIGRP automatically summarizes addresses at their network boundaries. This can be disabled using the `no auto-summary` command.

- EIGRP maintains the following tables:

  - Neighbor table stores information about EIGRP adjacent neighbors.

  - Topology table lists all known routes that have feasible successors or reachable next hops.

- Beginning with IOS 11.3, EIGRP packets can be authenticated using MD5 authentication. More detail will be provided later in this chapter.

The Five Path Vector Metrics for EIGRP

When EIGRP sends out route updates, five path vector metrics are sent to describe each destination prefix. As stated earlier, EIGRP uses the same path vector metrics as IGRP, but bandwidth and delay are multiplied by 256.

The composite metric, or EIGRP distance, is an integer number used to compare different routes toward the same destination subnet, allowing only the best path to each given prefix to be installed in the routing table. The composite metric calculated for each prefix and specified in the routing table is *never* sent to a neighbor. Only the path vector metrics, in relation to the router sending the route update, will be sent. Based on both the bandwidth and delay metrics sent, a neighbor is able to calculate the reported distance to a particular destination prefix and then calculate its own composite metric based on the interface it received the update. To help further explain which path metrics are sent and how the composite metric is calculated, we'll use Figure 9.7. As mentioned earlier, by default, only the bandwidth and delay metrics are used during computation.

FIGURE 9.7   EIGRP path metrics (A)

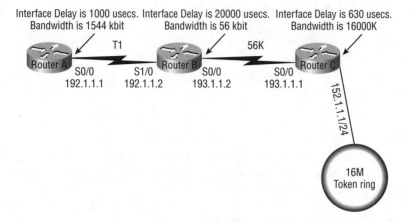

Router C has the following in its topology table:

```
P 152.1.1.0/24, 1 successors, FD is 176128
        via Connected, Tokenring0/0
```

Router B has the following in its topology table:

```
P 152.1.1.0/24, 1 successors, FD is 46242304
        via 193.1.1.1 (46242304/176128), Serial0/0
```

Router A has the following in its topology table:

```
P 152.1.1.0/24, 1 successors, FD is 46754304
        via 192.1.1.2 (46754304/46242304), Serial0/0
```

Router C will send an update to router B as follows:

```
Next-Hop IP Address = 193.1.1.1
Delay Metric = 160000
Bandwidth Metric = 16128
MTU = 1500
Hop Count = 0
Reliability = 255
Load = 1
```

And then router B will send the following update to router A:

```
Next-Hop IP Address = 192.1.1.2
Delay Metric = 528128
Bandwidth Metric = 45714176
MTU = 1500
Hop Count = 1
Reliability = 255
Load = 1
```

The bandwidth metric can be looked at as having two constituents:

Bandwidth   Interface bandwidth is referenced in kilobits and based on media type. To change media type defaults, you must use the interface `bandwidth` command. Use the `show interface` command to display the interface bandwidth:

```
Serial0/0 is up, line protocol is up
  Hardware is PowerQUICC Serial
  Internet address is 193.1.1.1/30
  MTU 1500 bytes, BW 56 Kbit, DLY 20000 usec,
      reliability 255/255, txload 1/255, rxload 1/255
```

$BW_{EIGRP (MIN)}$ The formula is 10^7 / smallest `bandwidth` statement of any *outgoing* interface along the path toward the destination prefix multiplied by 256. This bandwidth metric value is used to calculate the feasible distance (FD) to a destination prefix. Once calculated, this path metric is sent with each route prefix in the route update packet. The neighbor router will receive this path metric along with the delay metric and compute the reported distance (RD) to the destination prefix.

For example, based on the destination prefix to 152.1.1.0 /24, router B's serial 0/0 interface has a default of 1544Kbps and a default $BW_{EIGRP (MIN)}$ metric of 1657856.

The formula for $BW_{EIGRP(min)}$ is (10^7 / bandwidth statement = BW_{IGRP}) X 256:

```
(10,000,000 / 1544 = 6476) X 256 = 1657856
```

To change the bandwidth to 56Kbits, use interface command `bandwidth 56`. The $BW_{EIGRP (MIN)}$ metric will now equal the following:

```
interface Serial0/0
  bandwidth 56              10,000,000 / 56 = 178571 X 256 = 45714176
```

Also note in Figure 9.7 that even though router A has a T1 link (which is the path to reach 152.1.1.0/24) to router B it still computes the bandwidth portion of the smallest bandwidth reported along the path, 56K.

The delay metric can be looked at as having three constituent parts:

Delay (DLY)   Interface delay is referenced in microseconds and based on media type. Use the `show interface` command to display the interface delay:

```
Serial0/0 is up, line protocol is up
  Hardware is PowerQUICC Serial
  Internet address is 193.1.1.1/30
  MTU 1500 bytes, BW 56 Kbit, DLY 20000 usec,
     reliability 255/255, txload 1/255, rxload 1/255
```

Delay$_{EIGRP}$ To a given destination prefix, this is the outgoing interface delay (DLY), expressed in microsecond units (*usec*), divided by 10 microsecond units and multiplied by 256. If multiple hops exist to a given destination prefix, this value is used in addition to the reported delay received from a neighbor to calculate the total end-to-end delay.

For example, Based on destination prefix to 152.1.1.0 /24, router C's token 0/0 interface has a default delay (DLY) of 630 microseconds and a Delay$_{EIGRP}$ metric of 16128.

The formula for Delay$_{EIGRP}$ is (10^7 / bandwidth statement) / 10 = Delay$_{IGRP}$ X 256:

```
(10,000,000 / 16,000 = 625) /10 = 63 (rounded) X 256 = 16128
```

To change interface delay (DLY) defaults, you must use the interface `delay` command. Values for the `delay` command range from 1 to 16777215 microseconds, giving a maximum delay of 167 seconds. The maximum end-to-end delay must not be greater than 167 seconds:

```
interface Ethernet0/0
  delay 63                      63 X 10 (usec) = 630 usec (DLY)
```

Delay$_{EIGRP\,(SUM)}$ The Delay$_{EIGRP\,(SUM)}$ is the end-to-end delay (total sum) to any destination prefix. Each router along the path to a given destination prefix will calculate its own total delay to that destination prefix. The total delay is calculated by adding the router's own interface Delay$_{EIGRP}$ metric to the delay path metric received from a neighbor. Once calculated, this path metric is sent with each route prefix in the route update packet. The next neighbor router will receive this path metric along with the bandwidth metric and compute the reported distance (RD) to the destination prefix.

For example, based on destination prefix 152.1.1.0/24, router A's Delay$_{EIGRP(sum)}$ is based on the Delay$_{EIGRP(sum)}$ metric received from neighbor router B plus router A's interface delay cost:

```
Delay_EIGRP(sum) received from router B =      528128
Router A's Delay_EIGRP =                     + 512000 (2000 × 256)
Delay_EIGRP(sum) =                             1040128
```

Each enabled EIGRP interface will have the bandwidth and delay parameters associated with the type of interface. Table 9.6 includes a listing of common media types and their associated metric values. The values presented are based on IGRP metrics multiplied by 256. Use the formulas listed in the preceding section.

TABLE 9.6 Bandwidth and Delay Metric Table

Interface Media	Bandwidth Command Statement	$(BW_{IGRP} \times 256)$ BW_{EIGRP}	Default Interface Delay (usec)	$(Delay_{IGRP}/10)$ $Delay_{EIGRP}$
FastEthernet (100M)	100000	25600 (100 X 256)	100	2560 (10 X 256)
FDDI (100M)	100000	25600 (100 X 256)	100	2560 (10 X 256)
16M Token Ring	16000	160000 (625 X 256)	630	16128 (63 X 256)
10M Ethernet	10000	256000 (1000 X 256)	1000	25600 (100 X 256)
T1 (1.544M)	1544	1657856 (6476 X 256)	20000	512000 (2000 X 256)
512K	512	4999936 (19531 X 256)	20000	512000 (2000 X 256)
DS0 (64K)	64	40000000 (156250 X 256) 20000	512000 (2000 X 256)	
56K	56	45714176 (178571 X 256)	20000	512000 (2000 X 256)
Loopback	8000000	256 (1X 256)	5000	128000 (500 X 256)

The reliability metric reflects the total outgoing error rate on the interfaces along the route, calculated on a 5-minute weighted average. Values are 1–255; 255 (0xFF) is 100-percent reliable, and 128 (0x80) is 50-percent reliable). The lowest value along the path is used for this metric. This metric is not used in the composite metric calculation unless the metric weights command is used. To display route reliability, use show ip route A.B.C.D.

The load metric reflects the total load of outgoing interfaces along the route, calculated on a 5-minute weighted average. Values range from 1–255 (1[0x01]) being minimally loaded and 255 (0xFF) being a 100-percent loaded link. The highest load along the path is used for this metric. This metric is not used in the composite metric calculation unless the `metric weights` command is used. To display route load, use `show ip route A.B.C.D`.

IGRP tracks the minimum MTU along the entire path to the destination network. This metric is not used in the composite metric calculation. To display minimum MTU for a route, use `show ip route A.B.C.D`.

Although the Hop Count is not used as part of the five path vector metrics, it is included in each prefix update. The hop count is simply the number of gateways that a packet will have to go through to get to the destination. A router will advertise a directly connected interface with a hop count of 0 (zero). The default maximum hop count, or network diameter, is 100. It can be changed using the `metric maximum-hops` command. Values range from 1–255. To display hop count for a destination prefix, use the command `show ip route A.B.C.D`.

EIGRP Definitions

When we were describing EIGRP path vector metrics, we used terms such as *feasible distance* and *reported distance*. To provide further explanation of the functionality of EIGRP, we need to define some additional terms. Figure 9.8 is the same as Figure 9.7, but we've added an additional link between router A and router B to provide multiple paths to router C's destination prefix 152.1.1.0/24.

FIGURE 9.8   EIGRP path metrics (B)

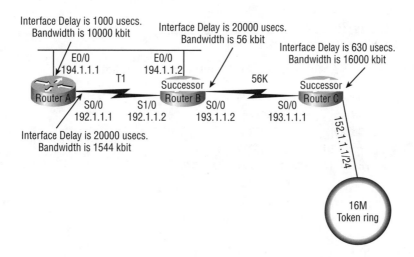

Router C has the following in its topology table:

```
P 152.1.1.0/24, 1 successors, FD is 176128
        via Connected, Tokenring0/0
```

Router B has the following in its topology table:

```
P 152.1.1.0/24, 1 successors, FD is 46242304
          via 193.1.1.1 (46242304/176128), Serial0/0
```

Router A has the following in its topology table:

```
P 152.1.1.0/24, 1 successors, FD is 46267904
          via 194.1.1.2 (46267904 /46242304), Ethernet0/0
          via 192.1.1.2 (46754304/46242304), Serial0/0
```

Router C has computed the feasible distance as follows:

$$BW_{EIGRP(min)} = 625 \times 256 = 160000$$
$$Delay_{EIGRP(sum)} = 63 \times 256 = 16128$$
$$Feasible\ Distance = 176128$$

Router B has computed the feasible distance as follows:

```
        Received route for 152.1.1.0/24
```
$$BW_{EIGRP(min)} = 160000$$
$$Delay_{EIGRP(sum)} = 16128$$
```
        Reported Distance = 176128
```

```
        --------------------
```
$$BW_{EIGRP(min)} = 178571 \times 256 = 45714176$$
$$Delay_{EIGRP(sum)} = 16128 + (2000 \times 256) = 528128$$
$$Feasible\ Distance = 46242304$$

And finally, router A will compute the feasible distance as follows:

```
    Received route for 152.1.1.0/24 via E0/0
```
$$BW_{EIGRP(min)} = 45714176$$
$$Delay_{EIGRP(sum)} = 528128$$
```
        Reported Distance = 46242304
    Received route for 152.1.1.0/24 via S0/0
```
$$BW_{EIGRP(min)} = 45714176$$
$$Delay_{EIGRP(sum)} = 528128$$
```
        Reported Distance = 46242304

            --------------------

        Feasible Distance via Serial0/0
```
$$BW_{EIGRP(min)} = 178571 \times 256 = 45714176$$
$$Delay_{EIGRP(sum)} = 528128 + (2000 \times 256) = 1040128$$
$$Feasible\ Distance = 46754304$$

```
        Feasible Distance via Ethernet0/0
```

$$BW_{EIGRP(min)} = 178571 \text{ X } 256 = 45714176$$
$$Delay_{EIGRP(sum)} = 528128 + (100 \text{ X } 256) = 553728$$
$$\text{Feasible Distance} = 46267904$$

Let's discuss the feasible distance.

Feasible distance (FD or fd)   The *feasible distance (FD)* is equal to the sum of the costs of the links to reach a destination network (the default calculation is based on bandwidth and delay metrics). The lowest calculated metric to each destination will become the FD to that destination and the route will be stored in the global routing table. The FD is calculated using the RD added to the local router's metric defined by the interface on which the route was learned (cost of reaching the directly connected neighbor). Using Figure 9.8, from router A's point of view, the FD (lowest cost) to 152.1.1.0 /24 is 46267904, via Ethernet 0/0:

```
Router A#show ip eigrp topology
P 152.1.1.0/24, 1 successors, FD is 46267904
        via 194.1.1.2 (46267904/46242304), Ethernet0/0
        via 192.1.1.2 (46754304/46242304), Serial0/0


Router A#debug ip eigrp
03:16:14: IP-EIGRP: Processing incoming UPDATE packet
03:16:14: IP-EIGRP: Int 152.1.1.0/24 M 46267904 - 45714176 553728
   SM 46242304 - 45714176 528128
```

Reported distance (RD)   The *reported distance (RD)* is also referred to as the advertised distance. It is the link cost of the path to a given destination prefix as advertised by a neighboring router(s) and can be displayed in the EIGRP topology table. As you can see in Figure 9.8, router A has two active EIGRP links to router B. Therefore, there are two route update packets seen for destination prefix 152.1.1.0 /24. However, using the following output, notice that the RD is exactly the same cost. The RDs that router A calculated from both updates is router B's point-of-view, or router B's FD, on how to reach 152.1.1.0 /24. Also note that router B does not send its calculated FD to router A. Router B's route update packet to router A only contains the path vector metrics. Router A will calculate the RD to 152.1.1.0/24 based on the path vector metrics received from router B:

```
Router A#show ip eigrp topology
P 152.1.1.0/24, 1 successors, FD is 46267904
        via 194.1.1.2 (46267904/46242304), Ethernet0/0
        via 192.1.1.2 (46754304/46242304), Serial0/0


Router A#debug ip eigrp
03:16:14: IP-EIGRP: Processing incoming UPDATE packet
03:16:14: IP-EIGRP: Int 152.1.1.0/24 M 46267904 - 45714176 553728
   SM 46242304 (Reported Distance) - 45714176 (B/W metric) 528128
   (Delay metric)
```

Successor   A *successor* is the next-hop router on the path to a given destination prefix. Based on the FD, it is the forwarding path to which packets are sent for a given destination network prefix. For every destination listed in the topology table, the route with the lowest FD metric is chosen and placed in the routing table along with the next-hop IP address. Using the following output, from router A's point of view, router B is the successor for destination prefix 152.1.1.0 /24:

```
Router A#show ip route
152.1.0.0/24 is subnetted, 1 subnets
D        152.1.1.0 [90/46267904] via 194.1.1.2, 01:12:57, Ethernet0/0

Router A#show ip eigrp topology
P 152.1.1.0/24, 1 successors, FD is 46267904
          via 194.1.1.2 (46267904/46242304), Ethernet0/0
          via 192.1.1.2 (46754304/46242304), Serial0/0
```

From router B's point of view router C is the successor for destination prefix 152.1.1.0 /24. The number of successors to a given destination prefix can be displayed in the EIGRP topology table using the show ip eigrp topology command.

Feasible successor (FS)   A *feasible successor (FS)* is an alternate path or alternate next-hop router on the path to a given destination prefix and can be used in case the path to the current successor goes down. To qualify as an FS, another next-hop router must have an RD less than the FD of the current route. In other words, for router A, the current FD to 152.1.1.0/24 is 46267904. If we connect another router, router D, between router A and router C as an alternate path to 152.1.1.0/24, router D must advertise 152.1.1.0/24 to router A with an RD of less than 46267904.

When no FS exist but neighbors are advertising the destination, a recompilation must occur. Through this process, a new successor or path is determined. The amount of time that it takes to recalculate the route affects the convergence time. The route is active during this time and no data can pass to the destination prefix. Once a new successor or path has been found and convergence has completed, the route becomes passive and may be used to route traffic.

FS routes are not marked in any way special when using show ip eigrp topology. Depending on the variance command, FS routes show up in the routing table as alternate routes. See the definition for *variance* for more explanation.

Router A does have an FS to reach destination prefix 152.1.1.0 /24, via the s0/0 link to router B. The route received via the s0/0 interface qualifies as the RD (46242304) and is less than the FD (46267904) of the current route . The output in the Passive section below shows an FS, which means if the current successor fails, the FS will be automatically selected.

Passive   A route is considered passive when a router has received a response to the query and is not performing recompilation on that route. Routes in the EIGRP topology table are marked with a *P*:

```
show ip eigrp topology
IP-EIGRP Topology Table for AS(1)/ID(5.5.5.5)

Codes: P - Passive, A - Active, U - Update, Q - Query, R - Reply,
       r - reply Status, s - sia Status
P 152.1.1.0/24, 1 successors, FD is 46267904
        via 194.1.1.2 (46267904/46242304), Ethernet0/0
        via 192.1.1.2 (46754304/46242304), Serial0/0
```

Active   When a router looses a route and does not have an FS in its topology table, it looks for an alternate path to the destination. The router that sent the route query must receive a response to come out of an active state. This flag serves to prevent routing loops. Routes in the EIGRP topology table are marked with an *A*.

Stuck in Active (SIA)   When a route goes active and queries are sent to neighbors to find an alternate path, the route will remain active until a reply is received for every query sent. However, what would happen if a neighbor that was queried for an alternate path goes down or for some reason cannot reply to the initial query? The route remains in an active state and the router originating a diffusing computation is blocked from completing the computation. To prevent a router from being in a continuous active state, an active timer is used. The timer is set for each query sent. If the timer expires, the route is declared *stuck-in-active (SIA)* and the neighbor is presumed dead. The neighbor is flushed from the neighbor table and any route associated with that neighbor is flushed from the route table. The computation proceeds as though these neighbors replied with an infinite metric, 4294967295.

When a router does not receive a reply to all outstanding queries within 3 minutes, the route goes to the stuck in active state. The router then resets the neighbor (or neighbors) that fails to reply by going active on all routes known through that neighbor. SIA can occur if the EIGRP network grows too large because the query range or query boundary grows as well. Alternatively, SIA can also be caused if there are links in the internetwork that are congested, low-bandwidth links, routers with low memory, or overutilized CPU. If there are numerous queries to handle, limited resources could delay the query response going back to the originator. If a neighbor goes down or is unreachable, the hello timer should expire prior to any route to that neighbor going SIA due to a neighbor failure.

The default active state time limit is 3 minutes. It can be changed or disabled using the `timers active-time [time-limit | disabled]` command. The time limit is specified in minutes. Values range from 1 to 4294967295.

Maximum paths   If multiple paths exist to the same network, by default up to four *equal* cost paths will be used. By using the maximum path statement, up to six equally good routes will be kept in the routing table.

Real World Scenario

Query Scope

Author Rob Payne tells about an experience he had with EIGRP query scope:

It is extremely important to understand the query scope or query range. Many people think that the EIGRP autonomous system (AS) is the boundary of the queries, but this is a totally incorrect assumption. In reality, EIGRP queries will span from one autonomous system to another as long as both of the autonomous systems contain part of the classful address boundary.

I worked on one network in the past in which the 10.0.0.0 Class A IP address space was deployed to two separate countries. Each country was implemented with EIGRP and each country was part of a separate autonomous system (the international circuits connecting the two autonomous systems belonged to the first country's AS).

The engineers started to notice that they were experiencing a lot of stuck in active (SIA) routes within these two EIGRP ASs. Now the common thought process was that they should not be getting SIA routes because each country is its own EIGRP AS. So, they started checking the latency on all the WAN circuits within each country, and they were not able to find any problems.

However, they realized that because the 10.0.0.0 Class A IP address space resided in both countries, the EIGRP queries were spanning across the international circuits and into the other EIGRP AS, thus creating a rather large query scope.

One solution to this problem would be to readdress the network in one of the EIGRP ASs so that they both did not have the same classful address space. Another solution, the one that we implemented, was to separate the two EIGRP ASs by making the international circuits connecting the two countries a different routing protocol. This solution, of course, separated the two EIGRP ASs and thus broke the query scope into two separate scopes. We used BGP across the international circuits, but you could use any other IGP as well to include static routes.

Variance   The amount of load balancing that is performed can be controlled by the `variance` command. To control how traffic is distributed among routes when there are multiple routes for the same destination network that have different costs, use the `traffic-share` command. With the keyword *balanced*, the router distributes traffic proportionately to the ratios of the metrics associated with the different routes. With the keyword *min*, the router uses routes that have minimum costs. More explanation is given later in this chapter in section "Load-Balancing Traffic."

EIGRP is a scalable and efficient protocol that has been deployed in global networks. Table 9.7 lists the features of EIGRP and their values. EIGRP is one of the best interior gateway routing protocols available today.

TABLE 9.7 The Features of EIGRP

Feature	Value
Category	Advanced distance vector (hybrid)
Class type	Classless
Advertising address	Multicast; 224.0.0.10
Metric	Composite (bandwidth, delay, reliability, loading)
Max hop count	224
Periodic interval	None (only trades routing information when a change occurs)

Manipulating Routes with EIGRP

As with any routing protocol, there must be mechanisms to allow the router to prefer one route to another route. With EIGRP, the offset-list command can be utilized for this purpose. An offset list is a method of increasing the inbound or outbound composite metric of routes learned by the router through EIGRP. You can specify only certain routes to apply the offset amount to by using an access list to specify the actual routes (networks) that the offset will be applied against. As mentioned earlier, the composite metric value is never sent with the prefix updates. The offset values actually increase the delay metric, whereby an offset of 1 will add an additional 10 microsecond units.

Let's take a look at some of the possible commands, which can be configured within the EIGRP routing process.

```
router eigrp 100

network 147.19.0.0

offset-list 1 out 37972 Serial0
```

Route metrics can be manipulated using the offset command. This command will add an additional 379720 microseconds to the delay metric to affect the overall composite metric for the route entry matched in Access List 1. If no ACL is called, by using a zero as the access list number all updates incoming or outgoing will be modified, offset-list 0 selects all networks

Out – Perform offset on outgoing updates.

In – Perform offset on incoming updates.

```
                      Offset - Values for offset are 0-2147483647.

                      Manipulate the delay metric.

                      If no interface is stated, the list
                      will modify all incoming or outgoing
                      updates specified by the ACL on any
                      interface

access-list 1 permit 147.19.2.0 0.0.0.255
```

Rule of Split-Horizon for EIGRP

Because EIGRP was developed from IGRP, it has to follow the rule of split-horizon, which states that any packets that enter a router through an interface cannot flow back out of the same interface. This is an important concept to keep in mind with everyday networking and in the CCIE lab examination. (Refer back to the beginning of this chapter for an explanation of split-horizon.) It is possible to disable split-horizon on an interface that is using EIGRP as its routing protocol. Apply the following command on the interface:

```
no ip split-horizon eigrp 100      Enabled on interfaces by default. When split
                                   horizon is enabled on an interface, routing
                                   updates and query packets are not sent for
                                   destinations for which this interface is the
                                   next hop.  This example is for AS 100.
```

Load-Balancing Traffic

EIGRP can load-balance traffic across multiple paths (up to six) to a destination. This will allow for greater throughput and reliability to a destination network. One method of allowing paths with different composite metrics to load-balance traffic across each other, is the use of the variance command. The variance command is a multiple of the configured router's composite metric. If the composite metric of the entire second destination path is within the variance (multiple) of the configured router's composite metric, then the router can use the second path along with the first path and load-balance traffic across both paths to the destination network.

If the load sharing is not equal, it is weighted by the metric of each alternate path. For example, if the metric for one path is 10 and the metric for another path is 20, 66 percent of the traffic is sent via the path with the metric of 10 and 33 percent will be sent via the other path. By default, the variance is equal to 1, which means that only equal cost load balancing can occur. The variance command is applied within the routing process on the router. To find the multiplier value, divide the highest FD with the lowest FD. In the configuration in Figure 9.8, the highest FD is 46754304, via serial 0/0, and the lowest is 46267904, via Ethernet 0/0. To use both paths, use this command:

```
46754304 / 46267904 = 1.01    Set the variance to 2, using the variance 2 EIGRP
                              process command, to allow both paths to be used.
```

Let's take a look at some of the possible commands, which can be used to configure load balancing across multiple paths.

```
router eigrp 1

network 192.1.1.0 0.0.0.3

network 194.1.1.0

no auto-summary
```

`variance 3`	Any path composite metric less than three times the routers composite metric is considered an equal path. Default multiplier or variance is 1. Traffic distributed proportionately based on FD metric.
`maximum-paths 2`	Limit the number of possible equal paths to two. The router can handle a value of 1 to 6 multiple paths. Default is 4 maximum paths.
`traffic-share balanced`	To balance traffic distribution among routes when there are multiple routes for the same destination networks that have different costs. Traffic is distributed proportionately to the ratios of the metrics. Default – Command not needed
`traffic-share min`	All traffic shared among minimum metric paths – All feasible paths should be entered into the routing table, even though no load balancing should occur. All packets should use the lowest-cost route and switch to the next-best path only if the primary fails. If there are multiple minimum-cost paths and this command is used, EIGRP will perform equal-cost load-balancing
`traffic-share min across-interfaces`	Use different interfaces for equal-cost paths

Configuring EIGRP on a Router

The first step to implementing EIGRP within your network is of course to configure the routing process on the routers. This is accomplished with the `router eigrp 100` command (in this example, the autonomous system is 100). It is not necessary to have a registered autonomous system number to use EIGRP. If you do not have a registered number, you are free to create your own. We recommend that if you do have a registered number, you use it to identify the EIGRP process. Either way, all routers within your network that are expected to share routing information must belong to the same AS. There are exceptions when performing route redistribution, but that is a topic for further discussion in Chapter 10 of this book. EIGRP will send routing updates out the interfaces that are within the specified networks. If any of the router interface IP addresses do not belong to the networks that are specified in the EIGRP routing process, they will not be advertised in any EIGRP routing update.

Let's take a look at the `eigrp stub` command, which can be configured within the EIGRP routing process.

`router eigrp 100`	Enable the EIGRP routing process and assign an AS number, AS = 100 in this example
`network 147.19.0.0`	Associate networks with an EIGRP routing process
`eigrp stub`	Available with 12.0.7(T). A router that is configured as a stub with the eigrp stub command shares connected and summary routing information with all neighbor routers by default. Any neighbor receiving stub information from a neighbor will not query those routers for any routes

EIGRP Commands

Let's take a look at some of the possible commands, which can be configured within the EIGRP routing process.

`router eigrp 100`	Enable EIGRP (Process ID = AS number: 1 - 65535)
`network 147.19.1.1 0.0.0.15`	Define interface(s) that will participate in EIGRP AS#100. Reverse mask option was introduced in IOS 12.0(4)T.
`no auto-summary`	By default EIGRP summarizes at network boundaries. Routing table indicates local routes with Null0 as the next-hop. —Disable summarization with this command - Summarized route with Null0 no longer listed

passive-interface Ethernet0/0	Stops EIGRP from establishing any neighbors | stops hello's.
passive-interface default	Optional whereby all interface are set to passive.
no passive-interface FastEthernet1/0	Used with passive-interface default command to allow this interface to establish neighbors and send hello's.
distance eigrp <internal weight> <external weight>	
	Change the administrative distance value for the internal and external eigrp routes

EIGRP Authentication

MD5 is an algorithm that takes a message (EIGRP packet) and shared secret (key) and then generates 128 bits of hash (fingerprint or message hash). The MD5 value generated is appended to the EIGRP packet and is sent to a neighbor. The receiving neighbor then compares the result with the MD5 fingerprint in the packet. If the results match, the packet is authentic; if not, then the packet is not authentic or has been tampered with.

Let's take a look at some of commands, which can be configured for EIGRP authentication.

interface Serial0

ip address147.19.1.1 255.255.255.240

ip authentication key-chain eigrp 100 josh	Enables EIGRP authentication on interface and specify the key-chain josh to be used
ip authentication mode eigrp 100 md5	Creates md5 authentication, command still needed even though MD5 is the only option
key chain josh	Defines key chain name josh. Has local significance only.
key 1	Defines key or keys on the key chain.
key-string chris	Specifies password chris - Must be same on both ends

To troubleshoot EIGRP MD5 authentication, use the following command:

```
debug ip eigrp packets verbose        EIGRP: ignored packet from x.x.x.x opcode
                                       = 5 (invalid authentication)

show key chain
```

Summarizing Addresses

With the EIGRP routing protocol, there are two forms of summarization that can be used. By default, EIGRP summarizes addresses at their classful network boundaries. (Refer back to the beginning of this chapter for an explanation of classful versus classless.) Automatic summarization can be disabled using no auto-summary command:

```
router eigrp 100
```

network 172.16.0.0	With auto-summary enable (default), this subnet does not have to originate as a directly connected network to be summarized. If this router is seeing 172.16.1.0/24, 172.16.50.0/24 from another neighbor, due to this network statement this router will propagate a 172.16.0.0/16 route to other adjacencies, adding the route to its table pointing to Null0 while still learning the more specifics from the original neighbor. (See auto-summary rules below)
auto-summary	Default auto-summarization. IGRP compatibility mode where only major networks are announced across network boundaries and the subnets are suppressed.
no auto-summary	Enables support for discontiguous networks in EIGRP.

Or, you can manually summarize address space on the outbound interface:

```
interface Serial0
  ip address 192.168.16.19 255.255.255.240
```

ip summary-address eigrp 10 172.0.0.0 255.0.0.0	Sends a summary route to AS #10 neighbors off of S0 interface - Route listed with next-hop of Null0. No current limit on the number of statements can be on an interface, as long as they don't overlap.

When you configure the summary address command, the EIGRP summary route is advertised as an internal route and therefore has an admin distance of 90. This can be used to remove external EIGRP routes by summarizing them into an internal summary route.

Default Network

Default candidate routes and the gateway of last resort are routes that mark the exit from the local routing table environment and the path toward another router that has more routing information. The default candidates are not used as default routes themselves; IOS evaluates all default candidates and chooses the one with minimum AD and the minimum routing metric as the best default candidate. The next hop router of the best default candidate becomes the gateway of last resort. EIGRP supports the IP default route (0.0.0.0/0) as well as default candidates. The default route (0.0.0.0/0) is considered to be just another default candidate in IOS.

There are several differences between EIGRP and other routing protocols such as RIP, OSPF, and IS-IS:

- EIGRP is the only classless routing protocol that supports default candidates.
- RIP always generates the default route as soon as the router itself has the gateway of last resort set.
- OSPF generates the default route in a stub or NSSA area.
- IS-IS generates the default route pointing toward the nearest Level 2 router on any Level 1 router.
- To insert the default route into EIGRP topology database, you have to manually configure redistribution of the default route.
- OSPF can generate a default route announcement by using `default-information originate` command.
- Whenever the default route is redistributed into the EIGRP topology database, the default candidate marker is set automatically in the topology database.
- EIGRP automatically redistributes a connected network (or subnets) marked as `ip default-network` into the EIGRP process. No other classless routing protocol performs redistribution behind the scenes; you have to configure it.

Example 1: IP Default Network

Here is an example of the `ip default-network` command:

```
interface Serial 0
  ip address 192.77.3.4 255.255.255.252
router eigrp 100
```

```
network 147.19.0.0

ip default-network 192.77.3.0
```
See item above, no network statement needed

Connected Network(s) - If the router has a directly connected interface onto the network specified in the ip default -network statement, a default candidate route will be generated to neighbors marked with a default candidate flag (*)

Non-connected – If the route is already in EIGRP topology database, mark the network with a default candidate flag (*)

Subnet – Insert the summary route for the major network into which the subnet belongs in the routing table

Example 2: Static Route

Here is an example of the ip route command:

```
router eigrp 100

  network 147.19.0.0

  redistribute static metric 64 20000 255 1 1500
```
See item above. Metrics can be changed from interface defaults

```
ip route 0.0.0.0 0.0.0.0 147.19.1.2
```

NOTE If the network is dual-homed, control the exit point out to the Internet by changing metrics to favor one router over the other for all internal users.

Example 3: Floating Static Route

In Figure 9.9, a floating static is added in case subnet 147.19.1.0/24 is gone. A default will still be propagated down to R3. The `network` statement is used for 147.19.0.0 on R2 to send the classful route of 147.19.0.0/16 to R3.

FIGURE 9.9   EIGRP with floating static

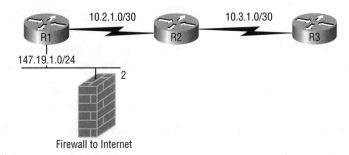

Router R1 has the following commands configured:

```
router eigrp 100
 network 147.19.0.0
 network 10.0.0.0
 redistribute static metric 64 20000 255 1 1500
 distribute-list DefaultOnly out

ip route 0.0.0.0 0.0.0.0 147.19.1.2
ip route 0.0.0.0 0.0.0.0 Null0 250
ip access-list standard DefaultOnly
 permit 0.0.0.0
```

Router R2 has the following commands configured:

```
router eigrp 100
 network 147.19.0.0
 network 10.0.0.0
 redistribute static metric 64 20000 255 1 1500

distribute-list DefaultOnly out Serial 0

ip route 0.0.0.0 0.0.0.0 Null0 250

ip access-list standard DefaultOnly
 permit 0.0.0.0
```

EIGRP Troubleshooting

The following are some of the recommended commands to assist in the troubleshooting of EIGRP routing issues:

`show ip eigrp topology`	Display EIGRP topology table (Successor, FS, FD, Active/Passive)
`show ip eigrp topology all-links`	The above command only displays the successors and feasible successors paths. To display all available paths to all known destination prefixes.
`show ip eigrp topology x.x.x.x`	Display the EIGRP topology information for an individual route.
`show ip eigrp topology summary`	Display EIGRP topology table summary.
`show ip eigrp neighbors`	Display neighbors discovered by EIGRP (neighbor table)
`debug eigrp packets`	Type of EIGRP packets sent/received. All defaults are turned on.
`debug eigrp neighbors`	Neighbor discovery and contents of hello packets
`debug ip eigrp`	Packets sent/received on an interface
`debug ip eigrp summary`	Summarized version of EIGRP activity

If you have a good understanding of the operation of EIGRP within the routing environment and how EIGRP derives its routing decision, then resolving any routing issues should be a quick process.

Intermediate System-to-Intermediate System (IS-IS)

In this section, we will discuss the Integrated *Intermediate System-to-Intermediate System (IS-IS)*, classless, link-state, VLSM routing protocol. IS-IS is an International Organization for Standardization (ISO) dynamic routing specification. The Cisco implementation of IS-IS allows you to configure IS-IS as an IP routing protocol, utilizing integrated IS-IS. IS-IS was not originally designed for the IP protocol; therefore, Integrated IS-IS was developed as an extension to IS-IS. This integrated protocol is still based on the OSI intradomain IS-IS routing protocols, but it's augmented with IP-specific information. RFC 1195 discusses the ability to integrate both Connectionless Network Service (CLNS) and IP protocols together, allowing Integrated IS-IS to be an interior gateway protocol (IGP) used to route IP traffic. Even as Integrated IS-IS, it is still a CLNS-based routing protocol, which means that it still utilizes CLNS protocol data units (PDUs) rather than IP packets to communicate routing information.

Integrated IS-IS is one of the two methods of allowing multiple network layer protocols within the same router because you can use pure CLNS to route DECNet Phase V traffic and also use CLNS to carry IP traffic. The other method of allowing multiple routing protocols to coexist on the same router is known as the "ships-in-the-night" approach. "Ships-in-the-night" routing (also a method of integrated routing) allows the use multiple routing protocols at the same time within the same router, each routing protocol supporting a separate, coexisting network layer protocol. The different types of routing protocol packets pass like ships in the night; each one has no knowledge of the other protocols. With integrated routing, multiple Network layer protocols are routed by utilizing routing tables, which are created by a single routing protocol, thus saving some router resources. Integrated IS-IS uses this approach.

The intradomain IS-IS routing protocol is intended to support many large routing areas, with each AS supporting many networks. These networks can consist of point-to-point links, multipoint links, X.25 subnetworks, and broadcast subnetworks such as ISO 8802 LANs. In order to support large routing ASs (domains), IS-IS supports a hierarchical architecture. A large AS (domain) may be segmented into areas. Each system must exist in one and only one area. Routing within an area is referred to as Level 1 routing. Routing between areas is referred to as Level 2 routing. Level 2 intermediate systems (ISs) keep track of the route paths to all the other destination areas. Level 1 ISs keep track of the routing within their own area. Refer to Figure 9.10.

FIGURE 9.10   IS-IS network

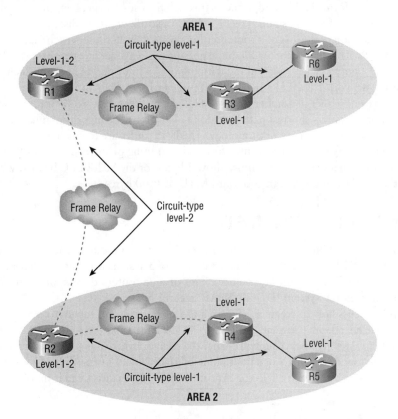

A Cisco router can perform as a Level 1 IS device, a Level 2 IS device, or a Level 1/Level 2 IS-device.. The Level 1/Level 2 IS device is used to interconnect each Level 1 area to the Level 2 backbone. Between areas, routers know how to reach the backbone, and the backbone routers (Level 2) know how to reach other areas. Routers establish Level 1 adjacencies to perform routing within a local area, known as intra-area routing. Routers establish Level 2 adjacencies to allow routing between Level 1 areas, known as interarea routing. Let's discuss the three types of routers used in IS-IS.

Level 1 (L1) routers   Similar to internal OSPF routers, talk to other Level 1 and Level 1/Level 2 routers

Level 1/Level 2 (L1/L2) routers   Similar to OSPF ABRs, talk to Level 1 routers in its area and other Level 2 routers

Level 2 (L2) routers   Similar to OSPF backbone routers, talk to other Level 2 routers only

Similar to OSPF, IS-IS uses areas to segment the network into smaller areas. An area defines the part of the network that a single router must have knowledge of. In ISO terminology, a router is an intermediate system (IS) and a workstation is an end system (ES). The foundation of IS-IS is the CLNS protocol instead of the IP protocol, so IS-IS uses ISO-defined protocol data units (PDUs) to communicate between routers. IS-IS uses several different types of PDUs, such as hello PDUs, link-state PDUs (LSPs), and sequence number PDUs (SNPs). Hello PDUs allow the IS-IS routers to form neighbor adjacencies through the use of Type, Length and Value (TLV) types 2, 22, 128. 130, 135, and so on. The hello PDUs also allow for the discovery of new routers and the determination of the loss of a router within the area. IS-IS routers exchange routing information with LSPs. These LSPs are used to build and maintain a link-state database (LSDB) in each router. An LSP identifies each router along with important information about it, such as its area and connected networks. The LSPs are reliably flooded to all routers through a process that uses complete or partial sequence number PDUs (CSNPs or PSNPs). Just like OSPF, IS-IS calculates routes based on Dijkstra's shortest path first (SPF) algorithm. The algorithm must be run whenever there is a change in the network topology. The IS-IS routes are then added to the IP routing table, where they may coexist with routes from other routing protocols. With IS-IS, there is an MTU size of 1497 bytes because you must allow 3 bytes for the 802.2 LLC header, which when added to the 1497 bytes provide the standard MTU of 1500 bytes.

Network Entity Title (NET)

The *Network Entity Title (NET)* is an ISO network address unique to each IS-IS router. The purpose of the NET is to identify the Network layer of a system without associating the same system with a specific transport layer entity. This unique router address, or router ID (RID), consists of the area ID, system ID, and NSAP selector byte.

Now we'll discuss how to create a NET on a Cisco router. It can range from 8 to 20 bytes in length written in hexadecimal format. The last byte is always the n-selector and must be 0 (0 in hexadecimal = 00). In actuality, the router will change the selector byte to a nonzero qualifier in order to represent a psuedonode on a LAN or a multipoint interface, but all you need to do is create the NET in the router configuration with a selector byte of 00. The 6 bytes directly in front of the n-selector are the system ID. The system ID is a fixed size of 6 bytes and cannot be changed (at least that is the rule for configuring Cisco routers). The system ID must be unique throughout each area (Level 1) and throughout the backbone (Level 2). In the following example, we have assigned a system ID of all 1s because this NET is configured on router R1, thus on router R2 the system ID will consist of all 2s. All bytes in front of the system ID are the area ID, which can range from 3 to 13 bytes including the authority and format identifier (AFI). In this example, router R1 belongs to Area 1, so we used an area ID value of 49.0001. For the Cisco Integrated IS-IS implementation, the NET begins with the AFI having a hexadecimal value of 49, followed by the remainder of the Area ID. Even when IS-IS is used to perform IP routing only (no CLNS routing such as DECNet Phase V enabled), a NET must still be configured to define the router system ID and area ID.

Figure 9.11 shows an example of the following NET. The Network Entity Title (NET) is comprised of the following: AFI(2 Hex)-AREA(4)-SYSTEM ID(12)-SELECTOR(2). In this example, Router R1 in Area 1. Let's explain the following NET: 49.0001.1111.1111.1111.00 (49.0001 = Area)(1111.1111.1111 = System ID)(00 = Selector). .

- Router ID: 49.0001. 1111.1111.1111.00

- Example: 49.0001.1111.1111.1111.00

FIGURE 9.11   IS-IS NET example

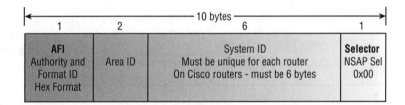

Table 9.8 lists the features of IS-IS and their values.

TABLE 9.8   The Features of IS-IS

Feature	Value
Category	Link state
Class type	Classless
Advertising address	Multicast
Metric	Arbitrary (can use delay, expense, and error)
Max hop count	None
Periodic interval	None (only trades routing information when a change occurs)

Configuring IS-IS

The first step to implementing IS-IS within your network is of course to apply the `clns routing` global command, which activates the CLNS protocol within the router. In our test lab, we found that if you do not configure the `clns routing` command, it will be automatically configured by the router as soon as you configure the `router isis` command. However, depending on the version of IOS you have loaded, sometimes the `clns routing` command will appear in the running configuration and other times it will not appear. Second, you must configure the routing process on the router. This is accomplished with the `router isis` command along with a `net` command. Then, using the `ip router isis` command, the IS-IS protocol must be configured on each interface that you want to route IS-IS traffic across.

Let's take a look at some of the possible commands, which can be configured within the IS-IS routing process.

`clns routing`	Enables CLNS routing

```
interface serial0/0
  encapsulation frame-relay
```

`frame-relay map clns 101 broadcast`	If this is a physical or multipoint Frame-Relay interface, then you must have a frame-relay map clns command, or IS-IS will never form an adjacency with the neighbor.
`ip router isis`	Configure an IS-IS routing process for IP on an interface and to attach an area designator to the routing process
`isis circuit-type level-2-only`	The proper way is to configure a router as an Level 1-only, Level 1-2 or Level 2-only system with the is-type command under the isis routing process. However, on all Level-1-2 routers, you should limit all interfaces to the correct level with the isis circuit-type command. Only on routers that are between areas (Level 1-2 routers) should you configure some interfaces to be Level 2-only to prevent wasting bandwidth by sending out unused Level 1 hellos. Note that on point-to-point interfaces, the Level 1 and Level 2 hellos are in the same packet

`isis hello-interval 10`	Specify the length of time between hello packets that the Cisco IOS software sends, the Default is 10 seconds
`isis hello-multiplier 3`	Specify the amount of seconds which a neighbor may miss IS-IS hello packets before the router should declare the adjacency as down. In this example, the hello-interval is 10 seconds, and the hello-multiplier is 3, so the router will wait for 30 seconds. Default is 3 with a possible range of 3 - 1000
`isis metric 34 level-2`	Metric assigned to the link and used to calculate the cost from each other router via the links in the network to other destinations. You can configure this metric for Level 1 or Level 2 routing. The range is from 0 to 63 for the narrow-style metric, and 0- over 16 million for the wide-style metric. The default value is 10. The lowest metric is preferred
`isis priority 64`	Sets the priority of a router and is a number from 0 to 127, Default value is 64. The highest priority is preferred. Priorities are used in determining the Designated Router (DR) and can be configured for Level 1 and Level 2 independently. Specifying the level-1 or level-2 keywords resets priority only for Level 1 or Level 2 routing, respectively
`router isis`	Activates an IS-IS routing process on this router
`net 49.0001.2222.2222.2222.00`	Within the NET, make each routers System ID unique with series of a number = 222...

```
is-type level-2-only          OPTIONAL, configures the entire router
                              as level-2 only. So this router will not
                              participate in any level-1 area.  The
                              default router type is level-1/level-2

metric-style wide             Allows 32-bits for metric values
                              (wide-style), instead of only 6-bits
                              (narrow-style)
```

If you are configuring IS-IS across a point-to-point link with PPP encapsulation, then after configuring the `ip router isis` command on the serial interface of each router at both ends of the link, you must shut down one of the interfaces and then reactivate it to force PPP to renegotiate the link. Once PPP renegotiates the link, IS-IS will be able to form an adjacency across the link.

Interface Authentication

IS-IS allows for the configuration of a password for a specified link, an area, or an AS (domain). Routers that want to become neighbors must exchange the same password for their configured level of authentication. Only clear text passwords are supported. Authentication information is encoded as a Type, Length and Value (TLV) type of Link State Packets (LSPs). By default, authentication is disabled.

When configuring IS-IS authentication on an interface, you can enable the password for Level 1, Level 2, or both Level 1/Level 2 routing. If you do not specify a level, the default is Level 1. The level of IS-IS interface authentication should match the type of adjacency on the interface. To find out the type of adjacency, use the `show clns neighbor` command. For area and domain authentication, you cannot specify the level of authentication.

Let's take a look at some of the commands required to configure IS-IS authentication on an interface.

```
interface serial0/0

  ip address 172.16.1.1 255.255.255.0

  ip router isis

  isis password josh level-1    Assigns josh as an authentication password on
                                this interface. Password must be the same for
                                all routers on the same network, otherwise
                                adjacencies will not be formed. All PDUs will
                                be authenticated. By default, authentication
                                is disabled. If enabled, default is level1,
                                if not specified. The password is carried in
                                the Hello PDU
```

Let's take a look at some of the commands required to configure IS-IS authentication on the routing process.

```
router isis
  net 49.0001.2222.2222.2222.00
```

area-password josh	Configures josh as a level-1 area authentication password. All L1 or L1/L2 routers must be in the same area and the password must be the same for all routers. Passwords are carried in L1 LSPs, CSNPs and PSNPs PDUs. Adjacencies will still form even if the passwords are not configured the same, but L1 LSPs will not be exchanged
domain-password josh	Configures josh as a level-2 routing domain authentication password. The password is carried in L2 LSPs, CSNPs and PSNPs PDUs. The password must be the same for all L2 and L1/L2 routers within the same IS-IS domain. Adjacencies will still form even if the passwords are not configured the same, but L2 LSPs will not be exchanged

Default Route Propagation

When a router is configured as a Level 1 type router, the LSDB will only contain Level 1 (intra-area) routes. In order for the Level 1 router to send interarea traffic, it must be connected to a Level 1/Level 2 router. The L1/L2 router uses the ATT (attached bit) to tell the L1 routers that it has interarea connections. The L1/L2 router will advertise a default route to all the L1 routers automatically if it has an attached area. Another method of sending a default route, but within an IP environment only, is to use the default-information originate command:

```
router isis
  net 49.0001.2222.2222.2222.00
  default-information originate
```

default-information originate	The Default Route to Null 0 (below) will be sent to all L1 adjacencies

```
ip route 0.0.0.0 0.0.0.0 Null0
```

It is also possible to configure a conditional default route, in which a route-map statement must be satisfied:

```
router isis

 net 49.0001.2222.2222.2222.00

 default-information originate route-map chris      Injects a Default Route if
                                                    the route-map statement is
                                                    satisfied



access-list 8 permit 2.2.2.0 0.0.0.255             The 2.2.2.0 route MUST
                                                   already exist in the
                                                   routing table

route-map chris permit 10

 match ip address 8
```

IS-IS Interarea Default Routes

If an area exists across an L2 link, then you want to ensure that R3 has a 0.0.0.0 route. The scenario in Figure 9.12 is only used to explain what happens when an L1/L2 router is configured in the same area as both of its adjacencies. As stated earlier, an L1/L2 router should generate a default route to all L1 routers in the same area as soon as the L1/L2 router becomes adjacent to another router outside of its area. In Figure 9.12, router R1 and router R2 are configured within the same area, and router R2 and router R3 are configured in the same area. Therefore, in the present configuration, router R3 will not receive the default 0.0.0.0 route.

FIGURE 9.12   Inter-area default routes

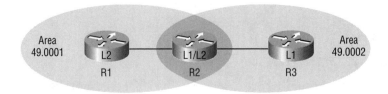

The existing router configurations for Figure 9.12 are as follows:

```
*********R1*************
router isis
net 49.0001.1111.1111.1111.00
is-type level-2

interface Serial 0
ip address 10.1.1.1 255.255.255.0
ip router isis

router isis
net 49.0002.3333.3333.3333.00
is-type level-1

**********R2************
router isis
net 49.0001.2222.2222.2222.00
net 49.0002.2222.2222.2222.00
is-type level-1-2

interface Serial 0
ip addresss 10.1.1.2 255.255.255.0
ip router isis

interface Serial 1
ip address 192.168.1.1 255.255.255.0
ip router isis

*********R3*************
router isis
net 49.0002.3333.3333.3333.00
is-type level-1

interface Serial 0
ip address 192.168.1.2 255.255.255.0
ip route isis
------------------------------------------------
```

You must fool router R1 into believing it has an ATTached area apart from 49.0001. Here is a suggested solution is to change the configuration on router R1:

```
router isis

net 49.0001.1111.1111.1111.00

net 49.0003.1111.1111.1111.00        This will cause the ATT Bit to be set
                                     and the 0.0.0.0 route to be forwarded
                                     to router R3
```

Router R2 will now see router R1's LSPs coming from an additional area (Area 3) and therefore sends a default route LSP to router R3 with the ATT bit set. You can verify this through the command show isis database and look under the ATT column.

Address Summarization for IS-IS

To create aggregate or summarized addresses for IS-IS, you use the same command as is used in OSPF. Use the summary-address router configuration command. The metric used to advertise the summary is the smallest metric of all the more specific routes. The correct command syntax is as follows:

```
summary-address address mask {level-1|level-1-2|level-2}
summary-address          Configure IP address summaries
  level-1                Summarize into level-1 area
  level-1-2              Summarize into both area and sub-domain
  level-2                Summarize into level-2 sub-domain


router isis
 net 49.0001.2222.2222.2222.00
 summary-address 172.16.0.0 255.255.252.0 level-1
```

Narrow-Style Metrics vs. Wide-Style Metrics

IS-IS by default utilizes the *Type, Length and Value (TLV)* type 128, or narrow-style metrics (shown in Figure 9.13), which allows for a possible metric value of 0–63 by providing 6 bits for the metric value. Cisco routers, by default, only use the default metric of the narrow-style metric, TLV 128. So, the 3 bytes carrying the delay, expense, and error metrics are not used, which equate to 3 bytes or 24 bits of overhead in the narrow-style metric, TLV 128. The default metric value is used to calculate the cost from each other router via the links in the network to other destinations. You can configure this metric for Level 1 or Level 2 routing. The default value is 10. The lowest metric is preferred. The metric value is set on a per-interface basis with the isis metric 34 level-2 command. Of course, you could specify the metric value for Level 1 instead of Level 2 if desired.

FIGURE 9.13 TLV 128 and TLV 135

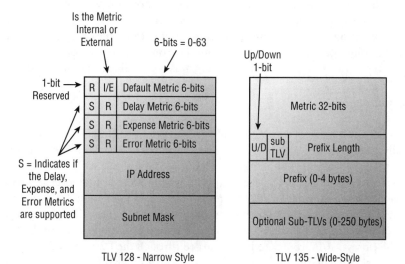

TLV 128 - Narrow Style   TLV 135 - Wide-Style

In order to provide for more granularity and to allow support for future applications such as traffic engineering, it is recommended that you implement the Type, Length and Value (TLV) type 135, or wide-style metrics (shown in Figure 9.13). The TLV 135 provides 32 bits to be used for the metric value instead of limiting you to the 6 bits provided for with the narrow style. However, due to TLV 22 providing only 24 bits for the metric value, TLV 135 uses only 24 bits out of the possible 32 bits for the metric value even though there are 32 bits provided in the TLV. So, with the 24 bits, you have 16,777,218 possible metric values. And now with more discrete metric values, you are able to properly cost or weight your links within your network to obtain optimum traffic flow efficiency. TLV 135 provides a 32-bit metric field (only uses 24 bits) and adds a bit for the "Up/Down" resulting from the route leaking of Level 2 to Level 1. Known as the Extended IP Reachability TLV, this TLV addresses the issues with both TLV 128 and TLV 130.

IS-IS also utilizes the TLV type 2 and the TLV type 22 to allow for the forming of IS-IS adjacencies between routers. TLV 2 is used with the narrow-style metric and allows 6 bits for the default metric value, and TLV 22 is used with the wide-style metric format and allows 24 bits for the default metric value. And because these TLVs are CLNS packets, always keep in mind that it is possible for CLNS to form an adjacency between routers but IP may not be communicating across the link. So even though the router may have an adjacency to its neighbor, you must still verify that your IP is configured correctly.

Understanding the Network Types

In IS-IS, there are two types of networks: point-to-point and broadcast. IS-IS does not have a point-to-multipoint network type or a nonbroadcast network type as Open Shortest Path First (OSPF) does. However, just as in OSPF, you must assure that both ends of a link are configured as the same type of network to allow the hello packets to pass across and form the adjacency.

Remember that IS-IS does not have a network type interface command as OSPF does, so you must be sure that you are using the proper type of interface on both ends of the link so that both interfaces are transmitting the same type of hello packet.

Also remember that a physical interface configured with Frame Relay encapsulation is by default a multipoint interface. Therefore, the interface on the other end of the link must also be a multipoint type of interface, or both interfaces must be a point-to-point type of interface.

Route Leaking

IS-IS allows for a two levels of routing: Level 1 (L1) and Level 2 (L2). There can be multiple L1 areas usually connected with a Level 2 area, also referred to as a backbone. A router can belong to L1, L2, or both (Level 1/Level 2). The L1 link-state database (LSDB) contains information about the L1 area only. The L2 LSDB contains information about that level as well as each of the L1 areas. A Level 1/Level 2 (L1/L2) router contains both the L1 and L2 databases. The L1/L2 router will advertise into the L2 area networks for the L1 area to which it belongs. Each L1 area is basically a stub area. Packets destined for a network that is outside of the L1 area are routed to the closest L1/L2 router to be forwarded through the L2 area to the destination network. However, in the destination area, which will be an L1 area, the L1 routers do not have specific routes in their routing tables; instead they have routes for only other L1 routers within the same area as themselves and a default route to the closest L1/L2 router. The L1/L2 router is the gateway out to the L2 area and all other L1 areas.

Route leaking will reduce suboptimal routing by providing a mechanism for leaking, or redistributing, L2 information into the L1 areas, which allows the L1 routers to have specific routes. This can be extremely useful when you may have redundant L1/L2 routers or exit points out of the L1 area. It will allow the L1 routers to make a better decision of which L1/L2 router to forward the packet to.

Route leaking can be used with either the narrow-style metric TLV type 128 or the wide-style metric TLV types 135. We recommend using the wide-style metric because it allows for Traffic Engineering. However, both metric types (TLV 128 and TLV 135) use the Up/Down bit to indicate whether or not the route defined in the TLV has been leaked. If the Up/Down bit is set to 0, the route was originated within that L1 area. If the Up/Down bit is set to 1, the route has been redistributed into the L1 area from the L2 area. The Up/Down bit is used to prevent routing loops because an L1/L2 router will not readvertise into the L2 area any L1 routes that have the Up/Down bit set.

Figure 9.14 shows a typical IS-IS network structure. Notice that router R1 is an L1/L2 router in Area 1. Also, it has a loopback interface configured with the 147.19.1.0 network. Area 2 has two separate Level-1-2 (L1/L2) routers R4 and R2. And router R5 is a Level-1 router inside Area 1. Router R5 has connectivity to both of the Level-1-2 (L1/L2) routers R4 and R2.

FIGURE 9.14   Route leaking

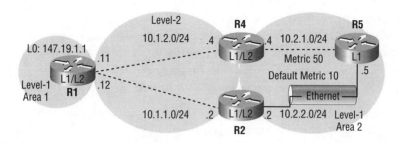

In Area 1, router R1 will propagate the 147.19.1.0 network across the L2 circuits to both routers R4 and R2. However, because routers R4 and R2 are L1/L2 routers, they will not propagate the 147.19.1.0 network inside Area 2, which is L1.

Remember that an L1 router will only have a default route to the closest L1/L2 router as an exit point out of its L1 area. And because the Ethernet connection from router R5 to router R2 has a default metric value of 10, it will be preferred as the L1/L2 exit point over the connection from router R5 to router R4, which has a set metric of 50. Thus, all packets that are destined to networks outside of Area 2 will be sent to the R2 L1/L2 router.

The following routing table from router R5 confirms that the preferred L1/L2 exit point router is router R2 via its Ethernet interface with IP address 10.2.2.2:

```
R5#show ip route

Gateway of last resort is 10.2.2.2 to network 0.0.0.0

     10.0.0.0/24 is subnetted, 2 subnets
C       10.2.1.0 is directly connected, Serial0/0
C       10.2.2.0 is directly connected, FastEthernet0/0
i*L1 0.0.0.0/0 [115/10] via 10.2.2.2, FastEthernet0/0
                [115/50] via 10.2.1.4, Serial0/0
```

And on routers R4 and R2, you will notice that the routing table shows that the 147.19.1.0 network has been received across the L2 circuits. The following routing table is the output from router R2 only because the routing table from router R4 is the same:

```
R2#show ip route

Gateway of last resort is not set
```

```
       147.19.0.0/24 is subnetted, 1 subnets
i L2     147.19.1.0 [115/20] via 10.1.1.12, Serial0/0.1
       10.0.0.0/24 is subnetted, 4 subnets
i L1     10.2.1.0 [115/20] via 10.2.2.5, FastEthernet0/0
i L2     10.1.2.0 [115/20] via 10.1.1.12, Serial0/0.1
C        10.2.2.0 is directly connected, FastEthernet0/0
C        10.1.1.0 is directly connected, Serial0/0.1
```

At this point, all packets from router R5 destined to any network outside of Area 2 will be sent to router R2. Now we want to perform route leaking on router R4 so that a specific route for the 147.19.1.0 network can be leaked from the L2 database of router R4 into the L1 database of router R4. This will allow router R4 to propagate the 147.19.1.0 network to router R5. So, we must configure router R4 for route leaking by first configuring an IP extended access list permitting the 147.19.1.0 network and then applying the `redistribute isis ip level-2 into level-1 distribute-list 100` command, which will leak the 147.19.1.0 network into the L1 database of router R4. The following are the actual commands added to the router R4 configuration:

```
router isis
 redistribute isis ip level-2 into level-1 distribute-list 100
 net 49.0002.4444.4444.4444.00

access-list 100 permit ip 147.19.1.0 0.0.0.255 any
```

With router R4 configured for route leaking, the 147.19.1.0 network should be propagated inside Area 2 to router R5. And router R5 will still have its preferred default route pointing to router R2 for all packets destined outside of Area 2. However, now there is the one exception that any packets destined to the 147.19.1.0 network will be routed to router R4 because router R5 has a specific route in its routing table for the 147.19.1.0 network. The following output of the router R5 routing table confirms this:

```
R5#show ip route

Gateway of last resort is 10.2.2.2 to network 0.0.0.0

       147.19.0.0/24 is subnetted, 1 subnets
i L1     147.19.1.0 [115/94] via 10.2.1.4, Serial0/0
       10.0.0.0/24 is subnetted, 3 subnets
C        10.2.1.0 is directly connected, Serial0/0
i L1     10.1.1.0 [115/94] via 10.2.1.4, Serial0/0
C        10.2.2.0 is directly connected, FastEthernet0/0
i*L1 0.0.0.0/0 [115/10] via 10.2.2.2, FastEthernet0/0
                [115/50] via 10.2.1.4, Serial0/0
```

Finally, the Up/Down bit will be set to a 1 inside the TLV advertising the 147.19.1.0 network indicating that this route was leaked into the L1 area (Area 2). So when router R2 receives the 147.19.1.0 route from router R5, router R2 knows that the route was leaked into this L1 area and to *not* propagate the 147.19.1.0 network back across the L2 circuit to router R1. This will stop any possible routing loop.

Route leaking can also be used to implement a crude form of traffic engineering. By leaking routes for individual host machines or services from specific L1/L2 routers, you can control the exit point from the L1 area used to reach these addresses. Route leaking is supported in IOS version 12.0S, 12.0T, and 12.1. The 12.0T and 12.1 versions use the `redistribute isis ip level-2 into level-1 distribute-list 100` command, and the 12.0S version uses the `advertise ip l2-into-l1 100` command and also requires the `metric-style wide` command. The `metric-style wide` command is not required for the 12.0T and 12.1 versions of the IOS, but it is strongly recommended. You must create an IP extended access list (shown as ACL 100 in the sample commands) to define which routes will be leaked from L2 into L1.

IS-IS Troubleshooting Commands

The following are some of the recommended commands to assist in the troubleshooting of IS-IS routing issues:

`show isis database [level-1	level-2]`	An asterisk (*) next to any entry indicates the LSP was originated by the local router
`show isis route`	IS-IS level-1 routing table
`show isis topology`	IS-IS paths to Intermediate Systems
`show clns is-neighbors`	View the IS-IS neighbor adjacency table
`show clns interface`	
`show clns protocol`	Information of the IS-IS routing process. (System ID, areas, interfaces, etc.)
`show ip protocols`	
`debug clns`	
`clear clns is-neighbors`	Clears IS-IS neighbor adjacencies
`clear isis *`	Clears the IS-IS LSDB and any neighbor adjacencies

Open Shortest Path First (OSPF)

This section deals with the configuration of the *Open Shortest Path First (OSPF)* routing protocol. OSPF is a link-state routing protocol and as such is probably the most widely used interior gateway protocol (IGP). This is primarily because of its ability to scale and its ability to converge quickly and because it is a nonproprietary routing protocol unlike EIGRP. OSPF allows for interoperability between multiple vendors and is standards based. The current version of OSPF that is available in Cisco IOS is version 2.

One of the major differences between distance vector and link-state protocols is that a link-state protocol generates a routing update only when there is a network or topology change. The change is sent or flooded to its neighbors instantly, and this is the reason that link-state protocols converge very quickly. When a distance vector routing protocol detects a change, the protocol has to wait for periodic updates, hold timers, and flush timers to stabilize the routing table.

The *Open* in *Open Shortest Path First* means open standard. OSPF is the open standard routing protocol based upon the Dijkstra algorithm. OSPF is a big topic to which several books have been dedicated. As you will see, however, the ideas and the implementation of the protocol are straightforward and easy to understand.

The shortest path first (SPF) algorithm is often called the Dijkstra algorithm in honor of its inventor, the late Edsger Wybe Dijkstra.

OSPF Interface Cost

OSPF is based on the shortest path first (SPF) algorithm. OSPF automatically assigns a cost to each router's interface. The default cost assigned to each interface is figured using the following formula:

```
OSPF cost = 100,000,000/Interface Bandwidth
```

Notice that the cost is 100,000,000 divided by the interface bandwidth in bps, *not* Kbps as is used in IGRP/EIGRP.

The OSPF cost for standard router interfaces is as follows:

- Fast Ethernet = OSPF cost 1
- Loopback = OSPF cost 1
- DS3 = OSPF cost 2
- 16M token ring = OSPF cost 6

- Ethernet = OSPF cost 10
- Serial port = OSPF cost 64

For a WAN interface, it is extremely important that the `bandwidth` command be defined under the interface or subinterface. Otherwise, the OSPF cost will automatically be the cost of the physical interface as shown in the preceding list. Optionally, the OSPF cost can be set using the `ip ospf cost` command, which is configured under the router's interface. Because routers support interface speeds higher that 100Mbps, a router can now be configured with the `auto-cost reference-bandwidth 1000 router configuration` command. This command allows the reference bandwidth to be changed from a default of 100MBits to a new reference of 1000MBits. With a new reference bandwidth of 1000MBits, a Fast Ethernet will now have an OSPF cost of 10 and an Ethernet an OSPF cost of 100.

Shortest Path First

OSPF differs considerably from distance vector routing protocols. Instead of passing routes to a neighbor router, as is the case in distance vector routing protocols, OSPF passes link-state advertisements (LSAs) to its neighbor. These LSAs are then used to populate a link-state database. Every router in an OSPF area will have an identical link-state database; this is a very important point to understand about the OSPF link-state database. The relevant information contained in an LSA is the originating router ID (RID), a link-state ID (such as a LAN subnet address or serial link subnet address with subnet mask), the LSA type, and the associated OSPF interface cost.

Each OSPF router has a complete link-state database. The link-state database is not the router's routing table but is used to generate the router's routing table. To do this, the router performs the Dijkstra algorithm, or the shortest path first calculation. The router performs this by putting itself as the root of a routing tree. It then uses the contents of the link-state table and does a step-by-step calculation to figure out the shortest path to each downstream router and its connected networks. This process is continued until a complete tree is built based on the shortest path link-state calculation.

To keep from continuously running the shortest path first algorithm, the OSPF process will wait for 5 seconds before performing the SPF after a network changes. This also allows other updates to be received. It is possible to configure the OSPF process with a different wait time after a network change, but this can have significant effects on the performance and convergence of the network. The following router configuration is used on each router in Figure 9.15:

```
interface Loopback1

  ip address 10.1.254.X 255.255.255.255    Assign a loopback address to each
                                           router where X is the router number
                                           ( 1,2 etc,). This is the highest
                                           loopback address on the router and
                                           will therefore be the OSPF RID
```

router ospf 1   Starts the OSPF process using
                                             process ID 1, (process ID is locally
                                             significant)

  network 10.1.0.0 0.0.128.255 area 0   All router interfaces with IP
                                             addresses from 10.1.0.0 –10.1.127.255
                                             will participate in OSPF Area 0. The
                                             Loopback 1 address will not be
                                             propagated as an OSPF network

FIGURE 9.15 OSPF network

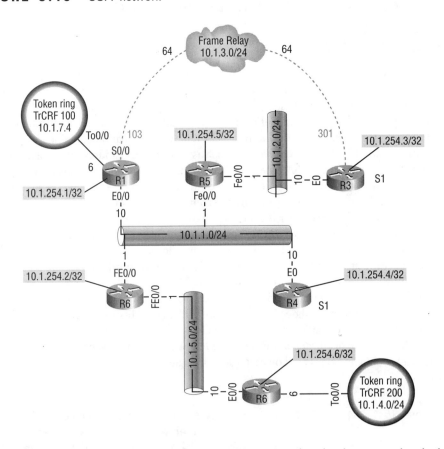

Assuming that all the routers are configured with OSPF, after the shortest path calculation is performed, the routing tree for router R3 would conceptually look like it does in Figure 9.16. Even though R3 and R1 are connected directly via a 1544K Frame Relay network, the shortest path is across the Ethernet connection to R5 and then to R1.

FIGURE 9.16   OSPF logical network

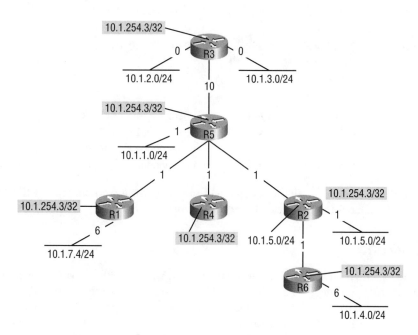

Here is the output from a show ip route command on router R3:

```
Gateway of last resort is not set

     10.0.0.0/8 is variably subnetted, 7 subnets, 2 masks
C       10.1.3.0/24 is directly connected, Serial
O       10.1.4.6/32 [110/18] via 10.1.2.5, 00:00:08, Ethernet0
C       10.1.2.0/24 is directly connected, Ethernet0
O       10.1.1.0/24 [110/11] via 10.1.2.5, 00:00:08, Ethernet0
O       10.1.7.0/24 [110/17] via 10.1.2.5, 00:00:08, Ethernet0
O       10.1.5.0/24 [110/12] via 10.1.2.5, 00:00:08, Ethernet0
C       10.1.254.3/32 is directly connected, Loopback1
```

The output shows both the administrative distance for OSPF (110) and the cost associated with each network.

Here is the output from a show ip ospf database command on router R3:

```
Link ID        ADV Router      Age      Seq#          Checksum Link count
10.1.254.1     10.1.254.1      61       0x8000002B 0x4602    3
10.1.254.2     10.1.254.2      44       0x80000028 0x396A    2
```

10.1.254.3	10.1.254.3	53	0x80000027	0x5546	2
10.1.254.4	10.1.254.4	62	0x80000025	0x5279	1
10.1.254.5	10.1.254.5	47	0x80000029	0xE6B4	2
10.1.254.6	10.1.254.6	39	0x80000030	0x5A36	2

```
                Net Link States (Area 0)


Link ID         ADV Router      Age       Seq#        Checksum
10.1.1.2        10.1.254.2      48        0x80000027  0xDB0
10.1.2.3        10.1.254.3      56        0x80000024  0x409D
10.1.5.2        10.1.254.2      44        0x80000001  0x7986
```

The output shows the RID of all the routers in the area and the advertising router (DR) for the link ID, which includes the broadcast Ethernet networks.

OSPF Areas

To provide scalability, OSPF can be broken into multiple areas. The OSPF area is a 32-bit number that can be represented by an integer such as 0 or 124023. OSPF areas can also be represented in dotted decimal—for example, 0.0.0.0 or 172.16.2.0. Either way, the router interprets it as a 32-bit number. The backbone area *must* always be Area 0, and all other areas must connect to Area 0. It is a violation in the OSPF model to connect two areas such as Area 2 and Area 3 together. The routers may have a physical network connection, but from an OSPF perspective, routers in Area 2 cannot communicate (form adjacencies or pass LSAs) with any router in another area other than routers in Area 0 or within its own area. In the OSPF model, traffic from Area 2 to Area 3 will always travel via the backbone (Area 0).

Another advantage of segmenting a network into multiple areas is to stabilize the network. Any network change that generates a topology database change will cause the shortest path first calculation to be performed. During the time it takes to perform Dijkstra, the router stops routing all packets. So, segmenting the network will ultimately stabilize the network if it is designed efficiently. The goal for the backbone (Area 0) in OSPF is to have a very stable area; all interarea traffic must flow through Area 0. Topology changes in other areas should not cause OSPF to recalculate within Area 0, and with the right design, this can be achieved.

In OSPF, there are intra-area routes, and interarea routes:

Intra-area routes Routes to other networks in a specific area. A router connected to Area 2 would have intra-area routes to all other networks within Area 2.

Interarea routes Routes to networks in other OSPF areas within the same OSPF domain. A router connected to Area 2 will have interarea routes to networks in Area 0, Area 1, and so on.

OSPF Link-State Advertisements

OSPF is a very structured protocol with different types of *link-state advertisements (LSAs)*. The different types of link-state advertisements assure that OSPF is populated into the link-state database in the appropriate place. Keep in mind how OSPF works. Every router *must* have an identical link-state database. Therefore, LSAs at the very least are sent to every router within a given area. The following is a list of LSAs:

LSA type 1 (Router LSA)   Generated by the router and describes the router and interfaces. It is sent to all other routers within an area and is not passed to routers outside the area

LSA type 2 (Network LSA)   Originates from a designated router (DR) in a multiaccess environment and contains a list of the routers connected to the network. This LSA is sent to all routers within the area and is not passed to routers in other areas

LSA type 3 (Summary LSA)   Generated by an area border router (ABR) and is sent to every router in the connected areas (not sent into totally stubby areas). It describes routes to get to networks outside of your own area. This LSA is sent to all other routers within an area

LSA type 4 (ASBR Summary LSA)   Generated by an area border router (ABR) but contains information about routes to get to an autonomous system boundary router (ASBR). This LSA is sent by the ABR to every router in its attached areas

LSA type 5 (AS External LSA)   Generated by an ASBR. This is sent to every router in the entire OSPF domain (not sent into stubby areas) and contains information about a route to a network in another autonomous system. LSA type 5 can also be used to send a default route for this OSPF autonomous system

LSA type 7 (NSSA External LSA)   Generated by an ASBR. This ASBR is connected in a not-so-stubby area (NSSA) and generates a LSA type 7. The ABR for this area will convert the LSA type 7 and send out an LSA type 5 to the rest of the OSPF domain

Figure 9.17 depicts the LSAs that would be sent by each router in an OSPF AS. R2 is configured as an ABR for Area 1 and also as an ASBR to another AS connected to the ATM network. Router R3 is configured as a ASBR in an NSSA area. Routers R1, R2, R4, and R5 are all connected to the backbone (Area 0). Router R2 is the ABR for Area 1. Router R4 is the ABR for Area 2 and the ASBR for the NSSA area. Every router in the OSPF AS will generate an LSA type 1. Routers R5 and R6 are the DR routers for each of the LANs. Therefore, they will generate LSA type 2 for the LAN segment. R2 and R4 will generate LSA type 3 to the routers in their respective areas; the LSAs will describe connectivity to Area 0 and the other areas in the OSPF domain. R2 is also configured as an ASBR, so it will therefore generate an LSA type 5 for every route that it sends into the OSPF AS and a type 4 into Area 1 describing R4 as an ASBR for the NSSA area. R3 is an ASBR in an NSSA area, therefore it will generate an LSA type 7. Router R4 will receive the LSA type 7; this type 7 is converted to an LSA type 5. R4 must send a type 5, and the function of sending out a type 5 makes R4 an ABR/ASBR.

FIGURE 9.17   OSPF LSAs

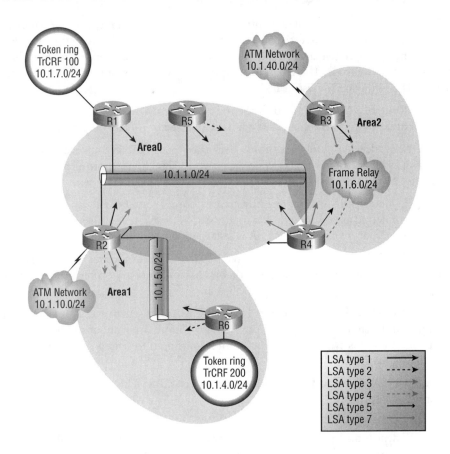

Here is the output from a show ip route command on R5:

```
Gateway of last resort is not set

     172.16.0.0/24 is subnetted, 1 subnets
C        172.16.34.0 is directly connected, Serial0/0
     10.0.0.0/8 is variably subnetted, 11 subnets, 2 masks
O E2     10.1.10.0/24 [110/20] via 10.1.1.2, 00:01:14, FastEthernet0/0
O        10.1.3.0/24 [110/65] via 10.1.1.1, 00:01:14, FastEthernet0/0
C        10.1.2.0/24 is directly connected, FastEthernet0/0
C        10.1.1.0/24 is directly connected, FastEthernet0/0
```

```
O        10.1.7.0/24 [110/7] via 10.1.1.1, 00:01:14, FastEthernet0/0
O IA     10.1.6.0/24 [110/65] via 10.1.1.4, 00:01:14, FastEthernet0/0
O IA     10.1.5.0/24 [110/2] via 10.1.1.2, 00:00:38, FastEthernet0/0
O E2     10.1.40.0/24 [110/20] via 10.1.1.4, 00:01:14, FastEthernet0/0
C        10.1.254.5/32 is directly connected, Loopback1
```

The output shows that router R5 will see interarea routes and external routers for the external networks that are connected. Use the `show ip ospf database` and `show ip ospf database router` commands to see information about the OSPF LSA information.

OSPF Hello Packet

An OSPF router sends out hello packets and expects to receive hello packets from its neighbors. In the event that a neighbor is declared down, the router will clear the topology database of all information regarding this OSPF router and recalculate the routing table. The hello packet is also used to form adjacencies between OSPF neighbors. The OSPF hello packet contains information that must match for both neighbors; otherwise, an adjacency cannot be formed. The hello packet includes the following information (the fields that must match are in bold):

Router ID   Must be unique across the entire OSPF domain
Router Hello Timer
Router Dead Timer
Router priority number   Used in the election process of the DR and BDR
OSPF Area
Network Mask of the outgoing interface
OSPF stub
OSPF authentication

If the routers agree on these five items (also the interface MTU must be agreed upon), they can form an adjacency. The routers then progress through the following states:

DOWN   No hello packets have been sent.

INIT   One router has sent a hello packet.

TWO-WAY   Both routers have sent a hello packet.

EXSTART   Routers determine who has the highest router ID. The router with the highest router ID begins the exchange.

EXCHANGE   The routers trade a summary of their routing tables.

LOADING   Routers exchange additional information if needed.

FULL   Complete.

Once all routers reach the FULL state, the network has converged.

Each router sends OSPF hellos to each of its neighbors. Depending on the OSPF network type, the hello timer and dead timer may have different values for the different type of OSPF network types. The following list shows the values for the different network types:

OSPF Network Type	Hello Timer	Dead Timer
Broadcast	10	40
Point-to-point	10	40
Nonbroadcast	30	120
Point-to-multipoint	30	120

For the broadcast network type, such as Ethernet, hello packets are sent using multicast address 224.0.0.5 and 224.0.0.6. Multicast is also used on point-to-point and multipoint network types. On other networks, unicast packets are used to send the hello packets. If two routers have their interfaces configured with different OSPF network types, the routers will not form an OSPF adjacency because the OSPF dead and hello timers will not match. A common misconception is that you can adjust the hello and dead timers to match each other and neighbors configured with different network types will form an adjacency. This is not the case because other features come into play—for example, some network types don't elect a DR.

OSPF Network Types

When OSPF is configured on a router, each interface in the router must be configured under the OSPF process to participate in the routing protocol. OSPF supports many network types, and each router interface in a Cisco router will automatically be assigned an OSPF network type. Table 9.9 shows each OSPF network type and the router interface type that will automatically be assigned.

TABLE 9.9   OSPF Network Types

OSPF Network Type	Router Interface
Point-to-point	Serial interface
	Frame Relay subinterface point-to-point
	ATM sub-interface point-to-point
Broadcast	Ethernet
	Token ring
	FDDI

TABLE 9.9   OSPF Network Types *(continued)*

OSPF Network Type	Router Interface
Nonbroadcast	Frame Relay physical interface
	ATM physical interface
Point-to-multipoint	Frame Relay subinterface point-to-multipoint
	ATM subinterface point-to-multipoint

Let's discuss the various types of OSPF networks.

OSPF point-to-point network   Has no DR and uses multicast (224.0.0.5) addressing to establish adjacencies with its neighbor.

OSPF broadcast network   Has a DR and BDR and uses multicast (224.0.0.5) to establish adjacencies with its neighbors and multicast (224.0.0.6) to talk to the DR.

OSPF nonbroadcast network   Has a DR but uses unicast packets to establish adjacencies. The OSPF Neighbor must be configured with this network type. The election of the DR needs to be controlled so that the hub router, with connectivity to all spokes, is set as the DR.

OSPF point-to-multipoint   Has no DR, routers send LSAs to other adjacent routers connected to the network, and OSPF figures out the correct path through the network. In a point-to-multipoint network, OSPF treats each router-to-router link as if it was a point-to-point link because host routes are installed for each spoke network to enable communications between spoke routers. The routers then exchange additional link-state updates that describe connectivity to the neighboring routers. This is the easiest OSPF network configuration for an NBMA network because OSPF does all the hard work.

The OSPF network type is one of the most confusing and misunderstood parts of the OSPF configuration process and is probably one of the main reasons why OSPF adjacencies do not get established. The most useful commands for troubleshooting OSPF neighbor adjacencies are `show ip ospf interface` and `debug ip ospf hello`. All routers connected to a network, whether Frame Relay or an Ethernet network, must agree on the OSPF network type; otherwise, OSPF adjacencies will not be established.

The following is the output from `show ip ospf interface` from router R3, which is a Frame Relay physical interface with its default OSPF network type:

```
Serial1 is up, line protocol is up
  Internet Address 10.1.6.3/24, Area 2
  Process ID 1, Router ID 10.1.254.3, Network Type NON_BROADCAST, Cost: 64
```

```
Transmit Delay is 1 sec, State WAITING, Priority 1
No designated router on this network
No backup designated router on this network
Timer intervals configured, Hello 30, Dead 120, Wait 120, Retransmit 5
  Hello due in 00:00:24
  Wait time before Designated router selection 00:01:54
Index 1/1, flood queue length 0
Next 0x0(0)/0x0(0)
Last flood scan length is 1, maximum is 1
Last flood scan time is 0 msec, maximum is 0 msec
Neighbor Count is 0, Adjacent neighbor count is 0
Suppress hello for 0 neighbor(s)
```

Here is the output from show ip ospf interface from router R4, which is a Frame Relay physical interface with its default OSPF network type:

```
Serial1.2 is up, line protocol is up
  Internet Address 10.1.6.4/24, Area 2
  Process ID 1, Router ID 10.1.254.4, Network Type POINT_TO_POINT, Cost: 64
  Transmit Delay is 1 sec, State POINT_TO_POINT,
  Timer intervals configured, Hello 10, Dead 40, Wait 40, Retransmit 5
    Hello due in 00:00:00
  Index 1/2, flood queue length 0
  Next 0x0(0)/0x0(0)
  Last flood scan length is 1, maximum is 3
  Last flood scan time is 0 msec, maximum is 0 msec
  Neighbor Count is 0, Adjacent neighbor count is 0
  Suppress hello for 0 neighbor(s)
```

From the preceding outputs, it can be seen that the default OSPF network types are not compatible between these interfaces and therefore one side of this connection must be changed for the two routers to form an OSPF adjacency.

The following output is from debug ip ospf events from router R3:

```
1d00h: OSPF: Mismatched hello parameters from 10.1.6.4
1d00h: OSPF: Dead R 40 C 120, Hello R 10 C 30  Mask R 255.255.255.0 C
255.255.255.0
```

The debug output shows the mismatched hello timers, hence an adjacency cannot be formed.

OSPF Designated Router (DR)

In OSPF, for broadcast and nonbroadcast multiaccess (NBMA), each network must have a *designated router (DR)*. This can be automatically elected by the OSPF Hello protocol (highest priority is selected), or it can be manually configured in the router. Once the DR is elected, no new election occurs, even if a new router that has a higher priority joins the network. Regardless of how many broadcast segments exist in an single area, each segment will elect a DR and a *backup designated router (BDR)*. If there are 10 Ethernet segments, each segment will elect a DR and a BDR. A router can be a DR/BDR for a single segment, or it can be the DR for multiple segments.

On a broadcast segment, the DR and BDR will form full OSPF adjacencies with each router connected to the segment, whereas all other routers connected to the segment will only achieve the TWO-WAY neighbor state with the other routers on the segment.

The following is the output of the `show ip ospf neighbor` command on R5, which is a DR, and on R2, which is a normal router. R5 will have a FULL state with all the routers connected to the Ethernet, while the same command entered on R2 shows a FULL state with only the DR and BDR and is in a TWO-WAY state with all the other routers on the Ethernet segment:

```
Router R5
Neighbor ID     Pri   State          Dead Time   Address      Interface
10.1.254.1      1     FULL/DROTHER   00:00:35    10.1.1.1     FastEthernet0/0
10.1.254.2      1     FULL/DROTHER   00:00:38    10.1.1.2     FastEthernet0/0
10.1.254.4      1     FULL/BDR       00:00:35    10.1.1.4     FastEthernet0/0


Router R2
10.1.254.6      1     FULL/DR        00:00:30    10.1.5.6     FastEthernet0/0.7
10.1.254.5      5     FULL/DR        00:00:35    10.1.1.5     FastEthernet0/0.8
10.1.254.1      1     2WAY/DROTHER   00:00:34    10.1.1.1     FastEthernet0/0.8
10.1.254.4      1     FULL/BDR       00:00:34    10.1.1.4     FastEthernet0/0.8
```

OSPF Router ID (RID)

The OSPF *router ID (RID)* is a very important part of the OSPF protocol. The RID is a 32-bit value and must be unique across the entire OSPF domain. The RID can be configured under the OSPF process. If it is not configured under the OSPF process, the OSPF process will select the highest IP address configured on the router and use this as the RID. If a loopback interface is configured, regardless of whether it is the highest IP address or not, the loopback address will be used as the RID. If multiple loopback addresses exist, the highest IP address will be used. Once the RID has been set by the OSPF process, the RID will not change.

For configuring virtual links, which is covered later in this chapter, the RID must remain constant. Otherwise, virtual links that have been configured and for which connectivity has been established will not recover if the RID changes on either of the routers.

It is important that the RID is kept consistent and is not changed in an active network. The RID is used and referenced by the OSPF process for virtually all calculations and operations.

Activating OSPF Interfaces

Making an interface participate in the OSPF domain requires that one or more network commands are configured under the OSPF process. The network statement uses a network address and a *reverse mask* along with an OSPF area that this network space is assigned to. The reverse mask is entered in decimal format but is actually used as a binary mask. Table 9.10 shows the binary-to-decimal conversion. When a bit is set to 1 in a reverse mask, the corresponding bit in the network is ignored. Where there is a 0 in the reverse mask, the corresponding bit in the network must match exactly. The bit assignment in the reverse mask must be contiguous. Table 9.10 shows the reverse mask for a single octet.

TABLE 9.10   Reverse Masking

Binary								Decimal
0	0	0	0	0	0	0	0	0
0	0	0	0	0	0	0	1	1
0	0	0	0	0	0	1	1	3
0	0	0	0	0	1	1	1	7
0	0	0	0	1	1	1	1	15
0	0	0	1	1	1	1	1	31
0	0	1	1	1	1	1	1	63
0	1	1	1	1	1	1	1	127
1	1	1	1	1	1	1	1	255

The following examples demonstrate reverse masks implementation. The first example is as follows:

```
Network     Mask              Reverse Mask
10.0.0.0    255.255.255.0     0.0.0.255

network 10.0.0.0 0.0.0.255 area 0
```

This would activate OSPF on any interface in the router that has an IP address from 10.0.0.0-0.0.0.255 and assign the interface in Area 0. It will not active OSPF on an interface with an IP address of 10.1.0.1 because this is not covered by the mask.

Here is the second example:

```
Network         Mask              Reverse Mask
192.64.10.64    255.255.224.0     0.0.31.255
```

```
network 192.64.10.64 0.0.31.255 area 0
```

Again, this statement will activate OSPF on any interface on the router with IP address of 192.164.0.0-192.64.31.255 and assign the interface in Area 0.

Here is the third example:

```
Network    Mask               Reverse Mask
10.1.1.1   255.255.255.255    0.0.0.0
```

```
network 10.1.1.1 0.0.0.0 area 3
```

This statement will activate only OSPF on a router interface with the specific IP address of 10.1.1.1 and assign this interface to Area 3.

The fourth example is as follows:

```
Network    Mask       Reverse Mask
0.0.0.0    0.0.0.0    255.255.255.255
```

```
network  0.0.0.0 255.255.255.255.255 area 0
```

This statement will activate OSPF on all router interfaces and assign every interface on the router to Area 0.

 OSPF network statements are executed sequentially by the router if the router has the following network statements configured: 0.0.0.0 255.255.255.255.255 area 0 and 10.1.1.0 0.0.0.255 area 3. All router interfaces will be assigned to Area 0 because the first network statement assigns all interfaces to Area 0, and the second network statement will subsequently be ignored.

OSPF Routers and Areas

As we've already discussed, OSPF can be segmented into multiple areas. The main reason for having a multiple area implementation is to allow networks to scale. Breaking the OSPF network into multiple areas will break up the shortest path first algorithm, and network changes in one area will have no impact on data packets passing between other areas. Again, when designing an OSPF network, you should make the backbone (Area 0) as stable as possible. No dial-up links or unstable serial links should be in Area 0. Any network changes that impact Area 0 will cause the SPF calculation to run, and during this process no traffic will be passed over the backbone. Depending on the network size, it can take several seconds for an area to converge after a network event has happened.

In a single-area environment, it is not necessary that an Area 0 exist. All routers within the domain must be configured with the same area. Therefore, in a single-area implementation, all routers can be configured to be in Area 1 because this is a perfectly valid configuration. However, it is more common that all the routers are configured for Area 0. In a multiple-area environment, routers fall into four different router type categories, discussed in the following section.

Router Types

There are four router type categories:

Internal router   The internal router has all interfaces assigned to one area. An internal router belonging to Area 0 will have all OSPF interfaces assigned to the backbone (Area 0). This router will have all `network` statements assigned to the same area.

Area border router (ABR)   The area border router has at least one interface configured in Area 0 and at least one other interface configured in a different area. This router will participate in multiple SPF calculations, and the router will independently perform an SPF calculation for each of the configured areas. This router will have multiple `network` statements and must have at least one network configured for Area 0 and one `network` statement for each other area.

Backbone router   All routers with at least one interface connected to the backbone are considered to be backbone routers. Routers with all interfaces in the backbone are considered to be internal routers.

Autonomous system boundary router (ASBR)   These routers exchange routes with routers from other Autonomous Systems, this is done by "redistribution" under the OSPF routing process. There is no restriction on where an ASBR can be configured, except in a stub area. A backbone, ABR or internal router in any Area can be an ASBR. An ASBR will have a `redistribute` command configured under the OSPF process. Routers from an ASBR will appear as "OSPF external" routes in a routers routing table.

When routes are redistributed from an external AS into the OSPF domain, the routers can advertise the routes as external type 1 or type 2. The difference in the two types of external routes is how the router's metric will appear in OSPF. If no metric is specified, the external metric is a value of 20 for all IGPs and a default value of 1 for BGP:

External type 1   The metric for external type 1 is the cost of the external route plus the cost of the internal route. Type 1 routes are preferred over type 2. External type 1 routes are usually used where there are multiple ASBRs advertising routes to the same external AS.

External type 2   The metric for external type 2 is the cost of the external route only. This is the default type applied to all redistributed routes. External type 2 routes are normally used when there is only one ASBR advertising routes to the external AS.

There are five types of areas possible in OSPF:

OSPF standard area   A standard OSPF area has only OSPF routers. The area routers will have a full OSPF routing table, which will contain area routes, all interarea routes, and all external routes. This is configured using the `network` command under the OSPF process. OSPF standard areas can have ASBRs configured.

OSPF stub area   The OSPF stub area will have all intra-area and interarea routes but will not have any external routes because type 5 LSAs will not be propagated into a stub area. A stub requires a default route to route outside of the OSPF domain. This is configured using the `network` command under the OSPF process. All routers in a stub area *must* also have the `area X stub` command entered under the OSPF process An ASBR cannot be configured in an OSPF stub area. A stub area is not a transit area, therefore it cannot be Area 0. A stub area cannot support virtual links.

OSPF totally stubby area   An OSPF totally stubby area is the same as an OSPF stub except that this area has only a default route propagated to all routers within the area from the ABR because no interarea or external routes are propagated into a totally stubby area. This is achieved by configuring the ABR with the `area X stub no summary` command; this command is not required on any other router within the totally stubby area.

OSPF not-so-stubby area   An OSPF not-so-stubby (NSSA) is a stub area that has an ASBR router. The ASBR generates external type 1 or type 2 routes. In an NSSA area, type 7 LSAs are permitted. In an NSSA area, you can permit type 7 LSAs by using the `redistribute` command under the OSPF process. The NSSA is configured using the `area X nssa` command. All routers in the area must be configured with this command. No default route is generated by the ABR in an NSSA, unlike for a stub area.

NSSA totally stubby area   When the ABR is configured with the `area X nssa no summary` command, the ABR will send out a default summary route, and this is referred to as an NSSA totally stubby area

Summary Addressing in OSPF

OSPF is a very scalable routing protocol, and as such, there are several techniques to help scale the network. The first is obviously the ability to segment the network into a multiple-area environment. Segmenting the network into multiple areas allows for the implementation of the stub and totally stub networks. These OSPF area types are essentially built-in summarization mechanisms to limit the routes that are sent from the OSPF backbone (Area 0) to the perimeter OSPF areas. The second method is to perform network summarization. There are two types of summarization that can be used. The OSPF area types listed in the preceding section help to reduce the size of the topology database and hence the routing table in the specified area, but they do not reduce the size of the topology database in the backbone. In a well-designed network, where the IP address space has been allocated in a structured manner and where the address space has been allocated sequentially, you can use the `area X range` command on an OSPF ABR. This command is used to summarize the address space of a given area. And you can also use the `summary-address` command on an ASBR to summarize external networks.

In Figure 9.18, the following are the associated router configurations to summarize and optimize the address space: Routers R3 and R5 are both ABRs. Router R6 is an ASBR connected to network 172.16.0.0/23, but it must be configured to announce a route for 10.1.4.0/24.

FIGURE 9.18   OSPF Summary Addressing

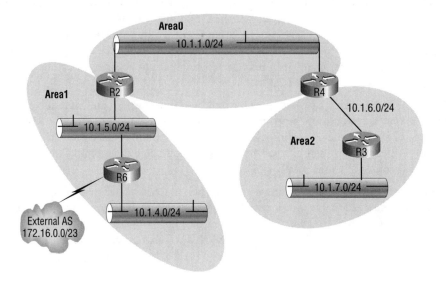

To simulate the external network, a loopback interface (172.16.1.6/23) was used on router R6:

```
Router R2
```

`router ospf 100`	Configure OSPF and use process ID 100, the process ID is locally significant
`network 10.1.1.0 0.0.0.255 area 0`	Assigns any router interface with an IP address in the range of 10.1.1.0-10.1.1.255 to Area 0
`network 10.1.5.0 0.0.0.255 area 1`	Assigns any router interface with an IP address in the range of 10.1.5.0-10.1.5.255 to Area 1. This covers both the Ethernet and Token-ring networks address space
`area 1 range 10.1.4.0 255.255.254.0`	This will generate a Summary route from R2 (ABR) for the address space 10.1.4.0/23

Router R3

router ospf 100

network 10.1.6.0 0.0.1.255 area 2   Assigns any router interface with an IP address in the range of 10.1.6.0-10.1.7.255 to Area 2. This covers the address space for both the Ethernet and Serial interfaces

Router R4

router ospf 100

network 10.1.1.0 0.0.0.255 area 0   Assigns any router interface with an IP address in the range of 10.1.1.0-10.1.1.255 to Area 0

network 10.1.6.0 0.0.0.255 area 2   Assigns any router interface with an IP address in the range of 10.1.6.0-10.1.6.255 to Area 2

area 2 range 10.1.6.0 255.255.254.0   This will generate a Summary route from R1 (ABR) for the address space 10.1.6.0/23

Router R6

router ospf 20   Configure OSPF and use process ID 20, the process ID is locally significant and does not have to match the process ID that is configured on R1

network 10.1.4.0 0.0.1.255 area 1   Assigns any router interface with an IP address in the range of 10.1.4.0-10.1.5.255 to Area 1. This covers the address space for both Ethernet LANs

redistributed connected subnets   This command will get the connected loopback interface which is connected to network 172.16.1.0/23 installed as an OSPF External type 2 route

summary-address 172.16.0.0 255.255.0.0   This will generate a Summary route for 172.16.0.0/16 from the ASBR, the route will appear as an external type 2

The following is the output from a `show ip route` command on router R2:

```
Gateway of last resort is not set

O E2 172.16.0.0/16 [110/20] via 10.1.5.6, 00:02:13, FastEthernet0/0.7
        10.0.0.0/8 is variably subnetted, 8 subnets, 3 masks
C       10.1.1.0/24 is directly connected, FastEthernet0/0.8
O IA    10.1.6.0/23 [110/65] via 10.1.1.4, 00:04:55, FastEthernet0/0.8
C       10.1.5.0/24 is directly connected, FastEthernet0/0.7
O       10.1.4.0/24 [110/7] via 10.1.5.6, 00:04:55, FastEthernet0/0.7
C       10.1.254.2/32 is directly connected, Loopback1
```

This output shows that network 172.16.0.0/16 is connected as OSPF E2. The OSPF cost (20) remains the same in both R2 and R5. R2 has specific routes inside Area 1 and has a interarea summary route from router R4.

The following is the output from a `show ip route` command on router R5:

```
Gateway of last resort is not set

O E2 172.16.0.0/16 [110/20] via 10.1.1.2, 00:00:19, FastEthernet0/0
        10.0.0.0/8 is variably subnetted, 9 subnets, 3 masks
C       10.1.1.0/24 is directly connected, FastEthernet0/0
O IA    10.1.6.0/23 [110/65] via 10.1.1.4, 00:02:56, FastEthernet0/0
O IA    10.1.4.0/23 [110/2] via 10.1.1.2, 00:02:56, FastEthernet0/0
C       10.1.254.5/32 is directly connected, Loopback1
```

Router R5 has an E2 route for network 172.16.0.0/16 and two interarea summary routes from both R2 and R4.

Configuring OSPF Authentication

OSPF authentication can be configured such that the hello packets that are exchanged between routers are verified to have the same authentication type and password. By default, routers send OSPF hellos out with a null authentication type, which means that no authentication is performed. There are two methods for configuring OSPF authentication:

- Simple password authentication or clear-text authentication

- Message-Digest authentication (MD5)

Rules for configuring OSPF authentication are as follows:

- All interfaces in an area must be configured to perform the same authentication type (null|simple|MD5).
- Routers must share a common password or key; multiple passwords can be supported in a single area using multiple keys.
- Simple authentication sends a clear-text password in the OSPF hello packets, therefore this method is easily compromised.
- With MD5, the key value is sent. The configured password is not sent in the hello packet, so it is inherently more secure than clear text.
- With MD5, the key value, encryption level, and password must match on all routers in the area.

The following are the associated commands needed to authenticate Area 1 in Figure 9.18 as simple password authentication and to authenticate Area 2 as MD5:

Let's look at the required configuration for router R2:

```
Router R2
router ospf 100                    The OSPF process ID

 area 1 authentication             Defines Area 1 to use simple password
                                   authentication

interface Ethernet0                This assumes that E0 is connected to
                                   network 10.1.5.0 network, which is
                                   part of Area 1

 ip address 10.1.5.2 255.255.255.0

 ip ospf authentication-key 3 chris   Configures an ospf authentication
                                   password of chris, this must match all
                                   other routers in the Area.  It also
                                   specifies the key number as 3, this is
                                   locally significant.  Multiple
                                   authentication keys can exist to
                                   support multiple passwords in an Area
```

Let's look at the required configuration for router R6:

```
Router R6
router ospf 20                     The OSPF process ID
```

`area 1 authentication`	Defines Area 1 to use simple password authentication, and enables authentication on every interface on Area 1
`interface Ethernet0`	This assumes that E0 is connected to network 10.1.5.0 network, which is part of Area 1
`ip address 10.1.5.1 255.255.255.0`	
`ip ospf authentication-key 1 chris`	Configures an ospf authentication password of chris, this must match all other routers in the Area. It also specifies the key number as 1, this is locally significant. Multiple authentication keys can exist to support multiple passwords in an Area

Let's look at the required configuration for router R3:

`Router R3`

`router ospf 100`	The OSPF process ID
`area 2 authentication message-digest`	Defines Area 1 to use MD-5 authentication
`interface Serial0`	This assumes that S0 is connected to network 10.1.6.0 network, which is part of Area 2
`ip address 10.1.6.3 255.255.255.0`	
`ip ospf message-digest-key 1 md5 2 josh`	Configures an ospf authentication type as message-digest for this interface. It also specifies the key number as 1, this MUST match the remote end. For this Key, the encryption is MD5, with a password of josh, the password is case sensitive.

The encryption type can be configured as follows: 1=unencrypted, 2=encrypted, 7= Cisco proprietary. This must match the configuration values set in router R4. Multiple authentication keys can exist to support multiple passwords and multiple encryption types.

Let's look at the required configuration for router R4:

Router R4	
router ospf 100	The OSPF process ID
area 2 authentication message-digest	Defines Area 1 to use MD-5 authentication
interface Serial0	This assumes that S0 is connected to network 10.1.6.0, which is part of Area 2
ip address 10.1.6.4 255.255.255.0	
ip ospf message-digest-key 1 md5 2 josh	Configures an ospf authentication type as message-digest for this interface. It also specifies the key number as 1, this MUST match the remote end. For this Key, the encryption is MD5, with a password of josh, the password is case sensitive.

The following is the output from the show ip ospf command on router R6:

```
Routing Process "ospf 1" with ID 10.1.254.6
 Supports only single TOS(TOS0) routes
 Supports opaque LSA
 SPF schedule delay 5 secs, Hold time between two SPFs 10 secs
 Minimum LSA interval 5 secs. Minimum LSA arrival 1 secs
 Number of external LSA 0. Checksum Sum 0x0
 Number of opaque AS LSA 0. Checksum Sum 0x0
 Number of DCbitless external and opaque AS LSA 0
 Number of DoNotAge external and opaque AS LSA 0
```

```
Number of areas in this router is 2. 2 normal 0 stub 0 nssa
External flood list length 0
   Area 1
       Number of interfaces in this area is 2
       Area has simple password authentication
       SPF algorithm executed 32 times
       Area ranges are
       Number of LSA 11. Checksum Sum 0x50C82
       Number of opaque link LSA 0. Checksum Sum 0x0
       Number of DCbitless LSA 0
       Number of indication LSA 0
       Number of DoNotAge LSA 0
       Flood list length 0
```

The following output is from a debug ip ospf adjacencies command on router R2 when authentication has not been configured on router R6:

```
1d00h: OSPF: Rcv pkt from 10.1.5.6, FastEthernet0/0 : Mismatch
   Authentication type. Input packet specified type 0, we use type 1
```

This output is from a debug ip ospf adjacencies command on router R3 when authentication has not been configured on router R3:

```
1d00h: OSPF: Rcv pkt from 10.1.6.4, Serial1 : Mismatch Authentication
   type. Input packet specified type 2, we use type 0
```

Configuring OSPF Virtual Links

OSPF has various limitations and criteria that must be met when implementing OSPF areas. One of the criteria is that all ABRs must have a connection to the backbone (Area 0). The backbone area is the transit area for all interarea communications. Therefore, all ABRs must be physically connected to the backbone. However, in today's networking environment, it is always possible to have an area not directly connected to the backbone. In this instance, an OSPF virtual link can be used to connect to the backbone. The *virtual link* is treated as an unnumbered point-to-point link.

The OSPF virtual link provides a logical path to Area 0 across an intermediate OSPF area. OSPF virtual links can be used to prevent Area 0 from becoming discontiguous in the event of a network failure. A virtual link can be used to provide a "back door" for Area 0 through another area.

Here are the rules for implementing a virtual link:

- A virtual link can only be created between two ABRs; one of them must be connected to Area 0.

- The two ABRs that the virtual link will be created between share a common OSPF area.

- The transit area across which the virtual link is built must not be a stub area.

The following are the router configurations for routers R1, R2, and R5 in Figure 9.19. All routers are configured with the loopback addresses shown in the figure. The OSPF process will then use the loopback address as the OSPF RID. To confirm the OSPF RID use the `show ip ospf` command.

FIGURE 9.19   OSPF virtual links

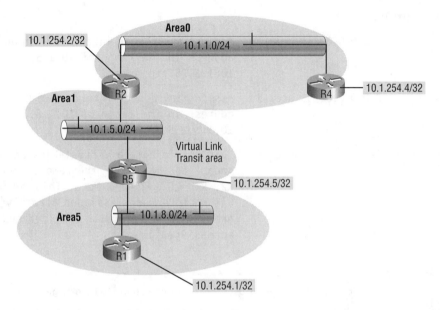

Here are the router configurations:

```
Router R1

router ospf 100

  network 10.1.8.0 0.0.0.255 area 5
```
Assigns any router interface with an IP address in the range of 10.1.8.0–10.1.8.255 to Area 5

```
Router R2

router ospf 100

  network 10.1.1.0 0.0.0.255 area 0
```
Assigns any router interface with an IP address in the range of 10.1.1.0–10.1.1.255 to Area 0

```
  network 10.1.5.0 0.0.0.255 area 1
```
Assigns any router interface with an IP address in the range of 10.1.5.0–10.1.5.255 to Area 1

`area 1 virtual-link 10.1.254.5`	This will create a Virtual-Link across Area 1 to the RID of the remote router R5 (RID=10.1.254.5)

Router R5

router ospf 100

`network 10.1.5.0 0.0.0.255 area 1`	Assigns any router interface with an IP address in the range of 10.1.5.0-10.1.5.255 to Area 1
`network 10.1.8.0 0.0.0.255 area 5`	Assigns any router interface with an IP address in the range of 10.1.8.0-10.1.8.255 to Area 5
`area 1 virtual-link 10.1.254.2`	This will create a Virtual-Link across Area 1 to the RID of the remote router R2, RID=10.1.254.2. Note: This router has no interfaces assigned directly to Area 0, only a Virtual-Link defined across Area 1

 You can use the show ip ospf neighbor command to quickly get the RID for a neighbor.

The following is the output of show ip ospf virtual-link command on router R5:

```
Virtual Link OSPF_VL0 to router 10.1.254.2 is up
  Run as demand circuit
  DoNotAge LSA allowed.
  Transit area 1, via interface FastEthernet1/0.7, Cost of using 1
  Transmit Delay is 1 sec, State POINT_TO_POINT,
  Timer intervals configured, Hello 10, Dead 40, Wait 40, Retransmit 5
    Hello due in 00:00:01
    Adjacency State FULL (Hello suppressed)
```

This output shows that the virtual link is Up, but the important piece of information is that the adjacency state is FULL.

The following is the output of show ip route command on router R1:

```
Gateway of last resort is not set

     10.0.0.0/8 is variably subnetted, 8 subnets, 3 masks
```

```
C       10.1.8.0/24 is directly connected, Ethernet0/0
O IA    10.1.1.0/24 [110/12] via 10.1.8.5, 00:00:17, Ethernet0/0

O IA    10.1.5.0/24 [110/11] via 10.1.8.5, 00:01:17, Ethernet0/0

C       10.1.254.1/32 is directly connected, Loopback1
```

OSPF Virtual Link Parameters

OSPF virtual links, like any other OSPF network type, sends hello packets to it adjacencies. As with any other OSPF hello packet, timers can be configured and authentication can be set on the virtual link. The following are the router configuration commands for manipulating virtual link parameters:

```
router ospf 1

area 1 virtual-link 10.1.254.1 authentication chris
```

> This will authenticate the Virtual-Link with a clear text password of chris across Area 1 to the RID of the remote router R1 (RID=10.1.254.1). The remote router must also have the same authentication type and password configured

```
area 1 virtual-link 10.1.254.1 message-digest-key 3 md5 2 josh
```

> This will authenticate the Virtual-Link with a MD5, using password josh. As with standard area authentication, the key number, password, and the encryption type MUST match with the configuration values set in the remote Virtual-Link router

```
area 1 virtual-link 10.1.254.1 hello 20
```

> This will change the hello timer to 20 seconds for the Virtual-Link. The remote router must also have the same authentication type and password configured

---

Real World Scenario

OSPF RIDs and Virtual Links

The important thing to remember about the OSPF RID is that if the interface that the IP address uses as the RID experiences a problem that causes the interface to transition to a DOWN state and then the interface IP address will no longer be the OSPF RID. This is why it is good network design practice to always use a loopback interface for your OSPF RID because the loopback interface will always be in an UP/UP state. Also, remember that when configuring a virtual link, the command you configure points to the OSPF RID at the other end of the virtual link.

We have actually seen networks in which the engineers implemented a virtual link between two routers and, unfortunately, the routers were both using one of the local Ethernet interfaces as the OSPF RID. Of course, when one of the routers encountered a problem on that specific Ethernet network, the Ethernet interface (which was also the OSPF RID for that router) went to a DOWN state. Consequently, the virtual link no longer functioned and part of the network become segmented. What a mess!!!

The engineers really felt bad when they realized what they had done in their design. If they had just configured loopback interfaces on both of the routers and used the loopback IP addresses as the OSPF RIDs, they would not have segmented the network because of an Ethernet LAN problem.

As you can imagine, they had a rough time explaining to their management why a single Ethernet LAN issue took down an entire region of the company network.

Configuring OSPF on the Router

In the following sections, we'll list some of the most common configuration commands for implementing OSPF.

Global Commands

This is a common global command:

router ospf 100   Enables OSPF on the router and uses process ID 100. The process ID is locally significant, and this is not the OSPF Autonomous System ID. This process ID is not sent in the OSPF Hello packet, and is not used in forming adjacencies, therefore the process ID can be different on every router in an OSPF Domain. This again is different from EIGRP, in which the EIGRP AS number is sent in the EIGPR Hello packet

OSPF Process Commands

The OSPF process commands are as follows:

network 10.1.0.0 0.0.0.255 area 0

Enables OSPF for Area 0 on all interfaces with an IP address in the range of 10.1.0.0–10.1.0.255

network 10.1.2.0 0.0.0.255 area 10

Enables OSPF for Area 10 on all interfaces with an IP address in the range of 10.1.2.0–10.1.2.255

area 10 Stub

Configured on an ABR and defines Area 10 as an OSPF Stub Area. This command must be entered on all routers that are part of Area 10

area 10 Stub no summary

The no summary command is entered on the ABR only. This command generates and sends a default summary route to all other Area routers, and is referred to as a Totally Stubby Area

area 11 nssa

Configured on an ABR and defines Area 11 as a Not So Stubby Area. This command must be entered on all routers that are part of Area 11

area 11 nssa no summary

The Optional no summary command is entered on the ABR only. This command generates and sends a default summary route to all other Area routers, and is referred to as a NSSA Totally Stubby Area

maximum-paths [1-6]

Defines the number of equal cost paths a router will install in its routing table. The default value is for 4 equal cost paths

neighbor 10.1.1.2	Specifies the IP address of an OSPF neighbor. This command is used in a Non-Broadcast configuration
default-information originate [always] [type1|Type2]	
	This commands generates a default route to the entire OSPF domain. The always command will stop the router from checking for the existence of the 0.0.0.0 route in the routers routing table. The type1|type2 defines how the default route will appear in all routers routing tables
area 11 virtual-link 10.1.1.1	Defines a Virtual-Link over Area 11, the address 10.1.1.1 is the OSPF RID of the router at the other out end of the Virtual-Link
area 1 range 10.1.1.0 255.255.252.0	This command is configured on an ABR and will generate a summary route for the address space specified. This summary will be sent to all routers in Area 0 and to all routers in all other Areas
summary address 172.16.0.0 255.255.0.0	This command will generate a summary route into OSPF for the specified address space, the Mask is a standard network mask. This is used to summarize routes for external AS routes. This command is only configured on an ASBR
area 0 authentication [Message digest]	Turn OSPF authentication on for Area 0. If the Authentication for this area is MD5, then the optional key words message-digest must be specified

Interface Commands

Here is a list of some common interface commands:

```
interface Ethernet0
```

`ip ospf priority 0`	This command sets the OSPF priority to 0. The priority range is 0–255. Priority 255 is the highest priority. If two routers have the same priority, the router with the highest RID value will be elected the DR. Priority 0 indicates that this router will not participate in the election of the DR or BDR. Priority 0 is the priority that is set on the spoke routers in a Non-Broadcast Frame-Relay network configuration
`ip ospf network [broadcast|Non Broadcast]`	Configures the OSPF network type. The network of all routers connected to the same point-to-point [point-to-Multipoint] network must have the same OSPF network type. Otherwise, OSPF adjacencies will not be formed
`ip ospf hello-interval`	Sets the time in seconds for the OSPF Hello interval. By default, the OSPF Dead timer is 4 times the hello interval. Both the OSPF Hello and Dead timers must match on all routers connected to the same OSPF network
`ip ospf dead timer`	The default value for the Dead timer is four times the hello timer, this command allows for the Dead timer to be independently set. While this allows for the Dead timer to be changed both the OSPF Hello and Dead timers must match on all routers connected to the same OSPF network
`ip ospf cost`	Changes the cost of an OSPF interface.

Summary

This chapter covered RIP versions 1 and 2, IGRP, EIGRP, IS-IS, and OSPF. Obviously, we had to omit some details, but you should now understand the essence and fundamentals of each protocol.

The development of RIP for IP was an important step that allowed the IP to grow in popularity. RIP version 2 addressed many of the problems of RIP version 1, but it still uses hop count for a metric.

Cisco developed IGRP as an improvement over RIP version 1. IGRP's use of a composite metric that defaults to a combination of bandwidth and delay helped the protocol gain support. When RIP version 2 was released, IGRP's lack of VLSM support made the protocol less desirable.

EIGRP was and is the answer for many organizations. This proprietary protocol is fast, efficient, and easy to configure and supports IP, IPX, and AppleTalk. Although EIGRP requires an all-Cisco-routed network, some consider it worth the price.

IS-IS is a fully functional link-state protocol that is not implemented much except for MPLS implementations. The failure of IS-IS to gain popularity stems mainly from the lack of vendor support.

Many consider OSPF the protocol of the present and the future. This link-state protocol is robust and an open standard. OSPF supports VLSM, has fast convergence, uses bandwidth in the metric calculation, and supports arbitrary summarization. OSPF configuration can be complex, but being an open standard is quite an advantage.

A CCIE candidate needs to understand how each of the protocols functions, paying particular attention to OSPF.

Exam Essentials

Know how static routes are manually configured on each router   They are required at each hop along a path so that each routing device knows where to forward to the next hop. Every time a change in the network topology is made, a network administrator must manually change the static routes throughout the entire network as required to correspond with the changes to the network topology.

Know the rule of split-horizon   The primary purpose of the split horizon algorithm is to prevent routing loops between adjacent routers. The basic premise is that "it's never useful to send information out the interface from which it was learned." Or, in other words, "don't tell me, what I told you."

Understand EIGRP   Classified as a hybrid distance routing protocol, EIGRP incorporates features that are exhibited in a distance vector routing protocol, but it also has more advanced features because it associates characteristics of a link-state routing protocol without the additional overhead.

Know what a feasible successor (FS) is   A feasible successor is an alternate path or alternate next-hop router to a given destination prefix that can be used in case the path to the current successor goes down. For a path or router to qualify as an FS, another next-hop router must have a reported distance (RD) that is less than the feasible distance (FD) of the current route.

Know the difference between Level 1 and Level 2   The intra-domain IS-IS routing protocol is intended to support many large routing areas, with each autonomous system (AS) supporting many networks. A large AS (domain) may be segmented into areas. Each system must exist in one and only one area. Routing within an area is referred to as Level 1 routing. Routing between areas is referred to as Level 2 routing. Level 2 intermediate systems (ISs) keep track of the route paths to all the other destination areas. Level 1 ISs keep track of the routing within their own area.

Describe distance vector versus link-state   One of the major differences between distance vector and link-state protocols is that a link-state protocol generates a routing update only when there is a network or topology change. The change is sent or flooded to its neighbors instantly, and this is the reason that link-state protocols converge very quickly. When a distance vector routing protocol detects a change, the protocol has to wait for periodic updates, hold timers, and flush timers to stabilize the routing table.

Know what the OSPF router ID (RID) is   The RID is a 32-bit value and must be unique across the entire OSPF domain. The RID can be configured under the OSPF process. If it is not configured under the OSPF process, the OSPF process will select the highest IP address configured on the router and use this as the RID. If a loopback interface is configured, regardless of whether it is the highest IP address of not, the loopback address will be used as the RID.

Key Terms

Before you take the exam, be certain you are familiar with the following terms:

administrative distance (AD)	Network Entity Title (NET)
backup designated router (BDR)	Open Shortest Path First (OSPF)
classful	reported distance (RD)
classless	reverse mask
default route	route leaking
designated router (DR)	router ID (RID)
distance vector	Routing Information Protocol (RIP)
Enhanced Interior Gateway Routing Protocol (EIGRP)	split-horizon
feasible distance (FD)	stuck-in-active (SIA)
feasible successor (FS)	successor
Interior Gateway Routing Protocol (IGRP)	Type, Length and Value (TLV)
Intermediate System-to-Intermediate System (IS-IS)	virtual link
link-state advertisements (LSAs)	

Review Questions

1. Which of the following is used by OSPF on Cisco routers to calculate the metric?

   A. Bandwidth

   B. Delay

   C. Reliability

   D. Loading

   E. MTU

2. What is the primary algorithm used by IGRP?

   A. DUAL

   B. SPF

   C. Bellman-Ford

   D. IS-IS

   E. Dijkstra

3. Which technology prevents routing updates from being sent out the same interface from which they were learned?

   A. Defining a maximum

   B. Poison reverse

   C. Holddown timer

   D. Split-horizon

   E. None of the above

4. Which of the following routing protocols are classless? (Choose all that apply.)

   A. RIP version 1

   B. RIP version 2

   C. IGRP

   D. EIGRP

   E. OSPF

5. Four routers are running IGRP on an Ethernet segment. All routers can ping each other. R1 and R2 are exchanging IGRP routes, and R3 and R4 are exchanging IGRP routes. No other IGRP routes are being exchanged. What is a likely problem?

   A. Different autonomous systems

   B. Invalid passwords

   C. Invalid network statements

   D. Cabling error

   E. Route exchange not possible

6. A router running EIGRP determines that the best path to network A is through R1 with an advertised distance of 100 and a feasible distance of 200. The second best path is through R2 with an advertised distance of 150 and a feasible distance of 250. What will happen to the route to network A if R1 fails?

   A. Nothing.

   B. The path through R2 will be immediately selected.

   C. The route will become active.

   D. The path through R2 will be used after the route becomes active.

7. In IS-IS, what term is given to a workstation?

   A. IS

   B. ES

   C. MAC

   D. LU

   E. PU

8. Which type of OSPF area will prevent type 3, 4, and 5 LSAs from entering an area?

   A. Backbone

   B. Summary

   C. Stub

   D. Totally Stubby

   E. Standard

9. In OSPF, where can a router get the router ID? (Choose all that apply.)

   A. From the loopback IP address

   B. From the lowest IP address of an active interface when OSPF starts

   C. From the highest IP address of an active interface when OSPF starts

   D. From the MAC address of Ethernet interface

   E. From the OSPF process ID

10. In OSPF, a router connected to the OSPF network and a RIP network at the same time is known as what?

   A. Backbone router

   B. Internal router

   C. ABR

   D. ASBR

   E. None of the above

Answers to Review Questions

1. A. By default, Cisco routers calculate the metric using the configured interface bandwidth, which is referred to as a cost.

2. C. IGRP is a Cisco-proprietary distance vector routing protocol based on the same algorithm used by RIP.

3. D. The rule of split horizon states, "Don't tell me what I told you."

4. B, D, E. IGRP and RIP version 1 are older classful protocols.

5. A. IGRP routers exchange information only with other IGRP routers in the same autonomous system.

6. B. The advertised distance of the feasible successor is less than the feasible distance of the successor, so the route will be used immediately.

7. B. A workstation is an end system (ES).

8. D. Totally Stubby areas prevent external LSAs and summary LSAs.

9. A, C. The router first looks for a loopback interface. If there is not one, it looks for the highest IP address on an active interface.

10. D. An autonomous system boundary router (ASBR) connects to a non-OSPF network.

Chapter 10

Protocol Redistribution and NAT

THE CCIE QUALIFICATION EXAM TOPICS COVERED IN THIS CHAPTER INCLUDE THE FOLLOWING:

- ✓ Route redistribution
- ✓ Configuring static NAT
- ✓ Configuring dynamic NAT
- ✓ Configuring inside global address overloading
- ✓ Configuring TCP load distribution
- ✓ Configuring translation of overlapping addresses

In this chapter, we will discuss the functionality of redistributing routes learned from one routing protocol into another routing protocol. This is actually a rather simple process to complete; the complexity comes into play when one of the routing protocols is *classful* and the other routing protocol is *classless*. (Refer to Chapter 9, "IP Interior Gateway Protocols," for an explanation of the difference between classful and classless and Fixed Length Subnet Mask (FLSM) and Variable Length Subnet Mask (VLSM).) We will discuss the specific methods of performing redistribution with each of the major IGPs: Routing Information Protocol (RIP), Interior Gateway Routing Protocol (IGRP), Enhanced Interior Gateway Routing Protocol (EIGRP), Open Shortest Path First (OSPF), and Intermediate System-to-Intermediate System (IS-IS).

Then we will discuss Network Address Translation (NAT), including the various methods of utilizing NAT, such as dynamic and static translations, Port Address Translation (PAT), TCP load sharing, and overlapping subnets.

Basic Redistribution

The basic mechanics of route redistribution are fairly simple and straightforward. You have a target routing protocol you want to bring routes into and the source routing protocol you want to get the routes from. In configuration mode, go into the target routing protocol's process and enter the `redistribute` command followed by the source routing protocol and optionally a metric value. In the following command, we are redistributing routes learned from EIGRP AS 1 into OSPF process 100 with a metric of 100:

```
router ospf 100
    redistribute eigrp 1 metric 100 subnets
```

So, we're taking all the routes learned from EIGRP AS 1 and injecting them into OSPF process 100 with a cost of 100. There are two items to note about the metric value:

- This value is arbitrary and decided by you; it is your estimation of how the metric/cost values of one protocol map into another.

- This value is essential for redistribution with some routing protocols; without it, routes will not be redistributed (unless a separate `default-metric` statement is configured under the target routing protocol).

Because there may be multiple sources of routing information on a router, you may need to redistribute routes from multiple routing protocols or even from other instances of the same routing protocol. This does not pose a problem; there is no limit to the number of routes that can be redistributed (provided you have enough memory and CPU), nor is there a limit on the number of routing protocols from which routes can be redistributed. In the following example, routes from multiple protocols are redistributed into OSPF process 100:

```
router ospf 100
   redistribute connected
   redistribute static
   redistribute eigrp 1 metric 100
   redistribute bgp 6500 metric 200
   redistribute isis level-1-2 metric 20
   redistribute ospf 200 metric 10
```

Although this is not a highly realistic example, it does show that it is possible to have multiple protocols redistributed at the same time. What we'll explore next is how to control exactly what routes you want to redistribute from one routing protocol into another and then examine each routing protocol in turn (except for BGP, which is covered in Chapter 12) to see what special requirements they have.

Controlling Redistribution

Sometimes more is not better. There are instances when only a few select routes are desired for redistribution or, conversely, all but a select few are desired. The example in the previous section showed all routes from the source routing protocols being redistributed into the target. To control the routes you want to redistribute, you can set up a route map in combination with an access list:

```
route-map EIGRPtoOSPF permit 10
    match ip address 10
    set metric 100

access-list 10 permit 172.16.0.0 0.0.255.255

router ospf 100
     redistribute eigrp route-map EIGRPtoOSPF
```

The route map in this example allows only 172.16.*x.x* routes to be redistributed from EIGRP to OSPF; all other EIGRP-learned routes will not be redistributed. Also, because of the `set` command in the route-map statement, the metric for these route will be 100, overriding the default-metric statement if one exists. Just as with access lists, route maps have an implicit deny at the end; if no match statements in the list are matched, the route falls through and no action is taken.

Another use of route maps in the redistribution process is to tag routes coming from one protocol to another. Protocols such as EIGRP and OSPF have fields in their route updates and databases that allow for an administrative tag to be applied to routes. Although this tag is optional and frequently left blank, it can be used to mark the routes' origins and also can be used as a method to block route redistribution if necessary. The following example shows routes being tagged upon entry into OSPF. The tags chosen are arbitrary; in real life, some administratively relevant values would be used:

```
route-map TAG_EIGRP permit 10
    set tag 101010
    set metric 10


route-map TAG_RIP permit 10
    set tag 202020
    set metric 50



router ospf 100
    redistribute eigrp route-map TAG_EIGRP subnets
    redistribute rip route-map TAG_RIP subnets
```

In the following sections on individual routing protocols, we'll show more examples of route maps being used to control redistribution. Route maps are also used extensively for BGP route manipulation as you'll see in Chapter 12. They are also used for policy-based routing (PBR) to override normal route table look-ups.

Another method of controlling redistribution is to use distribute lists. Here is an example of RIP route redistribution into EIGRP. The distribute list uses access list 10 to allow only 172.16.0.0/16 routes into EIGRP:

```
router eigrp 100
  redistribute rip 200 metric 56 2000 255 1 1500
  distribute-list 10 out rip

access-list 10 permit 172.16.0.0 0.0.255.255
```

RIP Redistribution

Because RIP version 1 and version 2 share the same database, there is no need for redistribution between them when they are running simultaneously on the same router. The only configuration needed is to enable or disable the sending and receiving of the appropriate version of the protocol. By default, Cisco routers send version 1 and listen to versions 1 and 2. Here's how to change this configuration:

```
interface serial0/0
 ip rip send version 1 2
 ip rip receive version 2

interface serial1/0
 ip rip send version 2
 ip rip receive version 1
```

As this example shows, you can configure the RIP version on a per-interface and per-direction basis. Once the information is learned, it is available to both versions of RIP.

The following commands are an example of redistributing routes sourced from IGRP into the RIP routing process. Static routes and connected networks are redistributed as well in the following example:

```
router rip

 version 2                                    Run RIP as version 2, allowing VLSM

 network 10.0.0.0

 redistribute connected metric 5             Metric is defined as hop count.
                                              Values = 1-15

 redistribute static metric 5                Static routes locally defined on
                                              router will be redistributed into
                                              RIP with a hop count of 5

 redistribute igrp 1 metric 5                IGRP process 1 routes are
                                              redistributed into the RIP routing
                                              table with a hop count of 5

ip route 10.1.2.0 255.255.255.0 10.1.4.1    Send all traffic destined to the
                                              10.1.2.0 network to a next-hop
                                              address of 10.1.4.1
```

RIP Redistribution Example 1

The same redistribution could also be performed along with route filtering by utilizing route maps:

```
router rip

 version 2                                    Run RIP as version 2, allowing VLSM

 network 10.0.0.0
```

`default-metric 3`	Specify default metric to be associated with routes redistributed into RIP
`redistribute igrp 1 route-map kyle`	Use a route-map named kyle to filter other routing protocols into RIP. Redistribute all routes from IGRP 1 that match the criteria of the Route-Map named kyle
`access-list 2 permit 10.30.4.0 0.0.0.255`	Matches IGRP route prefix in the routing table
`route-map kyle permit 10`	Creates the Route-Map named kyle
`match ip address 2`	Look for routes that match the criteria of access-list 2
`set metric 7`	If the route matches access-list 2, then assign a metric of 7
`route-map kyle permit 20`	All other routes that do NOT match access-list 2, redistribute using the default metric of 3

RIP Redistribution Example 2

The following example will redistribute IGRP 10 into RIP with a hop count of 2:

`router rip`

`redistribute igrp 10`	IGRP process 10 routes are redistributed into the RIP routing table
`default-metric 2`	Specify default metric (2) to be associated with routes redistributed into RIP

RIP Redistribution Example 3

The following example will redistribute IGRP and EIGRP into RIP and assign IGRP (172.16.0.0) routes a metric of 1, all other IGRP routes a metric of 3, and EIGRP routes a metric of 2:

`router rip`

`redistribute igrp 10 route-map katherine`	Use a route-map named katherine to filter other routing protocols into RIP. Redistribute all routes from IGRP 10 that match the criteria of the Route-Map named katherine

`redistribute eigrp 21`	EIGRP process 21 routes are redistributed into the RIP routing table using the default-metric of 2
`default-metric 2`	Specify default metric to be associated with routes redistributed into RIP
`access-list 2 permit 172.16.0.0 0.0.255.255`	Matches IGRP route prefix in the routing table
`route-map katherine permit 10`	Creates the Route-Map named katherine
`  match ip address 2`	Look for routes that match the criteria of access-list 2
`  set metric 1`	If the route matches access-list 2, then assign a metric of 1
`route-map katherine permit 20`	All other IGRP routes that do NOT match access-list 2, redistribute using a default metric of 3
`  set metric 3`	

RIP Redistribution Example 4

The following example will *only* redistribute the EIGRP internal routes to RIP:

`router rip`

`redistribute eigrp 10 route-map lynne`	Use a route-map named lynne to filter other routing protocols into RIP. Redistribute all routes from EIGRP 10 that match the criteria of the Route-Map named lynne
`route-map lynne permit 10`	Creates the Route-Map named lynne
`  match ip route-type internal`	Look for routes that match the criteria of EIGRP Internal routes

NOTE   Because there is no route-map lynne permit 20 statement, no other routes will be redistributed.

IGRP Redistribution

If you have both IGRP and EIGRP routing protocols configured and they both have the same autonomous system number, they automatically redistribute routes between themselves. However, if they have different autonomous system numbers, then redistribution *must* be manually configured. Remember, IGRP is a FLSM protocol and EIGRP is a VLSM protocol. When sending EIGRP routes into IGRP, only the natural class routes are sent.

The following commands are an example of redistributing routes from EIGRP 25 into the IGRP 10 routing process:

```
router igrp 10

  redistribute eigrp 25 metric 56 2000 255 1 1500
```

Redistribute the routes from the EIGRP 25 process into the IGRP 10 process. When redistributing IGRP routes into EIGRP, the IGRP metrics will be multiplied by 256. And, when redistributing EIGRP routes into IGRP, the EIGRP metrics will be divided by 256

Route filtering can also be applied to the above example by utilizing route maps (refer to the examples in the section on RIP redistribution earlier in this chapter because the process is the same with all the routing protocols).

EIGRP Redistribution

The following are the rules of redistribution that EIGRP must follow:

- Only routes from the source routing protocol that the router itself uses for packet forwarding are redistributed into the target protocol. Redistribution is done from the routing table, not from the EIGRP topology database or OSPF topology database. Use the show ip route *routing-protocol* command.

- EIGRP tries to calculate the proper EIGRP metric to advertise with the redistributed route, if possible. EIGRP can calculate the metric for routes imported from the following:

  - Other IGRP or EIGRP processes

  - Connected routes redistributed into EIGRP

  - Static routes that have a next hop for which EIGRP is computable

For all other protocols, the metric must be manually set using `metric` on the redistribute command, or by using the `default-metric` command. Routes for which the EIGRP metric cannot be computed are not redistributed into EIGRP.

- Redistribution into EIGRP is always classless.

- Redistributed information can be filtered using the `route-map` option or use the `distribute-list out` command in the target routing protocol.

- If the same subnet is being received through different routing processes, compare the administrative distance (AD) of the route(s). Refer back to Chapter 9 for a listing of routing protocols and their default administrative distance.

- If two routing processes are carrying the same information with the same AD and metric, usually the route appearing last in the topology database (the less stable) overwrites the previous route that came into the routing table from another routing process with the same AD and metric.

- The results are more predictable if both routing processes are EIGRP processes. The route with the best metric is inserted. It is even possible to load-share between routes received through different EIGRP processes if they have the same AD and the same metric.

The following example will redistribute BGP 25, OSPF 200, and all static routes configured on this router into EIGRP 42:

```
router eigrp 42
```

`redistribute bgp 25 metric 10000 1000 255 1 1500`	BGP 25 routes are redistributed into the EIGRP 42 routing table
`redistribute ospf 200 metric 56 2000 255 1 1500`	OSPF 200 routes are redistributed into the EIGRP 42 routing table
`redistribute static`	Static routes locally defined on router will be redistributed into EIGRP 42. If no metrics are defined, the "default-metric" command will be used
`default-metric 56 4000 255 1 1500`	Last three K values (metrics) are not used when deciding composite metric unless the "metric-weights" command is used

> If the redistribute command contains options like metric or route-map, the no redistribute command will not eliminate the entire command but only take out the options. You will have to issue the no redistribute command a second time to stop redistribution of a particular protocol's routes.

OSPF Redistribution

When an OSPF router is configured to redistribute its OSPF routes into another routing protocol, the OSPF router becomes an autonomous system boundary router (ASBR). As an ASBR, the router will generate LSA type 5 routes into the OSPF AS (or LSA type 7 routes if the router is in a not-so-stubby area, or NSSA). It also generates a type 4 ASBR Summary LSA to identify itself.

OSPF can utilize filtering techniques such as route maps and distribute lists in the same manner as other routing protocols. In chapter 16 we will discuss various filtering mechanisms that you can implement.

External routes default to a metric type of 2 (O E2), unless this is changed manually using the redistribute ospf 10 metric-type 1 command. Figure 10.1 shows the following two routes:

OSPF External Type 1 metrics (O E1)   Uses internal and external costs, meaning the cost or metric used in redistribution, along with the addition of each outgoing router interface cost along the path of the routers receiving the external route. Usually used when there are multiple ASBRs connecting to the same external domain, whereby the external routes are sent into the OSPF domain. Because O E1s are preferred over O E2s, this causes one ASBR router to be preferred over the other.

OSPF External Type 2 metrics (O E2)   Uses external cost only, meaning the cost or metric used in redistribution will remain the same throughout the OSPF domain. If there is only one ASBR connecting to the external domain, then leave the metric type as the default of O E2.

FIGURE 10.1   OSPF external routes type 1 and 2

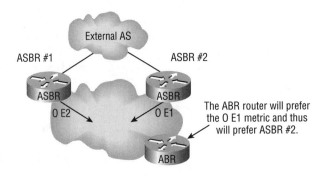

Also, if you redistribute BGP into OSPF and include the no default-metric command or do *not* put a metric at the end of the redistribution command, OSPF redistributes routes with a metric of 1. With all other sourced protocols, routes sent with a metric of 20 as O E2.

OSPF Redistribution Example 1

The following example will redistribute RIP into OSPF with a cost of 10. It should be second nature to use the subnets statement when redistributing routes into OSPF.

router ospf 10	Creates the OSPF routing process with a Process ID (PID) of 10
redistribute rip subnets	Redistribute the RIP routes into the OPSF routing process, and include its subnets
default-metric 10	Specify default metric to be associated with routes redistributed into OSPF

OSPF Redistribution Example 2

The following example will redistribute RIP with cost of 20 and IGRP with a cost of 10 into the OSPF process:

router ospf 10	Creates the OSPF routing process with a Process ID (PID) of 10
redistribute rip subnets metric 20	Redistribute the RIP routes (including the subnets) into the OPSF routing process and assignthem a metric of 20
redistribute igrp 10 subnets	Redistribute the IGRP routes (including the subnets) into the OPSF routing process and because no metric is specified, use the default-metric value
default-metric 10	Specify default metric to be associated with routes redistributed into OSPF

OSPF Redistribution Example 3

Redistribution can also be performed along with route filtering by utilizing route maps. The following example will redistribute all IGRP network 10.30.4.0 routes into OSPF with a cost of 25, and all other IGRP routes will be redistributed with a cost of 50:

`router ospf 10`	
` network 10.0.0.0`	
` default-metric 3`	Specify default metric to be used with routes redistributed into OSPF
` redistribute igrp 1 route-map kyle`	Use a route-map named kyle to filter other routing protocols into OSPF. Redistribute all routes from IGRP 1 that match the criteria of the Route-Map named kyle
`access-list 2 permit 10.30.4.0 0.0.0.255`	Matches routes with a destination address in the 10.30.4.0 network
`route-map kyle permit 10`	Creates the Route-Map named kyle
` match ip address 2`	Look for routes that match the criteria of access-list 2
` set metric 25`	If the route matches access-list 2, redistribute with a metric of 25
`route-map kyle permit 20`	
` set metric 50`	All other IGRP routes that do NOT match access-list 2, redistribute with a metric of 50

Real World Scenario

The Number of OSPF Type 5 LSAs vs. the number of Routes

Author Kevin Manweiler shares this experience:

"A key point with redistribution into OSPF is the difference between routes and type 5 LSAs. I was involved with a network transitioning from OSPF to EIGRP. The network was sizable and had thousands of routes due to some summarization issues. All told, there were around 4000 routes that were redistributed from the growing EIGRP section of the network back into the shrinking OSPF portion halfway through the migration. It was at about this point in time when some stability issues started plaguing the network—a few MALLOC messages in the syslog here, a few routers having slow convergence there, and so on—nothing to get too alarmed about. However, a week later, after more of the network had been migrated over to the EIGRP section, all [heck] broke loose in the OSPF side of the network. Instead of just a few MALLOC messages, there were lots, and dozens of key routers were not converging.

"The reason for this behavior was the memory requirements not only for the route table, but also for the OSPF link-state database. Although there were only 4000 OSPF external routes in the routing table, because there were 4 routers redistributing the EIGRP routes, there were over 16,000 type 5 LSAs in the OSPF routers' databases. Some of the older routers in the network didn't have enough memory to hold all the LSAs, and even some of the newer routers didn't have enough IO memory to deal with the number of packets used for the database exchange.

"When it was determined that the amount of redundancy for redistributed routes was killing the rest of the network, the number of routers redistributing EIGRP to OSPF was cut to two. A concerted effort to put better summarization in place was also made.

"The key point to remember is that each ASBR redistributing a route into OSPF generates a type 5 for that route whether or not it's used in other routers' route tables."

IS-IS Redistribution

Routes can be redistributed into IS-IS as either internal (default) or external routes and as either Level 1 or Level 2 (default) routes. The IS-IS metric needs to be between 1 and 63. There is no default-metric option in IS-IS, so you should define a metric for each protocol, as shown in the following examples:

```
router isis
 net 49.1234.1111.1111.1111.00        Configure the Network Entity Title - NET
 redistribute static ip metric 20 metric-type internal level-1

                                      Redistribute all IP Static Routes
                                      configured locally on this router as
                                      internal level-1 types with a metric of 20
```

```
redistribute rip metric 20 metric-type external level-2
```
> Redistribute all RIP routes as external level-2 types with a metric of 20

```
redistribute igrp 1 metric 20 metric-type internal level-1-2
```
> Redistribute all IGRP routes as internal level-1-2 types with a metric of 20

```
redistribute eigrp 1 metric 20 metric-type external level-2
```
> Redistribute all EIGRP routes as external level-2 types with a metric of 20

```
redistribute ospf 1 metric 20 metric-type internal level-1
```
> Redistribute all OSPF routes as internal level-1 types with a metric of 20

The following is an example of performing mutual redistribution between OSPF and IS-IS:

```
router ospf 1
redistribute isis level-1-2 metric 100 subnets
```
> Redistribute isis level-1 and level-2 routes with a metric of 100

```
network 150.10.10.0 0.0.0.255 area 0


router isis
net 49.1234.1111.1111.1111.00
summary-address 10.0.0.0 255.0.0.0 level-1-2
```
> All 10.0.0.0 routes learned from OSPF will be summarized

```
redistribute ospf 1 metric 32 metric-type internal level-1-2
```
> Redistribute OSPF as internal level-1 & level-2 routes with a cost of 32

Now that we've looked at some of the specifics of redistributing routes into the various routing protocols, we're ready to look at some of the more challenging aspects of route redistribution.

Redistributing between Classful and Classless Routing Protocols

There are a number of instances where a network can contain classful and classless routing protocols—a merger between two networks where one is running a classful routing protocol and the other a classless routing protocol, or a network running a classful routing protocol that is migrating to a classless routing protocol. In either case, there usually exists a boundary between the classful side and the classless sides where the redistribution of routes takes some consideration.

We'll look at two examples: one where the classless routing protocol has a longer mask than the classful routing protocol and one where the classless routing protocol has a shorter mask than the classful routing protocol. As with most network issues, there is more than one way to solve the problem. A few of the more straightforward solutions are presented here.

Classless Routing Protocol with a Longer Mask Redistributing Routes into a Classful Routing Protocol

Figure 10.2 shows a network with some routers using RIP as their routing protocol and some routers using OSPF. Router R2 is running both routing protocols and is performing redistribution between them. The problem is that RIP will not advertise routes from a major network (147.19.0.0, in this case) through an interface of the same major network, but with a different network mask. Therefore, either we have to change the mask of the OSPF learned routes or come up with a different solution.

One way to fix this is to define static routes to the OSPF routes using the same subnet mask as the RIP routes summarizing a number of routes at once. In Figure 10.2, all of the OSPF routes can be summarized by one route to 147.19.15.0/24, as shown in the configuration below. Notice that the next hop for the static route is to null0 which is local to router R2 and is always up.

FIGURE 10.2   Classless routing protocol with longer mask than classful routing protocol.

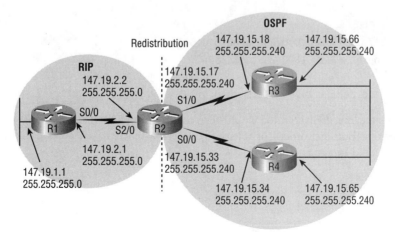

```
router ospf 100
 network 147.19.15.0 0.0.0.255 area 0.0.0.0
```
include all 147.19.15.x interfaces in OSPF

`redistribute RIP metric 100 subnets`   redistribute RIP learned routes into OSPF

```
router rip
 redistribute static
```
Static routes locally defined on router will be redistributed into RIP

```
  default metric 1
 ip route 147.19.15.0 255.255.255.0 null0
```

WARNING By default, there is no default metric! You must specify either a metric for each `redistribute` command or use the `default-metric` command for redistribution to occur.

Another possible solution is to summarize the OSPF routes in such a way that the mask of the summary route matches that of the RIP domain. The following code shows the 147.19.15.x routes from Figure 10.2 summarized on R2 and redistributed into RIP:

```
router rip
  redistribute ospf 100 metric 100
  distribute-list 10

router ospf 100
  network 147.19.15.0 0.0.0.255 area 0.0.0.0
  summary route 147.19.15.0 255.255.255.0

access-list 10 permit 147.19.15.0  0.0.0.255
```

Of course, the long-term solution would be to convert from RIP to OSPF, so that the network was running one routing protocol, or at least to convert from RIP to RIP version 2 so that subnet information could be propagated.

Classless Routing Protocol with a Shorter Mask Redistributing Routes into a Classful Routing Protocol

A similar problem to that of the last section arises if we try to redistribute from a classless routing protocol into a classful one where the subnet mask length is longer in the classful routing protocol. In Figure 10.3, we once again have RIP and OSPF routers that have a redistribution point at router R2. However, the subnet mask of the RIP routers' networks is longer than those on the interfaces of the OSPF routers.

FIGURE 10.3   Classful routing protocol with a longer mask than the classless routing protocol.

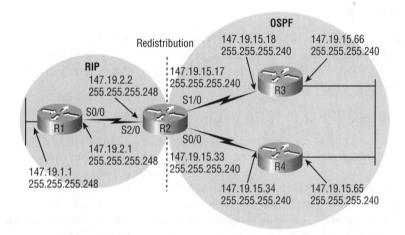

Static routes pointing to the OSPF networks can be added on router R2 that has the same subnet mask as the RIP routes. However, because the RIP masks are more specific, we have to use several static routes to cover each OSPF route as shown in the following configuration. Although this solution works, it is not scalable.

```
ip route 147.19.15.32 255.255.255.248 Serial0/0

ip route 147.19.15.40 255.255.255.248 Serial0/0

                              these routes cover 147.19.15.32/240

ip route 147.19.15.16 255.255.255.248 Serial1/0

ip route 147.19.15.24 255.255.255.248 Serial1/0

                              these routes cover 147.19.15.16/240

ip route 147.19.15.64 255.255.255.248 147.19.15.18
```

```
ip route 147.19.15.64 255.255.255.248 147.19.15.34

ip route 147.19.15.72 255.255.255.248 147.19.15.18

ip route 147.19.15.72 255.255.255.248 147.19.15.34
```
                                    these routes cover 147.19.15.64/240

```
router rip
```
```
redistribute static              Static routes locally defined on
                                 router will be redistributed into RIP
```
```
default metric 1
```

These solutions also work when you use EIGRP instead of OSPF and IGRP instead of RIP. This problem shouldn't happen if the masks of both protocols are the same or if all the protocols you're using support Variable Length Subnet Mask (VLSM). This fix is only considered a patch to cover the RIP and IGRP (FLSM) limitation.

Redistribute OSPF into IGRP (VLSM to FLSM)

What if you are not able to use static routes to perform the redistribution? Well, there are actually three methods of performing redistribution from an FLSM environment to a VLSM environment. You can use static routes as we have already done, but you can also use default routes and route summarization. Figure 10.4 will be used to demonstrate all three of the methods of performing route redistribution between these two autonomous systems: using static routes, using default routes, and performing route summarization. In the scenario we are using OSPF and IGRP. As stated in the previous examples, you can substitute the FLSM protocols and the VLSM protocols because the protocols do not matter in the scenarios as long as one is FLSM and the other is VLSM. The purpose is simply to demonstrate how to redistribute routes between an FLSM environment and a VLSM environment. In all three of the methods shown, we want router R4 to be able to ping all the interfaces within the OSPF domain.

FIGURE 10.4 Redistribute OSPF into IGRP

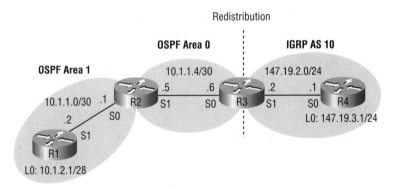

Redistribute OSPF into IGRP (VLSM to FLSM)

Option #1: Static Routes

R1

router ospf 1

network 10.1.0.0 0.0.255.255 area 1	This adds the Loopback "L0" interface and interface S1 to the OSPF process

R3

router ospf 1

redistribute igrp 10 subnets metric 100	Redistribute the IGRP routes (including the subnets) into OSPF

router igrp 10

redistribute static metric 100	Static routes locally defined on router (below) will be redistributed
ip route 10.1.2.0 255.255.255.0 S0	To get to network 10.1.2.0 go out the Serial 0 interface
ip route 10.1.1.0 255.255.255.0 S0	Go out interface Serial 0 to get to network 10.1.1.0

Option #2: Default Routes

R2

router ospf 1

area 1 range 10.1.2.0 255.255.255.0	Summarize the 10.1.2.0 to a 24-bit mask making it "classful"

R3

router ospf 1

redistribute igrp 10 subnets metric 100	Redistribute the IGRP routes (including the subnets) into OSPF

router igrp 10

```
redistribute ospf 1 metric 56 2000 255 1 1500      Redistribute the OSPF
                                                    routes into IGRP
```

R4

```
ip default-network 10.1.2.0                         Use the received "classful"
                                                    route 10.1.2.0 as the
                                                    Default-Network
```

In this case, R4 must receive the 10.1.2.0 in order to activate the `default-network` command. Using the `area range` command, R2 summarizes the 10.1.2.0 routes into a 24-bit mask route that gets redistributed by R3 into IGRP. R4 receives this route and can then route to 10.1.1.0 along the same path.

 The `ip default-network` command is mostly used for IGRP because IGRP does not understand quad zero (0.0.0.0). For other routing protocols, place the `default-information originate` command under the routing process on the router performing the redistribution. The `ip default-network` command can be placed on router R3 or router R4.

Option #3: Route Summarization

R1

`router ospf 1`

```
redistribute connected subnets                     Makes the router an ASBR, as
                                                    the Loopback interface
                                                    becomes an external OE2
                                                    network

summary-address 10.1.2.0 255.255.255.0             Summarize the external OE2
                                                    route

                                                    OR the loopback interface
                                                    can be changed to an OSPF
                                                    point-to-point network type
                                                    where its subnet is
                                                    advertised as a 24-bit mask
                                                    instead of a 32-bit mask.
```

`interface Loopback0`

`ip address 10.1.2.1 255.255.255.240`

```
ip ospf network point-to-point
```
Will advertise the Loopback as a 24-bit mask, NOT 32-bit mask since the network type has changed

R2

```
router ospf 1
  area 1 range 10.1.1.0 255.255.255.0
```
Summarize the 10.1.1.0 a single classful network on the ABR

```
  area 1 range 10.1.2.0 255.255.255.0
```
Summarize the 10.1.2.0 a single classful network on the ABR

R3

```
router ospf 1
  Redistrbute igrp 10 subnets metric 100
```
Redistribute the IGRP routes (including the subnets) into OSPF

```
Router igrp 10
  Redistribute ospf 1 metric 56 2000 255 1 1500
```
Redistribute the OSPF routes into IGRP

Summarize the address to a classful network on the interface (ABR) advertising the routes to you using the `area 1 range` command, or for networks external to OSPF, use the `summary-address` command on the router performing the redistribution.

Mutual Redistribution

Mutual redistribution occurs when routing protocol A's routes are redistributed to routing protocol B and routing protocol B's routes are redistributed into routing protocol A. Depending on the routing protocols involved and the number of routers involved in mutual redistribution, this could cause problems. Take for instance, the case shown in Figure 10.5.

FIGURE 10.5   Mutual Redistribution of EIGRP and OSPF

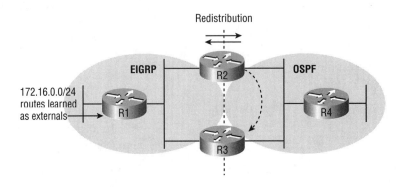

Routers R2 and R3 are both participating in OSPF and EIGRP routing and are both config-ured to redistribute routes from EIGRP to OSPF and OSPF to EIGRP. In this case, let's suppose that R2 redistributes the EIGRP routes into OSPF before R3. R3 will now see the 172.16.0.0 routes advertised as OSPF external routes in addition to EIGRP external routes. Because the OSPF routes have an *administrative distance* of 110 versus the administrative distance of 170 that the EIGRP external routes have, R3 will prefer them and point to R2 instead of R1 as its next hop for them.

Although there is no connectivity lost and R3 will have the correct routing if R2 crashes, this situation exhibits suboptimal routing. The fix for this would be to lower the administrative dis-tance of the EIGRP external routes using the `distance eigrp` command under the EIGRP glo-bal configuration.

Network Address Translation (NAT)

My 90 year-old grandmother using AOL Instant Messenger to communicate daily with my aunt has one thing in common with SNMP-controlled vending machines, IP phones, wireless PDAs, and even swarms of nanotechnology devices that communicate with each other: they all need IP addresses.

When the development on the TCP/IP protocol was started in 1969, no one could have envi-sioned its overwhelming popularity and exponential growth. Therefore, the four-octet IP addressing scheme encompassing nearly 4 billion addresses was thought to be more than adequate for all future needs. However, factors such as Class A and B depletion by corporations and other organizations and the Internet revolution have all but exhausted the capabilities of the 32-bit IP address.

Although IP version 6 and its virtually limitless address space will eventually solve such addressing limitations, it was not ready in the early to mid 1990s when the address space problem was manifesting itself. Therefore, *Network Address Translation* (NAT) was proposed in RFC 1631 as a method of con-serving address space. Together with the concept of private address space proposed in RFC 1918, NAT allows for devices to be coded with one IP address within a local scope but appear as a different address outside that scope. Therefore, addresses can be reused.

Although the syntax to configure NAT is quite different on the PIX firewall than for IOS, the basic concepts are the same. Because the source code is different, the PIX and IOS-based routers will have some variation in the NAT features they support and which IP applications they support. In general, a PIX should be used for NAT going to the Internet and a router should be used for NAT inside the corporate network. A router configured with NAT and IP access lists is no substitute for a correctly configured firewall such as the PIX.

Now that you know a bit more about NAT, we'll cover some of the advantages and disadvantages to using it in an IOS-based environment before reviewing how to configure it.

The Advantages of NAT

There are many advantages to using NAT. In this section, you will learn about some of the more important benefits. If your internal addresses must change because you have changed your ISP or have merged with another company, you can use NAT to translate the addresses from one network to the other.

The following list includes some of the advantages of NAT:

- NAT allows you to incrementally increase or decrease registered IP addresses without changes to hosts, switches, or routers within the network. (The only change necessary is to the NAT *border router*s connecting the inside and outside networks.)

- NAT can be used either statically or dynamically:

  - Static translation occurs when you manually configure an address table with IP addresses. A specific address on the inside of the network uses an IP address, manually configured by the network administrator, to access the outside network. This provides a consistent one-to-one mapping; the same outside address is always used for a specific inside address.

  - Dynamic mappings allow the administrator to configure one or more pools of registered IP addresses on the NAT border router. The addresses in the pools can be used by nodes on the inside network to access nodes on the outside network. The outside address is effectively random and may be different each time an inside device's traffic traverses the NAT router.

- NAT shares packet processing among routers using the Transmission Control Protocol (TCP) load distribution feature. NAT *TCP load distribution* can be accomplished by using one individual external address mapped to an internal router address. This round-robin approach is used between multiple routers distributing incoming connections across the routers. Each individual connection can be configured to use one individual router.

There is no limit to the number of NAT sessions that can be used on a router or route processor. The limit is placed on the amount of DRAM the router contains. The DRAM must store the configurable NAT pools and handle each translation. Each NAT translation uses approximately 160 bytes, which translates into about 1.6MB for 10,000 translations. This is far more than the average router needs to provide. CPU usage also becomes a limiting factor as the amount of NAT traffic increases, although this can be due to a large number of sessions or the heavy usage of a relatively few number of sessions.

The Disadvantages of NAT

You have learned about the advantages of using NAT, but you should also be aware of the disadvantages. The following is a list of some of the disadvantages of using NAT compared to using individually configured, registered IP addresses on each network host:

- NAT increases latency (delay). Delays are introduced in the switching paths due to the sheer number of translations of each IP address contained in the packet headers. The router's CPU must be used to process every packet to decide whether the router needs to translate and change the IP header.

- NAT hides end-to-end IP addresses, which renders some applications unusable. Some applications that require the use of physical addresses instead of a qualified domain name will not reach destinations when NAT translates the IP addresses across the NAT border router. Any application that embeds IP addresses inside its frames is likely to be broken when NAT'ed.

- Because NAT changes the IP address, there is a loss of IP end-to-end traceability. The multiple-packet address changes confuse IP tracing utilities. This provides one advantage from a security standpoint: it eliminates some of a hacker's ability to identify a packet's source. It also severely impedes entry into a network without traversing a NAT gateway and exploiting translation entries.

NAT Traffic Types

NAT supports many traffic types. We'll take a look at these types in the following two sections.

Supported Traffic Types

NAT supports the following traffic types:

- TCP traffic that does not carry source and destination addresses in an application stream
- UDP traffic that does not carry source and destination addresses in an application stream
- Hypertext Transfer Protocol (HTTP)
- Trivial File Transfer Protocol (TFTP)
- File Transfer Protocol (FTP)
- Archie, which provides lists of anonymous FTP archives
- Finger, a software tool for determining whether a person has an account at a particular Internet site
- Network Time Protocol (NTP)
- Network File System (NFS)

- rlogin, rsh, rcp (TCP, Telnet, and Unix entities to ensure the reliable delivery of data)
- Internet Control Message Protocol (ICMP)
- NetBIOS over TCP (datagram and name service only)
- Progressive Networks RealAudio
- White Pines CuSeeMe
- Xing Technologies StreamWorks
- DNS A and PTR queries
- H.323, versions 12.0(1)/12.0(1)T or later
- NetMeeting, versions 12.0(1)/12.0(1)T or later
- VDOLive, versions 11.3(4)/11.3(4)T or later
- Vxtreme, 11.3(4)/11.3(4)T or later
- Telnet
- Domain Name Service (DNS)
- IP multicast, source address 12.0(1) T or later

Unsupported Traffic Types

NAT does not support some traffic types, including the following:
- Routing table updates
- DNS zone transfers
- BootP
- Talk
- Ntalk
- Simple Network Management Protocol (SNMP)
- Netshow

NAT uses four types of addresses as shown in Figure 10.6 and defined as follows:

Inside local (IL) address   Used within an autonomous system. An example is a 172.16.0.0 address, nonroutable, used within your network.

Inside global (IG) address   A legitimate (registered) IP address that represents one or more inside local IP addresses to the outside world.

Outside local (OL) address   The IP address of an outside host as it appears to the inside network.

Outside global (OG) address   The IP address assigned to a host on the outside network by the host's owner.

FIGURE 10.6   NAT terminology

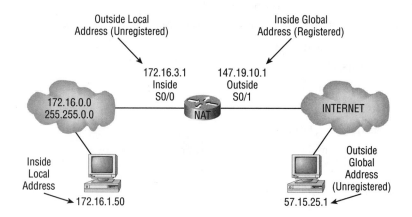

NAT: Inside Source

Use Figure 10.6 as a reference for the following configuration, which allows all packets with a source IP address that matches access list 10 to have the source IP address translated to an outside address from the pool named lynne. The `extendable` keyword in the example creates an extended NAT table entry where the TCP/UDP port numbers are kept as well. This makes the NAT statement more restrictive, requiring the exact port numbers to be matched for the translation to occur. Another keyword, `auto-alias`, can be used on NAT statements to cause the router to respond to ARP requests for translated addresses:

```
ip nat pool lynne 147.19.10.20 147.19.10.30 netmask 255.255.255.0
```
> Creates a pool of Inside Global (IG) addresses, named lynne

```
ip nat inside source list 10 pool lynne
```
> Specifies that a packet with an Inside Local (IL) address that matches access-list 8, can be NAT'd to an Inside Global (IG) address from the address pool named lynne

```
ip nat inside source static tcp 172.16.1.10 25 147.19.10.10 25 extendable
```
> Statically translating the inside address of 172.16.1.10 with TCP port 25 to the outside address of 147.19.10.10 with TCP port 25

```
access-list 10 permit 172.16.1.0 0.0.0.255
```

```
                                         Access-list defining the Inside
                                         Local (IL) address space to be
                                         NAT'd

interface Serial0/0

  ip address 172.16.3.1 255.255.255.0

  ip nat inside                          Serial0/0 belongs to the Inside
                                         Local (IL) address space of the NAT
                                         pool


interface Serial0/1

  ip address 147.19.10.1 255.255.255.0

  ip nat outside                         Serial0/1 belongs to the Inside
                                         Global (IG) address space of the
                                         NAT pool

router rip

  network 172.16.0.0
```

NAT: Outside Source

Use Figure 10.6 as a reference for the following configuration. The configuration allows all packets with an outside global (OG) IP address that matches access list 10 to have the source IP address translated to an outside local (OL) IP address from the pool named katherine. Traffic from 147.19.10.25 is translated specifically to 172.16.1.10, while traffic from 147.19.10.0/24 is translated using the pool of addresses 172.16.1.20 to 172.16.1.30:

```
ip nat pool katherine 172.16.1.20 172.16.1.30 netmask 255.255.255.0

                                         Creates a pool of inside addresses,
                                         named katherine

ip nat outside source list 10 pool katherine

                                         Specifies that a packet with an
                                         outside source address that matches
                                         access-list 10, can be NAT'd to an
                                         inside address from the address pool
                                         named katherine
```

```
ip nat outside source static 147.19.10.25 172.16.1.10
```

Statically translating the Outside Global (OG) address of 147.19.10.25 to the Outside Local (OL) address of 172.16.1.10

```
access-list 10 permit 147.19.10.0 0.0.0.255
```

Access-list defining the outside address space to be NAT'd

```
interface Serial0/0
 ip address 172.16.3.1 255.255.255.0
 ip nat inside
```

Serial0/0 belongs to the Inside Local (IL) address space of the NAT pool

```
interface Serial0/1
 ip address 147.19.10.1 255.255.255.0
 ip nat outside
```

Serial0/1 belongs to the Inside Global (IG) address space of the NAT pool

```
router rip
 network 172.16.0.0
```

NAT: Overloading or Port Address Translation (PAT)

Use Figure 10.6 as a reference for the following configuration, which allows all packets having a source IP addresses matching access list 10 to be translated to a single outside address from the pool named lynne. *Port Address Translation* (PAT) allows UDP and TCP traffic from multiple inside sources to use a single outside IP address. Each translation utilizes the same outside IP address, but with a different source port number, thus each socket will be unique. This type of translation is accomplished through the use of overloading. Basically, overloading provides the capability to use one outside (registered) address to replace multiple inside local (IL) addresses by mapping sessions by port numbers as well as the IP addresses. With overload (PAT), the pool can be a single IP address or a range of addresses:

```
ip nat pool lynne 147.19.10.21 147.19.10.22 netmask 255.255.255.255
```

```
                              Specifies the Inside Global (IG)
                              address as a pool named lynne
```

```
ip nat inside source list 10 pool lynne overload
```

```
                              Specifies that a packet with an Inside
                              Local (IL) address that matches access-
                              list 10 can be NAT'd [PAT] to the pool
                              lynne (IP address 147.19.10.21). Must
                              specify the keyword "overload" at the
                              end of the command for PAT to take place
```

The same functionality can be achieved using the outside interface's address instead of an address pool as follows:

```
ip nat inside source list 10 interface serial0/1 overload
```

```
                              With IOS 12.0, you can point to
                              the outside interface and use it's
                              IP address for PAT - NO pool is
                              required. Use this single command
                              in place of the two commands above
```

```
access-list 10 permit 172.16.1.0 0.0.0.255
```

```
                              Access-list defining the inside
                              address space to be NAT'd
```

```
interface Serial0/0
 ip address 172.16.1.1 255.255.255.0
 ip nat inside                Serial0/0 belongs to the Inside
                              Local (IL) address space of the
                              NAT pool
```

```
interface Serial0/1
 ip address 147.19.10.1 255.255.255.0
```

```
ip nat outside
```
                                    Serial0/1 belongs to the Inside
                                    Global (IG) address space of the
                                    NAT pool

```
router rip

network 172.16.0.0
```

NAT: TCP Load Sharing

TCP load sharing is used to make multiple servers appear as one server to your users. NAT can be used to map multiple individual host addresses to a single virtual host address used by the rest of the network. This is the same basic functionality you get when using Cisco LocalDirector.

Use Figure 10.7 as a reference for the following configuration. The configuration allows all packets (sessions) with a destination IP address that matches access list 8 (the virtual host address) to be distributed in a round-robin or rotary fashion to the multiple servers that belong to the pool named katherine. This allows you to distribute the user load across multiple servers using the single virtual host address. The users have no knowledge of the actual IP addresses of the multiple servers. With TCP load sharing, the pool can be a single IP address or a range of addresses, but the number of addresses in the pool should match the number of hosts participating in the TCP load share. A session from a host will be sent to the same server once a translation is made. Because the NAT translation includes information about the host address, the sessions will be "sticky."

FIGURE 10.7   TCP load sharing

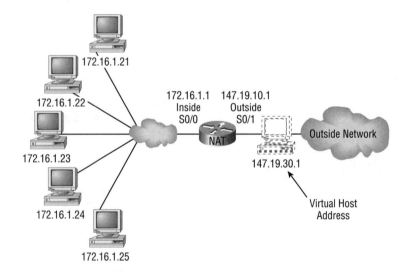

Here is the configuration for TCP load sharing:

```
ip nat pool katherine 172.16.1.21 172.16.1.25 prefix-length 24 type rotary
```

> Creates a pool of addresses named katherine - 5 shared hosts in pool

```
ip nat inside destination list 8 pool katherine
```

> Specifies that a packet (session) with an inside destination address that matches access-list 8, can be NAT'd to the pool katherine in a rotary fashion

```
access-list 8 permit 147.19.30.1
```

> Access-list defining the target Virtual IP Host Address

```
interface Serial0/0
 ip address 172.16.1.1 255.255.255.0
 ip nat inside
```

> Serial0/0 belongs to the Inside Local (IL) address space of the NAT pool

```
interface Serial0/1
 ip address 147.19.10.1 255.255.255.0
 ip nat outside
```

> Serial0/1 belongs to the Inside Global (IG) address space of the NAT pool

```
router rip
 network 172.16.0.0
```

NAT: Overlapping Subnets

As the term implies, *overlapping subnets* is the result of two or more separate networks choosing the same IP address space or portions of the same IP address space. This usually happens either when a registered IP domain is used inside another company or when the same RFC 1918 private addresses are used in multiple places within the same company, possibly after a merger or lack of communication between departments.

Figure 10.8 shows a network with overlapping address space with the 10.1.1.0 subnet provisioned on both R3 and R4. To enable the two networks to talk, R1 is configured with NAT. This is an example of bidirectional NAT, where both the inside and outside addresses are translated. In this case, 10.1.1.0/24 from R3 is translated using the pool "inside" to an address in the range 147.19.24.2 to 147.19.24.62. Because of the `ip nat inside source static` statement, 10.1.1.1 is specifically translated to 147.19.24.1 every time. Similarly, the 10.1.1.0/24 on R4 is translated using the pool "outside" to an address in the range 147.19.24.66 to 147.19.24.126. Because there is a static statement for this address, it is always translated to 147.19.24.65. The static statements are not essential to making bidirectional NAT work; they were used to help with the debugging output shown later to make sure the same addresses were used each time.

FIGURE 10.8   Overlapping subnets

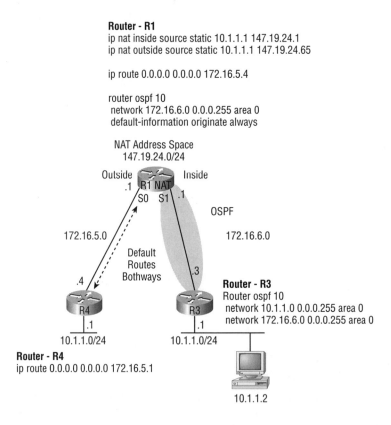

Using the dynamic NAT pools, the workstation off of router R3 with IP address 10.1.1.2 can ping the Ethernet interface of router R4. Notice that router R1 uses a dynamic routing protocol (OSPF) to communicate with router R3 and uses a default route to send traffic to router R4.

Required Commands on Each of the Three Routers in Figure 10.8

R1

```
interface Serial1
 ip address 172.16.6.1 255.255.255.0
 ip nat inside
interface Serial0
 ip address 172.16.5.1 255.255.255.0
 ip nat outside
router ospf 1
 network 172.16.6.0 0.0.0.255 area 0
 default-information originate always
```
Dynamic routing protocol must include the WAN serial link and the "default-information originate always" command, which will dynamically send a Default Route to router "R3"

```
ip route 0.0.0.0 0.0.0.0 172.16.5.4
```
Default Route pointing to the serial interface of router "R4"

```
ip nat pool inside 147.19.24.2 147.19.24.62 netmask 255.255.255.0
ip nat pool outside 147.19.24.66 147.19.24.126 netmask 255.255.255.0
ip nat inside source list 10 pool inside
ip nat inside source static 10.1.1.1 147.19.24.1
ip nat outside source list 10 pool outside
ip nat outside source static 10.1.1.1 147.19.24.65
access-list 10 permit 10.1.1.0 0.0.0.255
```

R3

```
interface Serial0
 ip address 172.16.6.3 255.255.255.0
interface FastEthernet0
 ip address 10.1.1.1 255.255.255.0
```

```
router ospf 1

 network 172.16.6.0 0.0.0.255 area 0

 network 10.1.1.0 0.0.0.255 area 0        Dynamic routing protocol must
                                          include the WAN serial link and the
                                          local Ethernet network

R4

interface Serial0

 ip address 172.16.5.4 255.255.255.0

interface FastEthernet0

 ip address 10.1.1.1 255.255.255.0

ip route 0.0.0.0 0.0.0.0 172.16.5.1      Default Route pointing to the serial
                                          0 interface of router "R1"
```

**Debug Information for an extended Ping from R3 Ethernet Interface to R4
Ethernet Interface**
```
R3 - debug ip icmp  (extended ping from 10.1.1.1 to 147.19.24.65)
20:11:47: ICMP: echo reply sent, src 10.1.1.1, dst 147.19.24.65
20:11:47: ICMP: echo reply sent, src 10.1.1.1, dst 147.19.24.65

R1 - debug ip nat
15:28:41: NAT: s=10.1.1.1->147.19.24.1, d=147.19.24.65 [2026]
15:28:41: NAT: s=147.19.24.1, d=147.19.24.65->10.1.1.1 [2026]
15:28:41: NAT*: s=10.1.1.1->147.19.24.65, d=147.19.24.1 [2026]
15:28:41: NAT*: s=147.19.24.65, d=147.19.24.1->10.1.1.1 [2026]

R4 - debug ip icmp
20:14:40: ICMP: echo reply rcvd, src 147.19.24.1, dst 10.1.1.1
20:14:40: ICMP: echo reply rcvd, src 147.19.24.1, dst 10.1.1.1
```

Troubleshooting NAT

Using the debug ip nat feature can greatly aid you when troubleshooting NAT problems. In the output from the example in Figure 10.8, you will notice that the source address of 10.1.1.1 is sending a packet to the destination address of 147.19.24.1. A -> indicates that a packet's source address was translated. An asterisk (*) indicates that the NAT'ed packet was fast-switched instead of process-switched. Typically, the first packet in a flow is process-switched and creates a NAT table entry. Subsequent packets will be fast-switched (or CEF-switched, depending on the mode enabled on the interface) using the NAT table entry. The IP identifier field is placed between the brackets [ ] in the output. More information is also given using the `debug ip nat detail` command.

Summary

Because it is rare for a company to run just a single routing protocol, route redistribution is an important and common configuration task to master. In the CCIE qualification and lab examinations, and in everyday networking, the process of redistributing routes from one routing protocol to another can get confusing, especially if one of the routing protocols is classful (FLSM). Although it is easier to accomplish this redistribution utilizing static or default routes, be sure to know how to accomplish it using route summarization. Basically, you have to make the classless (VLSM) protocol look like all of its routes are classful within the redistribution process. However, always be extremely careful when performing mutual redistribution between routing processes because it is very easy to create a routing loop. In chapter 16 we will discuss various filtering mechanisms that you can implement to stop routing loops.

Network Address Translation (NAT) can be implemented for multiple reasons and required functionality. Always keep in mind what you are attempting to accomplish because you must keep the inside and outside address spaces in perspective at all times. Also, always remember that if you have to implement NAT, be sure that all other previously implemented functionality has been accounted for. You may have to configure some static NAT statements to allow the previously implemented functionality to continue to perform properly.

Exam Essentials

Understand the basics of route redistribution.   Because different routing protocols keep the routes they learn separate, route redistribution is required for them to share routing information. Route redistribution is configured under each routing protocol's global configuration section. The `metric` command or addition to the `redistribute` command is used to translate between the different route comparators used by the various routing protocols. If a metric is not specified and there is no default-metric statement, redistribution will not occur.

Know the role of administrative distance.   Administrative distance is used by a router to determine which routing protocol to "believe" when two or more routing protocols deliver the same route. Although there is a routing protocol pecking order established by default, it is possible to change the administrative distance of any and all routing protocols. It is also possible to change the administrative distance for single routes or groups of routes using the `distance` command under any given routing protocol's global configuration.

Know what the `subnets` option under OSPF does.   OSPF by default will redistribute only classful routes from other protocols. In order to redistribute all routes from another routing protocol, the `subnets` option is required. The inclusion of the `subnets` option when redistributing into

OSPF should become as automatic as checking for the `metric` option or the `default-metric` command.

Understand the function of NAT.   NAT provides a mapping from one IP address space to another and was originally intended to preserve IPV4 addresses in the Internet. The NAT function on a router inspects incoming packets to see if they match configured criteria and changes the destination and/or source IP address based on configured mappings.

Know the difference between static and dynamic NAT.   Static NAT will assign the same translated address to the source address each time; dynamic NAT will generally be random. When static NAT is configured on the router, an entry is generated automatically in the NAT translation table. With dynamic NAT, entries are created when necessary and can age out of the table after a period of disuse.

Know what protocols NAT supports.   Although NAT supports most IP traffic—including TCP, UDP, ICMP—it must have special code to support protocols that embed either IP addresses or UDP/TCP port numbers in the data section of the frame. Examples of these protocols include DNS, CuSeeMe, StreamWorks, NetBIOS, Vxtreme, H.323, and ICMP packets with headers of other packets in them.

Know how to troubleshoot NAT.   Use the `show ip nat translations`, `show ip nat translations verbose`, and `debug ip nat` commands and output to help troubleshoot NAT.

Key Terms

Before you take the exam, be certain you are familiar with the following terms:

administrative distance	Network Address Translation (NAT)
border router	overlapping subnets
classful routing protocols	Port Address Translation (PAT)
classless routing protocols	TCP load distribution

Review Questions

1. A route is learned via the RIP version 1 protocol. This route should be advertised out Ethernet0 as a RIP version 2 route. What should be configured?

   A. Redistribute RIP 1 into RIP 2

   B. Redistribute RIP 2 into RIP 1

   C. Configure Ethernet0 to send RIP 2 updates

   D. Modify the distance of RIP 2

   E. Filter RIP 1 updates

2. A router is running EIGRP AS #1 on network 172.16.0.0 and IGRP AS #1 on network 10.0.0.0. The router learns about subnet 172.16.1.128/29 via EIGRP. An examination of other IGRP routers on the 10.0.0.0 network reveals that they have a route to 172.16.0.0/16 but not to the specific subnet. What must be configured so that the IGRP routers will have an IGRP route to the specific subnet 172.16.1.128/29?

   A. No auto-summary

   B. EIGRP summarization

   C. IGRP summarization

   D. Manual redistribution

   E. Not possible in this case

3. A router is running IGRP and EIGRP with the same autonomous system number. There is a single EIGRP route that you do not want shared into the IGRP system. Redistribution has not been configured. What should you do to prevent that route from being advertised to other IGRP routers?

   A. Nothing. No redistribution is configured.

   B. Modify EIGRP and IGRP so that they have the same administrative distance.

   C. Apply a route filter to EIGRP.

   D. Apply a route filter to IGRP.

   E. Configure partial mesh redistribution.

4. A router has been running OSPF, and now EIGRP has been added to it. OSPF routes should be advertised via EIGRP but are not. What is wrong in the following configuration?

```
router eigrp 200
  network 172.16.0.0
  redistribute ospf 1
!
router ospf 1
  network 10.1.1.1 0.0.0.0 area 0
!
```

   A. Needs the `redistribute` command in the OSPF section.

   B. Needs the `distance` command in the EIGRP section.

   C. Area must match AS #.

   D. OSPF must be enabled on 172.16.0.0.

   E. Need to specify EIGRP metric for redistribution.

5. A router learns about the network 172.5.0.0/16 via EIGRP AS #100. What would need to be configured to share this information via IGRP AS #300?

   A. Redistribution.

   B. EIGRP summarization.

   C. IGRP summarization.

   D. Nothing; automatic redistribution will occur.

   E. A static route.

6. What is the effect of setting the administrative distance to 255 for a protocol?

   A. That protocol is the first to be believed.

   B. That protocol is the last to be believed.

   C. That protocol is never believed.

7. Which of the following is a problem that NAT and PAT are designed to address?

   A. Assigning a DHCP address

   B. Assigning an IP address to a border router

   C. Translating nonroutable IP addresses to legal routable addresses

   D. Resolving IP addresses to fully qualified domain names

8. Which of the following types of NAT configurations would you implement if you were mapping all your inside IP addresses to one globally routable address?

A. TCP load distribution

B. Static NAT

C. One-on-one mapping

D. Overloading

9. Approximately how much DRAM on the NAT border router is used during each NAT translation?

A. 160 bytes

B. 100KB

C. 1MB

D. 64KB

10. Which of the following commands can be used to verify the NAT configuration? (Choose the two best answers.)

A. show ip nat statistics

B. show ip nat configuration

C. show ip nat all

D. show ip nat translation

Answers to Review Questions

1. C. RIP versions 1 and 2 share the same routing database, so redistribution is not needed. The Ethernet port should be configured to send RIP 2 updates.

2. E. IGRP is a classful protocol and does not include subnet information in the advertisements.

3. D. You want to prevent a route from being advertised via IGRP, so you must use a route filter because IGRP and EIGRP automatically redistribute for the same AS.

4. E. A metric or a default metric must be specified for redistribution to occur.

5. A. Redistribution would need to be configured because the autonomous system numbers are different.

6. C. The protocol would never be believed.

7. C. NAT and PAT provide functions that allow a nonroutable IP address to be translated into a routable IP address.

8. D. By enabling NAT overloading, you can map more than one inside IP address to a single IP address by using port information as a differentiator.

9. A. The NAT border router uses about 160 bytes per translation. This means that about 10,000 translations, which is far more than the average router should need to translate, will use about 1.6MB of DRAM.

10. A, D. The three commands that can be used to verify the NAT configuration are `show ip nat statistics`, `show ip nat translation`, and `show ip nat translation verbose`.

Chapter

11

Configuring the Layer 3 Network

This chapter is a hands-on scenario chapter, similar to Chapter 7. This chapter is not really aimed at preparation for the qualification exam; instead, it focuses on preparation for the lab examination, and it can also serve as a day-to-day layer 3 environment reference.

Because this chapter is not meant to be preparation for the qualification exam, we will not be specifying specific chapter objectives as they relate to the qualification exam. Likewise, you won't find the exam essentials or review questions at the end of the chapter.

For those of you who want to tackle both the written exam and the lab exam, this chapter takes what you've learned about layer 3 (IGP routing protocols, NAT, and redistribution) and applies it in practice in a way that's consistent with how you'll be tested during the lab examination. For those of you focusing solely on the written exam, this chapter will serve as an exercise, building on what you've learned thus far. It will help you solidify the concepts, and you'll see examples of how the protocols work in the real world.

In this chapter, we use the layer 2 scenarios built in Chapter 7 and overlay the routing protocols on top of these networks. The implementations of the routing protocols in these scenarios are by no means "best practices." They are intended to test your understanding of the interaction between layer 2 and layer 3 protocols and the customization of layer 3 routing protocols.

When implementing routing protocols, it is important to have a structured approach to configuring the protocols. We recommend that you break any configuration task down into manageable sections:

- Build the layer 2 networks before implementing any routing protocol.

- Configure each routing protocol across the entire network.

- Configure authentication, route summarization, or protocol redistribution.

- After completing each task, test and confirm that the connectivity is working as expected.

It is important to stick to this approach regardless of how simple the configuration task appears to be.

In each of the scenarios in this chapter, multiple protocols will exist. To simplify your understanding of the configuration of the protocols, each protocol will be configured individually across the network and tested. Once all the protocols are configured correctly, reachability (ping) issues across the network will be addressed.

This chapter covers the fundamentals associated with implementing routing protocols. As a CCIE candidate, your understanding of these fundamentals needs to be rock solid. If there's anything you don't understand, stop and research the topic until you do.

Being a CCIE candidate is about analyzing problems, stripping away the network veneer, eliminating guesswork, and providing solutions to many different technologies. A candidate must be able to focus on the individual technologies and their relationships with each other; this means understanding the effect of every router command at the most fundamental level.

By no means does this chapter provide definitive coverage of the internetworking issues that exist for routing protocols, but it certainly can be used as a self-assessment of your knowledge and understanding.

If you are preparing for the CCIE lab examination, it is crucial that you get as much time and experience on actual routers/switches as possible. If you are not able to physically get access to routers and switches, then it is a good idea to gain access to an equipment rack via Internet access. There are many websites that offer web and/or telnet access to routers and switches, usually on a pay-per-hour basis.

Lab Equipment List

Table 11.1 lists the equipment we used in our test rack to develop and verify the hands-on lab scenarios in this book.

TABLE 11.1 Test Rack Lab Equipment

Router	Model and Interface Type	Memory and Interface Name
R1	Cisco 2610 Router	48MB DRAM/16MB FLASH
	12.1.5 Enterprise Plus IPSEC 56	
	1 Ethernet	E0/0
	1 Serial WIC	S0/0
	1 ISDN BRI WIC	BRI0/0
R2	Cisco 3640 Router	64MB DRAM/32MB FLASH
	12.1.7 Enterprise Plus	
	1 FastEthernet	Fa0/0
	1 Serial WIC	S0/0
	1 ISDN BRI WIC	BRI0/0
	2 FXS VWIC	Voice-port1/0, Voice-port1/1
	1 ATM OC-3	ATM3/0
R3	Cisco 2501 Router	16MB DRAM/16MB FLASH

TABLE 11.1 Test Rack Lab Equipment *(continued)*

Router	Model and Interface Type	Memory and Interface Name
	12.1.5 Enterprise Plus IPSEC 56	
	1 Ethernet	E0
	2 Serial	S0, S1
R4	Cisco 2501 Router	16MB DRAM/16MB FLASH
	2.1.5 Enterprise Plus	
	1 Ethernet	E0
	2 Serial	S0, S1
R5	Cisco 2620 Router	64MB DRAM/32MB FLASH
	12.1.5 Enterprise Plus	
	1 FastEthernet	Fa0/0
	1 Serial WIC	S0/0
	1 NM-2V, 2 FXS VWIC, 1 FXO VWIC	Voice-port1/0, Voice-port 1/1, Voice-port1/2
R6	Cisco 2610 Router	48MB DRAM/16MB FLASH
	12.1.5 Enterprise Plus	
	1 Ethernet	E0/0
	1 Serial WIC	S0/0
S1	Cisco Catalyst 3550-24 Switch	64MB DRAM/16MB FLASH
	12.1.11.EA1 (EMI version)	
	2-port Gigabit Ethernet based on Gigabit Interface Converter (GBIC)	
	24-port 10/100Base-TX Ethernet	

We also used an additional separate router as our Frame Relay switch (FS). The equipment used for it is listed in Table 11.2.

TABLE 11.2 Frame Relay Switch

Router	Model and Interface Type	Memory and Interface Name
FS	Cisco 2522 Router	16MB DRAM/16MB FLASH
	12.1.5 Enterprise Plus	
	1 Ethernet	E0
	10 Serial	S0, S1, S2, S3, S4, S5, S6, S7, S8, S9

We used the equipment listed in Table 11.3 to fully develop the scenarios, but this equipment is not actually required to complete the scenarios.

TABLE 11.3 Additional Test Rack Lab Equipment

Equipment Type	Description
Terminal Access Server (TAS)	Cisco 2511 Router with 16 asynchronous ports
ATM Switch	Cisco LightStream 1010 with ATM OC-3 interfaces
ISDN Simulator Switch	Adtran Atlas 550 with 4-port BRI-U

As we stated in the beginning of this book, please keep in mind that although you are provided with partial router configurations within each chapter, they are not meant to be actual real-world router configurations. They are meant to show the possible commands that can be implemented and to provide a short description of the purpose of each command. Some of the commands that you will see within a configuration would never be implemented at the same time on a single router or even a single interface. However, within this book, they may be displayed together only as a means of showing the various commands within the fewest numbers of pages possible.

Likewise, the scenarios that we have developed for this book are by no means presented as real-world best practices. These scenarios have been designed to challenge you in as many aspects of the specified technologies as possible. They are intended to test your comprehension of the material and to aid you in your own self-assessment as you progress through this book. Hopefully, the scenarios will be helpful in your preparation for the CCIE lab examination and within your real-world job. Please remember that we do not recommend configuring your live network as we have done in the scenarios. Once again, these scenarios have been developed for this book to allow us to present as many complex routing and switching technology issues as possible.

Try to build these scenarios before reading the solutions. This chapter is intended to test your knowledge of layer 3 routing protocols. CCIE candidates must remember that 99-percent right is 100-percent wrong; there is no partial credit. If either the tasks themselves or the solution presented does not make sense, stop, investigate the problem, and do not move on until you have firm understanding of the problem and the solution.

Layer 3 Configuration Task 3.1

The first scenario that we will attempt is based on all the layer 3 technologies that have been presented to you in the previous chapters of this book. This scenario uses the network that was built in Task 2.1 (Chapter 7). Figure 11.1 shows the layer 3 network connectivity diagram that will be built in this scenario. The figure shows the configured interfaces, the network, and the IP addresses of each interface.

FIGURE 11.1   Network diagram for Task 3.1

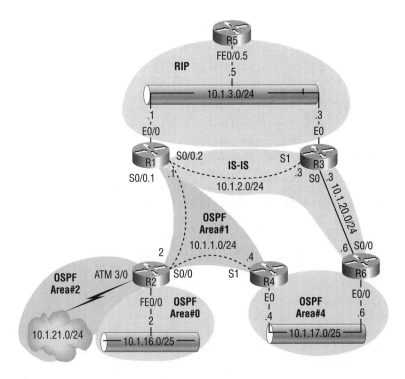

The requirements for this scenario are included in the following list, and then the solution to the scenario is presented. As stated earlier, try to complete the scenario without looking at the solution. Then review the solution to gauge your comprehension of the material presented thus far in the book. Here are the requirements:

- Configure OSPF Area 0 on network 10.1.16.0/25.

- Configure OPSF Area 1 on network 10.1.1.0/24. Configure this network using the OSPF network type point-to-multipoint. Authenticate Area 1 with clear text.

- Configure network 10.1.21.0/24 as OPSF Area 2. On router R2, add loopback 10 and assign it to network 10.1.76.0/24 and to OSPF Area 2. Ensure that all other routers in the network see a route to network 10.1.76.0/24.

- Configure OSPF Area 4 on network 10.1.17.0/25. Assign loopback 10 on router R6 and assign it to network 10.1.77.0/24 and to OSPF Area 4.

- On network 10.1.3.0/24, configure RIPv1. Ensure that routers R1, R3, and R5 are configured so that RIP updates are sent only on this network. On router R5, add loopback 10 to network 10.1.32.0/24. Ensure that all routers in the OSPF domain can ping this network.

- Make sure router R5 can ping the Ethernet address of router R2 as well as the Ethernet address of R6. Ensure that all routes that appear from the OSPF domain have a hop count of 2.

- Configure IS-IS on network 10.1.2.0/24 and on network 10.1.20.0/24.

- Configure R1 as an IS-IS Level 2 router. Configure router R3 as a Level 1/Level 2 router and configure router R6 as a Level 1 router. Ensure that all unnecessary IS-IS hello packets are not sent out across these networks.

- On router R3, configure loopback 11 and assign it to network 150.1.40.0/24. Assign this network to IS-IS.

- On router R6, configure loopback 11 and assign it to network 150.1.41.0/24. Assign this network to IS-IS. Make sure all IS-IS networks are reachable from all other routers in the network. R3 must see all the routes from the OSPF domain as IS-IS learned routes.

- Provide full network connectivity and configure route redistribution on only one router.

Solution 3.1: Configuring RIP on the Network

In this section, we'll show you the required router configurations for each of the routers to implement the RIP routing protocol and fulfill the requirements for Task 3.1.

Configure RIP on Network 10.1.3.0/24

RIP needs to be configured on routers R1, R3, and R5. Because RIPv1 is a classful protocol and because the network statement under the RIP process is also classful, `passive-interface` statements will be needed on routers R1 and R3 to limit the interfaces out of which RIP updates will be transmitted.

Router R1 Configuration

Router R1 is configured with two subinterfaces. You do not want RIP route advertisements to be advertised out of these two subinterfaces:

`router rip`	Enables the RIP routing process
`network 10.0.0.0`	Assigns all interfaces with an IP address of 10.x.x.x to participate in RIP
`passive-interface Serial0/0.1`	Stops the router from sending out RIP updates out this interface, which is connected to R2
`passive-interface Serial0/0.2`	Stops the router from sending out RIP updates out this interface, which is connected to R3

Router R3 Configuration

Router R3 is configured with two serial interfaces. You do not want RIP route advertisements to be advertised out of these two serial interfaces:

`router rip`	Enables the RIP routing process
`network 10.0.0.0`	Assigns all interfaces with an IP address of 10.x.x.x to participate in RIP
`passive-interface Serial1`	Stops the router from sending out RIP updates out this interface that is connected to R1
`passive-interface Serial0`	Stops the router from sending out RIP updates out this interface that Is connected to R6

Router R5 Configuration

Router R5 is configured with only one FastEthernet interface; there is no need to configure any passive interfaces:

`router rip`	Enables the RIP routing process
`network 10.0.0.0`	Assigns all interfaces with a IP address of 10.x.x.x to participate in RIP

For router R1, the serial subinterfaces must be specified as passive interfaces. Otherwise, RIP updates will be sent to R3 over the Frame Relay point-to-point interface. The following is the output of a debug command on R1 with a `passive-interface Serial0/0` command configured only on the physical interface. It can be seen that the RIP updates are still sent out each subinterface:

```
01:04:09: RIP: sending v1 update to 255.255.255.255 via Serial0/0.1 (10.1.1.1)
01:04:09: RIP: build update entries
01:04:09:        subnet 10.1.2.0 metric 1
```

```
01:04:09:        subnet 10.1.3.0 metric 1
01:04:09:        subnet 10.1.20.0 metric 2
01:04:09:        subnet 10.1.32.0 metric 2
```

After RIP has been configured correctly, the output for the `show ip protocol` command on router R1 is as follows:

```
Routing Protocol is "rip"
  Sending updates every 30 seconds, next due in 22 seconds
  Invalid after 180 seconds, hold down 180, flushed after 240
  Outgoing update filter list for all interfaces is
  Incoming update filter list for all interfaces is
  Redistributing: rip
  Default version control: send version 1, receive version 1
    Interface              Send  Recv  Triggered RIP  Key-chain
    Ethernet0/0              1     1
  Automatic network summarization is in effect
  Routing for Networks:
    10.0.0.0
  Passive Interface(s):
    Serial0/0.1
    Serial0/0.2
  Routing Information Sources:
    Gateway         Distance      Last Update
    10.1.3.3             120      00:00:06
    10.1.3.5             120      00:00:05
  Distance: (default is 120)
```

After RIP has been configured correctly, the output from the `show ip route` command on router R3 is as follows:

```
Gateway of last resort is not set

     10.0.0.0/8 is variably subnetted, 6 subnets, 2 masks
C       10.1.3.0/24 is directly connected, Ethernet0
C       10.1.2.0/24 is directly connected, Serial1
R       10.1.1.0/24 [120/1] via 10.1.3.1, 00:00:00, Ethernet0
C       10.1.20.6/32 is directly connected, Serial0
C       10.1.20.0/24 is directly connected, Serial0
R       10.1.32.0/24 [120/1] via 10.1.3.5, 00:00:26, Ethernet0
```

Now that the RIP protocol is configured and verified, we'll move on the configuring the OSPF protocol.

Solution 3.1: Configuring OSPF on the Network

In this section, we'll discuss the required router configurations for each of the routers to implement the OSPF routing protocol and fulfill the requirements for Task 3.1.

When configuring OSPF for this scenario, you need to break it down into tasks. Configure Area 0 and move logically through the other areas. After completing the basics of the OSPF configuration, move on to virtual links and then to authentication:

- Task 1: Configure OSPF areas.
- Task 2: Configure Area 2 to send a route out for 10.1.76.0/24.
- Task 3: Configure a virtual link for Area 4.
- Task 4: Authenticate Area 1 using clear text.

Task 1: Configure OSPF Areas

OSPF Area 1 (10.1.1.0/24) must be configured as an OSPF multipoint network. This will require that all routers with an interface(s) connected to Area 1 be configured with the `ip ospf network point-to-multipoint` command. On router R1, this command will have to be configured on the subinterface that is connected to the network. No other OSPF or interface configuration commands are needed for a multipoint configuration.

 /32 routes are generated for each interface configured with point-to-multipoint.

Task 2: Configure Area 2 to Send Route Out for 10.1.76.0/24

This scenario requires that all routers in the OSPF domain see a route for network 10.1.76.0/24. An `area 2 range` command must be used to send out a summary route. Without this command, the route will appear as 10.1.76.2/32. This is because loopbacks are treated as stub networks and are assigned an OSPF interface type of loopback. This network type will be sent out by OSPF with the host network mask (/32) regardless of the network mask assigned to the loopback interface. The /24 is required for RIP redistribution later on.

Here is the output from the `show ip route ospf` command on router R1:

```
10.0.0.0/8 is variably subnetted, 13 subnets, 3 masks
O        10.1.1.2/32 [110/781] via 10.1.1.2, 01:14:05, Serial0/0.1
O        10.1.1.4/32 [110/1562] via 10.1.1.2, 01:14:05, Serial0/0.1
O IA     10.1.17.0/24 [110/1572] via 10.1.1.2, 01:14:05, Serial0/0.1
O IA     10.1.16.0/25 [110/2344] via 10.1.1.2, 01:14:05, Serial0/0.1
O IA     10.1.16.0/24 [110/782] via 10.1.1.2, 01:14:05, Serial0/0.1
```

```
O IA    10.1.21.0/24 [110/782] via 10.1.1.2, 01:14:05, Serial0/0.1
O IA    10.1.76.0/24 [110/782] via 10.1.1.2, 01:14:05, Serial0/0.1
```

The output shows the summary route after the `area 2 range 10.1.76.0 255.255.255.0` command was configured. The virtual link has not yet been configured, so no route will exist for network 10.1.77.0/24.

Task 3: Configure a Virtual Link for Area 4

When configuring OSPF, one of the fundamental items that you must be aware of is the OSPF RID. In this configuration, the router R2 RID should be 10.1.76.2. However, the order in which the router was configured will depend on the assigned OSPF RID. This means that if OSPF is configured first and then loopback 10 is added, the RID of this router will be highest IP address of the router at the time the OSPF process was started, so the RID will be 10.1.21.2, which is the IP address of the ATM interface.

It is also possible to statically configure the RID using the `router-id` command. If router R2 was configured in this order, the output from `show ip ospf` command on router R2 will be as follows:

```
Routing Process "ospf 1" with ID 10.1.21.2
 Supports only single TOS(TOS0) routes
 It is an area border router
 SPF schedule delay 5 secs, Hold time between two SPFs 10 secs
 Minimum LSA interval 5 secs. Minimum LSA arrival 1 secs
 Number of external LSA 0. Checksum Sum 0x0
 Number of DCbitless external LSA 0
```

If this router is now rebooted, the RID will change to 10.1.76.2, which is the IP address of loopback 10. This is important because a virtual link between router R2 and R4 must be built. To build a virtual link, you must specify the RID using the `area 1 virtual-link Remote RID` command. If the virtual link was built and became operational when the R2 RID was 10.1.21.2 and after the routers were rebooted, the configured `virtual-link` command on router R4 would be incorrect. The virtual link that was previously working would now be down.

The following is the output of a `show ip ospf virtual-link` command after router R4 is rebooted:

```
Virtual Link OSPF_VL2 to router 10.1.17.4 is down
  Run as demand circuit
  DoNotAge LSA allowed.
  Transit area 1, Cost of using 65535
  Transmit Delay is 1 sec, State DOWN,
  Timer intervals configured, Hello 10, Dead 40, Wait 40, Retransmit
```

The following is the output of a `show ip ospf virtual-link` command after router R2 is rebooted:

```
Virtual Link OSPF_VL4 to router 10.1.76.2 is up
  Run as demand circuit
  DoNotAge LSA allowed.
  Transit area 1, via interface Serial0, Cost of using 781
  Transmit Delay is 1 sec, State POINT_TO_POINT,
  Timer intervals configured, Hello 10, Dead 40, Wait 40, Retransmit 5
    Hello due in 00:00:04
    Adjacency State INIT (Hello suppressed)
```

From the outputs, it can be seen that router R4's virtual link state is DOWN and that router R2's virtual link adjacency state is INIT. The adjacency state of a fully functioning virtual link is a FULL state.

Task 4: Authenticate Area 1 Using Clear Text

Finally, Area 1 must be authenticated using clear text. This requires that all routers connected to Area 1 have authentication turned on under the OSPF process and that OSPF authentication is configured on every Area 1 router interface.

Depending on the version of IOS in the router, to enable clear text authentication under the interface, both the following commands *may* need to be configured:

```
ip ospf authentication-key kelly
ip ospf authentication
```

The following router configurations show all OSPF commands used up to this point. Your configurations should look similar.

 NOTE   OSPF authentication can be enabled on a per-area or per-interface basis depending on IOS version (12.0.8 and higher).

Router R1 Configuration

Here is the configuration for router R1:

```
router ospf 1                     Enables the OSPF routing and uses process 1
 network 10.1.1.0 0.0.0.255 area 1

                                  Assigns interface in network 10.1.1.0/24 to
                                  Area 1
 area 1 authentication            Enables clear text authentication on Area 1
interface Serial0/0.1 multipoint
```

```
ip ospf network point-to-multipoint
```
Changes the OSPF network type from its default (non broadcast) to an OSPF multipoint

```
ip ospf authentication
```
Enables clear text authentication

```
ip ospf authentication-key kelly
```
Sets the clear text password to kelly

Router R2 Configuration

The configuration for router R2 is as follows:

```
router ospf 1
```
Enables the OSPF routing and uses process 1

```
network 10.1.16.0 0.0.0.127 area 0
```
Assigns interface in network 10.1.16.0/25 to Area 0

```
network 10.1.1.0 0.0.0.255 area 1
```
Assigns interface in network 10.1.1.0/24 to Area 1

```
network 10.1.21.0 0.0.0.255 area 2
```
Assigns interface in network 10.1.21.0/24 to Area 2

```
network 10.1.76.0 0.0.0.255 area 2
```
Assigns interface in network 10.1.76.0/24 to Area 2

```
area 0 range 10.1.16.0 255.255.255.0
```
Sends a summary route for network 10.1.16.0/24

```
area 2 range 10.1.76.0 255.255.255.0
```
Sends a summary route for network 10.1.76.0/24

```
area 1 virtual-link 10.1.17.4
```
Creates a virtual-link across Area 1 to router R4; the RID of R4 is 10.1.17.4

```
area 1 authentication
```
Enables clear text authentication on Area 1

```
interface Serial0/0
```

`ip ospf network point-to-multipoint`	Changes the OSPF network type from its default (nonbroadcast) to an OSPF multipoint
`ip ospf authentication`	Enables clear text authentication
`ip ospf authentication-key kelly`	Sets the clear text password to kelly

`interface Loopback10`	Creates the interface Loopback 10
`ip address 10.1.76.2 255.255.255.0`	

Router R4 Configuration

Here is router R4's configuration:

`router ospf 1`	Enables the OSPF routing and uses process 1
`network 10.1.1.0 0.0.0.255 area 1`	Assigns interface in network 10.1.1.0/24 to Area 1
`network 10.1.17.0 0.0.0.127 area 4`	Assigns interface in network 10.1.17.0/25 to Area 4
`area 1 virtual-link 10.1.76.2`	Creates a virtual-link across Area 1 to router R2; the RID of R2 is 10.1.76.2
`area 1 authentication`	Enables clear text authentication on Area 1
`area 4 range 10.1.17.0 255.255.255.0`	

`interface Serial1`	
`ip ospf network point-to-multipoint`	Changes the OSPF network type from its default (nonbroadcast) to an OSPF multipoint
`ip ospf authentication-key kelly`	Sets the clear text password to kelly

Router R6 Configuration

Here is the configuration for router R6:

```
router ospf 1
  network 10.1.17.0 0.0.0.127 area 4        Assigns interface in network
                                            10.1.17.0/25 to Area 4

  network 10.1.77.0 0.0.0.255 area 4        Assigns interface in network
                                            10.1.77.0/24 to Area 4

interface Loopback10                        Creates the interface Loopback 10

  ip address 10.1.77.6 255.255.255.0
```

The following is the output on R6 for the show ip route ospf command:

```
10.0.0.0/8 is variably subnetted, 12 subnets, 3 masks
O IA    10.1.1.2/32 [110/782] via 10.1.17.4, 01:11:11, Ethernet0/0
O IA    10.1.1.1/32 [110/1563] via 10.1.17.4, 01:11:11, Ethernet0/0
O IA    10.1.1.4/32 [110/1] via 10.1.17.4, 01:11:11, Ethernet0/0
O IA    10.1.16.0/25 [110/783] via 10.1.17.4, 01:11:11, Ethernet0/0
O IA    10.1.21.0/24 [110/783] via 10.1.17.4, 01:11:12, Ethernet0/0
O IA    10.1.76.0/24 [110/783] via 10.1.17.4, 01:11:12, Ethernet0/0
```

Now that the OSPF protocol is configured and verifies, we'll move on to configuring the IS-IS protocol.

Solution 3.1: Configuring IS-IS on the Network

When configuring IS-IS for this scenario, you need to break it down into tasks:

- Task 1: Enable Connectionless Network Service (CLNS) routing on all routers.
- Task 2: Configure IS-IS between R1 and R3 across Frame Relay.
- Task 3: Configure IS-IS between R3 and R6 across a point-to-point connection.
- Task 4: Limit IS-IS hello (IIH) packets.

Task 1: Enable CLNS Routing on All Routers

When configuring IS-IS on a router, the first step is to enable CLNS routing on the router. This is a global command, clns routing. If you do not configure this command, the router will automatically configure it when the IS-IS routing process is configured. Each router interface that participates in IS-IS routing must have the ip router isis command configured under the interface.

Router R1 will be configured in Area 0 as an L2 router. Routers R3 and R6 will be configured in Area 1, with R3 defined as an L1/L2 router and R6 as an L1 router.

Using the command `net 49.0000.1111.1111.1111.00` as an example, starting from left-to-right, the first three octets of the CLNS network contain the authority and format identifier (AFI) and the area ID (49.000x, where x will equal the specified area). The next six octets are the system ID and must be unique for each router. The last octet is the selector byte, which for Cisco implementations will be 00.

Task 2: Configure IS-IS between R1 and R3 across Frame Relay

The first issue that needs to be addressed is establishing a neighbor IS-IS relationship between router R1 and router R3. The issue here is that R1 is configured as a Frame Relay point-to-point and router R3 is configured with a Frame Relay physical interface. The IS-IS hello PDUs sent by each router are incompatible and an IS-IS adjacency will never establish. There are two ways to solve this problem; both require that the layer 2 network be changed:

- Change the interface on R1 to a point-to-multipoint. This will require that the subinterface on R1 be changed from a point-to-point to a multipoint subinterface. If the interface on R1 is configured as a point-to-point, the subinterface must be deleted and the router must be rebooted. When you're configuring IS-IS on a Frame Relay multipoint network, there must be a `frame-relay map clns dlci broadcast` command configured on each Frame Relay interface.

- The second option is to change the interface on R3 to use a subinterface point-to-point. However, Task 3.1 required that no subinterfaces be configured on any R3 interface.

The first option is the one that we have used. The following is the output from router R3 of the `show clns neighbors` command after the Frame Relay network has been configured correctly:

```
System Id        Interface   SNPA       State  Holdtime  Type Protocol
R1               Se1         DLCI 301    Up     26        L2   IS-IS
6666.6666.6666   Se0         *HDLC*      Up     21        L1   IS-IS
```

When using multipoint interfaces with IS-IS, a designated IS (DIS) will be elected. Because the default IS-IS interface priority of 64 was not changed on either R1 or R3, R3 will become the DIS for 10.1.2.0/24 network, because R3 has the highest system ID. Use the `show isis database` command to verify.

Task 3: Configure IS-IS between R3 and R6 across a Point-to-Point Connection

When IS-IS is configured on a PPP network, PPP negotiates the connection when an interface first initializes the protocols, which will run across this network. To enable IS-IS to work across a PPP link, the link must be restarted after IS-IS is configured on the interface. Assign loopback 10 to the 150.1.40.0/24 network on R3, make it a Level 1 interface, assign loopback 10 to the

150.1.41.0/24 network on R6, and make it a Level 1 interface. The following is the output from the show ip route isis command on router R6:

```
150.1.0.0/24 is subnetted, 2 subnets
i L1    150.1.40.0 [115/20] via 10.1.20.3, Serial0/0
i*L1 0.0.0.0/0 [115/10] via 10.1.20.3, Serial0/0
```

Router R6, which is an IS-IS Level 1 router, will only learn a default route and a route from network 150.1.40.0/24, which is from router R3. The following is the output from the show ip route isis command on router R1:

```
10.0.0.0/24 is subnetted, 4 subnets
i L2    10.1.20.0 [115/20] via 10.1.2.4, Serial0/0.2
       150.1.0.0/24 is subnetted, 2 subnets
i L2    150.1.41.0 [115/30] via 10.1.2.4, Serial0/0.2
i L2    150.1.40.0 [115/20] via 10.1.2.4, Serial0/0.2
```

This output shows that R1 will see all routes from R3 as Level 2 routes.

Task 4: Limit IS-IS Hello (IIH) Packets

The scenario requires that unnecessary IS-IS hellos are not sent out on the network. This is achieved by configuring on a per-interface basis the hello types it will send out. To do so, use the interface command isis circuit-type level-x. This command is usually only required on an L1/L2 type router, R3 in this example. The isis circuit-type command is entered on all IS-IS routers in the following IS-IS configurations as an example only. The router configurations show all IS-IS commands used up to this point. Your configurations should look similar.

Router R1 Configuration

Here's the configuration for router R1:

clns routing	Enables CLNS routing, which is required by IS-IS
interface Serial0/0.2 multipoint	
ip router isis	Specifies this interface will participate in IS-IS
isis circuit-type level-2-only	Optional - This interface is an IS-IS level-2 interface only; therefore, it will only process level-2 PDUs
frame-relay map clns 103	This frame-relay map statement is mandatory to allow CLNS packets to be sent over this Frame-Relay multipoint interface

router isis	Enables IS-IS on the router
net 49.0000.1111.1111.1111.00	Assigns the IS-IS network, to Area ID 0000 and a System ID of 1111.1111.1111
is-type level-2	Makes this router a level-2 only router

Router R3 Configuration

Here is router R3's configuration:

clns routing	Enables CLNS routing
interface Loopback 10	Adds the interface Loopback 10
ip address 150.1.40.3 255.255.255.0	
ip router isis	Specifies this interface will participate in IS-IS
isis circuit-type level-1	Allows only IS-IS level-1 PDUs on this interface – Required to limit PDUs on L1/L2
interface Serial1	
ip router isis	Specifies this interface will participate in IS-IS
isis circuit-type level-2-only	Allows only IS-IS level-2 PDUs on this interface– Required to limit PDUs on L1/L2
frame-relay map clns 301	This is needed to allow CLNS packets to be sent over this frame relay multipoint interface
interface Serial 0	
ip router isis	Specifies this interface will participate in IS-IS
isis circuit-type level-1	Allows only IS-IS level-1 PDUs on this interface– Required to limit PDUs on L1/L2
router isis	Enables IS-IS routing process
net 49.0001.3333.3333.3333.00	Assigns the IS-IS network, to Area ID 0001 and a System ID of 3333.3333.3333

Router R6 Configuration

The configuration for router R6 is as follows:

`clns routing`	Enables CLNS routing
`interface Loopback 10`	Adds the interface Loopback 10
`  ip address 150.1.41.6 255.255.255.0`	
`  ip router isis`	Specifies this interface will participate in IS-IS
`  isis circuit-type level-1`	Optional - Allows only IS-IS level-1 PDUs on this interface
`interface Serial 0/0`	
`  ip router isis`	Specifies this interface will participate in IS-IS
`  isis circuit-type level-1`	Optional - Allows only IS-IS level-1 PDUs on this interface
`router isis`	Enables IS-IS on the router
`  net 49.0001.6666.6666.6666.00`	Assigns the IS-IS network, to Area ID 0001 and a System ID of 6666.6666.6666
`  is-type level-1`	Makes this router a level-1 only router

Solution 3.1: Configuring Redistribution on the Network

Once all the routing protocols have been independently configured, network connectivity between all the routers needs to be completed. Redistribution must only be carried out on one router, and the only router on which full network connectivity can be achieved is router R1. The reason for this is that router R1 has all three routing protocols configured. This solution is broken down into three tasks:

- Task 1: Configure RIP redistribution
- Task 2: Configure OSPF redistribution
- Task 3: Configure IS-IS redistribution

Task 1: Configure RIP Redistribution

The first task is to redistribute OSPF into RIP. This is done using the `redistribute ospf` command under the RIP process. The second task is to redistribute IS-IS into RIP. The output from `show ip route rip` on R5 is shown here:

```
Gateway of last resort is not set

10.0.0.0/8 is variably subnetted, 12 subnets, 3 masks
R        10.1.1.2/32 [120/2] via 10.1.3.1, 00:00:10, FastEthernet0.5
R        10.1.2.0/24 [120/1] via 10.1.3.3, 00:00:03, FastEthernet0.5
                     [120/1] via 10.1.3.1, 00:00:10, FastEthernet0.5
R        10.1.1.0/24 [120/1] via 10.1.3.1, 00:00:10, FastEthernet0.5
R        10.1.1.4/32 [120/2] via 10.1.3.1, 00:00:10, FastEthernet0.5
R        10.1.21.0/24 [120/2] via 10.1.3.1, 00:00:10, FastEthernet0.5
R        10.1.20.0/24 [120/1] via 10.1.3.3, 00:00:03, FastEthernet0.5
R        10.1.77.0/24 [120/2] via 10.1.3.1, 00:00:10, FastEthernet0.5
R        10.1.76.0/24 [120/2] via 10.1.3.1, 00:00:13, FastEthernet0.5
R        150.1.0.0/16 [120/3] via 10.1.3.1, 00:00:13, FastEthernet0.5
```

Notice that network 10.1.16.0/25 and network 10.1.17.0/25 are not present. This is due to the fact that RIP will only forward routes that have the same mask as the outgoing interface, which is a /24. To resolve this issue, an `area x range` command needs to be configured on the originating ABR, which are routers R2 and R4, respectively. These routes will now appear in R5's routing table.

Routes redistributed from IS-IS appear with the true classful mask of the network (150.1.0.0/16), this is because 150.1.0.0/16 subnets are not known to the RIP domain. Also, Task 3.1 requested that all routes that appear in the OSPF domain have a hop count of 2 when redistributed into RIP. This was accomplished using a `metric 2` on the redistribution command.

Router R1 Configuration

Here is the configuration for router R1:

```
router rip
 redistribute ospf 1 metric 2
 redistribute isis level-2
 default-metric 3
```

Notice that under RIP there must be a metric command associated with each redistribution statement; otherwise, routes will not be redistributed into RIP. So, for the IS-IS redistribution, we have used a `default-metric` command.

Task 2: Configure OSPF Redistribution

To provide network connectivity from the OSPF domain to RIP and IS-IS, you must make sure redistribution of the RIP and IS-IS protocols happens under the OSPF process. Because the routes that are being redistributed from both RIP and IS-IS do not have a classful mask, the keyword `subnets` must be used to allow OSPF to send the redistributed routes out to the rest of the OSPF domain. These routes will appear inside of the OSPF domain as OSPF External Type 2 routes. Here is the output from the `show ip route ospf` on router R6:

```
O E2    10.1.3.0/24 [110/20] via 10.1.17.4, 00:01:38, Ethernet0/0
O IA    10.1.1.2/32 [110/782] via 10.1.17.4, 00:01:38, Ethernet0/0
O E2    10.1.2.0/24 [110/20] via 10.1.17.4, 00:01:38, Ethernet0/0
O IA    10.1.1.1/32 [110/1563] via 10.1.17.4, 00:01:38, Ethernet0/0
O IA    10.1.1.4/32 [110/1] via 10.1.17.4, 00:01:38, Ethernet0/0
O IA    10.1.16.0/25 [110/783] via 10.1.17.4, 00:01:38, Ethernet0/0
O IA    10.1.21.0/24 [110/783] via 10.1.17.4, 00:01:38, Ethernet0/0
O E2    10.1.32.0/24 [110/20] via 10.1.17.4, 00:32:22, Ethernet0/0
O IA    10.1.76.0/24 [110/783] via 10.1.17.4, 00:01:38, Ethernet0/0
        150.1.0.0/24 is subnetted, 2 subnets
O E2    150.1.40.0 [110/20] via 10.1.17.4, 00:01:39, Ethernet0/0
```

The one thing that needs to be noted in the preceding output is that the route for network 150.1.40.0/24 is now being learned by router R6 from OSPF and not from IS-IS. The reason for this is that the administrative distance of OSPF (110) is preferred over the administrative distance for IS-IS (115).

Router R1 Configuration

The configuration for router R1 is as follows:

```
router ospf 1
 redistribute rip subnets
 redistribute isis level-2 subnets
```

Notice that under OSPF, no metric or metric-type command is configured for each redistribution statement. Therefore, RIP and IS-IS routes will be sent out with a metric of 20 and as an External Type 2 (OE2) metric type.

Task 3: Configure IS-IS Redistribution

Because router R2 is an IS-IS Level-2-only router, the routes from both OSPF and RIP must be redistributed into IS-IS as Level 2 routes.

Router R1 Configuration

Here is the configuration for router R1:

```
router isis
 redistribute ospf 1
 redistribute rip
```

IP routes redistributed will be seen as IP external routes in the IS-IS link-state database (LSDB). Notice that under ISIS, there is no metric or metric-type command for each redistribution statement. Therefore, RIP and OSPF routes will be sent out with a metric of 0 and as an internal route. R3 will add its interface cost of 10 and install routes in the routing table as an i L2. There is no `default-metric` option in IS-IS, so you should define a metric, metric type, and level for each source protocol.

Solution 3.1: Testing the Network

The final test, as always, is to ensure that IP packets can route through the network. And this again can be achieved using ping:

- R5 should be able to ping the Ethernet addresses of R2 (10.1.16.2) and of R6 (10.1.17.6). Also, it should be able to ping the loopback addresses of R2 (10.1.76.2), R3 (150.1.40.3), and R6 (150.1.41.6).

- R2 should be able to ping the Ethernet address of R5 (10.1.3.5). Also, it should be able to ping the loopback addresses of R3 (150.1.40.3), R5 (10.1.32.5), and R6 (150.1.41.6).

Solution 3.1: Troubleshooting the Network

The following commands are used to troubleshoot this network:

```
show ip route [ospf | rip | isis]
show ip protocol
show ip ospf database
show ip ospf database router
show ip ospf virtual-link
show clns
show clns neighbor

debug frame-relay packet
debug ip rip
debug ip ospf events
debug ip ospf adjacencies
```

The reason for segmenting the configuration of the network is so that the testing and verification is simplified and can happen throughout the configuration process.

Layer 3 Configuration Task 3.2

The second scenario that we will attempt is based on all the Layer 3 technologies that have been presented to you in the previous chapters of this book. This scenario uses the network that was built in Task 2.2 (Chapter 7). Figure 11.2 shows the Layer 3 network connectivity diagram that will be built in this scenario. The figure shows the configured interfaces, the network, and the IP addresses of each interface.

FIGURE 11.2   Network diagram for Task 3.2

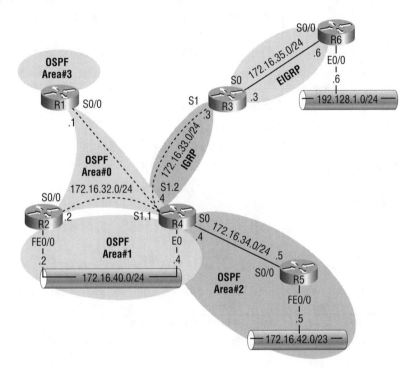

The requirements for this scenario are included in the following list, and then the solution to the scenario is presented. As we mentioned earlier, try to complete the scenario without looking at the solution. Then review the solution to gauge your comprehension of the material presented thus far in the book.

In this scenario, static routes can be configured where they are needed. Here are the requirements:

- Configure OSPF Area 0 on network 172.16.32.0/24. Configure this network using the OSPF network type of nonbroadcast.

- On router R1, add loopback 1 and assign it to network 172.16.2.0/24, and then assign this network to OSPF Area 3. Ensure that a route for 172.16.2.0/24 appears in all other OSPF routers; do not use an `area 3 range` command.

- Configure OPSF Area 1 on network 172.16.40.0/24. Authenticate this area using MD5.

- Configure network 172.16.34.0/24 as OSPF Area 2. Make this an OSPF totally stubby area.

- On router R5, add loopbacks 10 and 11 and assign these loopbacks to networks 172.16.4.0/24 and 17.16.5.0/24, respectively. Assign these networks to OSPF Area 2. Make sure that only the routers in OSPF Area 2 see these networks. Also on router R5, assign network 172.16.42.0/23 to Area 2. This should be visible to all routers in the entire network.

- On network 172.16.33.0/24, configure IGRP. Make sure that IGRP updates are sent out only on network 172.16.33.0/24 network. Router R3 must have routes for the entire OSPF domain, apart from routes to R5's loopback 10 and 11.

- For the IGRP domain, set a default route to R6. Do not use a static route on R3.

- Configure EIGRP on network 172.16.35.0/24. All routers in the network must have a route to network 192.128.1.0/24. Do not use a network statement under the EIGRP process. Authenticate the connection between router R3 and R6 using MD5.

- IGRP must have access to the EIGRP domains.

- EIGRP must have access to both the IGRP and OSPF domains.

- No redistribution commands can be used on router R3.

- Routers R3 and R6 must be able to ping the Ethernet interface of router R5.

- Router R5 must be able to ping the Ethernet interface of R6 (192.128.1.6) and the loopback 1 of R1 (172.16.2.1).

Solution 3.2: Configuring OSPF on the Network

In this section, we'll discuss the required router configurations for each of the routers to implement the OSPF routing protocol and fulfill the requirements for Task 3.2. When configuring OSPF for this scenario, it needs to be broken down into tasks:

- Task 1: Configure OSPF areas. Configure Area 0 as an OSPF nonbroadcast network.

- Task 2: Configure Area 2 as a totally stubby area.

- Task 3: Restrict R5's loopback routes from Area 2 to the rest of the OSPF domain.

- Task 4: Configure R1 so it will send out a route for 172.16.2.0/24.

- Task 5: Configure authentication on Area 1.

Task 1: Configure OSPF Areas and Configure Area 0 as an OSPF Nonbroadcast Network

OSPF Area 0 is configured on the Frame Relay network 172.16.32.0/24 using the nonbroadcast network type. When configuring a nonbroadcast network in a hub-and-spoke environment, the hub router must be configured as the DR and must also have a `neighbor` command configured for each spoke router.

It is also a good practice to configure the spoke router interfaces with an OSPF priority of 0, so that the spokes will never become the DR, and thus the hub router will always be elected as the DR.

Task 2: Configure Area 2 as a Totally Stubby Area

Area 2 must be configured as a totally stubby area. This requires that all routers in the area (R5) have an `area 2 stub` command configured under the OSPF process. R4, which is the ABR, must be configured with the `area 2 stub no-summary` command to make this area a totally stubby area.

The following output is from the `debug ip ospf events` command on router R5 when no `area 2 stub` command was configured on R5:

```
01:04:50: OSPF: Rcv hello from 172.16.34.4 area 2 from Serial0/0 172.16.34.4
01:04:50: OSPF: Hello from 172.16.34.4 with mismatched Stub/Transit area
   option bit
```

Here is the output from `show ip route ospf` on R5 after being configured with the `area 2 stub` command:

```
Gateway of last resort is 172.16.34.4 to network 0.0.0.0

     172.16.0.0/16 is variably subnetted, 5 subnets, 2 masks
C       172.16.42.0/24 is directly connected, FastEthernet0/0
C       172.16.34.4/32 is directly connected, Serial0/0
C       172.16.34.0/24 is directly connected, Serial0/0
C       172.16.4.0/24 is directly connected, Loopback10
C       172.16.5.0/24 is directly connected, Loopback11
O*IA 0.0.0.0/0 [110/782] via 172.16.34.4, 00:09:43, Serial0/0
```

The only route that R5 receives from R4 is a default route. This is due to the fact that it is in the totally stubby area.

Task 3: Restrict R5's Loopback Routes from Area 2 to the Rest of the OSPF Domain

Task 3.2 also requires that loopback 10 and 11 be defined on router R5, and they must not be propagated to the rest of the OSPF domain. R5's loopbacks must be known only to Area 2. To prevent these networks from being propagated, use the `area 2 range` command with the `not-advertise` option on the ABR, which is R4. These loopback interface networks must also be configured as OSPF network type point-to-point to propagate the correct network mask to router R4.

This issue was not addressed in Chapter 9 in which OSPF was covered. In the real CCIE lab, candidates will have to be prepared to deal with unexpected issues, hence the reason for this little wrinkle in the scenario.

Task 4: Configure R1 to Send Out the Route 172.16.2.0/24

R1 must send out a route for network 172.16.2.0/24. Because this network is assigned to a loopback, OSPF automatically sends it out as a host route (/32). To send this route out with a /24 mask, the OSPF network type needs to be changed to point-to-point using the `ip ospf network point-to-point` command under the loopback interface. The following shows the output from show ip route on router R2:

```
Gateway of last resort is not set

172.16.0.0/24 is subnetted, 5 subnets
C       172.16.40.0 is directly connected, FastEthernet0/0
O IA    172.16.42.0 [110/1563] via 172.16.32.4, 00:24:28, Serial0/0
C       172.16.32.0 is directly connected, Serial0/0
O IA    172.16.34.0 [110/1562] via 172.16.32.4, 00:27:58, Serial0/0
O IA    172.16.2.0 [110/782] via 172.16.32.1, 00:27:58, Serial0/0
```

Router R2 will see 172.16.2.0 with a /24-bit mask as expected. Also note from Task 3 that R2 does not receive routes for R5's loopback 10 and 11 networks.

Task 5: Configure Authentication on Area 1

Finally, Area 1 must be authenticated using MD5. This requires that both routers connected to Area 1 have message digest authentication turned on under the OSPF process and that OSPF message digest authentication is configured on each Area 1 router interface. The key value, encryption level, and password must match on all routers in the area. Depending on the version of IOS in the router, the router *may* need both of the following interface commands:

```
ip ospf authentication message-digest
ip ospf message-digest-key 5 md5 josh
```

Router R1 Configuration

Here is the configuration for router R1:

interface Loopback1	Creates interface Loopback1
ip address 172.16.2.1 255.255.255.0	
ip ospf network point-to-point	Changes the OSPF network type. The network will now be announced with the network mask that is configured
interface Serial0/0	
ip ospf priority 0	Sets the OSPF priority to 0, this router will not participate in the DR election
router ospf 1	Starts OSPF and uses process ID 1

network 172.16.2.0 0.0.0.255 area 3	Assigns interface in network 172.16.2.0/24 to Area 2
network 172.16.32.0 0.0.0.255 area 0	Assigns interface in network 172.16.32.0/24 to Area 0

Router R2 Configuration

Router R2's configuration is as follows:

interface Serial0/0

ip ospf priority 0	Sets the OSPF priority to 0, this router will not participate in the DR election

interface FastEthernet0/0

ip ospf authentication message-digest	Enables authentication using MD5 on this interface
ip ospf message-digest-key 5 md5 2 josh	
	Sets the key value, encryption level and password josh for authentication.
router ospf 1	Starts OSPF and uses process ID 1
network 172.16.32.0 0.0.0.255 area 0	Assigns interface in network 172.16.32.0/24 to Area 0
network 172.16.40.0 0.0.0.255 area 1	Assigns interface in network 172.16.40.0/24 to Area 1
area 1 authentication message-digest	Area 1 is now configured to perform authentication using MD5

Router R4 Configuration

Following is the configuration for router R4:

interface Serial1.1 multipoint

ip ospf priority 5	Sets the designated router. Router R4 must be the DR router in the non-broadcast network

interface Ethernet0

```
ip ospf message-digest-key 5 md5 1 josh
```
Enables authentication and set the key value, encryption level and password josh for authentication

```
router ospf 1
```
Starts OSPF and uses process ID 1

```
network 172.16.32.0 0.0.0.255 area 0
```
Assigns interface in network 172.16.32.0/24 to Area 0

```
network 172.16.34.0 0.0.0.255 area 2
```
Assigns interface in network 172.16.34.0/24 to Area 2

```
network 172.16.40.0 0.0.0.255 area 1
```
Assigns interface in network 172.16.40.0/24 to Area 1

```
neighbor 172.16.32.2
```
Manually define R2 as a neighbor using router R2's multipoint interface (not R2's RID)

```
neighbor 172.16.32.1
```
Manually define R1 as a neighbor using router R1's multipoint interface

```
area 1 authentication message-digest
```
Area 1 is now configured to perform authentication using MD5

```
area 2 stub no-summary
```
Configured Area 2 as a Stub Area. The no summary option makes this a Totally Stubby Area

```
area 2 range 172.16.4.0 255.255.254.0 not-advertise
```
Stops R4 from advertising this address space to all other area's in the OSPF domain

Router R5 Configuration

Here is router R5's configuration:

```
router ospf 1
 area 2 stub
 network 0.0.0.0 255.255.255.255 area 2
```

Solution 3.2: Configuring EIGRP on the Network

In this section, we'll discuss the required router configurations for each of the routers to implement the EIGRP routing protocol and fulfill the requirements for Task 3.2. When configuring EIGRP for this scenario, you need to break it down into the following tasks:

- Task 1: Configure EIGRP on both router R3 and R6.
- Task 2: Configure authentication.

Task 1: Configure EIGRP on Both Router R3 and R6

On router R3 and R6, EIGRP must be configured to run on network 172.16.35.0. R6 must announce its Ethernet network but the **network** command must not be used. This is achieved as by using the `redistribute connected` command under the EIGRP process. This route appears in router R3 as an EIGRP external. The following line shows the output from R3 for the `show ip route eigrp` command:

```
D EX 192.128.1.0/24 [170/21024000] via 172.16.35.6, 00:00:53, Serial0
```

Task 2: Configure Authentication

The connection between R3 and R6 must be authenticated; therefore, the following commands must be configured on each router (EIGRP process 100 as well as key chains chris and josh, with a password of kelly, were used in the examples that follow):

```
ip authentication mode eigrp 100 md5
ip authentication key-chain eigrp 100
key chain
```

Router R3 Configuration

The configuration for router R3 is as follows:

```
interface Serial0
 ip authentication mode eigrp 100 md5     Enables MD5 authentication for EIGRP
                                          AS 100

 ip authentication key-chain eigrp 100 chris

                                          EIGRP will use key chain chris

 ip summary-address eigrp 100 172.16.0.0 255.255.0.0 5
```

	This will cause EIGRP to send a summary route out Serial 0 for the 172.16.0.0/16 network, will also install a summary route in this router to Null0
key chain chris	Creates a key chain with a name of chris
key 1	Creates a key value of 1, this value must match on EIGRP neighbors for authentication to be successful
key-string kelly	String value must match on each EIGRP neighbor = password kelly
router eigrp 100	Starts EIGRP routing process for AS#100
network 172.16.0.0	Assigns network 172.176.0.0
no auto-summary	EIGRP by default is a classful protocol, and automatically summaries to the classful boundary. This command turns classful summarization off
passive-interface Serial1	Disables EIGRP outbound updates for interface serial1. Listens for inbound updates

Router R6 Configuration

Here is the configuration for router R6:

```
interface Serial0/0
```

ip authentication mode eigrp 100 md5	Enables MD5 authentication for EIGRP AS 100
ip authentication key-chain eigrp 100 josh	
	EIGRP will use key chain josh
key chain josh	Creates a key chain with a name of josh
key 1	Creates a key value of 1, this value must match on EIGRP neighbors for authentication to be successful

`key-string kelly`	String value must match on each EIGRP neighbor = password kelly
`router eigrp 100`	Starts EIGRP routing process for AS#100
`network 172.16.35.0 0.0.0.255`	Assigns network 172.16.35.0 to EIGRP 100. This is entered in an inverse wildcard bit mask just like OSPF uses
`redistribute connected`	Redistribute the connected Network 192.128.1.0/24 into EIGRP. This network will appear as an EIGRP external network to the rest of the EIGRP AS100
`passive-interface Ethernet0/0`	Disables EIGRP outbound updates for interface ethernet0/0. Listens for inbound updates.
`no auto-summary`	This command turns classful summarization off

Solution 3.2: Configuring IGRP on the Network

In this section, we'll discuss the required router configurations for each of the routers to implement the IGRP routing protocol and fulfill the requirements for Task 3.2. When configuring IGRP for this scenario, you need to break it down into tasks:

- Task 1: Configure IGRP to provide automatic redistribution between IGRP and EIGRP.
- Task 2: Customize IGRP on R3 and R4.
- Task 3: Configure R3 to propagate a default route.

Task 1: Configure IGRP to Provide Automatic Redistribution between IGRP and EIGRP

To allow automatic redistribution between IGRP and EIGRP, on every router the routing process must use the same AS number. Therefore, routers R3, R4, and R6 must us the same AS number. Remember, AS 100 was already defined for EIGRP.

Task 2: Customize IGRP on R3 and R4

IGRP must be configured on router R3 and R4, and updates must be limited to the network connection between these routers. This is achieved by configuring `passive-interface` on both routers for all interfaces there other than the 172.16.33.0/24 network.

Task 3: Configure R3 to Propagate a Default Route

The IGRP domain must have a default route pointing to R6. IGRP does not support a 0.0.0.0 default route but can use a gateway of last resort. The gateway of last resort is set by using the global command ip default-network. This command must be configured to use a learned classful network. R3 is learning a route from R6 for network 192.128.1.0/24, which is the classful route we'll use. From the point of view of R3 and R4, route 192.128.1.0 /24 will now become an IGRP exterior route.

The following output is from the show ip route command on router R4 after the ip default-network command was configured on R3. The gateway of last resort is set, and the router is learning the 192.128.1.0/24 network from R3:

```
Gateway of last resort is 172.16.33.3 to network 192.128.1.0

        172.16.0.0/16 is variably subnetted, 10 subnets, 2 masks
C       172.16.40.0/24 is directly connected, Ethernet0
O       172.16.42.0/23 [110/782] via 172.16.34.5, 02:09:26, Serial0
C       172.16.34.5/32 is directly connected, Serial0
C       172.16.32.0/24 is directly connected, Serial1.1
C       172.16.33.0/24 is directly connected, Serial1.2
C       172.16.34.0/24 is directly connected, Serial0
I       172.16.35.0/24 [100/82125] via 172.16.33.3, 00:00:19, Serial1.2
O       172.16.5.5/32 [110/782] via 172.16.34.5, 02:09:26, Serial0
O       172.16.4.5/32 [110/782] via 172.16.34.5, 02:09:27, Serial0
O IA    172.16.2.0/24 [110/782] via 172.16.32.1, 02:09:27, Serial1.1
I*   192.128.1.0/24 [100/84125] via 172.16.33.3, 00:00:20, Serial1.2
```

Solution 3.2: Configuring Redistribution on the Network

Once all the routing protocols have been independently configured, network connectivity between all the routers needs to be set up. Redistribution between IGRP and EIGRP was achieved automatically using the same AS number. To configure redistribution, the following needs to be completed:

- Task 1: Configure OSPF redistribution.
- Task 2: Configure IGRP redistribution.

Task 1: Configure OSPF Redistribution

To provide network connectivity from the OSPF domain to IGRP and EIGRP, redistribution of the IGRP process must happen under the OSPF process. Because the routes that are being redistributed from IGRP are not classful major networks, the keyword `subnets` must be used to allow OSPF to send the redistributed routes out to the rest of the OSPF domain. These routes will appear inside of the OSPF domain as OSPF External Type 2 routes:

```
Gateway of last resort is not set

O IA    172.16.40.0 [110/782] via 172.16.32.2, 00:00:00, Serial0/0
O IA    172.16.42.0 [110/1563] via 172.16.32.4, 00:00:00, Serial0/0
C       172.16.32.0 is directly connected, Serial0/0
O IA    172.16.34.0 [110/1562] via 172.16.32.4, 00:00:00, Serial0/0
C       172.16.2.0 is directly connected, Loopback1
O E2 192.128.1.0/24 [110/20] via 172.16.32.4, 00:00:00, Serial0/0
```

This shows the output from R1 when the `show ip route` command is used. Route 192.128.1.0 /24 shows an External Type 2. Notice that no other OSPF External Type 2 routes except for 192.128.10/24 appear in the routing table. This output was taken when the `subnets` command was not appended to the `redistribute igrp 100` command on router R4 and is used as a demonstration. Add the keyword `subnets` as stated earlier and look at R1's routing table again.

Task 2: Configure IGRP Redistribution

To configure the required IGRP for this scenario, you must accomplish the following three tasks:

- Task A: Redistribute OSPF routes into IGRP.
- Task B: Solve the split-horizon problem.
- Task C: Provide accessibility from router R5 to network 172.16.42.0/23.

Task A: Redistribute OSPF Routes into IGRP

When OSPF is redistributed into IGRP, if the redistribution command is entered as `redistribute ospf 1` and no metric is specified, the networks will be sent with a metric of 4,294,967,295, which means that the network is inaccessible. Therefore, when performing redistribution of OSPF under IGRP, a metric must be specified. Here is the output from a `debug ip igrp transactions` on router R3:

```
18:20:37: IGRP: received update from 172.16.33.4 on Serial1
18:20:37:      subnet 172.16.40.0, metric 80225 (neighbor 1100)
18:20:37:      subnet 172.16.32.0, metric 82125 (neighbor 8476)
18:20:37:      subnet 172.16.34.0, metric 82125 (neighbor 8476)
18:20:37:      subnet 172.16.2.0, metric 4294967295 (inaccessible)
```

Following is the output from a debug ip igrp transactions on router R3 when the metric is specified with the redistribution:

```
18:52:28:        subnet 172.16.40.0, metric 80225 (neighbor 1100)
18:52:28:        subnet 172.16.32.0, metric 82125 (neighbor 80125)
18:52:28:        subnet 172.16.34.0, metric 82125 (neighbor 80125)
18:52:28:        subnet 172.16.2.0, metric 82125 (neighbor 80125)
```

Task B: Solve the Split-Horizon Problem

Strange anomalies then appear in the routing table of router R3. Some of the learned networks will be reported periodically as possibly down. Here is the output of the show ip route command from R3:

```
Gateway of last resort is 172.16.35.6 to network 192.128.1.0


     172.16.0.0/16 is variably subnetted, 7 subnets, 2 masks
I       172.16.40.0/24 [100/80225] via 172.16.33.4, 00:00:11, Serial1
C       172.16.35.5/32 is directly connected, Serial0
I       172.16.32.0/24 [100/82125] via 172.16.33.4, 00:00:11, Serial1
C       172.16.33.0/24 is directly connected, Serial1
I       172.16.34.0/24 [100/82125] via 172.16.33.4, 00:00:11, Serial1
C       172.16.35.0/24 is directly connected, Serial0
I       172.16.2.0/24 is possibly down,routing via 172.16.33.4, Serial1
D*EX 192.128.1.0/24 [170/21024000] via 172.16.35.6, 00:50:13, Serial0
```

These routes will also appear and disappear from the routing table of router R6. The problem that is arising is the issue of split-horizon between router R4 and R3. Chapter 3 discussed the default configuration of split-horizon on the different Frame Relay interface types. R3 is configured with a Frame Relay physical interface; split-horizon is disabled by default on this interface. Therefore, R3 will send every learned route it receives from R4 back to R4, and because the IGRP administrative distance is 100 for IGRP, R4 will prefer these learned networks via R3. The following output is from show ip interface serial1 on R3:

```
Serial1 is up, line protocol is up
  Internet address is 172.16.33.3/24
  Broadcast address is 255.255.255.255
  Address determined by setup command
  MTU is 1500 bytes
  Helper address is not set
  Directed broadcast forwarding is disabled
  Multicast reserved groups joined: 224.0.0.10
```

```
Outgoing access list is not set
Inbound  access list is not set
Proxy ARP is enabled
Security level is default
Split horizon is disabled
ICMP redirects are always sent
```

R4, on the other hand, is configured with a Frame Relay subinterface; split-horizon is enabled by default on this interface. Therefore, R4 cannot send out a route on the same interface that it received the route on. In this instance, R4 will poison the route by setting the metric to 4294967295. This shows the output from `show ip interface serial1.2` on R4:

```
Serial1.2 is up, line protocol is up
  Internet address is 172.16.33.4/24
  Broadcast address is 255.255.255.255
  Address determined by setup command
  MTU is 1500 bytes
  Helper address is not set
  Directed broadcast forwarding is disabled
  Outgoing access list is not set
  Inbound  access list is not set
  Proxy ARP is enabled
  Security level is default
  Split horizon is enabled
  ICMP redirects are always sent
```

The solution to this problem is to change the default `split-horizon` configuration on R3:

```
2w1d: IGRP: received update from 172.16.33.4 on Serial1/1
2w1d:       subnet 172.16.40.0, metric 80225 (neighbor 1100)
2w1d:       subnet 172.16.42.0, metric 82125 (neighbor 80125)
2w1d:       subnet 172.16.32.0, metric 82125 (neighbor 80125)
2w1d:       subnet 172.16.34.0, metric 82125 (neighbor 80125)
2w1d:       subnet 172.16.2.0, metric 82125 (neighbor 80125)
2w1d: IGRP: edition is now 9
2w1d: IGRP: sending update to 255.255.255.255 via Serial1/1 (172.16.33.3)
2w1d:       subnet 172.16.35.0, metric=80125
2w1d:       exterior 192.128.1.0, metric=82125
```

In the preceding output, router R3 no longer sends back the learned routes from R4 and the routes will no longer become inaccessible.

ROUTER R4 CONFIGURATION

Here is the configuration for router R4:

```
router igrp 100

 redistribute ospf 1 metric 128 2000 255 1 1500
```

> Redistributes the routes from OSPF
> process 1 with the assigned metrics

ROUTER R3 CONFIGURATION

The configuration for router R3 is as follows:

```
interface Serial 1

 ip split-horizon
```

> Change the split-horizon configuration from its
> default of disabled, to enabled

Task C: Provide Accessibility from Router R5 to Network 172.16.42.0/23

Task 3.2 requests that router R6 must be able to ping R5's Ethernet interface (172.16.42.5). Router R6 is not learning a route for the 172.16.42.0 network. Here is the show ip route from R6:

```
Gateway of last resort is not set

172.16.0.0/16 is variably subnetted, 8 subnets, 2 masks
D EX    172.16.40.0/24 [170/21049600] via 172.16.35.3, 00:00:11, Serial0/0
D       172.16.35.5/32 [90/21024000] via 172.16.35.3, 00:00:48, Serial0/0
D EX    172.16.32.0/24 [170/21536000] via 172.16.35.3, 00:00:11, Serial0/0
C       172.16.35.3/32 is directly connected, Serial0/0
D       172.16.33.0/24 [90/21024000] via 172.16.35.3, 00:00:48, Serial0/0
D EX    172.16.34.0/24 [170/21536000] via 172.16.35.3, 00:00:11, Serial0/0
C       172.16.35.0/24 is directly connected, Serial0/0
D EX    172.16.2.0/24 [170/21536000] via 172.16.35.3, 00:00:12, Serial0/0
C    192.128.1.0/24 is directly connected, Ethernet0/0
```

In the preceding output, router R6 is learning routes from the OSPF domain but is not learning a route for 172.16.42.0/23. The reason for this is that a VLSM-to-FLSM issue exists. IGRP is an FLSM routing protocol and for major networks it is running on, it will only send out routes that appear in its routing table with the same network mask as the outgoing interface. Therefore, only routes from the classful network 172.16.0.0 with a mask of /24 will be sent by IGRP to router R3.

The solution is to install routes in R4's routing table for network 172.16.42.0/23 with a mask of /24. This is achieved using static routes. Two static routes are configured on router R4. These static routes are then redistributed under the IGRP process.

> **NOTE** An area range command couldn't be used to resolve this, because the classless network has a shorter mask than the classful mask.

ROUTER R4 CONFIGURATION

Here is router R4's configuration:

```
router igrp 100

 redistribute static metric 128 2000 255 1 1500
                                                  All configured static
                                                  routes will get
                                                  redistributed into IGRP
ip route 172.16.42.0 255.255.255.0 Serial0        Add static route for
                                                  172.16.42.0/24 out Serial 0
ip route 172.16.43.0 255.255.255.0 Serial0        Add static route for
                                                  172.16.43.0/24 out Serial 0
```

Solution 3.2: Testing the Network

After configuring the scenario, it is important to verify your work:

- R3 should be able to ping R5's Ethernet interface (172.16.42.5).
- R5 should be able to ping R6's Ethernet interface (192.128.1.6) and the loopback 1 interface of R1 (172.16.2.1).
- R6 should be able to ping R5's Ethernet interface (172.16.42.5) and should not be able to ping R5's loopback 10 (172.16.4.5) and loopback 11 (172.16.5.4) addresses. Also, R6 should be able to ping R1's loopback 1 address (172.16.2.1).

Solution 3.2: Troubleshooting the Network

The commands useful in troubleshooting this network are as follows:

```
show ip route [ospf | igrp | eigrp]
show ip ospf interface
show ip ospf database
show ip ospf neighbor
show ip eigrp neighbor
```

```
show ip protocol

debug ip frame-relay packet
debug ip ospf events
debug ip ospf adjacencies
debug ip igrp transactions
debug ip eigrp packet
```

Summary

It is truly important to have a strong understanding of how to implement layer 3 technologies. This chapter tests your knowledge and understanding of configuring routing protocols. It also presents issues involving the interaction of these protocols with one another.

You can look at internetworking as a building process. The layer 2 infrastructure is the foundation of all networking; it is difficult to build on top of this foundation if it is weak and brittle. Layer 3 frames the network. You need to know how to tie the layer 2 and layer 3 networks together, and you need to understand the dependencies and relationships between the different routing protocols.

Again, use these scenarios as a measuring stick of your networking knowledge. Understand how to make layer 2 and layer 3 networks work correctly and efficiently.

Chapter 12

Border Gateway Protocol (BGP)

THE CCIE QUALIFICATION EXAM TOPICS COVERED IN THIS CHAPTER INCLUDE THE FOLLOWING:

- ✓ Autonomous system (AS) numbers
- ✓ Border Gateway Protocol (BGP) overview
- ✓ Internal Border Gateway Protocol (iBGP)
- ✓ External Border Gateway Protocol (eBGP)
- ✓ BGP synchronization
- ✓ BGP reachability and next hop
- ✓ BGP message types
- ✓ BGP attributes
- ✓ The BGP route selection process
- ✓ Configuring BGP communities, confederations, route reflectors, and peer groups
- ✓ BGP route dampening

As you have learned, there are two types of routing protocols: interior gateway protocols (IGPs) and exterior gateway protocols (EGPs). IGPs exchange routing protocols within autonomous systems (ASs). Routing protocols for IP can include IGRP, EIGRP, RIP, and OSPF in a network. BGP is an exterior gateway protocol, which allows routes to be shared between different autonomous systems if both autonomous systems know about each other and agree on the routes to be shared.

This means that autonomous systems use BGP to share internal routes to the outside world (the other autonomous systems). This happens mostly within large companies to connect their networks to the network belonging to their ISPs if there are multiple connections to the same or different ISPs.

In this chapter, we will discuss the Border Gateway Protocol (BGP). We'll look at it first from an academic viewpoint and then discuss how to configure and implement the protocol. We will finish this chapter with a hands-on scenario (Task 1) for you to complete, which will allow you to verify your understanding of the material presented in this chapter.

But first, we'll discuss why BGP is even needed in the networking environment.

When Should I Use BGP?

There are many reasons to use BGP and many reasons not to use BGP. ISPs are a perfect example of when to use BGP because they usually have multiple connections to their own long-distance companies, their customers, and other phone providers. In this situation, you have many autonomous systems connected together, so you will want to allow routing between the client's autonomous systems and the other connected autonomous systems, as shown in Figure 12.1.

FIGURE 12.1 Multiple autonomous systems connected to an ISP

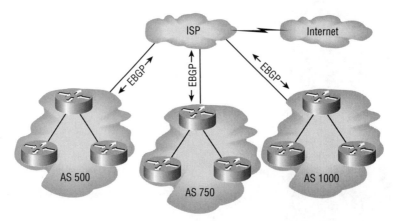

BGP is also useful in an enterprise situation as shown in Figure 12.2. If your company has multiple connections to the Internet for redundancy, there are multiple paths for data to travel. BGP can also be used to load-balance data traffic over those redundant links. Use BGP when you want to do the following:

- Route data through your network to other connected autonomous systems.

- Have more than one physical connection between autonomous systems.

- Control the path data takes between autonomous systems.

FIGURE 12.2 Multiple physical connections between autonomous systems

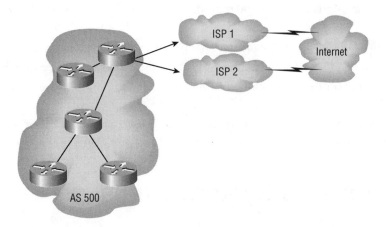

BGP also allows use of policies that allow you to determine the best path data will take to reach its destination. In Figure 12.3, take a look at the use of policy routing related to bandwidth with BGP.

FIGURE 12.3 Bandwidth policy routing

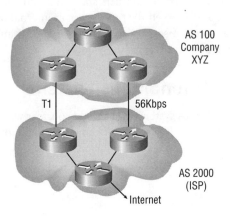

You now know when to use BGP, but there are also many reasons why you shouldn't use it.

When Shouldn't I Use BGP?

There are many situations in which BGP should not be used. When you have a single connection between two different autonomous systems, you should not use BGP. In this case, it is best to configure a static route and redistribute this static route through your autonomous system using an IGP. We will discuss this further as the chapter progresses.

By not using BGP, you also reduce the size of the routing tables and the amount of RAM needed to support routers using BGP. It is recommended that you have a router with at least 128MB of RAM and an adequate processor to allow for processing and storage of the large BGP routing tables (approximately 120,000 routes). Here are the scenarios in which you should *not* use BGP:

- When there is a single connection between two autonomous systems

- When you don't have a suitable router to handle the extra processing requirements

- When you don't have enough bandwidth between your autonomous systems to support BGP

We have spoken a lot about autonomous systems in a network. In the next sections, we'll review what an autonomous system is and the types you may find in a BGP environment.

Autonomous System Types

By definition, an autonomous system number (ASN) is a number logically assigned to all the routers that fall under a single administrative control. These routers then share routing tables that allow updates on a regular basis.

There are standards for assigning autonomous system numbers. First of all, the Internet Assigned Numbers Authority (IANA) assigns the BGP autonomous system numbers. The total number of available autonomous system numbers starts at 1 and ends at 65,535; however, the range from 64,512 to 65,535 is reserved for private use in internal networks.

In the following section, we'll discuss two different types of autonomous systems: stub autonomous systems and transit autonomous systems.

Stub and Transit Autonomous Systems

There are two types of autonomous systems you should consider when deciding whether or not to use BGP. A *stub AS,* as shown in Figure 12.4, is a network with one link in from and out to the outside world.

FIGURE 12.4 Stub AS

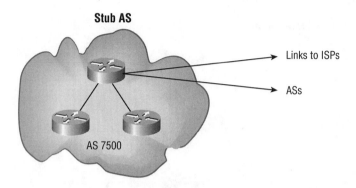

Another option (rather than assigning static routes) is to use an IGP. This allows your IGP to announce its routes to BGP and have BGP announce the routes to its peers.

A *transit AS* is an autonomous system the data must transit to get to another autonomous system. Figure 12.5 shows a transit AS. If AS 10 wants to send data to AS 50, it must go through AS 30, which is the transit AS.

FIGURE 12.5 Transit AS

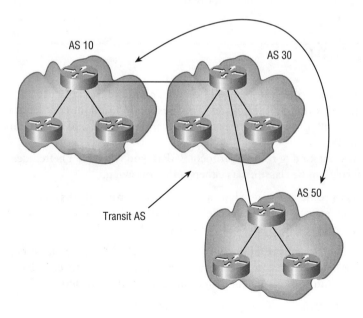

Figure 12.6 shows a non-transit AS. This is where an AS can pass data to and from multiple autonomous systems but never passes it between them.

FIGURE 12.6 Non-transit AS

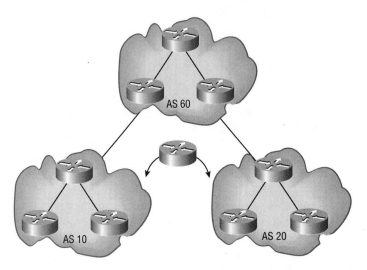

Next, we'll take a look at the basics of BGP.

BGP Basics

As with all routing protocols, you must have a strong foundation in the basics of BGP before we can look at the more complex features. You must understand the configuration of BGP peer connections, both eBGP and iBGP, the issue of synchronization, and the resolution of the next hop reachability.

If you know what kind of routing protocol BGP is, you will have a better idea of its function. Routing protocols can be classified as either as the following:

Interior gateway protocol (IGP)   These are the routing protocols that have been discussed in the previous chapters, the routing protocols that run within an autonomous system. Examples of these routing protocols are RIP, IGRP, EIGRP, OSPF, and IS-IS.

Exterior gateway protocols (EGP)   EGP is used to exchange information between different autonomous systems. BGP is an EGP protocol and is used to connect different autonomous systems together and to exchange information between these different ASs.

Figure 12.7 depicts three different autonomous systems communicating with each other. Within each AS, various IGP routing protocols are running. These IGPs may be redistributed between each other within a specific AS, but they are still classified as being contained within a single autonomous system. The demarcation from one AS to another AS is the BGP connection between them.

FIGURE 12.7   Typical BGP environment

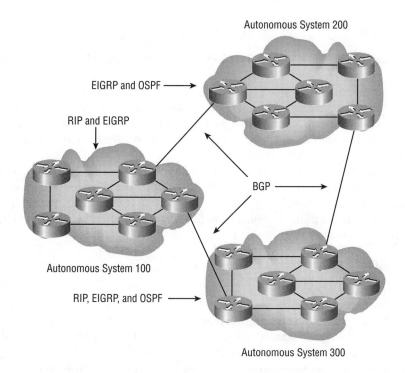

BGP is classified as an EGP, but what exactly is BGP? We'll discuss the protocol in the next section.

BGP Operation

BGP version 4 (BGP4) is the latest and greatest version of BGP and is defined in RFC 1771. The primary function of BGP is to provide inter-AS routing between different autonomous systems. BGP is a path vector routing protocol. The path information transferred via BGP from one AS to another AS contains all transit ASs that must be traversed to get to a destination. The path information also has associated attributes, which will be discussed later on in this chapter.

BGP is a stateful protocol and uses TCP port 179 to communicate between two adjacent BGP peers. The terms *BGP peers, BGP speakers,* and *BGP neighbors* all mean the same thing. Two BGP speakers establish a single TCP session between each other. Once this session is established, all BGP information and routing tables are exchanged across this connection.

Because the connection is over TCP, it is reliable. Once a BGP session is established, each BGP neighbor sends its full BGP routing table. After initialization, BGP will send only changes to its neighbors. Unlike other distance vector routing protocols, no periodic updates are sent. BGP uses TCP, which is reliable and connection oriented. If a change to a BGP filter, weight, distance, version, or timer is made, or if a similar configuration change is made, you must reset BGP connections for the configuration change to take effect. Use one of the following commands:

```
clear ip bgp *              This will clear all BGP connections

clear ip bgp 131.2.1.1      Only clears the BGP connection to this neighbor
```

BGP sends hello packets to its neighbors through the established TCP connection. By default, hello packets are sent every 60 seconds but are configurable under the BGP process using the `neighbor x.x.x.x timers 10` command, where *x.x.x.x* is the IP address of the neighbor and 10 is for 10 seconds. The configured timers for BGP can be viewed using the `show ip bgp neighbor` command.

BGP has two administrative distances associated with the protocol. eBGP learned routes will be assigned an administrative distance of 20, and iBGP learned routes will be assigned an administrative distance of 200. Routes learned from an IGP (OSPF=110, EIGRP=90, etc.) will always be preferred over routers learned from iBGP, assuming that the default administrative distances are not altered.

Internal BGP (iBGP)

Internal BGP (iBGP) connections are used within a single AS. iBGP is used to distribute BGP routes and route attributes between BGP neighbors within the same AS. iBGP is also used to transmit BGP information across an AS so that it can be passed to other connected BGP ASs. An iBGP router will not propagate routes learned from one iBGP neighbor to other iBGP neighbors; therefore, for an iBGP router to learn all routes, it must have an iBGP connection to every other iBGP router within the AS, so the requirement is that all iBGP neighbors must be fully meshed. This is referred to as the iBGP split-horizon rule, and its function is to avoid loops in an iBGP network. This does not allow iBGP to scale very well because the number of iBGP connections increases exponentially with the number of iBGP routers. The following is the formula for calculating the number of iBGP connections, where N is the number of iBGP routers: $N \times (N-1)/2$. With this formula, the scaling issue can be seen; 10 iBGP routers will require 45 iBGP connections, and 20 iBGP routers will require 190 iBGP connections. iBGP can operate without any IGP (RIP, OSPF, etc.) configured in the AS, but to get this configuration to work will require that every router is an iBGP speaker.

External BGP (eBGP)

External BGP (eBGP) connections are used to connect BGP neighbors from different ASs. One of the assumptions about eBGP connections is that the BGP neighbors share a common network (point-to-point, Ethernet segment, etc.). For a TCP connection to be established between the neighbors, both neighbors must have IP reachability to each other. If the neighbors share a common network, this can be achieved because the neighbors are directly connected. If the neighbors are not directly connected, then some routing protocol must exist to establish reachability to allow the TCP session to be established.

Let's discuss how BGP handles IP address space as well as how to perform route summarization in BGP.

Classful, Classless Inter-Domain Routing and Summarization

In older versions of IOS (before IOS 12.0), BGP by default was a classful protocol. Therefore, when BGP is acting in a classful manor, it automatically sends a classful route to its neighbors for any network that appears in its routing table without its appropriate classful mask. The default classful operation can be changed by configuring the `no auto summary` command under the BGP process. BGP supports Classless Inter-Domain Routing (CIDR). CIDR is best described as a mechanism to cross classful boundaries for the purpose of aggregating routes. Variable-Length Subnet Masking (VLSM) is a mechanism that is used to break up a classful network and allow multiple different network masks to be used inside of that classful network. Figure 12.8 shows two examples of CIDR summarizing classful networks and sending an aggregate route for the address range.

FIGURE 12.8   Route aggregation

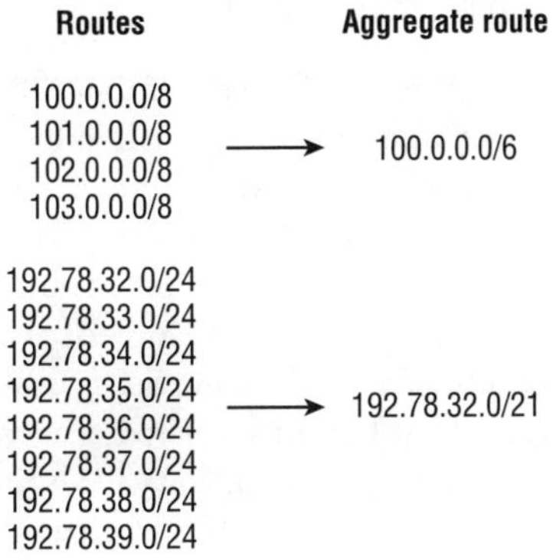

Routes	Aggregate route
100.0.0.0/8 101.0.0.0/8 102.0.0.0/8 103.0.0.0/8	100.0.0.0/6
192.78.32.0/24 192.78.33.0/24 192.78.34.0/24 192.78.35.0/24 192.78.36.0/24 192.78.37.0/24 192.78.38.0/24 192.78.39.0/24	192.78.32.0/21

With BGP it is also possible to aggregate (summarize) routes that are sent to neighbors. An aggregate address will be added to the BGP table and sent to neighbors if at least one or more specific entries exist in the BGP table.

To create an aggregate address in the routing table, use one of the following commands under the BGP process:

```
aggregate-address 131.1.0.0 255.255.0.0
```
Send an aggregate route for network 131.1.0.0/16 and all specific routes

```
aggregate-address 131.1.0.0 255.255.0.0 summary-only
```
Send a summary route ONLY for network 131.1.0.0/16, and suppress advertisements for the specific routes

Just as you can add the summary-only keyword at the end of the aggregate command, you can also add the as-set keyword to include a list of all of the ASNs that the more specific routes have passed through. When you use the as-set keyword, the BGP router will advertise the route as coming from your autonomous system and will set the atomic aggregate attribute to show that information regarding the route may be missing. Depending on your configuration, as-set might be needed to avoid routing loops

You now know how to summarize routes with BGP. But how does BGP learn routes (prefixes) so that it can advertise them? We'll explain in the next section.

Advertising Networks into BGP

Redistribution of routing information occurs in a number of ways. The network command allows BGP to advertise a network that is already in the IP table. When using the network command, you must identify all the networks in the autonomous system that you want to advertise.

You can also use the ip route command to create a static route. The static route is then redistributed into BGP. It is called *redistribution* when a router uses different protocols to advertise routing information received between the protocols. BGP considers a static route to be a "protocol." Static route information is advertised to BGP. This can be accomplished by redistributing the static routes into bgp or by using a network statement.

Just as you can redistribute static routes into bgp, you can also redistribute dynamically learned routes (routes learned through an IGP). In Chapter 10, "Protocol Redistribution and NAT," you learned the commands to enable this; however, Cisco does not recommend that this approach be used because of convergence issues. Convergence is the time it takes for the network to recover from a change in the network's topology.

Now we'll discuss how to configure BGP on a Cisco router.

Configuring BGP Peers

When configuring BGP peers, the neighbor statement is used to configure both iBGP and eBGP neighbors.

Figure 12.9 is a simple BGP design: AS 100 is connected to AS 200, AS 200 has iBGP running on all routers within the AS, and AS 200 is connected to AS 300. The following are the router configurations needed to define the BGP peering. For the iBGP configuration, a full mesh must be configured, therefore two iBGP peers exist on routers R1, R3, and R4. The complete router configurations are not provided, only the portion that pertains to the configuration of BGP. The end goal of this exercise is for router R5 to have routes and reachability to AS 300 and for R6 to have routes and reachability to AS 100.

FIGURE 12.9   Configuring BGP peers

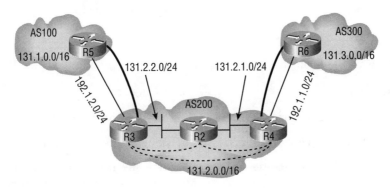

Router R2 Configuration

The following are the commands required to configure BGP on router R2:

```
router BGP 200                              Enable BGP AS 200

  network 131.2.1.0 mask 255.255.255.0

                                            Assign a network that will be
                                            announced to iBGP neighbors.
                                            Router R2 will install a route
                                            in BGP for 131.2.1.0/24.

  network 131.2.2.0 mask 255.255.255.0

                                            Assign a network that will be
                                            announced to iBGP neighbors.
                                            Router R2 will install a route
                                            in BGP for 131.2.2.0/24

  neighbor 131.2.1.4 remote-as 200          Define iBGP neighbor to router
                                            R1, specifying the AS 200 will
                                            make this an iBGP connection
```

neighbor 131.2.2.3 remote-as 200	Define iBGP neighbor to router R3, specifying the AS 200 will make this an iBGP connection
no synchronization	This command is required, but do not configure this command initially. Leaving synchronization on, will demonstrate the issue with synchronization

Router R3 Configuration

The following are the commands required to configure BGP on router R3:

router BGP 200	Enable BGP AS 200
neighbor 131.2.2.2 remote-as 200	Define iBGP peer to router R2
neighbor 131.2.1.4 remote-as 200	Define iBGP peer to router R4
neighbor 192.1.2.5 remote-as 100	Define eBGP peer to router R5 in AS 100. The remote AS is different from the AS that the router is participating in, which automatically makes this an eBGP connection
no synchronization	This command is required, but do not configure this command initially. Leaving synchronization on, will demonstrate the issue with synchronization

Router R4 Configuration

The following are the commands required to configure BGP on router R4:

router BGP 200	Enable BGP AS 200
neighbor 131.2.1.2 remote-as 200	Define iBGP peer to router R2
neighbor 131.2.2.3 remote-as 200	Define iBGP peer to router R3
neighbor 192.1.1.6 remote-as 300	Define eBGP peer to router R6 in AS 300
no synchronization	This command is required, but do not configure this command initially. Leaving synchronization on, will demonstrate the issue with synchronization

Router R5 Configuration

The following are the commands required to configure BGP on router R5:

router BGP 100	Enable BGP AS 100
network 131.1.0.0 mask 255.255.0.0	Assign network address space that will be announced to neighbors
neighbor 192.1.2.3 remote-as 200	Define eBGP peer to router R3 in AS 200

Router R6 Configuration

The following are the commands required to configure BGP on router R6:

router BGP 300	Enable BGP AS 300
network 131.3.0.0 mask 255.255.0.0	Assign network address space that will be announced to neighbors
neighbor 192.1.1.4 remote-as 200	Define eBGP peer to router R4 in AS 200

The following output is from a show ip bgp summary command on router R3 after the entire network has been configured with the configuration shown earlier:

```
Neighbor        V   AS MsgRcvd MsgSent   TblVer  InQ OutQ Up/Down State/PfxRcd

131.2.1.4       4   200      0       0        0    0    0 never     Active
131.2.2.2       4   200      8       9        4    0    0 00:04:21         2
192.1.2.5       4   100      8       9        4    0    0 00:04:08         1
```

What must be noted is that the peer session with router R4 has not ever been established. The reason for this is that no route exists in either R3 or R4 for the respective network that the routers are connected to. Here is the output from the show ip bgp command on router R3:

```
BGP table version is 5, local router ID is 192.1.2.3
Status codes: s suppressed, d damped, h history, * valid, > best, i - internal
Origin codes: i - IGP, e - EGP, ? - incomplete

   Network          Next Hop          Metric LocPrf Weight Path
*> 131.1.0.0        192.1.2.5              0            0 100 i
*> 131.2.0.0        0.0.0.0                0        32768 i
*  i131.2.1.0/24    131.2.2.2              0    100     0 i
*>i131.2.2.0/24     131.2.2.2              0    100     0 I
```

What needs to be understood is that router R3 is learning, via iBGP, about network 131.2.1.0/24 from router R2. What also needs to be understood is what exactly this command is displaying. The show ip bgp command is not showing the router's routing table but is showing the learned routes

534 Chapter 12 · Border Gateway Protocol (BGP)

from BGP. BGP learned routes are installed in the router's routing table. BGP routes that are installed are marked as best. In the preceding output, the route for network 131.2.1.0/24 is not marked as best. The following output is from a `show ip route` command on router R3, confirming that this route is not in the routing table. Router R3 is unable to ping router R4 and is therefore unable to establish the required TCP session for BGP. The reason this route is not being marked as best, and therefore the reason that this route is not installed in the router's routing table, involves the issue of synchronization. (See the next section for an explanation of synchronization.) The following output shows that no route exists in the router's routing table for network 131.2.1.0/24:

```
B    131.1.0.0/16 [20/0] via 192.1.2.5, 00:01:16
     131.2.0.0/24 is subnetted, 1 subnets
C       131.2.2.0 is directly connected, Ethernet0
     192.1.2.0/24 is variably subnetted, 2 subnets, 2 masks
C       192.1.2.0/24 is directly connected, Serial0
C       192.1.2.5/32 is directly connected, Serial0
```

The resolution is to turn off synchronization under the BGP process on routers R2, R3, and R4. This is achieved using the `no synchronization` command. Once synchronization is off, the routes on the routers may need to be cleared or the BGP process may need to be cleared to get the iBGP learned routes installed in the router's routing table. Here is the output from `show ip route` on router R3:

```
Gateway of last resort is not set

B    131.1.0.0/16 [20/0] via 192.1.2.5, 00:00:02
     131.2.0.0/24 is subnetted, 2 subnets
B       131.2.1.0 [200/0] via 131.2.2.2, 00:00:02
C       131.2.2.0 is directly connected, Ethernet0/0
     192.1.2.0/24 is variably subnetted, 2 subnets, 2 masks
C       192.1.2.0/24 is directly connected, Serial1/0
C       192.1.2.5/32 is directly connected, Serial1/0
```

The iBGP learned route is now installed in the routing table, and the route is also marked as best in the BGP route table.

We know that this synchronization thing is confusing. Let's see if we can clear it up a bit.

BGP Synchronization

There is a lot of confusion about synchronization and next hop reachability. The first thing that must be clearly understood is that they are completely independent issues that solve different problems. First we'll look at the issue of synchronization; the first thing that must be clearly understood is that synchronization is only an issue for routers that have iBGP connections. This is not an issue or concern for routers that have eBGP connections only. If a router has both eBGP and iBGP connections, there will be a synchronization issue for iBGP learned routes.

By default, synchronization is on when BGP is configured. When synchronization is turned on, a router will not install a route learned from an iBGP neighbor unless that route is local (a connected network) or unless that route is also learned by the router from an IGP. When the no synchronization command is used under the BGP process to turn synchronization off, the router will install all iBGP learned routes, for both local AS routes and external AS routes. The only caveat to this is that the router must have a valid route in its routing table to the next hop address that is specified in BGP. There are two ways to resolve the issue of synchronization:

- The first is to use the no synchronization command under the BGP process. This is also the recommended method, and it's only option if no IGP exists within the iBGP AS.

- If the AS is running an IGP through the entire network, the second option is to redistribute the BGP learned routes into the IGP somewhere within the AS. This will manually synchronize the routing tables of all the routers in the AS.

The issue of synchronization is as clear as mud, right? It may take a few times reading the description for it to become clear. In the meantime, another extremely important concept to clearly understand is that of the next hop reachability. It is imperative that you understand the two-step routing process that BGP utilizes.

BGP Two-Step Routing Process

BGP has essentially a two-step routing process. When BGP routes are installed in a router's routing table, the routes' next hop is an IP address and not a directly connected interface. The following output is from the show ip route command on router R3. The BGP learned routes all show a next hop of the IP address of the originating BGP peers. Network 131.2.1.0 is known via IP address 131.2.2.2, which is the IP address of router R2. Network 131.1.0.0/16 is known via 192.1.2.5, the IP address of router R5, which is in AS 100. Because these BGP installed routes do not have an outgoing interface assigned, the router must first match a route that is assigned to an outgoing interface that matches the next hop address. You may recall from our discussion in Chapter 9 that this is a recursive route.

The following shows the output of a show ip route command. This shows the routing table for the next hop address of the BGP learned routes:

```
Gateway of last resort is not set

B    131.1.0.0/16 [20/0] via 192.1.2.5, 00:31:26
     131.2.0.0/24 is subnetted, 2 subnets
B       131.2.1.0 [200/0] via 131.2.2.2, 00:02:34
C       131.2.2.0 is directly connected, Ethernet0
     192.1.2.0/24 is variably subnetted, 2 subnets, 2 masks
C       192.1.2.0/24 is directly connected, Serial0
C       192.1.2.5/32 is directly connected, Serial0
```

This is the two-step routing process that exists for all BGP learned routes. The reason that this is such an important issue is because the router will not install a BGP learned route unless a valid route that specifies an outgoing interface exists for the BGP next hop address.

As shown in the following output, there is no route to network 131.3.0.0/16. This network is being learned by router R4 and is being sent by R4 via iBGP. Here is the output from a show ip bgp command on router R3:

```
Status codes: s suppressed, d damped, h history, * valid, > best, i - internal
Origin codes: i - IGP, e - EGP, ? - incomplete
```

Network	Next Hop	Metric	LocPrf	Weight	Path
*> 131.1.0.0	192.1.2.5	0		0	100 i
* i131.2.0.0	131.2.1.4	0	100	0	i
*>	0.0.0.0	0		32768	i
*>i131.2.1.0/24	131.2.2.2	0	100	0	i
*>i131.2.2.0/24	131.2.2.2	0	100	0	i
* i131.3.0.0	192.1.1.6	0	100	0	300 I

It can be seen that router R3 is learning a route from R4, but it is not marked as best. The BGP next hop address is 192.1.1.6, and as you saw earlier, no route exists to network 192.1.1.0/24 or host 192.1.1.6/32. The rules of BGP routing state that a route will not be installed in the routing table of the router unless a route exists to the next hop address. Hence the route is not installed in the routing table of Router R3.

To further clarify the issue of BGP routing rules, a BGP speaker will not propagate a BGP update to a neighbor unless the route is installed in the router's routing table. Network 131.3.0.0/16 is not installed in router R3's routing table, so this route will not be propagated to router R5 because this route did not conform to the rules of BGP routing. The following shows the output from the show ip bgp command on router R5:

Network	Next Hop	Metric	LocPrf	Weight	Path
*> 131.1.0.0	0.0.0.0	0		32768	i
*> 131.2.0.0	192.1.2.3	0		0	200 i
*> 131.2.1.0/24	192.1.2.3			0	200 i
*> 131.2.2.0/24	192.1.2.3			0	200 I

Note that a route for network 131.3.0.0/16 is not being learned from BGP, therefore it can not be in the router's routing table.

The issue that needs to be solved is the issue of the next hop address reachability. For R3 to install a BGP learned route for 131.3.0.0/16, either of the following must be true:

- R3 must have a route to network 192.1.1.0/24 in its routing table.

- Network 131.3.0.0/16 must have a BGP next hop address to which R3 already has an existing route (if it doesn't, you need to change the next hop address).

The following is the output from the `show ip bgp` command on router R3 after the issue of next hop reachability has been resolved:

```
   Network          Next Hop          Metric LocPrf Weight Path
*> 131.1.0.0        192.1.2.5              0             0 100 i
*  i131.2.0.0       131.2.1.4              0    100      0 i
*>                  0.0.0.0                0         32768 i
*>i131.2.1.0/24     131.2.2.2              0    100      0 i
*>i131.2.2.0/24     131.2.2.2              0    100      0 i
*  i131.3.0.0       192.1.1.6              0    100      0 300 i
```

Router R3 is unable to install a route for network 131.3.0.0 because it does not have a valid path to IP address 192.1.1.6. Therefore, this route will not be forwarded to router R5 from R3. This next hop reachability issue exists for all iBGP routers in AS 200, and subsequently, routes are not forwarded to external ASs.

Solving Reachability to the Next Hop Address

As mentioned in the previous section, the next hop address that is specified in the BGP update must have a valid route out a local interface. If the next hop address does not have a valid route, the route will be neither installed in the router's routing table nor forwarded to other BGP neighbors. There are two ways to solve this issue for the network depicted in Figure 12.9. On router R4, we need to provide reachability to the next hop address. The reachability can be achieved by advertising the network using the `network 192.1.1.0 mask 255.255.255.0` command under the BGP process on Router R4 or by redistributing the connected networks under the BGP process. In the rest of this section, we'll show you the additional configuration commands of router R4:

```
router bgp 200
 network 192.1.1.0
```

or

```
router bgp 200
 redistribute connected
```

The BGP peers will need to be cleared using the `clear ip bgp *` command to ensure that this network is advertised from R4 to both R2 and R3. Here is the output from a `show ip route` command on router R4 after this configuration has been completed:

```
Gateway of last resort is not set

     131.2.0.0/24 is subnetted, 2 subnets
C       131.2.1.0 is directly connected, Ethernet0
B       131.2.2.0 [200/0] via 131.2.1.2, 16:48:10
```

```
B    131.3.0.0/16 [20/0] via 192.1.1.6, 16:49:04
     192.1.1.0/24 is variably subnetted, 2 subnets, 2 masks
C       192.1.1.0/24 is directly connected, Serial0
C       192.1.1.6/32 is directly connected, Serial0
B    192.1.2.0/24 [200/0] via 131.2.2.3, 00:00:11
```

You can see that a route for network 192.1.1.0/24 is installed with the next hop address of router R4. A route is also installed for network 131.3.0.0/16 with the next hop address of 192.1.1.6. This route will also be propagated to router R3 from router R4. The output of a show ip bgp command on router R6 is shown here:

```
Status codes: s suppressed, d damped, h history, * valid, > best, i - internal
Origin codes: i - IGP, e - EGP, ? - incomplete

    Network         Next Hop         Metric LocPrf Weight Path
*> 131.1.0.0        192.1.1.4                         0 200 100 i
*> 131.2.0.0        192.1.1.4           0             0 200 i
*> 131.2.1.0/24     192.1.1.4                         0 200 i
*> 131.2.2.0/24     192.1.1.4                         0 200 i
*> 131.3.0.0        0.0.0.0             0         32768 i
*> 192.1.2.0        192.1.1.4                         0 200 i
```

What needs to also be noted and understood from the preceding output is the next hop address on R6. The rules for eBGP learned routes state that the advertising router R4 must install its IP address as the next hop address when the route is being propagated to an eBGP peer. This can be seen in the preceding output because routes to both AS 100 and 200 all have the next hop address set to R4's IP address.

The second solution to resolving the next hop address issue is to change the advertised next hop address for all eBGP learned routes to be the IP address of the advertising iBGP peer. The following output is from a show ip bgp neighbor 131.2.1.4 routes command on router R3. This command shows the advertised routes from router R4 to router R3. The advertised next hop address is the IP address of the advertising eBGP router R6:

```
   Network         Next Hop         Metric LocPrf Weight Path
* i131.3.0.0        192.1.1.6           0    100      0 300 i I
```

To change the advertised next hop address for network 131.3.0.0/16 (AS 300) on router R4 under the BGP process, use the neighbor x.x.x.x next-hop-self command. This will change the advertised next hop address for all eBGP learned routes. This command must be configured under the BGP process for all iBGP neighbors. Let's look at more configuration commands for router R4.

```
router bgp 200
 neighbor 131.2.1.2 next-hop-self
 neighbor 131.2.2.3 next-hop-self
```

The following output is from a `show ip bgp neighbor 131.2.2.3 routes` command on router R3 after the `next-hop-self` commands have been configured on router R4. The BGP peers will need to be reset using the `clear ip bgp *` command. This is to ensure that this network is advertised with the new next hop address from R4 to both R2 and R3:

```
Network          Next Hop          Metric LocPrf Weight Path
*>i131.3.0.0     131.2.1.4              0    100      0 300 i
```

The next hop address in router R3 is now the IP address of router R4. This route is now installed in the routing table and will also be propagated to router R5. The following output is from a `show ip route` command on router R5. Router R5 has not installed a route for network 131.3.0.0/16, and the next hop address is the IP address of router R3. Again, the next hop address is the IP address of router R3 because on an eBGP learned route, the IP address is that of the eBGP peer:

```
Gateway of last resort is not set

     131.1.0.0/24 is subnetted, 1 subnets
C       131.1.1.0 is directly connected, Loopback20
     131.2.0.0/16 is variably subnetted, 3 subnets, 2 masks
B       131.2.1.0/24 [20/0] via 192.1.2.3, 00:58:24
B       131.2.0.0/16 [20/0] via 192.1.2.3, 00:57:54
B       131.2.2.0/24 [20/0] via 192.1.2.3, 00:58:24
B    131.3.0.0/16 [20/0] via 192.1.2.3, 00:02:54
     192.1.2.0/24 is variably subnetted, 2 subnets, 2 masks
C       192.1.2.3/32 is directly connected, Serial0
C       192.1.2.0/24 is directly connected, Serial0
```

It is *imperative* that you understand how BGP routing is carried out! The BGP features that allow routes to be manipulated rely completely on the fact that all issues with next hop address and synchronization have been resolved.

Next we'll discuss briefly how BGP can be configured to use loopback interfaces to form the neighbor connections.

Using Loopback Interfaces for Peering

When building either an iBGP or an eBGP neighbor, it is common to use a loopback interface to establish the peer connection. Loopback interfaces are not directly connected networks, so when they are used, an IGP (RIP, OSPF, static) must be used to provide reachability from the peers to connect. You generally only configure BGP neighbors using loopbacks when multiple paths exist between BGP peers. If peers are directly connected, there is no point in configuring loopbacks.

Under the BGP process, you must use the `neighbor x.x.x.x remote-as 100` command to specify the remote peer loopback address as the loopback IP address. What needs to be understood is the way BGP initiates a TCP connection. BGP will initiate the TCP connection using the IP address of the outgoing interface. Therefore, to ensure that the router sends the correct IP address in the TCP request, the command `neighbor x.x.x.x update-source Loopback 0` must be specified to ensure that the TCP connection is sourced using the correct IP address (Loopback 0 IP address).

If the connection is an eBGP connection, the TCP time to live (TTL) must also be changed using the `neighbor x.x.x.x ebgp-multihop 255` command; otherwise, the connection will not be established. The TTL, by default for eBGP connections, is set to 1. The `neighbor x.x.x.x ebgp-multihop 255` command will set the TCP TTL to 255. This is required for all eBGP connections that are not directly connected, including connections using the loopback interface.

Various message types are used for all interneighbor communication within BGP. These message types are the topic of the next sections.

BGP Update Messages

The biggest difference between an IGP and BGP is the amount of additional information passed between protocol-running devices. RIP is a simple IGP that carries only a few attributes, such as metric information and the next hop. OSPF is a much more complex routing protocol that has path attributes such as intra-area, interarea, and the external status. BGP has the ability to attach many attributes to a given route.

When two routers running BGP begin a communication process to exchange dynamic routing information, they use a TCP port at layer 4 of the OSI reference model. Specifically, TCP port 179 is used. BGP uses TCP so that it does not have to provide a component that controls the orderly delivery of messages, recognizes when data packets have been lost, detects duplicates, and controls buffering for both ends of the reliable session. Before a session between two or more BGP routers has been initiated, the endpoints are considered to be in the *Idle* state.

As soon as one endpoint tries to open a TCP session, the endpoint is considered to be in the *Connect* state. If there is a problem in establishing a connection between two endpoints, the router trying to initiate the session will transition to the *Active* state, where it will periodically try to establish a TCP session.

When the TCP connection has been established, the endpoints can be assured that as long as the session is active, there is a reliable connection-oriented path between the endpoints. TCP provides all Session layer functions—such as guaranteed delivery, handling of out-of-order packet delivery, flow-control, and so on—reducing the overhead of BGP.

BGP must rely on the connection-oriented TCP session to provide the reliable connection, because BGP cannot use a keepalive signal but sends a message with a KEEPALIVE type in a common header to allow routers to verify that sessions are active. When the TCP connection has been established, the endpoints can be assured that as long as the session is active, there is a reliable connection-oriented path between the endpoints. Messages between the endpoints can be sent reliably. This connection allows BGP messages to be very simple and include only the information necessary with little overhead.

Once the TCP connection has been established, BGP sends messages back and forth in a specific format. The first message is an identification message from the endpoints identifying themselves. As soon as this message is sent, the router transitions to the *OpenSent* state. When the router receives a reply to the identification message, it transitions to the *OpenConfirm* state. If a connection is received and accepted by the endpoints, the Connection state then becomes the *Established* state. From then on, when a message is sent to the endpoint routers, the routers can respond to the sent message, update their routing table with new information in the message, or have no reaction to the sent message whatsoever.

Endpoints typically stay in the Established state until there is a loss of the session or an error in the communication process, such as when a notification message is sent. If this occurs, then the connection returns to the Idle state and all the information that the BGP endpoints have learned from their neighboring endpoint will be purged from the BGP routing table.

BGP Common Header

A common header precedes all BGP messages. The header shown in Figure 12.10 shows the following fields:

- Marker
- Length
- Type

We will briefly discuss those fields following Figure 12.10.

FIGURE 12.10   The BGP common header

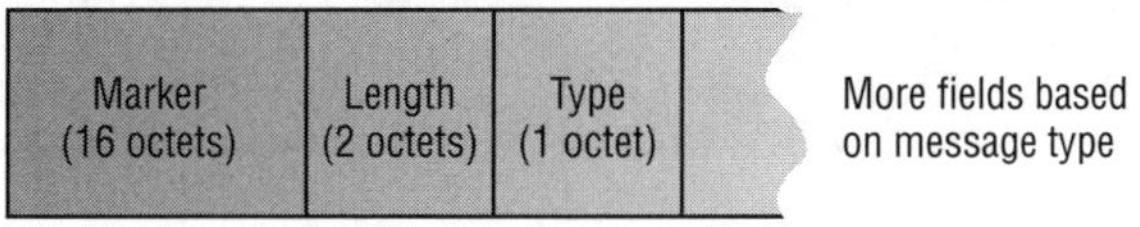

The Marker field is a field up to 2 bytes long. It is used for authentication and synchronization. The value of this field depends on the type of message being sent. The Length field indicates the size of the entire BGP message, including the header. The Type field indicates the type of message being sent. There are four possible values:

Type Value	Message Type
1	OPEN message
2	UPDATE message
3	NOTIFICATION message
4	KEEPALIVE message

Let's look at the different message types:

OPEN Message   This is the first message sent after a TCP session has been established between one or more peers. This message is used to identify the autonomous system that the router is a member of and to agree on protocol parameters and the protocol timers the session will use. Figure 12.11 shows the additional fields included in the BGP header for an OPEN message.

FIGURE 12.11   The additional fields added to the BGP common header for an OPEN message type

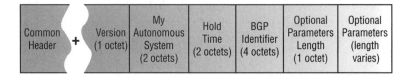

UPDATE Message   This type of message is the actual topology information sent between two BGP speakers. An UPDATE message can contain a new route, routes to be withdrawn, or both. However, only one new route can be advertised by an UPDATE message. The UPDATE message adds additional fields to the BGP common header, as shown in Figure 12.12.

FIGURE 12.12   The additional fields added to the BGP common header when the UPDATE message type is used

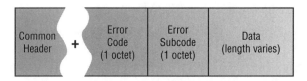

NOTIFICATION Message   If an error occurs during a BGP session, a BGP NOTIFICATION message is generated. As soon as the BGP speaker sends the NOTIFICATION message, it immediately terminates its BGP connection. This message can be used by the administrator to help troubleshoot why the connection was terminated.

There are two types of error codes in NOTIFICATION message fields to watch for. These are the error codes and the error subcodes (see Figure 12.3).

FIGURE 12.13   The NOTIFICATION message fields added to the BGP common header

KEEPALIVE Messages   BGP neighbors use a KEEPALIVE type message to confirm that the connection between the neighbors is still active. A BGP speaker sends a KEEPALIVE to each peer, usually at an interval of one-third of the agreed hold time, which is no more than once per second. If an UPDATE message is not sent during the established hold time, a KEEPALIVE message is sent in its place. A KEEPALIVE message consists of only a 19-byte header and can be turned off by setting the hold time to zero. The default keepalive time is 60 seconds on Cisco routers.

Now that we have discussed the various BGP message types, we'll discuss how to actually configure and implement each of these attributes. So that you do not have to continuously refer back to the earlier part of the chapter, we will provide a quick review of each attribute as we show how to configure it with a Cisco router.

Some attributes appear only in iBGP or in eBGP. For this book, we are going to state that iBGP and eBGP are the same protocol but just have differences in the peering points and the types of attributes. Remember where each is used. In iBGP, each peer communicates between speakers in the same autonomous system, and in eBGP, peers communicate between speakers in different autonomous systems.

Path attributes can be considered the metrics used by BGP routers that are passed in UPDATE messages to other BGP peers. The information in these messages can contain notifications of local routes, foreign routes, or route topology changes.

BGP Attributes

BGP *attributes* are the most powerful features of BGP. They are what allows BGP to be completely customizable. It is possible with attributes to solve a problem many different ways. For instance, you can influence the routing path taken using local preferences, multi-exit discriminators (MEDs), communities, or AS paths for a specific route or routes.

Each BGP route update that is sent to a BGP neighbor contains detailed information about the network. The information contained in an update about a destination is called the BGP attribute. In BGP, an attribute is either well known or optional, mandatory or discretionary, transitive or nontransitive.

The following sections describe a subset of the BGP attributes. These are the attributes that are most used when dealing with BGP:

Well-Known Mandatory

A well-known mandatory attribute is used by a totally compliant BGP implementation to propagate all the network's BGP neighbors. Well-known mandatory attributes must appear in all BGP update messages. Autonomous system path, next hop address, and origin are well-known mandatory attributes.

Autonomous System Path (AS Path)

AS_PATH (Type Code 2) is a well-known mandatory attribute. The AS_PATH attribute is composed of a variable-length series of autonomous system path segments. Each autonomous system path segment contains a path type, a length, and a value.

The AS_PATH's fields are modified only by eBGP speakers that advertise the route outside the local autonomous system. These eBGP speakers prepend their own autonomous system numbers to the end of the path vector in each of the fields. When a BGP speaker originates a route, it should include its own ASN in UPDATEs sent to other autonomous systems. The field is empty for an AS_PATH attribute advertised to iBGP speakers belonging to its own ASN. For this reason iBGP must avoid data loops by implementing a rule that specifies that each iBGP router must ignore any route learned from an iBGP peer.

The AS_PATH attribute makes BGP a path vector protocol. BGP messages carry the sequence of autonomous system numbers indicating the complete path a message has traversed. Thus, the AS path allows for loop detection, because BGP routers that receive a route that includes the local BGP router AS number will discard the route.

Next Hop Address

The NEXT_HOP (Type Code 3) attribute is a well-known mandatory attribute that indicates the IP address of the next hop destination router. The BGP speaker should never advertise the address of a peer as the NEXT_HOP of a route the current speaker is originating to that peer. NEXT_HOP_SELF configures an eBGP speaker to advertise routes to iBGP routers listing itself as the next hop rather than the BGP speaker that the route was learned from. The advertising eBGP speaker does not change the next hop of the route in its local routing table.

For eBGP, the next hop is the IP address of the eBGP neighbor that sends the updates. For iBGP, the next hop is the IP address of the eBGP peer that sent the routes to its AS. A BGP speaker can advertise any internal BGP router as the next hop as long as the IP address of the iBGP border router is on the same subnet as the local and remote BGP speakers. This means that one router can handle all the announcements on the same subnet.

Origin

The ORIGIN (Type Code 1) attribute is a well-known mandatory attribute used to tell the receiving BGP router the BGP type of the original source of the NLRI information. The ORIGIN type can be one of the following type codes:

IGP   If the route was learned from an IGP in the originating AS. This is achieved using a `network x.x.x.x` command under the BGP process. The route is indicated with an *i* in the router's BGP table.

EGP   If the route originated from the exterior gateway protocol. EGP learned routes will appear as *e* in the router's routing table.

Unknown Origin   If the origin of the route is unknown, the most common cause is due to routes being redistributed into BGP from another routing protocol. This route appears as *?* in the router's BGP table.

Well-Known Discretionary

A well-known discretionary attribute might be included in a route description, but it doesn't have to be. However, they must be understood, hence the term *well-known*. Local preference and atomic aggregate are well-known discretionary attributes.

Local Preference

The LOCAL_PREF (Type Code 5) attribute is a well-known discretionary attribute that can contain only a single autonomous system and can be used only with iBGP. Local preference is only applicable within an AS and to iBGP peers. In a multi-exit environment, local preference can be used to specify which path is used to exit the AS. A path with a higher local preference is preferred. The local preference is generally configured using route maps. The configured values for the local preference range from 0 to 4,294,967,295. Higher values are preferred over lower values. The default local preference is 100.

Atomic Aggregate

The ATOMIC_AGGREGATE (Type Code 6) is a well-known discretionary attribute that is used to indicate that route aggregation has occurred and the path information of the route may be incomplete. This is basically used as a flag to indicate that a prefix is or is not to be used. Therefore, the ATOMIC_AGGREGATE has a path length of 0.

Optional Transitive

An optional transitive attribute may not be recognized by some implementations of BGP but is not expected to be. These attributes are used in many private BGP-enabled networks. If an implementation of BGP does not recognize the optional transitive attribute of a message, it will mark the message as a partial message but still propagate the message to its neighbors. The aggregator and communities are optional transitive attributes.

Aggregator

The AGGREGATOR (Type Code 7) attribute is an optional transitive attribute with a length of 6 octets: 2 octets identify the ASN and 4 octets identify the IP address. This attribute identifies the autonomous system and router that performed the aggregation. This attribute is also transitive, so it will be forwarded by all BGP speakers to every peer.

Communities

The COMMUNITIES (Type Code 8) attribute is an optional transitive attribute that allows a given route to belong to one or more communities. *Communities* identify routes that share some common property. This attribute was included in BGP to simplify the configuration of complex BGP routing policies. Community attributes are optional, transitive, and variable in length. Current communities are 32 bits long, structured as two 16-bit fields. By convention, the first 16 bits are either 0 (zero), denoting a "well-known" community known to the Internet, or the ASN that "owns" the community value. The second 16 bits are meaningful either as defined by the owning autonomous system or, in the case of well-known communities, by the IETF. Communities perform the same function as route tagging in IGPs. In fact, route tags can be used by an IGP to carry community information between two nonconnected BGP speakers.

Optional Nontransitive

An optional nontransitive attribute may not be recognized by some BGP implementations. These attributes are used in many private BGP-enabled networks. Even if the implementation of BGP does recognize the optional nontransitive attribute of the message, it is not passed on. Multi-exit discriminator, originator ID, and cluster list are optional nontransitive.

Multi-Exit Discriminator (MED)

The MULTI_EXIT_DISCRIMINATOR (Type Code 4) is an optional nontransitive attribute that is used by BGP as an extensive route selection component. This component starts to work before the general route selection process begins, using a BGP attribute called multi-exit discriminator (MED), which was originally called the Inter-AS metric or the BGP metric. While the previous metrics tell the local autonomous system routers which path to select when leaving the autonomous system, MEDs tell the neighboring autonomous system which link to use to receive traffic. The lower the MED, the more preferred the path is.

The MED attribute influences how traffic is routed into an AS, and the local preference attribute influences how traffic is routed out of an AS.

Originator ID

Both the ORIGINATOR_ID (Type Code 9) and CLUSTER_LIST (Type Code 10, see next item) optional nontransitive attributes are used to support the route reflector feature used to scale iBGP meshes. The ORIGINATOR_ID is 4 octets long, and a CLUSTER_LIST attribute can vary in length in multiples of 4 octets. The ORIGINATOR_ID attribute is used to identify the router that originated a particular route into an iBGP mesh.

Cluster List

The CLUSTER_LIST attribute is used to detect updates that are looping inside the cluster. This way, if a route has already been advertised to a cluster, the advertisement message will be rejected.

Network Layer Reachability Information

The *Network Layer Reachability Information (NLRI)* field lists the prefixes that must be updated. One thing to understand is that all the prefixes listed in this field must match all the attributes listed in the Path Attributes field.

This means that more than one route can be withdrawn in the same UPDATE message, but if you want to add a route, it must be done in another UPDATE message. As opposed to the length of the overall Withdrawn Routes field, prefix lengths apply to specific routes. A length of 0 (zero) here implies the default route.

Each prefix in the NLRI field contains a 1-octet prefix length and a variable-length prefix, which does not necessarily have to contain an IP address.

Now we will discuss the route selection process that BGP uses to decide which routes are the best path to a destination network (prefix).

BGP Route Selection

BGP builds a BGP routing table (this is not the IP routing table but a separate table). You can use the `show ip bgp` command to look at the table. Before the BGP learned route is installed in the router's BGP routing table, the router goes through a route selection process. In the event that multiple routes exist to a destination network, BGP determines the route to install based on the attributes discussed in the previous section.

The following list includes BGP route selection criteria:

- If the route is learned via iBGP and synchronization is on, the route *must* be known by an IGP. If the route is not known by the IGP, the route will not be installed in the router's routing table. All eBGP learned routes are eligible to be installed in a router's routing table.

- The next hop address must be reachable from all iBGP routers; otherwise, the route will not be installed in the routing table.

- If multiple routes exist to an end destination, the highest weight is preferred (this is Cisco proprietary and is locally significant to a router).

- If multiple routes exist and have the same weight, prefer the route with the highest local preference. This can be only for routes learn via iBGP because local preference is valid *only* within an AS.

- If local preference is equal, prefer the route that was locally originated.

- If the route was not locally originated, prefer the route with the shortest AS path.

- If the AS path is the same, prefer the lowest origin code. The order of preference is IGP (i), then EGP (e), and then INCOMPLETE (?).

- If the origin code is still equal, prefer the lowest MED. Again, remember that the MED is sent by another AS peer.

- If the MEDs are equal, prefer eBGP learned routes over iBGP learned routes.

- Prefer the path with the lowest IGP metric to the BGP next hop.

- If the routes are learned the same, then prefer the route with the lowest BGP router ID.

- If the BGP router IDs are the same, prefer the lowest neighbor IP address.

The selection criteria is lengthy, but notice that in the first criteria, synchronization was mentioned. To understand the first and most important rule, it is extremely import that synchronization is understood. The second rule states that, for a route to get installed, the router must have a route to the next hop address that is specified in the BGP update. This was previously discussed at length in the section "Solving Reachability to the Next Hop Address" earlier in this chapter.

Now let's discuss how to configure the BGP attributes on a Cisco router.

Configuring BGP Attributes

Now that you have a good understanding of the workings of BGP, including the various message types and categories of attributes, we'll discuss how to configure and implement them on a Cisco router.

Implementing the Weight Attribute

The weight attribute is a Cisco-proprietary attribute. The weight is assigned locally to the router and will make sense only to that specific router. This attribute is not propagated to either iBGP or eBGP peers. A weight can be a number from 0 to 65535. Paths that the router originates have a weight of 32768 by default, and other paths have a weight of 0 (zero).

Routes with a higher weight are preferred when multiple routes exist to the same destination. In Figure 12.14, router R2 is configured to set the weight attribute for all routers learned via R4 to 1000 and for all routes learned from R3 to be 2000. This will make R3 the preferred path for all routes from AS 100.

FIGURE 12.14   Weight attribute

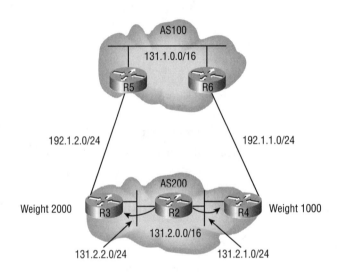

Router R2 Configuration

The following is the router configuration on router R2. The neighbor x.x.x.x weight 1000 command does not specify either in | out because the weight is a local attribute and is applied only to routes learned from a peer. Likewise, it will only influence the routes installed in router R2:

`router BGP 200`	Enable BGP AS 200
`  neighbor 131.2.1.4 remote-as 200`	Define iBGP neighbor to router R4
`  neighbor 131.2.1.4 weight 1000`	Set the weight for all routes learned from router R4 to 1000
`  neighbor 131.2.2.3 remote-as 200`	Define iBGP neighbor to router R3
`  neighbor 131.2.2.3 weight 2000`	Set the weight for all routes learned from router R3 to 2000

Here is the output on router R2 after the neighbor has been configured with a weight command:

```
   Network              Next Hop             Metric LocPrf Weight Path
*>i131.1.0.0/24         131.2.2.3                    100    2000 100 i
* i                     131.2.1.4            0       100    1000 100 i
*> 131.2.1.0/24         0.0.0.0              0              32768 i
*> 131.2.2.0/24         0.0.0.0              0              32768 I
```

The route from router R3 has a weight of 2000 and is the installed route because it has a higher weight than router R4. The weight for locally originated routes is by default set to 32768. It is also possible to configure a certain weight for a specific route through the use of a route map, which will be discussed in Chapter 17, "Route Filtering Capabilities."

Implementing Local Preference

Local preference is a BGP attribute associated with iBGP connections. This attribute is not sent from eBGP peers to other eBGP peers. Therefore, local preference is used to influence the path taken from within one AS to an external destination. Local preference is also only of use when there are multiple paths to an external destination because it allows one path to be preferred over another path. As stated earlier, Local Preference is an iBGP attribute used to influence the path taken to an external network. iBGP peering must be configured in a full mesh; this is the iBGP split-horizon rule. Therefore, the local preference attribute must be configured on the iBGP router that originated the route update. The route with the highest local preference is preferred. The default value is 100. As shown in Figure 12.15, two ASs are connected and multiple paths exist between AS 100 and AS 200.

FIGURE 12.15   Local preference attribute

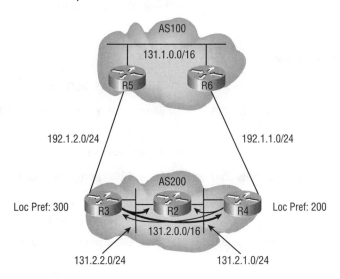

Let's look at the configuration commands required to configure the local preference for AS 200 such that the BGP advertised route for AS 100 is preferred via router R3. Notice that in Figure 12.15, we have implemented a configuration that makes the link via R3 always preferred.

Router R3 Configuration

Here is the configuration for router R3:

router BGP 200	Enable BGP AS 200
neighbor 131.2.2.2 remote-as 200	Define iBGP peer to router R2
neighbor 131.2.2.2 next-hop-self	Send all route update with the next-hop-address set to R3's IP address
neighbor 131.2.1.4 remote-as 200	Define iBGP peer to router R4
neighbor 131.2.1.4 next-hop-self	Send all route update with the next-hop-address set to R3's IP address
neighbor 192.1.2.5 remote-as 100	Define eBGP peer to router R5 in AS 100, the remote AS is different from the AS that the router is participating in which automatically make this an eBGP connection
no synchronization	This command is required to synchronize the iBGP learned routes
bgp default local-preference 300	Changes the default Local Preference value from 100 to 300 for all routes sent to iBGP neighbors

Router R4 Configuration

Here is router R4's configuration:

router BGP 200	Enable BGP AS 200
neighbor 131.2.1.2 remote-as 200	Define iBGP peer to router R2
neighbor 131.2.1.2 next-hop-self	Send all route update with the next-hop-address set to R4's IP address
neighbor 131.2.2.3 remote-as 200	Define iBGP peer to router R3
neighbor 131.2.2.3 next-hop-self	Send all route update with the next-hop-address set to R4's IP address
neighbor 192.1.1.6 remote-as 100	Define eBGP peer to router R6 in AS 100

```
no synchronization              This command is required to synchronize
                                the iBGP learned routes

bgp default local-preference 200  Changes the default Local Preference
                                value from 100 to 200 for all routes
                                sent to iBGP neighbors
```

The following output is from a **show ip route** command on router R2 before the local preference has been manipulated. The path preferred by router R2 for 131.1.0.0/16 is via router R4:

```
     17.32.16.0.0/24 is subnetted, 1 subnets
C        172.16.32.0 is directly connected, Serial0
     131.2.0.0/24 is subnetted, 3 subnets
C        131.2.2.0 is directly connected, FastEthernet0.2
C        131.2.1.0 is directly connected, FastEthernet0.1
     131.1.0.0/24 is subnetted, 3 subnets
B        131.1.0.0 [200/0] via 131.2.1.4, 00:00:25
```

Here is the output from a **show ip bgp** command on router R2. This shows that R2 has learned two routes, one from each iBGP neighbor. Each route has the default local preference set to 100, and each shows the same path AS 100:

```
   Network          Next Hop          Metric LocPrf Weight Path
*>i131.1.0.0/24     131.2.1.4              0    100      0 100 i
* i                 131.2.2.3                   100      0 100 i
* i131.2.0.0        131.2.1.4              0    100      0 i
* i                 131.2.2.3              0    100      0 i
*>                  0.0.0.0                0          32768 i
*> 131.2.1.0/24     0.0.0.0                0          32768 i
*> 131.2.2.0/24     0.0.0.0                0          32768 i
```

The deciding criteria for installing the route via router R4 is the BGP router ID. The route selection rule states that the router with the lowest router ID will be selected. The output that follows is from a **show ip bgp neighbor** command. This output confirms that router R4 has the lowest BGP router ID; therefore, this route is installed in router R2's routing table. Remember, when deciding the lowest IP address, the router will first compare the first byte of the IP addresses. If they are the same, it will compare the second byte of the IP addresses, and so on.:

```
BGP neighbor is 131.2.1.4,  remote AS 200, internal link
 Index 1, Offset 0, Mask 0x2
  BGP version 4, remote router ID 192.1.1.4
  BGP state = Established, table version = 7, up for 00:16:40
```

```
Last read 00:00:41, hold time is 180, keepalive interval is 60 seconds

BGP neighbor is 131.2.2.3,  remote AS 200, internal link
 Index 2, Offset 0, Mask 0x4
  BGP version 4, remote router ID 192.1.2.3
  BGP state = Established, table version = 7, up for 00:19:43
  Last read 00:00:43, hold time is 180, keepalive interval is 60 seconds
```

The default local preference on a router can be changed using the `bgp default local-preference` command. This will change the default local preference that is sent to all iBGP neighbors for all eBGP learned routes. Here is the output from router R2 after the default local preference has been changed:

```
    Network          Next Hop          Metric LocPrf Weight Path
* i131.1.0.0/24      131.1.1.4              0    200      0 100 i
*>i                  131.1.2.3                   300      0 100 i
*> 131.2.0.0         0.0.0.0                0          32768 i
* i                  131.2.1.4              0    200      0 i
* i                  131.2.2.3              0    300      0 i
*> 131.2.1.0/24      0.0.0.0                0          32768 i
*> 131.2.2.0/24      0.0.0.0                0          32768 i
```

Notice that R4 will also prefer the route for 132.2.2.0/24 via R3 due to the higher local preference advertised by R3.

The second option that can be used to change the Local Preference is a route map. This is a much more scalable and flexible solution because route maps can be used to change the local preference on specific routes. Route maps, distribute lists, filter lists, prefix lists, and so on will be discussed in Chapter 17.

Configuring Multi-Exit Discriminator (MED)

In an eBGP multipath environment, multi-exit discriminators (MEDs) are configured on the originating eBGP peers and sent to the adjacent eBGP peers. MEDs are used to influence the path that the adjacent AS uses to route traffic back to the originating AS.

The lowest MED is preferred, and the default MED value that is set on all eBGP updates is 0. Because the default MED value is 0, unmanipulated routes will always be preferred over manipulated routes. Therefore, when configuring MEDs, it is recommended that the MEDs are changed on all eBGP peer connections, and all routes should have their MEDs changed from the default.

In route selection, it is important to understand that the local preference is preferred over MEDs. Therefore, if the local preference is set, MEDs will not be used for route selection. Figure 12.16 shows three ASs connected together. MEDs are configured on the eBGP speakers of AS 100 to influence the route selection of routes in AS 200. MEDs will be sent by the eBGP peers in AS 200 to all of its iBGP peers in AS 200. The MED attribute is a nontransitive attribute; therefore, the MEDs that are received by routers R3 and R4 will not be sent to other eBGP neighbors within AS 300. The

MEDs that are sent by the eBGP speakers of AS 100 will make the route via R6 the more preferred route. The following sections include the configurations needed to achieve this.

FIGURE 12.16 Multi-exit discriminator attribute

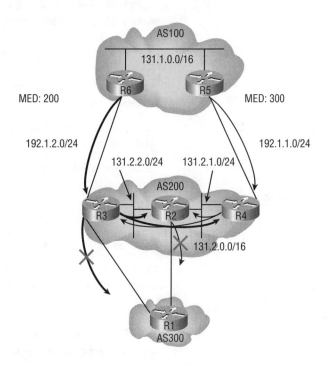

Router R5 Configuration

Here is the configuration for router R5:

router BGP 100	Enables BGP AS 100
no synchronization	This command is required to synchronize the iBGP learned routes
network 131.1.0.0 mask 255.255.0.0	
	Assigns network address space that will be announced to neighbors
neighbor 131.1.0.6 remote-as 100	Defines iBGP peer to router R6
neighbor 131.1.0.6 next-hop-self	Sends all route updates to R6 with the next-hop-address set to R5's IP address

neighbor 192.1.1.4 remote-as 200	Defines eBGP peer to router R5 in AS 100, the remote AS is different from the AS that the router is participating in which automatically makes this an eBGP connection
neighbor 192.1.1.4 route-map set-med out	Applies an outbound route-map called set-med to neighbor 192.1.1.4
route-map set-med permit 10	Creates a route-map called set-med and applies a sequence number of 10
set metric 300	Sets the BGP MED to 300 for all routes

Router R6 Configuration

Here is router R6's configuration:

router BGP 100	Enables BGP AS 200
no synchronization	This command is required to synchronize the iBGP learned routes
network 131.1.0.0 mask 255.255.0.0	Assigns Network address space that will be announced to neighbors
neighbor 131.1.0.5 remote-as 200	Defines iBGP peer to router R5
neighbor 131.1.0.5 next-hop-self	Sends all route update with the next-hop-address set to R6's IP address
neighbor 192.1.2.3 remote-as 100	Defines eBGP peer to router R3 in AS 100
neighbor 192.1.2.3 route-map set-med out	Applies an outbound route-map called set-med to neighbor 192.1.2.3
route-map set-med permit 10	Creates a route-map called set-med and applies a sequence number of 10
set metric 200	Sets the BGP MED value to 200 for all routes; metric is the key word used to set the MEDs under route-maps

The preceding configurations apply a simple outbound route map on each router. These route maps will simply set the MED on each router to send all routes to their specific eBGP neighbor with the configured metric (MED).

Here is the output of a `show ip bgp` command on router R4 before the MEDs are sent by the eBGP speakers in AS 100:

```
    Network          Next Hop          Metric LocPrf Weight Path
*  i131.1.0.0        131.2.2.3                100      0 100 i
*>                   192.1.1.5          0                 0 100 i
*  i131.2.0.0        131.2.2.3          0      100      0 i
*>                   0.0.0.0            0            32768 i
*  i                 131.2.1.2          0      100      0 i
*>i131.2.1.0/24      131.2.1.2          0      100      0 i
*>i131.2.2.0/24      131.2.1.2          0      100      0 I
```

The route to network 131.1.0.0/16 out of router R4 is the preferred route. The metric (MED) is also set to its default of 0. Here is the output on router R4 after the route maps have been applied on the eBGP speakers in AS 100:

```
    Network          Next Hop          Metric LocPrf Weight Path
*>i131.1.0.0         131.2.2.3          200    100      0 100 i
*                    192.1.1.5          300               0 100 i
*  i131.2.0.0        131.2.2.3          0      100      0 i
*>                   0.0.0.0            0            32768 i
*  i                 131.2.1.2          0      100      0 i
*>i131.2.1.0/24      131.2.1.2          0      100      0 i
*>i131.2.2.0/24      131.2.1.2          0      100      0 i
```

The preferred route out of router R4 is now via 131.2.2.3 (router R3) and the metrics are set on both routes. By default, MEDs are compared only for routes from neighbors within the same AS. To compare MEDs for routes from different ASs, the `bgp always-compare-meds` command must be configured under the BGP process.

Configuring AS Path Prepending

With the BGP route selection rules, if no BGP weight or local preference is configured, then the AS path is usually the first attribute that will influence the route selection. The route with the shortest AS path will be selected to be installed in the router's routing table. This path may not necessarily be the best or preferred path through the network, so a technique called *AS path prepending* is used to increase the AS path so that a more preferred path can be used. Another feature of AS path prepending is that the AS path is a transitive attribute, therefore every AS will pass the AS path attribute through the entire network.

Figure 12.17 shows three different ASs connected together. Routers in AS 200 will prefer a route for network 131.1.0.0/24 using the AS path attribute, and the installed route will be via router R4. Using AS path prepending, we will be able to change the path so that the preferred route from AS 200 to AS 100 will be the route via AS 400.

FIGURE 12.17 · AS path prepending

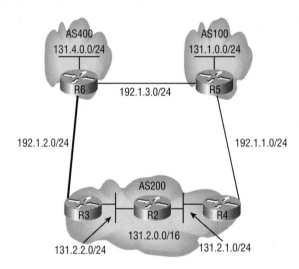

The output of a `show ip bgp` command on router R2 is shown here. Router R2 is learning only one BGP route, and this is the route from router R4. It is important that you understand why router R2 is not learning two BGP routes for AS 100:

Network	Next Hop	Metric	LocPrf	Weight	Path
*>i131.1.0.0/24	131.2.1.4	0	100	0	100 i
*> 131.2.1.0/24	0.0.0.0	0		32768	i
*> 131.2.2.0/24	0.0.0.0	0		32768	i
*>i131.4.0.0/24	131.2.2.3	0	100	0	400 i

From this output, it can be seen that router R2 is learning only one route for network 131.1.0.0/24, and this is from router R4. Router R2 does not receive two BGP routes (one from router R3, and one from router R4) because the installed route in R3 to get to 131.1.0.0/24 is via router R4. Therefore, because router R3's installed route in its routing table is an iBGP learned route via R4 (the shortest AS path), router R3 will not send an update to router R2 for network 131.1.0.0/24. Router R3 will send a route update only if the installed route in its routing table for network 131.1.0.0/24 is via router R6 (AS 400 100).

The issue that needs to be solved is to prepend the AS path attribute so that the received routes on both routers R3 and R4 will prefer the path via AS 400. Therefore, for the 131.1.0.0/24 network, the route that will be sent to router R2 is the route preferring router AS path 400 100.

Router R5 Configuration

The following is the router configuration on router R5 to change the AS path:

```
router bgp 100
 no synchronization
 network 131.1.0.0 mask 255.255.255.0
 neighbor 192.1.3.6 remote-as 400
 neighbor 192.1.1.4 remote-as 200
 neighbor 192.1.1.4 route-map as-add out

route-map as-add permit 10
 set as-path prepend 100 100
```

Here is the output from router R2 after the preceding changes have been implemented on R5:

Network	Next Hop	Metric	LocPrf	Weight	Path
*>i131.1.0.0/24	131.2.2.3		100	0	400 100 i
*> 131.2.1.0/24	0.0.0.0	0		32768	i
*> 131.2.2.0/24	0.0.0.0	0		32768	i
*>i131.4.0.0/24	131.2.2.3	0	100	0	400 i

This output shows that the path to network 131.1.0.0/24 is now preferred via AS 400 100.

The BGP route is being received from router R3, and this can be confirmed using the show ip bgp neigbbor 131.2.2.3 advertise command. Router R4 also sent an update to router R2 to withdraw the route via the prepend path (AS 100 100 100).

Router R2 will receive the route via R4 only if a problem exists with the path via router R3. In the event of a network failure on this path, R3 will send an update to withdraw the route, and router R4 will send a route update for the prepended path once this is the installed route in router R4's routing table. Here is the output when router R3's serial interface was shut down. Notice that the AS path for 131.1.0.0/24 has the prepended 100 100. Also, to get to 131.4.0.0/24, the path must go through R5, which also shows the prepended 100 100:

Network	Next Hop	Metric	LocPrf	Weight	Path
*>i131.1.0.0/24	131.2.1.4	0	100	0	100 100 100 i
*> 131.2.1.0/24	0.0.0.0	0		32768	i
*> 131.2.2.0/24	0.0.0.0	0		32768	i
*>i131.4.0.0/24	131.2.1.4		100	0	100 100 100 400 I

Let's now discuss what a community is and how it can be used within the BGP network environment.

Configuring and Using Communities

The community attribute provides a way of grouping destination networks into a community and applying routing decisions based on the community. A *community* is a group of network destinations that share some common attribute. Autonomous system administrators can define the communities to which a destination network belongs.

By default, all network destinations belong to the general Internet community. This is a "well-known" community. A number of well-known communities exist:

Internet   Advertise this route to the Internet community. All routers belong to it. This community does not need to be set.

No-export   Do not advertise this route to eBGP peers.

No-advertise   Do not advertise this route to any peer (internal or external).

Local-AS   Do not advertise this route outside of this AS (internal). This is extremely useful when implementing confederations.

A destination network can be assigned a well-known community or it can be assigned a custom community.

A community is a transitive attribute, therefore communities will be sent throughout the network. Communities can be used to influence routing decisions throughout the entire network. The exception to this rule is that Cisco routers will by default strip the community attribute if the router is not configured to send communities. To send communities, you must configure the command `neighbor x.x.x.x send community` on every neighbor to which the community attribute is to be sent out.

A community attribute is a 32-bit value. The format of the BGP community attribute is a value in the range from 1 to 4294967295 in a decimal format, or 0xFFFFFFFF in hexadecimal. To configure and display a community attribute in the aa:nn format, where the first part is the AS number and the second part is a 2-byte number, use the `ip bgp-community new-format` global configuration command.

Route maps can be used to set the community attributes. The route map set command has the following syntax: `set community community-number [additive]`. If you specify the `additive` keyword, the specified community value is added to the existing value of the community attribute. Otherwise, the specified community value replaces any community value that was previously set.

The following `set community` commands achieve the same outcome in respect to setting a community:

- `set community 30:20`
- `set community 0x1E0014`
- `set community 1966100`

Displaying Communities

To display communities in a router, use the `show ip bgp community aa:nn` command, where aa:nn is the community value. This can be used to see BGP routes and updates that match a specific community criteria.

Let's look at a description of some community types:

aa:nn	Community number
exact-match	Exact match of the communities
local-AS	Do not send outside local AS (well-known community)
no-advertise	Do not advertise to any peer (well-known community)
no-export	Do not export to next AS (well-known community)

Using Well-Known Communities

Now let's discuss two of the well-known communities (No-Export and Local-AS), as well as custom communities.

No-export Community

In Figure 12.18, the no-export community can be used in AS 100 to advertise 131.1.0.0/24 to AS 200 with the community attribute no-export. AS 200 will propagate the route throughout AS 200 but will not send this route to AS 400 or any other external AS.

FIGURE 12.18   No-export community

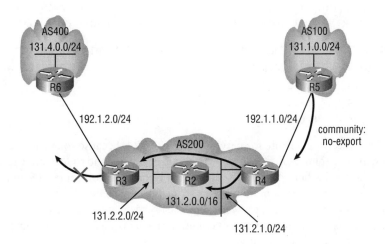

All routers must be configured to forward communities by configuring each neighbor with the `neighbor x.x.x.x send-community` command.

ROUTER R5 CONFIGURATION

The following is the router configuration on router R5 to set the no-export community:

```
router bgp 100

  network 131.1.0.0 mask 255.255.255.0

  neighbor 192.1.1.4 remote-as 200

  neighbor 192.1.1.4 send-community        Send communities to neighbor
                                           192.1.1.4

  neighbor 192.1.1.4 route-map set-community out

                                           Use route-map set-community on
                                           all outbound routes


route-map set-community permit 10          Creates a route-map and assigns it
                                           a sequence of 10

  set community no-export                  All routes will have the community
                                           attribute set to no-export
```

This shows the output from a `show ip bgp` command on router R6 before the `neighbor x.x.x.x send-community` command was configured on AS 200:

```
   Network          Next Hop           Metric LocPrf Weight Path
*> 131.1.0.0/24     192.1.2.3                        0 200 100 i
*> 131.2.1.0/24     192.1.2.3                        0 200 i
*> 131.2.2.0/24     192.1.2.3                        0 200 i
*> 131.4.0.0/24     0.0.0.0            0              32768 I
```

Router R6 is receiving a route for network 131.1.0.0/24, because router R3 has not been configured with a `neighbor x.x.x.x send-community` command to forward the community attribute. The `show ip bgp community no-export` command on router R6 will have no matching criteria because the community was striped out by router R4.

The following output is from a `show ip bgp community no-export` command on router R3 after AS 200 was configured to support communities. This shows that the route for network 131.1.0.0/24 matches this community:

```
BGP table version is 5, local router ID is 192.1.2.3
Status codes: s suppressed, d damped, h history, * valid, > best, i - internal
Origin codes: i - IGP, e - EGP, ? - incomplete

    Network         Next Hop          Metric LocPrf Weight Path
*>i131.1.0.0/24     131.2.1.4              0    100      0 100 i
```

And here again is the output on router R6 after the community support was added in AS 200 on both routers R3 and R4:

```
    Network          Next Hop            Metric LocPrf Weight Path
*> 131.2.1.0/24      192.1.2.3                            0 200 i
*> 131.2.2.0/24      192.1.2.3                            0 200 i
*> 131.4.0.0/24      0.0.0.0                0         32768 I
```

Network 131.1.0.0/24 is no longer being learned from AS 200.

Local-AS

In Figure 12.19, router R2 has been configured with a network 131.2.20.0/23. This network must be sent only to peers within AS 200. The well-known community local-AS will ensure that this route is sent to only routers in AS200, and the route will not be advertised by eBGP speakers to other ASs.

FIGURE 12.19   Local-AS community

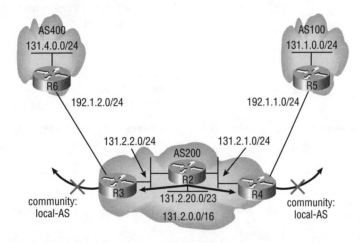

Router R2 Configuration

The following are the router configuration commands on router R2:

```
router bgp 200
 no synchronization
 network 131.2.1.0 mask 255.255.255.0
 network 131.2.2.0 mask 255.255.255.0
 network 131.2.20.0 mask 255.255.254.0    Network 13.2.20.0/23 will be
                                          advertised by router R2 to BGP
                                          neighbors
```

```
neighbor 131.2.1.4 remote-as 200
```

```
neighbor 131.2.1.4 send-community
```
Sends community attributes to router R4, must be configured to both iBGP peers

```
neighbor 131.2.1.4 route-map set-local-com out
```
Applies set-local-com route-map to all outbound routes

```
neighbor 131.2.2.3 remote-as 200
```

```
neighbor 131.2.2.3 send-community
```
Sends community attributes to router R3, must be configured on both iBGP peers

```
neighbor 131.2.2.3 route-map set-local-com out
```
Applies set-local-com route-map to all outbound routes

```
access-list 1 permit 131.2.20.0 0.0.1.255
```
Create access-list 1, allowing network 131.2.20.0/23 only, and denies all other routes

```
route-map set-local-com permit 10
```
Creates a route-map called set-local-com with a sequence of 10

```
 match ip address 1
```
Matches the contents of access-list 1

```
  set community local-AS
```
Sets the community to local-AS for all routes that match access-list 1

```
route-map set-local-com permit 20
```
There is an explicit deny at the end of a route-map, therefore without this command the only routes that will be sent are the routes that match. This is needed to send updates for networks 131.2.1.0/24 and 131.2.2.0/24

Here is the output on router R4 for a `show ip bgp community local-AS` command:

```
BGP table version is 15, local router ID is 192.1.1.4
Status codes: s suppressed, d damped, h history, * valid, > best, i - internal
Origin codes: i - IGP, e - EGP, ? - incomplete

   Network          Next Hop          Metric LocPrf Weight Path
*>i131.2.20.0/23    131.2.1.2              0    100      0 i
```

The route for network 131.2.20.0/23 has the well-known community local-AS applied, and neither router R3 nor R4 will forward this route to their respective eBGP neighbors. This can be confirmed using the `show ip bgp neighbor 192.1.1.5 advertise` command on router R4. This command shows the advertised networks to router R5, which is router R4's eBGP peer to AS 100. The output of this command is as follows:

```
   Network          Next Hop          Metric LocPrf Weight Path
*>i131.2.1.0/24     131.2.1.2              0    100      0 i
*>i131.2.2.0/24     131.2.1.2              0    100      0 i
*>i131.4.0.0/24     131.2.2.3              0    100      0 400 i
```

This output shows the networks that router R4 is advertising to router R5. Notice that network 131.2.20.0/23, which is part of the well-known community local-AS, is not being advertised to router R5.

Using Custom Communities

Custom communities can be set using route maps to group destination networks. But unlike with well-known communities, there is no predefined action. When using custom communities, there are two steps:

- Defining the community using a route map
- Defining an action for the community

In Figure 12.20, a community of 200:200 will be set for all routes originating from router R2. On router R5, this community will be used to change the local preference such that routes learned via R6 will be preferred. This will be accomplished by changing the local preference on R6 to 200. The following sections include the router configurations on router R2 and R5 to complete this.

FIGURE 12.20   Custom communities

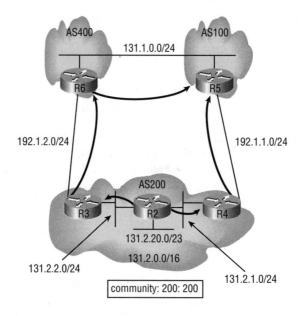

Router R2 Configuration

The following shows the commands required to set a custom community, which we have named 200:200 on router R2:

```
router bgp 200

no synchronization

network 131.2.1.0 mask 255.255.255.0        Advertise network 131.2.1.0/24

network 131.2.2.0 mask 255.255.255.0        Advertise network 131.2.2.0/24

network 131.2.20.0 mask 255.255.254.0       Advertise network 131.2.20.0/23

neighbor 131.2.1.4 remote-as 200

neighbor 131.2.1.4 send-community           Sends community to R4

neighbor 131.2.1.4 route-map set-local-cust out

                                            Applies set-local-cust route-map
                                            to all outbound routes

neighbor 131.2.2.3 remote-as 200

neighbor 131.2.2.3 send-community

neighbor 131.2.2.3 route-map set-local-cust out
```

	Applies set-local-cust route-map to all outbound routes
`route-map set-local-cust permit 10`	Creates route-map set-local-cust with sequence of 10
` set community 200:200`	Applies community 200:200 to all routes
`ip bgp new-format`	Displays the BGP custom communities in aa:nn format

Router R5 Configuration

The following shows the commands required to set the local preference on router R5, based on matching the community 200:200, which was set on router R2:

`router bgp 100`	
` network 131.1.0.0 mask 255.255.255.0`	Advertise network 131.1.1.0/24
` neighbor 131.1.0.6 remote-as 400`	
` neighbor 131.1.0.6 send-community`	Sends community to R6 in AS 400
` neighbor 131.1.0.6 route-map set-pref-200 in`	
	Applies set-pref-200 route-map to all inbound routes
` neighbor 192.1.1.4 remote-as 200`	
` neighbor 192.1.1.4 send-community`	Sends community to R4 in AS 200
` neighbor 192.1.1.4 route-map set-pref-150 in`	
	Applies set-pref-150 route-map to all inbound routes
` no auto-summary`	
`ip bgp-community new-format`	Displays the communities in new format
`ip community-list 1 permit 200:200`	Creates a community list 1 which matches community 200:200 only, this list is used in the route-maps below
`route-map set-pref-150 permit 10`	Creates a route-map set-pref-150 and assigns a sequence 10
` match community 1`	Matches community list 1 which is defined above

`set local-preference 150`	For all matched community set the local-preference to 150
`route-map set-pref-150 permit 20`	This creates a catch all for all other routes to be accepted, with out this routes from As 400 will not be accepted by R5
`route-map set-pref-200 permit 10`	Creates a route-map set-pref-200 and assigns a sequence 10
`match community 1`	
`set local-preference 200`	For all matched community set the local-preference to 200
`route-map set-pref-200 permit 20`	This creates a catch all for all other routes to be accepted, in this instance no route will match this, but it is good practice to configure a catch all with route-maps

This shows the output from a `show ip bgp community 200:200` command on router R5 before the route map was applied:

```
    Network           Next Hop         Metric LocPrf Weight Path
*>  131.2.1.0/24      192.1.1.4                         0 200 i
*                     131.1.0.6                         0 400 200 i
*>  131.2.2.0/24      192.1.1.4                         0 200 i
*                     131.1.0.6                         0 400 200 i
*>  131.2.20.0/23     192.1.1.4                         0 200 i
*                     131.1.0.6                         0 400 200 I
```

This output shows that router R5 receives routes via both AS 200 and AS 400 200. The preferred path is via AS 200 (192.1.1.4) because it is the shortest AS path, which in this case is the deciding factor in the route selection.

The following output is from a `show ip bgp community 200:200` command after the route maps have been applied to the inbound neighbors:

```
    Network           Next Hop         Metric LocPrf Weight Path
*   131.2.1.0/24      192.1.1.4               150     0 200 i
*>                    131.1.0.6               200     0 400 200 i
```

```
*   131.2.2.0/24      192.1.1.4                    150        0 200 i
*>                    131.1.0.6                    200        0 400 200 i
*   131.2.20.0/23     192.1.1.4                    150        0 200 i
*>                    131.1.0.6                    200        0 400 200 I
```

The preferred route, because of local preference, to get to the networks in AS 200 is now via AS 400 (131.1.0.6).

Communities are an extremely powerful tool that can be used to customize BGP routing. The examples we discussed are very simple, but we used them primarily to explain the different uses of the various communities and to try to give you a clear understanding of the operation of communities. Now we will shift gears a little and discuss regular expressions and how they can be used in conjunction with AS path access lists.

Using BGP Regular Expressions

The sending and receiving of BGP updates can be controlled by using a number of different filtering methods. BGP updates can be filtered based on route information, on path information, or on communities.

A regular expression is a pattern used to match against an input string. You specify the pattern that a string must match when you compose a regular expression. Matching a string to the specified pattern is called *pattern matching*. In the case of BGP, you are specifying a string that consists of path information that an input should match. Certain characters have special meaning when used in regular expressions. The following is a list of the regular expression special characters:

.	Match any character, including white space.
*	Match zero or more sequences of the pattern.
+	Match one or more sequences of the pattern.
?	Matches zero or one occurrence of the pattern.
_	Match the following.
[ ]	Match a single value in range.
-	Separate the endpoints of a range.

To match a regular expression pattern against the beginning or the end of the input string, the regular expression uses the concept of an anchor. You "anchor" regular expressions to a portion of the input string using the special characters listed here:

^	Begins with
$	Ends with

The following are examples of using the regular expression to create pattern matches:

_300_	Match any routes that pass via AS 300.
_300$	Match any routes that originated in AS 300.
^300_	Match only routes received via AS 300.
^300$	Match only routes that originated from AS 300 and did not pass through any other AS.
^$	Match all routes originating in your own local AS.
.*	Match all routes.

Configuring Regular Expressions

Regular expressions are configured using an AS path access list to specify matching criteria. A route map or filter list is then created and applied to the BGP peer. The route map or filter list uses the AS path access list to identify matching criteria. (Route maps, distribute lists, filter lists, prefix lists, and so on will be discussed in Chapter 17.)

In Figure 12.21, router R4 must be configured to receive only the routes originated from AS 100 and that have not passed through any other AS. Therefore, routes from AS 400 must be blocked.

FIGURE 12.21 Regular expressions

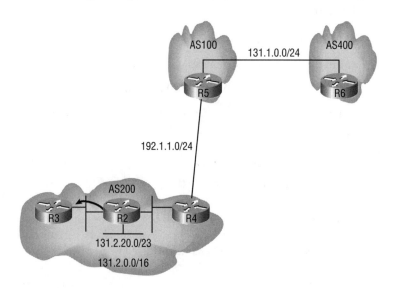

Router R4 Configuration

In this example, we will utilize a filter list. The following are the configuration commands in router R4 to achieve this:

```
router bgp 200
```

```
 neighbor 192.1.1.5 remote-as 100
```

`neighbor 192.1.1.5 filter-list 1 in`	Applies an inbound filter-list 1, which references as-path access-list 1. All routes from this neighbor will be passed through this AS-path access-list and only routes that match will be installed in the BGP route table
`ip as-path access-list 1 permit ^100$`	This creates an AS-path access-list 1. This list permits all routes originating from AS100 ONLY

This configuration ensures that router R4 will accept only routes originated from AS 100 that are sent from router R5.

Here is the output from a `show ip bgp regexp _100_` command entered on router R4:

```
   Network          Next Hop          Metric LocPrf Weight Path
*> 131.1.0.0/24     192.1.1.5             0           0 100 I
```

This output shows all routes in router R4 that match the regular expression for any routes that pass via AS 100. Once the filter list is applied, the only routes that will match the criteria are the routes originating from AS 100.

Now we can move on to the topic of iBGP scalability. By iBGP scalability, we mean the various methods of dealing with the full-mesh iBGP requirement, especially how to configure and implement many iBGP neighbors.

iBGP Scalability

iBGP has a significant scaling issue in large networks because a full mesh must be configured. In an iBGP network with 100 iBGP peers, a classic iBGP implementation would require that each iBGP neighbor have 99 configured neighbors, which is a total of 4950 configured peers across the network—$(100 \times 99) \div 2 = 4950$. The maintenance and configuration of this network can become unmanageable. Some scaling techniques exist to help scale iBGP in large networks:

- Confederations
- Route reflectors
- Peer groups

The third technique—peer groups—really does not reduce the number of required configured peers, but it will help reduce the amount of required configuration commands when multiple peer groups share the same configuration parameters.

Confederations

Confederations reduce the number of peers within the AS by dividing the network into multiple sub-ASs. Each sub-AS is fully meshed and iBGP is run among its peers, just as in a standard iBGP implementation. To connect the sub-ASs in the confederation, an eBGP connection is configured between them.

Even though the sub-ASs have eBGP peers to other sub-ASs within the confederation, these eBGP peers exchange routing updates as if they were using iBGP peers; the next hop, MED, communities, and local preference information is preserved in the updates as it would be in any iBGP update. Any confederation eBGP speaker can be configured with the `neighbor x.x.x.x next-hop-self` command to send updates to iBGP peers in the same AS to overcome next hop reachability, as is the case in a standard implementation. To the outside world, the confederation looks like a single AS. So all routes that are sent to an external AS will not see any of the confederation AS path information.

Building a confederation requires that each eBGP speaker in the confederation has the `bgp confederation identifier 100` command (AS 100 is the actual AS that the confederation belongs to in this example). These eBGP routers must also have a `bgp confederation peers 65100 65200` command that specifies all other sub-ASs that are part of the confederation. This is how the router identifies real eBGP connections as opposed to other confederation sub-ASs.

You only need to configure the AS numbers of the sub-ASs that an iBGP peer directly connects to. You don't need to configure all sub-ASs within the confederation.

When configuring a confederation, the issues associated with synchronization and next hop address reachability are still valid issues that need to be addressed. Figure 12.22 shows a confederation configuration for AS 100. Three sub-ASs make up the confederation. The confederation has two eBGP connections to AS 222. No IGP is installed in the confederation AS, so each router in the confederation is advertising the connected networks. This is needed to resolve next hop address reachability. Alternatively, an IGP such as OSPF can be used to provide next hop address reachability for the entire confederation.

FIGURE 12.22   Confederations

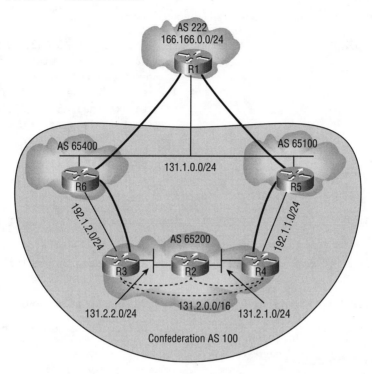

The following sections include the router configuration commands for all routers shown in the network in Figure 12.22.

Router R1 Configuration

The following are the router configuration commands on router R1:

`router bgp 222`	Enable BGP routing for AS 222 on router R1
`network 166.166.0.0 mask 255.255.255.0`	Advertise network 166.166.0.0/24 to BGP
`neighbor 131.1.0.5 remote-as 100`	Configure an eBGP neighbor to AS 100, this is the real AS of the confederation
`neighbor 131.1.0.6 remote-as 100`	Configure an eBGP neighbor to AS 100, this is the real AS of the confederation
`no auto-summary`	

Router R2 Configuration

The following are the router configuration commands on router R2:

`router bgp 65200`	Enables BGP AS 65200 on router R2, because router R2 has no eBGP connection to either other sub-AS in the confederation, or to external AS's. R2 believes that it is part of AS 65200
`no synchronization`	Router R2 needs synchronization turned off to allow iBGP learned routes to be installed in its routing table
`network 131.2.1.0 mask 255.255.255.0`	Advertise networks 131.2.1.0/24 to BGP
`network 131.2.2.0 mask 255.255.255.0`	Advertise networks 131.2.2.0/24 to BGP
`neighbor 131.2.1.4 remote-as 65200`	Define R4 as an iBGP neighbor
`neighbor 131.2.2.3 remote-as 65200`	Define R4 as an iBGP neighbor

Router R3 Configuration

The following are the router configuration commands on router R3:

`router bgp 65200`	Enables BGP routing for AS 65200
`no synchronization`	Router R3 needs synchronization turned of to allow iBGP learned routes to be installed in its routing table
`no auto-summary`	Turns classful summarization off
`bgp confederation identifier 100`	This must be configured on each router that has an eBGP connection to either a sub-AS in the confederation or to an external AS. This command identifies the real BGP AS that will be announced to any external eBGP connections

bgp confederation peers 65100 65400	Identifies all other sub-ASs that are participating in the confederation
network 131.2.2.0 mask 255.255.255.0	Advertises network 131.2.2.0/24 to BGP
network 192.1.2.0	Advertises network 191.1.2.0/24 to BGP
neighbor 131.2.1.4 remote-as 65200	Defines router R4 as an iBGP neighbor
neighbor 131.2.2.2 remote-as 65200	Defines router R2 as an iBGP neighbor
neighbor 192.1.2.6 remote-as 65400	Defines router R6 as an eBGP neighbor in AS 65400, which is part of the confederation
no auto-summary	Turns classful summarization off

Router R4 Configuration

The following are the router configuration commands on router R4:

router bgp 65200	Enables BGP routing for AS 65200
no synchronization	Router R4 needs synchronization turned off to allow iBGP learned routes to be installed in its routing table
bgp confederation identifier 100	This command identifies the real BGP AS number that will be announced to any external BGP connections
bgp confederation peers 65100 65400	Identifies all other sub-ASs that are participating in the confederation
network 131.2.1.0 mask 255.255.255.0	Advertises network 131.2.1.0/24 to BGP
network 192.1.1.0	Advertises network 191.1.1.0/24 to BGP
neighbor 131.2.1.2 remote-as 65200	Defines router R2 as an iBGP neighbor
neighbor 131.2.2.3 remote-as 65200	Defines router R3 as an iBGP neighbor
neighbor 192.1.1.5 remote-as 65100	Defines router R5 as an eBGP neighbor in AS 65100. AS 65100 is part of the confederation
no auto-summary	Turns classful summarization off

Router R5 Configuration

The following are the router configuration commands on router R5:

```
router bgp 65100
```

`bgp confederation identifier 100`	This command identifies the real BGP AS number that will be announced to AS 222
`bgp confederation peers 65200 65400`	Identifies all other sub-ASs that are participating in the confederation
`network 131.1.0.0 mask 255.255.255.0`	Advertises network 131.1.0.0/24 to BGP
`network 192.1.1.0`	Advertises network 192.1.1.0/24 to BGP
`neighbor 131.1.0.1 remote-as 222`	Defines an eBGP peer to AS 222, this AS is not part of the confederation
`neighbor 131.1.0.6 remote-as 65400`	Defines R6 as a eBGP confederation peer
`neighbor 192.1.1.4 remote-as 65200`	Defines R4 as a eBGP confederation peer
`no auto-summary`	Turns classful summarization off

Router R6 Configuration

The following are the router configuration commands on router R6:

```
router bgp 65400
```

`bgp confederation identifier 100`	This command identifies the real BGP AS number that will be announced to AS 222
`bgp confederation peers 65100 65200`	Identifies all other sub-ASs that are participating in the confederation
`network 131.1.0.0 mask 255.255.255.0`	Advertises network 131.1.0.0/24 to BGP
`network 192.1.2.0`	Advertises network 192.1.2.0/24 to BGP
`neighbor 131.1.0.1 remote-as 222`	Defines an eBGP peer to AS 222, this AS is not part of the confederation
`neighbor 131.1.0.5 remote-as 65100`	Defines R5 as a eBGP confederation peer

```
neighbor 192.1.2.3 remote-as 65200        Defines R3 as a eBGP
                                          confederation peer

no auto-summary                           Turns classful
                                          summarization off
```

The following output is from a show ip bgp command on router R2. The AS path contains the path required to get through the confederation AS. To get to the network 166.166.0.0/24, the path exists via confederation AS 65100 and AS 65400. Notice that the next hop addresses for network 131.1.0.0/24 are that of the originating routers (R5 and R6). For network 166.166.0.0/24, the next hop address is that of R1 (131.1.0.1). With confederation eBGP neighbors, the next hop address does not change, so routers R5 and R6 will not change the next hop address that they send to the confederation eBGP peers:

```
   Network              Next Hop        Metric LocPrf Weight Path
*  i131.1.0.0/24        192.1.1.5            0   100      0 (65100) i
*>i                     192.1.2.6            0   100      0 (65400) i
*> 131.2.1.0/24         0.0.0.0              0          32768 i
*  i131.2.2.0/24        131.2.2.3            0   100      0 i
*>                      0.0.0.0              0          32768 i
*  i166.166.0.0/24      131.1.0.1            0   100      0 (65400) 222 i
*>i                     131.1.0.1            0   100      0 (65100) 222 i
*>i192.1.1.0            131.1.0.5            0   100      0 (65400 65100) i
*  i                    192.1.1.5            0   100      0 (65100) i
*>i192.1.2.0            131.1.0.6            0   100      0 (65100 65400) i
*  i                    131.2.2.3            0   100      0 i
```

Here is the output from a show ip bgp command on router R1 (AS 222). All routes that are learned appear from AS 100, with no AS path information to indicate that AS 100 is configured as a BGP confederation:

```
   Network              Next Hop        Metric LocPrf Weight Path
*  131.1.0.0/24         131.1.0.6            0          0 100 i
*>                      131.1.0.5            0          0 100 i
*  131.2.1.0/24         131.1.0.6                       0 100 i
*>                      131.1.0.6                       0 100 i
*  131.2.2.0/24         131.1.0.6                       0 100 i
*>                      131.1.0.6                       0 100 i
*> 166.166.0.0/24       0.0.0.0              0      32768 i
*  192.1.1.0            131.1.0.5                       0 100 i
*>                      131.1.0.5            0          0 100 i
*  192.1.2.0            131.1.0.6            0          0 100 i
*>                      131.1.0.6                       0 100 I
```

Route Reflectors

Another solution for the scalability issue of iBGP peering within an autonomous system is using route reflectors (RRs). An iBGP speaker will not advertise a route learned via another iBGP speaker to a third iBGP speaker. This is to avoid loops in the network. By relaxing this rule and by providing additional control, you can allow a router to reflect iBGP learned routes to other iBGP speakers. The router that reflects the routes is called a route reflector.

 Route reflectors reduce the number of BGP neighbor peering relationships in an autonomous system by maintaining a single central update source for updates to their route reflector clients.

Using route reflectors will reduce the number of iBGP peers within an AS. To configure a router as a route reflector, the command `neighbor x.x.x.x route-reflector-client` must be configured for every RR client. The combination of the RR and its clients is called a cluster. When route reflectors are used, clients should only peer to RRs in their cluster and should not peer to iBGP speakers outside their cluster. Usually, a cluster of clients will have a single RR. In this case, the cluster will be identified by the router ID of the RR. To increase redundancy, a cluster might have more than one RR. All RRs in the same cluster must be configured with a common 4-byte cluster ID so that an RR can recognize updates from RRs in the same cluster. Configure the command `bgp cluster-id` on all RRs in the same cluster.

In an AS with multiple RR clusters, the RRs must be configured as an iBGP full mesh just like a standard iBGP implementation. A cluster list is a sequence of cluster IDs that the route has passed through. When a RR reflects a route from its clients to nonclients (BGP routers not participating in an RR cluster) outside of the cluster, it will append the local cluster ID to the cluster list. If this update has an empty cluster list, the RR will create one. Using this attribute, an RR can identify whether the routing information is looped back to the same cluster due to poor configuration. If the local cluster ID is found in the cluster list, the advertisement will be ignored.

 Nonclient refers to any iBGP peer that is not participating in the route reflector cluster as a client.

Because the next hop of reflected routes should not be changed, the `neighbor next-hop-self` command only affects the next hop of eBGP learned routes when used with route reflectors. Route reflectors do not solve the issue of synchronization or next hop address reachability. RRs will forward all BGP attributes such as local preference, MED, AS path, and communities as any other iBGP speaker would. Figure 12.23 shows a conceptual implementation of route reflectors.

FIGURE 12.23   Complex route reflector design

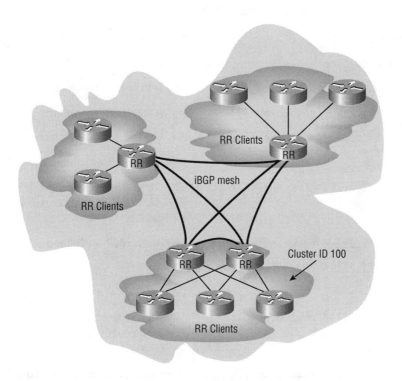

Figure 12.24 shows a simple route reflector implementation. R3 is configured as an RR for router R2 and R4.

FIGURE 12.24   Simple route reflector design

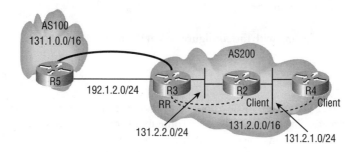

Router R3 Configuration

Here is the router configuration for router R3:

Router bgp 200	Enables BGP routing for AS 200
no synchronization	
network 131.2.2.0 mask 255.255.255.0	Advertises network 131.2.2.0/24
neighbor 131.2.2.2 remote-as 200	Defines iBGP neighbor
neighbor 131.2.2.2 route-reflector client	
	Defines iBGP neighbor as a RR client
neighbor 131.2.2.2 next-hop-self	Sets the advertised Next-Hop-Address for all routes sent to this neighbor as itself
neighbor 131.2.1.4 remote-as 200	Defines iBGP neighbor
neighbor 131.2.1.4 route-reflector client	
	Defines iBGP neighbor as a RR client
neighbor 131.2.1.4 next-hop-self	Sets the advertised Next-Hop-Address for all routes sent to this neighbor as itself
neighbor 192.1.2.5 remote-as 100	Defines eBGP neighbor to AS 100
no auto-summary	Turns classful summarization off

 If you have more than one route reflector, do not forget to peer route reflectors with one another.

A third method of dealing with the configuration of the many iBGP neighbors is through peer groups.

Peer Groups

A BGP *peer group* is a group of BGP neighbors that share the same update policies. A peer group is like a peer template. The template contains route maps, distribute lists, filter lists, and other common configuration options. Instead of defining the same policies for each individual neighbor, you define a peer group name and assign policies to the peer group. Members of a peer group inherit all of the configuration options of the peer group. The following are two sample peer-group configurations we have named them Internal-Peer and External-Peer. First, let's look at the Internal-Peer peer-group configuration:

```
router bgp 300
  neighbor Internal-Peer peer-group          Creates a peer group called
                                             Internal-Peer

  neighbor Internal-Peer remote-as 300       Peer group members are
                                             configured as iBGP peers

  neighbor Internal-Peer route-map INTERNAL out
                                             Assigns an outbound route-map
                                             INTERNAL to all peer members

  neighbor Internal-Peer next-hop-self       Sets the Next-Hop-Address for
                                             all peer members

  neighbor 131.2.1.2 peer-group Internal-Peer   Makes this neighbor a member of
                                             the Internal-Peer peer group

  neighbor 131.2.1.3 peer-group Internal-Peer   Makes this neighbor a member of
                                             the Internal-Peer peer group

  neighbor 131.2.2.2 peer-group Internal-Peer   Makes this neighbor a member of
                                             the Internal-Peer peer group
```

And the following is the External-Peer peer-group configuration:

```
router bgp 200
  neighbor External-Peer peer-group          Creates a peer group called
                                             External-Peer

  neighbor External-Peer route-map set-med out
                                             Assigns an outbound route-map
                                             set-med to all peer members

  neighbor External-Peer route-map loc-pref in
                                             Assigns an inbound route-map
                                             loc-pref to all peer members

  neighbor External-Peer next-hop-self       Sets the Next-Hop-Address for
                                             all peer members

  neighbor 172.2.1.2 remote-as 300           Define eBGP neighbor to AS 300
```

neighbor 172.2.1.2 peer-group External-Peer	Make this neighbor a member of External-Peer peer group
neighbor 166.22.1.3 remote-as 400	Define eBGP neighbor to AS 400
neighbor 166.22.1.3 peer-group External-Peer	Make this neighbor a member of External-Peer peer group
neighbor 140.44.2.2 remote-as 500	Define eBGP neighbor to AS 500
neighbor 140.44.2.2 peer-group External-Peer	Make this neighbor a member of External-Peer peer group

You can clear the BGP connection of a peer on any BGP router using the clear ip bgp peer-group peer-group-name command in privilege mode. Using this command is not recommended because it can take a great deal of time for a large network to renew all its BGP sessions after they are cleared.

That solves the problem of how to mange all those neighbors. Is there anything that can be implemented to assist with making the interconnection between routers more stable? That is a good question, and we have an answer. It is called route dampening.

Route Dampening

Route dampening is a BGP mechanism that minimizes the instability caused by route flapping. The following terms are used to describe route flap dampening:

Penalty   The penalty is a numeric value that is assigned to a route when it flaps.

Half-life time   This is a configurable numeric value that describes the time required to reduce the penalty by one half. The default value is 15 minutes.

Reuse limit   If the penalty for a flapping route falls below this value, a suppressed route that is up will no longer be suppressed. The range is from 1 to 20000. The default is 750.

Suppressed   A route is suppressed when the penalty reaches this limit. The range is 1 to 20000. The default is 2000.

Max-suppress-time   This is the maximum time a route can be suppressed. The range is from 1 to 20000. The default is four times the half life, which is 60 minutes. If the penalty is greater than the suppress limit, the route is suppressed.

History entry   A history entry is an entry that is used to store flap information about a route that is down.

A route that is flapping receives a penalty of 1000 for each flap. When the accumulated penalty reaches a configurable limit (default = 2000), BGP will suppress the advertisement of the route even if the route is up. The penalty is decremented by the half-life time (default 15 minutes). When the accumulated penalty is less than the reuse limit (750), the route is advertised again, if it is still up.

The command to configure route dampening is as follows:

```
bgp dampening [half-life | reuse | suppress | Max-suppress-time] [route-map]
```

Another good functionality that you can implement on the eBGP peers is the ability to limit the number of prefixes that you will accept from the peer. After all, you do not want an eBGP neighbor (peer) to overrun your router with too many prefixes.

Maximum Prefix

A BGP neighbor can be configured such that the router will accept only a certain number of routes/prefixes. To configure this, use the `neighbor x.x.x.x maximum-prefix 3000 80` command. This example command will configure the neighbor to accept 3000 routes (prefixes) and will send a message to the console if the number of received prefixes reaches 80 percent of the configured maximum.

At this point, we have concluded our discussion of BGP. The next section is a hands-on scenario for you to configure to see how well you comprehended the material presented in this chapter.

Try to build this scenario before reading the solutions. This section is intended to test your knowledge of BGP. CCIE candidates must remember that 99-percent right is 100-percent wrong; there is no partial credit. If either the tasks themselves or the solution presented does not make sense, stop, investigate the problem, and do not move on until you have firm understanding of the problem and the solution. Also, if you would like to try to implement a second BGP scenario, refer to "Chapter 12 Supplement" on the CD-ROM that accompanies this book.

Building BGP Networks

This section focuses on building BGP networks. In the real world, building networks from the ground up may not be a luxury you'll have. But in a lab environment, a structured approach is the most efficient and quickest way to building a network. Breaking the network configuration down into manageable sections is an important task that, when not implemented, can cause no end of pain. It is very easy to overlook something very simple. So, although it may take an extra few minutes to break a configuration into different segments, this is a good practice to get into. In the long run a structured, step-by-step, methodical approach will prove to be the most efficient and quickest method because it will help eliminate mistakes. This approach should be applied to both simple and complex network configurations because it will help you to both isolate and resolve problems.

The scenario in this section does not cover simple configurations, such as configuring loopback interfaces (you should know how to configure them at this point in the book). This section focuses on the configuration of BGP.

BGP Configuration Task 1

This scenario will use Layer 2 Configuration Task 2.1 from Chapter 7. Figure 12.25 shows the BGP layout that must be built.

FIGURE 12.25   BGP configuration Task 1 diagram

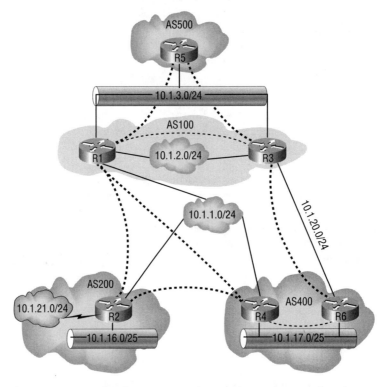

Here are the requirements for this scenario (the solution is presented in the next section):

- AS 200 must peer with both AS 100 and AS 400, and AS 100 must peer with both AS 200 and AS 400. Use the 10.1.1.*x* IP addresses (with *x* being the router number) to establish these connections.

- Define three loopback addresses on router R2 that are part of the following networks: 132.17.29.0/24, 132.17.30.0/24, and 132.17.31.0/24. Ensure that all AS 200 networks are distributed to routers in AS 100 and AS 400 only. Router R5 in AS 500 must not receive any routes for AS 200. No outbound policies can be applied in either router R1 or router R3 to achieve this.

- Announce the 10.1.1.0/24 network via BGP from router R2 only.

- In AS 400, configure two loopback interfaces on router R6 that are part of the following networks: 134.4.1.0/24 and 134.4.2.0/24.

- On router R4, configure two loopback interfaces that are part of the following networks: 134.4.4.0/23 and 134.4.6.0/23. Send only one summary route to all other ASs for this address space. This route should be the smallest summary route that covers all the address space in AS 400. In AS 400, on either router R4 or R6, do not configure any 10.0.0.0 address space using the network command under the BGP process.

- In AS 100, define an interface loopback 2 on router R1 that is part of network 133.3.32.0/24, and on router R3, define an interface loopback 2 that is part of 133.3.33.0/24. Announce only these routes to all other ASs. Ensure that R1 and R3 can receive routes and can route traffic from each other in the event that either the Ethernet or Frame Relay network has a connectivity problem.

- Router R3 must not receive routes from router R6 for AS 200.

- Define an interface loopback 2 in router R5 that is part of network 132.6.0.0/16. This route must appear as an "Origin incomplete" to all other routers. Router R5 must use a loopback interface for establishing its BGP connections to R1 and R3.

- Announce network 10.1.3.0/24 as part of AS 500 using the network command under the BGP process.

- From AS 500, ensure that all routes to AS 400 only are preferred via router R3 in AS 100; do not use MEDs or local preference to achieve this.

Solution for BGP Configuration Task 1

When configuring any network, the tasks have to broken down into manageable portions. The configuration of BGP has been broken down into the following tasks:

- BGP connectivity and reachability
- BGP route advertisement and filters

BGP Connectivity and Reachability

When working with BGP, the first and most important thing to do is to build the network connectivity and make sure that all the neighbors are communicating correctly. As with any network, a strong, stable foundation is necessary. Once this is achieved, BGP can be manipulated to influence and/or change the routing.

Connectivity

In BGP Configuration Task 1, AS 100 routers R1 and R3 must both be able to maintain BGP neighbors and route traffic in the event that either the Ethernet or Frame Relay network experiences a problem. To do this, R1 and R3 must peer using a loopback address to form iBGP neighbors. And to use a loopback address, each router must have a route to get to the loopback address on the other. The best way to achieve this is to run an IGP; the IGP will also detect network failures and route around the failures. OSPF is used as the IGP in this scenario, but any IGP can be used to perform this function.

Router R5 must also use a loopback for its eBGP neighbors to routers R1 and R3. Therefore, R5 must also participate in the IGP to both learn and send routes to routers R1 and R3. When configuring eBGP to use loopback addresses, you must specify the `neighbor x.x.x.x ebgp-multihop` command on all neighbor statements in all the routers.

Router R1 has an eBGP connection to both AS 200 and AS 400. These peers are defined using the connected interface IP address to the Frame Relay network. Even though the eBGP connection to router R4 is across the same network (10.1.1.0/24), the network is actually a Frame Relay hub and spoke. All IP traffic from routers R1 to R4 will go via R2 (the hub). The neighbor definition on routers R1 to R4 will need the `neighbor x.x.x.x ebgp-multihop` command because router R2 will decrement the TTL in the TCP packet and the neighbor will never establish a connection. Remember, eBGP has a default TTL value of 1. iBGP neighbors do not need to be specified as multihop because the default TTL for all iBGP neighbors is 255. The rest of the iBGP and eBGP neighbor definitions are straightforward.

BGP Reachability

All routers that have iBGP neighbor connections must have the `no synchronization` command configured under the BGP process. Router R2 is the only router that can advertise a network 10.1.1.0/24. Therefore, R1 will not advertise this network to R3, so R3 will not install any iBGP learned routes from R1 that have a next hop address of 10.1.1.*x*. This same issue needs to be resolved for R3, R4, and R6.

 Unless you have been explicitly told that you cannot do so, don't be afraid to turn off synchronization in the CCIE lab.

It is important to ensure that reachability is working correctly. Shut down the Ethernet interface of router R3 and make sure that the loopback address of R1 is still reachable using Ping. Shut down the Serial 1 interface of router R3 and ensure that R6 and R3 have installed routes to all ASs. Once both BGP peer connectivity and reachability issues are all resolved, you can move on to BGP route advertisement and filtering.

ROUTER R1 CONFIGURATION

Here is the configuration for router R1:

`router ospf 1`	Enable OSPF process 1
`  network 10.1.3.0 0.0.0.255 area 0`	Assign network 10.1.3.0/24 to area 0
`  network 10.1.2.0 0.0.0.255 area 0`	Assign network 10.1.2.0/24 to area 0
`  network 133.3.32.0 0.0.0.255 area 0`	Assign network 133.3.32.0/24 to area 0, the configured interface Loopback 2

router bgp 100	Enable BGP routing for AS 100
no synchronization	Disable IGP synchronization
network 133.3.32.0 mask 255.255.255.0	Advertise network 133.3.32.0/24
neighbor 10.1.1.2 remote-as 200	Define R2 as an eBGP neighbor
neighbor 10.1.1.4 remote-as 400	Define R4 as an eBGP neighbor
neighbor 10.1.1.4 ebgp-multihop 255	Specify that R4 is a multi-hop neighbor (set TTL=255)
neighbor 132.6.0.5 remote-as 500	Define R5 as an eBGP neighbor
neighbor 132.6.0.5 ebgp-multihop 255	Specify that R5 is a multi-hop neighbor (set TTL=255)
neighbor 132.6.0.5 update-source Loopback2	Source the TCP connection using a source IP address of Loopback 2 (IP address 132.2.32.1)
neighbor 133.3.33.3 remote-as 100	Define R3 as an iBGP neighbor
neighbor 133.3.33.3 update-source Loopback2	Source the TCP connection using a source IP address of Loopback 2 (IP address 132.2.32.1)
neighbor 133.3.33.3 next-hop-self	Change the next hop address of all eBGP learned routes that are forwarded to R3
no auto-summary	Turn off classful summarization

ROUTER R2 CONFIGURATION

Here is router R2's configuration:

router bgp 200	Enable BGP routing for AS 200
network 10.1.1.0 mask 255.255.255.0	Advertise network 10.1.1.0/24
network 132.17.29.0 mask 255.255.255.0	Advertise network 133.17.29.0/24
network 132.17.30.0 mask 255.255.255.0	Advertise network 133.17.30.0/24
network 132.17.31.0 mask 255.255.255.0	Advertise network 133.17.31.0/24
neighbor 10.1.1.1 remote-as 100	Define R1 as an eBGP neighbor
neighbor 10.1.1.4 remote-as 400	Define R4 as an eBGP neighbor
no auto-summary	Turn off classful summarization

ROUTER R3 CONFIGURATION

The configuration for router R3 is as follows:

router ospf 1	Enable OSPF process 1
network 10.1.3.0 0.0.0.255 area 0	Assign network 10.1.3.0/24 to area 0
network 10.1.2.0 0.0.0.255 area 0	Assign network 10.1.2.0/24 to area 0
network 133.3.33.0 0.0.0.255 area 0	Assign network 133.3.33.0/24 to area 0, the configured interface Loopback 2
router bgp 100	Enable BGP routing for AS 100
no synchronization	Disable IGP synchronization
network 133.3.33.0 mask 255.255.255.0	Advertise network 133.3.33.0/24
neighbor 10.1.20.6 remote-as 400	Define R6 as an eBGP neighbor
neighbor 132.6.0.5 remote-as 500	Define R5 as an eBGP neighbor
neighbor 132.6.0.5 ebgp-multihop 255	Specify that R5 is a multi-hop neighbor (set TTL=255)
neighbor 132.6.0.5 update-source Loopback2	Source the TCP connection using a source IP address of Loopback 2 (IP address 133.3.33.3)
neighbor 133.3.32.1 remote-as 100	Define R1 as an iBGP neighbor
neighbor 133.3.32.1 update-source Loopback2	Source the TCP connection using a source IP address of Loopback 2 (IP address 133.3.33.3)
neighbor 133.3.32.1 next-hop-self	Change the next hop address of all eBGP learned routes that are forwarded to R1
no auto-summary	Turn off classful summarization

ROUTER R4 CONFIGURATION

Here is router R4's configuration:

router bgp 400	Enable BGP routing for AS 400
no synchronization	Disable IGP synchronization
network 134.4.4.0 mask 255.255.254.0	Advertise network 133.4.4.0/23
network 134.4.6.0 mask 255.255.254.0	Advertise network 133.4.6.0/23
neighbor 10.1.1.1 remote-as 100	Define R1 as an eBGP neighbor
neighbor 10.1.1.1 ebgp-multihop 255	Specify that R1 is a multi-hop neighbor (set TTL=255)
neighbor 10.1.1.2 remote-as 200	Define R2 as an eBGP neighbor
neighbor 10.1.17.6 remote-as 400	Define R6 as an iBGP neighbor
neighbor 10.1.17.6 next-hop-self	Change the next hop address of all eBGP learned routes that are forwarded to R6
no auto-summary	Turn off classful summarization

ROUTER R5 CONFIGURATION

Here is the configuration for router R5:

router ospf 1	Enable OSPF process 1
network 10.1.3.0 0.0.0.255 area 0	Assign network 10.1.3.0/24 to area 0
network 132.6.0.0 0.0.255.255 area 0	Assign network 132.6.0.0/16 to area 0, the configured interface Loopback 2
router bgp 500	Enable BGP routing for AS 400
network 10.1.3.0 mask 255.255.255.0	Advertise network 10.1.3.0/24
neighbor 133.3.32.1 remote-as 100	Define R1 as an eBGP neighbor
neighbor 133.3.32.1 ebgp-multihop 255	Specify that R1 is a multi-hop neighbor (set TTL=255)
neighbor 133.3.32.1 update-source Loopback2	Source the TCP connection using a source IP address of Loopback 2 (IP address 132.6.0.5)

neighbor 133.3.33.3 remote-as 100	Define R3 as an eBGP neighbor
neighbor 133.3.33.3 ebgp-multihop 255	Specify that R1 is a multi-hop neighbor (set TTL=255)
neighbor 133.3.33.3 update-source Loopback2	Source the TCP connection using a source IP address of Loopback 2 (IP address 132.6.0.5)
no auto-summary	Turn off classful summarization

ROUTER R6 CONFIGURATION

Here is router R6's configuration:

router bgp 400	Enable BGP routing for AS 400
no synchronization	Disable IGP synchronization
network 134.4.1.0 mask 255.255.255.0	Advertise network 133.4.1.0/24
network 134.4.2.0 mask 255.255.255.0	Advertise network 133.4.2.0/24
neighbor 10.1.17.4 remote-as 400	Define R4 as an iBGP neighbor
neighbor 10.1.17.4 next-hop-self	Change the next hop address of all eBGP learned routes that are forwarded to R6
neighbor 10.1.20.3 remote-as 100	Define R1 as an eBGP neighbor
no auto-summary	Turn off classful summarization

After BGP connectivity has been configured, ensure that all the routes are learned in all the routers. The following shows the output from a show ip bgp command on router R6:

```
Status codes: s suppressed, d damped, h history, * valid, > best, i - internal
Origin codes: i - IGP, e - EGP, ? - incomplete


     Network          Next Hop          Metric LocPrf Weight Path
*    10.1.1.0/24      10.1.20.3                          0 100 200 i
*>i                   10.1.17.4              0    100    0 200 i
*>   10.1.3.0/24      10.1.20.3                          0 100 500 i
* i                   10.1.17.4                   100    0 100 500 i
*    132.17.29.0/24   10.1.20.3                          0 100 200 i
*>i                   10.1.17.4              0    100    0 200 i
```

* 132.17.30.0/24	10.1.20.3				0 100 200 i
*>i	10.1.17.4	0	100		0 200 i
* 132.17.31.0/24	10.1.20.3				0 100 200 i
*>i	10.1.17.4	0	100		0 200 i
*> 133.3.32.0/24	10.1.20.3				0 100 i
* i	10.1.17.4	0	100		0 100 i
* i133.3.33.0/24	10.1.17.4		100		0 100 i
*>	10.1.20.3	0			0 100 i
*> 134.4.1.0/24	0.0.0.0	0		32768 i	
*> 134.4.2.0/24	0.0.0.0	0		32768 i	
*>i134.4.4.0/23	10.1.17.4	0	100	0 i	
*>i134.4.6.0/23	10.1.17.4	0	100	0 i	

The important things to note are that the router has an installed (best) route for all learned routes and that two paths exist to all routes in AS 100, AS 200, and AS 500. This is how the network should appear to router R6 when all connectivity is functioning correctly. Note the advertising AS for 10.1.1.0/24 and 10.1.3.0/24; both these networks should be learned from AS 200 and AS 500, respectively.

BGP Route Advertisement and Filtering

Restrict route advertisement from AS 200 to AS 100 and 400 only. In BGP Configuration Task 1, routes from AS 200 must be sent only to all routers in AS 100 and AS 400. This must be achieved using no outbound policy on R1 and R3. With this restriction in place, the way to resolve this issue is to use the well-known community no-export. This community is set on router R2 and is applied to all routes originating from AS 200. For communities to function correctly in the network, the `neighbor x.x.x.x send community` command must be configured on all routers in every AS. A Cisco router by default will strip communities off if the neighbor is not specifically configured to send communities. The following output shows the routes learned by router R5 before any communities are implemented on the network. Router R5 has two paths to all routes via both routers R1 and R3, and both routers show the path AS 100 200:

* 132.17.29.0/24	133.3.33.3		0 100 200 i
*>	133.3.32.1		0 100 200 i
* 132.17.30.0/24	133.3.33.3		0 100 200 i
*>	133.3.32.1		0 100 200 i
* 132.17.31.0/24	133.3.33.3		0 100 200 i
*>	133.3.32.1		0 100 200 i

The following are the configuration commands to configure router R2 to send all routes that originated from its AS with the no-export community. This configuration is using an AS path access list. The access list, which specifies all routes that originated from its local AS, is using regular expressions. A route map then matches this criteria and sets the no-export community. The route map is then applied to each neighbor as an outbound policy:

```
router bgp 200
  neighbor 10.1.1.1 send-community          Enables R2 to send communities to
                                            defined neighbor R1

  neighbor 10.1.1.1 route-map comm-no-export out

                                             Apply outgoing route-map comm-no-
                                             export
  neighbor 10.1.1.4 send-community          Enables R2 to send communities to
                                            defined neighbor R4

  neighbor 10.1.1.4 route-map comm-no-export out

                                            Apply outgoing route-map comm-no-
                                            export
ip as-path access-list 1 permit ^$         Create AS-path permitting all paths
                                           that have Local AS-path Origin

route-map comm-no-export permit 10         Creates route-map
  match as-path 1                          Match AS-path access list 1
  set community no-export                  All routes that match AS-path access
                                           list set community to no-export

route-map comm-no-export permit 20         For all other router permit these
                                           routes to be sent
```

From router R3, here is the output of the show ip bgp community no-export command, which shows all routes that match this well-known community and therefore will not be sent to router R5:

```
Status codes: s suppressed, d damped, h history, * valid, > best, i - internal
Origin codes: i - IGP, e - EGP, ? - incomplete

   Network          Next Hop       Metric LocPrf Weight Path
*>i10.1.1.0/24      133.3.32.1          0    100      0 200 i
*>i132.17.29.0/24   133.3.32.1          0    100      0 200 i
*>i132.17.30.0/24   133.3.32.1          0    100      0 200 i
*>i132.17.31.0/24   133.3.32.1          0    100      0 200 i
```

You could verify that none of these routes from AS 200 are advertised to router R5, by doing a show ip bgp command on router R5 and viewing the received BGP routes.

Summary Route for AS 400

A summary route needs to be generated from AS 400 for its entire address space. AS 400 must send only a summary route and not the specific routes. AS 400's address space is as follows:

- 134.4.1.0/24
- 134.4.2.0/24
- 134.4.4.0/23
- 134.4.6.0/23

Therefore, a summary route for 134.4.0.0/21 must be generated. This covers the entire address space that is propagated from AS 400. To send a summary route, you must configure only the following command under BGP on both routers R4 and R6:

```
aggregate-address 134.4.0.0 255.255.248.0 summary-only
```

Here is the output from a show ip bgp command on router R5. This confirms that the aggregate-only route is received from AS 400:

	Network	Next Hop	Metric	LocPrf	Weight	Path
*>	10.1.3.0/24	0.0.0.0	0		32768	i
*>	132.6.0.0	0.0.0.0	0		32768	?
*	133.3.32.0/24	133.3.33.3			0	100 i
*>		133.3.32.1	0		0	100 i
*	133.3.33.0/24	133.3.33.3	0		0	100 i
*>		133.3.32.1			0	100 i
*	134.4.0.0/21	133.3.33.3			0	100 400 i
*>		133.3.32.1			0	100 400 i

Incomplete Origin from AS 500

Network 132.6.0.0/16 must be sent with the BGP origin set to incomplete. This is achieved by advertising this network using the redistribution connected command under the BGP process on router R5.

The following shows the output of a show ip bgp regexp _500$ command on router R2. This is using the regular expression to show only the router that originated in AS 500:

```
Status codes: s suppressed, d damped, h history, * valid, > best, i - internal
Origin codes: i - IGP, e - EGP, ? - incomplete
```

	Network	Next Hop	Metric	LocPrf	Weight	Path
*>	10.1.1.0/24	0.0.0.0	0		32768	i
*	10.1.3.0/24	10.1.1.1			0	400 100 500 i
*>		10.1.1.1			0	100 500 i

```
*  132.6.0.0        10.1.1.1                        0 400 100 500 ?
*>                  10.1.1.1                        0 100 500 ?
```

As can be seen from this output, two paths exist to network 132.6.0.0/16, but the origin is shown as incomplete.

Routes to AS 400 Preferred via Router R3

Without any route manipulation, router R5's (AS 500) preferred path to AS 400 is via R1 in AS 100. This is because the deciding factor is the lowest BGP router ID (RID). To manipulate these routes, MEDs or local preferences cannot be used. There are many ways to influence the routing decision to get router R5 to prefer R3. The method that we will use is the Cisco-proprietary attribute weight.

The weight attribute is locally significant to the configured router, and the higher weight is preferred. If we use the `neighbor x.x.x.x weight` command, which applies a default weight to all learned routes, R3 will be preferred for routes to all ASs, and this is *not* what was requested. Here is the output on router R5 from the `show ip bgp` command after a default weight was configured on the R3 neighbor. All routes to both AS 100 and AS 400 are preferred via R3:

```
    Network        Next Hop        Metric LocPrf Weight Path
*> 10.1.3.0/24     0.0.0.0              0         32768 i
*> 132.6.0.0       0.0.0.0              0         32768 ?
*  133.3.32.0/24   133.3.32.1           0     100     0 i
*>                 133.3.33.3                 32000 100 i
*  133.3.33.0/24   133.3.32.1                 100     0 i
*>                 133.3.33.3           0     32000 100 i
*  134.4.0.0/21    133.3.32.1                 100     0 400 i
*>                 133.3.33.3                 32000 100 400 I
```

To prefer routes to AS 400 only, a route-map must be used to selectively set the weight. The following is the router configuration on router R5 to prefer R3 for all routes to AS 400:

`router bgp 500`	
`neighbor 133.3.33.3 route-map set-weight in`	Apply incoming route-map set-weight
`ip as-path access-list 1 permit _400$`	Create AS-path access-list permitting all routes originated from AS 400
`route-map set-weight permit 10`	Create route-map set-weight
`match as-path 1`	Match AS-path access list 1

```
set weight 32000                        Set the weight to 32000
                                        for all matched routes

route-map set-weight permit 20          Allow all other router
                                        to be received and
                                        installed in BGP table
```

The following output is from router R5 after the route-map was applied. The only route that has a preferred path via R3 is the route to AS 400; all other routes prefer router R1:

```
    Network          Next Hop        Metric LocPrf Weight Path
*>  10.1.3.0/24      0.0.0.0              0         32768 i
*>  132.6.0.0        0.0.0.0              0         32768 ?
*>  133.3.32.0/24    133.3.32.1           0             0 100 i
*                    133.3.33.3                         0 100 i
*>  133.3.33.0/24    133.3.32.1                         0 100 i
*                    133.3.33.3           0             0 100 i
*   134.4.0.0/21     133.3.32.1                         0 100 400 i
*>                   133.3.33.3                     32000 100 400 i
```

BGP Troubleshooting

You need to troubleshoot BGP in a methodical fashion. When you're building a BGP network, it is important to understand how everything fits together and how to break the configuration down into different configuration sections. BGP is complex, and there are many ways to achieve the same results. It is important that you have a fundamental understanding of the route selection criteria in BGP and all the various ways to manipulate the route selection process. The following list includes commands that can be used to troubleshoot BGP:

```
ping

show ip bgp summary                     Summary of all neighbors and their
                                        connection state

show ip bgp neighbor                    Detailed information of all neighbors

show ip bgp                             Display all learned routes and
                                        installed routes from all BGP
                                        neighbors

show ip bgp neighbor x.x.x.x advertise  Routes that router is advertising
                                        to the neighbor

show ip bgp neighbor x.x.x.x  routes    Routes that this router is
                                        receiving from the neighbor
```

show ip bgp community	Display routes that match a BGP community
show ip bgp regexp	Display matched routes for a regular expression
show ip route	Display the router's routing table

Use these debug commands to troubleshoot peer connection issues. The debug ip bgp command can be used to display events as they occur. There is one drawback to this command: not only does the BGP process being used to advertise ASNs across the Internet use considerable processing power, but the debug command is assigned a high priority on the router and can kill your processing power. To stop all debugging on a router, use the undebug all command or the no debug all command. Here's a short summary of the debug commands:

debug ip bgp dampening	Displays BGP dampening events
debug ip bgp events	Displays all BGP events as they occur
debug ip bgp keepalives	Displays all events related to BGP keepalive packets
debug ip bgp updates	Displays information on all BGP update packets

That's it. We have discussed BGP and given you a chance to verify your understanding of the material with a hands-on scenario. Hopefully, you are feeling comfortable with BGP. If you would like to try to implement another BGP scenario, refer to "Chapter 12 Supplement" on the CD-ROM that accompanies this book.

Summary

Congratulations—if you have a completely photographic memory, you're now an expert on BGP. But if you're like the rest of us, this refresher of what was covered in this chapter will come in handy. There are many items to remember when configuring BGP. If you implement BGP incorrectly, not only can you disrupt your own internal network you can wreak havoc on neighboring organizations' networks as well. This can also include your own ISP's network. If you do not know how to configure or maintain BGP in a network, you should not implement BGP in your network.

After reading this chapter, you should have a firm understanding of how to configure BGP to include communities, peer groups, synchronization, confederations, and route reflectors. Here's a quick review of what was covered in this chapter:

- Autonomous systems are used to identify routers operating in a common network with a common administration.

- Transit autonomous systems are autonomous systems between two other autonomous systems.

- BGP peers are two routers running BGP and connecting through a TCP session to exchange messages. BGP peering is a reference to a specific relationship at the policy level.

- Internal BGP (iBGP) is BGP operating in an internal autonomous system, and external BGP (eBGP) operates between autonomous systems.

- Don't use BGP when you have a single connection to the Internet or a lack of bandwidth or when your networking equipment can't handle the processing of large routing tables.

- BGP message types identified in the BGP common header are the OPEN, UPDATE, NOTIFICATION, and KEEPALIVE message types.

- BGP path attributes are associated with the UPDATE message type and added to a common header.

- The weight attribute is a proprietary Cisco attribute.

- Communities and peer groups allow you to put one or more routers with identical policies into a single group.

- Configuring route reflectors and confederations are ways of reducing the number of neighbor statements configured on each router and avoiding the full-mesh peering rule.

BGP is definitely a topic that you must know extremely well for the CCIE lab examination. Likewise, it is essential to have a thorough understanding of BGP for real-world implementations. The entire Internet is operating through the implementation of BGP. And if you work for a large company, there is no doubt that, if you haven't already, you will be asked to design and implement a multihomed (multiple paths) to the Internet solution. Remember that with BGP, there are approximately three ways to accomplish just about any task, whether the task pertains to route filtering or traffic modeling. You should be familiar enough with BGP to be able to configure all possible methods for any given task because you never know when other limitations will negate some of the options.

Again, if you would like to try to implement another BGP scenario, refer to "Chapter 12 Supplement" on the CD-ROM that accompanies this book.

Exam Essentials

Know what an autonomous system number is.   An autonomous system number is a number logically assigned to all the routers that fall under a single administrative control.

Know what IGPs and EGPs are.   Interior gateway protocols (IGPs), discussed in previous chapters, are routing protocols that run within an autonomous system (AS). Exterior gateway protocols (EGPs) are used to exchange information between different autonomous systems.

Understand the difference between iBGP and eBGP and how to configure them.   Internal BGP (iBGP) is BGP operating in an internal autonomous system, and external BGP (eBGP) operates between autonomous systems. Make sure you have a good understanding of these concepts and that you know how to configure them.

Know what synchronization is.   When synchronization is turned on, a router will not install a route learned from an iBGP neighbor unless that route is local (a connected network) or unless that route is also learned by the router from an IGP.

Understand the BGP next hop.   When BGP routes are installed in a router's routing table, the route's next hop is an IP address and not a directly connected interface. The BGP learned routes all show a next hop of the IP address of the originating BGP peers. Because these BGP installed routes do not have an outgoing interface assigned, the router must first match a route that is assigned to an outgoing interface that matches the next hop address.

Know the BGP route selection process.   If the route is learned via iBGP and synchronization is on, the route *must* be known by an IGP. If the route is not known by the IGP, the route will not be installed in the router's routing table. All eBGP learned routes are eligible to be installed in a router's routing table. The next hop address must be reachable from all iBGP routers; otherwise the route will not be installed in the routing table. If multiple routes exist to an end destination, the following criteria are used to determine the best route.

Prefer the highest weight (this is Cisco proprietary and is locally significant to a router). If multiple routes exist and have the same weight, prefer the route with the highest local preference. This can only be for routes learned via iBGP because local preference is valid *only* within an AS. If local preference is equal, prefer the route that was locally originated. If the route was not locally originated, prefer the route with the shortest AS path. If the AS path is the same, prefer the lowest origin code. IGP (i) is the more preferred, then EGP (e), and then INCOMPLETE (?). If the origin code is still equal, prefer the lowest MED. Again, remember that the MED is sent by another AS peer. If the MEDs are equal, prefer eBGP learned routes over iBGP learned routes. If the routes are learned the same, then prefer the route with the lowest BGP router ID. If the BGP router IDs are the same, prefer the lowest neighbor IP address.

Understand BGP attributes and know how to configure them on Cisco routers.   BGP attributes are the most powerful features of BGP because they allow BGP to be completely customizable. There are different types of attributes: well-known or optional, mandatory or discretionary, transitive or nontransitive. Know the attributes that are most used when dealing with BGP and how to configure them on Cisco routers.

Understand communities, confederations, route reflectors, and peer groups.   You can use communities to group destination networks and apply routing decisions based on the community. Likewise, confederations, route reflectors, and peer groups are techniques you can use to help scale iBGP in large networks. Know how and when to use each one of these mechanisms.

Key Terms

Before you take the exam, make sure you are familiar with the following key terms:

AS path prepending	internal BGP (iBGP)
attributes	Network Layer Reachability Information (NLRI)
BGP neighbors	peer group
BGP peers	redistribution
BGP speakers	stub AS
communities	transit AS
external BGP (eBGP)	

Review Questions

1. When should BGP be used? (Choose all that apply.)

    A. When multihoming

    B. When connecting multiple ISPs

    C. When connecting routers within the same AS

    D. When configuring backup links

2. When an autonomous system (AS) must traverse another autonomous system to get to its destination, the traversed autonomous system is called which of the following?

    A. Transfer AS

    B. Forwarding AS

    C. Transit AS

    D. Transmitting AS

3. Which of the following describes an autonomous system between two other autonomous systems?

    A. A middle AS

    B. A stub AS

    C. A transit AS

    D. A transmitting AS

    E. A non-transit AS

4. The BGP hold timer is established in which of the following BGP message types?

    A. OPEN

    B. UPDATE

    C. NOTIFICATION

    D. KEEPALIVE

5. If an external autonomous system is not receiving updates from your autonomous system, which of the following show commands can be used to troubleshoot this? (Choose all that apply.)

    A. `show ip bgp events`

    B. `show ip bgp neighbor`

    C. `show ip bgp all`

    D. `show ip bgp`

6. Which of the following commands will begin a BGP process on a router and place you in BGP configuration mode?

    A. `router enable bgp`

    B. `router ip bgp 45323`

    C. `router bgp 32455`

    D. `router enable bgp 34657`

7. Which of the following is the valid range of BGP ASNs?

    A. 1 through 59,000

    B. 1 through 65,535

    C. 1 through 32,128

    D. 1 through 65,012

8. A grouping of BGP routers that share the same common policies is called which of the following?

    A. Policy group

    B. Peer group

    C. Identi-Group

    D. Access group

9. Which of the following commands can be used on a router to make sure that a route has stabalized before it is advertised after route flapping has occured?

    A. `ip bgp as-path`

    B. `ip bgp hold time`

    C. `set as-path extended`

    D. `bgp dampening`

10. BGP uses which of the following TCP ports to open a session with another BGP peer?

    A. Port 20

    B. Port 21

    C. Port 179

    D. Port 23

Answers to Review Questions

1. A, B. BGP should be used when multihoming and when connecting multiple ISPs.

2. C. A transit AS is an autonomous system through which data from one autonomous system must travel to get to another autonomous system.

3. C. A transit AS is an autonomous system through which data from one autonomous system must travel to get to another autonomous system. A stub AS is an autonomous system in which the exit point and entry point are the same. A non-transit autonomous system is an autonomous system that does not pass data through to another autonomous system. There is no such thing as a transmitting or middle autonomous system.

4. A. The OPEN message is used to establish a connection between BGP peers and to negotiate the hold time. An UPDATE message is used to advertise topology updates and changes, a NOTIFICATION message is used to advertise errors, and a KEEPALIVE message type is sent to keep a session active when no UPDATE messages are exchanged during the established hold time.

5. B, D. The `show ip bgp neighbor` command displays all the advertised routes, and the `show ip bgp` command looks at all the connections.

6. C. The `router bgp 32455` command is the only valid command listed to place the router in BGP configuration mode, which is identified by the `(config-router)` prompt.

7. B. The valid range of BGP numbers is 1 through 65,535.

8. B. Peer groups allow you to assign configurations to a group instead of to each individual router.

9. D. The `bgp dampening` command is used by BGP to set a hold time before a route can be readvertised.

10. C. Port 179 is used by BGP to establish a session with another BGP peer. Ports 20 and 21 are used by FTP, and port 23 is used by Telnet.

Chapter

13

Non-IP Protocols

THE CCIE QUALIFICATION EXAM TOPICS COVERED IN THIS CHAPTER INCLUDE THE FOLLOWING:

✓ Internetwork Packet Exchange (IPX), NetWare Link Services Protocol (NLSP), IPX Routing Information Protocol (IPX RIP), IPX Service Advertising Protocol (IPX SAP), IPX Enhanced Interior Gateway Routing Protocol (IPX EIGRP), Sequenced Packet Exchange (SPX), Network Control Protocol (NCP), IPXWAN, IPX addressing, Get Nearest Server (GNS)

✓ Windows NT (NetBIOS, browsing, domain controller [e.g., WINS], ACLs)

In this chapter, we'll consider two popular non-IP protocols: Novell NetWare's IPX and Microsoft's implementation of NetBIOS. We will not be discussing AppleTalk or DECnet because they are no longer included on the qualification (written) exam or in the lab exam for CCIE. The IPX and Microsoft Windows NetBIOS are listed objectives for the qualification (written) examination, but they are not included in the CCIE lab examination. And because they are not objectives of the lab examination, we will not have a hands-on scenario at the end of this chapter. This chapter is intended to present the material to assist you in preparing for the qualification exam and to assist in the day-to-day networking environment.

We'll start by discussing the IPX protocol.

Internetwork Packet Exchange (IPX)

NetWare is a network operating system (NOS) and related support services environment created by Novell, Inc. It was introduced to the market in the early 1980s. At that time, networks were small, local area network (LAN) workgroup communication was new, and the idea of a personal computer (PC) was just becoming popular. Most of NetWare's networking technology was developed from Xerox Network Service (XNS), a networking system created by Xerox Corporation in the late 1970s. By the early 1990s, NetWare's NOS market share had risen to between 50 percent and 75 percent. With more than 500,000 NetWare networks installed worldwide and an accelerating movement to connect networks to other networks, NetWare and its supporting protocols often coexisted on the same physical channel with many other popular protocols, including TCP/IP, DECnet, and AppleTalk. Although networks today are predominantly IP, there is some legacy Novell Internetwork Packet Exchange (IPX) traffic out there. Novell also offers Internet Protocol (IP) support in the form of User Datagram Protocol (UDP)/IP encapsulation of other Novell packets, such as IPX packets. IPX datagrams are encapsulated inside UDP/IP headers for transport across an IP-based internetwork. NetWare 5 runs native IP, but the previous versions of NetWare implement IP as the Novell-specific form we just referred to, also known as NetWare/IP.

IPX is a connectionless layer 3 protocol that provides the functionality of layer 3 and layer 4 of the OSI reference model. In many ways, you can think of it as providing the same services that IP and UDP provide in the TCP/IP world.

Sequenced Packet Exchange (SPX) is a connection-oriented protocol occurring at layer 4 of the OSI model and is the NetWare counterpart to TCP. An SPX constraint is that it is limited to a window size of 1.

NetWare provides file and printer sharing services, support for various applications such as electronic mail transfer and database access, and other services. Like other Operating Systems/File Systems, such as the Network File System (NFS) from Sun Microsystems, Inc. and Windows NT from Microsoft Corporation, NetWare is based on a client/server architecture. In such architectures, clients (sometimes called workstations) request certain services such as file and printer access from servers. A primary characteristic of the client/server system is that remote access is transparent to the user. This is accomplished through remote procedure calls (RPCs), a process by which a local computer program running on a client sends a procedure call to a remote server. The server executes the remote procedure call and returns the requested information to the local computer client. With the appropriate drivers, NetWare can run on any media-access protocol, such as Ethernet/IEEE 802.3, Token Ring/IEEE 802.5, Fiber Distributed Data Interface (FDDI), and Copper Distributed Data Interface (CDDI). NetWare also works over synchronous wide area network (WAN) links using the Point-to-Point Protocol (PPP) or Frame Relay encapsulation.

Now that you have an understanding of the IPX protocol, we need to discuss the various encapsulation types (which Novell refers to as frame types).

IPX Encapsulation Types

Although IPX was derived from XNS, it has several unique features, especially in the functionality of encapsulation. Encapsulation is the process of packaging upper-layer protocol information and data into frames. You can configure multiple framing types on the same Cisco router. In fact, you can configure multiple framing types on the same interface of a router. But, for two hosts (nodes) on a network to communicate with each other, they must have at least one frame type in common. However, the drawback of using multiple frame types is the broadcast traffic, because each frame type will transmit service advertisements, IPX RIP, and other NetWare administration packets. This will consume more of your bandwidth because you will have twice as many broadcast packets being transmitted. Table 13.1 shows the various forms of what Cisco refers to as encapsulation and Novell refers to as framing.

TABLE 13.1   Cisco and Novell encapsulation types

Cisco Encapsulation	NOVELL Framing	Description
arpa	ethernet_II	IPX Ethernet_II
novell-ether	802.3	IPX Ethernet_802.3
sap	802.2	IEEE 802.2 on Ethernet, FDDI, Token Ring
snap	ethernet_snap	IEEE 802.2 SNAP on Ethernet, Token Ring, and FDDI

TABLE 13.1   Cisco and Novell encapsulation types *(continued)*

Cisco Encapsulation	NOVELL Framing	Description
novell-fddi	novell-fddi	IPX FDDI RAW
hdlc	hdlc	HDLC on serial links

*Novell Netware versions 3.11 and earlier implement 802.3 framing by default

*Novell Netware versions 3.12 and later implement 802.2 framing by default

Internetwork Packet Exchange (IPX) is Novell's original Network layer protocol. If a destination device to be communicated with is located on a different network, IPX routes the packets to the destination network. To route packets between networks, IPX uses dynamic routing protocols such as an IPX version of RIP, EIGRP, or NLSP. IPX can also be routed through the use of static routes. We will discuss these various routing mechanisms later on in this chapter; for now let's move on to discuss how the IPX protocol works.

IPX Addresses, Protocol, and Socket numbers

An IPX logical address is 10 bytes or 80 bits in length, and it is presented in the typical Network.Node format. The characters are displayed in hexadecimal format, so each character is actually 4 bits, thus two characters equal 1 byte. The first 4 bytes, or 32 bits, must be a hexadecimal number between 1 and FFFFFFFD (the FFFFFFFF network is reserved for a broadcast, and the FFFFFFFE network is reserved for an NLSP default route) and represent the Network portion of the address, and the last 6 bytes, or 48 bits, represent the Node (host) portion of the address. The Node, or host, portion of the IPX address is usually the MAC address of the network interface card (NIC), thereby providing a unique address for each node. Figure 13.1 shows the basic format of a typical Novell IPX address.

FIGURE 13.1   Novell IPX address

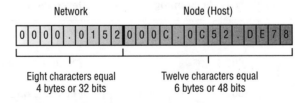

When displaying an IPX address, you can drop any leading 0's in the address, as shown below. For this reason, it is best to always look at an IPX address right to left

WAN interfaces do not have a MAC address association. The router assigns the address of the first LAN interface that is active at the time IPX initializes to the IPX routing process and uses the LAN MAC address for all WAN interfaces. To statically define a node address for all WAN interfaces, use the `ipx routing 0002.0002.0002` command. In this example, we have set all WAN interfaces to use the MAC address of 0002.0002.0002.

IPX has the capability to carry several various protocol types just as IP can. Likewise, IPX utilizes unique protocol numbers to identify the various protocols it carries, the same way IP does. This allows IPX to properly identify what protocol a packet belongs to. Table 13.2 shows a list of protocols. This is *not* a list of all possible protocols, however; these are protocols you should be familiar with.

TABLE 13.2   Novell IPX protocol numbers

IPX protocol numbers		Description
0	=	ANY/unknown
1	=	IPX RIP
4	=	SAP
5	=	SPX
17	=	NCP
20	=	NetBIOS

IPX utilizes socket numbers in much the same way that TCP and UDP utilize port numbers. Sockets distinguish specific functions or types of packets that are being transported by the IPX protocol. Socket addresses are used to describe the OSI upper-layer software application or processes, such as file/print server application, SAPs, NCP, IPX RIP, NLSP, SPX, NetBIOS, and so on. Novell's well-known static sockets start at 0x800, and dynamic sockets begin at 0x4001–0x7FFF (client socket numbers). Table 13.3 shows a list of socket numbers. This is *not* a list of all possible socket numbers; however, these are the socket numbers you should be familiar with (also, 0 matches all sockets).

TABLE 13.3   Novell IPX socket numbers

IPX socket numbers		Description
451	=	Netware Core Protocol (NCP)
452	=	Service Advertisement Protocol (SAP)

TABLE 13.3 Novell IPX socket numbers

IPX socket numbers		Description
453	=	IPX RIP
455	=	NetBIOS
457	=	serialization
4001 - 7FFF	=	Client socket numbers
85BE	=	IPX EIGRP
9001	=	Netware Link Service Protocol (NLSP)
9004	=	IPXWAN
9086	=	IPX ping

*Serialization packets (457)—transmitted every 66 secs. Protects against NetWare copyright violations.

Novell added a protocol called the Service Advertising Protocol (SAP) to its IPX protocol family. We also mentioned NCP; the *NetWare Core Protocol (NCP)* is a series of server routines designed to carry out application requests coming from, for example, the NetWare shell. These application requests are for services such as file access, printer access, name management, accounting, security, and file synchronization.

Next, we'll discuss how SAP and Get Nearest Server (GNS) work in the IPX network.

Service Advertising Protocol (SAP) and Get Nearest Server (GNS)

SAP allows nodes that provide NetWare services (such as file servers and print servers) to advertise their addresses and the services that they provide to other IPX servers and clients. Novell IPX uses SAP and RIP broadcasts to build a list of available services and routes. A *Service Advertising Protocol (SAP)* packet carries information on the type of service available, the name of the server, and its IPX address. A single SAP can carry a maximum of seven services. These updates are sent out every 60 seconds by devices on the network that provide a service for others, such as file servers and print servers. A router will listen to these SAP updates and build a SAP table cache that shows all known services. Routers do not forward individual SAPs; routers collect SAPs and place them in the SAP table. The router then forwards a consolidated list of SAPs every 60 seconds. This can greatly reduce the number of SAP advertisements traversing the WAN. The router can include multiple SAPs in a single packet.

Clients broadcast out *Get Nearest Server (GNS)* packets to locate the nearest active server of a particular type. An IPX network client issues a GNS request to solicit either a direct response from a connected server or a response from a router that tells it where on the internetwork the service can be located. Clients are not configured with a network number; they learn the network number through the GNS process. When an IPX client first boots, the client sends a GNS broadcast on the local segment. If a NetWare server is on that segment, the server replies, giving the client the network number as well as information about the server itself. On a segment with multiple NetWare servers, all the servers reply. The client accesses the first reply as the nearest server.

The SAP and GNS protocols work together to provide reliable services from the servers to the clients. GNS queries and responses are considered part of SAP. If the SAPs equal 20 percent or more of the traffic, you should reduce the SAPs using the methods described later on in this chapter, such as adjusting the `ipx sap-interval`. In a NetWare 4.1 or later environment, do not filter SAP type 0x4, 0x278, and 0x26B. If these SAP types are filtered, the NetWare Directory Services (NDS) server database will be unable to synchronize, and the other servers and clients will have difficulty logging on and gaining access to the required services. Figure 13.2 depicts IPX servers and clients and how the SAPs and GNS communicate. Notice that the servers are connected locally off of router R1.

FIGURE 13.2   Novell IPX SAPs and GNSs

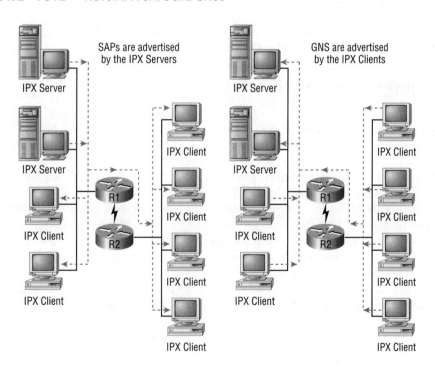

Table 13.4 shows a list of SAPs. This is *not* a list of all possible SAPs, but they are the ones you should be familiar with.

TABLE 13.4   Novell IPX SAP numbers

IPX SAP numbers		Description
0×0	=	All Services
0×4	=	File server
0×5	=	Job server
0×7	=	Print server
0×9	=	Archive server
0×47	=	Advertising print server
0×26B	=	Time synchronization
0×278	=	NDS server

Now that you have a good understanding of the IPX protocol, let's discuss how to configure it in the Cisco environment, starting with IPX RIP.

Configuring IPX with IPX RIP

IPX Routing Information Protocol (RIP) carries information on the route or path to take to get to a specific destination network. IPX RIP updates, which are broadcast every 60 seconds, contain the destination network number, the hop count, the delay (tick), and the next hop gateway information. As with SAP updates, a router will listen to the IPX RIP updates and build a routing table that lists all known destination routes or networks. Valid entries remain in the routing table for three multiples of the RIP interval (180 seconds). During this time, if a route entry is not refreshed by the RIP updates, the route is marked with an infinite hop count (16). Depending on the SAP entries and RIP routing table entries, the SAP entries will remain in the SAP table only if the associated IPX address is in the IPX routing table.

The first step to implementing IPX within your network is of course to apply the `ipx routing` global command, which activates the IPX protocol within the router as well as IPX RIP. When you specify the `ipx routing` command, if you do not include a node address at the end of the command, then the first active LAN interface MAC address will be used. We recommend that you specify a simple node address, such as the 0002.0002.0002 used in the sample configuration later in this section, which designates this router as router number 2. Second, you must specify the IPX networks that you wish IPX RIP to route under the routing process on the routers. Then, the IPX network must be configured on each interface that you want to route IPX traffic across.

IPX RIP is not compatible with the IP version of RIP. Just as the IP version of RIP uses the hop count metric to make routing decisions, the IPX version of RIP uses ticks to make the routing decisions. Ticks are displayed in the IPX RIP routing table as the amount of delay associated with each link in the path to the destination network (a tick is 1/18 of a second, or approximately 55 ms). If there is a tie in the delay (number of ticks) between two possible paths to a destination, then the hop count is used to break the tie. This is actually more efficient than the IP version of RIP because the IPX version of RIP, is actually taking into account the performance of the network to make its routing decisions in the form of the actual delay within the network from one point to another.

 The tick value of 1/18 second was derived from the original IBM PCs that ran at 4.77MHz. A tick was the smallest measurement of time that could be calculated at that time.

By default, all LAN interfaces have a RIP delay of 1 and all WAN interfaces have a RIP delay of 6. Leaving the delay at its default value is sufficient for most interfaces. However, you can adjust the RIP delay field by setting the tick count with the `ipx delay 36` command on the desired interface. This example will set the IPX RIP delay to 36 ticks (36 × 1/18 of a second, or 2 seconds) on the configured interface. The actual entries in the routing table that are exchanged with other routers are the network number, the hop count, and ticks.

The following router configuration example shows how to implement the IPX protocol and IPX RIP on a Cisco router, with some *optional* commands added for good measure:

```
ipx routing 0002.0002.0002            Enables the IPX protocol, the IPX RIP
                                      protocol, and specifies the Node address
                                      for all WAN interfaces

ipx default-output-rip-delay 65       OPTIONAL, sets 65 ms inter-packet delay
                                      on all interfaces for IPX RIP.  The
                                      default setting is 55 ms


ipx default-output-sap-delay 65       OPTIONAL, sets 65 ms inter-packet
                                      delay on all interfaces for IPX SAP.
                                      The default setting is 55 ms


interface Ethernet0/0

 bandwidth 10000                      OPTIONAL, changes the reference
                                      bandwidth for the interface
```

ipx network 25   Configures the IPX network number of 25
                                        on this interface

ipx network 31 encapsulation snap secondary

                                        OPTIONAL, in order to use a different
                                        type of encapsulation than the default,
                                        you must specify the encapsulation type.
                                        If you are adding a second or multiple
                                        IPX addresses to a single interface,
                                        then you must specify that it is a
                                        secondary network. Another possible
                                        solution, and the preferred solution,
                                        would be to use a sub-interface for each
                                        IPX network

ipx output-rip-delay 85   OPTIONAL, sets 85 ms inter-packet
                                        delay on this interface for IPX RIP.
                                        The default setting is 55 ms. This
                                        commands overrides the global command
                                        above

ipx output-sap-delay 85   OPTIONAL, sets 85 ms inter-packet
                                        delay on this interface for IPX SAP.
                                        The default setting is 55 ms. This
                                        commands overrides the global command
                                        above

ipx gns-response-delay 2000   OPTIONAL, adjusts the amount of time
                                        allowed for this interface to receive
                                        a GNS response to 2000 ms

ipx update interval sap passive   OPTIONAL, this will reduce/eliminate
                                        unnecessary SAP traffic on this
                                        interface

ipx update interval sap 300   OPTIONAL, configures SAP updates to be
                                        sent (and expected) on this interface
                                        every 300 seconds (5 minutes) to reduce
                                        periodic update overhead. Default is
                                        60 seconds. The minimum interval is 10
                                        seconds

```
ipx update interval rip 90          OPTIONAL, adjusts the interval at which
                                     RIP updates are sent to every 90 seconds.
                                     Default is 60 seconds.  The minimum
                                     interval is 10 seconds


ipx router rip                       Automatically implemented with the ipx
                                     routing command
  network 25                         Allows IPX network 25 to be routed by
                                     IPX RIP
  network 31                         Allows IPX network 31 to be routed by
                                     IPX RIP
```

Next we'll briefly discuss how the router handles (switches) the IPX packets internally.

Disabling IPX Fast Switching

Fast switching allows higher throughput by switching a packet using a cache created by previous packets. Fast switching is enabled by default on all interfaces that support it. Packet transfer performance is generally better when fast switching is enabled. (However, you might want to disable fast switching to save memory space on interface cards and to help avoid congestion when high-bandwidth interfaces are writing large amounts of information to low-bandwidth interfaces.) You will also need to disable fast switching if you decide to implement packet-by-packet load balancing. Packet-by-packet load balancing means that packets will be transmitted (evenly distributed) across all equal-cost paths. You can disable fast switching with the no ipx route-cache command on the desired interface. Turning off fast switching increases system overhead. Use the show ipx interface command to verify whether the interface is configured for IPX fast switching.

Fast switching is one way of manipulating the IPX packet flow in the router environment. Another way is to implement load balancing.

Configuring Load Balancing

If multiple best path routes are present for a destination network, IPX RIP will keep only one of them and insert the route into the routing table. If that route is lost, the router will send out an unreachable network RIP broadcast. The router must then wait for the next RIP broadcast update to arrive for the alternate route.

By default, a router will learn and use only one path to a given IPX network. However, Cisco routers support multiple equal-cost, parallel paths to a destination network instead of only one path. By using the ipx maximum-paths 4 command in global configuration mode, you can set the maximum number of equal-cost, parallel paths to a destination. The router will then distribute the output packets on a packet-by-packet basis in a round-robin fashion across the number of allowed paths because IPX can perform round-robin or per-host load sharing. The sample command earlier will allow four equal-cost paths, but you can specify up to a maximum of 512 paths. Use the show ipx route command to display the maximum number of paths that can be used for load balancing.

Now we will discuss how to implement the IPX EIGRP routing protocol instead of IPX RIP.

Configuring IPX with IPX EIGRP

IPX EIGRP is an enhanced version of the Interior Gateway Routing Protocol (IGRP) developed by Cisco. EIGRP uses the same distance vector algorithm and distance information as IGRP. However, the convergence properties and the operating efficiency of EIGRP have improved significantly over IGRP. The IPX version of EIGRP does not have all the advanced features that the IP version has. This is due to the fact that IPX EIGRP was developed solely for overcoming the large bandwidth consumption requirement that IPX RIP has. In fact, the common design is to run IPX EIGRP on WAN links and IPX RIP on the LAN. However, IPX EIGRP has some benefits:

Fast convergence The DUAL algorithm allows routing information to converge extremely quickly.

Partial updates EIGRP sends incremental routing updates and SAPs when the state of a destination changes instead of sending the entire contents of the routing table. This feature minimizes the bandwidth required for EIGRP packets.

Neighbor discovery mechanism This feature is a simple hello mechanism used to learn about neighboring routers.

Scaling EIGRP scales to large networks.

Redistribution Automatically redistributes with IPX RIP.

Let's take a look at some of the possible global, interface, and routing process commands, which can be used to configure IPX RIP.

ipx routing 0002.0002.0002	Enables the IPX protocol, the IPX RIP protocol, and specifies the Node address for all WAN interfaces
ipx maximum-hops 85	OPTIONAL, sets the maximum number of hops of an IPX packet reachable by non-IPX RIP routing protocols. Also sets the maximum number of routers that an IPX packet can traverse before being dropped. Maximum hop count = 254
interface Serial0/0.1 point-to-multipoint	
	Configures a multipoint sub-interface
encapsulation frame-relay	Configures this interface for Frame-Relay encapsulation

bandwidth 10000	OPTIONAL, changes the reference bandwidth for the interface
ipx network 15	Configures the IPX network number of 15 on this interface. Notice this network is specified under ipx router rip
ipx hello-interval eigrp 10 30	OPTIONAL, this sets EIGRP AS 10 to use a hello interval of 30 seconds on this interface. By default, hello packets are sent every 5 seconds. The exception is on low-speed, nonbroadcast multi-access (NBMA) media, where the default hello interval is 60 seconds
ipx hold-time eigrp 10 120	OPTIONAL, EIGRP AS 10 uses a hold time of 120 seconds on this interface. By default, the hold-time is three times the hello interval (15 or 180 seconds)
ipx bandwidth-percent eigrp 10 25	OPTIONAL, limits the IPX EIGRP Autonomous System 10 traffic to 25 percent of bandwidth on this interface. By default, EIGRP packets consume a maximum of 50 percent of the link bandwidth, as referenced to the configured bandwidth command on the interface
ipx router eigrp 10	Designates the IPX EIGRP routing process as Autonomous System 10
network 15	Allows IPX network 15 to be routed by IPX EIGRP
ipx router rip	Automatically implemented with the ipx routing command
no network 15	REQUIRED, instructs IPX RIP to NOT advertise network 15. If you have more than one IPX network to turn off, then use the no network all command

There are some *optional* commands that can be configured in order to fine-tune the IPX EIGRP routing protocol. We'll take a look at some of them in the following two sections.

Disabling Split-Horizon with IPX

Split-horizon controls the sending of IPX EIGRP update and query packets. If split-horizon is enabled on an interface, these packets are not sent for a destination if this interface is the next hop to that destination. Split-horizon is enabled on all physical interfaces by default.

Split-horizon blocks information about routes from being advertised by the router out any interface from which that information originated. This behavior usually optimizes communication among multiple routers, particularly when links are broken. However, with nonbroadcast networks (such as Frame Relay), situations in which you do not want this to happen can arise. For these situations, you can disable split-horizon with IPX EIGRP. It is extremely important to remember that you *cannot* disable split-horizon for IPX RIP or SAP advertisements, *only* IPX EIGRP. To disable split-horizon, use the following command in interface configuration mode:

`interface serial0/0.1 point-to-multipoint`	You will usually want to disable split-horizon on multipoint interfaces
`no ipx split-horizon eigrp 10`	Disable split-horizon for the EIGRP Autonomous System 10, on this interface

You can also disable split-horizon for incremental SAPs on a specific interface with the following command:

`interface serial0/0.1 point-to-multipoint`	You will usually want to disable split-horizon on multipoint interfaces
`no ipx sap-incremental split-horizon`	Disables split-horizon for SAPs, on this interface

Controlling SAP Updates

If IPX EIGRP peers are found on an interface, you can configure the router to send SAP updates either periodically (every 60 seconds) or when a change occurs in the SAP table (incrementally). When no IPX EIGRP peer is present on the interface, periodic SAPs are always sent. On serial lines, by default, if an EIGRP neighbor is present, the router sends SAP updates only when the SAP table changes. On Ethernet, token ring, and FDDI interfaces, by default, the router sends SAP updates periodically (every 60 seconds). To reduce the amount of bandwidth required to send SAP updates, you might want to disable the periodic sending of SAP updates on LAN interfaces. This should be disabled only when all nodes out of this interface are EIGRP peers; otherwise, loss of SAP information for the other nodes will result. To send SAP updates only when a change occurs in the SAP table, use the following command:

```
interface ethernet0/0
```

`ipx sap-incremental eigrp 10`	Sends SAP updates only when a change in the SAP table occurs within EIGRP Autonomous System 10. SAPs are advertised periodically (every 60 seconds) by default on a LAN interface. Only use on a LAN with no other IPX devices

```
interface serial0/0
```

`no ipx sap-incremental eigrp 10`	By default, on a WAN interface, SAP updates are sent only when a change in the SAP table occurs within EIGRP Autonomous System 10. However, this can be disabled with the no form of the command

There is a third method of IPX dynamic routing that can be implemented; it is called NetWare Link Services Protocol (NLSP).

Configuring IPX with NLSP

NetWare Link Services Protocol (NLSP) is, of course, a link-state routing protocol based on the Open System Interconnection (OSI) *Intermediate System-to-Intermediate System (IS-IS)* protocol; thus it uses the shortest path first (SPF) algorithm. The main purpose for which NLSP was designed was to replace the bandwidth-intensive broadcast associated with IPX RIP, SAPs, and GNS. It also increased the maximum hop count to 127. NLSP is far more efficient with SAPs, because it will send a SAP only when the network changes instead of periodically broadcasting out SAPs every 60 seconds as IPX RIP does. NLSP was designed to be used in a hierarchical routing environment in which networked systems are grouped into routing areas. Routing areas can then be grouped into routing domains, and domains can further be grouped into an internetwork. NLSP was actually designed after the same model as IS-IS; thus each router can be assigned to a particular level and area.

Level 1 routers connect networked systems within a given routing area. Areas are connected to each other by Level 2 routers, and domains are connected by Level 3 routers. Although NLSP is designed for hierarchical routing environments containing Level 1, 2, and 3 routers, only Level 1 routing with area route aggregation and route redistribution has been defined in an accepted specification.

Similar to OSPF, NLSP elects a designated router (DR) on multiaccess segments to limit the amount of adjacency traffic. Unlike OSPF, a backup designated router is not elected. The designated router represents all routers that are connected to the same LAN segment. It creates a virtual router called a *pseudonode,* which generates routing information on behalf of the LAN and sends it to the remainder of the routing area. The routing information generated includes adjacencies and RIP routes. The use of a designated router substantially reduces the number of entries in the LSP database. Designated routers are elected automatically. After a router has been a DR for 60 seconds, it increases its priority by 20. However, you can manually affect the identity of the designated router by changing the priority of the system; the system with the highest priority is elected to be the designated router. By default, the priority of the system is 44. To change this priority, configure the `ipx nlsp priority` command on the outbound interface. NLSP *cannot* be configured on loopback interfaces or on physical/multipoint Frame Relay interfaces. It can be configured on Frame Relay point-to-point interfaces and *tunnel* interfaces (use a Generic Route Encapsulation tunnel, or GRE tunnel). Also, when enabling NLSP and configuring multiple encapsulations on the same physical LAN interface, you must use subinterfaces. You cannot use secondary networks. NLSP routers will update routing tables when a change occurs or every two hours.

Let's take a look at some of the possible commands, which can be configured within the IPX NLSP routing process.

`ipx routing 0002.0002.0002`	Enables the IPX protocol, the IPX RIP protocol, and specifies the Node address for all WAN interfaces
`ipx internal-network 17`	REQUIRED, an IPX network number assigned to the router, the number must be unique on each router, same as a Router ID
`interface Serial0/0.1 point-to-point`	
`ipx network 25`	Configures the IPX network number of 25 on this interface
`ipx nlsp enable`	Enables NLSP on this interface
`ipx nlsp priority 50`	Sets this interface priority value to 50. Determines this interfaces priority in being elected the Designated Router (DR). Default value is 44, and the highest priority is preferred

`ipx nlsp metric 35`	Assigns a metric of 35 to the link and used to calculate the cost from each other router via the links in the network to other destinations. Just like IS-IS, the range is 0 to 63. The default value is 10. The lowest metric is preferred
`ipx nlsp rip off`	OPTIONAL, this interface will never generate RIP periodic traffic
`ipx nlsp sap off`	OPTIONAL, this interface will never generate SAP periodic traffic
`ipx router nlsp`	Enables NLSP
`area-address AAAABBB1 FFFFFFF0`	Defines a set of network numbers to be part of the current NLSP area. Network and Mask - area address that includes networks AAAABBB1 through AAABBBF. Use the area-address 0 0 command for no summarization, as 0's are open or anything

Because the FFFFFFF0 mask was used, the last digit defined the local network address, thereby making 16 local networks available. If the mask was FFFFFF00, then there would be 254 local networks.

We've now covered all three IPX dynamic routing protocols: IPX RIP, IPX EIGRP, and NLSP. Now would be a good time to discuss how to redistribute routes between these three routing protocols.

Configuring IPX Route Redistribution

Route redistribution between IPX RIP and IPX EIGRP is automatic because you do not have to manually configure any commands. Route redistribution between IPX RIP and NLSP is also automatic. The Cisco router will automatically redistribute the IPX RIP routes into EIGRP and NLSP as soon as you configure the IPX EIGRP or NLSP routing process. And remember that the IPX RIP routing protocol is automatically invoked as soon as you apply the `ipx routing` global command.

Remember this aspect of IPX RIP and IPX EIGRP and NLSP routing protocols. When you set up IPX EIGRP or NLSP routing for IPX in part of your network, you will actually have both IPX EIGRP and IPX RIP routing protocols or both NLSP and IPX RIP running concurrently.

In order to stop the IPX RIP routing protocol so that you are only running IPX EIGRP or NLSP in your specified part of the network, you must apply the no network all command under the ipx router rip routing process.

So, redistribution is automatically configured as soon as you enable an IPX routing protocol. One exception is NLSP and IPX EIGRP. You must configure the redistribution of IPX EIGRP into NLSP and NLSP into IPX EIGRP. Once you enable IPX EIGRP and NLSP redistribution, the router makes path decisions based on a predefined, nonconfigurable administrative distance and prevents redistribution feedback loops without filtering via a stored, external hop count.

The following is an example of mutual redistribution between IPX EIGRP and NLSP on the same router:

ipx router nlsp	Enables NLSP
redistribute eigrp 10	Enables redistribution of IPX EIGRP Autonomous System 10 into NLSP
ipx router eigrp 10	
redistribute nlsp	Enables redistribution of NLSP into IPX EIGRP Autonomous System 10
ipx router rip	IPX RIP is automatically implemented with the ipx routing command
no network 100	Instructs IPX RIP to NOT advertise the Network 100. Likewise, the no network all command will cause IPX RIP to not advertise any network

Configuring the IPXWAN Protocol

Cisco routers support the IPXWAN protocol, as defined in RFC 1634. *IPXWAN* allows a router that is running IPX routing to connect via a serial link to another router, possibly from another manufacturer, that is also routing IPX and using IPXWAN. IPXWAN is a connection startup/ negotiation protocol. Once a link has been established, IPXWAN incurs little or no overhead. You can use the IPXWAN protocol over PPP. You can also use it over High-Level Data Link Control (HDLC). However, the devices at both ends of the serial link must be Cisco routers; remember that the Cisco implementation of HDLC is proprietary. Likewise, by default, IPX assigns a "tick" delay value of 6 to all WAN links. By implementing the ipx ipxwan command on your WAN serial interfaces, you will be able to get an accurate "tick" delay value for the WAN link connected to the configured interface.

To use the `ipx ipxwan` command, you must first configure an `ipx internal-network` command on the router. Then verify that there is *not* already an `ipx network` command on the desired WAN interface. Finally, apply the `ipx ipxwan` command on both WAN interfaces at each end of the WAN link:

`ipx routing 0002.0002.0002`	Enables the IPX protocol, the IPX RIP protocol, and specifies the Node address for all WAN interfaces
`ipx internal-network 17`	REQUIRED, an IPX network number assigned to the router, the number must be unique on each router, same as a Router ID
`interface Serial0/0`	
`no ipx network`	Verify that NO IPX network is configured on this interface
`ipx ipxwan`	Configures IPXWAN protocol. It must be applied to both ends of the WAN link. This interface is using the default HDLC encapsulation

Configuring IPX through a GRE Tunnel

One of the methods of transporting IPX across an IP-based network is to encapsulate the IPX packets inside an IP-based Generic Route Encapsulation (GRE) tunnel. To configure a GRE tunnel, you must have a source interface for one end of the tunnel and a destination interface for the opposite end of the tunnel (the destination interface will be on the router at the other end of the tunnel you are configuring). You must configure the tunnel interface on both routers at each end of the tunnel. The GRE tunnel uses the IP protocol number 47, so if you have the tunnel flowing through any interfaces that have an access list implemented, configure the access list to permit IP protocol 47 to pass through both directions. After the configuration is complete, use the **show interface tunnel** command to verify that the tunnel is operational and the **debug tunnel** command to verify that traffic is flowing across the tunnel. Figure 13.3 shows a GRE tunnel between router R1 and router R2, across an Ethernet link, which is only configured for the IP protocol, *not* the IPX protocol. However, the IPX network 500 traffic will be able to flow across the Ethernet link because the IPX packets are encapsulated in IP packets. So, we say that the IPX traffic is being tunneled through the IP network.

FIGURE 13.3 IPX through a GRE tunnel

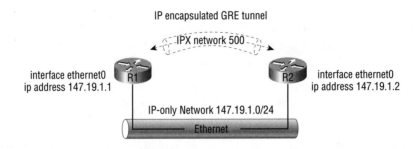

The following are the commands that would be required in the router R1 configuration to support the tunnel shown in Figure 13.3. Router R2 would require the same commands, but the tunnel source and tunnel destination addresses would have to be reversed. Remember that the tunnel source must be an active local interface name or IP address on the local router and the tunnel destination must be an active IP address on the remote router:

```
interface ethernet0
 ip address 147.19.1.1 255.255.255.0      Active IP address on this router


interface tunnel0                         Creates a virtual tunnel interface
 ipx network 500                          Specify the IPX network
                                          associated with this interface
                                          (tunnel)

 tunnel source 147.19.1.1                 The source can be a local
                                          interface name or local IP
                                          address on this router

 tunnel destination 147.19.1.2            The destination end of the
                                          tunnel.  Must be an IP address
                                          on the remote router


ipx router rip
 network 500
```

Static Routes, Default Routes, and SAPs

IPX uses RIP, EIGRP, or NLSP to determine the best path to route packets across when several routes to a destination exist. The routing protocol then dynamically updates the routing table. However, just like in the IP world, it is possible to add static routes to the routing table to explicitly specify routes to certain destinations. Static routes always override any dynamically learned routes.

Configuring IPX Static Routes

Be careful when assigning static routes. An IPX static route can be configured by specifying the next hop address or a local interface within the static route command.

The following example command is stating to send IPX packets to the destination IPX network AAA, with the next hop being the IPX host address (router) of 300.1234.1234.1234:

```
ipx route AAA 300.1234.1234.1234
```
Configure next-hop with either a host address 300.1234.1234.1234 or a local interface. You can also adjust the route metric by adjusting the tick (delay) at the end of the static route command. The tick value can be 1-65534

You can also configure static routes that have a lower priority (higher administrative distance) than the dynamically learned routes. These routes are referred to as floating static routes. You can use a floating static route to create a path of last resort that is used only when no dynamic routing information is available. To create a floating static route, simply add `floating-static` to the end of a static route:

```
ipx route AAA 300.1234.1234.1234 floating-static
```
The word floating-static changes the static route to a floating static route

By default, floating static routes are not redistributed into other dynamic routing protocols. In order to redistribute the floating static routes into a dynamic routing protocol, you must configure the `redistribute floating-static` command on the routing process into which you want the floating static routes redistributed.

Just as in IP, you can configure a default route in IPX. In the next section, we'll take a look at how to configure a default route for IPX on a Cisco router.

Configuring IPX Default Routes

The default route is used when a route to any destination network is unknown. All packets for which a route to the destination address is unknown are forwarded to the default route. By default, IPX treats network number–2 (0xFFFFFFFE) as the default route. A default route is enabled by default in IPX. Original IPX RIP implementations allowed the use of network –2 (0xFFFFFFFE) as a regular network number in a network. With the inception of NetWare Link Services Protocol (NLSP), network –2 is reserved as the default route for NLSP and RIP. Both NLSP and RIP routers should treat network –2 as a default route. You should implement network –2 as the default route regardless of whether you configure NLSP in your IPX network. You can configure a default route manually, if you wish. The following is an example of an `ipx route default` command:

`ipx route default 300.1234.1234.1234`   Creates a static entry for the default route. The router forwards all non-local packets for which no explicit route is known via the specified next hop address 300.1234.1234.1234 or local interface

IPX servers use Service Advertising Protocol (SAP) to advertise their services via broadcast packets. Cisco routers store this information in the SAP table, which is also known as the server information table. This table is updated dynamically. You might want to statically add a SAP to the server information table so that clients always use the services of a particular server. Let's take a look at how to configure static SAPs.

Configuring IPX Static SAPs

Static SAP assignments always override any identical entries in the SAP table that are learned dynamically, regardless of the hop count. If a dynamic network route that is associated with a static SAP entry is lost or deleted, the router will not advertise the static SAP entry until it relearns the lost route. There is no need to redistribute static SAP entries because static SAPs are automatically advertised. The suppression is due to the split-horizon rule, which states that RIP and SAP broadcast learned from a particular interface will not be advertised out the same interface. Use the `show ipx servers` command to display SAP entries. Static SAPs will be marked with an *S* next to the entry.

 When creating a static SAP, do *not* associate it with the address of an interface that you want the SAP to be transmitted out of or it will get suppressed.

The command syntax for configuring IPX static SAP is as follows:

```
ipx sap <service-type> <server name> <network.node> <socket> <hop-count>
```

Here is a command configuration example of an IPX static SAP:

```
ipx sap 4 server8 AAA.0000.0c12.1234 451 1
```
Specifies a static SAP table entry for the service type of 4 (file server), the servers name being server8, the IPX address of the server is AAA.0000.0c12.1234, utilizing socket 451 (NCP = NetWare Core Protocol), and the IPX server is 1 hop away from this router

The following is a brief example of how to use SAP access list range of 1000 through 1099 to filter SAPs based on the IPX server names. Remember that you can use the * as a wildcard to represent multiple characters within the IPX server name. For example, the following access list will deny all SAPs with an IPX server name beginning with *chris* and permits everything else:

```
access-list 1000 deny -1 0 chris*
access-list 1000 permit -1
```

We'll show you how to properly implement access lists later on in Chapter 16. For now, we have completed our discussion of the IPX protocol. In the next section, we'll briefly discuss how to troubleshoot the IPX environment.

IPX Troubleshooting

In troubleshooting Novell IPX services, you must first verify that there is reachability to the server that is providing the services that are required. If the server is not on your local network, then you must verify that your local router knows how to get to the remote IPX network where the server is located. A show ipx route command will list all networks known to the router, the interface to use, and the next hop gateway. A show ipx servers command will list the type of service, the name of the server, and the network address. Remember that a Novell server has what is known as an internal IPX network number, which is different than the LAN IPX network number. Your local router must know how to get to both of these networks because the network address associated with some services is the internal IPX network address, not the LAN IPX network address. Figure 13.4 shows a typical IPX network with all the required IPX networks shown.

FIGURE 13.4   IPX troubleshooting

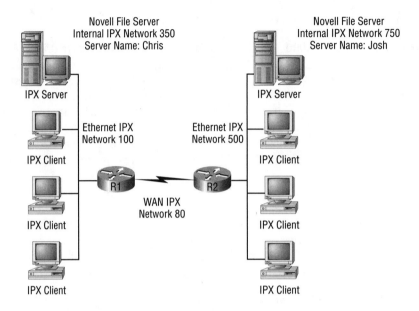

Notice that even though there are only two Ethernet LANs shown, there are actually five IPX networks (two Ethernet LANs, one WAN serial link, and two internal networks for the two servers).

Viewing IPX Routes and Services

Use the `show ipx route` command to verify that the local router is aware of all IPX networks. In Figure 13.4, router R1 will have networks 100 and 80 as directly connected networks and networks 350, 500, and 750 as learned networks. Router R2 will have networks 500 and 80 as directly connected networks and networks 750, 100, and 350 as learned networks. Use the `show ipx servers` command to verify that the router knows about the servers. Both router R1 and router R2 will have two servers listed, Chris and Josh.

Each IPX network must have a unique IPX network number (address). All devices on the LAN segment must agree on the IPX network address of the local LAN segment. So, the local LAN number (address) *cannot* be in use anywhere else within the internetwork. Remember that an IPX server also has its own internal IPX network number (address) and this internal IPX network address must also be unique. Each Novell server will have at lease two addresses assigned to it, the LAN IPX network address and an internal IPX network address. Also, remember that the default internal node (host) address of an IPX server is 0000.0000.0001. In Figure 13.4, the two servers will have default full IPX addresses of 350.0000.0000.0001 and 750.0000.0000.0001.

IPX Ping

To verify IPX connectivity between Cisco routers, use the `ping ipx 750.0000.0000.0001` command. In this sample command, a ping would be initiated to the device with a node (host) address of 0000.0000.0001 on the 750 network. This will help verify that a remote router or host device is reachable with the IPX protocol. IPX PING uses socket number 9086.

Monitoring and Maintaining IPX

The following are some of the recommended commands to assist in the troubleshooting of IPX routing issues:

`show ipx interfaces`	Displays the status of the IPX interfaces configured in the router and the parameters configured on each interface
`show ipx servers`	Lists the servers discovered through SAP advertisements
`show ipx route`	Displays the contents of the IPX routing table
`show ipx traffic`	Displays information about IPX traffic
`clear ipx route *`	Deletes all entries in the IPX routing table
`clear ipx traffic`	Clears IPX traffic counters

Monitoring and Maintaining IPX EIGRP

The following are some of the recommended commands to assist in the troubleshooting of IPX EIGRP routing issues:

`show ipx eigrp interfaces`	Displays information about interfaces configured for IPX EIGRP
`show ipx eigrp topology`	Displays the contents of the IPX EIGRP topology table
`show ipx route`	Displays the contents of the IPX routing table, including IPX EIGRP entries
`show ipx traffic`	Displays information about IPX traffic, including IPX EIGRP traffic

Monitoring and Maintaining NLSP

The following are some of the recommended commands to assist in the troubleshooting of NLSP routing issues:

`clear ipx nlsp neighbors`	Deletes all NLSP adjacencies from the adjacency database
`clear ipx nlsp traffic`	Clears NLSP traffic counters
`show ipx nlsp database`	Displays the entries in the NLSP database
`show ipx nlsp neighbors`	Displays the NLSP neighbors of the device and their states
`show ipx nlsp traffic`	Displays cumulative traffic statistics for NLSP traffic counters

It's time now to shift gears and discuss the Microsoft Windows environment, as it pertains to the Cisco router world.

Windows NT Support

Windows NT provides many challenges for the network administrator, including NetBIOS, browsing, domain controllers, and access lists. The primary cause of most problems is that Windows NT 4 and earlier all use an encapsulated NetBIOS (Session layer protocol). Windows 2000 does not use encapsulated NetBIOS (unless connecting to an older NT 4 or earlier domain controller), which resolves most of these problems. And Windows 2000/XP uses the common interface file system (CIFS). Windows NT groups servers and clients into NT domains. Each domain has a *primary domain controller (PDC)* and one or more *backup domain controllers (BDCs)*, which control functions such as user logon authentication within the domain. Resources, such as servers, are given names that clients use to access them. There are four methods for a device to resolve the resource (server) device names to IP addresses. Well, there is also a fifth method, domain name service (DNS); however, we will not be discussing DNS in this chapter, as it was discussed in Chapter 8:

- NetBIOS broadcast
- NetBIOS local cache
- LMHOSTS file
- Windows Internet Naming Service (WINS)

The LMHOSTS file is a statically configured file that resides on the local computer.

Windows NT uses the Session (layer 5) NetBIOS protocol for file and print services, messaging, and name resolution. In the next section, we'll discuss the NetBIOS name resolution functionality.

NetBIOS and NetBEUI

NetBIOS is a Session layer protocol, and must be transported by either TCP/IP, IPX, or NetBEUI. Now, let's discuss NetBIOS as it is carried by TCP/IP. All Windows computers send out NAME_ QUERY broadcasts to all other devices on the same LAN segment, and the device with the NetBIOS name being requested responds with its IP address. This process is known as a NetBIOS broadcast. Likewise, a device can keep a table of NetBIOS names and corresponding IP addresses in NetBIOS local cache. A device can also use a static file that is manually configured and maps NetBIOS names to known IP addresses. This local static file is known as the LMHOSTS file. The final method of Net-BIOS name resolution is WINS, which we will discuss in the next section.

NetBIOS can also run on top of *NetBIOS Extended User Interface (NetBEUI),* which is a nonroutable protocol because it has no logical network portion. To propagate this protocol between segments, the administrator has two choices: bridging or encapsulation.

Bridging allows all frames to propagate across the network; however, it must be supported throughout the network for two remote stations to communicate. All broadcasts are propagated throughout the entire network, which is not a practical solution for large networks.

Data-link switching (DLSw) provides a mechanism to encapsulate NetBEUI packets into IP packets. This allows two remote NetBEUI segments to communicate via an IP network.

The NetBEUI protocol is being phased out of all but the smallest of networks. You should consider bridging and DLSw as temporary solutions. We will discuss both bridging and DLSw in Chapter 14.

The most scalable solution is to operate NetBIOS over TCP/IP (NBT). With NBT, the NetBIOS broadcasts are still utilized, but they run using TCP and UDP port 137 for name services. The Net-BIOS datagram service uses TCP and UDP port 138, and the NetBIOS session services use TCP and UDP port 139. And for Windows 2000/XP, CIFS runs on TCP port 445. So, it is possible to filter the NetBIOS broadcast using IP access lists. We will discuss access lists in Chapter 16.

WINS

Windows can also encapsulate NetBIOS packets into IP packets. These packets are treated as normal IP packets and can be routed throughout the internetwork. To allow browsing of remote resources, Microsoft created the *Windows Internet Naming Service (WINS).* A WINS server builds a dynamic NetBIOS name registration database by collecting name information about machines on the internetwork. This service is very similar to the service that DNS provides for name resolution on the Internet.

Windows devices (hosts) register their NetBIOS names with the WINS server upon startup and then send unicast requests directly to the WINS server in order to resolve the NetBIOS names to IP addresses. This process basically eliminates the need for the NetBIOS NAME_QUERY broadcasts.

In problem situations, the `ip helper-address` command can ensure that name advertisements are forwarded to the WINS server. It is especially important that the clients be able to resolve the IP address of their domain controller (PDC and BDC).

Just as NetBIOS can operate with IP, it can also operate with IPX.

IPX

Windows machines can be configured with IPX for Microsoft file and print sharing because NetBIOS can also run over IPX. In the Windows NT environment, this is known as NWLINK. Again, NetBIOS is being encapsulated, but this time inside an IPX packet. These packets are treated as normal IPX packets with one caveat: Windows uses IPX type-20 broadcast packets for protocol services, such as browsing. To browse across the routers, IPX type-20 propagation (forwarding) must be enabled.

Summary

In this chapter, we discussed two popular desktop protocols: Novell NetWare's IPX and Microsoft's implementation of NetBIOS.

IPX at one time boasted more than 500,000 networks, but its use is declining. IPX is still used extensively in many corporations but primarily in conjunction with IP. The newest NetWare servers support TCP/IP natively. The Novell IPX protocol can be cumbersome because it is extremely reliant upon utilizing broadcast traffic (SAP and GNS) to allow the servers and clients to communicate with each other. Also, by default IPX uses the IPX RIP routing protocol (which is also broadcast intensive), periodically advertising the entire routing table to all neighbor routers every 60 seconds. But keep in mind that the IPX protocol was developed for a LAN environment in which the broadcast nature of the protocol was not a major problem.

Microsoft's implementation of NetBIOS is the most popular file- and print-sharing protocol in the world. It is implemented in three flavors: NetBEUI, NetBIOS over IPX, and NetBIOS over IP. These protocols each have their unique problems in a WAN environment. As Windows 2000 and its successors eliminate NetBIOS in favor of native IP, these protocols will also be used less.

As TCP/IP becomes more and more dominant, these desktop protocols will become less and less important. However, understanding them can give you great insight into the strengths and weaknesses of particular implementations of TCP/IP.

Exam Essentials

Know what IPX and SPX are.   Internetwork Packet Exchange (IPX) is a connectionless layer 3 protocol that provides the functionality of layer 3 and layer 4 of the OSI reference model. In many ways, you can think of it as providing the same services that IP and UDP provide in the TCP/IP world. Sequenced Packet Exchange (SPX) is a connection-oriented protocol occurring at layer 4 of the OSI model and is the NetWare counterpart to TCP. An SPX constraint is that it is limited to a window size of 1.

Understand encapsulation, or frame types.   Encapsulation is the process of packaging upper-layer protocol information and data into frames. NetWare refers to encapsulation as frame type.

Know what an IPX address is.   An IPX logical address is 10 bytes or 80 bits in length and it is presented in the typical Network.Node format. The characters are displayed in hexadecimal format, so each character is actually 4 bits, thus two characters equal 1 byte. The first 4 bytes, or 32 bits, must be a hexadecimal number between 1 and FFFFFFFD (the FFFFFFFF network is reserved for a broadcast, and the FFFFFFFE network is reserved for an NLSP default route) and represent the Network portion of the address. The last 6 bytes, or 48 bits, represent the Node (host) portion of the address. The Node (or host) portion of the IPX address is usually the MAC address of the network interface card (NIC), thereby providing a unique address for each node.

Be able to explain SAP and GNS.   A Service Advertising Protocol (SAP) packet carries information on the type of service available, the name of the server, and its IPX address. A single SAP can carry a maximum of seven services. Clients broadcast out Get Nearest Server (GNS) packets to locate the nearest active server of a particular type.

Understand the IPX RIP tick metric.   The IP version of RIP uses the hop count metric to make routing decisions. The IPX version of RIP uses ticks to make the routing decisions. Ticks are displayed in the IPX RIP routing table as the amount of delay associated with each link in the path to the destination network (a tick is 1/18 of a second, or approximately 55 ms). If there is a tie in the delay (number of ticks) between two possible paths to a destination, then the hop count is used to break the tie.

Know how split-horizon is implemented with IPX routing protocols.   It is extremely important to remember that you *cannot* disable split-horizon for IPX RIP or SAP advertisements, *only* IPX EIGRP.

Know what a GRE tunnel is.   One of the methods of transporting IPX across an IP-based network is to encapsulate the IPX packets inside an IP-based Generic Routing Encapsulation (GRE) tunnel.

Understand the purpose of the PDC and BDC. Each domain has a primary domain controller (PDC) and one or more backup domain controllers (BDCs), which control functions such as user logon authentication within the domain.

Know the four methods of NetBIOS name resolution. There are four methods a device can use to resolve the resource (server) device names to IP addresses: NetBIOS broadcast, NetBIOS local cache, LMHOSTS file, and Windows Internet Naming Service (WINS). (And DNS is actually a fifth method.)

Key Terms

Before you take the exam, be certain you are familiar with the following terms:

backup domain controllers (BDCs)

NetWare Link Services Protocol (NLSP)

data-link switching (DLSw)

primary domain controller (PDC)

Get Nearest Server (GNS)

IPX Routing Information Protocol (RIP)

Intermediate System-to-Intermediate System (IS-IS)

Sequenced Packet Exchange (SPX)

Internetwork Packet Exchange (IPX)

Service Advertising Protocol (SAP)

IPXWAN

tunnel

NetBIOS Extended User Interface (NetBEUI)

Windows Internet Naming Service (WINS)

NetWare Core Protocol (NCP)

Review Questions

1. Which of the following describes an IPX address?

   A. 32 bits: 16 bits for network, 16 bits for node

   B. 32 bits: 8 bits for network, 24 bits for node

   C. 64 bits: 32 bits for network, 32 bits for node

   D. 80 bits: 32 bits for network, 48 bits for node

   E. 80 bits: 16 bits for network, 64 bits for node

2. When an IPX client first boots, it has no knowledge of the network. How does the client acquire initial information about the network?

   A. RIP

   B. SAP

   C. GNS

   D. Network administrator

   E. DHCP

3. There are three NetWare file servers on a segment. Each has two services to advertise. How many SAP advertisements will a Cisco router forward from that segment every 10 minutes?

   A. 1

   B. 10

   C. 20

   D. 30

   E. 60

4. IPX RIP is a distance-vector routing protocol. How does IPX RIP determine the best path?

   A. The number of ticks plus the number of hops

   B. The number of ticks only

   C. The number of hops only

   D. Considers hops first and uses ticks for a tiebreaker

   E. Considers ticks first and uses hops for a tiebreaker

5. Which of the following protocols are based on the shortest path first algorithm?

    A. IPX EIGRP

    B. IPX RIP

    C. NLSP

    D. IPX IGRP

    E. IPX SAP

6. A Cisco router has two interfaces, an Ethernet and an FDDI. IPX EIGRP is enabled on the FDDI interface. How often are SAP updates sent out the FDDI interface?

    A. Once every 30 seconds

    B. Once every 60 seconds

    C. Once every 2 hours

    D. Only when changes occur

    E. Only once

7. Which of the following is true regarding IPXWAN?

    A. Reduces bandwidth utilization on LAN links

    B. Reduces bandwidth utilization on WAN links

    C. Is a startup negotiation protocol only

    D. Requires NLSP

    E. Provides incremental updates

8. A Novell server has what is known as an internal IPX network number, which is different than the LAN IPX network number. What is the default internal IPX address for a server that belongs to the internal network 500?

    A. 500. 0001.0001.0001

    B. 500. 0500.0500.0500

    C. 500. 0000.0000.0001

    D. 500. 0500.0500.0001

9. In order to browse NT resources on an IPX network, what must be enabled on the router? (Choose all that apply.)

  A. NLSP

  B. IPX type-20 propagation

  C. SAP filters

  D. GNS

  E. IPX routing

10. Two Microsoft NT networks are running NetBEUI. These remote networks want to connect via the Internet. Which of the following are possible solutions? (Choose all that apply.)

  A. Enable NetBEUI on Internet backbone.

  B. Enable bridging on Internet backbone.

  C. Convert network to TCP/IP.

  D. Use DLSw.

Answers to Review Questions

1. D. An IPX address contains a 32-bit network address, assigned by an administrator, and a 48-bit node address composed of the MAC address.

2. C. When a client first boots, it issues a Get Nearest Server (GNS) request to locate a NetWare server.

3. B. Routers collect individual SAPs into a consolidated SAP table. That SAP table is advertised every 60 seconds.

4. E. IPX RIP considers delay (ticks) first. Only in the event of a tie is hop count used.

5. C. The NetWare Link Services Protocol (NLSP) is a link-state protocol based on the shortest path first algorithm.

6. B. EIGRP treats FDDI interfaces as LAN interfaces by default.

7. C. IPXWAN negotiates the parameters during the initial startup.

8. C. The default internal node (host) address of an IPX server is 0000.0000.0001.

9. B, E. IPX type-20 propagation allows for encapsulated NetBIOS packets to propagate through the network.

10. C, D. DLSw encapsulates NetBEUI packets inside IP packets.

Chapter 14

Bridging and Data-Link Switching (DLSw)

THE CCIE QUALIFICATION EXAM TOPICS COVERED IN THIS CHAPTER INCLUDE THE FOLLOWING:

- ✓ Transparent bridging
- ✓ IEEE/DEC Spanning-Tree Protocol (STP)
- ✓ Multi-Instance Spanning-Tree Protocol (MISTP)
- ✓ Source-route bridging
- ✓ Remote source-route bridging (RSRB)
- ✓ Source-route translational bridging (SR/TLB) and source-route transparent (SRT) bridging
- ✓ Translational bridging, integrated routing and bridging (IRB), concurrent routing and bridging (CRB)
- ✓ Basic data-link switching (DLSw)
- ✓ Advanced data-link switching (DLSw)

This chapter starts by looking at bridging in its various forms: transparent bridging, source-route bridging (SRB), source-route transparent (SRT) bridging, source-route translational bridging (SR/TLB), remote source-route bridging (RSRB), concurrent routing and bridging (CRB), and integrated routing and bridging (IRB). Bridging is compared with routing, and the Spanning-Tree Protocol and its roles in transparent and source-route bridging are investigated as well.

The chapter finishes with a look at data-link switching (DLSw) and how it's used to transport Systems Network Architecture (SNA) and NetBIOS traffic. The different WAN transport methods of DLSw are covered, as are the topics of peer redundancy, filtering, and scalability.

Bridging and DLSw are important subjects for the CCIE routing and switching candidate to study for three main reasons: First, these two topics make up a small but significant portion of both the written and lab exams. Second, transparent bridging is the foundation for switch operation. And third, although SNA traffic is diminishing and changing, its transport is still a very vital function in most enterprise networks.

Bridging Overview

Bridging is a method of transporting network traffic based on information in the Data Link layer of the packet.

Bridges control data flow, handle transmission errors, provide physical addressing, and manage access to the physical medium for many layer 2 protocols, including Ethernet, token ring, and FDDI (Fiber Distributed Data Interface).

Bridges, like routers and other networking devices on Ethernet segments, have the ability to limit the collision domain and hence improve network scalability and performance. They also allow for device connectivity across a greater distance (including WANs). Here is a brief synopsis of each major type of media bridging:

Transparent bridging (TB)   Found primarily in Ethernet environments and mostly used to bridge networks that have the same media types. Bridges keep a forwarding table that is learned from source MAC addresses and associates the outbound interface on which the end station resides or is reachable.

Source-route bridging (SRB)   Found primarily in token ring environments. Bridges forward frames based only on the routing information contained in the frame. End stations are responsible for determining and maintaining the table of destination addresses and routing indicators.

Source-route transparent (SRT) bridging   Resolved a large part of the incompatibility in bridging token ring and Ethernet by supporting the functions of transparent bridging and source-route bridging on the same network device. However, token ring end stations using source-route bridging cannot communicate with the Ethernet end stations and vice versa.

Source-route translational bridging (SR/TLB) and encapsulation bridging   Provides the ability to bridge dissimilar LANs, usually token ring and Ethernet or Ethernet and FDDI, by allowing the translation between both the media and the bridging types.

Bridging vs. Routing

Perhaps a dozen or more years ago this would have been a hotly debated subject; today it is merely a space filler in certification guides. Few, if any, networks these days bridge traffic that could be routed instead. That said, the primary reason bridging is configured these days is to transport unroutable traffic like SNA, NetBIOS (NetBEUI), and local area transport (LAT) traffic. From that standpoint, bridges have a capability that routers don't have.

The biggest advantage bridges have over routers is that they are protocol independent. Because they only rely on information at the Data-Link layer of the OSI model, all upper-layer protocol information is irrelevant. Forwarding of all packets is accomplished in the same manner; therefore, there is no additional configuration information necessary each time another type of traffic is added to the network. Furthermore, bridge configuration is simple, and for the most part, plug and play. There are no network addresses to configure and no routing protocols to configure and manage as with routers.

The biggest advantage routing has over bridging is scalability. Consider an IP network with users on two segments, A and B. A host that wants to ping device 1 on segment B must know the MAC address of that device. Similarly, when the host on segment A wants to ping device 2 on segment B, it must send an Address Resolution Protocol (ARP) request and find out the MAC address of device 2. For each device on another segment, host A must have an ARP entry and broadcast out an ARP request. If routing were configured between segments A and B, the host on segment A needs to know only the MAC address of the router and the router finds and stores the MAC address of the target device(s) on segment B.

If you examine the frames of bridged traffic, you'll see that the source and destination MAC addresses are those of the end devices. You won't see the MAC address of any bridge in the frame, and the frame looks the same

Bridges don't fragment packets. If a bridge receives a packet that is too large for one of its interfaces, the packet is discarded. Bridges do not share information such as reachability tables with one another as routers do with route tables.

Now that you've seen some of the advantages and disadvantages of bridging as well as how it compares with using routers, we'll look at each type of bridging in more detail, starting with transparent bridging.

Transparent Bridging

The following three items summarize the main functioning of a transparent bridge:

- Look up the destination MAC address of the incoming frame in the filtering database and forward the packet out the port listed. If the port listed in the table is the same as the incoming port, the frame is dropped.

- If the MAC address is not in the table or is a multicast or broadcast address, forward a copy of the frame out on all ports except the incoming bridge port. This practice is also known as *flooding*.

- Inspect the incoming source MAC address to see if it is already in the filtering database. If it's not, add it and the incoming port to the database.

At a fundamental level, transparent bridging is just table lookup. When a packet comes into the bridge, its destination MAC address is looked up in a table to see which port it's associated with and then forwarded out that port—nothing complicated or mystical. In the case of Figure 14.1, when host 1 sends a packet to host 3, bridge B1 looks up host 3's MAC address in its forwarding table. It sees that host 3 is associated with port P2, so it forwards the frame out there. If the frame's destination MAC address arrives on the same port it is associated with, the packet is dropped by the bridge. This is why a transparent bridge is also known as a filtering bridge; it selectively filters which frames it will forward and which ones it will drop. In Figure 14.1, if host 1 sends a frame to host 2, bridge B1 sees that the frame comes in on port P1 and that host 2's MAC address is also off of port P1, so it does nothing with the frame. The MAC address/port number forwarding table that the transparent bridge uses to forward packets is also known as the filtering database.

FIGURE 14.1   Transparent bridge performing table lookup

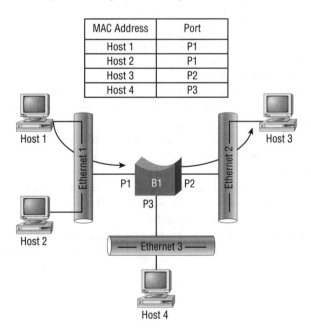

MAC Address	Port
Host 1	P1
Host 2	P1
Host 3	P2
Host 4	P3

The transparent bridge is also known as a learning bridge. This is because it learns where network devices (the MAC addresses more specifically) are in relation to it. Transparent bridges do not share reachability information with one another, so there must be some mechanism for them to populate their filtering database. In the scenario shown in Figure 14.2, assume that bridge B1 has just booted up and its filtering database is empty. When host 1 sends a frame to host 3, the bridge does not know where host 3 is located so sends a copy of the frame out all ports other than P1 where the frame first arrived. The bridge does look at the source MAC address of the frame and learns that host 1 is associated with port P1.

FIGURE 14.2   Transparent bridge with empty filtering database

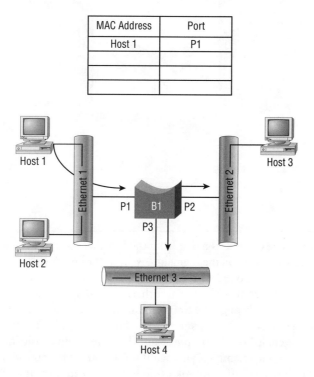

When host 3 sends a response to host 1's frame, bridge B1 looks up host 1's MAC address in its forwarding table. Because bridge B1 has already seen a frame from host 1, there is an entry in the table and the response can be sent out port P1, as seen in Figure 14.3. Bridge B1 also inspects the incoming frame's source MAC address and sees host 3's MAC address, which it puts in the forwarding table associated with port P2. Now subsequent traffic can take the correct path to host 3 without being forwarded out all bridge ports.

FIGURE 14.3   Transparent bridge learning host 3's location

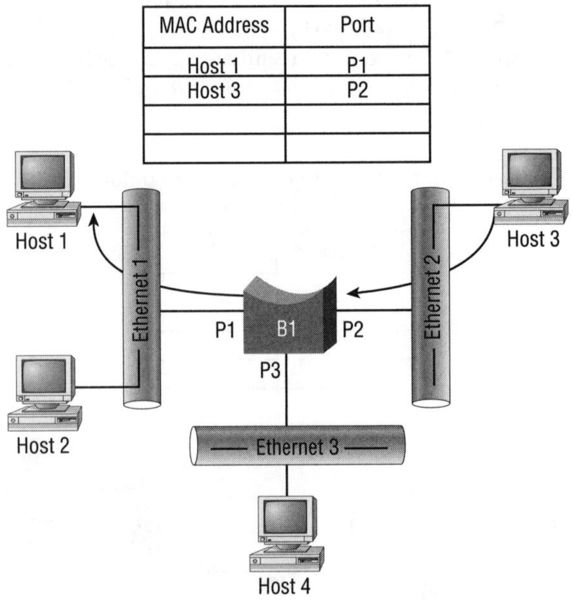

The transparent bridge derives its name from the fact that the end devices have no idea it is there; it functions transparently on the segment. As far as the end devices know, they are on the very same segment—there is no indication of how many segments away the other device is or whether any WAN links are traversed. The Ethernet, FDDI, or token ring frames are not changed in any way passing through the transparent bridge (technically, this is not true because one segment could be using 802.3 encapsulation and another ARPA, or in the case of token ring, the Monitor bit is not copied on the output frame, but you get the basic idea).

That's good for a simple example. Now we'll show you what happens when we grow the network and add redundancy. If you look at Figure 14.4, you'll see that we've added a few bridges and Ethernet segments to the path between host 1 and host 3. This should be good, right? If you look at the network after it's just powered up, all four bridges' forwarding tables are empty. When host 1 sends a frame to host 3, bridge B1 and bridge B2 both receive the frame and, because they don't know where host 3 is, forward out a copy out on all other ports (in this case, to Ethernet segment 2). Until host 3 responds to host 1's frame, bridge B1 and bridge B2 don't have host 3 in their forwarding tables. Therefore, when they receive the copy of the frame on Ethernet segment 2, they forward copies out again on segment 1, which starts the process all over again. This continues until the wires turn a dull red, then bright orange....

FIGURE 14.4   Transparent bridging with redundancy

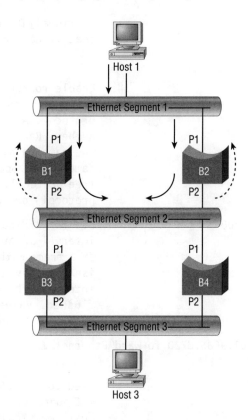

But let's say that somehow host 3 is able to respond to host 1 while this loop is raging out of control melting down the network. Bridge B1 and bridge B2 now learn about host 3 and update their forwarding tables to reflect that host 3 is off of their P2 ports. The loop ends and life is good, right? Well, let's say it's slightly better. We have no more loops with unicast traffic between host 1 and host 3, but now because there are four unique paths to get from Ethernet segment 1 to Ethernet segment 3, for every packet host 1 sends to host 3, there will be four copies. Although some protocols like TCP can deal with duplicate packets, protocols like SNA do not fare as well. Note also that broadcast and multicast frames will still loop endlessly. What can be done about this problem? We'll get to that right after we take a short break to show you how to configure transparent bridging on Cisco routers.

Configuring Transparent Bridging

The following lines show how to configure transparent bridging on a router. Note that any protocols configured for routing will not be bridged:

no ip routing

[Optional] Disables IP routing so that it can be bridged.

bridge 1 protocol ieee

Enable router to function as a bridge and assign a spanning tree protocol. Assign a bridge-group number. Range <1-255>; must be the same on all bridges in the same group. Specify the spanning tree protocol: ieee (IEEE 802.1D protocol) or dec (DEC protocol).

bridge 1 aging-time 200

Set forwarding aging time interval of entire bridge table. If a frame with a source address isn't received within age interval, the entry will be flushed. Values <10-1000000> seconds. Default 300 seconds

bridge 1 address 0001.9685.d720 forward Ethernet 1/0

Used to block/forward a certain MAC Address. The address can be a host, multicast or broadcast. Options include to forward or discard the frame as well as to specify the interface on which the address can be reached.

interface Ethernet 0/0

 no ip address

```
bridge-group 1
```
Associate interface with the appropriate bridge-group. By default all layer 3 protocols except IP are bridged. To route IP and bridge all other protocols, globally enable IP and assign this interface an IP address. Frames are bridged only among interfaces in the same group

```
interface Serial 1/0
```
On a Frame Relay multipoint interface allow bridging to be encapsulated over frame relay

```
encapsulation frame-relay

 bridge-group 1

 frame-relay map bridge 100 broadcast
```
Enable bridging over frame relay DLCI 100. On physical or sub-interfaces which have been configured for multi-point, use the frame-relay map statement. Broadcast capability is required for bridging but is not explicitly configured on point point-to-point interfaces.

The Spanning-Tree Protocol (STP) and Algorithm

Although the *Spanning-Tree Protocol* was covered with Ethernet in Chapter 6, "Ethernet LAN Technologies," a quick refresher never hurts. The answer to the problems in Figure 14.4 is the spanning-tree algorithm, which transforms the meshed, redundant topology into one with only a single path between segments (a "spanning tree"). This prevents loops and assures that packets arrive in order and have only one copy.

The basics of the STP are simple: elect a *root bridge* and select only one bridge port to forward packets back toward the root bridge on each Ethernet segment. The bridge with the lowest bridge priority becomes the root bridge, and the port with the lowest aggregate path cost back to the root bridge forwards on each segment. Each bridge has a bridge identifier, and each of its ports has an associated path cost and port priority value. The *bridge identifier* is used to select the root bridge, and the path cost, bridge identifier, and port priority are used to determine which bridge port on a segment is in a forwarding state. Both the root bridge election and forwarding port selection are accomplished with special packets called bridge protocol data units (BPDUs).

The root bridge "election" is fairly simple and is based on the root bridge priority value in the BPDU. The *bridge priority* is an 8-byte value composed of a 2-byte priority value and the 6-byte MAC address identifier of the bridge. The priority value defaults to 32768 (0x8000) and the MAC address is usually chosen from one of the bridge interfaces. The bridge with the *lowest* bridge priority value becomes the root bridge. When a bridge powers up, it sends out BPDUs advertising itself as the root bridge. When it receives a BPDU from another bridge, it checks the root bridge priority value. If it is numerically lower than its own (higher priority), it will stop transmitting its own BPDUs and transmit BPDUs with the root bridge's priority (although it will still put its own bridge identifier in the BPDU packets it sends out). If the bridge receives a BPDU with a root bridge identifier with a priority lower than its own priority, it will ignore this and continue sending its own BPDUs. BPDUs are generated at regular intervals by the root bridge, the default value being every 2 seconds.

Each port has a path cost associated with it that can be configured but defaults to a tabulated value based on interface bandwidth settings. The BPDU the root bridge generates will have a path cost of 0. As the BPDU is regenerated by each successive bridge in turn, the path cost of the bridge's receiving port is added to the path cost. Each bridge on a segment listens to the BPDUs sent out by the other bridges. If the receiving bridge's path cost is higher than that in the BPDU, the bridge will stop forwarding on that port. If a bridge hears no path cost lower than its own, it will continue forwarding traffic and BPDUs on that port. One exception to this is that every bridge has a root port, which is its closest port to the root bridge and must be in the forwarding state. The bridge port on a segment that forwards traffic back toward the root bridge is called the designated port.

If you look at Figure 14.5 as an example, you'll see that bridge B1 has the lowest bridge identifier and therefore becomes the root bridge and forwards out on all ports. Bridge B2 chooses its port P1 to be its root port and blocks on its port P2 because bridge B1 advertises a path cost of 0 to the root bridge for Ethernet segment 2. Bridges B3 and B4 select their port P1s as their root ports because these ports receive BPDUs with the lowest root bridge path cost. On Ethernet segment 3, both bridge B3 and bridge B4 advertise a root path cost of 19, which is the value of the incoming path cost (0) from the root bridge, bridge B1, plus the value of the incoming interface's port cost, 19. To break the tie, the bridge identifier is used. In this case, bridge B3 has the lower identifier, 8000:0200.3333.0003, based on its MAC address and forwards packets on Ethernet segment 3 while bridge B4's port goes into a blocking state.

FIGURE 14.5   Root bridge election and path cost determination

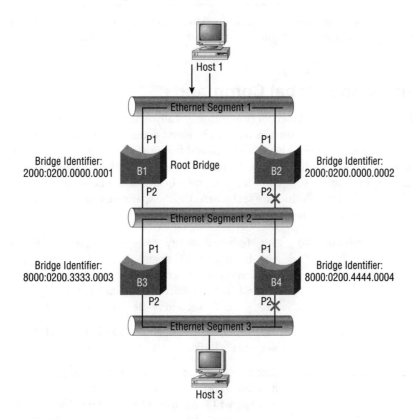

When configuring the Spanning-Tree Protocol, there are different options that can be chosen. Which STP algorithm is used will depend on the bridged environment and bridging methods used:

IEEE STP 802.1D   This type of spanning tree supports bridge domains and allows the bridge to construct a loop-free topology across an extended LAN. Specifically, the IEEE 802.1D STP supports the following IEEE bridge modes: transparent bridging (TB), source-route bridging (SRB), and source-route transparent bridging (SRT). Configurable using the keyword `ieee` when defining the bridge group.

IBM STP   This type of spanning tree was developed to manage the limited broadcast path through source-route bridges. Configurable using the keyword `ibm` when defining the bridge group.

DEC STP   The original spanning-tree algorithm implementation developed by DEC. The STP BDPU formats are different. This version will not be used in this chapter but can be configured using the keyword `dec` when defining the bridge group.

Cisco STP   The IEEE 802.1D STP was used as a basis for creating the Cisco STP and primarily used in a token ring environment. This version will not be used in this chapter.

Always make sure you know what bridge is going to be root. Set the bridge priorities appropriately on all routers doing bridging.

Spanning Tree Global Commands

Although the Spanning-Tree Protocol runs automatically when transparent bridging is configured, there are a number of parameters that can be tuned as the following commands show. The network diameter or number of bridges end to end from the root bridge should be taken into consideration when setting these values. It is recommended that the max-age is greater than or equal to 2 * (hello-time + 1 sec.) and the forwarding delay should be greater than or equal to (max-age/2 − 1 sec.). If these values are set incorrectly, the spanning tree could become unstable.

Here are some spanning tree global commands:

bridge 1 forward-time 40	Set forward delay time to indicate how long the bridge will spend listening for topology information after an interface has been brought up and before forwarding actually begins. Value <10 – 200> seconds. Default is 15 seconds
bridge 1 hello-time 5	Set interval between hello BPDUs. Values <1 – 10> seconds. Default is 2 seconds
bridge 1 max-age 22	Max allowed age of received Hello BPDUs. Must see a BPDU from Root Bridge within this time or bridge will assume the network has changed and recomputes the spanning tree algorithm. Values <6 – 200> seconds. Default is 20 seconds
bridge 1 priority 100	Configure Bridge priority value for spanning tree to affect root bridge election. Default = 32768 for IEEE, Values <0 – 65535>. Default for DEC = 128

Although the BPDU hello interval, forwarding delay, and max-age parameters can be changed on the router, they will only take effect if the router is the root bridge; otherwise, they follow what is set on the root bridge.

Spanning-Tree Interface Commands

At the interface configuration level, the Spanning-Tree Protocol port priority and path cost can be adjusted to influence the spanning tree topology and which bridge ports forward for a given segment and which enter the blocking state. The following commands show what can be changed at the interface level:

```
interface Ethernet 0/0
```

bridge-group 1 path-cost 30   Adjust this port's additive Path Cost to the Root Bridge. Values <0 – 65535>. The default cost is 1 Gbps divided by the interface's bandwidth setting.

bridge-group 1 priority 1   The port priority serves as a tie breaker if two bridges advertise the same Root Path cost and Bridge ID's on a segment. The port with the lower priority wins. In the event of a tie, the port with the lower port index wins. Values <0 – 255>. Default: 128

Source-Route Bridging (SRB)

Source-route bridging (SRB) was developed by IBM as a way to allow token ring attached devices to talk to one another if they are on separate rings. SRB has a few advantages over transparent bridging, such as improved scalability and the capability to have multiple active paths between the same endpoints. The cost of these benefits is that the token ring end stations must be aware that source-route bridging is taking place and are involved in the SRB process.

The basic concept of SRB is that the entire path through the network between two devices communicating with one another is coded within the *Routing Information Field (RIF)* in the token ring frame itself. Therefore, the bridges do not have to consult any lookup tables to make a forwarding decision; they merely find their place in the RIF and then forward the frame out the next ring. The RIF is built by the bridges when stations send out special broadcast frames that travel throughout the network. Each ring in the network is given its own unique identifier called a ring number, and each bridge is labeled with a bridge number. Ring numbers can be in the range 1–4095, and bridge numbers can be 0–15. Unlike ring numbers, bridge numbers are not unique.

Consider the internetwork shown in Figure 14.6. When station A wants to talk to station B, it assumes it is on the same ring and sends a local test frame to station B. (Note that all numbers in the diagram and RIFs are presented in decimal as configured in IOS. Normally these values are expressed in hexadecimal elsewhere.) When there is no response, station A assumes that station B is off-ring and builds a special test frame called an all-routes *explorer frame*. This frame is similar to the local test frame but with a few differences. Namely, station A sets the most significant bit of the source MAC address (Routing Information Indicator, or RII) to a 1 signifying that this frame contains a RIF. The most significant bit is reserved for use as the RII, which is why the locally administered MAC address range ends at 0x7fff.ffff.ffff. It also inserts the Routing Control field of the RIF after the source MAC address and sets the three Broadcast bits to 100 to indicate that this frame is an all-routes explorer (ARE) frame.

FIGURE 14.6   Source-route bridging

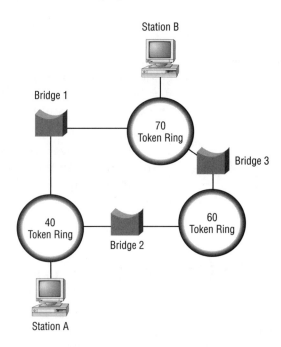

When bridge 1 sees the ARE frame, it inspects the RII bit to see if it is set. Because it is set, the bridge knows that the bytes following the source MAC address in this frame contain the RIF and not the 802.2 header. Bridge 1 looks at the Broadcast bits of the Routing Control field in the RIF and notes that this frame is an ARB. This tells the bridge to forward a copy of the frame out all ports other than the port on which the frame was received. Therefore, a copy of the ARE explorer is transmitted on ring 70 and reaches station B. As the ARE passes through the bridge, its RIF is updated to reflect that it arrived off of originating ring 40, was forwarded by bridge 1, and was sent out ring 70.

> The first bridge that receives the all-routes explorer (ARE) frame must append the receiving ring number to the RIF. Subsequent bridges append only the local bridge number and the ring number onto which the ARE is being forwarded. The destination station places a value of 0 in the bridge field to terminate the RIF.

Station B will reply to station A's explorer with a nonbroadcast specifically routed return packet. The RIF is copied from the received explorer, the Direction bit is set to a 1 (which indicates that the bridges are to read the RIF from right to left), and the RII is set in the source MAC address to denote that this is a bridged frame. The response travels along the path 70-1-40-ring 70 through bridge 1 to ring 40.

Simultaneously, bridge B2 receives a copy of the original ARE frame and, because the RII is set and the Broadcast bit indicates it is an ARE frame, forwards out a copy onto ring 60 after it has modified the RIF to read 40 2 60. The explorer frame reaches bridge B3, which updates the RIF to 40 2 60 3 70 and puts the frame out on ring 70. Station B receives the ARE frame and responds with a specifically routed frame using the RIF in the frame. So station A receives two responses to its explorer frame because there are two unique paths through the network between ring 40 and ring 70. If the network were larger and more complex, say, with 15 unique routes between ring 40 and ring 70, station A would receive 15 responses to the test frame and pick 1 to use.

There are a few points about the RIF chosen by the originating end station you should keep in mind. The most important is that only one RIF is used to forward frames between the pair of devices. This ensures that the packets arrive in order. The RIF used may have been the fastest path when it was originally chosen, but it may be less optimal depending on network traffic conditions. Although the originating end station usually chooses the first returned RIF, it could also choose the RIF with the least number of hops or the RIF indicating the largest maximum transmission unit (MTU) size. A bridge will inspect the RIF of the broadcast frame it is forwarding to make sure the frame has not already been on the outgoing port's ring. If it has, it will not be forwarded out that port. This prevents broadcast frames from looping around the network. One last point is that the MTU bits in the Routing Control field indicate the largest frame the path will support. The end station makes note of this when sending frames because anything larger will be dropped by at least one of the bridges in the path.

In the example in this section, the explorer frame that was used was an all-routes explorer frame. Although the replies were sent as nonbroadcast, specifically routed frames, there can still be a large amount of broadcast traffic. In order to cut down on the amount of broadcast frames, the IBM developers of SRB came up with the idea of spanning tree explorer (STE) frames, which make use of the spanning-tree algorithm to ensure that there is only a single path between any two segments. When a station originates an STE frame, only one copy will be seen on any given ring. When the target station responds, it sends back its reply as an all-routes explorer frame instead of a specifically routed frame, which enables the source station to receive replies traversing all paths in between. The net result is that there are fewer frames traversing the network due to the explorer process. The difference between the spanning-tree algorithm implementation in a source-route bridging environment and in a transparent bridging environment is that in the SRB environment, it blocks only spanning tree explorer (STE) frames, not all frames as in transparent bridging.

RIF Calculation

The key to understanding source-route bridging is knowing what the different fields in the Routing Information Field (RIF) mean. The only hard part about decoding RIFs is that, like IP VLSM addressing, the fields don't always fall on byte boundaries so you have to break the hex into binary to interpret.

The RIF has two main components: the Routing Control (RC) field and a list of routing descriptor (RD) fields. Both the RC and RDs are 2 bytes in length. The RC field tells us four things: the type of bridged frame, the length of the RIF, the direction to read the RIF, and the MTU of the bridged path. Figure 14.7 shows an exploded view of the RIF that can help us decode what each part means.

FIGURE 14.7 The token ring Routing Information Field (RIF)

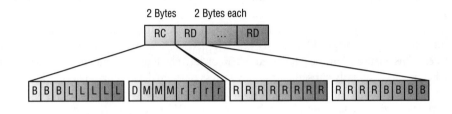

Routing Control (RC)

B - Broadcast bits
    100 - All Routes Explorer
    110 - Spanning Tree Explorer
L - Length Bits
    Length of RIF (including the RC itself)
D - Direction Bit
    0 - Read RIF left to right
    1 - Read RIF right to left
M - MTU Bits (Maximum Transmission Unit)
    000 - 516 Bytes
    001 - 1500 Bytes
    010 - 2052 Bytes
    011 - 4472 Bytes
    100 - 8144 Bytes
    101 - 11407 Bytes
    110 - 17800 Bytes
    111- Unknown
r = reserved (should be set to 0)

Route Descriptor (RD)

R - Ring bits (12 bits)
    Rings 1 - 4095 (decimal)
    0x001 - 0xFFF (hex)
B - Bridge Bits (4 bits)
    Bridges 0 - 15 (decimal)
    0x0-0xF (hex)

As an example, we'll take the following token ring frame snippet and decode it:

4000 1234 0001 C000 1111 0001 08A0 064A 0C83 0010 0404

This is a frame destined for a station with MAC address 4000.1234.0001 coming from station 4000.1111.0001. Notice that the Routing Information Indicator (RII) bit is set in the source MAC address, making the first hex digit a C rather than a 4 and signaling that there is a RIF following the SMAC address. The 0x08A0 is the Routing Control field, which breaks into binary 0000 1000 1010 0000. This can then be grouped more appropriately into the RC's five fields: 000 01000 1 010 0000. Decoding gives us the following:

Broadcast bits	000	Nonbroadcast
Length bits	01000	RIF is 8 bytes long with (8 − 2)/2 = 3 RD fields
Direction bit	1	Read RIF right to left
MTU bits	010	MTU size is 2052 bytes

Following the RC portion of the RIF are three routing descriptors (RDs): 064A, 0C83, and 0010. The first translates to ring 0x064 (100 decimal) crossing bridge 0xA (10). The second translates to ring 0x0C8 (200) via bridge 3. The last RD is easy because it's just ring 1. The last bridge number should always be 0 because the traffic ends up on a ring. The 0x0404 represents the DSAP and SSAP values. In this example, the traffic type is SNA.

So to put it all together, this is an SNA frame traveling from station 4000.1111.0001 on ring 1 and to station 4000.1234.0001 on ring 100 by way of bridge 3 on ring 1, transiting across ring 200, then being forwarded by bridge 10, and ending up on ring 100. The largest data payload accepted along this path is 2052 bytes. If either station tries to send a larger frame, it will be dropped somewhere along the bridged path. Although there may be other paths through the network between rings 1 and 100, this was apparently the fastest path at session startup. Because the Direction bit is a 1, we can assume that station 4000.1234.0001 initiated the session.

Here's another example:

4000 C286 0523 C012 8217 0336 8610 12C2 1900 00 0C

Decoding the Routing Control field (0x8610, binary 1000 0110 0001 0000) gives the following:

Broadcast bits	100	all-routes explorer
Length bits	00110	RIF is 6 bytes long with (6 −2)/2 = 2 RD fields
Direction bit	0	read RIF left to right
MTU bits	001	MTU size is 1500 bytes

Station A (4012.8217.0336) is searching for station B (4000.C286.0523) using an all-routes explorer test frame. Station A is on ring 400 (0x190), but we can't tell from this frame what ring station B is on. We can tell that the trace tool is on ring 300 (0x12C), that the frame passed through bridge 2 between rings 300 and 400, and that bridge 2's MTU size is 1500 bytes.

Configuring Local Source-Route Bridging

When configuring source-route bridging (SRB) on a router/bridge, you'll need to understand the concept of a virtual ring. A virtual ring is an imaginary ring that is built logically within the router and used to overcome the two-ring limitation on Token Ring chipsets. It also plays a vital role in source-route translational bridging and remote source-route bridging as well as data-link switching. We will use one configuration example to help introduce the concept, but later on in this chapter, we will deal with RSRB and DLSw in more detail.

The first configuration uses only two Token Ring ports, making the router a two-port bridge. These two ports cannot communicate with any other source-route bridge interfaces on this router/ bridge. End stations on either of these two interfaces cannot communicate with other end stations on other SRB interfaces, only between themselves. IP will be routed, and all other protocols will be bridged.

Two-Port Source-Route Bridge

The following lines of configuration provide an example of how to configure a router as a two-port bridge. Because there are only two ports involved, there is no requirement to have a virtual ring:

```
interface TokenRing 0/0
```

`ip address  10.1.1.1 255.255.255.0`	Because no iprouting is not globally specified, IP will be routed and all other protocols will be bridged
`ring-speed 16`	
`source-bridge 10 1 20`	Configure interface for SRB.
	Assign a local ring 10 (SRN) - This is the ring number attached to local interface Tok 0/0. SRN = Source Ring Number (in Decimal, not Hex)
	Assign a bridge number 1 (BN) - identifies the SRB connecting the local ring and the target ring. Values <1 - 15>
	Assign the target ring 20 (TRN)- which in this case is the ring attached to interface Tok 0/1. TRN = Target Ring Number

```
source-bridge spanning
```
This command allows the bridge interface to forward single-route explorer frames. Without this command single-route explorer frames are dropped. Required for DLSw.

```
interface TokenRing0/1
  ip address 10.2.2.1 255.255.255.0
  ring-speed 16
  source-bridge 20 1 10
```
Same explanation used above, but from Tok 0/1's perspective

```
  source-bridge spanning
```

   The first option provides a port limitation when defining the SRB environment. The second option allows more than two ports to be used within the same SRB network, by using the concept of a ring group. The ring group is a collection of token ring interfaces in one or more Cisco routers that are collectively treated as a virtual ring. Using the configuration in the next section, the virtual ring allows all four token ring interfaces to participate in the same SRB network. We will utilize IBM's Spanning-Tree Protocol. Figure 14.8 is used for the second configuration.

FIGURE 14.8   SRB with a virtual ring

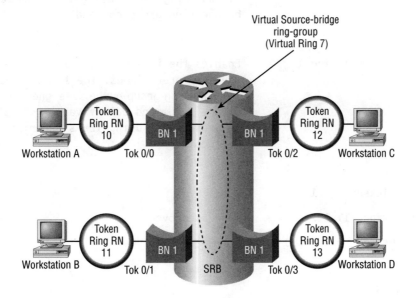

Four-Port Source-Route Bridge (Using a Virtual Ring)

The following example shows source-route bridging being set up between four different ports. In this case, a virtual ring must be configured. Note that the virtual ring shows up in the RIF of packets passing through this router and adds a hop:

source-bridge ring-group 7	Create a SRB virtual ring inside router. Valid range is in decimal format <1 – 4095>
interface TokenRing0/0	
source-bridge 10 1 7	Configure interface for SRB.
	Assign a local ring - This is the ring number attached to local interface Tok 0/0
	Assign a bridge number - identifies the SRB connecting the local ring and the target ring. Values <1-15>
	Assign the target ring - in this case is the virtual ring number assigned in the source-bridge ring-group command
source-bridge spanning 1	Enables the interface to forward spanning tree explorer frames. The 1 indicates the SRB spanning group number assigned with the bridge 1 command below. Values <1-255>. Only used when using IBM's spanning tree protocol
interface TokenRing0/1	
source-bridge 11 1 7	Same as above
source-bridge spanning 1	
interface TokenRing0/2	

```
source-bridge 12 1 7           Same as above

source-bridge spanning 1


interface TokenRing0/3

source-bridge 13 1 7           Same as above

source-bridge spanning 1


bridge 1 protocol ibm          Assign a Bridge Group number for Bridging
                               Values <1-255>. Specify that the bridge
                               will use the IBM spanning tree protocol
```

Introduction to Remote Source-Route Bridging (RSRB)

Remote source-route bridging (RSRB) allows you to bridge traffic between two token rings from separate routers across a WAN internetwork. RSRB is very similar to DLSw, but Logical Link Control (LLC2) information, such as acknowledgments, flows across the WAN. So, with RSRB, we are extending the source-route bridging from one Token Ring LAN environment and, through the implementation of a virtual ring, extending it across a WAN internetwork to a remote router supporting another Token Ring LAN source-route bridging environment. A virtual ring is created to make the IP backbone appear as another ring to all RSRB neighbors. RSRB performs RIF passthrough—the RIF that is seen by the end stations contains all the ring and bridge information end to end. Therefore, the virtual ring and its underlying IP backbone appear as another hop in the source-route bridge network. All RSRB peers *must* use the same virtual ring number.

RSRB supports multiple types of encapsulation, such as Fast Sequenced Transport (FST), Transmission Control Protocol (TCP), and direct encapsulation.

Virtual Rings

Virtual rings and ring groups are mechanisms for bridging together two or more rings. Virtual rings can be extended between multiple routers across a WAN internetwork so that all of the rings on multiple routers are able to communicate with each other. This extension is done with the source-route remote-peer command. There are some things to keep in mind when setting up virtual rings. In order to pass source-route bridging (SRB) traffic between them, routers must be part of the same ring group (virtual ring). Also, routers being peered together must have source-route remote-peer statements pointing to each other.

Configuring RSRB

As we just stated, RSRB supports multiple encapsulation methods. The process of configuring RSRB is very similar to the process for configuring DLSw. First, you must configure a `source-bridge remote-peer` command, in which you will specify the local router. Second, you must configure a `source-bridge remote-peer` command, in which you specify each of the remote peer routers. At least one side of a peer connection must be configured as a remote peer. Finally, you must configure the `source-bridge ring-group` command, in which you will specify the virtual ring number. Remember that each router (including all the remote peer routers) must have the identical virtual ring number configured in order to communicate across the WAN internetwork.

Figure 14.9 shows an internetwork topology over which we will implement RSRB. All routers are using the Enhanced Interior Gateway Routing Protocol (EIGRP) 10 routing process.

FIGURE 14.9 RSRB diagram

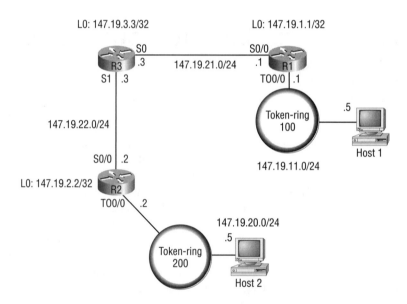

Configuring RSRB with TCP Encapsulation

The most commonly used encapsulation type is TCP. This encapsulation has greater overhead than direct encapsulation and FST because every RSRB packet gets encapsulated within a full IP and TCP header and in the routers, where there is additional processor overhead for maintaining a TCP session for every remote peer required. The advantage of TCP encapsulation is the reliable delivery of packets, which lessens the recovery responsibility of end stations in the case of a lost or corrupted packet. TCP is very simple to configure because, instead of a unique command to represent the local peer as in DLSw, the local peer in RSRB is defined with a `source-bridge remote-peer` command, the same as the remote peers.

In the internetwork shown in Figure 14.9, we will not be configuring router R3 with RSRB; it does not have a local Token Ring SRB environment supporting hosts that require communication across the WAN to other remote Token Ring SRB LAN environments. Router R1 and router R2 will be configured to allow remote bridging across the virtual ring of the WAN.

Routers R1 and R2 have connected token rings, which means that all the token ring traffic must be source-route-bridged from the local ring to a source-route ring group to allow remote bridging across the virtual ring of the WAN. Therefore, we must configure a `source-bridge ring-group` command with a virtual ring number, and the token ring interfaces require a `source-bridge` command directing traffic from the token ring interface to the virtual ring.

Router R1 Configuration

Here is the configuration for router R1:

`source-bridge ring-group 75`	Specifies a virtual-ring of 75
`source-bridge explorerQ-depth 100`	OPTIONAL, limits the source-bridge to 100 explorer packets
`source-bridge remote-peer 75 tcp 147.19.1.1`	Defines local peer using tcp encapsulation and is a member of virtual ring 75
`source-bridge remote-peer 75 tcp 147.19.2.2`	Defines a remote peer with tcp encapsulation and is a member of virtual-ring 75

```
interface Loopback0
  ip address 147.19.1.1 255.255.255.255


interface Serial0/0
  ip address 142.19.21.1 255.255.255.0


interface Tokenring0/0
  ip address 142.19.11.1 255.255.255.0
```

`source-bridge 100 1 75`	Specifies local ring 100 connects to local bridge 1, which then connects to the virtual ring 75
`source-bridge spanning`	Specifies that the local ring is using spanning-tree [single-route] explorer packets

Router R2 Configuration

Here is the configuration for router R2:

`source-bridge ring-group 75`	Specifies a virtual-ring of 75
`source-bridge remote-peer 75 tcp 147.19.2.2`	
	Defines local peer, with tcp encapsulation, and is a member of virtual-ring 75
`source-bridge remote-peer 75 tcp 147.19.1.1`	
	Defines remote peer, with tcp encapsulation, and is a member of virtual-ring 75

```
interface Loopback0
  ip address 147.19.2.2 255.255.255.255


interface Serial0/0
  ip address 142.19.21.1 255.255.255.0


interface Tokenring0/0
  ip address 142.19.20.2 255.255.255.0
```

`source-bridge 200 1 75`	Specifies local ring 200 connects to local bridge 1, which then connects to the virtual ring 75
`source-bridge spanning`	Specifies that the local ring is using spanning-tree [single-route] explorer packets

Configuring RSRB with FST Encapsulation

Fast Sequenced Transport (FST) encapsulation is similar to TCP encapsulation but has less packet header overhead. Like TCP, it allows you to extend over multiple hops, encapsulates SRB packets into an IP packet, and relies on a Level 3 protocol (IP) to know how to reach the remote peers across the virtual ring of the WAN. Unlike TCP encapsulation, FST is its own IP protocol (90) and does not handle retransmissions. Therefore, if there are dropped or corrupted frames across the WAN, it is up to the end devices to perform error recovery and retransmission. Now we will configure the exact same scenario as before, but this time using FST encapsulation. The only real difference in configuring RSRB for FST encapsulation is that each router using FST peering must have a `source-bridge fst-peername` command configured to identify the local peer. Then, just as with TCP encapsulation, you configure the `source-bridge remote-peer` command to identify all the remote peers.

Router R1 Configuration

Here is the configuration for router R1:

`source-bridge fst-peername 147.19.1.1`	Defines local peer
`source-bridge ring-group 75`	Specifies virtual-ring of 75
`source-bridge remote-peer 75 fst 147.19.2.2`	Defines remote peer, with fst encapsulation, and is a member of virtual-ring 75

Router R2 Configuration

Here is router R2's configuration:

`source-bridge ring-group 75`	Use virtual-ring 75
`source-bridge remote-peer 75 fst 147.19.1.1`	Defines remote peer, with fst encapsulation and is a member of virtual-ring 75

Configuring RSRB with Direct Encapsulation

Direct encapsulation is the simplest type of remote peering. When serial lines are slow, or not completely clean, FST or TCP are better choices for encapsulation types. Use direct encapsulation in point-to-point connections. In a point-to-point configuration, using TCP or FST encapsulation adds unnecessary processing overhead.

Now we will configure the exact same scenario, but this time we will use the direct encapsulation. The only real difference in configuring RSRB for direct encapsulation is that you do *not* have to configure any commands to designate the local peer. You only have to configure a `source-bridge remote-peer` command to identify all the remote peers. And if you are implementing this across a Frame Relay cloud, then the Frame Relay interfaces require a `frame-relay map` command with the keyword `rsrb` specified. And remember that this is direct encapsulation on top of the layer 2 protocols, so there are no IP addresses involved in the router configurations. Figure 14.10 shows a different core topology for our routers. We have removed the IP protocols from the core and inserted a Frame Relay core. Now we must configure our RSRB peers using the Frame Relay Data Link Connection Identifiers (DLCIs).

FIGURE 14.10   RSRB with direct encapsulation

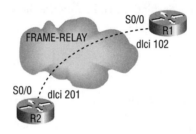

Router R1 Configuration

Here is the configuration for router R1:

```
source-bridge ring-group 75          Specifies a virtual-ring of 75

source-bridge remote-peer 75 frame-relay interface serial0/0 102


                                     Defines the remote peer using the
                                     local DLCI 102



interface Serial0/0

  encapsulation frame-relay

  frame-relay lmi-type ansi

  frame-relay map rsrb 102           Send all rsrb traffic out this interface
                                     on DLCI 102. Required on all Multipoint
                                     Frame-Relay interfaces
```

Router R2 Configuration

Here is R2's configuration:

```
source-bridge ring-group 75                    Specifies a virtual ring of
                                               75

source-bridge remote-peer 75 frame-relay interface serial0/0 201


                                               Defines the remote peer
                                               using the local DLCI 201


interface Serial0/0

  encapsulation frame-relay

  frame-relay lmi-type ansi

  frame-relay map rsrb 201                     Maps all RSRB traffic out this
                                               interface to use DLCI 201.
                                               Required on all Multipoint
                                               Frame Relay interfaces.
```

RSRB Advanced Features

RSRB includes additional features to enhance its functionality, such as local acknowledgments, passthrough, keepalive timers, and largest-frame adjustment capabilities.

Configuring the Keepalive interval

Use the source-bridge keepalive interface configuration command to assign the keepalive interval of the remote source-bridging peer. The keepalive interval is configured in seconds. The valid range is 10 through 300. The default is 30 seconds. Here's a command syntax example:

```
source-bridge keepalive 60             Define the keepalive interval of 60
                                       seconds for this RSRB peer
```

Configuring Local Acknowledgment

Use the local-ack keyword at the end of the source-bridge remote-peer command to enable local acknowledgments. Local ack specifies that the LLC2 session is split into two pieces, one at the local router and the other at the remote. Each side sends acknowledgments on behalf of the far side and is responsible for retransmitting in case of a problem on the WAN. Local acknowl-edgment also applies back pressure to sessions in the form of receiver not ready (RNR) frames if there is congestion on the WAN. Here's a command syntax example:

```
source-bridge remote-peer 75 tcp 147.19.1.1 local-ack
```

> Enable LLC2 local acknowledgment on a per-remote-peer basis. Specifies to locally acknowledge LLC2 for all traffic destined to the 147.19.1.1 remote peer on virtual-ring 75

Configuring Passthrough

Use the `source-bridge passthrough` global configuration command to configure some sessions on a few rings to be locally acknowledged and the remaining to pass through. The specified ring number is either the start ring or destination ring of the two end devices (hosts) for which the passthrough feature is to be configured. The ring group number must match the number you have specified with the `source-bridge ring-group` command. The valid range is 1 through 4095. Here's a command syntax example:

```
source-bridge passthrough 75     Configures the router for passthrough on ring 75
```

Configuring Largest Frame

RSRB gives you the capability to transport large source-route-bridged frames across the WAN between two token ring segments; however, there are reasons to limit the size of these frames in some cases. If one of the RSRB peers is connected via Ethernet to its WAN router or if the WAN connection's MTU size is limited to 2052 or 1500 bytes, the RSRB peers or intervening routers will have to fragment 4k or 8k packets. In order to prevent this, you can configure the largest-frame parameter, which will override the MTU bits in the returned RIF and cause the end stations to use a smaller packet size. Here's a command syntax example:

```
source-bridge largest-frame 75 1500     Limit the RIF MTU size for all
                                         peers using virtual-ring 75 to
                                         a maximum of 1500 bytes.
```

Source-Route Transparent (SRT) Bridging

Source-route transparent bridging (SRT) enables transparent bridging between Token Ring and Ether-net segments. It also provides transparent bridging between Ethernet segments, transparent bridging between Token Ring segments, and source-route bridging between Token Ring segments. However, it does not allow bridging from a source-routing device to a non-source-routing device. If an incoming frame on a Token Ring segment has the Routing Information Indicator (RII) bit set in the source MAC address, it will not be transparently bridged onto a Token Ring or Ethernet segment.

SRT is defined in the IEEE 802.1d specification and uses a mutual Spanning-Tree Protocol implementation between Token Ring and Ethernet to ensure that there are no loops in the combined environment.

Bridging between token ring and Ethernet requires that certain frame translations occur and other items be taken into account as outlined in the following list:

- Ethernet frames can use different frame formats, such as 802.3 and Ethernet II, compared with Token Ring, which uses the 802.5 frame format.

- Ethernet uses a canonical MAC address format and token ring uses a noncanonical MAC address format. These terms will be explained later.

- Ethernet uses broadcast frames (FFFF.FFFF.FFFF) and token ring uses functional addressing (C000) to broadcast information.

- The MTU is 1500 for Ethernet, whereas Token Ring can support much larger frame sizes.

- Ethernet is contention based and token ring is token frame based

We'll look at an example of how to configure SRT and then learn about source-route translational bridging (SR/TLB). SR/TLB enables the translation of frames from devices using source-route bridging to those in the transparent bridging realm that don't.

Configuring Source-Route Transparent (SRT) Bridging

Source-Route Transparent bridging is easy to configure. It involves enabling transparent bridging groups on both Ethernet and token ring interfaces as well as source route bridging on the desired token ring interfaces. If more than two token ring interfaces are to perform SRB, a ring-group needs to be configured. The *Spanning Tree Protocol* must be set for the transparent bridge group(s).

```
interface TokenRing0/0

  source-bridge 1 1 2                perform source route bridging from
                                     ring 1 to ring 2 as bridge 1

  ip address 147.19.16.1 255.255.255.0   IP will be the only routed protocol.
                                     All other protocols will be bridged


bridge-group 1                       Enables transparent bridging on the
                                     token ring interface.

interface TokenRing0/1

  source-bridge 2 1 1                perform source route bridging from
                                     ring 2 to ring 1 as bridge 1
```

```
ip address 147.19.66.1 255.255.255.0
source-bridge 2 1 1                    Same as above, except local ring and
                                       target ring are reversed

bridge-group 1                         Enables SRT on the  token ring
                                       interface.



interface Ethernet0/0                  Same commands used for Transparent
                                       bridging

  bridge-group 1                       Associate interface with a bridge-
                                       group assigned in bridge command
                                       below



interface Ethernet0/1

  bridge-group 1                       Associate interface with a
                                       bridge-group assigned in bridge
                                       command below



  bridge 1 protocol ieee               Assign a bridge-group and select
                                       spanning tree algorithm
```

Source-Route Translational Bridging (SR/TLB)

Like source-route transparent (SRT) bridging, *source-route translational bridging (SR/TLB)* allows bridging between Token Ring and Ethernet devices. Unlike SRT, SR/TLB enables bridging between source-route-capable and non-source-route capable devices. The SR/TLB bridge is responsible for discovering and remembering RIFs for devices in the source-route portion of the network and accomplishes this by becoming a proxy source-route-bridge-capable device for hosts in the transparent environment. The forwarding table for MAC addresses includes a section for Routing Information Fields (RIFs) so that as source-route-enabled device MAC addresses are learned, any accompanying RIFs are stored as well.

SR/TLB makes use of the source-route virtual Token Ring and a pseudo ring when translating between transparent and source-routing segments. Like the virtual ring, the pseudo ring is an internal construct rather than a physical interface but shows up in the RIF going to and from a device on the source-route bridging side. Figure 14.11 has a sample network that we can use to show you how SR/TLB operates and where the virtual and pseudo rings come into play.

FIGURE 14.11   Source-route translational bridging (SR/TLB)

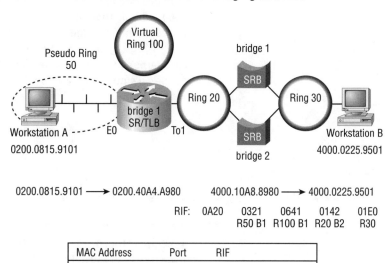

Let's assume that workstation A knows workstation B's MAC address and sends a frame to workstation B. Let's also assume that the router configured as an SR/TLB bridge has not heard anything from workstation B in a while and therefore has no entry in its forwarding table. When the frame arrives at port E0, the bridge inspects its forwarding table for an entry. As with a normal transparent bridge, if there is no entry, a copy of the frame is forwarded out on all other ports. In this case, the SR/TLB bridge "proxies" an all-routes explorer frame searching for workstation B. The RIF that goes out port To1 shows the pseudo ring 50 being bridged onto virtual ring 100 through bridge 1 and then onto ring 20 via bridge 1. Two copies of the explorer reach workstation B through bridge 1 and bridge 2 onto ring 30. Workstation B responds to both explorers with specifically routed frames. When the SR/TLB bridge receives the responses, it associates workstation B's MAC address with port To0 and records the portion of the RIF from the bridge out to workstation B. The RIF is removed from the frame as it is sent out port E0.

Let's look at how to configure the SR/TLB router in Figure 14.11.

Configuring Source-Route/Translational Bridging

The key to configuring source-route translational bridging is the `source-bridge transparent` statement, which defines the pseudo ring and links the transparent domain to the source-route bridging domain:

`source-bridge ring-group 100`	Create a SRB virtual ring inside router. Valid range is in decimal format <1 - 4095>
`source-bridge transparent 100 50 1 1`	Create the association between the virtual ring (100), pseudo ring (50), SR Bridge number (1) and the transparent bridge group number (1) The bridge-group number can be used as the pseudo ring number if the ring number is not in use elsewhere in the network.

`interface TokenRing 0`
   `ring-speed 16`
   `source-bridge 20 1 100`
	Configure interface for SRB.

	Assign a local ring - This is the ring number attached to interface Tok 0
	Assign a bridge number - identifies the SRB connecting the local ring and the target ring
	Assign the target ring - which in this case is the virtual ring created above using the source-bridge ring-group command
`interface Ethernet 1`	Used to transparently bridges the ethernet segment

```
bridge-group 1                          Associates the interface with the
                                        transparent bridge-group number
                                        created below using the bridge-group
                                        1 command


bridge 1 protocol ieee                  Assign a bridge-group and select
                                        spanning tree algorithm
```

The `multi-ring` command under the Token Ring interface is used to enable a routed protocol such as IP or IPX to coexist in a bridged environment. Much like the proxy function in SR/TLB, `multi-ring` sends out broadcast/multicast traffic using all-routes explorers and associates MAC addresses with the necessary RIFs to reach them in the SRB environment.

Canonical vs. Noncanonical Bit Ordering

The standard way of describing the order of binary bits in a byte is known as *canonical* bit ordering, in which the least significant bit (LSB) of a byte in a frame is transmitted first. IBM usually writes the binary values in reverse order, known as *noncanonical* (nonconforming) bit ordering, whereby the most significant bit (MSB) of a MAC address is transmitted first. The token ring MAC hardware address utilizes the noncanonical format, which is different from the format used by an Ethernet MAC, which is canonical. As the Ethernet frame is sent, the Ethernet source and destination MAC addresses are transmitted with the LSB of each byte first; on a token ring environment, the token frame source and destination MAC addresses are sent with the MSB of each byte first.

A source-route translational bridge must be able to swap the frame address formats as the frame passes through the bridge so that each media type can understand the MAC addresses within the frame.

Figure 14.12 is used to help explain the difference between the canonical and noncanonical format. Workstation A has an Ethernet NIC, which means that its MAC address is canonical. Let's see how the MAC address of workstation A is reversed to become noncanonical. Figure 14.12 shows Station A's SA address being bit-swapped before it is sent on to the token ring side. The easiest way to do this is to take the Ethernet MAC address in hexadecimal (canonical) format and break up each byte into its binary format. Stations A's Ethernet MAC address is 0004.7bd5.78af (separated = 00 04 7B D5 78 AF). If the order of each byte's bits is reversed so that the least significant bit becomes the most significant bit, the non-canonical representation then becomes 0020.deab.1ef5. Remember, only the bits of each byte are flipped; each byte remains in its original sequential order.

FIGURE 14.12 Canonical versus noncanonical bit ordering

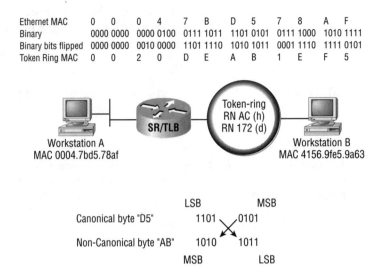

Concurrent Routing and Bridging (CRB) and Integrated Routing and Bridging (IRB)

The default behavior for the router is to only route a given protocol if routing for that protocol is enabled even on bridged interfaces where a network address is not specified. To enable the router to both route and bridge the same protocol, *Concurrent Routing and Bridging (CRB)* and *Integrated Routing and Bridging (IRB)* were developed. Although they provide similar functionality, they cannot be configured on the router at the same time.

Concurrent Routing and Bridging (CRB) allows the same Network protocol, such as IPX, to be bridged across some interfaces and routed between others. However, traffic from the bridged domain cannot reach the traffic in the routed domain except through an external router. Therefore the behavior is akin to having separate routers and bridges in the same box.

Integrated Routing and Bridging (IRB) was developed to overcome the lack of communication between the routing and bridging domains within a single router. IRB enables the communication between the routed interfaces of a protocol with the bridged interfaces using a special construct called the Bridge-Group Virtual Interface (BVI). The BVI is basically a routed interface in the bridged domain. It is configured with an IP address that is in the same subnet as that used by the IP devices being bridged. The BVI uses a MAC address taken from one of the other physical interfaces on the router. Devices in the bridging domain that point to the BVI send traffic to this MAC address and traffic from the routed domain sent to the bridged domain will appear to be sourced from this MAC address.

Configuring Concurrent Routing and Bridging (CRB)

To configure CRB, you use the same commands you use to configure transparent bridging, with only a few exceptions. In the following configuration example, IP is routed on Ethernet0/0 and Ethernet 0/1, and all other protocols are bridged on Ethernet 0/2 and Ethernet 0/3:

`bridge crb`	Enables concurrent routing and bridging. The default behavior is to bridge all protocols that are not explicitly routed in a bridge group
`bridge 1 protocol ieee`	Assign a bridge-group and select spanning tree algorithm
`bridge 1 bridge ip`	Bridge IP traffic on interfaces in bridge group 1
`interface Ethernet 0/0`	
`  ip address 147.19.160.65 255.255.255.0`	Only route IP traffic here
`interface Ethernet 0/1`	
`  ip address 147.19.161.1 255.255.255.0`	Only route IP trafic here
`interface Ethernet 0/2`	
`  no ip address`	
`  bridge-group 1`	Bond interface with bridge-group 1 to bridge all other traffic
`interface Ethernet 0/3`	
`  no ip address`	
`  bridge-group 1`	Bond interface to bridge-group 1 to bridge all other traffic

Configuring Integrated Routing and Bridging (IRB)

To configure IRB, use the same commands you use to configure transparent bridging with the addition of configuring the BVI interface. The BVI interface number is the same as the bridge group number it supports. In the following configuration, Ethernet 0/0, Ethernet 0/1, and Ethernet 0/2 bridge

IP traffic using bridge group 2; therefore, the BVI interface will be BVI2. Ethernet 0/3 routes IP traffic. Figure 14.13 is used for this configuration.

FIGURE 14.13 Integrated Routing and Bridging (IRB)

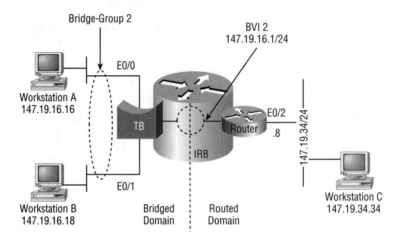

An important command to note with IRB is the `bridge x route` command that tells IRB which protocols to route off of a given bridged domain. Without it, traffic does not cross the routed/bridged boundary even with a BVI configured,. The command can be used at the global configuration level, in which case it applies to all interfaces in a given bridge group. It can also be configured at the interface level to either include or exclude bridged traffic from being routed via the BVI interface. In the following example, the `bridge 2 route ip` command directs the router to route any IP traffic on bridge group 2 directed to the BVI2 interface. However, say we don't want traffic from interface E0/2 to cross over to the rest of the routed IP world. In this case, we keep it in bridge group 2 using the `no bridge 2 route ip` command at the interface level.

`bridge irb`	Enable Integrated routing and bridging
`bridge 2 protocol ieee`	Assign a bridge-group and select spanning tree algorithm
`bridge 2 route ip`	Allow routing to occur for IP in bridge group 2
`no bridge 2 bridge ipx`	[optional] disables bridging of IPX traffic in bridge group 2, since the default behavior is to bridge all protocols.

```
interface Ethernet 0/0
  no ip address
  bridge-group 2

interface Ethernet 0/1
  no ip address
  bridge-group 2

interface Ethernet 0/2
  no ip address
  bridge-group 2
    no bridge 2 route ip
```
prevent traffic from using the BVI interface and being routed.

```
interface Ethernet 0/3
  ip address 192.168.10.1 255.255.255.0
```

```
interface BVI 2
```
The BVI interface number is the same number as the defined bridge group. Range <1-255>. IRB must be configured first using the bridge irb command. If there are no active interfaces in bridge-group 2 the BVI is shut down

```
  ip address 192.168.15.1 255.255.255.0
```
IP is used in this example so the BVI interface is also assigned an IP address that represents the corresponding bridge group subnet. It uses a MAC Address from one of the bridge-group interfaces.

Bridging: Troubleshooting Commands

The following are some useful commands for troubleshooting bridging issues:

`show spanning-tree`	Display global spanning tree parameters, along with port specific parameters
`show interfaces crb`	Display interface routing/bridging info for CRB
`show interfaces irb`	Display interface routing/bridging info for IRB
`show interfaces bvi 2`	Display the status of the BVI interface
`show bridge`	Display all entries in the bridge forwarding database
`show bridge 00b3.6f54.7c85`	Display MAC entry in the bridge forwarding database
`show bridge ethernet 0/0`	Display MAC entries in the bridge forwarding database for a particular interface
`show source-bridge`	Used to see the source-route bridging (SRB) side
`show source-bridge interfaces`	Displays information about all SRB enabled interfaces
`show bridge verbose`	Used to see the transparent side
`show rif`	Display RIF cache entries
`show arp`	Display ARP table information
`show tcp`	Display tcp session details-useful for monitoring RSRB with TCP encapsulation
`clear bridge group`	Clear bridging table / forwarding table of any learned entries. Specify bridge group
`clear source-bridge`	Clear the SRB statistical counters
`clear rif-cache`	Clear all entries in the RIF cache
`debug token ring`	Note: some of these debugs may require the use of an ACL to limit the output

```
debug spanning-tree events

debug spanning tree-all

debug source bridge

debug rif
```

Data-Link Switching (DLSw)

Data-link switching (DLSw) is a method of transporting SNA and NetBIOS traffic across WAN connections. At a high level, DLSw is a combination of bridging and IP encapsulation; however, it is more than this, as you'll soon see. IBM released DLSw in 1992 for its ill-fated 6611 routers and, breaking with tradition, made it an open standard by publishing RFC 1434, which defined DLSw's switch-to-switch protocol. The purpose of DLSw was twofold: allow for the integration of SNA and NetBIOS traffic with other multiprotocol traffic and prevent session time-outs across the WAN.

At the time DLSw was developed, many SNA and NetBIOS networks were using bridges to connect remote sites back to the mainframe and home office servers over 56Kbps circuits. Often these circuits would become congested and user sessions would drop. These large bridged networks were also susceptible to broadcast storms, which could rage through large portions of the network and take sessions down. Also, because these networks were on Token Ring using source-route bridging, the network diameter became constrained with the seven *hop count* limitation. The following list outlines some of the benefits of Data Link Switching primarily as compared with RSRB:

Overcomes the SRB hop count limit RSRB passes the RIF end-to-end, hence RSRB is still governed by the SRB limitation of a maximum of 7 hops (IBM) or 13 hops (IEEE 802.5). DLSw terminates the RIF, meaning that a new RIF is constructed at each receiving peer, allowing the SRB network to span a greater distance.

Support for Ethernet DLSw provides transparent support for bridged Ethernet (and other encapsulations) networks.

Smarter communications between peers Peers are able to exchange capabilities, which provides enhanced functionality.

Broadcast reduction mechanisms DLSw provides mechanisms to reduce explorer traffic. DLSw uses CANUReach messages to query peers if the destination MAC address contained in an explorer is reachable via the peer. DLSw supports the use of manual ICANReach configuration statements that are exchanged upon initialization. The ICANReach message contains either a destination MAC address or a NetBIOS name. DLSw also offers *explorer firewalls*, which eliminate duplicate explorers being sent across the DLSw backbone network.

Internet Protocol (IP) and Internetwork Packet Exchange (IPX) are protocols whose datagrams are expected to be best-effort delivery and that use Transport layer protocols to implement reliable delivery. In contrast to this, SNA and NetBIOS expect reliable transport at the Data-Link layer. Therefore, one of the design challenges of DLSw is to ensure the reliable delivery of SNA and NetBIOS traffic to its destination and handle any retransmissions or error conditions.

In Figure 14.14, you see the traditional way of bridging SNA/NetBIOS traffic. All traffic is passed over the WAN and LLC2 acknowledgments and error recovery is handled end to end.

FIGURE 14.14 Traditional LLC acknowledgments

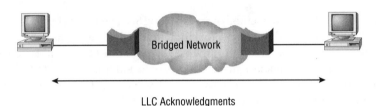

LLC Acknowledgments

In DLSw, the LLC session between the endpoints is broken into two separate pieces: one between the originating station and its DLSw router and the other between the target and its DLSw router as shown in Figure 14.15. This is also known as spoofing or local acknowledgment because each end device believes the acknowledgments are coming from the other device. The LLC termination also allows for devices using source-route bridging to be up to six hops away on both sides because the RIF is terminated by the DLSw router's virtual ring. It also keeps receiver ready/receiver not ready (RR/RNR) traffic off of the WAN. If the WAN link becomes congested, DLSw will send RNRs to end devices to keep the session alive but prevent them from sending additional traffic.

FIGURE 14.15 DLSw LLC acknowledgments

LLC Acknowledgments   LLC Acknowledgments

The benefits of using TCP/IP as a transport for DLSw are similar to those for its use as a transport method by RSRB; namely, the fact that all intervening routers don't have to be configured for bridging, IP can be rerouted in case of a link failure, and TCP can handle out-of-sequence packets if there are multiple paths between peers. In addition, for token ring attached devices, TCP segments larger source-route-bridged packets into multiple frames for transmission across Ethernet and WAN segments with smaller MTU sizes.

Figure 14.16 shows how a DLSw circuit gets started. A DLSw circuit is simply defined as a 4-tuple consisting of a source MAC address, a source SAP, a destination MAC address, and a destination SAP in the case of SNA traffic. For NetBIOS, the 4-tuple is defined by the source MAC address, the source NetBIOS name, the destination MAC address, and the destination NetBIOS name. In the figure, Host 1 sends an explorer frame, which Router A receives. Router A then sends to its DLSw peers a special frame called a CANUReach message, which causes the peers to send out test frames locally. The peer that has the target resource sends back an ICANReach message to Router A, and the rest of the session bring-up proceeds.

FIGURE 14.16   DLSw explorers and CANUReach frames

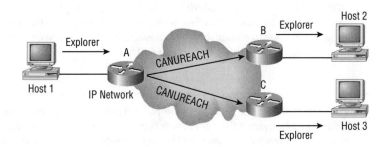

One important point to note is that Router A caches the location of the target MAC address or NetBIOS name for subsequent session initiations. If another host wants to start a session to the same target 5 minutes later, Router A sends a CANUReach message just to the cached peer, not all other peers. Similarly, if there are multiple devices wanting to start sessions to the same target simultaneously, Router A sends only one CANUReach frame to its peers instead of a barrage. This is known as explorer firewalling.

This section has given you an overview of DLSw. Next, we'll look more closely at the different options you have for DLSw peer connectivity.

DLSw Transport Methods

There are multiple methods of configuring the transport connection between DLSw routers. The method you select will probably be determined by the needs of the network and is not tied to TCP/IP as is the standard DLSw. Cisco supports four transport protocols between DLSw routers:

TCP/IP   Transports SNA and NetBIOS traffic across the WAN when local acknowledgment is required to minimize unnecessary traffic and prevent data-link control time-outs. Also provides automatic rerouting around link failures.

FST/IP   Transports SNA and NetBIOS traffic across the WAN with an arbitrary topology. This solution allows rerouting around link failures, but recovery may be disruptive depending on the time required to find an alternative path. This option does not support local acknowledgment of frames and uses a proprietary frame format that is assigned to IP protocol 91.

Direct   Transports SNA and NetBIOS traffic across a point-to-point or Frame Relay connection. Use this method if automatic rerouting around link failures is not required. This option does not support local acknowledgment of frames.

DLSw Lite   Transports SNA and NetBIOS traffic across a point-to-point connection (currently only Frame Relay is supported) when local acknowledgment and reliable transport are important but when automatic rerouting around link failures is not required. DLSw Lite uses RFC 1490 encapsulation of Logical Link Control type 2 (LLC2).

When using TCP/IP encapsulation, be aware that RFC 1795 introduces the use of UDP for CANUReach and ICANReach explorer traffic. On by default, this feature can be turned off using the dlsw udp-disable command. This is important to know if you have to establish DLSw sessions through a firewall as well as if you are blocking or prioritizing traffic with ACLs.

With IOS 12.0 and later, RFC 1191 compliance is on by default and causes the TCP MSS to be 576 bytes if the peer router is not on the same subnet. Use the ip tcp path-mtu-discovery command to allow the router to determine the largest MTU size for its peer(s).

Configuring DLSw

Setting up a basic configuration in DLSw is very easy. Although there are a myriad of configuration options available to tune DLSw, it takes very few commands to get DLSw up and running between a pair of routers. In the following example we have two routers, peer 1 and peer 2, that have users needing to establish SNA sessions. Devices on Peer 1 are Token Ring attached while devices on peer 2 are attached via Ethernet.

Here is the configuration for peer 1:

```
source-bridge ring-group 500
dlsw local-peer peer-id 1.1.1.1
dlsw remote-peer 0 tcp 2.2.2.2
 int to1/0
        source-bridge 301 1 500
```

Here is the configuration for peer 2:

```
dlsw local-peer peer-id 2.2.2.2
dlsw remote-peer 0 tcp 1.1.1.1
```

```
dlsw bridge-group 1
 int f0/0
         bridge-group 1
bridge 1 protocol ieee
```

The process of configuring DLSw is not difficult. First, you must configure a `dlsw local-peer` command. Second, you must configure a `dlsw remote-peer` command. As a minimum, at least one side of a peer connection must be configured as a remote peer. If you decide to not configure the `dlsw remote-peer` command, you must specify the `promiscuous` keyword at the end of the `dlsw local-peer` command. If you have used RSRB in the past, you need to know what not to configure. With DLSw, you do not need proxy explorer, NetBIOS name caching, Synchronous Data Link Control (SDLC) to LLC2 conversion (SDLLC), or source-route translational bridging (SR/TLB). All of these features are built into DLSw. Figure 14.17 shows a topology on which we will implement DLSw. All routers are using the EIGRP 10 routing process.

FIGURE 14.17   DLSw diagram

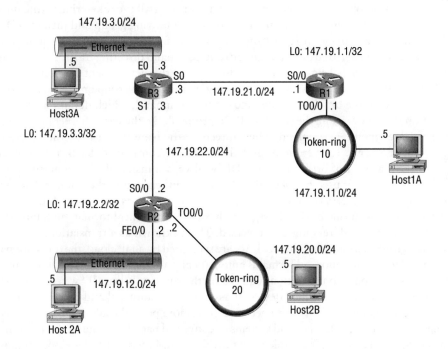

Configuring DLSw as Promiscuous with Local Translational Bridging

In the topology shown in Figure 14.17, we will configure router R3 as the hub, or border peer router and router R1 and router R2 will be spokes, or local peer routers. Router R3 will not have any `dlsw remote-peer` commands configured because it will use the `promiscuous` command option. Also, all DLSw connections will be configured based on the loopback addresses of each router. The number following `dlsw remote-peer` is the ring list number. Ring lists are an advanced topic, which we will cover later on in this chapter. So for now, specify 0 (zero) in this space, which indicates that ring lists are not in use.

Router R1 has a token ring connected, which means that all the token ring traffic must be source-route-bridged from the local ring to a source-route ring group and then into DLSw. Therefore, we must configure a `source-bridge ring-group` command with a virtual ring number, and the token ring interface requires a `source-bridge` command directing traffic from the token ring interface to the virtual ring. Router R3 has an Ethernet segment connected from the Ethernet 0 interface. So, we must first configure the bridge group on the router from the global prompt with the `bridge 1 protocol ieee` command, which defines bridge group number 1 on this router using the standard IEEE protocol. On the Ethernet interface, configure a `bridge-group 1` command that directs traffic from the Ethernet interface to the number 1 bridge group. Next, from the global prompt, we must configure a `dlsw bridge-group 1` command; this command allows the traffic from the bridge group to be carried by DLSw across the WAN.

Router R2 has a token ring connected, which means that all the token ring traffic must be source-route-bridged from the local ring to a source-bridge ring group and then into DLSw. We must configure a `source-bridge ring-group` command with a virtual ring number, and the token ring interface requires a `source-bridge` command directing traffic from the token ring interface to the virtual ring. Router R2 also has an Ethernet segment connected from the FastEthernet 0/0 interface. So, we must first configure the bridge group on the router from the global prompt with the `bridge 1 protocol ieee` command, which defines bridge group number 1 on this router using the standard IEEE protocol. On the FastEthernet interface, configure a `bridge-group 1` command, which directs traffic from the FastEthernet interface to bridge group number 1. Then from the global prompt, we configure `dlsw bridge-group 1`; this links DLSw as part of bridge group 1. DLSw always transfers data in noncanonical format, which is the format used by token ring. However, Ethernet uses the canonical format. In order for the MAC address of an Ethernet device (host), which is in canonical format, to be understood by a token ring device (host), which uses noncanonical format, all 8 bits of each byte within the MAC address must be reversed. This is known as a translation.

If a Token Ring LAN and an Ethernet LAN are separated by an IP cloud, the translation from noncanonical format to canonical format is automatically accomplished by the DLSw protocol, so there is no additional configuration required on the routers. When DLSw receives a MAC address from an Ethernet-attached device, it assumes it is canonical and converts it to noncanonical for transport to the remote peer. At the remote peer, the address is either passed unchanged to token ring–attached end systems or converted back to canonical if the destination media is Ethernet. However, if the token ring LAN and an Ethernet LAN are both connected to the same router, as is the case with router R2, then you must configure SR/TLB using the `source-bridge transparent 50 3 1 2` command from the global prompt. This command configures the routers to perform the translation of the noncanonical format to the canonical format. The command syntax specifies the virtual ring, the pseudo ring (a ring to represent the

Ethernet LAN), the source-route bridge number, then the transparent bridge-group number. So, the previous sample command configures the Ethernet bridge group number 2 to be known as the pseudo ring number 3 and allows the bridge group to communicate with the token ring source-bridge number 1 through the virtual ring number 50.

Router R1 Configuration

Here is the configuration for router R1:

```
source-bridge ring-group 50                Specifies a virtual-ring of 50

source-bridge explorerQ-depth 100          [optional] limit the queue to
                                           100 explorer frames

dlsw local-peer peer-id 147.19.1.1 group 40 promiscuous

                                           Sets the local peer as a member
                                           of group 40 and to operate in
                                           promiscuous mode. A group must
                                           be configured if implementing a
                                           Border peer.

dlsw remote-peer 0 tcp 147.19.3.3 lf 1500  Defines the remote peer's IP
                                           address. The lf 1500 keyword only
                                           accepts ICANReach responses
                                           indicating an MTU of 1500 bytes
                                           or less.


interface Loopback0

   ip address 147.19.1.1 255.255.255.255


interface Serial0/0

   ip address 142.19.21.1 255.255.255.0


interface Tokenring0/0

   ip address 142.19.11.1 255.255.255.0
```

`source-bridge 10 1 50`	Specifies the local ring is 10, the bridge number is 1, and connects to virtual ring 50.
`source-bridge spanning`	Enable the local ring to forward spanning-tree [single-route] explorer frames.

Router R3 Configuration

Here is router R3's configuration:

`dlsw local-peer peer-id 147.19.3.3 group 40 border promiscuous`

	Set the local peer as a Border Peer in group 40. A Border Peer must be configured in the group to allow the spokes to peer with each other. There are NO remote peer statements since it is in promiscuous mode.
`dlsw bridge-group 1`	Allows bridge-group 1 traffic to go across the DLSw connection.

```
interface Loopback0
   ip address 147.19.3.3 255.255.255.255


interface Serial0
   ip address 147.19.21.3 255.255.255.0


interface Serial1
   ip address 147.19.22.3 255.255.255.0


interface Ethernet0
   ip address 147.19.13.3 255.255.255.0
```

bridge-group 1	Include this interface's traffic in bridge-group 1
bridge 1 protocol ieee	Creates bridge-group 1 on this router for transparent bridging and use the ieee spanning tree protocol

Router R2 Configuration

Router R2's configuration is as follows:

source-bridge ring-group 75	Specifies a virtual-ring of 75
source-bridge transparent 75 3 1 2	Allows translational bridging on this router ONLY. Traffic from the Token-Ring source-bridge 1 can be translated to the FastEthernet bridge-group 2 (using pseudo-ring 3), through the virtual-ring 75
dlsw local-peer peer-id 147.19.2.2 group 40 promiscuous	Defines local peer, as a member of group 40. And the Hub is operating in promiscuous mode. group must be configured if you are implementing border peers this allows the spokes to communicate with each other
dlsw remote-peer 0 tcp 147.19.3.3	Defines the remote peer IP address
dlsw bridge-group 2	Allows bridge-group 2 traffic to travel across the DLSw connection. Also, automatically performs translational bridging bridge-group 2

```
interface Loopback0
  ip address 147.19.2.2 255.255.255.255

interface Serial0/0
```

```
    ip address 142.19.21.1 255.255.255.0


interface Tokenring0/0

    ip address 142.19.20.2 255.255.255.0

    source-bridge 20 1 75          Specifies the local ring as 20 using
                                   the bridge number of 1 and connecting
                                   to virtual ring 75

    source-bridge spanning         Allows this port to participate in the
                                   source route bridging spanning tree.


interface FastEthernet0/0

    ip address 147.19.12.2 255.255.255.0

    bridge-group 2                 Specifies that this interface is a
                                   member of bridge-group 2


bridge 2 protocol ieee            Creates bridge-group 2 on this router
                                   for transparent bridging
```

Configuring Standard DLSw with Translational Bridging and FST Encapsulation

Now we will configure the exact same scenario, but this time we will not use the promiscuous mode. The hub, router R3, will need to have dlsw remote-peer commands pointing to the two spokes, routers R1 and R2, and the promiscuous keyword will not be used. So, the only commands that need to be changed are the dlsw local-peer commands and the dlsw remote-peer commands.

Router R1 Configuration

Here is the configuration for router R1:

```
dlsw local-peer peer-id 147.19.1.1 group 40      Defines local peer, as
                                                 a member of group 40

dlsw remote-peer 0 fst 147.19.3.3Set R3 as a
remote peer  using fst encapsulation
```

Router R3 Configuration

Here is router R3's configuration:

```
dlsw local-peer peer-id 147.19.3.3 group 40 border
```

> Defines local peer, as a Border
> Peer and as a Member of group 40

```
dlsw remote-peer 0 fst 147.19.1.1
```

> Defines router R1 as a remote
> peer using fst encapsulation

```
dlsw remote-peer 0 fst 147.19.2.2
```

> Defines router R2 as a remote
> peer using fst encapsulation

Router R2 Configuration

Here is the configuration for router R2:

```
dlsw local-peer peer-id 147.19.2.2 group 40
```

> Defines local peer, as a
> member of group 40

```
dlsw remote-peer 0 fst 147.19.3.3
```

> Defines router R3 as a remote
> peer using fst encapsulation

Configuring DLSw with Direct Encapsulation

Direct encapsulation is a minimal-overhead option for transporting traffic across point-to-point lines when rerouting is not required. Direct encapsulation is supported over High-Level Data Link Control (HDLC) connections and Frame Relay virtual circuits. It includes a DLSw 16-byte header and the Data Link Control header. Direct encapsulation is fast-switched, not process-switched, so using this encapsulation allows DLSw to process more packets per second than TCP encapsulation. Direct encapsulation provides neither reliable delivery of frames nor local acknowledgment. It is supported only when the end systems reside on token ring, because Ethernet LANs are *not* supported with this encapsulation. Direct encapsulation does not provide any rerouting. It is sometimes considered for very low-speed lines to minimize overhead, but TCP encapsulation with payload compression may offer lower WAN overhead without the limitations of direct encapsulation.

All keepalive frames flow end to end, so you must specify the `pass-thru` keyword at the end of the `dlsw remote-peer` command. The Frame Relay interfaces require a `frame-relay map` command with the keyword `dlsw` specified. And remember that this is direct encapsulation on top of the layer 2 protocols, so there are no IP addresses involved in the router configurations. Figure 14.18 shows a different core topology for our routers. We have removed the IP protocols from the core and inserted a Frame Relay core. Now we must configure our DLSw peers utilizing the Frame Relay DLCIs.

FIGURE 14.18   DLSw with direct encapsulation

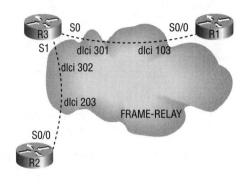

Router R1 Configuration

Here is the configuration for router R1:

```
dlsw local-peer                          Defines local peer
dlsw remote-peer 0 frame-relay interface serial 0/0 103 pass-thru
```

Defines the remote peer using the
local DLCI 103, and the pass-thru
command to allow the keepalives to
flow across the WAN

```
interface Serial0/0
  encapsulation frame-relay
  frame-relay lmi-type ansi
  frame-relay map dlsw 103
```

Specifies to map all DLSw traffic
out this interface to DLCI 103.
Required on all Multipoint Frame-
Relay interfaces

Router R3 Configuration

Here is router R3's configuration:

```
dlsw local-peer           Defines local peer
dlsw remote-peer 0 frame-relay interface serial 0/0 302 pass-thru
```

| | Defines the remote peer using the local DLCI 302, and the pass-thru command to allow the keepalives to flow across the WAN |

```
dlsw remote-peer 0 frame-relay interface serial 0/0 301 pass-thru
```

| | Defines the remote peer using the local DLCI 301, and the pass-thru command to allow the keepalives to flow across the WAN |

```
interface Serial0
 encapsulation frame-relay
 frame-relay lmi-type ansi
 frame-relay map dlsw 301
```

| | Specifies to map all DLSw traffic out this interface to DLCI 301. Required on all Multipoint Frame-Relay interfaces |

```
interface Serial1
 encapsulation frame-relay
 frame-relay lmi-type ansi
 frame-relay map dlsw 302
```

| | Specifies to map all DLSw traffic out this interface to DLCI 302. Required on all Multipoint Frame-Relay interfaces |

Router R2 Configuration

Here is the configuration for router R2:

```
dlsw local-peer                          Defines local peer
dlsw remote-peer 0 frame-relay interface serial 0/0 203 pass-thru
```

| | Defines the remote peer using the local DLCI 203, and the pass-thru command to allow the keepalives to flow across the WAN |

```
interface Serial0/0
```

```
encapsulation frame-relay

frame-relay lmi-type ansi

frame-relay map dlsw 203                    Specifies to map all DLSw
                                            traffic out this interface
                                            to DLCI 203.  Required on all
                                            Multipoint Frame-Relay
                                            Interfaces
```

 DLSw sessions are not transitive. If A is peered with B and B is peered with C, there are no sessions established from A to C through B. A must be peered with C to have circuits.

Configuring DLSw Lite over Frame Relay

DLSw with LLC2 encapsulation is also known as DLSw Lite. It supports many DLSw features, including local acknowledgment, media conversion, minimized LLC2 keepalive traffic, and reliable delivery of frames, but it uses less overhead (16 bytes of DLSw header and 4 bytes of LLC2). It is currently supported over Frame Relay and assumes a direct WAN connection to the peer. DLSw Lite supports end devices attached via token ring, SDLC, Qualified Logical Link Control (QLLC), and Ethernet. DLSw Lite traffic is process-switched and handles approximately the same traffic volume as DLSw using TCP encapsulation.

Now we will configure the exact same Frame Relay scenario in Figure 14.18, but this time we will use DLSW Lite encapsulation. Notice that the dlsw remote-peer commands do *not* have the pass-thru keyword anymore; The LLC2 keepalives are locally acknowledged. Also, the frame-relay map commands on the interfaces must now specify the keyword llc2 instead the of the keyword dlsw, which was used with direct encapsulation.

Router R1 Configuration

Here is the configuration for router R1:

```
dlsw local-peer                             Defines local peer

dlsw remote-peer 0 frame-relay interface serial 0/0 103


                                            Defines the remote peer
                                            using the local DLCI 103



interface Serial0/0

  encapsulation frame-relay
```

```
frame-relay lmi-type ansi

frame-relay map llc2 103
```
Specifies to map all DLSw traffic out this interface to DLCI 103. Required on all Multipoint Frame-Relay interfaces

Router R3 Configuration

Router R3's configuration is as follows:

```
dlsw local-peer
```
Defines local peer

```
dlsw remote-peer 0 frame-relay interface serial 0/0 302
```
Defines the remote peer using the local DLCI 302

```
dlsw remote-peer 0 frame-relay interface serial 0/0 301
```
Defines the remote peer using the local DLCI 301

```
interface Serial0

  encapsulation frame-relay

  frame-relay lmi-type ansi

  frame-relay map llc2 301
```
Specifies to map all DLSw traffic out this interface to DLCI 301. Required on all Multipoint Frame-Relay interfaces

```
interface Serial1

  encapsulation frame-relay

  frame-relay lmi-type ansi

  frame-relay map llc2 302
```
Specifies to map all DLSw traffic out this interface to DLCI 302. Required on all Multipoint Frame-Relay Interfaces

Router R2 Configuration

Here is router R2's configuration:

```
dlsw local-peer                           Defines local peer

dlsw remote-peer 0 frame-relay interface serial 0/0 203


                                          Defines the remote peer using
                                          the local DLCI 203


interface Serial0/0

  encapsulation frame-relay

  frame-relay lmi-type ansi

  frame-relay map llc2 203                Specifies to map all DLSw
                                          traffic out this interface to
                                          DLCI 203. Required on Frame-
                                          Relay Multipoint interfaces
```

> DLSw performance is not tied as closely to the number of peers or the number of circuits as it is to the transactions per second the router processes. This is equivalent to the traffic load. One mainframe to mainframe circuit to one peer has the potential to push a router's CPU higher than, say, 30 peers each with 10 circuits for data entry terminals.

DLSw Advanced Features

DLSw includes many additional features to enhance the implementation of the protocol functionality, such as backup peers, statically mapped reachability, statically mapping MAC addresses to remote peers, MAC-exclusive, costs, bridge groups and ring lists, queuing, and Dial-on-Demand capabilities.

Configuring Backup Peers

DLSw allows you to configure a backup peer, which the router will use to form a DLSw connection with in the event that the primary DLSw connection is lost. To configure a backup peer, you must first configure a dlsw remote-peer command for the backup remote router. Then add the backup-peer command at the end of your dlsw remote-peer command, pointing to the primary connection. In the backup-peer command, you must specify the IP address of the backup remote router. Also, in the event that you have lost the primary DLSw connection, the connection to the backup remote router (peer) is activated. Once the primary peer connection is active again, it is possible to have the backup connection wait a specified amount of time before tearing itself down. This is accomplished with the linger keyword at the end of the backup-peer command. With the linger command, you must specify the number of minutes the backup connection should remain active before tearing itself down. In the following example, the topology shown in Figure 14.17 is used, with a primary DLSw connection from router R3 to router R1. We will configure a backup connection from router R3 to router R2. The backup-peer command is applied to router R3. Here is the configuration for router R3:

```
dlsw local-peer peer-id 147.19.3.3          Defines local peer

dlsw remote-peer 0 tcp 147.19.2.2           Defines the remote peer IP
                                            address

dlsw remote-peer 0 tcp 147.19.1.1 backup-peer 147.19.2.2 linger 8


                                            Defines the remote peer IP
                                            address (147.19.1.1), and
                                            if remote-peer 147.19.1.1
                                            [primary] is unreachable,
                                            connect to 147.19.2.2
                                            [backup] as a remote-peer.
                                            When primary link is restored,
                                            wait 8 minutes before tearing
                                            down backup-peer
```

Statically Mapping Reachability

The DLSW reachability cache can be statically configured with global commands. This is sort of like a static route because it is a way of statically listing what network devices (either by NetBIOS name or by MAC address) the router can reach. These static mappings can be applied on the router with a local significance *only*, or they can be configured so that they are propagated to the router's remote peers.

Here is the configuration for local significance *only*:

```
dlsw mac-addr  4000.1234.5678               This router can reach MAC
                                            address 4000.1234.5678

dlsw netbios-name  HOST2                     This router can reach NetBIOS
                                            name HOST2
```

Here is the configuration in which they are propagated to remote peers:

```
dlsw icanreach netbios-name HOST1        This router will respond locally for
                                         any request to reach the NetBIOS name
                                         HOST1.  It will NOT send explorer
                                         frames for this host

dlsw icanreach mac-address 4000.0000.3745 mask FFFF.FFFF.0000

                                         This router will respond locally for
                                         any request to reach any of the MAC
                                         addresses within the range of
                                         4000.0000.3745 to 4000.0000.FFFF.  It
                                         will NOT send explorer frames for
                                         these MAC addresses.  Notice the 0's
                                         in the mask represent anything
```

If you want a host's NetBIOS name to remain in your cache even in the event that the host or even the remote router intermittently becomes unreachable, you can configure the `dlsw timer netbios-cache-timeout 300` and `dlsw timer sna-cache-timeout 300` commands. These commands specify in seconds how long the entry should remain in the cache after it is not heard from.

Statically Mapping MAC Addresses to Remote Peers

You can save bandwidth within the WAN by statically mapping a MAC address to its proper remote peer. This way, the router will not have to transmit broadcasts to every remote peer when it attempts to locate the specified MAC address. In the following example, let's say that the device with MAC address 4000.5c9e.3745 is connected off of router R2. Here is the configuration for router R3:

```
dlsw local-peer peer-id 147.19.3.3      Defines local peer

dlsw remote-peer 0 tcp 147.19.1.1       Defines the remote peer IP address

dlsw remote-peer 0 tcp 147.19.2.2       Defines the remote peer IP address

dlsw mac-addr 4000.5c9e.3745 remote-peer ip-address 147.19.2.2

                                         Specifies that to reach the MAC address
                                         4000.5c9e.3745 you must use the
                                         connection to remote peer 147.19.2.2
```

Configuring MAC-Exclusive Filters

DLSw routers have the ability to advertise reachability information to their peers using the `dlsw icanreach mac-address` command. If configured, the MAC addresses of devices reachable via this DLSw router are advertised during the peer capabilities exchange process. In this way, peer routers looking for a particular MAC address can send CANUReach messages only to the correct peer. A further enhancement to this process is the `dlsw icanreach mac-exclusive` command. This specifies to DLSw peers that only the devices reported are reachable via this router. Therefore, any unwanted explorer traffic is blocked at the peer router.

The `dlsw icanreach mac-address` command takes a MAC address in non-canonical format and a mask. In the mask, bits that are set to 1 are significant and those that are set to 0 are don't care. To specify a single MAC address a mask of FFFF.FFFF.FFFF is used. If all reachable devices at the local router have locally administered MAC addresses of the format 4000.3745.00xx, the command format could be: dlsw icanreach mac-address 4000.3745.0000 ffff.ffff.ff00, where the last byte of the address is not checked. Figure 14.19 shows a typical data center application of the `mac-exclusive` filter where the central DLSw router has only one mainframe it wants to establish circuits for.

FIGURE 14.19   DLSw with MAC-exclusive

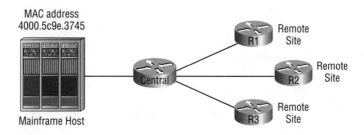

Here is the central router configuration:

```
dlsw icanreach mac-exclusive  [remote]
dlsw icanreach mac-address 4000.5c9e.3745 mask FFFF.FFFF.FFFF
```

The `dlsw icanreach mac-exclusive` command also limits local broadcasts that do not match the MAC address criteria to be sent out to peers. If the remote keyword is added to the `dlsw icanreach mac-exclusive` command, it allows local explorer frames to bypass the MAC address check and get sent to remote peers. It does not change the peer's behavior.

Configuring Cost

Cost can be specified on either the `dlsw local-peer` or the `dlsw remote-peer` command. When it is specified on the `dlsw local-peer` command, it is exchanged with remote DLSw peers as part of the capabilities exchange. The peer with the lower cost is always preferred. If you configure the `cost` on the `dlsw remote-peer` command, this allows different areas or parts of the internetwork to favor different central site gateways. Using the network in Figure 14.20, we can configure the routers to allow all traffic from router R2 to prefer the remote peer of router R4 and all traffic from router R1 to prefer the remote peer of router R3.

🌐 Real World Scenario

DLSw Filtering: The Key to Success

Possibly one of the most powerful public service announcements ever aired was one by Yul Brynner released after he had died of lung cancer. In it he stated, "If I could just say one thing I would say, "Don't smoke. Just… don't smoke." In a similar fashion, if we could just say one thing, it would be, "Just filter." We can't tell you the number of meltdown situations we've been paged on over the last 10 years that could have been avoided if the proper filtering had been in place. As a general rule, most SNA traffic uses SAP x04 (and to a lesser extent, x08 and x0C). A `dlsw icanreach sap 00 04` statement keeps peers from sending traffic other than the desired protocol. In addition, on the central peer, you can add an `ICANReach MAC exclusive` filter to tell remote peers to send explorer frames only for the designated hosts. In addition, bridging filters applied to input interfaces can eliminate broadcasts from reaching the DLSw process and wasting CPU cycles. It is usually very easy to configure DLSw and get it up and running; however, the key to having a stable network is proper filtering.

FIGURE 14.20   DLSw with cost

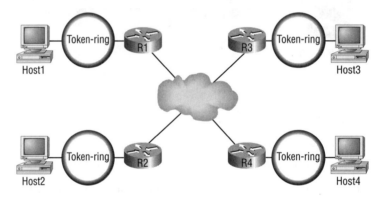

Router R1 Configuration

Here is the configuration for router R1:

`dlsw local-peer peer-id 147.19.1.1`	Defines DLSw local peer
`dlsw remote-peer 0 tcp 147.19.3.3 cost 2`	Defines the remote peer IP address. The cost 2 keyword at the end of the command sets the cost for this remote peer
`dlsw remote-peer 0 tcp 147.19.4.4 cost 4`	Define the remote peer IP address and its cost. Since cost 4 is higher than 147.19.3.3's it is not the preferred peer

Router R2 Configuration

Here is router R2's configuration:

```
dlsw local-peer peer-id 147.19.2.2          Define local peer id

dlsw remote-peer 0 tcp 147.19.4.4 cost 2    Defines the remote peer IP
                                            address. The cost 2 keyword at
                                            the end of the command sets the
                                            cost for this remote peer

dlsw remote-peer 0 tcp 147.19.3.3 cost 4    Define the remote peer IP
                                            address and its cost. Since cost
                                            4 is higher than 147.19.4.4's it
                                            is not the preferred peer
```

Router R3 and R4 Configuration

Here is router R3's configuration:

```
dlsw local-peer peer-id 147.19.3.3          Defines local peer
```

And the configuration for Router R4 is as follows:

```
dlsw local-peer peer-id 147.19.4.4          Defines local peer
```

Configuring Bridge Groups and Ring Lists

Another way of filtering your DLSw connections is through the use of bridge groups and ring lists. You can specify which bridge groups or ring lists a remote peer is allowed to access. This can be accomplished through the `dlsw bgroup-list` command and the `dlsw ring-list` command. Until now, we have always configured the list number in the `dlsw remote-peer` command as a 0. However, the list value can be any of the following values:

0	*no* lists applied to this remote peer
Bridge group list number	local bridge group
port list number	local interface
ring list number	local ring

Here is a sample configuration:

```
source-bridge ring-group 75        Specifies a virtual-ring of 75
dlsw local-peer peer-id 147.19.2.2  Defines local peer
dlsw remote-peer 1 tcp 147.19.3.3   Defines the remote peer IP address,
                                    and applies list 1 to this remote peer
                                    connection
```

`dlsw remote-peer 2 tcp 147.19.1.1`	Defines the remote peer IP address, and applies list "2" to this remote peer connection
`dlsw ring-list 1 rings 20`	Specifies that any remote peer with this list applied, can ONLY access the local Token-Ring 20
`dlsw bgroup-list 2 bgroups 2`	Specifies that any remote peer with this list applied, can ONLY access the local bridge-group 2
`dlsw bridge-group 2`	Allows bridge-group 2 traffic to travel across the DLSw connection. Also, automatically performs the translational bridging with bridge-group 2

`interface Tokenring0/0`

  `ip address 142.19.20.2 255.255.255.0`

`source-bridge 20 1 75`	Specifies local ring 20 connects to local bridge 1, which then connects to the virtual ring 75
`source-bridge spanning`	Specifies that the local ring is using spanning-tree [single-route] explorer packets

`interface FastEthernet0/0`

  `ip address 147.19.12.2 255.255.255.0`

`bridge-group 2`	Specifies that this interface is a member of bridge-group 2

`bridge 2 protocol ieee`	Creates bridge-group "2" on this router for transparent bridging

So, the remote peer 147.19.3.3 can access only the local Token Ring number 20, and the remote peer 147.19.1.1 can access only the local bridge group number 2.

Configuring Queuing

By default, a DLSw TCP peer connection uses port 2065 for all circuit traffic on a first come, first serve basis; no circuit's traffic is prioritized over another's. If there needs to be differentiation between DLSw circuits for traffic delivery, the `priority` keyword can be used at the end of the `dlsw remote-peer` statement. The `priority` keyword causes DLSw to establish four separate TCP connections with the specified peer using port numbers 2065, 1981, 1982, and 1983 representing high, medium, normal, and low priority traffic, respectively.

TCP port 2065   Defaults to high priority. In the absence of any other configuration, this port carries all circuit administration frames (CUR_cs, ICR_cs, contact SSP frames, disconnect SSP frames, XID, ICR_ex), peer keepalives, and capabilities exchange.

TCP port 1981   Defaults to medium priority. In the absence of any other configuration, this port does *not* carry any traffic.

TCP port 1982   Defaults to normal priority. In the absence of any other configuration, this port carries information frames (nonbroadcast datagram frames).

TCP port 1983   Defaults to low priority. In the absence of any other configuration, this port carries broadcast traffic (CUR_ex, Name_query_ex, SSP DATA/ DGRM broadcasts).

Here's a command syntax example:

```
dlsw remote-peer 0 tcp 192.168.15.91 priority
```
Defines remote peer's IP address and activates the 4 priority queues for traffic destined to this peer

```
dlsw tos map high 5 medium 4 normal 3 low 2
```
[optional] sets the IP precedence values for port 2065, 1981, 1982, and 1983, respectively

```
sap-priority-list 1 high ssap 08 dsap 08
```
assign traffic with source and destination SAPs 0f 08 to the DLSw high priority transport

```
sap-priority-list 1 low ssap F0 dsap F0
```
assign NetBIOS traffic to the DLSww low priority transport

```
dlsw  bridge 1 sap-priority 1
```
enable SAP traffic prioritization

DLSw Improved Scalability with Border Peers and Peer on Demand

Most traditional SNA networks are hierarchical and do not require any-to-any connectivity; devices at a remote location only need to reach the central mainframe. Therefore, each remote DLSw router needs only to peer with the central site DLSw peer. However, in some NetBIOS networks and some SNA networks using Advanced Peer to Peer Networking (APPN), there is need for any-to-any connectivity where one remote site may need to have sessions with multiple other remote sites. To achieve this, each remote site would have to peer with every other remote site. In a 100-site network, this would require configuring 99 peers per router. If the network expands and 5 new sites are added, each of the existing 100 routers would have to add them to their peer lists. Clearly this is not scalable.

Two DLSw+ features that overcome this scalability problem are border peers and Peer on Demand (PoD). The *border peer* feature allows for the network to be segmented into smaller pieces somewhat along the lines of Open Shortest Path First (OSPF) areas. The routers in a peer group all peer to one router called a border peer, which in turn peers to border peers in other peer groups, as shown in Figure 14.21. If a device off of one of the peer group 1 routers needs to connect to a device off of a peer group 2 router, its router sends a CANUReach frame to its border peer. The border peer forwards the explorer to all other peers in its peer group as well as to the other border peers it is peered with. In this case, the explorer reaches the border peer in peer group 2, which in turn sends out copies of the CANUReach frame to all of its peers in peer group 2. The remote router in peer group 2 that has the target device responds with an ICANReach frame to its border peer. The border peer in group 2 responds to the border peer of group 1 and includes the IP address of the responding router. The border peer for group 1 caches this information and forwards it to the originating router. This router then establishes a peer connection to the router in peer group 2 before the circuit can be set up. Note that the border peers only act as facilitators and do not handle the actual circuits.

FIGURE 14.21   DLSw+ peer groups

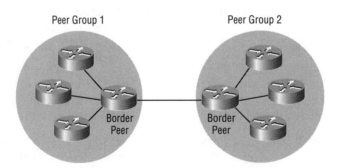

The Peer on Demand (PoD) feature allows for greater scalability as well. With any-to-any connectivity, the sessions are generally not persistent and may only last as long as a single file transfer. To keep the number of peer sessions that must be maintained to a minimum, PoD will tear down peer connections once there are no circuits going across them or when there is no traffic after a certain amount of time.

Configuring DLSw with Dial-on-Demand Routing (DDR)

Dial-on-Demand Routing (DDR) refers to the capability of DLSw to transfer data over a dial-up connection and automatically drop the dial connection when there is no data to send. To use DLSw DDR, you must first configure the `dlsw remote-peer` command and include the additional required syntax or keywords for the DLSw DDR functionality.

The `dynamic` keyword will prevent the remote peer connection from being established unnecessarily. The `keepalive` keyword is needed because DLSw locally acknowledges SNA (or more precisely, SDLC or LLC2) traffic, so no Data Link Control acknowledgments or receiver ready frames will bring up the dial connection. However, DLSw peers send peer keepalives to each other periodically, and these keepalives will bring up the dial connection. The `keepalive` option refers to how often DLSw peers send peer keepalives to each other. If you set this to 0 (zero), no keepalives will be sent and, therefore, the peer keepalive will not keep the dial line up. You must specify `keepalive 0` in *both* peers, the local and remote DLSw router. The `timeout` keyword is needed because without peer keepalives, DLSw is dependent on TCP timers to determine when the SNA session has come down. TCP will only determine that it has lost a partner if it does not get an acknowledgment after it sends data. By default, TCP may wait up to 15 minutes for an acknowledgment before tearing down the TCP connection. Therefore, when `keepalive 0` is specified, you should also set the `timeout` keyword, which is the number of seconds that TCP will wait for an acknowledgment before tearing down the connection. Time-out should be long enough to allow acknowledgments to get through in periods of moderate to heavy congestion but short enough to minimize the time it takes to recover from a network outage. SNA Data Link Control connections typically wait 150 to 250 seconds before timing out. We recommend a value of approximately 90 seconds. You can also specify an *optional* keyword, the `dest-mac` keyword. This keyword allows you to specify a single destination MAC address, which will allow the DLSw DDR connection to be brought up active only if the destination MAC address matches the MAC address that you have specified with the `dest-mac` keyword. Remember, this keyword is *optional*, because the DLSw DDR connection will function properly without it. Here is a quick review of the additional keywords for implementing DLSw DDR:

`dynamic`	Prevents the peer connection from being brought up automatically. When a circuit tries to connect, Dial-on-Demand Routing (DDR) dialing is initiated and the peer comes up.
`keepalive 0`	Specified as a number of seconds, sets how often the peers will exchange keepalive packets. Setting the value to 0 disables the keepalives, which allows the ISDN connection to drop when the line is idle.
`timeout 90`	Specified as a number of seconds, tears down the peer connection after 90 seconds of inactivity.
`dest-mac`	Optional. Specifies that the link will be brought up *only* for traffic destined to this specified MAC.

Here is a command syntax example:

```
dlsw remote-peer 0 tcp 147.19.2.2 dynamic keepalive 0 timeout 90
   [dest-mac 0c00.0000.aaba]
```

In order to completely implement the DLSw DDR connection, you must specify in the dialer list that the DLSw TCP port 2065 is identified as "interesting" traffic, in both directions of the traffic flow. The `dialer-list` command will be discussed in Chapter 15, "Integrated Services Digital Network (ISDN) and Dial Backup." Here's a command syntax example:

```
dialer-list 1 protocol ip list 101


access-list 101 permit tcp any eq 2065 any
access-list 101 permit tcp any any eq 2065
```

DLSW and NAT

You may remember from the beginning of this chapter (in the section "Establish Peer Connections") that DLSw peers establish two TCP connections between them. A Cisco router will drop the extra TCP connection (TCP port 2065) unless it is communicating with another vendor's router that requires two TCP connections. The TCP connection with the *highest* IP address will be the connection that must be torn down when building a connection between two Cisco routers. This can cause a problem if the DLSw connections are flowing through a router with Network Address Translation (NAT) being performed. Figure 14.22 shows router R1 and router R2 attempting to establish a DLSw connection between them. However, the connection must flow through an intermediate router that is performing NAT.

FIGURE 14.22   DLSw with NAT

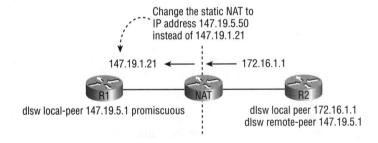

Router R1 thinks that its DLSw TCP session is between itself (147.19.5.1) and 147.19.1.21, which is the IP address of router R2 after it passes through the NAT router. Router R1 thinks it has the highest IP address, so it thinks it must tear down the TCP connection on its local TCP port 2065. Router R2 thinks that its DLSw TCP session is between itself (172.16.1.1) and 147.19.5.1. Router R2 thinks it has the highest IP address and that it must tear down the TCP connection on its local TCP port 2065. So now, both of the TCP connections have been torn down, leaving the routers in a DISCONNECT state. The routers will then both establish TCP port 2065 connections again, which they will in turn both tear down. Thus, you will see the session being established and then torn down over and over.

The solution is to make sure that the NAT statically translates the 172.16.1.1 address to a higher IP address, like 147.19.5.50, so both routers agree that router R2 has the highest IP address. Therefore, router R1 will always tear down its TCP port 2065 connection, and the TCP port 2065 connection from router R2 to router R1 will always be the higher IP address and remain active.

DLSw Troubleshooting

DLSw troubleshooting involves a number of different areas including peer connectivity, bridging, and end device configuration. It is generally a good idea to get the current configurations of both DLSw peers in order to make sure that all appropriate parameters match up between peers and that there are no access lists that would block peer traffic or end device traffic. For checking peer connectivity, the `show dlsw peers`, `show dlsw capabilities`, and extended `ping` commands are very helpful. The `show bridge` and `show source` commands are used to check the transparent and source route bridging components of a DLSw circuit. It should also be noted that a basic router health check looking at router CPU use, interface status, buffer usage, the IP route table, and traffic levels should always be done when investigating DLSw problems.

`show dlsw capabilities`	Displays the configuration of all peers
`show dlsw circuits`	Displays the individual SNA and NetBIOS sessions.
`show dlsw circuits detail`	Display SNA and NetBIOS session I- Frame, RIF, and pacing statistics
`show dlsw circuit history detail`	Displays circuit connect and disconnect times and reasons
`show dlsw peers`	Displays DLSw peer information
`show dlsw peers ssp`	Displays peer switch to switch statistics. Useful for evaluating filters
`show dlsw reachability`	Displays all reachable hosts by NetBIOS name and MAC address
`show dlsw statistics`	Displays the number of frames processed in the local, remote, and group cache
`show tcp`	Displays TCP session information
`show bridge`	Displays transparent bridging statistics
`show source`	Displays source-route bridging statistics

ping	Verifies IP connectivity between peers
debug dlsw peers	Enables debugging output for peer events
debug dlsw reachability	Enables debugging output for reachability events (explorer traffic). Event-level information is displayed for all protocols

 The DLSw process can be reset on the routers by issuing the dlsw disable command followed by the no dlsw disable command.

 The extended ping command is invaluable for debugging DLSw peer connectivity issues because it allows you to ping from the local DLSw IP address to the remote's DLSw peer ID. It also allows you to vary the packet size and data payload. Because SNA session data can contain long strings of binary 0s or 0x40s for screen displays, it is helpful to use these values in the ping payload.

SNA Transport: The Future

Although the following material is not included on either the written or lab CCIE Routing and Switching examinations, it is useful to know if you are going to be working in an environment with IBM hosts. The push to migrate to Ethernet with the withdrawal from sale of token ring network adapters and switches as well as the end of sales on IBM FEPs is changing the topology of mainframe connectivity. The new model both Cisco and IBM are endorsing has IBM mainframes connecting to the network using Open System Adapter (OSA) cards, APPN, and Enterprise Extender (EE). End devices will connect to routers running SNAsw, which translates the SNA traffic to UDP/IP packets bound for the host or other APPN devices. Cisco's CCO website contains a lot of good information about SNAsw and migration scenarios.

Summary

In this chapter, we explored different methods of bridging as well as data-link switching (DLSw). Although bridging is no longer widely used in networks as the primary means of conveying traffic, it is still necessary because SNA traffic is nonroutable and still very important to running most enterprise networks. Because Ethernet switching is basically transparent bridging, it is necessary to understand how transparent bridges work as well as how the Spanning-Tree Protocol works in order to understand the fundamentals of switching.

We studied the two main types of bridging, transparent and source-route, as well as their derivatives source-route transparent (SRT) and translational (SR-TLB) and remote source-route bridging (RSRB). Concurrent Routing and Bridging (CRB) and Integrated Routing and Bridging (IRB) were reviewed as well.

We covered the theory and benefits of using DLSw to transport SNA and NetBIOS traffic as well as the advanced features DLSw has to filter, scale, and handle redundancy. DLSw is easy to configure in a basic setup, but the CCIE candidate would do well to understand all the options DLSw supports, not only for the written and lab exams but also to optimize DLSw transport in real-world situations.

Some hands-on lab scenarios and material on bridging and DLSw that weren't covered in this chapter are presented in Chapter 14 Supplement on the CD-ROM that accompanies this book. It is well worth your time to check it out.

Exam Essentials

Know what transparent bridging is.   Transparent bridging forwards traffic by looking at the destination MAC address (DMAC) in a frame and performing table lookup on what port that MAC address is reachable. The transparent bridge populates its table by inspecting each incoming frame's source MAC address (SMAC) and associating it with the incoming port.

Know why the spanning-tree algorithm is used and how it is implemented.   The spanning-tree algorithm is used to take a redundant, meshed topology and turn it into a "spanning tree" in which there is only a single path between any two network segments. This prevents loops and multiple copies of frames from reaching a destination. The Spanning-Tree Protocol works by first electing a root bridge based on the lowest bridge identifier and then having the bridges on each network segment compare their path costs back to the root bridge. The bridge with the lowest path cost on a segment will forward traffic for the segment back to the root bridge; all other bridges' ports on that segment will enter a blocking state.

Understand the fields inside the source-route bridging RIF.   The RIF contains the list of rings and bridges (routing descriptors, or RDs) a frame has to travel through between two token ring stations. It also has the Routing Control field, which contains 3 Broadcast bits, 5 Length bits specifying the length of the RIF, 1 Direction bit indicating whether to read the RD list left to right or right to left, and 3 MTU bits, which indicate the largest frame size the bridged path is able to accommodate.

Understand the concepts of DLSw and how to configure basic DLSw.   Data-link switching (DLSw) is used to transport nonroutable SNA and NetBIOS traffic across an IP WAN infrastructure. In addition to IP encapsulation and reroutability around failed links, DLSw breaks the LLC2 session into two pieces and terminates both sides. This allows DLSw to control acknowledgments and error recovery and keeps this traffic off the WAN.

Know all of the encapsulation types supported by DLSw+. Besides the RFC 1795–compliant TCP/IP encapsulation with spoofing, DLSw+ allows for FST and direct encapsulation as well as DLSw Lite and RIF passthrough. Know which types of encapsulation support local acknowledgments, and know when the appropriate times to use each of them are.

Know the advanced filtering and peering features of DLSw+. DLSw+ supports a wide variety of features designed to provide redundancy and control the amount of broadcast explorer frames. Border peers allow for DLSw to scale in a large network where any-to-any connectivity is required rather than the traditional connectivity between remote site and data center. Back-up peers provide peer redundancy, as does configuring multiple peers with different costs. ICANReach/ICANNOTReach MAC address and SAP filters allow peers to communicate their reachability information so they won't receive extraneous explorer traffic.

Key Terms

Before you take the exam, be certain you are familiar with the following terms:

border peer	root bridge
bridge identifier	Routing Information Field (RIF)
bridge priority	source-route bridging (SRB)
data-link switching (DLSw)	source-route translational bridging (SR/TLB)
explorer frame	source-route transparent bridging (SRT)
flooding	Spanning-Tree Protocol (SPT)
Integrated Routing and Bridging (IRB)	

Review Questions

1. In the RIF C6A0 0047 00A0, in which direction should the route descriptor be read?

    A. Left to right

    B. Right to left

    C. Top to bottom

    D. Bottom to top

    E. None of the above

2. Bridge A has a priority of 100, has a MAC address of 0000.0C11.1111, and is running the DEC Spanning-Tree Protocol. Bridge B has a priority of 100, has a MAC address of 0000.0C22.2222, and is running the 802.1d Spanning-Tree Protocol. Which of the following is true of the root bridge election?

    A. Bridge A would be the root bridge.

    B. Bridge B would be the root bridge.

    C. There would not be a root bridge.

    D. Bridge A and bridge B would be root bridges.

    E. No election would occur because bridges A and B have invalid MAC addresses.

3. You have configured IRB between an Ethernet segment and a token ring segment. An Ethernet station has the MAC address 0000.0111.3333. What is the corresponding Token MAC address for this station?

    A. 0000.0111.1111

    B. 0000.8088.CCCC

    C. 3333.1110.0000

    D. 0000.0FFF.2222

    E. FFFF.F999.DDDD

4. In the RIF 0610 0157 0A00, what is the first ring encountered on the path in decimal?

    A. 1

    B. 4

    C. 21

    D. 57

    E. 100

5. Your router is configured for SR/TLB. A 5000-byte token ring frame is destined for an Ethernet segment with an MTU of 1500. What will happen to the 5000-byte frame?

A. It will be made into three Ethernet frames.

B. It will be made into four Ethernet frames.

C. The frame will be routed to a different segment.

D. The frame will be dropped.

E. The frame will be segmented into 568-byte frames.

6. SNA uses LLC2 to transmit data. Which of the following is true of LLC2? (Choose all that apply.)

A. Connectionless

B. Connection oriented

C. Variable time-outs

D. Routable

E. Fixed-length time-outs

7. A NetBIOS station wants to locate network resources. The NetBIOS station transmits an explorer frame that is received by the DLSw switch. The DLSw switch would send what kind of frame or packet to its DLSw peer?

A. All-routes explorer

B. Single-route explorer

C. RARP

D. ARP

E. CANUReach

8. DLSw+ adds many features to DLSw. Which feature allows for clustering routers in a region?

A. Border peer caching

B. Peer groups

C. IP proxy

D. SNA areas

E. APPN areas

9. Which of the following is implemented in DLSw? (Choose all that apply.)

A. Flow control

B. NetBIOS Pass-thru

C. IPX spoofing

D. IP Intercept

E. SNA MAC address and NetBIOS name caching

10. Use the following configuration information to answer this question: On router R1, what is the virtual ring number?

```
Hostname R1
!
source-bridge ring-group 300
dlsw local-peer peer-id 172.16.2.1
dlsw remote-peer 0 tcp 172.16.1.1
!
interface Loopback0
 ip address 172.16.2.1 255.255.255.0
!
interface Serial0
 ip address 172.16.100.2 255.255.255.0
!
interface TokenRing0
 ip address 172.16.20.2 255.255.255.0
 ring-speed 16
 source-bridge 2 1 300
 source-bridge spanning
```

A. 1

B. 2

C. 300

D. 0

E. 172.16.20.2

Answers to Review Questions

1. B. The third character is 0xA. Because 0xA is greater than 0x8, the route descriptor must be read from right to left.

2. D. The two different Spanning-Tree Protocols do not interoperate. They would not even know the other exists. They would hold separate elections.

3. B. The MAC address needs to be converted from canonical to noncanonical.

4. C. The third character is less than 0x8, so the frame is read from left to right. The first ring is 0x015. Converting this to decimal yields 21.

5. D. The sending station is ignoring the largest frame indicator in the RIF field, so the frame will be dropped.

6. B, E. LLC2 is a connection-oriented protocol designed for use on the LAN. It has short, fixed-length time-outs.

7. E. The DLSw requesting switch would send a CANUReach. The remote DLSw switch uses explorer frames on the local segment to determine whether the resource is available. If it is available, the switch replies with an ICANReach message.

8. B. DLSw+ implements peer groups to allow for a hierarchically designed network.

9. A, E. DLSw uses TCP to mimic the flow control expected by LLC2 and will cache SNA MAC addresses and NetBIOS names.

10. C. The virtual ring is defined by the source-bridge ring group 300.

Chapter

15

Integrated Services Digital Network (ISDN) and Dial Backup

THE CCIE QUALIFICATION EXAM TOPICS COVERED IN THIS CHAPTER INCLUDE THE FOLLOWING:

- ✓ ISDN
- ✓ Understanding the difference between BRI and PRI
- ✓ ISDN signaling, reference points, and function groups
- ✓ LAPD
- ✓ Configuring T1/E1 PRI
- ✓ Configuring ISDN and dial backup services

Integrated Services Digital Network (ISDN) has gained quite a following over the past few years. It offers a switched high-speed data connection that can also be used to support voice, video, or fax calling. Some predict that Digital Subscription Service (DSL), which can also provide data, voice, and fax services to end users, is probably going to replace ISDN completely within the next few years because DSL is cheaper and faster, which means it must be better—maybe. Another competitor, the cable modem, has also been around for a few years, providing much of the same service as ISDN.

Data transmitted via ISDN is digital from end to end instead of going through an analog conversion as it does with a modem. Analog modems convert information from its digital state on the computer to analog through the modem and back to digital on the remote computer end.

In this chapter, you will learn about ISDN, beginning with the Physical layer and working up. Upon completion of this chapter, CCIE candidates will be able to successfully configure, test, and troubleshoot an ISDN connection.

What Is Integrated Services Digital Network (ISDN)?

Integrated Services Digital Network (ISDN) has been under development for a couple of decades but has been hampered by the lack of applications that could use its speed. ISDN switch technology was originally somewhat proprietary in nature, and the lack of a standard prevented widespread use. This obstacle was overcome when National ISDN-1 was made available in 1992, allowing vendors to interoperate between devices.

Before getting into what ISDN is, we'll take a look at how traditional telephone service, known as *plain old telephone service (POTS)* or *public switched telephone network (PSTN)*, operates. Typically, you pick up the telephone receiver and enter the number and the party answers at the other end. Your voice—which is an analog wave—is converted into a digital signal through a process called *pulse code modulation (PCM)*. PCM samples your voice 8000 times a second and converts the audio level into an 8-bit value, thus $8 \times 8000 = 64K$. This 64Kbps channel, or DS0 (digital signal level 0), is multiplexed with 23 other channels to form a T1. If you do the math, you'll notice that a T1 is 1.544MB, and 24 $\times$ 64KB is only 1.536MB. Where are the other 8KB? They are used by a single framing bit that is added to every 24-channel block. Now we have 1.544MB. However, *robbed-bit signaling* uses the lowest significant bit for signaling, or for indicating that the line is on or off the hook, leaving a practical channel bandwidth of 56Kbps (64K – 8K = 56K). Robbed-bit signaling is also known as *in-band signaling*.

ISDN differs from POTS in a couple of ways. First, ISDN starts off as digital, so there is no analog-to-digital conversion. Second, in the case of a basic rate interface (BRI), the call setup and teardown is accomplished through a dedicated 16KB channel, which is also known as a D (data) channel. By using out-of-band signaling, we have the entire 64KB for data. This leaves one or two B (bearer) channels for data or voice traffic. ISDN benefits include improved speed over analog modems, fast call setup (1 second or less), and lower cost compared to a dedicated point-to-point circuit. Likewise, a primary rate interface (PRI) uses a 64KB D channel for signaling and either 23 B channels (T1) or 30 channels (E1).

ISDN Line Options

ISDN is available in many different configurations or line options. In this section, you will learn about two of the most common—Basic Rate Interface (BRI) and Primary Rate Interface (PRI). Each option has one or more DS0s, or B channels, and a D channel. ISDN is characterized by the presence of a D channel, which carries control and signaling information, freeing up the B channels for voice and data transport. Table 15.1 shows the relationship between the DS level, speed, designations, and number of DS0s per channel.

TABLE 15.1   North America Digital Hierarchy

Digital Signal Level	Speed	Designation	Channels
DS0	64Kbps	None	1
DS1	1.544Mbps	T1	24
DS2	6.312Mbps	T2	96
DS3	44.736Mbps	T3	672

Another ISDN characteristic is the *Service Profile Identifier (SPID)*. A SPID identifies the characteristics of your ISDN line. SPIDs may or may not be needed, depending on the type of switch your service provider uses. An ISDN National-1 and DMS-100 switch require a SPID for each B channel, whereas it is optional with an AT&T 5ESS switch type. Outside of the United States, SPIDs aren't normally required. The format of a SPID is usually the 10-digit phone number plus a prefix and possibly a suffix. For example, let's say that your telephone number is (212) 555-8663. Adding a prefix of 01 and a suffix of 0100 gives you a SPID of 0121255586630100. To place an ISDN call, you will also need a directory number, or DN. A DN is the actual number you would call to reach that B channel (212558663).

Basic Rate Interface (BRI)

A *Basic Rate Interface (BRI)* uses a single copper pair of wires to provide up to 192Kbps of bandwidth for both voice and data calls. A BRI uses two 64Kbps B channels and one 16Kbps D channel. So, 144Kbps is the total bit rate, but only 128Kbps (data bit rate) can be used for data/voice.

BRI Switch Options

There are several different BRI switch options available for configuring your router. These switch options vary according to geographic location. The available switch types are shown in Table 15.2.

TABLE 15.2   ISDN BRI Switch Types

Switch Type	Typically Used
basic-1tr6	1TR6 switch type for Germany
basic-5ess	AT&T 5ESS switch type for the U.S.
basic-dms100	Northern DMS-100 switch type
basic-net3	NET3 switch type for U.K. and Europe
basic-ni	National ISDN switch type
basic-ts013	TS013 switch type for Australia
ntt	NTT switch type for Japan
vn3	VN3 and VN4 switch types for France

The D channel can also be used to transport packet-switched data communications, such as X.25. In fact, Cisco has enabled this feature in version 12.0 of its internetwork operating system (IOS) software. The feature is called Always On/Dynamic ISDN (AO/DI). Basically it allows low-bandwidth traffic to use the D channel and initiates a call using one or two B channels if the traffic warrants. This feature will be most useful for Point of Sale (POS) applications.

Primary Rate Interface (PRI)

Most Internet service providers use *Primary Rate Interface (PRI)* ISDN to connect to the public switched telephone network (PSTN). PRI allows providers to implement dial services to analog modem users as well as ISDN customers. If need be, ISDN calls can be routed to the analog modems after the access server receives the calling number's B channel, or *bearer capability*. PRIs have the following capacities:

- A T1-based PRI has 23 B channels and one 64Kbps D channel, which equals a band-width of 1.536Kbps. An 8Kbps channel for framing and synchronization is used as well to get a bandwidth for a U.S. T1/PRI of 1.544Mbps. The 24th channel is used for signaling.

- An E1-based PRI has 30 B channels and one 64Kbps D channel. An E1 uses channel 15 for signaling (D channel). An E1 has 2.048Mbps of bandwidth.

PRI Switch Options

As with BRI, you can use several switch types with PRI. Check with your provider to get the correct one. If you change any ISDN switch-type setting, you may have to reboot your router for the change to take effect. PRI switch options are shown in Table 15.3.

TABLE 15.3   PRI Switch Types

Switch Type	Typically Used
primary-5ess	AT&T 5ESS switch type for the U.S.
primary-4ess	AT&T 4ESS switch type for the U.S.
primary-dms100	Northern DMS-100 switch type
primary-net5	NET3 switch type for U.K. and Europe
vn3	VN3 and VN4 switch types for France

T1- and E1-based PRIs use different line coding and framing schemes. A T1-based PRI uses B8ZS encoding and ESF for framing. An E1-based PRI uses High-Density Bipolar with 3-zeros (HDB3) for encoding and cyclic redundancy check, level 4 (CRC-4) for framing.

ISDN Function Groups

It is important to understand the different function groups when you design and troubleshoot your ISDN network. By having a firm understanding of the functions, you can more easily troubleshoot an ISDN line. Figure 15.1 shows the different function groups and their placement in an ISDN network.

FIGURE 15.1 ISDN function groups

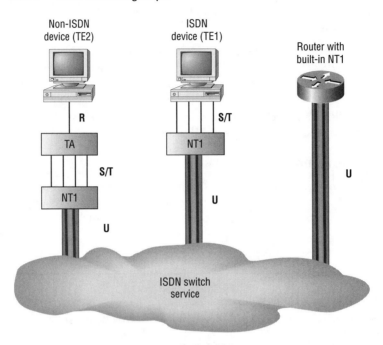

The following are definitions and examples of ISDN BRI functional groups as they relate to Figure 15.1.

Terminal equipment 1 (TE1)   A device that understands ISDN digital signaling techniques. Examples of TE1 devices are digital telephones, routers with ISDN interfaces, and digital facsimile equipment. TE1 devices are four-wire (two-pair) but need to be two-wire (one-pair) to communicate with an ISDN network. A TE1 can connect into a network termination type 1 (NT1) in order to connect the four-wire subscriber wiring to the two-wire local loop facility.

Terminal equipment 2 (TE2)   Equipment that does not understand ISDN signaling standards. Examples of TE2 devices are X.25 interfaces and serial interfaces on a router. TE2 needs to be converted to ISDN signaling, which is provided by a terminal adapter (TA). After that, it still needs to be converted to a two-wire network with an NT1 device.

Network termination type 1 (NT1)   Used to convert a four-wire ISDN connection to the two-wire ISDN used by the local loop facility.

Network termination type 2 (NT2)   Used to direct traffic from ISDN devices (TEs) to an NT1. This is probably the most intelligent device in the ISDN network: it provides switching and concentrating and can sometimes even be a PBX.

Terminal adapter (TA)   Allows a TE2 device to communicate with the telco's network by providing any necessary protocol and interface conversion. In essence, a TA adapts the unipolar signal coming from a non-ISDN device into a bipolar signal to be used by the ISDN network.

Local termination (LT)   The same device as an NT1, but located at the provider's site.

Exchange termination (ET)   The connection into the ISDN switch, which is typically an ISDN line card. Both the LT and the ET are typically just referred to as the local exchange (LE).

ISDN Reference Points

A reference point defines a connection point between two functions; it may also be referred to as an interface but not actually represent a physical interface. The reference point is where data is converted between device types. Figure 15.2 shows the different reference points defined in an ISDN network.

FIGURE 15.2   ISDN reference points

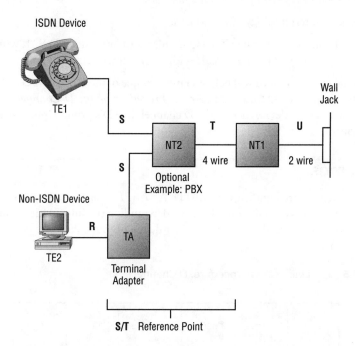

The reference points shown in Figure 15.2 are described in detail in the following list:

R   Defines the reference point between non-ISDN equipment and a TA. The R reference point allows a non-ISDN device to appear on the network as an ISDN device.

S   The point between the user terminals and NT2, or in other words, between a TE1 or a TA and the network termination (which is either an NT1 or an NT2).

T   Defines the reference point between NT1 and NT2 devices.

S/T As the name implies, combines both the S and the T interfaces. This interface is governed by the International Telecommunications Union (ITU) I.430 standard, which defines the connection as a four-wire connection. The S/T interface is typically an RJ 45, 8-pin cable using pins 3 and 6 to receive data and pins 4 and 5 to transmit data.

U Also known as a U interface. This is a two-wire connection between the NT1 and the telephone company (LE).

ISDN Protocols

ISDN protocols define how information is transferred between devices. Currently, the ITU-T has established three types of protocols to handle this information transfer:

E Specifies ISDN on the existing telephone network.

I Specifies concepts, terminology, and services.

Q Specifies switching and signaling. Two Q standards of interest are Q.921, which deals with layer 2 interfacing, and Q.931, which deals with layer 3 interfacing.

Understanding the Q standard will help you use a couple of the IOS debug commands we'll go over later in this chapter. Q.921 uses *Link Access Procedure on the D Channel (LAPD)* to communicate with other ISDN devices across the D channel. LAPD's primary purpose is to transport signaling information.

LAPD Frames

Layer 2 and 3 functions are handled with LAPD. An *LAPD frame* has six parts: Flag, Address, Control, Information, CRC, and a final Flag. Understanding the information contained in this frame will help you understand Q.921 and Q.931 debug outputs. Please refer to Figure 15.3 as you read about each part.

FIGURE 15.3 Link Access Procedure, D Channel

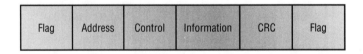

The following list includes more detailed information about the parts of the LAPD frame:

Flag This 1-octet field starts and ends the frame with a value of 7E (0111 1110).

Address   This 2-octet field identifies TE and has four parts: Service Access Point Identifier (SAPI), Command/Response, Address Extension 0, and Terminal Endpoint Identifier.

SAPI   This is a 6-bit field. Table 15.4 lists the available values.

TABLE 15.4   SAPI Values

SAPI	Description
0	Call control procedures
1	Packet mode using Q.931 call procedures
16	Packet mode communications procedures
32–47	Reserved for national use
63	Management procedures
Others	Reserved for future use

Command/Response (C/R)   This 1-bit field identifies the frame as either a command or a response. The user side always sends commands with this bit set to 0 (zero) and responds with it set to 1. The network side sends a command with this bit set to 1 and responds with this bit set to 0 (zero).

End Address 0 and 1 (EA0 and EA1)   This is 1-bit field. Setting this bit to 0 (zero) and EA1 to 1 identifies the frame as an LAPD frame.

Terminal Endpoint Identifier (TEI)   These values uniquely identify each TE on an ISDN S/T bus. A TEI can be either dynamically or statically assigned. Table 15.5 lists and describes the available values.

TABLE 15.5   Terminal Endpoint Identifier (TEI) Values

TEI	Description
0–63	Fixed TEI assignments
64–126	Dynamically assigned (assigned by the switch)
127	Broadcast to all devices

Control   This field has 11 available values. Each is shown in Table 15.6, along with its application. You will see one of three types of information here: Information Transfer, Supervisory, or Unnumbered.

TABLE 15.6   Control Field Values

Format	Message Type	Control/Response
Information Transfer	I (information)	Control
Supervisory	RR (receiver ready)	Control/response
Supervisory	RNR (receiver not ready)	Control/response
Supervisory	REJ (reject)	Control/response
Unnumbered	SAMBE (Set Asynchronous Mode Balanced Extended)	Control
Unnumbered	DM (disconnected mode)	Response
Unnumbered	UI (unnumbered information)	Control
Unnumbered	DISC (disconnect)	Control
Unnumbered	UA (unnumbered acknowledgment)	Response
Unnumbered	FRMR (frame reject)	Response
Unnumbered	XID (exchange identifier)	Control/response

Information   This field carries the Q.931 protocol data and user data.

Protocol Discriminator   This is a 1-octet value that identifies the layer 3 protocol.

Length of CRV   This is a 1-octet value that indicates the length of the call reference value.

Call reference value (CRV)   This value is 1 or 2 octets and is assigned to each call at the beginning and used to distinguish between other simultaneous calls. This value is released after the call is torn down.

Message type   This is 1 octet.

Mandatory and optional information elements   These variable-length options are based on the message type.

Channelized T1/E1 (PRI)

Large businesses have typically used point-to-point connections with channel service units/data service units (CSUs/DSUs) to connect two sites together. In turn, the CSUs/DSUs are connected to low- and high-speed serial interfaces on routers—usually Cisco routers.

However, the T1 and E1 circuits do not only have a use as point-to-point WAN circuits, they are also utilized to provide voice/dial services through the use of the PRI signaling. T1s providing voice/dial services are called a Primary Rate Interface (PRI), and also run at 1.544Mbps and use 24 channels in contrast to E1PRIs, which use 30 channels and run at 2.048Mbps. E1 is mainly used in Europe, and both T1 and E1 are considered wide area digital transmission schemes.

Configuring T1 ISDN PRI

The serial links connect into either a private data network or a service provider's network. Both the line encoding and the framing must match the service provider's equipment. To configure a PRI on a serial link, you must supply the following information:

Channel type   Either T1 or E1.

Frame type   When using a T1, this can be either *Super Frame* or *Extended Superframe Format (ESF)*. Super Frame can also be referred to as D4 framing, which consists of 12 frames, each with 193 bits. The last bit is used for error checking. Extended Superframe Format is an enhanced version of Super Frame that uses 24 frames, each with 192 bits. ESF is typically used in the U.S.

Linecode   This will be either *alternate mark inversion (AMI)* or binary 8-zero substitution (B8ZS). B8ZS is typically used in the U.S.; however, most legacy phone systems still use AMI.

Which time slots the T1 uses   By using the `pri-group` command on your subchannel, you can define the subchannels associated with each time slot.

In the following example, we chose to configure Controller 0 to support a PRI, and we opted for ESF framing with B8ZS line coding. Likewise, since this is the only PRI circuit configured, it will get its timing from the line and act as the primary timing source for the router. The `pri-group timeslots 1-24` indicates that we are utilizing all 24 channels of the circuit. Here's a look at the output:

```
controller T1 0
 framing esf
 clock source line primary
 linecode b8zs
 pri-group timeslots 1-24
```

The D channel will be automatically generated and will appear as a Serial interface identical to the controller number (which in this example is 0). It will also be identified with a :23 depicting that this serial interface is the D channel for the PRI (channel 24, 0 through 23). When you configure ISDN PRI, you only ever configure Layer 2 and Layer 3 parameters on the D channel, as shown in the following example:

```
interface serial 0:23
 encapsulation ppp
 ip address 172.16.30.5 255.255.255.252
 isdn switch-type primary-5ess
```

Configuring E1 ISDN PRI

The E1 configuration is similar to the T1 configuration, with a few differences:

- The E1 framing types available are crc4, no-crc4, and australia. The default is crc4, and it specifies CRC error checking; no-crc4 specifies that CRC checking is (surprise) disabled. The australia framing method is used when configuring an E1 in (another surprise) Australia.

The linecode is either AMI or HDB3 when configuring an E1, with AMI as the default.

In the following example, we chose to configure Controller 0 to support a PRI, and we opted for crc4 framing, with hdb3 line coding. Likewise, since this is the only PRI circuit configured, it will get its timing from the line and act as the primary timing source for the router. The pri-group timeslots 1-31 indicates that we are utilizing all 31 channels of the circuit. But remember from Chapter 3 that with an E1, one 64Kbps DS0 channel is used for framing, so we are actually left with 30 DS0s. Here's a look at the output:

```
controller E1 0
 framing crc4
 clock source line primary
 linecode hdb3
 pri-group timeslots 1-31
```

The D channel will be automatically generated and will appear as a Serial interface identical to the controller number (which in this example is 0). It will also be identified with a :15 depicting that this serial interface is the D channel for the PRI. When you configure ISDN PRI, you only ever configure Layer 2 and Layer 3 parameters on the D channel, as shown in the following example:

```
interface serial 0:15
 encapsulation ppp
 ip address 172.16.30.5 255.255.255.252
 isdn switch-type primary-net5
```

Configuring Dial Backup with IP

Now let's discuss *dial-on-demand routing (DDR)*, which is often implemented for dial backup functionality. DDR is used to provide network connections across the public switched telephone network (PSTN). Usually, WAN links are implemented on leased lines or other options (such as Frame Relay or ATM) from the service providers. However, you can also provide temporary connectivity from site to site through the use of DDR or dial-up connections.

Dial backup is the most popular form of fault tolerance. Dial backup protects against WAN downtime by permitting a network administrator to simply configure a backup serial line through a circuit-switched connection. Dial backup is extraordinarily cost effective because the secondary line is almost never used. The principle is simple: when the primary connection fails, a secondary line is brought up and stays active until the primary line is functional again. The three most frequently implemented methods of accomplishing this are backup interfaces, floating static routes, and OSPF on-demand circuits.

DDR can be used over synchronous serial interfaces, Integrated Services Digital Network (ISDN) interfaces, or asynchronous serial interfaces (such as your standard telephone line). Asynchronous serial interfaces are supported in certain serial interfaces for routers; they are also available as the auxiliary port on Cisco routers. DDR is also supported over ISDN using either Basic Rate Interface (BRI) or Primary Rate Interface (PRI). Specific uses and requirements are different for each type of interface.

Synchronous serial interfaces   Dialing on synchronous serial lines can be initiated using V.25bis dialing or data terminal ready (DTR) dialing. V.25bis is the ITU standard for in-band dialing. With in-band dialing, dialing information is sent over the same connection that carries the data. With DTR dialing, the DTR signal on the physical interface is activated, which causes some devices to dial a number configured into that device. DTR dialing allows lower-cost devices to be used in cases in which only a single number needs to be dialed. Synchronous serial lines support PPP, HDLC, and X.25 encapsulation. To convert a synchronous serial interface into a dialer interface, use the `dialer in-band` command.

ISDN interfaces   All ISDN devices subscribe to services provided by an ISDN service provider, usually a telephone company. ISDN DDR connections are made on B channels at 56 or 64Kbps, depending on the bearer capabilities of the end-to-end ISDN switching fabric. Multilink PPP is often used to allow BRI devices to aggregate both B channels for great bandwidth and throughput. ISDN BRI and PRI interfaces are automatically configured as dialer in-band interfaces. ISDN can support PPP, HDLC, X.25, and V.120 encapsulation. Usually, PPP encapsulation is used for DDR solutions.

Asynchronous serial interfaces   Asynchronous connections are used by communication servers or through the auxiliary port on a router. Asynchronous DDR connections can be used to support multiple Network layer protocols. When considering asynchronous DDR solutions, designers should consider if the internetworking applications can tolerate the longer call setup time and lower throughput of analog modems (in comparison with ISDN). For some design applications, DDR over asynchronous modem connections may provide a very cost-effective option.

Encapsulation Methods

When a connection is established between two DDR peers, the data must be encapsulated and framed for transport across the Dialer media. The encapsulation methods available depend on the physical interface being used. Cisco supports Point-to-Point Protocol (PPP), High-Level Data Link Control (HDLC), Serial Line Internet Protocol (SLIP), and X.25 data-link encapsulations for DDR:

PPP Recommended encapsulation method because it supports multiple protocols and is used for synchronous, asynchronous, or ISDN connections. In addition, PPP performs address negotiation and authentication and is interoperable with different vendors.

HDLC Supported on synchronous serial lines and ISDN connections only. HDLC supports multiple protocols. However, HDLC does not provide authentication.

SLIP Works on asynchronous interfaces only and is supported by IP only. Addresses must be configured manually. SLIP does not provide authentication and is interoperable only with other vendors that use SLIP.

X.25 Supported on synchronous serial lines and a single ISDN B channel.

Dialer Maps

It is possible to translate next hop protocol addresses to telephone numbers through the use of the `dialer map` command. If you are configuring dial-up on a physical interface, then a `dialer map` command is required; without it, DDR call initiation cannot occur. This is because when the routing table points at a dialer interface and the next hop address is not found in a dialer map, the packet is dropped. As we move forward through this chapter, remember that broadcasts and multicasts propagate by default with dialer profiles using `dialer string` commands instead of the `dialer map` command. But for Legacy DDR, which use the `dialer map` commands, the word `broadcast` *must* be appended to the end of the `dialer map` command. We will discuss the specific functions of each of these dialer types later on in this chapter.

In this command syntax example, we are configuring a dialer map for router R1 in Figure 15.4:

```
interface BRI0/0
  ip address 172.16.1.1 255.255.255.252
  dialer map ip 172.16.1.2 name R2 5551212
```

```
                                Packets are routed to a next-hop
                                address of 172.16.1.2, which is
                                statically mapped to telephone
                                number 555-1212, which is the
                                remote device named R2
```

FIGURE 15.4   Dial backup reference diagram

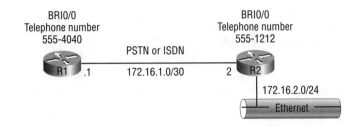

If you want broadcast packets transmitted to remote sites defined by dialer map commands, use the broadcast keyword at the end of the dialer map command. This is very important if you are configuring an IGP across a DDR circuit. Also, when setting up DDR between more than two sites, it is necessary to use PPP authentication and to use the name keyword with the dialer map command because dialer maps for inbound calls are maps between protocol addresses and authenticated usernames.

Static Routing

You can enter your required network routing manually through the use of static routes. This will eliminate the need for a routing protocol to broadcast routing updates across the DDR connection. Static routes can be effective in small networks that do not change often. The problem with dynamic routing protocols is that the periodic updates and neighbor adjacency hellos are traffic that will cause the dial connections to be made unnecessarily.

Here are command syntax examples for router R1 in Figure 15.4. And remember that the static route could be configured either of the two ways shown:

```
ip route 172.16.2.0 255.255.255.0 172.16.1.2
```

> For packets to get to the 172.16.2.0 24-bit mask destination network, the next hop IP address on the remote router is 172.16.1.2

        OR

```
ip route 172.16.2.0 255.255.255.0 Bri0/0
```

> For packets to get to the 172.16.2.0 24-bit mask destination network, route them out the local Bri0/0 interface

It is usually necessary to configure redistribution of static routes into the backbone dynamic routing protocol to ensure end-to-end connectivity. This redistribution can be accomplished with the redistribute static command configured in the required routing protocol process in the router configuration.

Floating Static Routes

Floating static routes are probably the most popular way to implement dial backup. They give you the ability to handle breaks in connectivity regardless of interface state changes, because floating routes rely on existence or lack of reachability information between the routers.

Floating static routes are static routes that have an administrative distance greater than the administrative distance of any configured dynamic routing protocols. Administrative distances can be configured on a static route so that the static route is less desirable than a dynamically learned route. In this manner, the static route is not used when the dynamically learned route is available. However, if the dynamic route is lost, the static route can take over and traffic can be sent through this alternate route. If this alternate route is provided using a DDR interface, then that interface can be used as a backup mechanism.

Here are command syntax examples for router R1 in Figure 15.4:

```
ip route 172.16.2.0 255.255.255.0 172.16.1.2 240
```

This static route will be used in routing decisions as long as there is no other learned route for the 172.16.2.0 network, with an administrative distance lower than 240. All dynamic routing protocols have an administrative distance less than 240, so as long as a dynamic routing protocol is operating, this floating static route will NOT be used

Dynamic Routing

Dynamic routing can be used in a DDR network design, although you will most often find static routes used. However, if dynamic routing is required, the routing protocol selected for DDR is typically a distance vector protocol such as RIP, EIGRP, or IGRP. OSPF can be implemented across a DDR link efficiently through the use of the `ip ospf demand-circuit` command (this command will be discussed later on in this chapter). Selecting the simplest protocol that meets the needs of the internetwork design and that is supported by the DDR routers is recommended. Also, dynamic routing can be used with snapshot routing, which we will discuss later on in this chapter, to cache routes learned by dynamic routing protocols, thus allowing the automation of static routing maintenance. In order to prevent a dynamic routing protocol from advertising routes across the DDR link, you can cause the dialer interface to not advertise any dynamic routing updates. This is accomplished with the `passive-interface` command. Remember, if you are using legacy DDR (dialer map commands), then be sure to add the keyword `broadcast`.

Backup Interfaces

You can configure your dialer interface to act as a redundant standby connection to be activated in the event that your primary network connection is lost. This can be accomplished by configuring a `backup interface` command on the primary network connection interface in which you want the backup to be performed. If you implement this approach in a Frame Relay environment, you should use a point-to-point subinterface because the main or multipoint interface can remain in an up/up state even if permanent virtual connections (PVCs) go down. The `backup interface` command places the specified dialer interface into the standby mode until such time as the primary interface goes down.

You can also configure the dialer interface to be activated if the primary network connection exceeds a configured bandwidth utilization threshold. This is commonly referred to as *Bandwidth on Demand (BoD)*. The traffic load (bandwidth) is monitored and a 5-minute moving average is computed. If the average exceeds the configured threshold value for the primary network connection, the backup (dialer) line is activated. This is configured with the `backup load` command, which specifies the traffic threshold at which the backup (dialer) interface is to be activated and deactivated.

Here are command syntax examples for the `backup interface` command:

```
interface Serial 0/0

  ip address 172.16.1.1 255.255.255.252
```

`backup interface bri 0/0`	BRI 0/0 is activated only when serial0/0 interface (the primary line) goes down. You should configure this command on one end of a dial backup link – NOT both ends of the link
`backup delay 10 20`	Configures the backup connection to activate 10 seconds after serial0/0 interface goes down and to remain activated for 20 seconds after the serial0/0 interface comes up
`backup load 75 5`	BRI 0/0 is activated when the load on serial0/0 (the primary line) exceeds 75 percent of its bandwidth. The backup line is deactivated when the aggregate load between the primary and backup lines is within 5 percent of the primary line's bandwidth

Dialer Filtering

The term *dialer filtering* is used to represent the process of classifying all packets traversing the DDR interface as either *interesting* or *uninteresting*. This is accomplished by using access control lists (ACLs) to specify with the `permit` keyword which types of protocols are allowed to activate the DDR connection. These permitted packets are known as interesting. Only interesting packets can bring up and keep up DDR connections. All of the packets that were denied by the ACL are known as uninteresting. The uninteresting packets must not be allowed to cause unnecessary DDR connections. If a packet is uninteresting and there is no connection established, the packet is dropped. If the packet is uninteresting but a connection is already established to the specified destination, the packet is sent across the connection but the idle timer is not reset. If the packet is interesting and there is no connection on the available interface, the router attempts to establish a connection. Each packet arriving at a dialer interface is filtered and determined to be interesting or uninteresting based on the `dialer-group` and `dialer-list` commands.

Here are command syntax examples of the `dialer-group` and `dialer-list` commands:

```
interface BRI0/0
```

`dialer-group 5`	Configure the dialer-group command on the dialer interface. Specifies that the global command dialer-list number 5 will be used to specify the interesting traffic
`dialer-list 5 protocol ip permit`	Specifies that all ip traffic is interesting

Defining Interesting Packets with Access Lists

You can be even more specific in identifying interesting traffic by configuring your `dialer-list` command to invoke an access list. The access list will actually specify the protocols, which are interesting. The `dialer-list` command and the `access-list` commands are all configured in the global mode. Chapter 16 will cover access lists and how to properly implement them. Here is a quick example of using an access list command in conjunction with the `dialer-list` command:

`dialer-list 5 protocol ip list 101`	Specifies that all packets that are permitted by the ip extended access-list 101 are classified as interesting
`access-list 101 deny udp any any eq snmp`	
	Deny all packets which are the UDP protocol port number 161, which is snmp
`access-list 101 deny eigrp any any`	Deny all packets which are the EIGRP routing protocol

```
access-list 101 permit ip any any
```

Permit all IP protocol packets which did not meet any of the above access-list 101 criteria

Optional Timer Commands

Here are some optional timer commands, which can be used to fine tune the dial session parameters:

`dialer idle-timeout [seconds]`	Specifies the idle timer value to use for the call. This timer disconnects the call if no interesting traffic has been transmitted for the specified time. The default is 120 seconds
`dialer fast-idle [seconds]`	Specifies a quick disconnect time if there is another call waiting for the same interface and the interface is idle. The waiting call will not have to wait for the idle timer to expire. The default is 20 seconds

Configuring Dialer Watch

With the dialer watch process, a router monitors the existence of a specified route, and if that route is not present in the routing table, the router activates backup (dial) connection. Unlike the other backup methods (such as backup interface or floating static routes), dialer watch does *not* require interesting traffic to trigger the dialing. It requires RIP, IGRP, or EIGRP (will work with the OSPF demand circuit) and can only be implemented with the IP protocol. Following is a description of the dialer watch process:

NOTE Unlike a backup interface, you can use dialer interfaces for other purposes when they are not being used by dialer watch.

1. The dialer watch process is configured to watch for a specified route in the routing table, the specified route is removed from the routing table, then the primary WAN interface is considered to be down and unusable.
2. When the *watched* route is removed from the routing table, and the primary WAN interface is considered down, the dial interface will initiate a call to connect to the remote end, which will allow for the exchange of routing information and network traffic.
3. Once the dial link is operational, the dialer watch process will continue to check the routing table for the *watched* route at the end of each idle-timeout period. If the *watched* route is not present in the routing table, then the primary WAN interface continues to be considered down, and the idle-timeout is reset. If the *watched* route does appear in the routing table,

then the primary WAN interface will be considered up and be used for primary routing. And since no traffic will be flowing across the dial link anymore, the idle-timeout will expire and the router will deactivate the dial link.

Dialer Watch Commands

Here is a command syntax example of the `dialer group-watch` command:

`dialer watch-group [group-number]`   Configure this command on the backup (dialer) interface. The group number used here matches the group number of the dialer watch-list command, which is defining the routes to be watched

Here is a command syntax example of applying dialer watch to a interface:

`interface bri 0/0`

  `dialer watch-group 1`   Configures this interface to use the dialer watch-list number 1 to specify the routes to be watched

`dialer watch-list [group-number] ip [ip-address] [address-mask]`

Defines the IP addresses or networks to be watched. The address or network (with the correct mask) that is configured must exist in the routing table. You can also watch multiple routes with the dialer watch-list command

Here are some examples of the `dialer watch-list` command syntax:

`dialer watch-list 1 ip 10.1.1.0 255.255.255.0`

Configures dialer watch-list number 1, which is watching for the existence of the 10.1.1.0 IP network with a 255.255.255.0 mask in the routing table

`dialer watch-list 1 ip 10.1.2.0 255.255.255.0`

Configures dialer watch-list number 1, which is watching for the existence of the 10.1.2.0 IP network with a 255.255.255.0 mask in the routing table

`dialer watch-disable [seconds]`   Configures a disable delay time for the backup (dialer) interface. After the primary interface recovers, this delay prevents disconnecting the backup interface for the specified time period. This delay timer is started when the idle timer expires, and the status of the primary route is checked and found to be up. This delay can ensure stability, especially for flapping interfaces or interfaces experiencing frequent route changes

`Dialer watch-list 1 delay route-check initial 90`

Configures the router to activate the backup connection 90 seconds after the router boots up, even though the watched route has never existed in the routing table

Snapshot Routing

With snapshot routing, the router is configured with a distance-vector, dynamic routing protocol, such as RIP, IGRP, or IPX RIP. Snapshot routing controls the update interval of the routing protocols. Normally, these routing protocols broadcast routing updates every 30 to 90 seconds, so an ISDN/PSTN connection would be made every 30 to 90 seconds simply to exchange routing information. This is not efficient, as the cost is too great. Snapshot routing solves this problem.

Snapshot routing utilizes a client/server design. When snapshot routing is configured, one router is designated as the snapshot server and the other routers are designated as snapshot clients. The server and clients exchange routing information during an active period, which is a configurable time value. At the beginning of the active period, the client router dials the server router to exchange routing information. At the end of the active period, each router takes a snapshot of the entries in its routing table. These entries remain frozen during a quiet period, which is also a configurable time value. At the end of the quiet period, another active period begins, which means that the client router will dial the server router again to receive the latest routing information; this will update the routing table in the client. The client router determines the frequency at which it calls the server router. The quiet period can be as long as 100,000 minutes (approximately 69 days).

Configuring snapshot routing is an easy task because all the required commands are configured on the interface. For this example, refer to Figure 15.4: The server router (router R1) needs to be configured for snapshot routing by having the `snapshot server` command applied to its BRI0/0 interface. The `snapshot server` command specifies the length of the active period and whether the router is allowed to dial remote sites to exchange routing updates in the absence of regular traffic. The client router (router R2) needs to be configured with the `snapshot client` command on its BRI0/0 interface. The `snapshot client` command specifies the following variables:

- The length of the active period (which must match the length specified on the server router)

- The length of the quiet period

- Whether the router can dial the central router to exchange routing updates in the absence of regular traffic

- Whether connections that are established to exchange user data can be used to exchange routing updates

If the routing protocol is not supported by snapshot routing (for example, OSPF or EIGRP), standard routing redistribution techniques can be used to ensure that routing updates are propagated between routing protocols. So, redistribute your OSPF routes into RIP to travel across the ISDN connection; then at the remote end, redistribute the RIP routes back into OSPF. Remember to include subnets in your redistribution, and look out for routing loops.

Here is a command syntax example for router R1:

```
interface BRI0/0

 ip address 172.16.1.1 255.255.255.252

 snapshot server 5 dialer          Configures this interface as the server,
                                   designating a 5 minute active period. The
                                   dialer keyword allows a DDR call to be
                                   made to initiate a snapshot session
```

Here is an example of the syntax for configuring router R2:

```
interface BRI0/0

 ip address 172.16.1.2 255.255.255.252

 dialer map snapshot 1 name R1 5554040

                                   Configures this interface to dial the specified
                                   number 5554040 to reach the remote end router
                                   named R1. And designates that this is the first
                                   1 dialer map snapshot on this interface
```

```
snapshot client 5 600 supress-statechange-updates dialer
```

Configures this interface as a client,
designating a 5 minute active period and a 600
minute quiet period. The OPTIONAL keyword
supress-statechange-updates specifies to NOT
update the routing table when interesting
traffic has activated the snapshot interface.
And the OPTIONAL keyword dialer allows this
client to initiate a call to the server

Multilink PPP

Multilink PPP is a method for spreading traffic across multiple physical WAN links while providing packet fragmentation and reassembly, proper sequencing, multivendor interoperability, and load balancing on inbound and outbound traffic. Multilink PPP allows packets to be fragmented. These fragments are sent simultaneously over multiple point-to-point links to the same remote address. The multiple physical links come up in response to a user-defined load threshold. The used-defined load threshold is configured using the `dialer load-threshold` command. This command dictates the percentage of bandwidth utilization on the first PPP connection should the second PPP connection be activated. Or, for example, with an ISDN BRI connection with two B channels, only the first B channel is activated when the ISDN connection is initiated, and you can specify that exceeding the bandwidth utilization level of the first B channel will cause the second B channel to be activated. This load threshold is specified using the range of 1 through 255. So, if you desire a 10-percent load threshold, you would specify a load threshold of 26. If you want the second B channel to be activated immediately, specify a `dialer load-threshold 0` command. Here is a guide to follow:

10% load	26
20% load	51
50% load	128
75% load	192
100% load	255

This load can be measured on just inbound traffic or on just outbound traffic; however, it cannot be measured on the combined load of both inbound and outbound traffic. Multilink PPP is configured on the physical interface with the `ppp multilink` command, and you must also configure the `dialer load-threshold` command to designate the load threshold to activate the second B channel.

Here is the syntax for configuring Multilink PPP:

```
dialer load-threshold 128 either
```
Configures this interface, that MUST have the ppp multilink command applied, to activate the second B-channel if either the inbound or outbound traffic load on the first B-channel exceeds 50% utilization (128)

```
ppp multilink
```
Allows the two B-channels to be bundled

OSPF Demand Circuit

If an *Open Shortest Path First (OSPF)* link is configured as a demand circuit, the OSPF hellos are suppressed and the periodic link-state advertisement (LSA) refreshes are not flooded across the link. The hellos and LSAs will bring up the link only when they are exchanged for the first time or any time a change occurs in the information they contain, such as a change in the network topology. An OSPF demand circuit will allow the Data-Link layer to remain stable as long as there are no network changes. An OSPF demand circuit that goes up and down indicates a problem that needs to be investigated. An OSPF demand circuit is configured on an interface with the `ip ospf demand-circuit` command. Only one side of the link (it doesn't matter which end is configured) needs to have the `ip ospf demand-circuit` command configured because, if the other side is capable of understanding the demand circuit, it automatically negotiates this capability in the hello packet. If it is not capable of understanding the demand circuit, it ignores this option. A demand circuit will suppress the periodic hellos on a point-to-point and point-to-multipoint network type. On any other network type, OSPF hellos are still sent over the interface.

Periodic LSA refreshes that normally take place every 30 minutes do not occur with an OSPF demand circuit. When a demand circuit link is established, a unique option bit (the DC bit) is exchanged between neighboring routers. If two routers negotiate the DC bit successfully, they mark a specific bit in the LSA Age field called the DoNotAge (DNA) bit. The DNA bit is the most significant bit in the LSA Age field. When this bit is set, the LSA stops aging and no periodic updates are sent.

Here is an example of the command syntax for configuring an OSPF demand-circuit link:

```
ip ospf demand-circuit
```
Configures this interface as an OSPF demand circuit. No Hellos or periodic LSAs will be transmitted across this link, which would be continually activating the link

Remember that if you are implementing OSPF across a DDR connection and the OSPF area that the DDR interfaces belong in are being authenticated, the authentication *must* be applied to the DDR interfaces on both ends of the DDR connection.

PPP Authentication

PPP Authentication via *Challenge Handshake Authentication Protocol (CHAP)* or *Password Authentication Protocol (PAP)* is described in RFC 1334 and should be used to provide security on DDR connections. PPP Authentication occurs after link control protocol (LCP) is negotiated on the DDR connection but before any network protocols are allowed to flow. PPP Authentication is negotiated as an LCP option and is bidirectional, meaning each side can authenticate the other. Sometimes it may be necessary to enable PPP Authentication on the call-in side only. You can configure your PPP Authentication so that the calling side does not authenticate the called side. This is accomplished with the `callin` keyword, which we will discuss later on in this chapter.

CHAP and PAP

With CHAP, a remote device attempting to connect to the local router is presented with a CHAP challenge containing the hostname and a challenge seed. When the remote router receives the challenge, it looks up the hostname received in the challenge and replies with the hostname and a CHAP response derived from the challenge seed and the password for that hostname. The passwords must be identical on the remote device and the local router. The names and passwords are configured using the `username` command. PAP is another authentication protocol used with PPP. However, PAP is less secure than CHAP. CHAP does not exchange the password whatsoever in an unencrypted or encrypted format—rather the password is used to encrypt the challenge seed + other information, which generates a hash. The receiving end uses the generated hash to authenticate, but PAP passes the password in clear text, which makes it less secure than CHAP. CHAP is identified as Authentication Protocol c223, which is carried in the Information field of a PPP packet. When being authenticated with PAP, the router looks up the username that matches the dialer map used to initiate the call. In the following example we are using CHAP, and router R1 will allow router R2 to call in using the password cisco (by default, the hostname of the router is used as the username, and the enable password of the router is used as the CHAP authentication password):

Here are the commands on Router R1 for CHAP authentication:

`hostname R1`	Configures this router as hostname R1, which means that router R2 must have a username statement for the hostname R1
`username R2 password cisco`	Configures a username statement to verify authentication of the hostname R2 with the password cisco
`interface BRI0/0`	
`  encapsulation ppp`	Configures this interface for layer 2 encapsulation of PPP
`  ppp authentication chap`	Configures this interface to use CHAP authentication with the router at the remote end of the DDR connection

Here are the commands on router R2 for CHAP authentication:

`hostname R2`	Configures this router as hostname R2, which means that router R1 must have a username statement for the hostname R2
`username R1 password cisco`	Configures a username statement to verify authentication of the hostname R1 with the password cisco
`interface BRI0/0`	
`encapsulation ppp`	Configures this interface for layer 2 encapsulation of PPP dialer map ip 172.16.1.1 name R1 5554040
`ppp authentication chap`	Configures this interface to use CHAP authentication with the router at the remote end of the DDR connection

PPP Authentication Using *Callin*

You can configure your PPP authentication so that the calling side does not authenticate the called side. This is accomplished with the `callin` keyword appended to the end of the `ppp authentication chap` command. Using the scenario in Figure 15.4 as an example, router R1 will be the router initiating the call. Router R1 is configured with the `ppp authentication chap callin` command, but router R2 will be configured with the `ppp authentication chap` command. When the keyword `callin` is appended to the end of the authentication command on router R1, router R2 can authenticate router R1, but router R1 will *not* authenticate router R2. This is also known as one-way authentication. The authentication command with the keyword `callin` appended to it *must* be configured on the physical interface of the router initiating the call.

Configuring Legacy DDR

Legacy DDR is the original method of configuring dial-up services within a router. This method utilizes the physical interface, which means that in a dial backup scenario, the physical dialer interface *cannot* be used for any other purpose because it will be in a spoofing state (dedicated to the dial backup role). As you will see later on in this chapter, the concept of dialer profiles is far more efficient because you do *not* have to dedicate your physical dialer interface. Legacy DDR is much easier to configure than dialer profiles are.

Here is a command syntax example for Legacy DDR:

`hostname R1`	Configures this router as hostname R1, which means that router R2 must have a username statement for the hostname R1
`enable password cisco`	Configures this router with the enable password of cisco
`username R2 password cisco`	Configures this router to authenticate router R2 with password cisco
`interface BRI0/0`	
`  ip address 172.16.1.1 255.255.255.252`	
	Configures the local IP address on this interface
`  encapsulation ppp`	Configures this interface for layer 2 encapsulation of PPP
`dialer map ip 172.16.1.2 name R2 broadcast 5551212`	
	Packets are routed to a next-hop address of 172.16.1.2, which is statically mapped to telephone number 555-1212, which is the remote end device named R2. Also, specify the keyword broadcast to allow broadcast and multicast packets to flow across the DDR connection
`  dialer-group 1`	Specifies that the global command dialer-list number 1 will be used to specify the interesting traffic
`  isdn switch-type basic-ni`	Specifies the Central office or ISDN service provider switch type which is providing the ISDN service to this interface

`isdn spid1 30355540401111`	Used in North American BRI implementations. SPID's allow multiple ISDN devices, such as voice and data, to share the local loop. SPID's identify the services that are ordered from the carrier. If you are connecting to a DMS-100 or NI-1 switch-type, you will most likely need to configure spids. Most 5ess switches don't require spids
`isdn spid2 30355540411111`	See above, you require a SPID for each B-channel
`ppp authentication chap`	Configures this interface to use CHAP authentication with the router at the remote end of the DDR connection
`ppp multilink`	Allows the two B-channels to be bundled
`dialer-list 1 protocol ip permit`	Specifies that all ip traffic is interesting

Configuring Legacy DDR with Callback

DDR environments can be configured for callback operations. When PPP callback is configured on the participating routers, the calling router (the callback client) passes authentication information to the remote router (the callback server), which uses the hostname and dial string authentication information to determine whether to place a return call. If the authentication is successful, the callback server disconnects and then places a return call. The remote username of the return call is used to associate it with the initial call so that packets can be transmitted. This functionality provides enhanced security by ensuring that the remote site can connect only from a single location as defined by the callback number and can also enhance administration by centralizing billing for remote DDR connections. Using the scenario in Figure 15.4 for this example, router R1 is the callback client and router R2 is the callback server. Here is the command syntax for router R1:

hostname R1	Configures this router as hostname R1, which means that router R2 must have a username statement for the hostname R1
enable password cisco	Configures this router with the enable password of cisco
username R2 password cisco	Configures this router to authenticate router R2 with password cisco
interface BRI0/0	
ip address 172.16.1.1 255.255.255.252	Configures the local IP address on this interface
dialer map ip 172.16.1.2 name R2 broadcast 5551212	Packets are routed to a next-hop address of 172.16.1.2, which is statically mapped to telephone number 555-1212, which is the remote end device named R2. Also, specify the keyword broadcast to allow broadcast and multicast packets to flow across the DDR connection
dialer-group 1	Specifies that the global command dialer-list number 1 will be used to specify the interesting traffic
ppp callback request	Configures the interface to request ppp callback from the server
ppp authentication chap	Configures this interface to use CHAP authentication with the router at the remote end of the DDR connection
encapsulation ppp	Configures this interface for layer 2 encapsulation of PPP

ppp multilink	Allows the two B-channels to be bundled
isdn switch-type basic-ni	Specifies the Central office or ISDN service provider switch type which is providing the ISDN service to this interface
isdn spid1 30355540401111	Used in North American BRI implementations. SPID's allow multiple ISDN devices, such as voice and data, to share the local loop. SPID's identify the services that are ordered from the carrier. If you are connecting to a DMS-100 or NI-1 switch-type, you will most likely need to configure spids. Most 5ess switches don't require spids
isdn spid2 30355540411111	See above, you require a SPID for each B-channel
dialer-list 1 protocol ip permit	Specifies that all ip traffic is interesting

Here's the command syntax for router R2, the called router:

hostname R2	Configures this router as hostname R2, which means that router R1 must have a username statement for the hostname R2
enable password cisco	Configures this router with the enable password of cisco
username R1 password cisco	Configures this router to authenticate router R1 with password cisco
interface BRI0/0	
ip address 172.16.1.2 255.255.255.252	
	Configures the local IP address on this interface
dialer map ip 172.16.1.1 name R1 class dial1 broadcast 5554040	

	Packets are routed to a next-hop address of 172.16.1.1, which is statically mapped to telephone number 555-4040, which is the remote end device named R1, using the dial1 map-class established for PPP callback on this interface. Also, specify the keyword broadcast to allow broadcast and multicast packets to flow across the DDR connection
dialer-group 1	Specifies that the global command dialer-list number 1 will be used to specify the interesting traffic
ppp callback accept	Allows this interface to accept a callback request from a remote client
ppp authentication chap	Configures this interface to use CHAP authentication with the router at the remote end of the DDR connection
encapsulation ppp	Configures this interface for layer 2 encapsulation of PPP
ppp multilink	Allows the two B-channels to be bundled
isdn switch-type basic-ni	Specifies the Central office or ISDN service provider switch type which is providing the ISDN service to this interface
isdn spid1 30355512121111	Used in North American BRI implementations. SPID's allow multiple ISDN devices, such as voice and data, to share the local loop. SPID's identify the services that are ordered from the carrier. If you are connecting to a DMS-100 or NI-1 switch-type, you will most likely need to configure spids. Most 5ess switches don't require spids
isdn spid2 30355512131111	See above, you require a SPID for each B-channel

`dialer-list 1 protocol ip permit`	Specifies that all ip traffic is interesting
`map-class dialer dial1`	Map class dial1 is used in the dialer map command for the callback
`dialer callback-server username`	Identify the return call dial string using the authenticated username

Configuring Dialer Profiles

Dialer profiles separate logical configurations from the physical interfaces that receive or make calls. Because of this separation, interfaces such as ISDN, asynchronous modems, or synchronous serial connections can be shared by multiple dialer profile configurations at the same time. Dialer profiles allow logical and physical configurations to be bound together dynamically on a per-call basis, allowing physical interfaces to take on different characteristics based on incoming or outgoing call requirements. Dialer profiles can define encapsulation, access control lists, and minimum or maximum calls and can toggle features on or off. A dialer interface essentially defines a single connection to a remote destination.

Components

Let's discuss the components that are utilized in a dialer profile configuration:

Dialer interfaces   Logical entities that use a per-destination dialer profile. Any number of dialer interfaces can be created in a router. All configuration settings specific to the destination go in the dialer interface configuration. Each dialer interface uses a dialer pool.

Dialer pool   A group of physical interfaces (ISDN BRI and PRI, asynchronous modem, and synchronous serial) associated with a dialer profile. A physical interface can belong to multiple dialer pools. Contention for a specific physical interface is resolved by configuring the optional priority command.

Physical interfaces   Interfaces in a dialer pool that are configured for encapsulation parameters. The interfaces are also configured to identify the dialer pools to which they belong. Dialer profiles support PPP and High-Level Data Link Control (HDLC) encapsulation.

Dialer map-class (optional)   Define a group of shared configuration parameters, which can be supplied to dialer interfaces (for example, ISDN speed, dialer timers parameters, and so on). A map-class can be referenced from multiple dialer interfaces.

Here is an example of the command syntax for configuring a dialer profile:

hostname R1	Configures this router as hostname R1, which means that router R2 must have a username statement for the hostname R1
enable password cisco	Configures this router with the enable password of cisco
username R2 password cisco	Configures this router to authenticate router R2 with password cisco
interface BRI0/0	
no ip address	This interface will get its IP address from the virtual dialer interface
encapsulation ppp	Configures this interface for layer 2 encapsulation of PPP
ppp authentication chap	Configures this interface to use CHAP authentication with the router at the remote end of the DDR connection
isdn switch-type basic-ni	Specifies the Central office or ISDN service provider switch type which is providing the ISDN service to this interface
isdn spid1 30355540401111	Used in North American BRI implementations. SPID's allow multiple ISDN devices, such as voice and data, to share the local loop. SPID's identify the services that are ordered from the carrier. If you are connecting to a DMS-100 or NI-1 switch-type, you will most likely need to configure spids. Most 5ess switches don't require spids
isdn spid2 30355540411111	See above, you require a SPID for each B-channel
ppp multilink	Allows the two B-channels to be bundled
dialer pool-member 1	This interface is a member of dialer pool 1 which is defined under the Interface Dialer 0

`interface Dialer0`	Creates the virtual interface template
`ip address 172.16.1.1 255.255.255.252`	
	Configures the IP address which will be assigned to the physical interface BRI0/0
`encapsulation ppp`	Configures this interface for layer 2 encapsulation of PPP. This command MUST be configured on the virtual interface AND the physical interface
`dialer remote-name B00`	Specifies the remote router's CHAP authentication name. For the Calling router, the dialer remote name is irrelevant, for the Called router the dialer remote name MUST match the ppp chap hostname of the Calling router
`dialer string 5551212`	Specifies the number of the remote router to call
`dialer pool 1`	Specifies to use a physical interface that belongs to the dialing pool number 1 to use for initiating calls to a remote router
`dialer-group 1`	Specifies that the global command dialer-list number 1 will be used to specify the interesting traffic
`ppp authentication chap`	Configures this interface to use CHAP authentication with the router at the remote end of the DDR connection. This command MUST be configured on the virtual interface AND the physical interface
`ppp chap hostname chris`	OPTIONAL, use the hostname chris, instead of the R1 configured hostname. Router R2 will require a username/password command for this alternate hostname
`ppp chap password kelly`	OPTIONAL, use the password kelly, instead of the cisco configured password. Router R2 will require a username/password command for this alternate password
`ppp multilink`	Allows the two B-channels to be bundled
`dialer-list 1 protocol ip permit`	Specifies that all ip traffic is interesting

Configuring Dialer Profiles with Callback

DDR environments can be configured for callback operations. When PPP callback is configured on the participating routers, the calling router (the callback client) passes authentication information to the remote router (the callback server), which uses the hostname and dial string authentication information to determine whether to place a return call. If the authentication is successful, the callback server disconnects and then places a return call. The remote username of the return call is used to associate it with the initial call so that packets can be transmitted. This functionality provides enhanced security by ensuring that the remote site can connect only from a single location as defined by the callback number. It can also enhance administration by centralizing billing for remote DDR connections. Using the scenario in Figure 15.4, router R1 is the callback client and router R2 is the callback server. Here is the configuration for router R1:

`hostname R1`	Configures this router as hostname R1, which means that router R2 must have a username statement for the hostname R1
`enable password cisco`	Configures this router with the enable password of cisco
`username R2 password cisco`	Configures this router to authenticate router R2 with password cisco
`interface BRI0/0`	
`  no ip address`	This interface will get its IP address from the virtual dialer interface
`  encapsulation ppp`	Configures this interface for layer 2 encapsulation of PPP
`  ppp authentication chap`	Configures this interface to use CHAP authentication with the router at the remote end of the DDR connection
`  ppp callback request`	Configures the interface to request ppp callback from the server
`  isdn switch-type basic-ni`	Specifies the Central office or ISDN service provider switch type which is providing the ISDN service to this interface

isdn spid1 30355540401111	Used in North American BRI implementations. SPID's allow multiple ISDN devices, such as voice and data, to share the local loop. SPID's identify the services that are ordered from the carrier. If you are connecting to a DMS-100 or NI-1 switch-type, you will most likely need to configure spids. Most 5ess switches don't require spids
isdn spid2 30355540411111	See above, you require a SPID for each B-channel
ppp multilink	Allows the two B-channels to be bundled
dialer pool-member 1	This interface is a member of dialer pool 1 which is defined under the interface Dialer 0
interface Dialer0	
ip address 172.16.1.1 255.255.255.252	
	Configures the IP address which will be assigned to the physical interface BRI0/0
dialer remote-name BOO	For the Calling router (which is this router in this scenario) the dialer remote-name is irrelevant, for the Called router the dialer remote-name MUST match the ppp chap hostname of the Calling router. So, in this example, you can make this name whatever you like, as it does not matter
dialer string 5551212	Specifies the number of the remote router to call
dialer pool 1	Specifies to use a physical interface that belongs to the dialing pool number 1 to use for initiating calls to a remote router

encapsulation ppp	Configures this interface for layer 2 encapsulation of PPP. This command MUST be configured on the virtual interface AND the physical interface
dialer-group 1	Specifies that the global command dialer-list number 1 will be used to specify the interesting traffic
ppp callback request	Configures the interface to request ppp callback from the server. This command MUST be configured on the virtual interface AND the physical interface
ppp authentication chap	Configures this interface to use CHAP authentication with the router at the remote end of the DDR connection. This command MUST be configured on the virtual interface AND the physical interface
ppp chap hostname josh	Specifies to use the hostname josh, instead of the R1 configured hostname. Router R2 will require a username/password command for this alternate hostname of josh
ppp multilink	Allows the two B-channels to be bundled
dialer-list 1 protocol ip permit	Specifies that all ip traffic is interesting

Here's the configuration for router R2, the called router:

hostname R2	Configures this router as hostname R2, which means that router R1 must have a username statement for the hostname R2
enable password cisco	Configures this router with the enable password of cisco

username R1 password cisco	Configures this router to authenticate router R1 with password cisco
username josh password cisco	Configures this router to also authenticate the alternate hostname of josh which is configured on the virtual interface of router R1
interface BRI0/0	
no ip address	This interface will get its IP address from the virtual dialer interface
encapsulation ppp	Configures this interface for layer 2 encapsulation of PPP
ppp authentication chap	Configures this interface to use CHAP authentication with the router at the remote end of the DDR connection
ppp callback accept	Allows this interface to accept a callback request from a remote client
isdn switch-type basic-ni	Specifies the Central office or ISDN service provider switch type which is providing the ISDN service to this interface
isdn spid1 30355512121111	Used in North American BRI implementations. SPID's allow multiple ISDN devices, such as voice and data, to share the local loop. SPID's identify the services that are ordered from the carrier. If you are connecting to a DMS-100 or NI-1 switch-type, you will most likely need to configure spids. Most 5ess switches don't require spids
isdn spid2 30355512131111	See above, you require a SPID for each B-channel
ppp multilink	Allows the two B-channels to be bundled
dialer pool-member 1	This interface is a member of dialer pool 1 which is defined under the interface Dialer 0
interface Dialer0	

```
ip address 172.16.1.2 255.255.255.252
```

Configures the IP address which will be assigned to the physical interface BRI0/0

`dialer remote-name josh`

For the Calling router (which is the R1 router in this scenario) the dialer remote-name is irrelevant, for the Called router the dialer remote-name MUST match the ppp chap hostname of the Calling router. So, in this example, the remote-name MUST be josh, as that is the ppp chap hostname configured on the virtual interface of router R1

`dialer string 5554040 class dial1`

Specifies the number of the remote router to call, also using the dial1 map-class established for PPP callback on this interface

`dialer pool 1`

Specifies to use a physical interface that belongs to the dialing pool number 1 to use for initiating calls to a remote router

`dialer-group 1`

Specifies that the global command dialer-list number 1 will be used to specify the interesting traffic

`encapsulation ppp`

Configures this interface for layer 2 encapsulation of PPP. This command MUST be configured on the virtual interface AND the physical interface

`dialer callback-secure`

OPTIONAL, provides for a secure callback process

`ppp authentication chap`

Configures this interface to use CHAP authentication with the router at the remote end of the DDR connection. This command MUST be configured on the virtual interface AND the physical interface

`ppp multilink`

Allows the two B-channels to be bundled

`map-class dialer dial1`

Map class dial1 is used in the dialer string command for the callback

```
dialer callback-server username    Identify the return call dial string
                                   using the authenticated username

dialer-list 1 protocol ip permit   Specifies that all ip traffic is
                                   interesting
```

Troubleshooting

The following output is from a show isdn status command. Notice that layer 1 shows an ACTIVE status, and layer 2 shows a MULTIPLE_FRAME_ESTABLISHED status with the terminal endpoint identifier (TEI) set to 64. Layer 3 will show that there are no active calls if the ISDN interface if not active:

```
The current ISDN switchtype - basic-ni
ISDN BRI0/0 interface
    Layer 1 Status:
        ACTIVE
    Layer 2 Status:
        TEI = 64, SAPI = 0, State = MULTIPLE_FRAME_ESTABLISHED
    Layer 3 Status:
        0 Active Layer 3 Call(s)
    Activated dsl 0 CCBs = 0
    Total Allocated ISDN CCBs = 0
```

If you issue a show interface command for the ISDN interface, you can see that it is in the spoofing state (pretending to be up/up so the routing table can point to this interface):

```
R1#show interface bri 0/0
BRI0/0 is up, line protocol is up (spoofing)
```

When troubleshooting DDR, it is always beneficial to use the show dialer command because it will show you general diagnostic information for interfaces configured for DDR. This command also displays the timer's configuration and the amount of time before the connection times out:

```
R1#show dialer
BRI0/0 - dialer type = ISDN
Dial String      Successes    Failures    Last called    Last status
5551212              0            0          never            -
```

```
0 incoming call(s) have been screened.
BRI0/0:1 - dialer type = ISDN
Idle timer (60 secs), Fast idle timer (20 secs)
Wait for carrier (30 secs), Re-enable (5 secs)
Dialer state is idle
BRI0/0:2 - dialer type = ISDN
Idle timer (60 secs), Fast idle timer (20 secs)
Wait for carrier (30 secs), Re-enable (5 secs)
Dialer state is idle
```

Another good command to use in troubleshooting is the show dialer map command. This command will display configured dynamic and static dialer maps:

```
R1#sh dialer map
Static dialer map ip 172.16.1.2 name R2 (5551212)
on BRI0/0
```

Debug Commands

Here are some good troubleshooting commands:

debug isdn q931	Displays call setup and tear down of the ISDN network connection (Layer 3)
debug isdn q921	Displays data link layer messages (Layer 2) on the D channel between the router and the ISDN switch. Use this debug if the show isdn status command does not display Layer 1 and Layer 2 up
debug dialer	Displays DDR debugging information about the packets received on a dialer interface
debug ppp negotiation	Displays information on PPP traffic and exchanges while negotiating the PPP components including Link Control Protocol (LCP), Authentication, and NCP. A successful PPP negotiation will first open the LCP state, then Authenticate, and finally negotiate NCP
debug ppp authentication	Displays the PPP authentication protocol messages, including Challenge Authentication Protocol (CHAP) and Password Authentication Protocol (PAP) packet exchanges

Real World Scenario

Preventing Routing Loops with Dial Environments

Let's assume we have a remote site that will receive a default route (dynamic routing protocol) across its primary circuit (frame relay) from a core network. The remote site router is also configured with a floating static default route directed out the dial (async or ISDN) interface, weighted at a higher administrative distance than the dynamic routing protocol (Frame Relay circuit). Given this environment, when the primary circuit becomes unavailable and the site loses its dynamic default route from the core network, the floating static default route will initiate its dial backup circuit.

During recovery, depending on the duration of the idle timer configured on the dial interface, a routing loop is created in the core network due to the default being generated to the remote site and the remote site's floating static. A preferred method is to lock down the default route coming from the remote site. The logical place to do this is at the termination point of the dial backup connection (in this example an AS5300). Distribute lists could be applied inbound and outbound on the async and ethernet interfaces.

Example: AS5300 Configuration

router eigrp 100

 distribute-list 10 out Async1

 distribute-list 20 in Async1

 ....

 distribute-list 10 out Async192

 distribute-list 20 in Async192

 distribute-list 20 out Ethernet0

 distribute-list 30 in Ethernet0

access-list 10 deny any

access-list 30 permit 0.0.0.0

access-list 30 deny any

access-list 20 deny 0.0.0.0

access-list 20 permit any

This is a rather standard type of configuration used in most networks, as we are assured that we will not have a routing loop caused by improper propagation of multiple default routes within the network during convergence.

Summary

In this chapter, we delved into the details of ISDN. We discussed the differences between legacy ISDN configuration and the new dialer profile and then looked at the benefits of each by using some IOS debug and show commands. We also went into more detail about PPP authentication. We also described how to configure dial-on-demand routing (DDR), dial backup, and Bandwidth on Demand (BoD) and how to verify your configuration by using more IOS show commands.

Dial-up lines have traditionally been the most cost-effective way to implement fault tolerance on the WAN. However, selecting the appropriate type is important. Backup interfaces, floating routes, and OSPF each demand that circuits provide different advantages in this environment.

Following these guidelines will help you construct scalable DDR internetworks that balance performance, fault tolerance, and cost. If implementing the dialer profile method, remember which commands must be configured on the physical interfaces and which commands must be configured on the virtual "dialer" interface.

Also, if you would like to try to implement a dial backup scenario, we have developed a hands-on exercise. You'll find it in Chapter 15 Supplement on the CD-ROM that came with this book.

Exam Essentials

Know the difference between ISDN and POTS.   First, ISDN starts off as digital, so there is no analog-to-digital conversion as there is with POTS. Second, call setup and teardown is accomplished through a dedicated 16KB channel, which is also known as a D (data) channel, whereas with POTS all signaling is accomplished in-band.

Understand what a BRI and PRI are.   A Basic Rate Interface (BRI) uses a single copper pair of wires to provide up to 144Kbps of bandwidth for both voice and data calls. A BRI uses two 64Kbps B channels and one 16Kbps D channel. A T1-based Primary Rate Interface (PRI) has 23 B channels and one 64Kbps D channel, which equals a bandwidth of 1.536Kbps. An 8Kbps channel for framing and synchronization is used as well to get a bandwidth for a U.S. T1/PRI of 1.544Mbps. An E1-based PRI has 30 B channels and one 64Kbps D channel. An E1 uses channel 15 for signaling (D channel). An E1 has 2.048Mbps of bandwidth.

What is Multilink PPP.   Multilink PPP is method for spreading traffic across multiple physical WAN links while providing packet fragmentation and reassembly, proper sequencing, multivendor interoperability, and load balancing on inbound and outbound traffic. It allows packets to be fragmented.

Key Terms

Before you take the exam, be certain you are familiar with the following terms:

Bandwidth on Demand (BoD)

Basic Rate Interface (BRI)

bearer capability

Challenge Handshake Authentication Protocol (CHAP)

dial backup

dial-on-demand routing (DDR)

Integrated Services Digital Network (ISDN)

LAPD frame

Link Access Procedure on the D Channel (LAPD)

Open Shortest Path First (OSPF)

Password Authentication Protocol (PAP)

plain old telephone service (POTS)

Primary Rate Interface (PRI)

public switched telephone network (PSTN)

pulse code modulation (PCM)

Service Profile Identifier (SPID)

Review Questions

1. What does an NT1 do?

    A. Converts non-ISDN devices into a compatible signal

    B. Consolidates devices onto an ISDN line at a point between LE and TA

    C. Provides the conversion between a bipolar and unipolar signal

    D. Converts the unipolar signal from the NT2 into a bipolar signal before sending it to the network

2. Which of the following refers to a nonnative ISDN device such as a POTS phone or a fax machine?

    A. NT1

    B. NT2

    C. TA

    D. TE2

3. How long is the SAPI field?

    A. 1 octet

    B. 2 octets

    C. 3 bits

    D. 6 bits

4. Which ISDN switch type requires a Service Profile Identifier (SPID)?

    A. NTT

    B. 5ESS

    C. DMS-100

    D. NET3

5. Which of these is not a Primary Rate Interface (PRI) switch option?

    A. National-1

    B. DMS-100

    C. 4ESS

    D. NET5

6. CHAP is identified by which authentication protocol ID?

   A. 0xFFF

   B. 0xc223

   C. 0xEFF

   D. 0x89

7. Which command verifies that ISDN layer 3 is working?

   A. show ISDN status

   B. debug ISDN Q.931

   C. show dialer

   D. show IP interface brief

8. What is the format of the LAPD flag?

   A. 7E

   B. AF

   C. FF

   D. 9D

9. Which set of commands would configure the bri0 interface to back up the serial0 interface?

   A. int s0, backup interface bri0

   B. int bri0, backup interface serial 0

   C. int bri0, backup interface serial 0 delay 20

   D. int bri0, backup load 60

   E. int s0, backup load 60

10. Which command would change an interface into an OSPF demand circuit?

   A. suppress lsa

   B. ip ospf supress lsa

   C. ip ospf demand-circuit

   D. ip supress multicast

   E. ip ospf supress

Answers to Review Questions

1. C. The NT1 converts the telco's 2B1Q signal into a bipolar signal that the NT2 can understand. It also acts as a loopback device for network testing. An NT1's output is also known as the T interface.

2. D. A TE2 is any nonnative ISDN device, such as a POTS telephone or a fax machine. This device requires a TA to interface with the ISDN network.

3. D. The SAPI field is 6 bits. The values transported in the SAPI field identify the type of information in the packet.

4. C. National-1 and DMS-100 switches require a SPID for each B channel. It is optional with an AT&T 5ESS, but you still may need to set one.

5. A. National-1 is the BRI standard, not a PRI standard.

6. B. CHAP is identified as Authentication Protocol c223, which is carried in the Information field of a PPP packet.

7. C. The `show dialer` command verifies that ISDN layer 3 is working. This is indicated by `success` under `last status`.

8. A. An LAPD frame starts with 7E.

9. A. The `backup` command is configured under the primary interface.

10. C. The `ip ospf demand-circuit` command is the only command needed to configure a demand circuit.

Access Control Lists (ACLs)

THE CCIE QUALIFICATION EXAM TOPICS COVERED IN THIS CHAPTER INCLUDE THE FOLLOWING:

- ✓ Access control lists (ACLs)
- ✓ Standard and extended IP access lists
- ✓ Named, dynamic, timed, and reflexive ACLs
- ✓ IPX access lists
- ✓ MAC access lists
- ✓ LSAP access lists
- ✓ NetBIOS access lists

This chapter introduces the operation and utilization of Cisco access control lists (ACLs), also referred to as access lists, and how they pertain to Cisco routers. This is an extremely important topic to understand because access lists are used in many different features. This chapter should give you a basic understanding and overview of some of the more common types of access lists and gives a few examples on how to configure them. However, we won't cover all available types and all possibilities that may exist when configuring an access list; this kind of coverage would deserve a book all of its own. For the most part, when people hear the term *access control list*, they think of providing network security filters to allow (permit) or block (deny) certain traffic patterns. Although this is true, Cisco has also provided extended features to its IOS to allow access lists to be used for quite a few different applications. Here are just a few:

- As a traffic filter applied to an interface

- Under the routing processes to filter certain route updates, implement router preference, change the metric values using offset lists, or change route attributes before they are redistributed into another routing process

- To control Telnet access to virtual terminal (vty) ports.

- As packet classification for queuing mechanisms, such as custom queuing (CQ), priority queuing (PQ), low-latency queuing (LLQ), committed access rate (CAR), and so on

- To apply traffic shaping and policing tools, such as Generic Traffic Shaping (GTS), Frame Relay Traffic Shaping (FRTS), and rate limiting

- To allow Encryption and IPSEC applications.

- To support Dialing applications, such as Dial-on-Demand and Dialer-Watch.

- To allow Network Address Translation.

- To control which SNMP servers are allowed to read only and read and write to SNMP MIBs.

What Is an Access Control List?

Access control lists (ACLs) are made up of access control entries (ACEs), which are criteria used for identifying certain traffic flows, along with instructions for what action to take when a match in the traffic pattern is found. The action taken is to deny (drop the packet) or to permit (allow the traffic to pass through the router). Traffic flow patterns will be compared to the applied list and read in sequential order, line by line, top-down, until either a match is found, in which case no further comparison is made, or until the end of the list is reached. Implicitly, the end of an ACL will always deny traffic. The order in which the access list criteria is listed is very important to keep in mind when creating one. Any new additional criteria statement that is applied to an already existing ACL is appended to the end of the access list statements. If there is a requirement to change the order in which the lines are read, the access list must be deleted and reentered in that particular order of requirement. Some important caveats should be kept in mind when dealing with ACLs:

- Place the most commonly used entries near the beginning of the access list. And although the order of the entries in the ACL is important, access lists are processor intensive for the router; therefore, you should also take into consideration where to place the access list itself.

- Standard access lists should be placed close to the destination so that traffic can be filtered where it is unwanted and still reach other areas of the network. This is because standard ACLs only filter on the source, effectively permitting or denying access to *all* destinations.

- Extended access lists should be placed close to the originating source of the traffic. Allowing or denying traffic from entering the network will save on unnecessary traffic across the network.

- If you delete an access list that has already been applied to an interface, all packets will be forwarded by the router as if no access list association was applied to the interface. This could cause a big security hole.

 Deleting an IPSec ACL will leave a crypto map sequence incomplete and will prevent evaluation of that and subsequent crypto map sequences. Additionally, if the first crypto sequence is the one that is incomplete, all incoming traffic to the router will be dropped (depending on IOS version).

- When creating an access list, caution should also be taken to not explicitly permit all traffic prior to any deny statements.

- In addition, do not create an access list that contains only deny statements. The ACL should contain, at the most, one permit statement. If it doesn't, all traffic will essentially be denied.

- Which leads us to the last point. At the end of every access list is an implied "deny all traffic" criteria statement. Therefore, if a packet does not match any of your criteria statements, the packet will be denied. If the point of the ACL is to deny certain criteria, then include an explicit "permit everything" entry at the end of the list.

Next, we'll show you how to implement access lists in the Cisco networking environment.

Applying the Access List

As mentioned earlier, access lists, for the most part, are made up of a number of criteria that will be used for comparison. Once an ACL is created, there are quite a few ways to apply it, depending on its purpose.

Applying Access Lists to an Interface as Traffic Filters

An access list can be applied to an interface as either an inbound or outbound filter:

- If an access list is applied to an interface as an inbound, or ingress' filter, when the router receives a packet, it checks the access list's criteria for a match. If the packet is permitted, the router continues to further process and forward the packet. If the packet is denied, the router discards the packet.

- If an access list is applied to an interface as an outbound, or egress' filter, the router will receive a packet, determine its next hop, and forward it to an outbound interface; the router will then check any criteria statements in the access list for a match. If the packet is permitted, the router transmits the packet. If the packet is denied, the router discards the packet.

Multiple access lists can be created on the router, and the same access list can be applied to multiple interfaces. However, the interface can have only one inbound and one outbound list applied to it for the same protocol.

IP access lists are applied to an interface using the `ip access-group [in | out]` command. IPX access lists are applied to an interface using the `ipx access-group [in | out]` command.

If the optional direction `in` or `out` keyword is not specified, the default direction is out. The direction is always from the interface's point of view with respect to the traffic flow. For example, if the traffic comes into a network via Serial 0/0, an inbound filter can be applied using the keyword `in`. If the traffic left a network via Serial 0/0, then an outbound filter can be applied using the keyword `out`.

Let's briefly discuss the various methods of implementing ACLs.

Applying Access Lists under the Routing Processes

Access lists can be used to prevent certain routes from being sent out or from entering the routing table or another routing process altogether

- Access lists are applied to the routing process with a `distribute-list` command.
- Routing metric adjustments use offset-list statements.
- Access lists can be used within route maps to perform a variety of filtering and metric adjustments.

Distribute lists and route maps will be further explained in Chapter 17, Route Filtering Capabilities.

Applying Access Lists to Control Access to Vty Lines

IP access lists are applied on vty lines using the `access-class` command. This is a mechanism to restrict TELNET/SSH acces to a router.

Applying Access Lists for Queuing Mechanisms

Let's discuss how ACLs can be utilized within various types of queuing.

- Access lists are applied to custom queuing techniques using the `queue-list` command. They are applied to an interface using the `custom-queue-list` command.

- Access lists are applied to priority queuing techniques using the `priority-list` command. They are applied to an interface using the `priority-group` command.

- Access lists are used to classify traffic into class-maps for use in Low Latency Queueing policy maps.

Further explanation can be found in Chapter 18, Quality of Service (QoS).

Applying Access Lists for Traffic Shaping and Policing Tools

Let's discuss how ACLs can be utilized with traffic shaping.

- An access list for IP policy routing is applied using the `ip policy` command.

- Standard or extended ACLs are used for generic traffic shaping and applied to an interface using the `traffic-shape group` command.

- An access list for rate limiting is applied using the `access-list rate-limit` command and to an interface using the `rate-limit access-group` command.

Further explanation can be found in Chapter 18.

Applying Access Lists for Cisco Encryption and IPSEC

When creating IPSEC crypto maps, you can define extended ACLs to provide a `match address` list to specify traffic that is to be encrypted. Further explanation can be found in Chapter 19, Network Security.

Applying Access Lists for Dialing Applications

Let's discuss how ACLs can be utilized with dial applications.

- An access list is applied to Dial-on-Demand using the `dialer-list` command.

- An access list is applied to Dialer Watch applications using the `dialer-watch` command

Further explanation can be found in Chapter 15, Integrated Services Digital Network (ISDN) and Dial Backup.

Applying Access Lists for Network Address Translations (NAT)

An access list can be used when defining dynamic NAT pools. They are applied using the `ip nat [inside | outside] [source | destination] list` command. Further explanation can be found in Chapter 10, Protocol Redistribution and NAT.

Now we'll look at the many different types of access lists that exist.

Types of Access Lists

There are only two types of access lists that are supported by Cisco: standard and extended. The difference between the two is based on the amount of packet information criteria that will be evaluated when the filter is applied. There are many ACLs to choose from, and which one to choose and how simple they will be to create will depend on your requirements. ACLs are protocol specific, and they allow the administrator to filter on different protocols such as TCP/IP, SAP, IPX/SPX, NetBIOS, and so on. Access lists can be created using unique numbers that identify which access list is going to be defined, or they can be created using only names that uniquely define them. With IOS release 11.2 and later, you can use names rather than numbers for some numbered access lists, depending on the type that is being created.

Table 16.1 includes the predefined list of numbers that the IOS will use to interpret what kind of access list you are defining.

TABLE 16.1   Access lists number ranges.

Access List Number	Description
1–99	IP standard access list
100–199	IP extended access list
200–299	Protocol type-code access list
300–399	DECnet access list
400–499	XNS standard access list
500–599	XNS extended access list
600–699	AppleTalk access list
700–799	48-bit MAC address access list
800–899	IPX standard access list
900–999	IPX extended access list
1000–1099	IPX SAP access list
1100–1199	Extended 48-bit MAC address access list
1200–1299	IPX summary address access list

TABLE 16.1   Access lists number ranges. *(continued)*

Access List Number	Description
1300–1999	IP standard access list (expanded range)
2000–2699	IP extended access list (expanded range)

Both numbered and named access list will be discussed in further detail. However, as mentioned earlier, all possible variations dealing with each access list and protocol will not be covered in this chapter.

We'll begin by discussing the IP access lists.

Configuring IP Access Lists

The next few sections will deal with IP access lists and how to filter traffic based on information within the IP header fields. To control access to IP networks, there are several types of IP access lists that can be used to filter various kinds of traffic. IP provides the ability to define what type of access lists are being created: numeric standard or extended access lists or named access lists. IP access lists can be classified into the following categories:

- IP standard access lists can restrict traffic based on a specific source host IP address or source network address. They are defined by using a numeric range from 1 to 99 or by using a unique name to identify the access list.

- IP extended access lists provide further enhancements by filtering traffic not only on source IP address but also based on other IP header information, such as IP destination addresses, source and destination sockets, type of service, and protocol type fields. They are defined by using a numeric range from 100 to 199 or by using a unique name to identify the access list.

IP Standard Access Lists

Compared to the other IP access lists we will cover, IP standard access lists are limited in function because they restrict traffic based only on the source IP address within the IP packet header. IP standard access lists can be identified by using a number within the range from 1 to 99 or defined by assigning a unique name. Named access lists will be discussed later. The format to create standard access-list is as follows:

```
access-list [access-list-number] [deny | permit] source address [source- wildcard]
```

Here are explanations of some of the components of the command:

`access-list`   Use a number within the range from 1 to 99 to define IP standard access lists. Each access list statement with the same numeric value will be read as one entity and they will be read in the order they are entered.

`deny | permit`   These keywords specify the action to take if the criteria is meet.

`source address`   The source address can be specified by using a network number, identifying a range of host addresses, or identifying only one specific host address:

A network subnet   Look for packets within a particular subnet range. Must supply a reverse (wildcard bit) mask.

The host keyword   Use the `host source` command as an abbreviation for a source address (IP address of individual host) and source wildcard (0.0.0.0).

The any keyword   Use the any keyword as an abbreviation for any source address and source wildcard (0.0.0.0 255.255.255.255).

`source-wildcard`   The source wildcard indicates a mask to apply to the source IP address in order to specify which bits in the address you care about matching. The mask must be entered as a *wildcard mask,* which means that the subnet mask and the wildcard mask must be entered in reverse (inverse) order:

- When defining the wildcard mask, use a binary 0 to represent an exact match.
- When defining the wildcard mask, use a binary 1 to represent the "don't care" condition.

To further explain, an example will be used. Let's look at wildcard mask using the network range 192.168.16.0 /20 (consisting of 16 Class Cs):

```
IP subnet range and mask:        192.168.16.0 255.255.240.0
Subnet          192       168       16        0
Binary          11000000  10101000  00010000  00000000
Subnet Mask     255       255       240       0
Binary          11111111  11111111  11110000  00000000

IP subnet range using a reverse mask:    192.168.16.0 0.0.15.255
Subnet          192       168       16        0
Binary          11000000  10101000  00010000  00000000
Reverse Mask    0         0         15        255
Binary          00000000  00000000  00001111  11111111
Range allowed   192       168       16 - 31   any
```

Standard Access List Example 1

In this example, any packets inbound with a source IP address of 192.168.12.1 will be blocked; all other packets sourced from the 192.168.12/24 subnet will be allowed. Any other source addresses in the 192.168.0.0/16 subnets will be denied. Any other source address outside of those listed in the ACL will be permitted:

```
interface Serial 0
  ip access-group 1 in


access-list 1 deny host 192.168.12.1
```

```
access-list 1 permit 192.168.12.0 0.0.0.255
access-list 1 deny 192.168.0.0 0.0.255.255
access-list 1 permit any
```

Standard Access List Example 2

In this example, a Standard ACL will be used to allow all *even* networks into RIPv2. This example is used to help clarify how the reverse masks can be used and will check only the last bit in the third octet in the mask:

```
router rip
  version 2
  distribute-list 1 in
```

```
access-list 1 deny 192.168.1.0 0.0.254.255
```

```
                                 Deny all 192.168.0.0 ODD networks
access-list 1 permit any         Permit all other networks, which
                                 will equal all EVEN networks
```

```
        OR
access-list 1 permit 192.168.0.0 0.0.254.255
```

```
                                 Permit all EVEN networks, from all
                                 subnets, using one command line
```

Using the first two statements, break down the subnets into binary bits and compare them against the wildcard mask. Using any odd subnet (192.168.13.0) and even subnet (192.168.68.0), compare the third octet with the wildcard mask. All odd addresses in the third octet range will have the last bit set to a 1. As stated previously, the 0 in the wildcard mask is a match, and the 1 is a "don't care" bit.

IP Extended Access Lists

Standard access lists are limited to filtering only on the source IP address in the packet IP header. IP extended access lists, as implied by their name, provide more flexibility when looking into the IP header and can provide further filtering capabilities based upon the following:

- Source and destination IP addresses
- Protocol type (Based on the Protocol Type field in the IP header, layer 4 application packets can be filtered.)
- Source and destination ports

- Type of service (ToS) byte field (IP precedence and ToS bits)
- Using other optional keywords, such as `log` and `established`

IP extended access lists can be defined by using a number in a range or defined by assigning a unique name. Named access list will be discussed later. The format to use extended an access list is as follows:

```
access-list  access-list-number{deny | permit} [protocol protocol]
   [source address] [source-wildcard] [source port] [destination
   address] [destination-wildcard] [destination port]
```

Here are explanations of some of the components of the command:

`access-list` Use a number in a range from 100 to 199 to define IP extended access lists. Each access list statement with the same numeric value will be read as one entity and they will be read in the order they are entered.

`deny| permit` These keywords specify the action to take if the criteria is meet.

`protocol` Defines the protocol type field number in the IP header that will be filtered. The value range is 0–255. Certain IP protocol numbers are well known and cannot be used by any other application. The mnemonic name can be specified when entering the protocol. Options with IP extended access lists include ah, `eigrp`, esp, gre, `icmp`, `igmp`, `ip`, nos, `ospf`, pim, `tcp`, or udp. Because the IP header identifies the protocol type, the keyword `ip` it encompasses the keywords `tcp`, udp, esp, gre, and `icmp`.

Source or destination address The source/destination address can be specified by using a network number, identifying a range of host addresses, or identifying only one specific host address:

A network subnet Look for packets within a particular subnet range. Must supply a reverse mask.

The host keyword Use the `host source` command as an abbreviation for a source/destination address (IP address of individual host) and source/destination wildcard (0.0.0.0).

The any keyword Use the `any` keyword as an abbreviation for any source/destination address and source/destination wildcard (0.0.0.0 255.255.255.255).

Source or destination wildcard The source/destination wildcard indicates a mask to apply to the source IP address in order to specify which bits in the address you care about matching. The mask must be entered as a wildcard mask, which means that the subnet mask and the wildcard mask must be entered in reverse (inverse) order:

- Use a binary 0 to represent an exact match.
- Use a binary 1 to represent the "don't care" condition.

Source or destination port For the most part, this keyword field is used when the protocol type being filtered is TCP or UDP. You can enter the port as one of a variety of decimal numbers, from the range of 0 through 65535, or as a recognized mnemonic name. TCP and UDP well-known port numbers will be converted to a mnemonic name when entered. For example,

TCP port 23 is used to describe the Telnet application. It can be entered as the name *Telnet* or as a port number of 23. If it's entered as a numeric value of 23, the IOS software will convert to a mnemonic name of telnet. Port numbers are divided into three distinct categories:

Well-known ports   Well-known, standards-based ports are port numbers that are assigned by the *Internet Assigned Numbers Authority (IANA)* and are documented in RFC 1700. The range is from 0 to 1023.

Registered ports   Vendors who wish to avoid conflict with other server port numbers may register these ports. The range is from 1024 to 2047.

Undefined ports   These are usually used for client-based applications. The range is from 2048 to 65536.

Before identifying the source/destination TCP or UDP ports, you can use other keywords to help match against the port number, as shown here:

eq	Match only packets for a given port number.
established	Match established connections. See "Extended Access List Example 2" for more details.
gt	Match only packets that are greater than the port specified.
lt	Match only packets that are less than the port specified.
neq	Match only packets that are not on a port number that's specified.
range	Match only packets in the inclusive range of ports provided. Requires two port numbers.

Here are some additional points to remember when defining socket port numbers:

- The following are some common port numbers with *no* associated name:

Application	Protocol number
DLSw+ TCP (read)	2065
DLSw+ TCP (write)	2067
FST/IP, used in DLSw+ and RSRB	91

- When filtering FTP (ftp-data = 20, ftp = 21), it is important to keep in mind that File Transfer Protocol (FTP) is performed in multiple modes of operation that can affect the way the access list criterion is set up as well as the direction in which the ACL is placed on the interface.

- The first FTP mode is known as standard FTP, also referred to as active or normal mode FTP. This is the default mode of operation used between an FTP client and server. The client opens a control connection from a random port number greater than 1023 to the FTP server using port 21. The client then informs the server of a second port the client is listening to for the data connection, again a random port number greater than 1023. The FTP server opens port 20 as the source port number and sends any FTP destination data traffic using the second port.

- The second FTP mode in known as passive FTP. In passive mode, the client opens a control connection on port 21 to the server, just as in the standard FTP mode, but this time the client requests to use passive mode through the use of the PASV command. If the server agrees to this mode, the server allocates a random port, greater than 1023, which the client will use for data transmission.

- When trying to filter HTTP traffic, be aware of the HTTP traffic being redirected.

Extended Access List Example 1

This example will be used to show clearly that if the ACL is built incorrectly, certain unwanted results can occur. The first line in the ACL denies communication from any IP source address/any port to any destination address/any port on subnets 192.168.0.0/16. The second line permits any source address with TCP port 80 (WWW) web traffic to communicate with any 192.168.12 device also using port 80. The first line overrides the second line and any destination address with 192.168.12.0/24 will still be denied:

```
access-list 101 deny ip any 192.168.0.0 0.0.255.255
access-list 101 permits tcp any eq 80 192.168.12.0 0.0.0.255 eq www
access-list 101 permit ip any any
```

Extended Access List Example 2

This example uses the `established` keyword and deals with TCP-based sessions only. Within the TCP header, the Flags field is used to carry a variety of control information, including the SYN and ACK bits used for connection establishment and the FIN or RST bits used for connection termination. If an internal host sets up a connection to another external device, the first part of the TCP connection handshake is to send a connection request with the SYN bit set to 1 in the TCP header. The external device acknowledges the SYN and replies with a SYN_ACK, with the SYN and ACK bits set to a 1. All subsequent traffic for this TCP connection from the external device will either have the ACK bit set or will have the RST bit set (indicating connection termination). The `established` keyword monitors for the ACK or RST bits being set on the arriving or returned packet and if there is a match, forwards the packet. Therefore, from a security standpoint, essentially only TCP connections that were originated internally are allowed. The below access lists allow return packets from any source IP address that are part of an FTP conversation initiated by the FTP client, internal host 147.19.12.1. This is a standard mode FTP connection; FTP port 20 is used for the FTP data transfer. All other traffic will be denied:

```
interface Serial0/0
  ip access-group 102 in

access-list 102 permit tcp any eq ftp host 147.19.12.1 gt 1023 established
access-list 102 permit tcp any eq ftp-data host 147.19.12.1 gt 1023
```

You also have the option of creating IP access lists using names instead of the numbers, as described earlier.

Configuring Named IP Access Lists

When you're dealing with numbered IP standard and extended access lists each type is limited to only 100 lists per filter type. In most circumstances, this allows for enough access lists of each type to accomplish what you need. In some circumstances (for example, in the ISP world), this may not be enough. IP named access lists allow the administrator to create an unlimited number of IP access lists as well as provide a way to quickly and easily identify access lists that may be applied to an interface or within a routing process. As with numbered IP standard and extended access lists, there are some rules and caveats that must be applied when using named access lists:

- The name uniquely identifies the access list but does not specify the access list type. You must specify the type (standard or extended) when creating the list.

- When named access lists are created on a single router, no two names can be the same even if the lists are different types.

- With numbered access lists, you must delete the entire ACL if different criteria is needed. A big advantage to named access lists is that the entire list does not need to be deleted if an existing line(s) needs to be deleted. However, if you need to change the order or add new lines, just as with numbered access list you'll need to delete the entire existing list and reapply the new ordered list. Use caution because this may cause a security hole.

The format to use a standard named access list is as follows:

```
ip access-list standard name
{deny | permit} source [source-wildcard]
```

Here is the format to use an extended named access list:

```
ip access-list extended name
{deny | permit} protocol source address [source-wildcard] destination
    address [destination-wildcard]
```

Example of a Named Access List

Here is an example of a named ip extended access list:

```
interface Ethernet 0/0
   ip access-group Deny-Inbound-Traffic in

ip access-list extended Deny-Inbound-Traffic
   deny tcp any any eq snmp
   deny tcp any any eq ftp log
   deny tcp any any eq ftp data log
   deny tcp any any eq domain
   deny tcp any any eq smtp
```

```
deny udp any any eq tftp
permit tcp any any
```

There are certain types of access lists that provide special functionality. In the next sections, we'll discuss dynamic (lock-and-key), timed, and reflexive access lists.

Dynamic Access Lists (Lock-and-Key Security)

From an IP traffic filter security standpoint, dynamic access lists, also known as lock-and-key security access lists, provide further traffic filtering enhancements than that used with normal IP standard and extended access lists. When the lock-and-key feature is configured, only certain designated users can gain temporary access to devices that would normally be blocked by the router using other access list methods. As the name, the access list entries are created dynamically via a temporary opening on limited-time basis. A designated user is required to first telnet to the router and authenticate access through the use of a local database configured on the router or through the use of a *RADIUS* or *TACACS* server. Once the user authenticates, the Telnet session is closed and the router places a dynamic entry as an access list criteria that will permit IP packets from the source IP address of the authenticated user. The user can gain access only to defined destination hosts and only for a predefined period of time. Dynamic ACLs are placed on an interface and used in conjunction with other static extended access lists, which would normally filter external, "untrusted" traffic from entering internal, "trusted" hosts. You can also use dynamic ACLs to allow certain subnets internally to gain temporary access to external devices. One additional step must be covered to allow dynamic access lists to function properly. As mentioned earlier, the user must authenticate with the router via Telnet; in addition, the user must execute the access-enable command to trigger the temporary permissions. Through the use of the autocommand parameter under vty lines, this temporary function (autocommand access-enable) can be accomplished. As with any vty Telnet session, you can authenticate the login process by using a local internal router database, performed using the `username`/`password` statement, or by using a RADIUS or TACACS server. Some rules and caveats for using dynamic (lock-and-key) access lists need to be explained before configuring them.

Dynamic access lists can be created using numeric IP extended access lists mentioned earlier. The syntax to create dynamic ACLs is as follows:

```
access-list [100 - 199] permit tcp source [source-wildcard]
    destination [destination wildcard] eq telnet
access-list [100 - 199] dynamic [dynamic-name] [timeout minutes] [deny | permit]
    [protocol source] [source-wildcard] destination [destination-wildcard]
    [established]
```

Here is an explanation of the purpose of the two access lists:

- The first ACL criterion is used to allow a designated user to telnet to the router; set the protocol keyword to `telnet`. The destination/destination wildcard mask should match a router interface closest to the designated user that is allowed access.

- The second ACL criterion is always ignored until the lock-and-key feature is triggered. It defines the access criteria that will be used by the designated user. Because dynamic ACL use IP extended access list commands, refer to the section "IP Extended Access List" earlier in this chapter.

The following list includes the keywords associated with dynamic access lists:

`dynamic`   Keyword used to define a globally unique alphanumeric name for the dynamic access list.

`timeout`   Optional keyword to define the absolute time period, measured in minutes, that a user is allowed access to destination addresses. Timer is not reset. The user will be required to log back in and reauthenticate. To define the time period that a user is allowed access, an absolute time-out period or an idle time-out period, used with the autocommand, must be set to remove any dynamic entries from the access list once they are created. If both timers are used, make sure the absolute time period is greater than the autocommand time-out period.

Define one or more vty ports for lock-and-key support using the following commands:

`login local`   Define access authentication using a local username and password database on router (if aaa new model is not used).

`login tacacs`   Define access authentication using TACACS or XTACACS. For TACACS+ or RADIUS, aaa new-model is required.

`password`   Define the same password for all access to the vty port, not for individual users.

When implementing aaa new-model, the proper command syntax is `login aaa method`.

The EXEC line entry to use is the `access-enable` parameter to enable the creation of temporary access-list entries. The following two keywords can be configured in conjunction with the `autocommand access-enable` command:

`host`   This is a required parameter that is used to substitute the source IP address of the authenticating host in the dynamic entry. Without this keyword, all hosts on the entire network are allowed to set up a temporary entry.

`timeout`   This parameter is optional if the absolute timer was specified within the dynamic access list statement. This keyword specifies the idle-timeout value used if no traffic is seen. The timer is reset every time a packet matches the dynamic list entry. This timer and the absolute timer can both be set, but if this timer is set, its value must be less that the absolute time-out value.

Example of a Dynamic Access List

In this example, one external user will be allowed access to internal hosts' subnet 192.168.12.0 / 24 off of interface Ethernet 0/0. As well, the internal users off of Ethernet 0/1 will be allowed external connectivity to all devices, but only allowing Web-related access:

```
username chris password josh


interface Ethernet 0/0
  ip address 192.168.12.1 255.255.255.0
```

```
interface Ethernet 0/1
  ip address 192.168.13.1 255.255.255.0

  ip access-group 100 in

interface Serial 1/0
  ip address 147.19.16.1 255.255.255.252

  ip access-group 101 in

access-list 100 permit udp any eq 53 192.168.13.0 0.0.0.255 gt 1023
```

> This statement allows DNS queries from source addresses from the 192.168.13.0/24 subnet

```
access-list 100 permit tcp any eq www 192.168.13.0 0.0.0.255 gt 1023
```

> This statement allows Web browsing from source addresses from the 192.168.13.0/24 subnet

```
access-list 101 permit tcp any host 147.19.16.1 eq telnet
```

> This statement will allow telnet access to Serial 1/0 to allow external users to authenticate

```
access-list 101 dynamic kelly timeout 120 permit tcp any 192.168.12.0 0.0.0.255 log
```

> This statement allows any external source address to access any host on the 192.168.12.0/24 subnet. Absolute timer set to 2 hours or120 minutes

```
line vty 0 1                    VTY ports 0 and 1 will be used for
                                dynamic access-list authentication

  login local                   Requires a local database assignment
                                on router

  autocommand access-enable host
```

Time-Based Access Lists

Prior to Cisco IOS release 12.0, access list statements were always in effect once they were applied. The ability to implement access lists based upon a time period will allow a network administrator to have more control over when to permit or deny certain traffic patterns; you can configure access based on the time of day, the day of the week, or both. Currently, only IP and IPX extended access lists can provide the time range function. This section will cover only IP time-based access lists; however, IPX time-based access lists are roughly the same. Both named and numbered access lists can reference a time range.

Some rules and caveats need to be explained before configuring time-based access lists:

- When you're defining a time range, the router's internal clock will be used. It is important that the clock time is correct prior to initiating time-based access lists. Through the use of a Network Time Protocol (NTP) server, a more accurate time source can be used to synchronize the router's clock.

- When you're defining time lines using the time range command, if you're using the `absolute` and `periodic` keywords within the same time range, the periodic statements are evaluated only after the absolute start time begins. In addition, the periodic statements are not evaluated after the absolute time has expired.

- Only one absolute statement can be used per time-range command; however, multiple periodic statements are allowed.

Example of a Time-Based Access List

Here is the configuration to apply the time range command to a named IP extended access list:

```
interface serial0/0

  ip access-group test1 in        Applies the named access-list test1 to
                                   the interface

ip access-list extended test1      Extended ACL named test1 to apply on
                                   Serial0/0

  deny tcp any any eq www time-range my-time
```

Identifies the time-range with the
name my-time

permit ip any any

From 5:01 PM to 7:59 AM Monday - Friday
and from Friday 5:01 PM to Monday 7:59
AM all access is permitted

time-range my-time

periodic weekdays 8:00 to 17:00

From 8:00 AM to 5:00 PM Monday -Friday
no access to any Web Server internal
to Serial0/0, from any external
address, will be allowed

IP Reflexive Access Lists

IP reflexive access lists were introduced in Cisco IOS Release 11.3. IP reflexive access lists are called IP session filters because they allow the router to filter IP packets based on upper-layer session information. The only other conventional access list that allows filtering based on an upper-layer protocol is the IP extended access list, but it's limited to TCP-based traffic only, and only when the established keyword is used. Basically, reflexive access lists are used to enable a router to filter based upon the bidirectional nature of connections. Although you may define permitted traffic on the client-side of a connection, you must also consider return traffic from the server-side. Reflexive ACLs detect TCP, UDP and ICMP "sessions or connections" and dynamically open up entries in the ACL that filter return traffic to permit only return traffic associated with the connection. IP reflexive access lists extend the filtering capabilities further by allowing the access list to filter on upper-layer protocols, such as IP, TCP, UDP, ICMP, thus providing a greater degree of network security. Through the use of reflexive access lists, it is much harder to spoof incoming traffic because more filtering criteria must be matched before a packet is permitted through. When the established keyword is used with extended access lists, the filtering criteria is only looking for an ACK or RST bit within the TCP packet to allow the traffic to pass through to the internal, protected network. With reflexive filtering, source and destination addresses and protocol and ports numbers are checked against the reflexive access list entries to permit traffic.

Another significant improvement when using a reflexive access list is that the router creates temporary, dynamic openings. Based on the reflexive access list criteria, these temporary entries are dynamically created when an internal network host initiates an IP upper-layer session with the packet destined for another host on the external side of the network. Because the session was initiated from the inside and the reflexive entry was created based on these predefined criteria, any inbound traffic that is originated from the outside network and that is not part of an existing session entry will not be allowed to pass through to the internal network. The temporary entry will be removed when the session request is terminated by either end of the session, in the case of TCP-related sessions, or if no more packets are seen within a predefined period, as in the case of UDP, ICMP, or IGMP related sessions. The term *reflexive access list* refers to the fact that when an IP session is initiated and the packet matches the permit reflexive access list criteria, a temporary entry is created. The temporary entry is a mirror image, or reflection, of the permit reflect access list statement. In other words, the packet source and destination IP addresses along with their related source and destination ports are entered as a temporary entry in reverse order of the originating packet. Incoming traffic will now be evaluated against the temporary entry or entries. To help clarify this, we'll use an example.

The following access list entry creates a reflexive access list called test that allows all internal users on the 130.16.64.0 /24 subnet to initiate Telnet sessions to the outside (the extended access list would be placed as an outbound filter on the outside interface toward the Internet):

```
permit tcp any any eq telnet reflect test
```

The reflexive temporary entry will be created upon an internal session request and will be entered in the reverse order:

```
Reflexive IP access-list test
    permit tcp host 172.16.2.4 eq telnet host 130.16.64.2 eq 11088 (25 matches)
    (time left 82)
```

This allows incoming sessions associated with the originating outbound session to be evaluated against the incoming filter and forwarded into the internal network. The example in the next section shows the configuration and diagram that was used to provide the preceding output. Just like all the other access lists mentioned, reflexive access lists have certain characteristics that must be dealt with:

- To create reflexive access lists, you must use extended named IP access list statements. All related protocols can be applied when creating a session filter.

- Because the reflexive statement will be included with other extended named IP access list statements, the order in which entries are placed is important because the ACL will be read in sequential order. When including a reflexive access list statement, make sure the packets that need to be evaluated in the reflexive statements are not allowed in previously nonreflexive extended permit or deny named list statements.

- When defining FTP passive mode filtering, keep in mind changing port numbers.

Because reflexive access list commands are nested within extended named IP access list statements, the majority of the command syntax is related to the extended named IP access list. Refer to the section "Configuring Named IP Access Lists" earlier in this chapter for further explanation. Apply the extended named IP access list to an interface using the `ip access-group` command.

Example of a Reflexive Access List

This example uses a reflexive access list to filter incoming external traffic based on any initiated session from inside the network. Any other interfaces on the router with traffic destined for the Internet will be verified against the outbound filter, `out-traffic`, and any return traffic will be verified against the inbound filter, `in-traffic`. Refer to Figure 16.1 below for the following configuration. A Telnet session is initiated from workstation A to router R2. The output of the reflexive access list was shown previously. The configuration doesn't show all possible ACL criteria to allow or disallow other criteria; it shows only possibilities that can occur.

FIGURE 16.1 Reflexive ACL

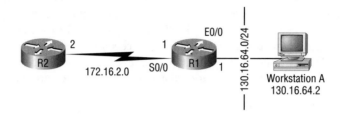

Here is the configuration for router R1:

```
interface Ethernet0/0
 ip address 130.16.64.1 255.255.255.0
```

```
interface Serial0/0                     Interface connected to the Internet
 ip address 172.16.2.1 255.255.255.0
```

```
 ip access-group in-traffic in          Apply the IP Extended access-list to
                                         the interface to filter inbound
                                         traffic
```

```
 ip access-group out-traffic out        Apply the IP Extended access-list to
                                         the interface to filter outbound
                                         traffic
```

```
ip access-list extended out-traffic     Specifies the outbound IP access-
                                         list, named out-traffic
 permit eigrp any any
 permit tcp any any eq www reflect test
```

```
                                         Allows the creation of the reflexive
                                         dynamic ACL entries to watch incoming
                                         www based traffic. The reflexive ACL
                                         is named test
 permit tcp any any eq telnet reflect test
```

	Allows the creation of the reflexive dynamic ACL entries to watch incoming telnet based traffic. The reflexive ACL is named test
`permit tcp any any eq domain`	This command was entered to show that the above reflexive statements could be inserted above or below conventional IP Extended list statements. Use Caution when ordering the list and also remember the implicit deny at the end of any list
`ip access-list extended in-traffic`	Specifies the inbound IP access-list, named in-traffic
`permit eigrp any any`	
`evaluate test`	The evaluate command is placed at the end of the list. Because the out-traffic filter is based on the outbound session criteria, incoming traffic will now be checked against any reflexive entries with the name of test. Remember the implicit deny
`ip reflexive-list timeout 120`	Dynamic ACL entries will timeout in 120 seconds. Default is 300 seconds

As you saw, there are many various functions for IP access lists, but IP is not the only protocol that can utilize access-lists. We'll briefly discuss the IPX access lists.

Configuring IPX Access Lists

The previous sections dealt mainly with filtering IP-based traffic. The next few sections will deal with *Internetwork Packet Exchange (IPX)* access lists and how to restrict traffic based on information within the IPX header fields. When you compare the configuration of IPX access list filters to the configuration of IP access list filters, you'll find that there are some similarities and some major differences. If you have read the previous section, these similarities and differences will be obvious.

To control access to IPX networks, there are several types of IPX access lists that can be used to filter various kinds of traffic. As with IP access lists, IPX provides the ability to define what type of access lists are being created: numeric standard and extended access lists as well as named access lists. IPX access lists can be classified into the following categories:

- IPX standard access lists
- IPX extended access lists

IPX Standard Access Lists

IP standard access lists restrict the filtering capabilities to only source-destination IPX networks-addresses. They restrict traffic based on source and destination address information contained in the IPX header. IPX standard access lists can be used to filter data packets that are routed in or out of interfaces, for controlling IPX network route updates, and to filter IPX broadcast-related traffic. They can be identified by using a numeric range from 800 to 899 or defined by assigning a unique name.

Example of an IPX Standard Access List

Here is an example of an IPX standard access list; notice that IPX ACLs use hex addressing and wildcard masks:

```
access-list 800 deny -1 2
```
Denies access to traffic from all IPX networks (-1) to destination network 2

```
access-list 800 deny 1.0000.0c00.1111
```
Denies access to all traffic from IPX address 1.0000.0c00.1111

```
access-list 800 deny 1.0000.0c00.0000 0000.00ff.ffff
```
Denies access from all nodes on network 1 that have a source address beginning with 0000.0c

IPX Extended Access Lists

IPX extended access lists extend the functionality of IPX standard ACLs by filtering IPX header information based on not only source and destination addresses but also IPX protocol type and IPX socket information. They can be identified by using a numeric range from 900 to 999 or defined by assigning a unique name. If you use numbers to identify your access lists, you are limited to 100 access lists per filter type.

Example of an IPX Extended Access List

The following example denies access to all RIP packets from the RIP process socket on source network AA that are destined for the RIP process socket on network BB. It permits all other traffic. This example uses protocol and socket names rather than hexadecimal numbers.

```
access-list 903 deny any AA rip BB rip
access-list 903 permit any
```

Remember from Chapter 13 that IPX relies on the broadcast of SAPs and GNSs to provide communication between the server and the clients. In the next section, we'll discuss how to implement the SAP access list.

SAP Access Lists

As mentioned in Chapter 13, Novell servers often send *Service Advertising Protocol (SAP)* broadcasts every 60 seconds, which can consume a large amount of bandwidth, on both LANs and WANs. SAPs allow servers that provide NetWare services to advertise their addresses and the services that they provide to other IPX servers and clients. A router will listen to the SAP updates and advertise these known services to other routers so that all clients can see the service messages. SAP access lists provide one means of controlling the amount of advertisements by prohibiting routers from advertising services from certain Novell servers based on the source network address of a SAP entry, the type of SAP entry (file server, print server), and the name of the SAP server. One other method described in Chapter 13 was to configure IPX EIGRP; instead of periodic SAP updates being sent across the WAN interfaces, EIGRP sends incremental updates that include SAP broadcasts only when changes occur to the SAP table, thereby conserving bandwidth. This section will only cover configuring access lists to filter SAP updates.

Get Nearest Server (GNS) queries and responses are also part of the SAP protocol. Clients broadcast out GNS packets to locate the nearest active server of a particular type. An IPX network client issues a GNS request to solicit either a direct response from a connected server or a response from a router that tells it where on the internetwork the service can be located.

Just a reminder, in a NetWare 4.1 or later environment, do not filter SAP type 0x4, 0x278, and 0x26B. If these SAP types are filtered, the NetWare Directory Services (NDS) server database will be unable to synchronize and the other servers and clients will have difficulty logging into and gaining access to the required services. SAP access lists can be configured as either numeric (1000 to 1099) or named access lists. The syntax to create either one is exactly the same.

Example of Applying a SAP Access List

The following example allows all print server SAP entries from PrinterB, all file server entries, and all other SAP entries from network ABA except those from a server called ServerA; all other entries will be denied:

```
interface Ethernet0/0
 ipx network ABA
 ipx-input-sap-filter Accounting_Server

ipx access-list sap Accounting_Server
 permit -1 47 PrinterB
```

```
permit -1 4
deny ABA 0 ServerA
permit ABA
```

 Notice that -1 means "any" for some parameters (e.g. source address), while 0 means "any" for other parameters (e.g. socket)

So far we have discussed the IP and IPX protocols, which are both layer 3, routable protocols. But what about nonroutable protocols? These are protocols that must live in a bridged, layer 2 environment. There are access lists designed for this environment, such as MAC, LSAP, and Net-BIOS access lists.

Nonroutable Traffic Access Lists

We've covered IP and IPX access lists, which give you the ability to filter packets based on layer 3 packet information. The next few sections will provide an overview on how to configure and apply bridged layer 2 nonroutable traffic filters, such as the following:

MAC access lists   MAC address access lists filter bridged traffic based on a specific source and/ or destination MAC address, by vendor type codes (OUI) prefixes, or by specifying arbitrary bytes in the frame.

LSAP access lists   LSAP access lists filter bridged traffic based on 802.2 Link Service Access Point (LSAP) information.

NetBIOS access lists   NetBIOS is a programming interface that allows service applications to communicate with each other via names rather than by hardware station addresses. NetBIOS access lists can be configured to filter traffic based on these names, thereby limiting application session establishments.

To help explain the concept behind why the ACL is needed, in each of the following sections, we will provide a brief overview prior to configuring and applying the respective access lists statements. We won't cover each ACL in its entirety.

MAC Access Lists

When filtering bridged traffic, you are dealing with filtering traffic based on Data-Link layer (layer 2) information. The IEEE standard separates the Data-Link layer into two sublayers known as the MAC sublayer and the LLC sublayer. The first of these is the *Media Access Control (MAC)* sublayer, which provides the logic that controls the transmission to the shared access medium independent of the access method (i.e., Token Ring, Ethernet, FDDI, etc.) and provides each frame with an address that identifies the sending and receiving station addresses. A manufacturer uses an Organizationally Unique Identifier (OUI) or vendor code to generate a unique MAC address for each device it produces. The LLC sublayer and corresponding filters will be discussed using Protocol Type and LSAP access lists. Media Access Control (MAC) access lists filter transmission by filtering the MAC-layer address, whether it is by a specific MAC address, a vendor code, or a protocol type. MAC address are defined using a dedicated numeric ACL value:

Numeric ACL	Definition
700–799	Standard 48-bit MAC address access lists filter traffic based on a single source or destination MAC layer address or vendor code.
1100–1199	Extended 48-bit MAC address access lists filter traffic based not only on source or destination MAC but also on an arbitrary byte value in the packet.

When defining MAC access lists, keep the following in mind:

- MAC addresses within an Ethernet frame use canonical bit-ordering, meaning each byte of the address is bit-swapped, whereas MAC addresses on Token Ring and DLSw use noncanonical bit-ordering. When you're using different media and building access lists to filter on MAC addresses, always use the canonical Ethernet representation for the access lists.

- Caution should be taken to not filter specific multicast or broadcast MAC destination addresses.

- After an access list is created initially, any subsequent additions (possibly entered from the terminal) are placed at the end of the list. In other words, you cannot selectively add or remove access list command lines from a specific access list.

A 48-Bit MAC Address Access List (Standard)

In a bridged environment, if more than one particular source or destination address needs to be filtered, using 48-bit MAC address access lists allows the administrator to filter groups of MAC addresses, including those with particular vendor codes. The vendor code is the first three bytes of the MAC address (read left to right). For example, in the MAC address 00e0.1eae.ff78, 00e0.1e is the OUI or vendor code; in this case, 00e0.1e defines a Cisco Systems, Inc. hardware address.

MAC address access lists can be used in environments in which transparent bridging is used to filter bridged traffic based on the source or destination MAC address. They can also be used in environments in which *data-link switching (DLSw)* is used. Introduced in IOS 11.2, the `dmac-output-list` option permits (or denies) an established TCP connection only when the explorer frame matches output destination MAC addresses specified by the access list.

 DLSw ACLs *always* use non-canonical addressing, even if frames from Ethernet networks are being filtered.

You can apply 48-bit MAC address access lists to a particular bridged interface to filter frames based on the MAC source addresses received on that interface or the MAC destination addresses that would be forwarded out that interface. Source or destination filtering is based on which interface command is used on a particular interface.

To filter by source or destination addresses, apply one of the following commands. To assign an access list to an Ethernet interface for filtering by MAC source addresses, use this command:

```
bridge-group [bridge-group-number] input-address-list [access-list-number]
```

To assign an access list to an interface for filtering by the MAC destination addresses, use this command:

```
bridge-group [bridge-group-number] output-address-list [access-list-number]
```

In a DLSw+ environment, use this command to establish the TCP connection only when the explorer frame passes the specified access list:

```
dlsw remote-peer [ring-group-list-number] tcp [remote peer IP address]
    dmac-output-list [access-list-number]
```

Example of Applying a MAC ACL on a Transparent Bridge

In this example, the filter will match MAC destination addresses, permitting a group range starting with 00e0.1e as well as permitting any broadcast traffic, such as ARP. All other destination addresses will be discarded:

```
interface Ethernet0/0

 bridge-group 1 output-address-list 701       Filter frames based on
                                               destination addresses


access-list 701 permit 00e0.1e00.0000 0000.00ff.ffff


access-list 701 permit ffff.ffff.ffff 0000.0000.0000


                                               Allows broadcast related traffic
access-list 701 deny 0000.0000.0000 ffff.ffff.ffff


                                               Every other destination address
                                               is denied. Any MAC
                                               0000.0000.0000 ffff.ffff.ffff
```

Extended 48-bit MAC Address Access List

Standard 48-bit MAC access lists provide the capability to filter only on source or destination MAC addresses. Extended 48-bit MAC address access lists allow the bridge administrator to filter on more values that are within the frame to allow for finer control of bridged traffic. These lists allow you to still filter frames on a particular source or destination MAC address, but they also allow you to filter on arbitrary byte patterns in the frame itself, using a byte offset. When filtering frames based on the offset values, you must understand how different media encapsulation types require different offset values to access particular fields. As with 48-bit MAC ACLs, extended 48-bit MAC ACLs (1100–1199) are applied to a particular bridged interface to filter frames based on the MAC source addresses received on that interface or the MAC destination addresses that would be forwarded out that interface. Source or destination filtering is based on which interface command is used on a particular interface. To filter frames using an extended access list, apply one of the following interface commands to a bridged interface in which transparent bridging is used.

The following command applies an extended access list to the packets being received by an interface:

```
bridge-group [bridge-group-number] input-pattern-list [access-list-number]
```

This command applies an extended access list to the packet being sent by an interface:

```
bridge-group [bridge-group-number] output-pattern-list [access-list-number]
```

Protocol Type and LSAP Access Lists

The previous section allowed you to filter traffic based MAC sublayers by matching on source and/or destination MAC hardware address fields within the frame. *Link Service Access Point (LSAP)* access lists are used to filter traffic based on the second sublayer, the LLC sublayer, by matching the source and/or destination SAP fields found in the IEEE 802.2 header portion of the frame as well as filtering Ethernet II frames based on the frame Type field. LLC is placed between the MAC layer of the Data-Link layer and the Network layer. Service access points identify the upper-layer network protocol type or services that resides on the station and are used to tell the Network layer which network process is to accept the frame and which network process submitted the frame. IEEE 802 defines three types of implementations for LLC; only the first two are of importance when configuring LSAP ACLs:

- 802.2 LLC Type 1 is a connectionless-oriented protocol that relies on upper-layer protocols to control sequencing and acknowledgements for session establishment and traffic sent between end stations. The most common application used with LLC1 is called Sub-network Access Protocol (SNAP). SNAP was implemented with LLC to enable network protocols to transition to new frame formats introduced by the IEEE 802.2 committee. Protocols such as TCP/IP and SPX/IPX use LLC Type 1.

- 802.2 LLC Type 2 is a connection-oriented protocol that provides link layer acknowledgment, sequencing, and flow control between end stations. NetBIOS and SNA traffic rely on LLC Type 2.

Both 802.2 LLC1 (SNAP) and LLC2 headers contains two 1-byte SAP fields, represented in hexadecimal format, that identify the source SAP (SSAP) address and a destination SAP (DSAP) address:

LLC1 802.2 SNAP header   The SSAP and DSAP fields are always be set to AA, followed by the Control field which is set to 03 to indicate unnumbered information packets. What distinguishes the different network protocols is a 5-byte field that follows the Control field, known as the Protocol Discriminator (PD) field. The first 3 bytes of the PD field identifies the OUI (vendor) and the next 2 bytes indicate the type of packet it is, (e.g., IP over Ethernet = 0x0800, AppleTalk = 0x809B and 0x80F3, DEC = 0x6000 – 0x6007, etc). Some of the type identifiers are the same protocol identifiers used in the Ethernet II frame Type field. LSAP ACLs filter traffic based on the 2-byte Type field when LLC1 Type 1 encapsulation is used. The AA fields are ignored and the type identifier is read.

LLC2 802.2 header   The SSAP uses 7 bits to identify the address and 1 bit to indicate whether the frame is a command or response (C/R) type frame. If the C/R bit is set to 0, the frame is a command frame, and if the C/R bit is set to 1, it is a response frame. LSAP ACLs will filter traffic based on the C/R bit value when LLC Type 2 encapsulation is used. See the list in the following paragraph for examples of common IEEE SAP assignments.

The IEEE registers SAPs for the most common known protocols that implement the 802.x protocols. Commonly used SAP addresses in hexadecimal format are as follows:

SAP ID	Description
00	Null LSAP addresses (all 0s in the SSAP and DSAP fields)
AA	802.2 SNAP header information
04,05,08,0C	SNA Path Control
06	Internet Protocol (IP)
42	IEEE 802.1 Bridge Spanning-Tree Protocol
E0	Novell NetWare IPX
F0	IBM NetBIOS
FF	Global DSAP

To help clarify the function of LSAP ACLs, we'll use an LLC2 encapsulated frame. As stated previously, LSAP access lists filter traffic by allowing or denying a particular protocol based on their respective C/R SSAP value. When defining the ACL, the SSAP and the DSAP values will be paired together, the first pair representing the SSAP and the second pair representing the DSAP. Consider a NetBIOS encapsulated frame as an example. NetBIOS uses 0xF0 to indicate a command message and 0xF1 to indicate a response message. This is important because the ACL is going to require a wildcard mask to determine which SAPs are allowed or based off of the SSAP/DSAP pairs. Therefore, in order to filter NetBIOS traffic, the ordered pair would be represented using 0xF0F0, with a mask of 0x0101. Once again, write down the SAP values and the mask in binary format. When you're defining the mask, a binary 0 indicates an exact match and a binary 1 indicates the "don't care" position:

```
SSAP|DSAP:      F    0           F     0
 Binary:        1111 0000        1111  0000
 Wildcard Mask: 0000 0001        0000  0001
 Allowed Binary: 1111 000(0 or 1) 1111  000(0 or 1)
 Allowed Hex:    F    0 or 1      F     0 or 1   F0 = Command, F1 = Response
```

SAP ACLs can be applied to Ethernet interfaces to filter transparent bridge traffic or between DLSw peer routers.

When you're applying an LSAP ACL to an bridged Ethernet interface, to filter incoming Ethernet Type II frames based on type code, use the following command on the end of the bridge-group command:

```
bridge-group [bridge-group-number] input-type-list [access-list-number]
```

To filter incoming 802.3/802.2 encapsulated frames, use the following command on the end of the bridge-group command:

```
bridge-group [bridge-group-number] input-lsap-list [access-list-number]
```

When you're applying an LSAP ACL to a DLSw peer, for DLSw+, you can only filter based on output IEEE 802.5 encapsulated packets to a remote peer:

```
dlsw remote-peer [ring-group-list-number] tcp [remote peer IP address]
lsap-output-list
    [access-list-number]
```

NetBIOS Access Lists

Network Basic Input/Output System (NetBIOS) is a Session layer protocol, most commonly referred to as an applications programming interface (API) that provides a method for two stations to communicate with each other across the network using their respective NetBIOS names rather than their station MAC addresses. When an application establishes a session or sends traffic to another station, the application relies only on the respective node name. An application that is supported by a node will be assigned a unique NetBIOS name. If multiple applications exist, each application will also be identified by an application NetBIOS name. A node that provides an application service(s) will also be administratively assigned a unique name or assigned internally by the NetBIOS software to uniquely identify the node itself. On startup, the node will register all NetBIOS names it wants to use by broadcasting an ADD_NAME_QUERY to find out if any other node on the network is using the same name. Each station is responsible for finding out the name of the other station before an application can establish a session with another NetBIOS application. In a SRB environment, the originating station must broadcast a Name-Query spanning-tree explorer (STE) frame to determine the path or route in the network to the required destination node. When the destination end station recognizes the name as belonging to one of it applications, the station replies back with a Name-Recognized frame. The returned frame will contain the name and any RIF information to reach the end destination. The application is now capable of establishing a new connection to the destination station. NetBIOS was initially designed for a LAN environment, in which NetBIOS traffic was locally bridged or switched between segments. Because NetBIOS is a non-routable protocol and in order to pass NetBIOS traffic across the WAN infrastructure to other stations on remote LANs, RSRB or DLSw can be used. As mentioned, NetBIOS relies mainly on broadcast-related traffic; WAN links can easily get overwhelmed with this broadcast traffic and soon congest the link to other remote stations.

If a Cisco router is used to support the bridging function, the software allows you to set up Net-BIOS filters to filter traffic based on source and/or destination NetBIOS hostnames or by filtering arbitrary byte patterns contained in the frame. NetBIOS access lists do not filter an all frames in and out of the router. They filter packets that are used to establish and maintain client/server connections, thereby eliminating any new service requests, which in turn may reduce any traffic that transverses across a WAN to a remote LAN network. The router also maintains a NetBIOS name cache, either by statically defining the NetBIOS MAC address and any RIF association or by listening for Name-Query and Name Recognized messages sent between each node. The NetBIOS name, related MAC address, and interface on which the message was learned are stored in the name cache for a predefined time-out period. If no traffic is seen within that time, the cached entry is deleted. The router can also use this information to alleviate some of the broadcast traffic used by NetBIOS end stations when they are trying to find each other. Any duplicate Name-Query messages are reduced to one frame and are resent on a predefined time period. The router can also forward broadcast requests sent by clients to find servers, as well as servers' responses to a client's request, rather than forward them for broadcast across the entire bridged network. NetBIOS access lists have certain characteristics when being configured:

- Similar to any access list statements we covered, the order in which they are created is important. New lines will be added to the bottom of the list, but the implied deny any statement is always added to the very bottom of the list. If the order of the list needs to change, you must first delete the ACL and reenter the new list.

- NetBIOS access lists use a name rather than a numeric value to distinguish each ACL. When defining a hostname in the filter, match the case letters of the actual server/client name listed in the router's NetBIOS name cache. In most cases, the names will be all uppercase letters.

- If you are creating a NetBIOS host ACL or an ACL that filters on a byte pattern, the same name can be used for both. The two ACLs have no relationship to each other when they are configured.

- NetBIOS access lists are applied to an interface. The messages are filtered based on the direction the ACL is applied.

Example of Applying a NetBIOS ACL on a DLSw Peer

NetBIOS ACLs use wildcard bits, such as the "?" to represent any single character and the "*" to represent any string of characters. In this example, the ACL will deny any devices with a NetBIOS hostname that begins with *FLA* or a NetBIOS hostname that has three characters beginning with a *C*. All other NetBIOS hostnames will be permitted on the DLSw remote peer 149.17.10.2:

```
netbios access-list host accounting deny FLA*
netbios access-list host accounting deny C??
netbios access-list host accounting permit *

dlsw remote-peer 0 tcp 149.17.10.2 host-netbios-out accounting
```

When DLSw remote-peer statements are used, all filters are outbound only.

We have completed our discussion on the various types of access lists to be implemented in the Cisco networking environment. Next, we'll briefly discuss a few commands that can be helpful in troubleshooting access list issues.

ACL Troubleshooting Commands

Here are some commands that can be useful in troubleshooting ACLs:

`show [ip | ipx] interface`

`show ip protocol`

`show access-lists`

`show ip access-list [access-list number]`

`show running configuration`

`show access-expression`

`clear access-list counters [access-list number]`	Used to clear counters on all access-lists, or a specified access-list
`clear access-template`	Used to clear dynamic access-list entries

Summary

Hopefully, you have a good understanding of the various types of access lists and how to implement them based on the desired functionality. It's extremely important that you become thoroughly knowledgeable on the operation and configuration of access lists. You will find that access lists are utilized in almost every fine-tuning and packet/route filtering implementation. There are many optional keywords that can be used in the configuration of access lists. It will be helpful (but not necessary) to know all of the possible keywords. Although, knowing the keywords will most certainly be helpful in the

CCIE lab examination and in the everyday networking environment. Be sure to understand the correct masking (wildcard bit) mechanism for each type of access lists (i.e., is it configured in decimal or hexa-decimal)? Also, be sure to have a good understanding of how to apply the various access-lists to the appropriate interface, routing process, and so on.

In the next chapter, we will discuss how to utilize ACLs as distribution lists to filter routes in the routing table.

Exam Essentials

Know what an ACL is.   Access control lists (ACLs) are made up of access control entries (ACEs), which are criteria used for identifying certain traffic flows, along with instructions for what action to take when a match in the traffic pattern is found. The action taken is to deny (drop the packet) or to permit (allow the traffic to pass through the router).

Know how to implement standard versus extended IP ACLs.   Standard access lists should be placed closed to the destination in order to filter the traffic where it is unwanted and make sure it can still reach other areas of the network. Extended access lists should be placed close to the originating source of the traffic. Allowing or denying traffic from entering the network will save on unnecessary traffic across the network.

Understand how many ACLs can be implemented per router interface.   Multiple access lists can be created on the router, and the same access list can be applied to multiple interfaces. However, the interface can have only one inbound and one outbound list applied to it for the same protocol.

Know what the wildcard mask is.   A wildcard mask is a mask to apply to the source IP address in order to specify which bits in the address you care about matching. The mask must be entered as a wildcard mask, which means that the subnet mask and the wildcard mask must be entered in reverse (inverse) order. When defining the reverse mask, use a binary 0 to represent an exact match and a binary 1 to represent the "don't care" condition.

Key Terms

Before you take the exam, be certain you are familiar with the following terms:

access control lists (ACLs)	Media Access Control (MAC)
data-link switching (DLSw)	Network Basic Input/Output System (NetBIOS)
Get Nearest Server (GNS)	RADIUS
Internet Assigned Numbers Authority (IANA)	Service Advertising Protocol (SAP)
Internetwork Packet Exchange (IPX)	TACACS
Link Service Access Point (LSAP)	wildcard mask

Review Questions

1. Which of the following are uses for an ACL? (Choose all that apply.)

    A. As a traffic filter

    B. To control Telnet access to vty lines

    C. To allow Encryption and IPSEC applications

    D. To allow Network Address Translation

2. Where is the proper placement for a standard IP ACL within a network as it pertains to the source and destination?

    A. Close to the source

    B. Close to the destination

    C. Close to the middle

    D. On the local LAN interface

3. An IP extended access list is identified by which number range?

    A. 1 to 99

    B. 100 to 199

    C. 800 to 899

    D. 900 to 999

4. When defining a wildcard mask, what do the binary 0 and binary 1 represent? (Choose all that apply.)

    A. Use a binary 1 to represent an exact match.

    B. Use a binary 0 to represent the "don't care" condition.

    C. Use a binary 0 to represent an exact match.

    D. Use a binary 1 to represent the "don't care" condition.

5. What is the correct wildcard mask to deny all odd networks for the 192.168.0.0 network?

    A. 0.0.1.255

    B. 255.255.254.0.0

    C. 0.0.254.255

    D. 255.255.1.0

6. In an extended IP access list, what keyword can be used to represent a source address (IP address of individual host) and source wildcard (0.0.0.0)?

   A. `device`

   B. `host`

   C. `any`

   D. −1

7. Which of the following are true regarding IPX standard access lists? (Choose all that apply.)

   A. Occur in the range 800–899

   B. Occur in the range 900–999

   C. Filter on source address only

   D. Filter on source and destination addresses

   E. Filter based on protocol and socket

8. A IPX SAP access list is identified by which number range?

   A. 1 to 99

   B. 100 to 199

   C. 800 to 899

   D. 900 to 999

   E. 1000 to 1099

9. In an IP access list, what keyword can be used in conjunction with the ACL to provide security by monitoring the ACK flag?

   A. `established`

   B. `host`

   C. `any`

   D. −1

10. You want to control which servers a router replies with when responding to a client's GNS query. Which type of access list would you create?

    A. Standard IPX access list

    B. Extended IPX access list

    C. IPX SAP access list

    D. IPX GNS access list

    E. Not possible

Answers to Review Questions

1. A, B, C, D. All four of the options are uses for ACLs.

2. B. Standard access lists should be placed close to the destination in order to filter the traffic where it is unwanted and make sure it can still reach other areas of the network.

3. B. IP extended access lists filter traffic not only on source IP addresses but also based on other IP header information, such as IP destination addresses, source and destination sockets, type of service, and protocol type fields. They are defined using a number in the range 100 to 199.

4. C and D. When defining the wildcard mask, use a binary 0 to represent an exact match and a binary 1 to represent the "don't care" condition.

5. C. Use `deny 192.168.1.0 0.0.254.255` to deny all 192.168.0.0 odd networks.

6. B. Use the `host` keyword as an abbreviation for a source address (IP address of individual host) and source-wildcard (0.0.0.0).

7. A, D. IPX standard access lists permit or deny traffic based on source and destination address. Standard IPX access lists can be named, or they can be numbered in the range 800–899.

8. E. SAP access lists can be configured using either numeric (1000 to 1099) or named access lists.

9. A. The `established` keyword monitors for the ACK being set on the arriving or returned packet and, if there is a match, allows the connection to continue. Therefore, from a security standpoint, only those connections that originated internally should match this criterion.

10. C. GNS filters use SAP access lists to permit or deny GNS replies.

Chapter 17

Route Filtering Capabilities

THE CCIE QUALIFICATION EXAM TOPICS COVERED IN THIS CHAPTER INCLUDE THE FOLLOWING:

- ✓ IP and IPX route filtering
- ✓ Distribute lists
- ✓ Policy-based routing (PBR)
- ✓ Configuring prefix lists
- ✓ Understanding and configuring route maps
- ✓ Regular Expressions
- ✓ BGP route filtering
- ✓ Configuring AS_PATH attribute filters
- ✓ Configuring community lists

Routing and switching packets is the foundation of a router. A packet arrives on an interface and the router must decide, by verifying the destination address against a forwarding table, which next hop and appropriate outgoing interface to forward the packet to. In order to populate the forwarding table, an administrator defines which routing protocols to enable on each router within an autonomous system. Routing policies are also determined on how and where to route certain packets in or out of the administered network. There are going to be times when you have no control over which routes are being sent to you from another administrative domain or how packets are forwarded outside of your domain. Whether you are administering the network or the routes are received from another network, you have to decide how to apply both inbound and outbound routing policies within your own control.

In this chapter, we will discuss various methods of filtering route updates, as well as how to use these methods to influence which prefix will be placed into the router's routing table.

Route Filters

Routing protocols advertise network reachability information to known neighboring or adjacent routers. To help control which routes are placed in the routing table and advertised out of the routing table, policies, known as route filters, can be implemented between such neighbors. The filters covered in this chapter are ones that provide the following services:

- Prevent the advertisement and/or receipt of updates through particular router interfaces

- Control which routes are placed in route advertisements and which routes are placed in the routing table based on updates received globally or on a per-neighbor basis

- Further influence routing decisions and manipulate route characteristics, values, or parameters prior to sending routing table updates as well as receiving routes.

- Control the path the traffic may take by implementing route preferences

Route filtering has a different effect on link-state routing protocols than they do on distance vector protocols. A router running a distance vector protocol advertises and receives routes based on information stored in its route table. As a result, a route filter influences which routes the router advertises to or receives from a neighbor. Routers running link-state protocols (for example, OSPF and IS-IS) exchange topology database information, which includes link-state status, through the use of link state update messages. Exchanged updates messages are then stored locally in a topology database. After SPF is run against the database, the routing table is then built and maintained based upon the best route for each destination prefix. Certain route filters, such as distribute lists, have no effect on routes exchanged in Link State Updates. Further explanation will be provided when we discuss filters and link-state protocols.

Policy Routing

The terms *policy routing* and *routing policy* are sometimes used to describe route filtering. However, the term *policy routing* as it's used in this chapter refers to *policy-based routing (PBR),* whereby policies are used to help identify a packet and forward the packet based on a predefined policy. Policy-based routing can be used to influence routing decisions as follows:

- By deciding where the traffic should be routed based on specific or different paths
- By applying Quality of Service (QoS) to identify packets to allow preferential services
- By identifying certain characteristics of a packet and forwarding the packet based on those parameters

Policy-based routing is applied only to incoming packets on a particular interface(s) and never to outgoing packets. Packets that match a policy are forwarded or routed based on criteria defined using route maps.

We'll come back to policy-based routing (PBR) later on in this chapter when we cover route maps.

Applying Route Filters and Policies

In this section, we'll cover various ways to apply routing filters and policies. In the routing protocol environment that deals with IP and IPX network reachability, distribute lists are mainly used. To further enhance filtering and defining policies, other options are available for IP. In the BGP environment, there are multiple ways to perform route filtering:

- IP and IPX route filtering
  - Distribute list
- IP routing policies and filtering
  - Prefix list
  - Route map
  - Policy-based routing (PBR)
- BGP routing policies and filtering
  - Distribute list
  - Prefix list
  - Route map
  - Filter list (AS path access list)
  - Community list

Let's get started by discussing the route filtering method that is most predominantly implemented: the distribute list.

Distribute Lists

The first concept that we'll use to control route advertisement and route updates, which is essentially route filtering, involves the `distribute-list` command. *Distribute lists* filter routes based on the content of route update messages that are either sent to a neighboring router or received from a neighboring router. Distribute list statements are placed under the routing process, where you can assign them with the aid of access list or prefix list statements and apply them to all interfaces, individual interfaces, or both.

When dealing with the distribute lists, keep the following in mind:

- Distribute list statements are placed within the routing process configured on the router. Which syntax to use will depend on whether the routing process is an IGP (RIP, IGRP, EIGRP, OSPF, etc.) or an EGP (BGP). There will be more explanation for dealing with OSPF later in this section.

- Distribute list statements can be applied in an IP and an IPX environment to filter routing updates.

- Distribute lists can be used in conjunction with the redistribution of routes from one routing process into another to limit the routes that are redistributed.

- If the distribute list is applied on an individual interface as well as globally, the route update messages are filtered against both distribute list statements. If the route update filter permitted a defined prefix on an interface level, it will then be checked against the globally defined filter as well. If both distribute lists allow the prefix, it is put in the routing table.

When using dynamic routing protocols and distribute lists to control filtering, there are some caveats to deal with:

- The most common IGP filtering mechanism prior to IOS release 12.0 was the use of distribute lists in combination with access lists. One of the biggest disadvantages with access list statements is the fact that the internal router's CPU must process each route update by comparing it against any ACL criteria. If the ACL criteria was lengthy or grew over time, then the CPU could be adversely affected. Some routing protocols, such as RIP and IGRP, must periodically send their full routing table every 30 and 90 seconds, respectively. This can also impact the router's CPU if there are a large number of routes and route updates to process. Prefix lists are more efficiently evaluated and were created to replace access lists and help alleviate CPU load.

- Distribute lists may not be the best solution for defining a routing policy in some cases. The section "Applying a `distribute-list out` (Example 3)" later in this chapter shows one solution that may not work using distribute lists.

- One possible way to control routing updates on an interface is to apply a `passive-interface` command under the specified routing process. In the case of EIGRP, RIP, and IGRP, also valid for OSPF, this would block not only the routes being sent but also any neighbor adjacencies from forming (unless unicast neighbors are configured). The section "Applying a `distribute-list out` (Example 4)" later in this chapter shows a possible solution using distribute lists to allow neighbor adjacencies to form but still deny routing updates.

When dealing with link-state IGP routing protocols, such as OSPF, distribute lists can filter routes based only on the following criteria:

- Using the `distribute-list in` command and an associated access list, you can filter routes from the local topology database from entering the local routing table.

- Neither the `distribute-list in` nor the `distribute-list out` command prevents routes from being advertised within Link State Update packets. There is one exception, and that involves OSPF autonomous system boundary routers (ASBRs).

- When dealing with OSPF area border router (ABR) routes between areas, an administrator can use the `area filter-list` command, based on prefix lists, to filter inbound or outbound interarea routes. See Cisco's CCO website for more details.

- OSPF ASBRs can use distribute lists only on routes being redistributed by the ASBR into the OSPF domain. They can be applied to External Type 1 (O E1) and External Type 2 (O E2) routes but not to intra-area (O) and interarea (O IA) routes.

Standard access lists (1–99) and extended access lists (100– 99) can be used to filter routing updates. However, standard access lists do not provide the ability to filter on a prefix range when dealing with Classless Inter-Domain Routing (CIDR) blocks. Extended access lists allow the use of wildcard bit masking to filter network prefixes and their associated masks to provide further filtering capabilities. Extended access lists can also be used to filter addresses or prefixes based on the prefix length, but you must have a solid understanding of how to use wildcard masks to filter prefixes. Because of their complexity, IP prefix lists are easier to use when filtering prefix ranges.

There are two ways to apply the distribute list command, using the `distribute-list in` and the `distribute-list out` commands. Each is very similar in syntax, but the purpose of each is very different as well as the available options:

- The `distribute-list in` command is used to control which routes will be filtered in incoming route message updates.

- The `distribute-list out` command is used to control which routes are included in outgoing route message updates.

As mention earlier, you can use numeric or named access lists with distribute lists. You can also use prefix lists with them to apply appropriate filters. The use of access lists and their syntax were covered in Chapter 16. The use of prefix lists will be covered later in this chapter.

The *distribute-list in* Command

Define an inbound routing policy using the `distribute-list in` command to control which routes will be filtered when incoming route message updates are received. To use the `distribute-list in` command, use the following syntax:

```
distribute-list [access-list-number] in [interface-name]
```

Applying a *distribute-list in* (Example 1)

In the following example, one inbound interface filter and one global distribute list filter are defined. Any inbound RIP update messages on Serial 0.2 are checked against access list 10 and any routes that match 147.19/16 to /32 are entered in the routing table. The same prefix(es) will also be checked against access list 11, which is globally defined to check all interfaces that are receiving RIP updates. Because of the `permit any` statement, any route prefix from 147.19/16 to /32 will be installed in the routing table:

```
router rip
  version 2
  distribute-list 10 in Serial 0.2
  distribute-list 11 in


access-list 10 permit 147.19.0.0 0.0.255.255
access-list 11 deny 10.0.0.0 0.255.255.255
access-list 11 deny 172.16.0.0 0.0.15.255
access-list 11 deny 192.168.0.0 0.255.255.255
access-list 11 permit any
```

Applying a *distribute-list in* (Example 2)

Inbound filtering policies can also be defined for an IPX environment. In this example, networks AAA and BBB will be allowed to enter the IPX routing table from any IPX-enabled interface:

```
ipx router rip
  network CCC
  distribute-list 810 in
  distribute-list 811 out


access-list 810 permit AAA
access-list 810 permit BBB
access-list 811 permit CCC
```

The *distribute-list out* Command

Define an outbound routing policy using the `distribute-list out` command to control which routes will be filtered when advertising route message updates. For the most part, the syntax is the same as the syntax for the `distribute-list in` option. The only difference is that the `out` option provides additional filtering based on routing protocol arguments that can be used when redistribution from another specified routing process or autonomous system takes place. To use the `distribute-list out` command, use the following syntax:

```
distribute-list [access-list-number] out [interface-name | routing process]
```

Applying a *distribute-list out* (Example 1)

In the following example, routes sourced from IGRP 100 are being redistributed into RIP. Any RIP outbound routing updates are compared against ACL 10; in this case, only networks in 147.19.0.0/16 are sent to neighboring routers:

```
router rip
  version 2
  default-metric 1
  redistribute igrp 100
  distribute-list 10 out Serial 0/0

access-list 10 permit 147.19.0.0 0.0.255.255
```

Applying a *distribute-list out* (Example 2)

The biggest difference between this example and the preceding example is based on when RIP advertises redistributed sourced IGRP routes. RIP, by default, will advertise routes every 30 seconds, IGRP every 90 seconds. If the commands in Example 1 were used, all IGRP sourced routes will be sent every 30 seconds to neighboring RIP routers. If there were a lot of 147.19 subnets being sent in the RIP update, you could possibly encounter a CPU load trying to process the distribute list ACL/route update every 30 seconds. This example illustrates a cleaner method that allows sourced IGRP routes to be sent only every 90 seconds based on when IGRP updates are redistributed into RIP:

```
router rip
  default-metric 1                Routes redistributed into RIP will have
                                  a hop-count metric of 1

  redistribute igrp 100           Redistribute IGRP AS 100 routes into RIP

  distribute-list 1 out igrp 100  Advertise only prefixes defined by ACL 1,
                                  which are derived from the IGRP AS 100
                                  redistribution process, every 90 seconds.
                                  Possible CPU load is reduced

access-list 1 permit 147.19.0.0 0.0.255.255


                                  Send only 147.19.0.0/16 networks to
                                  neighboring RIP routers
```

Applying a *distribute-list out* (Example 3)

When you're defining routing policies, distribute lists statements may not be the best solution. Figure 17.1 shows a RIP-enabled environment in which next-hop reachability is based on hop count and not bandwidth. To reach 147.19.2.0 /24, R1 will prefer the 64K link via Serial 0.1 to the T3 links via Serial 0.2. You could possibly define a route policy using the distribute list command allowing all traffic destined for R2 to prefer the three hops via Serial 0.2. Bandwidth- and delay-wise, this would be the best path, but this method would not allow for any failover situation if any of the T3 links fail. Other possible solutions, such as an offset list, can better control any routing policies.

FIGURE 17.1 distribute-list out Example 3

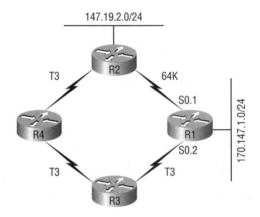

Here is the configuration from router R1:

```
router rip
 version 2
 distribute-list 11 in Serial 0.1
 distribute-list 11 out Serial 0.1
 distribute-list 12 in Serial 0.2
 distribute-list 13 out Serial 0.2

access-list 11 deny any
access-list 12 permit 147.19.2.0 0.0.0.255
access-list 13 permit 170.147.1.0 0.0.0.255
```

Applying a *distribute-list out* (Example 4)

In most IGP routing environments, the passive-interface statement is a possible method for stopping routing updates from being sent out an interface. However, for EIGRP, this statement will also block any EIGRP neighbor adjacencies from happening. Using the commands in this example will allow EIGRP neighbor adjacencies to form across interface Serial 0/0 and still block any updates from being sent. EIGRP routes inbound will still be received:

```
router eigrp 100
 distribute-list 10 out serial 0/0


access-list 10 deny any
```

Using a Distribute List in BGP

BGP autonomous system (AS) route advertisements can be filtered to or from a particular External Border Gateway Protocol (eBGP) neighbor by using route filters such as neighbor distribute-list (used with filter lists), neighbor filter-list, and neighbor route-map commands. This section covers the use of distribute lists to filter routes based on individual eBGP neighbors or routes defined for multiple neighbors using peer group statements. Filtering routes using filter lists and route maps will be covered later in this chapter. To use the neighbor distribute-list command, use the following syntax:

```
neighbor [ip-address|peer-group-name] distribute-list
    [access-list] [in|out]
```

Applying a Distribute List with a Standard Access List

In this example, router R1 is receiving network 147.23.10.0 /24 from peer 147.20.1.2, AS 65011. A distribute list filter is being applied to peer 147.21.1.2 to stop this route from being advertised to AS 65012. All other networks will be advertised:

```
router bgp 65010
 network 147.19.0.0
 neighbor 147.20.1.2 remote-as 65011
 neighbor 147.21.1.2 remote-as 65012
 neighbor 147.21.1.2 distribute-list 10 out


access-list 10 deny 147.23.10.0 0.0.0.255
access-list 10 permit any
```

Once the BGP TCP session and peering have been established between two BGP neighbors, routing information will be exchanged. Any filters applied to a neighbor will be applied at the time of peering. If subsequent changes to the filter are made by altering the ACL criteria, a BGP neighbor must be reset using a soft or hard reset command in order for the new filter list to take effect.

Applying a Distribute List with an Extended Access List

Configuring distribute lists using extended access lists can be confusing at first. Wildcard bits are used to mask against prefixes as well as the network mask. Wildcard bit masks are similar to the bit masks used with other access lists. When used to compare against a prefix or mask, a binary 0 equals a match and a binary 1 is an ignore or a "don't care" match. The following extended access list example will permit route 147.19.1/24 but deny 147.19/16 and all other subnets of 147.19.0.0:

```
router bgp 65010
 network 147.19.0.0
 neighbor 100.100.100.1 distribute-list 110 out

access-list 110 permit ip 147.19.1.0 0.0.0.255 any
access-list 110 deny ip 147.19.0.0 0.0.255.255 any
access-list 110 permit ip any any
```

Filtering Routes Based on Prefix Length

Extended access list configuration can be used to filter prefixes based on the prefix length. The following extended access list example will deny all prefixes that are longer than 25 bits and permit all of shorter prefixes:

```
router bgp 65010
 network 147.19.0.0
 neighbor 100.100.100.1 distribute-list 110 in

access-list 110 deny   ip any 255.255.255.128 0.0.0.127
access-list 110 permit ip any any
```

IP Prefix Lists

In the previous sections, we used distribute lists in conjunction with access lists to define which incoming routes to receive or which outgoing routes to advertise. By far, distribute lists are most commonly used when defining a routing policy because they cover both IGP and BGP routing protocols. However, the biggest disadvantage when using distribute lists is the fact that they require the use of access list, which can be very CPU intensive as the access list criteria grow.

IP *prefix lists* are yet another way to define and restrict routing information by defining which routes to advertise and which routes to receive. With their introduction in IOS release 12.0, prefix lists can be used to replace access lists when defining filters. They are a vast improvement, with both CPU and route lookup, over ACLs when large filter lists have to be defined. Another big advantage when using prefix lists is that they support incremental changes by allowing the administrator to add or delete individual entries without adversely having to change the entire policy.

In this section, we'll cover the different ways to define prefix lists and how they are applied within an IGP and BGP policy. When applying prefix lists, the rules are very similar to the rules for applying access list criteria. When defining prefix list statements, the following rules should be used:

- If no prefix list statements are defined but they are being called by another configuration statement (see Applying Prefix Lists in BGP below), all prefixes will be accepted and installed in the routing table for use. An empty prefix list permits all prefixes.

- Sequence prefix lists criteria are in the order they should be processed. The router begins the search for a match at the top of the prefix list, which is indicated by the statement with the lowest sequence number.

- When a match occurs, the router doesn't need to go through the rest of the prefix list. Put the most commonly used matches (permits or denies) near the top of the list by specifying a lower sequence number.

- As with access lists, an implicit deny is defined at the end of each prefix list for any given prefix that does not match any entries of any prefix list. To help define what filter action should be taken if no other prefix list statement matches, whether the intent is to deny or allow all other prefixes, the last prefix list statement should define a default list.

- Prefix lists can be used in conjunction with route maps, which will be discussed later in this chapter.

The syntax used to define prefix list statements is as follows:

```
ip prefix-list [list-number] seq [seq-value] [deny|permit]
   network/length] [ge ge-value] [le le-value]
      OR
ip prefix-list list-name [seq seq-value] [deny|permit] IP prefix
   <network>/<length> [ge ge-value] [le le-value]
```

It's important to understand certain parts of the command:

sequence-number   As with standard and extended access lists, a numeric value can be used to identify prefix lists. However, sequence numbers are not limited to 1–199.

list-name   The list-name value must be unique per prefix list, per type, and per router. Assign a meaningful name that describes the function the prefix list is going to perform and that everyone else can easily understand. Names are case sensitive. Within the name, characters such as -, _, ., !, @, #, $, &, (,), [,], {, and } can be used. No spaces should be included between any characters.

seq-value   This is an optional keyword that defines the order in which the prefix list criteria is to be processed. Sequence numbers are 32 bits in length, and if no value is specified, the default is to start at sequence number 5 and increment each subsequent statement by 5 (5, 10, 15, etc.) unless otherwise defined by an administrator. Values range from 1 to 4294967294. If you define your own sequencing numbers, leave numeric space between each statement to allow any additional prefix list statements to be added in the future, if required. If you define the first sequence number (for example, 4) and do not specify any subsequent sequence entries, the sequence values will still increment by 5 (9, 14, 19, etc.). Individual statements can be deleted by using the no command in front of the ip prefix-list list-name seq seq-value command.

ge-value   This is an optional keyword. The ge keyword means greater than or equal to the value of value, which is the range of the prefix length to be matched. The range of the prefix length to be matched for prefixes that are more specific than network/len. The range is assumed to equal the value of ge-value up to 32 if only the ge attribute is specified. You may optionally use this keyword in combination with the le keyword to define a lesser range. When using ge and/or le values, make sure len < ge-value <= le-value.

le-value   This is an optional keyword. The le keyword means lesser than or equal to the value of value, which is the range of the prefix length to be matched. The range of the prefix length to be matched for prefixes that are more specific than network/len. The range is assumed to be from the len argument to the le-value if only the le attribute is specified.

Applying Prefix Lists in BGP

Filter incoming or outgoing route updates to and/or from a defined neighbor or peer group. For any given neighbor, do not apply both a neighbor distribute-list and a neighbor prefix-list command in any given direction, inbound or outbound. Either command applies the same function. Only one in or out command can be applied to each inbound or outbound direction. Let's look at the command syntax for applying a prefix-list to a BGP neighbor:

```
neighbor [ip-address|peer-group-name] prefix-list-name [in|out]
```

Now, let's look at a more realistic example of applying a prefix-list to a BGP neighbor:

```
router bgp 200
 neighbor 100.100.100.1 remote-as 100
 neighbor 100.100.100.1 prefix-list Filter_AS100 in
```

> Used in the same way as distribute-list
> with access-list statements

```
ip prefix-list Filter_AS100 description Filter routes from AS100

ip prefix-list Filter_AS100 seq 5 deny 0.0.0.0/0
```

> Deny any default route

```
ip prefix-list Filter_AS100 seq 7 deny 0.0.0.0/0 ge 25
```

> Deny any prefixes that match a Length
> of /25 or greater

```
ip prefix-list Filter_AS100 seq 9 permit 0.0.0.0/0 le 24
```

> Permit everything else

Applying Prefix Lists with Route Maps

In the following example, a route map is used to apply an outbound policy and filter. Any route prefix with a length of /24 or less will have a BGP MED value of 200 added. Any other route prefix that matches a length of /25 to /32 will not be sent (see the next section for further details on how to apply route-map statements):

```
router bgp 200
 neighbor 100.100.100.1 remote-as 100
 neighbor 100.100.100.1 route-map PREFIX out
```

```
ip prefix-list Filter_out seq 1 permit 0.0.0.0/0 le 24
```

```
route-map PREFIX permit 10
 match ip address prefix-list Filter_out
```

```
 set metric 200                          Apply a MED value of 200 to all routes
                                         defined by the prefix-list
```

Route Maps

We have dealt with two ways to manipulate which route prefixes are sent or received during the route update processes and how filtering is related to specific routing protocols, both in an IGP and BGP environment. As well, we have covered ways to filter routes when redistributing from one routing process into another.

This next topic is *route maps*, which provide a more robust approach when dealing with managing routing policies and route redistribution. When dealing with route maps, you must be able to identify which routes or packets, based on certain values or attributes, must match before you can define which routing policy(ies) to apply. Route maps provide a way for you to define these conditions by using the match argument within the route-map statements. Multiple match statements are applied using AND logic to help identify packets or routes even further. In most cases, once the prefixes have been identified by using the set argument, you can define the routing policy by manipulating certain routing information or defining packet forwarding. Use the following syntax when defining route-map statements:

```
route-map route-map-tag [permit|deny] [seq-number]
 match [condition]
 set [parameters]
```

It's important to understand certain parts of the command:

route-map-tag   The route-map-tag keyword defines the name of the route map. The name must be unique per route map. Assign a meaningful name that describes the function the route map is going to perform and that everyone else can easily understand. Names are case sensitive.

seq-number   Indicates the position that a new route-map statement will have in the list of route-map statements already configured with the same name. If the initial sequence number is not applied after the permit or deny keywords, the default will start with sequence number 10.

Subsequent sequence numbers will not be automatically incremented. When defining route-map statements in the same route map policy, you may want to do the following:

- Include a default behavior for all remaining route prefixes that have not been matched in the prior route-map statements. The default behavior will be listed as the last route map sequence number.

- Leave numeric space between sequence numbers (for example, 10, 20, 30) to allow for additional route maps statements to be added if the need arises.

- Put the most-used `match` arguments at the top. Route-map statements are read in sequential order based on the sequence number provided.

Defining the Match Criteria

Route-map match statements are used to define the conditions to be checked:

- A match statement may have several conditions. Only one condition must be true for that match statement to be considered a match (for example, match community 101 102).

- A single `route-map` command may include one or more match statements; however, all match statements must be true for the `route-map` command to be considered a match and any set commands to be invoked.

- If no match statement is specified under the route-map statement, the default is to match everything.

- If the packet is being policy routed, the following applies:
  - If permit | match is used, a packet that matches the applied route map will invoke any set commands and be policy routed.
  - If deny | match is used, a packet that does not match the applied route map is forwarded through normal routing processes.
  - If no further match statements are used or if there is an implicit deny, a packet will not be policy routed and will be forwarded through normal routing processes.

- If the route is being redistributed, the following applies:
  - If permit | match is used, a route that matches the applied route map will invoke any set commands and be redistributed.
  - If deny | match is used, a route that matches the applied route map is not redistributed.
  - If no further match statements are used or if there is an implicit deny, the route will not be redistributed.

- If the route is being applied to a BGP policy, the following applies:
  - If permit | match is used, a route that matches the applied route map will invoke any set commands.

- If deny | match is used, a route that matches the applied route map will not be advertised.

- If no further match statements are used or if there is an implicit deny, the route will not be advertised.

There are many optional methods of specifying the match criteria, such as by AS path, community list, extcommunity (extended community), interface, IP address, next hop, length, metric, and so on.

Defining the Set Criteria

The set criteria is used to define the actions to be followed if there is a match:

- In some conditions, match statements may not require the use of the `set` argument.

- One or more set commands can be used. Each set will be applied.

There are many optional methods of specifying the set criteria, such as by AS path, community list, community, dampening, default interface, extcommunity, interface, ip default next hop, next hop, precedence, local preference, metric, origin, weight, and so on.

Next we'll discuss how route maps can be utilized to perform policy-based routing (PBR).

Policy-Based Routing (PBR)

Route maps can be used in conjunction with the `ip policy` interface command to perform PBR on an inbound interface basis or with the `ip local policy` global command to affect all traffic generated locally by the router leaving any interface.

Use route maps to define routing policies (the use of routing polices is known as policy-based routing, or PBR. PBR allows packets to be forwarded based on when they match a predefined source IP address, protocol type, port number, and so on. The router will forward the packet to a specified next hop address or out a specified interface. You can enable PBR on a particular interface or globally using the following commands:

- Use the `ip policy route-map map-tag` interface command to match packets entering the router.

- Use the `ip local policy route-map map-tag` global command to match packets that are generated from the router itself, such as routing protocol packets.

Remember that when you create a route map to be used in PBR, there are many match and set options that you can choose from, as you'll see in the examples in the following sections.

Policy-Based Routing (Example 1)

In this example, we will apply PBR on the inbound interface (Ethernet0/0). We want all traffic with a destination IP address of 192.1.1.0/24 to be routed out of the router's serial0/0 interface and all traffic with a destination IP address of 192.1.2.0/24 to be routed out of the router's serial0/1 interface:

```
interface Ethernet0/0
 ip policy route-map kelly

route-map kelly permit 10
 match ip address 101
 set interface serial0/0
route-map kelly permit 20
 match ip address 102
 set interface serial0/1


access-list 101 permit ip any 192.1.1.0 0.255.255.255
access-list 102 permit ip any 192.1.2.0 0.255.255.255
```

This is actually providing the same functionality as a static route because it is directing the specified destination traffic out of a specified interface toward the destination. Let's look at another example.

Policy-Based Routing (Example 2)

In this example, we want all IP packets inbound on interface Ethernet0/0 with a packet length of 3 to 500 bytes to be directed to a next hop of 150.1.1.2 and all IP packets inbound on interface Ethernet0/0 with a packet length of 501 to 1500 bytes to be directed to a next hop of 150.1.1.6:

```
interface Ethernet0/0

 ip policy route-map chris


route-map chris permit 10

 match length 3 500             Packet length 3 to 500 bytes

 set ip next-hop 150.1.1.2      Direct these packets to the next-hop at
                                other end of the serial link
route-map chris permit 20

 match length 501 1500          Packet length 501 to 1500 bytes

 set ip next-hop 150.1.1.6      Direct these packets to the next-hop at
                                other end of the serial link
```

What if we want to affect all traffic locally generated within a router? In that case, we will have to use the `ip local policy` global command. Let's look at an example of this command.

Policy Based Routing (Example 3)

In this example, we want to set all Telnet-based packets generated by the router itself to an IP precedence level of critical (IP precedence level 5):

```
route-map josh permit 10

 match ip address 199

 set ip precedence critical                    Set IP Precedence to 5


ip local policy route-map josh                 Apply as a GLOBAL command


access-list 199 permit tcp any eq 23 any
access-list 199 permit tcp any any eq 23
```

Notice that access list 199 specifies all Telnet-based (tcp port 23) packets in either direction (as the source or the destination).

Policy-based routing (PBR) is a useful tool for influencing a routing decision within a router. Remember that the PBR will affect only the router on which it is implemented because it is locally significant. It will *not* affect a routing decision of any other routing device in the network.

In the next section, we'll discuss regular expressions; you'll need a good understanding of these before we can discuss the AS path access list.

Using Regular Expressions (*regexp*)

Before we get into configuring BGP-related filters, it is important that you have a solid understanding of how to define regular expressions because they are a prerequisite to configuring AS_PATH access lists or community list filters. When dealing with a Unix shell operating system, you can use regular expressions to search for files by specifying filenames or partial filenames, to search for content within a file(s), or to change file contents. A *regular expression* is a pattern string that can be composed of letters, numbers, and special symbols that are used to match against one or more strings. When regular expressions are defined, some characters have special meaning; these characters are called *metacharacters*. Other characters are interpreted as themselves; they are known as literals. You construct a regular expression by combining literals with one or more metacharacters:

- Metacharacters are special characters that have specific meanings. They are used in regular expressions as wildcards, delimiters, and other special pattern-matching characters. (Examples have been provided in Table 17.1.)

- Literals are letters and numbers that are interpreted as themselves. Examples of literals are 1–9 and A–Z. They can be grouped together using metacharacters, such as commas, hyphens, braces, and so on, or used by themselves.

With an understanding of regular expressions, you can define simple or complex filters to search for database information stored on the local router. BGP AS_PATH access list filters and community list filters can use regular expressions to search the BGP table for a set of strings or characters that match on AS_PATH or COMMUNITIES attribute information, respectively. Each will be covered further in the next few sections.

The best way to learn and define regular expressions is by seeing them as examples. The intent of this section is to show many examples of regular expressions and the metacharacters that are used within them. The examples match on examples of AS_PATH attribute information but can also be applied based on COMMUNITIES attributes as well. Table 17.1 includes a list of metacharacters used in regular expressions.

TABLE 17.1   Metacharacters

Metacharacter	Name	Meaning
.	Period	Match any single character against an input string, including white space.
*	Asterisk	Match zero or more occurrences of the character or pattern.
+	Plus sign	Match one or more occurrences of the character or pattern.
?	Question mark	Match any one character that may or may not be included. Note: Use Ctrl+V prior to entering the ?. Otherwise, the ? will be interpreted as a command-line question.
^	Caret	Match the character(s) at the beginning of the string of characters or that the string of characters starts with.
$	Dollar sign	Match the character(s) at the end of the string of characters or that the string of characters ends with.
_	Underscore	Match a specific character at the beginning of string (^), end of a string ($), left or right parenthesis (( )), left or right brace ({}), comma (,), or just white space ( ).

TABLE 17.1 Metacharacters *(continued)*

Metacharacter	Name	Meaning
[ ]	Brackets	Match any character value(s) listed between the brackets; one character or a range of characters may be listed.
[^]	Caret within brackets	Match any character value(s) except those listed between the brackets.
-	Hyphen	Match any character in the range between the two literals separated by the hyphen.
|	Pipe or vertical bar	Perform an OR operation by using either of the literals separated by this metacharacter.
( )	Parentheses	Match on all character value(s) listed between the parentheses, taken together as a unit.
\	Backslash	Remove the special character meaning and match on the next single character that precedes the backslash. Each of the other characters in this table has a special meaning when defining regular expression. If you are searching a string that may contain one of these characters, use the backslash character to match

Examples of Regular Expressions

Let's look at some syntax examples of Regular Expressions:

60	No metacharacters, match not only 60, but also 600, 6000, 460, etc., if in AS_PATH
_700_	Match any routes that passes through AS 700, match on a single instance of AS 700 anywhere in AS_PATH. AS 700 would be a transit AS, or was prepended to the AS_PATH somewhere along the route to the destination prefix
_700_400_	Match AS_PATH with 700, 400 in path (200 700 400), (200 700 400 750), etc

^700_	Match AS_PATH that begins with AS700, (700, 400) (700 400 750) and so on
_700$	Match AS_PATH that ends with, or originated from AS700, (400 700) (660 400 700) and so on
^700_400$	Must match AS_PATH (700 400) only
^$	All routes originating in your AS (no literals / internal routes will have an empty AS_PATH information; therefore, only internal AS subnets will be forwarded)
^700$	Only routes that originated from AS 700 and did not pass through any other AS
^84[01359]$	Filter matches AS_PATH with any single AS number (840,841,843,845,or 849)
^84[0-4]$	Filter matches AS_PATH with any single AS number (840,841,842,842,843,or 844)
^[2-6]00$	Filter matches AS_PATH with any single AS number (200,300,400,500 or 600)
^[246]00$	Filter matches AS_PATH with any single AS number (200, 400 or 600)
^84[^0-4]$	Filter matches AS_PATH with any single AS number except 840-844 (i.e. match 845 - 849)
^(841| 842)$	Filter matches AS_PATH with any single AS number, match 841 or 842
^(840)?$	Filter matches AS_PATH with any single AS number or an empty list, matches what is listed in brackets, AS 840, if no AS 840 then empty AS_PATH list. The 840 may or may not be there
_840?$	Filter matches AS_PATH with an AS number that matches 84 or 840 at the end. The question mark is questioning the last character. The 0 may or may not be there. (100 84) or (100 840)
.*	Using the . and the * together can be used to indicate all routes. Usually used at end of an ACL if using prior deny statements. Can be used to indicate a permit any

Verifying Regular Expressions

Now let's briefly discuss the `show ip bgp regexp` command, which allows the verification of BGP prefixes, which match a specified Regular Expression.

```
show ip bgp regexp [regular expression]
```
This shows all the paths that have matched the configured regular expression

Regular expressions are utilized heavily with BGP, so now that you have a good understanding of regular expressions, we'll move on to discuss BGP route filtering.

BGP Route Filtering

The primary function of a Border Gateway Protocol (BGP) speaker is to exchange Network Layer Reachability Information (NRLI) with other BGP speakers. Included within each update message, each NRLI network prefix/prefix length pair contains information about the list of autonomous system paths as well as other path attributes. Both inbound and outbound BGP updates can be controlled by using different filtering methods that filter based on route information, on AS path information, or on communities. BGP updates can be filtered using the following types of lists:

- Distribute lists based on applied access lists, which are filtered based on identifying a network prefix or prefixes
- Alternatively, IP prefix lists in place of access lists in many BGP route filtering policies
- AS path access lists to filter routes based on BGP's autonomous system (AS) paths, defined by identifying the AS_PATH attribute
- Community list filters based on identifying the BGP's COMMUNITIES attribute

Distribute lists and IP prefix lists were mentioned earlier in this chapter; the next two sections describe how to configure BGP router filters using regular expressions to help identify BGP AS_PATH and COMMUNITIES attributes.

AS Path Access Lists

The BGP *AS_PATH* is a well-known, mandatory attribute that must be recognized by all BGP implementations and is one of the main deciding factors when choosing the best route/path to a given prefix. This attribute identifies the autonomous systems (ASs) through which the routing information (carried in an update message) has passed in order to reach a destination. When an eBGP speaker propagates a route that it has learned from another eBGP neighbor, it will modify the route's AS_PATH attribute to include its own AS information. If the route prefix originated from within its own AS, the route update message will contain only the originating speaker's AS. Route updates within an iBGP environment remain unchanged.

Using *AS path access lists* or BGP AS path filters, you can define routing policies based on the AS path information contained in the update messages. Prefixes containing AS_PATH information can be identified using regular expressions. AS path filters can be applied using a route map or filter list applied on a per-neighbor basis using the `neighbor` command. Routes that do not match the AS path access lists are unaffected. Use the following syntax when defining AS path filters (`as-regular-expression` is a regular expression to match the BGP AS paths):

```
ip as-path access-list access-list-number [permit|deny] as-regular-expression
```

Applying AS Path Filters

Use these commands to establish BGP policies using BGP neighbor statements:

```
neighbor [ip-address|peer-group-name] filter-list as-path access-
   list-number [in|out]
neighbor [ip-address|peer-group-name] filter-list as-path access-
   list-number weight
```

Use this command to establish BGP policies using route-map statements:

```
neighbor [ip address | peer-group] route-map [route-map-name] [in|out]

route-map map-name

match as-path   [as-path access-list number]      Multiple lists can be used
```

AS PATH FILTERS (EXAMPLE 1)

The following example defines policies and filters based on using AS path access lists. BGP peer groups are used to define the same update policy, with the exception of one BGP neighbor, 147.19.16.9. All outbound updates defined by a peer group and that originate from AS 307 will have a BGP *multi-exit discriminator (MED)* of 200 applied. No other outbound routes will be changed. All inbound routes defined by a peer group will allow only those routes that have AS 306, 316, 326, 336, 346, or 356 in the update. One neighbor in the peer group, 147.19.16.13, will override the inbound update policy by applying its own AS path filter:

```
router bgp 307

 network 147.19.1.1 mask 255.255.255.255

 neighbor externalAS peer-group

 neighbor externalAS ebgp-multihop 2

 neighbor externalAS update-source Loopback0

 neighbor externalAS route-map applyMED out

                              Apply a MED of 200 for all outbound
                              bound routes that originated from
                              this AS, leave MED alone for all
                              other routes

 neighbor externalAS filter-list 10 out
```

Update outbound filter applied to all peers

```
neighbor externalAS filter-list 11 in
```

Update inbound filter applied to all peers

```
neighbor 147.19.3.1 remote-as 346

neighbor 147.19.3.1 peer-group externalAS

neighbor 147.19.5.1 remote-as 306

neighbor 147.19.5.1 peer-group externalAS

neighbor 147.19.7.1 remote-as 316

neighbor 147.19.7.1 peer-group externalAS

neighbor 147.19.7.1 filter-list 12 in
```

By applying and individual filter-list you can override filter-list 11 inside the peer group. You can only affect inbound route updates

```
neighbor 147.19.9.1 remote-as 308

neighbor 147.19.9.1 ebgp-multihop 2

neighbor 147.19.9.1 update-source Loopback0

ip as-path access-list 10 permit _30[8-9]_
```

Send only those routes that have an AS 308 or 309 anywhere in the AS path. Routes that originate from AS 307 will not be sent

```
ip as-path access-list 11 permit _3[0-5]6$
```

Receive only those routes that have originated from AS 306, 316, 326, 336, 346 or 356

```
ip as-path access-list 12 permit .*        Permit everything

ip as-path access-list 20 permit ^$        Applied on routes from AS 307

route-map applyMED permit 10

 match as-path 20
```

```
set metric 200
```
Those routes that originated from this AS will have a BGP MED attribute of 200 added

```
route-map applyMED permit 20
```
All other routes will be sent unaffected

AS PATH FILTERS (EXAMPLE 2)

In the following example, routes that have passed through any of these ASs (840, 841, 843, 845, or 849) will have a weight of 300 applied. Routes that begin with AS 842 or 844 will have a weight of 400 applied. Those routes that do not match the filter-list statements within the AS path will have a weight of 500 applied:

```
router bgp 847

 neighbor 147.19.16.1 remote-as 846

 neighbor 147.19.16.1 filter-list 10 weight 300

 neighbor 147.19.16.1 filter-list 11 weight 400
```
Multiple filter-list weight commands to a neighbor may exist

```
 neighbor 147.19.16.1 weight 500
```
Both the commands can be used together. Any route not covered in the above filter-list statements will be covered with this command. The neighbor filter-list weight takes precedence over this command

```
ip as-path access-list 10 permit _84[01359]_
```
Transit AS 840, 841, 843, 845 or 849 in the AS_PATH

```
ip as-path access-list 11 permit ^(842 | 844)_
```
AS 842 or 844 at the beginning of the AS_PATH

Now that you understand AS path access list, we'll discuss the BGP community list. Using BGP communities is an efficient method of controlling routes within a large BGP environment. We discussed what a BGP Community was back in Chapter 12, so now we'll show you how you can use the communities you create to affect routing decisions.

BGP Community Lists

You have already seen route filtering based on route maps and AS path filtering based on AS path access lists. Another method for controlling routes is community filtering. The BGP COMMUNITIES attribute is defined as an optional, transitive attribute. Administrators can tag routes with the COMMUNITIES attribute to identify them as belonging to a certain community. Once the route has been identified as belonging to a member of a community, routers can watch for communities on route advertisements and apply routing policies, such as filtering incoming/outgoing routes or redistribution policies, based on the COMMUNITIES attribute.

Once the COMMUNITIES attribute has been applied using route maps, another router, either external or internal to the BGP domain, can use *community-list* statements to identify which routes to look for and take certain action against those routes. Use the following global command when defining community-list statements:

```
ip community-list [community standard-list-number]
```

Standard Numeric Community List

In the following example, any route that matches community-list 1, which identifies any route that has either COMMUNITIES attribute 100:20 or 200:10 or both, has its weight set to 40. Any route whose COMMUNITIES attribute matches only 300:40 and 400:50 (using the **exact** keyword) has its weight set to 60:

```
ip community-list 10 permit 100:20 200:10
```

One statement to identify two different communities

OR

```
ip community-list 11 permit 300:40
```

Two statements to identify two different communities

```
ip community-list 11 permit 400:50


ip bgp-community new-format


router bgp 100
  neighbor 147.19.16.1 remote-as 200
  neighbor 147.19.16.1 route-map apply-weight in
```

```
route-map apply-weight permit 5

 match community 10

 set weight 40


route-map apply-weight permit 10

 match community 11 exact

 set weight 60
```

Extended Numeric Community List/Regular Expression

In the following example, regular expressions will be used to identify communities. Any route that matches community list 110, which identifies any community attribute of $100.x0$ (x = any numeric value), will be sent with a local preference of 200. Any route that matches community list 120, which identifies any community attribute of x:10 (x = any AS numeric value), will be sent with a local preference of 300. Any route that matches community list 10, which identifies any community attribute of no-export, will not be advertised. All other communities will be permitted by community list 130 with a local preference of 100 (default):

`ip community-list 110 permit 100:.0`	Match communities such as 100:10, 100:20, 100:30, etc.
`ip community-list 120 permit :10`	Match communities such as 300:10, 4:10, 65000:10, etc.
`ip community-list 10 permit no-export`	Match any route with the community attribute of no-export
`ip community-list 130 permit .*`	Match any other community attribute

```
ip bgp-community new-format


router bgp 100

 neighbor 147.19.16.1 remote-as 100

 neighbor 147.19.16.1 route-map apply-LP out

route-map apply-LP permit 10

 match community 110
```

```
set local-preference 200


route-map apply-LP permit 20

 match community 120

 set local-preference 300


route-map apply-LP deny 30

 match community 10


route-map apply-LP permit 40

 match community 130
```
                                           `Match routes with any other`
                                           `community attribute. Local`
                                           `preference will default to 100`

That completes our discussion of various route filtering mechanisms. There are other route filtering mechanisms available, but we discussed only the main methods utilized in the networking industry.

Summary

In this chapter, we discussed various methods to filter routes within the IP environment. We also briefly discussed route filtering in the IPX environment. It is extremely important that you understand this functionality, because no matter which networking environment you're working in, you will most likely be required to filter routes. You may have to filter routes in order to prevent a routing loop within the route redistribution, or perhaps you will need to filter routes to create a desired routing environment. Therefore, it is imperative that you understand the use of distribute lists to provide route filtering.

Likewise, you need to understand the use of prefix lists, community lists, and AS path access lists to specify certain routes for filtering, and you need to understand how to use them in the route selection process.

And finally, we discussed using route maps to create match/set statements. Match/set statements are similar in concept to what in the programming world is known as if/then statements, meaning that *if* a certain criteria is met, *then* perform a certain action. Route maps are extremely versatile and useful, and as you get more comfortable using them, you may wonder how you ever made routing work without them.

Exam Essentials

Know what a distribute list is.   Distribute lists filter routes based on the content of route update messages that are either sent to a neighboring router or received from a neighboring router. Distribute-list statements are placed under the routing process, where you can globally assign them.

Understand how prefix lists are used.   Prefix lists are used to define and restrict routing information by defining which routes to advertise and which routes to receive. Prefix lists can be used to replace access lists when defining filters. In terms of both CPU usage and route-lookup, they are a vast improvement over ACLs when large filter lists have to be defined. Another big advantage when using prefix lists is that they support incremental changes by allowing the administrator to add or delete individual entries without adversely having to change the entire policy.

Know what a route map is.   A route map provides a more robust approach when dealing with managing routing policies and route redistribution. When dealing with route maps, you must first be able to identify which routes or packets, based on certain values or attributes, must match before you can define which routing policy(ies) to apply. Route maps provide a way for you to define these conditions to by using the `match` argument within the route-map statements. Several match arguments can be used to help identify packets or routes even further.

Understand how to use regular expressions.   A regular expression is a pattern string that can be composed of letters, numbers, and special symbols that are used to match against one or more strings. When defining regular expressions, some characters have special meaning (metacharacters), and others are interpreted as themselves (literals).

What is the purpose of an AS path access list.   An AS path access list is used for routing policies based on the AS path information contained in the update messages. Prefixes containing AS_PATH information can be identified using regular expressions. AS path filters can be applied using a route map or applied on a per-neighbor basis using the `neighbor` command.

Key Terms

Before you take the exam, be certain you are familiar with the following terms:

AS path access lists	policy routing
AS_PATH	policy-based routing (PBR)
community-list	prefix lists
distribute lists	regular expression
metacharacters	route maps
multi-exit discriminator (MED)	

Review Questions

1. Distribute lists filter routes based on what?

    A. Source IP address of the neighboring router

    B. Destination IP address of the neighboring router

    C. Content of route update messages

    D. Source and destination port number

2. What are two ways to apply the `distribute-list` command?

    A. `distribute-group in`

    B. `distribute-group out`

    C. `distribute-list in`

    D. `distribute-list out`

3. Once the BGP TCP session and peering have been established between two BGP neighbors, routing information will be exchanged. What must be done if subsequent changes to the filter are made by altering the ACL criteria? (Choose all that apply.)

    A. Shut down the neighbor interface

    B. Perform a hard reset

    C. Perform a soft reset

    D. Use `clear ip route *`

4. If no prefix list statements are defined but they are being called by another configuration statement, what prefixes will be permitted?

    A. None. All prefixes are denied.

    B. Odd prefixes *only*.

    C. All prefixes will be permitted.

    D. Even prefixes *only*.

5. What prefix list criteria defines the order in which the prefix-list statements will be processed?

    A. `sequence-number`

    B. `seq-value`

    C. `ge-value`

    D. `le-value`

    E. `list-name`

6. Which route filtering mechanism utilizes match and set commands?

   A. Distribute list

   B. Prefix list

   C. AS path access list

   D. Route maps

   E. Community list

7. A route-map statement can be configured to contain how many match statements?

   A. One

   B. Two

   C. More than one

   D. All of the above

8. Which of the following is a pattern string that can be composed of letters, numbers, and special symbols that are used to match against one or more strings?

   A. Match statement

   B. Regular expression

   C. Set statement

9. Which of the following AS path statements will match only routes that originated from AS 700 and did not pass through any other AS?

   A. $^700_

   B. *700^

   C. _700_

   D. ^700$

10. Once the COMMUNITIES attribute has been applied using route maps, what would you use to identify which routes to look for so certain action can be taken against those routes?

   A. Distribute list

   B. Prefix list

   C. AS path access list

   D. Route maps

   E. Community list

Answers to Review Questions

1. C. Distribute lists filter routes based on the content of route update messages that are either sent to a neighboring router or received from a neighboring router.

2. C, D. There are two ways to apply the `distribute-list` command: `distribute-list in` and `distribute-list out`.

3. B, C. Once the BGP TCP session and peering have been established between two BGP neighbors, routing information will be exchanged. Any filters applied to these neighbor pairs will be applied at the time of peering. If subsequent changes to the filter are made by altering the ACL criteria, the BGP neighbor pair must be reset using a soft or hard reset command in order for the new filter list to take effect.

4. C. If no prefix list statements are defined but they are being called by another configuration statement all prefixes will be accepted and installed in the routing table for use. An empty prefix list permits all prefixes.

5. B. The optional keyword `seq-value` defines the order in which the prefix list criteria is to be processed. Sequence numbers are 32 bits in length, and if no value is specified, the default is to start at sequence number 5 and increment each subsequent statement by 5 (5, 10, 15, etc.) unless otherwise defined by an administrator.

6. D. Route maps provide a way to define match and set conditions by using the `match` argument within the route-map statements. Several `match` arguments can be used to help identify packets or routes even further. In most cases, once the prefixes have been identified, you can use the `set` argument to define the routing policy by manipulating certain routing information or defining packet forwarding.

7. D. A single `route-map` statement may include one or more match statements; however, all match statements must be true for the `route-map` command to be considered a match and any set commands to be invoked.

8. B. A regular expression is a pattern string that can be composed of letters, numbers, and special symbols that are used to match against one or more strings.

9. D. The statement ^700$ permits only routes that originated from AS 700 and did not pass through any other AS.

10. E. Once the COMMUNITIES attribute has been applied using route maps, another router, either external or internal to the BGP domain, can use community-list statements to identify which routes to look for and take certain action against those routes.

Chapter 18

Quality of Service (QoS)

THE CCIE QUALIFICATION EXAM TOPICS COVERED IN THIS CHAPTER INCLUDE THE FOLLOWING:

- ✓ Queuing techniques: first in/first out (FIFO), priority queuing (PQ), custom queuing (CQ), weighted fair queuing (WFQ), class-based WFQ (CBWFQ), low latency queuing (LLQ), Weighted Round Robin (WRR), and Weighted Random Early Detection (WRED)

- ✓ Frame Relay Traffic Shaping (FRTS) and Generic Traffic Shaping (GTS)

- ✓ CAR, RSVP, Traffic Coloring (IP Precedence), and NBAR

- ✓ RTP priority and header compression

- ✓ Packet Marking with DSCP and 802.1p

- ✓ Policy-based routing (PBR)

- ✓ Multiprotocol Label Switching (MPLS) QoS marking

Quality of service (QoS) has traditionally been used to prioritize interactive traffic over batch/bulk transfer across resources where bandwidth is scarce, such as low-speed serial links. With the convergence of voice, video, and data in the same network, QoS becomes even more critical because the delay and jitter tolerances of voice and video demand greater attention than even interactive session traffic.

Cisco routers and switches include many features that are used to implement quality of service, and we'll discuss them in this chapter. In particular, queuing methods such as first in/first out (FIFO), priority queuing (PQ), custom queuing (CQ), weighted fair queuing (WFQ), class-based weighted fair queuing (CBWFQ), and low latency queuing (LLQ) are covered.

Although queuing methods are at the heart of QoS, packet classification, rate limiting, compression, and shaping are also important. Among the topics covered in this area are policy-based routing (PBR), committed access rate (CAR), FRF.9 compression, Generic Traffic Shaping (GTS), and Frame Relay Traffic Shaping (FRTS). Other features like Network Based Application Recognition (NBAR) and Multiprotocol Label Switching (MPLS) are reviewed as well.

Delivering Network Services

All networks can take advantage of aspects of QoS to improve network efficiency, and not all QoS mechanisms need to be implemented on every network. IP networks can be classified from a QoS perspective as falling into one of the following three categories:

- Best effort services
- Integrated Services (IntServ)
- Differentiated Services (DiffServ)

We'll take a look at each of these categories in the following sections.

Best Effort Services

Generally, generic IP networks are viewed as best effort delivery services; the network delivers data if it can without guaranteeing any reliability, delay, or throughput. Best effort service is first in/first out (FIFO) queuing and is suitable for a wide range of networked applications, such as file transfers (FTP), e-mail, or applications that are not time sensitive.

Integrated Services

Integrated Services (IntServ) can accommodate multiple QoS requirements. In the IntServ model, QoS is integrated not only in the network but also in the end stations requiring a set quality of service. The application requests a specific kind of service from the network before it sends data. The request can encompass QoS requirements such as bandwidth and delay and uses explicit signaling across the entire network. The network in turn performs administration control and commits to meeting the QoS requirements of the server/application as long as the traffic remains within the requested profile specifications.

IntServ is a connection-orientated service. The edge router performs an admission control to ensure that available resources are sufficient in the network before a session is established. The IntServ standard assumes that all routers along a path set and maintain state for each individual communication. IntServ is a very useful tool to assure strict QoS requirements for application-level traffic such as VoIP.

IntServ uses RSVP to signal QoS requirements across a network. RSVP is discussed in the next section.

Resource Reservation Protocol (RSVP)

The *Resource Reservation Protocol (RSVP)* is used by applications to request and allocate bandwidth and other QoS parameters across a session's path. RSVP has its own IP protocol for communications (IP protocol 46, as described in RFC 2205), although there are provisions for use of UDP as well. RSVP relies on the underlying IP routing of the network to reach its destinations; it does not keep a separate routing table or use special multicast/broadcast messages to communicate.

RSVP Mechanics

RSVP uses seven different message types: Path, Resv, Path Teardown, Reservation Teardown, Confirmation, Path Error, and Reservation Error. These messages are used to set up, maintain, and tear down QoS reservations. Inside the Path and Resv messages are flow descriptors that are composed of a flow spec and a flow filter. The flow filter is used to identify the packets of the traffic flow being reserved, and the flow spec details the traffic characteristics of the flow. The flow spec includes a service class along with an Rspec that describes the QoS requested and a Tspec that describes the traffic flow. Rspec and Tspec parameter formats are described in RFC 2210.

Figure 18.1 shows a simple network with some IP phones. When phone 2 calls phone 1, phone 1 as the sender transmits a Path RSVP message to reserve bandwidth along the path to the receiver, phone 2. As each router receives the Path message, it adds itself in the path list and sends the updated copy out. When phone 2 receives the Path message, it sends back a Resv message containing the path information so that the message travels back along the original path. The routers along the path check to see if they have sufficient resources to grant the request. If they do, they propagate the Resv message. If they don't, they transmit a Reservation Error message to the sender to indicate that there is a problem. When the Resv message makes it back to phone 1, phone 1 knows that the proper bandwidth and latency have been reserved and starts its session with phone 2.

RSVP relies on symmetrical routing. If asymmetric routing is present, RSVP does not work correctly because the return path is different.

FIGURE 18.1 RSVP reservation setup

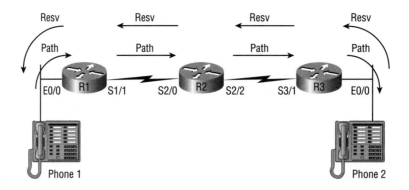

The routers set timers to make sure that unused reservations are canceled. Active sessions periodically send Path and Resv messages along the path to maintain the circuit reservation. This process of periodically sending messages also helps if there are routing or other changes in the network.

Although RSVP in and of itself does not enforce QoS, it ties into the queuing mechanisms of IOS to provide QoS. For instance, RSVP causes weighted fair queuing (WFQ) to set up individual queues for reserved traffic. These queues are then given preferential service.

RSVP Router Configuration

Configuring RSVP on a router is straightforward and consists mainly of the one interface level command:

```
rsvp <max reservable total bandwidth> <max reservable per session>
```

The command's two parameters specify the total amount of bandwidth that can be allocated for Integrated Services sessions and the maximum amount of bandwidth that can allocated to any single session. The interface maximum allocation parameter is limited to 75 percent of the interface's total bandwidth to ensure that RSVP reserved sessions don't monopolize the entire link. This percentage can be modified; however, it is not recommended. Therefore, it is a good idea to define the bandwidth on the interface explicitly. The following commands show how to configure RSVP on a router's interface:

`(config)#interface serial 2/1`	`outbound interface in session path`
`(config-if)#bandwidth 1536`	`inform interface of total bandwidth`
`(config-if)#rsvp bandwidth 512 64`	`enable RSVP. 512 = maximum total bandwidth RSVP can reserve on this interface (in Kbps). 64 = maximum bandwidth allowed to be reserved by any single flow (in Kbps)`

RSVP can be monitored using the following commands:

```
show ip rsvp interface
show ip rsvp neighbor
show ip rsvp sender
show ip rsvp host receivers
show ip rsvp host senders
show ip rsvp request
show ip rsvp reservation
```

The `ip rsvp reservation` and `ip rsvp sender` global command can be used on routers to test RSVP configurations in a lab environment because it is sometimes difficult to find an RSVP-enabled application. The following configuration lines show how to configure two routers to simulate a UDP session between the addresses of 172.16.8.15 and 172.16.2.25 using port numbers 20000 and 22000. A rate of 16Kbps is requested with a 1KB burst:

```
R1
ip rsvp reservation-host 172.16.8.15 172.16.2.25 udp
     20000 22000 172.16.2.26 f0/0 ff rate 16 1

R2
ip rsvp sender 172.16.2.25 172.16.8.15 udp 22000
     20000 172.16.8.16 f2/0 16 1
```

Differentiated Services

Differentiated Services (DiffServ) is a service model that can satisfy differing QoS requirements. However, unlike with IntServ, an application using DiffServ does not explicitly signal the router before sending data.

For Differentiated Services, the network tries to deliver a particular kind of service based on the QoS specified for each IP packet. This packet-by-packet QoS first requires classification, which can occur in different ways:

- Using the IP Precedence or DiffServ bits in the IP headers
- By source and destination IP addresses
- By application using well-known TCP and UDP port numbers

The network can then use the classification to shape and police traffic as well as to perform intelligent queuing. Traffic can be classified and then marked using the following:

- Committed access rate (CAR)
- Policy-based routing (PBR)
- Modular QoS CLI (MQC)

Packet Classification and Marking

Queuing and shaping mechanisms must be able to distinguish one type of traffic from another in order to accomplish their set tasks. Although access lists can be used by routers to look at packets and classify them, it makes more sense for a packet to be labeled in a special way to denote its QoS characteristics. This is the purpose of marking or coloring packets. A packet only has to be classified at the edge of the network and marked so that routers farther in the network can focus on routing and queuing.

There are several methods of marking or coloring packets. At layer 2, packets can be colored using fields in the 802.1q and ISL trunking tags. At layer 3, IP packets can be marked using the IP Precedence or *Differentiated Service Code Point (DSCP)* fields.

For security and efficiency reasons, marking and classification should be performed at the edge of the network. This relieves core routers of an unnecessary burden and allows them to concentrate on their primary task of routing large numbers of packets very quickly. It also places the administrative control as close to the source as possible and is the only real way to provide true end-to-end QoS.

Now we'll look at some of the methods to mark packets for QoS.

IP Precedence

The Type of Service (ToS) field in the IPv4 packet, shown in Figure 18.2, has two 3-bit fields that allow for the classification of traffic. The higher-order 3 bits define the IP Precedence, and the next lower three the type of service. Table 18.1 lists the IP Precedence bit values and their meanings as assigned in RFC 791.

FIGURE 18.2   IP header with IP ToS and DS fields

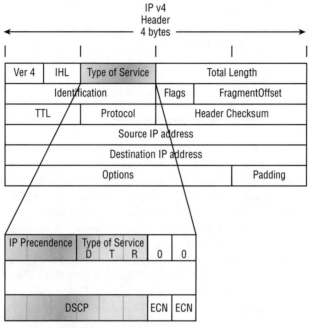

Differentiated Services (DS) Field

TABLE 18.1   IP Precedence Values

Value	Name
7	Network override
6	Internetwork control
5	Critical/ECP
4	Flash override
3	Flash

TABLE 18.1 IP Precedence Values *(continued)*

Value	Name
2	Immediate
1	Priority
0	Routine

As you can see, the higher the precedence number, the more important the traffic. Therefore, packets with a precedence of 6 or 7 should be transmitted before packets with lower precedence values. Likewise, if a router experiences congestion on a link and needs to drop queued packets, it should drop packets with lower precedence values before discarding traffic with higher values. VoIP and DLSw traffic are marked with IP Precedence 5 by default. IP Precedence values 6 and 7 should be used only for inter-router control communications, not for data communications.

The three Type of Service bits are used to further indicate traffic needs. Table 18.2 lists the ToS bits and their meanings. Typically, these bits are not set and are generally not considered when providing QoS. It should be noted that the 3-bit ToS field was redefined in RFC 1349 to incorporate bit 6, which was previously unused and set to 0. The new 4-bit field defines only five new values because the value can be 0 or only 1 bit can be set at a time.

TABLE 18.2 ToS Bits (RFC 791)

Bit	Name	Traffic Requirements
D	Delay	0 = Normal delay
		1 = Low delay
T	Throughput	0 = Normal throughput
		1 = High throughput
R	Reliability	0 = Normal reliability
		1 = High reliability

Differentiated Services (DiffServ) and DSCP

A method of delivering Differentiated Services (DiffServ) for IP traffic is defined in RFCs 2474 and 2475. DiffServ is a way to mark packets and have consistent per-hop behavior (PHB) within an administrative domain. It evolved as an alternative to IntServ, which was considered hard to implement and poor at scaling. Rather than reserve explicit bandwidth for traffic along a path as IntServ does, DiffServ marks packets at the ingress to the network and lets routers make queuing decisions based on these markings. Central to the DiffServ model is the Differentiated Services (DS) field in the IP header.

The DS field is shown in Figure 18.2 as an overlay to the ToS field and is composed of two fields: the 6-bit Differentiated Services Codepoint (DSCP) field and the 2-bit Explicit Congestion Notification (ECN) field. The two 3-bit ToS and IP Precedence fields are now combined into the 6-bit DSCP field, allowing for 64 different traffic levels as opposed to the 8 with IP Precedence. The least significant 2 bits were originally unused but were defined in RFC 3168 to signal congestion. The DS field is also used with IPv6 in the Traffic Class field.

Although Cisco IOS can mark packets with a strictly numeric DSCP value (0–63), the RFCs define categories of DSCP values. Namely, there are four classes of DSCP PHBs:

- Default PHB
- Class selector PHB
- Assured Forwarding (AF) PHB
- Express Forwarding (EF) PHB

Default PHB

The default PHB has a DSCP value of 0x000000. It is used for backward compatibility as well as for marking packets for best effort delivery. RFC 2474 does not define any special behavior for this class of traffic other than the regular IP routing behavior called out in RFC 1812.

Class Selector PHB

The class selector PHBs are defined for partial backward compatibility with IP Precedence and take the form xxx000. It is assumed that class selectors with higher numeric values will deliver better service than class selectors with lower numeric values.

Assured Forwarding (AF) PHB

RFC 2597 defines the Assured Forwarding (AF) PHB codepoints. Four classes of PHBs are defined, each with three levels of drop precedence as shown in Table 18.3. It is presumed that traffic assigned to each higher class will be given better service than traffic assigned to the class below it. Likewise, within each class, the higher the drop precedence, the more likely traffic will be dropped during times of congestion.

TABLE 18.3   DSCP Codepoints

Drop Precedence	Class 1	Class 2	Class 3	Class 4
Low	001010 (10) AF11	010010 (18) AF21	011010 (26) AF31	100010 (34) AF41
Medium	001100 (12) AF12	010100 (20) AF22	011100 (28) AF32	100100 (36) AF42
High	001110 (14) AF13	010110 (22) AF23	011110 (30) AF33	100110 (38) AF43

Expedited Forwarding (EF) PHB

RFC 2598 defines a special PHB labeled the Expedited Forwarding (EF) PHB, which is given a value of 0x101110 (46). The per-hop behavior for this class of traffic corresponds to the highest service level agreement and is equated to a virtual circuit where the departure rate for this traffic is greater than the arrival rate. Jitter, loss, and latency are all to be minimized for EF traffic. A DiffServ-compliant device is not required to support this PHB class of traffic.

Next we'll look at some other marking techniques that can be used outside the IP header.

Multiprotocol Label Switching (MPLS) Experimental Field

IP traffic traveling though a network enabled with *Multiprotocol Label Switching (MPLS)* can be marked for QoS using the three experimental/Class of Service (CoS) bits in the MPLS tag. Although the IP Precedence or DSCP bits may be set in the IP header of a packet transported through an MPLS network, the exp/CoS field is used by the MPLS-enabled routers to make QoS decisions. Figure 18.3 shows the MPLS tag and its format. The MPLS exp/CoS bits can be set using route maps, CAR, or the Modular QoS CLI (MQC).

FIGURE 18.3 MPLS tag format

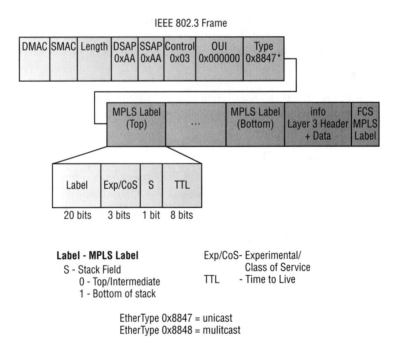

Class of Service (CoS)/802.1p

Layer 2 Ethernet traffic can be marked for QoS using the 3 priority bits in the IEEE 802.1p portion of the IEEE 802.1q VLAN trunking tag. Switches and routers can then make queuing decisions based on this marking or coloring. Like the 3 IP Precedence bits in the IP header, the 802.1p priority bits define eight levels of service, with 7 being the highest. Cisco IP phones mark their packets with 802.1p priority 5 by default. Figure 18.4 shows the 3 802.1p priority bits in the 802.1q tag; they are also referred to as the *Class of Service (CoS)* bits.

FIGURE 18.4   802.1p priority bits

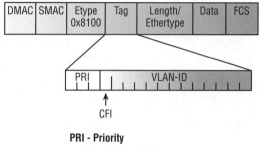

PRI - Priority
3 bits to denote 802.1p priority

The 802.1p priority of incoming packets can be set or changed on a Catalyst 3550 switch port or configured to let the CoS setting of a packet remain the same. The following commands mark incoming packets with a CoS of 4:

```
(config)#mls qos                                enable QoS on the switch

(config)#interface f0/14

(config)#switchport trunk encapsulation dot1q   port must be trunking to

(config-if)#switchport mode dynamic desirable   set the CoS value

(config-if)#mls qos cos 4                        set default CoS value to 4

(config-if)#mls qos override                     reset incoming packet's CoS
                                                 value to the default Value
                                                 regardless of what it
                                                 arrives with.
```

CoS can be used to classify incoming traffic on a router or to mark packets outbound. The outbound interface, of course, has to be configured for trunking.

Cisco Modular QoS CLI (MQC)

With IOS version 12.0(5)XE/12.1(2)T, Cisco introduced a method of configuring QoS functionality that was consistent across all platforms, making it easier to configure QoS. As shown in Figure 18.5, *Modular QoS CLI (MQC)* has three steps/levels of configuration: a class map, a policy map, and a service policy. Class maps assign traffic to different classes. Policy maps determine what to do with traffic in each class. And service maps are used to attach policy maps inbound or outbound to different interfaces.

FIGURE 18.5 Modular QoS CLI

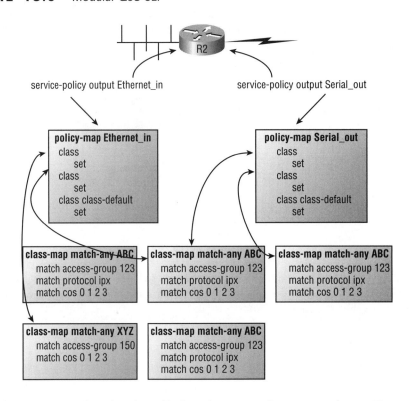

The class map is used to classify traffic based on access lists, protocol type, IP precedence, and so on, much in the same manner a policy-based routing match statement is used. A class map may have several criteria for traffic to adhere to in order to be included in the class. The keywords match-any and match-all are used to specify how stringent the requirements are. If match-any is used, a packet is in a class if it matches any of the criteria in the class compare list. If match-all is specified, a packet must match all the criteria in the class map to be selected for the class. The default value is match-all if there is more than one match statement for the class. Traffic cannot be put into more than one class on an interface; once it is selected for a class, there is no further classification done. There can be a maximum of 256 classes defined on a router.

After the class map assigns traffic to a class constructor, a policy map is used to determine what is done with/to the traffic in a class or set of classes. The IP Precedence or DSCP markings can be set or changed, the queuing strategy for the traffic chosen, shaping or policing enabled, bandwidth allocated, and random detection enabled among other things. A policy map is applied to an interface inbound or outbound using the service-policy input/output command.

In a way, MQC is like object-oriented programming in that classes are defined and can be reused. A class map defining a set of traffic can be used by several policy maps simultaneously.

The policy maps in turn can be attached inbound or outbound to one or more interfaces as well. A class map can include another class map in its match list, mimicking class inheritance. Policy maps can include other policy maps by using the `service-policy` statement.

The following simple example of MQC demonstrates how to mark traffic from a particular workstation (the boss's) with a high IP Precedence value. An access list is used to identify the boss's workstation:

```
(config)access-list 15 permit host 172.16.2.25    identify the boss's IP address

(config)class-map match-all TheBoss               create new class(case
                                                   sensitive)

(config-cmap)#match access-group 15               only let traffic passing
                                                   access list 15 in

(config)#policy-map SuckingUp                      create new policy

(config-pmap)#class TheBoss                        include class TheBoss

(config-pmap-c)set ip precedence 6                 mark traffic from Boss's work-
                                                   with critical precedence

(config)#int f0/0                                  interface Boss's vlan is
                                                   connected to

(config-if)#service-policy SuckingUp output

                                                   attach policy map SuckingUp
```

You can look at MQC configurations using the following commands:

```
show policy-map
show class-map
```

Now that you've learned how to mark and classify packets, we'll show you what can be done with them as we move on to queuing.

Queuing

Queuing is just a fancy way of saying "standing in line" (apologies to our British readers). Shop owners don't want new customers to go away when they're waiting on other customers; if a new customer can wait a bit, the shop owner will get to them. In a similar fashion, if the arrival rate of packets to go out an interface is greater than the available bandwidth, some packets will have to wait. Even though the average packet rate may be lower than the interface's bandwidth, the instantaneous rate may be such that packets have to wait before they are transmitted.

Because of the bursty nature of traffic, queuing helps to alleviate the problems that would occur if packets were just dropped when an interface is busy. If queuing was not in place, traffic would be dropped unnecessarily during momentary high traffic rates. However, on the converse side, queuing is not a cure for chronic lack of bandwidth. Also, setting queue depths too large may lead to lower overall throughput, particularly in the case of TCP traffic. As traffic waits on the queue, retransmission timers pop and cause more traffic to be sent. If a packet and its retransmission are sitting on a queue, there's no reason to send both.

Although queuing is mostly associated with WAN interfaces, voice and video traffic can require queuing on Ethernet interfaces as well. The issue on high-bandwidth interfaces like Ethernet is not deciding what traffic will be dropped, but deciding which gets sent the quickest. Because voice and video traffic are particularly sensitive to delay and jitter, it's essential that these packets are sent ahead of data packets.

As you'll see in the following sections on the different queuing methods, queuing involves not only how packets are selected and placed into different queues, but also in what order the queues are serviced and how many packets or how much data is taken at one time. This is what allows for QoS and different categories of service.

Packets are subjected to queuing mechanisms only when there is congestion on the interface. Otherwise they are queued on the interface's transmit queue in a first in/first out (FIFO) manner.

First In/First Out (FIFO)

The simplest queuing mechanism on routers is first in/first out (FIFO) queuing. Packets are sent out the interface in the order they arrive; there is no scheduling or prioritization between different types of packets. This queuing method places the least burden on the router's CPU and memory; however, it does little to ensure QoS.

For high-speed interfaces on the router (greater than E1 speed, 2.048Mbps), this is the default queuing method. Interfaces that are running Weighted Fair Queuing can revert to running FIFO by performing the `no fair-queue` interface command.

The actual output queue on an interface is implemented as a FIFO queue and is designated the tx-ring. When FIFO queuing is enabled on an interface, there will be an output hold queue, as shown in Figure 18.6. This queue holds packets that have been process-switched or locally originated in the router. If a packet is fast-switched and the driver's queue in full, the packet is dropped. One exception to this is on a 7500, which has the `transmit-buffers backing-store` command enabled on the interface.

FIGURE 18.6   FIFO queuing

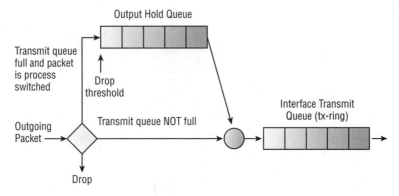

Note that the tx-ring implementation is hardware platform dependent and can be observed using the show controller command:

```
Mr.7200#show controller s5/0
M4T: show controller:
...
mxt_ds=0x634C28C8, rx ring entries=47, tx ring entries=64
txring=0x20061BC0, txr shadow=0x623AC650, tx_head=20, tx_tail=20, tx_count=0
...
tx_underrun_err=0, tx_soft_underrun_err=0, tx_limited=1(2)
```

Priority Queuing

Priority queuing (PQ) is a method of queuing traffic on an interface into one of four queues: high, medium, normal, and low. Traffic is drained from these queues in a strict order: all traffic is sent from the high queue, followed by all traffic from the medium queue, the normal queue, and finally the low queue, as shown in Figure 18.7. When a packet has been transmitted out the interface, PQ first looks to see if there are any packets in the high queue to place on the transmit queue. If there are none, it then checks the medium queue for any packets. If there is one, it's placed on the interface's transmit queue. If there aren't any packets in the medium queue, the normal queue is checked and finally the low queue. Note that the high queue is always checked first for packets by the scheduler. Therefore, it is possible for traffic in the lower queues to be deprived of bandwidth if there is constantly high traffic in the queues above them, and for this reason, priority queuing is sometimes referred to as starvation queuing.

FIGURE 18.7 Priority queuing

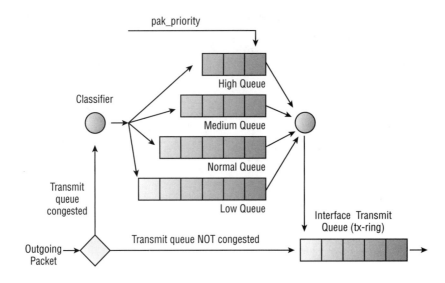

By default, all traffic is placed into the normal queue if there is no customization done to priority queuing. Packets can be assigned to the different queues based on criteria such as protocol, access lists, and packet size. In the case of IP traffic, source and destination addresses, protocol type, and UDP and TCP port numbers can be used when making a queue assignment.

Configuring Priority Queuing

Cisco IOS allows for up to 16 priority lists on a router. Each priority list can define a unique set of mappings to the four priority queues for an interface. Priority queuing is configured by assigning traffic types to a priority list in the global configuration mode and attaching the list to an interface or subinterface either by using the `priority-group` command directly or by assigning the traffic types in a map class.

The following example shows a router with some specific traffic requirements. All Telnet and DLSw traffic must be assigned a high priority. All IPX packets with a packet size greater than 750 bytes and any IPX packets sent to IPX network 300 and 400 must be assigned to the normal queue; all other traffic must be assigned to the low queue:

```
priority-list 5 protocol ip tcp high 2065        DLSw uses TCP port 2065

priority-list 5 protocol ip tcp high telnet      assign telnet traffic to the
                                                 high queue

priority-list 5 protocol ipx normal lt 750       ipx packets less than 750
                                                 bytes are assigned to the
                                                 medium queue
```

`priority-list 5 protocol ipx normal list 800`	packets matching access-list 800 are assigned to the normal queue
`priority-list 5 protocol default low`	make the low queue the new default queue for priority list 5.
`priority-list 5 queue-limit 10 15 20 25`	change the default queue depth packet limits from High 20 -> 10 Medium 40 -> 15 Normal 60 -> 20 Low 80 -> 25
`access-list 800 permit -1 300`	allow IPX traffic from any source destined to network 300
`access-list 800 permit -1 400`	allow IPX traffic from any source destined to network 400
`interface Serial 0`	
`  priority-group 5`	enable PQ on this interface and use priority-list 5 to classify traffic

To monitor priority queuing, you can use the `show interface`, `show queuing priority`, and `show access-list` commands:

```
Output queue (queue priority: size/max/drops):
high: 0/10/0, medium: 0/15/0, normal: 0/20/0, low: 0/25/0
```

> **NOTE** Reasonable values should be chosen for queue limits. A large size will help ensure that packets don't get dropped, but, as in the case of TCP, a retransmission may occur if the original packet sits in the queue too long. Sometimes it's better if some traffic is dropped. Too small a size will result in unnecessary drops during brief periods of congestion.

Custom Queuing

Custom queuing (CQ) is another queuing mechanism; it's similar to priority queuing and is shown in Figure 18.8. The main difference between custom and priority queuing is that queues are not serviced in a strict order with CQ. Instead, CQ services queues in a round-robin fashion. Therefore, there is little if any chance of traffic getting starved as there is with priority queuing, unless there is a gross misconfiguration.

FIGURE 18.8   Custom queuing

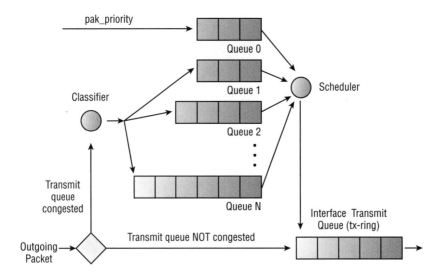

CQ can be configured to have up to 16 different queue list definitions, each having up to 16 user-configurable queues. Only one queue list can be attached to an interface at a time; however, the same queue list definition can be used by multiple interfaces concurrently. Each queue is assigned a byte count, either user configured or a default value. This byte count is used to determine how much traffic is to be drained from a queue each time it is serviced. On an interface, CQ transmits packets from each configured queue in the queue list in turn, transmitting the allocated number of bytes from that queue and moving on. Depending on the number of queues, link speed, and byte count specified for each queue, the latency for a packet could become significant.

The default byte count for each queue is 1500 bytes, and the default queue limit is 20 packets per queue. A default queue can be specified for traffic that does not match any of the configured queue criteria. If no default queue is configured, traffic is assigned to queue 1 regardless of what else is configured to go to queue 1. Queue 0 in each custom queue list is reserved for system traffic such as ARP, LMI, routing updates, and so on. This queue is serviced in a priority manner; queue 0 is always checked before packets are sent from any of the other queues. Although traffic can be configured to be placed in queue 0, this practice is strongly discouraged.

Calculating Custom Queuing Percentage Bandwidth

Before configuring custom queuing, it is important to make sure the expected bandwidth allocation is correct. CQ allows you to configure the byte count to send out per queue. You must translate the byte count values for each queue into an equivalent bandwidth.

As an example, take a case in which there are three categories of traffic to be sent: A, B, and C. We want A to have 50 percent of the bandwidth, B to have 35 percent, and C to have 15 percent. (for the moment, we'll ignore the default queue and queue 0). We could set the byte counts to 500, 350, and 150, respectively, to give the appropriate ratio. This would work well if category A traffic was made up of 500-byte packets, B was 350-byte packets, and C was 150-byte packets. Custom queuing would take a packet from A's queue, then from B's, then from C's, and start back at A's queue.

However, if the packet sizes were all 500 bytes, CQ would still transmit a packet from each queue in turn and the bandwidth ratio would fall to an even 33 percent for each category. This is because custom queuing will always transmit at least one packet from each queue as it is serviced; it can't transmit just the byte count and stop if the byte count is smaller than the queued packet. Also, as long as there is "credit" on the byte count for a queue, CQ will transmit packets. If a queue has a byte count of 1500 and CQ has transmitted four packets with a total count of 1400 bytes, if there is another packet in the queue, it will get transmitted as well, even if it is a 2000-byte packet.

Therefore, a better selection for the byte counts to maintain the 50/35/15 (3.3/2.3/1) ratio given an expected packet size of 500 bytes would be 1650 for A, 1150 for B, and 500 for C. Cisco recommends using the expected packet size as the lowest value.

If a packet size is larger than the allocated byte count for the queue, CQ will send the whole packet, skewing bandwidth percentage calculations. It is best to research traffic packet sizes and interface MTUs before making byte count assignments.

Configuring Custom Queuing

The process for configuring custom queuing is similar to that of configuring priority queuing: configure queue lists in the global configuration mode and enable CQ on an interface using the `custom-queue-list` command. The only real difference is that in addition to classifying which traffic is assigned to which queues, the byte count for each queue can also be specified.

In the following example, CQ queue list 1 is configured and attached to serial interface s3/2. There are five customized queues, and queue 10 is set as the default queue. DLSw traffic is assigned to queue 1, Telnet traffic to queue 2, IPX packets less than 150 bytes long to queue 3, IPX packets greater than 150 bytes long to queue 4, and traffic from host 172.16.20.15 to queue 5.

Queue 0 is used for layer 2 and layer 3 keepalive and control packets. It is not advisable to assign any traffic to this queue.

Here is the configuration:

```
(config)#queue-list 1 protocol ip 1 tcp 2065
(config)#queue-list 1 protocol ip 2 tcp telnet
```

```
(config)#queue-list 1 protocol ipx 3 lt 150
(config)#queue-list 1 protocol ipx 4 gt 150
(config)#queue-list 1 protocol ip 5 list 10
(config)#queue-list 1 default 10
(config)#queue-list 1 queue 0 limit 17
(config)#queue-list 1 queue 1 byte-count 2000
(config)#queue-list 1 queue 2 byte-count 1000
(config)#queue-list 1 queue 3 byte-count 750
(config)#queue-list 1 queue 4 byte-count 1200
(config)#queue-list 1 queue 5 byte-count 2000
(config)#queue-list 1 queue 10 byte-count 2000
(config)#access-list 10 permit 172.16.20.15

(config)#interface Serial3/2
(config-if)#custom-queue-list 1
```

Weighted Fair Queuing (WFQ)

Weighted fair queuing (WFQ) debuted in IOS version 11.0 as an alternative to priority and custom queuing. Its advantage over priority queuing is fairness and the ability to prevent traffic starvation. Its advantage over custom queuing is its ease of configuration: on interfaces with E1 bandwidth (2.048Mbps) and less, there is none; it is on by default. Although WFQ does have some configuration options, most of the time it is left with the default values.

WFQ works by assigning traffic to one of 2^n queues created dynamically as they are needed, as shown in Figure 18.9. Incoming traffic is classified based on a hashed value of fields in the packet header. A certain number of bytes in the header are added together then ANDed with a mask equal to the total number of queues. In the case of an IP packet, the source and destination IP addresses, IP protocol, and Type of Service bits (not precedence) are added and masked. If the packet is TCP or UDP, the source and destination port numbers are added to the hash as well. The hash value is used as an index into the list of traffic queues. Each queue is said to hold traffic for a unique conversation or flow. Although it is possible for two IP flows or conversations to share the same hash value, it does not happen often. Also, it is a common misconception that all non-IP traffic is sent to a single queue or shares a single queue based on protocol. IPX traffic, for instance, hashes to different queues based on the first 25 bytes in the IPX header: the IPX packet type, source and destination addresses, and source and destination socket numbers.

FIGURE 18.9 Weighted fair queuing

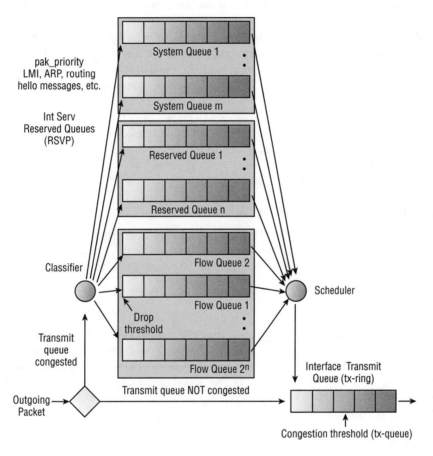

Fair queuing is the process of taking one packet from each queue in a round-robin fashion so that each flow gets serviced equally. The *weighted* in *WFQ* means that WFQ takes IP Precedence into account. Packets with higher IP Precedence are given a greater portion of the bandwidth than those with a lower precedence value. The portion of bandwidth per flow is calculated by adding 1 to the flow's IP Precedence value and dividing it by the sum of all the flows' adjusted precedence values. As an example, take five flows with IP Precedence values 0, 1, 2, 5, and 7, respectively. The sum of the adjusted precedence values is 20, calculated as follows:

```
Total = (0 + 1) + (1 + 1) + (2 + 1) + (5 + 1) + (7 + 1) = 20
```

Therefore, the different flows will get 5 percent, 10 percent, 15 percent, 30 percent, and 40 percent of the bandwidth, respectively. Note that all non-IP flows are assigned an IP Precedence value of 0.

Another feature of WFQ is that it gives priority to flows with lighter traffic. WFQ assigns an effective time stamp to packets as they arrive in a queue. The time stamp is based on an estimate of how long it will take before the last byte in the packet will be transmitted. Instead of servicing the queues in a round-robin manner, WFQ services the queues based on the queue with the smallest time stamp.

By default, weighted fair queuing allocates 256 queues each with a maximum depth of 64 packets. These values can be changed depending on traffic needs. The number of queues can be set to 16, 32, 64, 128, 256, 512, or 1024. The queue depth, or congestive discard threshold, can be adjusted to values from 1 and 4096 and lets WFQ know how many packets can be added to each queue before they are tail-dropped.

Configuring and Monitoring WFQ

As stated previously, WFQ is the default queuing mode on interfaces running E1 speeds and below. WFQ requires minimum configuration on the router. Access lists are not needed to classify traffic for queuing. To configure WFQ on a serial interface, the `fair-queue` command must be configured on the interface:

```
(config)#interface serial 1/0
```

```
(config-if)#fair-queue 64 512          set the congestive discard threshold to
                                       64 packets and the maximum number of
                                       hash queues to 512. The max number
                                       of hash queues must be a power of 2
```

To look at the performance of WFQ, use the following commands:

```
show interface
show queueing fair
```

```
Kurt#show queueing fair interface s1/0
Current fair queue configuration:
```

Interface	Discard threshold	Dynamic queues	Reserved queues	Link queues	Priority queues
Serial1/0	64	512	0	8	1

```
Kurt#show interface serial 1/0
Serial1/0 is up, line protocol is up
  Hardware is M4T
```

```
MTU 1500 bytes, BW 1544 Kbit, DLY 20000 usec,
    reliability 255/255, txload 25/255, rxload 15/255
  ….
Queueing strategy: weighted fair
Output queue: 0/1000/64/0 (size/max total/threshold/drops)
    Conversations  5/20/512 (active/max active/max total)
    Reserved Conversations 0/0 (allocated/max allocated)
    Available Bandwidth 1158 kilobits/sec
```

Weighted Random Early Detection (WRED)

Weighted Random Early Detection (WRED) is Cisco's implementation of Random Early Detection (RED) and is used as an alternative to default tail-drop behavior (dropping packets from the tail of a queue when the queue is full). WRED is used to provide congestion avoidance. RED addresses the problem of global synchronization, which can occur when multiple TCP streams are traversing a router and going out a common interface. As seen in Figure 18.10, multiple TCP sessions start up and build in transmission speed. When the aggregate rate of the sessions exceeds the outgoing line speed for a period of time, buffers fill up and packets are dropped. These dropped packets cause the adaptive TCP sessions to back off in their transmission rates. With severe enough drop rates, TCP backs its timers off significantly and effectively goes back into slow-start mode. Because the TCP sessions have all had their packets dropped at the same time, they all commence transmitting in slow-start mode, building to full rate at roughly the same time and pace. This leads to a cycle of transmitting at peak, throttling back, and building up as, shown in Figure 18.10

FIGURE 18.10   WRED in operation

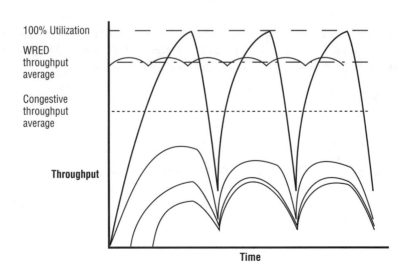

The average throughput in the congestive state is less than the theoretical 100 percent due to the turbulence of all the streams competing for the bandwidth. WRED alleviates this condition by spreading out the packet discards so that the impact on any single stream is much less and causes the overall throughput to increase.

WRED is most effective with TCP traffic that has adaptive back-off. If the majority of traffic on an interface is non-TCP, configuring WRED will do little to alleviate congestion.

Dynamic Buffer Limiting is a new feature that provides congestion avoidance for all types of traffic

WRED Operation

WRED works by checking set thresholds before queuing a packet. If the queue size is under the minimum threshold, the packet is queued. If the queue is over the maximum threshold, the packet is dropped. If the queue size is between the minimum and maximum threshold values, a probability factor is used to decide whether to drop the packet or not. The probability factor is based on an average derived from the average queue depth and current queue depth according to the following equation (where n is a weighting factor):

```
Average =  (previous-average * (1 - (1/2)ⁿ) + (current-queue-depth * (1/2)ⁿ)
```

The larger the value of n, the more the average value follows the moving average. The smaller the value of n, the more important the current queue size becomes and WRED reacts to bursty traffic.

WRED also takes IP Precedence and DSCP into account when deciding whether to drop packets. The minimum drop thresholds are progressively higher for traffic the higher the precedence or DSCP values are. Therefore, a packet with higher IP Precedence is much less likely to be dropped than one with the default precedence. The default value of n is 9.

Configuring WRED

WRED is enabled by using the `random-detect` interface command:

```
interface serial 0/0

    random-detect          enable WRED on the interface using default values
```

Using MQC, it can be applied in conjunction with other queuing methods, as you'll see in the section on class-based weighted fair queuing (CBWFQ).

Customizing WRED

WRED can be customized to change its performance characteristics. The following configuration customizes the WRED queue for IP Precedence; again, this is configured under the router interface. The command structure for customizing WRED for IP Precedence is as follows:

```
random-detect precedence value min-threshold max-threshold mark-prob-denominator
```

The following is a sample for customizing all WRED for all IP Precedence values:

```
interface serial 0/0
 random-detect
 random-detect precedence 0    20 200 100
 random-detect precedence 1    30 200 100
 random-detect precedence 2    40 200 100
 random-detect precedence 3    60 200 100
 random-detect precedence 4    80 200 100
 random-detect precedence 5    10 20 10
 random-detect precedence 6    10 20 10
 random-detect precedence 7    10 20 10
```

WRED can also be customized for DSCP using the `random-detect dscp-based` interface command and then using the `random-detect dscp` command to change the thresholds and probability denominators for each desired PHB. The following is a sample configuration for customizing WRED for DSCP values af12 and af42:

```
interface serial 0
 random-detect dscp-based
 random-detect dscp af12 20 50 20
 random-detect dscp af42 30 50 20
```

Weighted Round Robin (WRR)

Weighted Round Robin (WRR) can be configured on switch ports to provide a form of fair queuing. Each switch port queue is serviced in a round-robin fashion so that no queue is starved. By default, the amount of effective bandwidth is equal for each of the queues; however, different weights can be assigned to provide QoS differentiation. WRR can be configured using the `priority-queue out` command to designate one of the queues as an expedite queue. In this case, traffic in the expedite queue is always serviced first, and the remaining three queues are serviced in a proportional-round robin fashion with the remaining bandwidth. WRR uses CoS values to assign traffic to different queues. Table 18.4 lists the default CoS-to-queue mappings on a Catalyst 3550.

TABLE 18.4 WRR Default CoS to Queue Mappings

CoS	Queue
0, 1	1
2, 3	2
4, 5	3
6, 7	4

Weighted Random Early Detection (WRED) can also be configured in conjunction with WRR. As noted earlier, WRED is most useful if the majority of traffic is TCP or any other protocol that uses an adaptive back-off strategy.

WRR Configuration

Configuring WRR on a 3550 involves using the `wrr-queue` interface command on gigabit interfaces. Before WRR can be configured and enabled, QoS has to be enabled on the switch with the `mls qos` command. In the following example, the default queue bandwidths are modified from the defaults:

```
(config)#mls qos                              globally enable qos

(config)#interface g0/1

(config-if)#wrr-queue bandwidth 4000 3500 3000 2000

                                  assign bandwidth weights to
                                  each of the 4 queues

(config-if)#wrr-queue

(config-if)#wrr-queue random-detect max-threshold 1 20 40

(config-if)#wrr-queue random-detect max-threshold 2 30 50

(config-if)#wrr-queue random-detect max-threshold 3 50 75

(config-if)#wrr-queue random-detect max-threshold 3 50 75
```

Class-Based Weighed Fair Queuing (CBWFQ)

Class-based weighted fair queuing (CBWFQ) builds on the existing weighted fair queuing by adding user-definable traffic classes. Keep in mind that strict CBWFQ only exists in a small range of IOS versions, since in recent IOS it has been superseded by LLQ (covered later), which has the same functionality and configuration but also includes provisions for priority queuing. Up to 64 classes can be specified, and traffic can be assigned to these classes using access lists, CAR, DSCP, IP Precedence, or any other packet-classifying mechanism or criteria. All traffic assigned to a class is put into a single FIFO queue. Figure 18.11 shows the queue structure of CBWFQ.

FIGURE 18.11   Class-based weighted fair queuing (CBWFQ)

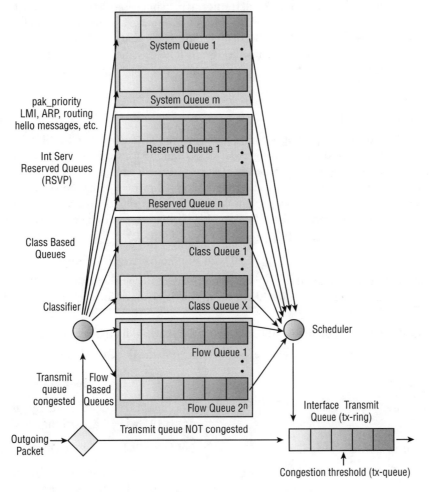

Each class can be assigned a bandwidth value or bandwidth percentage value to guarantee a minimum amount of bandwidth during periods of congestion. By default, CBWFQ is able to reserve only 75 percent of the bandwidth on an interface. This ensures that there is available bandwidth for layer 2 and layer 3 keepalives and routing protocol traffic. Therefore, if a class specifies a bandwidth of 32 percent, this translates to 24 percent of the interface's actual bandwidth. The maximum amount of bandwidth used by CBWFQ can be adjusted using the `max-reserved-bandwidth` interface command. However, it is recommended that you don't change this value unless all layer 2/3 requirements are guaranteed.

Traffic that does not match any of the user-defined classes and is not handled by an RSVP assigned queue or is not system traffic can be handled in one of three ways. If no default class is specified, the nonclassified traffic is treated in the same manner as WFQ; it is assigned to different queues based on packet header information and is given whatever bandwidth is not allocated to the user-defined classes or used by system traffic. If the default class (class-default) is specified and the fair-queue option is not used, all traffic not matching user-defined classes is assigned to a single queue, which can have a bandwidth value or percentage assigned to it as well as a queue drop strategy and depth configured. If the default class is specified and the fair-queue option is used, all traffic not assigned to user-defined classes is flow-classified, as in WFQ, into individual queues. This traffic is delivered in a best effort fashion and given the remaining bandwidth not assigned to other classes.

Configuring CBWFQ

Class-based weighted fair queuing is configured using the Modular QoS CLI (MQC). Traffic is classified and placed into a class using class maps. Bandwidth values or percentages, queue depths, and drop strategies are assigned to classes using policy maps. And finally, CBWFQ is enabled on an interface by attaching the appropriate policy map using the service-policy interface command. In the following example, four different classes are created. The interface is a serial T1 with 1536Kbps available bandwidth. The classes are to be configured as follows:

- Class 1 is all traffic to network 10.10.10.0/23 and should receive 200Kbps of the bandwidth.

- Class 2 is all traffic to network 10.20.20.0/24 and should receive 300Kbps of the bandwidth.

- Class 3 must be configured to drop based on IP-Precedence-aware WRED. Allocate 400 of the bandwidth to this class. WRED defaults will be changed for packets of precedence 1, 2, 3, and 4.

- Class 4 is all traffic bound for the Internet and is serviced by the default class.

The following are the commands necessary to achieve the these CBWFQ requirements:

`class-map class1`	Define a class map called class1
`  match access-group 101`	All traffic identified by access-list 101 will be assigned to class1
`class-map class2`	Define a class map called class2
`  match access-group 102`	All traffic identified by access-list 102 will be assigned to class2
`class-map class3`	Define a class map called class3
`  match access-group 103`	All traffic identified by access-list 103 will be assigned to class3

```
access-list 101 permit ip any 10.10.10.0 0.0.1.255
```

	Match all IP traffic to destination network 10.10.10.0/24, traffic in class1
access-list 102 permit ip any 10.20.20.0 0.0.0.255	
	Match all IP traffic to destination network 10.10.10.0/24, traffic in class2
access-list 103 permit ip any any precedence priority	
	Match all IP traffic with precedence set to 1, this is traffic in class3
access-list 103 permit ip any any precedence immediate	
	Match all IP traffic with precedence set to 2, this is traffic in class3
access-list 103 permit ip any any precedence flash	
	Match all IP traffic with precedence set to 3, this is traffic in class3
access-list 103 permit ip any any precedence flash-override	
	Match all IP traffic with precedence set to 4, this is traffic in class3
policy-map serial0/0	Create a policy-map called serial0/0
class class1	Assign class-map class1 to this policy
bandwidth 300	Assign 300Kbps of bandwidth, the default queuing mechanism is WFQ
class class2	Assign class-map class2 to this policy
bandwidth 200	Assign 200Kbps of bandwidth, the default queuing mechanism is WFQ
class class3	Assign class-map class3 to this policy
bandwidth 400	Assign 400Kbps of bandwidth

random-detect			This command configures WRED as the drop mechanism for class 3
random-detect precedence 1	10	60	Configure WRED parameters for IP precedence 1, with min threshold packets of 10 and a max threshold of 60, the mark probability is not specified and is therefore set to 9 (default)
random-detect precedence 2	20	60	Configure WRED parameters for IP precedence 2, min = 20, max = 60
random-detect precedence 3	30	60	Configure WRED parameters for IP precedence 3, min = 20, max = 60
random-detect precedence 4	40	60	Configure WRED parameters for IP precedence 4, min = 20, max = 60
interface serial0/0			
service-policy output serial0/0			attach policy map serial0/0 for use with outbound traffic

Strict Priority Queuing

Strict priority queuing is used to help deliver QoS to delay-sensitive data such as voice. Strict priority means that if packets exist in the priority queue, they are sent before packets in other queues. To avoid packet drop, when implementing a strict priority scheme, allocate to the priority queue the most optimum amount of bandwidth.

There are two mechanisms to help configure strict priority queuing using MQC: IP RTP priority in conjunction with CBWFQ or low latency queuing (LLQ).

Configuring IP RTP Priority

IP RTP priority is configured under the router interface. Only one IP RTP priority can be configured per interface (or subinterface). The following command allocates 50Kbps to all voice traffic:

interface serial 0	
ip rtp priority 16384 16383 50	Create a strict priority queue for all well known voice ports. VoIP packets are transported in UDP-based RTP packets using destination and source port numbers in the range from 16384 to 32767 (16384 + 16383)
max-reserved-bandwidth 100	Change the maximum bandwidth to 100%

Low Latency Queuing (LLQ)

Like IP RTP priority, *low latency queuing (LLQ)* also provides a priority queuing mechanism. However, LLQ allows for any traffic to be classified for priority queuing rather than just Voice over IP. LLQ is an enhancement that supersedes CBWFQ and is sometimes called priority queuing/class-based weighted fair queuing (PQ/CBWFQ).

Without a priority queuing mechanism, CBWFQ provides weighted fair queuing or WRED queuing to defined classes with no provision available for real-time traffic. CBWFQ determines the weight of a packet based on the bandwidth allocated to the class and the size of the packets that need to be sent. With delay-sensitive traffic such as voice, which is largely intolerant of delay and especially jitter, LLQ provides strict priority queuing that reduces jitter in voice conversations. Low latency queuing uses the same concept as priority queuing; the high priority queue will always get service over other lower queues, except with LLQ, a configurable amount of bandwidth can be allocated to the class. This is why LLQ is referred to as strict priority queuing. The bandwidth parameter both guarantees bandwidth to the priority class and restrains the flow of packets from the priority class to ensure that it does not starve all other classes.

When LLQ is configured and the interface is not congested, the priority class traffic is allowed to exceed its allocated bandwidth. However, when the interface is congested, the LLQ class will always be serviced until the point when the configured bandwidth has been exceeded if a packet exists in the queue. This is where LLQ and RTP priority queuing differ. With RTP priority queuing, the high queue always gets serviced as long as there are packets in the queue. With LLQ, traffic destined for the priority queue is metered and controlled to ensure that the bandwidth allocation to the class to which the traffic belongs is not exceeded. When the interface is congested, the router discards the traffic above the allocated bandwidth.

LLQ traffic is metered using a token system that is applied on a packet-by- packet basis; tokens are replenished as packets are sent. If there are an insufficient number of tokens, the packet is dropped. Therefore, under congestion, LLQ meters priority traffic to its allocated bandwidth to ensure that other classes are not starved of bandwidth. When you're configuring LLQ, all of the valid match criteria used to specify a class can be used to identify the priority traffic. Although it is possible to assign other types of traffic to the priority queue, it is recommend that LLQ is used for voice traffic only.

Configuring LLQ

Configuration of LLQ is performed using MQC and requires the following steps to be completed:

- Classify the traffic that will be serviced by the priority class. This is accomplished by creating a class map using the `class-map` command on the router.
- Allocate bandwidth to the priority class. This is achieved by creating a policy map using the `policy-map` command on the router. Under the policy map, the `class-map` is configured for priority queuing using the priority command and bandwidth is allocated to the queue.
- Assign the policy map to the interface using the `service-policy output` command under the interface on the router.

In the following example, four different classes have been created. The interface is a fractional T1 serial that has 768Kbps available bandwidth:

- Class voice-data matches all voice data assigned 300Kbps of interface bandwidth.

- Class immediate-data matches all packets that have IP Precedence 2 and 100Kbps of interface bandwidth and use WRED.

- Class priority-data matches all packets that have IP Precedence 1 and 200Kbps of interface bandwidth.

- Class default matches all other IP packets; use WRED on this class.

The following is the router configuration to achieve the these LLQ/CBWFQ requirements:

class-map voice-data	Create class map
match access-group 101	Match all traffic in access-list 101
class-map immediate-data	Create class map
match access-group 102	Match all traffic in access-list 102
class-map priority-data	Create class map
match access-group 103	Match all traffic in access-list 103
access-list 101 permit udp any any range 16384 32767	
	Allows all voice traffic which uses well known UDP port 16384 - 32767
access-list 102 permit ip any any precedence immediate	
	Allow all IP packets with IP precedence 2
access-list 103 permit ip any any precedence priority	
	Allow all IP packets with IP precedence 3
policy-map llq-policy	Create a policy map
class voice-data	Assign class-map voice-data to this policy
priority 300	Assign a this as a priority queue with 300Kbps of bandwidth
class immediate-data	Assign class-map immediate-data to this policy
bandwidth 200	Assign a this 200Kbps of bandwidth
random-detect	This command configures WRED as the dropping mechanism

class priority-data	Assign class-map priority-data to this policy
bandwidth 100	Assign a this 100Kbps of bandwidth, uses WFQ as the queuing mechanism.
class class-default	Configures the default class
random-detect	This command configures WRED as the drop mechanism for the default class
interface serial 0/0	
service-policy output llq-policy	Assign policy map llq-policy on interface serial0/0

Conversely, the same result can be achieved using IP RTP priority and legacy CBWFQ. The following is the router configuration in which IP RTP priority and CBWFQ are used to achieve the requirements listed earlier. The class maps and access lists remain the same for the classes defined for CBWFQ. The IP RTP priority is created under the interface and is allocated the same 300Kbps bandwidth:

policy-map no-llq-policy	Create a policy map
class immediate-data	Assign class-map immediate-data to this policy
bandwidth 200	Assign a this 200Kbps of bandwidth
random-detect	This command configures WRED as the drop mechanism
class priority-data	Assign class-map priority-data to this policy
bandwidth 100	Assign a this 100Kbps of bandwidth, uses WFQ as the queuing mechanism
class class-default	Configures the default CBWFQ class
random-detect	This command configures WRED as the drop mechanism for the default class
interface serial 0/0	
service-policy output no-llq-policy	Assign policy map llq-policy as a CBWFQ policy on interface serial0/0
ip rtp priority 16384 16383 300	Create strict priority queue, assign 300Kbps to voice RTP UDP ports

Displaying and Monitoring the Queues in LLQ

The following commands can be used to display the queues in LLQ. These commands are useful in troubleshooting LLQ:

```
show policy-map                      Show all policies configured on the
                                     router

show policy-map interface serial 0/0 Show policy applied to a specific
                                     interface

show queue serial 0/0                Show the status of the queue for
                                     interface serial 0/0
```

Now that we've looked at queuing, let's look at some other features used to enhance QoS.

Traffic Shaping and Policing

Traffic shaping and policing are features used to control ingress and egress traffic from interfaces. They are QoS features used to control ingress and egress traffic on an interface and are a powerful adjunct to queuing and marking. Both policing and shaping implement the concept of a token bucket, in which a packet must have enough tokens to be admitted or transmitted); however, the two features differ in how they handle packets that don't have enough credit. With shaping, traffic exceeding the set transmit rate is buffered, whereas with policing, excess traffic is dropped. In both cases, the upper traffic rate is controlled.

Traffic shaping is most widely configured on Frame Relay interfaces where the physical transmit speed of the interface is typically greater than the traffic rate the user pays for. Traffic shaping on Cisco routers can take one of two forms: Frame Relay Traffic Shaping (FRTS) or Generic Traffic Shaping (GTS) (MQC also has shaping mechanisms). As the names imply, FRTS is configured solely on Frame Relay interfaces and GTS can be configured on just about any interface except dial, X.25, and ISDN.

Policing controls the rate of traffic allowed in on an interface. Through the use of access lists or protocol statements, the admission of traffic or certain types of traffic on an interface can be controlled. Policing can be configured by using committed access rate (CAR) or by using the Modular QoS CLI (MQC).

Before launching into a discussion of traffic shaping and policing directly, a discussion of the token bucket paradigm is in order.

The concept behind a token bucket is simple. Every time a packet is to be processed, tokens are taken out of the bucket to "pay" for it. If there are not enough tokens in the bucket, the packet is either discarded in the case of policing or queued in the case of shaping. Tokens are added to the bucket in discrete time increments in the case of shaping and a continuous fashion in the case of policing. There are three parameters associated with a token bucket: the mean rate, burst size, and time interval. The mean rate is equal to the burst size divided by the time interval and is the rate at which tokens are added to the bucket. The burst size is equivalent to the size of the bucket and specifies the maximum amount of traffic that can be passed at one time. If more tokens than the bucket can hold are granted to a traffic stream, they are lost and cannot be used. Therefore, an inactive traffic stream can't hoard tokens beyond the bucket size and then suddenly transmit at an unrestricted speed.

Traffic Shaping

Frame Relay or ATM networks often have asymmetrical interfaces at either end of a network connection, and the access rate at one site may differ from the access rate at another. In such cases, it is common to use traffic shaping on the faster-rate interface to shape to the access rate of the slower-rate interface. If shaping is not configured, then it is possible to either queue or discard packets in the provider's (Frame Relay or ATM) network. The function of traffic shaping is to control the rate at which traffic is sent out an interface so that the output rate conforms to a committed information rate that the network can handle. Traffic shaping implies the existence of a queuing mechanism; the function of the queue is to buffer packets that are delayed because of traffic shaping.

Frame Relay Traffic Shaping (FRTS)

As its name implies, *Frame Relay Traffic Shaping (FRTS)* is used on Frame Relay interfaces. It can provide traffic shaping on either an interface or per-PVC (DLCI) basis. To understand how traffic shaping is implemented on Frame Relay interfaces, it is important to understand the Frame Relay traffic parameters and how they relate to the token bucket model:

Committed information rate (CIR)   This is the mean rate (bits per second) that the router sends to the Frame Relay network. It can be different (higher) from the contracted CIR that the Frame Relay provider is guaranteeing. The configured CIR on the router should be equal to the required CIR + burst rate. If the interface is 256Kbps and the contracted CIR from the provider is 128Kbps but the provider allows bursting to line rate, then one can configure CIR to 256Kbps. With this configuration, you must be willing to accept the consequence of possible data loss if the provider's network is congested. The provider is still contracted to delivering 128Kbps of traffic.

Minimum CIR (MINCIR)   MINCIR is the rate at which the traffic should be sent in a congestion situation. This is the contracted CIR that the network provider guarantees to deliver. (MINCIR is also the rate at which traffic will be throttled down to when adaptive shaping is used on FRTS.) This is the real purpose of MINCIR. When delivering voice services over a Frame Relay network, it is recommended that CIR equals MINCIR. This is to ensure that no voice packets are dropped regardless of whether the provider network is congested. During periods of congestion, frames with the BECN bit are received by the router.

Committed burst size (Bc)   This is the burst size expressed in bits that can be sent in a time interval and is used to calculate the time interval (Tc). CIR = burst / time interval.

Excess burst (Be)   This is the maximum number of bits the Frame Relay switch attempts to transfer beyond the Bc over the time interval (Tc).

Time interval (Tc)   This is the time period over which Bc or (Bc + Be) bits are transmitted. Tc is calculated as Tc = Bc / CIR.

Backward Explicit Congestion Notification (BECN)   When a Frame Relay switch in the provider's network detects congestion, it sets the BECN bit on frames destined for the source router. The BECN bit signals the router to reduce its transmission rate. The router can choose to ignore these bits and continue sending traffic over the CIR. If adaptive shaping is enabled, the router will throttle its rate incrementally down to the MINCIR value. If MINCIR is not configured, the router will assume a value of half the configured CIR.

Figure 18.12 is a 512Kbps circuit, the PVC has a contracted CIR (router value = MINCIR) from the Frame Relay provider of 96bbps. The router is configured for a CIR of 128Kps, which equated to the router sending 12800 bits per time interval of 100ms.

FIGURE 18.12   Frame Relay Traffic Shaping

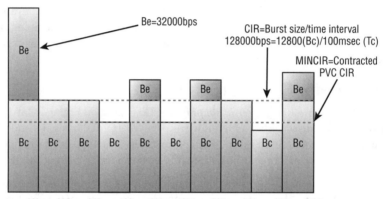

The router is also configured for a Be of 32000bps, which allows up to a maximum rate from the router of 44800 bits per 100ms. This is assuming that the router has the available Be token credits. The figure also shows that in the instance in which the router sends less than the Bc, the router in the next time interval has built up Be token credits and can "burst a little," but at this time, the router is unable to burst to the Be maximum because there are not enough token credits.

 Real World Scenario

Frame-Relay to ATM Service Interworking (FRF.8)

Many providers offer Frame Relay to ATM Service Interworking (FRF.8) when ATM is delivered at the head office and Frame Relay is delivered to each branch office, allowing high-speed branch access without oversubscription at the head office. With FRF.8, you may not be able to run FRF.12 because it is an end-to-end protocol that requires configuration on both ends of the Frame Relay PVC. However, you can run Multilink PPP (MLPPP) over Frame Relay and ATM because it allows end-to-end PPP fragmentation and interleaving.

Configuring Frame Relay Traffic Shaping

When FRTS is enabled on an interface, both traffic shaping and per-VC queuing are enabled for all the PVCs on the interface. Use the `frame-relay traffic-shaping` command on the physical interface to enable FRTS. The command needs to be configured on the physical interface. A router can be configured to automatically learn QoS parameters from a Cisco switch (BPX, MGX) using Enhanced Local Management Interface (ELMI). The Cisco switch must also be configured for ELMI (QoS autosense). The following is the router configuration to enable this:

```
interface serial 0

  frame-relay traffic-shaping          Enables FRTS

  frame-relay qos-autosense            This enables Enhanced LMI. ELMI
                                       allows a router and a Cisco frame
                                       Relay switch to automatically learn
                                       the CIR, Bc, and Be. The router
                                       will then use these parameters to
                                       traffic shape the VC output rate
```

Frame Relay Traffic Shaping and Class Maps

Frame Relay traffic shaping can be customized on a per-interface or per-subinterface basis. If a physical interface has a Frame Relay map class assigned, all subinterfaces inherit the parameters from the physical interface. In a typical hub-and-spoke network design, the hub router can be configured as a physical Frame Relay interface or a multipoint Frame Relay interface, or it could also be configured with multiple subinterfaces, one for each remote router connection.

The recommended design is to have individual subinterfaces configured because this allows for much more granular configuration of the traffic shaping parameters required for each remote site. If the head-end router is configured as a physical interface and Frame Relay Traffic Shaping is enabled, all the PVCs inherit the same traffic shaping parameters. This design does not adapt when different PVCs require different CIR, Bc, and Be parameters. If all the remote routers are connected at 128Kbps with CIR equal to 64Kbps, then this solution will provide traffic shaping that allows the head-end router, which is connected to the network at 1544Kbps, to shape the traffic to conform to the slow-speed remote ends. But there is no way to differentiate between different remote routers having different access speeds and output rates.

The following configuration is the head-end router configuration on the physical interface that allows a peak rate of 128Kbps on all PVCs with an average rate of 64Kbps:

```
interface serial 1

  frame-relay traffic-shaping          Enable traffic shaping

  frame-relay class multi_point        Assign a frame-relay class
                                       multi_point to this interface
```

```
map-class frame-relay multi_point          Create frame Relay class
                                            multi_point

 frame-relay traffic-rate 64000 128000     Set the traffic shaping rate to an
                                            CIR of 64000 bps and a peak rate of
                                            128000 bps. When the router receives
                                            a BECN it will reduce the output
                                            rate to 64000bps. The Tc is set to
                                            the default of 125ms
```

In Figure 18.13, the remotes are connected using point-to-point subinterfaces. Router R1 can then have a different Frame Relay class that gives custom characteristics to each PVC.

FIGURE 18.13 Frame Relay Traffic Shaping example

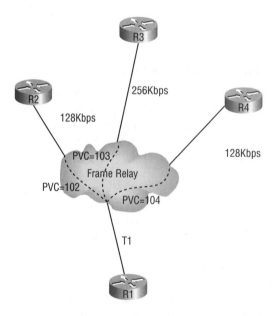

The following is the router configuration on the head-end router to provide per-PVC parameters. The interface uses the default queuing strategy of WFQ:

```
(config)#interface serial 0
(config-if)#frame-relay traffic-shaping
(config)#interface serial 0.1 point-to-point
(config-subif)#frame-relay interface-dlci 102
```

```
(config-fr-dlci)#frame-relay class 128_access
```
	Assign class 128_access to this sub interface

```
(config)#interface serial 0.2 point-to-point
(config-subif)#frame-relay interface-dlci 103
(config-fr-dlci)#frame-relay class 256_access
```
	Assign class 256_access to this sub interface

```
(config)#interface serial 0.3 point-to-point
(config-subif)#frame-relay interface-dlci 104
(config-fr-dlci)#frame-relay class 128_access
```
	Assign class 128_access to this sub interface

```
(config)# interface serial 0.1 point-to-point
(config-subif)# frame-relay interface-dlci 102
(config-fr-dlci)# class 128_access
```

`map-class Frame-relay 128_access`	Create map-class 128_access
`  frame-relay cir 128000`	Configures the sustained output rate to send at the clock rate of the remote router
`  frame-relay bc 10000`	Burst size is 10000bits, which sets the Tc = 78ms
`  frame-relay be 0`	The router is already sending at the maximum rate the network can deliver to the remote router, therefore setting a Be >0 will cause the Layer 2 network to queue
`  frame-relay mincir 64000`	When congestion is detected, the router will reduce the output rate to 64000bps
`  frame-relay adaptive-shaping becn`	The mechanism for detecting congestion is BECNs
`map-class Frame-relay  256_access`	Create map-class 256_access

`frame-relay cir 256000`	Configures the sustained output rate to send at the clock rate of the remote router
`frame-relay bc 20000`	Burst size is 20000bits, which sets the Tc = 78ms
`frame-relay be 0`	The router is already sending at the maximum rate the network can deliver to the remote router, therefore setting a Be >0 will cause the Layer 2 network to queue
`frame-relay mincir 128000`	When congestion is detected, the router will reduce the output rate to 128000bps
`frame-relay adaptive-shaping becn`	The mechanism for detecting congestion is BECNs

Configuring Frame Relay Traffic Shaping for Voice

The traffic shaping configuration on a Frame Relay interface supporting voice traffic differs slightly from the configuration on a data-only interface. When voice traffic is implemented over a Frame Relay network, there are some guidelines that should be followed. First, don't exceed the CIR of the Frame Relay PVC. This prevents any queuing delays inside the provider's cloud and ensures that no packets are dropped by the provider. Bc should be made as small as possible to help ensure that, if a large packet takes the available credits, the time frame to build up more credit to send a voice packet will be small. Be should generally be set to 0 to prevent the CIR from being overrun.

Frame Relay Voice-Adaptive Traffic Shaping and Fragmentation is a new feature in 12.2(15)T code that detects the presence of voice traffic on a PVC and lowers the shaping rate to MINCIR and activates fragmentation. If there is no voice traffic, shaping adheres to the normal burst values, and fragmentation is disabled. The `shape fr-voice-adapt` policy-map command and `frame-relay fragmentation voice-adaptive` interface command are used to configure this feature.

Generic Traffic Shaping (GTS)

Generic Traffic Shaping (GTS) allows you to configure traffic shaping not only on Frame Relay interfaces, but others as well. Like FRTS, GTS allows you to specify the traffic rate, burst size, and excess burst size. However, instead of specifying these values in Frame Relay terms like CIR, Bc, and Be, GTS uses bit rate, burst size, and excess burst size in bits rather than bytes.

🌐 Real World Scenario

The Case of the Mysterious EIGRP Neighbor Drops

We had a situation with our remote site routers in the U.K. dropping their Enhanced Interior Gateway Routing Protocol (EIGRP) neighbors once nightly during a server back-up operation. Although there were no resulting outages because the sites were closed, and the EIGRP neighbors and file transfers recovered quickly, the loss of routes caused everything to appear red on the network management map and was a constant source of worry for the Network Operations Center (NOC) personnel.

The remote sites were connected via 56Kbps Frame Relay circuits back to the termination routers. Each PVC had an 8Kbps CIR. Although the circuits had a very low CIR, the provider never seemed to drop any packets when traffic exceeded it. When the remote site router configurations were reviewed, it was found that priority queuing was enabled but not properly configured. After correcting the access lists for PQ, the EIGRP neighbor drops still occurred.

We were able to get a test window to see how the network behaved. Extended ping tests using large packets showed that the circuits were held to the 8Kbps CIR and no Internet Control Message Protocol (ICMP) packets were dropped during the test. But while testing, we were able to cause the EIGRP neighbor drop problem. We quickly checked the access lists and priority lists— they were correctly configured. We then noticed that there were very few, if any, hits on the access list counters. How could this be? We had congestion, didn't we? Wasn't traffic backing up between the remote site and the main site? The answer was yes, it was. However, it wasn't backing up on the routers. It was being buffered up inside the provider's cloud instead. We had to figure out how to keep the traffic buffered up on the routers during congestion so they could make the proper queuing decisions.

We decided that Frame Relay Traffic Shaping would do the job. After we configured shaping to the 8Kbps CIR, there were no more EIGRP neighbor drops and we could see hits on the priority queuing access lists. However, it was noticed that the nightly back-ups now took twice as long as before. Therefore, we experimented with some different values of MINCIR, Bc, and Be and arrived at a combination that provided good data transfer times and kept the EIGRP neighbors from dropping.

Configuring Generic Traffic Shaping

The following lines show how to configure GTS on a serial interface using the `traffic-shape group` command. In this case, there are two sets of traffic that we want to shape. The traffic could be destined either for two separate sites across two different DLCIs if the interface is a Frame Relay interface or for two different applications that have different traffic constraints.

Because the excess burst size is equal to the regular burst size, there is no excess burst capability for this traffic:

```
interface  Serial 0/0
 bandwidth 1544
 traffic-shape group 111 128000 12000 12000
```
> All traffic matching access-list 111 is shaped with CIR = 128000bps, burst size = 12000 bits and excess burst of 12000 bits

```
 traffic-shape group 112  64000 8000 8000
```
> All traffic matching access-list 112 is shaped be shaped with CIR = 64000bps burst size = 8000 bits and excess burst size of 8000 bits

```
access-list 111 permit ip any 10.10.10.0 0.0.0.255
```
> Identifies all traffic to network 10.10.10.0/24

```
access-list 112 permit ip any 10.10.20.0 0.0.0.255
```
> Identifies all traffic to network 10.10.20.0/24

Generic Traffic Shaping and Frame Relay

On a Frame Relay interface, GTS can be configured to respond to Frame Relay BECNs and adapt the output rate of the interface. As with FRTS, GTS has a graduated response to BECNs and limits the output incrementally as BECNs are received down to the MINCIR rate. The commands to configure this are as follows:

```
interface serial 0
 bandwidth 1544
 traffic-shape rate 512000          Shape the output rate to 512000 bits
 traffic-shape adaptive 128000      In the event of that BECN's are
                                    received, throttle back to actual
                                    CIR = 128000
 traffic-shape fecn-adapt           When this command is configured at
                                    both ends of the link, for received
                                    FECNs at the far end, the far end
                                    sends BECNs in the Q.922 message
                                    response
```

I/F	Access List	Queue Depth	Packets	Bytes	Packets Delayed	Bytes Delayed	Shaping Active
Se0/0	111	0	195	123180	55	66620	no
Se0/0	112	0	15	1560	0	0	no

Committed Access Rate (CAR) and Policing

Committed access rate (CAR) has two functions within the QoS model. First, it is a traffic policer, controlling the rate at which traffic enters or leaves an interface. Second, CAR has the capability to mark or color packets. CAR, like traffic shaping, looks at the traffic rate on an interface and limits it. However, instead of buffering traffic exceeding the set threshold, CAR drops the traffic, performing policing instead of shaping/buffering. As with traffic shaping, CAR loosely uses the paradigm of a token bucket to control traffic flow but drops anything that "spills over" rather than buffering it.

Configuring Policing

Policing can be configured using CAR and the legacy interface command `rate-limit` or by using the Modular QoS CLI (MQC) method with the `police` statement under policy maps. The MQC method is preferred and gives the extra feature of violate-action. Cisco has stated that no new additions to the legacy `rate-limit` command will be made and that all new features will be added solely to MQC. The following example shows the policing of inbound HTTP traffic on an Ethernet interface to 1Mbps with a burst size of 10,000 bytes and an excess burst size of 20,000 bytes. The example is first configured using CAR and then shown using MQC:

```
interface fa 0/0

rate-limit input access-group 101 1000000        limit traffic matching

10000 20000 conform-action transmit             access-list 101 (http)

exceed-action drop                              to 1Mbps with a burst size
                                                of 10000 bytes and an excess
                                                burst size of 20000 bytes.
                                                Anything over these limits
                                                gets dropped.

access-list 101 permit tcp any any eq www   match http traffic
```

NOTE   CAR requires interfaces to be configured with CEF.

Here is the example using MQC:

`class-map match-all simpleHTTP`	use class-map to classify
`  match protocol http`	http traffic
`policy-map rateLimit_HTTP`	create policy-map to set up
`  class simpleHTTP`	rate limiting of the http
`    police 1000000 10000 20000`	traffic. Rate set to 1Mbps
`      conform-action transmit`	with burst of 10K bytes and
`      exceed-action drop`	an excess burst size of 20K
	bytes. Anything over is dropped.
`interface fa 0/0`	
`  service-policy inbound rateLimit_HTTP`	attach policy-map for inbound
	traffic

Network Based Application Recognition (NBAR)

Network Based Application Recognition (NBAR) is used to identify and classify IP traffic beyond the UDP/TCP port layer. By looking up to 512 bytes within a packet (including IP and UDP/TCP headers), NBAR can differentiate traffic based on upper layer fields such as message types, return codes, and other application specific information. This Cisco IOS feature originated in 12.0(5)XE code and was more generally available in the 12.1(5)T and beyond.

 NBAR increases CPU usage in the neighborhood of 15–20% and uses 1MB DRAM by default.

Although NBAR has built-in recognition for numerous applications and types of traffic, its capability can be extended to recognize new applications through one of two ways. The first is to define and map custom applications using the `port-map` option, and the second is by loading Packet Description Language Modules (PDLMs). The port-map function can be used to map up to 16 TCP/UDP port numbers to a custom protocol. There can be up to 10 custom protocols defined using NBAR. Although access lists could be used to perform this same classification, NBAR is considered to be easier to configure and implement than access lists and provides enhanced statistics reporting.

PDLMs are classification templates that can be downloaded from the CCO Cisco website and loaded into flash memory on a router running NBAR. Once on the router, PDLMs can be loaded into running memory dynamically to begin classification of traffic; no reboot is required. The use of PDLMs keeps you from having to upgrade IOS to incorporate new applications into NBAR. Cisco posts new PDLMs periodically to CCO, so if you're running NBAR, it's a good idea to check once in awhile.

In the same manner that access lists can be used as a poor-man's firewall, NBAR can act as a poor-man's intrusion detection system (IDS) and can be used to detect worms such as Slammer and Code Red, although it does not send out alarms as an IDS would. However, if you're serious about security, a dedicated appliance is almost always preferable to using a router.

 NBAR requires Cisco Express Forwarding (CEF) to be enabled. NBAR does not run on dialer interfaces, VLANs, interfaces configured with Multilink PPP (MLPPP), etherChannel, tunneling, or encryption. NBAR does not work on non-IP traffic, fragmented packets, multicast packets, locally originated packets, or asymmetric flows with stateful protocols.

Here is an example of NBAR used to classify and block HTTP traffic going to a particular gambling website. It is assumed that traffic enters interface f0/0 and attempts to exit interface f1/0:

```
(config)#class-map match-all noGambling
(config-cmap)#match protocol http url "*JoesCasino*"
(config)#policy-map sorryJoe
(config-pmap)#class noGambling
(config-pmap-c)#set ip dscp 5
(config)#policy-map dropUnwantedTraffic
(config-pmap)#class noGambling
(config-pmap-c)#police 8000 1500 1500 conform-action
        drop exceed-action drop violate-action drop
(config)#interface f0/0
(config-if)#service-policy inbound sorryJoe
(config)#interface f1/0
(config-if)#service-policy outbound dropUnwanted Traffic
```

Compression

Compression is the technique of removing redundant information from a packet in order to make it smaller so that less bandwidth is taken to transmit it. Compression can also decrease the overall latency of traffic on a low-speed link by reducing the queuing delay. Compression does, however, increase router CPU usage.

RTP Header Compression (cRTP)

The need for *RTP header compression (compressed RTP, or cRTP)* arises from the fact that the IP, UDP, and RTP headers attached to a VoIP packet can be much larger than the actual data payload and contribute to much greater bandwidth utilization, especially for slower links. By using cRTP on a G.729a VoIP stream, you can save nearly 50 percent of the bandwidth use; however, cRTP does add some latency that needs to be considered. The idea behind cRTP is to replace the IP, UDP, and RTP header with a smaller (compressed) header for transmission across a point-to-point link. Because most of the information in an RTP flow's headers remains constant, there is no need to transmit it across the link. The routers on both ends keep a copy of the full header to "reconstitute" the IP, UDP, and RTP headers for transmission to the end devices.

RTP header compression is defined in RFC 2508. It notes that there are fields in the IP, UDP, and RTP headers that do not change packet by packet as well as fields whose values change by a constant amount packet by packet. Therefore, the second order difference for these two types of fields is 0 (i.e., the incremental change for these fields is constant packet by packet).

RTP header compression can be enabled on a per-interface basis using the `ip rtp header-compression` command on non-Frame Relay interfaces and using the `frame-relay ip rtp header-compression` command on Frame Relay interfaces.

Frame Relay Compression (FRF.9)

Frame Relay interfaces can make use of FRF.9 compression using the `frame-relay payload-compression frf9 stac` interface command. Compression can be enabled on an interface or subinterface. Traffic is decompressed by the router on the other side of the Frame Relay link:

```
interface s3/2.1
frame-relay payload-compression frf9 stac
```

Cisco routers also support a proprietary compression method over Frame Relay that can be activated using the `frame-relay payload-compression packet-by-packet` interface command.

Summary

Previously, QoS was thought of as just a way to prioritize DLSw or interactive traffic like Telnet, and priority queuing and custom queuing were equal to the task. However, Quality of Service plays a crucial role in helping to converge voice, video, and data across one network. New queuing methods like low latency queuing (LLQ) and classification techniques like Network Based Application Recognition (NBAR) have evolved to help. QoS has moved into the switching realm as well with marking and queuing features supported on most Catalyst switches.

QoS covers a lot of topics but can be made manageable when grouped into classification, scheduling, policing/shaping, congestion avoidance, and link efficiency. In this chapter, wee covered how to mark layer 2 and layer 3 packets using the 802.1p and ISL priority bits, IP Precedence bits, the DSCP field, and the MPLS experimental/CoS field. We also looked at how to mark these fields using route maps, access lists, and the Modular QoS CLI (MQC). Legacy queuing methods such as priority queuing (PQ), custom queuing (CQ) and weighted fair queuing (WFQ) are still in use and valuable tools for QoS. Because of their importance to voice traffic, the low latency queuing (LLQ) and RTP priority queuing methods should be well understood as well as the underlying class-based queuing subsystem.

Traffic shaping and policing with committed access rate (CAR) are also important features and were shown to be useful in conjunction with queuing methods to provide QoS. Finally, we looked at reducing WAN load using Frame Relay compression and RTP header compression (cRTP).

Exam Essentials

Know the different queuing mechanisms, their strengths, and their weaknesses.   Cisco IOS has a number of queuing mechanisms including first in/first out (FIFO), priority queuing (PQ), custom queuing (CQ), weighted fair queuing (WFQ), Weighted Random Early Detection (WRED), class-based weighted fair queuing (CBWFQ), RTP priority, and low latency queuing (LLQ).

Understand the difference between Integrated Services and Differentiated Services and the different roles of DSCP and RSVP.   Both the Integrated Services (IntServ) and Differentiated Services (DiffServ) models apply to IP traffic, but IntServ is a QoS model in which bandwidth is "carved out" for applications in the network before session traffic starts, very similar to dedicated circuits in the PSTN world. IntServ is currently implemented using the Resource Reservation Protocol (RSVP) and reserved queues in certain methods of queuing (WFQ, LLQ, etc.). RSVP is also implemented on clients and servers (applications) to signal their QoS needs. Differentiated Services (DiffServ) takes a different approach to QoS. Instead of reserving explicit bandwidth, DiffServ marks IP packets using the Differentiated Services Codepoint (DSCP) field in the IP header to signal traffic's QoS needs. Queuing methods on routers are then tailored to meet the expected needs of different traffic classes on a per-hop basis on each router. DiffServ scales much better than IntServ but does not guarantee bandwidth and requires more configuration. DiffServ is also supported on switches. The Catalyst 3550 and other switches have the ability to translate CoS layer 2 markings to DSCP and vice versa with IP traffic.

Understand how to configure QoS using the Modular QoS CLI (MQC) method.   MQC has three parts: class maps, policy maps, and the `service-interface` command. Class maps are used to identify and classify traffic. Each class map is given a unique, case-sensitive name. Policy maps are then used to specify what is done to the traffic in the classes, such as mark, police, set queue limits, set bandwidth limits, and so on. Policy maps are then attached to interfaces either inbound or outbound using the `service-interface` command. Like class maps, policy maps are assigned unique, case-sensitive names.

Know the purpose of traffic shaping, how it works, and how to configure it.   Traffic shaping is used to rate limit traffic outbound on an interface. It is most commonly used on multi-access serial links where the physical line speed on one end exceeds the rate at the far end. For example, it might be used when a head-end Frame Relay router with a T1 link is sending traffic to remote sites with 64Kbps links and slower committed information rates. Traffic shaping is enabled at the main interface layer but can be tailored on a per-PVC basis using class maps. There are two categories of traffic shaping: Generic Traffic Shaping (GTS) and Frame Relay Traffic Shaping (FRTS). The meanings of the CIR, Bc, Tc, and Be parameters should be well understood.

Key Terms

Before you take the exam, be certain you are familiar with the following terms:

Class of Service (CoS)

class-based weighted fair queuing (CBWFQ)

custom queuing (CQ)

Differentiated Service Code Point (DSCP)

Differentiated Services (DiffServ)

Frame Relay Traffic Shaping (FRTS)

Generic Traffic Shaping (GTS)

Integrated Services (IntServ)

low latency queuing (LLQ)

Modular QoS CLI (MQC)

Multiprotocol Label Switching (MPLS)

Network Based Application Recognition (NBAR)

priority queuing (PQ)

Resource Reservation Protocol (RSVP)

RTP header compression (compressed RTP, or cRTP)

weighted fair queuing (WFQ)

Weighted Random Early Detection (WRED)

Weighted Round Robin (WRR)

Review Questions

1. Which queuing method requires the least amount of configuration on a T1 link?

   A. Class-based weighted fair queuing

   B. Custom queuing

   C. Weighted fair queuing (WFQ)

   D. Low latency queuing (LLQ)

   E. Weighted Random Early Detection (WRED)

2. Which of the following are used to mark/color/classify packets? (Choose all that apply.)

   A. DSCP

   B. WFQ

   C. 802.1p

   D. IP Precedence

   E. PQ

3. How many different priority levels can DSCP differentiate?

   A. 8

   B. 16

   C. 32

   D. 64

   E. 128

4. Which type of queuing is also referred to as "starvation queuing"?

   A. Priority queuing (PQ)

   B. Class-based weighted fair queuing (CBWFQ)

   C. Custom queuing (CQ)

   D. Weighted Random Early Detection (WRED)

   E. FIFO

5. Weighted Round Robin (WRR) is used on some Catalyst switches to _____.

   A. Mark CoS values on layer 2 packets

   B. Mark IP Precedence/DSCP values

   C. Dequeue packets

   D. Drop TCP packets to prevent synchronization

   E. Police ingress traffic

6. Which of the following is not an aspect of IOS MQC?

    A. Class map

    B. Route map

    C. Service-interface

    D. Policy map

7. Committed access rate (CAR) can be used to do which of the following? (Choose all that apply.)

    A. Mark IP packets

    B. Mark IPX packets

    C. Drop traffic above a set threshold

    D. Buffer traffic above a set threshold

    E. Route packets to a different interface based on DSCP settings

8. Weighted fair queuing (WFQ) assigns AppleTalk and DECnet traffic to which of the following?

    A. Separate queues based on hashed header values

    B. One queue for all non-IP traffic

    C. Reserved queues for non-IP traffic

    D. The same queues as IP traffic with IP Precedence of 0

9. NBAR can classify traffic based on which of the following? (Choose all that apply.)

    A. HTTP URL

    B. UDP port

    C. 802.1p CoS

    D. IP protocol

    E. All of the above

10. MPLS makes use of which field to make its QoS decisions?

    A. 802.1p

    B. 802.1q

    C. Experimental/CoS

    D. IP Precedence

    E. RSVP

Answers to Review Questions

1. C. Weighted fair queuing (WFQ) is enabled by default on interfaces with E1 (2.048Mbps) speeds and less and generally requires no additional configuration from a user.

2. A, C, D. DSCP and IP Precedence are used to mark IP packets, and 802.1p is used to mark 802.1q encapsulated packets.

3. D. Using 6 bits of the ToS field in the IP header, DSCP has 64 different priority levels.

4. A. Priority queuing (PQ) is referred to as "starvation queuing" because the amount of traffic assigned to the higher priority queues gets strict priority over the traffic in lower queues and can starve them out.

5. C. WRR is used to dequeue packets from switch queues.

6. B. Modular QoS CLI (MQC) uses class maps to classify traffic for policy maps to act upon. Policy maps are attached inbound or outbound on an interface using the `service-interface` command.

7. A, C. CAR is used to rate-limit inbound or outbound traffic and drops traffic above a set threshold; it does not buffer it. CAR can also be used to mark IP packets either via IP Precedence or DSCP. IPX packets do not have any provisions for QoS marking, so CAR cannot color them. Unlike route maps, CAR cannot make/affect routing decisions directly.

8. A. Weighted fair queuing (WFQ) assigns traffic to queues based on a hashed value of fields in the packet header. This hashed value is used as an index into a list of queues. Separate AppleTalk and DECnet traffic streams (flows) will more often than not hash into unique queues of their own. It is possible that a hash value could coincide with an IP flow's so that an AppleTalk flow could share the same queue with an IP flow.

9. A, B, D. NBAR inspects up to 512 bytes into a packet, including the IP and UDP/TCP headers. NBAR has capabilities to match URLs and other values within an HTTP packet.

10. C. MPLS uses a 3-bit experimental/CoS field in the MPLS tag to denote QoS priority settings.

Chapter 19

Network Security

THE CCIE QUALIFICATION EXAM TOPICS COVERED IN THIS CHAPTER INCLUDE THE FOLLOWING:

- ✓ Local user authentication
- ✓ Authentication, authorization, and accounting (AAA); Terminal Access Controller Access Control System (TACACS); and Remote Authentication Dial-In User Service (RADIUS)
- ✓ Understanding the syslog function
- ✓ Firewalls: Cisco Secure PIX Firewall, access control lists (ACLs), demilitarized zones (DMZ)
- ✓ IKE and IPSec
- ✓ Authentication hashes
- ✓ Encryption: public key/private key, Data Encryption Standard (DES)

Network security has grown in complexity in the past few years. Before the Internet, security was an internal matter and a network with poor security often went unharmed. In the age of the Internet, every network is a target and security is of supreme importance.

In this chapter, we will investigate subjects related to enhancing and maintaining network security, including how to manage a large number of users in your network with authentication, authorization, and accounting (AAA). Additionally, we will consider how Terminal Access Controller Access Control System (TACACS) and Remote Authentication Dial-In User Service (RADIUS) can be used to centralize administration. Logging will allow you to record events in a network. The PIX firewall, demilitarized zone (DMZ), and access list can be used to control what network traffic is allowed to traverse the network. Finally, we will discuss encryption and its uses.

Authenticating the User

First of all, you must ensure that the person connecting to a router is permitted access to it (in the case of a terminal server configuration). The most common way to do that is to use a password or a combination of username and password. The user submits the needed information to the router, and the router checks the information. If the information is correct, the user has been authenticated.

Line Authentication

The most common form of authentication is line authentication, which uses different passwords to authenticate users depending on the line they are connecting through. In Figure 19.1, a user who directly connects to the console port would need to submit the password florida to be allowed access. Alternately, a user connecting via a Telnet application would need to provide the password arkansas. Finally, a user connecting to the auxiliary (aux) port (e.g., over a modem connection) would need to provide the password colorado.

FIGURE 19.1   Line authentication

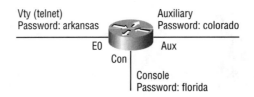

The usefulness of line authentication is limited, because all users have to know the same password to authenticate. The configuration is quite simple:

```
R1(config)#line con 0
R1(config-line)#login
R1(config-line)#password florida
R1(config-line)#line aux 0
R1(config-line)#password colorado
R1(config)#line vty 0 4
R1(config-line)#password arkansas
```

The only subtlety you may note is the `login` command under the console configuration. The `login` command instructs the router to check for a line password, and this is enabled by default on telnet (vty) and auxiliary lines.

Line authentication is acceptable in environments that have few administrators and few routers. If one administrator should leave the group, all passwords should be changed on all routers (for security reasons) and all the other administrators must be told the new passwords. Now we will discuss local authentication.

Local Authentication

Local authentication allows for separate usernames and passwords for additional password protection and logging. Not only do hackers need to guess the password, they now must also figure out the corresponding username. This increase in security permits for greater accountability and more exacting control. In the scenario in Figure 19.2, Chris and Josh both have access to router R1 and router R3. Chris has access to router R2, but Josh does not. If Chris were to leave the company, we would simply delete that username.

FIGURE 19.2   Local authentication

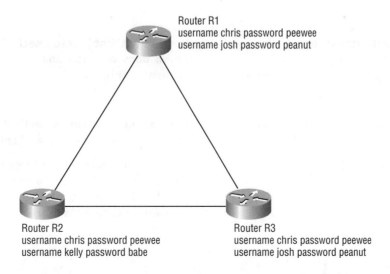

Router R1
username chris password peewee
username josh password peanut

Router R2
username chris password peewee
username kelly password babe

Router R3
username chris password peewee
username josh password peanut

Note that each user must be created on each router, and this can be a time-consuming task if there are a large number of routers or users. These users are stored locally in the router configuration, so the router must then be told to check this local list of users when authenticating:

```
username chris password peewee
username josh password peanut


line con 0
 login local
line aux  0
 login local
line vty 0 4
 login local
```

The `login local` command instructs the router to check the local list of users stored in the router configuration.

Now let's look at how to configure the vty lines (Telnet) to use the local database of username/password statements without using the `login local` command; the line con and line aux will not require any type of login:

```
aaa new-model
```

`aaa authentication login default local`	Uses the local database of username/ password statements
`aaa authentication login kelly none`	Group kelly does NOT require any aaa authentication
`username chris password josh`	Local database
`line con 0`	
`  exec-timeout 0 0`	
`  login authentication kelly`	Use aaa authentication method kelly, which does not use any authentication
`line aux 0`	
`  login authentication kelly`	Use aaa authentication method kelly, which does not use any authentication
`line vty 0 4`	Uses the default aaa authentication method, which is configured to use the local database of username/ password statements

Once the user has been authenticated, the user's actions can be more closely monitored:

```
R1>show users
    Line     User      Host(s)        Idle Location
*   1 vty 0  chris     idle           0 192.168.0.2

R1>en
Password:
R1#conf t
Enter configuration commands, one per line. End with CNTL/Z.
R1(config)#end
%SYS-5-CONFIG_I: Configured from console by chris on vty0 (192.168.0.2)
```

A show users command now reveals that a user authenticated as chris has logged into the router. When a change is made to the router, note that the user's name is associated with the change.

Local security is a step up from line security and is efficient if you have a small number of routers. As the number of routers increases, local security becomes more cumbersome because the user list on each router must be maintained separately. In a larger network environment, it is better to implement security servers.

Security Servers

Local and line security provide adequate security but require a large amount of administration. Imagine a network with 300 routers: Every time a password needs to be changed, the administrator would need to individually modify all 300 routers. The solution to this quandary is security servers. Security servers provide centralized management of usernames and passwords. When a router wishes to authenticate a user, the router collects the username and password information from the user and submits this information to the security server, as shown in Figure 19.3.

FIGURE 19.3   Security servers

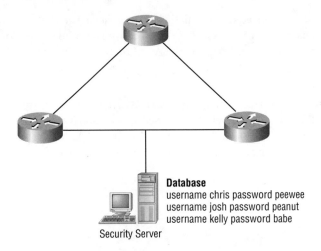

Database
username chris password peewee
username josh password peanut
username kelly password babe

Security Server

The security server compares the submitted information to the user database to determine if the user should be permitted access to the router. All usernames and passwords are stored centrally on the single security server. By consolidating administration to a single device, managing the users becomes almost trivial.

Security servers are able perform their administration function through the use of authentication, authorization, and accounting (AAA). The authentication component provides a method for identifying users, authorization uses a set of attributes that describe which actions the user is authorized to perform, and accounting collects security information and can be used for reporting, auditing, and billing. See "Authentication, Authorization, and Accounting (AAA)" later in this chapter for a detailed explanation. There are three primary types of security servers supported by Cisco routers, namely RADIUS, TACACS, and Kerberos. There are three primary types of security servers supported by Cisco routers, namely RADIUS, TACACS, and Kerberos.

RADIUS

Remote Authentication Dial-In User Service (RADIUS), developed by the Internet Engineering Task Force (IETF), is a security system that secures the network against unauthorized access. RADIUS implements a client/server architecture. The client is typically a router, and the server is a Windows NT or Unix server running RADIUS software.

Newer versions of RADIUS use UDP port number 1812. Older versions of RADIUS implement UDP port number 1645 for authentication plus UDP port number 1646 for accounting.

The authentication process has three distinct stages. First, the user is prompted for a username and password. Second, the username and encrypted password are sent over the network to the RADIUS server. The RADIUS server will reply with one of the following:

Accept	The user has been successfully authenticated.
Reject	The username and password are not valid.
Challenge	The RADIUS server requests additional information.
Change Password	The user should select a new password.

RADIUS only encrypts the password in the access-request packet. RADIUS is an open standard implemented by most major vendors and is one of the most popular types of security servers. Another popular method of authentication is TACACS.

TACACS+

Terminal Access Controller Access Control System (TACACS+) is a security server similar in many ways to RADIUS. TACACS+ was developed by Cisco Systems and is specifically designed to interact with Cisco's authentication, authorization, and accounting (AAA). The TACACS+ server handles authentication, authorization, and accounting separately. (There is more information on AAA later in this chapter). TACACS, which uses TCP, encrypts the entire body of the packet. TACACS has evolved through three different versions:

- The first standards-based implementation of the protocol was called TACACS.
- Enhanced TACACS is an extension of the protocol and provides additional router information.
- TACACS+ provides detailed accounting information and flexible administrative control over the authentication and authorization processes.

TACACS+ allows the full implementation of AAA features: Authentication includes messaging support in addition to login and password functions, authorization enables explicit control over user capabilities, and accounting supplies detailed information about user activities. TACACS+ does all that RADIUS does and more.

Example of TACACS+ and RADIUS Implementation

Let's look at a basic example of AAA commands utilizing RADIUS, TACACS+, and a local database:

`aaa new-model`	Enable AAA commands
`aaa authentication login default local`	Use local authentication for access to the router
`aaa authentication enable default enable`	Use enable password as the default method of authenticating privileged mode access
`aaa authentication ppp default radius`	Use radius for the default method of authentication ppp sessions
`aaa authentication ppp kelly tacacs+ local`	Try TACACS+, then the local database for any ppp chap sessions, which belong to the method list kelly
`enable password cisco`	
`username chris password josh`	Local database
`interface BRI 0/0`	
`  ip address 171.16.1.1 255.255.255.252`	
`  encapsulation ppp`	
`  ppp authentication chap kelly`	On this list all ppp sessions are authenticated via chap using method list kelly

```
tacacs-server host 147.19.24.10          TACACS+ server address

tacacs-server key francis                TACACS+ server key=francis

radius-server host 147.19.24.5 auth-port 1645 acct-port 1646

                                         RADIUS server address and the
                                         specified port numbers

radius-server key ken                    RADIUS server key=ken
```

Another form of authentication and encryption method that can be used by Cisco routers to ensure that data can't be "sniffed" off of the network is Kerberos.

 Real World Scenario

TACACS: Secure Administration Access and Accounting over WAN

A fellow Network Engineer, Dean Olson, has advice concerning TACACS deployment. During a very successful review of the new AAA/TACACS+ on the core equipment, management decided that it was time to push this control out to the remote locations to gain the same security authentication and accounting features for those devices. The engineering teams immediately started pushing the configuration changes to 100 sites for pilot. During the pilot quite a few calls were generated from the level 1 and level 2 support teams complaining that their telnet sessions to most of these test sites were slow.

At this point, Dean received a call from management asking "why are my support teams having issues with telnet sessions to these sites"? Dean started researching the configurations. After his audit was complete and didn't find any immediate issues with the implementation, Dean started reviewing the WAN statistics and discovered that the remote locations were bursting well over the CIR limit more often than not. And to make matters a little more difficult, they were using priority queuing to allow certain applications the high queue, a few others the normal queue, and everything else in the low queue, which included TACACS. So, in conclusion the support teams were falling into the bit bucket!

Dean's recommendation was to either remove TACACS for the remote sites including both Authentication and Accounting, install a remote ACS Server at the remote locations, or change the AAA configuration by removing accounting, adding the "tacacs-server timeout 10" and "tacacs-server retransmit 3" commands.

Management decided to audit all circuits and those that had available bandwidth are using TACACS for authentication with the server timeouts set to 10 seconds and TACACS will quit requesting after three attempts and to fall back default local logins. This allows some security without impacting the business. The real key is that centralized AAA should be thoroughly researched prior to deployment, especially over low CIR WAN connections. You may cause more damage than good! Thanks to Dean for that tip.

Kerberos

Kerberos was developed at MIT and was designed to provide strong security using the Data Encryption Standard (DES) cryptographic algorithm. Another key design goal of Kerberos is to provide single sign-on.

Kerberos can be used like RADIUS or TACACS+ for authenticating a user. However, after a user is authenticated with Kerberos, an admission ticket is granted. The ticket will allow the user to access other resources on the network without resubmitting the password across the network. These tickets have a limited life span, and upon expiration they require renewal to access resources again.

Cisco routers also support Kerberos for `telnet`, `rlogin`, `rsh`, and `rcp`. These Kerberized sessions allow encrypted communication between the end station and the router. This is especially useful for administrators who configure routers because Telnet messages are normally sent in clear text.

Kerberos will continue to gain popularity, particularly because it is now included with Windows 2000. Kerberos is currently one of the most secure methods of authenticating a user.

After the user has been successfully authenticated by the router, the next question to ask is which tasks or commands should the user be authorized to execute? Some users should be granted very limited permissions, whereas others should have complete control of the router.

Granting Permissions

There are a number of ways to control what a user is authorized to do. The most popular methods are using the default modes, controlling privilege levels, and employing security servers.

User Modes

One of the first commands taught in a course about Cisco routers is the `enable` command, which upgrades the access rights to the router from user level to privilege level. There are three default privilege modes.

The lowest level is actually the not logged in mode (privilege level 0), in which the only commands available are those required to log in. User mode is actually privilege level 1, and most show commands are available to the user (except those used for viewing the configuration). User mode also allows for Telnet, Ping, and some other fundamental commands. Router configuration cannot be accomplished from user mode.

Privilege mode (often called enable mode) maps to privilege level 15 (the highest level), and every command is available to the user. This is the equivalent of the administrator, supervisor, or root users in other operating systems. Figure 19.4 shows the relationships between the different modes.

FIGURE 19.4 User modes

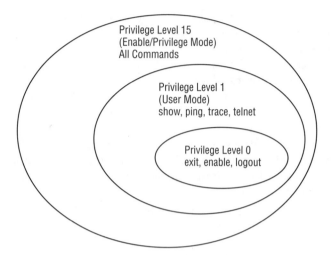

The default modes are useful, but they do not give you the fine control that is often needed. What if you have a user who needs to be able to clear Telnet sessions but you do not want this user to have configure permissions? In this case, the default user modes will not suffice. Privilege levels will need to be configured.

Privilege Levels

We have already discussed the three default privilege levels, so now we will investigate controlling privileges for specific users and specific commands. In the preceding section, we mentioned giving a user permission to clear lines but not permissions to configure. The global command to accomplish this is as follows:

```
privilege exec level 1 clear line
```

The command changes the privilege level for the clear line command to level 1, and the exec indicates that this command is executed in executive mode (i.e., Router> or Router#). The privilege level is changed without requiring the network administrator to grant the default level 15 privilege access. Now, any user in user mode has permission to clear the lines, which may not be the desired effect. Consider the following configuration:

```
enable secret level 2 kelly
privilege exec level 2 clear line
```

This configuration creates a separate password (kelly) requirement for privilege level 2 for the clear line command. Now a user in user mode level 1 would not be able to use the clear line command:

```
R1>clear line 10
     ^
```

```
% Invalid input detected at '^' marker.

R1>enable 2
Password:
R1#clear line 10
[confirm]
```

Once the user enters privilege level 2, the command becomes available for use. Privilege levels can also be associated with a user login so that when the user is authenticated, the user is immediately placed in the appropriate privilege level:

```
R1(config)#username chris privilege 2
R1(config)#username josh privilege 15
```

In this example, when Chris logs into the router, he will immediately be placed at privilege level 2, whereas Josh would be placed at privilege level 15. An advantage of this is that Josh would never need to know the enable password.

Privilege levels provide fine control over authorizing the use of commands, but they must be configured on a per-router basis. An AAA server can be used as a central repository to store the privilege levels for each individual user.

Security Servers and Authorization

Security servers once again provide the solution for reducing administration. Some security servers provide the ability to assign privilege levels in addition to restricting or permitting individual commands based on the username. This centralized authorization scales well for large networks.

Recording Activity

Often, the first step in troubleshooting is asking, "What did you change since the network last worked?" This inevitably draws the response, "Nothing!" Keeping an account of what has occurred on the routers can greatly reduce your troubleshooting effort and can also be used for security-related issues such as audits, billing, error-reporting, and so on.

Logging

Cisco routers provide the functionality to send syslog events to a syslog server. To configure a router to send the events to the server, you must use the `logging host` global command. The keyword `host` can be either the name or IP address of the host to be used as a syslog server.

Cisco routers provide system message logging (syslog) to several optional destinations, as shown in Figure 19.5. Table 19.1 lists the commands used to do so.

TABLE 19.1   Logging Command Syntax

Command	description
logging console	Outputs messages to the console port of the router (default)
logging buffered	Outputs messages into memory
logging monitor	Sends the messages to any session that has enabled monitoring (usually Telnet)
logging trap	Outputs messages to a remote server, making it the most useful and important logging destination

FIGURE 19.5   Logging messages to different destinations

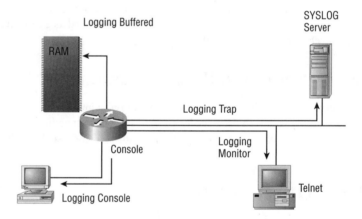

Syslog is a protocol defined for UDP on port 514. Messages are sent from the router to a server running the syslog service. The server will archive these messages for later analysis by the administrator.

The router provides several configuration options. Logging can be turned on or off for a particular destination. Messages are divided into the categories shown in Table 19.2.

TABLE 19.2   Syslog levels

Name	Level	Description	Syslog Event
Emergencies	0	System unusable	LOG_EMERG
Alerts	1	Immediate action needed	LOG_ALERT

TABLE 19.2   Syslog levels *(continued)*

Name	Level	Description	Syslog Event
Critical	2	Critical conditions	LOG_CRIT
Errors	3	Error conditions	LOG_ERR
Warnings	4	Warning conditions	LOG_WARNING
Notifications	5	Normal but significant condition	LOG_NOTICE
Informational	6	Informational messages only	LOG_INFO
Debugging	7	Debugging messages	LOG_DEBUG

The router can be configured to send logging messages that meet a specified minimum severity level. Logging provides an excellent way to record changes that are occurring within the router. When a specific syslog level is specified, all events for the selected level and all higher levels are logged (level 0 is the highest level).

Syslog requires network connectivity to deliver a message to the server. If the interfaces that are required to communicate with the syslog server fail, no message will be recorded.

SNMP

The *Simple Network Management Protocol (SNMP)* provides a myriad of features and abilities, one of which is the ability to record events. SNMP operates using UDP ports 161 and 162. When an SNMP-configured router encounters an error, an SNMP trap is generated and sent to the management server. The management server will record the event and can then notify the administrator graphically or even by pager. To configure SNMP on a Cisco router, the following command is configured:

```
snmp-server community <community-name> [RO|RW]
```

The RO at the end of the command is for the Read-Only access community (the default is Public), and the RW at the end of the command is for the Read-Write access community (the default is Private).

Authentication, Authorization, and Accounting (AAA)

In the previous section, we discussed authenticating the user (authentication), granting permissions (authorization), and recording activity (accounting). We also mentioned that each of these features could be implemented with security servers, such as RADIUS, TACACS, or Kerberos. In the past, when any of these security servers were implemented in the Cisco IOS, new commands had to be created. Cisco wanted to standardize that configuration regardless of which type of security was implemented.

Cisco thus created a standardized way to control access to the network, called *authentication, authorization, and accounting (AAA)*. A successful CCIE candidate needs to understand each component of AAA and how it interacts with the other components.

As we stated earlier in this chapter, the *authentication* component provides a method for identifying users that includes login, password, messaging, and encryption elements. In fact, there are two fundamental types of authentication that relate to AAA on a Cisco router: the first is authenticating access to the router itself; the second is authenticating access to the network protected by the router. Authentication identifies users before they are allowed access to the network. AAA supports several authentication methods, including local, TACACS, RADIUS, and Kerberos. These methods can be applied to Telnet logins, console logins, and enabling passwords.

Authorization uses a set of attributes that describe which actions the user is authorized to perform. These privileges can be granted to individuals or groups. TACACS and RADIUS can store this information, which is then read by the router during the login process.

Accounting collects security information and can be used for reporting, auditing, and billing. The accounting information may include data on when the user logged on and off and what commands were executed and provide statistical information such as the number of packets. This activity is reported to a TACACS or RADIUS security server.

AAA provides a standardized method of configuration that is independent of the security server used. Ideally, as new security methods are devised, AAA will support them.

Security Servers and Accounting

Security servers also have the capability to record events that occur on the router. On the security servers, this is known as *accounting*. One of the most useful features of accounting is the ability to record for billing purposes how long a user is logged onto the network. Because the security server is responsible for authenticating the user, it can also record the duration of the event as well.

Controlling Network Traffic

As private networks connect more and more frequently to the Internet, the need for controlling network traffic grows. Cisco provides two primary hardware devices to accomplish this: routers and the PIX. These devices can permit or deny traffic as needed to ensure the security of the network. In this section, we will investigate the PIX, IP access lists, NAT, the IOS Firewall feature set, and TCP Intercept. Finally, we'll consider multimedia issues.

Private Internet Exchange (PIX)

Cisco Secure PIX Firewall is a hardware/software security solution that can provide a flexible yet very secure connection to the Internet.

The PIX firewall is built around the *Adaptive Security Algorithm (ASA),* which provides packet analysis and handling. ASA supports stateful connection-oriented flows for today's multimedia applications. ASA also uses randomized TCP sequence numbers to prevent sequence number attacks.

PIX is typically implemented in conjunction with a *demilitarized zone (DMZ),* as shown in Figure 19.6. The DMZ is where publicly accessible devices such as Web and FTP servers are located.

FIGURE 19.6   PIX firewall with DMZ

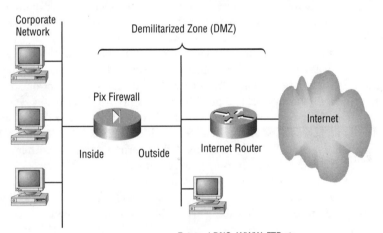

The PIX firewall provides many other features, including network address translation, URL filtering, user authentication, and other mechanisms to ensure network security. Table 19.3 depicts the various models of PIX available.

TABLE 19.3   PIX Firewall Models

Model	Number of Supported Sessions
PIX 535	500,000 concurrent connections
PIX 525	280,000 concurrent connections

TABLE 19.3 PIX Firewall Models *(continued)*

Model	Number of Supported Sessions
PIX 515-R	50,000 concurrent connections
PIX 515-UR	100,000 concurrent connections
PIX 506E	25 simultaneous VPN peers
PIX 501	3500 concurrent connections, 5 simultaneous VPN peers

IP Access Control Lists (ACLs)

Cisco supports a number of IP access lists. Although standard and extended access lists have been around for several years, dynamic and reflexive access lists are more recent introductions. For more information on these types of access lists, refer back to Chapter 16. *Context-Based Access Control (CBAC)* is the newest security feature and is included only with the firewall feature set.

Standard IP access lists have the capability to filter on source IP addresses only. Today, standard access lists have largely been replaced by extended access lists, which provide much greater control (but lower performance). An extended access list can filter on source addresses, destination addresses, protocols, and ports (even if the connection has not yet been established). For many environments, extended access lists deliver all the security that is required.

Dynamic access lists, also called lock-and-key access lists, provide temporary access for authenticated users. With dynamic lists, the user must first be authenticated by the router, which then implements a temporary access list allowing that user access to the network.

Reflexive access lists allow for session-based traffic filtering. When a user begins an outbound session, the router creates a reciprocal access list that will allow all packets that are part of this session through the router. This temporary access list will be deleted after a period of inactivity.

The main feature of CBAC is to enable connection-based filtering rather than packet-based filtering. CBAC recognizes connections and ensures return traffic or new dynamic connections are permitted by the security configuration of the router. CBAC analyzes Application layer information to determine whether to permit or deny TCP and UDP packets. It supports many protocols, such as File Transfer Protocol (FTP), Remote Procedure Call (RPC), and Structured Query Language (SQL). In addition to monitoring Application layer information, CBAC can perform Java blocking, real-time alerts and audit trails, and denial-of-service prevention. CBAC does not work for all protocols, but the most popular protocols are supported. It also provides NAT support for some Application layer protocols that are broken by NAT.

Network Address Translation (NAT)

Although *Network Address Translation (NAT)* was primarily designed to allow devices with private addresses to access the public Internet, it also provides a degree of security. Attacks cannot be directed at private addresses because the Internet will not forward packets destined for private addresses. (Refer back to Chapter 10 for more information on NAT.) There is no direct access to private addresses without going through a NAT gateway. However, an attacker could still try to attack devices that have existing translation entries on a NAT device (DMZ hosts or hosts with a current outgoing connection). NAT itself is not a sufficient security mechanism—stateful firewalling mechanisms should still be implemented.

IOS Firewall Feature Set

Standard and extended access lists have long been used on Cisco routers to control traffic. However, administrators have often needed to purchase an external firewall to provide greater protection and control. The Cisco IOS feature set implements CBAC, which provides security within the router itself.

In the following example, we will set up Cisco Secure (IP Firewall) so that Serial0/0 is the outside interface and FastEthernet0/0 is the inside interface. We will allow the firewall to inspect TCP, UDP, FTP, H323, RCMD, RealAudio, SMTP, SQLNet, and TFTP traffic. There is a mail, web, and FTP server inside at 172.26.1.10. We set up a NAT for this server to 172.28.1.10 / 28 and allow mail, Web, and FTP traffic that is initiated from the outside to reach the server inside:

```
interface FastEthernet0/0

 ip nat inside

 ip inspect FW in

interface Serial0/0 point-to-point

 ip access-group 104 in

 ip nat outside

ip inspect name FW tcp             Firewall will inspect these types
                                   of traffic

ip inspect name FW udp

ip inspect name FW ftp

ip inspect name FW h323

ip inspect name FW rcmd

ip inspect name FW realaudio
```

```
ip inspect name FW smtp

ip inspect name FW sqlnet

ip inspect name FW tftp

ip audit notify log

ip audit po max-events 100

ip nat inside source list 1 interface Serial0/0 overload

                                    NAT to the IP address on Serial0/0

ip nat inside source static 172.26.1.10 172.28.1.10

access-list 1 permit 172.26.1.0 0.0.0.255

access-list 104 permit tcp any host 172.28.1.10 eq smtp

access-list 104 permit tcp any host 172.28.1.10 eq www

access-list 104 permit tcp any host 172.28.1.10 eq pop3

access-list 104 permit tcp any host 172.28.1.10 eq ftp
```

TCP Intercept

TCP Intercept was designed to prevent the most common type of denial-of-service attack, known as *TCP SYN flooding*. The beginning of the TCP three-way handshake starts with a SYN (synchronize) request from a client. The server opens a socket and replies with a SYN/ACK (synchronize/acknowledgement). The client should then complete the three-way handshake by sending an ACK (acknowledgement). Refer back to Chapter 8, "IP Addressing and Subnetting," for more information on the TCP three-way handshake.

TCP SYN flooding exploits the three-way handshake by sending thousands of SYN requests. The server opens a socket for each of these requests. Eventually the server runs out of resources and cannot open new sockets. At this point, if a valid client were to attempt to connect to the server, there would be no services available.

TCP Intercept prevents SYN flooding attacks by intercepting TCP connection requests. The router establishes a connection on behalf of the server. If the connection to the client is successful, the router will open a session to the server and marry the two connections together.

Multimedia Considerations

Multimedia and multiservice applications provide a special challenge for network administrators. As in normal applications, a single connection is established between the client and server; most firewalls and routers do not have a problem allowing this connection. Where multimedia applications differ from normal is that, in order to improve their performance, they will open multiple sessions simultaneously. Typically, these sessions use high port numbers, which are dynamic in nature, making it impossible to define static ports that should be permitted.

Cisco's solution to this problem is to use the enhanced multimedia adaptive security available on the PIX firewall. The PIX firewall has the capability to identify certain types of multimedia traffic and monitor the connections needed. The IOS Firewall also supports multimedia applications.

Data Security

Encrypting data is one of the best ways to implement security on the network, and encryption schemes are constantly improving and changing. Encryption can be used in a variety of ways, from the simple idea of sending encrypted passwords to the more complex creation of a *virtual private network (VPN)*. In VPNs, data is encrypted, transmitted through the public network, and decrypted at the other end, effectively creating a private network.

Cisco offers numerous methods of encryption within the IOS. Initially, Cisco developed a number of proprietary encryption methods, primarily because there were not many public standard encryption methods available. As encryption evolved, Cisco implemented it within the IOS code. A few examples include IPSec, certificate authorities, and Internet Key Exchange.

Cisco Encryption

Cisco encryption technology provides for the encryption of IP packets. If an administrator wants to encrypt any other protocol, that protocol must first be encapsulated into an IP packet. Peer routers use *Digital Signature Standard (DSS)*, which uses public and private keys for authentication. The private key is not shared with any other device, and the public key is shared with other authenticating devices. A session key is generated for use in encrypting the data for that particular conversation. This type of encryption is secure but proprietary.

Open Standard Encryption

IP Security (IPSec) prevents packet replay by rejecting duplicate and old packets. It also guarantees that the data has not been altered and that the authenticated device sent the data. IPSec uses the *Internet Key Exchange (IKE)* for key management.

IKE is a key management protocol that is used in conjunction with IPSec to enhance security. IKE is a hybrid protocol that controls key exchange between authenticating devices during the initial key exchange. The keys are used for encryption.

Finally, *certificate authority (CA) interoperability* allows Cisco routers to participate in IPSec implementation using certificate authorities. CA allows for the centralized management of signatures. Digital signatures contain information to identify the device, company, or IP address as well as a copy of the public key. The certificate is signed by a certificate authority that is trusted by the receiver. This allows for the secure exchange of public keys. CA interoperability allows routers to participate in a public key infrastructure (PKI), in which parties use certificates to authenticate each other, provide data integrity, and provide data confidentiality.

IP Security (IPSec)

Without a doubt, one of the most utilized security mechanisms in networking today is *IP Security (IPSec)*. *IPSec* is an open standard developed by the Internet Engineering Task Force (IETF) and defined in RFC 2401. IPSec uses the Data Encryption Standard (DES) to encrypt the data, and the resulting 56-bit encryption is suitable for most purposes. Optionally, some platforms support Triple DES (3DES), which provides 168-bit encryption. IPSec can be implemented as a secure method of creating tunnels (tunnel mode) to interconnect geographically separated locations across a public network. IPSec is able to encrypt the data as it flows across the public network; this is typically referred to as a virtual private network (VPN). IPSec also operates in transport mode, where it provides only data security between two IPSec devices and does not provide VPN services. IPSec provides three major functions:

Confidentiality   Utilizing encryption algorithms such as DES allows data packets to flow from one location to another without allowing outside parties to view the information contained in the packets.

Integrity   Utilizing hashing algorithms such as Message Digest 5 (MD5) and Secure Hash Algorithm (SHA) allows the data packets to reach the destination location without any alteration.

Authentication   Utilizing mechanisms such as digital certificates ensures that the data that was transmitted by the sender was received by the destination location. Preshared keys are the most common form of IKE authentication.

Internet Key Exchange and IP Security

Now we'll discuss Internet Key Exchange (IKE) and IP Security (IPSec). You must have a good understanding of these items in order to design a good VPN security policy utilizing IPSec. IPSec offers a standard way of establishing authentication and encryption services between endpoints. It offers not only standard algorithms and transforms, but also standard key negotiation and management mechanisms, such as *Internet Security Association Key Management Protocol (ISAKMP),* which allows the interoperability between devices by performing the negotiation of services between these devices. By negotiation, we mean the establishment of policies or *security associations (SAs)* between devices. An SA establishes a trusted communications channel between two devices. Once this channel is established, data can be sent in a secure fashion. SAs are negotiated for both IKE and IPSec, and it is IKE that facilitates this SA establishment.

Internet Key Exchange (IKE)

IKE is defined in RFC 2409 and is a form of ISAKMP that was developed specifically for IPSec. In fact, IKE is basically ISAKMP with Oakley extensions. ISAKMP describes the phase of negotiation as well as the method to establish an authenticated key exchange. ISAKMP Phase 1 is used when two peers establish a secure, authenticated channel with which to communicate. ISAKMP Phase 2 is required to establish SAs on behalf of other services such as IPSec, which needs key material and/or parameter negotiation.

IP Security (IPSec)

IPSec is defined in RFC 2401. It provides IP Network layer encryption and defines a new set of headers to be added to the IP datagrams. The new headers will be placed after the IP header and before the encrypted payload. Through the use of Authentication Header (AH) and/or Encapsulating Security Protocol (ESP) services, the payload of the IPSec packet will be secured.

Authentication Header (AH)

The Authentication Header (AH) is defined in RFC 2402 and is a mechanism for providing strong integrity and authentication for IP datagrams. The Authentication Header (AH) appears after IP headers of the IPSec packet. The IPv4 or IPv6 header immediately preceding the Authentication Header will contain the value 51 in its Next Header (or Protocol) field.

Encapsulating Security Payload (ESP)

The Encapsulating Security Payload (ESP), defined in RFC 2406, may appear anywhere after the IPSec packet's IP header. ESP operates utilizing the assigned protocol number 50. The IP ESP provides security by encrypting the data and placing the encrypted data in the data portion of the IP ESP. ESP can operate in two modes:

Transport mode   Transport mode is used for end-system-to-end-system secure communication. Only the IP payload is encrypted, and the original IP headers are left intact. This allows the source and destination network addresses to be viewed by all routing devices within the network, thus special processing can be enabled such as quality of service (QoS) based on the information on the IP header. The layer 4 header will be encrypted, limiting the examination of the packet. This mode has the advantage of adding only a few bytes to each packet.

Tunnel mode   In tunnel mode, the entire original IP datagram is encrypted, and it becomes the payload in a new IP packet. This mode is typically used for router-to-router communication, which is also referred to as a virtual private network (VPN). The router will act as an IPSec proxy, which means that the router will perform the encryption on behalf of the hosts. The source's router encrypts packets and forwards them along the IPSec tunnel. The destination's router decrypts the original IP datagram and forwards it on to the destination system. Tunnel mode is the most commonly deployed method of IPSec. Implementing IPSec with tunnel mode allows security within the network without having to modify the operating system or any applications on your PCs, servers, and hosts.

Authentication Hashes

Authentication hashes are used as cryptographic checksums to determine if data has been modified during the transportation of the packets from the source to the destination. The two most popular hash types are MD5 and SHA:

- Message Digest 5 (MD5) is a one-way hash that combines a shared secret password and the message (the header and payload) to produce a 128-bit value.

- Secure Hash Algorithm (SHA) is similar to MD5 but produces a 160-bit hash value. SHA is more secure (but slower) than MD5.

AH and ESP algorithms

There is a choice of AH and ESP algorithms that may be used singly or combined:

ah-md5-hmac	AH-HMAC-MD5 transform
ah-sha-hmac	AH-HMAC-SHA transform
comp-lzs	IP Compression using the LZS compression algorithm
esp-3des	ESP transform using 3DES(EDE) cipher (168 bits)
esp-aes	ESP transform using AES cipher
esp-des	ESP transform using DES cipher (56 bits)
esp-md5-hmac	ESP transform using HMAC-MD5 auth
esp-null	ESP transform w/o cipher
esp-sha-hmac	ESP transform using HMAC-SHA auth

Summary

As security needs become more complex in our networking environments, Cisco continues to extend its features to meet demands. With authentication, authorization, and accounting (AAA), you can control users and what they are permitted to do. With RADIUS and TACACS, you can implement a centralized security plan in which the events that occur on a network are recorded to the security server or sent to a syslog server via logging.

Cisco has implemented firewall capability in two distinct ways. The Secure PIX Firewall is a hardware/software solution that meets the most demanding challenges in security today. The Cisco IOS firewall option provides many of the firewall features within the router itself.

Standard and extended access lists have long been used for security purposes. The addition of three new types of access control lists offers even greater control. Dynamic access lists create temporary but intentional holes in your security to allow a particular user access to the network. Reflexive access lists dynamically modify themselves to allow replies from any server in response to a client's contact. CBAC goes one step further by analyzing Application layer information. These access lists give a network administrator explicit control over network traffic.

Although not as stringent as a firewall, Network Address Translation (NAT) provides some security to network clients by limiting connectivity to private addresses. TCP Intercept prevents SYN flooding attacks. Cisco's enhanced multimedia adaptive security provides for multiservice access.

Even as security requirements become increasingly complex, the fundamentals of traffic control still apply. Using encryption can increase network security of traffic that is traversing an IP network. When implementing IPSec in your network, it is imperative that you understand all aspects of the required commands for proper implementation. If you happen to forget or even misconfigure a single command, the entire IPSec implementation can be doomed to failure.

Security has become critically important in the age of the Internet. Techniques continue to improve with time, but so do the tools used by hackers. The best security today will be considered weak three years from now. It is important for an administrator to stay current with security trends.

Also, if you would like to try to implement an IPSec scenario, we have developed a hands-on IPSec lab exercise. You will find it in Chapter 19 Supplement on the CD-Rom that came with this book.

Exam Essentials

Understand router authentication.   The most common way to ensure security is by using a password or a combination of username and password. The user submits the needed information to the router; the router checks this information. If the information is correct, the user has been authenticated.

Know what a security server is.   Security servers provide centralized management of usernames and passwords. When a router wishes to authenticate a user, the router collects the username and password information from the user and submits this information to the security server. The security server compares the submitted information to the user database to determine if the user should be permitted access to the router. All usernames and passwords are stored centrally on the single security server. There are three primary types of security servers supported by Cisco routers: RADIUS, TACACS, and Kerberos.

Know what IPSec and IKE are.   IP Security (IPSec) prevents packet replay by rejecting duplicate and old packets. It also guarantees that the data has not been altered and that the authenticated device sent the data. IPSec uses the Internet Key Exchange (IKE) for key management. IKE is a key management protocol that is used in conjunction with IPSec to enhance security. IKE is a hybrid protocol that controls key exchange between authenticating devices during the initial key exchange.

Know what Message Digest 5 (MD5) is.   MD5 is a one-way hash that combines a shared secret password and the message (the header and payload) to produce a 128-bit value. The destination device runs the same hash of the message and compares it with the inserted hash value. The resulting value should be the same, which indicates that nothing in the packet has been changed in transit.

Key Terms

Before you take the exam, be certain you are familiar with the following terms:

Adaptive Security Algorithm (ASA)

authentication, authorization, and
accounting (AAA)

Context-Based Access Control (CBAC)

demilitarized zone (DMZ)

Digital Signature Standard (DSS)

Internet Key Exchange (IKE)

Internet Security Association Key Management
Protocol (ISAKMP)

IP Security (IPSec)

Kerberos

Network Address Translation (NAT)

Remote Authentication Dial-In User
Service (RADIUS)

security associations (SAs)

Simple Network Management
Protocol (SNMP)

Syslog

Terminal Access Controller Access
Control System (TACACS)

virtual private network (VPN)

Review Questions

1. Which component of AAA provides for the identification of users?

   A. Accounting

   B. Authorization

   C. Authentication

   D. Administration

2. What protocol does a Cisco router use for sending logging information? (Choose all that apply.)

   A. TCP

   B. UDP

   C. Syslog

   D. IPX

   E. LAT

3. Which of the following products uses the Adaptive Security Algorithm (ASA)?

   A. Enterprise feature set for Cisco IOS

   B. Firewall feature set for Cisco IOS

   C. IPSec feature set for Cisco IOS

   D. CiscoWorks 2000

   E. Cisco Secure PIX Firewall

4. Which component of AAA controls the privileges a user is granted?

   A. Accounting

   B. Authorization

   C. Authentication

   D. Administration

5. Which of the following can help prevent a TCP SYN attack? (Choose all that apply.)

   A. TCP Intercept

   B. NAT

   C. Access list

   D. PIX firewall

6. Which of the following will best prevent a TCP SYN flooding attack?

A. Standard access list

B. Extended access list

C. NAT

D. TCP Intercept

E. AAA

7. A company wishes to bill clients based on network usage. Which technology would be the best solution?

A. Authentication

B. Authorization

C. Accounting

D. Logging

E. NDS

8. An administrator wishes to allow syslog messages to pass through the router. Which of the following lines should be added to the access list to allow this to happen?

A. `Access-list 100 permit ip any any eq 514`

B. `Access-list 100 permit tcp any any eq 514`

C. `Access-list 100 permit udp any any eq 514`

D. `Access-list 10 permit tcp any any eq 514`

E. `Access-list 100 permit tcp any any eq SYSLOG`

9. Which of the following security technologies can be implemented on a Cisco router? (Choose all that apply)

A. DSS

B. DES

C. IPSec

D. IKE

E. Certificate Authority

10. In an encrypted environment, what is the trusted entity that stores digital signatures?

A. Certificate authority

B. RADIUS

C. TACACS+

D. Kerberos

E. DES

Answers to Review Questions

1. C. Authentication identifies a user, including login, password, messaging, and encryption.

2. B, C. Syslog is a protocol defined for UDP on port 514.

3. E. The Cisco Secure PIX Firewall (PIX) uses the ASA algorithm.

4. B. Authorization determines what a user is permitted to do after logging on.

5. A, B, C, D. All of these mechanisms can be used to help prevent a TCP SYN attack.

6. D. TCP Intercept is specifically designed to prevent SYN flooding attacks.

7. C. Accounting allows for collecting information such as network usage.

8. C. Syslog uses UDP.

9. A, B, C, D, E. Cisco routers can support all of the technologies listed.

10. A. A certificate authority (CA) stores digital signatures that include public keys.

Chapter 20

Multiservice Technologies

THE CCIE QUALIFICATION EXAM TOPICS COVERED IN THIS CHAPTER INCLUDE THE FOLLOWING:

- ✓ Telephony interfaces and signaling
- ✓ SS7, H.323 (Voice/Video), SIP, and CODECs
- ✓ Real-Time Transport Protocol (RTP) and RTP Control Protocol (RTCP)
- ✓ Voice over IP, Frame Relay, ATM
- ✓ Voice ports and dial peers
- ✓ The basics of MPLS

Multiservice (voice and video packets transmitted over an existing data network) is one of the 11 major topics covered by the Routing and Switching Qualification Exam (350-001). There is enough emphasis placed on this technology (voice and video) that the topics listed in the chapter objectives will be covered in detail. This chapter covers the aspects of Cisco's multiservice configuration and support.

In today's network environment, cost effectiveness is a must. Legacy enterprises can often consist of two or three parallel networks. Figure 20.1 depicts a legacy enterprise. You will see that the company has three networks: a data network, a voice network, and a video network.

FIGURE 20.1 Legacy parallel networks

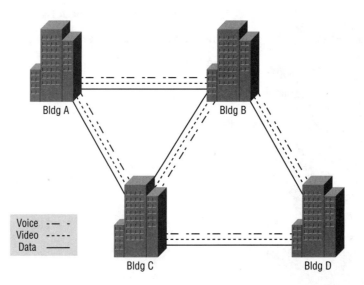

With today's multiservice technology, voice and video can also be carried across the data network. Today's enterprise can look something similar to Figure 20.2. Cisco's solution includes Architecture for Voice Video and Integrated Data (AVVID). This architecture implements a variety of hardware platforms specific to voice and video integration as well as multiservice applications. You can't just throw voice and video on a data network without specific devices that support those applications.

FIGURE 20.2   Integrated voice, video, and data network

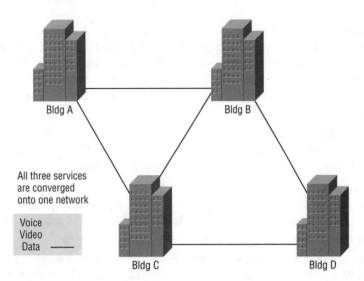

It is the focus of this chapter to introduce the types of equipment that must be used, how they function, and how they integrate to create a multiservice network.

In implementing Voice over IP (VoIP) technology, the analog voice signal is digitized (encoded) into IP packets. A dial plan must be created that will list all the IP destinations of all IP phones and outbound phones in the network. When a phone number is dialed for a phone connected off of a router, the router looks at the dialed digits and routes the calls (IP packets) to the appropriate IP destination.

Interfaces and Signaling

As with any technology, you should start at the beginning in order to achieve a good understanding of its underlying principles and operation. Upon learning legacy information about analog and digital voice implementation, you will be in a better position to build, configure, and deploy an integrated network. You will also be expected to know telephony vernacular for the exam. Several interfaces are used to connect the various types of voice equipment. You need to understand the different components of a legacy voice network in order to understand where Cisco equipment joins it and the role Cisco equipment plays in the network. Key system, *private branch exchange (PBX)*, and *public switched telephone network (PSTN)* connections demand accurate methods of seizing lines and signaling in today's multiservice networks, specifically for voice transmissions. By learning the principles of telephony interfaces and signaling types, you can more successfully integrate Cisco multiservice equipment, thus creating a multiservice network.

There are three main analog interfaces, which can be considered to be part of the access layer of a voice network:

Foreign Exchange Office (FXO)   This interface allows an analog connection to be directed at the PSTN's central office or to a station interface on a PBX. The FXO uses a standard RJ-11 jack and sits on the switch end of the connection. It plugs directly into the line side of the switch so the switch thinks the FXO interface is a telephone. The FXO voice interface card is not an FXS card and therefore will not provide dial tone. Do not plug a telephone set into an FXO voice interface card.

Foreign Exchange Station (FXS)   This is the standard interface that virtually every home in North America employs. It connects devices such as telephones, modems, fax machines, key systems, and analog PBXs. It has an RJ-11 two-wire jack that provides the dial tone and signaling needed by the FXO interface. In simple terms it is, or acts like, the PSTN.

Earth and Magneto (E&M)   This interface is commonly used for analog trunks or tie lines with PBX systems. There are several types of E&Ms (which is also referred to as Ear and Mouth). It uses an RJ-45 jack and six to eight wires, depending on the type of E&M being implemented.

An example of a digital interface is a channelized T1 (or E1), which is a digital trunk line that connects to a PBX system, and within this trunk line, each channel (DS0) supports an active phone call.

In order to determine the correct number of required trunk lines to handle the expected number of calls, Erlangs are used. An *Erlang* is a unit of telecommunications traffic measurement that represents the continuous use of one voice path. Actually, it is used to determine the total traffic volume within one hour, as well as the voice call usage in terms of bandwidth requirements for voice network design.

Once the interface to the network has been determined, the system needs to express the seizure of the line. The following sections discuss the type of seizure signaling used with the various interfaces.

FXS/FXO Signaling

Two types of signaling are used for seizure signaling with FXS/FXO interfaces: either loop start or ground start, depending on the application.

Loop Start Signaling

Loop start signaling is most often used in home telephone systems. When the handset is on-hook, the loop (or circuit) is open. When the handset is taken off-hook, the loop is closed.

The ring lead is connected to –48 volts (V) at the central office (CO), and the ground lead is connected to the ground at the CO. To initiate the call, you close the loop, allowing the current to flow through the circuit. The CO will then provide the dial tone.

A fairly common type of problem with this type of signaling is called *glare,* and almost everyone has experienced it at one time or another. Have you ever picked up your telephone and started to make a call only to realize someone is already on the line trying to talk to you? This is known as glare, which occurs when both sides of the link seize the line at the same time (or nearly the same time).

Ground Start Signaling

Ground start signaling virtually eliminates the possibility of glare. It is usually used when there are more trunks than there are in a home telephone system, typically for signaling between a CO and a PBX.

The ring lead is connected to –48V, and at the same time, the tip is monitored by the PBX for ground. When the line is seized, the PBX grounds the ring lead. This usually happens within approximately 100 milliseconds (ms). The CO senses the ground and grounds the tip lead. The PBX in turn senses the ground from the CO, so it closes the two-wire loop and removes the ring ground.

E&M Signaling

Unlike the other types of signaling, E&M uses separate leads for the voice and signaling. The M-lead sends the signal, and the E-lead receives the signal.

When a call is placed, the PBX raises the M-lead by applying –48V, and the remote PBX detects the change on the E-lead. The dial tone is then attached to the trunk and the PBX. You dial the digits, and they are sent to the remote PBX. Once the circuit is complete, the remote PBX raises its M-lead. Table 20.1 shows the E&M signaling system.

TABLE 20.1   E&M Signaling and Pinouts

Signaling	Pinout	Description
Signal battery (SB)	1	Connects to –48V DC
M-lead (M)	2	Signal from PBX to trunk
Ring (R)	3	Audio in/out
Ring 1 (R1)	4	Audio in/out
Tip 1 (T1)	5	Audio from PBX side
Tip (T)	6	Audio from PBX side
E-lead (E)	7	Signal from CO
Signal ground (SG)	8	Connects to ground

E&M Cross Connecting

There are several Cisco products that can be used for E&M signaling. They are the 1750, 2600, and 3600 series routers with E&M voice interface cards. There are basic connections to PBXs like the Lucent G3R E&M trunk and the Nortel Option 11 E&M trunk.

E&M Signaling Types

There are five types of E&Ms used today that Cisco equipment supports: Types 1 through 5. These types vary in the way that they signal on-hook and off-hook conditions. To understand how Cisco equipment must work, it is important to understand how the signaling occurs:

Type 1   This is a two-wire interface that is most commonly used in North America. The two wires are the M-lead and the E-lead. The off-hook condition from the PBX is signaled by connecting the M-lead to the battery. The off-hook condition from the CO (or trunk) side is signaled by connecting the E-lead to the ground. Therefore, for the on-hook condition, the M-lead is connected to the ground and the E-lead is open.

Type 2   This is a four-wire interface that is used in North America, but to a lesser degree than Type 1. The four wires are the M-lead, E-lead, signal ground (SG), and signal battery (SB). The SG and SB are the return paths for the E-lead and M-lead, so no common ground is required. The off-hook condition from the PBX is signaled by connecting the M-lead to the SB at the CO side. The CO signals the off-hook condition by connecting the E-lead to the SG on the PBX side. For the on-hook condition, the SB for the M-lead and the SG for the E-lead are open.

Type 3   This type is not used in modern systems. It is a four-wire interface, similar to Type 2 but without the SG lead to provide a common ground. While on-hook, the M-lead is looped to the signal ground on the CO side. The PBX signals the off-hook condition by disconnecting the M-lead from the signal ground and connecting it to the SB on the CO side. The CO signals the off-hook condition by connecting the E-lead to the ground.

Type 4   This is a four-wire interface that does not require a common ground. Each side closes a current loop to the signal, and this flow is detected to indicate the presence of a signal. This type is not supported by Cisco router interfaces.

Type 5   This is a two-wire interface that is most commonly used in Europe. This interface requires a common ground and is a simplified version of Type 4. The PBX signals the off-hook condition by connecting the M-lead to the ground. The CO signals the off-hook condition by connecting the E-lead to the ground.

E&M Line Seizing

You now know how to identify on-hook and off-hook conditions with E&M signaling, but how do you know when it is time to send digits? There are three ways to complete this function: immediate start, wink start, and delay start.

Immediate Start

The immediate start trunk-supervision signaling method is the most basic of the three. Once the off-hook signal is set up, the originating PBX waits a minimum of 150ms before sending digits blindly to the other end. The remote PBX acknowledges the calling PBX after the called party answers. Here's the sequence:

1. The calling PBX seizes the line.
2. The local PBX waits a minimum of 150ms and then sends the digits. It does not wait for an acknowledgment from the remote PBX.
3. The remote PBX acknowledges after the called party answers.

Wink Start

Wink start is the most common line seizing protocol. This protocol waits for a special acknowledgment, called a *wink*, from the remote PBX. The wink is a toggle of the off-hook signal. Once the sending PBX hears the wink, it sends the digits. Here's the sequence:

1. The calling PBX seizes the line.
2. The called PBX does not return an acknowledgment.
3. The calling PBX waits for a digit register.
4. The called PBX sends a wink.
5. The calling PBX recognizes the wink and then sends the digits.
6. The called party answers.
7. The called PBX raises the M-lead.

Delay Start

Delay start is used in the CO to allow it a way to delay the calling PBX until the receiving switch is ready. Here's the sequence:

1. The calling PBX seizes the line.
2. The calling PBX waits 200ms.
3. During that time, the CO (receiving switch) detects the off-hook signal and returns an off-hook condition to the calling PBX.
4. After the 200ms period, the calling PBX checks the E-lead for the on-hook condition, signaling the PBX to send the digits.

   Now let's discuss digital signaling, both in-band and out-of-band, and how it operates.

Digital Signaling

Digital signaling is accomplished in one of two ways: in-band or out-of-band. *In-band signaling* uses bits in the voice stream to carry the signaling information. *Out-of-band signaling* uses a separate channel to carry the signaling.

In-Band Signaling

Channel associated signaling (CAS), also known as *robbed-bit signaling (RBS)*, is the procedure for in-band signaling. It uses bits in Super Frame (SF) or Extended Superframe Format (ESF) as follows:

- In SF, bits from the 6th and 12th frames are used. These bits are called the A and B bits.

- In ESF, bits from the 6th, 12th, 18th, and 24th frames are used. These bits are called the A, B, C, and D bits. The A and C bits are taken from the 12th and 24th frames, and the B and D bits are taken from the 6th and 18th frames.

SF has A and B robbed-bit signaling. ESF has A, B, C, and D robbed-bit signaling. This signaling contains the on-hook/off-hook signaling as well as Automatic Number Identification (ANI) and Dialed Number Identification Service (DNIS) information.

Out-of-Band Signaling

Common-channel signaling (CCS) is the method for out-of-band signaling. Anyone using Integrated Services Digital Network (ISDN) is familiar with CCS. The signaling on an ISDN circuit is carried on the D channel. E-1 and Signaling System 7 (SS7) are some of the other systems that use CCS. To explain how out-of band signaling works, we will examine the SS7 system.

Signaling System 7 (SS7) is an out-of-band, International Telecommunication Union Telecommunication Standardization Sector (ITU-T) standard originally developed for the general switched telephone network (GSTN). It covers call establishment, billing, routing, and information exchange. There are three components that make up an SS7 network, and they are connected by six different types of links. It also provides fast call setup and is a redundant signaling architecture.

SS7 Components

The three components are the signal points:

- The Signal Transfer Points (STPs) are responsible for the packet switching of the network and are configured in pairs for redundancy. These points also measure traffic and usage.

- The Signal Control Point (SCP) element provides advanced services, such as an 800 database. It also is responsible for providing additional routing information.

- The Signal Switching Point (SSP) is the end office. The SSP is the place where all the calls originate, terminate, or are switched.

SS7 Links

SS7 uses the following six link types for its connections:

- A links connect SSPs and SCPs to STP pairs.

- B (Bridge) links connect the two mated pairs of STPs and carry the signaling messages.

- C (Cross) links connect the STP pairs together. They are used only when congestion occurs on the B links. Normally, they carry only management information.

- D (Diagonal) links connect STP pairs at one level to another pair of STP pairs on another level. They are identical to B links.

- E (Extended) links connect an SSP to another STP. They are only used if a failure occurs in the home STP.

- F links connect endpoints and are used if the STP is not available or is congested.

SS7 Layers

The SS7 architectures consists of four layers:

- The Physical layer contains the DS0 format at 56Kbps or 64Kbps.

- The Message Transfer Part, Level 2 (MTP-L2) layer is the link layer for two endpoints. It also provides for flow control, error control, and sequencing. This layer creates reliable point-to-point links.

- The Message Transfer Part, Level 3 (MTP-L3) layer is the network layer. Addressing, routing, and congestion control operate here.

- The Signaling Connection Control Part (SCCP) layer provides additional routing, management, and communications to applications on end nodes.

SS7 Messages

SS7 using the following message types to exchange information:

- ISDN User Part (ISUP) messages are responsible for call setup and tear down.

- Transaction Capabilities Application Part (TCAP) messages provide the applications in the nodes with a standard protocol to communicate between each other. TCAP uses SSCP to communicate between the applications.

- Operations, Maintenance, and Administration Part (OMAP) messages provide the functions to troubleshoot link problems and check the routing tables.

Telecommunication Standards

Now we will discuss the typical protocols that are implemented in the VoIP environment, such as Real-Time Transport Protocol (RTP) and RTP Control Protocol (RTCP), H.323, and Session Initiation Protocol (SIP).

Real-Time Transport Protocol and RTP Control Protocol

Real-Time Transport Protocol (RTP) was a necessary addition to the protocol suite for voice and video traffic on an IP network. Due to the lack of reliability of a normal network, RTP was designed to provide services that would allow better end-to-end responses. It does this via some very specific flow control methods, such as time stamps, sequence information, and payload identification:

Time stamps   The time stamp is placed within a 32-bit field of the RTP header indicating the exact time of the sampling.

Sequence information   This information is used so that arriving packets in a buffer can be identified according to the sequence in which they were sent.

Payload ID   This allows the RTP to identify which CODEC was used for the data conversion and compression.

RTP Control Protocol (RTCP) is a companion protocol to RTP. It takes on the responsibility of source/recipient reporting, or delivery monitoring. As the name indicates, it is responsible for gathering reports from sources as well as recipients. RTCP packets contain information regarding the session. This information can be used to try to enhance performance.

To implement voice in a data network, you must configure the use of new protocols, such as Real-Time Transport Protocol (RTP). RTP, which is defined in RFC 1889, runs over User Datagram Protocol (UDP) because UDP has less delay than TCP. Also, RTP Control Protocol (RTCP), which is also defined in RFC 1889, monitors the delivery of data and provides the control and identification functions required for the operation of the call. Like any IP-based technology, supporting voice means that you must utilize certain TCP, UDP, and RTP ports. The following ports are required for voice:

TCP port 1720   Used by H.225 for call establishment. H.245 activates after H.225 establishes the call. H.245 uses ports 11000 through 11999.

UDP ports 16384 through 32767   The *even* port numbers are used by RTP to transport the actual voice traffic, and the *odd* port numbers are used by the RTCP to provide statistical reporting information to the RTP data source on traffic flow statistics.

Keep these port numbers in mind because, if you happen to have a requirement for your voice traffic to flow through an ACL, these ports must be permitted to flow through the ACL. As you can see in Figure 20.3, a typical RTP packet carrying a 20-byte voice sample comprises a lot of overhead bytes. Figure 20.3 shows a G.729 packet; to carry a 20-byte voice sample, a 40-byte header is required.

FIGURE 20.3   RTP header

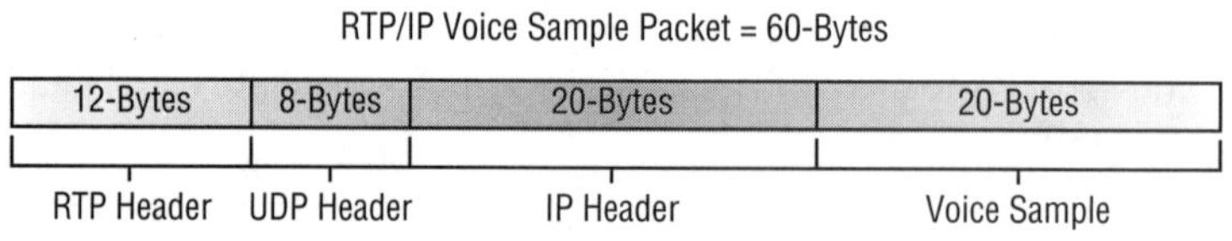

RTP/IP Voice Sample Packet = 60-Bytes

12-Bytes	8-Bytes	20-Bytes	20-Bytes
RTP Header	UDP Header	IP Header	Voice Sample

There are also a few mechanisms that can be implemented to improve the bandwidth utilization in a VoIP network. You can use RTP header compression on WAN links to reduce the size of the voice IP packets; this is referred to as Compressed RTP (CRTP). RTP header compression is enabled on serial interfaces with the `ip rtp header-compression` command. The maximum number of active RTP compression sessions is controlled through the use of the `ip rtp compression-connections` command. Keep in mind that CRTP is performed on a hop-by-hop basis, meaning that the compression and decompression occur on every link in the path to the destination. CRTP is discussed in further detail in Chapter 18, "Quality of Service (QoS)."

Other mechanisms, such as Multilink PPP with Interleaving, allows large packets to be multilink-encapsulated and then fragmented into smaller packets. Also, keep in mind that several queuing techniques can be implemented to provide guaranteed bandwidth utilization and voice call performance.

Now let's discuss the H.323 standard.

The H.323 Standard

H.323 is the ITU-T standard for carrying audio, video, and data across an IP network. When voice signals are transferred across a network, they must be encoded and decoded for analog-to-digital conversion and digital-to-analog conversion. Cisco supports this standard for audio/video transport over IP. You will need to understand H.323 and which devices support it for an end-to-end audio/video solution. You will be expected to answer questions regarding H.323 on the exam.

H.323 provides standards for Registration, Admission, and Status (RAS), encoding (CODECs), bandwidth management, and connections to other devices. Assuming a vendor complies with the H.323 standard, that vendor's equipment should interoperate with other H.323-compliant devices.

H.323 consists of the following components and standards:

Terminal   These are machines used for real-time multimedia presentation. The transfer of data is bidirectional.

Gateway   These are used to bridge two disparate networks. Communication is established via translating protocols and media format conversions. Gateways are not required when two H.323 terminals wish to communicate on an H.323 network.

Gatekeeper   These devices provide addressing, call routing, authentication, authorization, and bandwidth utilization information.

Multipoint control units (MCUs)   When more than two H.323 terminals are involved (conference) in communication, MCUs are used to establish the connection with all terminals in a "hub-and-spoke" type of topology. It also handles the streaming and CODEC to be used for the conference.

CODECs (coder-decoder)   CODECs, which are Presentation layer protocols, are hardware devices or software packages that encode audio and video from analog waveforms to digital signals for transmission. Once it has reached its destination, the digital signal is converted back to an analog waveform.

H.225   This protocol is used by H.323 for call signaling and call setup.

H.245   Negotiation of terminal capabilities is performed by H.245. It is also responsible for the creation of media channels.

RAS   The acronym stands for Registration, Admission, and Status. These control functions are done with the gatekeeper.

Real-Time Transport Protocol/RTP Control Protocol (RTP/RTCP)   These protocols, which were discussed earlier in this chapter, are used within H.323 to create and transmit audio packets on an IP network.

Now let's discuss the SIP standard.

Session Initiation Protocol

Session Initiation Protocol (SIP) is defined in RFC 2543 and is an alternative multimedia framework to H.323, as it was developed specifically for IP telephony. SIP is an Application Layer protocol which is used for creating, modifying, and terminating Internet multimedia conferences, IP telephone calls, and multimedia distribution.

SIP incorporates the following protocols:

- Resource Reservation Protocol (RSVP), which is defined in RFC 2205, for reserving network resources

- RTP for transporting real-time data and providing QoS feedback

- Session Announcement Protocol (SAP) for advertising multimedia sessions with multicast

- Session Description Protocol (SDP), which is defined in RFC 2327, for describing multimedia sessions

SIP is implemented with a modular architecture that includes the following components:

SIP User Agent   Endpoints that create and terminate sessions, SIP phones, SIP PC clients, and gateways.

SIP Proxy Server   Routes messages between the SIP user agents.

SIP Redirect Server   Call control device that provides routing information to SIP user agents.

SIP Registrar Server   Stores the location of all SIP user agents in the domain or subdomain.

SIP Location Services   Provides the logical location of SIP user agents. These services are used by the proxy, redirect, and registrar servers.

Back-to-back User Agent   Call-control device that allows centralized control of the network.

This completes our discussion of the various protocols that are implemented in the VoIP network. Next, we'll discuss how an analog voice signal becomes a digital signal.

Analog-to-Digital Signal Conversion

Because voice is an analog signal, it must be coded into a digital signal using one of many coding schemes. After the signal reaches its destination, it must be decoded to re-create the analog signal. This is called digitization.

Several steps must take place to convert an analog signal to a digital signal before it can be transmitted to the final destination:

1. Sample the analog signal.

2. Quantize the sample.

3. Encode the data.

These steps are described in the following sections.

Sampling the Data

To create a sample that is a fairly close representation of the original analog signal, you must sample at a rate two times the highest frequency. This procedure is called the Nyquist Theorem. Because voice generally falls in the range of 300Hz to 3400Hz, a maximum value of 4000Hz is used to determine the sampling rate. So, the sampling rate must be 8000 times a second. The output created by the sampling step is called a Pulse Amplitude Modulation (PAM) signal.

Quantization

Quantization is the method by which each step in the analog signal is assigned a digital code word. How this is done depends on which quantization method is used, either mu-Law or a-Law. Both methods generate an 8-bit code word and a 64Kbps stream.

Each code word is divided as follows:

Word	Length	Description
Polarity	1 bit	Represents a positive or negative position along the quantizing line.
Segment	3 bits	There are 16 segments (0–7), 8 positive and 8 negative.
Step	4 bits	Represents the division in each segment (0–15).

Encoding the Data

The following methods, or CODECs, can be used for encoding data:

Pulse Code Modulation (PCM), or G.711   The process of sampling at 8000 times per second and quantizing the analog signal into an 8-bit code word is known as PCM. Notice that 8 bits times the sample rate of 8000 times a second equals 64,000 bits per second, or 64Kbps, which is a DS0. G.711u is the mu-law version implemented in North America and Japan, and G.711a is the a-law version, which is implemented in Europe and other international countries. This method is supported by Cisco equipment.

Adaptive Differential PCM (ADPCM), or G.726   ADPCM calculates the difference between one sample and the next by looking at the last sample and predicting the encoding. Because

ADPCM is "adaptive" and only calculates the difference between each sample, the bandwidth is greatly reduced. This method is supported by Cisco equipment.

Code Excited Linear Predictor (CELP)   CELP is a hybrid coder that converts an 8-bit PCM sample to a 16-bit linear PCM sample. Then a codebook is used to learn and predict the waveform. The coder is excited by a white noise generator, and a mathematical value is sent to the far end decoder to regenerate the voice signal.

Low Delay CELP (LD-CELP), or G.728   LD-CELP uses a smaller codebook than CELP uses, with no lookahead, to minimize the delay to from 2ms to 5ms. This encoding format is supported by Cisco equipment.

Conjugate Structure Algebraic CELP (CS-ACELP), or G.729a, b, ab   CS-ACELP codes on 80 PCM frames and maps them to 10 8-bit code words. CS-ACELP also provides noise reduction and pitch synthesis to enhance voice quality. Cisco's implementation bundles two code words into a single frame. This is also a Cisco-supported CODEC. In fact, g729r8 is the default CODEC setting for VoIP.

Multi-Pulse Excitation-Maximum Likelihood Quantization (MP-MLQ), or G.723.1(a), and Algebraic Code Excited Linear Prediction (ACELP)   These methods use digitations and compression at different rates, as shown in Table 20.2. It is also the audio component of the H.323 standard.

As a standard method of determining the expected quality of the audio signal produced by each of the CODECs, a rating known as the Mean Opinion Score (MOS) was developed, A 1 is a low (bad) score and a 5 is a high (good) score. Table 20.2 also provides the MOS for each the compression techniques.

TABLE 20.2   Compression Techniques

Coding	ITU-T	Kbps	MOS
PCM	G.711	64	4.10
ADPCM	G.726	32	3.85
LD-CELP	G.728	16	3.61
CS-ACELP	G.729	8	3.92
CS-ACELP	G.729a	8	3.70
MP-MLQ	G.723.1	6.3	3.90
ACELP	G.723.1	5.3	3.65

Now that you understand about signaling and data compression standards used by Cisco equipment, you can begin the configuration process.

Voice-over-Network Configuration

Configuring Voice over IP (VoIP), Voice over Frame Relay (VoFR), or Voice over ATM (VoATM) is accomplished through voice ports and *dial peers*. First, we will explain how to configure voice ports, then we'll cover the dial peer configuration, and finally we'll go into some of the optional capabilities that can be configured on voice ports and dial peers.

Configuring a Voice Port

We'll use Figure 20.4 as a reference for all of the configuration examples we discuss in this chapter.

FIGURE 20.4   Network diagram for voice

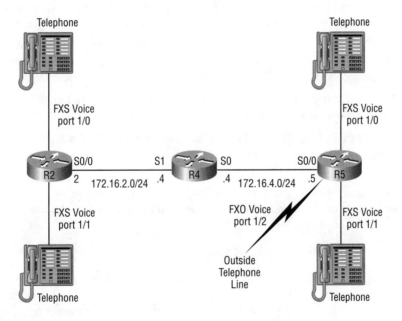

Before you will be able to use the voice port on the router, you *must* perform a `no shutdown` command on each voice port you want to connect devices to. It is also possible to configure other optional functionality on the voice ports, such as Private Line Automatic Ringdown (PLAR), CODEC type, and signaling. Some of these options will be discussed later on in this chapter.

Configuring a Dial Peer

We will discuss the three main types of dial peers that can be configured: IP based, Frame Relay based, and ATM based. The type of dial peer that you implement will depend on the layer 2 infrastructure that you have within your network. Refer to Figure 20.4 for all three of the following dial peer configuration examples.

Types of Dial Peers

It is possible to configure two types of dial peers on a Cisco router:

- *Plain old telephone service (POTS)* dial peers define the characteristics of a traditional telephone network connection. The POTS dial peer maps a dial string to a specific voice port on the local router. Normally, the voice port connects the router to the local public switched telephone network (PSTN), private branch exchange (PBX), or telephone. POTS dial peers do *not* automatically forward digits.

- Voice-Network dial peers define the attributes of a packet voice network connection. They map a dial string to a remote network device.

The specific type of Voice-Network dial peer you must configure depends on the layer 2 packet network technology used. Different technologies are used by dial peers:

Voice over IP (VoIP)   The dial peer is mapped to the IP address, Domain Name System (DNS) name, or server type of the destination VoIP device that terminates the call. This applies to all VoIP protocols, such as H.323, SIP, and Media Gateway Control Protocol (MGCP).

Voice over Frame Relay (VoFR)   The dial peer is mapped to the Data Link Connection Identifier (DLCI) of the interface from which the call exits the router.

Voice over ATM (VoATM)   The dial peer is mapped to the ATM virtual circuit for the interface from which the call exits the router.

When configuring a dial peer, you must first create the dial peer with the `dial-peer voice` command. The `dial-peer voice` command has the following syntax:
To configure an interface on a fixed configuration router, you always use the command `interface type number`.

```
dial-peer voice [sequence number] [type of dial-peer]
```

Once you create the type of dial peer you need, you can configure various other options for it. We will not cover every possible configurable option for a dial peer in this chapter. However, we will discuss three items that you will need to configure: the destination pattern, the session target, and the port option, which you must specify if you have created a POTS type of dial peer.

Destination Pattern

You must configure the `destination-pattern` command to specify the prefix or the full E.164 telephone number (depending on your dial plan) to be used for this dial peer. When the router identifies a match for this configured destination pattern, it will direct the call to the configured local voice port (if this dial peer is a POTS type) and will direct the call to the configured Session

Target (if this dial peer is a VoIP, VoFR, or VoATM type). The `destination-pattern` command has the following syntax:

```
destination-pattern [string]
```

The [string] variable is a series of digits that specify the E.164 telephone number. A . (period) can be used in the destination pattern as a wildcard representing a single character. For example, to identify the destination pattern as any seven-digit number that begins with 593, you would enter the following command:

```
destination-pattern 593....
```

Session Target

You must configure the `session target` command to specify a network-specific address for a dial peer. The session target syntax is different depending on whether the dial peer is a VoIP, VoFR, or VoATM type:

- For a VoIP type:

  ```
  session target ipv4:[IP address of the remote router interface]
  ```

- For a VoFR type:

  ```
  session target [outbound-frame-relay-interface] [outbound-frame-relay-interface dlci]
  ```

- For a VoATM type:

  ```
  session target [outbound-atm-interface] [outbound-atm-interface vpi/vci]
  ```

Port

If you have created a POTS type of dial peer, then you must configure the `port` command to specify a local voice port to which associate the dial peer should be associated. The `port` command has the following syntax:

```
port [local voice-port]
```

POTS Dial-Peer Example

Let's look at a command syntax example for configuring a dial peer:

`dial-peer voice 5 pots`	Creates a Dial-Peer as a POTS type, with a sequence number of 5
`destination-pattern 5551212`	This assigns the telephone number 555-1212 to the standard POTS phone connected to voice-port 1/0
`port 1/0`	This dial-peer configuration is attached to the local voice port 1/0

IP Dial-Peer Example

To configure VoIP, first the dial-peer command must be configured. Second, configure the destination pattern. And finally, configure the session target:

dial-peer voice 2 voip	Creates a Dial-Peer as a VoIP type, with a sequence number of 2
destination-pattern 5551212	This assigns the telephone number 555-1212 to the device that is specified in the session target command
session target ipv4:147.19.1.2	Specifies the Session Target as the remote router interface with an IP Version 4 address of 147.19.1.2

Frame Relay Dial-Peer Example

VoFR is configured in basically the same way as VoIP is configured. The biggest difference is the session target. Because this is Frame Relay, you need to use the local interface and DLCI pair:

dial-peer voice 3 vofr	Creates a Dial-Peer as a VoFR type, with a sequence number of 3
destination-pattern 5551212	This assigns the telephone number 555-1212 to the device that is specified in the session target command
session target Serial0/0 204	Specifies the Session Target as the local Serial 0/0 interface, which is assigned 204 DLCI

When implementing a Frame Relay dial peer, it is best to also implement traffic shaping on the Frame Relay interface. The Frame Relay map class that you configure *must* have the voice bandwidth command specified. Also, if this is a point-to-point Frame Relay interface, which uses the interface-dlci command, then you *must* also specify the vofr cisco command under the DLCI configuration.

Normally, a packet must wait its turn before being serialized and sent out. This can be a major problem with voice because it is very time sensitive. Suppose that our target end-to-end time is 150ms. What happens if we send a 1500-byte packet down a 64Kbps line? It takes more than 180ms—(1500 * 8)/64Kbps = 187.4ms—for this big packet to get out of the way before the small VoFR packet can even get on the wire. We've already exceeded our goal.

FRF.12 (FRF Standard for Fragmentation for VoFR) provides an industry-standard method of fragmenting Frame Relay packets. FRF.12 is not enabled by default. Because this is a Frame Relay command, you must enable Frame Relay encapsulation. Here is a short configuration example:

```
interface serial 0/0.1
 encapsulation frame-relay
 frame-relay traffic-shaping
 frame-relay interface-dlci 100
  class kelly

map-class frame-relay kelly
 frame-relay fragment 80
```

Frame Relay traffic shaping enables traffic shaping and per-virtual-circuit queuing on the interface. The default queuing strategy is first in/first out (FIFO).

The command `frame-relay interface dlci 100 voice-encap 80` enables FRF.12 on Data Link Connection Identifier (DLCI) 100. The `voice-encap 80` sets the packet segment size to 80 bytes. Cisco's recommended segmentation sizes are calculated on a maximum serialization delay of 10ms and shown in Table 20.3. Select your segmentation size based on the smaller of the two ends of the connection. Otherwise, you may overutilize the slower of the two.

TABLE 20.3   FRF.12 Data Segmentation Sizes

Interface Access Speed	Recommended Segmentation Size
64Kbps	80 bytes
128Kbps	160 bytes
256Kbps	320 bytes
512Kbps	640 bytes
1.536Mbps	1600 bytes
2.048Mbps	1600 bytes

Remember the 1500-byte packet that delayed our VoFR packet? It now waits 10ms before being serialized and sent out the interface. That is a major improvement.

ATM Dial Peer example

VoATM is configured in basically the same way as VoFR and VoIP are configured. The biggest difference is the session target. Because this is ATM, you need to use the local interface and the virtual path identifier/virtual channel identifier (VPI/VCI) pair:

`dial-peer voice 4 voatm`	Creates a Dial-Peer as a VoFR type, with a sequence number of 4
`destination-pattern 5551212`	This assigns the telephone number 555-1212 to the device that is specified in the session target command
`session target ATM0/0 40/100`	Specifies the Session Target as the local ATM 0/0 interface, which is assigned the VPI/VCI pair of 40/100

Optional Voice Port Capabilities

Now we'll discuss some of the optional type of functionality that can be configured on voice ports. We will discuss the Private Line Automatic Ringdown (PLAR) option, the option of configuring a router to provide a standard "dial 9 to access an outside line" function, and the ability to associate multiple telephone numbers with a single voice port.

Private Line Automatic Ringdown

The Private Line Automatic Ringdown (PLAR) function is basically the Hotline or "Bat Phone" functionality: as soon as a configured telephone is taken off-hook, the remote end telephone automatically rings. The following example is configured on router R5 in the network shown in Figure 20.4:

`voice-port 1/0`

`connection plar 5111`	Configures this voice-port for PLAR, when the telephone connected off of this port goes off-hook, the telephone number 5111 will be dialed immediately
`dial-peer voice 5000 pots`	Remember that POTS dial peers do NOT automatically forward digits
`destination-pattern 5000`	This assigns the telephone number 5000 to the standard POTS phone connected to voice-port 1/0
`port 1/0`	This dial-peer configuration is attached to the local voice port 1/0
`dial-peer voice 5111 pots`	Remember that POTS dial peers do NOT automatically forward digits

destination-pattern 5111	This assigns the telephone number 5111 to the standard POTS phone connected to voice-port 1/1. So, when the telephone connected off of voice-port 1/0 goes off-hook, the call is directed to voice-port 1/1
port 1/1	This dial-peer configuration is attached to the local voice port 1/1

With this configuration, when the telephone connected to voice port 1/0 is taken off-hook, the telephone connected to voice port 1/1 will automatically ring.

Off-Net: Dial 9 with an FXO Port

It is possible to configure a router to provide a standard "dial 9 to access an outside line" function as you encounter in most businesses with their own PBX. This is accomplished through the use of an FXO port on the router that is connected to an outside telephone line. This functionality will allow multiple telephones inside the building to use the same outside telephone line (however, only one phone can use the outside telephone at a time). The following example is configured on router R5 in the network shown in Figure 20.4:

voice-port 1/1	Router R5 FXS Voice-port 1/1, has a standard POTS phone connected
voice-port 1/2	Router R5 FXO Voice-port 1/2, is connected to outside PSTN line
ring number 1	This is an FXO-only command, which specifies the number of rings before the FXO port answers the call
dial-peer voice 5111 pots	Remember that POTS dial peers do NOT automatically forward digits
destination-pattern 5111	This assigns the telephone number 5111 to the standard POTS phone connected to voice-port 1/1
port 1/1	This dial-peer configuration is attached to the local voice port 1/1
dial-peer voice 5222 pots	
destination-pattern 9	This assigns the telephone number 9 to the outside PSTN or POTS line connected to voice-port 1/2. So, when the number 9 is dialed, the call is directed to voice-port 1/2
port 1/2	This dial-peer configuration is attached to the local voice port 1/2

With this configuration, when the telephone connected to voice port 1/1 goes off-hook and the number 9 is dialed, the call will be directed to voice port 1/2. Voice port 1/2 is connected to the outside PSTN line, so the telephone connected off of voice port 1/1 will receive dial tone from the outside PSTN line.

Associating Multiple Numbers with a Single Voice Port

It is possible to configure a router so that a telephone connected to a single voice port is able to have multiple telephone numbers associated with it. The following example is configured on router R2 in the network shown in Figure 20.4:

`voice-port 1/0`	Router R2 FXS Voice-port 1/0, has a standard POTS phone connected
`voice-port 1/1`	Router R2 FXS Voice-port 1/1, has a standard POTS phone connected
`dial-peer voice 2000 pots`	Remember that POTS dial peers do NOT automatically forward digits
`destination-pattern 2000`	This assigns the telephone number 2000 to the standard POTS phone connected to voice-port 1/0, which also has telephone numbers 2001 and 2002 associated with it
`port 1/0`	This dial-peer configuration is attached to the local voice port 1/0
`dial-peer voice 2001 pots`	Remember that POTS dial peers do NOT automatically forward digits
`destination-pattern 2001`	This assigns the telephone number 2001 to the standard POTS phone connected to voice-port 1/0, which also has telephone numbers 2000 and 2002 associated with it
`port 1/0`	This dial-peer configuration is attached to the local voice port 1/0
`dial-peer voice 2002 pots`	Remember that POTS dial peers do NOT automatically forward digits
`destination-pattern 2002`	This assigns the telephone number 2002 to the standard POTS phone connected to voice-port 1/0, which also has telephone numbers 2000 and 2001 associated with it

port 1/0	This dial-peer configuration is attached to the local voice port 1/0
dial-peer voice 2111 pots	Remember that POTS dial peers do NOT automatically forward digits
destination-pattern 2111	This assigns the telephone number 2111 to the standard POTS phone connected to voice-port 1/1
port 1/1	This dial-peer configuration is attached to the local voice port 1/1

With this configuration, the telephone connected to voice port 1/0 is associated with telephone numbers 2000, 2001, and 2002. If we take the telephone connected off of voice port 1/1 off-hook and dial telephone number 2000, 2001, or 2002, the telephone connected off of voice port 1/0 will ring.

Optional Dial Capabilities

The following two examples demonstrate how to implement the number expansion functionality and how to configure a router to automatically set all voice packets flowing through the router to a preconfigured IP precedence level.

Number Expansion

In most corporate environments, the telephone network is configured so that you can reach a destination by dialing only a portion (possibly an extension number) of the full E.164 telephone number. Voice over IP can be configured to recognize extension numbers and expand them into their full E.164 dialed number. This is accomplished with the num-exp command, which has the following syntax:

```
num-exp [extension-number] [extension-string]
```

In the this example, the full E.164 telephone number 408-555-XXXX will be dialed if the number 5-XXXX is dialed:

```
num-exp 5.... 408555....
```

And in the following example, if any 10-digit telephone number that begins with 303-593 is dialed, the 4-digit extension 3600 will actually be dialed (remember that the . is a single character wildcard):

```
num-exp 303593.... 3600
```

Other Optional Commands

The following are some of the optional commands that can be configured on a dial peer:

ip precedence 5

Specifies that this Dial-Peer will generate all packets as an IP precedence level of 5, which will give the voice packets a higher priority over the other packets

no vad

Specifies that this Dial-Peer will NOT use Voice Activity Detection (VAD), which will increase the quality of the voice call, but use more bandwidth

Voice Activity Detection (VAD) is used to suppress IP packets that represent silence during a phone conversation. Because you listen and pause between words and sentences in a typical voice conversation, up to 60 percent of a voice conversation can be silence. In a standard telephone network, all the voice calls are a full 64Kbps (DS0) channel regardless of how much of the bandwidth is carrying voice or silence portions of the conversation. In the multiservice, or VoIP, network the entire conversation, voice and silence, is encoded into IP packets, so VAD will suppress (or not transmit) the IP packets of silence, thus saving the bandwidth. VAD is enabled by default on all VoIP calls. VAD is not recommended for toll quality voice applications because clipping occurs after a silent period.

Voice Troubleshooting

Here are a few of the possible commands that can be used to troubleshoot Voice:

show call active voice brief

Display active call information for voice calls in progress

show dial-peer voice summary

Checks the validity of the dial peer configuration

`show voice port`	Displays the current configuration of the voice-ports on the router
`show dialplan number [digit_string]`	Displays the dial-peer that is matched by a string of digits
`show queue`	Displays fair queueing configuration and statistics
`show ip rtp header-compression`	Displays RTP header compression statistics
`debug priority`	Displays priority queueing output if packets are dropped from the priority queue
`debug voip ccapi inout`	Used to debug end-to-end VoIP calls
`Debug vpm`	Used to debug the Voice Processor Module
`debug vtsp`	Used to debug Voice Telephony Service Provider (VTSP) commands
`Debug vtsp dsp`	Shows the digits as they are received by the voice-port

Now that we have completed our discussion of voice-related multiservice technologies, we'll briefly discuss a newer and rapidly growing multiservice technology: Multiprotocol Label Switching.

Multiprotocol Label Switching

Multiprotocol Label Switching (MPLS), which is described in RFC 2547, provides a common mechanism to combine the intelligence of the routing environment with the power of the switching environment while also allowing the implementation of router-based virtual private networks (VPNs). One major benefit of MPLS is that it can be layer 2 independent, meaning that it will allow the layer 3 packets to be carried over almost any layer 2 technology, such as Packet over Synchronous Optical Network (Packet over SONET, or PoS), Ethernet, Frame Relay, Point-to-Point Protocol (PPP), and asynchronous transfer mode (ATM).

How does MPLS work? It works through the implementation of MPLS labels, because the labels contain specific routing (label switch path) information that tells the routers and switches in the network where to forward the packets based on predetermined IP routing information. The use of the label is highly efficient because the layer 3 routing decision only has to be made at the edge of the MPLS network, thus the layer 3 routing decision does not have to be performed at each hop through the network. Labels are inserted at the edge of the MPLS network and removed when the packets leave the MPLS network. The MPLS network applies services and forwards packets that are based on the information contained in the label. With MPLS, service providers can provide VPN services and scale those services for many customers.

MPLS Label

The MPLS label is inserted between the layer 2 (LLC sublayer) header and the layer 3 (IP) header in a layer 2 frame. In ATM networks with label switching, the label is mapped into the virtual path identifier/virtual channel identifier (VPI/VCI) fields of the ATM header. The MPLS label field is 4 bytes (32 bits) in length; the actual label (tag) is 20 bits. Figure 20.5 shows the MPLS label header. Table 20.4 describes how the 32 bits of the MPLS label header fields are utilized.

FIGURE 20.5 MPLS label header

TABLE 20.4 MPLS Label Header Fields

Field	Bits
Label	20
Experimental	3
Bottom of Stack	1
Time to Live	8

The actual label is 20 bits long, providing 1,048,576 possible label switched paths through a single label switch router (LSR) if assigned on a per-platform basis. The Experimental bits are planned for congestion control and are often used to map the IP header Type of Service (ToS) value into, thus carrying the ToS value across the MPLS network. Because MPLS labels can be stacked on top of each other as the switch path is built, the Bottom of Stack bit is used to specify the label residing at the bottom of the label stack. The label immediately after the layer 2 header is the top label, and the label with the S bit set to a 1 is the bottom label. The Time to Live (TTL) 8 bits, which is used to protect against forwarding loops, is copied from the IP header and decremented at each LSR hop.

The label, which is put on a packet as the packet enters the MPLS network, will represent which *Forwarding Equivalence Class (FEC)* the packet will belong to. The LSRs will direct traffic based on the FEC, which is basically a group of IP packets meant to be forwarded in the same manner and over the same path through the network. The FEC can be based upon multiple criteria, such as the destination IP address, the IP precedence of the packets, and so on. All the packets within the same FEC will be treated in the same manner within the MPLS network.

MPLS Label Switch Routers

All routers within an MPLS network are *Label Switch Routers (LSRs),* which forward packets based on the MPLS label and not based on the common routing protocols. If the MPLS network uses ATM, the LSRs are called ATM LSRs. The Edge Label Switch Router (Edge LSR) is responsible for adding the label to or removing it from the packet as the packet enters or exits the MPLS network. Routers that are not part of the MPLS network are referred to as non-LSRs. Figure 20.6 shows these router types within a MPLS network.

FIGURE 20.6   Label Switch Routers

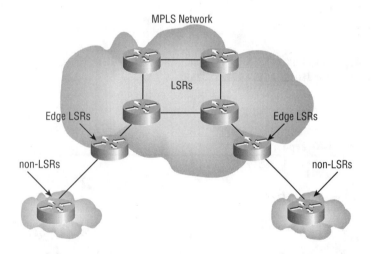

The LSRs communicate with each other about what labels to assign to the packets through the use of the *Label Distribution Protocol (LDP).* Cisco also supports a prestandard version of LDP, known as the Tag Distribution Protocol (TDP).

An LSR can also route non-MPLS (native IP) packets it receives on an MPLS-enabled interface within the network. As long as an IP address is enabled on the router interface, native IP packets can be transmitted and received as usual. Remember that IP is just another protocol. The receiving router (LSR) will analyze the received packets and verify whether it contains MPLS encoding at layer 2. If the IP packet does not contain the MPLS layer 2 encoding, it will be handled as a native IP packet. However, an LSR cannot transmit or receive an MPLS packet unless the router interface is MPLS enabled. If an MPLS packet is received on an interface that is not MPLS enabled, the packets will be dropped.

Enabling MPLS on LSRs

To enable MPLS, Cisco Express Forwarding (CEF) must first be enabled on all routers running MPLS. You can accomplish this with the `ip cef` global command. Remember, CEF is utilized in the VPN routing and forwarding (VRF) table.

To enable MPLS on the router interfaces, use the `mpls ip` command. When this command is applied to a router interface, TCP port 646 (LDP) and TCP port 711 (TDP) are automatically opened on that interface. The `mpls ip` command must be configured on every interface of the LSR that is participating in the MPLS network. A simple configuration of a LSR in a MPLS network is shown here:

```
ip cef

interface Loopback0
 ip address 192.168.1.1 255.255.255.255

interface Serial0/0
 encapsulation frame-relay

interface Serial0/0.1 point-to-point
 ip address 192.168.50.1 255.255.255.252
 mpls ip
 frame-relay interface-dlci 100

interface Serial0/0.2 point-to-point
 ip address 192.168.50.5 255.255.255.252
 mpls ip
 frame-relay interface-dlci 200
```

As we stated previously, MPLS can be used (and most often is) to implement virtual private networks (VPNs).

MPLS Virtual Private Networks

The MPLS-enabled routers will hold a *VPN routing and forwarding (VRF)* table for each VPN. A VRF comprises the IP routing table, the Cisco Express Forwarding (CEF) table, and a description of the router interfaces using this forwarding table. Because the router holds a separate VRF for each VPN, MPLS VPNs are secure in that packets will never be sent outside of the configured VPN (unless that functionality is explicitly configured). Another benefit of the router holding a separate VRF for each VPN is that each VPN is unique unto itself, thus different VPNs can use duplicate IP addresses, and because the packets for a VPN will never be sent outside of the configured VPN, each VPN can utilize the same IP addresses and never conflict with the others.

To implement MPLS-based VPNs within the MPLS network, Provider (P) routers and Provider Edge (PE) routers need to be implemented inside the service provider network. Likewise, the customer's network, which is not part of the MPLS network, is made up of Customer (C) routers and

Customer Edge (CE) routers, which connect to the service provider's PE routers. Descriptions of these four types of routers are in Table 20.5.

TABLE 20.5   MPLS Router types

Type	Description
P router	The internal routers within the service provider's network. These core routers do not maintain VRF tables, thus they have no knowledge of the MPLS VPN.
PE router	The edge routers within the service provider's network that connect to the customer's CE routers. PE routers maintain VPN routing and forwarding (VRF) tables for the VPNs associated with the connected interfaces.
C router	The internal routers within the customer's network. They do not connect to the service provider's network. These routers do not maintain VRF tables, thus they have no knowledge of the MPLS VPN.
CE router	The edge routers within the customer's network. They connect to the service provider's PE routers. These routers do not maintain VRF tables, thus they have no knowledge of the MPLS VPN.

Figure 20.7 shows a diagram of these routers in an MPLS VPN network.

FIGURE 20.7   MPLS VPN

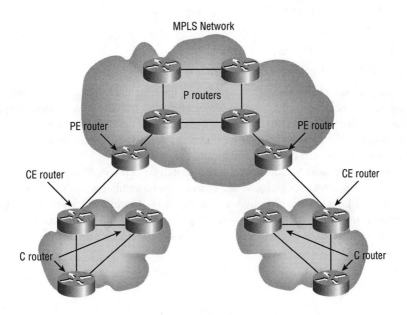

MPLS VPNs are also referred to as layer 3 VPNs or BGP VPNs because the Border Gateway Protocol (BGP) is used to establish peering relations and signal the VPN-associated labels with each of the corresponding PE routers. This results in a highly scalable implementation because core (P) routers have no information about the VPNs inside the MPLS network. BGP VPNs are useful when subscribers want layer 3 connectivity and would prefer to offload their routing overhead to a service provider.

Layer 3 VPNs have been deployed in networks that have as many as 700 PE routers. Service providers are currently providing up to 500 VPNs, with each VPN containing as many as 1000 sites. A wide variety of routing protocols are available to provide connectivity on the subscriber access link (i.e., CE-router-to-PE-router link). These include static routes, BGP, Routing Information Protocol (RIP), and Open Shortest Path First (OSPF). Most VPNs have been deployed utilizing static routes for the CE-router-to-PE-router connectivity.

MPLS is emerging as a widely acceptable technology, evidenced by the 100+ customer deployments of Cisco MPLS. It is important to note that MPLS is not a replacement for IP. The IP control plane is a fundamental component of MPLS, which makes MPLS extremely attractive to both service providers and enterprises.

Summary

This chapter has covered some legacy telephony information so you can understand how Cisco voice technologies can be integrated. We discussed some standard signaling and encoding methods that Cisco equipment supports.

In this chapter, you learned about the requirements for voice communications over a network. We covered the following topics:

- Interfaces and signaling
- RTP/RTCP, H.323, SIP, SS7, and CODECs
- Configuration of Voice over IP, Frame Relay, and ATM

The industry is only starting to see the migration of traditional telephony services to the IP-based networking environment. The configuration of voice services on a Cisco router, in its simplest form, is a very easy task. Basically, you just have to configure the required POTS and Voice-Network dial peers. Remember to always keep in mind which voice port each POTS dial peer is associated with and which session target each dial peer is associated with.

We also briefly discussed Multiprotocol Label Switching (MPLS). Many service providers are implementing MPLS, often on a global scale. You need to be familiar with the information we presented because MPLS is a listed objective within the CCIE Routing and Switching Blueprint.

Also, if you would like to try to implement a multiservice technology scenario, we have developed a hands-on voice lab exercise. You'll find it in Chapter 20 Supplement on the CD-ROM that came with this book.

Exam Essentials

Know the difference between in-band and out-of-band signaling.   Digital signaling is accomplished in one of two ways: in-band or out-of-band. In-band signaling uses bits in the data stream to carry the signaling information. Out-of-band signaling uses a separate channel to carry the signaling.

Know what SS7 is.   Signaling System 7 (SS7) is an out-of-band ITU-T standard originally developed for the GSTN (general switched telephone network). It covers call establishment, billing, routing, and information exchange.

Understand RTP and RTCP.   Real-Time Transport Protocol (RTP) was a necessary addition to the protocol suite for voice and video traffic on an IP network. Due to the lack of reliability of a normal network, RTP was designed to provide services that would allow better end-to-end responses. RTP runs over UDP because UDP has less delay than TCP. Also, RTP Control Protocol (RTCP), which is also defined in RFC 1889, monitors the delivery of data and provides the control and identification functions required for the operation of the call.

Understand H.323 and SIP.   H.323 is the ITU-T standard for carrying audio, video, and data across an IP network. When voice signals are transferred across a network, they must be encoded and decoded for analog-to-digital conversion and digital-to-analog conversion. Session Initiation Protocol (SIP) is an alternative multimedia framework to H.323 because it was developed specifically for IP telephony. SIP is an Application layer protocol that is used for creating, modifying, and terminating Internet multimedia conferences, IP telephone calls, and multimedia distribution.

Know what FRF.12 is.   FRF.12 (FRF Standard for Fragmentation for VoFR) provides an industry-standard method of fragmenting Frame Relay packets. Normally, a packet must wait its turn before being serialized and sent out. This can be a major problem with voice because it is very time sensitive. FRF.12 solves this problem.

Key Terms

Before you take the exam, be certain you are familiar with the following terms:

channel associated signaling (CAS)	Multiprotocol Label Switching (MPLS)
common-channel signaling (CCS)	out-of-band signaling
Erlang	plain old telephone service (POTS)
Forwarding Equivalence Class (FEC)	private branch exchange (PBX)
glare	public switched telephone network (PSTN)
in-band signaling	quantization
Label Distribution Protocol (LDP)	robbed-bit signaling (RBS)
Label Switch Routers (LSRs)	VPN routing and forwarding (VRF)

Review Questions

1. What is the A link used for in Signaling System 7 (SS7)?

   A. Associates two COs so they can exchange voice traffic

   B. Connects hierarchical pairs of STPs

   C. Interconnects STPs to an endpoint in the network

   D. Mates two matched pairs of STPs

2. How much traffic does MP-MLQ produce?

   A. 8.3Kbps

   B. 16Kbps

   C. 6.3Kbps

   D. 5.3Kbps

3. How much traffic does Pulse Code Modulation (PCM) produce?

   A. 26.4Kbps

   B. 6.3Kbps

   C. 64Kbps

   D. 32Kbps

4. Which CODEC is defined by the ITU as the standard H.323/H.324 to encode voice traffic?

   A. G.729

   B. G.711

   C. G.728

   D. G.723

5. Which E&M type is most frequently used in North America?

   A. Type 1

   B. Type 2

   C. Type 3

   D. Type 4

6. Which of the following is *not* used for E&M line seizing?

   A. Immediate start

   B. Wink start

   C. Delay start

   D. Loop start

7. What does Frame Relay Forum 12 (FRF.12) define?

    A. Maximum MTU sizes for Voice over Frame Relay (VoFR)

    B. The VoFR packet format

    C. A router's response to a Backward Explicit Congestion Notification (BECN)

    D. Data frame segmentation

8. Which command can be used under a POTS `dial-peer` statement?

    A. `session target port`

    B. `session target DNS`

    C. `session target VCD`

    D. Both A and C

9. In a `dial-peer` statement, which destination pattern will the number 1991 match?

    A. `1T`

    B. `1`

    C. `199.`

    D. `1991`

10. G.729 uses which coder type?

    A. PCM

    B. ADPCM

    C. CELP

    D. CSA-CELP

Answers to Review Questions

1. C. An A link interconnects Signal Transfer Points (STPs) to either a Signal Control Point (SCP) or a Signal Switching Point (SSP), which is the endpoint in a network.

2. C. ACELP uses 5.3Kbps. The value of 16Kbps is for LD-CELP. 8.3 is not a valid answer.

3. C. G.711 uses PCM to produce a 64Kbps stream.

4. D. Two different methods are defined by G.723: MP-MLQ, and ACELP. Either one works within H.323.

5. A. E&M Type 1 is the most commonly used type in North America.

6. D. Wink, delay, and immediate start are all used by E&M for trunk supervision.

7. D. FRF.12 is the standard for fragmentation for VoFR.

8. D. You may use either the port or ATM VCD when configuring a POTS dial peer.

9. D. Options A, C, or D will work, but the router will select D because it is the longest match.

10. D. G.729 uses CSA-CELP to produce an 8Kbps voice stream.

IP Multicast

THE CCIE QUALIFICATION EXAM TOPICS COVERED IN THIS CHAPTER INCLUDE THE FOLLOWING:

- ✓ Unicast, broadcast, and multicast addresses
- ✓ Group address, admin group, and link local L3 to L2 mapping
- ✓ Internet Group Management Protocol (IGMP) versions 1 and 2
- ✓ Cisco Group Management Protocol (CGMP)
- ✓ Distribution trees (shared and source)
- ✓ Protocol Independent Multicast (PIM): dense mode, sparse mode, and sparse-dense mode
- ✓ PIM mechanics: joining, pruning PIM state, Mroute table
- ✓ Rendezvous points (Auto-RP and BSR)

Today's web and enterprise applications are directed toward larger audiences on the network than ever before because voice and video are being sourced for larger and larger audiences. One-on-one communications can overwhelm both servers and network resources. However, multicast services can eliminate these problems.

This chapter will aid you in understanding the differences in the communication methods of unicast, broadcast, and multicast. It is imperative that you understand how multicast addressing spans both layer 3 and layer 2 of the OSI model. You will also learn about the protocols and tools used to implement and control multicast traffic on your network. As with any service that runs on your network, you must understand the resources needed and the implications of enabling multicast on your network.

Multicast Overview

Blue, yellow, and red are different and have their own place within the spectrum of visible light. Similarly, unicast, broadcast, and multicast are different but each is used to achieve a specific purpose or fulfill requirements of a specific part of the communication spectrum. It is important to know where each falls within the spectrum as well as the potential applications of each.

RFC 1112 is an older RFC, but the material is very relevant because it discusses multicast in great detail, specifically host extensions and groups and the methods by which hosts are entered into multicast groups and how they are able to leave those groups. RFCs 2236 (IGMPv2), 3376 (IGMPv3), and 2362 (PIMv2) are some of the new RFCs that describe multicast technology.

Unicast Communications

Unicast is used for direct host-to-host communication. When the layer 3 protocol data unit (PDU) is formed, two layer 3, IP addresses are added to the IP header. These are the source and destination IP addresses. They specify a specific originating and receiving host. After the layer 3 PDU is formed, it is passed to layer 2 to create the layer 2 PDU, or frame. The frame consists of all of the previous layer's headers in addition to the layer 2 header and trailer. With an Ethernet frame, for example, the two 48-bit source and destination MAC addresses are specified in the layer 2 header. Other protocols such as IEEE 802.5 (Token Ring) and FDDI also have headers that contain specific host source and destination addresses.

Unicast communication is used when two hosts need to exchange data with only one another and are not concerned with sharing the data with everyone. A MAC address must uniquely identify a host. No two hosts MAC addresses are the same. Therefore, unicast capitalizes on the unique MAC address for each host. With a specific address, any source host should be able to contact the destination host without confusion.

One of the caveats to unicast communication is that the source host *must* know the destination layer 3 address or name. After that, with Ethernet the host either sends an ARP request for the default gateway (if the network mask indicates it is *not* on the same subnet) or sends an ARP request for the host (if the network mask indicates it is on the same subnet).

This may not be done on a host-by-host basis in a routed environment. The normal operation is that the host has a default gateway assigned for use when the logical destination address does not reside on the same subnet as the source host. Figure 21.1 depicts how unicast traffic works on the same subnet.

FIGURE 21.1   Unicast communication

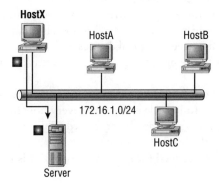

This is a two-way communication. These two hosts are interested only in communicating with one another. So what happens when one host wants to talk to multiple hosts or all of the hosts on the same network segment. That is one instance where broadcast communications can be used.

Broadcast Communications

With a good understanding of unicast, you can understand the principle of broadcast communication on networks. Whereas unicast messages target a single host on a network, broadcast messages are meant to reach all hosts on a broadcast domain. Figure 21.2 depicts a broadcast message sent from Host X to all machines within the same broadcast domain.

FIGURE 21.2   Broadcast message on a network

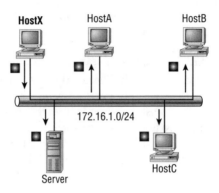

A good example of a broadcast message is an Address Resolution Protocol (ARP) request. When a host has a packet destined for a logical address that is not located on the same network, the host must ARP for the default gateway's MAC address so it can create the layer 2 frame and in turn send the datagram to the router. The MAC address is obtained via an ARP request. The ARP request is a broadcast message sent to all devices in the broadcast domain. The router will be the device that responds to the broadcast message, whereas other stations will evaluate the frame but not respond.

This brings up another good point: broadcasts can cause problems on networks. Because the broadcast frame is addressed to include every host, every host must process the frame. CPU interruption occurs so that the frame may be processed. This interruption affects other applications that are running on the host. When unicast frames are seen, a quick check is made to identify whether the frame is intended for the host or not. If it isn't, the frame is discarded.

Multicast Communications

Multicast is a different beast entirely. At first glance it appears to be a hybrid of unicast and broadcast communication, but that isn't quite accurate. Multicast does allow point-to-multipoint communication similar to broadcasts, but it happens in a different manner. The crux of multicast is that it allows multiple recipients to receive messages without flooding them to all hosts on a broadcast domain. Thus, multicast is a one-to-many communications mechanism (i.e. only one source, many receivers).

Multicast works by sending messages or data to multicast group addresses. Multicast routers then forward copies of the packet out every interface that has hosts subscribed to those group addresses if IP multicast routing is configured. This is where multicast differs from broadcast messages because routers do not forward broadcasts. Copies of packets are sent only to subscribed hosts, whereas broadcasts are sent to all hosts. This can be paralleled with mailing lists and spam. You subscribe to a mailing list when you want to receive mail from a specific group regarding specific information, such as a Cisco user group mailing list, for example. You expect to get messages only from other members of the group regarding topics related to the group's purpose. Spam is unsolicited mail that is sent to everyone. When it arrives in your inbox, you aren't expecting it from the sender, nor are you likely to be interested in the content.

Multicast works in much the same way. You, as a user, or an application will subscribe to a specific IP multicast group to become a member. Once you're a member of the group, IP multicast packets containing that group address in the destination field in the header will arrive at your host and be processed. If you don't subscribe to the group, your host will not process packets addressed to the group. Refer to Figure 21.3 for a visual reference on how multicast works.

FIGURE 21.3 Multicast communication

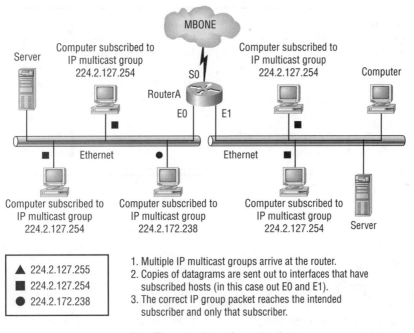

1. Multiple IP multicast groups arrive at the router.
2. Copies of datagrams are sent out to interfaces that have subscribed hosts (in this case out E0 and E1).
3. The correct IP group packet reaches the intended subscriber and only that subscriber.

Note: The router did not forward packets belonging to 224.2.127.255.

The key to multicast is the addressing structure. This is key because all communication is based on addressing. In unicast communication, there is a unique address for every host on a network. With broadcast communication, a global address that all hosts will respond to is used. A multicast group is assigned an address that only hosts subscribed to the group will respond to. The next section will cover multicast addressing in detail.

Multicast Addressing

Similar to mailing lists, with multicast there are several different groups that users or applications can subscribe to. The range of multicast addresses starts with 224.0.0.0 and goes through 239.255.255.255. As you can see, this is IP Class D address assignment based on classful IP assignment. This is denoted by the fact that the first 4 bits in the first octet are 1110. Just as with regular IP addresses, there are some addresses that can be assigned and there are ranges of reserved addresses.

It is important to recognize that the reserved addresses are categorized. Table 21.1 depicts some of the reserved addresses and their corresponding categories.

TABLE 21.1   IP Multicast Reserved Addresses

Multicast Address	Purpose
224.0.0.0–224.0.0.18	Use by network protocols
224.0.0.1	*All hosts*
224.0.0.2	*All routers*
224.0.0.4	*DVMRP routers*
224.0.0.5	*All OSPF routers*
224.0.0.6	*All OSPF DR routers*
224.0.0.9	*RIPv2 routers*
224.0.0.10	*EIGRP routers*
224.0.0.13	*All PIM routers*
224.0.0.105–224.0.0.250 and 252-255	Local network control block
224.0.1.0–224.0.1.177	Internetwork control block
224.0.1.1	*NTP*
224.0.1.39	*Cisco-RP-Announce*
224.0.1.40	*Cisco-RP-Discovery*

TABLE 21.1   IP Multicast Reserved Addresses *(continued)*

Multicast Address	Purpose
224.0.1.178–224.0.1.255	Unassigned
224.0.2.0–224.0.255.0	AD-HOC block
239.0.0.0–239.255.255.255	Private multicast domain

Each of these address ranges is managed by the Internet Assigned Numbers Authority (IANA). Due to the limited amount of multicast addresses, there are very strict requirements for new assignments within this address space. The 239.0.0.0–239.255.255.255 range is equivalent in purpose to the private networks defined by RFC 1918.

Let's discuss the multicast *scope*, which defines in terms of hops the number of multicast routers a multicast packet will be transmitted. This is implemented by setting the TTL of the multicast packet. The difference between the IP multicast ranges of 224.0.0.0–224.0.0.255 and 224.0.1.0–224.0.1.255 is that the first range will not be forwarded by an IP router, as the TTL will be set to 1. Both ranges of addresses are used by applications and network protocols. The first group, classified as local-link, is meant to remain local to the subnet or broadcast domain on which the system resides. The second group is a global address that can be routed and forwarded through IP routers. Scope is important in ensuring private multicast packets are not forwarded outside an organizations administrative domain.

Mapping IP Multicast to Ethernet

As networks grew, so did the need for a way to use multicast. This growth required that there be a way to use multicast across routers instead of being limited to the physical segment where hosts were located. In regular unicast, MAC addresses are layer 2 addresses, and to reach remote hosts, layer 3 logical IP addresses are used to route data to the remote subnet. Once the packet reaches the remote subnet, the Address Resolution Protocol (ARP) is used to find the MAC address of the host. Using an existing ARP table, or via an ARP request, the MAC address that is associated to the layer 3 IP address is found and the packet is forwarded to the destination host.

IP multicast generates a MAC address based on the layer 3 IP multicast address. All devices that are subscribed to the IP multicast group will listen to frames with the appropriate multicast MAC address. A MAC address is a 48-bit address (6 bytes), but a multicast MAC frame has a standard prefix, or organizational unique identifier (OUI) of 24 bits. This prefix is used for all Ethernet multicast addresses: 0x01005e. When the remaining portion of the MAC address is generated, the 24th bit, or high order bit, is set to 0 and then the last 23 bits of the IP address are mapped in to the remaining 23 bits of the MAC address. Figure 21.4 depicts how this looks.

FIGURE 21.4   IP multicast mapped to MAC multicast

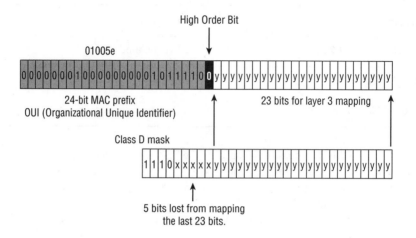

Let's look at some examples for mapping layer 3 multicast addresses to layer 2 multicast addresses. A local IP multicast address is 224.0.0.1. Refer to Figure 21.5 to see how this is mapped. The conversion from binary to hex reveals the MAC multicast address. The prefix was 01-00-5e. The last 23 bits and the high order bit give you 00-00-01. Put them together and you get 01-00-5e-00-00-01 as the MAC address.

FIGURE 21.5   Example #1 for mapping IP multicast to MAC multicast addresses

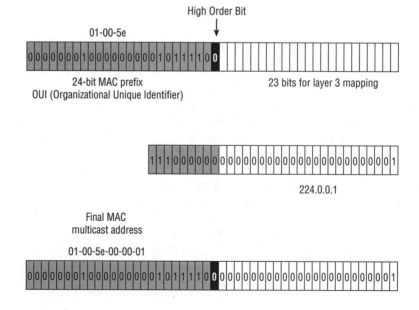

Now let's try one that's a little harder. Suppose you have the IP multicast address of 225.1.25.2. Follow along with Figure 21.6. Only the first 23 bits map into the MAC layer. Convert the first 3 Class D octets to binary, set the 24th bit to 0, convert to hex, and concatenate to 01-00-5e, resulting in 01-00-53-01-19-02.

FIGURE 21.6   Example #2 for mapping IP multicast to MAC multicast addresses

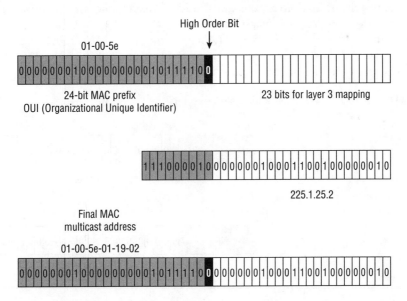

After you do the math and map the last 23 bits, the MAC address becomes 01-00-5e-01-19-02. The easiest way to map layer 3 to layer 2 manually is to do the math and make the binary conversion so you can see what the last 23 bits of the layer 3 IP address is. Once you have that number, all you have to do is insert it into the MAC address and then calculate the remaining 3 hex octet values. The first three octets will always be the same, 01-00-5e.

It is important that you spend time studying this procedure and the steps needed to convert a layer 3 IP multicast address to a layer 2 MAC multicast address.

One last method of determining the last 23 bits that will work on some addresses is to keep in mind that 127 is the highest value you can get in the second octet and still have it be included in the 23 bits that will map to the MAC address. You know that the last two octets (three and four) will map no matter what. So you will have 7 bits from the second octet and a total of 16 bits from the last two octets for a total of 23 bits. Once your value goes above 127 in the second octet, simply subtract 128 and convert to hex.

Layer 3 to Layer 2 Overlap

After you have done a few of these conversions you'll notice, or maybe you already have, that there is a problem with this conversion scheme. By not using all available bits for a Class D address, you cannot get an accurate map of layer 3 to layer 2 addresses. If you look at properties of a Class D address, you will see that the high order bit lies in the first octet and is in the 16 value position, the first four bits are always fixed (1110), leaving 28 bits for host specification. This leaves 28 bits for host specification. However, if only 23 bits of the layer 3 IP address are used, 5 bits are left out of the mapping. This causes an overlap of 2^5, or 32 layer 3 addresses for every 1 layer 2 address. With a ratio of 32:1, you can expect to see a significant amount of address ambiguity. It is safe to say that any IP address that has the same values in the last 23 bits will map to the same MAC multicast address.

For example, 224.0.1.1 and 225.128.1.1 map to the same MAC address. Figure 21.7 shows why this is true. You can see that the bits that differ between 224.0.1.1 and 225.128.1.1 are all within the lost 5 bits. The last 23 bits are identical.

FIGURE 21.7 Multicast addressing overlap

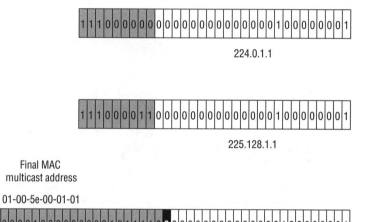

The impact of this can be significant. It creates a window for multiple multicast groups' data to be forwarded to and processed by machines that didn't intentionally subscribe to the groups. To give another example, a machine that subscribes to a multicast group 224.2.127.254 will receive packets for a MAC address of 01-00-5e-02-7f-fe. These host will also process packets that come from multicast group 225.2.127.254 because the layer 2 MAC address is identical.

The problem this creates is that the end host must now process packets from both multicast groups even though it is only interested in data from 224.130.127.254. This causes unwanted overhead and processor interrupts on the host machine. It also reduces network efficiency as multicast frames are forwarded unnecessarily.

Managing Multicast in an Internetwork

Reverting a little to the differences between broadcast and multicast communication, one of the major differences that we discussed is that broadcast traffic goes to all hosts on a subnet whereas multicast traffic goes only to the hosts that request it. The distinguishing factor that puts multicast traffic so far ahead of broadcast traffic in utility is the ability to specify which multiple hosts will receive the transmission on a layer 2 basis. However, hosts still have the last word on deciding whether to listen or not once the information is received on the host interface.

This decision isn't made magically, and it isn't simply because it's multicast traffic that it knows who and where the recipients are. As with any application, protocols are needed to make things happen. Multicast works on the basis of host subscription to groups. Several methods and protocols have been developed and implemented to facilitate multicast functionality within the internetwork. Each of these protocols and methods is used for specific tasks or to achieve specific ends within the multicast environment.

We will now look at these protocols and learn just where they fit in and what they are needed for. We will begin with the most important, subscription and group maintenance, and then move on to enhancements for multicast deployment and distribution.

Subscribing and Maintaining Groups

For multicast traffic to reach a host, the host must be running an application that sends a request to a multicast-enabled router informing the router that it wishes to receive data belonging to the specified multicast group. If this request were never to take place, the router wouldn't be aware that the host was waiting for data for the specified group.

The router listens on all interfaces waiting for a request from a host to forward multicast group traffic. Once a host on an interface makes a request to become a member of a group, the requested group is activated on that interface and only on that interface. While the host is a member, multicast data will be forwarded to that interface and any host subscribed to the group will receive the data. Multicast routers don't constrain traffic on the LAN, they simply determine whether or not a particular group must be sent on to the LAN. Multicast-aware switches are required to limit the Layer 2 ports out which a multicast is forwarded within the LAN.

That was a simple overview. Now we'll go into more detail on how this is accomplished. We will start by discussing the host subscription protocol: Internet Group Management Protocol (IGMP).

IGMPv1

As the name indicates, *Internet Group Management Protocol version 1 (IGMPv1)* was the first version of the protocol. This resulted from RFC 1112. The purpose of this protocol is to allow hosts to subscribe or join specified multicast groups. By subscribing to groups, the hosts notify the router that listeners for certain multicast groups exist on a given interface.

IGMP has several processes that it executes to manage multicast group subscription and maintenance. We will discuss them in greater detail so you can get an understanding of what happens.

IGMPv1 Processes

An important process is the query process, which is a kindred to a keepalive procedure. Because the router needs to keep tabs on which multicast groups need to remain active, it sends a Membership Query out each interface. The query is directed to the reserved address of 224.0.0.1, and all multicast hosts will respond to it.

Once the query is received, the hosts report (Membership Report) back with their group subscription information. Once a specific group has been reported to the router, subsequent reports from different hosts will be suppressed for that IP multicast group. This is done because only one host on a subnet/VLAN needs to request the membership for the router to activate it on that interface. Once the multicast group is active on the router interface, any host of the subnet/ VLAN wanting to receive data for that group may receive it. Figure 21.8 depicts how this process works.

FIGURE 21.8 IGMPv1 query routine

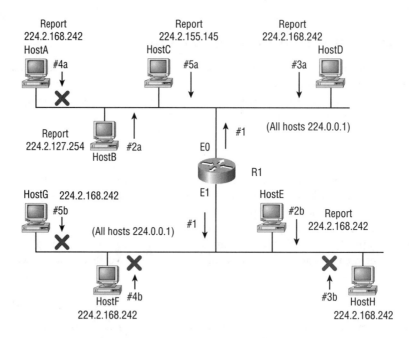

You can follow the numbers indicated in the figure. First, the query to 224.0.0.1 is sent. The hosts begin to report back within 10 seconds. The first host to respond is host B (#2a) requesting data for the multicast group 224.2.127.254. Host D (#3a) responds next with a request for the group 224.2.168.242. The next host to reply is host A (#4a), but because the report from host

D was already multicast to the 224.2.168.242 group, host A heard the report and suppressed it to the group.

The protocol is smart enough to understand that once one host has reported its membership to the group, no other hosts need to report. This avoids unwanted and unnecessary bandwidth and processor utilization.

Host C (#5a) responds with a different group number, 224.2.155.145. Once all of the hosts have responded to the query, R1 will maintain activity for these groups on interface E0.

Notice that this description applied to interface E0 on R1. A multicast flood to 224.0.0.1 was sent out interface E1 simultaneously. The first host to respond on this segment is host E (#2b) and it is reporting membership to 224.2.168.242. Notice that this report was not suppressed, even though host D had already multicast a report to this group. The router queries the local all hosts address 224.0.0.1, which is not forwarded by the router. That is why the same query is sent out all interfaces on the router. Now that host E has multicast to the group for this segment, none of the other hosts on this segment will report because they are all members of the 224.2.168.242 group.

The other processes that remain are joining and leaving multicast groups. Both of these processes are quite simple and straightforward. You understand how interfaces are maintained in an active state through Membership Queries. The Membership Query process only runs every 60 seconds. If a host desires to join a multicast group between Membership Queries, it may simply send an unsolicited report to the multicast router stating that it wants to receive data for the specified multicast group. Figure 21.9 depicts how this occurs.

FIGURE 21.9   Unsolicited join requests

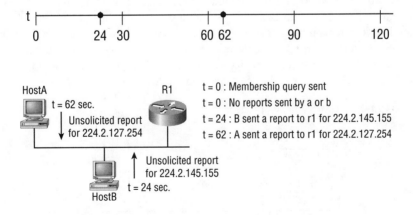

Withdrawal from a group is not initiated by the host as one would imagine. The router maintains a timer that is reset every time a response is received from a host on the subnet. The timer runs for 3 minutes, which is equivalent to three Membership Query cycles (every 60 seconds). If the timer expires and no response is received from a host for that group on the interface, the router disables multicast forwarding on that interface.

IGMPv2

As with any software revision, things are made better. *Internet Group Management Protocol version 2 (IGMPv2)* provides enhancements over version 1. For example, a leave process was included to avoid long time-outs that are experienced in version 1. This version is defined by RFC 2236.

As a whole, IGMPv2 provides the same functionality as version one did, with a few enhancements. In the following paragraphs, these enhancements will be discussed.

IGMPv2 Processes

One enhancement that was made to IGMPv2 processes is a new query type. The Membership Query message, as it was called in IGMPv1, was renamed General Query message, and the new type is Group-Specific Query. The new query type is used to query a specific multicast group (kind of obvious from the name). The overall procedure is the same as it is in IGMPv1.

When multiple IGMPv1 routers existed on the same segment, a multicast routing protocol made the decision as to which of all the multicast routers would perform the membership queries. Now, the decision is made using features added to IGMPv2.

The frame for the query was changed to enable a Maximum Response time that may allow the hosts on the segment less time to respond to the query. This reduces the leave latency.

Finally, IGMPv2 implemented the capability for hosts to remove themselves from the multicast group immediately (a matter of seconds) instead of having to wait up to 3 minutes. The two new additions of the Leave and Group-Specific messages work together to allow a host to remove itself from the multicast group immediately.

Figure 21.10 depicts how the process works. First (#1), host A sends a Leave message to the all multicast routers (224.0.0.2) to withdraw from the multicast group. Because R1 doesn't know how many hosts on the segment belong to group 224.2.155.145, it must send a Group-Specific Query (#2) to see if there are any hosts that remain members of the group. If no responses are received, the router disables multicast forwarding for that group out of the interface. If any hosts respond back to the query, the router leaves the interface status-quo. In the figure, you can see that host B responds (#3) as still participating in the group 224.2.155.145. Hence, the interface is left active for that group.

FIGURE 21.10   IGMPv2 Leave process

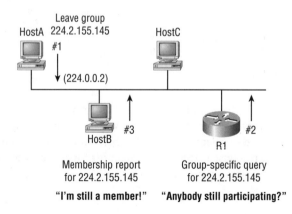

It is important to be aware of issues when both versions of IGMP are present on the network. Version 2 is backward compatible with version 1, but the functionality of version 2 is lost when operating with version 1 devices. A version 2 host has to use version 1 frame formats when talking with a version 1 router. The same is true when a version 2 router tries to communicate with a version 1 host; it must use the version 1 format.

A multicast querying router sends out host Membership Query messages in order to discover which multicast groups have active members left on it's locally attached networks. The hosts will respond with IGMP reports, which indicate that they want to remain a member of the multicast group. Host query messages are addressed to all hosts within multicast groups with the address 224.0.0.1 and a TTL of 1.

Configuring IGMP on a Router

To configure IGMP on a router, you must first have IP multicast enabled on the router with the global `ip multicast-routing` command. Then you must configure one of the following commands on the interface that is connected to the hosts that are participating in the multicast group: `ip pim sparse-mode` or `ip pim sparse-dense-mode`. Enabling Protocol Independent Multicast (PIM) on an interface enables IGMP operation on that interface. An interface can be configured to be in dense mode, sparse mode, or sparse-dense mode. (These various modes will be discussed later in this chapter.) Then you can optionally specify the `ip igmp version X` command; the *X* value represents either a 1 or 2 for IGMP version 1 or version 2. This will enable the configured version of IGMP on the interface. The default version of IGMP is set to version 2.

Configuration Command Syntax

Let's look at the command syntax to configure a router:

```
ip multicast-routing            Enable IP multicast routing


interface FastEthernet0/0

 ip address 147.19.1.1 255.255.255.0

 ip pim sparse-mode             Configures interface for sparse-mode
```

CGMP

We have discussed open standard protocols for host membership of multicast groups: IGMPv1 and IGMPv2. When multicast is run at layer 2, things get a little complicated for the switch. It doesn't know which packets are Membership Report messages or which are actual multicast group data packets because all of them have the same MAC address. *Cisco Group Management Protocol (CGMP)* was implemented to fill this void. It runs on both Cisco routers and switches (i.e., it is proprietary).

CGMP makes use of two MAC addresses: the Group Destination Address (GDA), and Unicast Source Address (USA). The GDA is the multicast group address mapped to the MAC multicast address. The USA is the unicast MAC address of the host. The two addresses allow the host to send multicast Membership Reports to the multicast router and still tell the switch which port needs to receive the multicast data using the USA.

In addition to being able to make port assignments on the switch, CGMP also handles the interface assignment on the router. If a switch doesn't have any ports that need to receive multicast data, CGMP will inform the router that it doesn't need to forward multicast group data out the router interface.

CGMP Processes

Hosts do not use CGMP; only the switches and routers can implement it. When a host sends an IGMP Report (Membership Report) advertising membership of a multicast group, the message is forwarded to the router for processing. The router sees the request and processes it accordingly. The multicast group is set up. The router then sends the switch a CGMP join message. With the CGMP join message, the switch can assign the multicast group to the port of the requesting host. You can see the entire process in Figure 21.11.

FIGURE 21.11 CGMP Join process

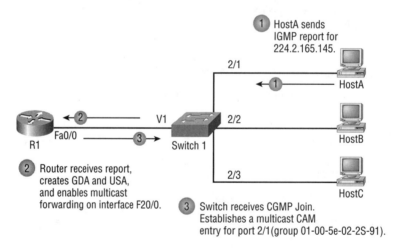

Host management is performed by the router. The router continues to solicit and receive IGMP messages from the host. Then the router responds with a CGMP message and sends it to the switch. The switch then performs the appropriate port maintenance.

This process is followed for the multiple types of message that the host can generate. The Leave process is done in the same manner. The router receives the request and then informs the switch that this USA has left *the* group and the port associated with this USA should be deleted form *the* group's port list.

Here is the CGMP configuration command syntax for a router:

```
interface FastEthernet0/0
```

```
ip cgmp                            Configures this interfaces for cgmp to
                                   communicate with a Catalyst switch
```

Here is the CGMP configuration command syntax for a switch:

```
set cgmp enable                    Enables cgmp on this Catalyst switch
```

```
set multicast router 2/8           Configures port 2/8 on this switch
                                   for communicating with a connected
                                   router
```

In these example commands, the Cisco router has the FastEthernet 0/0 interface connected to the 2/8 port of the Catalyst switch, and they are both configured to allow CGMP communication between them. Remember, Cisco routers send CGMP messages and Cisco switches receive CGMP messages. It is a unidirectional communication. Depending on context, all routers talk CGMP and IGMP. However, CGMP is essentially a "legacy" protocol and is mainly supported on the older low-end Cisco switches. For example, the Catalyst 3550 does not support CGMP. Non-IGMP Snooping switches will have CGMP, and usually IGMP snooping switches don't have CGMP.

 Real World Scenario

CGMP saves the day

A fellow Cisco Network Engineer, Mark Breedlove, has implemented IP Multicast as a very efficient means to distribute video, streams of e-learning content, and to distribute files to multiple hosts across the network. Keep in mind that multicast is flooded throughout a switch because the multicast address is not used as the source address. The switch looks at the source address in order to learn the MAC address. Since the multicast MAC will not be in the MAC address table, the switch can't learn it. By default, a LAN switch will flood the multicast packets throughout a broadcast domain, which could be quite large if you have VLANs spanning several switches.

Mark recently ran into a problem where sections of a school's network were losing connectivity during the day. Initially this appeared to be a Spanning Tree problem, based on the description. So, Mark went out to the site to troubleshoot the problem. For the previous two weeks, at about 2:00 P.M., particular sections of the network would have either severely degraded performance or loss of connectivity. Then, the network started having problems earlier in the morning between 8:00 and 9:00 A.M.

Sure enough, at about 8:30, the network started experiencing problems. A quick examination of the switches showed an enormous amount of traffic on the uplinks and out the connected ports of those switches. A closer examination showed it to be multicast traffic. Using a sniffer, Mark traced the source of the traffic to a test server. A quick poll of the technical staff revealed that they had started to demo/test a new PC inventory and imaging application. The tester had been coming into work in the afternoon, but recently started working the mornings. This application was using multicast to inventory the PCs in the network and then update or image them with changes.

Mark first evaluated putting static MAC address entries in the switch configurations, but decided it wouldn't scale for the environment. He then decided to implement CGMP to prune the multicast traffic back to only those devices needing the streams. Mark configured multicast routing on the router interfaces for those subnets and enabled CGMP on the switches. This allowed the switch to send the multicast traffic only to the clients that had requested it. Now when the tester fired up the same application, the network ran smoothly and the application performed even better. Thanks to Mark for that tip.

Routing Multicast Traffic

Up to this point, we have been discussing the host side of multicast. You have learned how hosts interact with switches and routers to join multicast groups and receive the traffic. It is now time to move on to how multicast traffic gets from a source on a remote network, across the Internet or intranet, to a local router and host.

The following sections describe the tree structures that can be implemented to allow multicast routing. In addition to trees, several different protocol methods can be used to achieve the desired implementation of multicast.

Distribution Trees

Two types of trees exist in multicast: source and shared. Source trees use the architecture of the source of the multicast traffic as the root of the tree. Shared trees use an architecture in which multiple sources share a common rendezvous point.

Each of these methods is effective and allows sourced multicast data to reach an arbitrary number of recipients of the multicast group. We'll discuss each of them in detail.

Source Tree

Source trees are formed using the *shortest path* between the source and each receiver. Source trees use special notation. This notation is used in what becomes a multicast route table. Unicast route tables use the destination address and next hop information to establish a topology for forwarding information. Here is a sample from a unicast routing table:

```
B    136.142.0.0/16 [20/0] via 208.124.237.10, 3d07h
B    202.213.23.0/24 [20/0] via 208.124.237.10, 1w2d
     202.246.53.0/24 is variably subnetted, 2 subnets, 2 masks
B       202.246.53.0/24 [20/0] via 208.124.237.10, 1w2d
B       202.246.53.60/32 [20/0] via 208.124.237.10, 1w2d
```

Multicast route tables (MRoutes) are somewhat different. Here is a sample of a multicast table. Notice that the notation is different. Instead of listing the destination address and then the next hop to get to the destination, a source tree uses the notation (S, G). This notation specifies the source host's IP address and the multicast group address. Take the first one, for example. This is seen as (198.32.163.74, 224.2.243.55), which means the source host is 198.32.163.74 and it is sourcing traffic for the multicast group 224.2.243.55. With multicast forwarding, the interface closest to the source is the RPF interface and then each interface is either in a forwarding or non-forwarding state, depending on where receivers are located in the network. Figure 21.12 gives you a good picture of how source trees work. Here is the sample multicast table:

```
(198.32.163.74, 224.2.243.55), 00:01:04/00:01:55, flags: PT
  Incoming interface: POS1/0/0, RPF nbr 208.124.237.10, Mbgp
  Outgoing interface list: Null
(198.32.163.74, 224.2.213.101), 00:02:06/00:00:53, flags: PT
  Incoming interface: POS1/0/0, RPF nbr 208.124.237.10, Mbgp
  Outgoing interface list: Null
(207.98.103.221, 224.2.127.254), 00:00:40/00:02:19, flags: CLM
  Incoming interface: POS1/0/0, RPF nbr 208.124.237.10, Mbgp
  Outgoing interface list:
    FastEthernet4/0/0, Forward/Sparse, 00:00:41/00:02:53
    FastEthernet4/1/0, Forward/Sparse, 00:00:41/00:02:19
(128.39.2.23, 224.2.127.254), 00:04:43/00:02:06, flags: CLMT
  Incoming interface: POS1/0/0, RPF nbr 208.124.237.10, Mbgp
  Outgoing interface list:
    FastEthernet4/0/0, Forward/Sparse, 00:04:43/00:02:43
    FastEthernet4/1/0, Forward/Sparse, 00:04:43/00:03:07
```

FIGURE 21.12   Source tree forwarding

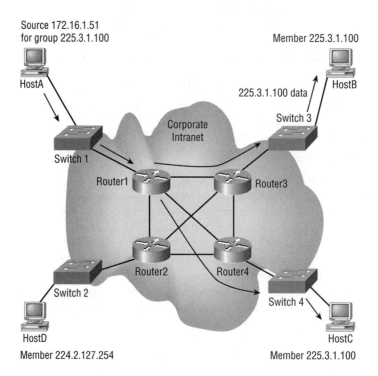

Shared Tree

There are two types of shared tree distribution: unidirectional and bidirectional. They both work a little differently than source tree distribution. Shared tree architecture lies in the characteristic that there may be multiple sources for one multicast group. Instead of each individual source creating its own shortest path tree (SPT) and distributing the data apart from the other sources, a shared root is designated. Multiple sources for a multicast group forward their data to a shared root, or *rendezvous point (RP)*. The rendezvous point then forwards the data to the members of the group on the shared tree. A shared tree is represented as (*,G). Figure 21.13 depicts how the shared tree distribution works.

FIGURE 21.13   Shared tree forwarding

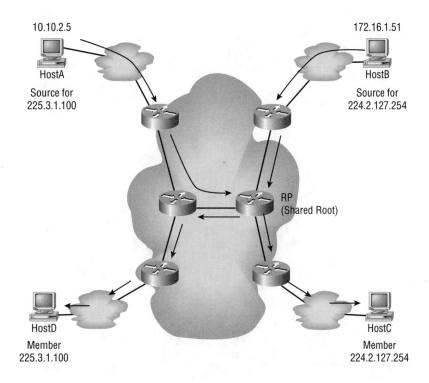

Unidirectional shared tree distribution operates as shown in Figure 21.13. All recipients of a multicast group receive the data from a rendezvous point (RP) no matter their place in the network.

Bidirectional shared tree distribution operates somewhat differently. If a receiver lives upstream of the RP, it can receive data directly from the upstream source. Figure 21.14 depicts how this works. As you can see, Host A is a source for group 224.2.127.254 and Host B is a receiver of that same group. In a bidirectional shared tree, data goes directly from Host A to Host B without having to come from the RP.

FIGURE 21.14   Shortest path tree (SPT)/rendezvous point tree (RPT) shared tree

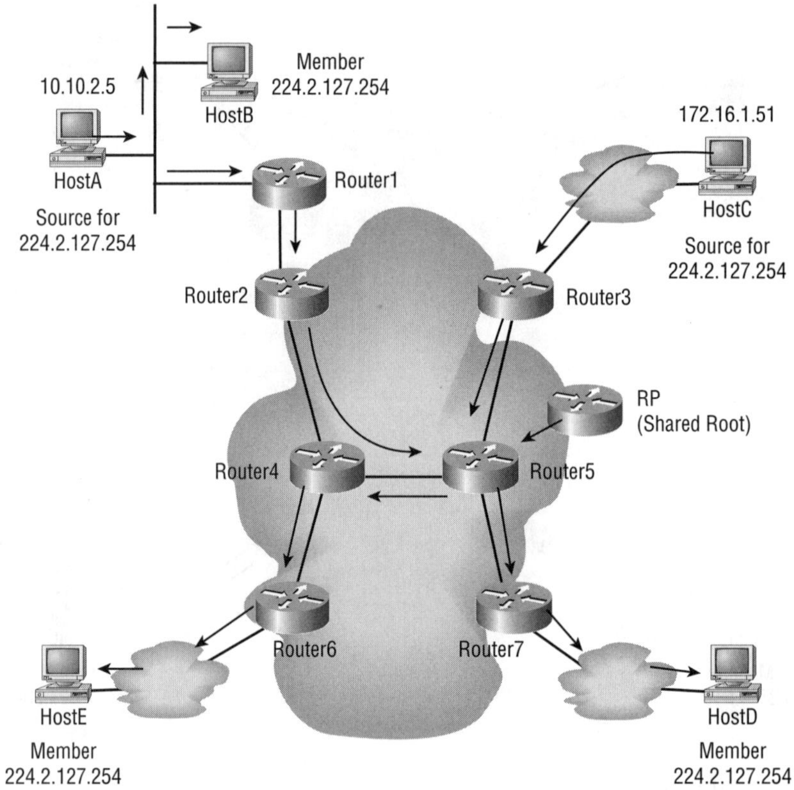

Managing Multicast Delivery

Even though the tree distributions explain how source information is managed, we must now discuss how the actual data delivery is managed. There are several methods of making sure that delivery is as efficient as possible. The ones that will be discussed here are Reverse Path Forwarding (RPF), time-to-live (TTL) attributes, and routing protocols.

RPF works in tandem with the routing protocols, but it will be described briefly here. As you have seen in the figures, specifically Figures 21.13 and 21.14, the traffic goes only to the multicast group receivers. We also mentioned that bidirectional distribution eliminates the need to build a separate tree to forward data upstream. You may ask, "How do you define *upstream*?" It is easy to clarify. By means of the routing protocols, routers are aware of which interface leads to the source(s) of the multicast group. That interface is considered upstream.

Reverse Path Forwarding is based on the upstream information. When it receives an incoming multicast packet, the router verifies that the packet came in on an interface that leads back to the root of the tree. The packet is forwarded by the router if the RPF check passes; otherwise, the packet is discarded. This check eliminates loops. To avoid increased overhead on the router's processor, a multicast forwarding cache is implemented for the RPF lookups.

Time to Live (TTL)

Another method of controlling the delivery of IP multicast packets is the use of *scopes*, which are comprised of the time-to-live (TTL) counter and TTL thresholds. The TTL counter is decremented by one every time the packet hops a router. Once the TTL counter is decremented to zero, the packet is punted to the CPU and may be discarded.

Thresholds are used for higher granularity and greater control within one's own network. They are applied to specified interfaces of multicast-enabled routers. The router compares the threshold value of the multicast packet with the value specified in the interface configuration. If the TTL value of the packet is greater than or equal to the TTL threshold configured for the interface, the packet will be forwarded through that interface.

TTL thresholds allow network administrators to bound their network and limit the distribution of multicast packets beyond their boundaries. This is accomplished by setting high values for outbound external interfaces. The maximum value for the TTL threshold is 255. Refer to Figure 21.15 to see how network boundaries can be set to limit distribution of multicast traffic.

FIGURE 21.15   TTL threshold utilization

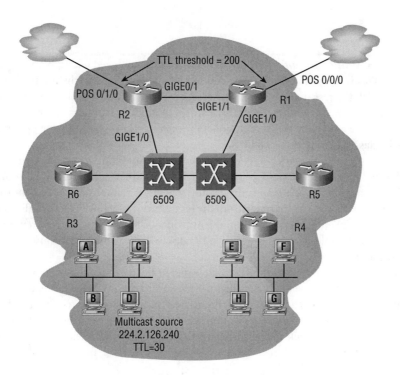

The multicast source initially sets the TTL value for the multicast packet and then forwards it on throughout the network. In this scenario, the TTL threshold values have been set to 200 on both of the exiting Packet over SONET (POS) interfaces. The initial TTL value has been set to 30 by the application. There are three to four router hops to get out of the campus network. R3 will decrement by one, leaving a TTL value of 29, the Catalyst 6509's multilayer switch feature card (MSFC) will decrement by one as well, leaving the value set to 28. Once the packet gets to R2 or R1, the value will be 27 or 26 respectively. Both of these values are less than the TTL threshold of 200, which means the routers R1 and R2 will drop any outbound multicast packets.

Routing Protocols

We now need to turn our attention to the variety of multicast routing protocols. Unicast has several routing protocols that build route tables that enable layer 3 devices such as routers and some switches to forward unicast data to the next hop toward its final destination. We have also discussed some of the methods that multicast, in general, uses to distribute multicast data. Similar to unicast, multicast has a variety of routing protocols, including distance vector and link-state protocols.

Protocols are used to enhance the efficiency by which multicast application data is distributed and to optimize the use of existing network resources. This section will cover Distance Vector Multicast Routing Protocol (DVMRP), Multicast Open Shortest Path First (MOSPF), and Protocol Independent Multicast (PIM), although PIM is a state machine rather than a routing protocol.

DVMRP

Distance Vector Multicast Routing Protocol (DVMRP) has achieved widespread use in the multicast world. This is the primary multicast routing protocol utilized in the multicast backbone (MBONE), which the research community uses. As the name indicates, this protocol uses a distance vector algorithm. It uses several of the features that other distance vector protocols, such as RIP, implement: a 32 max hop count, poison reverse, and 60-second route updates. It also allows for IP classless masking of addresses.

Just like some routing protocols, DVMRP-enabled routers must establish adjacencies in order to share route information. Once the adjacency is established, the DVMRP route table is created. Route information is exchanged via route reports. It is important to remember that the DVMRP route table is stored separately from the unicast routing table. The DVMRP route table is more like a unicast route table than the multicast route table that was shown previously in this chapter. A DVMRP table contains the layer 3 IP network of the multicast source and the next hop toward the source.

Because the DVMRP table has this form, it works perfectly in conjunction with source tree distribution as discussed earlier. Using the information in the DVMRP table, the tree for the source can be established. In addition, the router uses this information to perform the Reverse Path Forwarding check to verify that the multicast data coming into the interface is coming in an interface that leads back to the source of the data. DVMRP uses SPT for its multicast forwarding.

Figure 21.16 shows how DVMRP works. You can see that not every router in the network is a DVMRP router. You should also notice that the adjacencies are established over tunnel interfaces. DVMRP information is tunneled through an IP network. On either end of the tunnel, information is learned and exchanged to build a multicast forwarding database or route table.

FIGURE 21.16   DVMRP

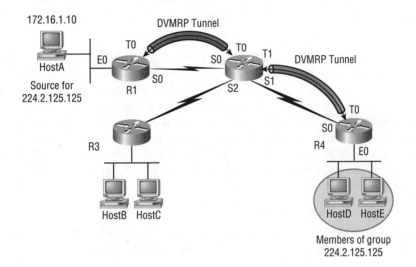

MOSPF

Now we will concentrate on *Multicast Open Shortest Path First (MOSPF)*, which is a link-state protocol. Some changes were made to OSPFv2 to allow multicast to be enabled on OSPF-enabled routers. This eliminates the need for tunnels like those used for DVMRP.

To completely understand the full functionality of MOSPF, you must have a good understanding of OSPF itself. However, here we will attempt to cover only the basic functionality of MOSPF, so you should be fine with just a basic understanding of OSPF.

MOSPF's basic functionality lies within a single OSPF area. Things get more complicated as you route multicast traffic to other areas (interarea routing) or to other autonomous systems (inter-AS routing). This additional complication requires more knowledge of OSPF routing. We will briefly discuss how this is accomplished in MOSPF, but most detail will be given regarding MOSPF intra-area routing.

Intra-Area MOSPF

OSPF route information is shared via different link-state advertisement (LSA) types. LSAs are flooded throughout an area to give all OSPF-enable routers a logical image of the network topology. When changes are made to the topology, new LSAs are flooded to propagate the change. In addition to the unicast routing LSA types, in OSPFv2 there is a special multicast LSA

(Type 6) for flooding multicast group information throughout the area. This additional LSA type required some modification to the OSPF frame format.

Here is where you need to understand a little about OSPF. Multicast LSA flooding is done by the designated router (DR) when there are multiple routers connected to a multiaccess media, such as Ethernet. On point-to-point connections, there is no DR and backup designated router (BDR). Look at the following code from a Cisco router running OSPF over point-to-point circuits:

```
Neighbor ID  Pri  State       Dead Time  Address      Interface
172.16.1.2    1   FULL/  -    00:00:31   172.16.1.2   Serial3/0
192.168.1.2   1   FULL/  -    00:00:39   192.168.1.2  Serial3/1
```

On a multiaccess network, the DR must be multicast enabled, that is, running MOSPF. If there are any non-MOSPF routers on the same network, their OSPF priority must be lowered so they do not become DRs. If a non-MOSPF router were to become the DR, it would not be able to forward the multicast LSA to the other routers on the segment.

Inside the OSPF area, updates are sent describing which links have active multicast members on them so that the multicast data can be forwarded to those interfaces. MOSPF also uses (S, G) notation and calculates the SPT using the Dijkstra, or shortest path first (SPF), algorithm that is used for calculation of unicast routes. You must also understand that an SPT is created for each source in the network.

Interarea and Inter-AS MOSPF

When discussing the difference between intra-area and Inter-AS MOSPF, you must remember that all areas connect through Area 0, the backbone. In large networks, having full multicast tables in addition to all the unicast tables flow across Area 0 would cause a great deal of overhead and possibly latency.

Unicast OSPF uses a summary LSA to inform the routers in Area 0 about the networks and topology in an adjacent area. This task is performed by the area's area border router (ABR). The ABR summarizes all the information about the area and then passes it on to the backbone (Area 0) routers in a summary LSA. The same is done for the multicast topology. The ABR summarizes information about which multicast groups are active and which groups have sources within the area. This information is then sent to the backbone routers.

In addition to summarizing multicast group information, the ABR is responsible for the actual forwarding of multicast group traffic into and out of the area. Each area has an ABR that performs these two functions within an OSPF network.

OSPF implements autonomous system boundary routers (ASBRs) to be the bridge between different autonomous systems. These routers perform much the same as an ABR but must be able to communicate with non-OSPF speaking devices. Multicast group information and data is forwarded and received by the multicast autonomous system border router (MASBR). Because MOSPF runs natively within OSPF, there must be a method or protocol by which the multicast information can be taken from MOSPF and communicated to the external AS. Historically, DVRMP has provided this bridge.

PIM Dense Mode

We briefly mentioned *Protocol Independent Multicast (PIM)* previously. Now we will dedicate some time to learning how it is used in conjunction with the other multicast routing protocols. PIM DM (Dense Mode) maintains several functions. The ones that will be discussed here are flooding, pruning, and grafting.

PIM is considered "protocol independent" because it actually uses the unicast route table to determine where the source is in the network. And then, which interfaces a multicast group is forwarded out of is determined by PIM messages exchanged between PIM routers. *Protocol Independent Multicast Dense Mode (PIM DM)* understands classless subnet masking and uses it when the router is running an IP classless unicast protocol.

PIM DM routers establish neighbor relationships with other routers running PIM DM. It uses these neighbors to establish an SPT and forward multicast data throughout the network. The SPT created by PIM DM is based on source tree distribution.

Flooding

When a multicast source begins to transmit data, PIM runs the RPF using the unicast route table to verify that the interface leads toward the source. It then forwards the data to all PIM neighbors. Those PIM neighbors then forward the data to their PIM neighbors. This happens throughout the network whether there are group members on the router or not. This is why it is considered flooding.

When multiple, equal-cost links exist, the router with the highest IP address is elected to be the incoming interface (used for RPF). Every router runs the RPF when it receives the multicast data.

Figure 21.17 depicts the initial multicast flooding in a PIM DM network. You can see that the data is forwarded to every PIM neighbor throughout the network. Once a PIM neighbor does the RPF, it will forward the data to interfaces that have active members of the group.

FIGURE 21.17   PIM DM flooding

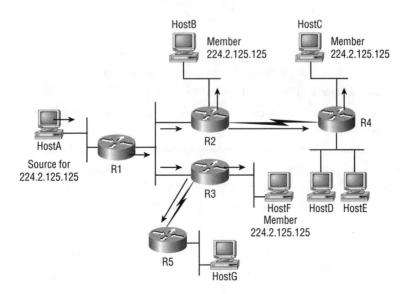

Pruning

After the initial flooding through the PIM neighbors, pruning starts. *Pruning* is the act of trimming down the SPT. Because the data has been forwarded to every router, regardless of group membership the routers must now prune back the distribution of the multicast data to routers that actually have active group members connected.

Figure 21.18 shows the pruning action that occurs for the PIM DM routers that don't have active group members. R5 does not have any active group members, so it sends a prune message to R3. Even though R4 has a network that does not have members, it does have an interface that does, so it will not send a prune message.

FIGURE 21.18 PIM DM pruning

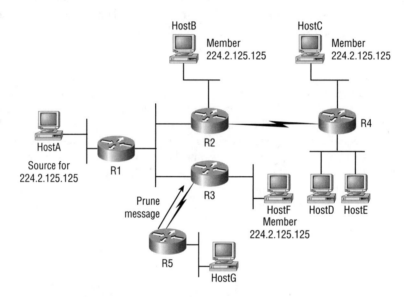

There are four criteria that merit a prune message being sent by a router:

- The incoming interface fails the RPF check.
- If a router has no directly connected active group members and no PIM neighbors, then it is considered a leaf router.
- Point-to-point non-leaf router receives a prune request from a neighbor.
- LAN non-leaf router receives a prune request from another router and no other router on the segment overrides the prune request.

If any of these criteria are met, a prune request is sent to the PIM neighbor and the SPT is pruned back.

Grafting

PIM DM is also ready to forward multicast data once a previously inactive interface becomes active. This is done through the process of *grafting*. When a host sends an IGMP group membership report to the router, the router then sends a Graft message to the nearest upstream PIM neighbor. If the upstream neighbor is not part of the desired multicast stream, it will forward a Graft message to its upstream neighbor and so on until a router receiving the multicast flow can forward it downstream to the original host reporting membership. Figure 21.19 depicts the grafting process.

FIGURE 21.19   PIM DM grafting

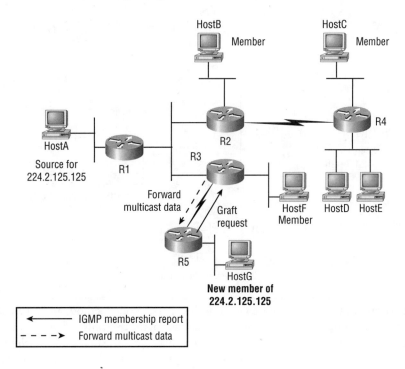

Sparse Mode Routing Protocols

Sparse mode protocols use shared tree distribution as their forwarding methods. This is done to create a more efficient method of multicast distribution. There are two sparse mode protocols that will be discussed in this section, Core-Based Trees (CBTs) and Protocol Independent Multicast Sparse Mode (PIM SM).

Core-Based Trees

When we discussed shared trees, you learned that there were two types, unidirectional and bidirectional. CBT utilizes the bidirectional method for its multicast data distribution. Because CBT uses a shared tree system, it designates a core router that is used as the root of the tree, allowing data to flow up or down the tree.

Data forwarding in a CBT multicast system is similar to the shared tree distribution covered earlier. If a source to a multicast group sends multicast data to the CBT-enabled router, the router then forwards the data out all interfaces that are included in the tree, not just the interface that leads to the core router. In this manner, data flows up and down the tree. Once the data gets to the core router, the core router forwards the information to the other routers that are in the tree. Figure 21.20 depicts this process.

FIGURE 21.20 CBT data distribution

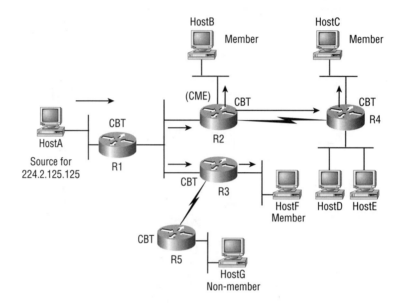

It is important to see the difference between this sparse mode method, and the dense mode method. In sparse mode operation, routers are members of the tree only if they have active members directly connected. Dense mode operates on the initial premise that all PIM neighbors have active members directly connected. The tree changes when the directly connected routers request to be pruned from the tree.

A CBT router may become part of the tree once a host sends an IGMP Membership Record to the directly connected router. The router then sends a Join Tree request to *core* router. If the request reaches a CBT tree member first, that router will add the *leaf* router to the tree and begin forwarding multicast data.

the tree is pruned in much the same way. Once there are no more active members on a router's interfaces, the router will send a Prune request to the upstream router. The answering router will remove the interface from the forwarding cache if it is a point-to-point circuit, or it will wait for a timer to expire if it is on a shared access network. The timer gives enough time for other CBT routers on the segment to override the prune request.

PIM Sparse Mode

Protocol Independent Multicast Sparse Mode (PIM SM) uses the architecture of SPT and shared tree distribution. There is a rendezvous point (RP) router that acts as the root of the shared tree.

Unlike CBT, PIM SM uses the unidirectional shared tree distribution mechanism. Because PIM SM uses the unidirectional method, all multicast source routers for any group must register with the RP of the shared tree. This enables the RP and other routers to establish the RP tree, or RPT (synonymous with SPT in source tree distribution).

Just as with CBT, PIM SM routers join the shared tree when they are notified via IGMP that a host requests membership of a multicast group. If the existing group entry (*, G) does not already exist in the router's table, it is created and the Shared Tree Join request is sent to the next hop toward the RP. The next router receives the request. Based on whether or not it has an exiting entry for (*, G), two things can happen:

- If an entry for (*, G) exists, the router simply adds the interface to the shared tree and no further Join requests are sent toward the RP.

- If an entry for (*, G) does not exist, the router creates an entry for the (*, G) group and adds the link to the forwarding cache. In addition to doing this, the router sends its own Join request toward the RP.

This happens until the Join request reaches a router that already has the (*, G) entry or a Join request reaches the RP.

The next facet of PIM SM is the shared tree pruning. With PIM SM, pruning turns out to be just the opposite of the explicit Join mechanism used to construct the shared tree.

When a member leaves a group, it does so via IGMP. When it happens to be the last member on a segment, the router removes the interface from the forwarding cache entry and then sends a Prune request toward the RP of the shared tree. If there is another router with active members connected to the router requesting the prune, it is removed from the outgoing interface list and no additional Prune messages are sent to the RP. See Figure 21.21 for a visual description.

FIGURE 21.21   PIM SM pruning

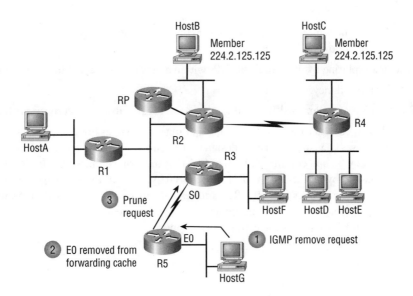

R5 receives an IGMP message requesting the removal of host G from the group. Because host G was the last active member of the group, the (*, G) entry is set to null 0 and a Prune request is sent by R5 to R3. When R3 receives the request, it removes the link for interface S0 from the forwarding table. Because host F is a directly connected active member of the group, the entry for (*, G) is not null 0, so no Prune request is sent to R2 (the RP for this example).

If host F were not active, the entry for (*, G) would have been set to null 0 also and a Prune request would have been sent to the RP.

Because PIM SM uses shared trees (at least initially), it requires the use of a rendezvous point (RP). The RP may be manually configured in the network. This is accomplished with the `ip pim rp-address` global command. Sources register with the RP, an SPT is built, and then data is forwarded down the shared tree to the receivers. If the shared tree is not an optimal path between the source and the receiver, the routers may dynamically create a source tree and stop traffic from flowing down the shared tree. By default, this happens immediately on Cisco routers configured for PIM sparse or sparse-dense mode operation. Sparse mode scales well to a network of any size, including those with WAN links.

PIM Sparse-Dense Mode

Cisco has developed an third mode of PIM operation, PIM sparse-dense mode. Basically, the sparse-dense mode allows for sparse mode or dense mode to be chosen on a per-group basis instead of a per-router basis, which is the only method for the first two modes. You can configure sparse-dense mode on a router interface. This configuration option will allow an individual group to be run in either sparse mode or dense mode depending on whether RP information is available for that group. If the router learns RP information for a particular group, it is treated as a sparse mode group. Otherwise, the group is treated as dense mode. To configure PIM sparse-dense mode on a router interface, use the `ip pim sparse-dense-mode` command.

Auto-RP

Auto-RP is a feature that automates the distribution of group-to-RP mappings in a PIM network. This feature has the following benefits:

- It allows load splitting by using multiple RPs within a network to serve different group ranges.
- It provides redundancy.
- It avoids inconsistent manual RP configurations that can cause connectivity problems.

Multiple RPs can be used to serve different group ranges or serve as hot backups of each other. To make Auto-RP work, a router must be designated as an RP-mapping agent with the `ip pim send-rp-discovery scope` command. Remember, that the *scope* defines how far RP advertisements are propagated, by modifying the TTL appropriately. The RP-mapping agent will receive the RP-announcement messages from the RPs and resolve any conflicts. The RP-mapping agent then sends the consistent group-to-RP mappings to all other routers. Thus, all routers automatically discover which RP to use for the groups they support.

If you configure PIM in sparse mode or sparse-dense mode and do not configure Auto-RP, you must statically configure an RP using the `ip pim rp-address` global command. Remember that RPs discovered dynamically through Auto-RP take precedence over statically configured RPs.

Auto-RP utilizes the sparse-dense mode. This allows the Auto-RP groups to operate in DM. If an RP is known in the group-to-RP cache, then the group mode is in sparse mode. Otherwise, it defaults to dense mode. RP information is conveyed to the routers by the auto RP mechanism that uses two well-known multicast groups, 224.0.1.39 (RP discovery) and 224.0.1.40 (RP announce). The advantage of this is that any change to the RP designation will need to be configured only on the routers that are RPs and not on the leaf routers as in the static configuration.

ANNOUNCING THE RP

When implementing Auto-RP, it is necessary to designate router(s) as the CandidateRPs. This can be accomplished with the `ip pim send-rp-announce` global command. The syntax for this command is as follows:

```
ip pim send-rp-announce [interface advertised as RP] scope [TTL]
    group-list [access-list-number specifying the multicast group]
```

The following example advertises the IP address Loopback0 as the RP to all routers within a time to live or hop count of 10 hops for the multicast group address of 239.12.0.1:

```
ip pim send-rp-announce loopback0 scope 10 group-list 1
access-list 1 permit 239.12.0.1
```

ASSIGNING THE RP MAPPING AGENT

The RP mapping agent is the router that sends the authoritative Discovery packets telling other routers which group-to-RP mapping to use. Such a role is necessary in the event of conflicts (such as overlapping group-to-RP ranges).

Find a router whose connectivity is not likely to be interrupted and assign it the role of RP-mapping agent. All routers within the time to live (TTL) or number of hops from the source router receive the Auto-RP Discovery messages. To assign the role of RP mapping agent in that router, use the following command in global configuration mode:

```
ip pim send-rp-discovery scope [TTL]
```

PIMv2 Bootstrap Router

Instead of Auto-RP, a PIMv2 Bootstrap Router (BSR), which is defined in RFC 2362, can be implemented to automatically select an RP for a multicast network. You must configure BSR candidates (C-BSRs) with priorities ranging from 0 to 255 and a BSR address. C-BSRs exchange bootstrap messages, which are sent to multicast address 224.0.0.13 (all PIM routers). If a C-BSR receives a bootstrap message, it compares the received message's bootstrap priority with its own. The highest priority C-BSR is selected as the BSR. In the event of a tie, the highest IP address is selected. To assign the role of C-BSR in that router, use the following command in global configuration mode:

```
ip pim [bsr-candidate] [interface] [hash-mask-len] [pref]
```

After the BSR is selected for the network, it will collect a list of all candidate RPs. The BSR will collect all C-RP sets and send them to all routers using group address 224.0.0.13; then each router creates the group-to-RP cache.

NBMA Mode Solution

What if you are required to implement IP multicast within a Frame Relay environment? You will need to configure nonbroadcast multiaccess (NBMA) mode. This PIM feature allows you to configure a router to send packets only to those neighbors that want to receive them. A router in PIM NBMA mode treats each remote PIM neighbor as if it were connected to the router through a point-to-point link. In a Frame Relay network that uses IP multicast, NBMA mode improves router performance for the following reasons:

- Traffic is fast-switched rather than process-switched.
- PIM neighbors are tracked via switched virtual circuits (SVCs) or Data Link Connection Identifiers (DLCIs).
- Routers receive traffic only for the multicast groups to which they are joined.

To configure the PIM NBMA mode on an interface, use the `ip pim nbma-mode` command. This command allows the router to track the IP address of each neighbor when a PIM Join message is received from that neighbor. The router can also track the interface of the neighbor in the outgoing interface list for the multicast groups that the neighbor joins. This information allows the router to forward data destined for a particular multicast group to only those neighbors that have joined that particular group. Remember that this command is only used with sparse mode because it is dependant upon receiving a join message and only sparse mode uses join messages.

If your network can support both the point-to-point subinterfaces and NBMA mode solutions, we recommend point-to-point subinterfaces because of their simplicity and ease of use with Auto-RP. If you are utilizing the `ip pim sparse-dense-mode`, then the `ip pim nbma-mode` command is *not* recommended.

IP Multicast Troubleshooting

It is possible to have a router join a multicast group. This is accomplished with the `ip igmp join-group` interface command. If all the multicast-capable routers and access servers that you have configured are members of a multicast group, pinging that group causes all routers to respond. So, the interface that you configured the `ip igmp join-group` command on will respond to the ping. This can be a useful administrative and debugging tool. Another time to have a router join a multicast group is when other hosts on the network have a bug in IGMP that prevents them from correctly answering IGMP queries. Having the router join the multicast group causes upstream routers to maintain multicast routing table information for that group and keep the paths for that group active. The syntax for this command is as follows:

```
ip igmp join-group [multicast group address]
```

The following are other commands that can be helpful in troubleshooting IP multicast issues:

`show ip mroute`	Displays the contents of the IP multicast routing table
`show ip igmp groups`	Displays the multicast groups that are directly connected to the router and were learned by IGMP
`show ip igmp interface`	Displays multicast-related information about an interface
`show ip pim rp mapping`	Displays active RPs that are cached with associated multicast routing entries. Information learned by configuration or Auto-RP
`sh ip pim interface`	
`sh ip pim neighbor`	
`debug ip igmp [group]`	Displays Internet Group Management Protocol (IGMP) packets received and transmitted, as well as IGMP-host related events
`debug ip pim [group]`	Displays Protocol Independent Multicast (PIM) packets received and transmitted as well as PIM related events
`debug ip mrouting [group]`	Displays changes to the IP multicast routing table

IP Multicast Configuration Examples

Let's look at an example of configuring PIM Dense Mode:

`ip multicast-routing`	Enables IP Multicast Routing on this router
`interface Ethernet0/0`	
`  ip pim dense-mode`	Configures this interface for dense-mode
`  ip igmp join-group 239.12.0.1`	Allows this interface to join the multicast group 239.12.0.1

Let's look at an example of configuring PIM Sparse Mode (with 147.19.1.1 as a Rendezvous Point):

`ip multicast-routing`	Enables IP Multicast Routing on this router
`ip pim rp-address 147.19.1.1`	Statically points this router to 147.19.1.1 as the Rendezvous Point
`interface Serial0/0`	
`  frame-relay map ip x.x.x.x dlci xxx`	
`  ip pim sparse-mode`	Configures this interface for sparse-mode
`  ip pim nbma-mode`	Configures the routers to treat each DLCI participating in IP Multicast as a point-to-point connection, even through this is a multipoint interface
`interface Ethernet0/0`	
`  ip pim sparse-mode`	Configures this interface for sparse-mode

Let's look at an example of configuring PIM Sparse-Dense Mode (with Auto-RP):

`ip multicast-routing`	Enables IP Multicast Routing on this router
`interface loopback0`	
`  ip pim sparse-dense-mode`	Configures this interface for sparse-dense-mode
`  ip igmp join-group 239.12.0.1`	Allows this interface to join the multicast group 239.12.0.1
`interface Serial0/0`	
`  encapsulation frame-relay`	
`interface Serial0/0.1 multipoint`	
`  frame-relay map ip x.x.x.x dlci xxx`	
`  ip pim sparse-dense-mode`	Configures this interface for sparse-dense-mode
`interface Serial0/0.2 point-to-point`	
`  frame-relay interface-dlci xxx`	
`  ip pim sparse-dense-mode`	Configures this interface for sparse-dense-mode

```
ip pim send-rp-announce Loopback0 scope 12 group-list 10
```

>   Makes this router the Rendezvous
>   Point, using the IP of Loopback0 as
>   the RP. The multicast group is
>   239.12.0.1, and reaches a maximum of
>   12 hops

```
ip pim send-rp-discovery Loopback0 scope 12
```

>   Assigns this router the role of RP
>   mapping agent

```
access-list 10 permit 239.12.0.1
```
>   The IP address of the multicast group
>   is 239.12.0.1

Summary

In this chapter we described some of the many different facets of IP multicast. We started out with an overview and comparison of multicast with unicast and broadcast communications. We then showed you which IP addresses are multicast addresses and how to convert them to layer 2 MAC address.

The implementation of multicast can have significant impact on a network. This merited the topics regarding managing multicast distribution. We covered the basics of multicast and how hosts and sources participate before moving on to the different types of routing protocols that were made for multicast routing. We also discussed PIM DM, PIM SM, CBT, MOSPF, and DVMRP. These are independent protocols that use tree distribution to manage multicast data delivery in a network.

If you would like to try to implement an IP multicast scenario, we have developed a hands-on IP multicast lab exercise that can be found in Chapter 21 Supplement on the CD-ROM that came with this book.

Exam Essentials

Know which IP addresses are used for multicast.   Just like mailing lists, there are several different multicast groups that users or applications can subscribe to. The range of multicast addresses starts with 224.0.0.0 and goes through 239.255.255.255. As you can see, this is the IP Class D address assignment based on classful IP assignment. This is denoted by the fact that the first 4 bits in the first octet are 1110. Just as with regular IP addresses, there are some addresses that can be assigned and there are ranges of reserved addresses.

Know the purpose of IGMP and CGMP.   IGMP allows hosts to subscribe or join specified multicast groups. By subscribing to groups, the hosts are thereby enabled to receive multicast data forwarded from the router. CGMP runs on Cisco routers and switches and allows switches to prune ports that do not have multicast members.

Know how PIM DM and PIM SM work.   PIM DM transmits multicast packets out all of the router's interfaces, and PIM SM utilizes a rendezvous point (RP) to determine how to distribute the multicast streams.

Key Terms

Before you take the exam, be sure you're familiar with the following terms:

Cisco Group Management Protocol (CGMP)

Distance Vector Multicast Routing Protocol (DVMRP)

Internet Group Management Protocol version 1 (IGMPv1)

Internet Group Management Protocol version 2 (IGMPv2)

grafting

Multicast Open Shortest Path First (MOSPF)

Protocol Independent Multicast (PIM)

Protocol Independent Multicast Dense Mode (PIM DM)

Protocol Independent Multicast Sparse Mode (PIM SM)

rendezvous point (RP)

Review Questions

1. Which of the following is the valid range of IP multicast addresses? (Choose all that apply)
    A. 223.0.0.0–239.255.255.255
    B. 224.0.0.0–225.255.255.255
    C. 224.0.0.0–239.0.0.0
    D. 224.0.0.0–239.255.255.255

2. What is the main difference between broadcast and multicast communications?
    A. Multicast data is distributed to subscribed hosts on specific groups.
    B. Broadcast data is distributed to subscribed hosts on specific groups.
    C. Multicast data uses unicast route tables to flood the network instead of the network's broadcast address.
    D. There really is no difference.

3. What is the purpose of the reserved IP multicast address 224.0.0.2?
    A. All DVMRP routers
    B. All multicast routers
    C. All hosts
    D. All CGMP-enabled routers

4. How many bits of the layer 3 IP address are used to map to the layer 2 MAC address?
    A. 24
    B. 22
    C. 25
    D. 23

5. What is the layer 2 MAC address for the layer 3 IP address 224.2.127.254?
    A. 01-00-5E-02-7E-FF
    B. 01-00-5E-02-7F-FE
    C. 01-00-5E-00-7E-FF
    D. 01-00-5E-00-7F-FE

6. What is the layer 2 MAC address for the layer 3 IP address 224.215.145.230?
    A. 01-00-5E-57-91-E6
    B. 01-00-5E-D7-91-E6
    C. 01-00-5E-5B-91-E6
    D. 01-00-5E-55-91-E6

7. Why do some Cisco Catalyst switches use CGMP instead of just using IGMP snooping?

   A. Cisco's proprietary code is easier to compile into IOS.

   B. Cisco catalysts don't understand IGMP packets.

   C. Routers need switches to translate IGMP requests into CGMP requests in order to process them.

   D. Hardware is required to implement IGMP Snooping and some older Catalysts switches do not have them.

8. What two values does CGMP use from the IGMP report packet?

   A. CGMP utilizes the USA and GDA.

   B. CGMP utilizes the MAC address and IP address.

   C. CGMP utilizes the GSA and UDA.

   D. CGMP uses the MAC address and switch port.

9. What are two types of shared root tree distributions?

   A. Unidirectional

   B. Unicast

   C. Multidirectional

   D. Bidirectional

10. Which of the following are attributes of PIM sparse mode or PIM dense mode? (Choose all that apply.)

   A. PIM DM assumes that all PIM neighbors have active members directly connected and initially forwards multicast data out every interface.

   B. PIM SM requires an explicit join from a router before the router is added to the shared tree.

   C. PIM DM is based on a source root tree distribution mechanism.

   D. PIM SM is based only on bidirectional shared root tree distribution.

Answers to Review Questions

1. D. The valid range of IP addresses for multicast start at 224.0.0.0. Anything lower than that is not within the specified range. The range continues until 239.255.255.255. The range 224.0.0.0–239.255.255.255 specifies the entire Class D network. That makes D the correct answer.

2. A. Broadcast communications use the broadcast IP or MAC address to communicate information to all hosts. Multicast data is sent only to hosts that subscribe to groups active on the network.

3. B. IANA reserved the address to indicate all local multicast routers. Again, this address is not forwarded by any routers in the network.

4. D. Because only one half of one OUI was allocated for individual multicast MAC addresses, only 23 bits transfer from the layer 3 IP address.

5. B. The MAC prefix is 01-00-5E. You know you don't have to worry about the lost bits because the second octet of the IP address is less than 128. Therefore, the value is 02. The last two octets are mapped with no problem.

6. A. Again, the MAC prefix is 01-00-5E. Now that the second octet is greater than 127, you need to remember that it is possible that the value in the high order bit will be discarded. In this case it was, which leaves a binary value of 1010111 that needs to be converted to hex. In turn that leaves 57 as the value for the fourth octet of the MAC address.

7. D. Newer Catalyst switches have ASICs to implement IGMP snooping. The router must run CGMP in order to translate the IGMP requests received from the hosts into something the switch can process.

8. A. The USA is the Unicast Source Address (the unique MAC address of the machine) and the GDA is the Group Destination Address (the newly mapped layer 2 multicast MAC address). By using these two values, the switch knows which port on the switch to make a CAM entry for.

9. A, D. We are discussing multicast here, so obviously, unicast is not a valid answer. Because there are only two directions on a tree, the correct answers are bidirectional and unidirectional.

10. A, B, C. The problem with D is that PIM SM is based on unidirectional shared root tree distribution.

Chapter 22

IP Services

THE CCIE QUALIFICATION EXAM TOPICS COVERED IN THIS CHAPTER INCLUDE THE FOLLOWING:

- ✓ Internet Control Message Protocol (ICMP)
- ✓ Proxy Address Resolution Protocol (ARP)
- ✓ ICMP Router Discovery Protocol (IRDP)
- ✓ Hot Standby Router Protocol (HSRP)
- ✓ Dynamic Host Configuration Protocol (DHCP)
- ✓ Domain name service (DNS)
- ✓ Hypertext Transfer Protocol (HTTP)
- ✓ Network Time Protocol (NTP)

In this chapter we'll discuss some router features that either do not fit conveniently in any of the other chapters or provide ancillary functions that are not critical to network operation. With some features, such as DNS and NTP, the router acts as a client of IP services. With others, like HTTP and DHCP, the router acts as a server. Because any topic is fair game on the CCIE written and lab exams, it is beneficial to spend some time familiarizing yourself with some of the lesser-known features on the router. More importantly, there are times in the real world where a feature is needed to fulfill a special requirement.

Internet Control Message Protocol (ICMP)

The primary purpose of the *Internet Control Message Protocol (ICMP)* is to report packet delivery problems and issues back to the originating host. Originally defined in RFC 792, ICMP has evolved to include more functionality and options over time. It is perhaps best known for its role in the `ping` command sending echo and echo reply packets.

ICMP uses the standard layer 3 IP header to send its packets. It is IP protocol 1 and does not use Transmission Control Protocol (TCP) or User Datagram Protocol (UDP) port numbers. Instead, it differentiates its messages and functions using a 1-byte type field that is the first byte of the ICMP header. The type code determines the format of the rest of the ICMP fields. The ICMP types are listed in Table 22.1. Many ICMP types have a 1-byte code field that further defines the ICMP message. For example, ICMP type 3 messages are to alert the sender that the destination of its packet is unreachable. The value returned in the code field lets the sender know whether the IP address, TCP/UDP port number, or network is unreachable.

TABLE 22.1 ICMP Message Types

Type	Name	Codes
0	Echo Reply	
1, 2, 7	Unassigned	
3	Destination Unreachable	0 Net unreachable

TABLE 22.1   ICMP Message Types *(continued)*

Type	Name	Codes
		1 Host unreachable
		2 Protocol unreachable
		3 Port unreachable
		4 Fragmentation needed and Don't Fragment was set
		5 Source route failed
		6 Destination network unknown
		7 Destination host unknown
		8 Source host isolated
		9 Communication with destination network is administratively prohibited
		10 Communication with destination host is administratively prohibited
		11 Destination network unreachable for type of service
		12 Destination host unreachable for type of service
		13 Communication administratively prohibited
		14 Host precedence violation
		15 Precedence cutoff in effect
4	Source Quench	
5	Redirect	0 Redirect datagram for the network (or subnet)
		1 Redirect datagram for the host

TABLE 22.1 ICMP Message Types *(continued)*

Type	Name	Codes
		2 Redirect datagram for the type of service and network
		3 Redirect datagram for the type of service and host
6	Alternate Host Address	0 Alternate address for host
8	Echo	
9	Router Advertisement	0 Normal router advertisement
		16 Does not route common traffic
10	Router Solicitation	
11	Time Exceeded	0 Time to live exceeded in transit
		1 Fragment reassembly time exceeded
12	Parameter Problem	0 Pointer indicates the error
		1 Missing a required option
		2 Bad length
13	Timestamp	
14	Timestamp Reply	
15	Information Request	
16	Information Reply	
17	Address Mask Request	
18	Address Mask Reply	
19	Reserved for Security	
20–29	Reserved for Robustness Experiment	

TABLE 22.1   ICMP Message Types *(continued)*

Type	Name	Codes
30	Traceroute	
31	Datagram Conversion Error	
32	Mobile Host Redirect	
33	IPV6 Where-Are-You	
34	IPV6 I-Am-Here	
35	Mobile Registration Request	
36	Mobile Registration Response	
37	Domain Name Request	
38	Domain Name Reply	
39	SKIP	
40	Photuris	0 Bad SPI
		1 Authentication failed
		2 Decompression failed
		3 Decryption failed
		4 Need authentication
		5 Need authorization
41–255	Reserved	

ICMP is not something that can be enabled or disabled as a whole on the router. It is an inherent IP function. However, there are some ICMP parameters that can be tuned on the router. At the global configuration level, the number of ICMP unreachable messages can be tuned by using the `ip icmp unreachables` command. By default, the number of ICMP unreachable messages is limited to two per second per interface. This prevents the router from becoming the victim of denial of service (DoS) attacks. However, in some cases, this can cause problems, particularly for the traceroute and TCP MTU path discovery (RFC 1191) functions that rely on the router sending out ICMP unreachable messages.

The following interface level configuration commands can be used to alter some of ICMP's behavior:

`ip redirects`   `enable sending ICMP redirects on this interface.`

`ip unreachables` `enable sending ICMP unreachable messages on this interface`
                  `[on by default]`

The sending of ICMP redirects and unreachables is enabled by default. However, for security reasons or to prevent undesired interaction with other features such as HSRP, these commands may be used to disable the sending of ICMP redirects and unreachables.

The following output is the ICMP portion of the `show ip traffic` command, which lists packet counts of the ICMP message types sent and received by the router:

```
ICMP statistics:
  Rcvd: 0 format errors, 0 checksum errors, 0 redirects, 7 unreachable
        500895 echo, 25 echo reply, 0 mask requests, 0 mask replies, 210 quench
        0 parameter, 0 timestamp, 0 info request, 0 other
        0 irdp solicitations, 0 irdp advertisements
  Sent: 0 redirects, 13909 unreachable, 55 echo, 500895 echo reply
        0 mask requests, 0 mask replies, 0 quench, 0 timestamp
        0 info reply, 357760 time exceeded, 0 parameter problem
        0 irdp solicitations, 0 irdp advertisements
```

The `debug ip icmp` exec command can be used to gain further information about ICMP functioning on the router. It does not apply to ICMP traffic passing through the router; it applies only to ICMP packets originated or received by the router. The following debug output is generated by a ping from the router. As with any debug command, extreme care should be taken when turning on debugs:

```
Feb 25 22:48:55 est: ICMP: echo reply rcvd, src 1.1.1.250, dst 1.1.1.251
Feb 25 22:48:55 est: ICMP: echo reply rcvd, src 1.1.1.250, dst 1.1.1.251
Feb 25 22:48:55 est: ICMP: echo reply rcvd, src 1.1.1.250, dst 1.1.1.251
Feb 25 22:48:55 est: ICMP: echo reply rcvd, src 1.1.1.250, dst 1.1.1.251
Feb 25 22:48:55 est: ICMP: echo reply rcvd, src 1.1.1.250, dst 1.1.1.251
```

In addition to `ping`, a useful troubleshooting tool on the router is the `traceroute` command, which prints out a list of next hops a packet can take to reach a destination. On the router, `traceroute` works by sending out UDP packets with a set Time to Live (TTL) field and monitoring the responses that come back. When an intervening router tries to forward the UDP packet and the TTL value decrements to 0 (zero), it sends an ICMP Time Exceeded message back to the sending router. `Traceroute` records the intervening router's IP address as a hop. `Traceroute` sends out UDP packets with the TTL increased during each iteration until it receives an ICMP Destination Unreachable message from the end device.

By default, `traceroute` on a router sends out three packets with the TTL set to 1 and UDP port 33434, chosen as a likely unused port by end devices. Because these packets originate within the router, they are process-switched and are therefore sent to the next hop routers for the given destination IP address. When a next hop router receives the UDP packet, it decrements the TTL value to 0 (zero) and sends an ICMP type 11 (Time Exceeded) message back to the originating router. `Traceroute` then sends out three more UDP packets, this time with the TTL set to 2, and waits a default 3 seconds for the responses. It proceeds in this manner until the UDP packet reaches the destination device. The TTL value is decremented but is nonzero, so the end device does not send back a Time Exceeded ICMP message. Instead, because it is most likely not listening on UDP port 33434, the end device generates a type 3 ICMP (Destination Unreachable) message with subcode 3 (port unreachable). When `traceroute` receives this back from the destination device, it stops sending packets.

Microsoft Windows has a facility similar to `traceroute` called `tracert`; it also modifies the TTL value in outgoing packets to check the devices in the path to the end destination. However, unlike `traceroute`, `tracert` uses ICMP type 8 (echo request) packets (`ping`) instead of UDP packets. `Tracert` looks for the ICMP Echo Reply from the destination to know when to stop.

Now let's look at one of the uses of ICMP: IRDP, the ICMP Router Discovery Protocol used by hosts to find next hop routers.

ICMP Router Discovery Protocol (IRDP)

Instead of running a routing protocol, IP hosts can learn about next hop gateways via the *ICMP Router Discovery Protocol (IRDP)*. Routers configured for IRDP advertise their presence and available interfaces using router advertisement packets. These packets contain a list of router interfaces and associated preferences. A host running IRDP listens for these packets and determines which router interface to use based on the preference value. The host chooses the router interface with the highest preference value.

RFC 1256 defines the operation and packet formats of IRDP. As its name implies, the ICMP Router Discovery Protocol uses ICMP packets to advertise routers to hosts. A router advertisement packet uses ICMP type 9 packets, and a router solicitation packet uses ICMP type 10 packets. Routers send the router advertisement ICMP packets out at regular intervals to the 224.0.0.1 all hosts multicast address. If a router does not support multicast on an interface, the advertisement packets are sent to the local broadcast address of 255.255.255.255. The advertisements have a lifetime value that prevents black-holing of packets in case the advertising router goes down.

Instead of waiting for the periodic IRDP router advertisements, a host may request router information by sending solicitation packets. These packets are sent to the all routers multicast IP address of 224.0.0.2. The responses can be either unicast back to the requesting host or sent via the usual 224.0.0.1 multicast.

Figure 22.1 shows a lab implementation of IRDP. Routers R1 and R2 are configured as IRDP routers. Router R1 is configured with a preference value of 50; router R2 is configured with a preference value of 10. Router R3 is configured as an IRDP host. Because router R1 advertises the higher preference value, router R3 uses it as its default router.

FIGURE 22.1 IRDP example

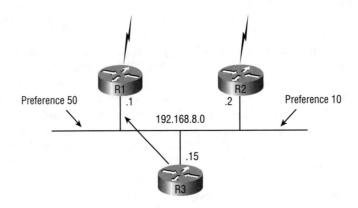

Below are the router configurations used in Figure 22.1. By default, the IRDP preference value on Cisco router interfaces is 0.

Router R1 Configuration

Here is the configuration for router R1, which is given the highest preference and has its advertisement interval lowered from 10 minutes to 20 seconds:

```
interface Ethernet0/0
 ip address 192.168.8.1 255.255.255.0
  ip irdp                          Configures this interface for IRDP
  ip irdp maxadvertinterval 20     Maximum interval in seconds between
                                   advertisements. The default is 600 seconds
  ip irdp minadvertinterval 15     Minimum interval in seconds between
                                   advertisements. The default is 0.75 times
                                   the maxadvertinterval
  ip irdp preference 50            The allowed range is -231 to 231. The
                                   default is 0. A higher value increases the
                                   router's preference level
```

Router R2 Configuration

Here is router R2's configuration:

```
interface Ethernet0/0
 ip address 192.168.8.2 255.255.255.0
```

`ip irdp`	Configures this interface for IRDP
`ip irdp maxadvertinterval 20`	Maximum interval in seconds between advertisements. The default is 600 seconds
`ip irdp minadvertinterval 15`	Minimum interval in seconds between advertisements. The default is 0.75 times the maxadvertinterval
`ip irdp preference 10`	The allowed range is -231 to 231. The default is 0. A higher value increases the router's preference level

Router R3 Configuration

Router R3 is configured to act as an IP host in this example:

```
no ip routing
interface Ethernet0/0
 ip address 192.168.8.15 255.255.255.0
 ip directed broadcast
 no ip proxy-arp
 no ip route-cache
ip gdp irdp
```
Configures the Router Discovery feature using the Cisco GDP routing protocol

Note that for hosts running Microsoft Windows, if DHCP is enabled then IDRP is enabled by default. On hosts running Solaris, IRDP is enabled by running the in.rdisc daemon.

Proxy ARP

Proxy Address Resolution Protocol (proxy ARP) is a variation of ARP in which an intermediate device such as a router sends an ARP response on behalf of an end node to the requesting host. The requesting host configures its own interface address as its default gateway. The proxy ARP has been defined and referenced in a number of RFCs, including 1027, 950, 925, 922, and 826, and is also referred to as a transparent subnet gateway. This technology once had a strong following, and one of the benefits is that it can reduce bandwidth usage on slow-speed WAN links. Proxy ARP worked well when the network was small, but it did not scale well as networks grew.

The Advantages and Disadvantages of Proxy ARP

Proxy ARP has the following advantages:

- Simple configuration, no need to configure clients with a default gateway
- Load balancing (although it's somewhat random)
- Immediate fault tolerance, if addresses have not been recently contacted

Using proxy ARP involves the following disadvantages:

- Increase in broadcast traffic
- Waiting for ARP cache on the workstation to time out in event of failure
- Lack of control over which router is primary and which is secondary

Proxy ARP does provide some fault tolerance on a multiaccess segment, but it does not give the level of control that most administrators want. A more robust and flexible method is needed. In response to this need, Cisco developed the Hot Standby Router Protocol (HSRP), which is discussed later in this chapter.

Enabling Proxy ARP on Cisco Routers

By default, proxy ARP is enabled on Cisco routers, as displayed by using the show ip interface command:

```
R1#show ip interface fastethernet2/0
FastEthernet2/0 is up, line protocol is up
  Internet address is 1.1.1.2/24
  Broadcast address is 255.255.255.255
  Address determined by non-volatile memory
  MTU is 1500 bytes
  Helper address is not set
  Directed broadcast forwarding is disabled
  Secondary address 161.163.50.2/25
  Secondary address 161.163.50.130/25
  Multicast reserved groups joined: 224.0.0.2 224.0.0.10
  Outgoing access list is not set
  Inbound  access list is not set
  Proxy ARP is enabled
  Security level is default
  Split horizon is enabled
  ICMP redirects are never sent
  ICMP unreachables are always sent
  ICMP mask replies are never sent
  IP fast switching is enabled
  IP fast switching on the same interface is disabled
```

```
IP Flow switching is disabled
IP CEF switching is enabled
IP Feature Fast switching turbo vector
IP Feature CEF switching turbo vector
IP multicast fast switching is enabled
IP multicast distributed fast switching is disabled
IP route-cache flags are Fast, CEF
Router Discovery is disabled
IP output packet accounting is disabled
IP access violation accounting is disabled
TCP/IP header compression is disabled
RTP/IP header compression is disabled
Probe proxy name replies are disabled
Policy routing is enabled, using route map GLOBAL_TRAFFIC
Network address translation is disabled
WCCP Redirect outbound is disabled
WCCP Redirect inbound is disabled
WCCP Redirect exclude is disabled
BGP Policy Mapping is disabled
IP multicast multilayer switching is disabled
R1#
```

Disabling Proxy ARP on Cisco Routers

Disabling proxy ARP is sometimes recommended for security reasons. To disable proxy ARP on a Cisco router, use the `no ip proxy-arp` command, as follows:

```
R1(config)#interface ethernet 0
R1(config-if)#no ip proxy-arp
R1(config-if)#^Z
R1#
```

Now that we've shown you two older ways of dynamically finding a default gateway, we'll look at HSRP and how it assists IP hosts in routing packets.

Hot Standby Router Protocol (HSRP)

The *Hot Standby Router Protocol (HSRP)* is a way that routers can project and share a virtual IP address. This HSRP virtual IP address is most often used by host devices that do not have a routing protocol configured; they point to the HSRP address as their default gateway. One router is the active router and responds to ARP requests for the virtual IP address, and one or more routers are standby routers that can take over for the active router if it fails. A router may have HSRP configured on multiple interfaces as well as having multiple HSRP groups configured on a single interface.

HSRP was a Cisco-proprietary protocol that was patented and then published in RFC 2281. Routers participating in HSRP communicate with each other with HSRP packets, as shown in Figure 22.2. HSRP packets use UDP port 1985 and are sent to the multicast IP address of 224.0.0.2 with a time to live (TTL) value of 1. By default, the HSRP virtual MAC address on Ethernet segments takes the form 0x0000.0C07.AC*xx* where *xx* is the group number. For instance, devices sending packets to the HSRP group 1 virtual IP address would use the destination MAC address of 0x0000.0C07.AC01 to reach the active HSRP router, and devices sending packets to the HSRP group 2 virtual IP address would use the MAC address of 0x0000.0C07.AC02 to reach the active HSRP router for group 2. Token ring interfaces support HSRP and use a functional address as the HSRP MAC address. However, they are limited to the following three functional addresses: 0xC000.0001.0000, 0xC000.0002.0000, and 0xC000.0004.0000.

FIGURE 22.2   HSRP packet

Version	Op Code	State	Hello Time
Holdtime	Priority	Group	Reserved
Authentication Data			
Authentication Data			
Virtual IP Address			

Since its inception, HSRP has undergone continual improvement with new features added to it. One major addition is Multiple HSRP (MHSRP), which allows a router's interface to have more than one HSRP group configured on it. A router's interface can be active for multiple groups or can be active for some and stand by for others. Another improvement is that HSRP is supported on Ethernet interfaces configured for ISL and 802.1q encapsulation. By default, the hello timer value is 3 seconds and the hold timer value is 10 seconds. HSRP was modified to allow for millisecond values to be used for the hello and hold timers.

Configuring HSRP

HSRP is primarily configured using the `standby` interface command. The `standby` command is used to select the HSRP virtual IP address, the group, timer values, priority values, preemption capability, authentication string, and tracking. The only required command is `standby x ip x.x.x.x`, which sets the virtual IP address. All other commands are optional. If the group number is not specified in the `stand` command, group 0 is the default value. The default priority is 100 and the default tracking decrement value is 10. Both of these values can be changed per group.

Figure 22.3 shows a possible deployment of HSRP. Routers R1, R2, and R3 all have addresses configured for the 10.1.1.0/24 subnet: 10.1.1.2, 10.1.1.3, and 10.1.1.4, respectively. The HSRP virtual IP address is set to 10.1.1.1, and the hosts on the segment are configured to use it as their default gateway. Initially, router R1 is the active HSRP router because it advertises a priority of 120 and responds to ARP requests for the virtual MAC address of 0000.0C07.AC01. If router

R1's serial interface goes down, its reported priority gets decremented by 30 so it is 90. Router R2 then has the highest priority and becomes the active router and sends a gratuitous ARP to make sure the CAM entry in any switches is correct. Router R3 then has the second highest priority and becomes the standby HSRP router. Router R1 goes into the listen state. If router R1's serial link were to come up at this point, router R1 would become the HSRP active router because it has the `preempt` tag at the end of the `standby priority` command; otherwise, router R2 would remain the active router even though router R1 has a higher priority.

FIGURE 22.3   HSRP Example

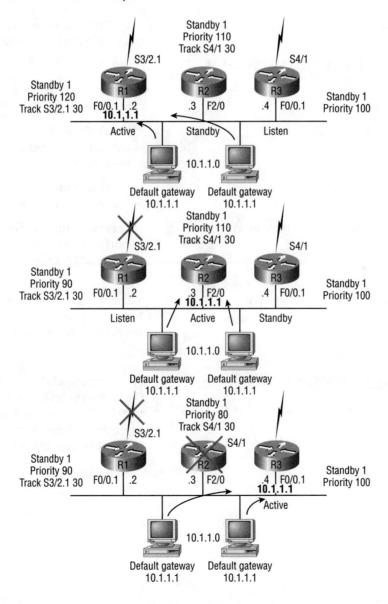

If router R2 goes down and router R1's serial interface is down, router R3, because its priority of 100 is higher than router R1's priority of 90, becomes the active HSRP router. Should router R2 come back up or router R1's serial interface come up, these routers would preempt router R3 as the active router.

Router R1 Configuration

Here is the configuration for router R1:

Interface f0/0.1

encapsulation isl 1	interface is using ISL encapsulation for VLAN 1
ip address 10.1.1.2 255.255.255.0	set real IP address on router interface
standby 1 ip 10.1.1.1	virtual IP address. Should not be an IP address in use by a host or router.
standby 1 timers 2 6	set hello time to 2 seconds and dead timer to 6 seconds
standby 1 priority 120 preempt	increase priority from default of 100 to 120 to make R1 more attractive as active router.
standby 1 authentication lynne	authentication string of lynne prevents inadvertant intrusion by another router.
standby 1 track Serial3/2.1 30	if interface s3/2.1 goes down, the priority will go from 120 to 90. If 90 is greater than any other advertisement, this router becomes the active hsrp router.

Router R2 Configuration

Here is router R2's configuration:

Interface f2/0

ip address 10.1.1.3 255.255.255.0

> set real IP address on router interface

standby 1 ip 10.1.1.1

> virtual IP address. Should not be an IP address in use by a host or router.

standby 1 timers 2 6

> set hello time to 2 seconds and dead timer to 6 seconds

standby 1 priority 110 preempt

> increase priority from default of 100 to 110 to make R2 more attractive as active router.

standby 1 authentication lynne

> authentication string of lynne prevents inadvertant intrusion by another router.

standby 1 track Serial4/1 30

> if interface s4/1 goes down, the priority will go from 110 to 80. If 80 is greater than any other advertisement, this router becomes the active hsrp router.

Router R3 Configuration

Router R3's configuration is as follows:

interface f0/0.1

encapsulation isl 1

> interface is using ISL encapsulation for VLAN 1

ip address 10.1.1.4 255.255.255.0

> set real IP address on router interface

standby 1 ip 10.1.1.1	virtual IP address. Should not be an IP address in use by a host or router.
standby 1 timers 2 6	set hello time to 2 seconds and dead timer to 6 seconds
standby 1 priority 100 preempt	default priority is 100 but this makes it clear. Take over as active if our priority is higher when we come back.
standby 1 authentication lynne	authentication string of lynne prevents inadvertant intrusion by another router.

 Although not recommended in general use, the use-bia command can be useful in some troubleshooting cases and as a workaround for some HSRP bugs.

The following commands are useful in troubleshooting HSRP and evaluating its status:

show standby brief	lists the basic HSRP status
show standby	shows the HSRP status of all interfaces including virtual IP addresses, active router for each group, timer values, virtual MAC addresses, etc.
show standby all	lists all HSRP state information including interfaces in the disabled state.
show standby f2/0	shows the HSRP information for just one interface
show standby internal	lists HSRP hit counters, and other hsrp statistics

Now we'll look at how the router assists hosts obtain their IP addresses dynamically using DHCP.

Dynamic Host Configuration Protocol (DHCP)

The *Dynamic Host Configuration Protocol (DHCP)* is an enhancement of the BootP function used to convey configuration information stored on a server to a client that has just booted up.

Real World Scenario

HSRP with Multiple Tracking

When implementing HSRP, it is important to remember the basis on which HSRP fails over. The router in a standby group that has the highest HSRP priority will become the primary and use the HSRP group address. In order to cause a failover to the standby router, the interface or interfaces the primary router is tracking must go into a DOWN state, causing the HSRP priority to be deducted by the default amount of 10. As long as the standby router's HSRP priority is higher than the new HSRP priority of the primary, HSRP will fail over. This is an example of how HSRP will fail over when tracking a single interface.

How then does HSRP fail over when tracking multiple circuits? Intuition would lead an engineer to believe that for each tracking statement, HSRP would deduct 10 from the HSRP priority. This instinct, however, is incorrect. HSRP by default will deduct 10 from the priority if either interface fails but not 10 for both. To allow HSRP to deduct an amount from the HSRP priority for both tracking statements, the priority decrement must be specified at the end of the `standby track` command. The question may be asked as to why this information is pertinent. When implementing a network, there will be instances when the network engineer has multiple circuits terminating on multiple routers. If the engineer wants HSRP to fail over only if both circuits go into a DOWN state, they must add the priority decrement. See the following graphic and example.

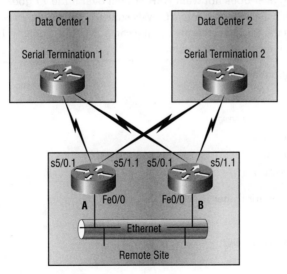

Here is the configuration for router A in the figure:

```
FastEthernet 0/0
standby 1 priority 100 preempt
standby 1 ip 10.10.10.1
```

```
    standby 1 track Se5/0.1 10
    standby 1 track Se5/1.1 10
```

Here is the configuration for router B:

```
    FastEthernet 0/0
    standby 1 priority 85 preempt
    standby 1 ip 10.10.10.1
    standby 1 track Se5/0.1 10
    standby 1 track Se5/1.1 10
```

The preceding configuration is simply saying that if serial interface 5/0.1 goes into a DOWN state, deduct 10 from its HSRP priority. If serial interface 5/1.1 goes into a DOWN state, deduct an additional 10. If the A router's priority drops below 85, then the B router takes over. Note that the tracking statements are tracking the *sub*interface of the serial interfaces. This is extremely important because there are many instances in which the subinterface can go down but the interface itself can still be up. An example of this is when there are multiple fractional T1s terminating to a single physical serial interface.

Using the priority decrement can also be useful if an engineer has two circuits of different sizes terminating to the same router. For example, say there are a DS3 and a T1 terminating to the same router. The engineer does not want HSRP to fail over if the T1 goes down. They want HSRP to fail over only if the DS3 goes into a DOWN state. By simply increasing the priority decrement on the end of the tracking statement, they can solve this problem. The following configuration provides an example of the solution.

Here is the configuration for router A:

```
    FastEthernet 0/0
    standby 1 priority 100 preempt
    standby 1 ip 10.10.10.1
    standby 1 track Se5/0.1 20 (This is the DS3 circuit)
    standby 1 track Se5/1.1 10
```

Here is the configuration for router B:

```
    FastEthernet 0/0
    standby 1 priority 85 preempt
    standby 1 ip 10.10.10.1
    standby 1 track Se5/0.1 10
    standby 1 track Se5/1.1 10
```

This way, configuration information can be centrally administrated. The most common configuration item requested is the client's IP address.

DHCP is defined in RFC 2131 and uses UDP ports 67 and 68. UDP port 67 is used for messages from the client to the server, and UDP port 68 is used for messages from the server to the client. The DHCP packet format is shown in Figure 22.4, and the fields are defined in Table 22.2.

FIGURE 22.4   Dynamic Host Configuration Protocol (DHCP) packet format

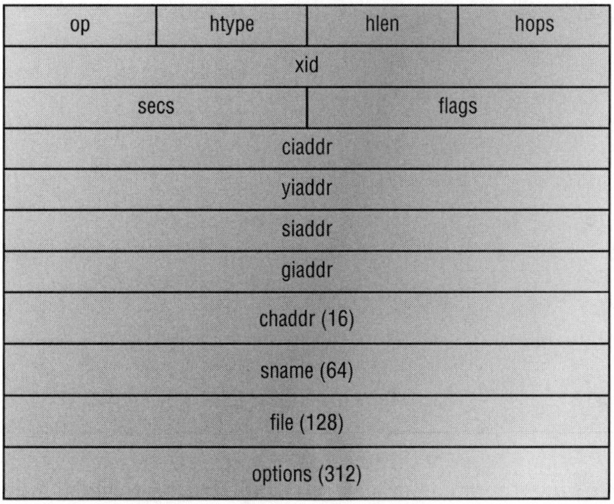

op	htype	hlen	hops
xid			
secs		flags	
ciaddr			
yiaddr			
siaddr			
giaddr			
chaddr (16)			
sname (64)			
file (128)			
options (312)			

TABLE 22.2   DHCP Packet Fields

Field	Size (bytes)	Name
op	1	Message op code
htype	1	Hardware address type
hlen	1	Hardware address length
hops	1	Set to 0 by the client or optionally used by relay agents when booting via a relay agent
xid	4	Transaction ID; random number used to associate messages and responses between client and server
secs	2	Seconds since client started trying to boot
flags	2	Flag values

TABLE 22.2 DHCP Packet Fields *(continued)*

Field	Size (bytes)	Name
ciaddr	4	Client IP address
yiaddr	4	"Your" (client) IP address
siaddr	4	IP address of next server to use in bootstrap; returned by the server
giaddr	4	Relay agent IP address
chaddr	16	Client hardware address
sname	64	Optional server hostname
file	128	Boot file name
options	312	Optional parameter field

Although a router's most common interaction with DHCP is to act as a forwarding agent for DHCP requests using the `ip helper-address` interface command, a router can also act as a DHCP server for hosts on directly connected segments. The following are the commands required to implement the DHCP server functionality on a Cisco router:

`ip dhcp pool IP4Sale`	Creates a DHCP server address pool named IP4Sale
`network 192.168.2.0 255.255.255.0`	Specifies the subnet network number and mask of the DHCP address pool
`default-router 192.168.2.1`	Specifies 192.168.2.1 as the IP address of the Default-Gateway for a DHCP client
`dns-server 192.168.8.15`	Specifies 192.168.8.15 as the IP address of a DNS server that the DHCP client will use
`domain-name ccie.org`	Specifies the DNS domain name for the client as ccie.org
`lease 0 0 15`	Specifies the duration of the lease. The default is a one-day lease. In this command the lease is for 0 days, 0 hours, 15 minutes

By using the `ip dhcp excluded-address` global command, you can exclude specific IP addresses within the DHCP address pool. These specific IP addresses are not issued to hosts. In the following example command, the router has been configured to exclude 192.168.2.1 from the DHCP address pool:

```
ip dhcp excluded-address 192.168.2.1
```

It is possible to manually bind a specified MAC address to a predetermined IP address. The following example creates a manual binding for a client named kyle. The MAC address of the client is 0200.7bb5.7df7 and the IP address of the client is 192.168.2.25:

`ip dhcp pool kyle`	Creates a DHCP server address pool named kyle
`host 192.168.2.25`	Specifies the IP address of the client = kyle
`hardware-address 0200.7bb5.7df7 01`	Specifies the distinct identification (MAC address) of the client in dotted-hexadecimal notation, and the 01 represents the Ethernet media type
`client-name kyle`	Specifies the name of the client using standard ASCII characters. The client name should NOT include the domain name

A Cisco router can also act as a DHCP client receiving interface addresses from a DHCP server. For the most part, this feature is only available on Ethernet interfaces, although newer code versions also allow for its use on PPPoE (PPP over Ethernet) and certain ATM interfaces. The DHCP client feature is enabled with the `ip address dhcp` command. It has two options, `hostname` and `client-id`, that can be used to pass information up to the server. The `client-id` option is used in current code to send a router interface MAC address as the identifier; in older versions of code, it could be entered as an ASCII string. The `hostname` option allows for sending a hostname that's different than the hostname entered at the global configuration level. The following lines show how to configure the DHCP client feature on a router interface:

```
interface fastethernet 0/0
```

`    ip address dhcp`	obtain this interface's IP address from a DHCP server instead of user configured. Optional parameters include client-id and hostname

Domain Name Service (DNS)

Because it is generally far easier to remember names than IP addresses, the *domain name service (DNS)* facilitates telnets, FTPs, and other applications by allowing a user to enter names rather than IP addresses. A host running DNS as a client sends a request to a configured server to look up a given name. The server responds with the configured IP address associated with the name. DNS servers are connected in a hierarchical and distributed fashion so that each server does not have to store the names of all devices in a particular network or for the Internet. If a DNS server does not have an association for a particular name, it forwards the query to a server that has a higher probability of knowing.

The basic DNS client function on a Cisco router consists of entering the `ip domain-lookup` command followed by the `ip name-server` command. The `ip name-server` command allows you to enter from 1 to 6 name server addresses to query to resolve a name. They are tried sequentially in the order they are entered. The following commands outline how to configure a DNS client on Cisco IOS:

`ip domain-lookup`	enable the DNS client function on the router to resolve names into IP addresses
`ip name-server 192.168.8.15 192.168.2.25 192.168.10.15 192.168.4.23`	specify the list of name servers to query to find the IP address of the name.
`ip domain-name routerLab.com`	sets the domain name to routerLab.com. All name queries will assume that the domain is routerLab.com so the fully qualified name does not have to be entered.

Note that when working in the lab, one of the first commands you should enter in the configuration is `no ip domain-lookup`. Otherwise, if you mistype a command, you'll have to wait for the router to try to have the command resolved as the name of a device to telnet to and you'll see something similar to the following output:

```
R1>enbTranslating "enb"...
domain server (1.5.7.8) (7.7.7.2) (2.2.8.16)
(1.5.7.8) (7.7.7.2) (2.2.8.16)
Translating "enb"...domain server (1.5.7.8) (7.7.7.2) (2.2.8.16)
%Unknown command or computer name, or unable to find computer address
```

Hypertext Transfer Protocol (HTTP)

The *Hypertext Transfer Protocol (HTTP)* is defined in RFC 2616 and is an application-level protocol for communication between distributed information systems. It uses TCP as its transport mechanism, although it is not explicitly tied to TCP; HTTP assumes reliable network transport. By default, it uses TCP port 80 but can use other ports as well.

Most Cisco routers and switches support the use of HTTP to access the router and perform configuration tasks. The following lines of global configuration information enable HTTP access to the router. To help prevent unauthorized use, the default HTTP port number of 80 is changed to 31465 and access is restricted only to a single device, presumably a centralized management station.

`ip http server`	Allows this router to be monitored or have its configuration modified from a standard Web browser
`ip http port 31465`	Specifies the port to be used by the internal Cisco Web browser interface. The default port = 80
`ip http access-class 14`	allow only the devices passing the access-list criteria to access the http server.
`access-list 14 permit host 10.1.1.1`	only allow the specific device 10.1.1.1 to access the http server.

Because of the number of security vulnerabilities associated with the HTTP server function on routers and switches, network administrators are generally discouraged from enabling this feature.

Network Time Protocol (NTP)

The *Network Time Protocol (NTP)* is used to synchronize all the device clocks in a network to a master clock source. This master clock source is considered to be more accurate than the individual devices. Borrowing from telephony terminology, clock sources are classified in terms of a stratum number. A stratum 1 device, such as an atomic clock or a radio clock, is considered the most reliable, possesses the greatest accuracy, and is referred to as a primary reference. Devices with higher stratum numbers (2–255) are referred to as secondary references. The higher the stratum number, the less reliable the time information is perceived to be.

Defined in RFC 1305, NTP uses UDP packets with port 123 as both the source and destination to transport time information. At the heart of the NTP packet is the 64-bit time stamp. The time stamp is composed of two 32-bit fields and is used to denote the number of seconds since 00:00 January 1, 1900. The first field defines the number of whole seconds and reached its halfway point in 1968. Therefore, it will roll over to 0 sometime in 2036. The second 32-bit field of the time stamp is used to define the fractional seconds and has a resolution on the order of 200 picoseconds.

NTP packets are transmitted at regular intervals that can be set anywhere from 64 seconds to 17 minutes. RFC 2030 defines the Simple Network Time Protocol (SNTP), which is a stateless version of NTP.

Higher-end Cisco routers can act as NTP clients or servers. It is possible to use a router as the master clock source for a network. The following are the commands for implementing NTP:

`clock timezone CST -6`	Set this router for Central Standard Time = Greenwich Mean time minus 6 hours
`clock summer-time CDT recurring`	Configures this router for summer time (daylight savings time)
`ntp update-calendar`	Configures this to update its internal calendar
`ntp master 2`	Configures this router as an authoritative NTP server as a Stratum level 2
`ntp server 192.168.1.1`	Configures this router as a client, which will synchronize to a Master at address 192.168.1.1
`ntp peer 192.168.1.2`	Configures this router as a client, which will synchronize to other clients or Master, and allow other routers to synchronize to this router. So this command allows bi-directional NTP synchronization
`ntp disable`	This is an INTERFACE command, which will disable NTP on this interface

In Figure 22.5, all three routers are configured for NTP synchronization. Router R1 is the master as a stratum level 5. Router R2 is configured with an `ntp server` command pointing to router R1 and an `ntp peer` command allowing router R3 to synchronize timing with it. Router R2 also has an access list implemented that allows only router R3 to synchronize with it. All of these routers are configured for authentication, which means that they must all authenticate with each other in order to synchronize time with one another.

FIGURE 22.5   NTP example

Here is the configuration for router R1:

`ntp master 3`	Configures this router as a Master with a stratum level of 3. Notice that authentication does not have to be configured on the Master

Here is router R2's configuration:

`ntp authenticate`	Enables Network Time Protocol (NTP) authentication
`ntp authentication-key 1 md5 thyme`	Defines authentication key 1 for NTP, using the MD5 encryption with the password thyme
`ntp trusted-key 1`	uthenticate the identity of a router to which NTP will synchronize using key number 1
`ntp server 192.168.1.1`	This router synchronizes to the Master at address 192.168.1.1
`ntp peer 192.168.2.3 key 1`	Let 192.168.2.3 synchronize with this router using authentication key 1
`ntp access-group peer 14`	Limits access to this router's NTP services. Only matches to ACL 14 are allowed

`access-list 14 permit 192.168.2.3`

The configuration for router R3 is as follows:

`ntp authenticate`	Enables Network Time Protocol (NTP) authentication
`ntp authentication-key 1 md5 thyme`	Defines authentication key 1 for NTP, using the MD5 encryption with the password thyme
`ntp trusted-key 1`	Authenticate the identity of a router to which NTP synchronizes using key number 1

Notice that router R3 does not require an `ntp server` or an `ntp peer` command because router R2 is allowing it to synchronize. Communications between routers running NTP (these communications are known as associations) are usually statically configured; each router is given the IP addresses of all routers with which it should form associations. Accurate timekeeping is possible by exchanging NTP messages between each pair of machines with an association.

Here is the output of a `show ntp status` command on router R2:

```
R2#show ntp status

Clock is synchronized, stratum 4, reference is 192.168.1.1
nominal freq is 250.0000 Hz, actual freq is 250.0000 Hz, precision
 is 2**24
reference time is BB944312.4451C9E7 (23:11:30.266 PDT Wed Mar 27 2002)
clock offset is 0.5343 msec, root delay is 13.26 msec
root dispersion is 18.02 msec, peer dispersion is 0.09 msec
```

If NTP is not configured on a router, `show ntp status` reveals the following:

```
R5#show ntp status
Clock is unsynchronized, stratum 16, no reference clock
nominal freq is 250.0000 Hz, actual freq is 249.9958 Hz, precision is 2**24
reference time is 00000000.00000000 (18:00:00.000 CST Thu Dec 31 1899)
clock offset is 0.0000 msec, root delay is 0.00 msec
root dispersion is 0.00 msec, peer dispersion is 0.00 msec
```

Summary

The feature-rich Cisco IOS code contains a wide array of features and functionality. A portion of this functionality is dedicated to IP services that enhance the operation of the network and provide convenience to the network administrator and host devices. Some of the features we've examined, such as IRDP and proxy ARP, allow for hosts to find routers or other devices. In a similar fashion, HSRP enables failover of a statically configured default gateway address from one router to another. Features such as the HTTP server and NTP do not help the router forward packets, but they contribute to the router's administration and maintenance. Finally, because it wasn't given treatment anywhere else in the book, and because of its many and varied functions, ICMP was covered as an IP service.

Exam Essentials

Understand ICMP's role in an IP network.   The Internet Control Message Protocol is for more than just sending pings. ICMP helps keep an IP network running smoothly by signaling problems back to the packet's source. ICMP is IP protocol 1 and has its own packet format. A 1-byte type field differentiates ICMP packets. Many ICMP packet types use a 1-byte code field to further specify information.

Know what proxy ARP is and how it functions.   If a device does not have a default gateway configured, it sends ARP requests for other devices that it is trying to reach even if they are on different subnets. The proxy ARP function enables the router to answer these ARP requests with its own MAC address. When packets are sent to the router's MAC address, the router forwards them to the destination IP address.

Be aware of how the ICMP Router Discovery Protocol (IRDP) enables routers and hosts to find routers.   IRDP is used by hosts to find next hop routers to forward their packets. This frees them from having to configure a default gateway or routing protocol. Routers configured for IRDP use ICMP message type 9 (router advertisements) and multicast address 224.0.0.1 to advertise a list of their interfaces. Each interface has a priority associated with it; the higher the value/priority of an interface, the more likely it will be used by hosts. Hosts may use ICMP message type 10 and multicast address 224.0.0.2 to solicit router advertisements.

Know what the purpose of HSRP is and how it works.   The Hot Standby Router Protocol (HSRP) is used to provide hosts with a virtual IP address that is backed up by one or more other routers in the event of an outage. Routers configured for HSRP communicate with one another via multicast packets sent at regular intervals. One router is in the active state, one router is in the standby state, and any other routers are in the listen state.

Understand how a router can act as a DHCP server.   Although a router is more often configured with `ip helper-address` to facilitate clients accessing dedicated DHCP servers, it can also be set up as a DHCP server to allocate IP addresses to local devices. A pool of addresses is configured on the router and can then be allocated to end devices.

Know how the router makes use of DNS.   The domain name service (DNS) enables the use of names instead of IP addresses, which is generally easier for human interfaces. Routers can be configured to translate names into IP addresses by enabling `ip domain-lookup`, which causes the router to send requests to a DNS server.

Understand the HTTP server function in the router.   In addition to Telnet and serial console connections, Cisco routers and switches can be interfaced using the Hypertext Transfer Protocol (HTTP).

Know what the Network Time Protocol (NTP) does. The Network Time Protocol (NTP) is used to keep router clocks in sync. Clock sources are classified as stratum devices; the lower the stratum number, the more reliable the source. A stratum 1 device usually sources its time from an atomic clock. Routers communicate using UDP port 123 to maintain synchronization.

Key Terms

Before you take the exam, be certain you're familiar with the following terms:

domain name service (DNS)

ICMP Router Discovery Protocol (IRDP)

Dynamic Host Configuration Protocol (DHCP)

Internet Control Message Protocol (ICMP)

Hot Standby Router Protocol (HSRP)

Network Time Protocol (NTP)

Hypertext Transfer Protocol (HTTP)

Proxy Address Resolution Protocol (proxy ARP)

Review Questions

1. What is the default TCP port used by the Hypertext Transfer Protocol (HTTP) server function on Cisco routers?

    A. 21

    B. 67

    C. 80

    D. 520

    E. 1024

2. The primary role of the Internet Control Message Protocol (ICMP) is to do which of the following?

    A. Send ARP requests to the proper proxy servers

    B. Send routing update messages between routers

    C. Send error messages to originating hosts

    D. Send network management data back to NMS stations

3. NTP uses what type of packets to synchronize routers?

    A. ICMP

    B. IGMP

    C. TCP

    D. UDP

    E. None of the above

4. A router configured as a Dynamic Host Configuration Protocol (DHCP) server can issue which classes of addresses? (Choose all that apply)

    A. Class A

    B. Class B

    C. Class C

    D. Class D

    E. IPV6

5. HSRP hello packets are sent to which of the following IP multicast addresses?

    A. 224.0.0.1

    B. 224.0.0.2

    C. 224.0.0.5

    D. 224.0.0.6

    E. 224.0.0.10

6. The ICMP Router Discovery Protocol (IRDP) uses what ICMP message types for its router advertisement and router solicitation messages?

    A. 1, 2

    B. 20, 21

    C. 2065, 2067

    D. 9, 10

    E. None of the above

7. A router can be configured to do which of the following with the domain name service (DNS)?

    A. Act as a DNS server

    B. Act as a DNS client

    C. Act as a DNS root

    D. Act as a DNS supplicant

8. Which UDP port number does ICMP use for port unreachable messages?

    A. 1985

    B. 1991

    C. 162

    D. None; uses TCP to deliver unreachable messages

    E. None of the above

9. What HSRP state is a router's interface in if it is not the active or the standby router but knows the virtual IP address and who the active and standby routers are?

    A. Listen

    B. Learn

    C. Preempt

    D. Forwarding

    E. Texas

10. A router running the Network Time Protocol (NTP) would most likely pick which of the following as its time source?

    A. A stratum 0 device

    B. A stratum 1 device

    C. A stratum 2 device

    D. A stratum 3 device

Answers to Review Questions

1. C. HTTP uses TCP port 80 by default, as does the HTTP server operating on Cisco routers.

2. C. ICMP is responsible for sending error and information messages back to the host that sent the packet. ICMP has other uses and roles, such as sending echo and Echo Reply packets for Ping, sending router advertisement as in IRDP, and sending time stamps.

3. D. NTP uses UDP packets to communicate between routers.

4. A, B, C. The router acting as a DHCP server can issue Class A, B, and C addresses. At this time it cannot issue IPV6 addresses.

5. B. HSRP hello packets are sent to the all multicast routers multicast address.

6. D. IRDP uses ICMP message type 9 for router advertisements (sent to the multicast IP address 224.0.0.1) and ICMP message type 10 for router solicitations (sent to the multicast IP address 224.0.0.2).

7. B. The router can function as a DNS client but not as a server or root server.

8. E. ICMP is IP protocol 1 and hence does not use UDP or TCP port numbers.

9. A. A router's interface can be in one of the following states: initial, learn, listen, speak, standby, or active. In the listen state, the router knows the virtual IP address and knows it is not the active or standby router for this group.

10. B. A router running NTP will seek the lowest stratum device to synchronize with. A stratum 1 device is a master clock source and lowest stratum device; there is no stratum 0.

Index

Note to the Reader: Page numbers in **bold** indicate the principle discussion of a topic or the definition of a term. Page numbers in *italic* indicate illustrations.

M

in IP Precedence fields, 830–832, *831*
in ISL tag priority bits, 214, *214*
at layers 2 and 3, 830
using Modular QoS CLI, 835–837, *836*, 871
in MPLS exp/CoS bits, 834, *834*
queuing
class-based weighted fair queuing, 850–854, *851*, *855*, *857*
custom queuing, 841–844, *842*
defined, **837–838**
first in/first out queuing, 838–839, *839*
IP RTP priority, 854, *855*, *857*
low latency queuing, 855–858
priority queuing, 839–841, *840*
strict priority queuing, 854–857
weighted fair queuing, 844–847, *845*
Weighted Random Early Detection, 847–849, *847*
Weighted Round Robin, 849–850
review question answers, 875
review questions, 873–874
traffic policing
with committed access rate, 867
configuring, 867–868
defined, **858**
token bucket paradigm, 858–859
traffic shaping, *See also* FRTS; GTS
defined, **858**, **859**, **871**
Frame Relay Traffic Shaping, 858, 859–864, *860*, *862*
Generic Traffic Shaping, 858, 864–867
token bucket paradigm, 858–859
QSAAL (Q.2931 signaling AAL), **157**, *See also* ATM
quantization, **917**
query scope in EIGRP, 382
queuing, *See also* QoS
access lists for, *758–759*

class-based weighted fair queuing, 850–854, *851*, *855*, *857*
configuring in DLSw, 695
custom queuing, 841–844, *842*
defined, **837–838**
first in/first out queuing, 838–839, *839*
IP RTP priority, 854, *855*, *857*
low latency queuing, 855–858
priority queuing, 839–841, *840*
strict priority queuing, 854–857
weighted fair queuing, 844–847, *845*
Weighted Random Early Detection, 847–849, *847*
Weighted Round Robin, 849–850

R

R reference points in ISDN, *713*, **713**
RADIUS (Remote Authentication Dial-In User Service), 768, 769, **882**, 883–884
Random Early Detection. *See* WRED
RARP (Reverse Address Resolution Protocol), *290*, *295*, *See also* ARP
RAS (Registration, Admission, and Status), **915**
RBS (robbed-bit signaling), **708**, **912**
RC (Routing Control) field in token frames, **172–173**, *173*
RD (reported distance), *377*, **379**
RD (Route Descriptor) field in token frames, **172–173**, *173*
Real-Time Transport Protocol. *See* RTP
recording activity, *See also* security
using AAA, 890
overview of, 887
in security servers, 890
using SNMP protocol, 889
syslog logging, 887–889, *888*
recursive static routes, **341–342**

X